The Later Iron Age in Britain and Beyond

The Later Iron Age in Britain and Beyond

edited by

Colin Haselgrove and Tom Moore

Oxbow Books

Published by
Oxbow Books, Park End Place, Oxford OX1 1HN

ISBN 978-1-84217-252-0 1-84217-252-0

A CIP record for this book is available from the British Library

This book is available direct from

Oxbow Books, Park End Place, Oxford OX1 1HN
(*Phone: 01865-241249; Fax: 01865-794449*)

and

The David Brown Books Company
PO Box 511, Oakville, CT 06779, USA
(*Phone: 860-945-9329; Fax: 860-945-9468*)

or from our website

www.oxbowbooks.com

Cover by Christina Unwin based on an idea by Rachel Pope; reconstruction of burial by Simon James

Printed in Great Britain at
Short Run Press, Exeter

Contents

New narratives of the Later Iron Age

Colin Haselgrove and Tom Moore

The nature and causes of the changes that took place in the last centuries of the Iron Age, particularly in southern Britain, have been a major focus of interest ever since Evans' (1890) pioneering study of the Aylesford cemetery and its continental antecedents. The idea of a culturally distinct Late Iron Age in south-east England triggered by Belgic immigrants ('Iron C') was formalised in the earlier twentieth century (e.g. Hawkes and Dunning 1931) and retained its significance even after Roy Hodson deconstructed invasion as the primary agent of change in Iron Age Britain. Emphasising the long trajectory of insular groups, Hodson (1964) replaced the by now over-complex ABC system (Hawkes 1959) with a simpler binary opposition, between an essentially indigenous early pre-Roman Iron Age lasting up to *c.* 100/50 BC, followed by a late pre-Roman Iron Age, defined by the introduction of La Tène D metalwork to Britain, and by the inception of the Aylesford culture – acknowledged as a distinctive, foreign element – in south-east England.[1] Elsewhere, the 'Woodbury Culture (Late)' held sway up to, and 'in many highland areas' beyond, the Roman conquest, although now subject to strong continental influences, reflected in innovations like coinage, rotary querns, and wheel-made pottery. Owing to the late dating in vogue in the 1960s, Hodson attributed several features to his 'late' phase which Hawkes and his generation associated with Iron B – and which we too would now see as much earlier – including currency bars, elaborate multivallation and decorated saucepan pottery.

Hodson's model of steady development from the Bronze Age followed by a short period of continentally-induced changes was adopted by Barry Cunliffe (1974a) for his highly influential *Iron Age Communities in Britain*, both in his initial presentation of the material (chs 2–9) and in the interpretation (ch. 16), which emphasised the social and economic dynamism of Late Iron Age groups linked to the resurgence of external contacts, contrasting this with the primacy of endogenous factors and more static nature of society over much of the first millennium BC. For Cunliffe, the Late Iron Age was also intrinsically different from what had gone before, as first coinage and then literacy encroached on south-east England, generating new sources of evidence through which to view pre-Roman (and Roman) Iron Age societies, whilst at the same time attesting to the major social and economic changes then taking place (*ibid.*, ch. 5). Following Allen's (1960) reappraisal of the imported coinage, Cunliffe put the onset of these changes a little earlier than Hodson, in the second century BC, at the same time correcting the dating of saucepan pottery and related pottery styles. Whilst Cunliffe's book has undergone various changes over the years as new data and ideas have emerged, and he has more recently subdivided the earlier pre-Roman Iron Age into 'Earliest', 'Early' and 'Middle' phases, the underlying structure has been retained in all three subsequent editions (Cunliffe 1978; 1991; 2005).[2]

Since the 1970s, most discussions of Late Iron Age developments have followed Cunliffe's lead, firstly by focusing on south-east England,[3] and secondly, by invoking mainly external causes. What the relevant changes actually represented has been largely a matter of theoretical fashion: in the brief heyday of processualism, they were construed as urbanisation linked to the intensification of external trade (Cunliffe 1976; 1978; Haselgrove 1976); in the 1980s, they became the rise and fall of paramount chiefdoms fuelled by Roman trade in prestige goods, as in the core–periphery model (Haselgrove 1982; 1984; 1987; Cunliffe 1988; 1991); nowadays, they are viewed as dynasty building and the adoption of continental-style identities, driven by Roman political agency and cultural imperialism, and even migration (Millett 1990; Creighton 2000; 2006; Hill 2002). There have been some attempts to explain the changes of the Late Iron Age in more local terms and to play down the role of external trade, but these have been in the minority, and, perhaps significantly, have been directed at areas outside south-east England (e.g. Fitzpatrick 1989; 2001; Sharples 1990).

Partly under the growing influence of post-processual approaches, disquiet about the then current models of the Late Iron Age and especially the focus on south-east England began to be voiced in the late 1980s and continued to mount up through the 1990s. As Haselgrove (1989, 1–3) noted, little attention was given to the formative role of the Middle Iron Age, despite growing evidence to suggest that many supposedly 'Late' Iron Age changes began earlier or were rooted in changes prior to the first century BC. The prevailing orthodoxy was also at variance with Iron Age studies in continental Europe, where the Middle La Tène period is widely regarded as marking a radical realignment in social structures (e.g. Duval 1976; Bintliff 1984; Haselgrove 1990; Pion 1990; Collis 1995; Kristiansen 1998). Haselgrove (1989) called for more research on the social and economic changes in the rest of Britain, which the new settlement data being generated by rescue archaeology suggested were more far reaching and extensive than had hitherto been thought, a view that subsequent work has reinforced (e.g. Hill 1995; 2002; Armit 1999; Haselgrove 1999a; 2004). It is now apparent that the archaeological record left by Iron Age communities outside the pottery- and burial-'rich' areas of southern Britain, far from being 'impoverished', has been distorted by complex cultural and depositional factors, whilst the apparent coexistence of culturally 'Middle' and 'Late' Iron Age groups in parts of southern Britain has cast further doubt on this terminology (Hill 1995), even where it once seemed to make sense

Reflecting these concerns, the recent review of research on Iron Age Britain called for new narratives to be developed to explain the widespread transformation in settlement, social structure, and material culture from *c.* 400–300 BC onward (Haselgrove *et al.* 2001, 28–31). The present book has its origins in a seminar on this theme held at the University of Durham in March 2002. The meeting also sought to set British developments in a wider geographical context by inviting papers on neighbouring countries such as Denmark, Ireland and the Netherlands. Further papers have since been added to enhance the regional coverage (Cripps; Davies; Frodsham *et al.*; Hamilton; Haselgrove), or to address other topics (Collis; Macdonald; Van der Veen and Jones). As we will see, the contributors offer a diversity of approaches and many papers also eschew traditional boundaries, instead seeking an integrated analysis of community and identity. While not excluding the highly visible changes in south-east England (e.g. Bryant; Carr; Hamilton; Hill), the majority of contributions focus on regions and topics that have received less attention in the past. We will begin with a brief discussion of terminology and of the new theoretical directions that have started to take shape in Iron Age studies, before going on to examine the specific themes in more detail.

Chronologies and terminologies

In this book, the Later Iron Age is taken to cover the period from *c.* 400–300 BC onward until the Roman conquest.[4] Such a framework is more appropriate to the many regions of the British Isles and north-west Europe that lack a distinctive Late Iron Age horizon characterised for example by *oppida* or wheel-made pottery, and where significant changes can be argued to have begun rather earlier and/or to have been played out well into the first millennium AD (e.g. papers by Armit; Hunter; Webley). Whilst the traditional terminology is retained in some papers, there is nonetheless a mood not to be constrained by rigid chronological divisions wherever other temporalities are implied by the material, and general agreement that 'Late Iron Age' developments can only be fully understood in a wider temporal and geographical context.

Later prehistoric archaeologists are also becoming increasingly aware that the landscapes we examine are not just geographical entities but temporal constructs (Gosden and Lock 1998; Bradley 2002). We need to explore how Iron Age communities interacted and negotiated with landscapes, both of their present and their past. As Cripps and Hey remind us, Later Iron Age communities did not live in a temporal vacuum, but were indebted to the monuments of the Neolithic and the Bronze Age. Later Iron Age communities created their worlds with reference to genealogical or mythical histories of the past. Such relationships with earlier landscapes can inform us about the negotiation of power and social organisation in the Later Iron Age.

As other recent studies have noted (e.g. Gwilt and Haselgrove 1997a; Hill 1999), the continued use of certain terms to define specific types of landscapes, settlements, and material culture can only inhibit attempts to build new social models and interpretative frameworks. As a number of contributors argue, labels like 'enclosure', 'hillfort' and 'round' are fraught with conceptual difficulties and have connotations that are at variance with the results of recent research (e.g. Cripps; Frodsham *et al.*; Wigley). Equally, as Albarella points out, the major cultural or chronological divisions tend to be based on very specific aspects of the material record. A faunal perspective, for instance, would provide very different divisions, but just as valid. Even such taken-for-granted elements of the Later Iron Age as La Tène art styles are being reassessed, providing new insights into the nature and timing of change (Macdonald). Instead, the wealth of material now available is giving researchers the confidence and ability to construct new models and frameworks through which to examine Iron Age societies.

Theoretical perspectives

The last 15 years have seen a major shift in Iron Age studies. Once criticised as dull and familiar (Hill 1989), the period is now at the forefront of theoretical debate. Recent analyses have been dominated by post-processual approaches (e.g. Cumberpatch and Hill 1995; Gwilt and Haselgrove 1997b; Bevan 1999). These have stressed the inter-relatedness of material culture, deposition practices, and settlement form with social practices, emphasising individuals as active agents in the shaping and structuring of these processes. The ways in which Iron Age people structured their settlement space has proved a particularly fruitful area for study (e.g. Hill 1996; Parker Pearson 1996; Fitzpatrick 1997; Giles and Parker Pearson 1999), as have the various changes in lifestyle and material culture in the Later Iron Age seemingly linked to new ideas about being and personal appearance (e.g. Hill 1997; 2002).

Whilst recognising the important advances that have resulted from this work, an increasing number of researchers have expressed concern over the failure of these approaches to engage with the broader scale changes and patterns present in the Later Iron Age and to address the causes and processes of regional and inter-regional change (e.g. Gerritsen 2003; Pope 2003; Moore 2006). Thus, whilst few of the papers see any necessity to assert the role of the individual agent, several of them have begun to stress, overtly or implicitly, the need to develop broader narratives of landscape and social change. At the same time, Collis warns us against the danger of first caricaturing and then rejecting previous models, without regard for the context in which they were formed or their possible merits. As Collis reminds us, in their time some of the approaches that now stand in disfavour were bold attempts at formulating new models of social organisation and change, leaving him a firm advocate of a pluralistic approach, a position that we entirely endorse.

Alongside theoretical debates, many of the papers respond to the call in national and regional agendas (e.g. Bryant 1997; Haselgrove *et al.* 2001; James and Millett 2001; Willis 2006) to engage with the data generated by developer-funded excavations (e.g. Bryant; Gwilt; Hey; Hamilton; Knight; Moore; Rylatt and Bevan). Following the implementation of PPG 16 in England in 1990 and its analogues in the rest of the United Kingdom, most 'new' Iron Age material comes to light as a result of contract archaeology and there has been a breathtaking rise in the amount of evidence in many areas (Bradley forthcoming; Moore 2006). At the same time, extensive metal-detecting and the launching of the Portable Antiquities Scheme in England to record this material has opened up whole new avenues for material culture and landscape research (Gwilt; Hutcheson; Worrell), to say nothing of spectacular individual discoveries (e.g. Hill *et al.* 2004). These developments are not restricted to the UK, with similar increases in metal detecting apparent, for example, in France and the Low Countries, where rescue archaeology is also providing a wealth of new site data (Haselgrove; Roymans).[5] Not only is the research potential of developer-funded and metal-detected material now abundantly clear almost everywhere – highlighting the need for more integration between academic research and the work of contract units and Finds Liaison officers – but we may expect it to yield some very different perspectives on later prehistoric societies (Yates 2001; Willis 2006; Bradley forthcoming).

Moving settlements: the new landscapes of the Later Iron Age

The period from the fourth century BC to the first century AD was one of dynamic change in settlement patterns and landscapes. Here, papers are characterised by their focus on the landscape as a whole, as an arena for display and as a place of visual references bound in with expressions of identity, social bonds, status, and ritual, reflecting a phenomenological approach to examining communities' relationships, perceptions and dialogues with the landscape (Tilley 1994; Bradley 2000; 2002; Chapman 2000). Through these themes, several papers emphasise the extent to which changes in settlement form, and manipulation and perceptions of the landscape, can inform us about the changing nature of social relations.

Studies of *oppida* demonstrate some of these new approaches in settlement studies. Despite long-standing interest in the sites and allowing for the failings of the nomenclature itself (Woolf 1993; Haselgrove 1995), we still understand remarkably little about the nature of these monuments, how they 'worked' or even their chronology (Burnham *et al.* 2001, 67; Haselgrove *et al.* 2001, 31). Bryant's re-examination of '*oppida*' in Hertfordshire demonstrates the varied and multiple roles of such sites, a phenomenon which is also apparent on the Continent (Haselgrove; Hill). A particular problem, at odds with the dominance of environs projects in Iron Age studies (e.g. Cunliffe 2000), has been the failure to examine *oppida* in relation to their wider landscapes. Bryant, Hill, Haselgrove (for northern France), and Moore attempt to redress this by placing these sites in a wider context, also emphasising the need to investigate other poorly understood settlement types, from banjo enclosure complexes such as Gussage Down to complexes like Braughing or Dragonby, which form part of the same wider developments.

The extent of the link between Iron Age landscapes and 'Roman' settlement patterns also needs exploring. Both Mark Corney (at the seminar) and Moore, for example, have identified a relationship between possible high-status (for want of a better term) Late Iron Age sites and early Roman villas, yet we remain largely ignorant of the implications this may have for the nature of power in both periods. It is no longer sufficient to couch this argument in terms of the 'Romanisation' of native elites; a more sophisticated understanding of how Late Iron Age groupings became 'Roman' communities needs to be developed. For instance, why did early villas develop on some sites but not others? What was the status of such communities prior to the conquest? Too often this crucial phase of social, settlement, and landscape change is interpreted from a Roman perspective and is regarded as marking the evolution of a hierarchical tribal system that was essentially fossilised by the Roman occupation and administrative structure (Millett 1990; Cripps *et al.* forthcoming).

In an inversion of the core–periphery model, Hill and Moore suggest that some of the sites and communities often regarded as central to Late Iron Age developments were once peripheral in their region, only later constructing their own distinctive identities. These studies also examine in more detail the observation that many British *oppida* emerged in areas of the landscape which were seemingly under-utilised prior to the first century BC or AD (Haselgrove and Millett 1997). Both Bagendon and Verulamium are now seen as emerging in this way, on the edge of existing social networks, but the significance of this has so far been underplayed, with the rise of *oppida* more usually being ascribed a functionalist explanation, such as a move to better trading locations. More research is needed on the use of these landscapes prior to the emergence of the *oppida*, and to explain how why these potential centres of power, status, production, exchange, and ritual are where they are, not elsewhere. These questions have major implications for how we understand the transition from earlier settlement patterns and social structures to the development of new modes of power and authority.

How Iron Age people themselves perceived 'marginal' and 'peripheral' areas is key to this debate. Whether marginality was recognised at the time and was crucial to the purpose and meaning of sites in such locations – or is instead a construct of our own making – is vital to understanding their role in wider social systems. This is pertinent not only to discussion of the *oppida*, but also for sites like Hengistbury Head or the Somerset Lake Villages, whose distinctive status has been linked to their supposed marginality (Sharples 1990). Hill shows how modern perceptions of which parts of the landscape were central and which were peripheral may mask the complex realities of prehistory; the East Anglian Fens, for example, were far from 'marginal' in the Later Iron Age, as Chris Evans noted at the seminar, but have often been treated as such by archaeologists, based on their perceived status today. As far as possible, we would be better to avoid using dichotomies like 'central' and 'peripheral', as these both oversimplify the archaeological record and are often based on anachronistic perceptions.

The heterogeneity and complexity of Late Iron Age landscapes is now much better appreciated. The British Isles and other areas of north-west Europe were far from uniformly settled, and even allowing for the unevenness of research, it is clear that many of these variations reflect particular forms of land use and differences in social organisation. Moore and Wigley both note a clustering of visible settlement in the West Midlands, implying that certain areas of the landscape were favoured for occupation, and a similar phenomenon is apparent in eastern Britain (e.g. Haselgrove 1999b; Hill 1999). Once again, the evidence points to new settlement forms having emerged in areas that were previously sparsely inhabited, although other explanations cannot be entirely discounted.

The clustering of settlement, representing either static or shifting communities, has implications for the social expression of these groups. If many houses and enclosures were only occupied for relatively short periods, the process of rebuilding them nearby has repercussions for concepts of community identity, their sense of place, and the transfer of social labour. This is especially true if we accept Wigley's argument that constructing these monuments was beyond the means of individual households and that the process of construction was intertwined in social relations between communities. Giles goes further still, suggesting that the collective labour of digging and cleaning out enclosure ditches helped ingrain lineage and a history of place into people, an affirmation of their identity in society and in the landscape.

Landscape locales

There is widespread agreement that the Later Iron Age was characterised by increasing specialisation of the landscape and the intensive use of sites and locations away from the normal areas of settlement for specific activities, as notably in the case of the Somerset Lake Villages with their apparent role as regional centres of production and exchange (Sharples 1990; Henderson 1991). As Bryant points out, the variety of sites collected together under the umbrella term *oppidum* might indicate an increased specialisation in the landscape for exchange, elite centres, and ritual practices. Such specificity of action can also be suggested for other activities such as salt making, quern provenance, and pottery manufacture, which were often focused on distinctive locations in the landscape (Morris; Moore; Willis). Morris suggests that there may well be a link between the magical character of these places in Iron Age eyes, situated well away from 'everyday life', and the magic needed to transform substances like salt from one state to another. As Hutcheson shows, other distinctive topographic areas were selected as the place for acts involving the repeated ritual deposition of high-status metalwork. Such locales of ritual activity were generally devoid of settlement activity, as at Snettisham. In some cases, these locations remained important well into the Roman period.

We have to remember, however, that landscapes were not static, but instead dynamic elements of the social environment. Willis and Hamilton examine the often neglected 'landscapes' of coastal zones and estuaries, recognising them as liminal interfaces between land and sea. Resonating with Morris' discussion of salt making in Lincolnshire, Willis shows that the coastline was the focus for a range of important activities, reinforcing previous studies which see the emergence of powerful industrial communities in liminal environments as one of the most significant developments of the Later Iron Age (Sharples 1990; Henderson 1991). There is considerable scope for further research in this area, using new technologies like GIS to understand why specific places were marked out for particular practices. Moore, for example, suggests that prominent landscape features could act as foci for production and be an expression of social relations. Similar associations between landscape features and locales of provenance or production have been noted elsewhere, for example associated with pottery production in Cornwall (e.g. Harrad 2003). We also need to explore the histories of such locations: why they became significant and how their meanings altered and developed in relation to mythical or genealogical histories (Gosden and Lock 1998) and to changing social contexts. Increasingly, landscapes are regarded as not just an economic resource or neutral backdrop, but as visual, evocative stimuli, in some senses social actors in their own right.

Different Iron Ages: the Later Iron Age beyond south-east England

A welcome re-orientation of research away from the traditional 'hotspots' of southern England, and, in Scotland, the Northern and Western Isles, towards areas of the British Isles where the changes of the Later Iron Age have received less attention, is seen in several papers. Regions examined in detail include south-west England (Cripps), the upper Thames valley (Hey), the Severn–Cotswolds (Moore), the Welsh Marches (Wigley), south Wales (Gwilt), the Trent valley (Knight), the Cheviots (Frodsham *et al.*), eastern Scotland (Davies) and Northern Ireland (Armit). Whilst emphasising the specificity of individual regional trajectories, which makes it to difficult to generalise across the island as a whole other than at a very superficial level (cf. Haselgrove 2004), these papers stress the vitality of the social and economic changes that occurred during the Later Iron Age and the long-term character of many of the relevant processes. The only reason that many of these regions have not figured more heavily in previous narratives has been a relative lack of excavation and research, not because of any inherent backwardness or conservativeness. Some lacunae remain, such as north-west England and some highland areas of Wales and Scotland, but even here developer-funded archaeology is causing a reassessment (e.g. Nevell 1999).

Those papers that focus on south-east England re-evaluate the uses and roles of many sites and artefacts that have long been recognised as 'typical' of the Late Iron Age (e.g. Bryant; Carr) and emphasise areas which were once perceived as peripheral to mainstream developments, such as the south coast and most of East Anglia (Hamilton; Hill). Comparison with material from the near Continent (Collis; Haselgrove; Roymans; Webley; Wells) also enables the Later Iron Age in Britain to be placed in a wider context. Although differences exist between these areas, similar themes emerge, in particular the growing importance of expressing both individual and regional identities alongside the development of larger socio-political groups. This further establishes the often unreal and unhelpful nature of the divisions drawn in the past between Britain and the Continent and the dangers in over-emphasising Britain's difference to the rest of Europe (Haselgrove 2001). Despite the diversity and strong sense of regionality in papers, broader inter-regional themes emerge – such as an increasing emphasis on enclosure – which hint at the wider preoccupations of Later Iron Age communities.

Bounding landscapes and people

The Later Iron Age is marked by radical developments in settlement form across north-west Europe. Whilst this should not be regarded as marking exactly the same process everywhere, it may reflect more widespread changes in the ways that modes of settlement space were negotiated. Several papers note the increasingly enclosed landscapes and communities of the Later Iron Age (Frodsham *et al.*; Giles; Haselgrove; Knight; Wigley; see also Moore 2007). This can be contrasted with an often more 'open' or unenclosed, and frequently less visible, Late Bronze Age and Earlier Iron Age pattern (Haselgrove and Pope 2007a). In the Later Iron Age, defining areas of landscape became increasingly important – from the dyke systems of the *oppida* to the smaller enclosures used to define individual groups or households. Such boundaries have been interpreted in various ways: as marking relative autonomy and independence from other communities (Hingley 1984) or as signifying status (Frodsham *et al.*; Wigley), but it is clear that their social meaning is still more complex.

Rather than signifying independence, many enclosure boundaries are simply too large for the enclosed community to have constructed unaided. The exchange of labour, and the relationships thus engendered, was of prime importance in the development of these settlement forms. As Giles, Moore, and Wigley indicate, settlement and landscape boundaries, along with 'natural' features, were used by Iron Age societies to construct social spaces and articulate relationships. Settlement patterning was not purely functional; instead, the construction of landscapes helped reproduce social relationships. By implication, the development of more physically bounded social spaces in the Later Iron Age marks the emergence of new forms of relationship.

The complexity of boundaries is well demonstrated by Rylatt and Bevan's discussion of pit alignments. These enigmatic features are increasingly being recognised throughout Britain, yet their roles remain hotly debated (Thomas 2003; Wigley 2007). Rylatt and Bevan argue that pit alignments can only be understood in their landscape context, in particular their location on routes leading to periodically waterlogged tracts of land. Any functional roles they possessed were combined with symbolic transitions. From wet to dry, from floodplain to land, from winter to summer, the role of these features was intimately tied to changing cycles of agricultural and social life. In other parts of Britain, pit alignments seem to be predominantly early in date, many being transformed into 'segmented' ditches or uninterrupted linear ditches in the course of the Later Iron Age (Moore 2006; Wigley 2007). In such instances, we may be seeing changing social relationships played out in these features – as a relatively permeable boundary became increasingly impassable.

Ireland provides a somewhat different picture. Boundaries marking the household or community appear to be generally absent from the settlement record of the later first millennium BC. Instead there is growing evidence that a number of large linear boundary systems existed, defining much larger social units or territories. The emphasis appears to be upon communal boundaries, of symbolic and territorial significance, at the expense of defining the smaller social unit. Ireland also contains the complex royal sites – combinations of monuments of varying forms and meanings combining perhaps secular and sacred power – discussed here by Armit. The use of space on these sites resonates with the Late Iron Age *oppida* or royal sites in Britain (Hill 1995). *Oppidum* boundaries also often appear 'illogical' and it is unclear what they demarcate or define. At Bagendon, for instance, they appear to form an elaborate 'entranceway' to the valley, whilst Bryant suggests some of the Verulamium earthworks acted as processional ways to be visualised in particular ways as well as used to control movement.

The association and definition of wet areas at many such sites (Verulamium, Stanwick, Bagendon) further implies that the areas of land thus demarcated were symbolic or ritual foci (Haselgrove and Millett 1997, 281; Haselgrove 2000). The form of these sites evidently had an important role in directing people around them, possibly projecting power but also demarcating symbolic space. This use of movement and visual messages might also be the key to explaining similar features, such as the banjo complexes of Wessex. Together these studies stress the use of landscapes and topography, as well as constructed space, to convey social messages, recognising that 'natural' landscapes are themselves 'constructed' through the reworking of physical and visual landscapes to create and maintain boundaries, themselves ingrained in social activities and the creation of relations between individuals and communities (e.g. Tilley 1994; Bradley 2000; Chapman 2000; Hamilton and Manley 2001).

Examining the 'household'

The house and household have been a major focus of research in recent years (e.g. Parker Pearson and Richards 1994; Giles and Parker Pearson 1999; Pope 2003) and continue to be a focus of many studies here. Those papers that discuss the smallest social unit, the household, stress the importance of not returning to generalised, monolithic 'Celtic' models, instead recognising the variation that existed through time and space (cf. Brück and Goodman 1999, 11). Giles, for example, notes that the household was not a monolithic entity and cannot be regarded as a simple building block for Iron Age societies. As many discussions of identity emphasise, the construction of the household may have been relative to different societies and groups. Nevertheless, despite the continued emphasis on the household and intra-spatial patterning on Iron Age sites, we still know little of these essential elements of Iron Age society. Whilst generalising models have rightly been rejected, the ensuing relativism has not replaced them with a sound understanding of Iron Age societies, either at the household level, or at the scale of the wider social group.

As Webley notes, changes at household level both influenced and replicated wider processes of change. In Denmark, modifications in house form, and the abandonment and rebuilding of houses elsewhere, reflect changes in the social role of the household and in the internal social relations of this group. Alterations in the form of enclosures used over a long period of time may also be linked to changes in the status and form of the household, as Wigley argues. Thus, discussion as to why settlements shifted or remained rooted to distinct locales is framed in a social debate about the nature of the household rather than purely in economic or subsistence terms. If, as recent research suggests, changes in the household were indeed in constant interplay with wider changes in society, it should be possible, by analysing this relationship, to explore how the different processes of change took place and manifested themselves on both a small and large scale.

Several papers reinforce the view that a fundamental shift in household form, and subsequently settlement patterns, occurred in many areas of north-west Europe in the later first millennium BC. In the Netherlands, Gerritsen (1998; 2003) has noted the increasing stability of social units, and a move from individual, 'wandering' households to larger, more stable units in the Later Iron Age. Webley notes a similar phenomenon in Jutland. Judging from the increased emphasis on enclosing the household and the greater permanence and stability of such units in the landscape, comparable changes took place in many parts of Britain (Giles; Knight; Wigley).

Other papers stress the crucial role of settlement space in constructing and engendering new social relationships, linking the appearance of new settlement forms to new forms of social relationship (e.g. Cripps). Webley emphasises the more restricted and structured use of space evident in Late Iron Age settlements in Jutland, related perhaps to an increasing sense of privacy and private ownership in this period. A neglected but potentially stark indicator of this changing perception may be the appearance of keys in the archaeological record at this time, indicative perhaps of a shift from a lack of need for closure, or one based on taboo and social practice, to one based on physical barriers. A different, but tantalisingly similar, process of increasing enclosure and restricted access apparent in the Later Iron Age in many parts of Britain may well mark similar social developments (Wigley). As Giles notes, physically defining enclosures creates a sense of outside/inside, creating notions of trespass and liminality as thresholds become more visible and meaningful.

All the papers are in broad agreement that the Late Iron Age is marked by a fundamental change in the use of settlement space, which points to new forms of social interaction between individuals and communities. Giles, for example, sees the rise of individuals or smaller social groups coinciding with a rejection of communal ceremonies, with the inhabitants of East Yorkshire no longer recognising group identity through cemeteries. As with much of the material culture, there is a sense of an increasing desire to define the individual and the household within the larger group. Among the factors that might have led individuals and communities to emphasise their identity and – in some cases – independence through the manipulation of landscapes and material culture, two that stand out at this time are rising population levels and contacts with larger 'corporate' entities such as Rome.

Artefacts and identity

Landscape and settlement studies have somewhat dominated discussion of the Iron Age in recent years and much of the material culture has been relatively neglected, not least the brooches and decorative metalwork that traditionally served as the 'linch pins' of both chronological and social models. In seeking to reintegrate this material into the mainstream of research, most of the studies offered here do not draw firm distinctions between artefact and landscape studies, seeing the relationship of artefact production, use, and deposition within the landscape as key to determining its different roles in society. This approach is leading to a far better understanding of artefact roles and distribution patterns. Hutcheson's analysis indicates strong links between Later Iron Age metalwork deposition and the construction of social relations and identities in northern East Anglia, whilst Worrell's research on the new Portable Antiquities data shows strong regional variations in the metalwork categories most often recovered – and thus by implication preferentially selected for deposition. This and the investigation of various British and European find sites for prestige metalwork and coin hoards (Priest *et al.* 2003; Hill *et al.* 2004; Haselgrove and Wigg-Wolf 2005) shows clearly that terms like 'stray find' are too simplistic, in danger of obscuring the complex relationships between artefact, form of deposition, and the wider natural and human landscape context. It was at sites like these that the construction and playing out of individual and community identities was taking place (Moore 2006). This is especially relevant in areas without obvious focal sites, where people came together periodically and where power and identity were negotiated, be they hillforts or *oppida*, or cemeteries and formal sanctuaries – as in parts of northern France (Wellington 2005).

Discussions of identity at various levels – from the household to the supra-regional – emphasise the often unreal division between artefact analysis and landscape studies. Identity may be expressed by very different means in different contexts and at different scales. A number of papers seek to unravel precisely what identity was being expressed and in what context. Hunter, for one, suggests that defining material culture in terms such as 'Celtic' and 'Roman' oversimplifies the construction of identities in the Roman Iron Age. Rather than seeing the continued use of 'Celtic' art as 'native' survival or even 'resistance', we might perhaps view it as indicating the formation of new, 'creolised' identities (cf. Webster 2001). Armit offers a similar perspective on Roman finds in Ireland. Long seen as evidence of either trade or raiding, he suggests a less prosaic explanation. Placed in the context of La Tène material culture, these imports might represent the articulation of new, potentially oppositional identities in the first century AD.

Wells, too, stresses the complexity of meanings that

material culture can possess, noting that the increased prevalence of swords and horse gear in Late Iron Age burials could express not only opposition to Rome, but also Roman influence and even a role in the Roman army. In all instances, the context of finds is paramount. It is time to stop treating all imports found in burials and on settlements as if they express one simple dichotomy, and allow for more complex manipulation of external influences by people set on articulating new social identities. We must not, however, expect to explain all such material as manifestations of identity. Often, such expressions are ones of power – some things were adopted, others were imposed.

Despite the prominence of La Tène art in early studies of the British and European Iron Age (e.g. Powell 1958), it has largely been neglected in recent reviews of the period. However, in reminding us of the metaphors and meanings expressed through the use not just of style and design, but also colour, in material culture, recent research in other branches of archaeology should inspire us to 'theorise' the study of La Tène art (e.g. Chapman 2002). Both Macdonald and Fitzpatrick seek to explore the meanings behind the artwork, whilst moving beyond interpreting the material as simply reflecting cultural or ethnic identities. Fitzpatrick's suggestion that colour as well as decorative form was used to express certain meanings – red for display, blue perhaps associated with the body – further underlines the complexity of expressions articulated through decoration. These studies are particularly enlightening in their discussion of the varied and changing visual world of the Later Iron Age. As material culture associated with the individual and the body became more prevalent, in the form of increasing quantities of brooches, horse harness, coinage, glass beads and so on, the colour and style of such objects became part of an expanding visual repertoire, which can tell us far more about identity, status, and perceptions of the body than mere origins and derivation.

The Later Iron Age also appears to be a period when the negotiation of identities at the opposite ends of the scale, the individual and the corporate group, became increasingly important. The changing organisation of space is matched by an increasing desire to negotiate social relations and construct new identities through changing modes of display and eating (e.g. Hill 1997; Creighton 2000). A number of papers have started to wrestle with what is perhaps the most difficult aspect of these developments: how can the varying levels – individual, household, community, and 'tribe' – be compared or related to one another? Wells regards the growing prominence of the sword in burials in Later Iron Age Europe as an expression of individual warrior identity. In contrast, changing depositional practices are seen as reflecting broader changes in social organisation. Hutcheson, for example, argues that the adoption of coinage marks the formation of wider social groups, with less restricted access to metalwork, in the latest Iron Age. In some instances, the same objects (such as coins) may attest personal relationships *and* inclusion in a larger group. There is no reason therefore why individual and corporate identity may not both have become more visible in the Late Iron Age. We may be witnessing a process of dialogue between these different scales of identity.

The distinct regional distributions of material culture discussed in a number of papers (Hunter; Hutcheson; Moore) also hint at the emergence of wider group identities. This area has been somewhat neglected in recent years. Whilst older interpretations suffered from a culture-historical approach, the broader material and depositional patterns themselves remain and require explanation, as Hunter notes.

Such distributions cannot be accounted for in purely functionalist or quasi-economic terms. Moore suggests that they were tied into symbolic landscapes and the creation of a set of wider, loose relationships and identities, embodied through exchange. Morris' study of salt making also emphasises how 'economic' activities were embodied within social and ritual practice. In many cases, material culture was bound into belief systems relating to the cultural biographies of artefacts, from production to deposition, themselves intimately tied to landscape biographies (Chapman 2000; Fowler 2004, 57). All the different elements of these biographies – production, exchange, use, fragmentation, and deposition – could have been important in communicating identities. By examining these biographies, for example from the extraction of a quernstone to its eventual discard, or the manufacture, use, and votive deposition of a La Tène sword, we should be able to learn more about the multiple and complex identities and meanings of these artefacts and the people associated with them. Overall, the emphasis of the papers is on seeing exchange processes and choices over material culture not in economic or ethnic terms, but as a part of social negotiation and reproduction, and intimately engaged in structuring the landscape.

New ways of living and dying

Communal and individual identities were increasingly reproduced through the foodstuffs people ate and the ways in which they were prepared and consumed. It has long been recognised that the material culture associated with eating and drinking changed markedly in the Later Iron Age, with the adoption of continental-style pottery linked to new habits of consumption, particularly the move to wine drinking (e.g. Hill 2002). New modes of drinking and feasting may have been important elements of Later Iron Age social relations and papers here explore the complexities of these foodways, in particular emphasising the absence of a simple dichotomy between 'Iron Age' and 'Roman' consumption patterns.

Choices over what was consumed were well defined. There is mounting evidence that these were not purely dictated by sustainability or geographical considerations, but by factors such as taboo, status and identity. Dobney and Ervynck indicate, for example, the extent to which Iron Age groups rejected the consumption of fish, even in areas where we might expect such resources to be exploited. The consumption patterns of particular foodstuffs may therefore have been engaged in expressing community or group identity as well as reflecting cultural mores or economic necessities. The holistic review of wetlands and seascapes undertaken by Willis may even imply that it was not just the fish that were taboo, but that water itself was a place of magic and transformation.

Albarella and Van der Veen and Jones offer a timely reminder that the conspicuous consumption of food as part of social identities and status, both within and between individuals and communities, was already part of Iron Age culture prior to the late first millennium BC. But it is in the Late Iron Age that major changes occur in production and consumption patterns. Albarella notes an increase in the numbers of sheep, and to some extent pig, with further dramatic changes taking place after the Roman conquest with a rise in cattle numbers, possibly part of an acculturation to foreign consumption patterns. The changes in eating habits appear complex, with hints of an increase in both arable and meat production, possibly part of the development of new foodways to express new power relations and identities. These changes cannot, however, be framed purely in terms of 'Romanisation' (or even 'Belgicisation'), as they differ from continental patterns. Thus the faunal evidence raises important questions about the extent to which these new foodways represented entirely new ways of feasting and expressing social identity distinctive to Britain, or were partly a continuation of the expression of power and status through production and consumption seen in earlier periods.

Debates over the existence and nature of the Germanic mode of production (e.g. Hingley 1984; Hill 1996) and existence of consumer and producer sites (e.g. Van der Veen 1992; Jones 1996) have meant that the nature and social impact of food production have figured prominently in Iron Age studies. Landscape studies suggest that the Later Iron Age saw an intensification of land use in many areas of Britain with heavier soils taken under cultivation (Haselgrove 1989; 1999a) and placing agricultural change in a wider social context remains crucial (Haselgrove *et al.* 2001, 10–11). Van der Veen and Jones explore how the production, storage and consumption of arable crops can be identified in the archaeological record and its implications for social organisation. They argue that detailed examination of the botanical and faunal remains is needed to understand Iron Age communities, stressing that a lack of attention to their context and taphonomy can lead to highly misleading interpretations of the nature and extent of production and thus social structures.

Alongside the changing foodways implied by the material culture, Van der Veen and Jones suggest an increasing emphasis on producing a surplus, accompanied by a decline in storage, possibly signifying more exchange of surplus beyond the immediate region. This may have been part of a move from communal feasting in the Earlier Iron Age to a more exclusive dining process, associated perhaps with new, imported material culture. It seems that whilst feasting was important throughout the first millennium BC, and continues to be regarded as a key element of the social changes evident in the Late Iron Age, the nature of such feasts may have changed markedly and was no longer a process of reciprocity (Dietler 1996; Hill 2002). Combined with the appearance of new material culture forms and the developments in settlement patterns and landscape discussed above, the emergence of very different forms of personal relationships is implied in the Late Iron Age.

Changes in material culture and foodways can be regarded as a social as much as an economic process, and cannot simply be attributed to levels of 'Romanisation'. Roymans stresses that the process of exchange, of gift giving, may have been as important as the nature and source of the 'things' themselves. As new forms of material culture appear, particularly coinage, it is the new relationships that these signalled and engendered – rather than their adoption *per se* – that informs us about the changing nature of society (Hill; Roymans; Van der Veen and Jones). These constituted social systems that were not necessarily 'Romanised', but were both new and distinctively regional within Belgic Gaul and southern England (Hill; Haselgrove; Roymans). Particularly clear in these accounts is the complex relationship between consumption and choices over material culture; practices vary regionally and are related to a range of specific community elements identifying, class, status and social choices.

Changes in the treatment of the dead in the Later Iron Age have long been regarded as crucial markers of ethnic (Hawkes 1959) or social change (Cunliffe 1991; Hill 1995). Carr, however, argues that rather than treating the adoption of cremation as a fundamental shift in perceptions of the dead, it may contain elements of continuity with Earlier Iron Age practices. We may also note the increased variation in mortuary practices apparent from the Middle Iron Age onward, not only regionally, but also at individual sites and within communities, illustrated by the recent discovery of cemeteries like Suddern Farm (Cunliffe and Poole 2000) and Yarnton (Hey *et al.* 1999). Later Iron Age societies are marked by their lack of homogeneity in the creation of new worlds for the living and the dead. Instead of the adoption of a Late Iron Age 'cultural package' (cf. Hodson 1964; Haselgrove 1984; Hill 2002), we should perhaps instead think in terms of the fracturing of societies, with individuals and communities responding in different ways to the social upheavals of the period (Barrett *et al.* 2000, 323; Moore 2006).

States and tribes

A theme to emerge throughout the volume is the extent to which all forms of living in the Later Iron Age were engaged in the expression and reinforcement of communal identities. The complexity and interaction of identities at different scales and in different forms of expression emphasises the difficulties in drawing simple boundaries around group identity. A major problem remains: we need to understand the ways in which the increased emphasis on individual and community identities during the Later Iron Age relates to the growth of larger socio-political groups. The formation of larger polities has been downplayed in recent studies. This is partly because of its past associations with 'tribes' interpreted from classical sources and uncritically coupled with archaeological evidence. However, as Collis notes, larger social groups, whether 'tribes', 'states', or something else, undeniably existed in the Late Iron Age, but the form and organisation of such entities and how this fits in with the increased emphasis on individual and household identities remains something of an unknown. Whilst recent studies have rightly stressed agency as key to understanding the processes of change (Gwilt and Haselgrove 1997a, 2; Barrett 2000), we need to explain why in the later first millennium BC there was a move towards larger – and more archaeologically visible – groupings.

A number of papers examine the larger scales of society. The form and even existence of the states and tribes alluded to in earlier accounts (e.g. Haselgrove 1987; Cunliffe 1991) is regarded as contentious, frequently bound up with questions of identity, the 'Celts', Classical sources, and questions of urbanism (Collis; Haselgrove; Roymans; G. Woolf 1993; A. Woolf 1998). It is interesting, however, that discussion of 'tribes' is still regarded as key in studies of Iron Age Gaul,[6] yet largely bypassed in studies of the British Iron Age. This perhaps marks an overdue need in European Iron Age studies as a whole thoroughly to re-examine the evidence pertaining to the nature and reality of tribal groups (Cripps *et al.* forthcoming). This should be tempered by the call not to reject their existence wholesale (Collis), recognising the need to explain why these entities, or names, emerged even if they were short-lived or merely represent Roman nomenclature.

The debate over tribal identities is inextricably bound up with questions about other forms of regional identity explored in some of the papers (Gwilt; Hunter; Roymans). Hunter examines how regional identities can be defined through material culture, asking the extent to which such regions have any validity. Whilst the provinces of Hawkes (1959) and Piggott (1966) and the tribal entities defined in Late Iron Age studies (e.g. Millett 1990; Cunliffe 1991; 2005) have attracted widespread criticism, there have been few attempts to explore the underlying reasons for the material culture patterns or to reconstruct wider, regional groups. On a broader scale, as Fitzpatrick (1996) and Kristiansen (1998) have argued, there is still a need to explain the similarities in metalwork across large areas of Europe. Do these relate to forms of supra-regional identities, as the employment of La Tène art may also suggest, or are local identities being submerged in our own broad generalisations of such phenomena, as Macdonald suggests? How did these identities influence each other in the development of new ones? Or did they work on such different levels of meaning and consciousness as to be distinct from each other? The papers by Webley and Roymans illustrate the problem and some possible solutions by showing the extent to which changes perceptible on one scale of social groupings affect those at other levels. It is surely in these processes where the reasons for social and cultural change in the period lie and the processes of structure and agency are at work (Giddens 1984; Barrett 2000).

Causality: what about the Romans?

Current research is moving away from the Romanisation paradigm that has dominated Later Iron Age research for the last twenty years, not just in south-east England but also in many other regions. For example, Cripps and Giles show how, in both Cornwall and East Yorkshire, settlement changes were attributed on minimal evidence to a 'Roman event horizon', as part of a widespread desire to equate archaeological developments across Britain to Roman influence. Other areas of Britain where Roman influence and causality are now being played down include Northumberland and eastern Scotland (Davies; Frodsham *et al.*). As Cripps comments, there was almost a 'need' to perceive Roman influence in areas where it is hard to identify. Now, however, as we have seen above, the focus of much current research is on longer-term processes of change and the contribution of indigenous factors, emphasising individual agency and regionality.

This shift in emphasis nevertheless runs a risk of ignoring the fundamental influence of Mediterranean societies on north-west Europe at this period (Collis; Wells). Growing recognition on the part of Iron Age and Roman archaeologists of the lack of a single 'Roman' social and cultural norm should lead to more sophisticated understanding of the impact and role of non-indigenous influences on Later Iron Age societies. The impact of Mediterranean societies on Iron Age groups was certainly far from straightforward, resulting in the articulation of a diverse range of ideas and material culture in different regional discourses (Collis; Hill; Haselgrove; Roymans). To take a single example, whilst the consumption of freshwater fish increased in England after the Roman conquest and remained significant in the Netherlands, Roman Belgium continues to show hardly any evidence for the exploitation of freshwater resources (Dobney and Ervynck). The debate over the relative influence of indigenous cultural factors and external forces on social change in Late Iron Age and Roman north-west Europe continues.

The proximity of Rome undoubtedly influenced material culture and the expression of identity, but this took a number of forms, sometimes including opposition. Examination of the impact of influences along the western seaboard (e.g. Cunliffe 2001) indicates that the forms could be varied and were manipulated in a variety of ways. It was seldom a 'one-way' process. Cripps' discussion of courtyard houses thus to some extent reflects Hunter's review of material culture: the courtyard house was an expression of indigenous and regional identity, but at the same time marked external, 'Roman' influences. Rather than focus on simplistic arguments of insular versus external, models of social change are becoming more dynamic, exploring the ways individuals and groups manipulated cultural, economic, ideological, and political influences to create new identities and forms of power.

Class and war

Within the debate over the nature of the changes in Later Iron Age societies, class and social divisions are emerging as important topics. At the seminar, John Barrett attempted to introduce class divisions into the period, arguing that it was in the Late Iron Age that such distinctions become more visible. The final centuries BC and the first century AD were characterised by the emergence of a new (or at least more visible) elite. For the first time, we have named individuals and places, and, in Britain at least, tangible manifestations of kingship in coin imagery and legends, permitting increasingly sophisticated insights into the nature of the relationship between these individuals and Rome (e.g. Creighton 2000; Williams 2005). However, there needs to be more discussion of how the role of high-status individuals within Late Iron Age society can be analysed archaeologically, along with that of named castes like the *druides*.[7] We need to explore their place and importance in the social and political changes that took place at this time in different parts of Europe and to ascertain their influence over the functions and form of the new types of site that emerge, such as *oppida* and sanctuaries. Were these individuals the prime instigators of the new forms and patterns of material culture and landscape developments that we see in these and other regions? What was their power base? And what lies behind the emergence of these new 'class divisions' in the first place?

Related to ideas of class and kingship is the issue of warfare. Despite the increasing prominence of inter-personal violence and warfare in other areas of later prehistory (e.g. Carman and Harding 1999; Osgood *et al.* 2000; Parker Pearson and Thorpe 2005) and some recent discussion relating to the Iron Age (e.g. Craig *et al.* 2005; James 2007), the subject is notably absent from most of the papers in this volume. Rather, the 'defensive' role of hillforts and enclosures continues to be questioned (Frodsham *et al.*; Wigley), in line with research over the last twenty years (e.g. Bowden and McOmish 1987; Hill 1996). This conflicts with the extensive evidence for trauma and weaponry from Later Iron Age Europe (Wells; Roymans),[8] possibly reflecting what James (2007) calls the 'pacifying' of the Iron Age. There is a need to explore the role of warfare in the Later Iron Age, accepting that violence may not be divorced from social or ritual practices (Ferguson 1990; Aijmer and Abbink 2000) and recognising that the securing of power could be violent. Giles, combining the burial, chalk figurine, and landscape evidence from East Yorkshire, leads the way, seeing an increasingly divided society in the Later Iron Age, but emphasising that distinct forms of conflict existed and that any understanding of inter-personal violence in the period needs to examine it within the broader context of the settlement and landscape evidence.

Warfare is far more prominent in discussions of the continental Iron Age. The Late Iron Age in Gaul, in particular, has been dominated by discussion of the Caesarian conquest, used both as a chronological marker and an impetus for change (extending to southern England). For Wells, martiality and warfare were a central preoccupation of Later Iron Age societies in northern Europe, the sword being of immense symbolic importance in conveying individual and community prowess (see also Hunter 2005). Wells sees warfare, the role of mercenaries, and the conflict with Rome as fundamental to the changing expressions of identity and power in the Late Iron Age. Similarly, Roymans regards the lower Rhine region as comprised of martial societies, challenging previous egalitarian interpretations. Haselgrove and Collis also view warfare as important, but suggest its impact was subtle and varied. Haselgrove's discussion of the limited and ambiguous nature of much of the 'evidence' left by even a major and well-chronicled conflict like the Gallic war reminds us just how difficult it is to recognise warfare in the protohistoric period. The division between a continental Iron Age, where warfare is regarded as a key social factor and cause of change, and a British Iron Age, where it is frequently conspicuously absent, increasingly appears to be one of archaeological approach, rather than a reflection of past levels of conflict.

Conclusions and future directions

The wealth of material now available for the Later Iron Age is at last enabling us to start writing the kinds of social histories called for by previous researchers. Combining material culture studies and landscape archaeology also allows for a far more multi-vocal Later Iron Age, one no longer perceived primarily through the lens of settlement hierarchies, economic forces and expanding empires. The individual has been placed centre stage as agent and locus of social change. At the same time, we have started to explore the complex interplay between individuals and the large-scale patterning and processes of change that we see at this period, necessitating new methodologies and heuristic devices, as John Collis notes. A healthy diversity of approaches is apparent, which had to a certain extent been lost during the processual/post-processual debate. Through such diversity a fuller picture of the nature of Later Iron Age societies will emerge. The themes of identity, causality, household structure, society, and class are all implicated in current debates about the nature of the dramatic social and material changes of the period and attempts to understand why they occurred.

We are conscious that the book does not reflect all aspects of the research currently under way on the Later Iron Age. In particular, there is no discussion of the developed hillforts of central southern England, the reasons for their demise, and of the settlements that grew up in the landscapes they had dominated (and physically, and perhaps conceptually, continued to dominate), despite much important work on these questions over the last decade (e.g. Barrett *et al.* 2000; Cunliffe 2000; 2005). The Danebury environs programme is now well into its second phase and it too promises – if the initial results (Cunliffe 2003) are any guide – to transform our understanding of society and landscape in Hampshire at the very end of the Iron Age and on into the Roman period. Nor do any of the papers deal with the intriguing developments apparent in the Northern and Western Isles of Scotland over the same period of time, on which there have similarly been important recent contributions (e.g. Sharples 1998; Parker Pearson and Sharples 1999).

Last but not least is the fresh data on Later Iron Age settlements and landscapes unearthed throughout Britain every week by developer-funded excavations and evaluations, which continues to confound and outpace even the most recent syntheses.[9] The trend toward closer research collaboration between individuals working in academic institutions, contract units, local authorities, and amateur groups is therefore not just beneficial, but increasingly vital, so that ideas and information flow freely between everyone concerned. At the same time, it is important not to overlook the enormous potential of the material culture now available for study, particularly now that metal detecting finds are being systematically recorded in many areas, if still not everywhere. While Iron Age landscape studies are thriving, the relative dearth of material culture specialists is, however, a concern (Haselgrove *et al.* 2001). It is vital that future research strikes an appropriate balance between all the different forms of evidence.

Acknowledgements

The authors would particularly like to thank Pam Lowther for her hard work in getting the volume to publication and Rachel Pope for her assistance in organising the Durham seminar. We would also like to thank all the referees for their time. The Rosemary Cramp Fund provided financial support for the seminar.

Notes

1. Hodson used the presence of imported Hallstatt C and La Tène A metalwork in Britain to subdivide his 'earlier pre-Roman Iron Age' into 'Earliest' and 'Earlier' phases, thereby further breaking with the ABC scheme, which attributed the inception of Iron A to a complex of folk movements in Hallstatt D, and linked Iron B to new incursions during La Tène B–C.
2. In the first two editions of *Iron Age Communities*, Cunliffe (1974a; 1978) defined various ceramic horizons prior to the Late Iron Age, without imposing strict subdivisions. In this, he differed both from Dennis Harding (1974), who split the insular material on continental lines into Earliest (Hallstatt), and Early, Middle and Late La Tène phases, and John Collis (1977), who in a response to both books, presented the Earliest, Early, Middle, and Late Iron Age framework, which has since become standard, pointing out that these divisions would have to be based on radiocarbon dates outside southern and eastern England, rather than on pottery styles. In another book published in 1974, Cunliffe (1974b) opted for a different approach, contrasting a 'phase of innovation' before 500 BC with a 'phase of development' lasting until the Roman conquest. For further discussion of the development of Iron Age terminology, see Haselgrove and Pope (2007a).
3. In surveying the Late Iron Age, the various editions of *Iron Age Communities* devote around four times more space to lowland Britain than to the north and west (cf. Cunliffe 1974a, chs. 5–8; 2005, chs. 6–9).
4. Strictly speaking, the later pre-Roman Iron Age. In Scotland, it is common to view the Iron Age as part of a much longer period of development, with the 'long Iron Age' being seen to continue until the Norse incursions. In his recent survey of northern Britain, Harding (2004, 3–5) reserves the term 'Later Iron Age' for the period from the second quarter of the first millennium AD, while his 'Earlier Iron Age' is equivalent to the entire pre-Roman Iron Age in England. In southern Scotland, though less so further north, the Roman interlude stands as the interface between these two main phases.
5. Figures illustrating the increase since the 1970s of Iron Age coin finds in northern France, Germany and the Low Countries due to metal detecting are given in Haselgrove (2005, 135–42). The proportion of finds currently being reported is very variable, depending on the archaeological regimes in place in the different countries. See also Roymans (2004).
6. See most recently Fichtl (2004).

7. See Crumley (1974) for an early attempt to do this within the framework of the New Archaeology.
8. As Craig *et al.* (2005) have recently shown, the mortuary remains from Danebury show ample evidence of killing and mutilation, and for the display of body parts, likely to be indicative of feuding and warfare.
9. To take just one example, whilst this book has been in preparation, a series of large-scale excavations have taken place in north-east England, which will necessitate a radical rethinking of the character of Later Iron Age society in the lowlands of Durham and Northumberland (e.g. at Faverdale, Darlington; Pegswood, Morpeth; and Newcastle Great Park).

Bibliography

Aijmer, G. and Abbink, J. 2000. *Meanings of Violence.* Oxford: Berg.

Allen, D.F. 1960. The origins of coinage in Britain: a reappraisal, in S.S. Frere (ed.), *Problems of the Iron Age in Southern Britain*, 97–308. London: Institute of Archaeology Occasional Paper 11.

Armit, I. 1999. Life after Hownam: the Iron Age in south-east Scotland, in Bevan 1999, 65–79.

Arnold, B. and Blair-Gibson, D. (eds) 1995. *Celtic Chiefdom, Celtic State.* Cambridge: Cambridge University Press.

Barrett, J. 2000. A thesis on agency, in M. Dobres and J. Robb (eds), *Agency in Archaeology*, 61–68. London: Routledge.

Barrett, J., Freeman, P. and Woodward, A. 2000. *Cadbury Castle, Somerset. The Later Prehistoric and Early Historic Archaeology.* London: English Heritage Archaeological Report 20.

Bevan, B. (ed.) 1999. *Northern Exposure: Interpretative Devolution and the Iron Ages in Britain.* Leicester: Leicester Archaeology Monograph 4.

Bintliff, J. 1984. Iron Age Europe in the context of social evolution from the Bronze Age to historic times, in J. Bintliff (ed.), *European Social Evolution: Archaeological Perspectives*, 157–225. Bradford: University of Bradford.

Bowden, M. and McOmish, D. 1987. The required barrier, *Scottish Archaeological Review* 4, 76–84.

Bradley, R. 2000. *An Archaeology of Natural Places.* London: Routledge.

Bradley, R. 2002. *The Past in Prehistoric Societies.* London: Routledge.

Bradley, R. forthcoming. *The Prehistory of Britain and Ireland.* Cambridge: Cambridge University Press.

Brück, J. and Goodman, M. (1999) Introduction: themes for a critical archaeology of prehistoric settlement, in J. Brück and M. Goodman (eds), *Making Places in the Prehistoric World. Themes in Settlement Archaeology*, 1–19. London: University College London Press.

Bryant, S. 1997. Iron Age, in J. Glazebrook (ed.), *Research and Archaeology: A Framework for the Eastern Counties*, 23–34. Norwich: East Anglian Archaeology Occasional Paper 3.

Burnham, B., Collis, J., Dobinson, C., Haselgrove, C. and Jones, M. 2001, Themes for urban research, c. 100 BC to AD 200, in James and Millett 2001, 67–76.

Carmen, J. and Harding, A. (eds) 1999. *Ancient Warfare: Archaeological Perspectives.* Stroud: Sutton.

Champion, T.C. and Collis, J.R. (eds) 1996. *The Iron Age in Britain and Ireland: Recent Trends.* Sheffield: J.R. Collis Publications.

Chapman, J. 2000. *Fragmentation in Archaeology: People, Places and Broken Objects in the Prehistory of South-Eastern Europe.* London: Routledge.

Chapman, J. 2002. Colourful prehistories: the problem with the Berlin and Kay colour paradigm, in A. Jones and G. MacGregor (eds), *Colouring the Past*, 45–72. Oxford: Berg.

Collis, J.R. 1977. An approach to the Iron Age, in J.R. Collis (ed.), *The Iron Age in Britain: A Review*, 1–7. Sheffield: Department of Prehistory and Archaeology, University of Sheffield.

Collis, J.R. 1995. States without centers? The Middle La Tène period in temperate Europe, in Arnold and Gibson 1995, 75–80.

Collis, J.R. (ed.) 2001. *Society and Settlement in Iron Age Europe (Actes du XVIIIe Colloque de l'AFEAF, Winchester, April 1994).* Sheffield: J.R. Collis Publications.

Craig, R., Knüsel, C. and Carr, G. 2005. Fragmentation, mutilation and dismemberment: an interpretation of human remains in Iron Age sites, in Parker Pearson and Thorpe 2005, 165–180.

Creighton, J. 2000. *Coins and Power in Late Iron Age Britain.* Cambridge: Cambridge University Press.

Creighton, J. 2006. *Britannia. The Creation of a Roman Province.* London: Routledge

Cripps, L., Moore, T. and Wigley, A. forthcoming. *Tribes and power: a re-examination of the tribes of Britain and Gaul.*

Crumley, C. 1974. *Celtic Social Structure: The Generation of Archaeologically Testable Hypotheses from Literary Evidence.* Ann Arbor: University of Michigan Museum of Anthropology Anthropological Papers 54.

Cumberpatch, C. and Hill, J.D. 1995. *Different Iron Ages: Studies of the Iron Age in Temperate Europe.* Oxford: British Archaeological Reports International Series 602.

Cunliffe, B. 1974a. *Iron Age Communities in Britain* (1st edn). London: Routledge and Kegan Paul.

Cunliffe, B. 1974b. The Iron Age, in C. Renfrew (ed.), *British Prehistory: a New Outline*, 233–262. London: Duckworth.

Cunliffe, B. 1976. *The origins of urbanisation in Britain*, in Cunliffe and Rowley 1976, 135–162.

Cunliffe, B. 1978. *Iron Age Communities in Britain* (2nd edn). London: Routledge and Kegan Paul

Cunliffe, B. 1988. *Greeks, Romans and Barbarians: Spheres of Interaction.* London: Batsford.

Cunliffe, B. 1991. *Iron Age Communities in Britain* (3rd edn). London: Routledge.

Cunliffe, B. 1994. After Hillforts, *Oxford Journal of Archaeology* 13, 71–84.

Cunliffe, B. 2000. *The Danebury Environs Programme. The Prehistory of a Wessex Landscape, Vol. 1. Introduction.* Oxford: Oxford University Committee for Archaeology Monograph 48.

Cunliffe, B. 2001. *Facing the Ocean: the Atlantic and its Peoples, 8000 BC–1500 AD.* Oxford: Oxford University Press.

Cunliffe, B. 2003. Roman Danebury, *Current Archaeology* 188, 344–351.

Cunliffe, B. 2005. *Iron Age Communities in Britain* (4th edn). London: Routledge.

Cunliffe, B. and Poole, C. 2000. *The Danebury Environs Programme. The Prehistory of a Wessex Landscape, Vol. 2 – Part 3. Suddern Farm, Middle Wallop, Hants, 1991 and 1996.* Oxford: Oxford University Committee for Archaeology Monograph 49.

Cunliffe, B. and Rowley, T. (eds) 1976, *Oppida: The Beginnings of Urbanisation in Barbarian Europe.* Oxford: British Archaeological Reports International Series 11.

Dietler, M. 1996. Feasts and commensal politics in the political economy: food, power and status in prehistoric Europe, in P. Wiessner and W. Schiefenhövel (eds), *Food and the Status Quest. An*

Interdisciplinary Perspective, 87–125. Oxford: Berghahn Books.

Duval, A. 1976. Aspects de La Tène moyenne dans le bassin Parisien, *Bulletin de la Société Préhistorique Française* 73, 457–484.

Duval, A., Le Bihan, J.P. and Menez, Y. (eds) 1990. *Les Gaulois d'Armorique. La fin de l'âge du Fer en Europe Tempérée (Actes du XIIe colloque de l'AFEAF, Quimper 1988)*. Rennes: Revue Archéologique de l'Ouest Supplément 3.

Evans, A.J. 1890. On a Late-Celtic Urnfield at Aylesford, Kent, *Archaeologia* 52, 315–388.

Ferguson, R.B. 1990. Explaining War, in J. Haas (ed.), *The Anthropology of War*, 26–55. Cambridge: Cambridge University Press.

Fichtl, S. 2004. *Les peuples gaulois. IIIe–Ier s. av. J.-C.* Paris : Éditions Errance.

Fitzpatrick, A.P. 1989. The uses of Roman imperialism by the Celtic barbarians in the later Republic, in J. Barrett, A. Fitzpatrick and L. Macinnes (eds), *Barbarians and Romans in North-West Europe*, 27–54. Oxford: British Archaeological Reports International Series 471.

Fitzpatrick, A.P. 1996. 'Celtic' Iron Age Europe. The theoretical basis, in P. Graves-Brown, S. Jones and C. Gamble (eds), *Cultural Identity and Archaeology: the Construction of European Communities*, 238–255. London: Routledge.

Fitzpatrick, A.P. 1997. Everyday life in Iron Age Wessex, in Gwilt and Haselgrove 1997b, 73–86.

Fitzpatrick, A.P. 2001. Cross channel exchange, Hengistbury Head and the end of hillforts, in Collis 2001, 82–97.

Fowler, C. 2004. *The Archaeology of Personhood: an Anthropological Approach*. London: Routledge.

Gerritsen, F. 1998. The cultural biography of Iron Age houses, in C. Fabech and J. Ringtved (eds), *Settlement and Landscape (Proceedings of a Conference in Åarhus, Denmark, May 4–7 1998)*, 139–148. Mooesgård: Åarhus University Press.

Gerritsen, F. 2003. *Local Identities. Landscapes and Community in the Later Prehistoric Meuse–Demer–Scheldt Region*. Amsterdam: Amsterdam Archaeological Studies 9.

Giddens, A. 1984. *The Constitution of Society: Outline of the Theory of Structuration*. Cambridge: Polity.

Giles, M. and Parker Pearson, M. 1999. Learning to live in the Iron Age: dwelling and praxis, in Bevan 1999, 217–232.

Gosden, C. and Lock, G. 1998. Prehistoric histories, *World Archaeology* 30, 2–12.

Gwilt, A. and Haselgrove, C. 1997a. Approaching the Iron Age, in Gwilt and Haselgrove 1997b, 1–9.

Gwilt, A. and Haselgrove, C. (eds) 1997b. *Reconstructing Iron Age Societies*. Oxford: Oxbow Monograph 71.

Hamilton, S. and Manley, J. 2001. Hillforts, monumentality and place: a chronological and topographic review of first millennium BC hillforts of south-east England, *European Journal of Archaeology* 4, 7–42.

Harrad, L. 2003. A sacred source? Investigating the phenomenon of Cornish clays, in Humphrey 2003, 11–16.

Harding, D.W. 1974. *The Iron Age in Lowland Britain*. London: Routledge and Kegan Paul.

Harding, D.W. 2004. *The Iron Age in Northern Britain. Celts and Romans, Natives and Invaders*. London: Routledge.

Haselgrove, C. 1976. External trade as a stimulus to urbanization, in Cunliffe and Rowley 1976, 25–50.

Haselgrove. C. 1982. Wealth, prestige and power: the dynamics of late Iron Age political centralization in south-east England, in C. Renfrew and S. Shennan (eds), *Ranking, Resource and Exchange*, 79–88. Cambridge: Cambridge University Press.

Haselgrove, C. 1984. 'Romanization' before the Conquest: Gaulish precedents and British consequences, in T.F.C. Blagg and A.C. King (eds), *Military and Civilian in Roman Britain*, 5–63. Oxford: British Archaeological Reports British Series 136.

Haselgrove, C. 1987. Culture process on the periphery: Belgic Gaul and Rome during the late Republic and early Empire, in M. Rowlands, M. Larsen, and K. Kristiansen (eds), *Centre and Periphery in the Ancient World*, 104–124. Cambridge: Cambridge University Press.

Haselgrove, C. 1989. The later Iron Age in southern Britain and beyond, in M. Todd (ed.), *Research on Roman Britain: 1960–89*, 1–18. London: Britannia Monograph 11.

Haselgrove, C. 1990. Later Iron Age settlement in the Aisne Valley: some current problems and hypotheses, in Duval *et al.* 1990, 249–259.

Haselgrove, C. 1995. Late Iron Age society in Britain and north-west Europe: structural transformation or superficial change?, in Arnold and Gibson 1995, 81–87.

Haselgrove, C. 1999a. The Iron Age, in J. Hunter and I. Ralston (eds), *The Archaeology of Britain: An Introduction from the Upper Palaeolithic to the Industrial Revolution*, 113–134. London: Routledge.

Haselgrove, C. 1999b. Iron Age societies in Central Britain: retrospect and prospect, in Bevan 1999, 253–278.

Haselgrove, C. 2000. The character of oppida in Iron Age Britain, in V. Guichard, S. Sievers and O.-H. Urban (eds), *Les processus d'urbanisation à l'âge du Fer*, 103–110. Glux-en-Glenne: Collection Bibracte 4.

Haselgrove, C. 2001. Iron Age Britain and its European setting, in Collis 2001, 37–72.

Haselgrove, C. 2004. Society and polity in late Iron Age Britain, in M. Todd (ed.), *The Blackwell Companion to Roman Britain*, 12–29. Oxford: Blackwell.

Haselgrove, C. 2005. A new approach to analysing the circulation of Iron Age coinage, *Numismatic Chronicle* 165, 129–174.

Haselgrove, C. and Millett, M. 1997. Verlamion reconsidered, in Gwilt and Haselgrove 1997b, 282–296.

Haselgrove C. and Pope R. 2007a. Characterising the Earlier Iron Age, in Haselgrove and Pope 2007b, 1–23.

Haselgrove C. and Pope R. (eds) 2007b. *The Earlier Iron Age in Britain and the Near Continent*. Oxford: Oxbow Books.

Haselgrove, C. and Wigg-Wolf, D. (eds) 2005. *Ritual and Iron Age Coinage*. Mainz: Studien zu Fundmünzen der Antike 20.

Haselgrove, C., Armit, I., Champion, T., Creighton, J., Gwilt, A., Hill, J. D., Hunter, F. and Woodward, A. 2001, *Understanding the British Iron Age: an Agenda for Action*. Salisbury: Trust for Wessex Archaeology.

Hawkes, C.F.C. 1959. The ABC of the British Iron Age, *Antiquity* 33, 170–182.

Hawkes, C.F.C. and Dunning, G. 1931. The Belgae of Gaul and Britain, *Archaeological Journal* 87, 150–335.

Henderson, J. 1991. Industrial specialisation in late Iron Age Britain, *Archaeological Journal* 148, 104–148.

Hey, G., Bayliss, A. and Boyle, A. 1999. Iron Age inhumation burials at Yarnton, Oxfordshire, *Antiquity* 73, 551–562.

Hill, J.D. 1989. Re-thinking the Iron Age, *Scottish Archaeological Review* 6, 16–24.

Hill, J.D. 1995. The pre-Roman Iron Age in Britain and Ireland: an overview, *Journal of World Prehistory* 9, 47–98.

Hill, J.D. 1996. Hillforts and the Iron Age of Wessex, in Champion and Collis 1996, 95–116.

Hill, J.D. 1997. 'The end of one kind of body and the beginning of another kind of body'? Toilet instruments and Romanization, in Gwilt and Haselgrove 1997b, 96–107.

Hill, J.D. 1999. Settlement, landscape and regionality. Norfolk and Suffolk in the pre-Roman Iron Age of Britain and beyond, in J.A. Davies and T. Williamson (eds), *The Land of the Iceni: the Iron Age in Northern East Anglia*, 185–207. Norwich: Studies in East Anglia History 4.

Hill, J.D. 2002. Not just about the potter's wheel. Making, using and depositing Middle and Late Iron Age pottery in south-east England, in A. Woodward and J.D. Hill (eds), *Prehistoric Britain: The Ceramic Basis*, 143–160. Oxford: Oxbow Books.

Hill, J.D., Spence, A., Niece, S. and Worrell, S. 2004. The Winchester hoard: a find of unique Iron Age gold jewellery from southern England, *Antiquaries Journal* 84, 1–22.

Hingley, R. 1984. Towards a social analysis in archaeology: Celtic society in the Iron Age of the Upper Thames valley, in B. Cunliffe and D. Miles (eds), *Aspects of the Iron Age in Central Southern Britain*, 72–88. Oxford: Oxford University Committee for Archaeology Monograph 2.

Hodson, R. 1964. Cultural groupings within the British pre-Roman Iron Age, *Proceedings of the Prehistoric Society* 30, 99–110.

Humphrey, J. 2003. *Re-searching the Iron Age*. Leicester: Leicester Archaeology Monograph 11.

Hunter, F. 2005. The image of the warrior in the British Iron Age – coin iconography in context, in Haselgrove and Wigg-Wolf 2005, 43–68.

James, S. and Millett, M. (eds.) 2001. *Britons and Romans: Advancing an Archaeological Agenda*. York: Council for British Archaeology Research Report 125.

Jones, M. 1996. Plant exploitation, in Champion and Collis 1996, 29–40.

Kristiansen, K. 1998. *Europe before History*. Cambridge: Cambridge University Press.

Millett, M. 1990. *The Romanization of Britain*. Cambridge: Cambridge University Press.

Moore, T. 2006. *Iron Age Societies in the Severn–Cotswolds: Developing Narratives of Social and Landscape Change*. Oxford: British Archaeological Reports British Series 421.

Moore, T. 2007. The Early to Later Iron Age transition in the Severn–Cotswolds: enclosing the household?, in Haselgrove and Pope 2007b, 259–278.

Nevell, M. (ed.) 1999. *Living on the Edge of Empire: Models, Methodology and Marginality. Late Prehistoric and Romano-British Rural Settlement in North-West England.* Manchester: Archaeology North-West 3.

Osgood, R., Monks, S. and Toms, J. 2000. *Bronze Age Warfare*. Stroud: Sutton.

Parker Pearson, M. 1996. Food, fertility and front doors in the first millennium BC, in Champion and Collis (1996), 117–132.

Parker Pearson, M. and Richards, C. 1994. Ordering the world: perceptions of architecture, space and time, in M. Parker Pearson and C. Richards (eds), *Architecture and Order: Approaches to Social Space*, 1–37. London: Routledge.

Parker Pearson, M. and Sharples, N. 1999. *Between Land and Sea. Excavations at Dun Vulan, South Uist*. Sheffield: Sheffield Academic Press.

Parker Pearson, M. and Thorpe, N. (eds) 2005. *Warfare, Violence and Slavery in Prehistory*. Oxford: British Archaeological Reports International Series 1374.

Piggott, S. 1966. A scheme for the Scottish Iron Age, in A.L.F Rivet (ed.), *The Iron Age in Northern Britain*, 1–15. Edinburgh: Edinburgh University Press.

Pion, P. 1990. De la chefferie à l'état? Territoires et organisation sociale dans la Vallée de l'Aisne aux âges des métaux (2200–20 av. J.-C.), in *Archéologie et Espaces (Xe Rencontres internationales d'archéologie et d'histoire, Antibes, Octobre 1989)*, 183–260. Juan-les-Pins: Éditions APDCA.

Pope, R. 2003. *Prehistoric Dwelling: Circular Structures in North and Central Britain c. 2500 BC–AD 500.* Unpublished Ph.D. thesis, University of Durham.

Powell, T.G.E. 1958. *The Celts*. London: Thames and Hudson.

Priest, V., Clay, P. and Hill, J.D. 2003. Iron Age gold from Leicestershire, *Current Archaeology* 188, 358–360.

Roymans, N. 2004. *Ethnic Identity and Imperial Power. The Batavians in the Early Roman Empire*. Amsterdam: Amsterdam Archaeological Studies 10.

Sharples, N. 1990. Late Iron Age society and continental trade in Dorset, in Duval *et al.* 1990, 299–304.

Sharples, N. 1998. *Scalloway: A Broch, Late Iron Age Settlement and Medieval Cemetery in Shetland.* Oxford: Oxbow Monograph 82.

Thomas, J. 2003. Prehistoric pit alignments and their significance in the archaeological landscape, in Humphrey 2003, 79–86.

Tilley, C. 1994. *A Phenomenology of Landscape*. Oxford: Berg.

Van der Veen, M. 1992. *Crop Husbandry Regimes: an Archaeobotanical Study of Farming in Northern England.* Sheffield: Sheffield Archaeology Monograph 3.

Webster, J. 2001. Creolizing the Roman Provinces, *American Journal of Archaeology* 105, 209–225.

Wellington, I. 2005. Placing coinage and ritual sites in their archaeological contexts: the example of northern France, in Haselgrove and Wigg-Wolf 2005, 227–246.

Williams, J. 2005. 'The newer rite is here': vinous symbolism on British Iron Age coins, in Haselgrove and Wigg-Wolf 2005, 25–41.

Wigley, A. 2007. Pitted histories: early first millennium BC pit alignments in the central Welsh Marches, in Haselgrove and Pope 2007b, 119–134.

Willis, S.H. 2006. The Later Bronze Age and Iron Age, in N. Cooper (ed.), *The Archaeology of the East Midlands. An Archaeological Resource Assessment and Research Agenda*, 89–136. Leicester: Leicester Archaeology Monograph 13.

Woolf, A. 1998. Romancing the Celts: a segmentary approach to acculturation, in R. Laurence and J. Berry (eds), *Cultural Identity in the Roman Empire*, 111–124. London: Routledge.

Woolf, G. 1993. Rethinking the Oppida, *Oxford Journal of Archaeology* 12, 223–234.

Yates, D. 2001. Bronze Age agricultural intensification in the Thames valley and estuary, in J. Brück (ed.), *Bronze Age Landscapes: Tradition and Transformation*, 65–82. Oxford: Oxbow Books.

The dynamics of social change in Later Iron Age eastern and south-eastern England *c.* 300 BC–AD 43

J.D. Hill

Introduction

Since the 1980s, little attention has been given to large-scale social explanations and narratives in British Iron Age archaeology. Debates over core–periphery models, the interpretation of hillforts, and the nature of social organisation, were – for good reasons – eclipsed by a focus on the symbolic meanings of space, structured deposition, and ritual. This shift in emphasis has, however, left a vacuum. Although the simple social evolutionary models of 'chieftains' and the use of core–periphery models for explaining change in the Late Iron Age were critiqued effectively in the mid 1980s, few alternatives have been put forward to replace them (cf. Creighton 2000).

This paper sketches a new narrative of change in south-east England from about 300 BC to the Roman conquest in AD 43. It also considers the East Midlands, although not in such great detail. Instead of offering an interpretation in terms of core–periphery relations with the expanding Roman world system, I argue that the marked changes seen in south-east England from *c.* 100 BC onwards were *not* caused by external factors (*contra* Haselgrove 1976; 1982; Cunliffe 1987; 1988; 1991). Rather, the evidence suggests that these changes should be understood in the context of long running internal developments in communities throughout central and eastern Britain. Indeed, in certain respects, what is usually seen as the 'core' might better be understood as originally a 'periphery', although the thrust of the paper is ultimately to reject such simple judgemental terms.

A basic narrative is offered here instead, with all the associated problems and weaknesses such a simple story line will contain. I would argue, however, that at present British archaeology has need of straightforward storyboards to arrange data around. We can criticise and test these later with the material, and with future theoretical perspectives.

Core–periphery models now

The core–periphery model to explain change in Late Iron Age south-east England was eloquently described by Colin Haselgrove (1982) and Barry Cunliffe (1988). At the heart of the model are clear patterns in the archaeological data, such as the limited distributions of cremation burials and imported material in south-east England, and the absence of these and apparent continuation of Middle Iron Age 'traditions' in surrounding areas. The model sees the presence of imported material in south-east England as the cause of change. In brief, there was an upsurge in commodity trade from Britain and Gaul to provide for the fast growing Roman world from 120 BC. This trade with an economically powerful 'core' economy led to major social changes in local Iron Age societies. In south-east England, existing elites quickly monopolised the control of this trade, providing raw materials to the Romans in return for wine and other luxuries. This led to economic development and increased political stratification in south-east England which, in its turn, developed into a local 'core' area, on which surrounding communities became economically – and hence politically – dependent: the periphery. In short, the model provides a simple narrative that was visually graspable in Colin Haselgrove's formulation (Fig. 1).

There have been extensive criticisms of this model, both because it is not effective in explaining social change and because the archaeological data do not support it

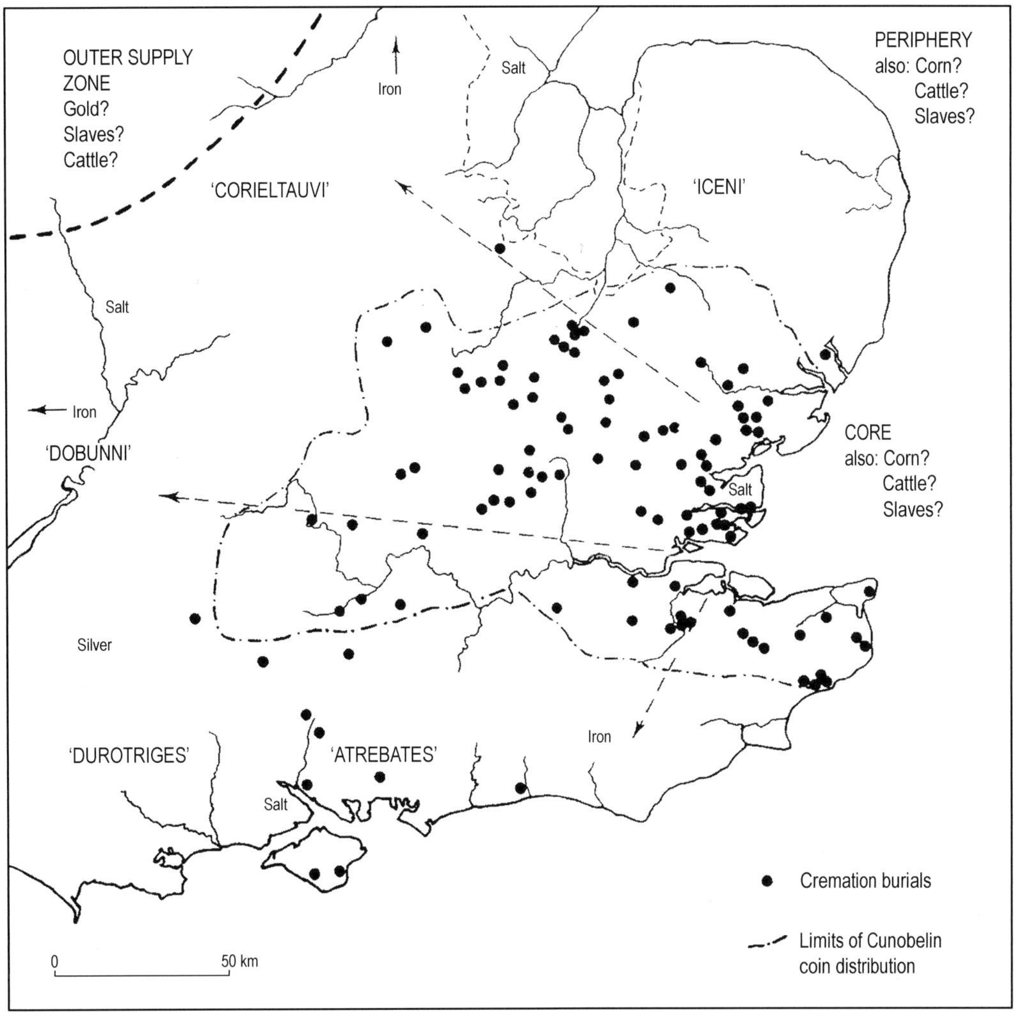

Fig. 1. The core–periphery model for explaining change in the Late Iron Age has an elegant simplicity to it that was immediately visually comprehensible in this map. Might the restricted geographical distributions of types of objects and graves that underlie this map also support other interpretations? (after Haselgrove 1982).

(Fitzpatrick 1989; 2001; Millett 1990; Sharples 1990; Woolf 1993a; Willis 1994). The core–periphery model used for Late Iron Age England was based on 1970s Structural Marxist concepts of how societies work. These ideas have been substantially modified in the last 30 years. At the same time, subsequent research on Iron Age cross-channel exchange indicates that it was not large-scale commodity trade, but took place on a more reduced scale, through pre-existing links of kinship, alliance, and gift exchange. The range of Gallic and Mediterranean objects entering southern Britain was limited, and the adoption of these objects and commodities depended on local cultural and political factors (Willis 1994; Hill 2002; cf. Dietler 1990).

Above all, the core–periphery models fail to understand the social context in which exchange and contacts with Gaul and Rome took place. They also assume that elites existed, and that these elites would naturally want wine and other Roman goods. Both are questionable assumptions. Finally, in the core–periphery models there is no time depth. No consideration is given to what was happening in either the core or the peripheral areas in Britain before the developments took place. The nature of the pre-existing societies is seen as being of little or no consequence to subsequent social changes. Ultimately the core–periphery models stand or fall on one crucial question: was the trade or exchange with the Continent evident in parts of Later Iron Age southern England the cause of social change, or simply a symptom of changes which had other causes? A recent reappraisal of the Wessex evidence by Andrew Fitzpatrick (2001) concluded that, while long-distance exchange was important in central southern England, it was not that important. This paper argues the same for eastern England.

There is also considerably more archaeological evidence for the Iron Age in eastern and south-eastern

England now than there was in the late 1970s. At that time, relatively little was known about the Middle Iron Age from the fourth to second centuries BC (broadly La Tène B–C; see Table 1) in the areas of Hertfordshire, Essex and Kent, which were identified as the 'core' in the first centuries BC and AD (La Tène D and the Julio-Claudian period). Surprisingly this is still largely the case for Hertfordshire and Kent, but much more is now known about the fourth to first centuries BC in the surrounding regions (the East Midlands, the upper Thames valley, Cambridgeshire).

This allows the development of the 'core' to be placed in a wider regional context, and within a longer time period. From examining eastern and south-eastern England as a whole over the Middle and Late Iron Age, two major patterns emerge:

1. The Late Iron Age of southern Anglia (taken here as comprising Bedfordshire, Buckinghamshire, southern Cambridgeshire, Essex, Hertfordshire, and southern Suffolk) and Kent was a very distinctive and regionally limited phenomenon. Features such as the widespread use of Gallo-Belgic coinage from *c.* 175/150 BC onwards; the later adoption of Aylesford–Swarling cremation burial rites from *c.* 100/75 BC; imported wine amphorae; and the so-called '*oppida*', are confined to this limited area of southern Anglia and Kent within the paper's study region – and to West Sussex and east Hampshire outside it.
2. This phenomenon flourished very late in the Middle/Late Iron Age. There is limited settlement evidence for many parts of southern Anglia and much of Kent before the first century BC (see also Bryant and Hamilton this volume). Most settlement and burial evidence dates to after 30/20 BC. This contrasts markedly with many parts of eastern and central England, where there is evidence of dense settlement by the fifth to third centuries BC, if not earlier. In other words, in the period from *c.* 300–100 BC, much of Kent and southern Anglia appears to have been relatively lightly settled. To the north and west, clusters of dense agricultural communities surrounded this region. In this sense, one can suggest that the 'periphery' existed and flourished before the 'core'.

	Continental chronology	*Coin Phase*	*Coin Period*			
200 BC						
c. 175–125 BC	La Tène C2	1	I	Gallo-Belgic A & B coins begin	Middle Iron Age	
c. 125–100 BC	La Tène D1	2				
c. 100–80 BC		3				
c. 80–60 BC	La Tène D2	4	II		Late Iron Age	
c. 60–50 BC		5		British gold coins begin		Caesar conquers Gaul, in south England
c. 50–20 BC		6				
c. 20 BC–AD 10	Early Roman	7	III	Classical imagery on coins		AUGUSTUS TASCIOVANUS
c. AD 10–40		8				TIBERIUS CVNOBELIN
c. AD 35–45		9				AD 43 Roman Conquest

Table 1. A chronology of change in eastern and south-eastern England in the Middle and Late Iron Age.

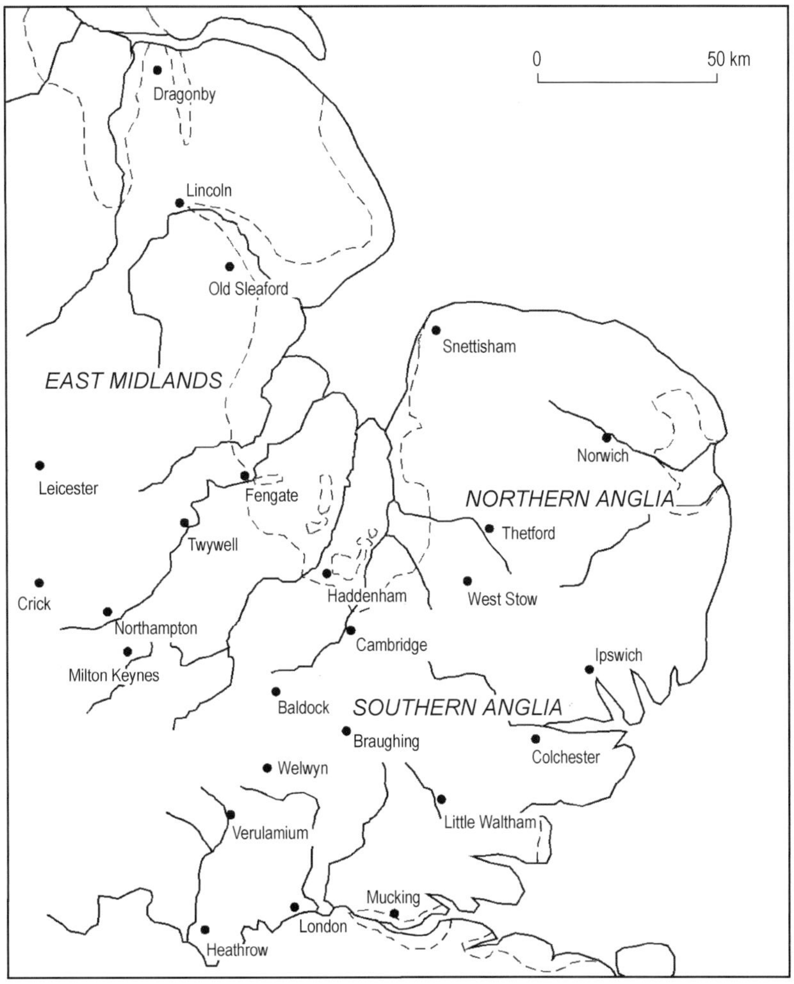

Fig. 2. Eastern England showing major rivers, wetlands, and the location of selected sites mentioned in this paper.

Middle and Late Iron Age eastern England

First, we must place developments in southern Anglia in the wider context of eastern England (Fig. 2). In the Middle and Late Iron Age, the East Midlands and northern Anglia (Norfolk, northern Suffolk etc.) had very different settlement patterns to other parts of Britain.[1] There were very few 'hillforts' or similar large enclosures, and most of these have little evidence for settlement or other activities inside them. The distribution of these large enclosures is patchy, and their functions may well have varied from one area to another. Circular and rectangular enclosures are found in north-west Norfolk on the apparent limits of a cluster of communities in that area (Davies 1996). A similar pattern of large enclosures 'on the edge' might explain the circular monuments of the Cambridge region, such as Arbury Camp, Belsar Camp and Wandlebury (Evans and Knight 2002). Large enclosures might have acted as a focus in some areas, such as Stonea Camp for communities on the southern Fen islands (Jackson and Potter 1996), or the rectangular enclosure at Fison Way, Thetford (Gregory 1992) – which probably originated earlier than the excavator realised.

The dominant settlement pattern is often described as open villages (e.g. Cunliffe 1991; 1995; Haselgrove 1999; 2004). This description covers many variations on the theme of large farms and hamlets that were not surrounded by a large bank and ditch. Settlement sizes also varied across the region. Many contained *c.* 3–4 contemporary round buildings – as at Twywell, Northamptonshire (Jackson 1975), Wardy Hill, Coveney, on the Isle of Ely (Evans 2003), or Bancroft and Wavendon Gate in Milton Keynes (Williams and Zeepvat 1994; Williams *et al.* 1996) – but larger agglomerations existed with 10–12 contemporary buildings, as at Cat's Water, Fengate near Peterborough (Pryor 1984), or even larger with 10–20 or more round buildings, like Dragonby, Lincolnshire (May 1996). Some of these large agglomerations may even have been seasonally occupied (e.g. Daventry International Rail Freight Terminal near Crick, Northamptonshire (Woodward and Hughes 2007), or, possibly, Mucking.

Fig. 3. One possible reconstruction of Cat's Water, Fengate. Variations on the theme of open agglomerated settlements – hamlets – were common across central and eastern England from c. 500 BC onwards. They varied in number of buildings, how tightly they were clustered, and their layout (drawing: Simon James).

The plans of these types of settlement varied. In some areas, very tight agglomerations of roundhouses existed, like Little Waltham, Essex (Drury 1978); in others they were more dispersed, such as West Stow, Suffolk (West 1990), or even scattered over a large area, as at Wetwang Slack, East Yorkshire (Giles this volume). Linear arrangements of 3–6 round buildings were common, as at Bancroft and Little Thetford, Ely, Cambridgeshire. For houses, pits and other structures to be located on one side of a major boundary marked by a pit alignment, ditch or track was relatively common, as for example at Twywell, and Wakerley, Northamptonshire (Jackson and Ambrose 1978;), or Pennyland, Milton Keynes (Williams 1993). Specific activity areas (e.g. D-shaped stock compounds, or clusters of pits or four-posters for storage) could be separated from one another and concentrations of houses by up to several hundred metres.

These activities, as well as round buildings ('domestic houses') would often shift location after some time (Hill 1999), creating complex histories of how a specific part of a landscape was used through the centuries. Enclosed settlement components and other enclosure types (e.g. D-shaped stock enclosures off boundaries) did exist, but usually were part of larger complexes of settlement and activity, and were often one phase in the complex history of settlement and other activity in one specific location; for example, the separate enclosures at different phases at Wakerley, Twywell, and Wardy Hill. Distinct individual enclosed settlements are found in eastern England, generally either as *de novo* settlements in previously less densely exploited areas, or – as a later development – as distinct components within the agglomerated settlements discussed above.

Communities, defined here as clusters of open agglomerated settlements in an area *c.* 10–15 km across, were widely distributed across the major river valleys of central and eastern England (e.g. the upper Thames, Ouse, and Nene), the Lincolnshire and East Yorkshire Wolds, and, probably, western Norfolk. Outside East Yorkshire, where inhumation cemeteries were common (Stead 1991a), these communities did not regularly bury their dead, and most dead people were probably either exposed or excarnated in other ways. Evidence for religious activities consists of the deliberate deposition of domestic objects, animals and occasionally human remains, focusing around the settlement (Gwilt 1997) and also at points in the landscape (Chadwick 1999; Hutcheson this volume). In the Middle Iron Age, such 'special deposits' on settlements were not usually as large or complex as those in Wessex. Human remains with cut-marks or other modifications occur in sparse quantities on a number of sites.

The settlements give the impression of successful agricultural communities practising mixed farming in landscapes with large open areas of arable and pasture suggesting that the land itself was communally owned or controlled. They tended to have undifferentiated ways of eating, few 'luxuries', and little overt indication of marked distinctions between households or individuals (Fig. 3). There is not much evidence for long-distance exchange, except for basic commodities such as iron, salt, or quernstones.

Although the material culture from these settlements appears 'poor', differences in the quantity and range of mundane items and agricultural products, or house size, may hint at relative differences in wealth and status between 'households' or larger communities (cf. Evans 2003). Overall, the impression is given of societies in which there were some differences in wealth and/or power between households/smaller groups, but these should not be exaggerated, and there was a strong emphasis on the larger community. They lack any clear evidence for the existence of a distinct elite status group or class (Hill 2003; 2006).

These societies are difficult to describe using traditional social categories. To classify these communities either as 'chiefdoms' – whether communally orientated or otherwise (Earle 1997) – or as 'hierarchical', may be very misleading (cf. Haselgrove 2004). It may be more accurate to see these groups as 'transegalitarian' (Hayden 2001), 'heterarchical' (Crumley 1995; 2001), 'segmentary societies' or 'corporate communities' (Hill 2006). Communities were probably led by a number of competing leading individuals/families – in some places few in number, in others most or all senior men/families. Power probably rested with the community and the positions of pre-eminence probably required constant negotiation. These were societies with 'leaders' but not 'rulers' (Haas 2001). It is difficult to assess how 'warlike' these societies were. It seems likely that there was a relatively high level of interpersonal violence and that carrying weapons was an important status symbol (of adult manhood); they may be better seen as communities of farmers who were warriors, rather than as warrior societies *per se*.

Eastern England is marked by an unusual concentration, in British terms, of fine metalwork including swords, shields, horse and chariot trappings, and torcs/neck-rings (Stead 1985; 1991b). These objects include the gold and silver torcs from north-west Norfolk and Ipswich; the large numbers of swords from the Thames and smaller numbers from rivers around the Fens, as at Orton Meadows near Peterborough, and Fiskerton (Field and Parker Pearson 2003); enamelled horse gear from across Norfolk (Hutcheson this volume; Worrell this volume); and unusual display objects, such as the Witham shield (from near Lincoln) or the Battersea shield and Waterloo helmet from the Thames.

Invariably described as 'prestige items', how such objects actually worked in their social settings is not as obvious as initially seems, and probably also changed over time (Hill 2003). Their existence need not indicate societies overtly acknowledging individual power, nor imply a 'simple' chiefly/aristocratic model of society. Rather than personal prestige, they may embody group wealth and power: the special paraphernalia of specific social and religious roles and offices representing or serving whole communities. Whatever the actual situation, such objects, especially the large number of gold torcs from north-west Norfolk, provide a crude measure of the wealth of these communities *c.* 400–100 BC (Fig. 4).

These dense clusters of agricultural settlement were not evenly spread over eastern England, nor were they all the same. A snapshot of the region in about 300 or 200 BC would reveal variations in material culture, settlement form, ritual, and social organisation between the clusters. The concentration of inhumation cemeteries in East Yorkshire, and of torcs and ringworks in north-west Norfolk, provide two obvious examples. Others include the very different styles of pottery found in East Yorkshire ('Arras Culture' pottery), Lincolnshire (Sleaford–Dragonby ware), Northamptonshire–Leicestershire–Bedfordshire (East Midlands Scored ware, with Hunsbury–Draughton bowls), and Norfolk–Suffolk–southern Cambridgeshire (East Anglian plain ware). By implication, these clusters of communities formed part of larger familial, political and cultural alignments or networks, some of which we might call tribes. However, few of the groupings seen archaeologically between 300–100 BC seem to equate to the 'tribes' or civitates apparent around the time of the Roman conquest. Similar settlement patterns, social forms, and trajectories to those found in the East Midlands can be seen in the upper Thames valley.

Transhumance and holes in the settlement pattern

The snapshot around *c.* 300–200 BC would also show that there were dense clusters of settlements in some areas, but not others (Fig. 5). These occur in the major river valleys (Ouse, Nene, Welland, Cam, Lark etc.), in the Lincolnshire and East Yorkshire Wolds, and in south-east Essex. West Norfolk is potentially another. Large areas of the region, however, have little evidence for densely settled communities, including parts of southern Anglia,

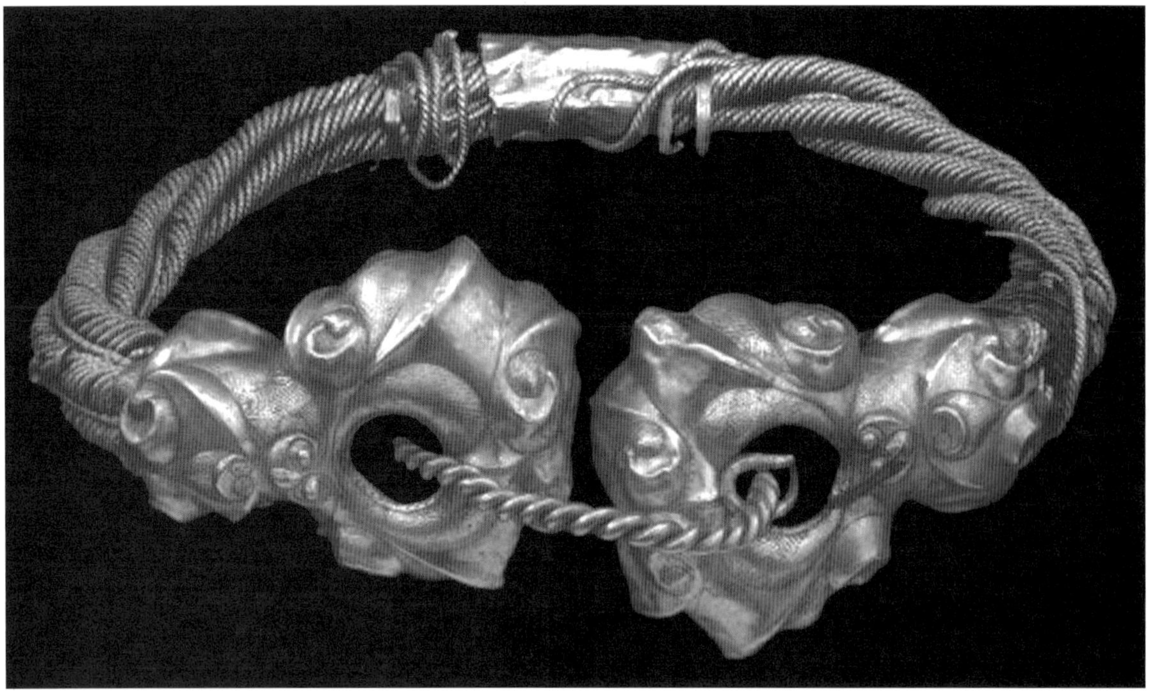

Fig. 4. The so-called grotesque torc from Snettisham hoard L (courtesy of the Trustees of the British Museum).

the Fens and lower Thames valley, and parts of Leicestershire, Nottinghamshire and south Yorkshire. These areas – and the smaller gaps between clusters – may have some settlement evidence or artefact findspots, but the character of Middle Iron Age 'occupation' is generally quite different from the areas with dense agglomerated settlements. It may consist of 'stray' metal artefacts, tiny quantities of pottery in the soil or accidentally found in features of a later date, individual isolated features, clusters of structures and features (four-posters, compounds, pits, salt production or other 'industrial' features), a few houses, or a few open or enclosed small settlements with one or two houses. There is evidence for specialist resource procurement sites in these areas, the best known being the salt making sites in the Fens, Essex marshes and other coastal marshes (Lane and Morris 2001).

Unlike the areas with communities of agglomerated 'villages' surrounded by intensively utilised agricultural landscapes, these apparently 'empty' areas were probably exploited economically and agriculturally in a much less intensive manner by the relatively few permanent settlements contained within them and, especially, by people visiting them, but not living there all year round. Interestingly, several of these areas possess evidence of Late Bronze Age settlements and field systems that continued into the Early Iron Age, but then appear to have been abandoned.

This evidence might suggest considerable seasonal transhumance of animal herds and their keepers along with other regular movements of people into these much less densely settled areas as part of the economic, social, and religious strategies of Iron Age communities. Seasonal movements with cattle and sheep over short (<10 km) but also long (up to 100 km or more) distances may have been commonplace. Salt making involved groups living away from home. Work parties travelling away from 'home' for short or long periods probably also exploited other specialist resources such as stone, iron, timber, fur, feathers, clay, and reeds (Evans and Serjeantson 1988).

These activities need not all have taken place in the summer. Reed harvesting, for example, is traditionally a winter activity. These movements would have had to be scheduled into the agricultural year, some fitting in with seasonal transhumance, others arranged on a separate work-party basis. People might regularly have travelled long distances for exchange, and to attend feasts, funerals and ceremonies held by other communities, or for similar social and ritual gatherings in 'empty areas', leading, for instance, to the ritual deposition of fine metalwork in parts of the Fens and lower Thames.

Within this broad scenario, a range of situations can be envisaged. It does, however, imply that the political and economic base of a community was not just the area immediately round about, and that potentially large numbers of people (possibly from specific age groups and genders) would be away from their permanent home base for parts of a year. It also envisages people, and sometimes their animals, moving through other communities as they travelled to and from their final destinations, and meeting members of other communities potentially far removed from their own. If correct, this scenario has implications for how we are to understand the relations between communities and the workings of exchange and marriage. It also raises questions about how issues of 'ownership' and 'rights' to graze, hunt, fell timber, or make salt were negotiated and organised in the less densely exploited and settled areas of the landscape.

In thinking about these types of movements, there is a tendency to concentrate on overland movement, but the potential for travelling long distances by river, around the coast, and across the Channel, should not be forgotten (cf. Cunliffe 1995).

Settlement expansion and moving people: a key feature of La Tène Europe?

An important feature of the Middle and Late Iron Age is the increasing amount of permanent settlement in many parts of Britain (Hill 1995; Haselgrove 1999). This process involved both local infilling of gaps around and next to existing settlement clusters and wholesale settlement of larger areas of landscape that previously only supported low densities of inhabitants all year round. Areas which witnessed this infill of permanent settlement often have small enclosed dwelling sites like Mingies Ditch, Oxfordshire (Allen and Robinson 1993) or Haddenham, Cambridgeshire (Evans 1997), whilst older areas still maintained open, agglomerated settlements. There is evidence for economic specialisation in some of the areas into which population expanded (Haselgrove 1989; Sharples 1990; Hill 1995). The majority of so-called Late Iron Age *oppida* in Britain appear to have emerged in areas with little evidence for dense occupation in previous centuries (Haselgrove 1976; Hill 1995).

Settlement and population expansion is potentially the key underlying social process for understanding change in Later Iron Age temperate Europe. Its causes can no longer simply be seen as an increasing number of people. Various studies indicate that a given society's perception of 'too many' people is relative, and provide examples of situations where 'too many' people have not produced migration and settlement expansion. They also show that even where population is growing rapidly, this is often a social strategy to cope with particular perceived problems or to achieve certain socially defined goals rather than a biologically determined given. For example, more children might be desired in order to have more family members to increase agricultural production, or to gain more marriage partners.

A simple notion of settlement expansion hides the potentially different realities of this process across Britain and other parts of Europe. Even if they are not directly answerable archaeologically, we need to think about these processes in the following terms:

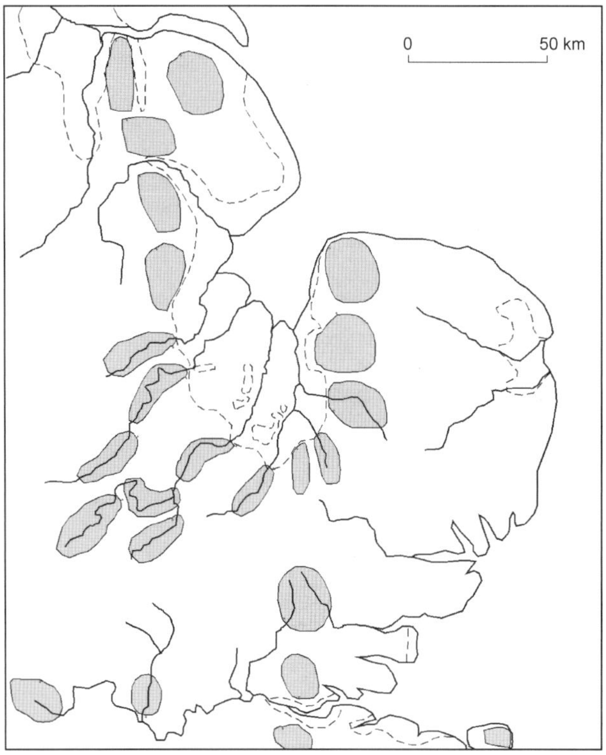

Fig. 5. Eastern England c. 200 BC: an approximation of where there were clusters of communities with agglomerated settlements and intense agricultural activities.

- Who was moving?
- Why were they moving?
- How far were they moving?
- How many people were moving at one time?
- What relationship did they have with the area they were moving to?
- What relationships did they maintain with the area they came from?
- What were their relations with people they moved through?

In southern and eastern England, the process was rarely one of whole communities or 'tribes' moving *en masse*. Rather, it generally seems to have been piecemeal, with small groups, perhaps one or a few families, moving. Their movement has also to be set in the context of the widespread transhumance and other travelling that was a regular part of social life in the region. In many cases, new settlements may have taken the form of permanent dwellings in areas that were previously only visited seasonally, albeit raising questions about the subsequent organisation of transhumance and other work-party journeys into these areas. In other instances, however, new settlements may have been established in areas

Fig. 6. Obverse and reverse of a Gallo-Belgic A gold stater. Gallo-Belgic A coins were in circulation c. 175/150 BC onwards and are probably contemporary with some of the Snettisham torcs (courtesy of the Trustees of the British Museum).

where the incomers may have had little or no previous links. Many of them were probably satellites, infill from and around existing permanent settlements, but there remains the possibility that some people travelled very long distances in the process. Some of them even probably crossed the sea. Similar social processes were at work in north-west Europe at the time and north-west Europeans – some of them from Belgic Gaul – could easily have settled in southern England. It certainly was not the case, however, that continental Europe was 'full' and that people consequently overflowed into England. It is just as likely that people born in England moved across the Channel in the opposite direction, and that people from one part of Britain moved to another.

The different reasons that led people to move are still unclear. Inheritance systems, property rights and types of agricultural/economic strategies are all potential causes of expansion. The movement of people and expansion of settlement could simply be due to a change that affected particular systems of inheritance and 'property ownership/rights' having spread across western Europe after *c.* 500–300 BC. Such a change might have created a need for those who did not inherit – or otherwise lost access to land or property rights – to move elsewhere. Another reason for the permanent settlement of previously underused areas may have been to increase production, or more easily to maintain 'control' of this resource for the community.

A particular tension in many Iron Age communities may have been the tendency or desire of certain elements – individuals, single households, and small kin groups – for more independence and control over resources. This might have been a major incentive for establishing new settlements. In southern Anglia, there almost seems to have been a tradition that to do something new – to create a new or different social form – was dependent on moving to a fresh location.

As noted above, large parts of Kent, Hertfordshire and Essex seem to have had relatively little permanent settlement *c.* 300–100 BC. People must have been moving into these areas, providing the background to the changes that took place there from 150/100 BC onwards. However, settlement expansion was not the sole cause of the developments seen in southern Anglia. Other parts of Britain experienced similar settlement expansion (e.g. the Trent valley, eastern Norfolk), but not the radical cultural and social changes seen in southern Anglia. What happened in the Late Iron Age there was one possible reaction to these processes, playing out another feature of Iron Age societies in Britain: regionality. The creation and maintenance of regionally distinct forms of material culture, settlement form, burial rites and, by definition, different ways of organising societies, was a major feature of Iron Age Britain. Such regionally limited social practices can be seen in southern Anglia and Kent from *c.* 150/100 BC.

It is these distinctive social practices – and the types of pottery and other objects they created – that set this area apart, and which led to older interpretations of invasion or core–periphery. At one level, the region was no different from the other areas of Mid to Late Iron Age Britain that had locally distinctive patterns of settlement, material culture and ritual. What was different, however, is that the inhabitants of southern Anglia and Kent adapted and borrowed parts of a cultural and social package from across the Channel to create their own particular identities.

New people and new societies: southern Anglia from 150 BC

The initial creation of these regional distinctions was not just a product of settlement expansion. The boundaries of the southern Anglian and Kentish cultural phenomenon can be seen archaeologically in the sharp limits to the distribution of its key features: Gallo-Belgic coinage, early wheel-turned pottery, cremation burials, imported pottery, and amphorae. The limits of this distribution are essentially the eastern watershed of the Great Ouse, the southern Fens and the southern watershed of the River Waveney. This boundary is initially seen with the appearance of the first gold coins to be used extensively in Britain: Gallo-Belgic A and B types from *c.* 175–150 BC onwards (Fitzpatrick 1992; Haselgrove 1993), probably closely contemporary with their appearance in Belgic Gaul (Fig. 6). There is evidence that Gallo-Belgic B coins were minted in Britain and it is likely that Gallo-Belgic A coins were produced both in southern Britain and Belgic Gaul.

The main distribution of Gallo-Belgic A coins – and also of later Gallo-Belgic types – is geographically limited. It includes parts of south Bedfordshire, south

Cambridgeshire, north-west Essex and southern Suffolk, as well as Kent and Hertfordshire (Fig. 7). The former areas are river valleys draining into the Fens with evidence of settlement agglomerations from *c.* 600 BC onwards. The distribution of Gallo-Belgic A, then, does not simply reflect a mixture of 'old' settlement 'hot-spots' with few coin finds and 'new areas' with many coins. Rather the invention/adoption – or just the deposition – of these coins was one way for some established communities to the south of the Fens to define themselves as different from other neighbouring groups to the north and west. This deposition of individual gold coins in the second century BC by people living to the south of the Fens contrasts markedly with the deposition of large quantities of gold and silver made into torcs in north-west Norfolk at essentially the same time.

Coins

Iron Age communities clearly had extensive and complex exchange and gift relations that did not need coins, since they functioned successfully for centuries without them. As such, coins were not required for these existing exchanges. Rather coins imply new types of relationship between groups and individuals, relationships that were different or additional to those already taking place in other parts of 'coinless' eastern England. Coins were probably not the means to facilitate the exchange of goods. Instead, they may have helped to articulate developing ties of clientage and dependency, and potentially to create new ancestral and familial links (Fitzpatrick 1992).

These new relationships might have been less socially and culturally encumbered than existing forms of social exchange, which involved the gift of labour, sharing food and feasting, marriage, or giving 'entangled' objects such as pots, swords, and torcs with their possibly complex biographies. The gift of a standard token such as a Gallo-Belgic stater from one person to another was potentially exactly that – a token of a relationship that had little other direct function, biography, or easy way to change into other goods or services.

A product of core–periphery thinking is the tendency to see foreign objects, such as Gallo-Belgic A coins – if indeed they were a foreign invention – and ideas as arriving first around the Thames estuary and the south coast, and then spreading outwards. There is no evidence, however, to support this idea. The deposition pattern could equally support a simultaneous adoption across the region, or even the view that Gallo-Belgic A coins were first used (and minted) by the old-established agricultural communities at the edge of their distribution in south-east England (*c.* 175–150 BC onwards), only later spreading to the south and east.

The latter model could imply that the initial impetus for links with north-east France came from the established communities of southern Bedfordshire,

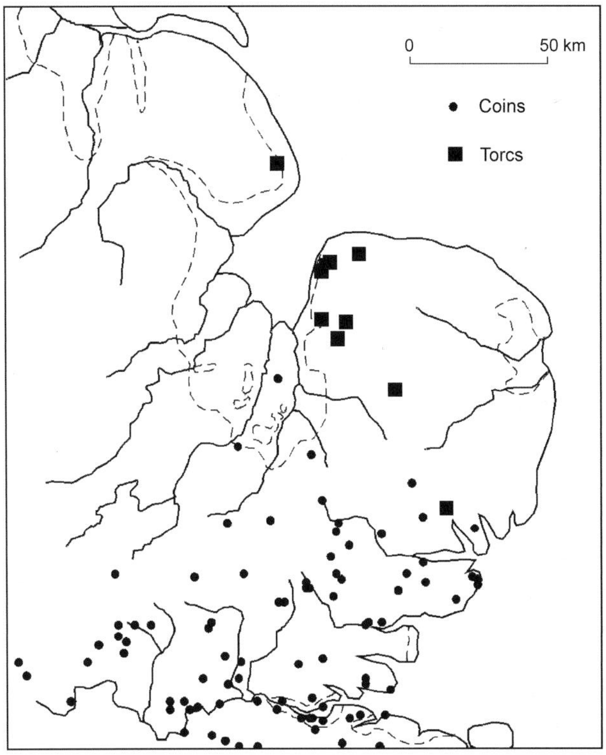

Fig. 7. The distribution of Gallo-Belgic A and B coins along with that of torcs (c. 175–150 to 75 BC). The limits of the main Gallo-Belgic A and B distribution are closely mirrored by later Gallo-Belgic coins, Aylesford-Swarling cremation burials, and the other defining features of the Late Iron Age in south-east England.

southern Cambridgeshire, and north-west Essex (and from similar communities in West Sussex and east Hampshire). If so, these contacts – and the tendencies associated with them – probably spread rapidly into the previously less densely settled north-western fringes of southern Anglia, since there are no fewer early coins there than elsewhere in other parts of the region (Haselgrove 1987). What specific factors drove – or allowed – the inhabitants of southern Bedfordshire, southern Cambridgeshire, and north-west Essex to use and deposit coins, whilst neighbouring groups of communities did not, is unclear, but hints at differences in social organisation.

This axis continued to mark a sharp 'border' for the Late Iron Age southern Anglian phenomenon in later years. The geographically restricted area where Gallo-Belgic A to D coin finds are common is closely mirrored by the later distribution of Aylesford–Swarling cremation burials, imported wine amphorae, and, ultimately, the limits of the Eastern Kingdom's main coin distribution (Haselgrove 1982). All follow the basic geographical limits set by the distribution of the earliest coins. Late Iron Age southern Anglia should not, however, be seen as an homogenous entity, nor as a single political unit before *c.* AD 10, and Cunobelin's kingdom. The Late Iron Age communities of southern Bedfordshire, southern Cambridgeshire, and north-west Essex differed in substantial ways from those found further south (Hill *et al.* 1999).

The use of coins, and by inference the new types of social relations they imply, intensified in Hertfordshire, Essex and Kent from 125/100 BC onwards. The numbers of coins appear to increase in these areas, and from *c.* 80 BC onwards new types of local coinages were minted in southern Anglia (Period II in Haselgrove's 1993 developmental scheme). Between *c.* 80–20 BC, a number of different entities or individuals issued coins in the region. Many of these local series were short-lived and do not equate with later coin issuing groups or personalities. Coins may give an appearance of large, stable political units or 'tribes', but the entities involved were more probably fluid networks of individuals and small groups – new 'tribes' that might cut across other existing affiliations – caused by creating and marking new types of power relationships and ties between the members of these networks – networks often articulated and created by powerful, or at least ambitious, individuals and small groups.

Settlement

From the late second to early first century BC, the 'centres of gravity' apparently moved from southern Bedfordshire, southern Cambridgeshire and north-west Essex further to the south and east. Rich burials, coin issuing, and exotic imported objects concentrate in Hertfordshire and southern Essex from the early to mid first century BC onwards. Only from 150/100 BC – perhaps even later – is a significant increase in permanent settlement evident in many parts of Hertfordshire. Sites with wheel-turned pottery are far more numerous than those with earlier hand-made pottery, and sites with early wheel-turned pottery (i.e. before 30/20 BC) are considerably less common than those with later pottery. In this context, the new forms of social relations shown in food and drink, burial, settlement and coins after 125/100 BC were related in some way to a potentially quite rapid influx of people to live permanently in the area. In this situation, tendencies already established in south Bedfordshire, south Cambridgeshire and north-west Essex, seen through the use of coins and the cross channel links that they reveal, were amplified and their trajectories potentially (radically) changed.

From this time, a different settlement pattern can be seen in much of southern Anglia, contrasting with the open agglomerated settlements of surrounding areas. Many settlements appear to be smaller units or single 'farmsteads' that are often enclosed. Some heavily enclosed units are known, as at Orsett Cock, Essex (Carter 1998), Gorhambury and Prae Wood, St Albans (Bryant and Niblett 1997), or Foxholes Farm, Hertford (Partridge 1989). There were also some larger enclosed communities in the first century BC or earlier, notably at Stansted Airport, Essex (Havis and Brooks 2004), and at Gatesbury, on the eastern side of the Braughing complex (Bryant this volume). The decision to enclose these new settlements with banks and ditches was a marked break with the unenclosed larger settlements in neighbouring regions, and these boundaries presumably played an important role in the self-definition of the (new) communities they contained (cf. Hingley 1990; Bevan 1997; Taylor 1997). Late Iron Age field systems have been suggested in several parts of southern Anglia (Williamson 1987), whilst excavations in the Ouse and Cam valleys indicate the existence of a greater number of paddocks, small enclosures and systems of tracks and boundaries from 50–1 BC – a marked compartmentalisation of space seen in other Late Iron Age landscapes. The more dispersed pattern of smaller settlement units and field systems might imply a different way of distributing and controlling/owning land than in the open agglomerated settlements with their lack of field systems and potentially communal ownership of land.

Many of these enclosed settlements belonged to larger agglomerations of settlements and activities. In the past these agglomerations have often been labelled *oppida* (e.g. Cunliffe 1991), with all the implications for proto-urbanisation and social complexity that word has come to carry.[2] However, *no* settlement or agglomeration in Late Iron Age southern Anglia is similar to the sites termed *oppida* in central France, southern Germany or the Czech Republic, such as Mont Beuvray, Manching or Stradonice (see also Bryant this volume). Nor do they resemble the rather different sites also called *oppida* in north-east France, such as Condé-sur-Suippe or Villeneuve-Saint-Germain (Haselgrove this volume), although Silchester and, perhaps, Abingdon are potentially more like these sites.

Rather, Late Iron Age large settlements in southern Anglia appear to be of two basic types. One comprises denser agglomerations of settlements and other specialist activities compared to surrounding areas, as much as *c.* 10–20 km across, as at Baldock or Welwyn (Bryant and Niblett 1997; Bryant this volume), and hence a variant on the clustering of communities of open settlements found elsewhere in eastern England. The other consists of smaller sites that seem to be variants of the individual open agglomerated settlements found elsewhere in the study region, as for example at Braughing or Heybridge, Essex.

Eating and drinking

Later developments seen in the pottery also point to new forms of social relationships. New shapes of pottery made using the wheel were adopted in southern Anglia from *c.* 125–75 BC onwards (Fig. 8), implying that new types of ceramic 'tools' were needed to prepare and serve foods and drinks in new ways. Drinking alcohol appears

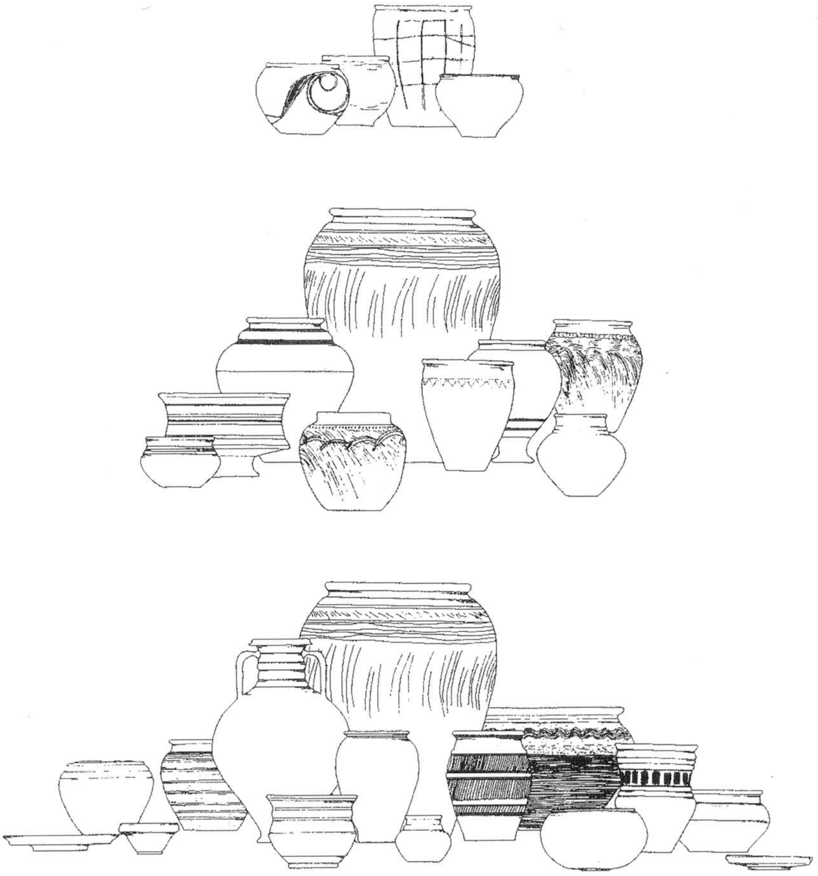

Fig. 8. The changing range and shapes of pottery used in southern Anglia from c. 200 BC onwards. The changes reflect increasing use of the wheel to make pottery and the growing presence of vessels made in France and Italy. More crucially, however, they reflect changes in the way foods and drinks were prepared, cooked, and served (drawing: S. Jundi).

to have taken on a new social role that required new specialised vessels to serve and drink from, such as pedestal urns and tall cylindrical jars. Food and drink were probably key means to creating and sustaining social relations in all Iron Age societies. What was different in southern Anglia was the exact ways – and on which social occasions – food and drink were used in these roles. Social drinking and eating in these communities took on new functions and needed new vessels as social props. This perhaps was associated with an increasing use of beer drinking to pay for mobilising work parties and for constructing and reinforcing relatively small social solidarities.

Eating and drinking became a key area in which southern Anglian communities differed from their neighbours. Meals may have become less communal in the sense of many sharing the contents of one or a few bowls at a Middle Iron Age meal. The types of cooking changed, especially from the later first century BC, with steaming, frying, and other methods increasingly replacing or augmenting the standard stews/soups and porridges of Middle Iron Age cuisine. These changes hint at potentially important increasing differences in gender, age, and servant/master relations between communities in southern Anglia compared to more 'traditional' areas elsewhere in England. The meal also increasingly became a tournament of value, an arena for competing in and overtly displaying differences in wealth and success between individuals, families and groups. Differentiated cuisine and styles of consumption became an important diacritical symbolic device to create and mark differences in social status or rank (cf. Dietler 2001).

It was this process that created the demand for the Gallic and Mediterranean objects, foods, and drink that crossed the Channel and drove the exchange relations with distant groups and individuals to acquire them – those key features so strong in core–periphery accounts. In reality, most of the imports found in Late Iron Age southern Britain belong to a very restricted range of meal-related objects: containers to enhance the serving of food and drink, objects for preparing beverages, for amusement at the dinner party, or exotic food stuffs and

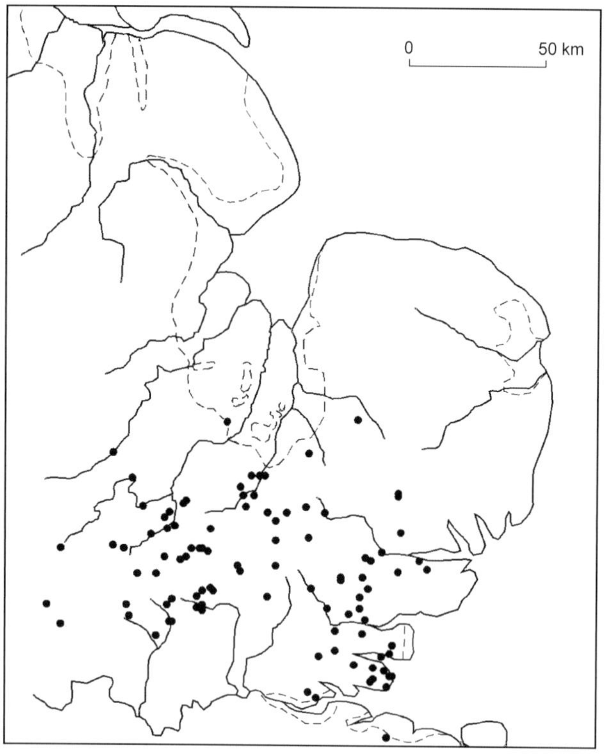

Fig. 9. The distribution of pre-Roman cremation burials of the first century BC and first century AD in eastern England.

drink itself. Many of the others relate to dress and appearance. Wine, Gallic finewares, and Roman metal vessels were present in some southern British communities because there was an internally driven demand for them generated by the changing social and cultural role that the meal played in these communities. Their absence from other parts of southern Britain probably has more to do with the lack or reduced scale of these internally driven processes, rather than the difficulty of obtaining imports.[3]

Cremation burial

This important diacritical symbolic role of the meal in southern Anglian and Kentish communities was also sanctioned through its central role in the new burial rite of cremation. The rite of burying (some of) the cremated remains of (some) people with accompanying grave goods is one defining characteristic of southern Anglia and Kent from 100/75 BC onwards. Small cemeteries away from settlements, often with no more than 10–12 burials made over only one or two generations, become common (Fig. 9). This is in marked contrast to traditional mortuary rites across eastern England that left no archaeological trace and probably involved exposure/excarnation. The new rite of Aylesford–Swarling type cremations was similar to mortuary rites in parts of Belgic Gaul. The burial rite, along with shared styles of ceramics, foodways, coins and other objects such as brooches point to strong links and shared social practices between parts of southern England and parts of north-east France (see also Hamilton this volume).

These links need not imply mass movements of people (in either direction) as the only possible explanation for this change in mortuary practice. Ethnography provides examples of rites, like dances and stories, featuring as items of exchange and gift in much the same way as tangible objects or people. It also provides examples of communities emulating the rituals of a group perceived as powerful or successful.

In addition, mortuary practice was often used as a strategy to mark or create social distinctions throughout Iron Age temperate Europe. Variations in mortuary ritual (inhumation *vs* cremation, barrow or flat grave, close to or away from other dead) were consciously used to define differences between individuals or communities, and equally to express similarities. In many cases the differences in burial rite marked or created differences between types of people in the same community such as elites or special individuals. In other situations, they were used to mark and create differences between large groups of people or communities, as with the geographically restricted use of inhumation burial in East Yorkshire, *c.* 400–100 BC. The Aylesford–Swarling cremations operated as a strategy in both ways. They clearly distinguished the communities using them from others in eastern and southern England who did not, but at the same time not everyone in the group appears to have been cremated, or – if they were cremated – then buried in exactly the same way.

Creating new or different communities of (some of) the dead that were visibly placed in the landscape in small discrete barrow cemeteries probably initially represented a conscious decision by some living people to break with existing mortuary rites. These new communities of the dead make very visible archaeologically the new communities of the living that had been evolving in southern Anglia and Kent over preceding generations. The limited geographical distribution of the new rite further emphasises the distinctly different ways of life in southern Anglia and Kent compared to surrounding communities. The cemeteries also hint at changes in land rights/ownership, and household/group organisation implied in other evidence. A relatively small community of the dead was now placed within the agricultural landscape. The small size of the burying group potentially reflected the smaller social group or basic household unit emphasised in southern Anglia compared to the larger household/kin groups/cultural alignments of earlier and still existing communities in other parts of eastern and southern England. The placing of a small burying community in the landscape might imply strategies to tie the dead of a specific living group (a household or lineage?) to particular parcels of land.

Social stratification

There is strong evidence for overtly, and potentially deliberately, different forms through which society was organised in these southern Anglian communities. In contrast to other parts of eastern England with their potentially group/community orientated power structures, Late Iron Age groups in southern Anglia appear more individualising, with greater emphasis on the small group (small family units) and individual power, aggrandisement and networking. Variations in wealth, rank or power between people and communities were certainly more clearly acknowledged, and probably were actually greater in southern Anglia.

The numbers and types of grave goods found in the burials provide the clearest evidence for the hierarchical, or at least well-differentiated, nature of these southern Anglia societies (cf. Haselgrove 1982). The variation in the type and quantity of objects buried in cremations reveals something of the disparity in wealth and success between small kin groups/families represented by the burial groups. The overt, archaeologically visible display of these differences in wealth begs the question of whether these divisions were present in earlier Iron Age communities – but were not previously visible – or whether they are a genuinely new development, as is the mortuary rite through which we can see them. I would suggest the latter, arguing that the increasing use of material culture and social practices to make and create distinctions between people in the same communities was a major change in Late Iron Age southern Anglia. This is a way of thinking about the world that makes it possible to establish more marked social inequalities, a mode of using material culture and practices not commonly expressed in earlier, Middle Iron Age communities. It also suggests that the communities of the Late Iron Age of southern Anglia were potentially unlike their ancestors in how they were organised.

The evidence from first-century BC burials in southern Anglia implies a burial hierarchy. First, there are a small number of 'wealthy' Welwyn-type graves, with Italian amphorae, firedogs, French pottery, and Roman bronze, silver and even glass vessels (Fig. 10). Second, there are potentially middle-ranking tiers of graves with fewer and

Fig. 10. A reconstruction of the Welwyn Garden City burial excavated in 1965. This grave exemplifies the changes that took place in first-century BC southern Anglia. It is a cremation burial of an individual who was buried c. 40–20 BC with substantially more objects than most people. It shows the new styles of eating and entertaining and the ways in which exotic foreign beverages and tableware could be used to mark or create social distinctions. The grave also contains possible evidence of close personal/political relationships between important Britons and Romans – in the form of a Roman silver cup (courtesy of the Trustees of the British Museum).

different objects, such as silver brooches, buckets and mirrors. Finally, there are burials with groups of local pots and brooches, and many graves with few or no items at all. Comparing whole cemeteries, the disparities in the 'wealth' buried with different small burial communities/families may not be as exaggerated before 20/10 BC as is sometimes assumed, although variations certainly do exist. Many cemeteries have one or two 'wealthy' graves with many pots that may not be too far removed from those with buckets, a few metal vessels or mirrors.

It may nevertheless be important that these first-century BC cemeteries are less well-equipped than the Welwyn-type graves with their imported wine amphorae. When assessing the wealth expressed in these graves, it is difficult to establish how 'rich' they are compared to other Iron Age individuals or communities. A decorated mirror or many amphorae might not constitute such 'expensive' grave goods as first appears. We do not know how much labour, surplus or extracted tribute was needed – if this is how it worked – to provide such items. In crude terms, would the Welwyn Garden City burial and its contents 'cost' more or less than a single Snettisham gold torc? This might suggest that, before 20/10 BC, there were differences in success, wealth and political influence between different families/burying communities in southern Anglia. However, these may not represent a rigid hierarchical or class system, and the gap between the most successful and averagely successful families may not (yet) have been that great.

The location of the richest Welwyn-type burials seems to have moved over time (Haselgrove 1982). A few of the rich burials with imported amphorae in south Cambridgeshire, south Bedfordshire and north-west Essex may date to the late second or early first century BC (e.g. Lord's Bridge, near Cambridge), as does the Baldock burial in north Hertfordshire with its Dressel 1A amphorae (Stead and Rigby 1986). But by the mid first century BC, the richest graves are in central Hertfordshire: at Welwyn A and B, Welwyn Garden City, and Hertford Heath, all with Dressel 1B amphorae (Stead 1967). This implies that the location of the most dominant and successful small groups in southern Anglia shifted rapidly in only a few generations. It also hints at the highly competitive and unstable nature of political success in these communities, and possibly at the novelty or creativity that typified their political economies. It may, however, be wrong to call the Welwyn-type graves prior to 20/10 BC, *Fürstengräber* or 'princely graves'. These groups might not have had this form of leadership and political institutions at all.

Contingency and not determinism

It is important not to see these developments as the product of a single evolutionary process. There is always a danger when we know the end point to a historical process that we construct everything that precedes it as inevitably leading to that moment. This teleological danger is particularly acute in studies of the Late Iron Age in eastern England, where the kingdom of Cunobelin (*c.* AD 10–40), the Roman conquest, and the political organisation of Roman Britain provide a known end point to which all previous history must logically, simply, and directly lead. However, as recent studies stress, in Wittgenstein's words, history is a curve whose direction is constantly changing. This is to view history as the product of human actions that are often at odds with each other, are internally contradictory, and have consequences unforeseen by their creators. Individuals also have the capacity to reflect on their situation and to accept the *status quo*, or try to change it. It is difficult when writing archaeological accounts, especially of the basic storyboard type offered here, to acknowledge individuals and human agency, but we can however recognise that there was no single, direct trajectory of social change that led inevitably to Cunobelin and the Roman conquest. Contingency, agency, dialectic, and accident all constantly operated, ensuring that the social trajectories in Later Iron Age Eastern England were neither predictable nor linear.

Kingship: a novel social experiment?

There may have been several radical shifts in those trajectories, cause by various factors between the third and first centuries BC and not simply by external forces or individuals such as Caesar, or the Roman conquest of southern Gaul. One such shift in these trajectories was the creation of kingship in southern Britain from *c.* 30/20 BC onward. This may be an example of a more general phenomenon in middle-order societies, where a social order with leaders changes to one led by rulers (Haas 2001). The different nature of Late Iron Age kingship has been emphasised by John Creighton (2000), who attributes many of its features to the rulers being client kings of Rome and having been hostages or 'apprentices' (*obsides*) in Rome itself.

The new political institution we may call kingship is visible archaeologically through coins, new types of site, and a massive increase in the quantity of material culture. These changes suggest a new political situation. It is not simply the social and political institutions present in the area *c.* 80–40 BC writ larger, more stable or more hierarchical. Nor was it an inevitable outcome of changes set in place a century or even 50 years before. Even if the increasing social stratification evident in parts of south-east England from the early first century BC onward was hard to stop, this need not have ended in a new political institution, nor taken the particular form it did. The political institutions created by Tasciovanus and Tincomarus in southern England in the 30s or 20s BC were potentially and deliberately very different forms of dominance and authority from those that existed before. Perhaps it was an attempt to free a dominant group from existing ideologies, obligations and religious institutions. This may also mean that the new kingdoms established in the 30s or 20s BC were potentially unstable up to AD 43, as the proliferation of named individuals issuing coins at the close of both Tasciovanus' and Cunobelin's coin sequences seems to suggest. They were new types of political entities that potentially made up the rules up as they went along.

To what extent Rome created these new entities is a key area for debate (Creighton 2000). The new political and cultural realities of Roman power in France, Julius Caesar's military expeditions to southern England, and the changing power structures of Gallo-Roman elites were clearly all factors shaping events in Britain. Augustus' creation of a new political entity in Rome could have provided an important model and inspiration for particular Britons to draw on to forge a politics of pre-eminent individual rulers. That the key changes in the emergence of kingship seem to take place after Augustus' succession implies that this, rather than any earlier political settlement with Rome after Julius Caesar's expeditions, was the key factor.

This need not, however, be a determining factor. It is difficult to see Roman influence being responsible for the precise forms of authority manifested in southern Britain after 20 BC. The first kings of the 'Eastern' and 'Southern' kingdoms, Tasciovanus and Tincomarus, may indeed have had close relationships with Rome and Romans. They may even have been clients and shared some features of ideology, dress and court paraphernalia with other client kings around the edges of the Roman Empire (Creighton 2000). However, even if Tasciovanus and Tincomarus were Roman clients, the particular forms of political institutions they created in southern Britain were unique inventions, intentional experiments with kingship by these British individuals and their associates. They did not directly copy either Roman or Gallo-Roman things, or previous institutions in Britain or Gaul. Rather they creatively borrowed elements from Rome, Gaul, and the past.

The altered nature of authority can be seen in new types of coins and also on the ground. The coins of the period show a marked concern with naming the ruler, their personal claimed ancestry, and a new symbolism of Roman images (Fig. 11; Creighton 2000; Williams 2001; 2002). These are clear breaks with the past, suggesting new power relations between an individual and others that did not exist – or exist in such a marked form – before. The concern with claiming an ancestry by stating X is 'son' of Y indicates how important it was for the position of authority to be passed within families. This preoccupation with indicating a real or claimed ancestry on (some of) the coins implies this was a new political concern and that the new rulers felt they needed to remind people (or least coin users) who they were (Williams 2002).

The use of classical imagery has many implications

Fig. 11. The material manifestations of kingship? A silver coin of Tasciovanus (BMC 1681) showing the classical-inspired imagery (courtesy of the Trustees of the British Museum).

(Creighton 2000). Important here is that these coins attest to the creative use of a new and changing iconographic language on a key material token to articulate the social networks through which the rulers operated.[4] This in turn may imply that a new or different ideological framework was evolved to justify and legitimate the new forms of dominance and power. Classical imagery and Latin names on the coins may give a misleading impression of the extent to which this ruling class emulated Roman ways of life and political culture. Some spoke Latin, even visited Rome, but other than the images on the coins and a few particular objects and practices, it is striking is how un-Roman and more Gallo-British were their deaths, daily lives and political arenas.[5] Royal burials like Lexden and Folly Lane (Foster 1986; Niblett 1999) are not Roman aristocratic graves, but variations on the existing rich burials of Gallia Belgica and southern Anglia. If pre-Roman Gorhambury at St Albans (Neal *et al.* 1990) is a typical royal or aristocratic settlement, it is not a Roman palace or villa, and the landscape of which it forms a part is definitely not paralleled in the Roman or even the Gallic world.

The sites often called 'territorial *oppida*' (e.g. Cunliffe 1991) are fundamentally associated with the political development of kingship. These are large tracts of landscape divided and structured with long banks and ditches, with enclosures, settlement and other activities of different kinds inside and around them. They occur at the known centres of both the Eastern (St Albans, Colchester) and Southern kingdoms (Chichester), and are also found beyond southern and eastern England, as at Bagendon, Gloucestershire (Moore this volume) and Stanwick, North Yorkshire (Haselgrove 1999). All date to after 20/10 BC.

St Albans is perhaps the best understood of these complexes (Bryant and Niblett 1997; Haselgrove and Millett 1997). It is not a major population centre, nor a proto-city, but an open landscape with settlements, dykes, mints, burial complexes, and other enclosures carefully sited to be visible or invisible from different parts of the

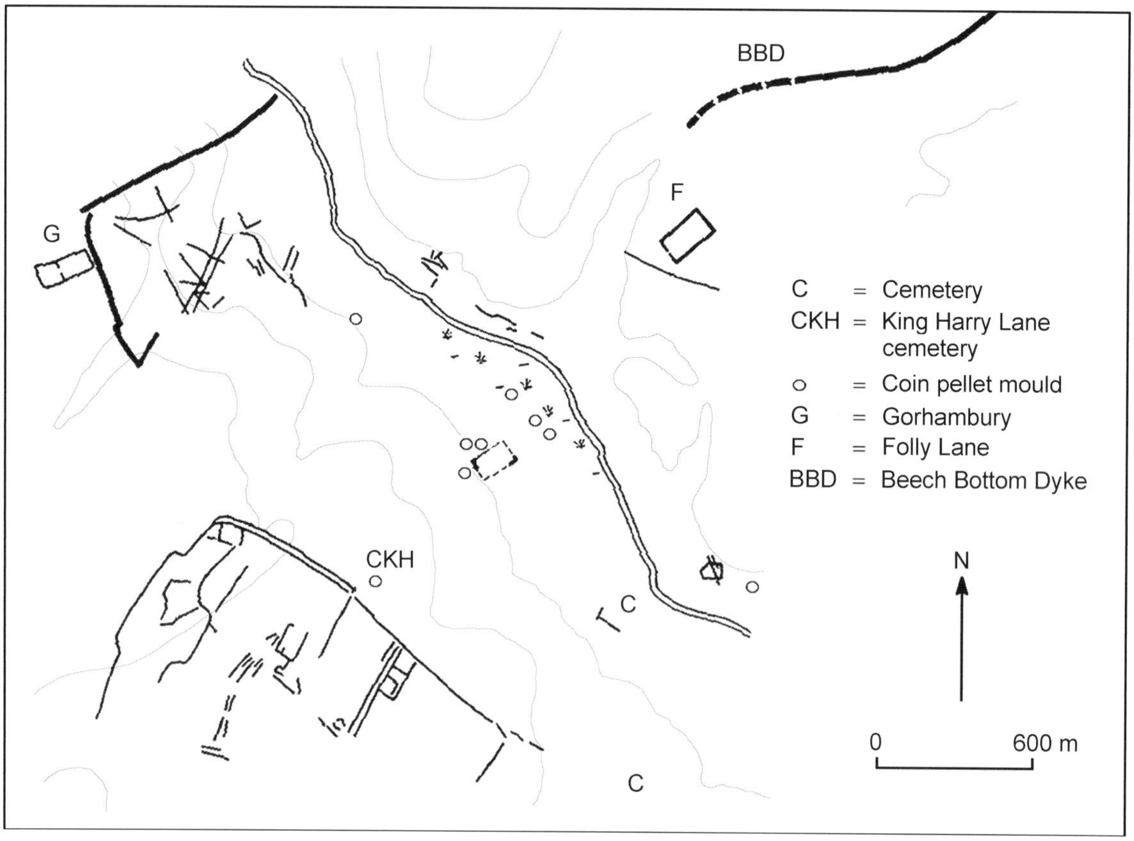

Fig. 12. The material manifestations of kingship? The 'royal site' at Verulamium – modern St Albans. The complex largely dates to after 10/1 BC, and would be better seen as a ceremonial landscape than either a royal estate or a town (after Bryant and Niblett 1997, fig 27.4)

complex (Fig. 12). This developed shortly after Tasciovanus apparently became paramount in Hertfordshire. This first king in the region minted coins there inscribed VER or VERLAMIO (for Verulamium, the Latin name of St Albans).

St Albans is perhaps better described as a 'royal site' than a territorial *oppidum* (Hill 1995), emphasising its role as an arena for the complex and changing realm of ceremonies and political, ritual, economic and agricultural activities associated with the new experiment of kingship. It appears to have been a new foundation, with little major settlement in the area before 30/20 BC. In the previous generation, rich burials suggest the Welwyn plateau, 10–15 km to the north-east (Bryant this volume), was the local political focus. The new institution of kingship perhaps needed a fresh location for its physical embodiment. It is interesting that St Albans and the other new 'royal sites' always had Latin names and indeed may never have had 'British' or 'Celtic' names (Williams 2002).

There is no space here to write a detailed narrative of the so-called Eastern kingdom, which Tasciovanus established. This polity has had less attention paid to it than to the so-called Southern kingdom, even though it appears to have been larger and more powerful. The 'history' of this eastern polity is witnessed through the coins issued by its apparent founder, Tasciovanus, and his successors, especially Cunobelin, although great care needs to be taken when reading the coins to this end. The kingdom appears to have incorporated several distinct smaller entities by the AD 20s, including Hertfordshire, southern Essex, and Kent. The principal geographical centre again needed to be moved – this time to Colchester – when Cunobelin was establishing himself, *c.* AD 10. Under him, the Eastern kingdom apparently had considerable influence over much of southern England. Although it is unclear if this was due to the use or threat of military force, much of this success might be attributable to this one man's efforts.

Socially and economically, the period from *c.* 30/20 BC marked a significant change across the region, if only because of the sheer increase in things of all types in the archaeological record (Table 2). Both Colchester and Verulamium acted as important centres, each with extremely rich burials (Lexden and Folly Lane) and

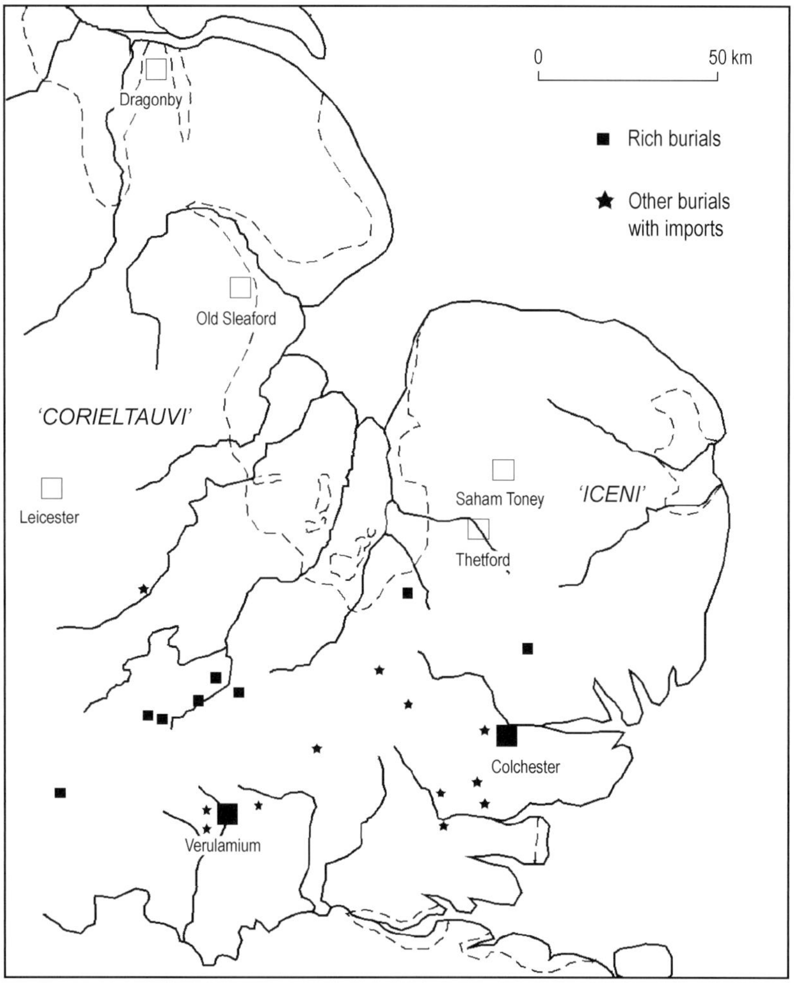

Fig. 13. The distribution of 'richly furnished' cremation burials in eastern England c. 20–10BC to AD 50–60, along with the location of selected key sites from this period.

surrounded by other graves with imports (Fig. 13), whilst Braughing flourished as a place where imported ceramics were consumed in large quantities. Stewart Bryant (Bryant and Niblett 1997; Bryant this volume) has observed how integrated the settlement patterns of Hertfordshire were from this time onwards. Further 'rich' burials with amphorae and other imports were distributed around the edge of the Eastern kingdom, for example at Snailwell, between Cambridge and Thetford, and a cluster including Stanfordbury from Bedfordshire (both graves are probably post-AD 43).

Earlier trends in changes in dress and cuisine also become far more marked at this time in southern Anglia and there was a major change in the volume of Gallic tablewares and other Gallo-Roman objects being used by people in the region; many of these forms were increasingly copied locally. How much these changes in daily life – and, presumably, increasing economic specialisation – in southern Anglia were due to the changing political situation, reflect the impact of the economic revival in the Roman world under Augustus, or were grounded in earlier indigenous factors, is unclear at present.

Northern Anglia and the East Midlands *c.* 100 BC onwards: backward, marginal and peripheral?

The previous sections have concentrated on southern Anglia. The following paragraphs sketch what was happening in the first centuries BC and AD in surrounding areas like the East Midlands and northern Anglia, since there is not space here to discuss these regions in the detail they deserve. In comparison to southern Anglia, the East Midlands and northern Anglia tend to be seen in a passive and negative light, and are often characterised more by what they lacked in the first centuries BC and AD than what they had. They did not have the characteristic features of southern Anglia, such as cremation burial, 'kings', or extensive evidence for trade and contacts with Gaul and Rome, whilst their coinages remained rooted in traditional designs. Instead of rapidly sharing the key features of the 'Late Iron Age', these regions appear to have continued an essentially 'Middle Iron Age' way of life and to have been slower in adopting elements of the Late Iron Age package such as coinage and wheel-made pottery (Table 3).

Northern Anglia and the East Midlands shared several broadly similar features and trends in the Mid to Late Iron Age, and by AD 43 they each housed large entities which can be seen through their coins. The coin-issuing entity in northern Anglia and the Fens was called the Iceni in AD 43, whilst the East Midlands group is now generally known as the Corieltauvi. Both these entities cross-cut a number of pre-existing smaller units that can be identified from limited distributions of pottery styles, settlement and monument types. The entities themselves are composites of potentially different individuals or groups issuing similar coins.

Archaeologically, however, the two regions provide different types of evidence. As yet, few Iron Age sites have been excavated in Norfolk and northern Suffolk, although there is now good evidence from the Fens. Instead, northern Anglia has an archaeology of metal-detected and other casual finds of coins, torcs and other metalwork (Davies 1996; 1999; Hutcheson 2004; this volume). In contrast, the East Midlands has a growing body of excavated settlement evidence (e.g. Knight this volume), although Lincolnshire has potentially equally high densities of metal-detector finds that remain to be synthesised (Worrell this volume). For both areas, the lack of a detailed chronology is a major problem that may mask social, cultural and economic change.

Across northern Anglia, the Midlands, and the upper Thames valley, there were important continuities through the period 300 BC–AD 43. In many places, the landscapes dominated by large successful populations living in unenclosed 'villages' continue. If these communities 'failed' to adopt new styles of pottery or were slow to adopt coinage, the explanation probably lies in a lack – or reduced nature – of the social factors and demands that led to these changes in southern Anglia. For example, the meal did not develop the same distinct social role in these other regions, so that they had no need to acquire new pot shapes, foreign dining utensils or exotic foods and drink (Hill 2002).

It would be wrong, however, to see these areas as unchanging. The large number of first century BC or AD tankard handles and possible bucket mounts from these areas points to some changes in the sphere of the meal. These might indicate greater differences in, or acknowledgement of, status or rank. So does the raised frequency of chariot-related metalwork in Norfolk (Hutcheson 2004) and possibly Lincolnshire, and of brooches, some of them in gold or silver. Some classes of metalwork show a broad distribution across northern Anglia, the East Midlands, and into the West Midlands, such as tankard handles or Birdlip brooches.

Settlement expansion and infill took place throughout the East Midlands and northern Anglia. A notable example is the increasing density of settlement and laying-out of field systems in the Trent valley and south Yorkshire (Knight this volume) and in parts of Norfolk (Williamson 1987). New sites that were the product of infill and expansion were often small, enclosed settlements, as at Enderby, Leicester (Clay 1992), or Haddenham V. If many of the established communities in the region were a source of the people moving into other areas, this process of fission and translocation must have had consequences 'at home'.

There is a tendency in some areas for the appearance of small, 'heavily enclosed' settlement units in the second and first centuries BC, like Haddenham V and Wardy Hill in north Cambridgeshire, or Aldwincle and Brigstock in Northamptonshire. These units have disproportionately large enclosing ditches and banks that have been argued to be defensive (Dix and Jackson 1989; Evans 2003). Some of these sites are part of larger agglomerated settlements, so the heavy enclosure may imply differences in the rank of their occupants (e.g. Haddenham V). In other cases, it might indicate a special status for the enclosed space (Gwilt 1997). Certainly, some of these sites are not dissimilar in size to the ditched enclosures at Fison Way, Thetford, and Barnham, near Thetford, which are potentially ritual foci. As in southern Anglia, there was also a trend in the first century AD in some areas towards paddocks, field systems and 'compartmentalised' landscapes, a trend that continued in most areas after the Roman conquest.

Agglomerated settlements and clusters of settlement agglomerations also continued. Sites like Saham Toney and Thetford in Norfolk, or Dragonby in Lincolnshire are potentially very similar to Baldock or Welwyn, and should no more be called *oppida* than their southern Anglian counterparts (cf. Bryant this volume). In Norfolk, there were changes through time in the dominant form of metalwork deposition, from torcs to coin hoards to chariot harness (Hutcheson 2004; this volume). The organisation of salt production in the Fens also altered significantly in the first centuries BC and AD (Morris this volume), hinting at other changes in production and agriculture.

Wheel-turned pottery generally appears late across these regions (*c.* 20 BC/AD 20 or even later) and the new technology was not normally used to make as wide a range of forms as in southern Anglia (Hill 2002). There are exceptions, notably the major agglomerations at Dragonby and Old Sleaford in Lincolnshire, and also Leicester, all of which have evidence for imported Gallic finewares from *c.* 20 BC/AD 20 (Willis 1996; 2005). The motivation for acquiring these imports and the changes in the meal that they imply need not be the same in all cases. As in Norfolk and northern Suffolk, there

Dates	*Continental chronology*	*Coin Phase*	*Coinage*	*Settlement*	*Burial*	*Major burials*	*Wheel-made pottery*	*Brooches & dress*	*Key sites*	*Political institutions*		*Dates*
250 BC				Little permanent settlement; probably seasonal & low intensity agricultural and economic exploitation								250 BC
200 BC				Some permanent settlement								200 BC
c. 175–125 BC	La Tène C2	1	Gallo-Belgic A & B in use & production: Serial imagery									c. 175–125 BC
c. 125–100 BC	La Tène D1	2		Increasing permanent settlement – often enclosed settlements of different sizes	? ??		? ? ??					c. 125–100BC
c. 100–80 BC		3			?? ???	Baldock	?? ???					c. 100–80 BC
c. 80–60 BC		4					Wheel-made pottery and new forms esp. pedestal urns, tazza bowls	Increasing numbers of brooches – Boss on Bow type brooches		Increasing evidence for social inequalities in burials		c. 80–60 BC
c. 60–50 BC	La Tène D2	5	British gold coins begin: localised issues of coin types			Welwyn A & B, Welwyn Garden City, Hertford Heath					Caesar in S England	c. 60–50 BC
c. 50–20 BC		6								Leaders but not Rulers		c. 50–20 BC
c. 20 BC–AD 10		7	Classical imagery on coins; NAMES and words on coins	Much settlement: large clusters of settlement & other activities Increasing evidence for multiple compounds and small enclosed units	Cremation burial	Lexden				**'Kingship'** a new political institution	TASCIOVANUS	c. 20 BC–AD 10
c. AD 10–40	Early Roman	8					**Increasingly more things:** new pottery forms, butt beakers, flagons, platters, cups. Gallo-Belgic imports and local copies	**Increasingly more brooches:** Colchester, Strip, Aucissa & Rosette types; personal grooming objects more common	Verulamium, Colchester, Braughing-Puckeridge	Rulers not Leaders The Eastern Kingdom	CVNOBELIN	c. AD 10–40
AD 43–60		9 Roman				Folly Lane, Snailwell, Stanway			London	Roman *civitas* political institutions	AD 43 Roman Conquest AD 60-61 Boudican Revolt	AD 43–60

Table 2. The principal changes seen in the archaeology of southern Anglia from c. 250 BC onwards.

Dates	Continental chronology	Coin Phase	Coinage	East Midlands settlement	Burial	Northern Anglia	Pottery	Brooches & dress	Major sites	Political institutions		Dates
250 BC				Many clusters of dense settlement & activity; unenclosed, wandering settlements;		?? ?? ??						250 BC
200 BC				seasonal & low intensity exploitation in marginal areas						Communal orientated polities; some differences in wealth & power, but no distinct elite social group;		200 BC
c. 175–125 BC	La Tène C2		Very few coins	As above with increasing permanent settlement in marginal areas	Almost no burials	Torcs	Hand-made pottery			Leaders not Rulers		c. 175–125 BC
c. 125–100BC	La Tène D1			Expansion of permanent settlement into many areas (Fens, eastern Norfolk, Trent valley etc.)								c. 125–100 BC
c. 100–80 BC										Some evidence for greater social distinctions;		c. 100–80 BC
c. 80–60 BC		4	Distinct silver coinage with serial imagery & local gold coins	Some 'heavily' enclosed small units		?? ?? ?? ??	Mostly hand-made pottery	Increasing numbers of brooches, but from very low base		Leaders not Rulers		c. 80–60 BC
c. 60–50 BC	La Tène D2	5									Caesar in S England	c. 60–50 BC
c. 50–20 BC		6				??	V small quantities of wheel-made pottery	Boss on Bow type brooches		2 large grouping emerge (one in EM, one in NA)		c. 50–20 BC
c. 20 BC–AD 10		7				?? ?? ?? ??		**Increasingly more brooches on some sites**			TASCIOVANUS	c. 20 BC–AD 10
c. AD 10–40	Early Roman	8	Distinct silver coinage with serial imagery continues; some names/words; almost no classical imagery	As above Increasing evidence for multiple compounds and small enclosed units in some areas	A very few cremation burials	Chariot gear	**Increasingly more things** Some wheel-made pot BUT still much hand-made pot	Colchester, Strip, Aucissa & Rosette & Birdlip types	Leicester, Saham Toney, Fison Way II	As above: some Leaders try to become Rulers; 2 large groupings continue: 'Corieltauvi' & 'Iceni'	CVNOBELIN	c. AD 10–40
AD 43–60		9 Roman						Personal grooming objects more common	Fison Way III	Roman *civitas* (EM) & client kingdom (NA)	AD 43 Roman Conquest AD 60–1 Boudican Revolt	AD 43–60

Table 3. The principal changes seen in the archaeology of northern Anglia and the East Midlands from c. 250 BC onwards.

are more brooches, chariot gear, and other small pieces of metalwork in all areas of the East Midlands from around the turn of the first centuries BC and AD.

Extensive use of coinage developed later in these regions than in southern Anglia. Distinctive northern Anglian and East Midlands coinages seem to appear only from *c.* 70/60 BC (Colin Haselgrove's Phase 5) and are of a different character from those of southern Anglia, being predominantly in silver and relatively constant in imagery from 70/60 BC up to AD 43 or later. Unlike the coinages associated with kingship in south-east England after *c.* 20 BC, these coins show little need to adopt Roman designs or constantly to present different images and messages on new issues.

Nor do they exhibit the same marked concern with named individuals. Writing and labels do appear on northern Anglian and East Midlands types from *c.* 20 BC or later, and might be personal names or something else. Even if they are individuals, there is a distinctly different feel about their positions and role in their communities compared to the rulers of the Southern and Eastern kingdoms. Or at very least, major differences in the iconographic and ideological 'languages' employed on the coins are apparent in the contrast between the standard northern Anglian and East Midlands issues and the few types that do employ 'Roman' portraiture and language more akin to those of southern Anglia, such as the rare issues inscribed ESVPRASTO/ESVPRASV or IISVPRASV (Williams 2001).

What can be made of the coin evidence? Clearly, the marked distinctions between these coin issues and those of southern Anglia confirm, continue, and reproduce the different social forms in these areas, whilst their distributions span pre-existing groups of 'communities' with different forms of settlements or pottery. This is most marked for the coins of the Corieltauvi in the East Midlands, but is also true for Norfolk and the Fens. On this basis, the northern Anglian and East Midlands coin-issuing entities might represent confederations or extensive networks of pre-existing 'tribes' or groups of communities. Or they could reflect an alternative form of social organisation co-existing with – and crossing through – pre-existing community groupings or 'tribes'.

It is not clear what forms of leadership and power these coins imply in northern Anglia and the East Midlands. But these regions did not possess the institution of kingship seen in the southern Anglia. These kings to the south, for their part, potentially asserted considerable diplomatic, kinship and military pressure or influence in these parts of Britain. They also may have provided a role model, which some East Midlands and northern Anglian individuals and families attempted to emulate before and at the time of the Roman conquest. As such, Prasutagus' role as client king of the Iceni after AD 43 need not imply the Iceni had kingship prior to this. Rather, this individual may have taken advantage of the Roman invasion to become a southern-style king. This might have followed similar, but unsuccessful, attempts by other people in previous decades.

Conclusions

This paper has sketched an alternative narrative for the history of south-eastern and eastern England over the three centuries before the Roman conquest. Most important, it sees the changes that took place towards the end of the Iron Age as driven by factors and forces within indigenous Middle Iron Age societies. The appearance of Mediterranean and Gallic material in graves and settlements in south-east England from *c.* 100 BC onwards was not the cause of the social changes seen in this area, but rather a symptom. Following Creighton (2000), the political changes in south-east England after *c.* 30/20 BC are viewed as the direct consequence of a series of British individuals redefining the nature of power in the light of political transformations in the Roman world.

Central to this paper has been the attempt to set developments in south-east England in a longer timeframe and broader regional context. In an even wider geographical setting, the changes in eastern and south-eastern England from 200 BC onward are part of a series of changes apparent across Britain and Ireland. These include the appearance of banjo enclosures in parts of southern central England (that often lacked hillforts); the changing function and sometimes abandonment of Wessex hillforts; settlement expansion and the appearance new small enclosed settlement units in north-east England; the building of brochs in the Northern and Western Isles; and the construction of 'royal sites' and other communal projects such as boundaries and trackways in eastern central and northern Ireland. Although all are different phenomena, they suggest that all over Britain and Ireland societies were facing broadly similar pressures that led to change and, in some cases, transformation, even if the (attempted) solutions were quite different. Set in this wider perspective, a very local model invoking external causes to explain Late Iron Age changes in south-east England appears even less likely.

Acknowledgements

This paper has had a long gestation. The essential ideas were first presented at a conference in Cambridge in 1994, and have been refined and altered through airings in seminars, conferences and public lectures ever since. Many people have helped shape this paper – often by disagreeing with it. I would especially like to thank Tim Champion, Colin Haselgrove, Elaine Morris, Mike Parker Pearson, Nico Roymans, Niall Sharples, Peter Wells, Ann Woodward, and – most importantly – Chris Evans, Natasha Hutcheson, and Jonathan Williams.

Notes

1. See Bryant (1997), Champion (1994), Davies (1996; 2003), Knight (1984), and especially Willis (1997; 2005), for different perspectives on these regions.
2. Woolf (1993b) provides a critique of these ideas.
3. For a fuller discussion of pottery and food, see Hill (2002).
4. In his recent study of the transfer of classical themes to British coin types, Williams (2005) shows how specific elements of Roman imagery were translated into indigenous categories to ensure that the representations could be read by their British audience.
5. Creighton (2000) offers a stimulating alternative view.

Bibliography

Allen, T. and Robinson, M. 1993. *The Prehistoric Landscape and Iron Age Enclosed Settlement at Mingies Ditch, Hardwick-with-Yelford, Oxon.* Oxford: Thames Valley Landscapes Monograph 2.

Bevan, B. 1997. Bounding the landscape: place and identity during the Yorkshire Wolds Iron Age, in Gwilt and Haselgrove 1997, 181–191.

Bryant, S. 1997. Iron Age, in J. Glazebrook (ed.), *Research and Archaeology: A Framework for the Eastern Counties,* 23–34. Norwich: East Anglian Archaeology Occasional Paper 3.

Bryant, S. and Niblett, R. 1997. The late Iron Age in Hertfordshire and the north Chilterns, in Gwilt and Haselgrove 1997, 270–281.

Carter, G.A. 1998. *Excavations at the Orsett 'Cock' Enclosure, Essex, 1976.* Chelmsford: East Anglian Archaeology Report 86.

Chadwick, A. 1999. Digging ditches but missing riches? Ways into the Iron Age and Romano-British cropmark landscapes of the north Midlands, in B. Bevan (ed.), *Northern Exposure: Interpretative Devolution and the Iron Ages in Britain,* 149–172. Leicester: Leicester Archaeology Monograph 4.

Champion, T.C. 1994. Socio-economic development in eastern England in the first Millennium B.C., in K. Kristiansen and J. Jensen (eds), *Europe in the First Millennium BC,* 125–144. Sheffield: J.R. Collis Publications.

Clay, P. 1992. An Iron Age farmstead at Grove Farm, Enderby, Leicestershire, *Transactions of the Leicestershire Archaeological and Historical Society* 66, 1–82.

Creighton, J. 2000. *Coins and Power in Late Iron Age Britain.* Cambridge: Cambridge University Press.

Crumley, C.L. 1995. Heterarchy and the analysis of complex societies, in R.M. Ehrenreich, C.L. Crumley, and J.E. Levy (eds), *Heterarchy and the Analysis of Complex Societies,* 1–5. Ann Arbor: Archaeological Papers of the American Anthropological Association 6.

Crumley, C.L. 2001. Communication, holism and the evolution of sociopolitical complexity, in Haas 2001, 19–36.

Cunliffe, B. 1987. *Hengistbury Head, Dorset, Vol. 1. The Prehistoric and Roman Settlement, 3500 BC–AD 500.* Oxford: Oxford University Committee for Archaeology Monograph 13.

Cunliffe, B. 1988. *Greeks, Romans and Barbarians: Spheres of Interaction.* London: Batsford.

Cunliffe, B. 1991. *Iron Age Communities in Britain* (3rd edn). London: Routledge.

Cunliffe, B. 1995. *Iron Age Britain.* London: Batsford.

Davies, J.A. 1996. Where eagles dare: the Iron Age of Norfolk, *Proceedings of the Prehistoric Society* 62, 63–92.

Davies, J.A. 1999. Patterns, power and political progress in Iron Age Norfolk, in Davies and Williamson 1999, 14–44.

Davies, J.A. and Williamson, T. (eds) 1999, *The Land of the Iceni: the Iron Age in Northern East Anglia.* Norwich: Studies in East Anglia History 4.

Dietler, M. 1990. Driven by drink: the role of drinking in the political economy and the case of early Iron Age France, *Journal of Anthropological Archaeology* 9, 352–406.

Dietler, M. 2001. Theorizing the feast: rituals of consumption, commensal politics, and power in African contexts, in M. Dietler and B. Hayden (eds), *Feasts: Archaeological and Ethnographic Perspectives on Food, Politics, and Power,* 65–114. Washington: Smithsonian Institution Press.

Dix, B. and Jackson, D. 1989. Some Late Iron Age defended enclosures in Northamptonshire, in A. Gibson (ed.), *Midlands Prehistory,* 158–179. Oxford: British Archaeological Reports British Series 204.

Drury, P. 1978. *Excavations at Little Waltham, Essex.* London: Council for British Archaeology Research Report 26.

Earle, T.K. 1997. *How Chiefs Come to Power: the Political Economy in Prehistory.* Stanford: Stanford University Press.

Evans, C. 1997. Hydraulic communities: Iron Age enclosure in the East Anglia fenlands, in Gwilt and Haselgrove 1997, 216–227.

Evans, C. 2003. *Power and Island Communities: Excavations at Wardy Hill Ringwork, Coveney, Ely.* Cambridge: East Anglian Archaeology Report 103.

Evans, C. and Knight, M. 2002. A Great Circle: investigations at Arbury Camp, Cambridge, *Proceedings of the Cambridge Antiquarian Society* 91, 23–53.

Evans, C. and Serjeantson, D. 1988. The backwater economy and excavation of a Fen-edge community in the Iron Age: the Upper Delphs, Haddenham, *Antiquity* 62, 381–400.

Field, N. and Parker Pearson, M. 2003. *Fiskerton: An Iron Age Timber Causeway with Iron Age and Roman Votive Offerings.* Oxford: Oxbow Books.

Fitzpatrick, A.P. 1989. The uses of Roman imperialism by the Celtic barbarians in the later Republic, in J. Barrett, A.P. Fitzpatrick and L. Macinnes (eds), *Barbarians and Romans in North-West Europe,* 27–54. Oxford: British Archaeological Reports International Series 471.

Fitzpatrick, A.P. 1992. The roles of celtic coinage in south-east England, in M. Mays (ed.), *Celtic Coinage: Britain and Beyond,* 1–32. Oxford: British Archaeological Reports British Series 222.

Fitzpatrick, A.P. 2001. Cross channel exchange, Hengistbury Head and the end of hillforts, in J. Collis (ed.) *Society and Settlement in Iron Age Europe (Actes du XVIIIe Colloque de l'AFEAF, Winchester, April 1994),* 82–97. Sheffield: J.R. Collis Publications.

Foster, J. 1986. *The Lexden Tumulus. A Re-appraisal of an Iron Age Burial from Colchester, Essex.* Oxford: British Archaeological Reports British Series 156.

Gregory, T. 1991. *Excavations in Thetford, 1980–1982: Fison Way.* Norwich: East Anglian Archaeology Report 53.

Gwilt, A. 1997. Popular practices from material culture: a case study of the Iron Age settlement at Wakerley, Northamptonshire, in Gwilt and Haselgrove 1997, 153–166.

Gwilt, A. and Haselgrove, C. (eds) 1997. *Reconstructing Iron Age Societies.* Oxford: Oxbow Monograph 71.

Haas, J. (ed.) 2001. *From Leaders to Rulers*. New York: Kluwer Academic.

Haselgrove, C. 1976. External trade as a stimulus to urbanization, in B. Cunliffe and T. Rowley (eds), *Oppida: The Beginnings of Urbanisation in Barbarian Europe*, 25–50. Oxford: British Archaeological Reports International Series 11.

Haselgrove. C. 1982. Wealth, prestige and power: the dynamics of late Iron Age political centralization in south-east England, in A.C. Renfrew and S. Shennan (eds), *Ranking, Resource and Exchange*, 79–88. Cambridge: Cambridge University Press.

Haselgrove, C. 1987. *Iron Age Coinage in South-East England: The Archaeological Context*. Oxford: British Archaeological Reports British Series 174.

Haselgrove, C. 1989. The later Iron Age in southern Britain and beyond, in M. Todd (ed.), *Research on Roman Britain: 1960–89*, 1–18. London: Britannia Monograph 11.

Haselgrove, C. 1993. The development of British Iron Age coinage, *Numismatic Chronicle* 153, 31–63.

Haselgrove, C. 1999. The Iron Age, in J. Hunter and I. Ralston (eds), *The Archaeology of Britain: an Introduction from the Upper Palaeolithic to the Industrial Revolution*, 113–134. London: Routledge.

Haselgrove, C. 2004. Society and polity in late Iron Age Britain, in M. Todd (ed.), *The Blackwell Companion to Roman Britain*, 12–29. Oxford: Blackwell.

Haselgrove, C. and Millett, M. 1997. Verlamion reconsidered, in Gwilt and Haselgrove 1997, 282–296.

Havis, R. and Brooks, H. 2004. *Excavations at Stansted Airport, 1986–91*. Chelmsford: East Anglian Archaeology Report 109.

Hayden, B. 2001. The dynamics of wealth and poverty in the Transegalitarian societies of South-east Asia, *Antiquity* 75, 571–581.

Hill, J.D. 1995. The pre-Roman Iron Age in Britain and Ireland: an overview, *Journal of World Prehistory* 9, 47–98.

Hill, J.D. 1999. Settlement, landscape and regionality. Norfolk and Suffolk in the pre-Roman Iron Age of Britain and beyond, in Davies and Williamson 1999, 185–207.

Hill, J.D. 2002. Not just about the potter's wheel. Making, using and depositing Middle and Late Iron Age pottery in south-east England, in A. Woodward and J.D. Hill (eds), *Prehistoric Britain, the Ceramic Basis,* 143–160. Oxford: Oxbow Books.

Hill, J.D. 2003. Is the Battersea Shield or the Snettisham Great Torc a material manifestation of an elite status group? Paper presented to the SAA Conference session, *Material and Symbolic Manifestations of Elite Status Groups*.

Hill, J.D. 2006. Are we any closer to understanding how Later Iron Age societies worked (or did not work)?, in C. Haselgrove (ed.), *Les Mutations de la fin de l'âge du Fer (IIe–Ier s. av. J.-C.)*, 169–179. Glux-en-Glenne: Collection Bibracte 12/4.

Hill, J.D., Evans, C. and Alexander, M. 1999. Hinxton Rings: a late Iron Age cremation cemetery from Hinxton, Cambridgeshire and a reassessment of the northern Aylesford–Swarling rite, *Proceedings of the Prehistoric Society* 65, 235–275.

Hingley, R. 1990. Boundaries surrounding Iron Age and Romano-British settlements, *Scottish Archaeological Review* 7, 96–103.

Hutcheson, N. 2004. *Later Iron Age Norfolk: Metalwork, Landscape and Society*. Oxford: British Archaeological Reports British Series 361.

Jackson, D.A. 1975. An Iron Age site at Twywell, Northamptonshire, *Northamptonshire Archaeology* 10, 31–93.

Jackson, D.A. and Ambrose, T. 1978. Excavations at Wakerley, Northamptonshire, 1972–75, *Britannia* 9, 115–242.

Jackson, R.A. and Potter, T.W. 1996. *Excavations at Stonea, Cambridgeshire 1980–85*. London: British Museum Press.

Knight, D. 1984. *Late Bronze Age and Iron Age Settlement in the Nene and Great Ouse Basins*. Oxford: British Archaeological Reports British Series 130.

Lane, T.W. and Morris, E.L. (eds) 2001. *A Millennium of Salt Making: Prehistoric and Romano-British Salt Production in the Fenland*. Lincoln: Lincolnshire Archaeology Heritage Report 4.

May, J. 1996. *Dragonby. Report on Excavations at an Iron Age and Romano-British Settlement in North Lincolnshire*. Oxford: Oxbow Monograph 61.

Millett, M. 1990. *The Romanization of Britain*. Cambridge: Cambridge University Press.

Neal, D.S., Wardle, A. and Hunn, J. 1990. *Excavation of the Iron Age, Roman and Medieval Settlement at Gorhambury, St Albans*. London: English Heritage Archaeological Report 14.

Niblett, R. 1999. *The Excavation of a Ceremonial Site at Folly Lane, Verulamium*. London: Britannia Monograph 14.

Partridge, C. 1989. *Foxholes Farm. A multi-period gravel site*. Hertford: Hertfordshire Archaeological Trust.

Pryor, F.M.M. 1984. *Excavations at Fengate, Peterborough, England: the Fourth Report*. Northampton: Northamptonshire Archaeological Society Monograph 2.

Sharples, N. 1990. Late Iron Age society and continental trade in Dorset, in A. Duval, J.P. Le Bihan and Y. Menez (eds), *Les Gaulois d'Armorique. La fin de l'âge du Fer en Europe Tempérée (Actes du XIIe colloque de l'AFEAF, Quimper 1988)*, 299–304. Rennes: Revue Archéologique de l'Ouest Supplément 3.

Stead, I.M. 1967. A La Tène III burial at Welwyn Garden City, *Archaeologia* 101, 1–62.

Stead, I.M. 1985. *Celtic Art in Britain before the Roman Conquest*. London: British Museum Press.

Stead, I.M. 1991a. *Iron Age Cemeteries in East Yorkshire*. London: English Heritage Archaeological Report 22.

Stead, I.M. 1991b. The Snettisham treasure: excavations in 1990, *Antiquity* 65, 447–465.

Stead, I.M. and Rigby, V. 1986. *Baldock: The Excavation of a Roman and Pre-Roman Settlement, 1968–72*. London: Britannia Monograph 7.

Taylor, J. 1997. Space and place: some thoughts on Iron Age and Romano-British landscapes, in Gwilt and Haselgrove 1997, 282–296.

West, S. 1990. *West Stow: The Prehistoric and Roman-British Occupations*. Ipswich: East Anglian Archaeology Report 48.

Williams, J. 2001. Coin inscriptions and the origins of writing in pre-Roman Britain, *British Numismatic Journal* 71, 1–17.

Williams, J. 2002. Pottery stamps, coin designs, and writing in late Iron Age Britain, in A. Cooley, *Becoming Roman, Writing Latin?*, 135–151. Portsmouth, Rhode Island: Journal of Roman Archaeology Supplement 48.

Williams, J. 2005. 'The newer rite is here': vinous symbolism on British Iron Age coins, in C. Haselgrove and D. Wigg-Wolf (eds), *Iron Age Coinage and Ritual Practices*, 25–41. Mainz: Studien zu Fundmünzen der Antike 20.

Williams, R.J. 1993. *Pennyland and Hartigans: Two Iron Age and Saxon Sites in Milton Keynes*. Aylesbury: Buckinghamshire Archaeological Society Monograph 4.

Williams, R.J. and Zeepvat, R. 1994. *Bancroft: a Late Bronze Age/Iron Age Settlement, Roman Villa and Temple Mausoleum*. Aylesbury: Buckinghamshire Archaeology Society Monograph 7.

Williams, R.J., Hart P.J., and Williams, A.T.L. 1996. *Wavendon Gate: a Late Iron Age and Roman Settlement in Milton Keynes*, 203–230. Milton Keynes: Buckinghamshire Archaeology Society Monograph 10.

Williamson, T. 1987. Early co-axial field systems on the East Anglian boulder clays, *Proceedings of the Prehistoric Society* 53, 419–431.

Willis, S.H. 1994. Roman imports into Late Iron Age British societies: towards a critique of existing models, in S. Cottam, D. Dungworth, S. Scott and J. Taylor (eds), *TRAC 94: Proceedings of the Fourth Theoretical Roman Archaeology Conference, Durham 1994*, 141–150. Oxford: Oxbow Books.

Willis, S.H. 1996. The Romanization of pottery assemblages in the east and north-east of England during the first century AD: a comparative analysis, *Britannia* 27, 179–221.

Willis, S.H. 1997. Settlement, materiality and landscape in the Iron Age of the East Midlands; evidence, interpretation and wider resonance, in Gwilt and Haselgrove 1997, 205–215.

Willis, S.H. 2005. The later Bronze Age and Iron Age, in N. Cooper (ed.), *The Archaeology of the East Midlands. An Archaeological Resource Assessment and Research Agenda,* 89–136. Leicester: Leicester Archaeology Monograph 13.

Woodward, A. and Hughes, G. 2007. Deposits and doorways: patterns within the Iron Age settlement at Crick Covert Farm, Northamptonshire, in C. Haselgrove and R. Pope (eds), *The Earlier Iron Age in Britain and the Near Continent*, 185–203. Oxford: Oxbow Books.

Woolf, G. 1993a. The social significance of trade in Late Iron Age Europe, in C. Scarre and F. Healy (eds), *Trade and Exchange in Prehistoric Europe*, 211–218. Oxford: Oxbow Books.

Woolf, G. 1993b. Rethinking the oppida, *Oxford Journal of Archaeology* 12, 223–233.

Life on the edge? Exchange, community, and identity in the Later Iron Age of the Severn-Cotswolds

Tom Moore

Introduction: Cores and peripheries

Recent discussions of the Later Iron Age[1] have signalled a need for the re-emergence of broad narratives of social change (e.g. Creighton 2001, 4; Haselgrove *et al.* 2001; Gerritsen 2003), but in Britain at least, no real alternative to the 1980s core–periphery model (Haselgrove 1982; 1987; Cunliffe 1988) has as yet emerged, although individual authors have offered important new perspectives on the changes in settlement and material culture seen in Late Iron Age southern Britain (e.g. Hill 1997; 1999; Willis 1997; Creighton 2000). Key to these re-interpretations is the role of individuals and communities as agents in the process of change. Alongside a greater awareness of the regional diversity of Iron Age Britain, this had led to reluctance to explain some of the broader patterns that exist in the archaeological record. This should not, however, prevent us from trying to explain these wider patterns. For example, why do some areas and sites contain imports, but not others? Why do regional pottery sources dominate at certain periods? How do we account for the appearance of new settlement forms? Whilst seeing individuals and communities as conscious agents, we need to explain why many communities apparently accepted or rejected broader cultural practices at much the same time.

In deconstructing the core–periphery model, Hill (1999; 2002; this volume) has expressed the view that the so-called 'core' area in Late Iron Age south-east England might actually be better understood as originally a 'periphery', since many *oppida* evidently developed at the margins of the existing social groupings. This inversion is in danger of misrepresenting some of the ideas underlying the model, since Cunliffe (1976) and Haselgrove (1982) also saw the new elements of Late Iron Age society developing around the peripheries of well-established social systems, as witnessed by the shift from the hillfort-dominated landscape of central southern England to south-east England and its *oppida*. The critical feature of the core–periphery model was the causal influence it accorded to external forces – especially those relating to Roman expansion – in stimulating indigenous social developments, even if some of the consequences were unintended or later developed a dynamism of their own (Cunliffe 1976, 149; 1991, 546; Haselgrove 1976, 26; 1987, 105). In contrast, Hill sees change as more dependent on factors internal to the social system, whilst at the same time emphasising the formation of new communities – whether from within existing societies or as a result of movement from outside (Hill 2002; this volume). Long a central tenet of Iron Age studies (e.g. Hawkes 1959), migration has been downplayed in recent decades, but there is an increasing awareness once again that people *did* move in later prehistory. What is different is that the processes are now seen as far more complex and not merely as simple replacement of one population by another.

Like the original core–periphery model, Hill's alternative narrative mainly concerns south-east England and the wider implications have yet to be considered. The aim of my own paper is to explore whether a similar approach can enhance our understanding of Later Iron Age developments elsewhere, particularly in regions previously seen as peripheral to a south-eastern 'core'. The area chosen for detailed study is the lower Severn–Cotswolds

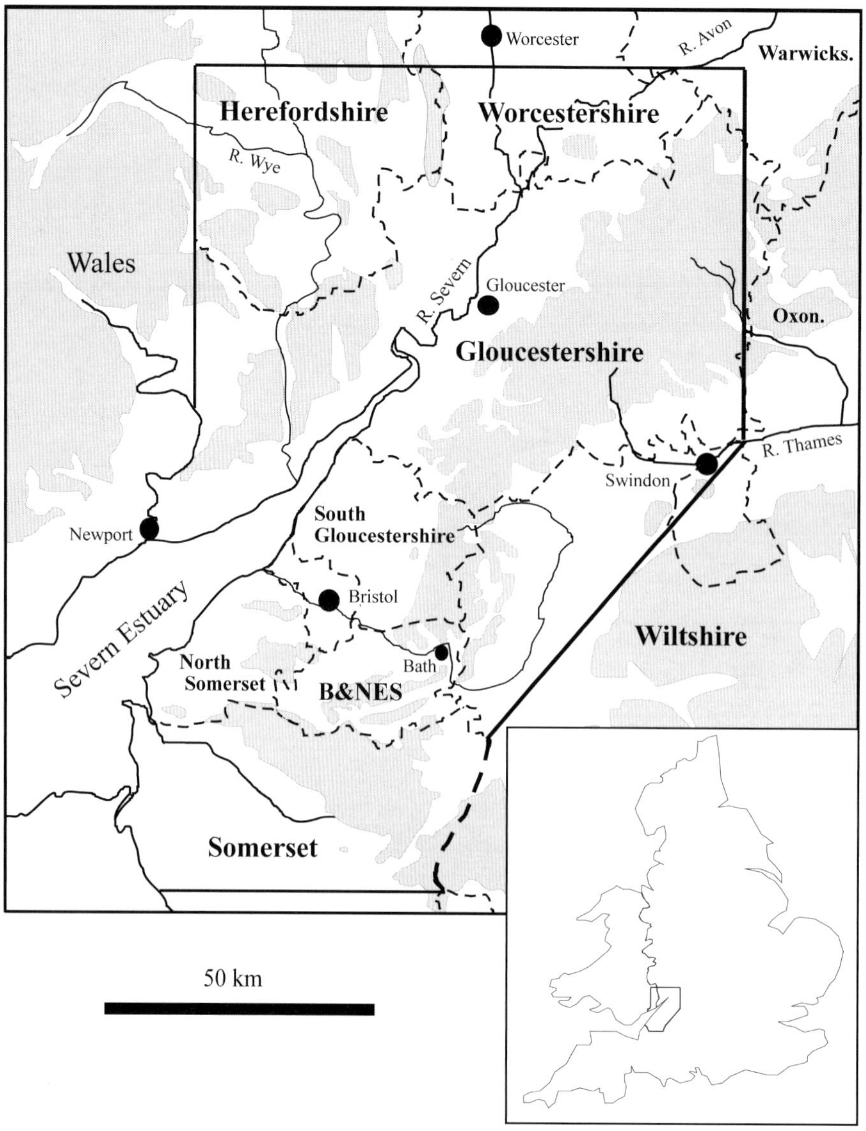

Fig. 1. The Severn–Cotswolds region.

(Fig. 1). This small region is not to be regarded as in any way representative of southern Britain as a whole, but rather as a specific case study of the relationship of Late Iron Age sites to social developments in the surrounding landscape. I will focus particularly on the problems raised by one site, the so-called '*oppidum*' at Bagendon (Clifford 1961), in the context of the wider changes evident in the Severn–Cotswolds. As I will show, although similar processes to those discussed by Hill can be identified, the precise factors behind the development of Bagendon are both complex, and regionally-specific; the nature of the existing settlement pattern and exchange systems, and how local and regional identities were constructed are all relevant. Simply reversing the core–periphery model runs the risk of establishing a new set of dichotomies that mask a far more complex and fractured picture.

The Severn–Cotswolds

The social and chronological models developed for the Iron Age in the Severn–Cotswolds have largely been adopted from elsewhere (Cunliffe 1984; Darvill 1987), emphasising features that are familiar from Wessex or south-east England, such as the many hillforts and enclosures, or the presence of Roman imports at sites like Bagendon. In effect, through sharing some of the 'classic' Iron Age features with these other areas, the Severn–Cotswolds has come to be regarded as an impoverished neighbour, where developments took place belatedly and to a lesser extent.

Whilst there are indeed similarities with other parts of southern Britain, many of them may be more apparent than real. As we will see, the Severn–Cotswolds has a distinctive settlement history, which has not been well-served by recent research. The general tendency to project the Roman *civitas* of the Dobunni backwards in time and treat the Severn–Cotswolds as synonymous with their tribal territory (e.g. Hawkes 1961; Cunliffe 1991),[2] merely compounds this by ascribing a cohesiveness to Later Iron Age settlement and society, which is not only potentially at odds with the coin evidence that has long been used to justify this equation (Haselgrove *et al.* forthcoming), but also ends up masking more subtle patterns in the archaeology (Moore and Reece 2001).

Later Iron Age settlement patterns

Before discussing the role of Bagendon, we need to begin by re-assessing the Later Iron Age settlement pattern in the Severn–Cotswolds as a whole, drawing on the wealth of new evidence that has become available in the last decade (Marshall 1995; 2001; Parry 1998a; 1998b; Mudd *et al.* 1999; Price 2000). The settlement record is dominated by enclosures, mainly known from cropmarks and under 1 ha in size; whilst varying in form, they are most commonly sub-rectangular (Webster and Hobley 1964; RCHME 1976; Moore 2003). Excavated examples suggest they date from the fourth century BC to the first century AD (Darvill 1987; Moore 2007). The landscape also contains a number of larger 'hillforts', some of which like Uley Bury seem to be densely occupied. Generalising about these sites is problematical, however. Smaller examples such as Conderton Camp potentially comprised communities little larger than some enclosures. On analogy with Wessex, commentators have tended to see the larger Severn–Cotswolds hillforts as central places, occupied by an elite to whom the inhabitants of the smaller enclosures were subservient (e.g. Darvill 1987; Thomas 2005), but as elsewhere in southern Britain (Hill 1996), there is little evidence to suggest that hillforts actually served such a role.

Far more relevant to the Severn–Cotswolds is the detailed model of Later Iron Age society proposed by Hingley (1984) for Oxfordshire. Hingley contrasted the open settlement pattern of the upper Thames valley with the isolated enclosures found on the Oxfordshire Cotswolds, which he interpreted as reflecting differences in social organisation; the boundary ditches of the enclosures in the latter region marking the relative social – and to some extent economic – independence of their inhabitants, compared with the more socially integrated communities of the Thames valley (Fig. 2). This view of enclosed communities as isolated, both socially and economically, has since been applied to other parts of Britain (e.g. Ferrell 1995; Hill 1996), although Hingley (1999, 244) has since stressed that those dwelling in enclosures were also integrated into wider social networks.

There is growing evidence indicating that the Severn–Cotswolds do not conform to Hingley's Oxfordshire model. Rather than being dispersed, Later Iron Age

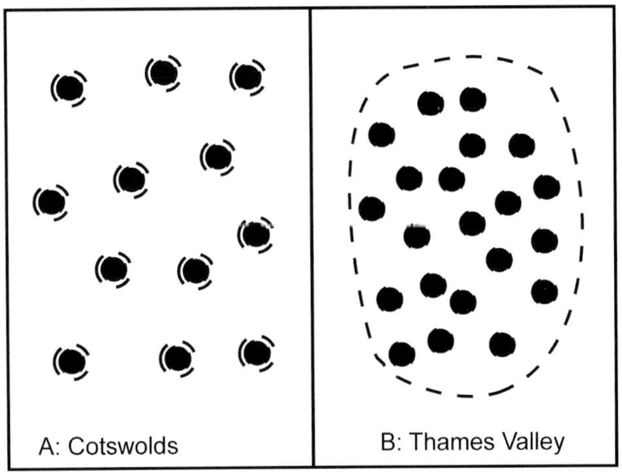

Fig. 2. Hingley's idealised settlement landscapes for the Oxfordshire Cotswolds and upper Thames valley. A. Enclosures on the Cotswolds as independent 'corporate social groups'. B. Unenclosed settlements in the Thames valley as part of larger corporate groups (after Hingley 1984, fig. 5.7).

enclosures in the Gloucestershire Cotswolds often seem to cluster, so that certain areas appear densely settled, with enclosures situated close to one another, as for example around Birdlip and Guiting (Fig. 3), whilst others seem much less densely occupied. Similar clusters exist in the lower Severn and (north) Avon valleys, often comprising a range of, sometimes multivallate, sub-rectangular enclosures, as for example at Broadway, Kempsey (Fig. 4), and elsewhere in southern Worcestershire (Webster and Hobley 1964; Dinn and Evans 1990; Moore 2003).

Overall, the cropmark evidence – reinforced by excavated sites such as Wyre Piddle (Napthan *et al.* 1997), Strensham (Parry 1998b), Throckmorton,[3] and south and east of Bredon Hill (Coleman and Hancocks forthcoming) – suggests a densely settled landscape in the lower Severn valley by the Later Iron Age, within which discrete clusters of enclosures existed in certain areas. Similar clusters of enclosures are known further up the Avon valley in Warwickshire (Hingley 1996) and are emerging elsewhere in Britain, for example in the central Welsh Marches, north-east England and south-east Scotland. In none of these instances is there any reason to suppose that the apparent clustering and associated 'gaps' are due to variable cropmark formation or flying patterns, rather than a real pattern. Many enclosures do not seem to have been 'isolated' in the landscape, which has important implications for how we view social relations between groups and wider community organisation.

Some Later Iron Age enclosures in the lower Severn valley and elsewhere in the West Midlands are apparently

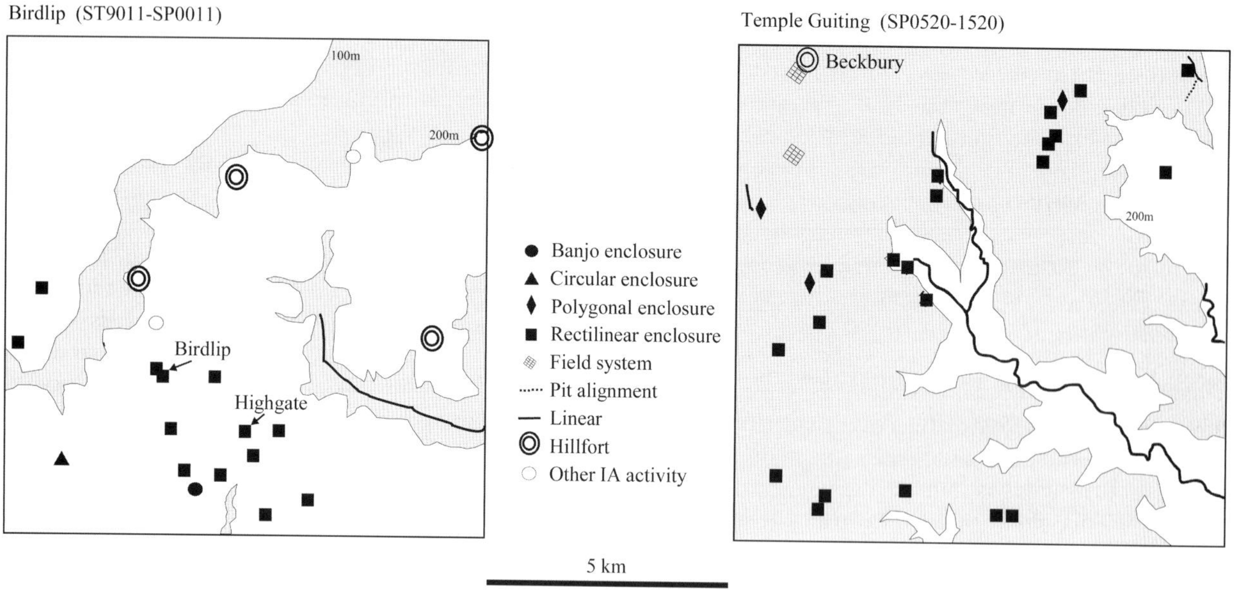

Fig. 3. Clusters of enclosures in the Birdlip and Guiting areas of the Gloucestershire Cotswolds.

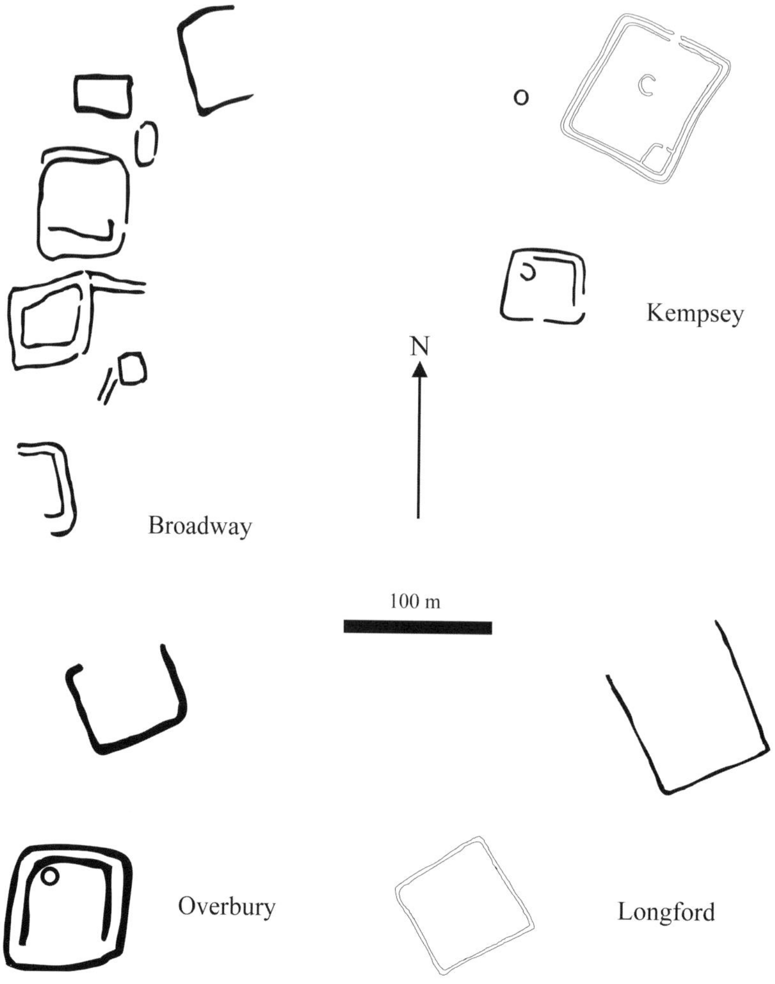

Fig. 4. Examples of clusters of enclosures from the lower Severn valley (after Moore 2003).

incorporated into larger field systems. At Aston Mill (Dinn and Evans 1990), Beckford (Oswald 1974) and elsewhere in the lower Avon valley, particularly around Bredon Hill, enclosures appear to be related to linears, trackways, and pit alignments; the pattern is repeated further up the Avon valley in Warwickshire (Hingley 1996). In the upper Thames valley, too, a densely occupied landscape existed by the Later Iron Age, here comprising a range of unenclosed and enclosed settlements (see e.g. Hey this volume), and in some areas, settlements were integrated into linears and other complex land divisions, as at Preston, where a polygonal enclosure is associated with contemporary segmented ditches (Mudd *et al.* 1999), and Ashton Keynes, where similar boundaries are associated with unenclosed settlement (Brossler *et al.* 2002).

There is an increasing sense of permanency of settlement in the Later Iron Age landscape compared to earlier periods (Moore 2007). The construction of small (household-sized?) enclosures from about the fourth century BC onwards indicates an increasing desire for communities to associate themselves visibly with particular locations (*ibid.*; Wigley this volume). A similar process may be argued for at least some upper Thames valley settlements, where houses acquired larger drainage gullies and an enclosure of their own within larger agglomerations (Moore 2007). By the later Iron Age, many parts of the region, particularly the northern Cotswolds and lower Severn valley (most visibly around Bredon Hill), possessed well-defined sets of landscape divisions and settlement clusters.

This evidence points to a highly organised and structured society, potentially very different from that envisaged either in the central place model or for Oxfordshire. At least in the northern Cotswolds and lower Severn valley, it seems likely that the occupants of enclosures, far from being isolated, participated in a variety of communal activities beyond the scope of the household to form wider communities. In addition, sites in the Avon and Severn valleys were integrated into wider systems of land divisions and in some areas there were dense clusters of enclosures. In such cases, groups were potentially bound into wider communities and a range of shared identities, as Hingley (1999, 244) has more recently suggested for the Stanton Harcourt area.

The nature of so-called 'Middle' and 'Late' Iron Age settlement patterns can also be reassessed on a wider scale (Fig. 5). For the purposes of this distribution map, Late Iron Age 'sites' are defined as having material such as Gallo-Belgic and early Severn Valley wares, Colchester brooches, or imports, and are conventionally dated to the early–mid first century AD, or slightly earlier. At 'Middle' Iron Age sites, such material is absent and only Middle Iron Age pottery forms and fabrics are represented. Essentially, then, this is a distribution of pottery types: sites with only hand-made pottery compared to those only or also producing wheel-thrown wares. Clearly there are major problems with such definitions, which I will return to later, but depicting the evidence in this way serves to illustrate the conceptual problems with previous models of the Later Iron Age in the region.

The most obvious point is the marked disparity in the distribution of Middle and Late Iron Age sites, implying a relationship between site location and chronology. In a number of cases, Late Iron Age sites seem to appear preferentially in areas where Middle Iron Age settlement is less apparent. The most striking example is around Bagendon in the southern Cotswolds. Apart from Bagendon itself (Clifford 1961; Trow 1982), this pocket of settlement includes the so-called 'hillfort' at Ditches (Trow 1988) and the recently excavated enclosures at Middle Duntisbourne and Duntisbourne Grove (Mudd *et al.* 1999), to which we may add the (first century BC?) burial near Baunton (*ibid.*) and a possible Late Iron Age site at Stratton just north of Cirencester (Wymark 2003). However, despite the density of first century AD occupation in the area, evidence for activity of earlier date is limited.[4] Equally, this area has produced very little evidence of cropmark enclosures compared to many parts of the Cotswolds or the upper Thames valley to the south (RCHME 1976; Moore 2003). This is in spite of the potential of Bagendon to act as a 'honey pot' for aerial survey, as has certainly happened with important Iron Age sites elsewhere.

In contrast, the other so-called *oppidum* at Salmonsbury, near Bourton-on-the-Water, is located in an area with plentiful Early and Middle Iron Age occupation, both in the immediate vicinity of the site (Dunning 1976; Marshall 1978; Barber and Leah 1998; Nichols 2001; 2004) and in the adjacent uplands around Guiting (Saville 1979; Marshall 1991; 1995), at Lower Slaughter (Timby 1998) and Naunton. Although there is some evidence of activity at Salmonsbury prior to the construction of the ramparts, the site probably emerged in the first century BC (Haselgrove 1997, 61), in close proximity to a densely settled and negotiated landscape.

Late Iron Age material is known elsewhere in the region,[5] notably at Frocester (Price 2000), Wycomb (Timby 1998), Uley–West Hill (Woodward and Leach 1993), Beckford (Oswald 1974), Weston-under-Penyard (Jackson 2000), and possibly Kings Stanley (Heighway 1989). In other cases, the nature of the evidence is much less clear. At Abbeymead and Brockworth in Gloucester (Atkin 1987; 1991; Thomas *et al.* 2003), there seems to be both Middle and Late Iron Age activity, but it is unclear if this represents direct continuity as is apparent at Frocester. Attributing material to before or after the Roman conquest remains particularly difficult. Finds such as the *terra rubra* sherd from Dorn (Timby 1998), the Dressel 1 amphorae from Kenchester (Wilmott and Rahtz 1985) or the brooches from Kingscote (Timby 1998; Moore 2003) could have been deposited on either side of the conquest, whilst

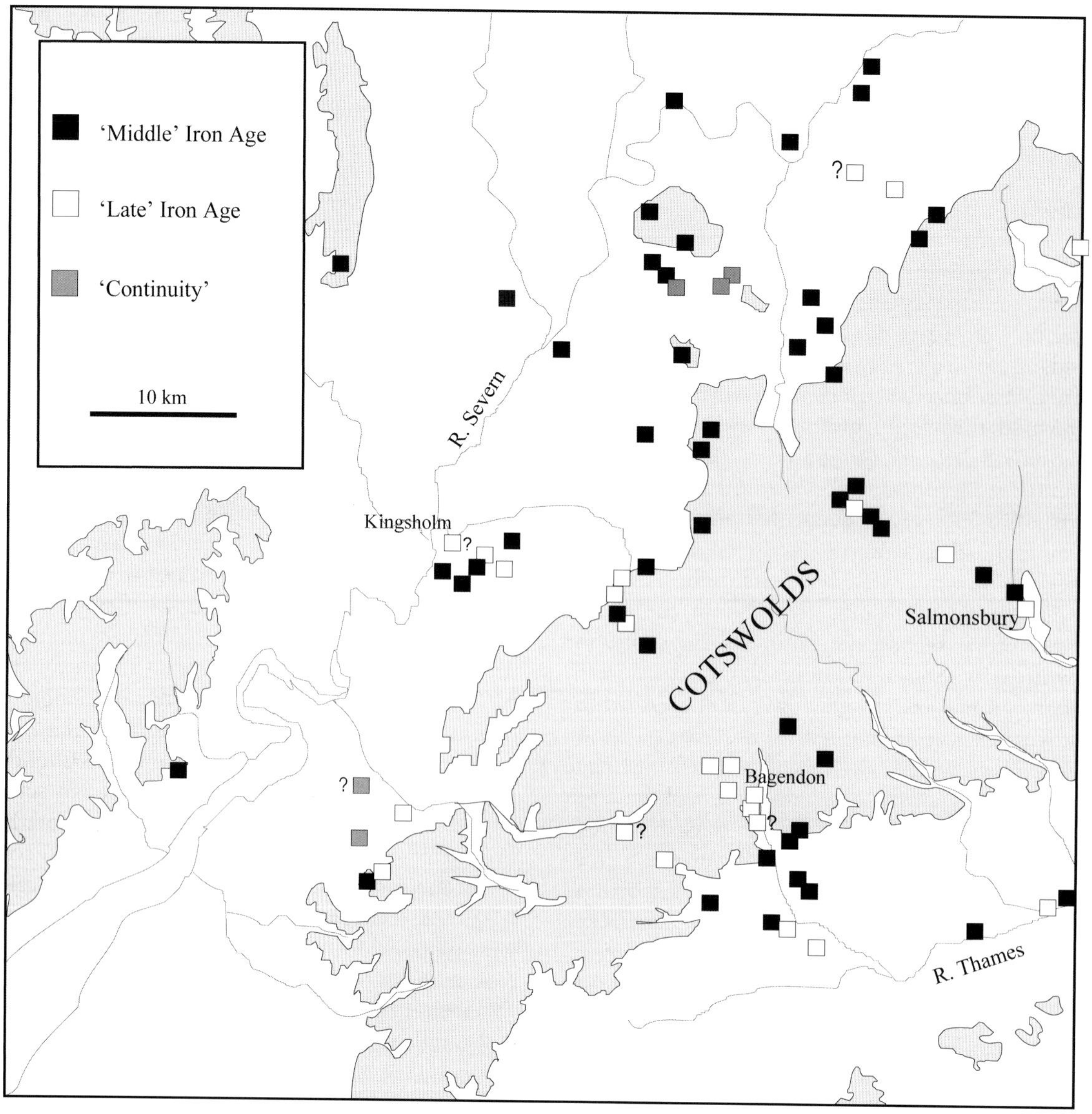

Fig. 5. The relationship between 'Middle' and 'Late' Iron Age sites in the north of the Severn–Cotswolds.

at Kingsholm, there is presently insufficient evidence to argue for continuity between the Mid–Late Iron Age settlements and the early Roman military site (Hurst 1999a; Timby 1999a).

A number of the sites yielding Late Iron Age material certainly represent settlements, including Beckford, Birdlip, and Frocester. Elsewhere, much of the evidence is ambiguous and could instead relate to ritual sites (Uley West Hill; Wycomb?) or exchange centres (Weston-under-Penyard?). In terms of both the landscape setting and the nature and quantity of finds, the Bagendon–Ditches complex may be regarded as regionally exceptional. Apart from Frocester (Price 2000) and Beckford – where the bulk of the excavations have yet to be published – remarkably few sites have good evidence of continuity between the Middle and Late Iron Age. Most sites with Late Iron Age material, as in the Bagendon area[6] and also elsewhere, such as Wycomb (Timby 1998), appear to possess little evidence of earlier activity. On the other hand, most 'Middle' Iron Age settlements, including the hillforts at Bredon (Hencken 1938), Conderton (Thomas 2005), and Uley Bury (Saville 1983); the enclosure at Guiting Power (Saville 1979); and the settlements at Aston Mill (Dinn and Evans 1990), Evesham (Edwards and Hurst 2000) and Gilder's Paddock (Parry 1999) are thought to have been abandoned by the second or first century BC, in other words, prior to the Late Iron Age. Is this picture real? Or is it a function of how 'Middle' and 'Late' Iron Age sites are identified?

New chronologies: a 'later' Iron Age?

A number of recent studies have suggested that as a distinct chronological entity the Late Iron Age has little meaning beyond certain areas of south-eastern England, and even in those 'core' areas cannot be regarded as a universal chronological horizon (Hill 1999; 2002; this volume). For a long time, finds of Middle Iron Age pottery, including Malvern wares, at sites like Bagendon and Cirencester, were seen as 'traditional hangovers', but there is a growing awareness that in the Severn–Cotswolds, as in other parts of southern Britain, such wares can persist into the first century AD, and that sites without wheel-thrown forms may post-date the first century BC. Regional hand-made wares (such as Peacock's B1 fabric) are now thought to continue as late as the 70s AD (Rigby 1982; S. Willis pers. comm.); conversely, certain 'early Roman' forms, particularly the early Severn Valley wares, may be pre-conquest in origin (Timby 1999a, 40; 2000, 363).

There are various reasons why this change in attitude was slow in coming. One is the continued reliance on a three phase Iron Age chronology which may not be relevant to the region (Darvill 1987; Saville 1984). Another is the assumption that by the first century AD communities had access to imported pottery, such as samian and Gallo-Belgic wares, or at least to wheel-thrown pottery. Sites like Uley Bury, where such material is absent, are therefore deemed to end by the first century BC (Saville 1983), whilst sites yielding wheel-thrown wares or imports in the same contexts as Middle Iron Age wares, are attributed to the Late Iron Age, the Middle Iron Age pottery usually being treated as a case of persistence into the later period, or in some cases as residual.

This method of dating has been adopted from south-east England, where both imports and wheel-thrown pottery are relatively common. In the Severn–Cotswolds region, however, the number of imports, in particular, is far lower (Fitzpatrick and Timby 2002, 168). At Frocester, for example, the identification of the Late Iron Age phase rests primarily on a handful of sherds of pre-Flavian finewares and the Iron Age coins (Price 2000, 63), and it may well be that at other sites, we are confusing an absence of evidence with evidence of absence. The Bowsings, for example, appears not to have produced wheel-thrown wares (Marshall 1991),[7] yet a radiocarbon date implies that the enclosure was not abandoned until the first century AD. Similarly at Birdlip, the envisaged hiatus between a Middle Iron Age and an early Roman (first century AD) phase of the enclosures may not be as well defined as the excavator believed (Parry 1998a, 55). This may imply that more Middle Iron Age enclosures continued to occupy the same location into the succeeding period and that many Late Iron Age sites possessed little or no wheel-thrown pottery.

Using pottery as a chronological indicator in this way ignores the role of the communities as active agents in the selection of pottery types and in the nature of the contacts and exchange between groups. As Steven Willis (1994; 1996) and others (Fitzpatrick and Timby 2002; Hill 2002, 144) have shown, the adoption of Roman and Gallo-Belgic imports and wheel-thrown pottery related as much to factors such as status, cultural identity and availability as to chronology. Consequently, the Middle and Late Iron Age are as much cultural constructs as chronological divisions (Willis 2005). The shift from one to the other should be seen not as a sharp break, but as a fluid process of cultural and technological change, reflecting individual communities' reaction to differing forms and sources of material, and ultimately dependent on the exchange networks, cultural traditions, status and choices by individuals and communities operating in a particular region. Rather than being purely a sign of Late Iron Age activity, the adoption of wheel-thrown technology and imports may in fact denote those groups that were willing – or able – to change both their consumption habits and their social practices.

Against this background, imposing a rigid chronological distinction between a Middle and a Late Iron Age in the Severn–Cotswolds is problematic and serves only to obscure the fluidity of changes in settlement and material culture over much of this period. For this reason, I employ the term Later Iron Age to cover the whole period from the mid fourth century cal. BC – which the associated radiocarbon dates suggest is when Middle Iron Age style pottery assemblages appeared in the region (Moore 2007) – until the first century AD, when these disappear from the record.

Freed of a purely chronological interpretation, the patterning in Figure 5 can be seen in a new light, as marking a cultural and/or socio-economic divide between sites with wheel-thrown wares/imports and those without. Three additional suggestions follow: First, we may in the first century AD be seeing the emergence of a group of new sites around Bagendon in an area of landscape devoid of earlier occupation. Second, some settlements classified as Middle Iron Age – and thus supposedly abandoned by the first century BC – might in fact be contemporary with later sites. Third, sites with wheel-thrown wares/imports may signify communities with different cultural links and connections from those that lack them.

Later Iron Age exchange networks

How does the Bagendon–Ditches complex relate to existing Later Iron Age social and economic networks? If we accept that material culture was embedded in exchange systems and employed in the construction of identities, we need to consider how such newly emergent sites fitted into the dominant exchange networks.

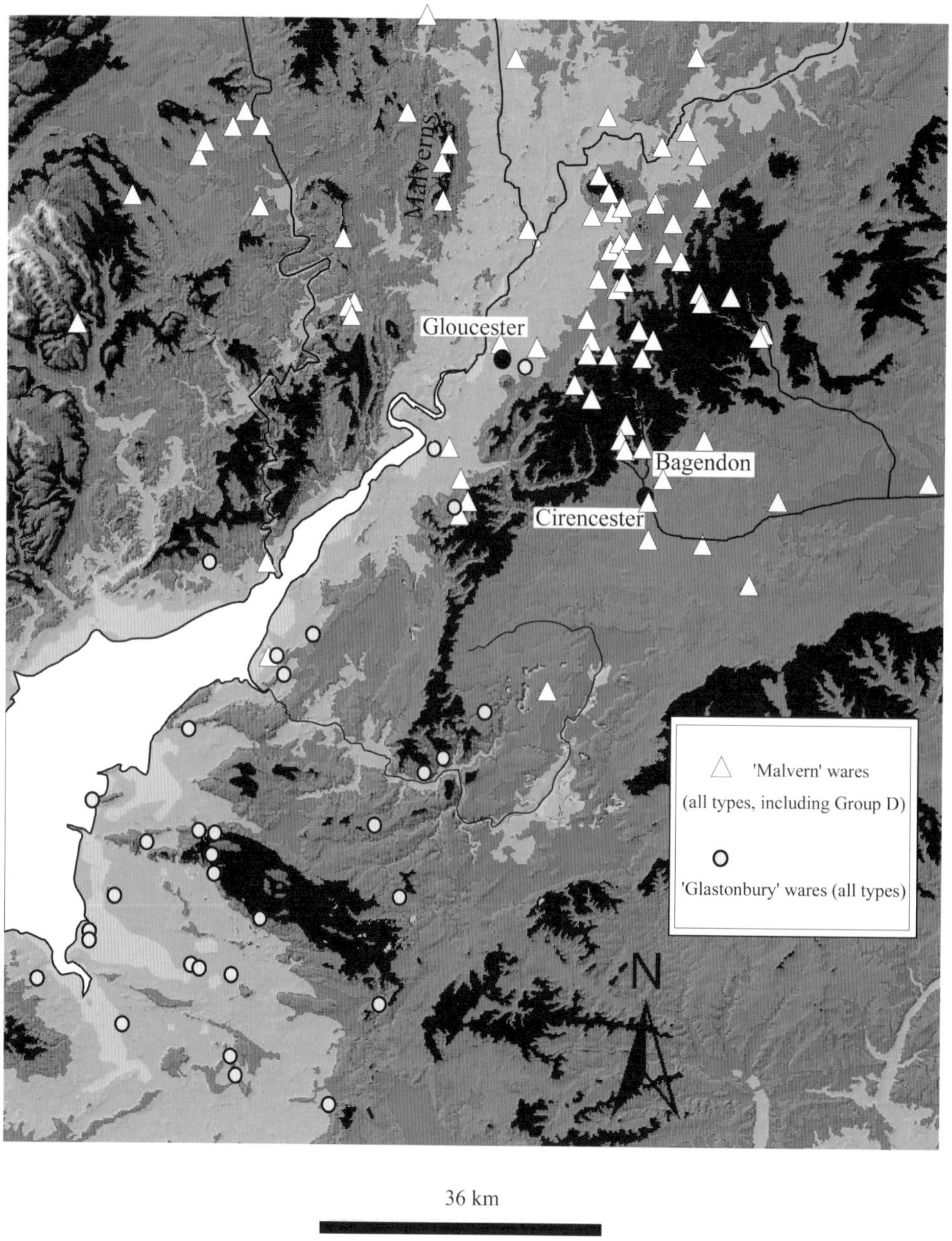

Fig. 6. Distribution of Malvern and Glastonbury wares in the Severn–Cotswolds. For full identification and discussion see Moore (2003). (Crown copyright/database right 2003. An Ordnance Survey/EDINA supplied service).

The existence of long-distance exchange systems in the region, involving Iron Age pottery and briquetage, has long been recognised (Peacock 1968; 1969; Morris 1983; 1994). More recently, specific locations for procuring stone for querns have also been identified, indicating that they too were involved in exchange systems. Many of these distribution networks appear to have been focused on distinct zones. The distribution of Malvern A and B1 wares,[8] for example, centres on the Severn valley and the Cotswold ridge (Fig. 6). Work by Fiona Roe on the lithology of querns has identified two distinct regional sources. In the northern Cotswolds, lower Severn valley and upper Thames many sites procured querns from May Hill, just to the south of the Malverns (Fig. 7), notably close to the various sources suggested for Later Iron Age Malvern wares (Peacock 1968; Morris 1983). Roe (1995) has also noted a distinct type of quern material, which probably derives from Beacon Hill, on the eastern end of the Mendips. Although fewer querns from this area

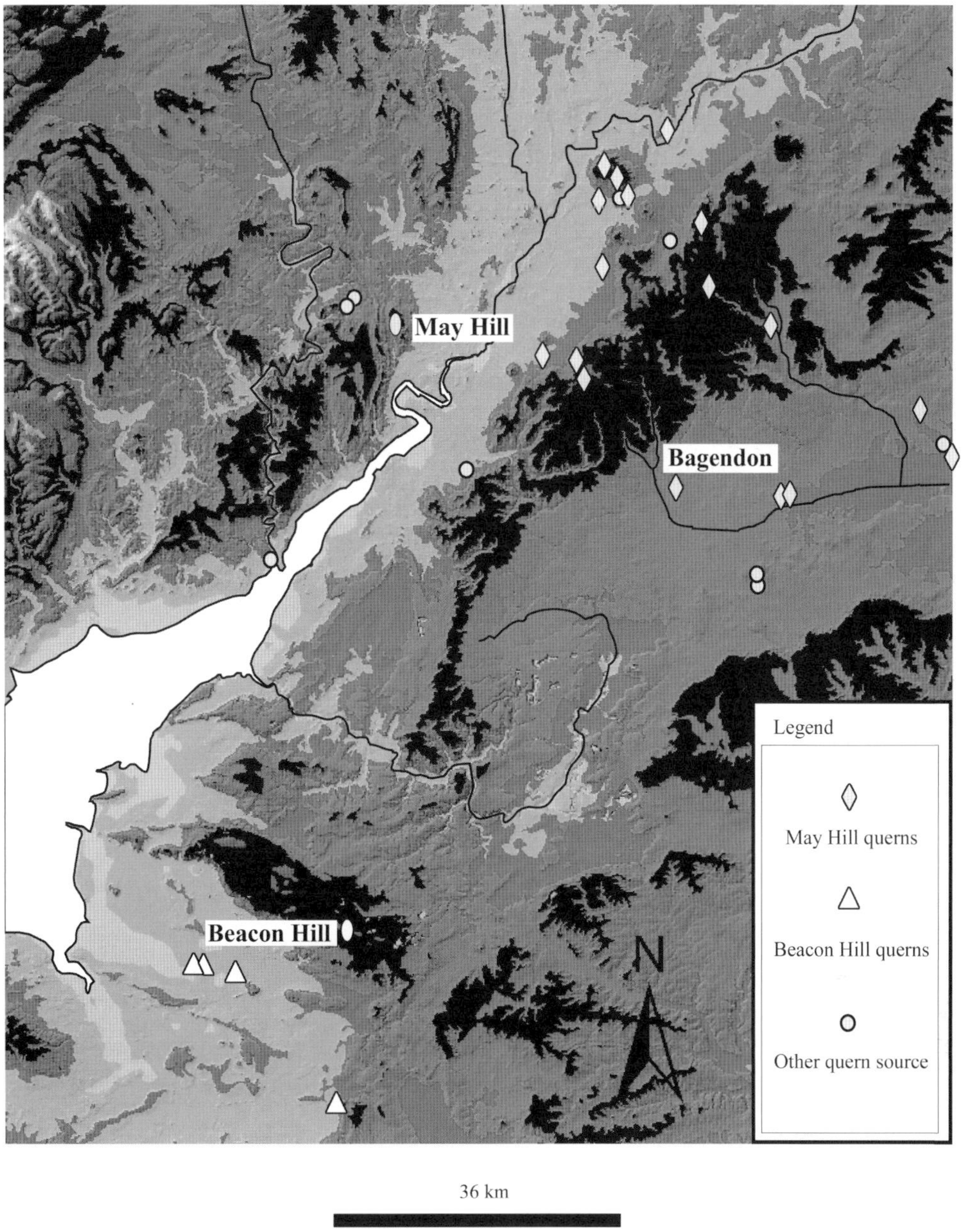

Fig.7. Distribution of quern types in the Severn–Cotswolds. For full identification and discussion see Moore (2003). (Crown copyright/database right 2003. An Ordnance Survey/EDINA supplied service).

have been sourced, the major find sites – which include the Lake Villages (Roe 1995) and Cadbury Castle (Roe 2000) – imply that this represents another defined exchange zone. The Beacon Hill area also appears to be the source of Glastonbury 2 ware, which has a similar distribution (Peacock 1969).[9]

These regional exchange systems emerged gradually around the mid first millennium BC. Malvern A and B1 ware (Peacock 1968) and Worcestershire Group D pottery (Morris 1983) probably began around the fourth century BC (Group D possibly slightly earlier), flourishing until the mid–late first century AD (Moore 2007). To the south, the Glastonbury wares deriving from the Mendips (Peacock 1969) appear roughly contemporary. May Hill querns on the other hand were already exploited in the Early Iron Age, as at Crickley Hill (P. Dixon pers. comm.) and may have started even earlier (Roe 1999), although the majority of sites with May Hill querns are of Later Iron Age date. Beacon Hill querns may start similarly early, but on current evidence flourished in the Late Iron Age, dominating, for example, the Late Cadbury assemblage (Fig. 8; Roe 2000, 263).

In both these cases the pottery and querns derive from closely related sources and apparently form similar relatively well-defined exchange areas, although too few other sites have sufficiently detailed reports to allow their querns to be sourced and many sites lack querns altogether. In addition, Droitwich briquetage was exchanged from the Early Iron Age throughout the northern half of the study area, although the full distribution extends right across the Welsh Marches and the West Midlands (Morris 1994). Finds of briquetage well beyond the limits of the distribution of the May Hill querns and Malvern pottery imply that its distribution relates to specific factors of supply and demand. However, it seems likely that the same networks operated in exchanging these different materials, since many sites with May Hill querns also have Malvern pottery and Droitwich briquetage.

Previous analyses have suggested that the distribution of pottery and briquetage related to economic patterns of exchange. Morris (1994; 1996) in particular, saw the evidence as reflecting down-the-line exchange. Others have sought to explain the distributions in terms of socio-cultural groupings (Blackmore *et al.* 1979), or quasi-political affiliations later reflected in the coinage (Cunliffe 1982; 1991, 172). In all these explanatory frameworks, the spheres of functional exchange and the relationship between material culture and cultural identity have largely been regarded as mutually exclusive.

None of these models fully explain either the distribution patterns or the choice of sources. Whilst the down-the-line-exchange model adequately accounts for the distribution of Malvern-sourced material (Morris 1994), it does not explain why communities would desire this material, or the popularity of these particular sources. Equally whilst reliance on regional exchanged material clearly increased in the Later Iron Age (Moore 2003), why this should come about is not considered. Nor is it explored why regional networks were such an important aspect of material culture in western and south-western Britain, or why in both the Malverns and the Mendips, the querns and pottery derive from closely related locations. In addition, the geographical fall-off in material may not be just about distance from source, but also about the extent to which different communities were integrated into the exchange networks.

Quasi-economic models rely on the assumption that the exchanged material was highly valued by other communities and was swapped for goods of equal value. In the absence of items appearing to travel in the

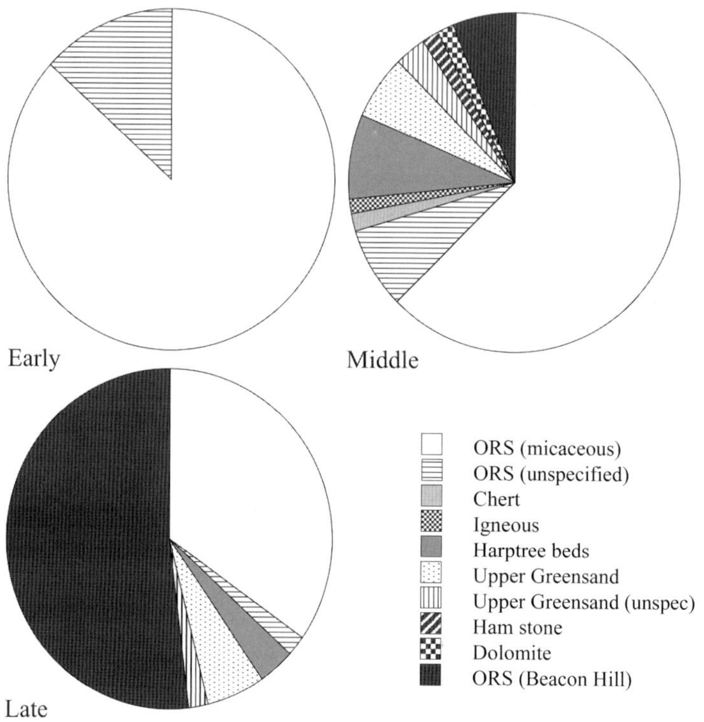

Fig. 8. Source of querns at Cadbury Castle by phase (numbers and quern identifications after Roe 2000).

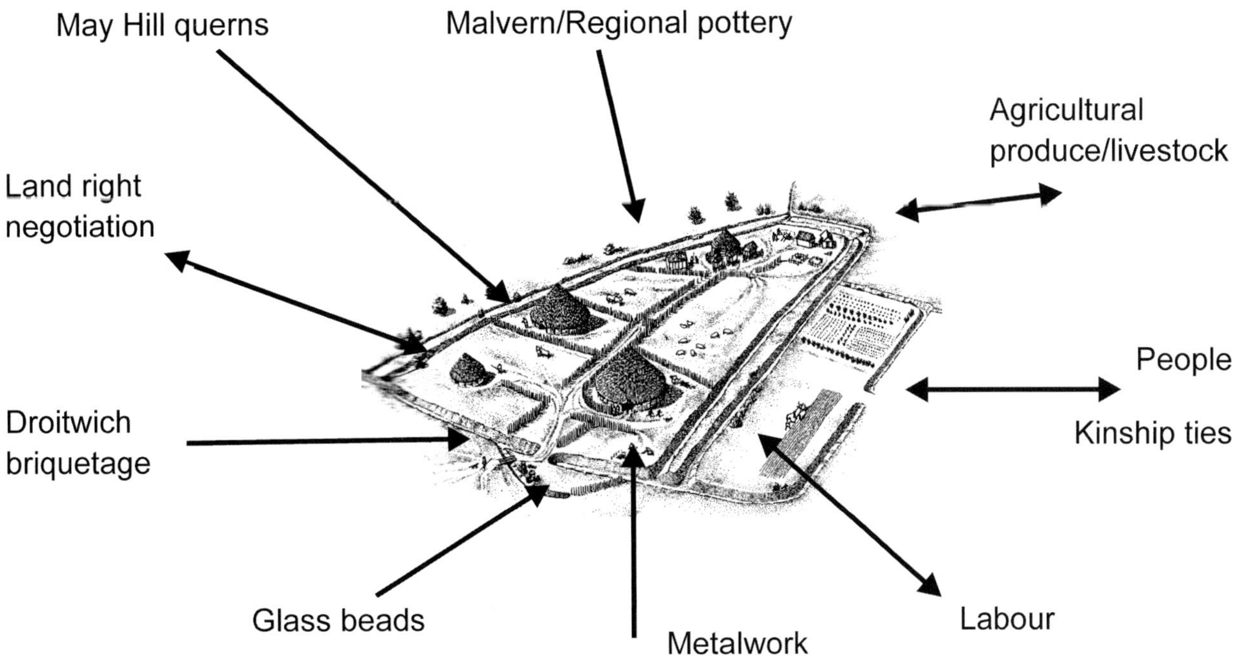

Fig. 9. Model of social relations engendered through exchange at an idealised enclosure community in the Severn–Cotswolds (Frocester reconstruction after Price 2000).

opposite direction, these are generally assumed to be materials that do not survive in the archaeological record, such as animals, foodstuffs and skins. Such models rarely explore the social processes of exchange, instead regarding it as essentially a functional requirement.[10] Other studies, however, have emphasised the role of exchange as a process of social interaction: for Cumberpatch, 'the exchange of utilitarian goods and food is an important, and in some senses primary, field of discourse, closely involved in the reproduction of social practices and the social formation' (Cumberpatch 1995, 82)

Anthropological studies suggest that exchanging material culture is often a form of social discourse, embodying the social relations and 'needs' of individual communities (Hodder 1982; Saitta 2000). As Le Blanc (2000, 55) suggests for the Yanomamo, 'the main goal of trade in some situations could have been to cement relationships between groups and the goods would thus have been a secondary benefit'. Can we, therefore, continue to regard the exchange of material like querns, pottery, briquetage and metalwork in Later Iron Age Britain as a purely functional or 'economic' process? To what extent might such finds reflect social relationships, such as forming alliances and marriages, as much as trade in the items themselves?

Exchanges might not have been restricted to material culture, but could also have involved the gift of labour. As indicated above, landscape and settlement boundaries are an important feature of the Later Iron Age in the Severn–Cotswolds, and their construction and maintenance may well have played a part in negotiations and exchange (cf. Sharples 2007; Wigley this volume). Other items may also have been exchanged, including food, drink, and people, particularly if we consider feasting as part of the social reciprocity taking place (Hill 2002). In this way, enclosure communities were potentially engaged in a range of exchanges and relationships outside the immediate household group (Fig. 9).

For some elements of material culture, the source may have been extremely important. Querns in particular, as powerful tools for transforming foodstuffs, were fundamental to Iron Age life. Although information is limited, there is tantalising evidence from the region that querns were treated in special ways upon deposition, such as those placed in the entrances at Conderton Camp, Croft Ambrey and Salmonsbury (Moore 2003). Similar observations have been made elsewhere in Britain (e.g. Hill 1995, 108; Willis 1999, 99). If we accept this as confirming the importance of querns in Iron Age life, their provenance also seems likely to have been of particular significance.

Obtaining items from specific sources may relate to more than just any perceived functional superiority of the material. One factor may have been the physical nature and landscape prominence of these localities. May Hill

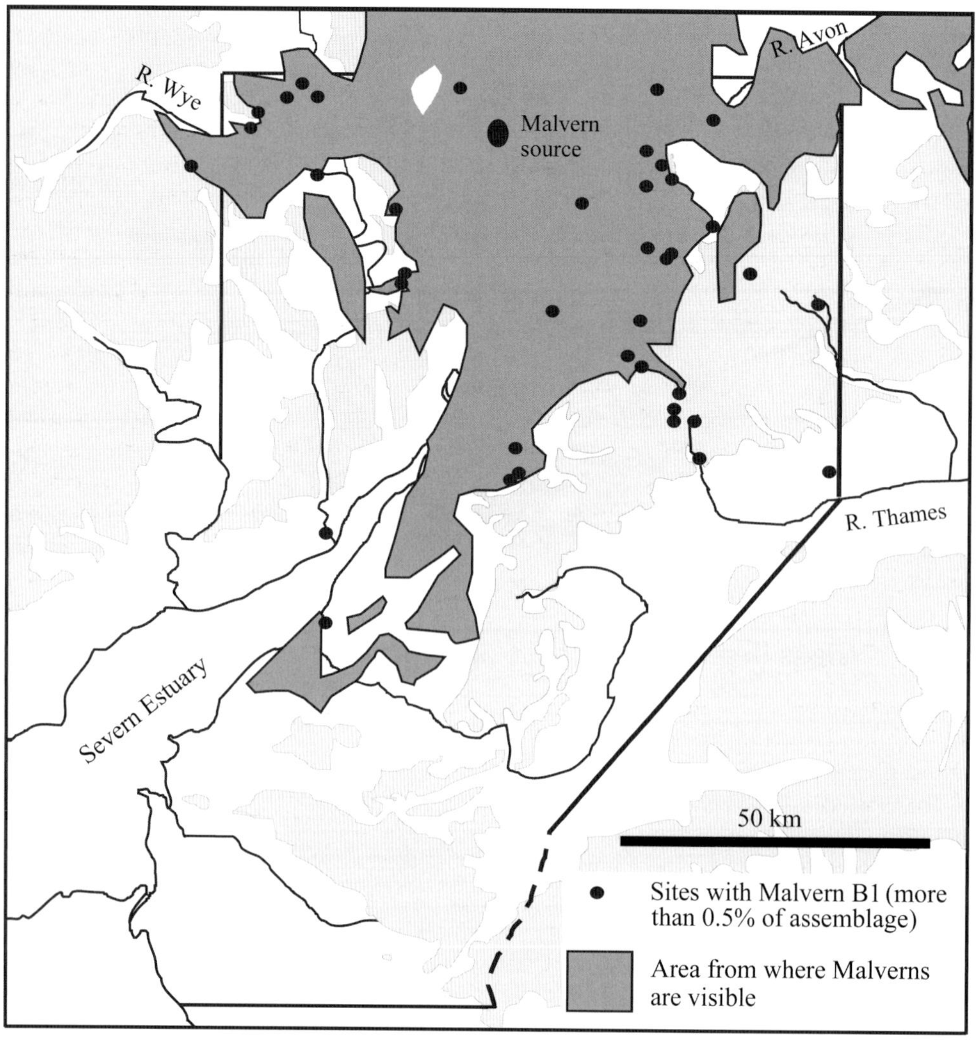

Fig. 10. The distribution of sites with Malvern B1 ware and visibility of the Malvern ridge (GIS viewshed Crown copyright/database right 2003. An Ordnance Survey/EDINA supplied service).

and the Malverns, for example, both dominate the lower Severn valley and can be seen from afar from the north, south and east, as well as from the Cotswold ridge. It is surely significant that the Malvern ridge was visible to a high proportion of the sites obtaining Malvern A and B1 in any quantity (Fig. 10). The very dominance of these locations may have led to them being regarded as special places, their symbolic role leading them in turn to be a focus for obtaining these materials. Similarly, their role as the source of superior querns and pottery may have consolidated the link to a special place and/or have imbued the artefacts themselves with a symbolism associated with the locations. Two large currency bar hoards deposited in rock fissures on the Malverns offer further testimony to the apparent symbolic importance of such natural features (Hingley 2005).

Such symbolic landscapes potentially had long and complex histories. Roe (1999) has noted early use of May Hill querns, potentially as far back as the Neolithic, and Bronze Age use of Malvern pottery temper has been suggested (Timby 2001), although not on the scale of the Later Iron Age. Whilst possibly marking a 'traditional' source (F. Roe pers. comm.), this does not sufficiently explain the increasing dominance of these sources. One possibility is that increased exploitation represented a conscious effort to perpetuate longer traditions of social exchange or to reference the cultural and landscape biographies of these localities. Another scenario is that pressure on land and resources and the growing complexity of social units generated a need to reinforce and negotiate the social bonds between communities through common relationships to the physical landscape. These shared visual references acted as part of the wider cultural biographies of the community.

It has been suggested that the Malvern clay sources were associated with particularly poor soil, leading local communities to specialise in pottery production (Jackson 1999). This may be too simplistic an explanation, but does reinforce the concept of these areas as somehow distinct from the rest of the landscape. The idea that 'marginal' landscapes formed distinct areas appropriate for specialised industries and exchange has already been suggested for the Somerset Levels (Sharples 1990), although with the crucial difference that Sharples regarded the Levels as a liminal zone between different social groups, whereas the quern and pottery sources may have acted as central foci. Unlike in many down-the-line exchanges, the high visibility of May Hill and the Malverns will have meant that most (if not all) of the communities obtaining their products were acutely aware of the source of this material and its significance. In this way, these sources may have been actively involved in creating and reinforcing social bonds.

These sources became increasingly important in the Later Iron Age. Increasing reliance on regionally distributed pottery at the expense of locally made material has been noted at many sites, including Beckford, Birdlip, Conderton, Evesham, Gilder's Paddock, and Uley Bury (Hancocks 1999; Morris 1994; 2005). By the latest phases at the first four of these sites, more than 50% of pottery was obtained from the non-local sources. The quern data does not permit such a detailed analysis, but there is some evidence that by the later centuries BC sites in the lower Severn–Cotswolds relied primarily on May Hill querns. To the south, a similar pattern emerges at Cadbury Castle, where a variety of sources were used in the earlier phases, whereas in the later phases Beacon Hill querns predominate (Roe 2000). This may partly relate to the increasing use of rotary querns (which were predominantly of this material), but implies a more firmly established exchange network with a single defined source, which (like May Hill and the Malverns) happens to be a prominent landscape feature, one of the highest points on the Mendip Hills.

The process of exchanging material – and having a visual reference for that process – may have been important in fostering a sense of shared identity between Later Iron Age communities in these two distinct areas of the Severn–Cotswolds. This need not have translated into defined social ties or membership of a wider corporate group; a number of sites were clearly able to engage in a variety of different exchange networks. Hallen (South Gloucestershire), for example, has produced Malvern B1 ware, Morris Group D pottery (from Martley, Worcestershire) and Glastonbury ware from the Mendips (Gardiner *et al.* 2002). The role of material culture in expressing cultural identity and ethnicity is highly complex (Jones 1997) and it would be wrong to suggest that these distributions necessarily represented tribal communities, or that possessing certain items of material culture necessarily reflected political or cultural affiliations (contra Blackmore *et al.* 1979; Cunliffe 1991, 171).

This does not, however, prevent us from examining the role of material culture – through production, exchange and interaction – in creating and sustaining social relations between communities. As Cumberpatch (1995) noted, whether or not linked to a knowledge of the source of the material, the physical process of exchange is important in forming, maintaining and manipulating social relationships between groups, and can in turn forge a sense of shared community and/or identity, however loose. This may be a part of – but not solely related to – the economic links fostered by such exchange. Where such relationships were concerned with obtaining such essential tools as querns and pottery – themselves probably bound into fertility and social rituals – they would have generated extremely strong socio-economic ties between communities, which would be broken only in extreme circumstances. If the model of enclosure communities enmeshed in an array of social obligations and relationships forged through local and regional exchanges presented above in Figure 9 is indeed valid, it suggests a far more complex and integrated Later Iron Age society in the Severn–Cotswolds than in previous accounts.

Exchange networks and the Bagendon–Ditches complex

It is noteworthy that the Bagendon–Ditches complex, and to some extent Salmonsbury, appear to be located on the peripheries of the existing exchange networks; for instance, although all the Bagendon sites have produced pottery from the Malverns (Timby 1999b; Trow 1988; Trow *et al.* forthcoming; Moore and Reece forthcoming), they are at the margins of the distribution. This may suggest that Bagendon was not as integrated into these networks and the social links generated by them as might have been expected. Freed of such ties, communities on the periphery were perhaps more able, socially and economically, to engage with new sources and forms of culture. The Bagendon–Ditches complex was thus better placed – or was deliberately placed – to develop new relationships to the east on account of its looser ties with communities to the north, south, and west. Similarly, its establishment in an area devoid of dense settlement and land divisions meant that it was not fixed into a set of local social obligations and land rights.

At this period, local identities must have been well established and integrated into wider socio-economic groupings. Rather than being central to such networks, Bagendon – at least – was peripheral. It would be wrong, however, to suggest that it was isolated from them. As I have noted, the constituent sites all had Malvern wares and it was in the Malvern area that the early Severn Valley wares emerged, possibly alongside continued production of traditional hand-made forms (Evans *et al.* 2000; Timby 1999a). The relationships were undoubtedly complex.

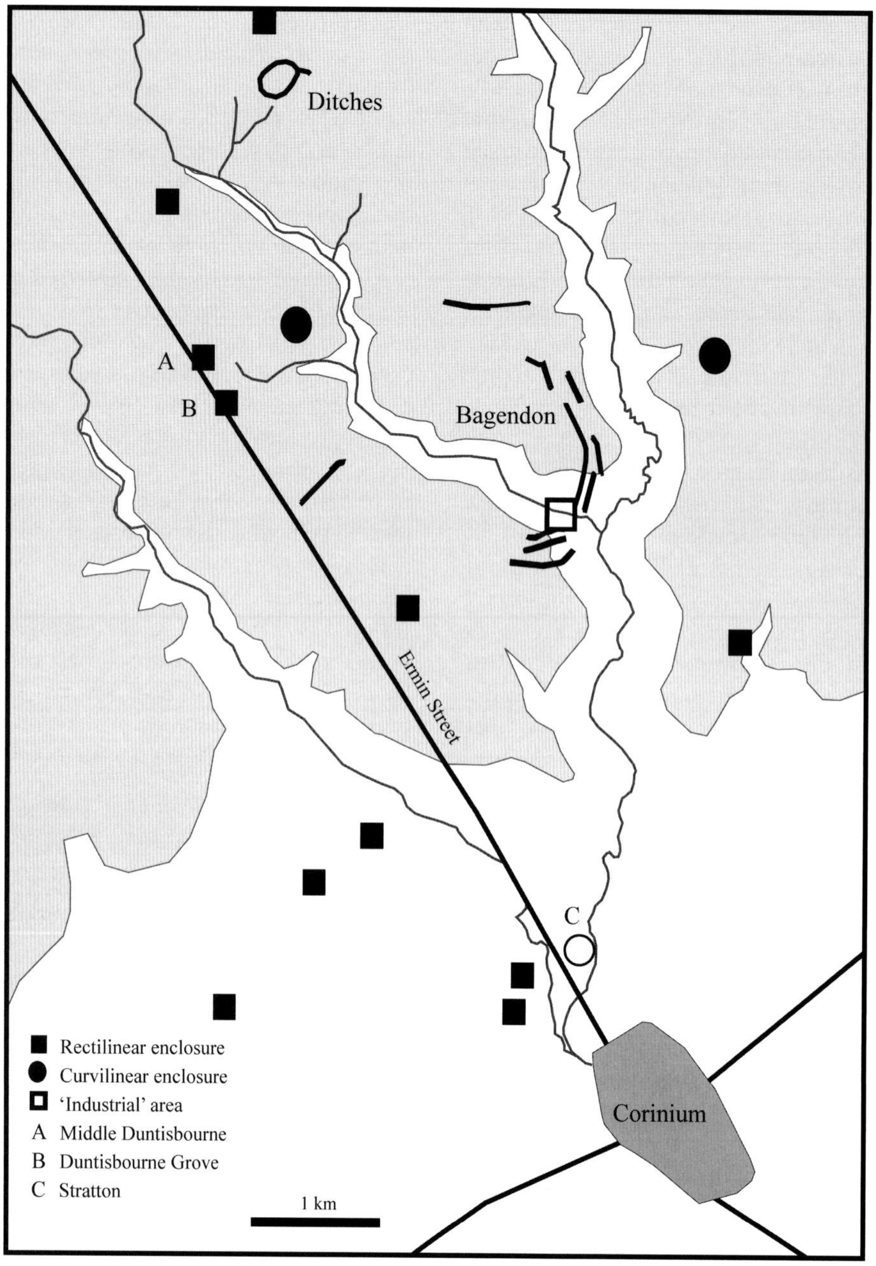

Fig. 11. The Late Iron Age complex at Bagendon–Ditches, Gloucestershire.

This is crucial for understanding the development of Bagendon: its inhabitants clearly were engaged with the communities to the north, even if the complex was deliberately sited to set it apart from existing ties.

Whether a discrete social group moved into the area (Hill this volume) or an existing elite seized a political and economic opportunity (Woolf 1993, 212), is uncertain; either way, placement between existing spheres of interaction and identity was highly significant. Whilst some have interpreted this location as the interface between a south-eastern 'core' and a western 'periphery' (Cunliffe 1991), what is in fact crucial is Bagendon's position between the densely occupied Later Iron Age landscapes of the Severn–Cotswolds and the upper Thames valley. We also need to examine the existing land use of the area. If the landscape was relatively empty prior to the construction of the Bagendon–Ditches complex, what does this mean? There is tantalising evidence of a banjo enclosure within the dyke complex (Fig. 11), which may hint at some kind of pre-existing focus. In addition, areas that were underused may have acted as 'neutral' foci for neighbouring Later Iron Age communities (cf. Haselgrove and Millett 1997; Hingley 1999, 244), as Sharples (1990) has suggested for the Lake Villages.

Crucial in this debate is the appearance in the later first century BC of a new regionally distributed exchange item: the so-called Western or 'Dobunnic' coinage (Haselgrove 1993; Van Arsdell 1994). Previous studies have tended to regard this coin series primarily as an expression of identity and as evidence of political or cultural unity in the Late Iron Age (Cunliffe 1984), whereas more recent studies stress the new sets of social relationships and messages implicit in coinage and its iconography (e.g. Creighton 2000; Hill this volume). The use of coinage could well indicate a move from the kind of social ties and obligations discussed above to more personal relationships between individuals or small groups.

The generally assumed relationship between coinage and *oppida* creates a misleading explanation for the role of these sites. Despite the large numbers of coins found there, Bagendon is, if anything, peripheral to the Western coin distribution. This same is true of other sites in the region with significant numbers of coin finds, such as Bath and Western-under-Penyard, and applies equally to several major sites in south-east England (Hill this volume). A second point to stress is that relatively few Western coins come from 'ordinary' Iron Age settlements; most are from *oppida*, temples, and early Roman sites in general (Haselgrove *et al.* forthcoming). This might imply that coins represent a set of relationships and activities associated only with particular types of sites and communities, although this of course assumes that coins were deposited where they were most frequently used; given that acts of deposition and/or 'losses' are only one part of a complex picture, this may not be so.

If we regard coins as expressing one-off, personal relationships, obligations and contracts[11] – and not necessarily as having any market function (e.g. Creighton 2000; Woolf 1993, 213) – the complexity of the Western issues and their distributions (Van Arsdell 1994) become more explicable. Together with the lack of direct correlation with other regionally distributed items, this suggests that is simplistic to see the coins as evidence of a unified (or bi-partite) territory (e.g. Cunliffe 1991, 171). Why should coinage be any more important than pottery or querns in expressing social and cultural identities? If anything, coins mark a move away from social relations bound into regionally recognised identities and cultural biographies to power relationships based primarily on individuals which came to the fore in the first century AD (Creighton 2000).

The nature of late Iron Age sites

Rather than being at the centre of previous developments, the Bagendon–Ditches complex was apparently peripheral, occupying a gap in the existing settlement pattern. Such a scenario has been suggested elsewhere, in particular for the emergence of Verulamium (St Albans) in an area largely devoid of previous occupation (Bryant this volume; Haselgrove and Millett 1997, 283). The existence of such gaps in the Later Iron Age settlement record remains somewhat controversial, contradicting the accepted view that by the mid first millennium BC, all areas of lowland southern Britain were densely settled (Cunliffe 1991, 533). Many gaps are argued to be the result of limited fieldwork, and where they seem genuine, expansion into them tends to be seen as part of a generalised process of population increase in the Later Iron Age. In contrast, Hill (1999; this volume) has sought to explain the emergence of Late Iron Age *oppida* in such areas in another way, linking it to the movement of new groups of peoples, or of communities marginalised in existing societies, into these areas. Hill sees these communities as more dynamic than those elsewhere and as the developers or bringers of new lifestyles, and more open to adopting exotic or foreign goods and habits.

The apparent lack of previous permanent settlement in these areas may be due to a number of factors, including possible special roles for these landscapes or their existence as liminal zones. As we have seen, some such areas, like the Malverns or Somerset Levels, supported specialised productive activities. Viewed in this light, Bagendon would be regarded not as peripheral, but playing a significant 'liminal' role between existing spheres of exchange and/or identity between the Thames valley to the south and the Severn–Cotswolds to the north and west. Here, the potential roles suggested for sites such as Bagendon – as production and exchange centres, meeting places, residences of new elites and potentially even as a ritual foci (Haselgrove 1995; 2001; Bryant this volume) – could exist outside the bonds of existing social networks and land rights. Such a model fits better with the evidence than an evolutionary model of social development that strives to see enclosures like Ditches and Salmonsbury as 'missing links' between the Middle Iron Age elites in their hillforts and Late Iron Age elites at *oppida*.

The morphology of sites such as Bagendon may well imply that they were involved in new activities, such as large-scale horse-rearing, as is suggested for Bury Hill, Hampshire (Creighton 2000). The possible banjo enclosure at Bagendon and the curving 'antenna' ditch at Ditches may well link the two in a specific function, perhaps stock corralling, as well as marking them out as distinct types of community. Potential parallels exist at Ashton Keynes, Barnsley Park, and Northleach, where complexes of banjo enclosures exist. Like Bagendon, these sites are peripheral to the exchange patterns noted above, being situated on the interface between the Cotswold dip-slope and the Thames valley (Fig. 12). Similar banjo complexes exist in Dorset and Hampshire and are dated to the Late Iron Age (Barrett *et al.* 1991;

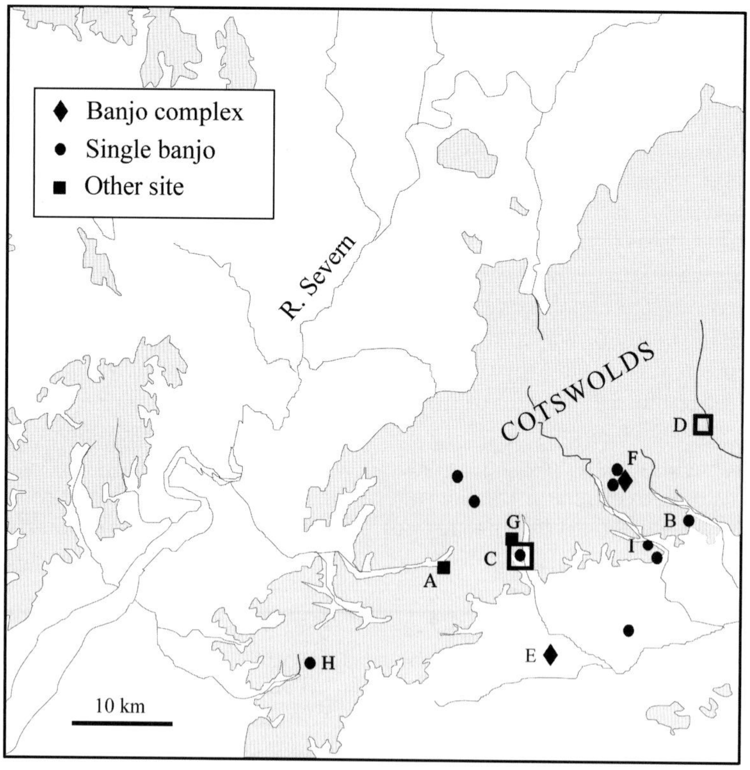

Fig. 12. The distribution of banjo enclosures in the northern Severn–Cotswolds. A. Frampton Mansell; B. Eastleach-Turville; C. Bagendon; D. Salmonsbury; E. Ashton Keynes; F. Northleach; G. Ditches; H. Lasborough; I. Barnsley Park.

Corney 1989); that at Gussage–Cow Down is particularly similar to Northleach. Several of these Wessex complexes have yielded imported pottery and Iron Age coinage, leading to the suggestion that they played a similar role to *oppida*; like their counterparts in the Gloucestershire Cotswolds, their distribution is discrete from the major hillforts (Barrett *et al.* 1991; Haselgrove 1994). Did these Wessex communities also operate on the margins of existing social networks and as a result were they able and/or more willing to engage in new relationships when the opportunity arose? Could the Bagendon *oppidum* have developed from such a complex and/or had similar roles?

How can the development of Bagendon be placed in the context of debates on 'Romanisation'? On the periphery and engaged in different activities from its neighbours, the inhabitants would have had more opportunity and indeed need or incentive to adopt the new lifestyles becoming available than communities economically and socially bound into existing exchange systems. Several Late Iron Age sites in the region have early villas, notably Ditches (Trow *et al.* forthcoming) and probably Waltham near Whittington (Hirst 2001), indicating rapid adoption of Roman 'lifeways' and building styles. The close relationship of many villas – including Barnsley Park,[12] Lasborough, and possibly Rodmarton – to banjo enclosures implies that their associated communities were also among the quickest to adopt Roman habits (Moore 2003). This phenomenon occurs elsewhere, particularly in parts of Wessex (M. Corney pers. comm.).

The tendency has been to regard sites like Ditches as the home of a new elite, who consciously opted for a Roman lifestyle, in contrast to the inhabitants of areas like the upper Thames valley who maintained a more traditional 'Iron Age' way of life (cf. Hingley 1989; e.g. Robinson 1981, 274). This may mask a more complex picture. It may be better to regard these Cotswold communities as better able to move to new lifeways than others in the region. This may mark a tension and difference – as suggested at Cadbury Castle – between those communities (and individuals?) that were able – or chose – to move away from existing traditions and could recast themselves as 'Roman', in contrast to those who were unwilling, unable, or did not comprehend the change to 'Roman' ways of life (Barrett *et al.* 2000, 323). These 'Romanising' communities need not have been the existing (or even new) elites, but simply those who were less integrated into existing social and economic networks.[13] We must be careful, however, that we do not simply replace one set of oppositions with another: 'Romanisers' versus 'native traditionalists'. The nature, meanings and reasons for the adoption of Roman-style buildings could be very different, even at two sites as close as Ditches and Frocester. What we appear to see in the Late Iron Age is a fracturing of society, with different groups and communities breaking away from existing well-defined relationships and adopting various attributes of different lifeways.

The treatment of human remains in the Severn–Cotswolds is one reflection of the complexity of identities being expressed in the Late Iron Age and shows that what was happening at this period was more than simple acceptance or rejection of a 'Roman' or 'Gallo-Belgic' cultural package. On the one hand, the rich inhumation burials at Birdlip mark a form of social expression not previously seen in the region, but visible elsewhere in southern England (Staelens 1982) and some individuals (but only very few) may have begun to engage in the cremation rites seen in south-east England (Moore 2003). On the other hand, the presence of disarticulated remains of skulls and long bones in settlements shows that other members of the population continued to be treated in 'traditional' ways, even at sites like Ditches and Bagendon that were using imported pottery (Trow 1988; Trow *et al.* forthcoming; Moore and Reece forthcoming).

One cultural package was not simply replaced by another, not even by individual groups. Instead, a previously relatively unified set of lifeways seems to have fragmented into a variety of different attitudes to food, social obligations, and death, with some communities (possibly new elites), as at Bagendon, adopting new lifestyles and economies, whilst other groups continued on trajectories already established in earlier centuries (cf. Hill this volume). The destabilising effect of influence from the south-east (Haselgrove 1982; 1987; Cunliffe 1988) must not be overlooked in the emergence of certain groups as dominant whilst others continued to operate on traditional terms. Some communities probably strongly resisted change to their lifestyles, some potentially violently. There is no evidence of a linear model of evolution from a Later Iron Age tribal society.

We must not assume that other major Late Iron Age sites in the region performed the same roles or reflect the same social processes as Bagendon. Salmonsbury, for instance, has some morphological similarities with banjo enclosures – the antenna ditches and presumed emphasis on stock control – but there are also significant differences in form and probable chronology between it and Bagendon, and it is located in an area with plentiful Middle Iron Age settlement. The apparent dense occupation of the interior and its division into defined areas may therefore mark a process of social aggregation reminiscent of that taking place in parts of northern France (Haselgrove 1995; this volume). In all probability, Salmonsbury was engaged in a quite different set of relations between communities than Bagendon, even if it too was peripheral to the major exchange networks of the Severn–Cotswolds.

Even within the region, the patterns discussed in this paper are localised. Continuity of material culture appears far more apparent in Avon and northern Somerset than it is further north, despite the apparent similarities of the exchange systems operating in each zone. More sites show continuity from the 'Middle' Iron Age through to the Roman period, amongst them Butcombe (Fowler 1968) and Cadbury Castle (Barrett *et al.* 2000).[14] Here too, the adoption of wheel-thrown wares and other Late Iron Age material was evidently variable and locally specific.

We should be careful, therefore, not to over-generalise about the development of Late Iron Age sites, when this evidently resulted from a complex combination of cultural choices, location and availability. It is important to question why developments to the south were different from those to the north and why no obvious parallel to Bagendon emerged,[15] or why Dorset is different yet again (cf. Blackmore *et al.* 1979; Sharples 1990). What is becoming clear is that the character of existing social systems had a crucial role everywhere and that the emergence of Late Iron Age phenomena – *oppida*, cremation burial, pottery and so on – relates to the choices made by existing communities (cf. Hill this volume), who selected and modified particular traits according to their existing cultural traditions, rather than adopting the whole 'package'.

Conclusions

This paper has suggested that current chronological models mask more subtle changes during the Later Iron Age. Individual communities were engaged in different sets of exchanges and social relations, which aided the construction of their cultural identity. These identities were influential in determining which communities became involved in the changes that took place from the first century BC onward. Rather than there being a clear break with the past, individual communities reacted to change in different ways and at different points in time, with those on the peripheries of existing exchange networks more willing – and often more able – to adopt new lifestyles and exploit new spheres of influence. Even before this period, important production centres were situated in parts of the landscape peripheral to existing groups. It is against this background that the emergence of Bagendon is best viewed – situated deliberately apart from existing communities and thus better able to exploit new resources and possibilities.

To achieve a better understanding of Later Iron Age societies, we need to go beyond simply reversing the core–periphery model and instead visualise how individual communities were involved in processes of change or stasis. Similarly, whilst rejecting quasi-economic models of exchange, we must now pay more attention to the sources of material culture and the social role of its exchange in creating wider regional identities and power structures.

Acknowledgments

I am grateful to J.D. Hill, Richard Reece and Mark Bowden for commenting on earlier drafts of this paper, to Colin Haselgrove and Richard Hingley for discussing many of the ideas presented here, and to Fiona Roe for comments on the quern evidence. My thanks also to those at the county HERs and units who assisted in searches of their archives, in particular to Neil Holbrook and the staff of Cotswold Archaeology for information on a number of ongoing projects prior to publication. Any errors or omissions remain my own. This paper is based on research for my Ph.D., which was funded by the AHRB.

Notes

1. The term Later Iron Age is used throughout this paper for the period from the fourth century BC to first century AD. The problems raised by applying the separate terms Middle and Late Iron Age are discussed later in the paper.
2. For a recent discussion of these issues, see Wigley (2001) on Shropshire and the Cornovii.
3. Information from Worcestershire County Council Archaeological Services.
4. The 1980s excavations yielded some evidence of a pre-first century AD ditch at Bagendon (Moore and Reece forthcoming), and there is possible Middle–Late Iron Age settlement continuity at Pheasant Way, Cirencester (R. Reece pers. comm.).
5. See Moore (2003) for a fuller discussion of sites with possible Late Iron Age activity.
6. The start date for Ditches remains contentious, but there is little to suggest a construction date before the late first century BC or early first century AD. Trow's (1988, 37) second/first century BC date for the initial enclosure is based on the presence of the currency bars and 'Middle Iron Age form pottery', although both could be slightly later.
7. Some caution must be noted here, as a full report on the pottery was not available from the excavator.
8. See Peacock (1968; 1969) and Timby (1999a) for fabric definitions.
9. For a fuller discussion of quern provenance and depositional practices see Moore (2003).
10. Morris (1996, 46) hints at the possible social implications.
11. Or between individuals and the gods, as indicated by the frequent presence of coins on Late Iron Age/early Roman ritual sites.
12. The Barnsley Park villa does not seem to be earlier than the second century AD (Webster 1981; 1982); however, the presence of Iron Age pottery and a coin, as well as circular structures which are almost certainly roundhouses rather than animals pens, could well point to Iron Age activity on or near the site.
13. Richard Reece has even suggested to me that we could envisage these as dynasties 'inserted' from elsewhere – yet who would manipulate such an insertion (and why) seems difficult to explain.
14. Although with all sites the evidence is complex. At Cadbury Castle, for example, there is some suggestion of a hiatus in occupation around the first century BC, although this is open to debate.
15. Both Camerton and Ilchester have been proposed as candidates (Cunliffe 1982; 1991), but no convincing evidence exists, almost certainly because different social and settlement systems existed in those areas.

Bibliography

Atkin, M. 1987. Excavation in Gloucester. An interim report, *Glevensis,* 21, 5–17.

Atkin, M. 1991. Archaeological fieldwork in Gloucester, 1990. An interim report, *Glevensis* 25, 4–33.

Barber, A. and Leah, M. 1998. Prehistoric and Romano-British activity at Bourton-on-the-Water Primary school, Gloucestershire. Excavations 1998. Unpublished Cotswold Archaeological Trust report.

Barrett, J., Bradley, R. and Green, M. 1991. *Landscape, Monuments and Society.* Cambridge: Cambridge University Press.

Barrett, J., Freeman, P. and Woodward, A. 2000. *Cadbury Castle, Somerset. The Later Prehistoric and Early Historic Archaeology.* London: English Heritage Archaeological Report 20.

Bevan, B. (ed.) 1999. *Northern Exposure: Interpretative Devolution and the Iron Ages in Britain.* Leicester: Leicester Archaeology Monograph 4.

Blackmore, C., Braithwaite, M. and Hodder, I. 1979. Social and cultural patterning in the late Iron Age in Southern England, in B. Burnham and J. Kingsbury (eds), *Space, Hierarchy and Society*, 93–112. Oxford: British Archaeological Reports International Series 59

Brossler, A., Gocher, M., Laws, G. and Roberts, M. 2002. Shorncote Quarry: excavations of a late Prehistoric landscape in the Upper Thames Valley, 1997–1998, *Transactions of the Bristol and Gloucestershire Archaeological Society* 120, 37–88.

Champion, T.C. and Collis, J.R. (eds) 1996. *The Iron Age in Britain and Ireland: Recent Trends.* Sheffield: J.R. Collis Publications.

Clifford, E. 1961. *Bagendon: A Belgic Oppidum.* Cambridge: Heffer and Sons.

Coleman, L. and Hancocks, A. F. forthcoming. *Excavations on the Wormington to Tirley Pipeline, 2000: Prehistoric, Romano-British and Anglo-Saxon Activity at five sites by the Carrant Brook and River Ishbourne, Gloucestershire and Worcestershire.* Cirencester: Cotswold Archaeology Occasional Paper 2.

Corney, M. 1989. Multiple ditch systems and late Iron Age settlement in Wessex, in M. Bowden, D. Mackay and P. Topping (eds), *From Cornwall to Caithness: Some Aspects of British Field Archaeology*, 111–121. Oxford: British Archaeological Reports British Series 209.

Creighton, J. 2000. *Coins and Power in Late Iron Age Britain.* Cambridge: Cambridge University Press.

Creighton, J. 2001. The Iron Age–Roman transition, in S. James and M. Millett (eds), *Britons and Romans: Advancing an Archaeological Agenda*, 4–11. York: Council for British Archaeology Research Report 125.

Cumberpatch, C. 1995. Production and Society in the Later Iron Age of Bohemia and Moravia, in Hill and Cumberpatch 1995, 67–94.

Cunliffe, B. 1976. The origins of urbanisation in Britain, in Cunliffe and Rowley 1976, 135–162.

Cunliffe, B. 1982. Iron Age settlement and pottery 650 BC–60 AD, in M. Aston and I. Burrow (eds), *Archaeology of Somerset*, 53–61. Taunton: Somerset County Council.

Cunliffe, B. 1984. The Iron Age in Gloucestershire, *Transactions of the Bristol and Gloucester Archaeological Society* 102, 2–9.

Cunliffe, B. 1988. *Greeks, Roman and Barbarians: Spheres of Interaction.* London: Batsford.

Cunliffe, B. 1991. *Iron Age Communities in Britain* (3rd edn). London: Routledge.

Cunliffe, B. and Rowley, T. (eds) 1976. *Oppida in Barbarian Europe.* Oxford: British Archaeological Reports International Series 11.

Darvill, T. 1987. *Prehistoric Gloucestershire.* Gloucester: Alan Sutton.

Dinn, J. and Evans, J. 1990. Aston Mill Farm, Kemerton: excavation of a ring ditch, middle Iron Age enclosure and a Grubenhaus, *Transactions of the Worcestershire Archaeology Society* (Ser. 3) 12, 5–66.

Dunning, G.C. 1976. Salmonsbury, Bourton on the Water, in D.W. Harding (ed.), *Hillforts. Later Prehistoric Earthworks in Britain and Ireland*, 76–118. London: Academic Press.

Edwards, R. and Hurst, D. 2000. Iron Age settlement and a medieval and later Farmstead: excavation at 93–97 High Street, Evesham, *Transactions of the Worcestershire Archaeological Society* 17, 73–111.

Evans, C.J., Jones, L. and Ellis, P. 2000. *Severn Valley Ware Production at Newland Hopfields. Excavation of a Romano-British Kiln Site at North End Farm, Great Malvern, Worcestershire in 1992 and 1994.* Oxford: British Archaeological Reports British Series 313.

Ferrell, G. 1995. Space and society: New perspectives on the Iron Age of North East England, in Hill and Cumberpatch 1995, 129–148.

Fitzpatrick, A.P. and Timby, J. 2002. Roman pottery in the Iron Age, in Woodward and Hill 2002, 161–172.

Fowler, P. 1968. Excavations of a Romano-British settlement at Row of Ashes Farm, Butcombe, Somerset: interim report 1966–7, *Proceedings of the Bristol Spelaeological Society* 11, 209–236.

Gardiner, J., Allen, M., Hamilton-Dyer, S., Laidlaw, M. and Scaife, R. 2002. Making the most of it: Late prehistoric pastoralism in the Avon levels, Severn Estuary, *Proceedings of the Prehistoric Society* 68, 1–40.

Gerritsen, F. 2003. *Local Identities. Landscapes and Community in the Later Prehistoric Meuse–Demer–Scheldt Region.* Amsterdam: Amsterdam Archaeological Studies 9.

Gwilt, A. and Haselgrove, C. (eds) 1997. *Reconstructing Iron Age Societies.* Oxford: Oxbow Monograph 71.

Hancocks, A. 1999. The Pottery, in Parry 1999, 104–110.

Haselgrove, C. 1976. External trade as a stimulus to urbanization, in Cunliffe and Rowley 1976, 25–50.

Haselgrove, C. 1982. Wealth, prestige and power: the dynamics of late Iron Age political centralisation in south-east England, in C. Renfrew and S. Shennan (eds), *Ranking, Resource and Exchange*, 79–88. Cambridge: Cambridge University Press.

Haselgrove, C. 1987. Culture process on the periphery: Belgic Gaul and Rome during the late Republic and early Empire, in M. Rowlands, M. Larsen and K. Kristiansen (eds), *Centre and Periphery in the Ancient World*, 104–124. Cambridge: Cambridge University Press.

Haselgrove, C. 1993. The development of British Iron Age coinage, *Numismatic Chronicle* 153, 18–62.

Haselgrove, C. 1994. Iron Age society in Wessex, in A.P. Fitzpatrick and E.L. Morris (eds), *The Iron Age in Wessex: Recent Work*, 1–3. Salisbury: Trust for Wessex Archaeology.

Haselgrove, C. 1995. Late Iron Age society in Britain and North East Europe: structural transformation or superficial change?, in B. Arnold and D. Blair Gibson (eds), *Celtic Chiefdom, Celtic State*, 81–87. Cambridge: Cambridge University Press.

Haselgrove, C. 1997. Iron Age brooch deposition and chronology, in Gwilt and Haselgrove 1997, 51–72.

Haselgrove, C. 2001. Iron Age Britain and its European setting, in J.R. Collis (ed.), *Society and Settlement in Iron Age Europe (Actes du XVIIIe Colloque de l'AFEAF, Winchester 1994)*, 37–72. Sheffield: J.R. Collis Publications.

Haselgrove, C. and Millett, M. 1997. Verlamion reconsidered, in Gwilt and Haselgrove 1997, 282–297.

Haselgrove, C. and Pope, R. (eds) 2007. *The Earlier Iron Age in Britain and the Near Continent.* Oxford : Oxbow Books.

Haselgrove, C., Armit, I., Champion, T., Creighton, J., Gwilt, A., Hill, J.D., Hunter, F. and Woodward, A. 2001. *Understanding the British Iron Age: An Agenda for Action.* Salisbury: Wessex Archaeology.

Haselgrove, C., Leins, I. and Moore, T. forthcoming. Don't mention the Dobunni! An archaeological study of the late Iron Age coinage of the Severn–Cotswolds, in P. Guest and J. Williams (eds), *Coins and an Archaeologist: A Symposium for Richard Reece.*

Hawkes, C.F.C. 1959. The A B C of the British Iron Age, *Antiquity* 33, 170–182.

Hawkes, C.F.C. 1961. The Western Third C culture and the Belgic Dobunni, in Clifford 1961, 43–74.

Hegmon, M. (ed.) 2000. *The Archaeology of Regional Interaction: Region, Warfare and Exchange across the American South-West and Beyond.* Boulder: University Press of Colorado.

Heighway, C. 1989. Excavations near the site of St Georges Church, Kings Stanley, *Glevensis* 23, 33–42.

Hencken, T. C. 1938. The excavation of the Iron Age camp on Bredon Hill, Worcestershire, 1935–1937, *Archaeological Journal* 95, 1–111.

Hill, J.D. 1995. *Ritual and Rubbish in the Iron Age of Wessex.* Oxford: British Archaeological Reports British Series 242.

Hill, J.D. 1996. Hillforts and the Iron Age of Wessex, in Champion and Collis 1996, 95–116.

Hill, J.D. 1997. 'The end of one kind of body and the beginning of another kind of body'? Toilet instruments and Romanization, in Gwilt and Haselgrove 1997, 96–107.

Hill, J.D. 1999. Settlement, landscape and regionality: Norfolk and Suffolk in the Pre-Roman Iron Age of Britain and beyond, in J. Davies and T. Williamson (eds), *Land of the Iceni: the Iron Age in Northern East Anglia*, 185–207. Norwich: Studies in East Anglia History 4.

Hill, J.D. 2002. Just about the potter's wheel? Using, making and depositing middle and later Iron Age pots in East Anglia, in Woodward and Hill 2002, 143–161.

Hill, J.D. and Cumberpatch, C. (eds) 1995. *Different Iron Ages: Studies on the Iron Age in Temperate Europe.* Oxford: British Archaeological Reports International Series 602.

Hingley, R. 1984. Towards a social analysis in archaeology: Celtic society in the Iron Age of the Upper Thames valley, in B. Cunliffe and D. Miles (eds), *Aspects of the Iron Age in Central Southern Britain*, 72–88. Oxford: Oxford University Committee for Archaeology Monograph 2.

Hingley, R. 1989. *Rural Settlement in Roman Britain.* London: Seaby.

Hingley, R. 1996. Prehistoric Warwickshire: a review of the evidence, *Transactions of the Birmingham and Warwickshire Archaeology Society* 100, 1–24.

Hingley, R. 1999. The creation of later prehistoric landscapes and context of the reuse of Neolithic and early Bronze Age

monuments in Britain and Ireland, in Bevan 1999, 233–252.
Hingley, R. 2005. Iron Age 'Currency bars' in Britain: items of exchange in liminal contexts?, in C. Haselgrove and D. Wigg-Wolf (eds), *Iron Age Coinage and Ritual Practices*, 183–205. Mainz: Studien zu Fundmünzen der Antike 20.
Hirst, K. 2001. *An Evaluation of Archaeological Remains at Waltham Roman Villa, Gloucestershire*. Unpublished Time Team report.
Hodder, I. 1982. Toward a contextual approach to prehistoric exchange, in J. Ericson and T. Earle (eds), *Contexts for Prehistoric Exchange*, 199–211. New York: Academic Press.
Hurst, H. 1999a. Topography and identity in *Glevum coloniae*, in Hurst 1999b, 113–135.
Hurst, H. (ed.) 1999b. *The Coloniae of Roman Britain: New Studies and a Review. (Papers of the conference held at Gloucester July 1997)*. Portsmouth, Rhode Island: Journal of Roman Studies Supplementary Series 36.
Jackson, D. 1999. *Settlement and Society in the Welsh Marshes during the 1st millennium BC*. Unpublished Ph.D. thesis, University of Durham.
Jackson, R. 2000. *The Roman Settlement of Ariconium, near Weston-under-Penyard, Herefordshire: an Assessment and Synthesis of the Evidence*. Unpublished Worcestershire County Council Archaeological Service Report 833.
Jones, S. 1997. *The Archaeology of Ethnicity*. London: Routledge.
Le Blanc, S. 2000. Regional interaction and warfare in the later prehistoric south-west, in Hegmon 2000, 41–70.
Marshall, A. 1978. The pre-Belgic Iron Age in the Northern Cotswolds, *Transactions of the Bristol and Gloucester Archaeology Society* 96, 9–16.
Marshall, A. 1991. *A defensively ditched, trapezoidal enclosure of later Iron Age date and Roman farmsteading area at The Bowsings, Guiting Power, Gloucestershire*. Cheltenham: Cotswold Archaeological Research Group Research Report 6.
Marshall, A. 1995. From Iron Age to Roman: The Park and Bowsings sites at Guiting Power, *Glevensis* 28, 13–19.
Marshall, A. 2001. Functional analysis of settlement areas: prospection over a defended enclosure of Iron Age date at the Bowsings, Guiting Power, Gloucestershire, *Archaeological Prospection* 8, 79–106.
Moore, T. 2003. *Iron Age Societies in the Severn–Cotswolds: Developing Narratives of Social and Landscape Change*. Unpublished Ph.D. thesis, University of Durham.
Moore, T. 2007. The Early to Later Iron Age transition in the Severn–Cotswolds: enclosing the household? in Haselgrove and Pope 2007, 259–278.
Moore, T. and Reece, R. 2001. The Dobunni, *Glevensis* 34, 17–26.
Moore, T. and Reece, R. forthcoming. *Excavations at Bagendon, Gloucestershire, 1979–81*.
Morris, E.L. 1983. *Salt and Ceramic Exchange in Western Britain during the First Millennium BC*. Unpublished Ph.D. thesis, University of Southampton.
Morris, E.L. 1985. Prehistoric salt distributions: two case studies from Western Britain, *Bulletin of the Board of Celtic Studies* 12, 336–379.
Morris, E.L. 1994. Production and distribution of pottery and salt in Iron Age Britain: a review, *Proceedings of the Prehistoric Society* 60, 371–393.
Morris, E.L. 1996. Artefact production and exchange, in Champion and Collis 1996, 41–66.
Morris, E.L., Marsden, P. and Williams, D. 2005. Pottery and briquetage, in Thomas 2005, 117–147.
Mudd, A., Williams, R. and Lupton, A. 1999. *Excavations alongside Roman Ermin Street, Gloucestershire and Wiltshire. The Archaeology of the A419/A417 Swindon to Gloucester Road Scheme, Vol. 2*. Oxford: Oxford Archaeological Unit.
Napthan, M., Hancocks, A., Pearson, E. and Ratkai, S. 1997. *Evaluation of Proposed Wyre Piddle Bypass*. Unpublished report, County Archaeological Services Hereford and Worcester County Council.
Nichols, P., 2001. Bourton on the Water, Primary school, in J. Wills (ed.), Archaeology Review 25, *Transactions of the Bristol and Gloucestershire Archaeological Society* 119, 187.
Nichols, P. 2004. Bourton on the Water. Primary school, in J. Wills (ed.) Archaeology Review 28, *Transactions of the Bristol and Gloucestershire Archaeological Society* 122, 175
Oswald, A. 1974. Excavations at Beckford, *Transactions of the Worcestershire Archaeology Society* 3, 7–54.
Parry, C. 1998a. Excavations near Birdlip, Cowley, Gloucestershire 1987–88, *Transactions of the Bristol and Gloucester Archaeological Society* 116, 25–92.
Parry, C. 1998b. The Strensham to Mythe water pipeline, 1991. The Worcestershire section, *Transactions of the Worcestershire Archaeology Society* 16, 69–78.
Parry, C. 1999. Iron Age, Romano-British and Medieval occupation at Bishops Cleeve, Gloucestershire; excavations at Gilder's Paddock 1989 and 1990–1, *Transactions of the Bristol and Gloucestershire Archaeological Society* 117, 89–118.
Peacock, D.P.S. 1968. A petrological study of certain Iron Age pottery from Western England, *Proceedings of the Prehistoric Society* 34, 414–427.
Peacock, D.P.S. 1969. A contribution to the study of Glastonbury Ware, *Antiquaries Journal* 49, 41–61.
Price, E. 2000. *Frocester: a Romano-British Settlement, its Antecedents and Successors, Vol. 1. The Sites; Vol. 2. The Finds*. Stonehouse: Gloucester and District Archaeological Group.
RCHME 1976. *Iron Age and Romano-British Monuments in the Gloucestershire Cotswolds. County of Gloucester, Vol. 1*. London: HMSO.
Rigby, V. 1982. The coarse pottery, in J. Wacher and A. McWhirr (eds), *Early Roman Occupation at Cirencester. Cirencester Excavations I*, 153–203. Cirencester: Cirencester Excavation Committee.
Robinson, M. 1981. The Iron Age to Early Saxon environment of the Upper Thames terraces, in M. Jones and G. Dimbleby (eds), *The Environment of Man: the Iron Age to the Anglo-Saxon Period*, 251–286. Oxford: British Archaeological Reports British Series 87.
Roe, F. 1995. 6.9 Stone, in J. Coles and S. Minnit (eds), *Industrious and Fairly Civilised. The Glastonbury Lake Village*, 161–167. Taunton: Somerset Levels Project and Somerset County Council Museums Service.
Roe, F. 1999. The worked stone, in Mudd *et al.* 1999, 414–421.
Roe, F. 2000. Worked stone, in Barrett *et al.* 2000, 262–265.
Saitta, D. 2000. Theorizing the political economy of southwestern exchange, in Hegmon 2000, 151–167.
Saville, A. 1979. *Excavations at Guiting Power, Gloucestershire 1974*. Cheltenham: CRAAGS Occasional Paper 7.
Saville, A. 1983. *Uley Bury and Norbury Hillforts. Rescue Excavations at Two Gloucestershire Iron Age Sites*. Bristol: Western Archaeological Trust Excavation Monograph 5.

Saville, A. 1984. The Iron Age, in A. Saville (ed.), *Archaeology in Gloucestershire; from the Earliest Hunters to the Industrial Age*, 140–178. Cheltenham: Bristol and Gloucester Archaeology Society.

Sharples, N. 1990. Late Iron Age society and continental trade in Dorset, in A. Duval, J.P. Le Bihan, and Y. Menez (eds), *Les Gaulois d'Armorique. La fin de l'âge du Fer en Europe Tempérée (Actes du XIIe colloque de l'AFEAF, Quimper 1988)*, 299–304. Rennes: Revue Archéologique de l'Ouest Supplément 3.

Sharples, N. 2007. Building communities and creating identities in the first millennium BC, in Haselgrove and Pope 2007, 174–184.

Staelens, Y. 1982. The Birdlip cemetery, *Transactions of the Bristol and Gloucester Archaeological Society* 100, 20–31.

Thomas, A., Holbrook, N. and Bateman, C. 2003. *Later Prehistoric and Romano-British Burial and Settlement at Hucclecote, Gloucestershire. Excavations in Advance of the Gloucester Business Park Link Road 1998*. Cirencester: Bristol and Gloucestershire Archaeological Reports 2.

Thomas, N. 2005. *Conderton Camp, Worcestershire: A Small Middle Iron Age Hillfort on Bredon Hill.* York: Council for British Archaeology Research Report 143.

Timby, J. 1998. *Excavations at Kingscote and Wycomb, Gloucestershire.* Cirencester: Cotswold Archaeological Trust.

Timby, J. 1999a. Pottery supply to Gloucester *colonia*, in Hurst 1999b, 37–44.

Timby, J. 1999b. Later Prehistoric and Roman pottery, in Mudd *et al.* 1999, 320–338.

Timby, J. 2000. Pottery (Roman, pre and post Roman), in Price 2000 Vol. 2, 125–162.

Timby, J. 2001. The pottery, in M. Leah and C. Young 2001. A Bronze Age burnt mound at Sandy Lane, Charlton Kings, Gloucestershire: excavation in 1971, *Transactions of the Bristol and Gloucestershire Archaeological Society* 119, 59–82.

Trow, S. 1982. The Bagendon Project 1981–82: A brief interim report, *Glevensis* 1, 26–29.

Trow, S. 1988. Excavations at Ditches hillfort, North Cerney, Gloucestershire, 1982–3, *Transactions of the Bristol and Gloucester Archaeological Society* 106, 19–86.

Trow, S., James, S. and Moore, T. forthcoming. *Excavations at Ditches 'hillfort' and Roman-British villa, North Cerney, Gloucestershire, 1984–5.*

Van Arsdell, R. 1994. *The Coinage of the Dobunni.* Oxford: Oxford University Committee for Archaeology Monograph 38.

Webster, G. 1981. The excavation of a Romano-British rural establishment at Barnsley Park: Part 1, *Transactions of the Bristol and Gloucester Archaeological Society* 99, 21–78.

Webster, G. 1982. The Excavation of a Romano-British rural establishment at Barnsley Park: Part 2, *Transactions of the Bristol and Gloucester Archaeological Society* 100, 56–89.

Webster, G. and Hobley, B. 1964. Aerial reconnaissance over the Warwickshire Avon, *Archaeological Journal* 71, 1–22.

Wigley, A. 2001. Searching for the Cornovii in the Iron Age: a critical consideration of the evidence, *West Midlands Archaeology* 44, 6–9.

Willis, S.H. 1994. Roman imports in Late Iron Age society: towards a critique of existing models, in S. Cottam, D. Dungworth, S. Scott and J. Taylor (eds), *TRAC 94. Proceedings of the Fourth Annual Theoretical Archaeology Conference, Durham 1994*, 141–150. Oxford: Oxbow Books.

Willis, S.H. 1996. The Romanization of pottery in assemblages in the east and north-east of England during the first century AD: a comparative analysis, *Britannia* 27, 179–218.

Willis, S.H. 1997. Settlement, materiality and landscape in the Iron Age of the East Midlands: evidence, interpretation and wider resonance, in Gwilt and Haselgrove 1997, 205–215.

Willis, S.H. 1999. Without and within: aspects of culture and community in the Iron Age of north-eastern England, in Bevan 1999, 81–110.

Willis, S.H. 2005. The later Bronze Age and the Iron Age, in N. Cooper (ed.), *The Archaeology of the East Midlands. An Archaeological Resource Assessment and Research Agenda,* 89–136. Leicester: Leicester Archaeology Monograph 13.

Wilmott, T. and Rahtz, S. 1985. An Iron Age settlement outside Kenchester, Herefordshire. Excavations 1977–79, *Transactions of the Woolhope Naturalists Field Club* 90, 36–185.

Woodward, A. and Hill, J.D. (eds) 2002. *Prehistoric Britain. The Ceramic Basis.* Oxford: Oxbow Books.

Woodward, A. and Leach, P. 1993. *The Uley Shrines.* London: English Heritage Archaeological Report 17.

Woolf, G. 1993. The social significance of trade in Late Iron Age Europe, in C. Scarre and F. Healy (eds), *Trade and Exchange in Prehistoric Europe*, 211–218. Oxford: Oxbow Monograph 33.

Wymark, C. 2003. *Thames Water Repairs to Public Sewers, Cirencester, Gloucestershire. Programme of Archaeological Recording.* Unpublished Cotswold Archaeology Report CA 03140.

Central places or special places? The origins and development of '*oppida*' in Hertfordshire

Stewart Bryant

Introduction

A previous review of the Late Iron Age of Hertfordshire and the North Chilterns (Bryant and Niblett 1997) assessed the 150-plus known sites, using data from published sources and Sites and Monuments Records, and attempted some basic spatial analysis. Most of the recorded evidence occurred within six large 'site-clusters', which are well known from the published literature: Braughing, Baldock, St Albans, Wheathampstead, Welwyn and the Bulbourne valley (Fig. 1). The article considered the evidence at each of the site-clusters for zoning, specialisation, and parallels elsewhere in Britain and Europe. However, few consistent patterns were apparent in the evidence, which was characterised amongst other things by its high diversity and variability in quality.

The present article summarises the key aspects of the author's Ph.D. thesis (Bryant 1999), which presented a more detailed analysis of the six Late Iron Age site-clusters as well as considering earlier and later periods of activity, and examining aspects of the local landscape as a factor in explaining origins and function. Each site-cluster will be examined in turn.

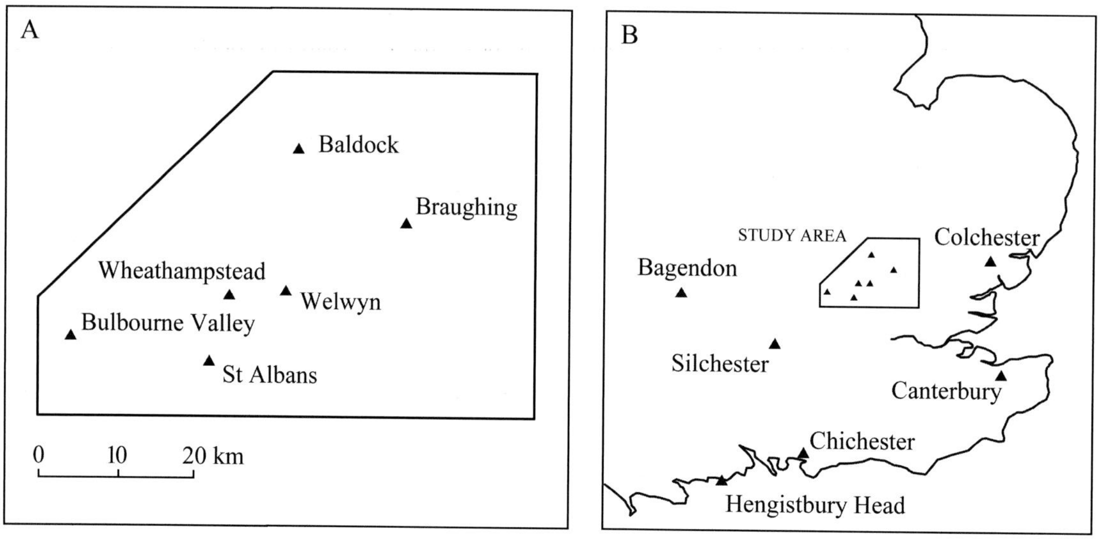

Fig. 1. A. Location of principal Late Iron Age site-clusters in the study area. B. Location of the study area in relation to other major sites in southern England.

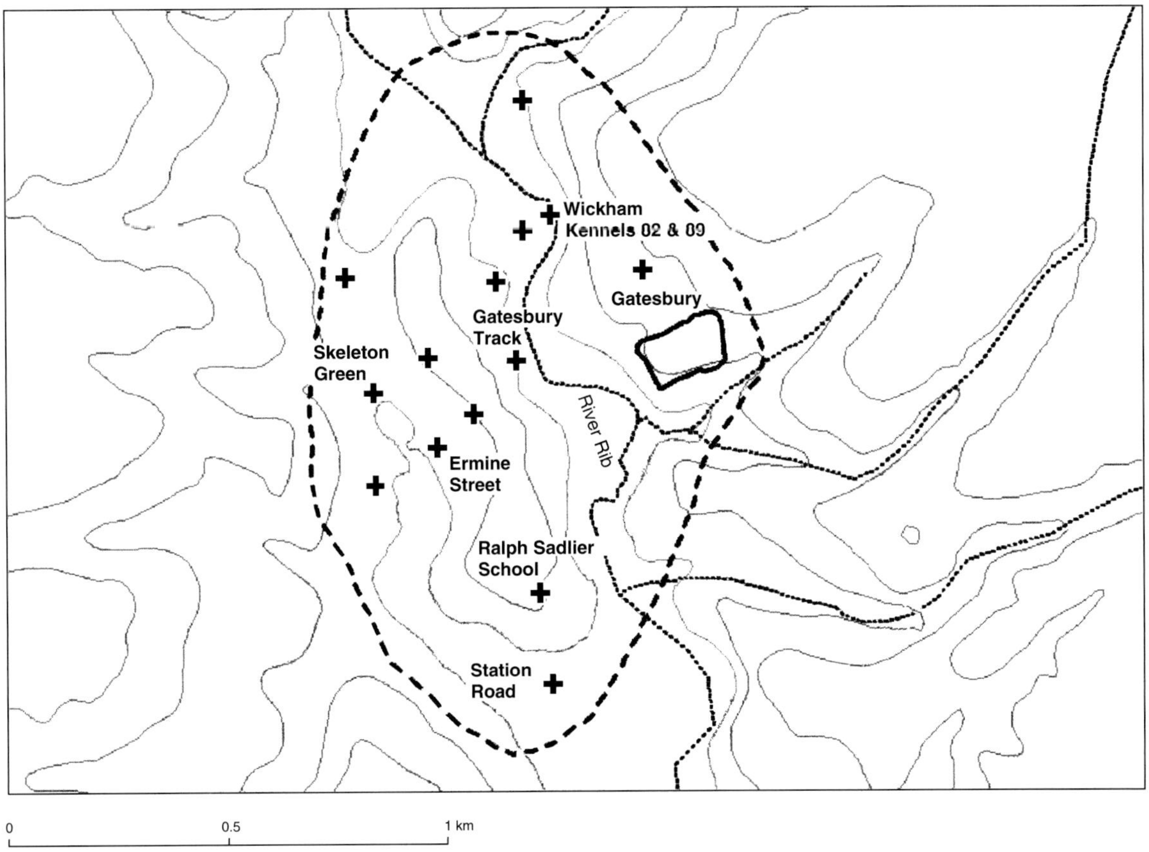

Fig. 2. The Braughing complex.

Braughing

Extent and survival of evidence

The broad limits of the Late Iron Age occupation at Braughing are reasonably well defined, comprising an oval area of 1.7 km^2 (Fig. 2). Watching briefs to the south of Station Road, Puckeridge (the most southerly site) have yielded no evidence of occupation. Likewise, no evidence has been forthcoming to the north of the boundary shown here (Thompson 2003).

The survival of evidence for Late Iron Age activity within this area is highly variable, due mainly to the extent of destruction caused by features associated with the subsequent Roman small town and erosion by ploughing. Of the 16 sites with Late Iron Age evidence, only two (Skeleton Green and Gatesbury Track) are relatively unaffected by these agencies. Skeleton Green occupies a low-lying area at the western base of Wickham Hill which has been protected from plough damage by a build-up of colluvium. Part of the area also appears to have been flooded in the early Roman period and was probably considered unsuitable for habitation. As a consequence, it was disturbed only by a few Roman cremation burials (Partridge 1981, 42). The Gatesbury Track site has also been unaffected by ploughing and, although there was Roman occupation, this does not appear to have disturbed the Late Iron Age deposits apart from a few post holes (Partridge 1979, 98, fig. 28). It is therefore no accident that these two sites provide the best structural and dating evidence of the 16 Late Iron Age sites at Braughing and figure strongly in past interpretations of the complex. However, it is important to note that less than one percent of the total area has been investigated and less than 0.2 % was well preserved or adequately excavated.

Chronology

Imported pottery from Italy and Gaul has been found at several Braughing sites, often (notably at Skeleton Green, Station Road, and Ermine Street) in large quantities (Partridge 1979; 1981; Potter and Trow 1988). Much of this pottery can be relatively accurately dated, as can other relatively abundant artefacts, such as brooches and coins. The coin evidence has also been used as an indicator of the relative intensity of occupation (Haselgrove 1988). The picture that emerges is, however, with a few exceptions, both complex and confusing, indicating that the focus of occupation and artefact deposition was relatively fluid between *c.* 30 BC and AD 40 (see Partridge 1975, fig. 4).

The possible pre-Caesarean phase

The one clear pattern identified by Partridge (1975) and Haselgrove (1988) is the early focus on the east side of the settlement area and to the north of the Gatesbury earthwork. Typologically early artefacts are known from the Gatesbury collection (Partridge 1981, 323–56), but the earliest stratified evidence comes from the small excavation at Gatesbury Track, where the earliest deposits were originally dated to *c.* 30–25 BC (Partridge 1979). There are, however, reasons for supposing they could be significantly earlier, since quantities of imported Italian Dressel 1 wine amphora were recovered, including the earlier Dressel 1A form, whose production is now dated to *c.* 150–75 BC (Loughton 2003).

Another indication of an early date for this phase at Gatesbury Track, including further possible evidence of links with Europe, is the presence of tall hand-made jars within the assemblage. These pots, which were replaced by wheel-made cordoned jars during the first century BC, suggest the early adoption of new specialised drinking forms from Gaul (Hill 2002). The variability of construction method and tempering used for the Gatesbury Track pottery also suggests experimentation at an early phase in the development of 'Belgic' pottery. The earliest deposits contained hand-made forms and wheel-turned pottery which was tempered with sand, a material more characteristic of earlier Iron Age pottery (Bryant 1995; Hill 2002). Hand-made, grog-tempered pottery was also found alongside early standard forms of grog-tempered, wheel-made 'Belgic' pottery in stratigraphically later deposits (Partridge 1979, 130; Thompson 1982, 644). The start of Gatesbury Track could therefore be conservatively placed within the bracket *c.* 120–70 BC.

The post-Caesarean phase

Figure 3 summarises the occupied periods at the eight Braughing sites for which close dating is possible. The dates for seven of the sites are taken from published reports; the eighth is based on a preliminary assessment of the pottery (Going 1980). The thick bars represent the estimated period of most intensive occupation and deposition; the thinner lines represent the total period of occupation. Some of the dates may need amending in the light of the general revision of continental Late La Tène chronology, particularly due to dendrochronology (Haselgrove 1996a), but nonetheless some clear observations can be made.

The general trends noted by Partridge, Haselgrove and others, are confirmed: the settlement was most active between *c.* 10 BC–AD 25, measured by the quantity of imports arriving and the extent of occupation, with both tailing off significantly after *c.* AD 30. Five of the eight sites were fairly intensively occupied during that period. A gradual decline in activity between AD 20 and 60 occurred, with just two sites occupied by *c.* AD 60. It should be emphasised that the dates are approximate and the specialist nature of the different dating techniques is such that most of the published dates could be subject to revision.

No clear chronological pattern can be related to the geography of the settlement, particularly the fact that

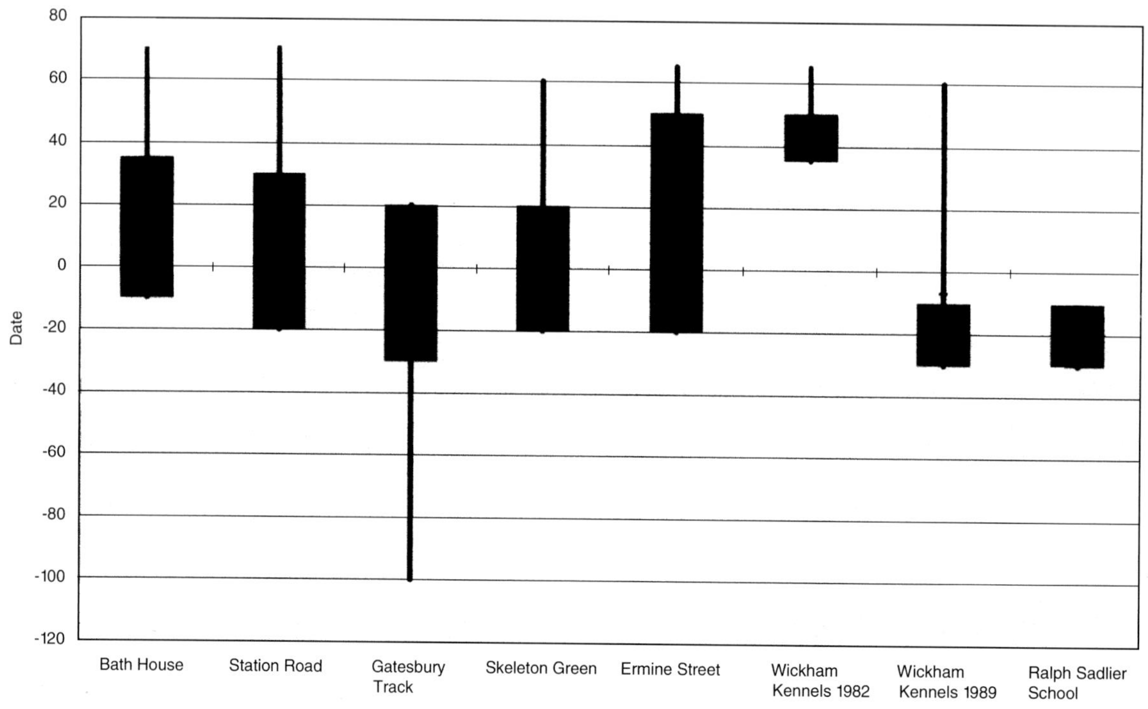

Fig. 3. Comparative dating of occupation at different sites in the Braughing complex.

the two adjacent sites at Wickham Kennels have produced significantly different occupation dates. The artefacts from the 1989 site have not been fully quantified, but Gallo-Belgic wares are absent and the native wares are of early character (Going 1990), which contrasts with the 1982 site (Partridge 1982). Similarly, the late dating of the Station Road site contrasts with the early date at Ralph Sadlier School 200 m to the north. The two most extensive excavated areas, at Skeleton Green and Ermine Street (which are also 200 m apart) also have significantly different occupation dates. These chronological variations over relatively short distances clearly represent substantial shifts in the focus of occupation, some reasons for which are explored below.

On the other hand, the evidence from Wickham Kennels suggests that some of the differences may be due to taphonomic processes, such as patterns of rubbish disposal and possible deliberate deposition of large quantities of artefacts within restricted parts of ditches. In situations where artefacts have been deposited in large quantities – whether as rubbish disposal or for ritual purposes – at a distance from their point of use, this could distort the observed geographical pattern across the settlement area. For large and complex settlements like Braughing, extrapolating the date of a site or part of the complex from a few dated deposits or features could therefore potentially be misleading.

The status and role of Braughing

The role of Braughing in the Late Iron Age has been considered by Trow (Potter and Trow 1988, 158–61) and Haselgrove (1987). Trow considers the evidence for Braughing as a royal centre, a port of trade and as a market, but does not reach any definitive conclusions as to which was most important. There are, however, several reasons for concluding that the role of Braughing as a political and administrative centre is the strongest and most consistent theme in the evidence.

A locally important political/administrative centre

The combination of imported Dressel 1A amphorae and the possible early use of the potter's wheel at Gatesbury Track is strongly suggestive of European contacts in the early first century BC. The probability that Braughing was receiving such contacts is significant in indicating that it was an important political centre at this time.

The possible status of Braughing as a tribal centre was considered by Rodwell (1976, 149–65), who argued that it was the residence of Addedomarus, who is named on coins of the later first century BC and whom Rodwell considered to be a leader of the Catuvellauni. The status of Addedomarus in relation to two other leaders named on coins of the same period – Tasciovanus and Dubnovellaunus – has, however, been the subject of some debate. Van Arsdell (1989, 349–62) concluded that the coinages of the Trinovantes and Catuvellauni should be considered as a single series, with the three named individuals ruling in sequence. However, Haselgrove (1993, 54–5) suggested that the three leaders may have ruled separate areas simultaneously. This is supported by a reassessment of site finds of coins of Dubnovellaunus and Addedomarus, which has shown that they have complementary but different distributions (Curteis 1997); moreover, of the two, Dubnovellaunus is the more likely to have been associated with Braughing. In addition, the coins of three slightly later leaders, Dias, Andoco, and Rues, show clustered distributions centred on Braughing, St Albans and Baldock, suggesting contemporary but separate minting and political centres (Curteis 1997; pers. comm.). The coin evidence therefore indicates that Braughing was probably a locally important political centre and possibly the residence of a tribal leader during the later first century BC.

The interpretation of Braughing as a locally important settlement is supported by the agricultural potential of the area (Bryant 1999). Whilst there is not a great difference between the estimated agricultural wealth available within a 10 km radius of the six site-clusters, Braughing and Welwyn each had a higher proportion of better-quality arable land. Agricultural wealth may therefore have been a factor in the rise of Braughing, although of the 13 known sites within 10 km of the complex, only Hadham Hall has good evidence for agricultural production (Walker 1994).

Evidence for a ritual and burial zone

Station Road yielded evidence of a possible area of ritual activity. The excavation of a small sample of a linear ditch revealed a substantial deposit of pottery, food refuse and human bone representing a minimum of 14 individuals, as well as the only *in situ* Late Iron Age burials from Braughing (Partridge 1979, 28–97). Geophysical survey and trial-trenching carried out over a large area to the north failed to reveal any further burials or occupation. Therefore, it is possible that the Station Road site was separated from the rest of the complex by an area devoid of occupation (*ibid.*, 33).

A politically controlled centre for exchange

The imported pottery which arrived at Braughing during its main period of activity (*c.* 20 BC to AD 25) forms one of the largest collections of Augustan and early Tiberian imports from Gaul and Italy found in Britain (Rigby 1981). A high proportion of the vessels are containers, including amphorae and jars from central Gaul in fabrics containing mica, or dusted with mica on the rim or shoulder (Rigby 1989; Tyers 1981).

No comparable early Gaulish or Italian imports are known from the study area, apart from a few sherds of Dressel 1B amphora and a few mica vessels from

Baldock (Stead and Rigby 1986). The Late Iron Age site at Hadham Hall, 6 km east of Braughing, did not produce any imports, although it was occupied during the later first century BC and first century AD (Walker 1994). This suggests that the contents of these containers were consumed within the Braughing settlement complex. The high proportion of imported tablewares and the dominance of pig bones from the excavated sites at Braughing also implies high-status consumption (Fifield and King 1988), as does the presence of exotic species such as the white-tailed eagle from Station Road, and the Spanish mackerel, other sea fish and numerous chicken from Skeleton Green (Ashdown 1979; 1981; Wheeler 1981). Domestic fowl in any quantity and fish are both unusual on Iron Age sites (see Dobney and Ervynck this volume); indeed the amount of chicken at Skeleton Green is almost as great as that from the *oppidum* of Manching in Bavaria (Ashdown 1981). Access to the products of the high volume of exchange which the imports represent is likely to have been under strong political control.

River boat would probably have been the favoured mode of transport for conveying the imports to Braughing. The River Rib, whilst not a major river, could have enabled the transport of commodities using the same type of log boat as was found at Hasholme in East Yorkshire (Millett and McGrail 1988), and may have attracted settlement for this reason. Other aspects of the evidence from Braughing also point to the importance of the River Rib. Five of the 16 sites are located within 70 m of the river, in areas which would have been prone to seasonal flooding. It is also reasonable to assume that the substantial ditches found at several sites – including Gatesbury Track and Wickham Kennels – were constructed primarily for drainage.

Braughing lies close to the northern limit of the Thames basin. If river transport was the primary means of transporting imported goods from Italy and central Gaul within southern England and easy access was sought to the Midlands and the Ouse basin, Braughing would have been a ideal location from which to exploit these areas, although there is currently no evidence that the imports arriving there found their way to the Midlands.

A proto-urban centre?

The high concentration of imported artefacts and buildings in the relatively small (1500 m^2) excavation at Skeleton Green indicates dense occupation in this part of the settlement. Little information is available to indicate the full extent of the occupation, but the absence of contemporary activity at the Ermine Street, Wickham Kennels, and Gatesbury Track sites implies a maximum size of *c.* 10 hectares. In terms of size, this is far too small to be described as urban, although it is noteworthy that the dominant activities were not concerned with agricultural production.

The contrast between the dense structural evidence from Skeleton Green and the lack of such evidence from the other sites within the complex means that it is difficult adequately to place it within a functional context. However, interpreting Braughing as a centre of politically controlled exchange, in which raw materials were brought to the settlement and almost all of the imports were consumed within it, could help explain the character of the Skeleton Green area and the apparently fluid nature of occupation.

The nature of the social and economic relations which governed the way in which the complex operated can only be guessed at, but it is likely that Braughing served as a magnet for the local population, who brought in the products which were exchanged for imports and took advantage of access to the imports and products manufactured at the site. Artisans, retainers, and opportunists would also have been attracted. The dominant role of imports as an economic basis for the site would have resulted in ebbs and flows in the physical extent of occupation, dependent upon the quantity and nature of the imported products. Any lengthy interruption in the flow of imports would have quickly reduced activity within the settlement, especially if access by the elite to wealth from other sources was limited. Fluctuations in the nature and chronology of occupation within the settlement may therefore be a consequence of variations in the quantity of imports over time. A marked and final decline in imports after AD 25 would have rapidly resulted in a reduction in the population and the area occupied.

A market?

A notable concentration of local and imported Iron Age bronze coins is recorded at Braughing, both in archaeological contexts and as stray finds (Haselgrove 1987; 1988), which would seem to imply a high frequency of transactions requiring coins (Haselgrove 1993, 57). One possibility is that the coins provide evidence for primitive market activity, but it is just as likely that they were used for payments to artisans, retainers or to other social or economic groupings residing within Braughing rather than for the trading of commodities. We should also consider the possibility that some of the coins were ritual deposits (Curteis 2005).

Implications

Several conclusions can be drawn from the above assessment. First, Braughing was probably a locally important political and administrative centre before the mid first century BC, possibly for a tribe or *pagus*. Locally available agricultural resources and the ability to communicate, via river and overland routes, with other major settlements in the region, may both have been factors in its location. The presence of Dressel 1A amphorae and indications of early use of the potter's wheel are suggestive of significant contacts with Gaul/Italy in the early first century BC, or even the later second century BC.

By the later first century BC, Braughing had become a regionally important centre for imports from Gaul and Italy, possibly due to the development of these contacts. However the exchange was probably under strong political control with few imports being redistributed beyond the confines of the settlement. The good communications offered by river and overland routes enabled Braughing to take advantage of the inter-regional contacts with Gaul and Italy and possibly also to benefit from the development of the ironworking and pottery industries in the local region. However, a number of alternative locations within the study area could have provided similar opportunities.

By the mid first century AD the quantity of imports had greatly declined and Braughing had reverted to the locally important settlement that it was earlier in the Late Iron Age. The reasons for this decline are unclear but may be related to the limited potential of the settlement and its hinterland to meet the economic and political aspirations of merchants and political contacts with the Roman Empire. The model which relates Braughing's fortunes to the advance of the Roman army probably provides the best explanation of these changes (Collis 1984a, 166–7).

Braughing existed as a small town throughout the Roman period. Significantly, there is both place-name and documentary evidence that the place continued to be a locally important centre until the later Anglo-Saxon period. The two names of Braughing itself (tribes of the Brehas) and Wickham Hill are early, and imply continuity of status from the Roman to the middle Saxon period (Bassett 1989; Gelling 1988; Gover *et al.* 1938). Braughing was also the name of the hundred and had a church in the ninth century (Gelling 1975), which was a Domesday minster (Morris 1976). This continuity of status over such a long period implies that Braughing was the centre of a stable and coherent administrative unit.

Baldock

Baldock lies at the north-eastern end of the Chiltern Hills at the watershed of the Ouse river system. The cluster of Late Iron Age evidence there can be reasonably be described as a large settlement (Fig. 4). However, several aspects of its interpretation are likely to be a consequence of sampling biases: the modern development which has led to excavation has been concentrated in areas which, according to Burleigh (1995a) were set aside for burial; the generally poor survival of the Late Iron Age structural evidence is due to the combination of damage from urban development (Roman to modern) and ploughing; and finally, Late Iron Age Aylesford-type cremation burial evidence is inherently easier to characterise than evidence of manufacturing and domestic habitation, particularly on sites with extensive plough-damage.

The burial evidence

A notable feature of Late Iron Age Baldock is the high proportion of burial and ritual evidence. This is concentrated in an area approximately six hectares in size lying mainly to the south of the Icknield Way and north of the Western Hills, which are the most prominent topographical feature in the area. Nine of the ten burial sites lie on the low ridge which Burleigh (1995a, 105) identified as a burial area. The tenth is the richly furnished Welwyn-type burial from The Tene, 400 m to the south-west of the ridge (Stead and Rigby 1986).

Another notable aspect of Baldock is the number and extent of the cemeteries, and the size of burial area as a whole, estimated at 6 ha. Other sizeable Aylesford-type cemeteries are known at King Harry Lane (*c.* 2 ha in extent; Stead and Rigby 1989) and Westhampnett in West Sussex (*c.* 1 ha; Fitzpatrick 1997), but both are substantially smaller than at Baldock. Several important aspects of the burial evidence, however, remain unclear, including the total number of burials, whether the cemeteries and enclosures form a defined functional burial and ritual zone, or if they are interspersed with areas which were left unoccupied or contained domestic occupation. Lastly, the presence of significant numbers of Late Iron Age inhumations should be noted.

Manufacturing

Evidence of manufacturing from Baldock is slight and small in scale, but suggests a workshop or specialist workshop mode of production (Cumberpatch 1995). Activities included brooch manufacture (Stead 1986, 122–3), cloth spinning (Foster 1986b, 170) and weaving (Burleigh 1995a; Foster 1986b, 168), and possible pottery production (Rigby and Foster 1986, 187–8). Unlike Braughing and St Albans, there are no finds of clay pellet moulds.

Habitation

As yet, Baldock lacks unambiguous evidence for habitation, although several structures of definite or probable Late Iron Age date are known. Two examples (one circular and one rectilinear) were found in Stead's Area A (Stead and Rigby 1986, figs 12–13), but the lack of domestic occupation evidence and their proximity to burial enclosures could indicate a possible ritual function (Curteis 2005). The rectangular structure, in particular, was situated between two Late Iron Age burial enclosures (Stead and Rigby 1986, fig. 4). Part of a ring gully was found at Hartsfield School (Burleigh 1995b),

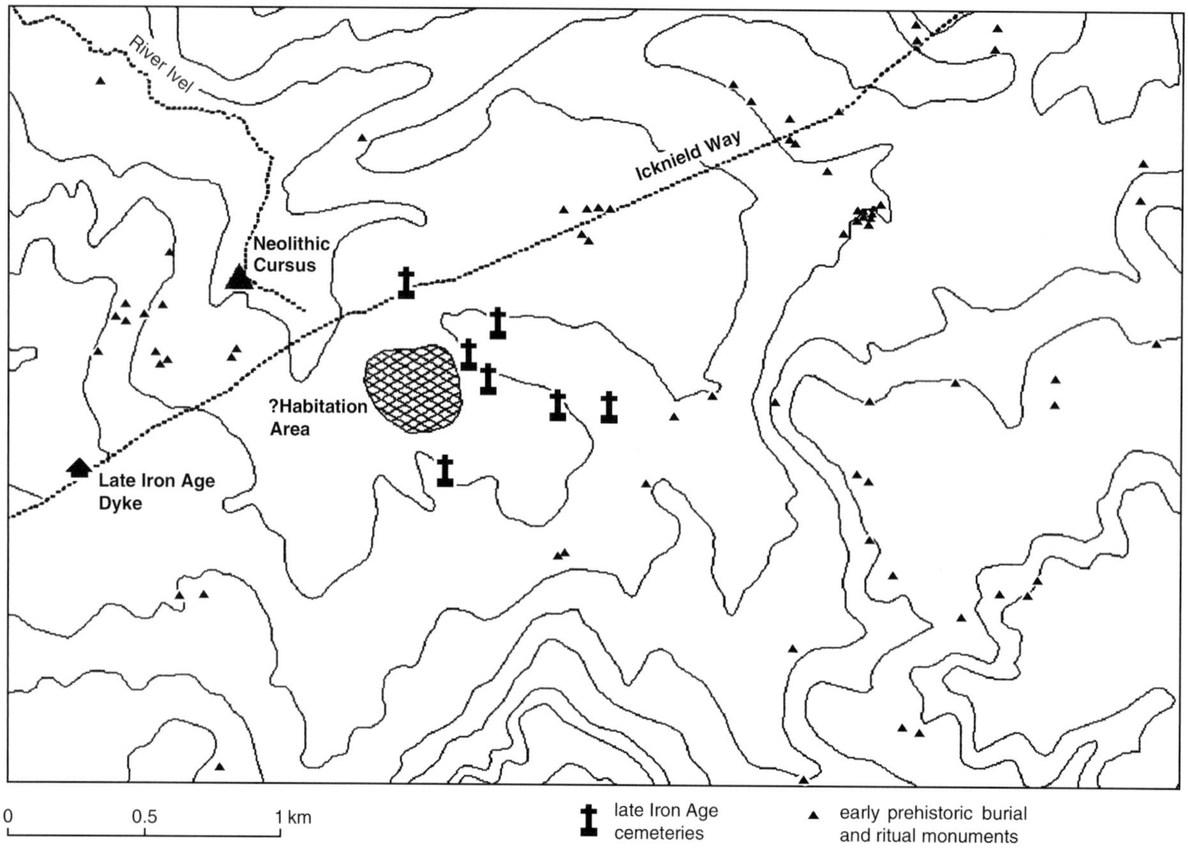

Fig. 4. Sites in the Baldock area.

but the absence of features such as surfaces, pits and ditches means that a domestic function is likewise unproved.

Domestic occupation is likely, given the overall size of the complex and the quantities of Late Iron Age features and finds, including ditch systems and trackways (Stead and Rigby 1986; Burleigh 1995a); the current lack of evidence is probably due in the main to the sampling biases referred to above. However, any domestic settlement may not have been large. A probable focus of settlement close to the Romano-Celtic temple at Baker's Close (east of the burial cluster and 200 m north of The Tene burial) seems to be the best candidate (Burleigh 1995a, 109; see Fig. 4). The presence of cemeteries to the east of this area and multiple ditches to the south would have restricted the size of any domestic area unless such occupation was interspersed with them. Haselgrove (1996b, 81) has suggested that a small elite focus may explain the concentration of Late Iron Age coins at Baldock, particularly the relatively large number of first century AD low-denomination bronzes. The status of any domestic settlement in the Baker's Close area is, therefore, likely to be high, based of the quality of the burial and artefact evidence.

Chronology

Possible earlier Iron Age occupation at Baldock is indicated by hand-made pottery with sand and shell temper (Stead and Rigby 1986) and by the high proportion of hand-made forms in the earliest deposits. Excavation of the Late Iron Age cremation cemetery at Hinxton, 25 km east of Baldock, has however suggested that the adoption of the potter's wheel was a complex process in the north Hertfordshire/south Cambridgeshire area, with many settlements possibly not using wheel-thrown pottery during the Late Iron Age (Hill *et al.* 1999). The nature and extent of any earlier Iron Age presence at Baldock is therefore uncertain based on the published evidence.

A significant presence at Baldock in the early first century BC is, however, clear from the inclusion of Dressel 1A amphorae with The Tene burial, and there are two possible La Tène D1b brooches from Area A (Stead and Rigby 1986; Haselgrove 1997, 69). The coins also indicate occupation no later than the second half of the first century BC, probably beginning to the south-west of the ridge on which the cemeteries lie (Walls Field) and subsequently moving onto the ridge (Upper Walls Common; Haselgrove 1987, 178). The most intensive period of occupation was during the first half of the first century AD, when large quantities of Gallo-Belgic pottery were arriving at the complex. The coin evidence also indicates a general expansion of the occupied area during this period (Haselgrove 1993, 54).

The role of Late Iron Age Baldock

A religious/cult centre

The evidence from Baldock is dominated by burial. Whilst the recovery of evidence has probably been significantly biased in favour of burials and against buildings and other elements of domestic occupation, the number and extent of the cemeteries strongly suggests that Baldock was primarily a centre at which burial and the associated funerary rituals were undertaken.

If this view is correct, a possible explanation could be provided by the Aylesford burials of the north Essex, north Hertfordshire and south Cambridgeshire area within which Baldock lies (Hill *et al.* 1999). The absence of such burials in excavations undertaken to the north of this area seems to confirm the reality of a northern boundary to the Aylesford burial complex in southern Cambridgeshire. It is also suggested that the unusual form of the Hinxton burials (which were demarcated and placed in grave pits within small round barrows) may be due to their location at the northern periphery of the Aylesford burial distribution (*ibid.*, 269). Hodder (1982) argued that enhanced symbolic display can be a feature of social boundaries. The same phenomenon may therefore explain the size of Baldock and the large number of its Late Iron Age burials. The situation of Baldock on an important long-distance communication route would also have served to maximise its impact. In this respect, the elaboration of the Icknield Way immediately to the west of Baldock by the building of a substantial bank and ditch and road surface (Moss Eccardt 1988) is significant, as is the large number of routes into the settlement from the south (Burleigh 1995a, 103).

The significance of earlier prehistoric ritual and burial activity in the Baldock area

Figure 4 shows the cluster of Late Iron Age burial and ritual sites at Baldock. No early prehistoric sites are located within the cluster, although Late Neolithic and Bronze Age pits were found in Stead's Area A (Stead and Rigby 1987, 82). However, a total of 56 burial and ritual monuments are known within a 1.7 km radius of the centre of the Iron Age burial cluster. These include three cemeteries – numbering 12, 7, and 17 barrows each – located along the route of the Icknield Way, which would have been clearly visible from the Late Iron Age burial focus to the south.

Adjacent to the westernmost of the three cemeteries lies a Late Neolithic trackway or cursus monument. Two parallel ditches 7 m apart have been traced over 244 m and sectioned at a number of points (Moss Eccardt 1988, 49–50). The eastern end of the cursus monument is located close to the source of the River Ivel, approximately 1.2 km west of the Late Iron Age burials, confirming that this was of ritual significance in the earlier prehistoric period. A possible connection between the Neolithic cursus monument and the Iron Age is provided by the cutting of two small ditches of Middle Iron Age date across the western end of the northern cursus ditch (Moss Eccardt 1988, 72 and fig.11).

There seems little doubt that the concentration of Late Iron Age burial and ritual sites at Baldock is in some way linked to the earlier prehistoric landscape and/or the ritual significance of the source of the River Ivel.

An administrative/elite centre

The suggested primary function of Baldock as a cult and burial complex fails adequately to explain some significant aspects of the evidence, especially that for specialised manufacturing and for the expansion of occupation in the earlier first century AD. The large collection of Gallo-Belgic tableware is indicative of 'Romanised' consumption, and the large number of coins – although some have been found in possible ritual contexts (Curteis 1997; 2005) – may represent some form of primitive market activity. These hint that Baldock was also a central place and possible elite residence by the first century AD.

In summary, Baldock was a major centre for Aylesford burials as well as the increasingly recognised Late Iron Age rite of inhumation burial. It was also probably a political/administrative centre.

St Albans

The cluster of Late Iron Age sites in and close to the Roman city of Verulamium in the valley of the River Ver (Fig. 5) can be identified with the place named as *Verlamion* on coins of Tasciovanus. It has been the subject of several major excavation campaigns (notably in the 1930s by the Wheelers, in the 1950s by Frere, and more recently by Niblett) and is probably the most intensively researched Late Iron Age settlement in England. The complex covers an area of approximately 7 km^2 of the Ver valley and the plateau edges to the east and west. Within this area several reasonably clear zones of activity can be recognised:

Habitation

In the Prae Wood/Mayne Avenue area on the clay plateau just beyond the valley edge to the south-west, a number of settlement compounds were apparently interspersed with agricultural and industrial activity (Hunn 1992;

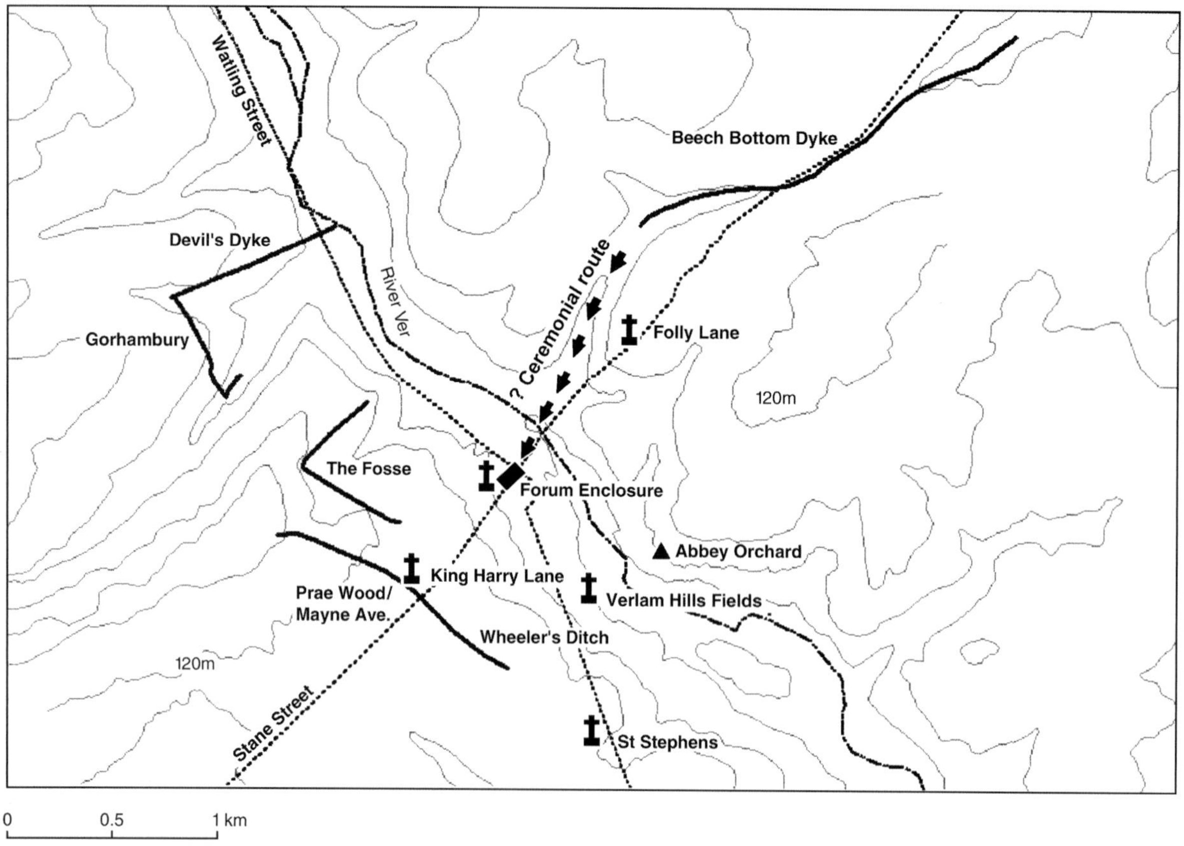

Fig. 5. The St Albans complex.

1994). The industrial activity includes cloth weaving, probable pottery manufacture, and the working of precious metals. The region is bounded to the north-east by a linear boundary (Wheeler's Ditch) which runs along the plateau edge parallel to the river valley for approximately 1450 m from north-west to south-east, falling gently by 20 m over its length. The boundary comprises a bank and ditch 6 m wide at the north-west end which diminishes to 3 m approximately half way along its length: the largest of the rectilinear enclosures appears to abut the ditch (Niblett 1999).

A kilometre north-west of the Prae Wood/Mayne Avenue area is a dyke system including the Devil's Dyke, New Dyke and White Dyke, with a rectilinear settlement enclosure to the west at Gorhambury. The dyke system appears to enclose two sides of an area of the south-western side of the Ver valley. The dykes have a total length of 1850 m and are generally larger than Wheeler's Ditch at Prae Wood. An excavated section of New Dyke adjacent to the Gorhambury enclosure had a width of 23 m, and a height of 10 m from bank top to ditch bottom (Neal *et al.* 1990, fig. 21). All of the dykes have the quarry ditch downhill of the bank (Hunn 1992; 1994).

The valley and Roman city

The fragmentary evidence from beneath the Roman city includes the working of precious metals, probably for coin blank manufacturing, associated with a rectilinear structure; some cremations and a probable ritual pit; a possible ritual focus in the marshy area next to the river; and a large rectangular enclosure beneath the Roman forum (Niblett 1999). The central location of the large enclosure and its spatial relationship to the Roman forum has led to its interpretation as the political centre of Verlamion, possibly a royal compound or palace site (Frere 1983; Hunn 1992; 1994).

Despite the partial nature of the evidence, there are potential similarities with the extensively excavated site at Fison Way, Norfolk. This comprised a large rectangular enclosure within which were two phases of large circular structures interpreted as shrines or temples (Gregory 1992). Outside were several subsidiary enclosures, within which the working of precious metals and cloth weaving took place. Inhumation burials were also located close to the enclosure. The juxtaposition of a large enclosure, burial and precious metalworking at Fison Way are all comparable to the evidence from Verulamium. Fison Way thus currently appears to be the best parallel for the forum enclosure, given the rarity of excavated examples with which to compare it.

Three further cemeteries are located within or overlooking the Ver valley. The Verulam Hills Fields enclosed cremation cemetery lies immediately to the south-east of the Roman town, the St Stephen's cemetery a further 700 m to the south-east, along Roman Watling Street (Anthony 1968; Niblett 1999). The King Harry Lane cemetery is situated on the north-eastern side of the 'Wheeler's Ditch' linear boundary (Stead and Rigby 1989), and scattered inhumation and cremation burials are known from the river floodplain and valley sides (Bryant and Niblett 1997, 273). Another large linear ditch known as 'The Fosse' in the river valley to the west of the Roman town has recently been interpreted as Late Iron Age (Niblett 1993). This follows the alignment of the Prae Wood ditch and turns at right angles to head towards the river, running on roughly the same course as Devil's Dyke 800 m to the north-west.

Redeposited Late Iron Age pottery and coin pellet mould fragments have been found in the valley bottom at St Albans Abbey orchard (Saunders and Havercroft 1982, 34, note 3).

Folly Lane

A richly furnished cremation burial was placed centrally within a large rectilinear enclosure on a hill at the north-east edge of the Ver valley in *c.* AD 50 (Niblett 1999). The burial was preceded by Late Iron Age occupation including a probable dwelling on the eastern side of a linear ditch which was traced for a distance of *c.* 200 m along the valley side. The presence of the linear ditch and occupation on the plateau side in the pre-burial phase has some similarities with Prae Wood on the opposite side of the Ver valley.

Verlamion as a ritual complex

Haselgrove and Millett (1997, 285–6) have argued that Iron age Verlamion developed as a ritual complex, possibly originating at a meeting place on the boundary of a number of territories. This interpretation is further developed by Niblett (1999), who suggests that the area including Folly Lane, the Roman town and the Ver valley, was probably a large religious cult complex, comparable in spatial organisation to the Gallo-Roman sanctuary complexes of northern Gaul, such as Ribemont-sur-Ancre (Brunaux 1999). The following evidence has been used as the basis for this interpretation:

1. The apparent zoning of activity areas, with ritual and burial activity occurring within the Ver valley, bounded to the south and west by the dyke complexes of Prae Wood and Gorhambury, beyond which settlement and agricultural activity was concentrated.
2. The cluster of Iron Age coins on the site of the Roman theatre. By analogy with Gallo-Roman sanctuaries, this may have been a ceremonial assembly area in the Late Iron Age (Haselgrove and Millett 1997; Niblett 1999).
3. The visibility of the cemeteries and the dyke system. The dykes face towards the valley area: if therefore the St Michael's/forum enclosure is assumed to be the centre of the ritual/cult complex, the other main features of the complex – including the dykes and the King Harry Lane and St Stephen's cemeteries and the Folly Lane site – would have all appeared as impressive skyline features.
4. The valley bottom close to the river was probably a wet, marshy area in the Late Iron Age, which would probably have been unsuitable for habitation but could well have provided a context for ritual activity including votive deposition (Haselgrove and Millett 1997, 284; Niblett 1999).
5. The spatial arrangement of the Folly Lane Romano-Celtic temple, the Roman theatre and forum resembles that of a Gallo-Roman sanctuary, many of which are known to have Iron Age origins (Niblett 1999; cf. Arcelin and Brunaux 2003).

The significance of Beech Bottom Dyke

The above interpretation is a logical and compelling explanation of the evidence, including the spatial arrangement of the key elements of Late Iron Age and early Roman Verlamion/Verulamion. It does not, however, adequately explain the presence and function of the largest and perhaps most visually impressive element of the complex, Beech Bottom Dyke. It is therefore worth looking afresh at the Dyke, especially its morphology, and how it relates spatially to the other elements of the complex.

Beech Bottom Dyke is a massive ditch located on the Stane Street between St Albans and Wheathampstead. It is up to 10 m deep and 30 m wide and is traceable for just under 2 km (Fig. 5). The ditch upcast appears on both sides although it is slightly higher on the south-eastern side. Topographically, the dyke is situated on the plateau between the Ver and Lea river valleys; at its south-western end, close to the Verlamion complex, it appears to run into a steep re-entrant dry valley (Saunders and Havercroft 1982, 36–7). The way the dyke cuts into the plateau is comparable to a small railway cutting. It is also morphologically similar to the shorter Devil's Dyke at Wheathampstead, 4.5 km to the north-east. The precise date of the Beech Bottom dyke is unclear. The only reasonably good dating evidence is provided by a hoard of Roman coins (dated to AD 120–140) found in 1932 in the ditch filling at the northern end (Wheeler and Wheeler 1936, 18), which would allow a Late Iron Age or early Roman date. Although the dyke lies outside the nominal area of Verlamion, there are good reasons for suggesting a connection with the complex.

Beech Bottom Dyke is traditionally interpreted as a boundary. Wheeler suggested that it formed the boundary between open country to the south-east and more wooded claylands to the north-west (Wheeler and

Wheeler 1936, 18). A relationship between the Dyke and various first century BC coin distributions is hinted at by Haselgrove (1987, 187; Haselgrove and Millett 1997, 283), suggesting that it could also have marked a territorial boundary. On the other hand, both the topographical situation and the absence of a large upcast bank militate against the idea that it was designed to be a prominently visible feature, suggesting that we should consider an alternative hypothesis: that the Dyke functioned as a routeway connected with the ritual complex at Verlamion.

The interpretation of Beech Bottom Dyke as a route comes from a rapid assessment of the ways in which the St Michael's enclosure might have been approached in the Late Iron Age. If Verlamion was indeed a ritual centre, it seems reasonable to assume that the spatial arrangement of its elements (dykes, enclosures, cemeteries) will reflect the ways in which people were required to move through the landscape. Figure 5 shows the main elements of the Verlamion settlement and Beech Bottom Dyke. A route to the St Michael's enclosure from the south or west seems unlikely given the presence of the dykes facing north and east on the skyline at Gorhambury and Prae Wood/ Mayne Avenue. In addition, the Fosse earthwork (if Late Iron Age in date) would have effectively blocked access from the west between the two aforementioned dyke systems, whilst an approach from the north-west would have been blocked by Devil's Dyke. Also, the dykes would not have been visible from the south-east (along the Watling Street or the Ver valley) until close to the St Michael's site. This leaves the north-east as the most likely general direction from which to approach the complex, along the dry re-entrant valley leading on from the southern end of Beech Bottom Dyke. The potential importance of this route is further supported by Niblett's (1999, 409–10) reinterpretation of the timber structure found close to the Ver to the north of the forum enclosure as a first century AD causeway across the river. The dating of the Colchester Road, which runs to the east of the Folly Lane site, to the later first century AD, means that this is unlikely to have been a Late Iron Age route.

If Saunders is correct in suggesting that the south-western end of the Beech Bottom Dyke lay at the point where the valley to the north-west of Folly Lane begins (Saunders and Havercroft 1982, 36–7), the valley would have served as a natural continuation of the Dyke whose direction was pointed straight at the river causeway and the St Michael's enclosure. The valley is narrow and steep and has a similar profile to the dyke, although much larger in size. An approach to Verlamion in the semi-darkness along the bottom of this valley would have added to the visual impact of the complex as the different elements eventually became visible about halfway along its course.

The similar form of the Wheathampstead Devil's Dyke also provides some support for the idea that Beech Bottom Dyke functioned as a route into the ritual complex from the north-east. Although much shorter than Beech Bottom Dyke (430 m), Devil's Dyke also lies on the route between the Ver and Lea rivers and is located in a natural dip in the land. The ends of the dyke, which seem to be original, terminate in gradual inclines which would have made for relatively easy access by foot. As we have already seen, the southern end of Beech Bottom dyke probably linked with a natural valley, whilst the surviving profile at the northern end implies that this was of a similar gradual incline to Devil's Dyke. In addition, the hearth found by Wheeler at the base of the deepest part of the Devil's Dyke could also be interpreted as ritual (see below).

Although based on very limited evidence, this hypothesis does provide an explanation for the unusually large size of these earthworks, together with their lack of defensive banks and unusual topographical location. Other parallels for Beech Bottom and Devil's Dykes are hard to find. Heath Farm Dyke at Colchester, which leads to the Gosbecks complex, may have had a similar function as there is no evidence for a significant bank, but it is much smaller in scale and does not lead directly to the heart of the complex in the same way as Beech Bottom Dyke (Hawkes and Crummy 1995).

Wheathampstead

Four Late Iron Age sites have been identified at Wheathampstead (Fig. 6). The Devil's Dyke was sectioned in the 1930s and was found to contain a Late Iron Age hearth at its base (Wheeler and Wheeler 1936, 16–22). Two smaller ditches nearby yielded pottery and other finds dating to the first century BC (Thompson 1979; Haselgrove and Millett 1997). Excavations in advance of the Wheathampstead bypass in 1974 and 1977 found scattered evidence of occupation dating to the first half of the first century AD at two sites in the Lea valley (Saunders and Havercroft 1982). A ditch containing a female inhumation and pottery dated to *c.* AD 60–70 was found at Wick Avenue on the southern edge of the river valley (Herts SMR 9795). Finally, an important Late Iron Age site has been recently discovered at Turners Hall Farm on the northern edge of the Lea valley, 3 km north-west of Devil's Dyke. Excavation in advance of a water pipeline revealed substantial evidence of occupation and industrial activity in the form of probable ironworking hearths and clay pellet moulds. The site appears to be of high status in the Late Iron Age and to have continued into the Roman period (Herts SMR 9913).

Role and status

Wheeler concluded that the area between Devil's Dyke and 'The Slad' – a natural ditch-like feature some 500 m to the east – housed a major Late Iron Age settlement. However, subsequent fieldwork and survey has indicated

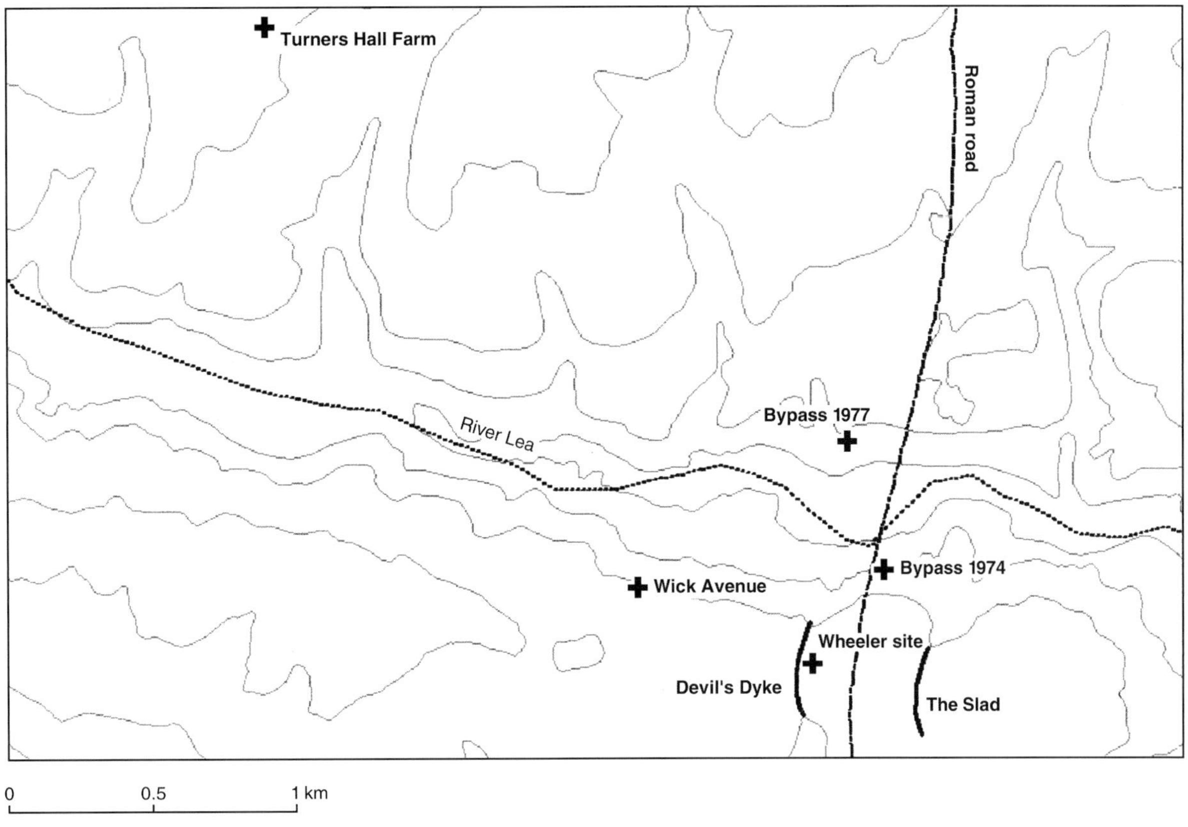

Fig. 6. Wheathampstead and the Lea valley.

that any occupation of this area was not extensive (Saunders and Havercroft 1982, 32–3), casting doubt on previous interpretations of Wheathampstead as an *oppidum*.

The later date of the two bypass sites has led to suggestions that the focus of occupation moved from the southern plateau edge to the river valley in the first century AD (Bryant and Niblett 1997, 275) but the new finds from Wick Avenue (also on the plateau edge) and Turners Hall Farm on the northern edge of the valley suggest that the situation is more complex. Some of the differences between the valley and plateau-edge sites may be due to status or function. The limited excavations at Devil's Dyke site yielded a La Tène D1b brooch, an iron knife, loomweights and a pair of bronze tweezers, indicative of fairly high-status activity (Wheeler and Wheeler 1936, 19), whilst the pottery from Wick Avenue includes imports (Herts SMR 9795).

In contrast, no imported pottery or other artefacts which might be indicative of high-status occupation were found at the valley sites (Haselgrove and Millett 1997, 286–7). There is also evidence for ritual activity at Wick Avenue and possibly Devil's Dyke, where the siting of the hearth at the base of the deepest point of the dyke (10 m) does not appear the most practical location for purely domestic or industrial activity. The Dyke would have provided shelter, but this would be offset by the risk of flooding and silting, and the necessity regularly to climb in and out of the ditch. There are shallower and more practical locations within the Dyke for domestic or industrial activity, implying that the deepest point was used for ritual purposes.

As I suggested above, it is possible that Devil's Dyke and the similarly constructed Beech Bottom Dyke served as a sunken, ceremonial route between the Ver and Lea rivers. The deeper parts of the Dyke may also have been a focus for specific rituals, as possibly evidenced by the hearth. In addition, the nearby ditches and absence of Late Iron Age remains further to the east may indicate that activity was concentrated close to the Dyke, possibly associated with its ritual function.

Despite the very limited evidence, several tentative conclusions can be drawn about Wheathampstead. There are no indications of an extensive Late Iron Age settlement, or of 'central place' functions in the form of mortuary or domestic/industrial activity comparable to the other five sites. Any occupation focus probably lay mainly to the west and north of the Devil's Dyke within an area of about one square kilometre, including the Lea valley and southern plateau edge. The significance of Wheathampstead is likely to be due to its location at the point where the routes from Verlamion both to Baldock

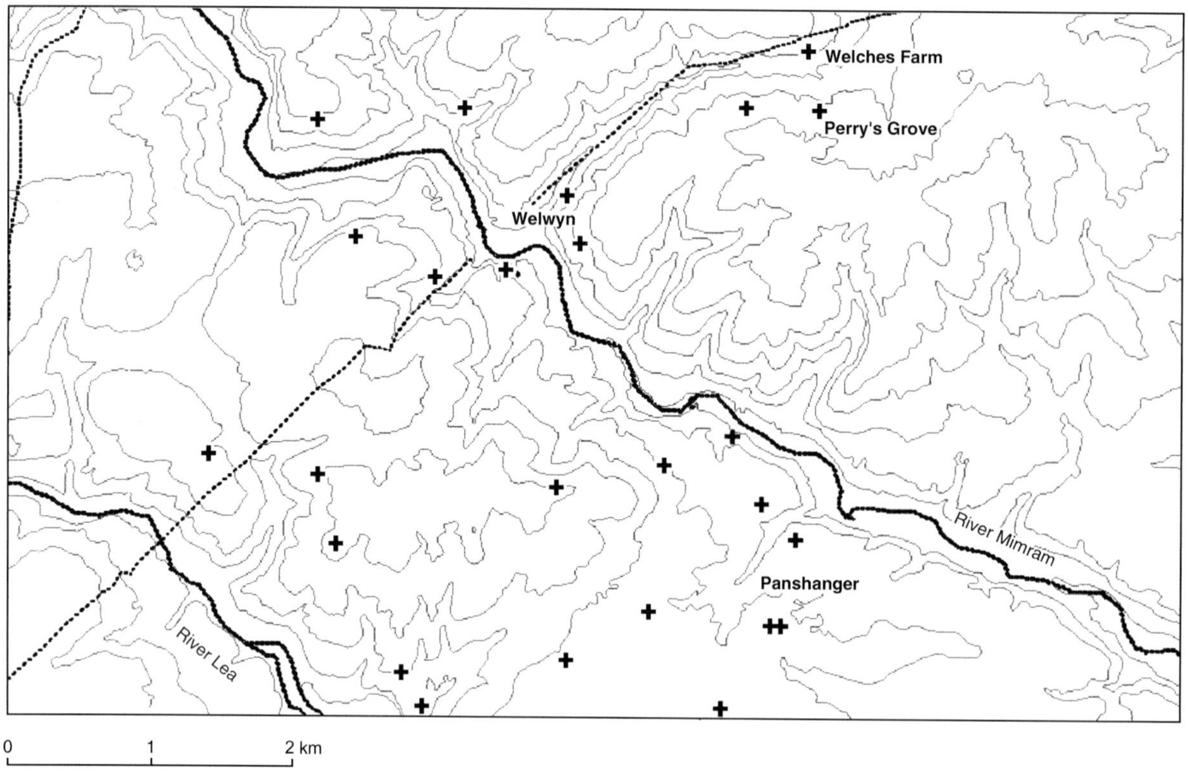

Fig. 7. Welwyn village and neighbouring sites.

and to Braughing/Colchester crossed the river. Arguably, the complex had a ritual or ceremonial function associated with the role of the Devil's Dyke. The discovery of the important site at Turners Hall Farm suggests that Wheathampstead may be only part of a much larger zone of Late Iron Age activity along the Lea valley.

Welwyn

The Welwyn complex comprises a cluster of 27 Late Iron Age sites located within an area of 20 km^2 which includes Welwyn Garden City (Fig. 7). They can be divided into three reasonably distinct groups:

The principal foci

Sixteen sites are known from the Welwyn Garden City plateau between the Lea and Mimram river valleys. These include the Welwyn-type burial and associated cemetery at Panshanger (Stead 1967); probable pottery manufacture nearby at Grub's Barn and Crookhams (Rook 1968a; 1970a); and enclosures at Panshanger golf course (Rook 1968b) and Stanborough School (Arnold 1952–54; Hunn forthcoming). This concentration of sites indicates that the plateau was a favoured area for settlement in the Late Iron Age, although much of the evidence is of low quality and not easily characterised. The lack of earlier Iron Age remains implies an expansion of activity in the Late Iron Age.

A second focus is indicated to the north of the Mimram valley at Welches Farm, where observation during the construction of a pipeline in the 1970s revealed continuous Late Iron Age occupation extending for over a kilometre (Rodwell 1976, 337; Rook 1974). This information has since been supplemented both by aerial photography and by fieldwalking (Herts SMR 2739). In addition, a large linear bank and ditch is known at 'Perry's Grove' 200 m to the south of Welches Farm; this is 120 m long and is aligned at right-angles to the route of Stane Street 500 m to the north. There is no direct evidence that the earthwork is of Late Iron Age date, but its size is comparable to the Verlamion earthworks. Finally, a probable richly furnished cremation burial is known 900 m to the west of Welches Farm (Rook 1968c; Stead 1967). The combination of occupation evidence, linear earthwork and burial suggests a major settlement focus.

A high-status Late Iron Age focus at Welwyn is implied by the two rich burials at Prospect Place (Smith 1912; Stead 1967) and remains of domestic habitation beneath the Roman villa at Lockleys 600 m to the west (Ward-Perkins 1937). The Lockleys villa dates from the mid first century AD, making it an important type-site for the early Romanisation of native elite residences. It is clear that Welwyn continued as a high-status focus in the Roman period. The villa at Dicket Mead, 500 m south of Lockleys, is the largest of the 40 known within the study area, and a temple/mausoleum, cemetery and small nucleated settlement are also attested. The presence of Greek craftsmen at Welwyn during the Roman period is indicated by several artefacts recovered from the villa and mausoleum (Rook 1983–6; Rook *et al.*1984).

Role and status

Although the density of Late Iron Age finds within the wider Welwyn area is much lower than at Baldock, Braughing or St Albans, aspects of the evidence, such as the apparent rapid expansion of settlement in the Late Iron Age, the richly furnished burials, the linear dyke, and the presence of imports at several sites, make it comparable to them. As with Braughing, a high-status/elite focus may well have acted as a magnet for settlement, although in Welwyn's case, there appear to be at least three: at Welwyn village, Panshanger and Welches Farm. Of the three, Welches Farm has evidence of extensive occupation, a probable rich grave nearby, and a linear dyke; Panshanger has a Welwyn-type burial and evidence of industrial activity; and Welwyn itself has two burials and was an important Roman focus. The last may also indicate that the village eventually became the single most important focus within the complex. It had a Minster church at Domesday, which suggests that it was a locally important administrative centre in the Late Anglo-Saxon period (Morris 1976). As discussed above, Welwyn, along with Braughing, was also surrounded by better quality agricultural land than any of the remaining settlement clusters (Bryant 1999). In all probability, the evidence for successive Late Iron Age, Roman, and Anglo-Saxon elite/administrative foci at Welwyn village indicates the existence of a relatively stable territory over a period of at least a millennium.

The Bulbourne valley

Compared to the other five Late Iron Age clusters, the quality of the excavated evidence in the Bulbourne valley is relatively low. All of the excavations have been either small in scale and/or have not been fully analysed. Of the two fully published sites, Dellfield was salvage recording in advance of development (Thompson and Holland 1974–6), whilst at Ward's Coombe the investigation was not extensive enough to understand the site (Dunnett 1973). However, this is to a great extent offset by the excellent results of the earthwork survey of the Ashridge Estate and Berkhamsted Common area, which enabled an extensive system of trackways, enclosures and field systems to be mapped (M. Solich pers. comm.). Although most of the earthworks are not directly dated, there is suggestive evidence of activity belonging to the relevant period in the form of associated surface scatters of Late Iron Age and Roman pottery (Morris and Wainwright 1995; Bryant and Niblett 1997).

Twenty Late Iron Age sites are known within a 45 km^2 area which includes the valley of the river Bulbourne and an upland area to the north comprising part of the Icknield Belt and the clay-with-flints dip slope (Fig. 8). The sites include four Aylesford-type cremation cemeteries (Wards Coombe, Aldbury, Dellfield, and Cow Roast); two sites with *in situ* ironworking (Dellfield, Tring); and a further five sites at which Late Iron Age ironworking is likely (Morris and Wainwright 1995). In addition to the various enclosures, field systems and trackways at Ashridge and Berkhamsted Common, the large linear earthwork known as Grim's Ditch at the south end of Berkhamsted Common is probably of Late Iron Age date. It is 1.3 km in length, 6 m wide and survives up to 3–4 m high, and lies across a spur on the north side of the Bulbourne valley close to its confluence with the Gade, overlooking Berkhamsted. This earthwork is significantly larger than the sections of the similarly named Grim's Ditch on the south side of the valley, which dates to the Late Bronze Age/Early Iron Age and, unlike them, does not follow the contours. It would have been an impressive feature on the skyline to anyone travelling up the valley from the south.

Ironworking

The most significant Late Iron Age and early Roman activity in evidence in the Bulbourne valley is iron-working. Five of the sites with ironworking evidence were found during the Ashridge Survey at the top end of the valley, each comprising surface scatters of smelting slag associated with Late Iron Age pottery (Morris and Wainwright 1995). The remaining sites both have evidence for smelting furnaces. Four shaft furnaces were found in 1970 at Dellfield and two more were found in 1974 during the construction of the Tring bypass, 15 km further up the valley (SMR 6069). The furnaces at Dellfield were recorded, but had been badly disturbed. Smelting slag and charcoal were recovered and three of the furnaces contained Late Iron Age pottery (Thompson and Holland 1974–6, 138–42).

Although the evidence of Late Iron Age ironworking from the Bulbourne valley is dispersed over 15 km and none of it is of high quality, it nevertheless currently provides one of the largest bodies of such material in southern England (P. Northover pers. comm.). The reason for the relative concentration of iron production in the valley is not entirely clear, as no local sources of ore are currently known. The area does however contain

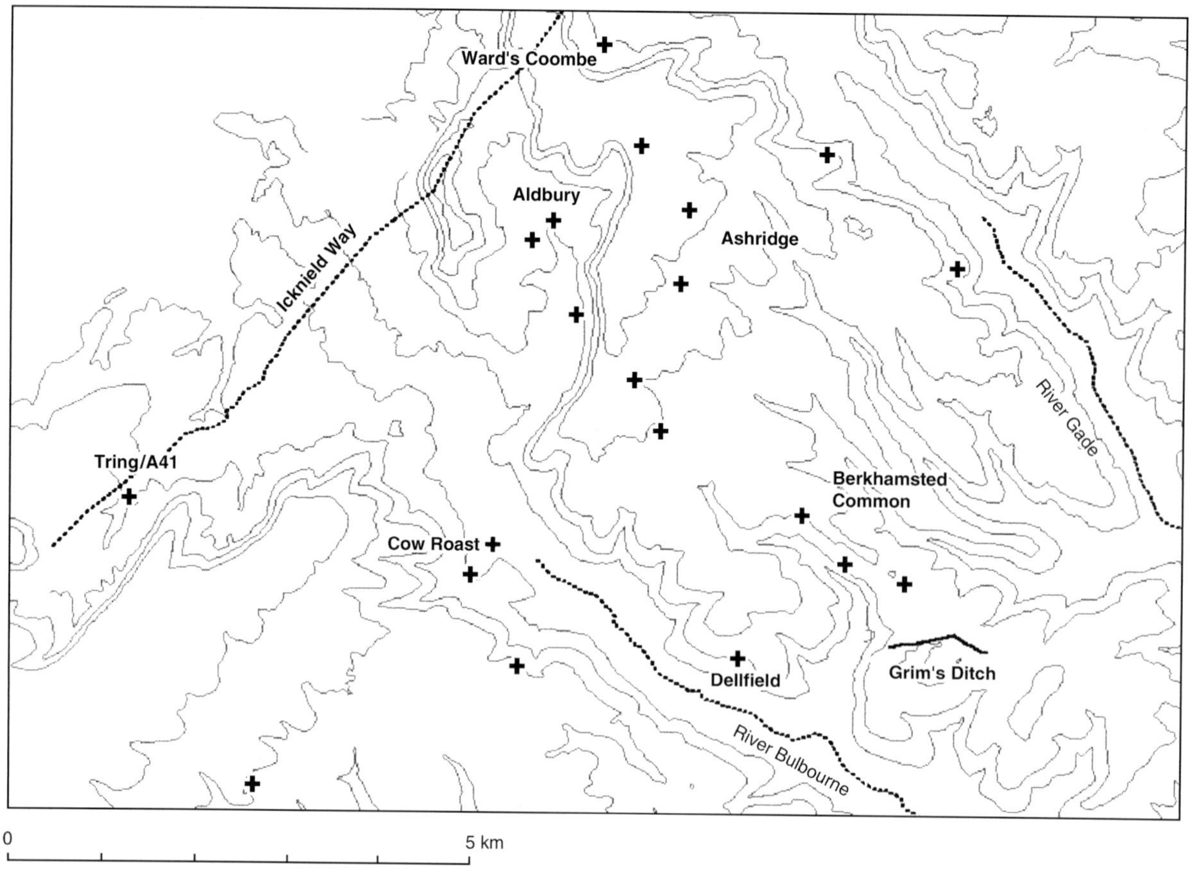

Fig. 8. Sites in the Bulbourne valley and Ashridge area.

plentiful supplies of the other two key material resources required for manufacturing iron, wood and clay, and it is entirely possible that the main resource being exploited was low-grade bog ore. This is effectively a very thick iron pan caused by percolating iron salts that accumulate between layers of soil, usually between peat and alluvium in valley floodplains.

The potential of the Bulbourne valley as a source of bog iron ore has not been investigated but it does contain extensive areas of alluvium and peat, which could have provided the right conditions for bog ore to form. The shaft furnaces at Dellfield and Tring may also indicate that low grade bog ores were being exploited. The shaft furnace is a more efficient and technologically advanced type than the simple bowl furnace used during the earlier Iron Age. The design of the shaft furnace enabled slag to be tapped and removed, thereby increasing the amount iron produced from each firing (Salter and Ehrenreich 1984, 146). Slag tapping furnaces do not seem to have a simple chronological relationship to bowl furnaces, and the distribution of the two types may relate partly to the quality of the available ores, with tapping furnaces enabling much lower-grade ores to be economically exploited (Salter 1987, 194).

The plateau areas to the north and south of the Bulbourne valley would have also provided an ample supply of the wood needed as fuel for the roasting of the ore and the production of charcoal. The Ashridge Estate is mostly ancient woodland and has been wooded since the Middle Ages. One particular area of 5 km^2 was devoid of Late Iron Age or Roman remains (A. Wainwright pers. comm.) and may therefore be a candidate for source of the wood required, although as we know nothing about the scale of the industry in terms of its potential iron output, the exact amount of woodland need to sustain it cannot be accurately calculated.

It can nevertheless reasonably be assumed that areas exploited for wood in the Late Iron Age would have been managed in a sustainable manner, probably by regular cutting of coppice on a rotational basis, as in the medieval and later periods. The alternative of simply clearing woodland would have necessitated chopping down large mature trees and cutting them up into manageable lumps of wood – both very labour-intensive tasks – and would have consumed inordinately large areas of woodland to maintain even a small iron industry. Coppiced woodland would not only provide sufficient supplies of timber, but would require much less labour input to cut and transport the poles.

If the model put forward here is correct, we would expect the sites where the iron was extracted to be situated in the zone between valley bottom, where the bog ore was obtained, and the plateau with its coppiced woodland, as seems to be the case. Another reason for the apparent concentration of ironworking in the Bulbourne valley is the easy communication it offers, both overland to the Midlands and eastern England, and by river to the Thames valley. Like the Rib at Braughing, the Bulbourne is relatively narrow and shallow, but would probably have been deep enough to float a laden Hasholme-style log boat, thus providing a relatively easy means of transporting the product (whether bloom or finished iron artefacts) to other areas within the Thames valley system.

Although the evidence is fragmentary, it suggests a thriving Late Iron Age iron industry in the Bulbourne valley. Given the presence of potentially contemporary field systems close to the ironworking sites, it is also quite likely that the inhabitants combined iron production and agriculture on a part-time or seasonal basis. The fact that the fields are located on heavy and stony clay-with-flints soils means that they are unlikely to have been productive in terms of crop or stock yields. A regime which combined ironworking and farming – albeit marginal – is therefore a possibility for the area.

Settlement status

It is not possible to reach firm conclusions about the relative status of the Bulbourne valley sites compared to the other five Late Iron Age site clusters, other than from the negative evidence that this area lacks richly furnished Aylesford burials and imports, which might suggest that it was less important than the others. This is however to some extent countered by the number of Iron Age bronze coins found at the Cow Roast site, which suggest some kind of Late Iron Age focus there (Haselgrove 1987, 181), and the site subsequently developed into a Roman roadside settlement. Another possible Late Iron Age focus is on Berkhamsted golf course, where there is a probable Romano-Celtic temple, a villa/temple, and a large rectilinear enclosure with evidence for Late Iron Age occupation (Morris and Wainwright 1995). The large Grim's Ditch earthwork lies 500 m to the south and may have served to mark the entrance to the site from the Bulbourne valley.

The six site-clusters as '*Oppida*'

Oppida appear in the Late La Tène of central and western Europe and are characterised *inter alia* by the presence of massive defences enclosing very large areas (over 25 hectares), zones of intensive settlement, large-scale manufacturing activity, and abundant evidence of long-distance trade (Collis 1984b, 6–8; Fichtl 2000). In England, few sites fulfil these criteria and the term '*oppidum*' has traditionally been used for settlements associated with large linear ditches or 'dykes', and evidence for industry, exchange, burial/ritual or other high status activity (Cunliffe 1976; 1991), although the use of the term remains confused (Collis 1984b, 6).

Attempts have been made to classify English *oppida* by dividing them on the basis of the morphology of the dykes into enclosed, territorial, and multiple dyke complexes (Cunliffe 1976; Edmonds 1989a–c). Territorial *oppida* have been further subdivided into (A) incomplete or 'unfinished' dyke systems and (B) rectilinear dyke systems (Edmonds 1989a). However, the dykes by which the sites are defined often occur in situations with little evidence of industry or high-status activity (e.g. Wheathampstead), or of nearby settlement (e.g. Chichester). The definition also excludes some obviously major settlements like Braughing, which lack dykes. In focusing on earthwork morphology, the English definition of *oppida* has therefore been of little use for understanding the key aspects of these sites and their role in Late Iron Age social and economic systems. Also, as Woolf (1993) has argued, the current definition is too general to be archaeologically useful.

Three of the clusters discussed here (Baldock, St Albans and Wheathampstead) are frequently described as *oppida*. The case for Baldock is based on the evidence of linear ditches, Welwyn-type burials, imports and other evidence of high-status activities (Burleigh 1995a). The presence of extensive dyke systems and high-status settlements and cemeteries at Verlamion has also made it widely accepted as an *oppidum* (e.g. Hunn 1992; Haselgrove and Millett 1997). Wheathampstead was originally described as an *oppidum* (Wheeler and Wheeler 1936), but its lack of internal occupation and unusual dyke morphology have thrown doubt upon its status (Saunders and Havercroft 1982).

Locational criteria

Collis has reviewed the major factors which influenced the location of continental *oppida* (Collis 1984b, 167–76). He concludes that control of long-distance trade routes was the most important factor in their siting, evidenced particularly by proximity to important routes along the major river valleys followed by the proximity to raw materials such as iron ore. Locally, a defensible situation was also a prime consideration, but access to areas of high population and to rich agricultural land were felt to be much less important (*ibid.*, 176).

The above discussion of factors affecting the location of the six clusters in the study area has concluded that communication was an important factor, although none of them appear to have been located with respect to the control of long-distance exchange. The best geographical location for this purpose within the study area is probably in the Hertford/Ware area of the Lea valley, which lies at the confluence of several rivers, and was later chosen as the site of the strategic military and trading centre at Hertford by Edward the Elder in AD 912–913 (Kiln and Partridge 1995). However, although several Late Iron Age sites are known from this area, and Braughing is not far away, there is no evidence for a major focus in the immediate locality.

As for access to agriculture and industrial resources, only the Bulbourne complex appears to have been influenced by the location of raw materials, whilst Braughing and Welwyn may have taken advantage of locally available agricultural wealth. None of the six clusters appears to have been situated for defensive purposes. Only the Gatesbury earthwork within the Braughing complex can be considered as probably defensive, and it only enclosed a very small proportion of the estimated area of the settlement. In sum, none of the six clusters within the study area which might potentially be classified as *oppida* fulfil the locational criteria defined by Collis.

Functional criteria

With its evidence of exchange, nucleation, and industry, Braughing is probably the closest of the six sites in functional terms to the continental definition, although the absence of defences is at variance with typical European *oppida* (Collis 1984b). The evident importance of Verlamion and Baldock as burial and ritual foci is also in contrast with the abundant traces of exchange and industrial activity at many continental *oppida*, and relative rarity of cemeteries. Religious sanctuaries are known within several *oppida* (Collis 1984b, 106; Fichtl 2000) and the internal ditches of others may have played a ritual role (Haselgrove 1996a). A more significant ritual function has been suggested for *oppida* in Moravia and Bohemia (Cumberpatch 1995), but as yet no-one has argued a dominant role for ritual in any western European *oppida*, although it is clear that we have underestimated the importance of sanctuaries in their development.

Parts of the Bulbourne and Welwyn settlement complexes may prove to fall within the more general English definition of *oppidum*. Both have evidence for dykes, industry, together with high status burial and imports in the case of Welwyn and possible market activity in the case of Cow Roast. However, although both clusters may have had some central place functions, the differences between them are too great for them to have had similar origins and roles.

In summary, the suggested origins and function of the six clusters are sufficiently distinct to conclude that they do not fall within a single settlement class and that the term *oppidum* is not a useful functional label for them.

Conclusions

Of the six Late Iron Age clusters, Braughing has the best evidence for high-status long-distance exchange and intensive occupation. It may have developed from an earlier settlement and remained a local centre of importance in the Roman and Anglo-Saxon periods. A not dissimilar sequence can be observed at Welwyn, although less is known about its origins. Both places had access to relatively good agricultural land and are likely to have performed a range of central place functions for their immediate areas. Baldock shows some similarities to the first two site clusters, but is dominated by burial and ritual activity and has yet to produce convincing evidence of contemporary settlement. The existence of an earlier prehistoric burial and ritual focus may have been an important factor in its location and development.

Verlamion also seems to have been a major burial and ritual centre (probably the *civitas* cult centre for the Catuvellauni) in the first century AD. There is as yet no evidence for significant earlier occupation, and the complex may even have been a deliberate foundation, intended to consolidate political developments, as Creighton (2000) has argued, although this seems less likely. There is nothing to suggest that Wheathampstead represents its predecessor as a major centre; if anything, it too seems to be part of the wider and ceremonial landscape focused on the Ver valley. Lastly, the Bulbourne valley complex of sites appears to have developed in the first century BC in an area where the processing of iron ore was a major activity. In contrast to Braughing, Welwyn, and Baldock, there is no evidence for imports or high-status burials and the agricultural potential of the area is relatively low.

The above analysis has shown that the six site-clusters have – based on current evidence – variable origins and functions. Some tentative grouping can however be suggested: Braughing and Welwyn village were existing central places; Verlamion (definitely) and Baldock (probably) originated as ritual/burial sites and became central places; and the Bulbourne valley develops as an iron processing area. However, this formulation will almost certainly need to be altered as the steady stream of new discoveries continues. Other potential high-status sites like Turner Hall Farm (West 2005) undoubtedly exist within the study area, whilst a number of important ritual sites have recently been discovered, at Essendon, Pegston, and Broadway Farm.

Bibliography

Anthony, I.E. 1968. Excavations in Verulam Hills Fields, St Albans, 1963–4, *Hertfordshire Archaeology* 1, 9–50.

Arcelin, P and Brunaux, J.-L. 2003. Cultes et sanctuaires en France à l'âge du fer, *Gallia* 60, 1–268.

Arnold, B.J. 1952–54. A Belgic settlement at Welwyn Garden City,

Transactions of the East Hertfordshire Archaeology Society 13, 128–137.

Ashdown, R. 1979. The avian bone from Station Road, Puckeridge, in Partridge 1979, 92–97.

Ashdown, R. 1981. The avian bone, in Partridge 1981, 235–241.

Bassett, S.R. 1989. In search of the origins of the Anglo-Saxon Kingdoms, in S.R. Bassett (ed.), *The Origins of Anglo-Saxon Kingdoms,* 3–27. Leicester: Leicester University Press.

Brunaux, J.-L. 1999. Ribemont-sur-Ancre, Somme. Bilan préliminaire et nouvelles hypothèses, *Gallia* 56, 177–283.

Bryant, S.R. 1995. The late Bronze Age to the middle Iron Age of the North Chilterns, in Holgate 1995, 17–27.

Bryant, S.R. 1999. *Settlement and Landscape in the Late Iron Age of Hertfordshire and the Northern Chilterns.* Unpublished Ph.D. thesis, University of Sheffield.

Bryant, S.R. and Niblett, R. 1997. The late Iron Age of Hertfordshire and the North Chilterns, in Gwilt and Haselgrove 1997, 270–281.

Burleigh, G. 1995a. A late Iron Age *oppidum* at Baldock, Hertfordshire, in Holgate 1995, 103–112.

Burleigh, G. 1995b. *Assessment Report Hartsfield School, Baldock, Hertfordshire.* Unpublished report, North Hertfordshire District Council.

Collis, J.R. 1984a. *The European Iron Age.* London: Batsford.

Collis, J.R. 1984b. *Oppida: Earliest Towns North of the Alps.* Sheffield: J.R. Collis Publications.

Creighton, J. 2000. *Coins and Power in Late Iron Age Britain.* Cambridge: Cambridge University Press.

Cumberpatch, C.G. 1995. Production and society in the Later Iron Age of Bohemia and Moravia, in J.D. Hill and C.G. Cumberpatch (eds), *Different Iron Ages: Studies on the Iron Age of Temperate Europe,* 67–94. Oxford: British Archaeological Reports International Series 602.

Cunliffe, B. 1976. The origins of urbanisation in Britain, in Cunliffe and Rowley 1976, 135–162.

Cunliffe, B. 1991. *Iron Age Communities in Britain* (3rd edn). London: Routledge.

Cunliffe, B. and Rowley, T. (eds) 1976. *Oppida: the Beginnings of Urbanisation in Barbarian Europe.* Oxford: British Archaeological Reports International Series 11.

Curteis, M. 1997. Iron Age Coinage, *The Archaeologist* (Spring 1997) 28, 21–22.

Curteis, M. 2005. Ritual coin deposition on Iron Age settlements in the south Midlands, in C. Haselgrove and D. Wigg-Wolf (eds), *Iron Age Coinage and Ritual Practices,* 207–225. Mainz: Studien zu Fundmünzen der Antike 20.

Dunnett, B.R.K. 1973. Report on the trial excavations at Wards Coombe, Ivinghoe, 1971, *Records of Buckinghamshire* 19, 141–156.

Edmonds, M. 1989a. *Monuments Protection Programme Single Class Monument Description: Territorial Oppida.* London: English Heritage.

Edmonds, M. 1989b. *Monuments Protection Programme Single Class Monument Description: Enclosed Oppida.* London: English Heritage.

Edmonds, M. 1989c. *Monuments Protection Programme Single Class Monument Description: Multiple Dyke Complexes.* London: English Heritage.

Fichtl, S. 2000. *La Ville Celtique. Les Oppida de 150 av. J.-C. à 15 ap. J.-C.* Paris: Editions Errance.

Fifield, P.W. and King, A. 1988. The faunal remains, in Potter and Trow 1988, 148–155.

Fitzpatrick, A.P. 1997. *Archaeological Excavations on the Route of the A27 Westhampnett Bypass, West Sussex, Vol. 2. The Cemeteries.* Salisbury: Wessex Archaeology Report 12.

Foster, J. 1986. Fired clay objects, in Stead and Rigby 1986, 168.

Frere, S.S. 1983. *Verulamium Excavations, Vol. II.* Oxford: Report of the Research Committee of the Society of Antiquaries of London 41.

Gelling, M. 1975. *Early Charters of the Thames Valley.* Leicester: Leicester University Press.

Gelling, M. 1988. *Signposts to the Past: Place-Names and the History of England.* Chichester: Phillimore.

Going, C.J. 1990. *Wickham Kennels Pottery Assessment Report.* Unpublished report, Hertfordshire Archaeological Trust.

Gover, J.E.B., Mawer, A. and Stenton, F.M. 1938. *The Place-Names of Hertfordshire.* Cambridge: English Place-Name Society Vol. 15.

Gregory, A. 1992. *Excavations at Thetford, 1980–82, Fison Way.* Gressenhall: East Anglian Archaeology Report 53.

Gwilt, A. and Haselgrove, C. (eds) 1997. *Reconstructing Iron Age Societies.* Oxford: Oxbow Monograph 71.

Haselgrove, C. 1987. *Iron Age Coinage in South-East England: The Archaeological Context.* Oxford: British Archaeological Reports British Series 174.

Haselgrove, C. 1988. The coins from the 1971–1972 excavations, in Potter and Trow 1988, 21–29.

Haselgrove, C. 1993. The development of British Iron-Age coinage, *Numismatic Chronicle* 153, 31–64.

Haselgrove, C. 1996a. Roman impact on rural settlement and society in southern Picardy, in N. Roymans (ed.), *From the Sword to the Plough: Three Studies in the Earliest Romanisation of Northern Gaul,* 127–187. Amsterdam: Amsterdam Archaeological Studies 1.

Haselgrove, C. 1996b. Iron Age coinage: recent work, in T.C. Champion and J.R. Collis (eds), *The Iron Age in Britain and Ireland: Recent Trends,* 67–86. Sheffield: J.R. Collis Publications.

Haselgrove, C. 1997. Iron Age brooch deposition and chronology, in Gwilt and Haselgrove 1997, 51–72.

Haselgrove, C. and Millett, M. 1997. Verlamion reconsidered, in Gwilt and Haselgrove 1997, 283–296.

Hawkes, C.F.C. and Crummy P. 1995. *Camulodunum II.* Colchester: Colchester Archaeological Report 11.

Hill, J.D. 2002. Just about the potter's wheel ? Using, making and depositing Middle and Later Iron Age pots in East Anglia, in A. Woodward and J.D. Hill (eds), *Prehistoric Britain: The Ceramic Basis,* 143–160. Oxford: Oxbow Books.

Hill, J.D., Evans, C. and Alexander, M. 1999. The Hinxton rings, a late Iron Age cemetery at Hinxton, Cambridgeshire, with a reconsideration of northern Aylesford–Swarling distributions, *Proceedings of the Prehistoric Society* 65, 243–273.

Hodder, I. 1982. *Symbols in Action.* Cambridge: Cambridge University Press.

Holgate, R. 1995. *Chiltern Archaeology: Recent Work.* Dunstable: The Book Castle.

Hunn, J.R. 1992. The Verulamium oppidum and its landscape in the late Iron Age, *Archaeological Journal* 149, 39–68.

Hunn, J.R. 1994. *Reconstruction and Measurement of Landscape Change: a Study of Six Parishes in the St Albans Area.* Oxford: British Archaeological Reports British Series 236.

Hunn, J.R. 1996. *Settlement Patterns in Hertfordshire: A Review of the*

Typology and Function of Enclosures in the Iron Age and Roman Landscape. Oxford: British Archaeological Reports British Series 249.

Hunn, J.R. forthcoming. Excavations on a first-century enclosure at Stanborough School, Welwyn Garden City, *Hertfordshire Archaeology.*

Kiln, R. and Partridge, C. 1995. *Ware and Hertford: the Story of Two Towns from Birth to Middle Age.* Welwyn Garden City: Castlemead.

Loughton, M.E. 2003. The distribution of Republican amphorae in France, *Oxford Journal of Archaeology* 22, 177–207.

Millett, M. and McGrail, S. 1988. The archaeology of the Hasholme logboat, *Archaeological Journal* 144, 69–155.

Morris, J. 1976. *Domesday Book, Vol. 12. Hertfordshire.* Chichester: Phillimore.

Morris, M. and Wainwright, A. 1995. Iron Age and Romano-British settlement, agriculture and industry in the Upper Bulbourne Valley, Hertfordshire: an interim interpretation, in Holgate 1995, 68–75.

Moss Eccardt, J. 1988. Archaeological investigations in the Letchworth area, 1958–1974, *Proceedings of the Cambridge Antiquarian Society* 87, 35–103.

Neal, D.S., Wardle, A. and Hunn, J. 1990. *Excavation of the Iron Age, Roman and Medieval Settlement at Gorhambury, St Albans.* London: English Heritage Archaeological Report 14.

Niblett, R. 1993. Verulamium since the Wheelers, in S. Greep (ed.), *Roman Towns: the Wheeler Inheritance. A review of 50 years research*, 78–92. York: Council for British Archaeology Research Report 93.

Niblett, R. 1999. *The Excavation of a Ceremonial Site at Folly Lane, Verulamium.* London: Britannia Monograph 14.

Partridge, C. 1975. Braughing, in W. Rodwell and R.T. Rowley (eds), *Small Towns of Roman Britain*, 139–157. Oxford: British Archaeological Reports British Series 15.

Partridge, C. 1979. Excavations at Puckeridge and Braughing 1975–79, *Hertfordshire Archaeology* 7, 28–132.

Partridge, C. 1981. *Skeleton Green. A Late Iron Age and Romano-British Site.* London: Britannia Monograph 2.

Potter, T.W. and Trow, S.D. 1988 *Puckeridge–Braughing, Herts. The Ermine Street Excavations, 1971–1972* (*Hertfordshire Archaeology* 10).

Rigby, V. 1981. The Gallo-Belgic Wares, in Partridge 1981, 159–195.

Rigby, V. 1989. Pottery from the Iron Age cemetery, in Stead and Rigby 1989, 112–204.

Rigby, V. and Foster, J. 1986. Building Materials, in Stead and Rigby 1986, 183–191.

Rodwell, W.J. 1976. Coinage, oppida and the rise of Belgic power in south-east Britain, in Cunliffe and Rowley 1976, 181–367.

Rook, A.G. 1968a. Investigation of a Belgic occupation site at Crookhams, Welwyn Garden City, *Hertfordshire Archaeology* 1, 51–65.

Rook, A.G. 1968b. A Belgic ditched enclosure at Nutfield, Welwyn Garden City, *Hertfordshire Archaeology* 1, 121–122.

Rook, A.G. 1968c. A note on the "rediscovery" of a Belgic chieftain burial, *Hertfordshire Past and Present* 8, 17–18.

Rook, A.G. 1970a. Investigation of a Belgic site at Grubs Barn, Welwyn Garden City, *Hertfordshire Archaeology* 2, 31–36.

Rook, A.G. 1974. Welches Farm, *Hertfordshire Archaeological Review* 9, 170–174.

Rook, A.G. 1983–6. The Roman villa site at Dicket Mead, *Hertfordshire Archaeology* 9, 79–175.

Rook, A.G., Walker, S. and Denston, C.B. 1984. A Roman mausoleum and associated marble sarcophagus and burials from Welwyn, Hertfordshire, *Britannia* 15, 143–162.

Salter, C. 1987 Ferrous metallurgy and other slags, in B. Cunliffe, *Hengistbury Head, Dorset, Vol. 1. The Prehistoric and Roman Settlement*, 197–205. Oxford: Oxford University Committee for Archaeology Monograph13.

Salter, C. and Ehrenreich, R.M. 1984. Iron Age iron metallurgy in central Southern England, in B. Cunliffe and D. Miles (eds), *Aspects of the Iron Age in Central Southern* England, 146–161. Oxford: Oxford University Committee for Archaeology Monograph 2.

Saunders, C. and Havercroft A.B. 1980–2. Excavation on the line of the Wheathampstead by-pass, 1974 and 1977, with some thoughts on the *oppida* at Wheathampstead and Verulamium, *Hertfordshire Archaeology* 8, 11–39.

Smith, R.A. 1912. On Late-Celtic Antiquities Discovered at Welwyn, Herts., *Archaeologia* 63, 1–30.

Stead, I.M. 1967. A La Tène III Burial at Welwyn Garden City, *Archaeologia* 101, 1–62.

Stead, I.M. and Rigby, V. 1986. *Baldock: the Excavation of a Roman and Pre-Roman Settlement 1968–75.* London: Britannia Monograph 7.

Stead, I.M. and Rigby, V. 1989. *Verulamium: the King Harry Lane Site.* London: English Heritage Archaeological Report 12.

Thompson, A. and Holland, E. 1974–6. Excavation of an Iron Age site at Dellfield, Berkhamsted, *Hertfordshire Archaeology* 4, 137–149.

Thompson, I. 1979. Wheathampstead revisited, *Bulletin of the University of London Institute of Archaeology 16*, 159–185.

Thompson, I. 1982. *The Grog-Tempered 'Belgic' Pottery of South-Eastern England.* Oxford: British Archaeological Reports British Series 108.

Thompson, I. 2002. *Braughing: Extensive Urban Survey Project Assessment Report.* Unpublished Report, Hertfordshire SMR.

Tyers, P. 1981. A note on the mica-dusted Jars, in Partridge 1981, 102–103.

Van Arsdell, R.D. 1989. *Celtic Coinage of Britain.* London: Spink.

Walker, C. 1994. *Hadham Hall, Little Hadham: Archaeological Excavations (west side).* Unpublished report, Hertfordshire Archaeological Trust.

Ward-Perkins, J.R. 1937. Romano-British Villa at Lockleys, *St Albans Architectural and Archaeological Society Transactions*, 131–139.

West, S. 2005. Life and Death on a Romano British Estate: Turners Hall Farm in Hertfordshire, *Minerva* 16 (1), 27–29.

Wheeler, A. 1981. Fish Bones, in Partridge 1981, 242–243.

Wheeler R.E.M. and T.V. 1936. *Verulamium. A Belgic and Two Roman Cities.* Oxford: Reports of the Research Committee of the Society of Antiquaries of London 11.

Woolf, G. 1993. Rethinking the Oppida, *Oxford Journal Of Archaeology* 14, 399–412.

Cultural choices in the 'British Eastern Channel Area' in the Late Pre-Roman Iron Age

Sue Hamilton

Introduction

The suite of changes that traditionally defines the Late Pre-Roman Iron Age of southern and eastern Britain is well known. It includes the adoption of coinage and wheel-made pottery, the appearance of visible burial rites and shrines, revitalised contacts with the Continent – evinced by imports and new fashions – and the emergence of large-scale settlements called *oppida*. This article reviews aspects of these defining features of the Late Iron Age, with particular respect to the areas of Britain which lie proximate to the English Channel, where in recent decades vastly increased numbers, and previously unknown categories, of site have been discovered.

My discussion centres on the highly distinctive settlement and burial evidence generated by the proliferation of fieldwork on the West Sussex coastal plain and coastal east Kent. Developer-funded archaeology impacted on the former area from the 1970s (Hamilton and Gregory 2000, 58), and recently yet more dramatically on east Kent, with the Channel Tunnel Rail Link work of the 1990s. These findings have yet to be incorporated into general syntheses; this article aims to collate these data, and explore some of their implications for our understanding of the Late Iron Age in south-east England.

I have coined the term 'British Eastern Channel Area' (hereafter BECA) for the zone encompassed by this recent archaeological activity – an area which geographically and topographically comprises the south coast and its hinterland from approximately Hayling Island, on the Hampshire border, to Ramsgate, east Kent (Fig. 1). The North and South Downs bound this area to the north and north-west, while on the south and east it is terminated by the sea – with its short crossings to Belgium and northern France (notably the Nord/Pas-de-Calais and Picardy regions). West of Hayling Island, southern Britain becomes increasingly distant from the Continent. This eastern Channel area lacked excavation in the past and does not correlate geographically with any single Late Iron Age cultural unit. Thus, the ceramic traditions of coastal east Hampshire/West Sussex fall within Cunliffe's (1991) Southern Atrebatic style zone, which continues beyond the current area of focus as far west as the Solent, as do the western limits of his Selsey socio-economic zone (defined on the basis of coinage; *ibid.*, fig. 7.2).

The south-east Kent Channel area remains necessarily ill-defined due to the wholesale lack of Iron Age evidence from present-day Romney Marsh, whilst Cunliffe (*ibid.*, fig. 7.1) subsumes the north Kent Channel area into his 'Aylesford–Swarling' zone. The newly emerging pattern of settlements and burials for the BECA, however, differs from those associated with either the Atrebatic or the Aylesford–Swarling traditions, in spite of elements of both being present. A primary remit of this article is therefore to contextualise the characteristics of the BECA finds, particularly when set against the better known Aylesford–Swarling material, on which our current understanding of the Late Iron Age of south-east Britain is largely founded. The nature of the continental context of the BECA is considered in the latter part of the article. My discussion is prefaced by a summary of the traditional view of the Late Iron Age in the area, and an outlining of the extant terminologies for its archaeology.

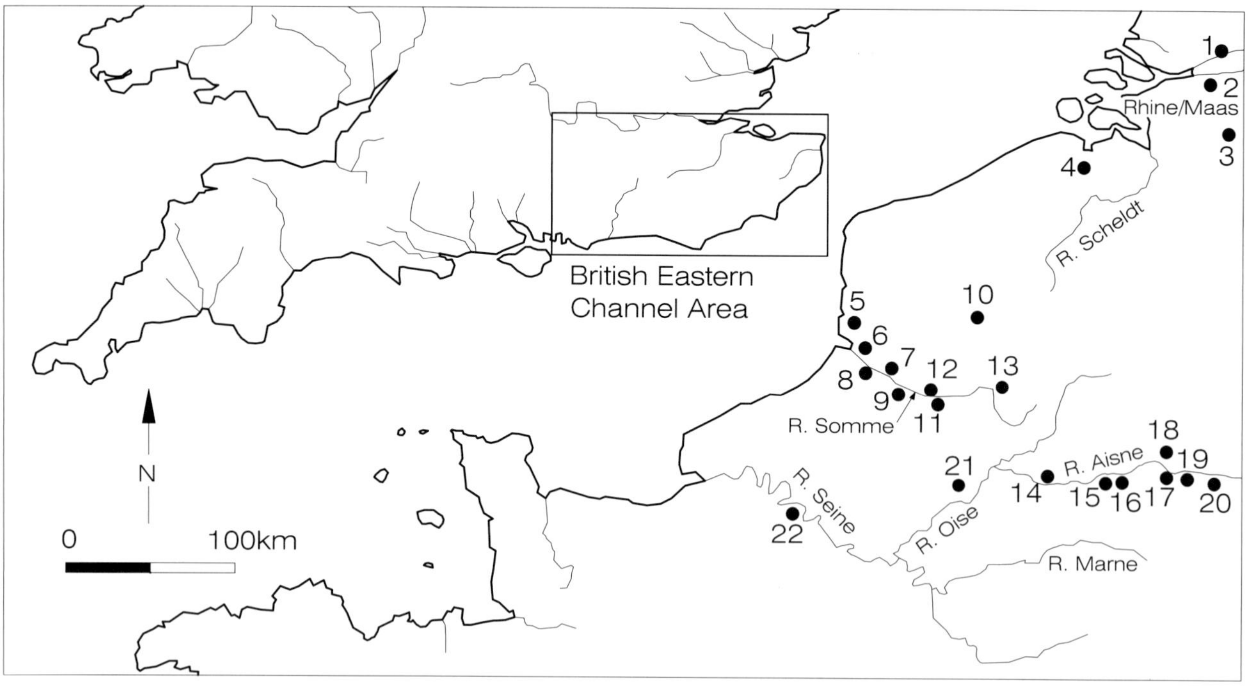

Fig. 1. Location map of the British Eastern Channel Area, with the locations of continental sites referred to in the text. 1. Wijk bij Duurstede; 2. Oss-Ussen; 3. Mierlo-Hout; 4. Destelbergen; 5. Nempont-Saint-Firmin; 6. Conchil-le-Temple; 7. Pont-Rémy, La Queute; 8. Bray-lès-Mareuil; 9. Condé-Folie, Les Garchettes; 10. Hénin-Beaumont; 11. Bayonvillers; 12. Ribemont-sur-Ancre; 13. Vermand, Champ des Lavoirs; 14. Bucy-le-Long; 15. Braine, La Grange des Moines; 16. Bazoches, Les Chantraines; 17. Nanteuil-sur-Aisne; 18. Château-Porcien; 19. Acy-Romance; 20. Thugny-Trugny; 21. Gournay-sur-Aronde; 22. Poses, Sur La Mare.

Traditional templates for the Late Iron Age of south-east Britain

Traditional interpretative templates for the British Iron Age are based on features that are typical of very limited areas of southern Britain, and particularly Wessex, for the Earlier Iron Age (Fitzpatrick 1997a). For the Late Iron Age, south-east England supersedes Wessex in providing the textbook version of Iron Age society. In such a scenario, the BECA is perceived as being peripheral to this hub of Late Iron Age action – which is presented as being focused in Essex, Hertfordshire, and north Kent. This situation is epitomised by Haselgrove's (1982) influential core-periphery model for south-eastern England. In this, the BECA lies within the 'periphery', which is characterised as being linked to a 'core' of intense, rapid social and economic development and continental contacts, but does not undergo significant structural change itself. Contact with the Continent is seen as prompting, or in current academic perspectives adding definition to, the Late Iron Age changes in the 'core zone' of south-east Britain. The BECA is paradoxically *geographically* nearer to the Continent, and the manner in which this proximity contributes in any way to its Late Iron Age development is unresolved.

Quagmire terminologies

Any student new to the British Iron Age will metaphorically wade through treacle if they attempt to unravel the spatial and cultural parameters, and academic baggage of the various names applied to the Late Iron Age artefactual (and supposed tribal) groupings of south-east England. For a start, the Late Iron Age archaeology of south-east England is irrevocably entwined with the problem of the Belgae. The origins of this 'marriage' lie in Sir Arthur Evans' (1890) linkage of his finds from the Aylesford cemetery in Kent with the peoples of Belgic Gaul. These are the people whom Caesar recorded as raiding the coastal regions of south-east England, and then staying to till the land (*Gallic War* V, 11–14; II, 4).

The wish to isolate the 'Belgae' in Britain by correlating burials, coins, pottery, and history fell apart in the 1960s (Fitzpatrick 1997b, 210) and we have long left behind the type of archaeology that neatly equates patterns of material culture with distinct groups of people. Current wisdom favours a mixture of cross-channel exchanges, limited migration (perhaps of specialists), and internal dynamics as contributing to the profound changes that took place at this period. Our texts, however, remain littered with archaic terminologies for the material culture groupings of south-east England, even though these no longer seem relevant to the essence of our concerns. There is no need fully to rehearse these here, except to indicate how these apply to the BECA in the extant literature.

In its adjectival form, the term 'Belgic' remains actively used for certain elements of Late Iron Age material in the BECA. It is particularly prevalent in pottery reports as a term for the high-shouldered, curvilinear wheel-made wares that, in varying degrees, dominate site assemblages in southern and eastern England. This designation is scrupulously avoided in many current texts, either in favour of the term Aylesford or Aylesford–Swarling (Cunliffe 1991; Fitzpatrick 1997b), or more simply Late Iron Age (Elsdon 1989; Hill 2002). Geographically, the BECA falls within Caesar's *pars maritima*. This is the area that he records as being settled with a new people, taken to be the Belgae (Harding 1974, 224; Cunliffe 1991), and is generally mapped as centring on West Sussex, East Sussex, and Kent (Harding 1974, fig 81). Collectively, however, these areas encompass *more than one* coeval tribal group/cultural tradition (e.g. Aylesford–Swarling, Eastern Atrebatic, and Western Atrebatic; Cunliffe 1991, 130–57). Additionally, some of the BECA's cultural practices, such as the use of cremation, are more particularly associated with the archaeology of Caesar's *pars interior*. This is located north of the Thames, and recorded by Caesar as inhabited by people who were proud of their native ancestry (Harding 1974, 224). This nexus of terminological ascription pre-eminently highlights the cultural complexity of the BECA in the Late Iron Age, and the need to study the data freed from such classificatory constructs.

Haselgrove's (1982) core–periphery synthesis effectively put to one side the hopeless problem of equating Caesar's spatial geography with archaeologically identified groupings by blocking together the Aylesford–Swarling/Belgic material to create a supra-regional 'core zone' of socio-economic change. Recent work has focused upon the smaller-scale, regional complexities of these changes, but interestingly has fallen back on modern county boundaries (perhaps reflecting the increased number of finds generated by the county-based planning frameworks within which commercial archaeology functions) to describe specific spatial patterns in the material. Thus, deposits of torcs and isolated finds of chariot equipment are recognised as being specific to Norfolk (cf. Hutcheson this volume), bucket cremations are thought characteristic of Kent and Hertfordshire, and so on. This breakdown in the geographical scale and cultural frameworks at which patterning is identified and explained makes it opportune to isolate less traditional geographies, such as the BECA, for analysis.

Settlement in the British Eastern Channel Area

The origins of Late Iron Age settlement patterns in south-east England, and the extent to which they resulted from the expansion, movement, or reconfiguration of communities, are poorly understood. The dramatic growth of evidence in the BECA provides an excellent opportunity to study the nascence and development of these settlement patterns. It is suggested below that the landscape uptake and morphological characteristics of Late Iron Age settlement in the BECA have their origins in the Middle Iron Age. This stands in contrast to the prevailing view of the Late Iron Age in much of south-east England, which is believed to be characterised by the expansion of communities into sparsely settled areas (Haselgrove 1999, 129; Hill 2002; this volume).

Middle Iron Age settlement

East Kent

The extent and nature of Middle Iron Age settlement in east Kent is still difficult to ascertain (Fig. 2). Dating relies predominantly on pottery associations, and the Middle Iron Age and the 'pre-Belgic' Late Iron Age phases of Kentish pottery production are ill-defined. This is due to the typological variability of the pottery assigned to the earliest Middle Iron Age and the absence of a 'saucepan-pot' continuum comparable to that which characterises the later Middle Iron Age elsewhere in southern Britain (Hamilton and Seager Thomas 2002). Additionally, many of the 'key' first millennium BC pottery assemblages from Kent are not yet published (notably Highstead, Beechbrook Wood, and the Hawkinge complex; a full list of Middle Iron Age findspots is given in Appendix 1).

The fact that east Kent lacks clearly defined pottery assemblages for the period *c.* 350–150 BC has been used to argue for settlement/population disruption in the later Middle Iron Age (Stevens 1999). A small number of saucepan-type forms are, however, present at east Kent sites, for instance in the 'waterhole assemblage' at Bigberry (Thompson 1983) and at Hawkinge (Stevens 1999). At both sites, the saucepan forms occur in association with 'pre-Belgic' S-profiled fineware jars with foot-rings, dated to *c.* 150/100 BC. These associations suggest a slightly earlier dating for the 'pre-Belgic' Late Iron Age assemblages, extending them and the sites where they occur back into what would be the Middle Iron Age elsewhere in southern Britain. On this basis the Late Iron Age sites on hilltops and south-facing hill slopes on the Chalk and Wealden geologies of east Kent have Middle Iron Age origins. For the Chalk, this includes Bigberry and the Mill Hill cemetery (Parfitt 1995, 153). At Saltwood, on a south-facing slope of the Wealden Greensand, a small group of Middle Iron Age inhumation graves was situated near the junction of two

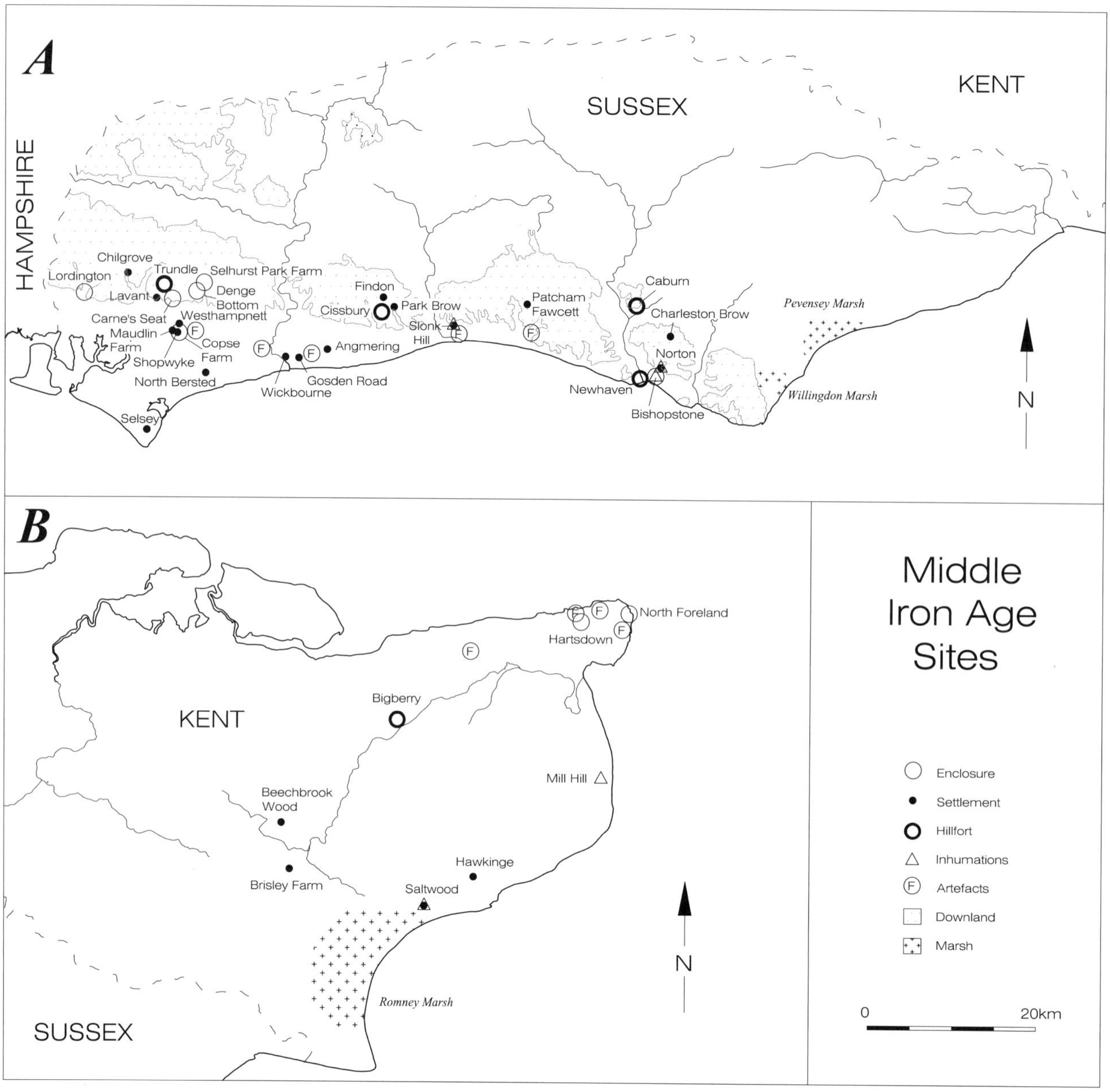

Fig. 2. Distribution map of Middle Iron Age sites in the British Eastern Channel Area.

hollow trackways – which later became the focus of a Late Iron Age settlement and field system (Union Railways South 2002a).

The recently discovered major Late Iron Age settlements on the lower-lying Wealden Greensand, such as Beechbrook Wood (Union Railways South 2002b), and on the Weald Clay, as at Brisley Farm (Johnson 2003) all have evidence of preceding, less intensive Middle Iron Age occupation (Appendix 1). Beechbrook Wood, just north-west of the Brisley Farm complex, provides an important sequence of expansion. From its establishment in the Late Bronze Age, the settlement sequentially shifts towards the lower-lying terrain to the east and south. This culminates in the construction of a double-ditched enclosure in the Middle Iron Age, which later became a focus for Late Iron Age activity. Such double-ditched enclosures are rare in south-east England. The Beechbrook Wood example has a funnel entrance and compares with Carne's Seat, West Sussex (below) and more generally to the Middle/Late Iron Age banjo enclosures of West Sussex, Hampshire, and Surrey (Bedwin 1984; Hanworth 1987, 265).

The Brisley Farm and Westhawk Farm evidence (pits and narrow ditches) suggests that later prehistoric expansion onto the east Kent Weald Clay dates to the

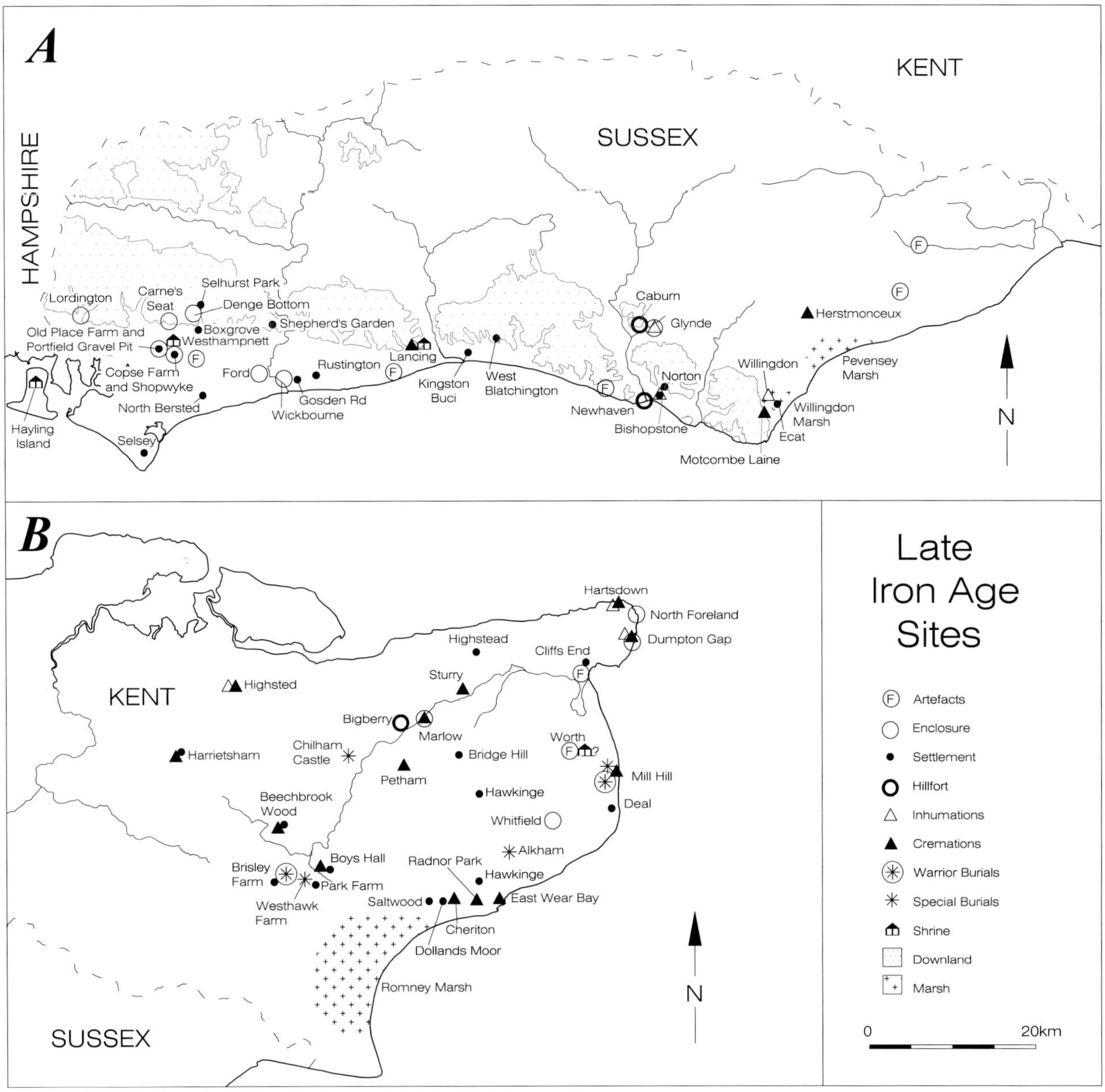

Fig. 3. Distribution map of Late Iron Age sites in the British Eastern Channel Area.

Middle/Late Bronze Age. As in the West Sussex Coastal Plain (below), there is then a 'gap' in the evidence for the Early Iron Age (but *not* for the Middle Iron Age). This uptake of the Weald Clay is then renewed in the Middle Iron Age (e.g. at Brisley Farm). In Kent, this may be a micro-pattern, distinct to the Channel area. It stands in apparent contrast to north Kent, where recent excavations suggest that sites with long prehistoric sequences were abandoned by the Middle Iron Age, and *new* sites were selected for settlement in the Late Iron Age, as at Thurnham and Whitehorse Stone (Union Railways South 2001a; 2001b).

Sussex coast and hinterland

At the beginning of the Middle Iron Age, distinct changes occurred in the number and locations of Sussex hillforts. The early first millennium BC hillforts went out of use and a reduced number of new hillforts were established in central, downland locations, notably the Caburn, Cissbury, and the Trundle (Hamilton and Manley 2001). These hillforts are positioned on hilltops of striking morphology that are highly visible, but lack evidence for centralised production, high-status goods, non-local goods, or concentrations of population (Drewett and Hamilton 1999; Hamilton and Manley 2001). There was some continued use of downland settlements on the crowns of hills that jut southwards into the coastal plain (e.g. Bishopstone and Slonk Hill; Appendix 1), but *contra* Wessex, these hillforts were co-eval with a paucity of local non-hillfort settlement (Bell 1977). 'Monumentalising' South Downs hills by conspicuously enclosing them may have had a key role in uniting dispersed communities, by creating a sense of topographic identity.

The choice of new topographic settings for these hillforts suggests a reworking of socio-political arenas in the Middle Iron Age. This is turn could well have been causal in the contemporary spread of settlement southwards, on to the West Sussex coastal plain. There are new sites on the south-west slopes of the Downs, such as the Carne's Seat banjo enclosure (Holgate 1986a), and at the heads of southerly orientated valleys, as at Norton (Seager Thomas 2005; Appendix 1). In recent years, it has become evident that the West Sussex coastal plain was resettled in the Middle Iron Age following an absence of sites earlier in the period (Bedwin 1983, 35). Farmsteads and associated square and rectangular ditched enclosures, linked by trackways, are a feature of the Late Iron Age in the coastal plain, but the excavated sites have Middle Iron Age origins, as at Copse Farm, Oving (Bedwin and Holgate 1985) and North Bersted (Bedwin and Pitts 1978). This re-impingement dates to the fourth or third century BC (Hamilton 2003), and is evidenced by saucepan pottery findspots and site assemblages, and radiocarbon dates from the excavated sites (Appendix 1). It formed the basis for the subsequent development of the coastal plain.

Late Iron Age settlement

East Kent

Many of the Late Iron Age sites are located on the low-lying Weald Clay (Fig. 3), and are hard to excavate due to their poor drainage, iron pans, and consequent difficulties in defining features and fills. A full list of Late Iron Age findspots is given in Appendix 2. Typically, the settlement architecture comprises roundhouses defined by ring-gully ditches, dispersed amongst these enclosure complexes. A notable feature is the emergence of larger foci of settlement. This is particularly apparent in the Ashford region. The Brisley Farm site was over two hectares in extent (Fig. 4), with the boundaries not reached in any direction by the excavations (Johnson 2003).

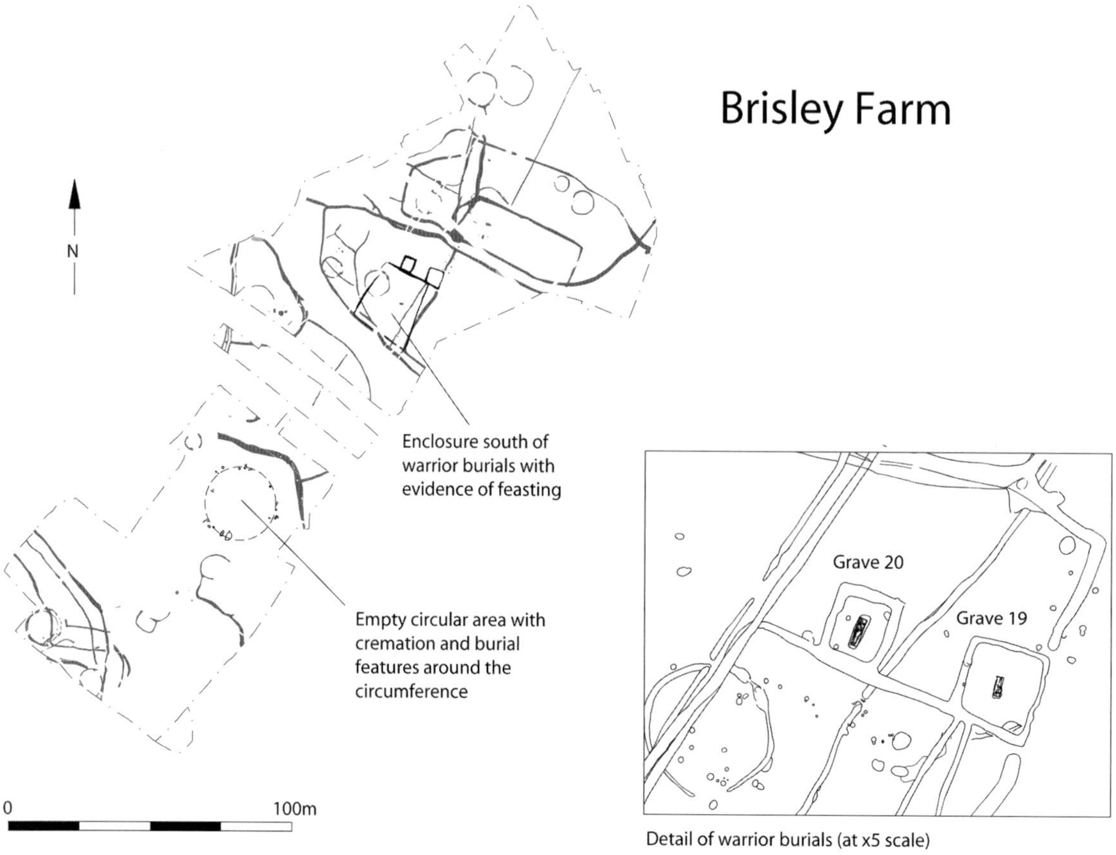

Fig. 4. Plan details of the locations of Brisley Farm cremations and 'warrior burials' (source: Field Archaeology Unit, UCL).

The settlement excavated by Wessex Archaeology at Park Farm, just north-east of Brisley Farm, appears to be an even larger exposure of ditch complex and circular houses with ring gullies. These two sites are sufficiently close to one another to suggest that they may be related. The rich pre-conquest cremation burial at Westhawk Farm, 750 m east of Brisley Farm, implies the possibility of yet another contemporary (but as yet unlocated) settlement (Booth and Lawrence 2000). It is beginning to look as if the Late Iron Age sites in the Ashford area formed a continuous landscape of ditched enclosures interspersed with larger-scale settlement foci.

A continuing trend towards the uptake of lower-lying land is clear at Brisley Farm. From its Middle Iron Age origins, the Late Iron Age and early Roman phases of Brisley Farm sequentially spread onto lower, wetter ground. Ditch complexes are central to the Late Iron Age drainage management of these low-lying areas of east Kent (as will also be discussed below for the West Sussex coastal plain). The Ashford sites are situated on a watershed (between the River Stour and the River Beault/ Medway), and there are no rivers or streams to channel ground water away. The sites do, however, pick out the most advantageous micro-topography with both Park Farm and Brisley Farm being situated on slight rises.

Elsewhere there are smaller, more contained sites, such as Beechbrook Farm, North Foreland, and Broadstairs. North Foreland (on the chalk) produced the remains of a small sub-rectangular enclosure of Middle to Late Iron Age date with a single entrance and at least six four-post buildings (Diack *et al.* 2000). Outside the enclosure there were settlement activity zones – including an area of large storage pits and clusters of post holes from at least one roundhouse as well as fence lines and palisades. At Beechbrook Farm the Middle Iron Age double-ditched enclosure remained a focus for deposition in the succeeding period, and two industrial plots, one associated with metalworking, were established. This small-scale zonation of activity is repeated on a larger scale at Park Farm and Brisley Farm, which have juxtaposed, distinct zones of mortuary/ritual activity, domestic activity, and industrial activity (including metalworking at Park Farm).

Sussex coast and hinterland

The Sussex evidence discussed above suggests that population changes in the Middle Iron Age were based on population dispersal rather than population pressure and expansion. The Sussex hillforts were abandoned at the end of the Middle Iron Age (Drewett and Hamilton 1999; Hamilton and Manley 2001), at the same time as the most extensive settlement of the West Sussex coastal plain occurred. The cemetery and religious site at Westhampnett lies at the beginning of this development. Fitzpatrick (1997b) estimates that this cemetery was used for 40 or 50 years (*c.* 90–50 BC) and represents a community of 90 people. No individual local settlement could have housed a population of this size, implying that the complex provided a central burial ground for dispersed settlements. It is seen as replacing the role of a regional focus previously provided by the Trundle hillfort.

By the mid first century BC an extensively ditched landscape, with repetitive elements was present on the West Sussex coastal plain (Appendix 2). These comprise rectangular/square settlement enclosures up to 40 m across, long trackways with ditches at either side, and associated systems of rectangular or square fields. On the evidence of Oving and North Bersted (Fig. 5), these systems were managed and exploited from single-unit farmsteads. These comprised a single roundhouse defined by a ring gully, associated working areas and hollows, and small pits with evidence of use as hearths or furnaces (Bedwin and Pitts 1978; Bedwin and Holgate 1985). The majority of these ditched sites are unexcavated, but are known from aerial photographs (e.g. Denge Bottom and Selhurst Park, Goodwood; Bedwin 1983). Accompanying this is an increasing density of pottery findspots (Fig. 3 above).

The small scale of the individual 'settlement' areas at these sites stands in marked contrast to the more extensive settlement complexes with their numerous roundhouses on the low-lying Kent Weald Clay, The large-scale development of drainage systems is however common to both regions. At North Bersted, over two hectares of ditch system are identified and the system was originally more extensive (Bedwin and Pitts 1978). The cumulative length of mapped ditch system is over 700 m, which directly compares with the ditches surrounding hillforts such as the Trundle (800 m perimeter; Bedwin and Pitts 1978). Evans (1997, 216) has stressed how the Iron Age settlements of East Anglia are similarly characterised by massive ditch digging projects. Such major drainage systems suggest communal organisation of landscape use, irrespective of the size of the individual settlement units. Additionally, the ditches would have required perhaps annual clearance of silts and rubbish in order to maintain free drainage; perhaps this was undertaken as a community event.

Late Iron Age oppida *in the British Eastern Channel Area?*

British *oppida*, or 'territorial *oppida*' are defined by imposing, embanked, discontinuous linear earthwork complexes enclosing often large areas within which there were important foci of activity – intense settlement, cemeteries, evidence of coin minting, and signs of involvement with long-distance trade with the Roman world. Two sites in the BECA are repeatedly classified as *oppida*: the area enclosed by the western part of the Chichester Entrenchments (specifically the Selsey peninsula) in West Sussex; and in east Kent, the site of

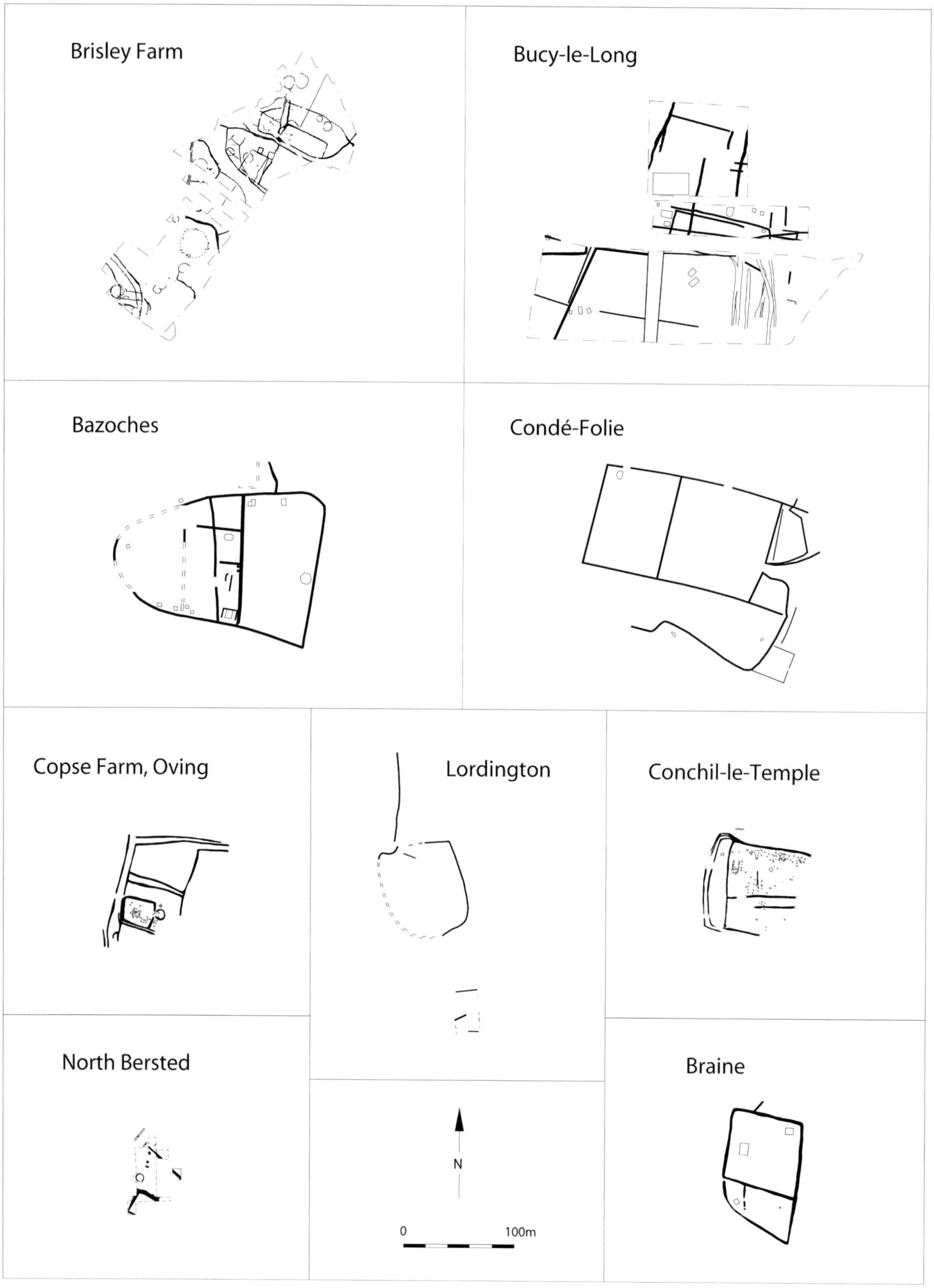

Fig. 5. Comparative settlement plans from the British Eastern Channel Area and northern France (redrawn to a common scale using the following sources: Braine: Auxiette et al. 2000; Brisley Farm: Field Archaeology Unit, UCL; Bucy-le-Long: Pommepuy et al. 2000; Bazoches 'Les Chantraines': Pommepuy et al. 2000; Conchil-le-Temple: Buchsenschutz 1984; Condé-Folie 'Les Garchettes': Buchenschutz 1984; Copse Farm, Oving: Bedwin and Holgate 1985; Lordington: Holgate 1986b; North Bersted: Bedwin and Pitts 1978).

Bigberry (Big*bury* in Cunliffe 1991 and Haselgrove 1999). The literature presents both sites as loci out of which the nearby Roman towns of Chichester and Canterbury respectively developed. This ascription is inappropriate for both sites, but a case can be made for heterogeneous, functionally *oppidum*-like developments in both West Sussex and east Kent.

Evidence for a major Late Iron Age settlement core in the Selsey peninsula is lacking (Bedwin 1983). Bigberry is likewise problematic. It is a plateau enclosure of hillfort dimensions (10.7 ha) and its designation as an *oppidum* relies largely on the discovery of an iron metalwork hoard, which included 'slave chains', agricultural tools, chariot and hearth equipment (Thompson 1983; Brockley and Brockley 1989). This suggests metalworkers' scrap or other high-status activities, but is insufficient to confirm the existence of an *oppidum* here (Hamilton and Manley 2001, 31). Instead, it is the presence of *integrated landscapes* that distinguish the Late Iron Age of the BECA. It is more productive to consider the West Sussex coastal plain as a whole and the totality of the Chichester Entrenchments, comprising the dykes to the east of the River Lavant and the 'War Dyke' in the vicinity of the River Arun, as well as those defining the Selsey peninsula (Hamilton and Manley 1999, 23). Collectively the West Sussex coastal plain has dispersed farmsteads within an organised, ditched landscape, together with mint debris (Ounces Barn, Boxgrove; Bedwin and Place 1995); a scatter of imports (amphorae, Arretine, and Gallo-Belgic ware) from settlements and other locations; shrines (below); and at least one focal cemetery/religious site (Westhampnett).

The low-lying landscape of east Kent was likewise linked by a network of ditched and drained trackways and enclosures, which were of particular intensity and extent in the Ashford area. But there are differences from the West Sussex coastal zone. The settlements are larger, and Beechbrook Wood, Westhawk Farm, and Brisley Farm all display zonation of activities; there is no evidence of shrines; and the funerary evidence is more diverse and suggests the emergence of cult or high-status individuals (see below). Imports are also present, but *contra* Sussex, are predominantly from burial contexts (see below). In east Kent, unlike West Sussex, territorial enclosure was apparently not of key importance to the collective definition of these sites.

These Late Iron Age settlement patterns suggest complex landscapes in the BECA, which have much in common with the territorial *oppida* of Essex and Hertfordshire, such as *Camulodunum* or *Verlamion* (Haselgrove and Millett 1997). The fact that the precise format of each of these BECA complexes is unique suggests individualistic resolutions of growing socio-economic complexity. The mortuary data of the BECA particularly exemplifies this pattern of individualism and will now be considered.

Late Iron Age mortuary and ritual practices in the British Eastern Channel Area

The BECA has a complex mix of 'old' traditions, and 'new', Aylesford–Swarling burial traditions. This is strikingly in evidence at Brisley Farm, where two 'warrior inhumations' occur alongside a range of formal (urned) and informally deposited cremations, and additionally with a small cremation cemetery to the east of the site. There is little apparent consistency from site to site. Both old and 'new' elements are taken from widely dispersed cultural traditions.

Does the 'BECA' mortuary evidence fit the perceived patterning for south-east England?

For south-east England, the perceived patterning of Late Iron Age burial traditions includes the following features:

- Burials and funerary rites are rarely directly associated with settlements.
- Cremation burial virtually replaced other modes of disposal.
- Inhumation was a very minor rite in Late Iron Age cremation cemeteries.
- Excarnation practices were deeply-rooted Iron Age traditions in southern Britain, and are distinct from the cremation rites of south-east Britain.

Many of these perceptions do not in fact hold true for the BECA, and are briefly outlined below.

Burials in settlements

It is rare in Britain to find Late Iron Age burials directly associated with settlements. The Late Iron Age of south-east England, in particular, is associated with an increasing separation of secular and ritual activities – through the provision of formal cemeteries and the construction of temples. Such a pattern is only partially evident in the BECA. *Some* cemeteries were indeed 'set apart'. The cremation cemetery of Westhampnett was located on a low but prominent hill, rising out of the West Sussex coastal plain (Fitzpatrick 1997b, 228). At Brisley Farm, a cemetery of eight cremations lay 60 m east of the settlement area on a low but conspicuous ridge. More commonly, as in east Kent, there is a greater interface between formal burial and settlement contexts than has been perceived for Late Iron Age Britain. Within the Brisley Farm complex, cremation burials, pyre bases, and the two 'warrior' inhumations formed elements of a complex of multiple ditch-enclosed spaces (Fig. 4 above). Other Kentish sites with formal burials in settlement contexts include Dumpton Gap, Broadstairs (Hurd 1909) and Glebe Lands, Harrietsham (Canterbury Archaeological Trust 1998).

Cremation

As noted, some discrete cremation cemeteries do occur in the BECA. Clusters of from one to nine cremations typically occur, typified by Herstmonceux (Norris 1956), Boys Hall Balancing Pond (Union Railways South 2000), and Brisley Farm (the cremation cemetery just outside the settlement). The size of the Westhampnett cemetery is exceptional – with 161 cremations (Fitzpatrick 1997b). Equally, at several cemeteries, cremation and inhumation burials were coeval, spatially intermixed traditions. Highsted, Sittingbourne – just east of the study area – has 20 inhumations and six cremations (Kelly 1978, 267), while Mill Hill, Deal yielded 42 inhumations and five cremations (Parfitt 1995). This suggests a fluidity of individual and community choice relating to the formal rites, ideologies, and ceremonies of death.

The cremation burial tradition was established by the 70s BC in south-east England, but the Westhampnett chronology suggests that it was established in parts of the BECA even earlier (Fitzpatrick 1997b, 204). It is possible that the rite was introduced into central southern England directly from France, possibly from Normandy where cremation was being practised by the mid second century BC, or from adjacent regions (Fitzpatrick 1997b). This offers the possibility that cremation is not a singular concept in the BECA. The beliefs and traditions on display at Westhampnett, for instance, need not be intimately related to those that guided the Aylesford cremation rituals. At Brisley Farm, in addition to formal cremation burials, quantities of cremated remains, mostly animal but also some human, occur in several of the ditched enclosures, suggesting a highly flexible approach to the rite. Indeed perhaps cremation was a technology that was open to and adaptable to more than one type of ceremony and concept of bodily entity.

Inhumation

It is often presumed that inhumation was a very minor rite in Late Iron Age cremation cemeteries in south-east England. Inhumation, however, continues to be of some importance in the BECA, but varies markedly in its occurrence and forms. There are a few individual burials, as at Bishopstone (Bell 1977), Dumpton Gap (Coy 1961), Glynde, Balcombe Quarry (Burstow and Norris 1962), and Willingdon (Budgen 1931). These continue the inhumation tradition that typifies Iron Age southern Britain as a whole, namely flexed/bound inhumations associated with domestic settlements, together with more casual burials in disused storage or rubbish pits (Whimster 1981). The rite of extended inhumation and the use of inhumation cemeteries lack parallel in south-east England. The 42 extended inhumations at Mill Hill are therefore exceptional. Brisley Farm has two – the 'warrior' burials discussed below. Extended inhumations are rare in Iron Age Britain as a whole and the tradition has been viewed as derived from the Continent. However, apart from imported Gallo-Belgic pottery, no non-local objects are associated with BECA extended burials.

Excarnation rites

The deposition of isolated human bones and body parts (probably as secondary burial post-excarnation) is widely attested at Iron Age settlements in southern Britain (Cunliffe 1991, 506). This practice is generally considered to be distinct from the cremation rites of south-east England (but see Carr this volume). What is particularly notable for the BECA is that these ideas occurred in tandem. A scatter of Late Iron Age settlements – Dumpton Gap, Broadstairs (Hurd 1909), Oving (Bedwin and Holgate 1985, 232), and North Bersted (Bedwin and Pitts 1978, 339) – have produced evidence of excarnated remains, in the form of leg and skull elements, near to sites with cremation burials.

Grave offerings in the British Eastern Channel Area

Non-food grave offerings in the BECA lack any distinct separation according to whether the rite is inhumation or cremation. Gallo-Belgic imported pottery is equally recurrent with *both* inhumations and cremation. Amphorae are lacking from all ritual contexts, as is imported metalwork, with the exception of the Westhawk Farm cremation (see below). Bronze, and occasionally iron, brooches are common grave goods irrespective of the rite, as for example at Mill Hill, Deal (Parfitt 1995).

At Mill Hill, three inhumations have highly specific grave goods. The 'warrior' and 'spoon' burials are discussed further below. The third (Grave X11) included a toilet set, comprising an ear scoop, tweezers, and a nail cleaner, all suspended from single wire (Fig. 6). Personal toilet items, which occur either singly or in sets, are particularly associated with Aylesford *cremations* (Stead and Rigby 1989). Hill (1997) has emphasised how the body – its dress and appearance – was a new focus of attention in the Late Iron Age. The Deal toilet set might therefore be a carrier of precise social meaning, which in this instance has been 'acquired' into an inhumation mortuary tradition. The mixing of elements from a range of burial traditions is a particular feature of the elite/special burials of the BECA (see below).

Animal food offerings are mostly associated with cremations, but their treatment varied. At Westhampnett, *c.* 22% of the graves contained cremated animal remains (lamb and piglets), implying that animal offerings were placed on the funerary pyre and later collected up with the human remains (Fitzpatrick 1997b). At Mill Hill, animal food offerings were restricted to two of the five cremation burials, and were absent from the inhumations. Here, the offerings were *un*burnt, each comprising a piece of pig, and a whole fowl. Pig offerings are inconsistently associated with the richest burials, irrespective of the rite. Each of the Brisley Farm 'warrior'

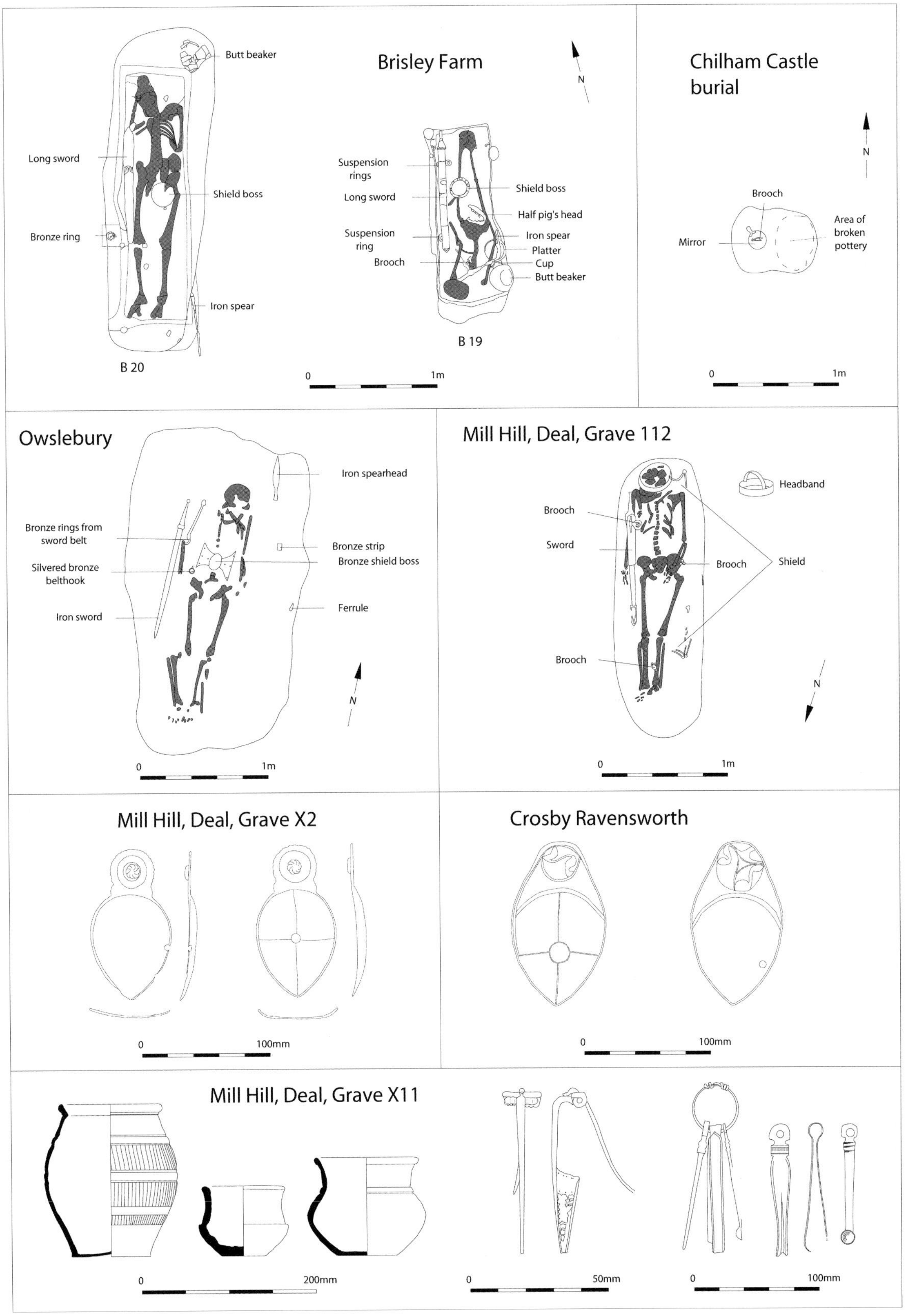

Fig. 6. Plans and finds relating to 'warrior' and other special burials in the British Eastern Channel Area. The Owslebury burial and Crosby Ravensworth (Cumbria) spoons are illustrated for comparison. The Crosby Ravensworth spoons were found by a spring in a bog. (Sources: Brisley Farm, Kent: Field Archaeology Unit, UCL; Chilham Castle, Kent: Parfitt 1998; Owslebury, Hampshire: Collis 1973; Mill Hill, Deal, Kent: Parfitt 1995; Crosby Ravensworth: Craw 1923–4).

inhumations had a pig's head placed in the grave, whereas the Mill Hill 'warrior' lacked animal offerings (as do other warrior burials south of the Humber; Table 1). The Westhawk Farm cremation contained both cremated and unburnt pig and sheep remains. Overall, the types of offering (particularly pig and domestic fowl) mirror those of the Aylesford cemeteries, as does the combination of unburnt and burnt animal offerings. The BECA evidence thus suggests an established repertoire of food offerings, but with no set formula of association with either the cremation or inhumation traditions, or as to the moment in the funerary proceedings when the offerings were made.

Elite burials in the east Kent Channel Zone: cult figures?

Compared to the Aylesford cemeteries in north Kent and north of the Thames, the cremation burials of the BECA are mostly characterised by their lack of wealth, as at Westhampnett (Fitzpatrick 1997b). A number of individually distinct, rich or exotic burials can, however, be defined. Amongst these, the Brisley Farm 'warrior' burials, together with the Westhawk Farm bucket burial, suggest a major focus of power and wealth in the Ashford area. This expression of wealth/status lacks a standard format, even at closely proximate sites. Additionally, the long-term veneration of the Brisley Farm 'warrior' burials, the regalia of the 'crowned warrior' from Deal, and the spoon burial from Deal have overtones of ritual status (see below). The inspirational sources of this regalia were therefore cross- or extra-cultural, being selected from a widely dispersed repertoire. In this respect, the BECA stands in significant contrast to the rather more regularised elite burials of the Aylesford zone (centered in north Kent, Hertfordshire, and Essex). Collectively, the east Kent elite/exotic burials are not well known and are disarmingly diverse. Their characteristics are further detailed below.

Bucket burials

Three 'bucket' burials are known from the east Kent Channel area. The recently discovered cremation at Westhawk Farm, Ashford (dated *c.* AD 20) is amongst the most richly furnished of the Aylesford type burials (Booth and Lawrence 2000). The cremated bones were placed in a wooden casket decorated with copper alloy fittings. Other grave goods were a yew-wood stave bucket, a *terra nigra* platter, and fragmentary copper alloy objects comprising an imported *patera*, a jug with a highly decorated handle depicting Silenus, and a bowl. Alkham, near Dover, has two further bucket burials. These

Key: E = extended; C = crouched; F = flexed; † = skeleton inferred; * = sword inferred.

Site	*spear*	*shield*	*food*	*pottery*	*brooch/es*	*imports*	*position*	*enclosure*	*Peculiarities*	*Reference*
Bradford Peverell, Dorset†				X						Whimster 1981, 345
Brisley Farm, Ashford, Kent B19	X	X	X	X	X	X	E	X	Bent spear	Johnson 2003
Brisley Farm, Ashford, Kent B20	X	X	X	X	X	X	E	X	Spear stuck into grave cut	Johnson 2003
Bryher, Isles of Scilly		X			X		C		Mirror	Johns 2002
Coleford, Glos.		X							2 bronze rings and a ring and button fitting from a sword belt	Webster 1990; Rawes 1988.
Gelliniog Wen, Anglesey							E			Whimster 1981, 353
Great Brackstead, Essex†	X	X		X		X			Bent spear and sword; Roman bronze bowl	Hunter 2005, 64.
Mildenhall, Suffolk							E		Gold torc and 'celt'; two horses	Fox 1923, 81.
Mill Hill, Deal, Kent		X			X		E		Headdress; ?folded shield	Parfitt 1995
Owslebury, Hants	X	X				X	E		Spear stuck into grave cut and ?broken	Collis 1973, 126–9
Shouldham, Norfolk						X	E			Clarke and Hawkes 1955, 198
St Lawrence, Isle of Wight		X					F			Jones and Stead 1969, 351–4
Sutton Courtenay, Oxon*		X		X	X		C		Five brooches	Whimster 1981, 135, 350–1
Whitcombe, Dorset	X				X		C		Craft tools	Aitken and Aitken 1990, 62

Table 1. Iron Age inhumations with swords from Britain south of the Humber estuary.

buckets again have ornate bronze mounts, but there are no imports and the grave goods are restricted to 'Belgic' style pedestal urns (Philp 1991; James and Rigby 1997, 70).

Warrior burials

The east Kent Channel area is remarkable for having produced three 'warrior' burials, all with swords (Brisley Farm: B19 and B20; and one from Mill Hill, Deal; Fig. 6). The term 'warrior burial' is commonly used for male burials accompanied by one or more of the following items: a sword, a shield, and knife, but there is no consistent application of the designation (Cunliffe 1991, 506; Parfitt 1995). Collis (1973) instead used the terminology 'burials with weapons', but more specific is Whimster's (1981) term 'sword burial'. Warrior burials are a regular feature in Early and Middle La Tène inhumation cemeteries from north-east France to Slovakia (Collis 1973, 121). Only 14 burials (all male) with swords had been found in England south of the Humber (Table 1; cf. Hunter 2005). Overall, the British examples lack an homogenous cultural or geographical patterning, leading Cunliffe (1991) to interpret them as representing a social class.

The Brisley Farm warrior burials, together with the one from Owslebury, Hampshire (Collis 1977) are exceptional in being situated within settlements (Johnson 2003). Each of the Brisley Farm 'warriors' lies within a square-ditched enclosure – this is assumed to have defined a barrow mound which originally covered the grave. Both were extended, with weapons and imported pottery – notably a butt beaker, a platter, and a small cup in B19. These are the latest examples of warrior burials from Britain. B19 is dated to between AD 20/25–40/45 and B20 to AD 30–70. Given their proximity in time, it is interesting that both burials show variations in what might be expected to be a standard rite. The B20 enclosure was the more monumental, but B19 was the more richly furnished. One warrior had his head to the north (B19), the other to the south (B20). Both of the burials had iron swords and spears, but in B19 the spear was deliberately bent and laid across the upper chest, while in B20 a long spear had been thrust into the south-east wall of the grave (which is reminiscent of Owslebury; Table 1). In B19, the shield was placed over the left knee, while with B20 the shield was laid over the body.

From the time of their placements, the Brisley Farm burials were central to the layout of the settlement complex. They were initially sited within a large irregular enclosure between the Middle and Late Iron Age settlements. By the mid/later first century AD, they had become the focal point for a new enclosure. At this time, the burial ditches were recut and these remained a focus for deposition (burnt animal bone and pottery) until the early second century AD (Johnson 2003). This continued veneration of the tombs of the warriors during the early Roman period is intriguing, and suggests that the 'warriors' may have had, or accrued, a cult status. Hero/ancestor worship may have been a significant feature of Late Iron Age life, and the Brisley Farm circumstances evoke the Folly Lane site, St Albans, where a high-status burial was succeed by a Romano-Celtic temple (Niblett 1999).

A cult status can also be argued for the Mill Hill 'warrior' burial. In addition to being furnished with an iron sword, scabbard, and hide-shaped shield, he had a so-called crown, a decorated bronze headband with a 'strap' running along top of the skull from side to side (Parfitt 1995). Based on the decoration on the metalwork, Stead (1995) dates the burial to the early second century BC. This would make it one of the earliest 'warrior' burials south of the Humber (although it would be helpful to have absolute dates to secure the chronology of decorative styles associated with British Iron Age ceremonial metalwork; see also Macdonald, this volume). The crown in particular raises the question of the basis of the status of the Deal 'warrior'. Approximately 20 bronze 'crowns' or head-dresses have been identified from Britain (Bird 1989; Parfitt 1995) These are occasionally associated with Iron Age and Roman inhumations, and more recurrently with Roman hoards and temples. The best parallel to Deal is the example from Hockwold, Norfolk, a site interpreted as a Roman ritual storehouse (Parfitt 1995, 75). Whilst the bronze bands of the Deal crown might conceivably be part of the superstructure to a hardened leather helmet, most of these head-dresses were evidently of little or no protective value. The Roman hoard and temple finds have led to them being interpreted as priestly regalia, and this may point to the Deal 'crown' being a signifier of cult status.

'Mirror burial'

Kent has a single 'mirror burial', a Late Iron Age cremation from near Chilham Castle, 10 km south-west of Canterbury (Fig. 6; Parfitt 1998, 350). Some 16 Late Iron Age mirrors are known from Britain, over half of which come from burials. The majority of mirror burials associated with cremations fall within the Aylesford tradition, whilst in western and south-western Britain, they are found with inhumations (Cunliffe 1991, 509). The Chilham mirror is associated with a matching pair of Late Iron Age 'boss on bow' brooches and 'Belgic' style grog-tempered pottery. The human remains are identified as female (Parfitt 1998); indeed mirror burials have long been considered to be the female counterpart of warrior burials – being likewise widely distributed, limited in occurrence, and lacking consistent funerary associations. The unique combination of both mirror and sword in the Bryher, Isles of Scilly, burial (extended inhumation, sex not determinable), however, defies simplistic sexual binaries (Johns 2002). This Bryher 'mix' can perhaps be better seen as part of the theme of active individualisation, through the selection of elements from a wide range of extant elite or cult options, which is here suggested for elite/exotic burials in the east Kent eastern Channel area.

'Spoon burial'

The pair of Iron Age bronze spoons from Mill Hill inhumation X2 is one of 23 such pairs found in diverse parts of Britain (Parfitt 1995). Their precise find contexts are mostly obscure, but several are from contexts that suggest an association with ritual procedures, such as bogs (Cunliffe 1991, 509). Only three spoon-pairs are known from burials (Craw 1923–4; Parfitt 1995). Typically the spoons have decorated handles and heart-shaped bowls. One of each pair has a plain bowl with a perforation at or near the edge, while the bowl of the other is marked with a cross, and sometimes a central circle, like the Mill Hill spoons (Fig. 6). Whether for personal purposes or religious rites (e.g. for distributing fine powder or oil), their presence in burials may again relate to a 'special' or cult persona.

Ritual architecture and rites in the British Eastern Channel Area

BECA ritual sites incorporate specific architectural elements and rites, although there do not appear to have been pre-set rules as to how these should be combined in specific contexts or at individual sites, implying that they were conceptualised separately. There is a marked concentration of shrine structures in West Sussex and east Hampshire, notably at Hayling Island, Lancing Down – where the small rectangular building is possibly a precursor to the later Romano-Celtic temple – and Westhampnett. Shrine buildings date to very late in the Iron Age and less than ten examples are known from southern Britain as a whole (Fitzpatrick 1997b, fig. 115). Their most overt architectural component is a square or sub-rectangular ditched enclosure or continuous bedding trench (for close-set planks). The square format of these shrines may be conceptually the same as for the enclosures surrounding the Brisley Farm 'warrior' burials, which effectively became shrines of deposition.

Circular space is another architectural element of BECA ritual traditions that likewise recurs in different forms. The second phase of the Late Iron Age shrine at Hayling Island was circular, whilst at Westhampnett, the burials were laid out around a large circular area with pyres lying beyond (Fig. 7). The Brisley Farm complex had a circular space in the southern settlement area with occasional cremations and other pit/post hole features around its circumference, and two pyre bases with X-shaped cuts very similar to those identified at Westhampnett (Fitzpatrick 1997b, 18). On a smaller scale, the five cremation burials at Herstmonceux Castle were placed in a circular arrangement (Norris 1956). This idea of circular space recurs through the Aylesford burial tradition, being noted for the type site by Evans (1890, 320–1), who evoked the term 'family circle'. Fitzpatrick (2000) suggests that this circularity echoed the format of Iron Age roundhouses and their suggested associations with cosmological referents (Oswald 1997).

The deposition of cultural material at the Hayling Island shrine exemplifies an adherence to a set of general principles concerning what was considered appropriate for religious/ritual deposition *irrespective* of the context of deposition. While the Westhampnett and Lancing Down structures (in common with most Late Iron Age shrines) yielded very few finds, the pit and the courtyard around the Hayling Island shrine were a major focus for deposition, particularly of coins, human remains and animal offerings, and mutilated (deliberately broken or bent) warrior equipment (King and Soffe 1998). Many of the coins are plated, and they may have been deliberately manufactured for ritual. The numerous Iron Age coins eroded out of the Selsey Bill cliffs have also been deemed votive deposits (Haselgrove 1987, 149, 458–61), as have those from the later Romano-Celtic temple at Wanborough, Surrey (Haselgrove 2005). Coins were occasionally placed in graves, as at Westhampnett (in a cremation; Fitzpatrick 1997b, 88) and at Mill Hill (in an inhumation; Parfitt 1997, 112).

Martial equipment forms a particularly important category of deposit at Hayling Island, notably numerous fragments of edge binding and terminal knobs for shields, and iron spearheads (King and Soffe 1998). At Worth, east Kent, a votive deposit of a small group of model shields suggests similarly orientated ritual activity preceding the Roman temple (Klein 1928), and this is borne out by the large number of Iron Age coins which have been recovered from the site in recent years (Holman 2005). The deposition and slighting of martial equipment at Hayling Island is repeated in southern Britain in the grave goods of 'warrior burials' (see above), and forms part of a wider north-west European tradition of deposition evinced in Britain at Llyn Cerrig Bach (Fox 1946), and at northern French sanctuaries such as Gournay-sur-Aronde (Oise: Brunaux *et al.* 1985).

Small quantities of human remains were also deposited at Hayling Island (cranium, mandible, and limb bone fragments; Fitzpatrick 1997b, table 30), together with sheep and pig joints. Sheep and pig are recurrent mortuary offerings (see above), and the presence of excarnated human remains has already been noted for settlement sites. Collectively, this suggests osmosis of ritual deposition between funerary, shrine, and settlement contexts.

These various repetitive mortuary and ritual elements were selected and customised from a very broad repertoire of concepts circulating in southern and south-east Britain and north-west Europe. Fitzpatrick (2000) has recently discussed the presence of a similar range and diversity of rites in northern France in the Middle and Late La Tène periods. In this respect the BECA is

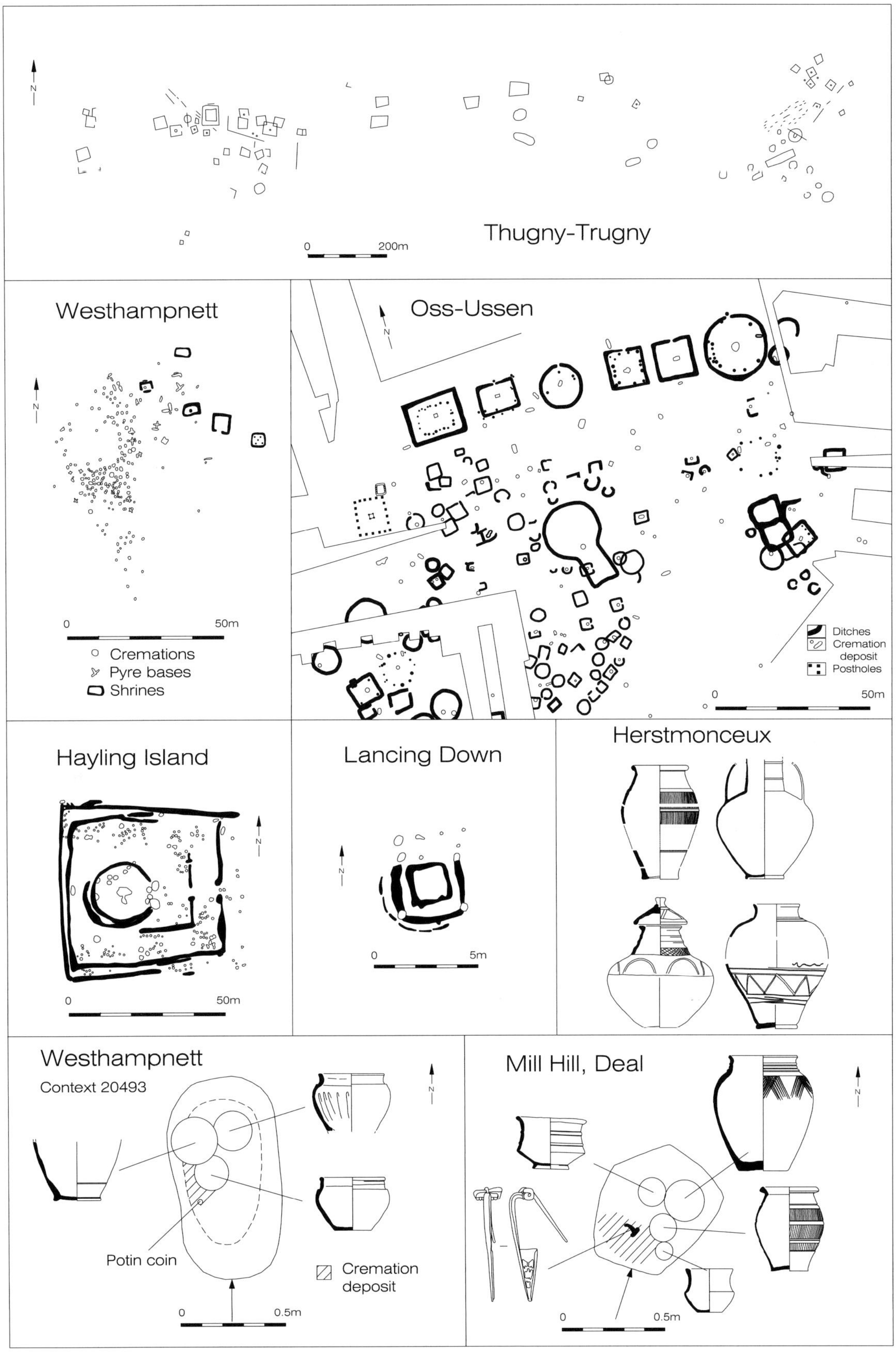

Fig. 7. Plans and finds relating to cremation burials and shrines in the British Eastern Channel Area, and comparable continental sites. The Herstmonceux cremation urns include Gaulish imports (top left – a butt beaker, and top right – a Cam. 161 lagena) and local hand-made East Sussex ware (bottom row). Herstmonceux scale: the Butt Beaker is 27.5 cm in height. (Sources: Thugny-Trugny: Lambot 1993; Westhampnett: Fitzpatrick 1997b; Oss-Ussen: Hessing 1993; Hayling Island: King and Soffe 1998; Lancing Down: Bedwin 1981; Herstmonceux: Green 1980; Parfitt 1995; Mill Hill, Deal: Parfitt 1995).

more continental in approach than the more sharply defined 'Aylesford' mortuary traditions.

The continental context

This paper has so far concentrated on the distinctive Late Iron Age settlement and burial finds from the BECA. The next section explores comparative continental settlement and burial data. As we will see, the BECA material seems to draw on a range of geographically discrete continental traditions, rather than on a specific region. Other apparently novel elements of BECA material culture are also considered, such as the introduction of coinage and presence of imported Gallo-Belgic pottery.

The Middle and Late La Tène settlement pattern of northern France, particularly on the alluvial terraces of the major river systems, is numerically dominated by enclosure complexes, often referred to as *fermes indigènes*, and frequently taken to correspond with the *aedificia* Caesar mentions in his *Gallic War* (e.g. Agache 1981). These sites were for long known primarily from aerial photographs and various attempts have been made to classify the wide range of enclosure forms on the basis of shape and size (e.g. Arbousse-Bastide 2000; Buchsenschutz 2000). Those belonging to settlements and field systems (as opposed to ritual and funerary sites) are distinguished by complex systems of multiple (exceptionally three or four) ditched enclosures, as in the case of Condé-Folie, Les Garchettes (Somme) and Conchil-le-Temple, La Frénésie (Pas-de-Calais) shown in Figure 5 above.

As a result of motorway construction and other development in the departments along the Channel coast, numerous examples have now been excavated and shown to date to the Middle and/or Late La Tène periods (e.g. Colin 2000; Rougier 2000; cf. Haselgrove this volume). At many of these sites, the complexity of the final plan can be shown to reflect a combination of gradual changes and accretions to the layout over a period of time (as with the BECA sites), punctuated by more comprehensive re-configurations of the spatial organisation, as for example at Hénin-Beaumont Sites 1 and 2 in Pas-de-Calais (Geoffroy and Thoquenne 2000), or Bayonvillers, Le Chemin d'Harbonnières (Prodéo 2000), and Pont-Rémy, La Queute (Prilaux 2000) in Somme.

The double-ditched enclosure of Brazy-les-Mareuil (Somme) with its ditched entrance funnel through into its inner kite-shaped enclosure (Buchsenschutz 1984, fig. 31) is interestingly reminiscent of the Beechbrook Wood enclosure in Kent. As Buchsenschutz (*ibid.*, 55) noted, an enclosure at Nempont-Saint-Firmin, Le Blanc Mont (Pas-de-Calais) contains the cropmark of what appears to be a roundhouse similar to those that characterise British later prehistoric building traditions. Since then, several circular buildings have been excavated on sites in Normandy suggesting the possibility, irrespective of uptake, of a common knowledge of vernacular architecture on both sides of the Channel. As yet, most of these French circular buildings appear to be Late Bronze Age or Early Iron Age date (Jahier *et al.* 2000), although the four examples found within an enclosure at Poses, Sur La Mare (Eure), on the lower Seine close to Rouen, do appear to be of Late Iron Age date (Dechezleprêtre *et al.* 2000).

The abundant evidence from the Aisne valley in southern Picardy (cf. Haselgrove this volume) implies that in the Late La Tène, settlements there became increasingly quadrilateral (square and rectangular) in plan, often with internal partitions, as at Bazoches, Les Chantraines; Braine, La Grange des Moines; and Bucy-le-Long, Le Fond du Petit Marais (Fig. 5 above). This trend is envisaged as evincing a more structured society, with designated areas for habitation, stock control and activities such as metalworking (Pommepuy *et al.* 2000, 203). This development is in line with the pattern observed in the BECA, particularly in terms of the increasing evidence for quadrangular site subdivision by ditched systems, associated with increasing zonation of activities. This is true both for farmsteads – as at Beechbrook Farm, North Foreland and Oving in the BECA, and Bazoches and Braine in the Aisne valley – and for extended settlements, such as Brisley Farm and Park Farm in the BECA, or Bucy-le-Long in the Aisne valley.

As in the BECA, the Late Iron Age settlement pattern in northern France seems in the main to have developed out of Middle Iron Age traditions and site locales, rather than involving any major resettling of the landscape. It is difficult, however, to ascertain to what extent integrated settlement landscapes like those inferred in the Brisley Farm–Park Farm and Chichester areas recur in the regions immediately across the Channel. The pattern of Late Iron Age settlement and other activity within the Chichester Dykes has been likened to a form of dispersed urbanism associated with scattered craft specialisation identified much further to the south, at Aulnat in the Auvergne, near Clermont-Ferrand (Bedwin and Holgate 1985), but convincing parallels have yet to be found in northern France. Easier to replicate on both sides of the Channel is the sometimes physically close juxtaposition of Late Iron Age settlement and funerary/ritual activity, as at the Brisley Farm–Park Farm–Westhawk Farm complex. Examples from across the Channel include Mierlo-Hout in the Netherlands (Leman-Delerive 2000) and Acy-Romance (Ardennes; Lambot and Méniel 2000); Bucy-Le-Long; Pont-Rémy, La Queute; and Vermand, Champ des Lavoirs (Aisne; Lemaire 2000) in northern France.

Mortuary and ritual traditions

The mortuary and ritual traditions of the BECA are marked by their diversity and the unique mixing of recurrent components of architecture, rite, and material culture at individual sites, including some outside the funerary sphere. Although rescue excavations in the last two decades have revealed numerous Iron Age cremation cemeteries in Somme and Pas-de-Calais, these appear to be predominantly of Middle La Tène date (e.g. Baray 1998), and for Late Iron Age comparisons, we must look further afield, to the Low Countries, to the Champagne–Ardennes region, and to the Moselle and Rhineland area.

The concept of circular sacred space present at Westhampnett, Brisley Farm, and Hayling Island, together with the more recurrent theme of square enclosure associated with burial and shrine sites, is mirrored in the small circular and square enclosures associated with Late Iron Age cremation burials in Flanders, as at Destelbergen and Mierlo-Hout (Leman-Delerive 2000), and in the alluvial areas of the Netherlands, for example at Oss-Ussen (Fig. 7 above) and Wijk bij Duurstede, Dorestad (Hessing 1993). Small square enclosures, presumed in the main to be burial enclosures, are numerous in northern France and the Moselle and Rhineland areas. The scale and longevity of some continental burial grounds – exemplified by Thugny-Trugny, Le Mayet (Ardennes), which extends for some 2 km from west to east and is between 300 and 600 m wide, and possesses numerous square (Iron Age, many of them Late La Tène), and circular (here, Bronze Age) enclosures surrounding cremation burials (Lambot 1993) – is not, however, repeated in the BECA, with the arguable exception of Mill Hill, Deal, with its earlier, Bronze Age barrow.

The *diversity* of the layout and content of the continental high-status/aristocratic grave formats and grave goods is particularly reminiscent of BECA status burials. The numerous isolated 'aristocratic graves' found in the region around the supposed *oppidum* at Château-Porcien (Ardennes) provide a good example, including as they do, burials with single examples (and also various combinations) of swords, Aylesford-type pans, Kelheim jugs, iron tripods, and amphorae (Lambot 1993; Lambot *et al.* 1994). With the exception of swords, however, such 'status' items are lacking from their BECA counterparts – apart from Westhawk Farm. Also, the BECA status burials are more fully integrated with or close to, settlements, as in the Brisley Farm–Park Farm–Westhawk Farm complex, or within cemeteries, as at Mill Hill, Deal. Late Iron Age inhumations are however rare on the opposite side of the Channel, although they do occur occasionally, for instance in the Netherlands (Hessing 1993). In this respect, the warrior burials of BECA share more in common with preceding traditions of the Marne, and indigenous southern British traditions.

The types of animal offerings, and emphasis on pig and domestic fowl, found in BECA burials and shrines are paralleled in cremation cemeteries and sanctuaries in northern France (Brunaux 1988; Méniel 1993). As in the BECA, excarnated human bone and – more exceptionally – burials are found within Late Iron Age settlements and shrines, as at Acy-Romance, La Warde, and the nearby sanctuary at Nanteuil-sur-Aisne (Lambot and Méniel 2000). In their structural form and in the types of deposits found at some of them – above all Hayling Island, with its mutilated military equipment, coins, and some human remains – the BECA shrines are clearly related to Brunaux's (1988, 11) 'sanctuaries of Belgic type', which originated in Middle La Tène, and occur throughout Picardy and Upper Normandy and in the surrounding regions. The amassed human bones at certain continental sanctuaries, notably Ribemont-sur-Ancre (Somme), however, have no British counterpart (Brunaux 1999).

Collectively the above suggests that BECA funerary and ritual traditions incorporated elements from a wide range of continental traditions, but are reliant on no single continental (or other) source.

Coinage

Whatever its role, the quantity of imported and copied coinage in the BECA suggests a prolonged, sustained, and diverse series of contacts with the Continent. There are notable concentrations of base metal Gaulish imports (beginning in the late second century BC) in east Kent and the Chichester area, and both Kent and Sussex developed early Gaulish-inspired silver and bronze coinages. The Kentish Primary and Flat-Linear potins (cast high-tin bronzes), starting in the second century BC, are the earliest British-minted coin series, and are found in great numbers in east Kent (Holman 2000), while southern East Sussex has a secondary cluster of Flat-Linear coins (20 from excavated contexts; Rudling 1999). Being of lower intrinsic value, potin coins may have facilitated new forms of exchange, but the Sussex evidence also suggests their use in hoarding and votive offerings (Haselgrove 1987; 1988; Rudling 1999).

Both Sussex and east Kent also have a number of coins originating in the Mediterranean region, notably bronze issues of Carthaginian Sicily and Ebusus, both dating between the fourth and second century BC (Holman 2000, 217). Whilst the idea that these Mediterranean coins are lost antiquities acquired by eighteenth-century travellers (Laing 1968, 15) cannot be wholly discounted, the numbers are great enough to suggest other possibilities (cf. Biddle 1975). Alternative explanations include mercenary activity, that the Roman army brought them in, or that they relate to Middle and Late Iron Age long-distance exchanges. At Archers Low Farm, Sandwich, two such coins were found with in excess of 50 Iron Age coins (including a high percentage of Gaulish types), together with imported *terra nigra* and *terra rubra* (Holman forthcoming). This is the strongest indication that at least some of the Mediterranean coin imports entered the BECA in the Iron Age through trade with Gaul.

The BECA displays an early and precocious development of coinage. However, given the evidence of immediately preceding contacts with the Continent (particularly from east Kentish Early/Middle Iron Age pottery, see below), this coinage cannot be seen either as having instigated trade contacts with the Continent, or as being a pre-requisite of those contacts. It is perhaps better seen as an uptake of a specific item of material culture, the use of which may have had multiple social, political, and status roles as much as a necessary economic role (Hamilton 1998; Rudling 1999).

Gallo-Belgic pottery

While the presence of imported Gallo-Belgic pottery in southern Britain is frequently emphasised, the evidence of an earlier tradition of small-scale pottery imports spanning much of the first millennium BC is often overlooked. In the case of east Kent, a fairly substantial body of evidence exists (Hamilton and Seager Thomas 2002). This includes occasional examples of early first millennium BC continental *jattes* and *assiettes tronconiques*, mid first millennium BC 'Marnian' pottery, and the parallel development of grog-tempering and 'rustication' in Kent, north-east France, and the Low Countries in the Middle Iron Age. Alongside this background, the distinctly diffuse presence of Late Iron Age imported pottery and metalwork in the BECA could be interpreted as a *lack* of interest in the elements of a continental lifestyle in which pottery had a role (cf. Hill 2002).

Gallo-Belgic platters, the commonest import in Aylesford–Swarling graves, are not as popular in the BECA, whilst Dressel 1 wine amphorae are hardly known in east Kent (Cunliffe 1982, 46), although they do have a limited presence in Sussex (Bedwin and Holgate 1985). All the confirmed Sussex examples are Dressel 1B, which has its main distribution north of the Thames. Interestingly, the Dressel 1B finds occur on small farmsteads and enclosures along the central south coast, such as Carne's Seat, North Bersted, and Oving, suggesting that the amphorae and their contents were not necessarily difficult to obtain.

The pottery assemblages of the BECA are strongly individual in their mixture of imports, and of local, continentally-inspired, and Aylesford traditions. Thus, the black cordoned ware from the Westhampnett cemetery has clear analogies with pottery from the lower reaches of the Seine in Normandy (Fitzpatrick 1997b, 131; 208), whilst at Copse Farm and Oving, similar cordoned ware occurs alongside occasional Aylesford style vessels (Hamilton 1985). At Herstmonceux Castle cemetery, one of the four cremations was associated with Gallo-Belgic imports, while the others are associated with local, hand-made East Sussex ware (Green 1980; Norris 1956).

Whilst the portable material culture of the BECA clearly needs more extensive synthesis against the patterns of intense cultural variability that are now apparent for the settlement and funerary data, it too suggests a fluidity of community and personal choices in which access to continentally-inspired and, less frequently, imported material culture was both feasible and recurrent, but not essential or new. It suggests that nearness to the Continent added to the diversity of available choices, but was not seminal to defining the Late Iron Age communities of the BECA.

Conclusion

This paper has characterised the nature of socio-economic change in the Late Iron Age in the British Eastern Channel Area. In particular, it has sought to synthesise the extensive and important findings of the developer-funded archaeology, which has taken place in region in recent decades. In spite of its location – facing the Continent – this zone has traditionally been considered to lie on the margins of the major continentally-inspired changes pre-eminently associated with the 'Aylesford–Swarling' zone. The British Eastern Channel Area is however the more cosmopolitan of the two zones in its active uptake of *choices* from a broad range of continental *and* southern British concepts and material culture. This development of heterogeneous rather than homogeneous traditions is not a sign of backwardness, impoverishment, or remnant archaism. I would see it rather as an index of a highly individualistic and dynamic society. Where distinct individuals can be recognised – as, for example, in the 'warrior' and bucket burials – there are indications that power or status was maintained as much through cult authority as through economic control.

Many of the Late Iron Age developments in the British Eastern Channel Area seem to have started in the Middle Iron Age and cannot be understood purely in terms of external causes. By the Late Iron Age, the intensely occupied landscape of the Ashford area in particular presents an almost suburban landscape of closely proximate and extensive sprawls of enclosures, houses, trackways, and ritual loci. This is on a scale that is currently unknown for the traditionally recognised *oppida* of the South-East. It is widely accepted that new models are required to explain archaeological change in southern and eastern Britain during the last two centuries BC (e.g. Hill this volume; Moore this volume), but such attempts will be impoverished if they focus too much on the landscapes of the territorial *oppida* and mainstream Aylesford–Swarling traditions. The idea of a tradition of eclectic individual choices, as opposed to adherence to corporate traditions, seems rather central to understanding the Late Iron Age in the British Eastern

Channel Area, and may be extremely relevant for understanding and contextualising contemporary trajectories elsewhere.

Acknowledgements

Figures 1–3 were drawn by Jane Russell; Figures 5 and 6 by Justin Russell. The Brisley Farm material was kindly made available by the Field Archaeology Unit, University College London, prior to its full publication. Casper Johnson, who directed the excavations, provided me with much useful information on recent finds from east Kent and commented upon the text. Railink Engineering gave me access to numerous assessment reports on the archaeology of the Channel Tunnel Kent Rail Link, for which particular thanks to Jay Carver and Helen Glass. Mike Seager Thomas provided many of the details in Appendices 1 and 2, and created the digital versions of Figures 5–7. I am grateful to Colin Haselgrove for updating me on recent French finds and for his helpful editing, and to Fraser Hunter for alerting me to the Coleford and Mildenhall sword burials.

Appendix 1: Middle Iron Age findspots in the Kent and Sussex Eastern Channel Area

Key: E = enclosure; H = hillfort; S = settlement finds such as pits and ditches; X = present or number unknown; ? = inconclusive evidence.

Site	*NGR*	*Settlement features*	*Burials*		*Other comments*	*Reference*
			Inhum.	*Crem.*		
KENT						
Beechbrook Wood, Ashford	TQ980455	S			key MIA pottery assemblage	Union Railways South 2002b
Bigberry	TR120575	H				Thompson 1983
Brisley Farm, Ashford	TQ990401	S			ditched enclosures	Johnson 2003
Mill Hill, Deal	TR363507		1 crouched		8–4th century BC ^{14}C date	Parfitt 1995
Dumpton Gap, Broadstairs	TR395668	?			pottery	Macpherson Grant 1996
Grenham Bay, Birchington	TR290699	?			pottery	Macpherson Grant 1991
Hartsdown, Margate	TR340690	E				Perkins 1996, 265–281
Hawkinge	TR213393	S				Stevens 1999
Highstead	TR210657	?			Pottery	Macpherson Grant 1991
Margate		?			Pottery	Elsdon 1989
North Foreland, Broadstairs	TR400700	?E			M/LIA date of enclosure uncertain	Diack, Mason and Perkins 2002
Saltwood	TR153369	trackway S?	X			Union Railways South 2002a
SUSSEX						
Angmering	TQ073036				pottery	M. Seager Thomas pers. comm.
Bishopstone	TQ467007	E	1 informal inhumation in a cut grave		originally dated to the MIA; now suggested to be Anglo-Saxon	Bell 1977; M. Seager Thomas pers. comm.
Caburn	TQ444089	H				Curwen and Curwen 1927
Carne's Seat	SU887094	E				Holgate 1986a
Charleston Brow	TQ484054	S				Parsons and Curwen 1933
Chilgrove	SU834124	S				Down 1979
Cissbury	TQ139080	H				Hamilton and Manley 2001
Copse Farm, Oving	SU895055	?E			M/LIA date of enclosure, & excarnated remains uncertain	Bedwin and Holgate 1985
Denge Bottom	SU916103	E			no dating; known from aerial photos	Bedwin 1984
Elm Grove, Brighton	TQ325054				Pottery	Curwen 1954
Findon	TQ141097	S				Fox and Wolseley 1928
Ford	SU994033				residual MIA pottery	Place 2000

Site	*NGR*	*Settlement features*	*Burials*		*Other comments*	*Reference*
			Inhum.	*Crem.*		
Gosden Road, Littlehampton	TQ039026	S				Gilkes 1993
Kingston Buci	TQ234057				unstratified MIA finds	Curwen and Hawkes 1931
Lavant	SU868095	S				Kenny 1993
Lordington	SU782101	E				Holgate 1986b
Maudlin Farm, Oving	SU887057	S				Browse and Kenny 1991
Newhaven	TQ449001	H				Hawkes 1939
North Bersted	SU927008	S			excarnated remains of M/LIA date	Bedwin and Pitts 1978
Norton	TQ473017	S	X			Seager Thomas 2005
Park Brow	TQ154086	S				Wolseley and Smith 1924
Patcham-Fawcett	TQ314090	2 pits			MIA pottery	C. Greatorex pers. comm.; Seager Thomas 2005
Rustington	TQ061031	unstratified MIA finds				Rudling 1990
Selhurst Park Farm	SU925113	ditched enclosures (aerial photos)			no dating	Bedwin 1984
Selsey	SZ857942	S?			unstratified MIA pottery	White 1934
Shopwyke	SU893055	S				Seager Thomas and Hamilton 2002
Slonk Hill	TQ226065	S	2 crouched inhumations			Hartridge 1978
Tote Copse, Aldingbourne	SU923048				stratified pottery	Pitts 1979
Trundle	SU877111	H			excarnated remains	Curwen 1931
West Blatchington	TQ275074	1 pit			MIA pottery	Norris and Burstow 1950; Seager Thomas 2005
Westhampnett, area 5	SU895065	S				Fitzpatrick 1997
Wickbourne, Littlehampton	TQ023027	S				Gilkes 1983

Appendix 2: Late Iron Age findspots in the Kent and Sussex Eastern Channel Area

Key: E = enclosure; H = hillfort; S = settlement finds such as pits and ditches; X = present/ number unknown; ? = not conclusive evidence.

Site	*NGR*	*Settlement features*	*Burials*		*Other comments*	*Reference*
			Inhum.	*Crem.*		
KENT						
Alkham, Dover	TR250430			4	2 of the cremations are 'bucket burials'	Philp 1991
Beechbrook Wood, Ashford	TQ980455	S		>4 & deposits in ditches	settlement has ditched enclosures and industrial plots	Union Railways South 2002b
Bigberry	TR120575	H				Thompson 1983
Boys' Hall	TR030406	S		>5	settlement has trackway and ditched field systems	Union Railways South 2000
Brisley Farm, Ashford	TR990401	S	2 warrior burials	X	settlement has ditched enclosures and trackways	Johnson 2003
Bridge Hill, Canterbury	TR189538	S				Watson 1963

Site	*NGR*	*Settlement features*	*Burials* Inhum.	Crem.	*Other comments*	*Reference*
Cheriton	TR193369			6+		Tester and Bing 1949
Chilham Castle	TR060540			1	LIA mirror	Parfitt 1998
Cliffs End, Ramsgate	TR340645	S			excarnation	T. Champion pers. comm.
Deal	TR370476	S				Parfitt 1985
Dolland's Moor	TR170370	S				Bennett 1988
Dumpton Gap	TR395668	E	possibly	X	excarnation	Hurd 1909; Coy 1961
East Wear Bay, Folkestone	TR240370			4–9		Whimster 1981
Ebbsfleet, Thanet	TR 337625	S				Perkins 1992
Harrietsham	TQ860540	S		11, plus 6 possible	ditches and possible enclosures	Canterbury Archaeological Trust 1998
Hartsdown, Margate	TR340690		poss. square ditched barrow	X		Perkins 1996
Hawkinge	TR213493	S				Stevens 1999
Highstead	TR210657	S				Tatton Brown 1996
Highsted, Sittingbourne	TQ914620		20	6		Kelly 1978
Marlow, Canterbury	TR150580	E		X		Macpherson-Grant 1991
Mill Hill, Deal	TR363507	slight evidence	*c.* 42	5	inhumations include 'warrior' and 'spoon' burials	Parfitt 1995
North Foreland, Broadstairs	TR400700	?E			M/LIA date of enclosure uncertain	Diack *et al.* 2002
Park Farm	TR019388	S			evidence of metalworking	C. Johnson pers. comm.
Petham, Swarling	TR127526			19		Whimster 1981; Birchall 1965
Radnor Park, Folkestone	TR218365			3		Whimster 1981
Saltwood	TR153369	S			settlement and field system	
Sturry	TR180610			at least 1 cremation		Union Railways South 2002a
Westhawk Farm, Ashford	TR998400			1	'bucket burial'	Booth and Lawrence 2000
Whitfield	TR300462	E				Macpherson-Grant 1996
Worth	TR338560				miniature bronze shields, pottery; coins; shrine site?	Klein 1928; Macpherson-Grant 1991; Holman 2005
SUSSEX						
Bishopstone	TQ467007	S	1 crouched inhum. in storage pit			Bell 1977
Broadwater	TQ150050				pottery findspot	Curwen 1954
Caburn	TQ444089	H			LIA pottery but post main phase of IA use of hillfort	Curwen and Curwen 1927; Drewett and Hamilton 1999
Carne's Seat	SU887094	E				Holgate 1986a
Charleston Brow	TQ484054	X				Parsons and Curwen 1933
Copse Farm, Oving	SU895055	E			excarnated remains, M/LIA	Bedwin and Holgate 1985
Crowhurst Park	TQ760138	ironworking site			possibly R-B	Piggott 1938
Denge Bottom	SU916103	E			no dating	Bedwin 1984
ECAT, Eastbourne	TV603997	S				Unpublished; Greatorex pers. comm.

Site	*NGR*	*Settlement features*	*Burials* *Inhum.*	*Crem.*	*Other comments*	*Reference*
Ford	SU994033	E			dated LBA, but has LIA pottery	Place 2000
Glynde, Balcombe Quarry	TQ461085	E	female with nearby baby in upper ditch fill			Wilson 1955; Burstow and Norris 1962
Gosden Road, Littlehampton	TQ039026	S				Gilkes 1993
Herstmonceux	TQ647104			5		Norris 1956
Kingston Buci	TQ324057	S?			unstratified pottery	Curwen and Hawkes 1931
Lancing	TQ179067			X	shrine	Bedwin 1081; Frere 1940; Rudling 1981
Lordington	SU782101	E				Holgate 1986b
Motcombe Laine (Pashley Road), Eastbourne	TV589989			4		Ray and Budgen 1916
Newhaven	TQ449001	H				Hawkes 1939
North Bersted	SU927008	S			excarnated remains, M/LIA	Bedwin and Pitts 1978
Norton	TQ473017	S				Seager Thomas 2005
Old Place Farm, Westhampnett	SU875062	E				Bedwin 1984
Ounces Barn, Boxgrove	SU922084	S			ditch with mint debris	Bedwin and Orton 1984
Portfield Gravel Pit	SU8705	S?				Curwen and Frere 1947
Rustington	TQ061031	S				Rudling 1990
Saltdean	TQ384025				pottery findspot	Curwen 1954
Selhurst Park Farm	TQ925113	S			no dating	Bedwin 1984
Sedlescombe	TQ780180				pottery finds; or R-B	Green 1980
Selsey	SZ857942	S				White 1934
Shepherd's Garden, Arundel	TQ010090	S			possibly R-B	Frazer-Hearne 1936
Shopwyke	SU893055	?E				Seager Thomas and Hamilton 2002
Sidlesham	SZ847978				pottery finds	Wilson 1955
Tote Copse, Aldingbourne	SU923048				pottery finds	Pitts 1979
West Blatchington	TQ275074	S				Norris and Burstow 1952
Westhampnett cemetery	SU896067			161	4 shrine structures	Fitzpatrick 1997b
Westhampnett, area 5	SU895065	S				Fitzpatrick 1997b
Wickbourne, Littlehampton	TQ023027	E				Gilkes 1983
Willingdon	TQ585005		1		accompanying butt beaker	Budgen 1931

Bibliography

Agache, R. 1981. Le problème de fermes indigènes pré-romaines et romaines en Picardie, in O. Buchsenschutz (ed.), *Les structures d'habitat à l'Age du Fer en Europe tempérée (Actes du colloque de Châteauroux, Bouges-le-Château, Levroux, 27–29 Octobre 1978)*, 45–50. Paris: Editions de la Maison des Sciences de L'Homme.

Aitken, G.M. and Aitken, G.N. 1990. Excavations at Whitcombe, 1965–1967, *Proceedings of the Dorset Natural History and Archaeological Society* 112, 57–94.

Arbousse-Bastide, T. 2000. Analyse et fonction des enclos protohistoriques de part et d'autre de la Manche, *Revue Archéologique de Picardie* 1/2, 77–96.

Auxiette, G., Desenne, F., Gransar, F. and Pommepuy, C. 2000. Structuration générale du site de Braine "La Grange des Moines" (Aisne) à La Tène finale et particularitiés: présentation préliminaire, *Revue Archéologique de Picardie* 1/2, 97–104.

Baray, L. 1998. Les cimetières à cremation de la basse vallée de la Somme d'après les découvertes de l'autoroute A16, *Revue Archéologique de Picardie* 1/2, 211–231.

Bedwin, O. 1983. The development of prehistoric settlement on the West Sussex coastal plain, *Sussex Archaeological Collections* 121, 31–44.

Bedwin, O. 1984. Aspects of Iron Age settlement in Sussex, in B. Cunliffe and D. Miles (eds), *Aspects of the Iron Age in Central Southern Britain*, 46–51. Oxford: University of Oxford Committee for Archaeology Monograph 2.

Bedwin, O. and Holgate, R. 1985. Excavations at Copse Farm, Oving, *Proceedings of the Prehistoric Society* 51, 215–245.

Bedwin, O. and Orton, C. 1984. The excavation of the eastern terminal of the Devil's Ditch (Chichester Dykes), Boxgrove, West Sussex, 1982, *Sussex Archaeological Collections* 122, 63–74.

Bedwin, O. and Pitts, M.W. 1978. The excavation of an Iron Age settlement at North Bersted, Bognor Regis, West Sussex, *Sussex Archaeological Collections* 116, 293–345.

Bedwin, O. and Place, C. 1995. Late Iron Age and Romano-British occupation at Ounces Barn, Boxgrove, West Sussex: excavations 1982–83, *Sussex Archaeological Collections* 133, 25–101.

Bell, M. 1977. *Excavations at Bishopstone* (*Sussex Archaeological Collections* 115).

Bennett, P. 1988. Channel Tunnel excavations, *Canterbury's Archaeology 1987–1988*, 46–69.

Biddle, M. 1975. Ptolemaic coins from Winchester, *Antiquity* 49, 213–215.

Birchall, A. 1965. The Aylesford–Swarling culture: the problem of the Belgae reconsidered, *Proceedings of the Prehistoric Society* 31, 241–367.

Bird, J. 1989. Romano-British priestly regalia from Wanborough, Surrey, *Antiquaries Journal* 69, 316–318.

Booth, P. and Lawrence, C. 2000. Ashford Westhawk Farm, *Current Archaeology* 168, 478–481.

Brockley, K. and Brockley, P. 1989. Excavations at Bigberry Camp, near Canterbury, 1981, *Archaeologia Cantiana* 107, 239–251.

Browse, R. and Kenny, J. 1991. *An Archaeological Evaluation near Dairy Lane, Oving, West Sussex*. Chichester: Chichester District Archaeological Unit.

Brunaux, J.-L. 1988. *The Celtic Gauls: Gods, Rites and Sanctuaries*. London: Seaby.

Brunaux, J.-L. 1999. Ribemont-sur-Ancre, Somme. Bilan préliminaire et nouvelles hypothèses, *Gallia* 56, 177–283.

Brunaux, J.-L., Méniel, P. and Poplin, F. 1985. *Gournay I. Les fouilles sur le sanctuaire et l'oppidum 1975–1984*. Amiens: Revue Archéologique de Picardie numero special.

Buchsenschutz, O. 1984. *Structures d'habitats et fortifications de l'Âge du Fer en France septentrionale*. Paris: Mémoire de la Société Préhistorique Française 18

Buchsenschutz, O. 2000. Traces, typologie et interprétation des enclos de l'âge du Fer, *Revue Archéologique de Picardie* 1/2, 1–11.

Budgen, W. 1931. A La Tène III inhumation, *Antiquaries Journal* 11, 71–73.

Burstow, G.P. and Norris, N.E.S. 1962. Excavations at Balcombe Quarry, Glynde, *Sussex Notes and Queries* 15/9, 307–309.

Canterbury Archaeological Trust. 1998. *An Archaeological Investigation at Glebe land, Harrietsham*. Unpublished interim report.

Clarke, R.R. and Hawkes, C.F.C. 1955. An iron anthropoid sword Shouldham, Norfolk with related continental and British weapons, *Proceedings of the Prehistoric Society* 21, 198–227.

Colin, A. 2000. Les habitats ruraux de l'âge du fer en Picardie nord-orientale, d'après les fouilles de l'autoroute A16, in Marion and Blancquaert 2000, 475–496.

Collis, J.R. 1973. Burials with weapons in Iron Age Britain, *Germania* 51, 121–133.

Collis, J.R. 1977. Owslebury, Hants, and the problem of burial in rural settlements, in R. Reece (ed.), *Burial in the Roman World*, 26–34. London: Council for British Archaeology Research Report 22.

Coy, J.G. 1961. Early Iron Age village at Dumpton Gap, *Archaeologia Cantiana* 76, lvi.

Craw, J.H. 1923–4. On two bronze spoon burials from an Early Iron Age grave near Burnmouth, Berwickshire, *Proceedings of the Society of Antiquaries of Scotland* 58, 143–160.

Cunliffe, B. 1982. Social and economic development in Kent in the pre-Roman Iron Age, in P.E. Leach (ed.), *Archaeology in Kent to AD 1500*, 40–50. London: Council for British Archaeology Research Report 48.

Cunliffe, B. 1991. *Iron Age Communities in Britain* (3rd edn). London: Routledge.

Curwen, E.C. 1931. Excavations in the Trundle. Second season, 1930, *Sussex Archaeological Collections* 72, 100–149.

Curwen, E.C. 1954. *The Archaeology of Sussex*. London: Methuen.

Curwen, E. and Curwen E.C. 1927. Excavations in the Caburn, near Lewes, *Sussex Archaeological Collections* 68, 1–56.

Curwen, E.C. and Frere, S. 1947. A Romano-British occupation site at Portfield Gravel Pit, Chichester, *Sussex Archaeological Collections* 86, 135–140.

Curwen, E. and Hawkes, C.F.C. 1931. Prehistoric remains from Kingston Buci, *Sussex Archaeological Collections* 72, 185–217.

Dechezleprêtre, T., Cousin, P., Leon, G., Paez-Rezende, L. and Rougier, R. 2000. Architecture des bâtiments de l'âge du fer en Haute-Normandie, in Marion and Blancquaert 2000, 321–338.

Diack, M., Mason, S. and Perkins, S. 2000. North Foreland, *Current Archaeology* 168, 472–473.

Down, A. 1979. *Chichester Excavations 4: The Roman Villas at Chilgrove and Uparden*. Chichester: Phillimore.

Drewett, P. and Hamilton, S. 1999. Marking time and making space: excavations and landscape studies at the Caburn hillfort, East Sussex, 1996–1998, *Sussex Archaeological Collections* 137, 7–36.

Elsdon, S.M. 1989. *Later Prehistoric Pottery in England and Wales.* Aylesbury: Shire Archaeology.

Evans, A.J. 1890. On a Late-Celtic urn-field at Aylesford, Kent, *Archaeologia* 52, 315–355.

Evans, C. 1997. Hydraulic communities: Iron Age enclosure in the East Anglian fenlands, in Gwilt and Haselgrove 1997, 73–86.

Ferdière, A. (ed.) 1993. *Monde des Morts et Monde des Vivants en Gaule rurale (Actes du colloque ARCHEA/AGER, Orléans, 7–9 Février 1992).* Tours: 6e supplément à la Revue Archéologique du Centre de la France.

Fitzpatrick, A.P. 1997a. Everyday life in Iron Age Wessex, in Gwilt and Haselgrove 1997, 73–86.

Fitzpatrick, A.P. 1997b. *Archaeological Excavations on the Route of the A27 Westhampnett Bypass, West Sussex, Vol. 2. The Cemeteries.* Salisbury: Wessex Archaeology Report 12.

Fitzpatrick, A.P. 2000. Ritual, sequence, and structure in Late Iron Age mortuary practices in north-west Europe, in J. Pearce, M. Millett and M. Struck (eds), *Burial, Society, and Context in the Roman World,* 15–29. Oxford: Oxbow Books.

Fox, C. 1923. *The Archaeology of the Cambridge Region.* Cambridge: Cambridge University Press.

Fox, C. and Wolseley, G.R. 1928. The Early Iron Age site at Findon Park, Findon, Sussex, *Antiquaries Journal* 8, 449–460.

Fox, C. 1946. *A Find of the Early Iron Age from Llyn Cerrig Bach, Anglesey.* Cardiff: National Museum of Wales.

Frere, S. 1940. A survey of archaeology near Lancing, *Sussex Archaeological Collections* 81, 141–172.

Frazer-Hearne, E.J. 1936. 'Shepard's Garden' Arundel Park. A pre-Roman and Romano- British settlement, *Sussex Archaeological Collections* 77, 223–245.

Geoffroy, J.-F. and Thoquenne, V. 2000. L'occupation du territoire à Hénin-Beaumont (Pas-de-Calais) à l'époque gauloise, in Marion and Blancquaert 2000, 371–394.

Gilkes, O.J. 1993. Iron Age and Roman Littlehampton, *Sussex Archaeological Collections* 131, 1–20.

Green, C. 1980. Handmade pottery and society in Late Iron Age and Roman East Sussex, *Sussex Archaeological Collections* 118, 69–86.

Gwilt, A. and Haselgrove, C. (eds) 1997. *Reconstructing Iron Age Societies.* Oxford: Oxbow Monograph 71.

Hamilton, S. 1985. Iron Age pottery, in Bedwin and Holgate, 220–228.

Hamilton, S. 1998. Using elderly data bases: iron Age pit deposits at the Caburn, East Sussex and related sites, *Sussex Archaeological Collections* 136, 23–40.

Hamilton, S. 2003. Sussex not Wessex: a regional perspective on southern Britain c. 1200–200 BC, in D. Rudling (ed.), *Sussex to AD 2000*, 69–88. Brighton: University of Sussex Press.

Hamilton, S. and Gregory, K. 2000. Updating the Sussex Iron Age, *Sussex Archaeological Collections* 138, 57–74.

Hamilton, S. and Manley, S. 1999. The end of prehistory, *c.* 100 BC–AD 43, in K. Leslie and B. Short (eds), *An Historical Atlas of Sussex*, 22–23. Chichester: Phillimore.

Hamilton, S. and Manley, J. 2001. Hillforts, monumentality and place: a chronological and topographic review of first millennium BC hillforts of south-east England, *European Journal of Archaeology* 4, 7–42.

Hamilton, S. and Seager Thomas, M. 2002. *Eight hundred years of Kent pottery, the first millennium BC pottery sequence from Canterbury Road, Hawkinge, and its continental affinities.* Unpublished client report for Archaeology South-East.

Hanworth, R. 1987 The Iron Age in Surrey, in J. Bird and D.G. Bird (eds), *The Archaeology of Surrey to 1540*, 139–164. Guildford: Surrey Archaeological Society.

Harding, D.W. 1974. *The Iron Age in Lowland Britain.* London: Routledge and Kegan Paul.

Hartridge, R. 1978. Excavations at the prehistoric and Romano-British site on Slonk Hill, Shoreham, Sussex, *Sussex Archaeological Collections* 116, 69–141.

Haselgrove, C. 1982. Wealth, prestige and power. The dynamics of Iron Age centralisation in south-eastern England, in C. Renfrew and S. Shennan (eds), *Ranking, Resource and Exchange*, 79–88. Cambridge: Cambridge University Press.

Haselgrove, C. 1987. *Iron Age Coinage in South-East England: the Archaeological Context.* Oxford: British Archaeological Reports British Series 174.

Haselgrove, C. 1988. The archaeology of British potin coinage, *Archaeological Journal* 135, 99–122.

Haselgrove, C. 1999. The Iron Age, in J. Hunter and I. Ralston (eds), *The Archaeology of* Britain, 113–134. London: Routledge.

Haselgrove, C. 2005. A trio of temples: a reassessment of Iron Age coin deposition at Harlow, Hayling Island, and Wanborough, in Haselgrove and Wigg-Wolf 2005, 391–418.

Haselgrove, C. and Millett, M. 1997. Verlamion reconsidered, in Gwilt and Haselgrove 1997, 282–297.

Haselgrove C. and Wigg-Wolf, D. (eds), *Iron Age Coinage and Ritual Practices.* Mainz: Studien zu Fundmünzen der Antike 20.

Hawkes, C.F.C. 1939. The pottery from Castle Hill, Newhaven, *Sussex Archaeological Collections* 80, 269–292.

Hessing, W.A.M. 1993. Nécropoles indigènes de la zone alluviale des Pays-Bas (50 av. J.-C.–300 ap. J.-C.), in Ferdière 1993, 105–112.

Hill, J.D. 1997. 'The end of one kind of body and the beginning of another kind of body'. Toilet instruments and 'Romanization', in Gwilt and Haselgrove 1997, 96–107.

Hill, J.D. 2002. Just about the potter's wheel? Using, making and depositing middle and later Iron Age pots in East Anglia, in A. Woodward and J.D. Hill (eds), *Prehistoric Britain: The Ceramic Basis,* 143–160. Oxford: Oxford University Press.

Holgate, R. 1986a. Excavations at the late prehistoric and Romano-British enclosure complex at Carne's Seat, Goodwood, West Sussex 1984, *Sussex Archaeological Collections* 124, 35–50.

Holgate, R. 1986b. Excavations at Lordington, Stoughton, West Sussex 1984, *Sussex Archaeological Collections* 124, 244–251.

Holman, D. 2000. Iron Age coinage in Kent, a review of current knowledge, *Archaeologia Cantiana* 120, 205–233.

Holman, D. 2005. Iron Age coinage from Worth and other possible evidence of ritual deposition in Kent, in Haselgrove and Wigg-Wolf 2005, 265–285.

Holman, D. forthcoming. Iron Age coins from Worth and Archer's Low Farm, Sandwich.

Hunter, F. 2005. The image of the warrior in the British Iron Age – coin iconography in context, in Haselgrove and Wigg-Wolf 2005, 43–68.

Hurd, C.E. 1909. On a Late-Celtic village near Dumpton Gap, Broadstairs, *Antiquaries Journal* 61, 427–438.

Ince, A.G. 1928. Pedestalled-urns in Kent, *Antiquaries Journal* 8, 93–94.

James, S. and Rigby, V. 1997. *Britain and the Celtic Iron Age*. London: British Museum Press.

Jahier, I., Besnard-Vauterin, C., Lepaumier, H., *et al.* 2000. Les bâtiments des habitats de l'âge du fer en Basse-Normandie: panorama des découvertes, in Marion and Blancquaert 2000, 339–357.

Johns, C. 2002. A sword and mirror grave from Scilly, *The Archaeologist* 44, 16.

Johnson, C. 2003. Two Late Iron Age warrior burials discovered in Kent, *Archaeology International 2002/2003*, 14–17. London: Institute of Archaeology, University College London.

Jones, J.D. and Stead, I.M. 1969. An Early Iron Age warrior burial found at St Lawrence, Isle of Wight, *Proceedings of the Prehistoric Society* 35, 351–354.

Kelly, D.B. 1978. Archaeological notes from Maidstone Museum, *Archaeologia Cantiana* 94, 264–268.

King, A. and Soffe, G. 1998. Internal organisation and deposition at the Iron Age temple on Hayling Island, *Proceedings of the Hampshire Field Club and Archaeological Society* 53, 35–47.

Klein, W.G. 1928. Roman temple at Worth, Kent, *Antiquaries Journal* 8, 76–86.

Laing, L. 1968. A Greek tin trade with Cornwall, *Cornish Archaeology* 7, 15–23.

Lambot, B. 1993. Habitats, nécropoles et organisation du territoire à La Tène finale en Champagne septentrionale, in Ferdière 1993, 13–38.

Lambot, B. Friboulet, M. and Méniel, P. 1994. *Le site protohistorique d'Acy Romance (Ardennes) – II: Les nécropoles dans leur contexte régional 1986–1988–1989*. Reims : Mémoire de la Société Archéologique Champenoise 8.

Lambot, B. and Méniel, P. 2000. Le centre communautaire et cultuel du village Gaulois d'Acy-Romance dans san contexte régionale, in S. Verger (ed.), *Rites et Espaces en pays celte et méditerranéen*, 7–139. Rome : Collection de l'Ecole Française de Rome 276.

Leman-Delerive, G. 2000. Enclos funéraires et cultuels dans la partie septentrionale de la Gaule Belgique, *Revue Archéologique de Picardie* 1/2, 67–76.

Lemaire, P. 2000. Un établissement enclos de La Tène moyenne à Vermand (Aisne); études preliminaries, *Revue Archéologique de Picardie* 1/2, 161–178.

Macpherson-Grant, N. 1991. A reappraisal of prehistoric pottery from Canterbury, *Canterbury's Archaeology 1990–91*, 38–48.

Macpherson-Grant, N. 1996. The Early Iron Age pottery, *Canterbury's Archaeology 1995–96*, 68.

Marion, S. and Blancquaert, G. (eds) 2000. *Les installations agricoles de l'age du fer en France septentrionale*. Paris: Etudes d'histoire et d'archéologie 6.

Méniel, P. 1993. Les animaux dans les pratiques funeraires des Gaulois, in D. Cliquet, M. Remy-Watte, V. Guichard and M. Vaginay (eds), *Les Celtes en Normandie. Les Rites Funeraires en Gaule (IIIeme–Ier siecle avant J.-C.)*, 285–290. Rennes: Revue Archéoloqique de l'Ouest Supplément 6.

Niblett, R. 1999. *The Excavation of a Ceremonial Site at Folly Lane, Verulamium*. London: Britannia Monograph 14.

Norris, N.E.S. 1956. Miscellaneous researches 1949–56, *Sussex Archaeological Collections* 94, 1–12.

Norris, N.E.S. and Burstow, G.P. 1950. A prehistoric and Romano-British site at West Blatchington, Hove, *Sussex Archaeological Collections* 89, 1–56.

Norris, N.E.S. and Burstow, G.P. 1952. A prehistoric and Romano-British site at West Blatchington, Hove, *Sussex Archaeological Collections* 90, 221–240.

Oswald, A. 1997. A doorway on the past: practical and mystical concerns in the orientation of roundhouse doorways, in Gwilt and Haselgrove 1997, 87–95.

Parfitt, K. 1985. Some Iron Age sites in the Deal area, *Kent Archaeological Review* 79, 206–219.

Parfitt, K. 1995. *Iron Age Burials from Mill Hill, Deal*. London: The British Museum.

Parfitt, K. 1998. A Late Iron Age burial from Chilham Castle, near Canterbury, Kent, *Proceedings of the Prehistoric Society* 64, 343–351.

Parsons, W.J. and Curwen, E.C. 1933. An agricultural settlement on Charleston Brow, near Firle Beacon, *Sussex Archaeological Collections* 74, 164–180.

Perkins, D. 1992. Archaeological evaluations at Ebbsfleet in the Isle of Thanet, *Archaeologia Cantiana* 110, 269–311.

Perkins, D. 1996. The Trust for Thanet Archaeology: evaluation work carried out in 1995 at Hartsdown Community Woodland Scheme, Margate, *Archaeologia Cantiana* 114, 265–284.

Philp, B.J. 1991. A major Iron Age site discovered near Alkham, Kent, *Kent Archaeological Review* 103, 50–52.

Piggott, C.M. 1938. The non-Roman pottery from Crowhurst Park, in E. Straker and B.H. Lucas, A Romano-British bloomery in East Sussex, *Sussex Archaeological Collections* 79, 229–232 (224–232).

Pitts, M. 1979. Some recent finds of Iron Age pottery on the West Sussex coastal plain, *Sussex Archaeological Collections* 117, 259–260.

Place, C. 2000. *Littlehampton and Bognor Regis UWWTD Ford Airfield Site (AT0374). Post-Excavation Assessment*. Report for RPS Consultants.

Pommepuy, C., Auxiette, G., Desenne, S., Desenne, F., and Hénon, B. 2000. Des enclos à l'Âge du Fer dans la vallée de l'Aisne: le monde des vivants et monde des morts, *Revue Archéologique de Picardie* 1/2, 197–216.

Prilaux, G. 2000. Une ferme Gauloise spécialisée dans le travail du sel à Pont-Rémy, La Queute et "Le Fond de Baraquin" (Somme). Evolution et particularités de l'espace enclos, *Revue Archéologique de Picardie* 1/2, 233–254.

Prodéo, F. 2000. Bayonvillers "Chemin d'Harbonnière" (Somme). Un petit habitat fortifié de La Tène moyenne et finale, *Revue Archéologique de Picardie* 1/2, 255–266.

Ray, J.E. and Budgen, W. 1916. Recent finds at Eastbourne, *Sussex Archaeological Collections* 58, 188–193.

Rougier, R. 2000. Les formes d'occupation du territoire à l'âge du fer en Pays-de-Caux, d'après les fouilles sur le tracé de l'autoroute A29, in Marion and Blancquaert 2000, 411–426.

Rawes, B. 1988. Archaeology review 12, *Transactions of the Bristol and Gloucestershire Archaeological Society* 106, 219–224.

Rudling, D. 1981. The pottery, in O. Bedwin, Excavations at Lancing Down West Sussex 1980, *Sussex Archaeological Collections* 119, 49–53 (37–55).

Rudling, D. 1990. Archaeological finds at Rustington, West Sussex 1986–88, *Sussex Archaeological Collections* 128, 1–20.

Rudling, D. 1999. Pits and potin coins: a report on a new potin coin find from the Caburn, in P. Drewett and S. Hamilton, Marking time and making space: excavations and landscape studies at the Caburn hillfort, East Sussex, 1996–98, *Sussex Archaeological Collections* 137, 28–29 (7–38).

Seager Thomas, M. 2005. Understanding Iron Age Norton, *Sussex Archaeological Collections*, 83–115.

Seager Thomas, M. and Hamilton, S. 2002. *Prehistoric pottery from Shopwyke and Merston*. Unpublished Client Report for Museum of London Archaeological Service.

Stevens, S. 1999. *Archaeological Investigations at Hawkinge Aerodrome, Hawkinge, Kent*. Unpublished client report prepared by Archaeology South-East.

Stead, I.M. 1995. The metalwork, in Parfitt 1995, 35–57.

Stead, I.M. and Rigby, V. 1989. *Verulamium. The King Harry Lane Site*. London: English Heritage Archaeological Report 12.

Tester, P.J. and Bing, H.F. 1949. A first century urn-field at Cheriton, near Folkestone, *Archaeologia Cantiana* 62, 21–36.

Thompson, F.H. 1983. Excavations at Bigberry, near Canterbury 1979–80, *Antiquaries Journal* 63, 237–278.

Union Railways South 2000. *Boys Hall Balancing Pond, Sevington, Kent. Post-Excavation Assessment Report*. Unpublished client report prepared by Oxford Archaeological Unit.

Union Railways South 2001a. *Thurnham Roman Villa. Post-Excavation Assessment Report*. Unpublished client report prepared by Oxford Archaeological Unit.

Union Railways South 2001b. *White Horse Stone. Post-Excavation Assessment Report*. Unpublished client report prepared by Oxford Archaeological Unit.

Union Railways South 2002a. *Saltwood Tunnel, near Folkestone, Kent. Post-Excavation Assessment Report*. Unpublished client report prepared by Canterbury Archaeological Trust and Wessex Archaeology.

Union Railways South 2002b. *Beechbrook Wood, Hothfield, Kent. Post-Excavation Assessment Report*. Unpublished client report prepared by Oxford Archaeological Unit.

Watson, M.B. 1963. Iron Age site on Bridge Hill, *Archaeologia Cantiana* 78, 185–188.

Webster, G. 1990. A late Celtic sword-belt with a ring and button found at Coleford, Gloucestershire, *Britannia* 21, 294–295.

Whimster, R. 1981. *Burial Practices in Iron Age Britain*. Oxford: British Archaeological Report 90.

White, G.M. 1934. Prehistoric remains from Selsey Bill, *Antiquaries Journal* 14, 40–52.

Wilson, A.E. 1955. Sussex on the eve of the Roman Conquest, *Sussex Archaeological Collections* 93, 59–77.

Wolseley, G.R. and Smith, R.A. 1924. Discoveries near Cissbury, *Antiquaries Journal* 4, 347–359.

Sea, coast, estuary, land, and culture in Iron Age Britain

Steven Willis

Introduction

This paper examines human relations with the sea and coasts in Iron Age Britain. Studies focussing on terrestrial landscape, ritual, space, and cultural life have become commonplace in the last 25 years, yielding valuable insights, but the sea, beaches, and shore margins, and human use and definition of these environs, have been of little concern, and receive only brief mention in the recent research framework for the British Iron Age (Haselgrove *et al.* 2001, 2). This is surprising given the now fairly general recognition of the significance of watery places in the social, symbolic and religious lives of Iron Age people, and the place of the sea itself as a physical constant in the economic and cultural lives of the island's inhabitants. It is true on the other hand that in prehistory at least much of the evidence for human interaction with the sea is indirect and thus not prominent in archaeological recovery or discourse. These latter characteristics are themselves of interest.

Tide, season, weather, and light bring forth change in the sea, while its actions transform coasts, sometimes spectacularly. These dynamic peculiarities clearly impact upon human consciousness. The coastline is immensely varied, reflecting differences in geomorphology, climate, currents, vegetation and flows of fresh water. Such microenvironments *may* be perceived and used in quite distinct ways depending on cultural and physical constraints, just as different cultures clearly have, and have had, varying attitudes to and contacts with the sea and coastline, relations moreover which have been subject to substantial change and re-interpretation over time. There is a striking contrast, for example, between modern-day attitudes to the sea, and the manner in which it was conceived and used in the Iron Age and Roman periods.

Beyond the patchwork of local physical variables and cultural attitudes, there are, however, also strong recurring elements within different perceptions and discourses of the sea and coasts in Britain, both now and in the past. In this paper, I will use both direct and indirect evidence to examine issues such as the sea as a potential economic resource; communication, contact and exchange; symbolic and ritual dimensions to the sea and coasts; and deposition of the dead and of cultural material in marine environments. It is not an exhaustive study; rather my aim is to outline some pointers to perceptions and 'uses' of the sea and coastlines during the Iron Age.

The sea and the shore as contexts in human experience

In this section I consider some dimensions of the relationships between people, the sea, and the coast that potentially pertained during the Iron Age. My aim is to define issues, parameters, and likelihoods, and create a framework from which to examine *specific* topics for which we have archaeological evidence in the rest of the paper. This section deals with perceptions and 'experiences' and is speculative and theoretical, employing a variety of expressions and events drawn from more recent times and/or different cultures, including visual art.[1]

Boundaries

Coasts and estuaries mark profound boundaries. The physical contrast of the land and the sea, and of their interface, has cultural implications. Such margins are often marked symbolically and otherwise by human actions past and present. Much rock art, for instance, in Scandinavia was apparently created beside ancient shorelines that became dry land as the land rose in the post-glacial period (Bradley 2002, 132–3). The Flag Fen 'barrier' may be understood as a symbolic interface between land and fresh water on the one side and an encroaching sea (Pryor 2001). To take a contrasting case, subsequent to their conquest of southern Britain, the Romans erected an elaborate triumphal monument at Richborough, marking emphatically the point of their arrival on British shores (Strong 1968). In the Roman mind the sea was occupied by a divine spirit, Oceanus (Braund 1996). Iron Age communities may have venerated the sea or a supernatural entity associated with it; shores would be the boundary to this power.

Coastal environments were different from agriculturally productive land: marine margins were rarely settled and were difficult to manage. Beaches and coasts, being 'wild' places, stood in great contrast to the increasingly controlled terrestrial landscapes of the Iron Age. On the other hand, they held potential in terms of resources (sea salt, marine life, reeds, and possibly stone for certain artefacts and minerals like sea coal). In addition the sea allowed access to and from other places, carrying possibilities for exchanges at many levels, contact, and migration (e.g. Owen 1999). The sea may have been a uniting medium, since communication across it may have been simpler than overland travel. An understanding that across the sea lay different and exotic places, prospect, and adventure is likely to have been strong in the past. This sense is evoked in J.E. Millais's classic painting, 'The Boyhood of Raleigh' in which the tanned seafarer points across the sea wall to the ocean beyond as his story captivates his audience.[2] Coasts and beaches will have been understood as real and symbolic boundaries, and as places of specific and uncertain status. They may have lain beyond the socially regulated 'normal' and have been domains in which a certain licence was possible (as in our contemporary world) or where taboos and other cultural mores were proscribed.

The phenomenology of the land–sea interface

Ingold (1986), Tilley (1994), Taylor (1997), Bradley (2002), and Thomas (2001) follow the cogent line that in order to decode the archaeology of landscapes and space, we need to understand the significance of those places in the minds, discourses, and experiences of past people and in their related actions. This view can hardly be contested and is now a fundamental premise in any theoretically-informed archaeological approach to landscapes.

Coastlines are often portrayed as carrying a 'spiritual charge' for humans. Here land, sea, and sky meet with ever-changing appearances day-to-day, and hour-by-hour, altered by the weather and by cosmological physics (tide, day and night etc.). They are places of movement and unique sounds. An extraordinary quality of seascapes is the strikingly open visibility they normally afford in contrast to many terrestrial places. Yet this openness fails at the horizon, beyond which lie uncertainties. Coasts are often places of dramatic scale, open to the elements, of changing light and colour; places in which people may feel small and dwarfed by their world. This sense is conveyed in Caspar David Friedrich's painting 'Monk by the Sea' in which the lonely figure seems infinitesimal against the boundless natural world; a sense of anomie is evoked.[3] It is a cliché to observe that these circumstances may give rise to fundamental questions about the nature of human existence and so forth. Religious and spiritual groups have often located themselves by the sea.

A counterpoint to the idea that the sea and the coast may bring forth doubts and questions of human being in the world may be found in the 1881–2 paintings by Winslow Homer of the fishing community at Cullercoats, just north of Tynemouth on the Northumberland coast. These works were produced in the Social Realism genre of the time; in them we typically see the 'everyday life of the community' in its embedded association with the sea (Cooper 1986). Watercolours such as 'Four Fisherwives' or 'Watching the Tempest' depict a peopled world of work, productivity, and shared experiences (divided by gender), but emphasising purpose, order, camaraderie, and location in the socially constructed world, with the sea the galvanising factor.[4] These may be common aspects in the lives of people living by the sea in the past.

In the modern Western world coasts have become prominent as socially constructed spaces. Through the twentieth century, they came to be presented, understood and consumed, from the Maldives to Minehead, as places of play, exercise, health, freedom, recreation, and relaxation, for re-making the mind and body: they *seem good* whether you are there for the sunshine, the golf links, or the heritage ship. These are all recent constructs – and now challenged by the Tsunami of 26th December 2004 – but they do highlight a fundamental: that coasts are places of difference. Differences are manifold and multiple; there are contrasts between coasts in terms of their topography, potential, and impact upon the senses, while to be just one hundred metres inland can place one in a very different terrestrial environment. Many people in the past, as presently, will have experienced their normal life away from the sea, and will have regarded the coast as markedly distinct from their mundane everyday environs of fields and settlements, particularly in the Iron Age when there was such an emphasis on arable cultivation.

On the other hand, for some people, most conspicuously in the Northern and Western Isles of Scotland, contact with the sea and coastline was intimate and normal, a key parameter in economic and social relations (cf. Cunliffe 1995, 11–14).

Perceptions of, and attitudes to, the sea will have been multi-layered during the Iron Age. Writing about ancient Greece, Buxton (1994, 102–3) notes that, 'in ritual, as in myth, contact with the sea can constitute a fresh beginning, a re-inauguration of hope… [the seashore] is the site for the transition between polluted and pure'. A sub-text to perceptions of the sea in the past will have been its 'strangeness': its tides, its unpleasant taste in contrast to fresh water, the extraordinary appearance of some of the creatures it contained as revealed by the stranding of marine mammals on the beach, its scale. Richard Hingley (pers. comm.) points out that detritus washed up from shipwrecks or from other cultures over the sea, and often modified by the action of the sea, will have engendered curiosity and intrigue. It is little wonder that the human mind has conjured up myths of sea beasts, as depicted, for instance, in Roman art on the Dolphin mosaic at Fishbourne (Cunliffe 1971), in the Neptune Baths at Ostia (Toynbee 1965, 259), and on samian ware (Oswald 1936–7). Iron Age communities may well have had similar myths and ideas, although these were not apparently translated into surviving art.

Coasts: questions of status and access

Shores and inter-tidal areas may have been subject to a different definition from other landforms in the Iron Age, not least in terms of ownership and rights. Nowadays different countries have contrasting patterns of ownership and access to beaches and the coast. In Britain, beaches are largely the possession of the Crown, whereas in New England, USA, much of the shoreline is privately owned. Land 'ownership' in the Iron Age is an uncertain area, but the extent of land divisions by the Later Iron Age show that control of agriculturally productive land was important in both lowland and upland, and indicate that ownership rights, whether or not periodically contested, were formally organised. It is conceivable, however, that coasts, beaches, and inter-tidal zones were outside normal definitions of access and land use. Their economic potential is likely to have been low in the first millennium BC compared to the land, so concern over ownership or control *may* have been limited around much of Britain, although a developed set of rights may have existed in Scotland, where settlements were often located close to the sea and many communities clearly had a close relationship with the sea. Other exceptions may have included sea-salt extraction.

In Britain today, rights and access to beaches are multi-layered and often complex due to several organisations such as the MOD, local authorities, the Environment Agency, harbour authorities, fishermen, and conservation organisations having formal relations with these environments, often over the same location. Within this framework, however, access to the shore is fairly unrestrained, if not always actively enabled, with a commonly articulated *belief* that coasts are shared property and that no one owns the shore below high-water mark (but see above). In the Iron Age, different people may have used these environments in distinct ways or could have had recognised rights to undertake certain tasks, or there may have been no sense of ownership of these places.

The sea and the coast as economic resource

The sea and its coasts have many economic dimensions in the present day. Here, I wish to note one particular field: the gathering of resources for consumption. As the archaeological and historical record shows, such resources have included fish, sea birds and their eggs, crustaceans, marine molluscs, sea mammals, salt, minerals, and reeds. A striking example is the life of the community on St Kilda (Steel 1994), while many of Winslow Homer's paintings of Cullercoats display this nexus, depicting, almost exclusively, women engaged in activities around fishing (Cooper 1986, 87–123).

The 'harvest of the sea' takes many forms and has been determined by cultural factors, combined with economic and subsistence options. Consumption of fish products has been an important part of popular culture in various societies: fish and fish sauces were evidently particularly significant in some diets in the Roman era, and fish is important in the modern Japanese diet. Sea mammals too have long been used (Gardiner 1997). Where fishing is an important economic activity, it is often culturally layered. Typically, rituals and religious practices are associated with a safe and successful fishing trip. Moreover, close communities develop where common experiences of risk, uncertainty and circumstance relating to fishing as a livelihood are shared, for instance, the Hessle Road community in western Hull in the nineteenth and twentieth centuries (Wild 1990).

The sea, coasts, and threat

A persistent sub-text of literature and material culture is that of the sea and coastlines as places of potential danger. This might be considered a universal aspect of human relations with the sea and its margins. The endemically varied, changeable, and unmanageable character of the sea and the coastline make these environments of risk, whilst the sea around Britain has been at the same time both a barrier and a potential conveyer of threat to its shores, whether from unwelcome and hostile others – of whom Caesar was but one of many – or merely of contagion from disease. Forts of many periods, Martello towers, and now well-researched pillboxes punctuate the shorelines of Britain. Texts such as Erskine Childers' 1903 novel *The Riddle of the Sands* play on and reinforce such perceptions. In 1940, Paul Nash produced a series of works encapsulating the real threat of Nazi aircraft and U-boats from across the sea,[5] whilst a recent exhibition celebrating the opening of the Channel Tunnel included life-sized models of Iron Age warriors gesturing in defence of the Kentish shores. Iron Age coastal forts and 'cliff castles' may be related to such aspects (although they are not prominent in Kent).

The sea, coasts, and death

An association of coasts and the sea with death is real enough in our present world. A series of news reports whilst this paper was being written are poignantly representative of the frequency of such incidents. Within the space of two days, it was reported that a further enquiry was underway into the loss of *The Gaul*;[6] and that a teenager had been tragically washed out to sea from a breakwater in County Down and three bodies had been found at the foot of Beachy Head, East Sussex.[7] It is not surprising that seashores, as the boundary between land and sea – that is to say, between security and risk – are often associated with ritual activity. Bradley (2002, 27), for instance, draws on Buxton's work (1994, 102–3) to observe that in the Classical world, 'the coastline was... the place to offer sacrifices before undertaking a hazardous journey' (see also below and Braund 1996, 12–21).

Ambiguities

Human relations with the sea and coasts are hence likely to be coloured with ambiguities. The sea is a process, both predictable and unpredictable. It intervenes physically to transform natural and cultural materials. Famous paintings by Paul Nash convey this ambiguity. 'Winter Sea', for example,[8] depicts a patchwork of light and dark sea with limited movement in which the order to the waves suggests fields that are at once familiar and potentially productive, but there is latent menace, foreshadowing a different destructive harvest seen in his later work. In a well-known series of views by Nash at Dymchurch, Kent, the great sea wall and breakwaters protecting Romney Marsh are prominent, showing a sea (temporarily) controlled.[9] Ultimately the sea cannot be definitively controlled, whether at Dymchurch or elsewhere (e.g. Robinson 1988); there is a stark contrast between human harnessing and managing of the land, and the 'ill-tamed' sea.[10]

Ambiguities exist at various levels today. The seaside is seen as a place of recreation, but the sea and its fish may be a source of contamination from pollutants of various kinds. Fish is suggested to be good for humans to eat, but perhaps not farmed fish, according to the latest research. To take a second example, eastern England is menaced by rising sea level, which threatens inhabitants, livelihoods, and property, but some argue that this could be of benefit in the long-term if it leads to the generation of salt marsh, which would be a better defence than the existing sea walls.

The use of coastal and maritime resources in Iron Age Britain

As I have sought to show, cultural and individual attitudes, engagements and experiences vis-à-vis the sea and coastlines are highly complex. Nevertheless, certain persistent themes in this interaction can be discerned, which might therefore assist us in thinking about Iron Age perceptions of the sea and the coast, and help to inform interpretation of the archaeology and material culture found in, or relating to, such contexts.[11] I will begin by outlining the nature of the archaeological material available for study.

Coastlines and sea margins are subject both to deposition and erosion (e.g. Allen and Gardiner 2000; O'Sullivan 2001). These processes may be sudden and dramatic – as with the history of Spurn Head, East Yorkshire, or further back in time, Doggerland (Coles 1998) – or gradual. In Holderness, for example, considerable erosion has occurred, leaving archaeology exposed in soft vulnerable cliffs (Van de Noort and Ellis 1995). In contrast, substantial deposition along the Lincolnshire coast to the south due to alluviation, colluviation, and wind-blown sand, has resulted in land surfaces and inter-tidal zones being buried. Yet by Ingoldmells, we again find erosion revealing significant later prehistoric remains (Warren 1932; Baker 1960; Palmer-Brown 1993; Robinson 2001). Prehistoric people will, too, have been aware of coastal changes.

Compared to other periods, there is a lack of Iron Age settlement adjacent to the sea in much of southern and eastern Britain, or indeed of definite ports or coastal trading points, the status of even Hengistbury Head being in some doubt (Cunliffe 1987; Sharples 1990; Fitzpatrick 2001). Although the coastline is, in places, much altered since later prehistory, there is no reason to suppose that this is a factor. In northern and western Britain, on the other hand, and particularly in Scotland, many Iron Age sites are located by the sea. This zone has a very long coastline in relation to its area, so it is not surprising to find a different pattern of settlement and practice here, whilst climate, geomorphology, latitude, topography, and soils all exercised major – although not exclusive – influences on food production and the siting of settlements. In sum, expediency evidently inclined Iron Age communities in these areas, especially in Scotland, to settle in coastal localities and hinterlands.

Fish in the Iron Age

As Dobney and Ervynck show (this volume), there is meagre evidence for the consumption of fish in Iron Age southern and central Britain. If this lack of evidence is a reliable index, the people of much of Iron Age Britain did not routinely consume fish, despite the temperate climate and at the time clean and probably well-stocked rivers and plentiful sea fish. Taphonomic factors should not however be completely discounted; fish remains could, for instance, have been processed to generate glue.

Sea fish *were* eaten in northern and western Scotland.[12] At Dun Vulan on South Uist, extensive evidence for a fishing economy was recovered (Parker Pearson and Sharples 1999). The habitats of several species recovered from Scottish sites indicate sea fishing from boats; both plaice and cod, for example, were recovered at Bu, Orkney. Given the environment of northern and western Scotland, consuming fish is likely to have been economically expedient. Yet across much of Britain, Iron Age peoples were not obliged to consume fish; animal husbandry and especially grain production seem to be pre-eminent (Haselgrove 1989; 2001; Hill 1995a).

The absence of fish from settlements implies that a cultural choice was being exercised (cf. Dobney and Ervynck this volume). Noting the general absence of wild animals from Iron Age assemblages, Hill (1995b, 104) suggests that they 'were probably surrounded by prohibitions, so that their occasional hunting... and consumption were probably heavily regulated or proscribed.' Wild animals may only have been brought onto settlements and consumed during feasting, perhaps as sacrifice. This possibility with regard to fish is considered further below.

Marine molluscs and crustaceans

Sea shells found on archaeological sites might indicate consumption, although it is well attested that shells also have other uses; they may, for instance, be fashioned into beads, form a currency, or as with oyster shells in particular be burnt for lime (Plant 1952, 139). A medieval inhumation burial on the Isle of May, at the mouth of the Firth of Forth, had a scallop shell inserted into the mouth, a sign that the deceased had been on a pilgrimage to Compostella (Yeoman and James 1999, 197).

Historically shellfish are known to have flourished in great numbers around the British coast. Sandy and/or rocky shores, and estuaries with limited or no deposition, provide suitable habitats. Local ecology, accessibility and the calendar will determine the chances of collecting them. According to Cunliffe (1991a, 382), 'shellfish were collected in great quantity' during the Iron Age, despite their low calorific value, also observing that on Scottish sites, 'limpets, winkles and whelks were well represented' (*ibid.*, 403). These statements perhaps engender an impression of large-scale exploitation, but on the whole the quantities of shellfish found at sites near to the coast and estuaries seem to be fairly limited, and marine shellfish are only occasionally found at inland sites. Again, the possibility of taphonomic biases must not be overlooked. Shellfish, for instance, might have been consumed at or near their collection point and hence not entered the archaeological record, which Cunliffe and Hawkins (1988, 36) refer to as 'eaten *in situ*'.

Marine molluscs were found in Iron Age features belonging to the settlement on Rookery Hill, Bishopstone, East Sussex (Bell 1977). This overlooks the English Channel east of Newhaven and the nearby shore is a suitable habitat for a range of species. The main species collected were mussels, common limpet, and edible/common periwinkle, together with some oysters and common cockle, and the relative proportions of different species brought to the site apparently remained broadly similar throughout the Iron Age (*ibid.*, table 21), although there was a significant increase in the proportion of oysters consumed in the Roman period. However, the absolute number of shells from Iron Age features is lower than for either Neolithic or for Roman and Anglo-Saxon deposits on the same site. Whilst other factors, including ecological changes, could have intervened, the volume of excavated soil appears to be comparable for the Iron Age, Roman, and Anglo-Saxon periods, suggesting this may be a reliable index of relative consumption. The remains of two cuttlefish were found in the Early Iron Age enclosure ditch (*ibid.*, 285) and probably represent consumption, although other uses of these shells are conceivable.

In Kent, shellfish are recorded from the site at Borden, near Sittingbourne (Worsfold 1948), whilst in East Anglia, shells of common edible mussel, oyster, scallop, cockle and whelk were recovered from the Early Iron Age site at Redgate Hill, Hunstanton, Norfolk, adjacent to the Wash, both by hand and from soil samples (Murphy 1986). Oysters and mussels were prominent in the assemblage, but whilst marine molluscs were apparently consumed, Murphy (*ibid.*, 296) makes a point of noting that the quantities of shells recovered were not large and that the importance of marine resources to the economy was not clear.

In south-west England, the excavations at Mount Batten, Plymouth, revealed Iron Age midden deposits including the remains of marine molluscs (Cunliffe and Hawkins 1988). All the species were probably collected locally. The assemblage is dominated by the edible/common periwinkle (1396 individuals) and limpets (603). It was concluded that shellfish contributed only in a minute way to the calorific intake of the community (*ibid.*, 38). Also in Devon, a large shell midden containing a variety of marine and estuarine species was discovered in 1959 at Stoke Gabriel, by the upper tidal estuary of the River Dart (Woolner and Woolner 1966). Whilst this deposit appears to be of Roman date, it may have begun in the Iron Age.

In southern Scotland, a large deposit of marine shellfish was recovered from a Late Iron Age enclosure ditch at Fishers Road West, Port Seton (Haselgrove and McCullagh 2000). It included nearly 1000 edible/common periwinkles; common limpet and mussel were also well represented, along with other species such as whelk and pod razor (Ceron-Carrasco 2000, table 12). Oysters occurred in a number of settlement contexts, but only as singletons. The shellfish were presumably collected from the rocky shore of the Firth of Forth less than 700 m away. They are interpreted as food remains, although fertiliser is admitted as a possibility (Haselgrove and McCullagh 2000, 73). Far fewer marine molluscs were found at the nearby Fishers Road East enclosure (Hambleton and Stallibrass 2000, table 30). The species list is varied, although once again all were locally available: oyster, edible/common periwinkle, and mussel were the commonest species. Here, the conclusion was that, despite the proximity of the sea, edible marine molluscs were not exploited as a significant food resource (*ibid.*, 155).

In general, marine molluscs are absent from inland sites, but not invariably. Marine creatures were represented at Staple Howe during the Early Iron Age (Brewster 1963), while Late Iron Age deposits at Silchester contained groups of edible oyster plus a small number of edible mussel shells (Grant 2000). At Dragonby, North Lincolnshire, however, none of the 1194 oyster shells are from Iron Age contexts, being confined to Roman deposits (Alvey 1996), emphasising the very different scale of oyster consumption in Roman Britain compared with the Iron Age.

A striking find at Slonk Hill, near Shoreham, West Sussex, close to the sea and the estuary of the river Adur must also be mentioned. This comprised a male Iron Age inhumation in a pit, resting on a sloping 'bed' of marine mollusc shells, mainly mussels (Hartridge 1978). The mussels were still in articulated pairs with sand within; winkles and barnacles were also present. Mussels appear to have been the main shellfish variety represented in other Iron Age deposits at this site (*ibid.*, 93). Iron Age burials containing small pockets of shells have been found at Knowe of Skea, Westray, Orkney (Moore and Wilson 2005).

Edible crustaceans rarely occur on Iron Age sites, especially outside Scotland. A crab claw, probably of the edible species *Cancer pagurus*, was recovered from a Late Iron Age pit at Bishopstone (Bell 1977, 287); the pit also yielded complete and near complete pottery vessels, as well as numerous mussel shells. At Fishers Road West, Port Seton, a burnt claw of *Cancer pagurus* was recovered from the same ditch fill as the edible periwinkles (Ceron-Carrasco 2000).

Sea birds

Domestic fowl apart, bird bones – like wild animal species – are far from common on Iron Age sites in southern and central Britain (Hill 1995b; Maltby 1995). Nevertheless, sea birds might be anticipated at sites near the coast, particularly in north-west Scotland, and do indeed occur. Two thirds of the birds represented at Dun Vulan were sea birds, as was the case at Crosskirk broch, Caithness (Fairhurst 1984; Cartledge and Grimby 1999). Most of the sea birds represented are edible species. Eggs and feathers may also have been collected but are unlikely to be preserved archaeologically (Serjeantson 1988). Further south, sea birds are no more common on coastal settlements than land birds are at inland sites. At Fishers Road East, only one bird bone was present, from a red-throated diver or similar (Hambleton and Stallibrass 2000, 154), and hardly any bird bones were found in the 1985–6 excavations at Maiden Castle (Armour-Chelu 1991).

At Dragonby, the Iron Age deposits yielded a small assemblage of bird bones, from a narrow range of species. These included a few gull bones and white-tailed sea eagle bones from at least two individuals (Harman 1996). The presence of the sea eagle is of note. Presumably always comparatively rare in Britain, these birds generally inhabit areas away from humans.[13] Another Iron Age example is recorded at Braughing–Puckeridge (Partridge 1979). Around 60% of the diet of these birds comprises fish. Harman (1996, 164) suggested that at Dragonby the eagles might have been kept as pets or trophies.

Amongst the pit deposits at Danebury were bones from four kittiwakes, including two articulated wings from separate pits that also yielded human bone and horse (Hill 1995b, 64). Hill notes that whilst bird bones at the site tend to be associated with articulated bone groups they are not usually associated with human bone. By comparison, only one of the 102 birds represented at Dun Vulan (above) was a kittiwake. Kittiwakes and one cormorant bone are the only sea birds recorded at the chalk downland Iron Age sites examined by Hill. They must have been brought to Danebury intentionally (*ibid.*, 64; Serjeantson 1991), as these birds are rarely seen inland and, apart from breeding, spend their lives at sea (Hayman and Burton 1982). Kittiwake is the only sea bird species recovered at Gussage All Saints, Dorset, another inland site (Harcourt 1979).

The presence of kittiwake remains is consistent with the pattern emerging from Danebury and other Wessex sites for wild species to appear in special deposits. Bird bones were found in all five contexts yielding human remains at Dun Vulan, although no further patterning was identifiable (Cartledge and Grimbly 1999, 288). Why kittiwakes were treated in this manner is unclear, although, nesting socially on cliffs, they may have been relatively easy seabirds to catch via netting (Hayman and

Coastal/marine resource	*Usage*
Fish	Minimal evidence
Shellfish	Modest exploitation by coasts
Crustaceans	Minimal exploitation by coasts
Sea birds	Minimal evidence; selected species?
Seaweed	Some utilisation by coasts
Sea mammals (e.g. whale, seal, etc)	Occasional finds; opportunistic use
Sea-salt	Intensive extraction in several regions
Salt marsh/wetland grazing	Intensive in at least several regions

Table 1. Summary of the use of coastal/sea resources during the Iron Age in southern and central Britain.

Burton 1982, 232). This relative 'ease of capture' might explain the absence of other members of the gull family; alternatively kittiwakes may have been selected for cultural or symbolic reasons.

Seaweed

Seaweed has long been used around Britain as sheep fodder, while sheep can graze seaweed strand-lines on beaches (Bell 1981). Another important use is as fertiliser (*ibid*; Smith 1999, 335), a function apparently attested in Roman Colchester (Crummy 1992, 33). Pliny notes its use as a root feed for cabbages (White 1970, 144). Other uses include dyeing cloth, and as fuel when dried, while selected types have been eaten or employed as a medicine (cf. Fenton 1978; 1986, 51–2; Plant 1952, 57, 80, 224–5; Smith 1999, 332).

All these uses are possible in Iron Age Britain. Seaweed does not normally survive unless it has been burnt, but indirect evidence can sometimes be found, as at Bishopstone, where Iron Age contexts produced marine barnacles and other inedible or very small marine mollusc species likely to have been introduced with seaweeds (Bell 1977; 1981, 122); such indicators are virtually absent from Roman contexts. Two Iron Age sites in East Lothian recently produced evidence for seaweed use: Fishers Road East, Port Seton, where charred remains, abundant in a few contexts, are thought to represent employment as a fertiliser (Hambleton and Stallibrass 2000, 155; Huntley 2000), and an enclosure at Whittingehame Tower, 8 km from the sea, where a deposit late in the occupation sequence yielded significant quantities of burnt seaweed and barley (J. Huntley pers. comm.). Fragments of charred seaweed were also recovered from a midden at Dun Vulan (Smith 1999, 332). In the early medieval period there is evidence for seaweed at inland sites.

Table 1 summarises potential Iron Age use of coastal and marine resources in southern and central Britain on the basis of the evidence discussed above.

Uses of sea life in the Roman era: social construction and social control

In contrast to the Iron Age pattern, fish, shellfish, and fish products were a not infrequent element in many people's diets in the Roman era (e.g. Edwards 1984). Fish sauces were widely manufactured and distributed in the Roman world and may have been produced in Roman Britain and elsewhere in the northern provinces (cf. Dobney *et al.* 1999, 24–5; Dobney 2001, 38; Van Neer *et al.* 2005).[14]

The quantity and variety of evidence for the use of sea-life in Roman Britain is striking compared to the Iron Age. Exotic imports apart (Dobney 2001, 38), fish seem a regular food for residents in Roman towns, although not a main food source. The range of fish is often more limited than might be anticipated, with fish from deeper marine environments not common (*ibid.*, 41); freshwater and estuarine species were, however, exploited. Fish from Roman deposits at Colchester include herring, plaice, flounder, and eel (Murphy 1992). Scales and bones from Leicester are mainly freshwater species, plus herring presumed to have arrived in a preserved state (Nicholson 1999). Cod is present at Hod Hill (Davies 1971). A strong iron fishhook from Richborough is presumed to be for sea fishing (Bushe-Fox 1949).

An element in the folklore of British archaeology is that oyster shells are commonly encountered on Roman sites. This belief has some truth, but requires qualification. Oysters were embedded in Roman culture and British oysters were highly regarded by Roman consumers (Stott 2004, 37–9). Roy Davies' (1971) study of Roman military diet identified oysters as the principal shellfish species consumed at forts and fortresses. Oyster shells are omnipresent at Colchester, but also well known from inland centres such as Alchester, Oxfordshire (Winder 2001) or Leicester. At the latter, Monckton (1999) has shown that many of the oysters found on The Shires and Causeway Lane sites almost certainly came from beds on the Essex coast, indicating an organised trade in these shellfish during the period.

In northern Gaul, edible mussels as well as oysters were traded inland in some quantity in the Roman period (Vanderhoeven *et al.* 1992; Van Neer and Ervynck forthcoming).

A characteristic of the Roman evidence for consumption of fish and shellfish is that many of the relevant deposits are structured or potentially votive. On Roman sites, oyster shells often occur in largish groups suggesting meals, feasts, or rituals. There is a particular connection with temples, such as Chanctonbury Ring and Lancing Down in West Sussex (Bedwin 1980, 188–9; 1981), and structured deposits. At the small town of Alcester, Warwickshire, a pit yielded an ensemble of oyster shells alongside 69 samian vessels, at least 6 unworn glass vessels, a complete Dressel 20 amphora minus rim, a dog skeleton, a copper alloy bracelet, a copper alloy plaque, and an iron stylus (Cracknell 1994, 252). As in the Iron Age, edible crustaceans are rare on Roman sites (Murphy 1992, 277), so that the occurrence of lobster claws in a second century AD deposit at St Albans (Wheeler and Wheeler 1936, 102–4) is conspicuous and implies high status consumption. The associated finds and the context of these claws – a well or shaft in an elaborate residence – indicate a structured deposit, perhaps related to feasting.[15]

At St Thomas Street, Southwark, the second-century AD timber-lined pit F28 may originally have been some kind of processing tank, but was subsequently used as a receptacle for an extraordinarily varied cultural, faunal, and palaeobotanical assemblage (Dennis 1978). Unfortunately the limited scale of the excavation restricted knowledge of the immediate functional milieu, although the pits lay at the back of a plot fronting the main Roman road through Southwark. A minimum of 11 fish species is represented in pit F28 – including freshwater fish like carp and pike and marine species such as haddock, herring and mackerel (Jones 1978) – reflecting the watery hinterland of London, together with the remains of ten dogs. The adjacent pit F29 was also timber-lined and yielded mussels.

The skull of a white-tailed sea eagle from a possible third-century AD well at Leicester is a further rare example of this species already encountered in Iron Age contexts at Dragonby and Braughing–Puckeridge. Understood to have a coastal preference in habitat, inland waters may also have attracted this species. Hence it is possible that this individual lived by the River Soar, although it may have come to Leicester in some way from the coast. An iconic creature in the Roman world, the eagle will have had a variety of potential uses, not least in connection with religion and imperial symbolism (Baxter 1992). There may have been a 'market' for such creatures that might have been procured from coastal groups. Another sea eagle comes from the shrine at Uley, Gloucestershire (Parker 1988), while the example from Leicester was evidently a part of a structured deposit (cf. Baxter 1992).[16] A Neolithic chambered cairn at Isbister, Orkney, housing the remains of over 300 humans contained other animal species, a remarkable 88% of the bird bones being carcasses and talons of sea eagles (Hedges 1984).[17]

In sum, the Romano-British evidence displays significant cultural and economic differences from the Iron Age pattern. The incorporation of southern Britain into the Roman empire resulted in an influx of people with a dietary tradition of eating fish and shellfish, and associated products. The consumption of fish and shellfish is more prominent at Roman sites of all types – not just the urban centres and *coloniae* – suggesting that elements of this 'Roman' diet were diffused into the wider British community. At the same time, however, much of the evidence comes from structured deposits,[18] implying that – whilst not as restrictive as in the Iron Age– there were social constructs relating to when fish or shellfish were appropriate to eat in Roman Britain and/or when they might be caught or taken. Egyptian religion exercised certain taboos with regard to fish (C. Chaffin pers. comm.), Roman soldiers were forbidden by military law from fishing or hunting except when officially sanctioned (see Suetonius, *The Twelve Caesars*, *Tiberius* 19; Davies 1971, 124, note 16), and many cultures, including Roman society, have regarded oysters as special (Stott 2004). Consumption of seafood in Roman Britain may even have been restricted mainly to feasts held to mark particular calendar dates or cultural events such as coming of age ceremonies, although, if so, the archaeological record suggests that they were normally eaten as one course or element in a bigger meal, rather than on their own. There is, therefore, clear evidence that the consumption of seafoods in the ancient world was socially constructed and socially regulated.

Settlement on the Margin

A changing relationship with wetlands?

Estuarine environments, brackish water, marsh and temperate wetlands are second only to tropical rain forest in terms of nutrients available to support plant life. The ecological richness of these environments is reflected in a range of exploitable resources. Francis Pryor (pers. comm.) has often stated that 'Bronze Age people loved water', not least, presumably, for this richness. This is apparent not just from the widespread scale of wetland exploitation, but also in the extent of monument building in wetlands and wetland margins at this time, as at Flag Fen (Pryor 2001). It is seen too in the concentration of settlement and artefact evidence in Lincolnshire around the lower Witham valley and the Fen edge.

Whether such attitudes endured in the Earlier Iron Age is less clear. In eastern England, for instance, a

Cultural phase	*Economy of the Fens/fen margin*
BA/LBA	Agricultural landscape focused with regard to wet ground
	Agriculture is livestock based (? predominantly sheep)
	Characterised by paddocks, other management features
	Dispersed settlement pattern
	Flag Fen – with 1 m diam. timbers
	'Sites' are numerous on the fen edge, and 'artefact-rich'
LBA/EIA	Flooding; marine incursion
	Creates advantages and disadvantages
	Coincides with other unfolding social and economic changes and attitudes
EIA & MIA	'Radical break and re-formation'
	Landscape focus away from the wet ground
	Mixed farming forms basis of economy with cereals
	Settlement 'nucleation begins'
	Sites concentrated on Fen margin and on islands of solid geology protruding from the peat in the Fens
	No settlement in the marsh proper

Table 2. The changing Fens of eastern England in the first millennium BC.

marine incursion occurred early in the first millennium BC, after which the nature of human activity on the coastal and estuarine margins alters. Watery places were still venerated, but there was markedly less monument building in the wetlands or evidence of settlement and exploitation. In East Anglia, for example, there was no settlement at all in the Fens and marsh proper, although sites do exist on the gravel fen-edge terraces and islands and sea-salt extraction took place on the silt fens (Evans 1997). The marine incursion was undoubtedly not the sole cause of these changes, as a whole range of social, economic and environmental factors affected Britain at this period. Further changes are apparent from early in the Middle Iron Age, when the increasing focus on intensive mixed farming rendered the wetland habitats of eastern England still more marginal to primary agricultural production, and as a result they began to be used in increasingly specialised ways (e.g. Haselgrove 1989; Hill this volume).

The picture in the wetlands and coastal margins of Holderness is broadly similar. Compared to the Bronze Age, Iron Age sites are distinctly lacking (Van de Noort and Ellis 1995). A number of possible later prehistoric sites have proved not to be wetland settlements at all, but the result of beaver action. Some Iron Age sites of considerable promise do nevertheless exist, as at Weldon's Plantation, Winestead, where artefacts and timber structures have been radiocarbon and luminescence dated to the Middle Iron Age, although this may have been a drier microenvironment (*ibid.*), or at Kelk, in north Holderness, where a Middle Iron Age enclosure beside a marshy area has yielded abundant evidence of bronze metalworking (Fenwick *et al.* 1999). West of Holderness, in the south-eastern Vale of York, extensive settlement colonisation occurred in the vicinity of the Foulness valley and estuary as this became a drier landscape from the Middle Iron Age; again there is evidence of metalworking, this time in the form of extensive smelting of bog ore at Welhambridge (Halkon and Millett 1999).

Table 2 summarises the changing pattern of fenland settlement in eastern England during the first millennium BC. Elsewhere along the coast of eastern and south-eastern England, most Iron Age sites seem to be located away from the marine margin. Summarising the results of the Langstone Harbour survey in Hampshire, for instance, Allen and Gardiner (2000) comment on the lack of Iron Age sites in the harbour itself, whilst noting the presence of the well-known shrine on Hayling Island as well as the hillfort at Tournerbury Camp. There are of course some exceptions, as in north-east England, where both South Shields (Hodgson *et al.* 2001) and Tynemouth (Jobey 1967) are close to the sea. Settlement away from the sea margin is likely to have been a function both of choice and of environmental factors. In some instances, pressure on land may have led to the settlement of marginal areas that were normally avoided, while specialisation, including livestock grazing, was also apparently a factor.

Use of the salt marsh

The Gwent Levels, in south-east Wales, provide one of the most intensively researched examples of the use of a coastal/estuarine environment at this time (Rippon 1996, 23–4; Bell *et al.* 2000; Murphy 2002, 55; Nayling 2002, 111). At Goldcliff, a number of rectangular buildings dating from the Middle Iron Age have been investigated and the evidence suggests humans and livestock were roofed within the same structures (Bell *et al.* 2000). In general, Iron Age sites found on the coastal margin to date seem to be specialised sites, often seasonal or temporary, associated with activities such as salt production and/or the grazing of sheep or cattle on salt marsh, alluvial grassland, the inter-tidal zone and other marginal lands.

Salt marshes on the east coast of England are likely to have supported sheep flocks on a large scale during the Iron Age (Wilkinson and Murphy 1995). Pryor (1996) argued cogently that this occurred in the Late Bronze Age on the western edge of the Fens, interpreting ditch systems and enclosures as flock management features, although in this case he did not see the regime extending into the Iron Age for environmental reasons. As an index of sheep management in Essex during the Iron Age, Sealey has emphasised Hilary Major's (1982, fig. 7) study of triangular loomweights, which shows a concentration of finds around Orsett beside the Thames estuary, with other examples from on or near to the coast and at the heads of estuaries. This distribution parallels the locations of sheep pasture reported in Domesday book (Sealey 1997, 63).

Preserved wooden hurdling and an Iron Age hurdle 'bridge' at The Stumble, Goldhanger, Essex, was of a type suitable for human and sheep movement across the marshes, possibly relating to tides (Wilkinson and Murphy 1995, 150), whilst Iron Age enclosure complexes at Chigborough Farm by the Blackwater estuary, were evidently for large-scale management of cattle and/or sheep (Wallis and Waughman 1998). Cattle were favoured on the Gwent levels at this time – at Goldcliff, they are attested by hundreds of hoof impressions – and Iron Age timber trackways, consisting of woven hurdles, are also known from the area (Rippon 1996, 22). Similar usage of the inter-tidal margins for seasonal livestock grazing is likely elsewhere during later prehistory, such as in north-west England and around estuaries in Ireland (O'Sullivan 2001).

The Iron Age saw the intensification of salt extraction from sea and estuarine waters at many locations around Britain (e.g. Morris 1994; this volume; Sealey 1995; Lane and Morris 2001; Willis forthcoming). Sea-salt extraction was undoubtedly an important industry involving many groups and communities, seemingly one of the few major avenues of economic articulation between Iron Age people and the sea. Work in recent years has related the salt industry to social structures, exchange and power. Salt will have been essential to the agricultural cycle in all sorts of ways – for flavouring foods, preserving meat, making cheese, curing hides, and for 'licks' for livestock – and could well have been an important ingredient of social reproduction (cf. Hingley 1997). Salt extraction was almost certainly a summer activity due to factors such as solar evaporation and marine saline levels, and may well have been combined with sheep rearing, with seasonal movement to suitable summer pastures in salt marsh and inter-tidal areas, including estuaries (Healey 1999; Chowne *et al.* 2001; Morris this volume).

Coastal hillforts and promontory forts

Coastal promontory forts are a particular feature of the coastline of parts of Wales (e.g. Pembrokeshire) and Scotland (e.g. Dumfries and Galloway) and the south-west peninsula (e.g. Griffith 1988), but occur elsewhere as well, as at Flamborough or Hengistbury Head. Hillforts also occur adjacent to the sea in the same areas. All told, over 100 promontory forts and coastal hillforts are known in Wales alone (Murphy 2002, 52), but the amount of work on them has been limited. Iron Age occupation in the form of circular buildings and other features is certainly attested within some sites, as at Porth y Rhaw and Tower Point in Pembrokeshire, or Carreg y Llam in Gwynedd, but it is unclear what, if any, use was made of specifically coastal resources. Research on Scottish promontory forts has been equally restricted (R. Hingley pers. comm.).

Any attempts at generalisation must therefore proceed with caution: these sites are not a uniform category, and evidently vary in date, scale, biography, and functions. Their location may have been determined more by a perceived need for 'defence' than by deliberate selection of a coastal site for cultural or economic reasons. In addition, many of the sites are in elevated positions high above the sea, which could have created a culturally significant separation from the sea. Some sites evidently enjoyed access to beaches – and thus the sea – in later prehistory, as with the fort at Mull of Galloway, but others apparently had no access for kilometres; the forts on Earn's Heugh, north-west of St Abb's Head, Berwickshire, may be a case in point, although erosion has altered the cliffs in this area.

The sea, boats, and trade in the Iron Age

The investigation of cross-Channel links with continental Europe has enjoyed a high profile in recent decades (e.g. McGrail 1983; 1995; Cunliffe 1987; 1991b) and maritime trade and contacts are often seen as playing a key formative role in Iron Age politics. In fact, few coastal sites can be confidently identified as 'ports' in any form in the Iron Age. Such a status has been attributed to Poole Harbour (Cunliffe 1991a), Meols on the Wirral (Matthews 1999),[19] Merthyr Mawr Warren in south Wales (Cunliffe 1991b; Gwilt this volume), Mount Batten, Plymouth (Cunliffe 1988a), North and South Ferriby on the Humber (Cunliffe 1991a; Millett 1990), as well as Hengistbury Head and, more speculatively, Dover and Folkestone, directly facing the Continent. Selsey in West Sussex might be bracketed with such a group, but the precise nature of the site is elusive and any pre-Roman port might instead lie at Fishbourne (or even as well). Both Hengistbury Head and Selsey lie on land projecting into the sea, connecting them to a range of hinterlands in Britain and across the Channel. There could well be a strong link between their geography, at a remove from the rest of society, and their apparent role as industrial and trading centres. In Essex, there was a point of entry at Colchester (see below), and there may have been another Iron Age port at Heybridge, on the Blackwater, but this is unclear (Atkinson and Preston 1998).

Quite what a 'port' would have been at this time is something over which to keep an open mind. The features revealed in Poole Harbour so far appear to represent some kind of Iron Age harbour installations (Markey *et al.* 2002), holding out the prospect that others may be found in the future. Elsewhere formal works may not have existed or been unnecessary, the practice being for ships simply to be beached along a designated stretch of shore or be anchored offshore with small craft employed to ferry goods. Cargoes may have been removed (and loaded) on the beach, and some items may have been consumed immediately without leaving any archaeological traces. Nor need there have been a permanently occupied site near the point of landing; people and goods could have moved directly to and from the interior (see also Gwilt this volume). The meagre direct evidence for ports or landing places has not, however, inhibited discussion of the possible significance of cross-Channel exchange. As Matthews (1996) reminds us, many 'archaeological invisibles' were probably being traded at this time, including, furs, slaves, dogs, lead, and other metals. Attention to imports remains high in some quarters of the archaeological literature, but critical approaches are warranted (cf. Willis 1994).

A first-century AD silver coin of Verica shows the prow of a Roman galley with a cornucopia (CCI 95.3428), perhaps implying that contact with Rome brought bounty and benefaction. Another coin of the period, this time a bronze issue of Cunobelin (BM 2010), depicts a distinctive high-sided ship with a sail (Muckelroy *et al.* 1978; Sealey 1997, fig. 8). The craft is not a galley and is probably a commercial, sea-going vessel. The general consensus is that the depiction of the ship evokes the significance of cross-Channel exchange at the time and that the boat itself is Gaulish or British – it is not Roman – quite possibly a kind of vessel used along both sides of the Channel. The distribution of the coin type focuses in east Kent (C. Haselgrove pers. comm.), the region nearest the Continent; in the circumstances, this is unlikely to be a coincidence.

Direct evidence of Iron Age shipping around the shores of Britain is, however, slight (Cunliffe 1991a; cf. Murphy 2002, 55), consisting of little more than the iron anchor and chain found in the interior of Bulbury Camp, Dorset (Cunnington 1884) and the lead anchor-stock from a small, late Republican vessel found at Porth Felen, off the Llŷn peninsula, Gwynedd (Boon 1977). Two possible Bronze Age wrecks are known, represented by metal finds of north French type (Muckelroy 1980): one off Moor Sand, Salcombe (Yates and May 2005), the other at Langdon Bay, immediately east of Dover (Clark 2004). The Dover boat, of Later Bronze Age date, is thought to have been a trading vessel, but, be that as it may, it may have ended its currency as a ritual deposit rather than being lost at sea or simply abandoned (Champion 2004). Comparatively few Iron Age vessels have been found in inland locations either and even the most impressive examples, such as the Brigg raft or the Hasholme logboat, were not suitable for use at sea (McGrail 1990). The only other relevant find perhaps is the remarkable gold model boat from Broighter, County Londonderry, dating to the first century BC (Warner 1991). This has a mast, benching and oars for nine sets of rowers, and a yardarm. It was deposited in an area of salt marsh by the old shoreline of Lough Foyle, together with the well-known torc and various other gold objects. Warner has argued that the hoard was a propitiatory offering to a sea god and interprets a motif on the torc as a 'sea horse'.

None of the putative 'ports' mentioned above seem to have been redistribution centres or what are often termed 'gateway communities' (cf. Cunliffe 1991a, 194). Hardly any of the imports they received reached their hinterlands, a phenomenon also observed at inland sites in 'contact' with the Continent, such as Braughing-Puckeridge (Bryant this volume). The number of imports from the Continent was probably, in any case, not that large, even in the century before the Claudian conquest (particularly away from Hertfordshire–Essex), their symbolic impact being of far more significance (cf. Haselgrove 1984; Fitzpatrick 1989; Willis 1994).

A significant amount of coastal trading along the shores of Britain is likely. Cunliffe (1988a) interprets the Mount Batten evidence to suggest such trading during the Later Iron Age, whilst Matthews (1996; 1999), building on Morris' work (e.g. 1994) has highlighted the coastal distribution of Cheshire salt transportation containers along the North Wales coast from the Dee estuary to Cardigan Bay, implying sea-borne supply.

The Hasholme logboat: a votive end?

Among the most spectacular Iron Age finds in Britain in the last 25 years is the Hasholme logboat. This was found in marine alluvium and peat within a former tidal creek system of the River Foulness, which fed into the Humber in East Yorkshire (Millett and McGrail 1987). This 12 m long vessel was constructed from the trunk of a tree felled *c.* 322–277 BC and apparently had a life of 30–50 years. Although impressive, it would have run a serious risk of capsizing in open water when conditions were other than calm. In consequence, McGrail and Millett (*ibid.*) suggest that the logboat was primarily used for conveying cargos such as local iron ore, processed iron, peat, meat, and grain within the tidal creek system, where it might even have been considered a 'symbol of power'. The place where it was lost may have been comparatively deep water at high tide.

McGrail and Millett suggested that the logboat may have been abandoned, become stranded ashore, or simply have sunk, favouring the latter. A fourth alternative is that it was a votive deposit.[20] Excavations at Fiskerton by the river Witham, Lincolnshire, have revealed fairly unequivocal evidence for the votive deposition of two modest sized Iron Age logboat dugouts (Pitts 2001), whilst in Iron Age Denmark there was a long-lived tradition of boat sacrifice associated with votive deposits (e.g. Randsborg 1995). A number of model boats dating to the first millennium BC are also known, including the sixth-century BC Roos Carr boat from Holderness, and are presumed to have had a symbolic function (Coles 1990).

The case for the Hasholme logboat being a votive deposit arises from several factors. She contained a 'cargo' of timber, was apparently riverworthy, and was found almost upright, albeit with a list. A single pottery rim sherd was found within her, perhaps a symbolic token, whilst bones thought to represent prime joints from two or more juvenile cattle were found tightly clustered outside the stern and the bow of the boat, along with a sheep skull. The fact that she was in good condition would have made her a more worthy gift than an unriverworthy vessel – at least one of the Fiskerton logboats appears to have been unused (Pitts 2001) – and, last but perhaps not least, her bow was orientated toward what was probably the nearest contemporary settlement (Millett and McGrail 1987, fig. 2).

Whether or not the logboat had a ritual end should not obscure its 'life role' as a cultural and technological expression and as an economic tool. The nature of its 'loss' is only part of a remarkable biography. It is appropriate that its resting place was in the tidal waters that had been its reason for existence and the context of its use. That this resting place became dry land is testimony to the dynamic nature of the sea–land interface.

Totes Meer (Dead Sea)?

As we have seen, the lack of marine remains from Iron Age sites in southern and central Britain would be easily explained by a shared belief that the consumption of fauna from watery environments was somehow inappropriate (cf. Dobney and Ervynck this volume). One way in which such a prohibition might conceivably have arisen in later prehistory would be if human remains were often disposed of in rivers, estuaries, and the sea, so that fish and sea birds were consequently perceived as feeding on the bodies of the dead.[21] The association of the sea with human dead undeniably affects its relationship with the living. Allied troops landing on the Gallipoli peninsula in the First World War experienced a chronic shortage of fresh water and desalination barges designed to condense sea water were deployed off the beaches to help solve the problem, but the method proved unpopular amongst the soldiers who knew that the sea here had 'been red with blood' during the contested landings earlier in the same year (Steel and Hart 1994, 308).

An association between the sea and the dead can be identified both historically and ethnographically (Bradley 2002). Despite arising separately at different times and places, this has become entwined with a number of broadly similar myths, such as the journey of the dead across water to an afterlife, and questions of water purity and corruption. In Arctic tradition, the sea was associated with the dead; prehistoric boat burials in southern Scandinavia imply a rite of burial at sea (Skaarup 1995); and some cultures associate the underworld with fish. Drawing on earlier studies, such as Kaul's (1997) analysis of Danish Bronze Age metalwork and Randsborg's (1993, 119–20) interpretation of burial iconography, Bradley (2002, 135) concludes that the association between sea and death 'was widely shared, although it might have been expressed in different ways in different regions'.

The idea that some human dead were disposed of in rivers in the British Iron Age is acquiring the status of an old chestnut, but in truth is an open question. If anything, the evidence implies that this was largely a Bronze Age practice. Many of the human skulls from the Thames are apparently of Bronze Age date (Bradley and Gordon 1988; Knüsel and Carr 1995) and skulls likely to be from Bronze Age deposits are known from the River Trent near Clifton (Knight and Howard 2004), and from the Gwent Levels (Nayling 2002). Explanation of the limited use of marine resources in much of Iron Age Britain need not therefore lie with notions of watery burial; other definitions and cultural attitudes may have been in operation.

To the land: the political economy of grain; empowerment and 'democracy'

Like fish and other marine resources (with the exception of salt), wild animals and birds apparently played a minor role in the food economies of much of Iron Age Britain, but unlike them, they do occur fairly regularly in structured deposits – not least in pits interpreted as former grain storage silos (Hill 1995b) – implying that they were in some way associated with rituals around food, fertility of the land, and the life cycle. Their inclusion in such deposits may be symbolic of attempts to manage and control nature. Bradley (2002, 152) touches on this area, noting a widespread change in the nature of votive deposits in north-west Europe during late prehistory, which he argues become more directly linked to food production, reflecting the growing importance of cereals as staples and of food storage, as well as cultural considerations of fertility. This can be seen in both the contexts of the finds and in the items chosen for burial, for instance quernstones (*ibid.*). Items from watery deposits may also relate to fertility, as with the Balachulish figurine, dating between 700–500 BC, which was found close to the sea (Armit 1997, 87–9), the idol from the Dagenham marshes (Drury 1980, 53) and the Roos Carr boat (Coles 1990).

During the first millennium BC, Iron Age societies seem to have become increasingly preoccupied with grain production, with other food sources, particularly those relating to unmanaged land, being largely marginalised. Grain was about power and empowerment. To produce it required land, labour, organisation, and suitable soils. It was readily processed to give life to humans and stock; it could be eaten, stored, traded, grown to produce next season's food, and was a means of wealth. In the apparently competitive world of the Iron Age with its expanding population there was a fundamental political economy to both grain and livestock. They could be *seen* in store or growing in fields; were managed by human input; and, within margins, their yields were both predictable and reliable: the immediate future for communities was assured. In contrast marine resources were far less flexible, more difficult to secure, and unquantifiable.

Agriculture is generally seen as increasingly controlled and centralised in the course of the Iron Age (Hill 1995a) and the ear of corn depicted on the gold staters of Cunobelin (BM 1772) could even be seen as symbolising the close association of grain with power and empowerment. At the same time, it might be suggested that there was a 'democracy' in arable production at this time, insofar as it was a common activity that was possible across much of Britain and temperate Europe; many could practise it and in doing so will have shared common experiences relating to the arable cycle and its benefits for individuals and communities.

Mixed waters: the venerated sea?

Ideology

The limited economic use of marine resources may explain why so few British Iron Age settlements are near the sea. This contrasts with the Roman period, when significantly more settlement was located close the coast, whilst the modern day settlement pattern bears striking testimony to contemporary perceptions of the sea and coast, as well as to economic factors.

As we have seen, Iron Age people may not have eaten seafood because of a cultural prohibition, and some of them may have associated the sea with the dead or disposal of the dead. This did not, however, prevent them from extracting sea-salt increasingly intensively. Hence relations with the sea may have been ideologically complicated – perhaps one could take the salt but not the fish? Alternatively, since extraction involved transforming water into salt, was it the alteration that enabled its consumption, as Richard Hingley (pers. comm.) has suggested? Or was it just that Iron Age people wanted salt from the sea but, in an uncomplicated way, were little interested in fish? One could also argue that where economically expedient – as with the acquisition of salt – groups may simply have enacted rituals to offset a normative prohibition and make the use of salt socially permissible. What is cast as sacred is often provisionally so. Today, old cemeteries may be built over and John Dent's (1982) interpretation of Iron Age burials in East Yorkshire suggests increasing economic pragmatism in the treatment of the dead there.

In their ideology and practice, Iron Age communities evidently had a complex relationship with watery contexts (e.g. Fitzpatrick 1984; Green 1989; Hedeager 1992; Willis 1997). It seems likely that in north-west Europe water in all its forms was venerated. This is not surprising given the properties and uses of water, and its symbolic potential. Our knowledge of this relationship mostly comes from freshwater environments in a terrestrial setting, where rivers may have held particular significance, e.g. as boundaries, but there is no reason why similar discourses should not have existed with regard to the sea. According to ethnographic evidence, headlands and the sea are amongst the natural places and environments assigned a sacred status by cultures (Bradley 2002). For Iron Age peoples the changing tides may have held significance, just as seasonal water courses like the Gypsey Race in East Yorkshire seem to have been important through prehistory (e.g. Fenton-Thomas 2003). The strange taste of the sea, its movement and 'life', and its ability, like other bodies of water, to reflect light, may also have set it apart.[22]

In the Graeco-Roman world, the sea was associated with deities and, as we have seen, religious significance was attached to the sea, coast, and estuaries (Braund 1996, 12–21). A pair of stone altars from the site of the Roman bridge at Newcastle-upon-Tyne, dedicated respectively to Neptune and Oceanus, exemplify this association (*RIB* 1319–1320). We will now examine the evidence suggesting that Later Iron Age communities likewise venerated the sea, or a super-natural being associated with it.

Coin iconography, Togidubnus, and Neptune

Scheers (1992) noted that a coin of Cunobelin (BM 1894) copies a Roman prototype depicting Neptune. Given the evident importance attached to the designs on Iron Age coins (Creighton 2000; Williams 2002; 2005), the selection of this specific image was presumably both intentional and culturally meaningful. As Creighton notes, several British coin types have a Neptune connection: the Cunobelin type has Neptune standing, while issues of Verica show a trident (VA 486) and a trident held in a hand (VA 487). Also of interest is the famous inscription from Chichester dedicating a temple to Neptune and Minerva and naming [T]ogidubnus client king (*RIB* 91); despite the early date, these gods were evidently known to the British king and to the guild of smiths who paid for the temple.

The coins and the inscription suggest an awareness of Roman gods amongst the native peoples of south-east England, synonymous, to a degree, with their own deities. Could it be that a linking of indigenous gods and the Roman pantheon (*interpretatio*) had occurred before AD 43 and that Roman gods were being honoured in Britain? Even if this was not the case, the references to Neptune strongly imply that a sea god was significant to Late Iron Age communities – or at least to those of them in south-east England whose territory bordered the sea.

Shrines and temples by the sea

Around the coast of southern Britain, a number of Iron Age shrines lie in close proximity to the sea, including Elms Farm, Heybridge; Hayling Island; Lancing Down, West Sussex; Worth, Kent. They appear to be Late Iron Age foundations, but may have earlier origins. In addition, several Roman temples adjacent to the coast, such as Brean Down, Somerset; Jordan Hill, Dorset; and Lydney Park, Gloucestershire, have potential Iron Age precursors. Another site that may be associated with this group is the earlier first millennium BC enclosure on Harrow Hill, West Sussex, which Manning (1995) identified as a site of ritual/religious activity.[23] Most of these sites are on elevated ground, by river estuaries and/or points where freshwater opens into the sea, locations which are known to have been of significance in past cultures (Tilley 1991, 130–3). Alexander the Great, for example, set up altars at the mouth of the Indus in 325 BC, whilst the Roman altars from the Tyne, noted above, are from the point where the river meets tidal waters. Around the coast of Britain, there is a similar tendency for early medieval churches and ecclesiastical establishments to be sited on higher ground close to where rivers issue into the sea, and indeed, at points where this confluence is visible (R. Cramp pers. comm.); this can be seen at Hartlepool, Jarrow, Seaham, Tynemouth, Wearmouth, and Whitby amongst others, although other factors such as safe anchorage may have contributed to the choice of location.

The Iron Age shrine at Hayling Island lay near to the sea, but also between the important estuaries that now constitute Langstone and Chichester harbours (King and Soffe 1991). Further east along the south coast, Lancing Down overlooks the English Channel and the estuary of the River Adur valley (Bedwin 1981). Elms Farm lies at the head of the Blackwater estuary, occupying a slight rise overlooking the river. The shrine appears to have been a key feature of the Late Iron Age site (Atkinson and Preston 1998), and as at Hayling Island and Lancing Down, a temple was constructed here in the Roman period. At Worth, the modern coastline and drainage pattern is much altered from that of late prehistory, but the site originally occupied a promontory projecting into the Wantsum Channel, which separated Kent from the Isle of Thanet until the medieval period (Holman 2005). A first-century BC enclosure ditch has been partly traced around the site and the abundant Iron Age coin finds include four examples of the ship type (BM 2010). The Roman temple here may not have been built until the fourth century AD.

The much earlier enclosure on Harrow Hill has only been subject to limited investigation. No firm evidence of occupation was forthcoming, but the faunal assemblage was highly unusual, leading Manning (1995) to suggest that it may be a ritual site. The enclosure overlooks the English Channel and in later prehistory the mouth of the Arun is likely to have been visible, although it is now 10 km away. Manning takes the view that the site was located on the hill due to the presence of earlier flint mine shafts.

The late Roman temple on Brean Down occupies an imposing spur projecting into the Bristol Channel and overlooking the mouth of the River Axe; in the Bronze Age, the site seems to have been an island, at least at high tide (Bell 1990). The location of Jordan Hill, overlooking Weymouth Bay, with the River Jordan entering the sea to the east and an extensive area of marginal wetland known as Lodmoor, to the west, is equally suggestive. No Iron Age material was found at Brean Down, almost giving the impression that the site was avoided at this period, but the discovery of two gold bracelets in a Late Bronze Age midden deposit strongly implies earlier cult activity on the promontory, whilst the finds from the preceding settlement phase included a large amount of salt-making equipment. Jordan Hill is mainly known from older work, but as well as the Roman temple, inhumations in the local Iron Age tradition and a Roman ironwork hoard have been found here, opening up the possibility of an Iron Age precursor.

Across the Channel, the Late La Tène hillfort of Bracquemont, above the chalk cliffs near Dieppe, contained the remains of a Romano-Celtic temple, since lost to erosion (Wheeler and Richardson 1957, 123–5; Fichtl 2005, 43). The site overlooks a valley draining into the sea at Puys and beyond that, just over a kilometre to the west, the Béthune issues into the sea at Dieppe; further, the enclosure itself contains a now dry but readily apparent watercourse opening to the Channel, perhaps once a seasonal waterfall or flow. The character of the finds from the site implies structured deposition and ritual practice during the Late La Tène period, hence this may be a further instance of a Late Iron Age coastal shrine at a meeting point of fresh and sea waters.

Judging from the topography and some of the finds, there may have been an Iron Age shrine at Fingringhoe Wick, Essex, on the River Colne below Colchester. This site occupies a gravel bluff on the west bank of the river south of its confluence with the Roman river and overlooking the tidal flats of the estuary (Crummy 1997). Fingringhoe is usually, probably correctly, interpreted as a conquest period supply base (Hawkes and Hull 1947; Willis 1990), but there could also have been a shrine at this location. Four Iron Age coins have definitely been found there – three bronzes of Cunobelin and a 'Dobunnic' silver coin – and a gold stater of Cunobelin is attributed to the site. Gold coins are not thought likely to be casual losses, and many seem to be votive (Haselgrove 1987), strengthening the possibility that there was some kind of cult site there. Also in Essex, but a little further down the coast, a cropmark at Langford on the bank of the River Blackwater has been interpreted as a possible Roman temple with Iron Age precursor (Wallis and Waughman 1998, 227). This site lies at the head of the Blackwater estuary, close to its confluence with the Chelmer; prior to modern silting, it may have been nearer still.

Pre-Roman shrines from Britain are generally of modest scale and rather ephemeral, and nearly all of them have been found during excavations on Roman temples and sanctuaries, which being monumentalised leave a more detectable footprint. A similar situation pertains in northern Gaul and Germany, where 'many Gallo-Roman temple complexes had a previous history as simple cult places' (Derks 1998, 177), both with and without timber structures. Such foci may be detected more easily through their associated material culture, particularly coins, than by other archaeological means. Worth and other coastal sites may belong to this latter category. The fact that we remain ignorant of many shrines that were not monumentalised in the Roman era merely underscores the significance to their local communities of those that were.

Each shrine is likely to have been instituted in the light of specific local factors, so the degree to which it is wise to generalise about them is uncertain. Nonetheless, there seem to be some shared attributes in site location and GIS analysis could well prove illuminating. The point where rivers met the sea was clearly of considerable symbolic importance, whilst it has long been recognised that many Iron Age shrines, both in Britain and northern Gaul, lie on or near what are believed to have been territorial boundaries (e.g. Roymans 1990). At a time of social change and growing threat from the Roman world, it not inconceivable that some shrines were founded specifically to reinforce acknowledged physical-territorial boundaries – which would have included the coast as much as rivers – and in other words to serve a political purpose as much as a religious one.

In the Zeeland area of the Netherlands, two temples of Roman date dedicated to Nehalennia, goddess of the North Sea are known (Green 1989; Derks 1998). Both sites, in the coastal dunes near Domburg, and near Colijnsplaat on the Oosterschelde estuary, lie in territory associated with the Morini. Nehalennia was evoked as a protector of seafarers, but is also known as a goddess of life and death. Monuments dedicated to the goddess include images of her below a sea-shell canopy, while she sometimes stands with one foot on the prow of a boat. The existing evidence is essentially second to third century AD and her origins are obscure, but the possibility that she was venerated in the region before the Roman era should certainly not be discounted, since the circumstances in which the archaeological material was recovered from the two temples were far from ideal (Green 1989).[24]

Sheepen, Camulodunum*: a place above the tide?*

The extensive Late Iron Age and early Roman site at Sheepen, Colchester, next to the River Colne, is generally seen as a major industrial and trading area, which formed the economic heart of Cunobelin's *oppidum* at *Camulodunum* (e.g. Hawkes and Hull 1947; Crummy 1997).

Whilst the report by Hawkes and Hull is exemplary for its time, the nature of some of the structural remains they found is somewhat enigmatic, even after the more recent excavations (Niblett 1985). I wonder if there is a further dimension to the emergence of such a site at this particular location. Firstly, no less than four Roman temples were constructed here after the Boudican revolt, perhaps more (Hull 1958; Crummy 1997). Was this a sacred area in the Late Iron Age as well? Several streams issuing from the spur to the south drain into the Colne at Sheepen, and could have had a religious significance. Feasting, festivals, and offerings may account for some, potentially most, of the extraordinarily rich brooch, ceramic and numismatic assemblage from the site, including a wide range of amphorae, samian and Gallo-Belgic pottery. In the Iron Age, metalworking and other productive activities were often associated with sacred locations, and religious intervention may have been considered crucial to the productive cycle (cf. Sharples 1990; Haselgrove and Millett 1997, 285–6). The archaeological record of Iron Age Britain shows that production, religion, and feasting were linked activities, and the evidence points to this being the case at Sheepen.

A second point also concerns the significance of the chosen location. Nowadays the River Colne is very modest, but it has altered since the Iron Age. The flood plain is very wide; two millennia ago there may have been areas of standing water here, whilst the river itself could have been tidal to a point not far below Sheepen (Hawkes and Hull 1947, 4).[25] Conceivably, the complex developed here precisely because this was the lowest point of the river that was not tidal. As I emphasised above, the freshwater–seawater interface seems to have

Fig. 1. The Humber estuary foreshore at South Ferriby, North Lincolnshire (photo: Steven Willis).

constituted a culturally meaningful boundary for Iron Age people. This might be because freshwater and seawater were associated with different deities; because seawater was regarded as unclean; or because of some other aspect of religious belief, any of which would nonetheless explain why Sheepen was located here and not further downstream.

In conclusion, I would suggest that the conventional economic interpretation of the rich remains found at Sheepen may *mask* the fundamental reason as to why the complex is where it is. This may have been a place of great religious significance, helping to explain why Colchester was to become the centre of the Imperial cult in the Roman province.

Votive deposits on shores and at coastal margins

Whilst many of the fine Iron Age objects from British rivers are uncontroversially regarded as votive deposits (e.g. Fitzpatrick 1984; this volume), Iron Age finds from the foreshore have had a lesser profile. In the past, many were assumed to have been eroded from terrestrial locations, whilst more recently numbers may have been artificially inflated by metal detectorists wishing to give a neutral provenance to their finds. It is beyond doubt, however, that some objects were deliberately deposited on the shore or coastal margin. O'Sullivan (2001, 127–8) notes likely Irish Late Bronze Age votive finds from the estuarine marshes of the Fergus and Shannon estuaries, proposing that it was in these liminal localities that later prehistoric peoples contacted and negotiated with spirits, deities or ancestors. The Broighter hoard may also belong to this category, as may the Dagenham idol.

An extensive haul of Iron Age coins and brooches has come from the Humber foreshore at South Ferriby (Fig. 1), a large proportion of which were gathered around a hundred years ago by a local man of keen eye and interest known as 'Coin Tommy' (e.g. Allen 1963; Creighton 1990). These objects are usually assumed to have come from an *oppidum* above the river cliff, washed down by the vigorously shifting channels of the Humber, which is over 1 mile across, tidal and often rough at this point, but an alternative explanation is that they were deposited on the beach as votive offerings. There are other possibilities, however: for instance, they could be from an eroded shrine or temple; indeed, it may be co-incidence, but a medieval 'holy well' lies just a few tens of metres inland from this foreshore.[26]

May's (1992) review of Iron Age coinage from East Yorkshire revealed the striking number of coin finds from the beach and coastal margin of Holderness, particularly between Bridlington Bay and Spurn, at least some of which are older discoveries, pre-dating metal detector use. Most – but not all – are beach finds, and May makes the point that the comparatively high number of coins from this shoreline compared to inland may arise in part from beach walking and collecting. Even so we have to account for how the coins got there, and the fact that bullion coins are present perhaps increases the possibility that some or all of them were votive items intentionally placed on or by the shore by Iron Age people. If on the other hand, all the coins have eroded from a site (or sites) along the Holderness coast, their source – as at South Ferriby – may have been a first-century AD shrine or temple by the shore.

Further south, the picture appears broadly similar. The numerous Iron Age coin finds from Selsey Bill are nearly all of gold and there is little doubt that they were intentionally deposited at the coastal margin, apparently at several separate locations and at different points in time (Haselgrove 1987, 119). Haselgrove also noted a higher than expected proportion of Iron Age gold coins from within one kilometre of the modern coastline of south-east England, particularly multiple finds, and inferred that a proportion of 'wet finds' were directly placed in the water (*ibid.*, 115–17). A significant number of coins deposited near the coast are of Gaulish origin, raising the intriguing question of whether coins from 'across the sea' were perceived and treated differently from those minted in Britain.

Conclusion: elements in the past

Iron Age Britain is characterised by its patchwork of regional and sub-regional differences and similarities. Given this background and the variation in the coastline itself, differing cultural attitudes and uses of the sea might be anticipated. At both individual and group level, a plurality of relations with marine environments must have existed, depending on both immediate and general circumstances. The extent to which such environments were 'taskscapes' (cf. Ingold 1986) is unclear given the lack of a direct Iron Age signature on all but a tiny minority of them; such changeable environments do not lend themselves to enduring signs that we can observe archaeologically in the same way as on managed land.

Although the relative neglect of the sea, beaches, and coastal margins in Iron Age studies is in part due to the partial nature of the evidence, the picture emerging from much of Britain is fairly clear. There was only limited exploitation of marine resources, even where sites lie close to the sea. Notable exceptions are sea-salt extraction and coastal grazing, both important seasonal activities. In northern and western Scotland, not least on the islands, fishing and perhaps the taking of birds and eggs, were evidently significant economic activities for some. Hingley (1992, 42) noted that because of this economic relevance, 'ritual acts probably also drew upon concepts linked with the acts of hunting and fishing', forming a marked contrast to the rest of Britain and thus a valuable topic for future research.

The rarity of marine life from structured deposits of Iron Age date is striking and contrasts with Roman Britain, where some of the most prominent assemblages testifying to the exploitation and consumption of seafood come from structured, potentially ritual, deposits. Although fish and shellfish were fairly widely consumed in the Roman period, much of the evidence may relate to specific events or festivals. Cultural factors were as key to when marine life was consumed in the Roman period as they were to its avoidance in the Iron Age. To paraphrase Hill (1995b), fish and shellfish might be 'good to eat but only at the right time'. Social regulation operated in the catching and consumption of seafood in Roman times in much the same way that it does in the contemporary world.

The resources of the sea and the sea margin were not centrally important in the economy of coastal areas in Iron Age central and southern Britain. Outside Atlantic Britain, people rarely seem to have chosen to live on the coast and then generally seasonally not permanently. The main activities attested are salt production and livestock grazing, often on quite a large scale; others probably included the collection of resources such as reeds and the procurement of peat for fuel. In some cases, these activities were probably closely integrated, just as they were restricted to certain environments.

The sea clearly had a place in the way that Iron Age people evaluated the world. Several Late Iron Age shrines are located with respect to the sea and the freshwater–seawater interface and reconsideration of Iron Age attitudes to the sea permits us to advance new interpretations of two icons of the period: the Hasholme logboat and the Sheepen site. Coasts may have been appropriate and even 'necessary' places for depositing votive material, and more detailed studies may elucidate how such practices evolved during the Iron Age.

Encouragingly a new interest is emerging in the archaeology of coastlines. To date this has been largely a product of heritage cataloguing and management programmes, but these have already led to some research initiatives. There is great potential for exploring past human relations with the sea and coastal margins; in the case of the Iron Age, pursuit of these aspects will help offset the hitherto landward gaze of so much of our work.

Acknowledgements

This paper evolved from my presentation at the Durham seminar. I would like to acknowledge the support of Colin Haselgrove, Tom Moore, and Rachel Pope. Richard Hingley and an anonymous referee made helpful comments on the text. Mark Curteis, J.D. Hill, Jacqui Huntley, Peter Murphy, and Niall Sharples all provided helpful pointers, which I followed up, whilst Keith Dobney, Anton Ervynck, and Wim Van Neer kindly made papers available to me in advance of publication. John Creighton supplied details of the Neptune coins and those with ship images. Nick Cooper, J.D. Hill, and

Rachel Seager Smith helped with queries. Martin Millett discussed the Hasholme logboat with me. I am grateful to Christopher Chaffin for reminding me of the significance of the Isiac finds from London.

Notes

1. The paintings cited in this paper illustrate ways in which humans understand and interact with the sea. These paintings are well known and familiar, and thus are not passive images but are today a mental reference point in how we conceive of the sea. Images of most of them can easily be found on the Web.
2. Oil, 1870, Tate Gallery, London.
3. Oil, 1809, Schloss Charlottenburg, Berlin.
4. 1881, Ruth Chandler Wilkinson Gallery, California, and Harvard University respectively.
5. 'Under the Cliff', 1940, Ashmolean Museum, depicts a ruined Nazi bomber below chalk cliffs and 'Raider on the Shore' 1940, Corporation Art Gallery Glasgow, shows another bomber on a beach below cliffs resembling a Dorset scene. Another wartime Nash watercolour entitled 'Deadmarch, Dymchurch', illustrating a downed aircraft in the sea, was lost when the ship conveying it to an exhibition in America was sunk by hostile action (Eates 1973, 77).
6. A Hull trawler that sank inexplicably in the Norwegian Sea in the mid 1970s with the death of all on board (BBC Radio 4 News, 17 Jan, 2004).
7. *The Independent*, 18 Jan, 2004.
8. Oil, 1925–37, York City Art Gallery.
9. Including 'Coast Scene, Dymchurch', oil, 1921, T.E. Lawrence Collection; 'The Wall Against the Sea', oil, 1922, Carnegie Institute; 'The Shore', oil, 1923, Leeds City Art Gallery; and 'Dymchurch Wall', watercolour, 1923, private collection.
10. The construction of sea defences at Dymchurch in 1844–6 led to the discovery of extensive Roman remains between the sea and the marsh, including burials, together with apparent salt working debris (Cunliffe 1988b); much evidence must now be lost to the sea. The British Museum collections include an intact Stanfield 67 samian flagon, recorded as found when making a sea wall at Dymchurch in 1844. Stanfield 67 flagons are uncommon and were presumably of some value; the type is closely associated with burials and structured deposits (Willis 2005). The findspot would appear to have been a natural boundary between land and sea in the mid Roman period.
11. The Ferens Art Gallery, Hull, has a fine collection of paintings with a maritime theme, as do many other coastal cities in Britain. Messages repeated by these paintings include boats and ships as magnificent creations; the sea as a source of wealth through harvest; the sea as a means to exchange and commerce; the role of coasts and the sea in warfare; danger and drama at sea; and the constitution of social inequalities around human relations with the sea.
12. A similar dichotomy exists in the Low Countries; the situation in Flanders mirrors southern Britain, whereas there is a fair amount of archaeological evidence for the later prehistoric consumption of fish in the Netherlands (see Dobney and Ervynck this volume and Van Neer and Ervynck forthcoming).
13. The species disappeared from Britain in the twentieth century, but has recently been re-introduced on the west coast of Scotland.
14. The archaeology of this consumption would benefit from further scrutiny, most obviously by reassessing the distribution of amphorae associated with these substances, although amphora re-use may complicate investigation.
15. Apart from the lobster claws, the fill of the shaft (in Insula 4, Building 8, Room 5) yielded 'large quantities of oyster-shells and a number of shells of mussel and whelk' and numerous artefacts including samian, coarse pottery, and glass vessels. The shaft was 11.5 m deep – not necessarily deep enough to have reached water in Roman times.
16. The faunal assemblage recovered from this feature (in Insula 24, possibly 25) was atypical of the site. It included a high proportion of wild species and immature domestic types (including barnacle goose, crow, jackdaw, young dogs, kittens, and piglets). Only the eagle skull was present, showing signs of decapitation and with the beak missing (Baxter 1992). A full list of finds of white-tailed sea eagle from Romano-British sites is given in Parker (1988).
17. According to recently obtained radiocarbon dates, the eagles died in the later third millennium BC, up to 1000 years after the tomb was built, although there is no doubt they represent a deliberate deposit (*British Archaeology* January–February 2006, 6). At least eight birds are represented, perhaps as many as 20.
18. Two further instances of structured deposition may be cited. Among the votive offerings in the third-century AD *mithraeum* at Tienen, Flanders, were the remains of fish sauce (*garum*), containing herring, flatfish, spratt, and other North Sea species (Vanderhoeven *et al.* 2001). At Richborough, a subterranean structure, which was interpreted as a cold storage cellar (Bushe-Fox 1949) but may be better seen as a shrine, yielded substantial deposits of oyster shells, presumably a residue from feasting.
19. Matthews (1999) notes a number of other possible 'port' sites in western Britain.
20. Martin Millett has also, independently, recently considered this possibility.
21. I am obliged to Niall Sharples for this suggestion.
22. As the anonymous referee observed, water may have been a medium to communicate with other worlds. This property may have been more important than any quality of water itself. Equally, if water was not itself sacred, making salt need not have been symbolically charged in the same way as eating fish.
23. As I noted above, the findspot of the much earlier Balachulish figurine lay in close proximity to the sea, whilst the context makes it likely that the figurine was a significant component of a shrine (Armit 1997, 87–9).
24. A Roman shrine to Isis appears to have existed by the Thames in London. Isis had many watery associations and her cult became popular across the empire. There was a close connection between the Isis myth, the Nile, and safe seafaring; the Tiber became a proxy Nile, while Nile water was extensively used in rituals (Witt 1997, 70). In 1912, a pot bearing the graffito LONDINI AD FANVM ISIDIS ('London at the temple of Isis') was found in Tooley Street, Southwark, close to the Thames (*ibid.*, fig. 21), whilst an altar recovered during work on the Roman riverside wall records that a propraetorian legate had ordered the temple of Isis to be restored after it had collapsed through old age (Wright *et al.* 1976, 378–9). Possibly by the Thames there is an instance of *interpretatio romana*?
25. Whether Sheepen could conveniently be reached by river boats is unclear, but this may not be particularly important, as river transport will certainly have been possible to a point no more than 1–2 km downstream.
26. See Creighton and Willis forthcoming; I am grateful to Colin Haselgrove for discussion of these finds.

Bibliography

Allen, D.F. 1963. Celtic coins from South Ferriby, *Hull Museum Publication* 214, 33–36.

Allen, M.J. and Gardiner, J. 2000. *Our Changing Coast: A Survey of the Intertidal Archaeology of Langstone Harbour, Hampshire*. York: Council for British Archaeology Research Report 124.

Alvey, R.C. 1996. Marine molluscs, in May 1996, 171.

Armit, I. 1997. *Celtic Scotland*. London: Batsford.

Armour-Chelu, M. 1991. The bird remains, in N. Sharples, *Maiden Castle: Excavations and Field Survey 1985–6*, 147. London: English Heritage Archaeological Report 19.

Atkinson, M. and Preston, S.J. 1998. The late Iron Age and Roman settlement at Elms Farm, Heybridge, Essex, excavations 1993–5: an interim report, *Britannia* 29, 85–110.

Baker, F.T. 1960. The Iron Age salt industry in Lincolnshire, *Lincolnshire Architectural and Archaeological Society Reports and Papers* 8, 26–34.

Baxter, I.L. 1992. An eagle skull from an excavation in High Street, Leicester, *Transactions of the Leicestershire Archaeological and Historical Society* 67, 101–105.

Bedwin, O. 1980. Excavations at Chanctonbury Ring, Wiston, West Sussex 1977, *Britannia* 11, 173–221.

Bedwin, O. 1981. Excavations at Lancing Down, West Sussex 1980, *Sussex Archaeological Collections* 119, 37–56.

Bell, M. 1977. *Excavations at Bishopstone* (*Sussex Archaeological Collections* 115).

Bell, M. 1981. Seaweed as a prehistoric resource, in D. Brothwell and G. Dimbleby (eds), *Environmental Aspects of Coasts and Islands*, 117–126. Oxford: British Archaeological Reports International Series 94.

Bell, M. 1990. *Brean Down. Excavations 1983–1987*. London: English Heritage Archaeological Report 15.

Bell, M., Caseldine, A. and Neumann, H. 2000. *Prehistoric Intertidal Archaeology in the Welsh Severn Estuary*. York: Council for British Archaeology Research Report 120.

Boon, G.C. 1977. A Graeco-Roman anchor-stock from north Wales, *Antiquaries Journal* 57, 10–30.

Bradley, R. 2002. *An Archaeology of Natural Places*. London: Routledge.

Bradley, R. and Gordon, K. 1988. Human skulls from the River Thames, their dating and significance, *Antiquity* 62, 503–509.

Braund, D. 1996. *Ruling Roman Britain*. London: Routledge.

Brewster, T.C.M. 1963. *The Excavation of Staple Howe*. Malton: East Riding Archaeological Research Committee.

Bushe-Fox, J.P. 1949. *Fourth Report on the Excavations of the Roman Fort at Richborough Kent*. Oxford: Report of the Research Committee of the Society of Antiquaries of London 16.

Buxton, R. 1994. *Imaginary Greece. The Contexts of Mythology*. Cambridge: Cambridge University Press.

Cartledge, J. and Grimbly, C. 1999. The bird bones, in Parker Pearson and Sharples 1999, 282–288.

Ceron-Carrasco, R. 2000. The marine fauna, in Haselgrove and McCullagh 2000, 56–57.

Champion, T. 2004. The deposition of the boat, in Clark 2004, 276–281.

Childers, E. 1998. *The Riddle of the Sands*. Oxford: Oxford University Press.

Chowne, P., Cleal, R.M.J. and Fitzpatrick, A.P. with Andrews, P. 2001. *Excavations at Billingborough, Lincolnshire, 1975–8: A Bronze–Iron Age Settlement and Salt-working Site*. Salisbury: East Anglian Archaeology Report 94.

Clark, P. (ed.) 2004. *The Dover Bronze Age Boat*. Swindon: English Heritage.

Coles, B.J. 1990. Anthropomorphic wooden figurines from Britain and Ireland, *Proceedings of the Prehistoric Society* 56, 315–334.

Coles, B.J. 1998. Doggerland: a speculative survey, *Proceedings of the Prehistoric Society* 64, 45–81.

Collis, J.R. (ed.) 2001. *Society and Settlement in Iron Age Europe* (*Actes du XVIIIe Colloque de l'AFEAF, Winchester, April 1994*). Sheffield: J.R. Collis Publications.

Connor, A. and Buckley, R. 1999. *Roman and Medieval Occupation in Causeway Lane, Leicester, Excavations 1980 and 1991*. Leicester: Leicester Archaeology Monograph 5.

Cooper, H.A. 1986. *Winslow Homer Watercolours*. New Haven: Yale University Press.

Cracknell, S. 1994. Discussion, in S. Cracknell and C. Mahany (eds), *Roman Alcester: Southern Extramural Area 1964–1966 Excavations Part 2: Finds and Discussion*, 249–259. York: Council for British Archaeology Research Report 97.

Creighton, J. 1990. The Humber frontier in the first century AD, in Ellis and Crowther 1990, 182–198.

Creighton, J. 2000. *Coins and Power in Late Iron Age Britain*. Cambridge: Cambridge University Press.

Creighton, J. and Willis, S.H. forthcoming. Excavations and survey at Redcliff-North Ferriby, East Yorkshire.

Crummy, P. 1992. *Excavations at Culver Street, the Gilberd School and other Sites in Colchester 1971–85*. Colchester: Colchester Archaeological Report 6.

Crummy, P. 1997. *City of Victory*. Colchester: Colchester Archaeological Trust.

Cunliffe, B. 1971. *Excavations at Fishbourne 1961–1969, Vols 1–2*. Leeds: Reports of the Research Committee of the Society of Antiquaries of London 26–27.

Cunliffe, B. 1987. *Hengistbury Head, Dorset, Vol. 1: The Prehistoric and Roman Settlement, 3500 BC to AD 500*. Oxford: Oxford University Committee for Archaeology Monograph 13.

Cunliffe, B. 1988a. *Mount Batten, Plymouth. A Prehistoric and Roman Port*. Oxford: Oxford University Committee for Archaeology Monograph 26.

Cunliffe, B. 1988b. Romney Marsh in the Roman Period, in Eddison and Green 1988, 83–87.

Cunliffe, B. 1991a. *Iron Age Communities in Britain* (3rd edn). London: Routledge and Kegan Paul.

Cunliffe, B. 1991b. Maritime traffic between the Continent and Britain, in Kruta *et al.* 1991, 573–578.

Cunliffe, B. 1995. *Iron Age Britain*. London: Batsford.

Cunliffe, B. and Hawkins, S. 1988. The shell midden deposits, in Cunliffe 1988a, 35–38.

Cunnington, E. 1884. On a hoard of bronze, iron and other objects found in Bulbury Camp, Dorset, *Archaeologia* 48, 115–120.

Davidson, A. (ed.) 2002. *The Coastal Archaeology of Wales*. York: Council for British Archaeology Research Report 131.

Davies, R.W. 1971. The Roman military diet, *Britannia* 2, 122–142.

Dennis, G. 1978. 1–7 St Thomas Street, in *Southwark Excavations 1972–*

1974, 291–422. London: London and Middlesex Archaeological Society and Surrey Archaeological Society Joint Publication 1.

Dent, J.S. 1982. Cemeteries and settlement patterns of the Iron Age on the Yorkshire Wolds, *Proceedings of the Prehistoric Society* 48, 437–457.

Derks, T. 1998. *Gods, Temples and Ritual Practices. The Transformation of Religious Ideas and Values in Roman Gaul.* Amsterdam: Amsterdam Archaeological Studies 2.

Dobney, K. 2001. A place at the table: the role of vertebrate zooarchaeology within a Roman research agenda for Britain, in S. James and M. Millett (eds), *Britons and Romans: Advancing an Archaeological Agenda*, 36–45. York: Council for British Archaeology Research Report 125.

Dobney, K., Hall, A. and Kenward, H. 1999. It's all garbage… A review of bioarchaeology in the four English *colonia* towns, in H. Hurst (ed.), *The Coloniae of Roman Britain: New Studies and a Review*, 15–35. Portsmouth, Rhode Island: Journal of Roman Archaeology Supplementary Series 36.

Drury, P.J. 1980. The early and middle phases of the Iron Age in Essex, in D.G. Buckley (ed.), *Archaeology in Essex to AD 1500*, 47–54. York: Council for British Archaeology Research Report 34.

Eates, M. 1973. *Paul Nash, the Master of the Image 1889–1946*. London: John Murray.

Eddison J. and Green C. (eds), 1988. *Romney Marsh: Evolution, Occupation, Reclamation.* Oxford: Oxford University Committee for Archaeology Monograph 24.

Edwards, J. 1984. *The Roman Cookery of Apicius Translated and Adapted for the Modern Kitchen.* London: Rider.

Ellis, S. and Crowther, D.R. (eds) 1990. *Humber Perspectives: A Region through the Ages.* Hull: Hull University Press.

Evans, C. 1997. Hydraulic communities: Iron Age enclosure in the East Anglia fenlands, in Gwilt and Haselgrove 1997, 216–227.

Fairhurst, H. 1984. *Excavations at Crosskirk Broch, Caithness.* Edinburgh: Society of Antiquaries of Scotland Monograph 3.

Fenton, A. 1978. *The Northern Isles: Orkney and Shetland.* Edinburgh: John Donald.

Fenton, A. 1986. *The Shape of the Past 2: Essays in Scottish Ethnology.* Edinburgh: John Donald.

Fenton-Thomas, C. 2003. *Late Prehistoric and Early Historic Landscapes on the Yorkshire Chalk.* Oxford: British Archaeological Reports British Series 350.

Fenwick, H., Fletcher, W., and Thomas, G. 1999. A new Iron Age Enclosure from Kelk, near Driffield; recent findings of the Humber Wetlands Project. Paper presented to the Iron Age Research Students Seminar, Southampton.

Fichtl, S. 2005. *La ville celtique. Les oppida de 150 av. J.-C. à 15 ap. J.-C* (2nd edn). Paris: Editions Errance.

Fitzpatrick, A.P. 1984. The deposition of La Tène Iron Age metalwork in watery contexts in southern England, in B. Cunliffe and D. Miles (eds), *Aspects of the Iron Age in Central Southern Britain,* 178–190. Oxford: Oxford University Committee for Archaeology Monograph 2.

Fitzpatrick, A.P. 1989. *Cross-Channel Relations in the British Later Iron Age.* Unpublished Ph.D. thesis, University of Durham.

Fitzpatrick, A.P. 2001. Cross-Channel exchange, Hengistbury Head, and the end of hillforts, in Collis 2001, 82–97.

Gardiner, M. 1997. The exploitation of sea mammals in medieval England: bones and their social context, *Archaeological Journal* 154, 173–195.

Grant, A. 2000. Diet, economy and ritual: evidence from the faunal remains, in M.G. Fulford and J. Timby, *Late Iron Age and Roman Silchester: Excavations on the Site of the Forum-Basilica, 1977, 1980–86*, 425–482. London: Britannia Monograph 15.

Green, M. 1989. *Symbol and Image in Celtic Religious Art.* London: Routledge.

Griffith, F.M. 1988. *Devon's Past: An Aerial View.* Exeter: Devon Books.

Gwilt, A. and Haselgrove, C. (eds) 1997. *Reconstructing Iron Age Societies.* Oxford: Oxbow Monograph 71.

Halkon, P. and Millett, M. 1999. *Rural Settlement and Industry: Studies in the Iron Age and Roman Archaeology of Lowland East Yorkshire.* Leeds: Yorkshire Archaeological Report 4.

Hambleton, E. and Stallibrass, S. 2000. Faunal remains, in Haselgrove and McCullagh 2000, 147–157.

Harcourt, R. 1979. The animal bones, in G. Wainwright, *Gussage All Saints: An Iron Age Settlement in Dorset*, 150–161. London: Department of the Environment Archaeology Report 10.

Harman, M. 1996. Birds, in May 1996, 163–164.

Hartridge, R. 1978. Excavations at the prehistoric and Romano-British site on Slonk Hill, Shoreham, Sussex, *Sussex Archaeological Collections* 116, 69–141.

Haselgrove, C. 1984. 'Romanization' before the Conquest: Gaulish precedents and British consequences, in T.F.C. Blagg and A.C. King (eds), *Military and Civilian in Roman Britain*, 5–63. Oxford: British Archaeological Reports British Series 136.

Haselgrove, C. 1987. *Iron Age Coinage in South-East England: The Archaeological Context.* Oxford: British Archaeological Reports British Series 174.

Haselgrove, C. 1989. The later Iron Age in southern Britain and beyond, in M. Todd (ed.), *Research on Roman Britain 1960–89,* 1–18. London: Britannia Monograph 11.

Haselgrove, C. 2001. Iron Age Britain and its European setting, in Collis 2001, 37–72.

Haselgrove, C. and McCullagh, R. (eds) 2000. *An Iron Age Coastal Community in East Lothian: The Excavation of Two Later Prehistoric Enclosure Complexes at Fishers Road, Port Seton, 1994–5.* Edinburgh: Scottish Trust for Archaeological Research Monograph 6.

Haselgrove, C. and Millett, M. 1997. Verlamion reconsidered, in Gwilt and Haselgrove 1997, 283–296.

Haselgrove, C. and Wigg-Wolf, D. (eds) 2005. *Ritual and Iron Age Coinage.* Mainz: Studien zu Fundmünzen der Antike 20.

Haselgrove, C., Armit, I., Champion, T., Creighton, J., Gwilt, A., Hill, J.D., Hunter, F. and Woodward, A. 2001. *Understanding the British Iron Age: An Agenda for Action.* Salisbury: Wessex Archaeology.

Hawkes, C.F.C. and Hull, M.R. 1947. *Camulodunum. First Report on the Excavations at Colchester 1930–1939.* Oxford: Report of the Research Committee of the Society of Antiquaries of London 14.

Hayman, P. and Burton, P. 1982. *The Birdlife of Britain.* London: Emblem.

Healey, H. 1999. An Iron Age salt-making site at Helpringham Fen, Lincolnshire: Excavations by the Car Dyke Research Group, 1972–7, in A. Bell, D. Gurney and H. Healey, *Lincolnshire Salterns: Excavations at Helpringham, Holbeach St Johns and Bicker Haven*, 1–19. Sleaford: East Anglian Archaeology Report 89.

Hedeager, L. 1992. *Iron-Age Societies: From Tribe to State in Northern Europe, 500 BC to AD 700*. Oxford: Blackwell.

Hedges, J. 1984. *Tomb of the Eagles*. London: John Murray.

Hill, J.D. 1995a. The pre-Roman Iron Age in Britain and Ireland: an overview, *Journal of World Prehistory* 9, 47–98.

Hill, J.D. 1995b. *Ritual and Rubbish in the Iron Age of Wessex*. Oxford: British Archaeological Reports British Series 242.

Hingley, R. 1992. Society in Scotland from 700 BC to AD 200, *Proceedings of the Society of Antiquaries of Scotland* 122, 7–53.

Hingley, R. 1997. Iron, ironworking and regeneration, in Gwilt and Haselgrove 1997, 9–18.

Hodgson, N., Stobbs, G.C. and Van der Veen, M. 2001. An Iron Age settlement and remains of earlier prehistoric date beneath South Shields Roman fort, Tyne and Wear, *Archaeological Journal* 158, 62–160.

Holman, D. 2005. Iron Age coinage from Worth, Kent, and other possible evidence of ritual deposition in Kent, in Haselgrove and Wigg-Wolf 2005, 265–285.

Hull, M.R. 1958. *Roman Colchester*. Oxford: Report of the Research Committee of the Society of Antiquaries of London 20.

Huntley, J. 2000. The charred and waterlogged plant remains, in Haselgrove and McCullagh 2000, 157–170.

Ingold, T. 1986. *The Appropriation of Nature*. Manchester: Manchester University Press.

Jobey, G. 1967. Excavation at Tynemouth Priory and Castle, *Archaeologia Aeliana* (Ser. 4) 45, 33–104.

Jones, A.K.G. 1978. The fish remains, in Dennis 1978, 414–416.

Kaul, F. 1997. Skibet og solhesten. Om nye fund af bronzealderens religiose kunst, *Nationalmuseets Arbejdsmark*, 101–114.

King, A. and Soffe, G. 1991. Hayling Island, in R.F.J. Jones (ed.), *Britain in the Roman Period: Recent Trends*, 111–113. Sheffield: J.R. Collis Publications.

Knight, D. and Howard, A.J. 2004. *Trent Valley Landscapes: The Archaeology of 500,000 Years of Change*. Great Dunham: Heritage Marketing and Publications Ltd.

Knüsel, C.J. and Carr, G.C. 1995. On the significance of the crania from the river Thames and its tributaries, *Antiquity* 69, 162–169.

Kruta V., Frey O.-H., Raftery B. and Szabó M. (eds.). 1991. *The Celts*. London: Thames and Hudson.

Lane, T. and Morris, E.L. (eds) 2001. *A Millennium of Saltmaking: Prehistoric and Romano-British Salt Production in the Fenland*. Sleaford: Lincolnshire Archaeology and Heritage Reports 4.

McGrail, S. 1983. Cross-channel seamanship and navigation in the late 1st millennium BC, *Oxford Journal of Archaeology* 2, 299–337.

McGrail, S. 1990. Early boats of the Humber basin, in Ellis and Crowther 1990, 109–130.

McGrail, S. 1995. Celtic seafaring and transport, in M. Green (ed.), *The Celtic World*, 254–281. London: Routledge.

Major, H.J. 1982. Iron Age triangular loomweights, *Essex Archaeology and History* 14, 111–132.

Maltby, J.M. 1995. Animal bone, in G.J. Wainwright and S.M. Davies, *Balksbury Camp, Hampshire. Excavations 1973 and 1981*, 83–87. London: English Heritage Archaeological Report 4.

Manning, W.H. 1995. Ritual or refuse: the Harrow Hill enclosure reconsidered, in B. Raftery (ed.), *Sites and Sights of the Iron Age*, 133–138. Oxford: Oxbow Monograph 56.

Markey, M., Wilkes, E. and Darvill, T. 2002. Poole Harbour: an Iron Age port, *Current Archaeology* 181, 7–11.

Matthews, K.J. 1996. Iron Age sea-borne trade in Liverpool Bay, in P. Carrington (ed.), *'Where Deva Spreads Her Wizard Stream': Trade and the Port of Chester*, 12–23. Chester: Chester City Council.

Matthews, K.J. 1999. The Iron Age of North-West England and Irish Sea trade, in B. Bevan (ed.), *Northern Exposure: Interpretative Devolution and the Iron Ages in Britain*, 173–195. Leicester: Leicester Archaeology Monograph 4.

May, J. 1992. Iron Age coins in Yorkshire, in Mays 1992, 93–111.

May, J. 1996. *Dragonby. Report on Excavations at an Iron Age and Romano-British Settlement in North Lincolnshire*. Oxford: Oxbow Monograph 61.

Mays, M. (ed.) 1992. *Celtic Coinage: Britain and Beyond*. Oxford: British Archaeological Reports British Series 222.

Millett, M. 1990. *The Romanization of Britain*. Cambridge: Cambridge University Press.

Millett, M. and McGrail, S. 1987. The archaeology of the Hasholme Logboat, *Archaeological Journal* 144, 69–155.

Monckton, A. 1999. Oysters, in Connor and Buckley 1999, 337–341.

Moore, H. and Wilson, G. 2005. An Iron Age 'shrine' on Westray, *Current Archaeology* 199, 328–332.

Morris, E.L. 1994. Production and distribution of pottery and salt in Iron Age Britain: a review, *Proceedings of the Prehistoric Society* 60, 371–393.

Muckelroy, K. 1980. Two Bronze Age cargoes in British waters, *Antiquity* 54, 100–109.

Muckelroy, K., Haselgrove, C. and Nash, D. 1978. A pre-Roman coin from Canterbury and the ship represented on it, *Proceedings of the Prehistoric Society* 44, 439–444.

Murphy, K. 2002. The archaeological resource: chronological overview to 1500 AD, in Davidson 2002, 45–64.

Murphy, P.L. 1986. Summary environmental report, in J.J. Wymer, Early Iron Age pottery and a triangular loomweight from Redgate Hill, Hunstanton, *Norfolk Archaeology* 39, 294–296 (286–296).

Murphy, P.L. 1992. Environmental studies: Culver Street, in Crummy 1992, 273–287.

Nayling, N. 2002. The Gwent Levels, in Davidson 2002, 109–104.

Niblett, R. 1985. *Sheepen: An Early Roman Industrial Site at Camulodunum*. London: Council for British Archaeology Research Report 57.

Nicholson, R. 1999. Fish remains, in Connor and Buckley 1999, 333–337.

O'Sullivan, A. 2001. *Foragers, Farmers and Fishers in a Coastal Landscape: An Intertidal Archaeological Survey of the Shannon Estuary*. Dublin: Royal Irish Academy Discovery Programme Monograph 5.

Oswald, F. 1936–37. *Index of Figure-Types on Terra Sigillata ('Samian Ware')*. Liverpool: University Press of Liverpool.

Owen, O. 1999. *The Sea Road: A Viking Voyage through Scotland*. Edinburgh: Historic Scotland.

Palmer-Brown, C. 1993. Bronze Age salt production at Tetney, *Current Archaeology* 136, 143–145.

Parker, A.J. 1988. The birds of Roman Britain, *Oxford Journal of Archaeology* 7, 197–226.

Parker Pearson, M. and Sharples, N. 1999. *Between Land and Sea. Excavations at Dun Vulan, South Uist*. Sheffield: Sheffield Academic Press.

Partridge, C. 1979. Excavations at Puckeridge and Braughing 1975–9, *Hertfordshire Archaeology* 7, 28–132.

Pitts, M. 2001. Fiskerton, *Current Archaeology* 176, 327–329.

Plant, M. 1952. *The Domestic Life of Scotland in the 18th Century*. Edinburgh: Edinburgh University Press.

Pryor, F.M.M. 1996. Sheep, stockyards and field systems: Bronze Age livestock populations in the Fenlands of eastern England, *Antiquity* 70, 313–324.

Pryor, F.M.M. 2001. *The Flag Fen Basin: Archaeology and Environment of a Fenland Landscape*. Swindon: English Heritage Archaeological Reports.

Randsborg, K. 1993. Kivik. Archaeology and iconography, *Acta Archaeologica* 64, 1–147.

Randsborg, K. 1995. *Hjortspring. Warfare and Sacrifice in Early Europe*. Aarhus: Aarhus University Press.

Rippon, S. 1996. *Gwent Levels: The Evolution of a Wetland Landscape*. York: Council for British Archaeology Research Report 105.

Robinson, D. 2001. Natural regions, in S. Bennett and N. Bennett (eds), *An Historical Atlas of Lincolnshire* (2nd edn). Chichester: Phillimore.

Robinson, G. 1988. Sea defence and land drainage of Romney Marsh, in Eddison and Green 1988, 162–166.

Roymans, N. 1990. *Tribal Societies in Northern Gaul*. Amsterdam: Cingula 12.

Scheers, S. 1992. Celtic coin types in Britain and their Mediterranean origins, in Mays 1992, 33–46.

Sealey, P.R. 1995. New light on the salt industry and Red Hills of prehistoric and Roman Essex, *Essex Archaeology and History* 26, 65–81.

Sealey, P.R. 1997. The Iron Age in Essex, in O. Bedwin (ed.), *The Archaeology of Essex*, 46–68. Chelmsford: Essex County Council.

Serjeantson, D. 1988. Archaeological and ethnographic evidence for seabird exploitation in Scotland, *Archaeozoologia* 11, 209–224.

Serjeantson, D. 1991. Bird bone, in B. Cunliffe and C. Poole, *Danebury: An Iron Age Hillfort in Hampshire, Vol. 5. The Excavations 1979–1988: The Finds*, 459–481. London: Council for British Archaeology Research Report 73.

Sharples, N. 1990. Late Iron Age society and continental trade in Dorset, in A. Duval, J.P. Le Bihan, and Y. Menez (eds), *Les Gaulois d'Armorique. La fin de l'âge du Fer en Europe Tempérée* (*Actes du XIIe Colloque de l'AFEAF, Quimper 1988*), 299–304. Rennes: Revue Archéologique de l'Ouest Supplément 3.

Skaarup, J. 1995. Stone Age burials in boats, in O. Crumlin-Pedersen and B. Thye (eds), *The Ship as Symbol in Prehistoric and Medieval Scandinavia*. Copenhagen: Nationalmuseet.

Smith, H. 1999. The plant remains, in Parker Pearson and Sharples 1999, 297–336.

Steel, N. and Hart, P. 1994. *Defeat at Gallipoli*. London: Macmillan.

Steel, T. 1994. *The Life and Death of St Kilda*. London: Harper Collins.

Stott, R. 2004. *Oyster*. London: Reaktion Books.

Strong, D.E. 1968. The monument, in B. Cunliffe, *Excavations of the Roman Fort at Richborough Kent, Vol. 5*, 40–73. Oxford: Report of the Research Committee of the Society of Antiquaries of London 23.

Taylor, J. 1997. Space and place: some thoughts on Iron Age and Romano-British landscapes, in Gwilt and Haselgrove 1997, 192–204.

Thomas, J. 2001. Archaeologies of place and landscape, in I. Hodder (ed.), *Archaeological Theory Today*, 165–186. Cambridge: Polity Press.

Tilley, C. 1991. *Material Culture and Text. The Art of Ambiguity*. London: Routledge.

Tilley, C. 1994. *A Phenomenology of Landscape*. Oxford: Berg.

Toynbee, J.M.C. 1965. *The Art of the Romans*. London: Thames and Hudson.

Van de Noort, R. and Ellis, S. (eds) 1995. *Wetland Heritage of Holderness: An Archaeological Survey*. Hull: Humber Wetlands Project, University of Hull.

Vanderhoeven, A., Martens, M. Ervynck, A., Cooremans, B. and Van Neer, W. 2001. Interdsiziplinäre Untersuchungen im Römischen Vicus von Tienen (Belgien). Die Integration von ökologischen und archäologischen Daten, in M. Frey and N. Hanel (eds), *Archäologie, Naturwissenschaften, Umwelt*, 13–32. Oxford: British Archaeological Reports International Series 929.

Vanderhoeven, A., Vynckier, G., Ervynck, A. and Cooremans, B. 1992. Het oudheidkundig bodemonderzoek aan de Kielenstraat te Tongeren (prov. Limburg). Interimverslag 1990–1993. Deel 1. De vóór-Flavische bewoning, *Archeologie in Vlaanderen* 2, 89–145.

Van Neer, W. and Ervynck, A. forthcoming. The zooarchaeological reconstruction of the development of the exploitation of the sea: a *status quaestionis* for Flanders, in M. Pieters, F. Verhaeghe and G. Gevaert (eds), *Fishery, Trade and Piracy. Fishermen and Fishermen's Settlements in and around the North Sea area in the Middle Ages and Later*. Brussels: Flemish Heritage Institute.

Van Neer, W., Wouters, W., Ervynck, A. and Maes, J. 2005. New evidence from a Roman context in Belgium for fish sauce locally produced in northern Gaul, *Archaeofauna* 14, 171–182.

Wallis, S. and Waughman, M. 1998. *Archaeology and Landscape in the Lower Blackwater Valley*. Chelmsford: East Anglian Archaeology Report 82.

Warner, R.B. 1991. The Broighter hoard, in Kruta *et al.* 1991, 617.

Warren, S.H. 1932. Prehistoric timber structures associated with a briquetage site in Lincolnshire, *Antiquaries Journal* 12, 254–256.

Wheeler, R.E.M. and Richardson, K.M. 1957. *Hill-forts of Northern France*. London: Report of the Research Committee of the Society of Antiquaries of London 19.

Wheeler, R.E.M. and Wheeler, T.V. 1936. *Verulamium: A Belgic and two Roman Cities*. London: Report of the Research Committee of the Society of Antiquaries of London 11.

White, K.D. 1970. *Roman Farming*. London: Thames and Hudson.

Wild, M.T. 1990. The geographical shaping of Hull from pre-industrial to modern times, in Ellis and Crowther 1990, 250–268.

Wilkinson, T.J. and Murphy, P.L. 1995. *The Archaeology of the Essex Coast, Vol. 1: The Hullbridge Survey*, Chelmsford: East Anglian Archaeology Report 71.

Williams, J. 2002. Pottery stamps, coin designs and writing in late Iron Age Britain, in A.E. Cooley (ed.), *Becoming Roman, Writing Latin? Literacy and Epigraphy in the Roman West*, 135–149. Portsmouth, Rhode Island: Journal of Roman Archaeology Supplementary Series 48.

Williams, J. 2005. 'The newer rite is here': vinous symbolism on British Iron Age coins, in Haselgrove and Wigg-Wolf 2005, 25–41.

Willis, S.H. 1990. Mould-decorated South Gaulish colour-coated cups from Fingringhoe Wick, Essex, *Journal of Roman Pottery Studies* 3, 30–34.

Willis, S.H. 1994. Roman imports into late Iron Age British societies: towards a critique of existing models, in S. Cottam, D. Dungworth,

S. Scott and J. Taylor (eds), *TRAC 94: Proceedings of the Fourth Annual Theoretical Roman Archaeology Conference, Durham 1994*, 141–150. Oxford: Oxbow Books.

Willis, S.H. 1997. Settlement, materiality and landscape in the Iron Age of the East Midlands: evidence, interpretation and wider resonance, in Gwilt and Haselgrove 1997, 205–215.

Willis, S.H. 2005. Samian pottery, a resource for the study of Roman Britain and beyond: the results of the English Heritage funded Samian Project, *Internet Archaeology* 17.

Willis, S.H. forthcoming. The briquetage containers from Stanwick, with a discussion of the Later Iron Age trade in salt in the north-east of England, in C. Haselgrove (ed.), *Cartimandua's Capital? The 1984–89 Excavations and Related Research on the Iron Age and Early Roman Site at Stanwick, North Yorkshire.*

Winder, J. 2001. Oyster shell, in P.M. Booth, J. Evans and J. Hiller, *Excavations in the Extramural Settlement of Roman Alchester, Oxfordshire, 1991: A41 (formerly A421) Wendlebury–Bicester dualling*, 416–417. Oxford: Oxford Archaeology Monograph 1.

Witt, R.E. 1997. *Isis in the Ancient World.* Baltimore: Johns Hopkins University Press.

Woolner, D. and Woolner, A. 1966. A midden at Borough, Stoke Gabriel, Devon, *Proceedings of the Devon Archaeological Exploration Society* 23, 31–34.

Worsfold, F.H. 1948. An early Iron Age site at Borden, *Archaeologia Cantiana* 61, 148–155.

Wright, R.P., Hassall, M.W.C. and Tomlin, R.S.O. 1976. Roman Britain in 1975. II. Inscriptions, *Britannia* 7, 378–392.

Yates, C. and May, J. 2005. A Bronze Age wreck? *Current Archaeology* 197, 212–213

Yeoman, P. and James, H. 1999. The Isle of May: St Ethernan revealed, *Current Archaeology* 161, 192–197.

Social landscapes and identities in the Irish Iron Age

Ian Armit

Introduction

Given its geographical proximity, the degree to which the study of Iron Age Ireland has become divorced from that of Iron Age Britain is quite remarkable. Few archaeologists have conducted primary research on both sides of the Irish Sea and, perhaps partly as a consequence, Iron Age archaeology has developed along quite different lines in both regions. The index to Barry Cunliffe's 550 page *Iron Age Communities in Britain* (1991), for example, contains only two references to Britain's nearest neighbour, both of which relate to Later Bronze Age cauldron production, and this has increased to just four in the newly published fourth edition (Cunliffe 2005). Ireland is also explicitly excluded from the recent research agenda for the British Iron Age (Haselgrove *et al.* 2001, 2).

This brief review presents a recent incomer's view of the Irish Iron Age, unashamedly biased by perspectives hauled across the North Channel. My main aim is to look afresh at some of the major issues relating to the period and to suggest some possible ways ahead. Throughout I will focus on the archaeology of the northern and eastern half of the island, thus avoiding the even thornier problems of the Iron Age in Munster and South Leinster (for a recent discussion of these see Raftery 1998a; Warner 1998; Woodman 1998).

As might be expected, the terminology covering the Irish Iron Age is rather different from that of much of Britain and the 'Later Iron Age' as understood for southern Britain is a largely meaningless concept in Irish terms. The Irish Iron Age is usually defined as the period from around 600 BC–AD 400 (Waddell 1998, 4), though, as ever, one could quibble with both start and end dates. The period from the earliest appearance of La Tène metalwork, in the third or second centuries BC, through to the end of the fourth century AD will be the focus of discussion here.

A truly 'different' Iron Age?

Sites that can be securely identified as Iron Age settlements are virtually unknown in Ireland. For an archaeologist used to the densely dotted distribution maps of the Scottish Iron Age, the eerie silence of the seemingly empty Irish equivalents can be a little disconcerting. It is clear that many of the Irish monument types which most closely parallel Scottish Iron Age forms in fact date several centuries later. Clear blue chronological water separates, for example, the latest dates for (Iron Age) Scottish souterrains (Armit 1999) and the earliest dates for their (Early Christian) Irish counterparts (Clinton 2001). The Iron Age crannogs of Scotland may be matched by some Irish examples on the basis of recent work (two in Lough Gara, on the border between Co. Roscommon and Co. Sligo, have been dated to the second half of the first millennium BC; Fredengren 2000), but the vast majority of Irish crannogs appear to be Early Christian in date. Similarly the 50,000 or so ringforts in Ireland, so similar in form and conception to the small, heavily enclosed settlements found widely across Iron Age Britain seem overwhelmingly to have been built in the sixth to eighth centuries AD (Stout 1997, although see below).

The lack of visible Iron Age settlement is not a problem peculiar to Ireland, but elsewhere it has tended to be remedied by the application of more intensive prospective techniques. In many areas of continental

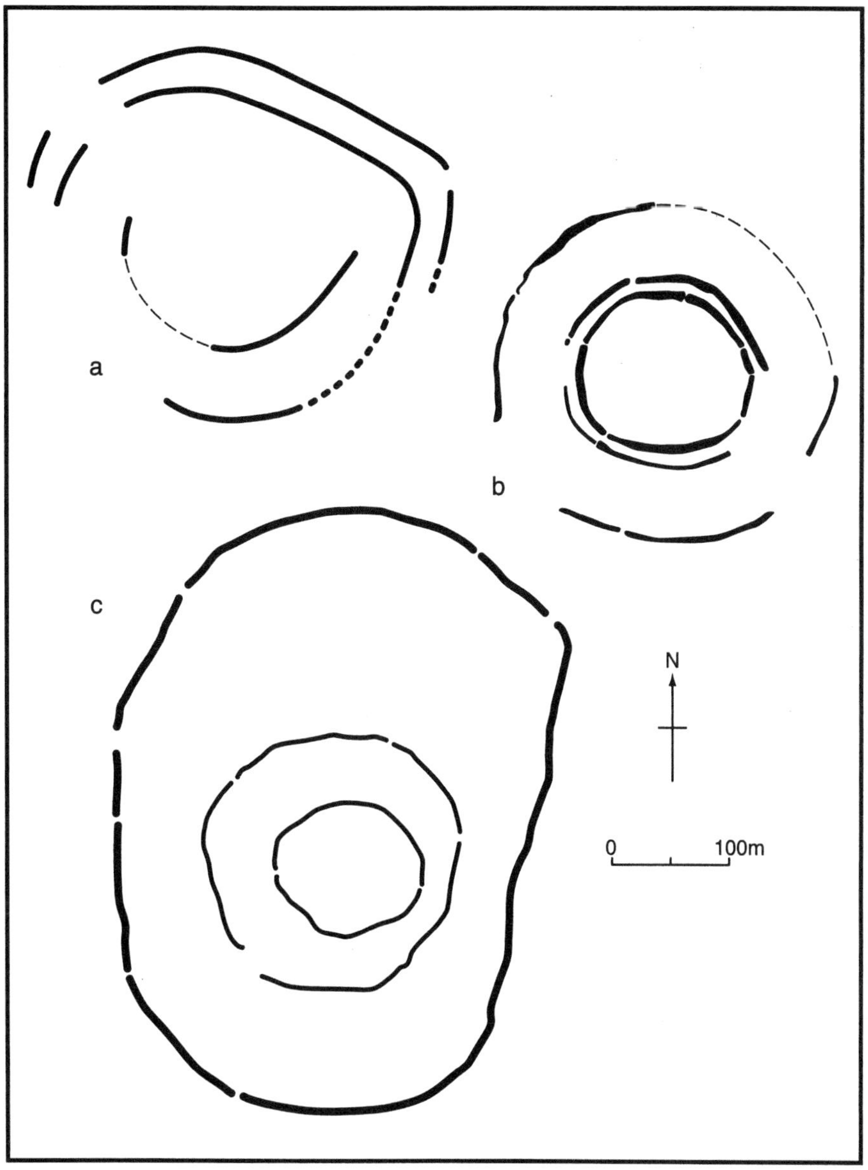

Fig. 1. Simplified comparative plans of Later Bronze Age hillforts: a. Haughey's fort; b. Rathgall; c. Mooghaun. Early medieval and later features have been removed from the plans.

Europe, the Aisne valley being an obvious example (Demoule and Ilett 1985), a combination of rescue opportunity and concerted academic effort have begun to overturn the traditional lack of settlement evidence. In Ireland, however, the employment of a battery of prospective techniques, both targeted and random, has failed to achieve similar results.

One of the principal aims of Ireland's state-funded Discovery Programme was to elucidate the notable gaps in Ireland's later prehistoric settlement sequence (Waddell 1997). While the various projects established under the aegis of the programme have produced a mass of exciting new evidence for Late Bronze Age settlement (e.g. Doody 1996; Grogan 1996; Cotter 2000), they have not yielded equivalent information for the Iron Age. Similarly, the vast upsurge in rescue excavation in the south of Ireland in particular has produced a massive increase in the numbers of known Neolithic, Bronze Age, and Early Christian settlement, but nothing comparable for the Iron Age.

Even the faith placed in the potential for Ireland's numerous hillforts to reveal Iron Age settlement evidence seems ever harder to sustain. Although excavations are still far from numerous, radiocarbon dates from hillforts such as Haughey's Fort, Co. Armagh (Mallory 1995), Rathgall, Co. Wicklow (Raftery 1976), Mooghaun, Co. Clare (Grogan 1996), and Knockdhu, Co. Antrim (Mallory pers. comm.), all suggest that hillfort building in Ireland was essentially a Later Bronze Age phenomenon, even though several have yielded evidence for some Iron Age presence (Fig. 1). Henderson (2000a) has argued that some of the generally small western stone forts may be of Iron Age date, but excavation, as at Dún Aonghasa, has so far singularly failed to yield definitive evidence of significant Iron Age activity (Cotter 2000).

Generally such evidence as there is for Iron Age settlement is scattered and fragmentary (Warner *et al.* 1991). At Lislackagh, Co. Mayo, for example, radiocarbon dates derived from three small circular foundation trenches, set within a ringfort, all suggest a date in the last two centuries BC or very shortly thereafter (Walsh 1995). These possible houses may or may not be associated with the ringfort itself. Elsewhere, a single radiocarbon date from one of a series of circular structures on the enclosed summit of Scrabo Hill, Co. Down, suggests construction in the last few centuries BC (Mallory and Hartwell 1997; Warner *et al.* 1991, 48). The list of isolated radiocarbon dates, associated with diverse pits and structural fragments, is extensive and varied, and no structural traditions or recurrent patterning of domestic deposits can yet be defined.

It may yet be the case that substantial classes of Iron Age settlement archaeology remain to be found. The best bet in this regard is probably the possibility that a relatively dispersed pattern of Iron Age settlements may be masked by the devastatingly dense distribution of Early Christian ringforts and miscellaneous undated 'enclosures'. Assessing this proposal (i.e. finding the right ringforts and enclosures), however, will not be an easy task.

One of the most important recent studies, which may suggest that Iron Age settlements will always remain fugitive in Ireland, is Weir's (1995) palynological analysis of a series of sites in Co. Louth, a region of high agricultural potential. This work appears to confirm the impression from numerous earlier studies, generally in more marginal areas, that the Iron Age, and especially the period from around 200 BC–AD 100, saw a marked decline in arable agriculture throughout much of Ireland. Weir suggests that this 'Iron Age hiatus' represents a genuine collapse in population levels and a major shift towards a pastoral farming regime (*ibid.*, 106–7). He further proposes that this state of affairs may have been brought about by an overall environmental decline, specifically a wetter climate, in the last few centuries BC, citing other environmental indicators from as far afield as Sweden and Germany (*ibid.*, 111). Given the marked increase in population densities and economic intensification which can be inferred for many parts of the British Later Iron Age, from Wessex to Atlantic Scotland, it is difficult to believe that environmental conditions across the whole of Ireland were so bad as to precipitate population collapse and the virtual abandonment of agriculture. Nonetheless, the existence of the 'hiatus' itself seems clear.

Taking all of the above into account, however, it seems clear that we can no longer maintain that Iron Age settlement evidence is so limited because of insufficient application, or inappropriate methodologies of prospection. Instead, we are forced to recognise that the Iron Age of Ireland simply does not accord with expectations based on analogy with intensively studied areas of Britain. This impression of difference drawn from the scarcity of Irish Iron Age settlement evidence is heightened by the lack of close British parallels for many of the sites and landscapes which do characterise the Irish Age; in particular the so-called 'royal sites', linear earthworks and routeways. Indeed, it could be argued that Ireland and Britain in the Iron Age share little more than large quantities of poorly contexted La Tène metalwork and a generally low incidence of archaeologically visible funerary ritual.

The 'Celtic paradigm'

Much more than in Britain the question of Celticism, and specifically Celtic immigration, continues to hold centre stage in Irish Iron Age studies. Ó Donnabháin (2000) has recently reviewed this subject in some detail, showing how thoroughly intertwined the concept of the Celts has become with perceptions of identity and nationhood in modern Ireland. In Barry Raftery's much-quoted phrase (1994, 228) it seems 'almost heretical to insist that a Celtic invasion of Ireland never happened'.

Yet few archaeologists in Ireland would now suggest that the arrival of the concepts associated with La Tène metalwork was accompanied by any massive folk migration, although there is still much debate regarding the nature and extent of prehistoric population movements and their role in the origins of the Irish language (Mallory 1991; Waddell 1991; Warner 1991; Mallory and Ó Donnabháin 1998). The debate in Ireland can be traced back to a seminar organised by Jim Mallory in 1984 (Waddell 1990, 360–1) and has latterly run in parallel to the tempestuous recent debates on the nature and existence of a pan-European 'ancient Celtic' identity played out in the pages of *Antiquity* and elsewhere (e.g. Megaw and Megaw 1996; 1998; Collis 1997; James 1999). What seems clear is that the archaeological dimension of the argument, at least with regard to the Irish Iron Age, has largely burnt itself out: there is plainly insufficient archaeological evidence for any substantial migration into Ireland during the period, but neither is there sufficiently strong evidence to demonstrate continuity. The debate over the origins of 'Celtic' languages in Ireland will continue, but as a structuring theme for the study of the Irish Iron Age, Celticism is a dead-end

Yet, as Ó Donnabháin (2000) points out, nothing has emerged to replace the 'Celtic paradigm'. A new framework for the archaeological study of the Irish Iron Age 'free from ethnic labels and preconceptions' (Waddell 1995, 158) is overdue. The challenge facing us is to find new ways of thinking about the Irish Iron Age which engage directly with the available data rather than trying to find archaeological answers to essentially linguistic or pseudo-historical questions. The Irish Iron Age should be studied not on the basis of what it appears to lack, but rather on the basis of what it actually comprises.

People and place

It is becoming ever clearer that Iron Age communities in Ireland did not routinely leave substantial traces of their presence in the landscape. Indeed the archaeology of Iron Age Ireland is essentially an archaeology of the non-routine; of ceremonial centres, routeways and boundaries, and rich metalwork offered up in bogs, rivers and pools.

'Royal' sites

The basic characteristics of the classic 'royal' sites of the Irish Iron Age are well known (e.g. Raftery 1994, 64–79; Waddell 1998, 325–54). Essentially these Iron Age centres of Navan, Co. Armagh (Waterman 1997; Mallory and Lynn 2002), Knockaulin, Co Kildare (Wailes 1990), Tara, Co. Meath (Newman 1997), and Rathcroghan, Co. Roscommon (Waddell 1998, 347–54), comprise an amalgam of monuments from many periods, including Neolithic and Bronze Age barrows. Although no two centres are exactly alike, the first three are dominated by large hengiform enclosures with evidence for complex ritual activity in their interiors. The ditch at Navan has recently been dated dendrochronologically to 94 ± 9 BC (Mallory *et al.* 1999) which accords remarkably well with the similarly dated construction and ritual destruction of the massive, timber '40 metre structure' on the summit of the enclosure. This burst of activity in the first century BC came late in a sequence extending back into the Later Bronze Age (Waterman 1997); broadly similar sequences can be discerned on the basis of excavations at Knockaulin (Wailes 1990), and inferred on the basis of more limited excavation and detailed survey evidence for Tara (Newman 1997; Roche 1999).

The concept of an exclusive set of 'royal' sites, operating as independent and competing 'neo-provincial' centres, has become rather reified largely because the archaeological evidence for these particular locations is augmented by the early written accounts, notably the *Martyrology of Oengus*, which identifies them collectively as royal residences, forts, and places of pagan worship. However, it is becoming increasingly clear that this rather tidy picture may be a distortion of a rather messier prehistoric reality (Fig. 2). Inevitably, the very fact that the known 'royal' sites are mentioned in the early literature has acted as a magnet for archaeological investigation. Raftery (1994, 80) has already suggested, however, that various unexcavated 'hillforts' with apparently hengiform enclosures and central mounds may well turn out to be similar, undocumented, centres. Similarly, Conor Newman's excavations at Raffin, Co. Meath, have shown the existence of a smaller centre displaying several of the traits of the classic 'royal' sites, including the hengiform ditch, evidence for monumental timber architecture, and votive deposition (Newman 1995). Others may include Uisneach in Co. Westmeath, where the complex of Early Medieval monuments seems to have originated in the early centuries AD, if not earlier (Grogan and Donaghy 1997), and Ballymount Great, Co. Dublin, with its hengiform ditch and internal mound, the latter now obscured by a seventeenth-century building (Stout 1998).

Linear earthworks and routeways

In the context of the Irish Iron Age, the term 'linear earthworks' covers monuments at a range of scales, from relatively short stretches of double banks and ditches such as the Mucklaghs, in the Rathcroghan 'royal' complex (Waddell 1998, 350), to boundaries like the Black Pig's Dyke which (on the most optimistic view) may run for more than 100 km, albeit incorporating natural features such as lakes and bogs. In general, the shorter earthworks have been interpreted either as ritual boundaries or processional ways, while the longer examples have been seen as defining territorial units associated with the major 'royal' centres.

An excavated section of the Black Pig's Dyke in Co. Monaghan revealed a complex boundary some 24 m wide incorporating a double bank with intervening ditch, as well as a palisade with timbers dating to 390–70 cal. BC (Walsh 1987). More precise dating was obtained from the Dorsey, the complex linear earthwork in Co. Armagh (Lynn 1989), which may form part of the same boundary system. Timbers from the southern part of the Dorsey were dated dendrochronologically to 100–90 BC: more or less the same time as the building of the Navan enclosure and '40 metre structure'. Not unnaturally, this has strengthened the widely held belief that the Dorsey/Black Pig's Dyke system formed a unitary frontier defining an ancient Ulster polity centred at Navan.

Although the identification of regional boundaries has been most enthusiastically pursued in an Ulster context, linear earthworks have been found in many parts of the island. The Doon of Drumsna, Co. Roscommon (Condit and Buckley 1989), and Claidh Dubh, Co. Cork (Doody 1995), for example, have both yielded Iron Age radiocarbon dates. While these cannot, by their very nature, match the precision of the dendrochronological dates from the Dorsey, it remains possible that the phenomenon of linear earthwork construction may have a narrow chronological horizon.

Almost matching the scale of effort represented by the linear earthworks are the few fortuitously discovered routeways preserved in the island's many peatland areas. Best known is the Corlea Road, Co. Longford (Raftery 1990), part of a system running for at least 2 km and with a 4 m wide surface of oak planks made from trees

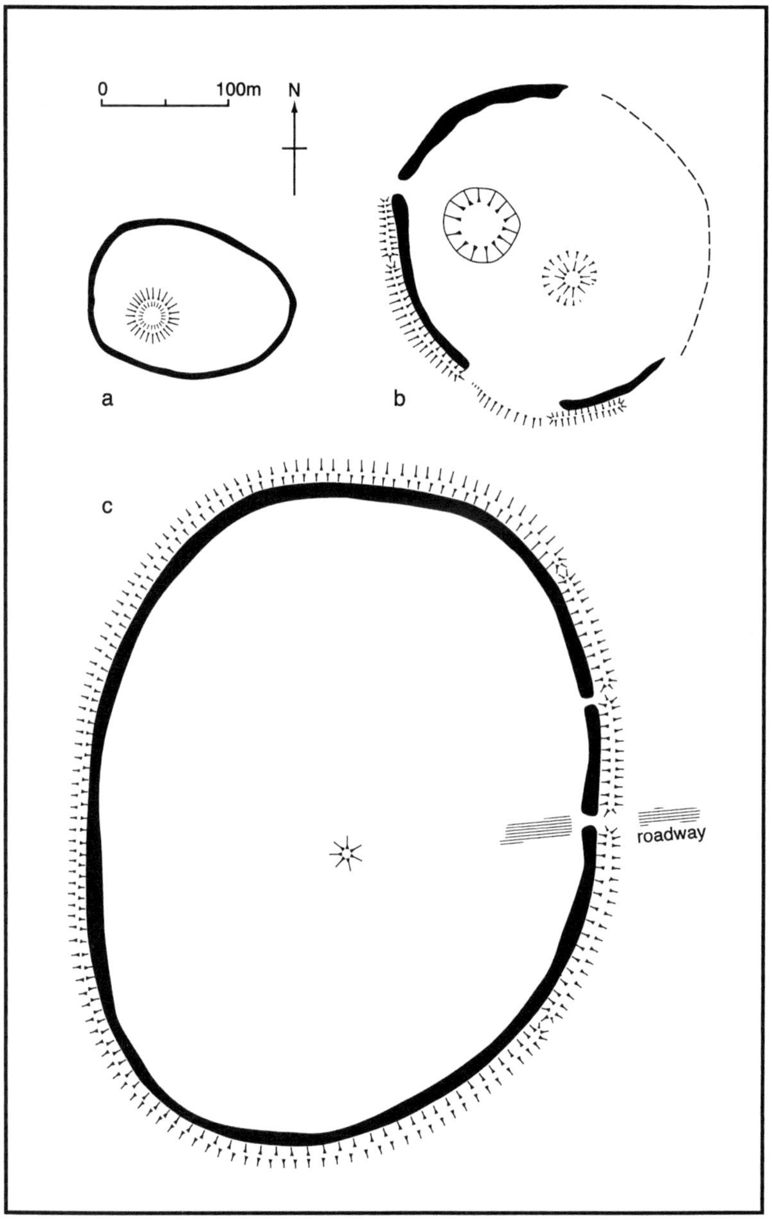

Fig. 2. Simplified comparative plans of hengiform enclosures: a. Ballymount; b. Navan; c. Knockaulin (the ditch at Knockaulin in particular has been simplified by removing the numerous internal quarries)

felled around 148 BC. Similarly, the largest of the numerous, multi-period routeways preserved in the peatland of Derryville Bog, Co. Tipperary, appears to be an Iron Age 'corduroy' road with a surface some 5 m wide (Gowen 1997, 29). As with the linear earthworks, these rare survivals point to the investment of enormous resources of both timber and labour in major communal projects, which would also seem to go against any idea of low population levels derived from Weir's (1995) palynological analysis.

It is notable that many of the known linear earthworks operate at the regional rather than the local scale. Boundaries were not routinely used to define Iron Age houses, farms, or fields (as they were in many areas of Britain), nor is there any evidence of 'ranch boundaries' or other economic land divisions like those of southern Scotland (Barber 1999). Instead, the building of boundaries, often of monumental proportions, seemingly addressed political and religious rather than economic objectives. Routeways like those at Corlea and Derryville Bog may reflect similar concerns. If landscape is the 'main locus of social memory' (Gosden and Lock 1998, 5), then social memory in Iron Age Ireland was apparently most concerned with the achievements, ambitions, and representations of corporate groups operating at a regional scale.

Archaeologists have expressed understandable frustration at the lack of Iron Age settlements (e.g. Raftery 1994, 112). Yet the sheer difference in scale between the fragmentary and transient remains of everyday life and the monumental scope of the major communal constructions in itself tells us something of the nature of these Iron Age communities. The absence of substantial settlement remains, the emphasis on pastoralism as seen through the palaeoenvironmental record, and the increasing importance of the horse, as suggested by the dominance of horsegear in the Irish La Tène metalwork record (Raftery 1983, 1984), combine to suggest a relatively mobile Iron Age population.

Chris Lynn (pers. comm.) has suggested a similar scenario on the basis that the light basketwork houses which appear on ringforts in the earliest part of the succeeding Early Christian period seem more appropriate in the context of a nomadic or semi-nomadic society than a settled agricultural one. At the same time, the vast communal works represented by the 'royal' centres, boundaries and routeways suggest that power structures existed which were capable of mobilising and directing labour on an enormous scale for building projects which seem to embody 'both sacral and secular authority' (Newman 1995, 131).

Continuity and change in the landscape

There has been a marked trend recently to point to a broad cultural continuity between the Later Bronze Age and the Iron Age in Ireland (see especially Cooney and Grogan 1991; 1999). In part this represents a welcome move away from the Celtic paradigm in which the Iron Age was seen as a period of Celtic immigration and Irish ethnogenesis. This new perspective lays stress on continuities in depositional practices (e.g. weapons in water), the use of particular locales (e.g. 'royal' sites like Navan and Tara), and the maintenance of regional identities (e.g. the use of distinct forms of personal adornment in the Later Bronze Age may reflect the emergence of distinct south-west and north-east identities that re-surface in the regional divisions of the Iron Age; Cooney and Grogan 1999, 202–3)

In other respects, however, the attempt to delineate continuity from the Bronze Age to the Iron Age is more problematic. For example, the relationship between people and the landscapes in which they lived seems to take on an entirely different aspect in the Iron Age. As we have seen, the creation of inscribed landscapes in the Iron Age reflected the importance of large-scale corporate groups and reinforced the relative invisibility of smaller-scale collectives such as households or kin-groups.

One area in which these smaller-scale identities may be maintained is in burial. The scattered examples of known Iron Age burials generally employ various forms of barrow which may derive from Bronze Age traditions. Richard Hingley (1999) has also drawn attention to the Iron Age re-modelling of certain Neolithic and Bronze Age monuments in Ireland, such as Knowth, Co. Meath, and Ballycarty, Co. Kerry. Such re-use of earlier monuments has again been suggested as indicating continuity of ritual practice (Cooney and Grogan 1999).

One specific example of continuity given by Cooney and Grogan (1999, 199) is the Iron Age cemetery at Kiltierney, Co. Fermanagh. The Kiltierney passage tomb forms part of a Neolithic and Bronze Age cemetery (Foley 1988). During the first century BC or AD, a ditch was excavated around the mound and the upcast used both to add to the mound and to create 19 small burial mounds circling the periphery. Under at least some of these smaller mounds were placed Iron Age cremation burials, while further cremations were dug into the side of the mound itself (*ibid.*, 25).

By the first century BC, the primary use of the Kiltierney passage tomb would have been well beyond the bounds of oral or genealogical history (to borrow the terminology used by Gosden and Lock; 1998): in other words it would have seemed immeasurably old. As a major feature in the landscape it would more likely have been explained and understood with reference to a 'pre-social' past of supernatural beings or undifferentiated ancestors. Thus the re-use of the tomb for Iron Age burial does not mark continuity with its earlier use, but rather represents a reclamation and incorporation into the Iron Age social landscape of a monument most probably understood in mythical or supernatural terms.

Cooney and Grogan's (1999) emphasis on the importance of landscape, further developed by Cooney (2000) in the context of Neolithic Ireland, is nonetheless a major step towards a contextual understanding of Iron Age communities in Ireland. The socialisation of the landscape was undoubtedly important to these communities, but the specific ways in which this was achieved marked particular concerns with regional identity and levels of authority.

Iron Age identities

The similar ways in which various Irish Iron Age communities socialised their landscapes with linear boundaries, routeways, and ritual centres suggests a fairly high degree of communication and shared traditions of sacred and monumental architecture. A communal grammar of hengiform enclosure, central mound, and timber circle, deployed in various combinations, characterises much of the most dramatic activity at the various 'royal' sites in the last century or so BC. In other ways, however, Irish Iron Age societies seem to have sought out means of displaying social difference.

The impacts of La Tène and Roman influence on

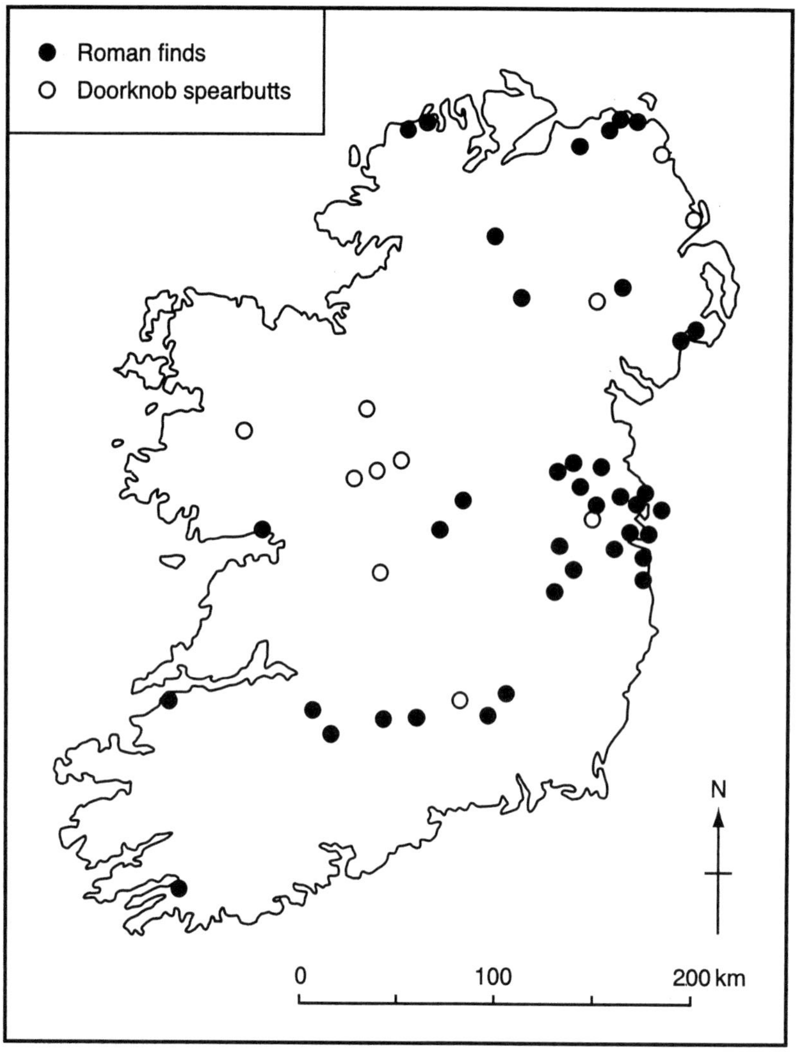

Fig. 3. Distribution of doorknob spearbutts (open circles) and finds of Roman material (solid circles). Based on distributions published by Heald (2001) and Raftery (1994) respectively.

Ireland have rarely been considered as comparable phenomena. La Tène art has long been equated with the arrival of Celtic colonists. Although alien in origin, La Tène material was subsequently 'nativised': La Tène objects were made in Ireland, where the style survived long after it had faded elsewhere. La Tène culture has, therefore, long been seen as a factor in the Celticisation of Ireland. By contrast, Roman material in Ireland has been relatively little-studied and, when it has, it has been seen largely as reflecting either trading or raiding on a rather limited scale (e.g. Freeman 2001, 11–12), or the activities of intrusive 'free-booters' (Warner 1991). In other words, La Tène material has been central to questions of developing Irish/Celtic identity, while Roman material has often been seen to have little more than curiosity value.

Yet, once we move beyond the Celtic paradigm, where La Tène material is seen as signalling an intrusive elite, the parallels between the adoption of La Tène and Roman material culture become more apparent. Both represent sets of ideas adopted from outside; from across the sea. In the case of La Tène art, which was most likely first adopted in the third century BC, its early applications seem to revolve around warfare and horsemanship, judging by the dominant forms of Irish La Tène metalwork. The exclusivity and exoticism of this material (at least at first) seem to have played a role in forging group identities within elite sectors of the population in the northern and eastern part of the island.

In the late first or second centuries AD, we see the adoption of Roman material in certain areas, notably in eastern central Ireland. Rather than view this material as the random spoils of raiders, the salvaged possessions of refugees, the stock of traders, or the signature of rampaging Romanised free-booters, it may be more helpful to consider how the adoption of Roman material in an Irish context played a role in the creation and maintenance of new social identities, much as La Tène art had done a few centuries earlier. Preliminary analysis has shown that the nature of the items adopted in Ireland differs markedly from what might be expected through mechanisms such as raiding. The inventory of Roman material in Ireland is quite unlike that found in Scotland north of the Antonine Wall, strengthening the view that native populations in both areas played an active role in selecting specific Roman forms (Magennis 2000). The preponderance of items such as toilet instruments in Ireland may even suggest a fairly significant change in attitudes to the body and personal identity, as has been suggested for southern England in the first century AD (Hill 1997).

The use of La Tène material culture clearly overlapped with that of Roman material, particularly in view of the extended chronology that may now have to be considered for certain traditional La Tène find types such as doorknob spearbutts (Heald 2001). Indeed, it is conceivable that the adoption of aspects of Roman material culture, including new modes of dress and personal display, may have been a deliberate strategy on the part of some Iron Age societies in Ireland to set themselves apart from what had become a more traditional way of living. Interestingly, the distribution of doorknob spearbutts markedly avoids the main east coast concentration of Roman artefacts (Fig. 3). Roman material may, in other words, have played a much more active role in the creation of new Irish identities than has previously been allowed.

Heterarchy and fragmentation

There were clearly several distinct arenas of depositional activity in Iron Age Ireland. For example, the deposition of La Tène metalwork is overwhelmingly biased towards wet locations, rivers, bogs, and lakes (Raftery 1983, 1984). By contrast, Iron Age burials are largely devoid of the finer material and grave goods are generally confined to small items of personal adornment such as bead necklaces (Raftery 1998b, 9). Even more surprising is the general paucity of La Tène material from 'royal' sites such as Tara and Navan. Although the activities on these sites clearly involved communal ritual on a large scale, there was little apparent role for the deposition of metalwork (although the pool of Loughnashade, close to Navan, did receive deposits of this kind). In contrast to the centralised impression given by the major building works, the small-scale, scattered nature of La Tène findspots suggests a proliferation of locally important places. Only the former lake of Lisnacrogher, Co. Antrim (O'Sullivan 1997, 98–9), stands out as a major centre for such deposition. This marks a sharp contrast with other parts of La Tène Europe where enclosed sanctuaries could be associated with substantial quantities of metalwork, as at Gournay-sur-Aronde (Brunaux *et al.* 1985; Brunaux and Rapin 1988).

Rather than being characterised by class-based, pyramidal 'Celtic' structures, with all-powerful kings ensconced in their 'royal' centres, it may be appropriate to see Irish Iron Age society as more closely related to Crumley's (1987; 1995) concept of heterarchy. In other words, social power may have been obtained and displayed in a multiplicity of ways, through separate and cross-cutting structures based on, for example, religious, military, or economic power. The over-arching regional authorities, responsible for the major constructional projects, and arguably based around concepts of sacral kingship (Newman 1995), may thus have cross-cut more localised structures based around kinship or military muscle associated with the localised deposition of La Tène metalwork.

Newman (1998) has suggested that the multiplicity of petty kingdoms which characterise Early Christian Ireland resulted from the fragmentation of much larger Iron Age polities of which the 'royal' sites were the ritual centres. Archaeologically this is manifested in the switch from an Iron Age dominated by the handful of 'royal' centres to an Early Christian period of 50,000 ringforts. Newman (1998, 133) has also suggested that a transitional period, when fragmenting social groups attempted to emulate traditional modes of authority, may have led to a proliferation of second tier 'royal' sites such as Raffin in the early centuries AD. What we may be witnessing, in the differential adoption of new identities associated with Roman material trappings, is part of a wider process in which 'traditional' notions of regional identity are being usurped by new ideologies based around the individual and the kin group. Thus the power balance between elements of the heterarchical Iron Age societies may have swung from regional to more locally-based structures.

Rather intriguingly, the social fragmentation which seems to characterise Ireland over the first few centuries AD is exactly the reverse of the process of political centralisation which was seemingly underway in Scotland at the same time (Armit 1997, 118–19). The archaeology of Early Christian Ireland, with its dense spread of enclosed settlements, its souterrains and crannogs, is almost a mirror image of Iron Age Scotland. Simple proximity to the Roman Empire thus had no predetermined outcome on the social development of societies on Europe's north-western fringe.

Conclusion

It is clearly time to move beyond the traditional Celtic paradigm and to recognise the particular character of the Irish Iron Age. As I have suggested, one avenue may be to examine how the different facets of the archaeological record relate to the activities of cross-cutting 'interest groups' within a broadly heterarchical society. This can be contrasted with the more traditional 'Celtic' hierarchical model for society with sacral kings, aristocratic La Tène warriors, and a mass of archaeologically invisible followers. I have also suggested that the Celtic paradigm has privileged the role of La Tène metalwork, obscuring what may be an equally important episode of identity-building using aspects of Roman material culture. A great deal of work remains to be done on the Irish Iron Age, both in terms of theory-building and the analysis and interpretation of primary data. The prospect of an Irish Iron Age without the Celts need not, however, be a barren one for archaeologists.

Acknowledgements

A number of colleagues kindly provided comments on an earlier draft, including Dr Chris Lynn, Professor Jim Mallory, Dr Philip McDonald, and Professor John Waddell. Responsibility for the views expressed remains, however, solely with the author.

Bibliography

Armit, I. 1997. *Celtic Scotland.* London: Batsford.

Armit, I. 1999. The abandonment of souterrains: evolution, catastrophe or dislocation? *Proceedings of the Society of Antiquaries of Scotland* 129, 577–596.

Barber, J. 1999. The linear earthworks of southern Scotland: survey and classification, *Transactions of the Dumfries and Galloway Natural History and Antiquarian Society* 73, 63–164.

Brunaux, J.-L., Meniel, P. and Poplin, F. 1985. *Gournay I: Les fouilles sur le sanctuaire et l'oppidum.* Amiens: Revue Archéologique de Picardie Numéro spécial.

Brunaux, J.-L. and Rapin, A. 1988. *Gournay II: Boucliers et lances, dépôts et trophées.* Paris: Editions Errance.

Clinton, M. 2001. *The Souterrains of Ireland.* Wicklow: Wordwell.

Collis, J.R. 1997. Celtic Myths, *Antiquity* 71, 195–201.

Condit, T. and Buckley, V.M. 1989. The 'Doon' of Drumsna – gateway to Connacht, *Emania* 6, 12–14.

Cooney, G. 2000. *Landscapes of Neolithic Ireland.* London: Routledge.

Cooney, G. and Grogan, E. 1991. An archaeological solution to the 'Irish' problem? *Emania* 9, 33–44.

Cooney, G. and Grogan, E. 1999. *Irish Prehistory: A Social Perspective* (revised). Wicklow: Wordwell.

Cotter, C. 2000. The chronology and affinities of the stone forts along the Atlantic coast of Ireland, in Henderson 2000b, 171–180.

Crumley, C.L. 1987. A dialectical critique of hierarchy, in T.C. Patterson and C.W. Gailey (eds), *Power Relations and State Formation*, 155–169. Washington: American Anthropological Association.

Crumley, C.L. 1995. Building an historical ecology of Gaulish polities, in B. Arnold and D.B. Gibson (eds.), *Celtic Chiefdom, Celtic State*, 26–33. Cambridge: Cambridge University Press.

Cunliffe, B. 1991. *Iron Age Communities in Britain* (3rd edn). London: Routledge.

Cunliffe, B. 2005. *Iron Age Communities in Britain* (4th edn). London: Routledge.

Demoule, J.-P. and Ilett, M. 1985. First millennium settlement and society in northern France, in T.C. Champion and J.V.S. Megaw (eds), *Settlement and Society: Aspects of West European Prehistory in the First Millennium BC*, 193–221. Leicester: Leicester University Press.

Doody, M. 1995. Ballyhoura Hills Project, *Discovery Programme Reports* 2, 12–45.

Doody, M. 1996. Ballyhoura Hills Project, *Discovery Programme Reports* 4, 15–25.

Foley, C. 1988. An enigma solved: Kiltierney, Co. Fermanagh, in A. Hamlin and C. Lynn (eds), *Pieces of the Past*, 24–26. Belfast: HMSO.

Fredengren, C. 2000. Iron Age crannogs in Lough Gara, *Archaeology Ireland* 52, 26–8.

Freeman, P. 2001. *Ireland and the Classical World.* Austin: University of Texas Press.

Gowen, M. 1997. Palaeoenvironment and archaeology: excavations at Derryville bog, *Archaeology Ireland* 42, 27–29.

Gosden, C. and Lock, G. 1998. Prehistoric histories, *World Archaeology* 30 (1), 2–12.

Grogan, E. 1996. Excavations at Mooghaun South 1994, interim report, *Discovery Programme Reports* 4, 47–57.

Grogan, E. and Donaghy, C. 1997. Navel-gazing at Uisneach, Co. Westmeath, *Archaeology Ireland* 42, 24–26.

Haselgrove, C., Armit, I., Champion, T., Creighton, J., Gwilt, A., Hill, J.D., Hunter, F. and Woodward, A. 2001. *Understanding the British Iron Age: an Agenda for Action.* Salisbury: Trust for Wessex Archaeology.

Heald, A. 2001. Knobbed spearbutts of the British and Irish Iron Age: new examples and new thoughts, *Antiquity* 75, 689–696.

Henderson, J. 2000a. Shared traditions? The drystone settlement traditions of Atlantic Scotland and Ireland 700 BC–AD 200, in Henderson 2000b, 117–154.

Henderson, J. (ed.) 2000b. *The Prehistory and Early History of Atlantic Europe.* Oxford: British Archaeological Reports International Series 861.

Hill, J.D. 1997. 'The end of one kind of body and the beginning of another kind of body'? Toilet instruments and 'Romanization' in southern England during the first century AD, in A. Gwilt and C. Haselgrove (eds.), *Reconstructing Iron Age Societies*, 96–107. Oxford: Oxbow Monograph 71.

Hingley, R. 1999. The creation of later prehistoric landscapes and the context of the reuse of Neolithic and Earlier Bronze Age monuments in Britain and Ireland, in B. Bevan (ed.), *Northern Exposure: Interpretative Devolution and the Iron Ages in Britain*, 233–251. Leicester: Leicester Archaeology Monograph 4.

James, S. 1999. *The Atlantic Celts: Ancient People or Modern Invention?* London: British Museum.

Lynn, C.J. 1989. An interpretation of 'the Dorsey', *Emania* 6, 5–10.

Magennis, C. 2000. *The Romanisation of Ireland.* Unpublished M.A. dissertation, Queen's University, Belfast.

Mallory, J.P. 1991. Two perspectives on the problem of Irish origins, *Emania* 9, 53–58.

Mallory, J.P. 1995. Haughey's Fort and the Navan complex in the Late Bronze Age, in Waddell and Shee-Twohig 1995, 73–86.

Mallory, J.P., Brown, D.M. and Baillie, M.G.L. 1999. Dating Navan Fort, *Antiquity* 280, 427–431.

Mallory, J.P. and Hartwell, B.N. 1997. Down in prehistory, in L. Proudfoot. and W. Nolan (eds), *Down: History and Society*, 1–32. Dublin: Geography Publications.

Mallory, J.P. and Lynn, C.J. 2002. Recent excavations and speculations on the Navan complex, *Antiquity* 76, 532–541.

Mallory, J.P. and Ó Donnabháin, B. 1998. The origins of the population of Ireland: a survey of putative immigrations in Irish prehistory and history, *Emania* 17, 47–82.

Megaw, J.V.S. and Megaw, M.R. 1996. Ancient Celts and modern ethnicity, *Antiquity* 70, 175–181.

Megaw, J.V.S. and Megaw, M.R. 1998. 'The mechanism of (Celtic) dreams?': a partial response to our critics, *Antiquity* 72, 432–434.

Newman, C. 1995. Raffin Fort, County Meath: Neolithic and Bronze Age activity, in E. Grogan and C. Mount (eds.), *Annus Archaeologiae: Proceedings of the OIA Winter Conference, 1993*, 55–66. Dublin: OPW, Organisation of Irish Archaeologists.

Newman, C. 1997. *Tara: an Archaeological Survey*. Dublin: Royal Irish Academy Discovery Programme Monograph 2.

Newman, C. 1998. Reflections on the making of a 'royal site' in early Ireland, *World Archaeology* 30 (1), 127–141.

Ó Donnabháin, B. 2000. An appalling vista? The Celts and the archaeology of later prehistoric Ireland, in A. Desmond, G. Johnson, M. McCarthy, J. Sheehan and E. Shee-Twohig (eds), *New Agendas in Irish Prehistory: Papers in Commemoration of Liz Anderson*, 189–196. Wicklow: Wordwell.

O'Sullivan, A. 1997. *The Archaeology of Lake Settlement in Ireland*. Dublin: Royal Irish Academy Discovery Programme Monograph 4.

Raftery, B. 1976. Rathgall and Irish hillfort problems, in D.W. Harding (ed.), *Hillforts. Later Prehistoric Earthworks in Britain and Ireland*, 339–357. London: Academic Press.

Raftery, B. 1983. *A Catalogue of Irish Iron Age Antiquities*. Marburg: Veröffentlichung des vorgeschichtlichen Seminars Marburg Sonderband 1.

Raftery, B. 1984. *La Tène in Ireland: Problems of Origin and Chronology*. Marburg: Veröffentlichung des vorgeschichtlichen Seminars Marburg Sonderband 2.

Raftery, B. 1990. *Trackways through Time*. Dublin: Headline.

Raftery, B. 1994. *Pagan Celtic Ireland: the Enigma of the Irish Iron Age*. London: Thames and Hudson.

Raftery, B. 1998a. Observations on the Iron Age in Munster, *Emania* 17, 21–24.

Raftery, B. 1998b. Knobbed spearbutts revisited, in M. Ryan (ed.), *Irish Antiquities: Essays in Memory of Joseph Raftery*, 97–109. Wicklow: Wordwell.

Roche, H. 1999. Late Iron Age activity at Tara, Co. Meath, *Riocht na Midhe* 10, 18–30.

Stout, G. 1998. The archaeology of Ballymount Great, Co. Dublin, in C. Manning (ed.), *Dublin and Beyond the Pale: Studies in Honour of Patrick Healy*, 145–154. Wicklow: Wordwell.

Stout, M. 1997. *The Irish Ringfort*. Dublin: Irish Settlement Studies 5.

Waddell, J. 1990. The Celticization of the west: an Irish perspective, in C. Chevillot and A. Coffyn (eds.), *L'Age du Bronze Atlantique*, 349–66. Beynac: Association des Musées du Sarladais.

Waddell, J. 1991. The question of the Celticization of Ireland, *Emania* 9, 5–16.

Waddell, J. 1995. Celts, Celticisation and the Irish Bronze Age, in Waddell and Shee-Twohig 1995, 158–169.

Waddell, J. 1997. Ireland's Discovery Programme: progress and prospect, *Antiquity* 71, 513–518.

Waddell, J. 1998. *The Prehistoric Archaeology of Ireland*. Galway: University of Galway.

Waddell, J. and Shee-Twohig, E. (eds) 1995. *Ireland in the Bronze Age (Proceedings of the Dublin Conference, April 1995)*. Dublin: The Stationery Office.

Wailes, B. 1990. Dun Ailinne: a summary excavation report, *Emania* 7, 10–21.

Walsh, A. 1987. Excavating the Black Pig's Dyke, *Emania* 3, 5–11.

Walsh, G. 1995. Iron Age settlement in Co. Mayo, *Archaeology Ireland* 32, 7–8.

Warner, R.B. 1991. Cultural intrusions in the Early Iron Age: some notes, *Emania* 9, 44–52.

Warner, R.B. 1998. Is there an Iron Age in Munster? *Emania* 17, 25–30.

Warner, R.B., Mallory, J.P. and Baillie, M.G.L. 1991. Irish Early Iron Age sites: a provisional map of absolute dated sites, *Emania* 7, 46–50.

Waterman, D. 1997. *Excavations at Navan fort 1961–71*. Belfast: Northern Ireland Archaeological Monograph 3.

Weir, D. 1995. A palynological study of landscape and agricultural development in County Louth from the second millennium BC to the first millennium AD, *Discovery Programme Reports* 2, 77–126.

Woodman, P. 1998. The Early Iron Age of South Munster: not so different after all, *Emania* 17, 13–20.

Re-situating the Later Iron Age in Cornwall and Devon: new perspectives from the settlement record

L. J. Cripps

Introduction

Visions of Iron Age society in Cornwall and Devon have remained largely unchanged in the forty or so years since the ABC scheme (Hawkes 1959), with its associated waves of invading 'Celts', was replaced by one which stressed the essentially 'indigenous' character of the British Iron Age. Unlike other regions such as Wessex (Hill 1996) or north-west England (Matthews 1999), where new work has unshackled us from the traditional characterisation of Iron Age social organisation, recent research in south-west England has been less challenging. Consequently, the 'Iron Age' there is still regarded as a somewhat lacklustre period in its prehistory.

Recent developer-funded and rescue excavations have provided tantalising glimpses into the wealth and diversity of Iron Age settlement in areas previously largely devoid of such information (e.g. Ratcliffe 1992; Nowakowski 1994; 2000; Jones 1996; Johns 2000; Craze *et al.* 2002; Lawson Jones 2003). Much of this work has yet to receive public dissemination, however, and most of these sites have not yet been situated within broader narratives for the region, or for Britain. Aerial reconnaissance has also resulted in the recognition of a vast number of previously unrecorded cropmark sites – over 1000 in Devon alone by the early 1990s (Griffith 1994, 87) – of which a number have been excavated and dated to the first millennium BC. In Cornwall, landscape surveys of Bodmin Moor (Johnson and Rose 1994) and the Lizard (Smith 1987) have increased the number of known earthwork sites, whilst the Cornwall and Isles of Scilly Mapping Project (Young 2001) has added significantly more detail to the settlement landscape. Particularly high densities of new enclosure earthworks and hut circles have been identified around the Camel estuary. Even so, and despite this continuing hard work, Late Bronze Age and Iron Age sites remain relatively elusive in Devon and Cornwall, and few have been the focus of large-scale excavation. This is one reason why views of the later prehistoric period of the region have remained relatively static.

The potential for new interpretation of the Iron Age of south-west England is vast. The location, wealth of extant monuments, and diverse range of natural resources result in a rich and unique regional archaeology, the nature of which owes much to the relationship with other maritime regions of the Atlantic seaboard. This is most visible in the presence of specific settlement forms, such as promontory forts or 'cliff castles', found along the coasts of Cornwall, Devon, Scotland, Wales, the Channel Islands, the Scilly Isles, the Isle of Man, Ireland, and Brittany (Lamb 1980, 4–6), or the courtyard houses, which for this period are unique to Cornwall and the Scilly Isles. Other aspects of social practice, such as the tradition of formal burial exhibited in Cornwall (e.g. Whimster 1977; Nowakowski 1991), also have few parallels elsewhere.

This paper reviews the nature of Later Iron Age settlement in Cornwall and Devon, highlighting some of the inconsistencies in current archaeological approaches to this material. The broader excavated record is considered in relation to recent interpretations and some alternative models offered. As a working paper written whilst my doctoral thesis is still in progress (Cripps forthcoming a), the discussion inevitably offers more questions for debate than solutions. Nevertheless I hope that by re-examining some key aspects of the

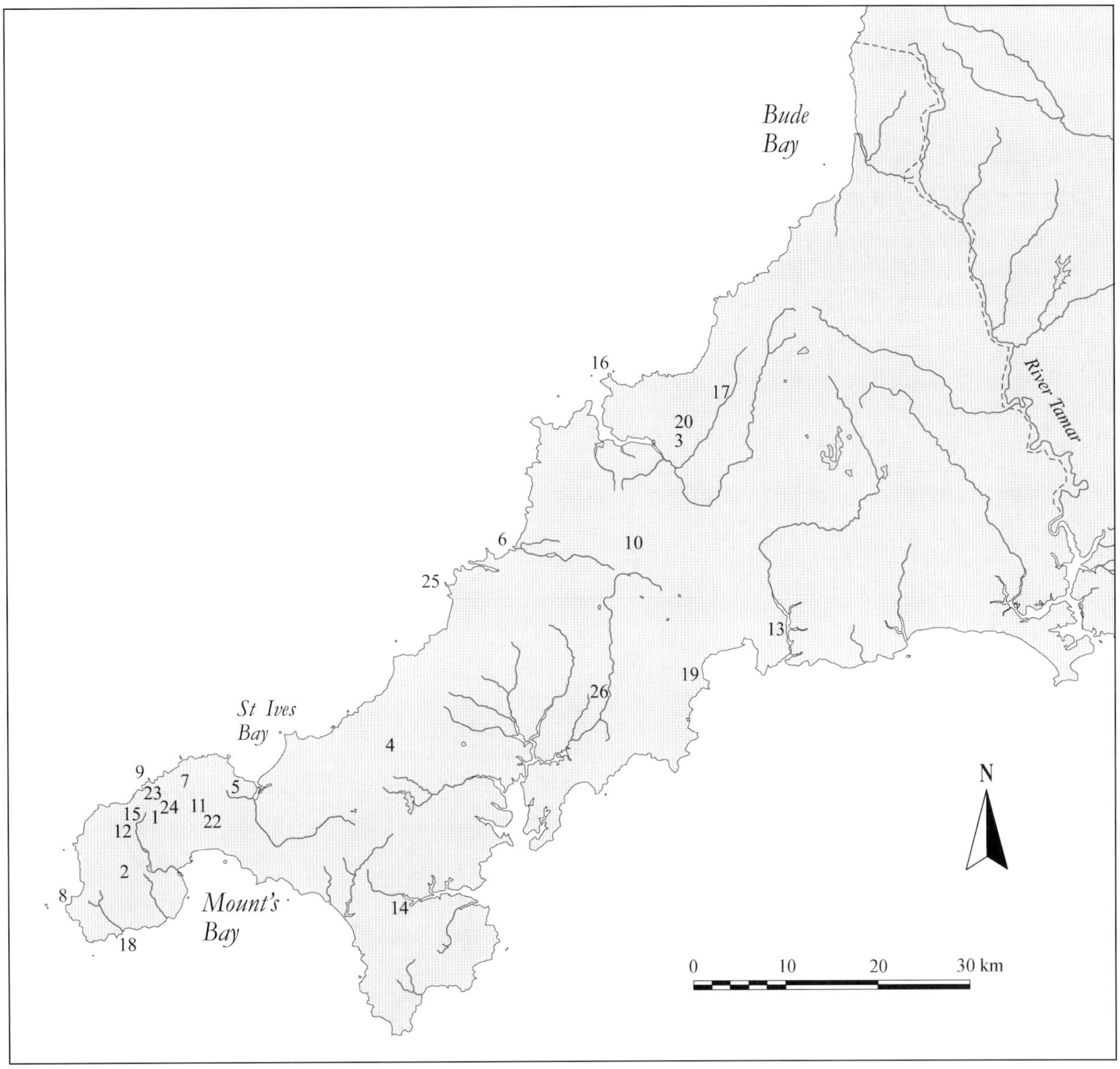

Fig. 1. Cornwall – principal sites: 1. Bodrifty; 2. Carn Euny; 3. Killibury; 4. Carn Brea; 5. Trencrom; 6. Trevelgue Head; 7. Wicca Round and Sperris Croft; 8. Maen Castle; 9. Gurnards Head; 10. Castle-an-Dinas (Restormel); 11. Castle-an-Dinas (Penwith); 12. Chun Castle; 13. Castle Dore; 14. Gear/Caer Vallack; 15. Bosullow Trehyllys; 16. The Rumps; 17. Tregeare Round; 18. Treryn Dinas; 19. Castle Gotha; 20. Tregilders; 21. Threemilestone; 22. Chysauster; 23. Porthmeor; 24. Mulfra Vean ; 25. Penale Castle; 26. Carvossa.

nature and interpretation of the Later Iron Age settlement record in south-west England, I can provide a more even platform from which future discussions can progress. Figures 1 and 2 show the location of the principal sites discussed in the text.

Current consensus

Current orthodoxy links a reduction in the visibility of settlement in the uplands of Cornwall and Devon toward the middle of the first millennium BC to a period of environmental deterioration which forced communities to evacuate marginal upland moors and move into the lowland areas of the peninsula. Considerable emphasis is placed on apparent 'continuity' between the Late Bronze Age and Early Iron Age prior to this shift, implied by the localised and largely standardised pottery and metalwork forms (see Todd 1987; Henderson 2007). Quinnell (1994) suggests the abandonment of higher land coincided broadly with an increase in hillfort numbers at the start of the Later Iron Age. Traditionally,

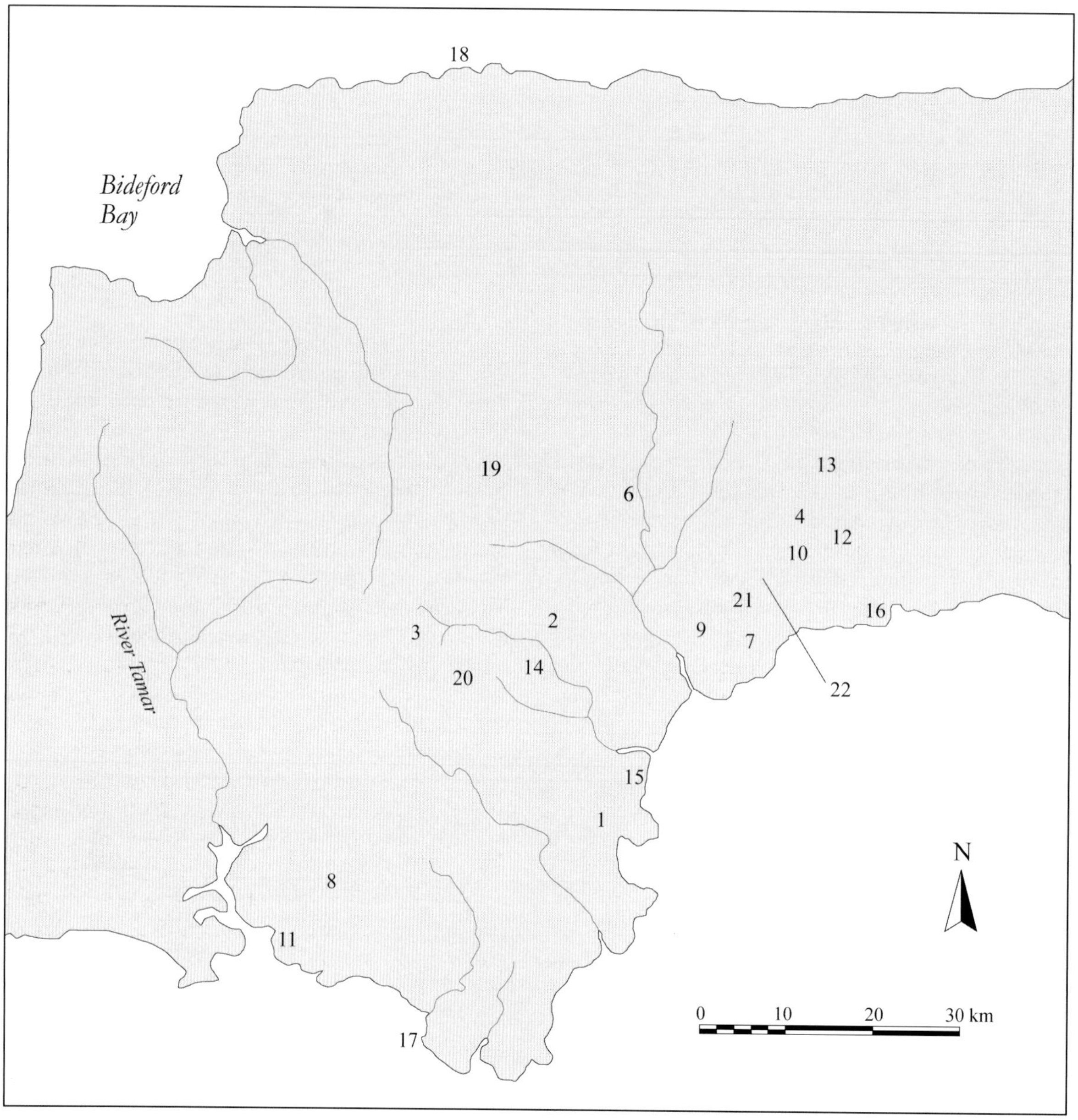

Fig. 2. Devon – principal sites: 1. Dainton; 2. Foale's Arrishes; 3. Kestor; 4. Hembury; 5. Embury Beacon; 6. Raddon Hill; 7. Woodbury Castle; 8. Shaugh Moor; 9. Blackhorse; 10. Castle Hill; 11. Mount Batten; 12. Hayne Layne; 13. Dumpdon; 14. Cranbrook Castle; 15. Milber Down; 16. Blackbury Castle; 17. Bolt Tail; 18. Wind Hill; 19. Rudge; 20. Gold Park; 21. Long Range; 22. Langland Lane.

these hillforts have been regarded as the linch pins of the Later Iron Age economy, situated on the interface between the uplands (seasonal grazing), and the lowlands (arable cultivation and pasture). Hillforts and cliff castles are seen as the residences of local elites, whose wealth may have been cattle-based and who controlled access to land, long-distance trade, and social ceremony as part of patron–client relationships with lower levels of society. The 'client' occupants of smaller enclosed settlements ('rounds') concentrated on arable cultivation and maintenance of animal stocks, some of which may have been on some form of loan from their elite patrons (see Todd 1987, 167; Cunliffe 1991, 312–70; Herring 1992; 1994; Quinnell 1994).

The most detailed application of this model to south-west England is that by Herring (1992; 1994) for West Penwith where, according to his model, four elite centres in the Early Iron Age – the cliff castles of Maen and Bosigran and the hillforts of Trencrom and Lescudjack – gave way to eight or ten smaller regional territories in the Later Iron Age, each of which was controlled by a new defended hillfort and its associated elite. Although

Herring raises the possibility that these later hillforts may have been an expression of community power, and not elite residences as such, their position at the top of a hierarchical social and settlement structure is clear:

> 'The higher levels of society, those probably responsible for building the defended sites, will have both exploited and served the farmers (of the rounds and open settlements)... Services provided by the higher levels will probably have centred on running local administration systems, ensuring local justice worked and guaranteeing security... and overseeing or organising both local trade or exchange and longer distance trade. Defended central places... would have served all these functions' (Herring 1994, 54).

More recently, Quinnell (2004) has proposed an alternative model of social organisation relating to the settlement evidence of Later Iron Age Cornwall. Within this interpretation, 'rounds' are seen as the residences of the controlling elite, whilst hillforts are viewed as places for broader communal activities. In line with Herring's suggestion (1994, 46–50) of fracturing territory, Quinnell proposes that at the beginning of the Later Iron Age, a system collapse lead to a breakdown of control by the elites occupying the larger hillfort centres and a resultant shift of power to a new elite situated within the rounds (Quinnell 2004, 214).

Chronology

Absolute chronologies for the Iron Age in Cornwall and Devon continue to be hindered by a relative lack of radiocarbon dates. Current consensus favours a twofold division: Early Iron Age (*c.* 800–400 BC) and Later Iron Age (400 BC–AD 43), largely derived from changes in pottery forms (Quinnell 1986). Pottery chronologies for the Early Iron Age are vague, and in some cases wares can only be identified to the first half of the first millennium BC. These are often termed 'Earlier Iron Age', meaning they could belong to the Late Bronze Age or Early Iron Age or both. The majority of pottery assemblages from this period consist of 'post-Trevisker wares', which evolved from the Middle Bronze Age Trevisker wares, which on current evidence terminated during the twelfth century BC in Cornwall (Nowakowski 1991, 102) and around the tenth/ninth century BC in Somerset (Quinnell 1994, 76). Post-Trevisker wares are largely undecorated, with shouldered jar and bowl forms being most common. Biconical urns, plainer and less recognisable than post-Trevisker wares, also appear in the Early Iron Age, although these have only been identified with certainty at Shaugh Moor enclosure 15 (Wainwright and Smith 1980).

The Later Iron Age is defined in part by the development of the so-called South-Western Decorated wares (Cunliffe 1991, 84–5). In Cornwall, their inception has been pushed back to the fourth century BC, based on the presence of developed examples with geometric designs in third-century BC contexts at Killibury in Cornwall and Meare Lake Village in Somerset (Quinnell 1986, 113). By the second century BC, raised slashed cordons, internal grooves, and incised curvilinear motifs are common. Slightly earlier and rarer are stamp-decorated wares, similar to fifth-century BC forms from Brittany, and found at sites such as Trevelgue and Carn Euny (Christie 1978, 402–3), the latter producing sherds with an associated radiocarbon date of 800–350 cal. BC.[1]

Cordoned wares, with developed curvilinear and 'cordon' designs, are generally thought to appear throughout Cornwall during the first century BC, when South-Western Decorated wares begin to die out. They are thinner and generally 'better made' than South-Western Decorated wares, but many still appear to have been hand-made. The extent of wheel-thrown pottery production in Cornwall in the Later Iron Age remains uncertain (Quinnell 2004, 109). A period of fusion between South-Western Decorated wares and Cordoned wares would seemingly reflect a short window of overlap during which both were produced simultaneously, although some authors have begun to suggest a longer life span for Cordoned wares, with an earlier inception within the Late Iron Age (Christie 1997, 6).

On current evidence, three phases of Cordoned ware can be distinguished (see Quinnell 2004, 109–11). Phase 1 wares, lasting from the first century BC to the mid/late first century AD, consist mainly of cups and bowls, large storage jars and some cooking pots (similar to the basic upright-necked form of South-Western Decorated wares, but without decoration). Phase 2 wares appear around the end of the first century AD and last until the latter half of the second century AD, when the less distinct, Phase 3 wares begin. Phase 2 wares mostly comprise the same large storage jars and cooking pots, as well as new styles copying Roman forms such as dishes with externally grooved rims. The cups and bowls typical of Phase 1 wares seem to have disappeared by Phase 2.

Earlier Iron Age developments

> 'Settlements of the mid first millennium... are few when compared with the preceding and following periods. What is known about them suggests no major change in settlement type had occurred' (Todd 1987, 155).

In order to understand the various changes of the Later Iron Age, it is necessary to offer a brief appraisal of the social landscape at the beginning of the first millennium BC. The Late Bronze Age–Early Iron Age in Cornwall and Devon is currently regarded as a period of continuity in settlement form but, as will be suggested below, this is more implied than real, relying largely on assumed typological bridges between settlement forms and weak pottery chronologies, rather than on excavated evidence.

Evidence of Early Iron Age settlement in Cornwall remains slight. At Bodrifty, one of the largest settlements of this period, occupation continued from the Late Bronze Age into the Early Iron Age when, possibly during the fifth century BC, eight huts were enclosed within a low wall (Dudley 1957a). At Garrow Tor, where there are approximately 100 hut circles, some of them enclosed, Early Iron Age post-Trevisker wares have been found, although occupation is thought to have begun earlier, in the Middle to Late Bronze Age (Dudley 1957b). Open and enclosed hut circles of Early Iron Age date have also been found at Sperris Croft, whilst the courtyard house village at Carn Euny represents the final phase of a settlement which is generally thought to have originated around the fifth century BC (Christie 1978, 385). On Bodmin Moor unenclosed settlements such as Catshole Tor, Stanning Hill, and Twelve Men's Moor (Johnson and Rose 1994) are traditionally grouped together as Late Bronze Age/Early Iron Age, but show significant variation in hut size and structure; without excavation, their date and contemporaneity should not therefore be assumed.

In Devon, evidence for open settlement is similarly sparse and – until recently – was heavily biased toward the uplands. At Dainton, discrete scatters of post-Deverel-Rimbury pottery and other debris such as querns around the site could indicate seasonal activity and/or continuing occupation associated with the field system (Silvester 1980). On Dartmoor, enclosures at Metherall and Foale's Arrishes (Silvester 1979) continued well into the first half of the first millennium BC, the latest phase at the latter being associated with ironworking, although not necessarily permanent occupation. Occupation at Shaugh Moor also seems to have continued across the Late Bronze Age–Iron Age transition; the latest radiocarbon date associated with a structural feature falls within the range 980–520 cal. BC, although a lack of obvious 'domestic' features such as hearths, drains and surfaces in the latest phases may indicate a shift toward occasional or temporary re-use of the site at this time (Wainwright and Smith 1980, 109). The scattered settlement and field system at Kestor apparently dates to the end of the Early Iron Age (Fox 1954), although Silvester (1979, 178–9) has since questioned whether the ironworking remains from within the circular structure at the centre of the enclosure known as the Round Pound may be of later date.

Few hillforts have been excavated in south-west England and in the last 35 years, only Hembury (1930–5 and 1980–3), Embury Beacon (1972–3) and Raddon Hill (1994) in Devon, and Killibury (1975–6) and Carn Brea (1981) in Cornwall, have undergone excavation on any scale. Although the majority of south-western hillforts seem to originate in the Later Iron Age, the use of many hilltop locations in preceding periods is becoming increasingly apparent. At Raddon Hill, a palisaded enclosure with a radiocarbon date of 810–410 cal. BC was identified pre-dating the hillfort ramparts (Gent and Quinnell 1999). A palisaded enclosure also pre-dates the hillfort phases at Woodbury Castle in Devon, whilst a Late Bronze Age enclosure has been suggested to precede the hillfort at Killibury (Miles 1977, 100). Late Bronze Age origins have also been proposed for other hillforts such as Cadonsbury, and 'Tor enclosures' such as Trencrom, but without further investigations, such suggestions can only be an assumption, one which could well be exaggerating the vision of continuity between the Late Bronze Age and Early Iron Age.

Whilst the evidence for Late Bronze Age and Early Iron Age settlement in Cornwall and Devon is limited, the suggestion that the period was stagnant, marked by similarity and continuity, is simply not tenable. If guided purely by pottery chronologies, it is difficult to discern changes in the settlement record during the early to mid first millennium BC. When focus returns to the nature and use of settlement, however, the picture is not so uniform, with more evidence of change over time. New forms of settlement do become visible in the Early Iron Age and traditional settlement forms are given new expression within a changing landscape. The grammar of the Early Iron Age settlement landscape is different from that of the Late Bronze Age.

There is some evidence for settlements which bridge the gap between the Late Bronze Age and Early Iron Age, and which often undergo a form of transformation towards the middle of the first millennium BC. Around 800–600 BC, ironworking became the focus at the established settlements of Foale's Arrishes and – less certainly – Kestor, as well as being evident at a much larger scale at the new cliff castle at Trevelgue Head (Nowakowski 2000). At the first two settlements, occupation does not appear to extend beyond the mid first millennium BC, and both sites are also unified by a decrease in, or lack of, apparent occupation, seemingly coinciding with the point at which the role of metal-working becomes more visible. At Shaugh Moor, occupation had also become less intense at the start of the Iron Age than in the Late Bronze Age, possibly even temporary or seasonal. Foale's Arrishes, Kestor, and Shaugh Moor are all situated on the periphery of Dartmoor, whilst the coastal location of Trevelgue can also be seen as spatially and conceptually 'liminal'. This has interesting implications for Hingley's (1997) consideration of the socially peripheral nature of ironworking during the Iron Age in Britain.

A shift thus appears to take place during the Early Iron Age, whereby specific upland sites are established or transformed, with limited or reduced evidence for intense occupation and the adoption of iron metal-working as their apparent focus. The introduction of iron does appear to have had an impact on the settlement record in the first half of the first millennium BC (*contra*

Todd 1987; Henderson 2007), with ironworking becoming the focus of activity at specific sites where 'domestic' settlement has been visibly reduced or is unapparent. Do these sites represent new communal foci for Early Iron Age communities who, in the midst of climatic deterioration, were re-establishing themselves in lowland areas and transforming their use of the upland landscape? It is notable, however, that only one of the three Iron Age sites excavated in the east Devon lowlands on the line of the A30 Improvement Scheme was occupied in the Earlier Iron Age: Blackhorse, near Exeter, where a post-built roundhouse found outside the later rectangular enclosure was radiocarbon dated to 770–370 cal. BC. Neither of the two Late Bronze Age settlements identified by the project – at Castle Hill and Hayne Lane west of Honiton – continued into the Early Iron Age (Fitzpatrick *et al.* 1999).

Whilst the upland areas of Devon may have become less permanently settled in the Early Iron Age, they were not, however, abandoned and indeed may have retained a significant power and importance within social consciousness as locales for ironworking. The site of Gold Park also gives a crucial indication of continued activity on Dartmoor well into the Later Iron Age (see below). The construction of stone cairns over earlier structures at this site – similar to, and most familiar within the Bronze Age moorland landscape – possibly relates to complex and reasoned perceptions of the longevity of the moorland's biography.

Increased enclosure of settlement also appears to be a feature of the Early Iron Age landscape. When viewed alongside the situations of new settlements such as Sperris Croft, the enclosure of sites such as Bodrifty and Wicca Round could be seen as part of a bigger transformation of settlement, which aimed to dominate and territorialise broader areas of space by making a deeper physical and visual impact on the landscape. New settlement forms *do* appear in the Early Iron Age: the hillfort at Raddon, the round at Wicca, and the cliff castles of Maen Castle and Trevelgue Head are all new 'types' of site, although the establishment of the two cliff castles is perhaps better seen as a transformation of place, given the continuity at these coastal venues of a tradition of veneration that can arguably be traced back to the Neolithic (Sharpe 1992). If so, this can be seen as part of a more general trend continuing into the Later Iron Age, whereby transformations in the settlement landscape developed with reference to mythical and/or genealogical understandings of earlier lived landscapes and the communities within them (see Gosden 1997; Gosden and Lock 1998; Brück and Goodman 1999): a past re-appropriated, transformed and maintained within social consciousness. As I argue elsewhere, this helped structure the organisation and control of power within Iron Age society (Cripps forthcoming b). It is from this social setting that the Later Iron Age settlement landscape developed.

Settlement of the Later Iron Age

Hillforts

Most hillforts in the peninsula are small and multivallate, although larger examples, more familiar in regions such as Wessex, are also found: Hembury, Dumpdon, Castle Carnuke, and Castle-an-Dinas, for example. In Devon, hillforts are most densely distributed in the south, many hugging the edge of the granite moorland, with an additional cluster on the north coast above Barnstaple. South-Western Decorated wares have been recovered from Cranbrook and Embury Beacon; at Hembury and Bury Castle these indicate a peak in activity from the second century BC, although occupation began earlier, probably during the fourth century BC (Todd 1984, 260). A small pottery assemblage from Berry Down indicates occupation from the third century BC (Gallant and Silvester 1985, 48), whilst at Milber Down occupation appears to have been briefer and later, first century BC to mid first century AD.

Fourth-century BC plainwares have been found at Blackbury Castle and, in greater numbers, at Woodbury Castle – which was apparently abandoned before South-Western Decorated wares were introduced. Increasing evidence for 'aceramic' activity at certain Later Iron Age sites, however, may require us to reappraise the nature of settlement after 400 BC. Four radiocarbon dates from a variety of post holes within the interior of Raddon Hill indicate that activity continued between the fifth century BC and second century BC, despite a total absence of pottery dating to this period. The enclosure circuit appears to have been abandoned at the same time, with the ramparts and ditches left unmaintained (Gent and Quinnell 1999, 24). This must cause us to question the nature of activity at other enclosures, particularly when sites such as Berry Down do have small assemblages dating to this period. In the latter case, this has led to the suggestion of temporary or seasonal occupation (Gallant and Silvester 1985), but other possibilities should be considered.

In Cornwall, hillforts are more densely scattered on the slopes of lower-lying land, although several can be found on the upland peripheries of Bodmin Moor and in West Penwith. Castle-an-Dinas (Wailes 1963), Killibury (Miles 1977), Chun Castle (Leeds 1926), and Castle Dore (Quinnell 1985) have all produced South-Western Decorated wares and Cordoned wares. The sequence at Castle Dore is the most complete, indicating relatively continuous occupation from the fourth century BC to the mid first century AD (*ibid.*, 123). Activity at Trencrom can also be attributed to the Late Iron Age, pottery sherds recovered from molehills having been dated to the second century BC.

It is frequently argued that south-western hillforts reflect an unusual 'absence' of activity and lack of occupation (e.g. Fox 1996), although the focus of excavation on ramparts and entrances rather than interiors has undoubtedly contributed to this impression. One similarity between the hillforts of Cornwall and Devon is an absence of storage pits. Killibury is the only site with possible examples and these appear to have been backfilled almost immediately with clean shillet (Miles 1977, 113). Grain is argued to have been stored above ground rather than below, although four- and five-post structures are suggested to be uncommon, as are roundhouses (Quinnell 1986, 115–17). This lack of evidence has dominated interpretation of the social role and function of hillforts in south-west England, particularly in terms of their proposed pastoral-based economies, in turn helping to underpin the current model of Late Iron Age social organisation for the region. However, to use a frequently coined phrase, is absence of evidence really evidence of absence?

Within Devon, the excavation of hillfort interiors has been limited to Blackbury Castle, Woodbury Castle, and Embury Beacon. Intriguingly, all three sites reportedly yielded structural evidence in the form of post-built 'rectilinear' structures (Fox 1996, 12–13; Todd 1987, 165), rather than the circular 'roundhouses' typical of Late Bronze Age and Iron Age settlement in the region. Whether these are indeed rectilinear structures, or simply groups of paired post holes and four-post arrangements, remains uncertain. In Cornwall, Castle Dore and Killibury produced evidence of dense multi-phase occupation, including roundhouses and four-post structures. At Castle-an-Dinas post holes, gullies and cobbled surfaces were recorded during minimal excavations in the interior, whilst at Chun Castle, numerous hut circles are visible, although excavations in the early twentieth century failed to achieve any relative chronology between them.

A range of pits, post holes, penannular gullies and 'domestic' debris have been found between the inner and outer ramparts at a number of hillforts such as Killibury and Milber Down, as well as at other forms of enclosure such as The Rumps cliff castle and Tregeare Round. In 2002, geophysical survey by Time Team within the interiors at the probable hillforts at Gaer and Caer Vallack on the Lizard revealed a palimpsest of features and 'activity', including probable Bronze Age barrows and circular structures; two of the latter were excavated and positively identified as Iron Age roundhouses. In 2004, geophysical surveys were undertaken of the interiors of a further seven partially excavated Iron Age enclosures, most of which showed indications of dense activity, in several instances contradicting the impression given by small-scale excavations previously undertaken at these sites (Cripps forthcoming a).

When considered in relation to the small area excavated within hillfort interiors, evidence of occupation is not so wholly absent. And whilst in some cases the 'settlement' of hillforts may appear to be less pronounced and less dense than that of other settlement types, this need not necessarily reflect the degree to which these sites were integrated within their representative communities.

Cliff castles

The majority of cliff castles in Cornwall and Devon are of Later Iron Age date and enclosed by multiple ditched ramparts. Maen Castle, near Sennen, and Trevelgue Head in Newquay, both appear to have originated in the Early Iron Age and, on current understanding, represent the earliest cliff castles in south-west England. The 1939 investigations at Trevelgue Head were never published, but an appraisal of the archive has shown that although the excavated area was small (perhaps only 2% of the interior), Trevelgue produced over 4000 sherds of pottery and evidence for relatively large-scale iron-working (see Nowakowski 2000). The pottery consisted of Early Iron Age, Late Iron Age and Roman wares and included a small collection of non-local sherds. Trevelgue was certainly a site of significance during the Iron Age, whilst the recovery of 88 Roman coins, the majority of which are late, indicates a continued importance of within the wider social landscape in the Roman period.

Excavation at Penhale revealed a single, circular, stone and post-built structure within the interior, along with several sherds of decorated pottery apparently from one vessel, and dating no later than the first century BC (Smith 1984). At Gurnards Head, several single- and double-walled hut circles with multiple occupation layers were found in the interior alongside fourth and third century BC pottery, including some stamped wares (Todd 1987, 163). More recent excavations at The Rumps in Wadebridge yielded a wealth of structural features and domestic debris, much of which came from between the inner and outer ramparts. A date range from the second century BC to the mid first century AD was originally suggested, but revised pottery comparisons from Castle Dore (Quinnell 1985) indicate that the initial occupation may have been as early as the fourth century BC. In Devon, fewer cliff castles have been excavated, although most, such as Bolt Tail in Malborough, Hillsborough in Ilfracombe, and Wind Hill near Lynmouth, are accepted as Iron Age in date.

There is circumstantial evidence to suggest that certain headlands were already of sites of significance during the Bronze Age. The enclosure of some of these sites during the Iron Age may have been part of a veneration of natural rocky landscapes associated with the past, mimicking Neolithic tor enclosures such as Carn Brea (Sharpe 1992). If this was indeed the case, one of the clearest examples would be the dramatic cliff castle of Treryn Dinas, where the outermost granite outcrop has yielded sherds of Bronze Age cremation urn and Iron Age pottery (*ibid.*, 66). Treryn is not the only cliff castle with evidence of earlier Bronze Age activity and a knowledge of the significance of these locations in the past is indicated by the re-use of Bronze Age landscape features at other cliff castles (Cripps and Giles forthcoming).

In current models, cliff castles are seen as having had the same 'function' as hillforts, either as the coastal retreats of an elite and/or a focus for communal activity (Herring 1994, 54). Their dramatic coastal location has also led to the suggestion that cliff castles were trading venues, but, although coastal, their frequently rocky nature would have made navigation tricky and actual evidence for trade remains ambiguous. Both the situation of these sites, with their impressive vistas, and the grand enclosure boundaries and entrances indicate places of high social significance and a ritual or religious function is often postulated (Cunliffe 2001, 346). As at hillforts, the practices undertaken at cliff castles appear to have varied, but as impressive liminal locales, we certainly should not be surprised that a number of these activities seem to have been associated with the exotic or unknown: with distant social contacts, technological innovation, death, and the past communities who lived within the landscape (see Cripps and Giles forthcoming).

Rounds and hill-slope enclosures

Two other forms of inland enclosure feature heavily in discussions of Later Iron Age Cornwall and Devon: the 'hill-slope enclosure' and the 'round'. Practically, the application of this distinction is problematic as the definition and use of each term varies between authors, and to a lesser degree, between the two counties. In his overviews of south-west England, Todd (1987, 157–68; 1998, 133) suggests that hill-slope enclosures are most common in west and north Devon and east and central Cornwall, but absent from west Cornwall, whilst rounds are common throughout Cornwall and north-west Devon. In more specific discussions of Iron Age Devon, hill-slope enclosures feature heavily but rounds are rare, whilst in accounts of Cornwall, rounds appear more frequently than hill-slope enclosures (Johnson and Rose 1994). For some authors, they are simply different names for the same settlement form: rounds in Cornwall are hill-slope enclosures in Devon (Silvester 1979, 181).

Such ambiguity arises partly from a lack of consensus upon the criteria used to distinguish rounds from hill-slope enclosures. Morphologically, both are very similar, displaying diversity in form but with circular and sub-circular univallate forms being most common. The main difference appears to be one of size, with rounds 'seldom exceeding a hectare in extent' (Cunliffe 1991, 256), whilst hill-slope enclosures are 'usually less than 3 hectares…[although] a number… cover up to 8 hectares' (Todd 1987, 165–6). On this basis, is the distinction between them – or for that matter between them and other non-hillfort enclosures – a valid and meaningful one? With no obvious differences between the assemblages found at the two forms of settlement, it would seem not. There is a large degree of overlap in the actual settlement record, where basic differences of size and form would appear insufficient and insignificant.

At one level, the argument may not be all that important. The categories and boundaries we create are only meaningful within the context of our own theorised settlement landscape and are always less distinct in reality. All attempts to categorise settlement have, to differing degrees, the effect of homogenising a diverse archaeological record. However, although excavations of both enclosure 'types' have failed to produce any obvious differences in the nature of activity *within* them, this has not prevented social distinctions being created *between* them, with hill-slope forts in Cornwall being suggested to represent a distinct stratum of society, somewhere between the hillfort elites and the inhabitants of the rounds (Quinnell 1986, 118). When unsupported assumptions of status are integrated into the settlement record in this way, classifications of settlement 'type' often gain undue significance, leading to over-simplistic social narratives based on a fictitious archaeological record. This model of settlement hierarchy has now been revised, with rounds becoming the new centres of elite control (Quinnell 2004), but before considering this model, the archaeology of rounds needs first to be summarised, along with that of the final Cornish settlement type, the Later Iron Age courtyard house.

Although rounds originated in the Late Iron Age, the majority appear to date to the Roman period. Excavations at Castle Gotha near St Austell revealed four circular structures, with occupation from the second century BC to the second century AD and evidence of a diverse range of agricultural practices and probable small-scale metal-working (Saunders and Harris 1982). Elsewhere, however, Late Iron Age structural evidence is sparse. No structures were found in limited excavations at Bodwen, although Later Iron Age pottery was found at the base of the topsoil. A Middle Bronze Age cord-impressed sherd, and an adze and rapier mould of contemporary date may indicate earlier activity at this site (Harris 1977, 46–56). Tregilders, a sub-rectangular enclosure close to Killibury hillfort, also failed to yield evidence of occupation in the interior, although a 'living area' was discovered just outside the enclosure, charcoal from there generating a radiocarbon date of 170 cal. BC–220 cal. AD (Trudgian 1977). The assemblage from this living area is curious: the 126 pottery sherds from this site were of gabbroic fabric and most, if not all, appeared to belong to jars with a rim diameter of 16–20 cm (*ibid.*, 126). Settlement activity has also been found outside the ditched enclosure bank of Threemilestone, Kenwyn, although here two oval enclosures and up to nine circular structures were found within the interior (Schwieso 1976). Evidence from the hill-slope enclosure at Rudge (Todd 1998), one of only a few in Devon to have been excavated, indicated

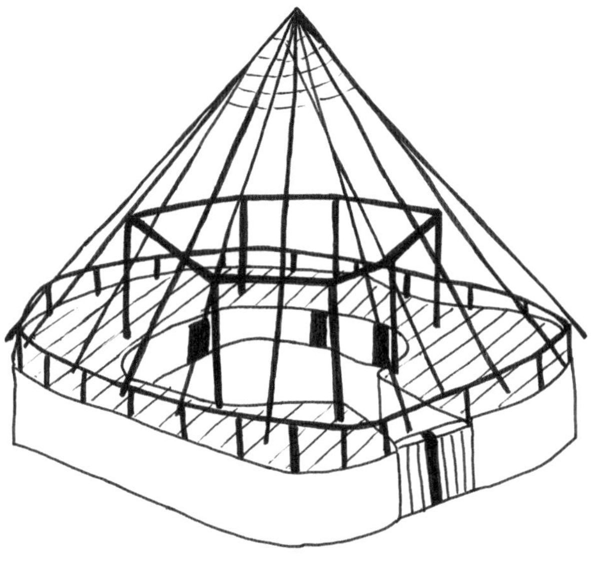

Fig. 3. Depiction of a single-roofed courtyard house (after Wood 1997, 104).

short-lived occupation in the later first century BC. The assemblage reflected extensive contacts, with a quarter of the pottery made up of Roman imports. Interestingly, Threemilestone and Rudge are also the only known rounds to have two outer ditches.

Excavations at Gold Park, on the eastern fringe of Dartmoor, have identified a palimpsest of Later Iron Age settlement (Gibson 1992), yielding invaluable insight into the environment and use of the moor during the later first millennium BC when, according to current models, permanent settlement had been abandoned. Central to Gold Park was a stone structure within an enclosure, situated in a network of prehistoric field systems which also contained a number of stone cairns and a banked trackway leading toward open land. A single sherd of late South-Western Decorated ware found in association with the stone structure would appear to indicate that, as at Raddon Hill, there was limited use of pottery at this time, for whatever reason. An internal hearth yielded a radiocarbon date of 360 cal. BC–cal. AD 60. Beneath the stone structure, the bedding trench, internal post holes and floor of an earlier timber structure were found, yielding a slightly earlier date of 390–90 cal. BC. Statistically, however, all five radiocarbon dates from the two structural phases are indistinguishable, implying that the stone house followed the timber phase with no appreciable time lapse (Gibson 1992). Bedding trenches, stake holes and post holes of four further timber structures were found underlying the cairnfield; these too appear to be of Later Iron Age date and thus comprise some of the only evidence for non-hillfort settlement and activity on Dartmoor during this period.

Similar palimpsest settlements, combining both open and enclosed phases, have been identified along the route of the A30 in east Devon. Post-built roundhouses and associated penannular gullies have been discovered at Langland Lane and Long Range, whilst at Blackhorse, several circular structures were found, one of which was situated in the centre of a square-ditched enclosure, as well as four-post structures. All three sites have radiocarbon dates falling between the fourth century BC and the first century AD. At Blackhorse, the enclosure was preceded by an open settlement, represented by the post-built roundhouse mentioned above.

Courtyard houses

Courtyard houses are only found in Cornwall and the Isles of Scilly. These structures are enclosed by a thick wall and typically include a paved entrance leading to a central 'courtyard', directly off which lie a series of circular, sub-circular and sub-rectilinear rooms. Current orthodoxy suggests that each room of a courtyard house was individually roofed with the central 'courtyard' left open, although it has been argued that one large hipped roof covering both courtyard and rooms would have been a more practical and viable method as well as allowing for the creation of a second floor gallery (Fig. 3; Wood 1997). This latter possibility is further supported by the reconstruction of a 'figure-of-eight' house on Great Bernera in the Western Isles (Neighbour and Crawford 2001), which is similar in plan to a courtyard house.

Eighty-two extant courtyard houses, most frequently found grouped in villages, have been identified in Cornwall. Only a small proportion have undergone any degree of excavation and most commentators follow Quinnell (1986, 120) in her view that courtyard house hamlets or villages belonged to the Roman period. This proposition is based upon two crucial readings of the archaeological evidence. The first of these concerns the stratigraphic context of the South-Western Decorated wares at Chysauster and Porthmeor. These are assumed to derive from non-secure contexts and as such relate to settlement on the site prior to the construction of the courtyard houses. At Porthmeor, some of the courtyard houses do indeed sit within the banks of an earlier round, but at Chysauster structural evidence for earlier settlement has not yet been found. Second, although the forms of Cordoned wares found at Carn Euny and Mulfra Vean are long-lived, originating in the first century BC and continuing throughout the Roman period, the vessels found at the two sites are assumed to be 'late' examples, post-dating the Iron Age (*ibid.*).

If we accept these arguments, the case for courtyard houses as a purely Roman phenomenon appears convincing, but by taking a more holistic approach to the evidence, a persuasive case can also be made for arrival of courtyard houses in the late second and early first centuries BC. First, there is no obvious reason to doubt the validity of the Iron Age contexts from which South-Western Decorated wares were recovered at

Chysauster and Porthmeor. The reports of both excavations, undertaken in the 1930s are, admittedly, ambiguous, but whilst the possibility of contamination or residuality cannot be ruled out at Porthmeor, the absence of any earlier settlement at Chysauster makes the argument for contamination at this site less convincing. Second, although the majority of excavated courtyard houses do indeed appear to date to the Roman period, we should not let this bias our reading of the archaeological record. If only the *origins* of courtyard houses rest in the Late Iron Age, it should not be particularly surprising that the evidence for Late Iron Age courtyard houses is minimal. Third, the fact that most courtyard houses are Roman does not make the assumption that the Cordoned ware vessels found at the above mentioned sites are 'Roman' any more valid.

The case for courtyard houses as a Late Iron Age development does not rest purely upon ambiguities within our excavation records and pottery chronologies. Several other courtyard houses have produced potential evidence of Late Iron Age origins. A number of unexcavated examples have yielded stray finds of Iron Age date: pottery and stone from Boddinar Crellas, and an Iron Age glass bead from Crankan, for example. In addition, sections of the field system within which the unexcavated courtyard house village at Bosullow Trehyllys lies have been excavated and yielded Late Iron Age South-Western Decorated wares (P. Herring pers. comm.). This material could all be residual from earlier settlement within or around the courtyard houses, but once again it is important to keep an open mind, and not let previous assumptions influence our interpretation and re-interpretation of the evidence.

Furthermore, courtyard houses are frequently found in association with 'fogous' – underground passages similar to the souterrains of Scotland and Brittany. Within Cornwall, fogous have nearly all been dated to the Late Iron Age; indeed, the only 'Roman' fogou is arguably the one from Bosullow Trehyllys, which as I have already noted, is unexcavated, and sits within a field system of Later Iron Age or earlier date; the Roman date is entirely down to its courtyard house status. When fogous are found in association with courtyard houses, they are generally attributed to 'earlier' settlement or activity, as most notably at Carn Euny (Cunliffe 1991, 236), but there is no reason why this should always be so.

Finally, the nature of courtyard houses, their construction, and their settlement biographies all indicate that they are very much a development founded within the social structures of the Late Iron Age. Several sites reflect a process of 'courtyardisation', whereby pre-existing roundhouse structures were incorporated into a larger courtyard house format, as at Bosporthennis houses 1 and 2; Croftoe house 1; Greenburrow; and Nanjullian. The plan of an established courtyard house can also be seen to evolve through accretion, whereby further rooms were added over time, as for example with Bosigran house 2; Bosporthennis houses 1 and 2; and Chysauster house 3. In addition, several courtyard houses apparently of single construction seem to have been used alongside standard roundhouse structures, such as Trevean houses 2 and 3. To this extent, courtyard house forms can be seen to grow up alongside, and within, traditional modes of living, a local, insular development derived from changes within the structure of Later Iron Age society. They were not brought by the Romans at the time of invasion.

The object of this discussion is to illustrate the proposition that courtyard houses in Cornwall can be traced back to the Late Iron Age, the implications of which are discussed below.

Settlement and society in the Later Iron Age

The above summary shows the variability and complexity of Iron Age settlement in Cornwall and Devon. The record remains biased toward upland areas where archaeological attention has traditionally been focused; partly because of the greater visibility of settlement due to the presence and use of stone for structures during prehistory; and partly because of the relatively low intensity of use of these areas during historic periods. In contrast, the lowlands have long been subject to cultivation and have suffered particularly from more recent intensive agriculture. Archaeological remains are also visibly harder to detect here, and are normally only found as part of developer-funded archaeology, the A30 Honiton to Exeter Improvement Scheme being the most obvious recent example. The Bronze Age and Iron Age sites examined in this project indicate the settlement numbers to be expected in other lowland areas of south-west England – sites that until recently we could not be sure existed – transforming our comprehension of later prehistoric settlement in the peninsula. Along with other sites like Gold Park, they also show that while enclosed sites became increasingly common in the later first millennium BC, open settlement did not disappear completely.

When placed against the settlement evidence, current models of Iron Age society and social organisation appear to raise more questions than answers. The nature of Early Iron Age society in the region is hardly discussed, tending to be regarded as a period defined by, and largely similar to, the Late Bronze Age (Henderson 2007), but as I noted above, this implied continuity misrepresents subtle changes in social dynamics at this time. Movement away from the uplands in the earlier first millennium BC is regarded as a turning point in the Iron Age of south-west England, but in reality, the certainty of this move is less than convincing. Settlement of the mid first millennium BC is now beginning to appear, bridging the gap between Earlier and Later Iron

Age communities and demanding a reappraisal of the social and settlement hierarchies suggested for the latter period and an explanation of the social shifts with which they were negotiated.

A number of inconsistencies are apparent within the current model of social organisation for Later Iron Age communities in Cornwall and Devon. There are major variations in hillfort use and the circumstantial evidence for pastoral hillfort economies – large enclosed areas, limited occupation, and a lack of apparent storage pits and/or four-post granaries – can no longer be upheld for many sites. At Castle Dore and Killibury for example, four-posters are available for 'storage' – if this is what they were indeed used for – the latter site also producing charred emmer and spelt grains, spikelet forks, and two pits, similar in size and form to storage pits identified elsewhere in England.

The size and intensity of hillfort use also varies greatly between sites. At Raddon there is activity from the fifth to the second century BC but archaeologically, the evidence is limited: pottery is absent and only one possible circular structure was identified to this phase. The defences were also neglected, no longer important in the context of use of the hilltop. Elsewhere, occupation is more abundant, but its nature remains varied and in some cases elusive: at Berry Down, for example, the limited animal bone and pottery assemblages alongside the nature and form of the enclosure banks imply pastoral and probably seasonal activity, as opposed to more intensive occupation at sites like Killibury and Castle Dore. Several hillforts – Castle Dore, Berry Down, St Mawgan in Pyder – have yielded rare, and presumably prestigious, objects such as glass beads or bangles; the bangles from Castle Dore are the earliest known examples in Iron Age Britain (Fitzpatrick 1985). These are not exclusive to hillforts, however, and are also found in other settlement and burial contexts, as for example at Carn Euny, Goldherring, and Harlyn Bay.

This evidence warns us against any generalised explanation of hillfort function, economic status, or role within the community. Particularly unconvincing is the suggestion that unfinished Devon hillforts like Cranbrook Castle, Natterdon, and Shoulsbury Castle represent attempts by a local community to build a defensive centre in reaction to an external threat that either subsided, or resulted in the subjugation of the hillfort builders, before the defences were completed (Quinnell and Silvester 1993). A lack of apparent occupation, or the seemingly 'unfinished' – to modern-day minds at least – nature of some hillfort defences, need not have made them redundant as a location of communal activity or, indeed, as a symbol of communal unity or identity (see Giles this volume).

The varied use of hillforts concurs with evidence from elsewhere in Britain, suggesting that they had different roles and functions within a community at different times (Stopford 1987; Hill 1996), a notion that the Danebury Environs Programme has reinforced (Cunliffe 2000, 178–96). Hillforts can be viewed as a reflection of community status, legitimacy and wealth, and as an active constituent in the re-affirmation and reiteration of social identity at a level beyond that of the individual household. The construction, maintenance, and repair of a hillfort as a communal space would have communicated the relations of the wider social group through their co-operation, in addition to providing a venue with specific economic and/or defensive roles within society over time. Thus, within broader notions of hillforts as emblems and expressions of community identity and focus, their use and role will have varied at a more localised level, a proposition reflected in their differing and changing morphologies and assemblages. Beyond this, to attempt to replace the generalising 'models' of hillfort function with further generalising interpretation, would defeat the purpose of deconstruction.

The nature of social structures

The importance of such focal centres for broader community identification should not be understated, particularly during a period when, as the archaeological record implies, the dominant economic and organisational unit was the extended household. The overriding impression generated by the Later Iron Age settlement record in Cornwall is of relatively small social groups operating at a largely local level. Enclosed settlements, particularly rounds of one, two, or three structures dominate the landscape, frequently situated within extensive field systems. Courtyard houses, too, cluster in small groups of two, three, or four, indicating small co-operative groups, possibly extended families. The vast majority of sites appear to have practiced a mixed farming regime, and on a day to day basis would have been largely self-sufficient.

This scale of social organisation, primarily at the scale of the extended household or small group, can also be inferred from the burial record. At Trethellan, the density and patterning of graves led Nowakowski (1991, 231) to suggest that they represent family groupings, with gaps being left deliberately for future interments. The Harlyn Bay cemetery also seems to have been organised along close kin lines (Whimster 1977). Here, a circular cist, divided down the centre and containing the skeletons of two adults and a child in the western half and one adult in the eastern half, may represent a family grave, periodically re-opened (*ibid.*, 73). The role of kin and of notions of genealogy and lineage exhibited in the burial record seem to reflect important and binding social conventions in the living world.

Cultural distinctions between local groups are also apparent in the burial record. Although cist cemeteries, such as those at Trevone and Harlyn Bay in Cornwall (Whimster 1977), Stamford Hill, Mount Batten, in Devon

(Cunliffe 1988) and Porth Cressa in the Isles of Scilly (Ashbee 1979), appear to reflect the most common Iron Age burial rite in south-west England, the discovery of a simple flat cemetery at Trethellan Farm suggests an element of local choice and/or differentiation in custom (Nowakowski 1991). The lack of cists and use of slate to line the graves cannot be simply written off as a difference in wealth. Slate was available locally at Trethellan and whilst this site was noticeably poor in grave goods, none of the cemeteries appear overly wealthy. And if the nature of the burial rite indicates localised and distinct social groupings, we must also remember that archaeologically visible burial was itself the preserve of the few in Iron Age Devon and Cornwall. Inhumation in itself seems likely to have been a cultural preference.

I suggested above that a desire for courtyard houses to be of Roman origin has hampered our ability to interpret the archaeological record without bias. Part of this desire, I believe, derived from a need to 'witness' the arrival of the Romans and the Roman period in Cornwall in particular. Courtyard houses have provided a convenient, visible marker to this effect. The appearance of rounds in the third or even fourth century BC and, arguably, courtyard houses around the late second or early first centuries BC represents a significant period of change in the settlement landscape prior to the Roman invasion of Britain. The next noticeable change is not until the second century AD, with the appearance of sub-rectangular enclosures and an increase in rounds (Quinnell 2004, 212). Although the intervening three or four centuries witnessed the arrival of the Romans in Britain, the settlement and material record changed very little. The ceramic record is marked by the onset of Cordoned wares in the early first century BC, perhaps earlier (Christie 1997, 6), but shows no major changes for some centuries after this. Only one Roman 'villa' is known in Cornwall, at Illogan, dating to the mid second to third century AD (O'Neil 1933), and only one Roman fort, at Nanstallon in the north of the region, which was occupied for a very short period from *c.* 50–70 AD (Fox and Ravenhill 1972). These appear to be a fair reflection of the extent of these Roman site types in Cornwall and in most of Devon as well, even for areas close to Exeter with its Roman fortress and then *civitas* capital. Other Roman military sites have from time to time been postulated in the peninsula, notably the rectilinear enclosure of Carvossa, although recent geophysical survey has shown that this interpretation to be unlikely (Fig. 4; Cripps forthcoming a).

Quinnell's re-interpretation of the Later Iron Age settlement hierarchy shifts elite control to the rounds, with hillforts now playing a communal role, more reflective of the archaeological evidence discussed above. This is a welcome attempt to stimulate debate about the nature of indigenous communities and certain elements of her model are particularly persuasive. The dramatic increase in the number of rounds in the second and third centuries AD is seen as a consequence of social and political stability (Quinnell 2004, 212) – as opposed to stress – and her view that Cornwall was allowed more autonomy that other parts of southern Britain during the Roman period is convincing.

Whilst the nature of social transformations during the Roman period are compelling, the idea of a hierarchical social structure of ruling elites, through which these transformations were negotiated, remains, in my opinion, less convincing. This interpretation derives more from Romano-centric expectations of Late Iron Age society than from the regional archaeological evidence. In effect, Quinnell's model for the origins of rounds and their role as seats controlling power in the Later Iron Age provides a convenient backdrop against which the growth in numbers in the second century AD can be understood. According to her hypothesis, a systems collapse in the fourth century BC led to the fragmentation of territory (indicated by increased number of small hillforts) and the emergence of rounds (Herring 1994). This shift saw local groups with some status, 'using the authority provided by the rounds in which they lived to maintain stability in their areas' (Quinnell 2004, 216).

Having accepted the weaknesses in the traditional model of a hillfort elite, this new model has simply transferred the elite to a new settlement type. At the same time, it meets the desire for a simpler social hierarchy in keeping with the 'relatively unsophisticated rural societies' (Herring 1994, 45) of Late Iron Age Cornwall – whilst still providing a platform for the socially more complex situation seen as existing in the Roman period, with local and regional distinctions and self-rule. The archaeological evidence from the rounds themselves is, however, ambivalent. Whilst certain rounds such as Trethurgy do appear long-lived and to reflect a degree of visible material wealth, this situation is distinctly not the case elsewhere, for instance at Bodwen or Threemilestone.

The arrival of courtyard houses provided a distinctly different way of living from the standard roundhouse. Notwithstanding the criticisms I made above with regard to the traditional Roman dating of this innovation, it is interesting that spatially, the layout of a courtyard house is very similar to that of early *atrium* houses of the late first millennium BC in Italy (Wallace-Hadrill 1997), albeit on a reduced scale (Fig. 5). The restricted distribution of courtyard houses in West Penwith would appear to indicate a distinct cultural tradition at the southernmost tip of the south-western peninsula. This may, in turn, be a reflection of particular links and influences this locality had with the Continent and beyond in the last couple of centuries BC. In this respect, the spatial distribution of courtyard houses, coinciding with the lodes of tin and gold in West Penwith, may be significant. Incorporation of elements of a shared spatial ideology within the courtyard house form could even reflect a 'duality of

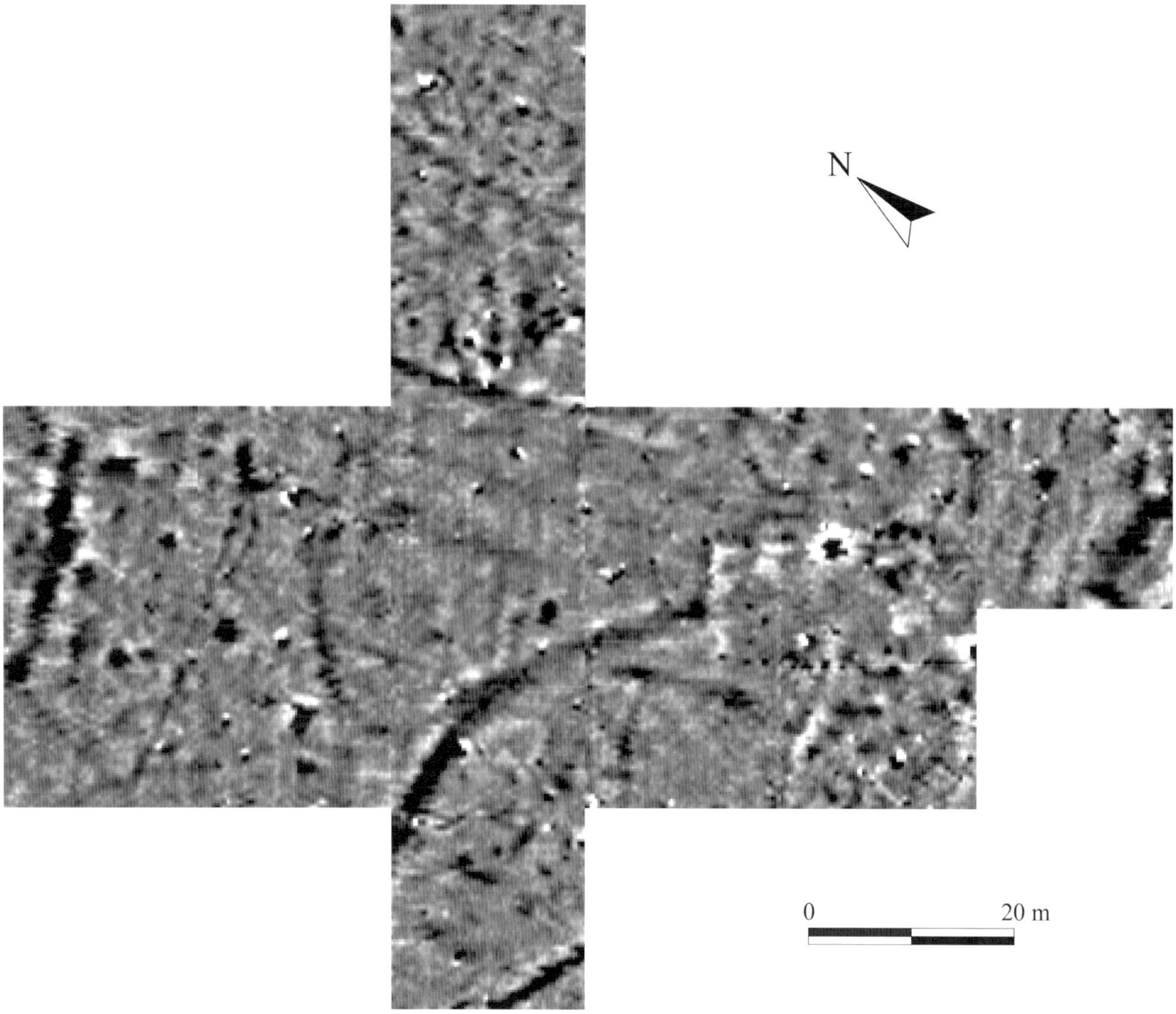

Fig. 4. Results of geophysical survey undertaken at Carvossa, near Probus, Cornwall. A palimpsest of features was revealed, none of which are obviously of Roman military character. Note the possible rectangular post-built structure on the right of the survey.

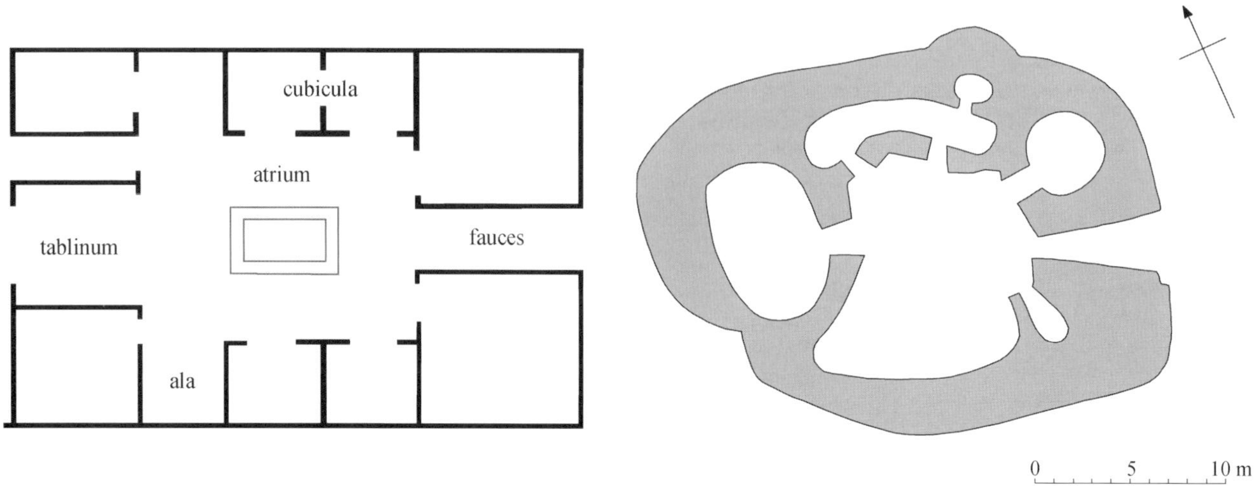

Fig. 5. Comparative plans of (left) a typical third century BC Roman atrium house (nts; adapted from Grahame 2000, 88) and (right) a Cornish courtyard house.

purpose' (Scott 1990, 170) whereby courtyard house communities sought to forge stronger cultural links with an expanding 'Roman' world, whilst in the process, distancing the household from a potentially hostile situation. The Dressel 1 amphora base from Carn Euny (Christie 1978) could conceivably be another reflection of such links, although it is perhaps more likely to have arrived via Armorica.

If, as I have argued, courtyard houses and rounds coexisted in the final centuries before the Roman conquest, this would seem to indicate very localised communities in Cornwall, with differing cultural outlooks, living side by side. Both courtyard houses and rounds were apparently relatively self-sufficient in terms of arable cultivation and access to pasture and were able to access trade networks, with their fair share of exotic finewares. This situation is also supported by the burial evidence, albeit tentatively. Social identities and social structures appear to be defined primarily at the level of the household and small social group.

Although cultural distinctions are apparent, evidence for formal hierarchies in terms of archaeologically visible material wealth and spatial divisions, are less clear. When considered as a whole, the settlement landscape of Late Iron Age Cornwall does not seem to fit any existing model of social hierarchy, and may instead point towards a more complex and localised organisation of communities for whom any inequalities operated horizontally within an overarching 'heterarchical' social structure (Paynter 1989; Crumley 1995, 30). As I have shown elsewhere the Later Iron Age in Cornwall was a period of social stratification, but not overarching hierarchy (Cripps forthcoming a), and similar models of Late Iron Age identities and social structures are now being proposed for other regions of Britain (e.g. Hill 2003; Moore 2005).

With social structures organised at a local scale and established trading links, negotiation with the new ruling power of Roman Britain need not have resulted in any overt regional hierarchy. Local centres such as Carvossa and St Mawgan in Pyder, where the assemblages have links to the Continent and where later structural developments show potentially Roman traits – as at Carvossa (Fig. 4 above) – could have had an important role in this interaction, but not necessarily as centres of a local elite (*contra* Quinnell 2004, 216). Such sites could instead have operated as community locales, where social relations beyond those of the household or small social group were periodically re-affirmed. In the process, continued interaction with Roman material would have allowed an acknowledgement and consolidation of the region's situation within an ever-expanding global context. In terms of the limited Roman military advance into Cornwall, the lack of any pre-existing overarching hierarchical power structure and a knowledge of particular social groups gained through established links with the Continent, may well have provided a strong, yet unthreatening localised social structure, which allowed Cornwall to develop, relatively independently, during the Roman period.

Conclusions

> 'The overall picture of later prehistoric settlement is one of a multitude of small fiefdoms, of which the hill-forts were the centres of power and the hill-slope enclosures the main repositories of wealth. No large central place is known to have developed, along the lines of the great *oppida* of other parts of Britain. No coinage was issued by any ruler or dynasty to proclaim authority or reward allegiance. Any unity that existed must have been expressed in intangibles' (Todd 1987, 167).

In this paper, I have tried to identify some of the problems inherent in the orthodox interpretation of the Iron Age of Cornwall and Devon and to highlight inconsistencies in the way that the topic is currently approached. Whilst great progress has been made in recognising and embracing notions of ritual occurring *within* the everyday since Hill (1989) first exhorted us to perceive a 'different' Iron Age (e.g. Parker Pearson 1996; Fitzpatrick 1997; Giles and Parker Pearson 1999), our own comprehension of the day to day structure and organisation of communities, and the language and notions we use to discuss them, remains largely familiar, couched in our own perceptions of society and social norms. Although I share Todd's impression of a largely 'localised' Cornish Iron Age, I disagree with the social and political context implicit in the above quotation. For me, the suggestion that any unity was expressed 'in intangibles' merely typifies an assumption of – or desire for – a Later Iron Age that is familiar and easy to explain in relation to the developments of the Roman period. The Iron Age of Cornwall was a complex and apparently diverse period, where society was organised primarily at local level, horizontally stratified but perhaps not hierarchical.

Acknowledgements

I would like to thank Colin Haselgrove, Tom Moore, and an anonymous referee for their helpful comments concerning earlier drafts of this paper, and Ed Cork for his technical support and hard work in helping prepare Figures 1–2. I am also extremely grateful to Colin Haselgrove, Pam Lowther, and Tom Moore for more general advice and support over numerous cups of coffee during the last few years. Naturally, all opinions expressed remain my own.

Note

1. 90.6% probability. Older radiocarbon dates have been recalibrated using OxCal 3.8 and unless otherwise specified are cited in the text at 2 sigma (95.4%).

Bibliography

Ashbee, P. 1979. The Porth Cressa cist graves, St Mary's, Isles of Scilly: a postscript, *Cornish Archaeology* 18, 61–80.

Bevan, B. (ed.) 1999. *Northern Exposure: Interpretative Devolution and the Iron Ages in Britain.* Leicester: Leicester Archaeology Monograph 4.

Brück, J. and Goodman, M. 1999. *Making Places in the Prehistoric World.* London: University College London Press.

Champion, T.C. and Collis, J.R (eds) 1996. *The Iron Age in Britain and Ireland: Recent Trends*, 95–116. Sheffield: J.R. Collis Publications.

Christie, P.M. 1978. The excavation of an Iron Age souterrain and settlement at Carn Euny, Sancreed, Cornwall, *Proceedings of the Prehistoric Society* 44, 309–434.

Christie, P.M. 1997. *Chysauster and Carn Euny.* London: English Heritage.

Craze N., Gossip J. and Johns C. 2002. *Tretherras School, Newquay, Cornwall.* Unpublished Cornwall Archaeological Unit Report R076.

Cripps, L.J. forthcoming a. *In Time and Space. Spatial Relations, Community and Identity in Cornwall, 800 BC–AD 200.* Ph.D. thesis, University of Leicester.

Cripps, L.J. forthcoming b. The past has a place: ancestral relations and identity in the Iron Age of Cornwall, in C. Peters (ed.), *Cornwall: A European Case Study in Identity.* Oxford: British Archaeological Reports British Series.

Cripps, L.J. and Giles, M. forthcoming. Cliff castles and the Cornish landscape, in G. Tregidga and B. Keys (eds), *People and Places.* Newbury: Threshold Press.

Crumley, C.L. 1995. Building an historical ecology of Gaulish polities, in B. Arnold and D.B. Gibson (eds), *Celtic Chiefdom, Celtic State*, 26–33. Cambridge: Cambridge University Press.

Cunliffe, B. 1988. *Mount Batten, Plymouth. A Prehistoric and Roman Port.* Oxford: Oxford University Committee for Archaeology Monograph 26.

Cunliffe, B. 1991. *Iron Age Communities in Britain* (3rd edn). London: Routledge.

Cunliffe, B. 2000. *The Danebury Environs Programme: the Prehistory of a Wessex Landscape, Vol. 1. Introduction.* Oxford: Oxford University Committee for Archaeology Monograph 48.

Cunliffe, B. 2001. *Facing the Ocean.* Oxford: Oxford University Press.

Dudley, D. 1957a. An excavation at Bodrifty, Mulfra Hill, near Penzance, Cornwall, *Archaeological Journal* 113, 1–32.

Dudley, D. 1957b. The Early Iron Age in Cornwall, *Proceedings of the West Cornwall Field Club* 2, 47–54.

Fitzpatrick, A.P. 1985. The Iron Age glass bracelets from Castle Dore, *Cornish Archaeology* 24, 133–140.

Fitzpatrick, A.P. 1997. Everyday life in Iron Age Wessex, in Gwilt and Haselgrove 1997, 73–86.

Fitzpatrick, A.P., Butterworth, C.A. and Grove J. 1999. *Prehistoric and Roman Sites in East Devon: the A30 Honiton to Exeter Improvement DBFO Scheme, 1996–9.* Salisbury: Wessex Archaeology Report 16.

Fox, A. 1954. Celtic fields and farms on Dartmoor, in the light of recent excavations at Kestor, *Proceedings of the Prehistoric Society* 20, 87–102.

Fox, A. 1996. *Prehistoric Hillforts in Devon.* Tiverton: Devon Books.

Fox, A. and Ravenhill, W.D. 1972. The Roman fort at Nanstallon, Cornwall, *Britannia* 3, 56–111.

Gallant, L. and Silvester, R.J. 1985. An excavation on the Iron Age hill-fort at Berry Down, Newton Abbot, *Proceedings of the Devon Archaeological Society* 43, 39–49.

Gent, T.H. and Quinnell, H. 1999. Excavations of a causewayed enclosure and hillfort on Raddon Hill, Stockleigh Pomeroy, *Proceedings of the Devon Archaeological Society* 57, 1–76.

Gibson, A. 1992. The excavation of an Iron Age settlement at Gold Park, Dartmoor, *Proceedings of the Devon Archaeological Society* 50, 19–46.

Giles, M. and Parker Pearson, M. 1999. Learning to live in the Iron Age: dwelling and praxis, in Bevan 1999, 217–231.

Gordon, A.S.R. 1940. The excavation of Gurnards Head, an Iron Age cliff castle in western Cornwall, *Archaeological Journal* 97, 96–111.

Gosden, C. 1997. Iron Age landscapes and cultural biographies, in Gwilt and Haselgrove 1997, 303–307.

Gosden, C. and Lock, G. 1998. Prehistoric histories, *World Archaeology* 30, 2–12.

Grahame, M. 2000. *Reading Space: Social Interaction and Identity in the Houses of Roman Pompeii: A Syntactical Approach to the Analysis of Built Space.* Oxford: British Archaeological Reports International Series 886.

Griffith, F.M. 1994, Changing perceptions of the context of prehistoric Dartmoor, *Proceedings of the Devon Archaeological Society* 52, 85–100.

Gwilt, A. and Haselgrove, C. (eds) 1997. *Reconstructing Iron Age Societies.* Oxford: Oxbow Monograph 71.

Harris, D. 1977. Bodwen, Lanlivery: a multi-period occupation, *Cornish Archaeology* 16, 43–60.

Hawkes, C.F.C. 1959. The ABC of the British Iron Age, *Antiquity* 33, 170–182.

Henderson, J.C. 2007. The Atlantic West in the Early Iron Age, in C. Haselgrove and R. Pope (eds), *The Earlier Iron Age in Britain and the Near Continent*, 306–327. Oxford: Oxbow Books.

Herring, P. 1992. The prehistoric landscape of Cornwall and west Devon: economic and social contexts for metallurgy, in P. Budd and D. Gale (eds), *Prehistoric Extractive Metallurgy in Cornwall*, 19–21. Truro: Cornwall Archaeological Unit.

Herring, P. 1994. The cliff castles and hillforts of west Penwith in the light of recent work at Maen Castle and Treryn Dinas, *Cornish Archaeology* 33, 40–56.

Hill, J.D. 1989. Re-thinking the Iron Age, *Scottish Archaeological Review* 6, 16–23.

Hill, J.D. 1996. Hill-forts and the Iron Age of Wessex, in Champion and Collis 1996, 95–116.

Hill J.D. 2003. Is the Battersea Shield or the Snettisham Great Torc a material manifestation of an elite status group? Paper presented to the SAA Conference session *Material and Symbolic Manifestations of Elite Status Groups.*

Hingley, R. 1997. Iron, ironworking and regeneration: a study of the symbolic meaning of metalworking in Iron Age Britain, in Gwilt and Haselgrove 1997, 9–18.

Johns, C. 2000. *St Austell North East Distributor Road. Archaeological Excavations at Trenowah, Cornwall 1997.* Unpublished Cornwall Archaeological Unit Report R014.

Johnson, N. and Rose, P. 1994. *Bodmin Moor: An Archaeological Survey.* London: English Heritage.

Jones, A.M. 1996. *An Archaeological Investigation at Stencoose, Cornwall, 1996. Archive Report.* Unpublished Cornwall Archaeological Unit Report R046.

Lamb, R.G. 1980. *Iron Age Promontory Forts in the Northern Isles.* Oxford: British Archaeological Reports British Series 79

Lawson Jones, A. 2003. *Little Quoit Farm, St Columb Major, Cornwall. Excavation of a Romano British Smithing Site.* Unpublished Cornwall Archaeological Unit Report R001.

Leeds, E.T. 1926. Excavations at Chun Castle, in Penwith, Cornwall, *Archaeologia* 76, 205–240.

Matthews, K.J. 1999. The Iron Age of north-west England and Irish Sea trade, in Bevan 1999, 173–195.

Miles, H. 1977. Excavations at Killibury Hillfort, Egloshayle 1975–6, *Cornish Archaeology* 16, 89–121.

Moore, T. 2005. Viewed through a Roman Kaleidoscope. Late Iron Age Tribal Identities and Early Roman Landscape Organisation. Paper presented at the Theoretical Roman Archaeology Conference.

Neighbour, T. and Crawford, J. 2001. Bernera: reconstructing a figure-of-eight house at Bosta, *Current Archaeology* 175, 294–300.

Nowakowski, J.A. 1991. Trethellan Farm, Newquay: the excavation of a lowland Bronze Age settlement and Iron Age cemetery, *Cornish Archaeology* 30, 5–242.

Nowakowski, J.A. 1994. *Bypassing Indian Queens: Archaeological Investigations along the A30.* Unpublished Cornwall Archaeological Unit Report.

Nowakowski, J.A. 2000. *Trevelgue Head, Cornwall. Appraisal of 1939 Excavations and Design for Assessment.* Unpublished Cornwall Archaeological Unit Report R067.

O'Neil, B.St J. 1933. The Roman villa at Magor Farm, near Camborne, Cornwall, *Journal of the British Archaeological Association* 39, 116–175.

Parker Pearson, M. 1996. Food, fertility and front doors in the first millennium BC, in Champion and Collis 1996, 117–133.

Paynter, R. 1989. The archaeology of equality and inequality, *Annual Review of Anthropology* 18, 368–399.

Quinnell, H. 1985. Castle Dore: the chronology reconsidered, *Cornish Archaeology* 24, 123–132.

Quinnell, H. 1986. Cornwall during the Iron Age and Roman period, *Cornish Archaeology* 25, 111–134.

Quinnell, H. 1994. Becoming marginal? Dartmoor in later prehistory, *Proceedings of the Devon Archaeological Society* 52, 75–84.

Quinnell, H. 2004. *Trethurgy: Excavations at Trethurgy Round, St Austell.* Truro: Cornwall County Council.

Quinnell, H. and Silvester, R.J. 1993. Unfinished hillforts on the Devon moors, *Proceedings of the Devon Archaeological Society* 51, 17–32.

Ratcliffe, J. 1992. *Initial Summary of the Excavation at Duckpool, Morwenstow: 3rd–18th August 1992.* Unpublished Cornwall Archaeological Unit Report R013.

Saunders, A. and Harris, D. 1982. Excavation at Castle Gotha, St Austell, *Cornish Archaeology* 21, 109–153.

Schwieso, J. 1976. Excavations at Threemilestone Round, Kenwyn, Truro, *Cornish Archaeology* 15, 51–67.

Scott, E. 1990. Romano-British villas and the construction of space, in R. Samson (ed.), *The Social Archaeology of Houses*, 149–172. Edinburgh: Edinburgh University Press.

Sharpe, A. 1992. Treryn Dinas: cliff castles reconsidered, *Cornish Archaeology* 31, 31–38.

Silvester, R.J. 1979. The relationship of first millennium settlement to the upland areas of the south-west, *Proceedings of the Devon Archaeological Society* 37, 176–190.

Silvester, R.J. 1980. Forts and farms: The Iron Age in Devon, in S.C. Timms (ed.), *Archaeology of the Devon Landscape*, 43–52. Devon: Devon County Council.

Smith, G.H. 1984. Penhale promontory fort, Perranzabuloe, 1983, *Cornish Archaeology* 23, 180.

Smith, G.H. 1987. The Lizard Project: landscape survey 1978–1983, *Cornish Archaeology* 26, 13–68.

Stopford, J. 1987. Danebury: an alternative view, *Scottish Archaeological Review* 14, 70–75.

Todd, M. 1984. Excavations at Hembury (Devon), 1980–83: a summary report, *Antiquaries Journal* 64, 251–268.

Todd, M. 1987. *The South-West to AD 1000.* London: Longman.

Todd, M. 1998. A hillslope enclosure at Rudge, Morchard Bishop, *Proceedings of the Devon Archaeological Society* 56, 133–152.

Trudgian, P. 1977. Excavation at Tregilders, St Kew, 1975–6, *Cornish Archaeology* 16, 122–128.

Wailes, B. 1963. Excavations at Castle-an-Dinas, St Columb Major: interim report, *Cornish Archaeology* 2, 51–55.

Wainwright, G. and Smith, K. 1980. The Shaugh Moor Project: second report – the enclosure, *Proceedings of the Prehistoric Society* 46, 65–122.

Wallace-Hadrill, A. 1997. Rethinking the Roman Atrium House, in R. Laurence and A. Wallace-Hadrill (eds), *Domestic Space in the Roman World: Pompeii and Beyond*, 219–240. Portsmouth, Rhode Island: Journal of Roman Archaeology Supplementary Series 22.

Whimster, R. 1977. Harlyn Bay reconsidered: the excavations of 1900–1905 in light of recent work, *Cornish Archaeology* 16, 61–88.

Wood, J. 1997. A new perspective on west Cornwall courtyard houses, *Cornish Archaeology* 36, 95–106.

Young, A. 2001. *The National Mapping Programme. Cornwall and Isles of Scilly Mapping Project: Annual Progress Report 2000/2001.* Truro: Cornwall Archaeological Unit.

Unravelling the Iron Age landscape of the Upper Thames valley

Gill Hey

Background

There has been a considerable amount of work on Iron Age sites in the Upper Thames valley since the pioneering work of Stephen Stone in the nineteenth century, and this has increased dramatically since the 1960s, with ever larger sites being investigated (Miles 1997). Atypically for his time, Stone focused his attention on ordinary settlement, attempting to understand the deep pits, post holes and ditches of an unenclosed site in the lower Windrush valley (Stone 1856–9) and making a scale model of the features he saw (Bradford 1942, pl. XXIX). His work set a trend for later prehistoric research in the region which has continued ever since, enabling a fairly detailed understanding to be gained of Iron Age settlement patterns and land use of some areas in the valley (e.g. Lambrick 1992). In this article I will examine our current perceptions of how individual communities articulated in the valley landscape, at the same time highlighting the value of looking at long time trajectories for the understanding of these societies.

Development has been the catalyst behind much research into the Iron Age of the region, principally gravel extraction; this was as much true in the mid nineteenth century as it is today. Large tracts of the countryside have been exposed in advance of some sizeable gravel quarries (Fig. 1), enabling the excavation of hectares of late prehistoric remains, largely by Oxford Archaeology (formerly the Oxford Archaeological Unit), but latterly by a wide range of archaeological groups. The scale of the work has encouraged a wider perspective to be taken of settlement patterns and land use; there has never been a narrow, site-based focus. In addition, there has been a long tradition of environmental archaeology and the investigation of the wider landscape context of excavated sites (Robinson 1992). Since the innovative work of Martin Jones, David Miles, and Mark Robinson unravelling the villa economy at Barton Court Farm in the late 1970s (Miles 1986), there has been a conscious effort to collect environmental data from archaeological and natural features both on- and off-site, and to integrate the evidence with data from the excavations. The results of research by, for example, George Lambrick, Mark Robinson, and Tim Allen in the lower Windrush valley, have shown how successful this can be; this article relies heavily on their work throughout the region.

Our understanding of late prehistoric settlement and landscape does not sit in a time vacuum, for exposure of large areas of gravel has revealed archaeological remains from the Neolithic to the present day. In particular, it has been possible to observe the development of communities from the Neolithic to the Iron Age in terms of settlement type, land use, the extent to which they transformed the landscape around them, and their response to changing environmental conditions. Although this pattern is more easily observed in some parts of the valley than others, it is apparent that differences can be observed along its length. These differences may be particularly revealing about mechanisms for social change and interaction in the later prehistoric period.

A word of caution should be introduced at this stage. In contrast to many parts of Britain, much less is known about Iron Age communal or higher-status sites than about ordinary settlements. Comparatively little work has been done on hillforts, for example, along with their valley counterparts, or on *oppida*, although all these site

Fig. 1. Gravelly Guy: a typical Iron Age unenclosed settlement in the context of gravel extraction (© Oxford Archaeological Unit).

types exist in the area. This situation has recently begun to be addressed by some major hillfort excavations on the Berkshire Downs (Miles *et al.* 2003; Lock *et al.* 2005; Gosden and Lock 2007), and by work at Castle Hill, Little Wittenham, and on the major late Iron Age defended settlement beneath modern Abingdon by Tim Allen of Oxford Archaeology (Allen 2000, 22–32). However, it is not yet possible to relate the changes observed among the small valley communities with events at a wider social level. Limited work has also been undertaken on the banjo enclosures and other enclosed sites on the higher Cotswold slopes, and how these relate to their valley counterparts is poorly understood, despite important research by Richard Hingley in the late 1970s and 1980s (Hingley 1984), and recent air photographic coverage (Featherstone and Bewley 2000).

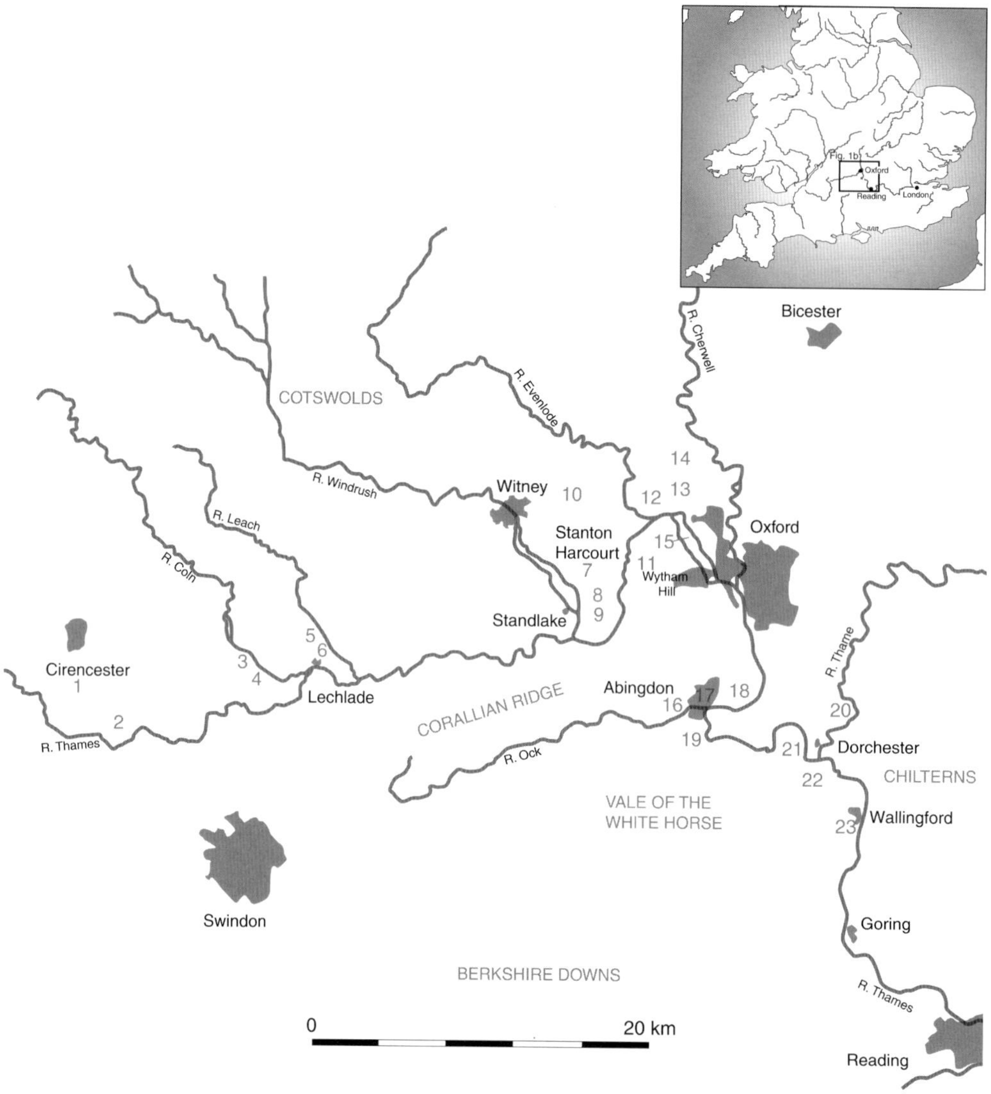

Fig. 2. The Upper Thames valley: geology and location of principal sites mentioned in the text. 1. Shorncote; 2. Ashton Keynes; 3. Thornhill Farm; 4. Claydon Pike; 5. Roughground Farm; 6. Butler's Field; 7. Mingies Ditch; 8. Gravelly Guy; 9. Watkins Farm; 10. Eynsham Hall Camp; 11. Farmoor; 12. Cassington; 13. Yarnton; 14. Bladon Camp; 15. Port Meadow; 16. Ashville; 17. Abingdon Vineyard; 18. Barrow Hills, Radley; 19. Drayton; 20. Mount Farm; 21. Dyke Hills; 22. Castle Hill, Little Wittenham; 23. Wallingford.

Geography and topography

The geographical scope of this article is the Thames valley and its major tributaries above the Goring Gap (Fig. 2). In this area, the Thames has incised its path through the Jurassic limestone of the Cotswolds uplands, from south of Cirencester to Lechlade and then between the Cotswolds and the Corallian ridge to a point just north of Oxford. Here the river cuts through the west–east trending ridge to flow southwards to the Goring Gap, where the chalk of the Berkshire Downs and the Chilterns is breached. A number of rivers flow into the Thames, including seven major tributaries along this part of the valley. Here gravel terraces are wider and these areas of free-draining soils were favoured for clearance and settlement in the past. They have seen widespread gravel extraction.

Although Iron Age sites are found throughout the region, they seem to be particularly common along the gravel terraces, with settlements known approximately every 2 km in some places. The tributary areas of the Coln, the lower Windrush valley, the Evenlode, and the Ock have been particularly prolific of Iron Age sites, and here the articulation of late prehistoric communities is seen most clearly. They are also areas with important concentrations of earlier prehistoric sites (Barclay *et al.* 1996). Iron Age sites are also present on the Cotswold slopes, the Corallian Ridge, the Berkshire Downs, and the Chilterns, and these are becoming increasingly evident as development pressure extends into these areas. Recent survey of 14 km^2 in the clay Vale of the White Horse, for example, revealed 11 new Iron Age sites (Hearne 2000) and housing development around

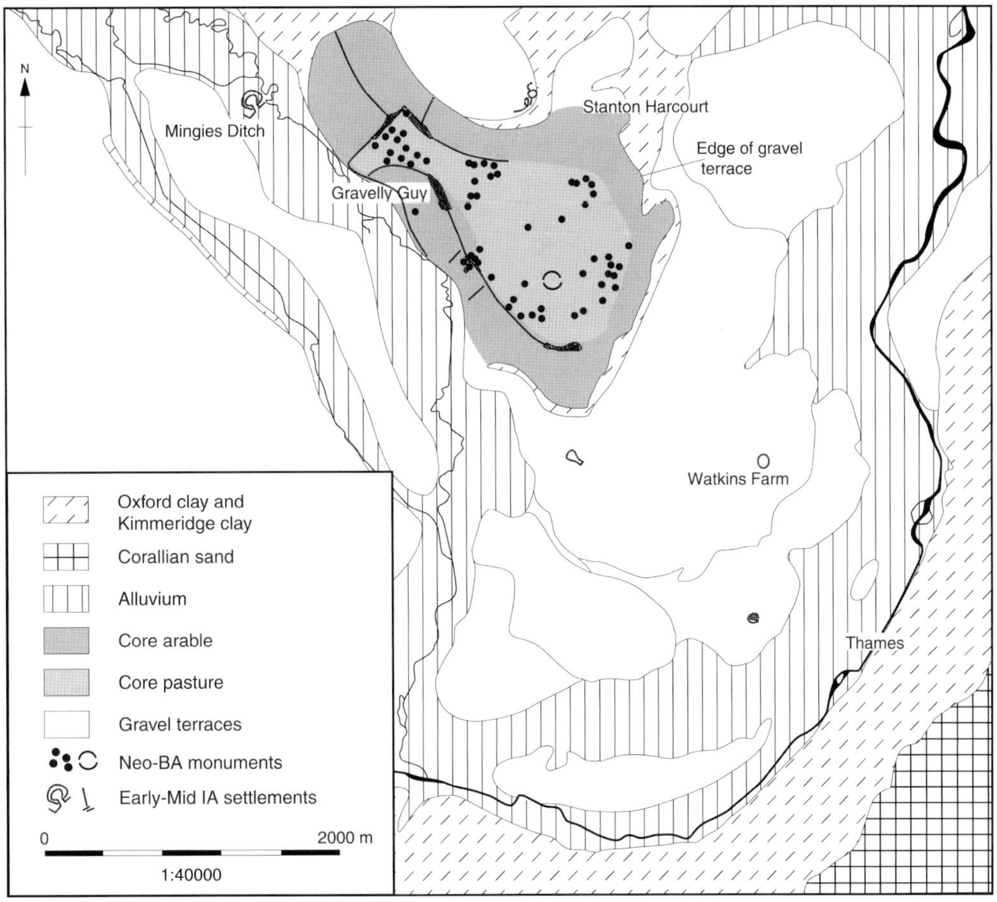

Fig. 3. Lower Windrush settlement and farming pattern in relation to early monuments.

Bicester has resulted in the discovery of several more (e.g. Mould 1996; Cromarty *et al.* 1999; Ellis *et al.* 2000). However, the distribution of sites seems genuinely sparser than on the gravels.

Different settlement types appear to be found in the different topographic zones. Enclosed settlements, usually of relatively small size, predominate on the upland slopes, as they do on the Thames floodplain, whereas unenclosed and larger settlements lie on the higher and drier gravel terraces. Two caveats must, however, be placed on this general pattern of differential site location and settlement size. The first is that the gravel terraces tend to be more susceptible to air photography and geophysical survey, and have seen more fieldwork than their higher and lower counterparts, thus unenclosed settlements may lie undiscovered in the other topographic zones. Nevertheless, enclosed sites are not common on the gravel terraces upstream of Dorchester, and there does appear to be a genuine contrast between enclosed, shifting farmsteads and permanent unenclosed sites where boundaries were presumably recognised through custom. Secondly, enclosed sites appear to have supported smaller numbers of people than the more sprawling gravel terrace settlements, but this may be a result of their relative duration of occupation. At least some gravel terrace sites may have been fairly small-scale establishments, which remained in the same place for generations, thus giving the appearance of greater density of use.

A considerable amount of gravel extraction has taken place in the lower Windrush valley since the 1930s, and it is here that a very detailed understanding is being acquired of Iron Age settlement patterns and land use. The idea that the settlements around Stanton Harcourt formed a distinct socio-economic group was proposed by Dennis Harding in the 1970s (1972, 16–9), but a more detailed understanding of relationships between different communities in the area and mechanisms for change has grown out of George Lambrick's excavations at Gravelly Guy, *c.* 4 km north of the confluence of the Windrush and the Thames (Lambrick and Allen 2004).

Inherited landscapes: settlement in the lower Windrush valley

Gravel terrace sites

Gravelly Guy is one of about five unenclosed settlements located around a spur of second terrace gravel, positioned approximately 200 m from the terrace edge (Fig. 3). The settlements surrounded a central area which was, in the Neolithic and Bronze Age, an important ceremonial and funerary landscape, focusing on the

Devil's Quoits circle henge monument. The evidence for this complex and its growth has been recovered piecemeal, but it is apparent that it developed from limited mid Neolithic activity, probably associated with forest clearance but including some funerary activity, to become a ceremonial centre around which developed an extensive barrow cemetery or group of cemeteries, with in excess of 70 barrows (Barclay *et al.* 1996). The Devil's Quoits henge was constructed in the Late Neolithic with the stone circle probably added in the Early Bronze Age (Barclay *et al.* 1995). Two hengiform ring ditches, a penannular post circle and scatters of Grooved ware pits probably also belong to this phase of activity. Subsequently, round barrows were constructed in the surrounding area, including important Beaker groups and double ring ditches at Gravelly Guy and Linch Hill Corner, and the Stanton Harcourt Wessex barrow (*ibid.*, 78–105). A number of 'flat', unmarked burials have also been exposed between the barrows over the years.

Snails from the lower fills of the Devil's Quoits henge ditch show that this was a cleared and grazed landscape from an early period (Evans 1995, 67), although environmental evidence from the nearby Mingies Ditch site demonstrates that, on the adjacent floodplain, there were areas of ancient woodland until the Late Bronze Age; widespread clearance only took place there in the Iron Age (Robinson 1993, 136–8). The absence of evidence for cultivated soils, the paucity of charred crop remains, and the preponderance of cattle in animal bone assemblages at the Devil's Quoits and in the Gravelly Guy pits all point to the pastoral use of this landscape.

Maintenance of an open landscape suggests that the area was fairly intensively grazed, although areas of scrub and small stands of trees may have existed. There are no surviving prehistoric land boundaries, and if there were small cultivated plots (and small quantities of cereals have been recovered) they seem most likely to have lain around the edge of the terrace, away from the burial mounds, and the flat graves that lay between them (Lambrick and Allen 2004). There is no evidence for occupation of this date and the extent of permanent settlement is uncertain, but it seems probable that large numbers of people would have congregated at this regionally important ceremonial centre seasonally or periodically with their herds, as has been suggested for cursus monuments in the Upper Thames (Barclay and Hey 1999). When and how people settled permanently in this landscape is not fully understood, although there is some evidence of increasing cereal cultivation at the end of the Bronze Age (Lambrick and Allen 2004, 479). It is interesting to speculate on the extent to which barrow clusters, proposed by Humphrey Case (1982, 111–13) to represent the cemeteries of individual communities, correspond to the subsequent Iron Age settlement sites.

Iron Age settlement in this area was located around the edge of the Neolithic/Bronze Age ceremonial core, as shown in Figure 3. Like the other sites, Gravelly Guy sits close to the edge of the terrace and has a tightly clustered linear layout, within which there is a striking cumulative density of features (Fig. 4). This suggests that there were acknowledged, if not physical, boundaries to the site. Five or six households can be recognised, which seem to have survived over a period of around 700 years, and there appears to have been a mixed farming regime (Lambrick and Allen 2004). Grain storage pits were dug in a tight row on one side of the settlement (towards the gravel terrace edge) and small enclosures opened out onto the centre of the terrace. Contrary to the expected pattern (Harding 1972, 18–19), it was the edge of the terrace that was cultivated, whereas the core remained as pasture (Lambrick 1992; Lambrick and Allen 2004). A scatter of pits was revealed beyond the ploughed fields, at the edge of the gravel terrace.

The other contemporary sites in this area show this same site layout and land distribution over *c.* 250 ha, and it is clear that they had a shared strategy for this landscape. As people gathered at sacred and ceremonial sites, it seems likely that a communal pattern of grazing would have become established. As these communities settled permanently, traditional land use patterns seem to have become fossilised as the agricultural pattern around intensified (Lambrick 1999); it is possible that the small Iron Age ploughed fields lay upon earlier plots. Whether this was the perpetuation of customary practices, or was because earlier ceremonial places retained ritual significance or were seen as ancestral burial grounds, is unknown. It is possible that other groups still retained access to grazing rights, even if they were not permanently settled in the immediate area, limiting options to change land use.

Richard Hingley has argued that Iron Age social organisation in the lower Windrush valley, with the continuing relevance of the Devil's Quoits monument complex, can be explained in terms of a 'Germanic mode of production' as proposed by Bonte (1981) for pastoralist societies (Hingley 1999, 242–5). In this model, property can be seen as being divided into 'wild' (in this case the central core with its landscape of grassland and water) and 'domesticated' property (in this case livestock and the increasingly settled fringe with appropriated land for animal enclosures and arable). It is through domestic property that communal relations come about, and they develop through social relations of exchange (*ibid.*, 244).

However, the evolution of settlement in this area from the fourth millennium BC suggests an alternative interpretation. In the Neolithic and Early Bronze Age, it was the core of this territory which formed the heart of social activity and interchange from which the relations between groups developed, an area of 'domesticated' landscape which could be contrasted with the uncleared 'wild' portion of the valley. A similar model has been suggested for the Drayton Cursus (Barclay *et al.* 2003, 237). It is not known how livestock would have been owned, possibly

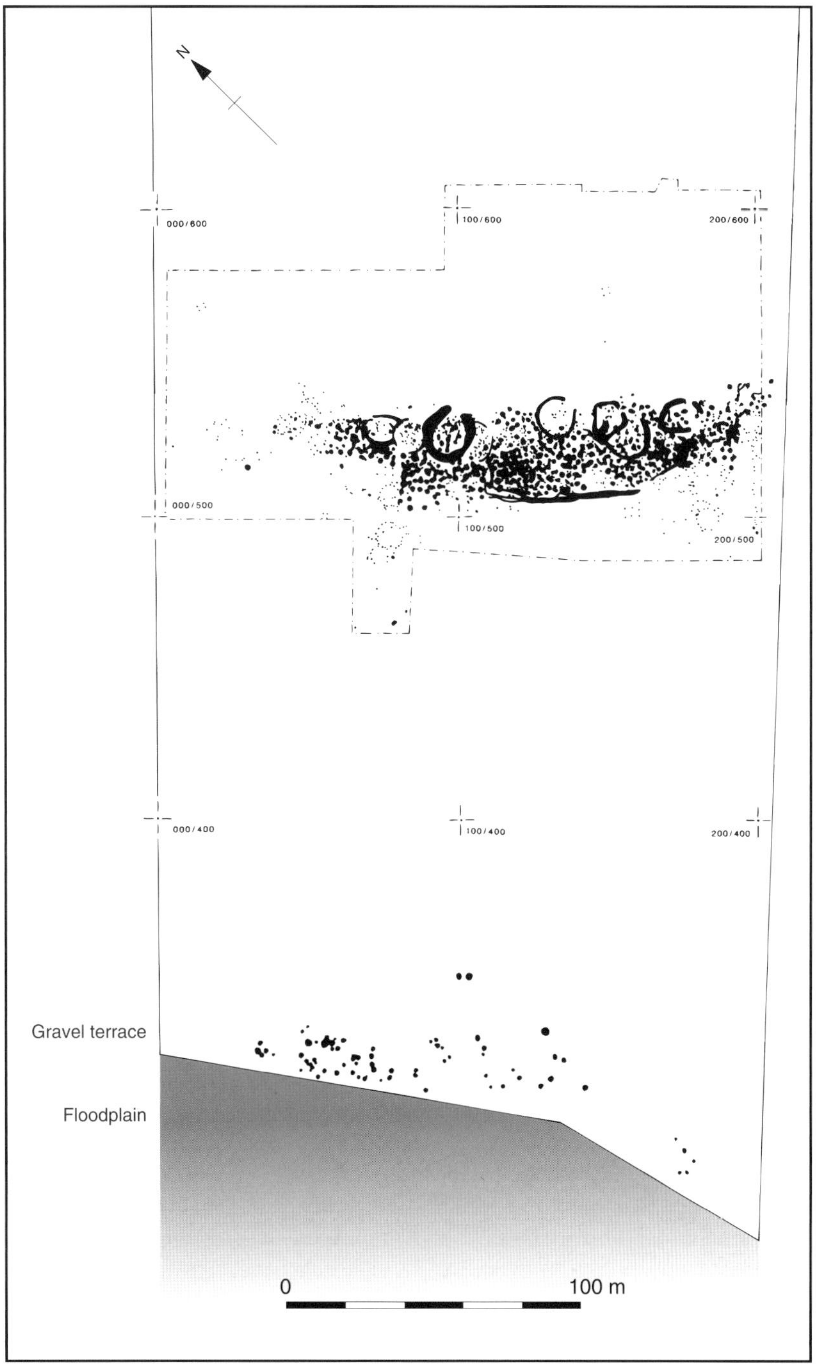

Fig. 4. Gravelly Guy excavation plan.

by small family groups, but it was the shared use of this area that created the open landscape upon which people traditionally grazed their animals; it was maintained during communal gatherings and may have been held in common. And so it is more likely that it was from this communal space that small groups carved out territories for their individual households and settlements, mediating relations with their neighbours and others who had been accustomed to use it in the process.

Other information regarding social organisation in this area has been unravelled as a result of the very detailed excavations at Gravelly Guy, in which it was possible to excavate virtually all of the Iron Age settlement, including around 800 pits. Lambrick has pointed out that this represents approximately one pit for every year of occupation, and has estimated that this would store enough seed for the site's arable fields (Lambrick and Allen 2004, chapter 12). He suggests that, although the house areas are clearly differentiated and the enclosures opening out from them indicate that each house had its own animal enclosures, crop husbandry was managed on a settlement level.

The wider landscape seems to have been organised or agreed on a much larger scale. There evidently was increasing pressure on arable, for at the very end of the Iron Age, certainly not much earlier that the last decades of the first millennium BC, each one of the settlements which surrounded the gravel terrace shifted their areas of occupation further into its core. At Gravelly Guy there was no overlap between the two areas and, according to the finds, the shift seems to have occurred in a very short space of time. This appears to have been undertaken to increase the area of cultivation on the edge of the terrace, for the ceremonial centre was not ploughed until later in the Roman period. These Late Iron Age sites were occupied until the early second century AD, when they were all abandoned.

Floodplain sites

The general pattern of intensification can also be seen on the adjacent floodplain. Clearance of low-lying areas probably reflects a need to extend pasture, especially as increasing arable cultivation on the gravel terrace would have put immediate pressure on pasture by limiting grazing on higher ground, particularly in the summer months. By the Middle Iron Age specialised pastoral settlements were established on the floodplain and lower gravel terraces. Unlike the higher sites, however, these settlements were often enclosed within banks and ditches, though whether for protection, for site definition within territory where land ownership was uncertain, for animal management purposes, or as a flood-relief measure is uncertain. Mingies Ditch, which lay to the north-west of Gravelly Guy (Fig. 3 above), was an enclosed site on the floodplain that seems to have been occupied year-round by one or two families (Allen and Robinson 1993). The economy was predominantly pastoral, with some emphasis on horses, and the plant remains indicate that the inhabitants imported processed crops (Jones with Robinson 1993); perhaps they were dependent upon the higher gravel terrace sites, or had close economic relationships with them. Watkins Farm is another example of a low-lying, enclosed pastoral settlement in the same area, this time on the first gravel terrace (Allen 1990).

Not all sites on lower topographies in the Thames valley were permanent, however, and not all were enclosed. A different strategy seems to have applied at Farmoor, on the floodplain of the Thames a little further downstream, 2.5 km east of Stanton Harcourt (Lambrick and Robinson 1979). Small, single-phase farmsteads, represented by a house and a few animal pens, seem to have been used seasonally, as suggested by occupation deposits interstratified with alluvial flood silts. Lambrick and Robinson suggest that these sites were specifically exploiting the summer grazing of the floodplain grassland.

The floodplain sites demonstrate a varied practical response to an increasing population and pressure on farm land, the use of which was constrained by customary practice.

Inherited landscapes: settlement in the Abingdon area

The area around the confluence of the Rivers Ock and Thames has also seen major gravel extraction in recent decades, but most modern development is associated with the growing town of Abingdon. This makes an understanding of the articulation of prehistoric communities more difficult to observe, but some interesting similarities with the lower Windrush valley are apparent.

The Abingdon area was also a centre of major ceremonial importance in the Neolithic and Bronze Age, focused on two separate areas of activity. The Abingdon causewayed enclosure was constructed to the north of the confluence and two oval barrows, a linear mortuary structure, and single graves lay to the east (Barclay and Halpin 1999). A linear barrow cemetery developed on its east side, with associated flat graves, pits, and cremation deposits.

To the south-west of the confluence, at Drayton, a cursus 1.5 km long was created in two sections on either side of a stream (Barclay *et al.* 2003). An oval barrow and an elongated enclosure lay nearby and, at a later date, a henge monument was built to the north and a barrow cemetery developed next to it. There is evidence that both of these monument complexes had been cleared of woodland, and that they remained largely open grassland throughout the Bronze Age, with some phases of woodland regeneration at Drayton (*ibid.*; Parker 1995). It is suggested that these areas were used in a particular cultural context which involved the herding and grazing of cattle, and that by these means the clearings created for ceremonial activities were maintained (Barclay and Hey 1999). Whilst the desire to create these monuments and the physical act of building them would have brought people together, so land use around them would have perpetuated contact during the daily routines of life.

As in the lower Windrush valley, Iron Age settlement avoided the monuments and ploughed fields were positioned between them (Fig. 5). The monument complexes remained as grazed grassland; much of Barrow Hills, Radley, was pasture well into the medieval period when it acquired its name.

There are two major concentrations of Iron Age settlement in the area. Although they were more sprawling than their upstream counterparts and less well understood, they too show evidence of a shared pattern of settlement development. Four Early Iron Age

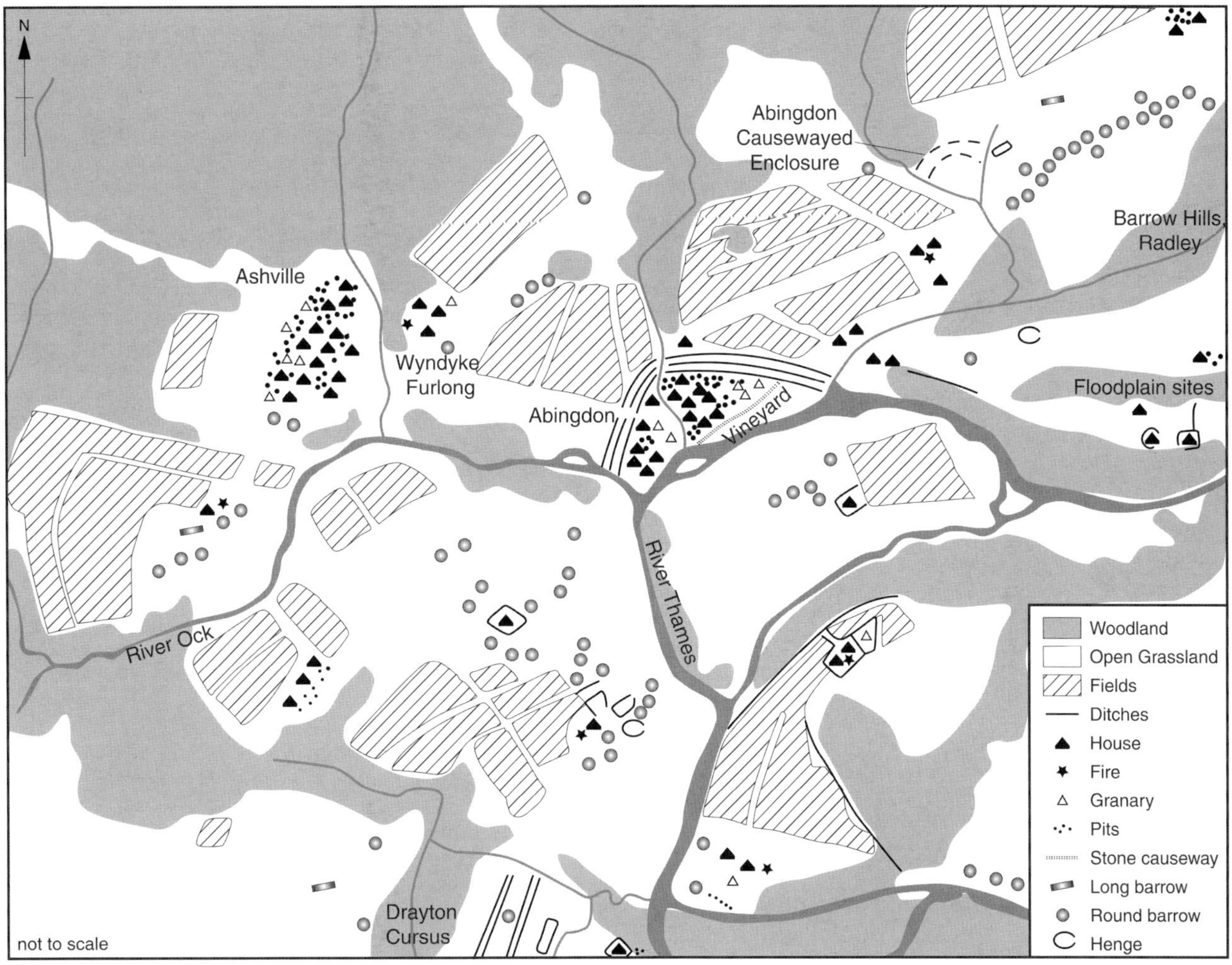

Fig. 5. Reconstruction of the Iron Age settlement pattern around Abingdon.

settlements divided by tributaries of the Ock and Thames merged in the Middle Iron Age into two nucleated settlements, one at Ashville/Wyndyke Furlong and the other beneath the town centre at Abingdon (Abingdon Vineyard; Allen 2000). In the Late Iron Age Ashville/Wyndyke Furlong was abandoned, as Abingdon became a major defended settlement and *oppidum*. As in the lower Windrush valley, small and relatively short-lived pastoral sites were established from the Middle Iron Age close to the Thames north of Abingdon (e.g. Everett and Eeles 1999).

Patterns of continuity: settlement at Yarnton

In many ways, settlement at Yarnton and Cassington resembles that in the lower Windrush valley. There are no visible early land boundaries or field systems in the area. Iron Age occupation sites were unenclosed; they lay at the edge of the second gravel terrace around a spur of higher ground (Fig. 6) and the settlement layout was characterised by post-built roundhouses and numerous pits. Recent work in the Cassington gravel pit suggests that these were, however, smaller settlements. The Yarnton site had one or two contemporary households despite the apparent density of features which is a factor of its longevity of use (Hey *et al.* forthcoming). Unlike the sites in the lower Windrush valley, settlement at Yarnton does not reveal the distinct shifts in location at the end of the Iron Age and in the early second century AD; rather, site location gradually drifted across the terrace through time. The Yarnton site is also unusual because it had its own small cemetery in the fourth or third century BC, with 35 crouched inhumation burials (Hey *et al.* 1999).

Work by Oxford Archaeology has not only concentrated on the gravel terrace but also on the adjacent floodplain in order to attempt a much more detailed reconstruction of later prehistoric and Roman land use and to reveal more fully earlier prehistoric activity in the area. The evidence demonstrates increasing intensity of

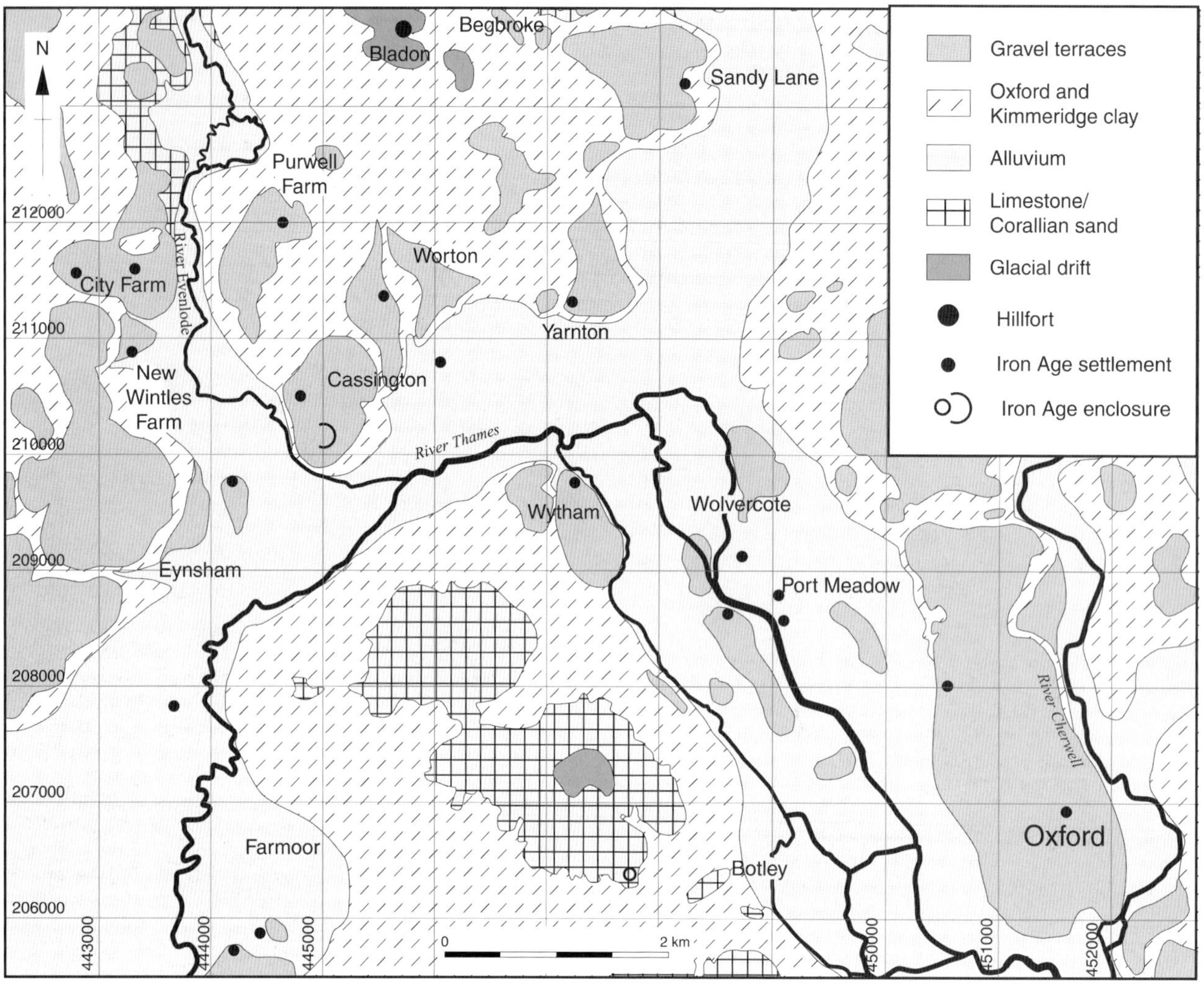

Fig. 6. Iron Age sites in the Yarnton–Cassington area.

land use (Fig. 7). In the Early Iron Age, cultivation was apparently undertaken in a series of shifting fields, probably situated on the adjacent areas of terrace between settlements, as occupation sites lay at the edge of the terrace. These fields may have been more permanently sited by the Middle Iron Age, leading to a decrease in perennial weeds and the increase of annuals (Stevens forthcoming).

In the Late Iron Age and early Roman period, old fields seem to have been better manured and weeded, but new fields were also laid out on wetter ground, and there was more focus on autumn-sown crops. The new fields were located on the floodplain, as can be attested by the physical survival of boundary ditches and ploughsoils beneath alluvium; an entire field system with droveways and river crossings was laid out here by the Roman period. This was an area that had traditionally been grassland from at least the Early Bronze Age, and there is continuing evidence of grazing by animals into the Iron Age. Indeed, an increase in dung beetles in the silting-up river channels which crossed this area reveals a general intensification of use of this zone. This occurred at a time when the water table was rising, and flooding was increasingly common, and it is probable that field ditches were dug to alleviate wet ground conditions within fields; a spill of alluvium through one field entrance demonstrates how effective these could be. There is no evidence for cultivation on higher clay lands and the interior of the gravel terrace until later in the Roman period.

Pressure on land may also be indicated by the digging in the Middle Iron Age of a substantial boundary ditch for the first time in this landscape. The ditch ran for over 300 m north-north-east from a palaeochannel across the floodplain between the settlements of Yarnton and Cassington.

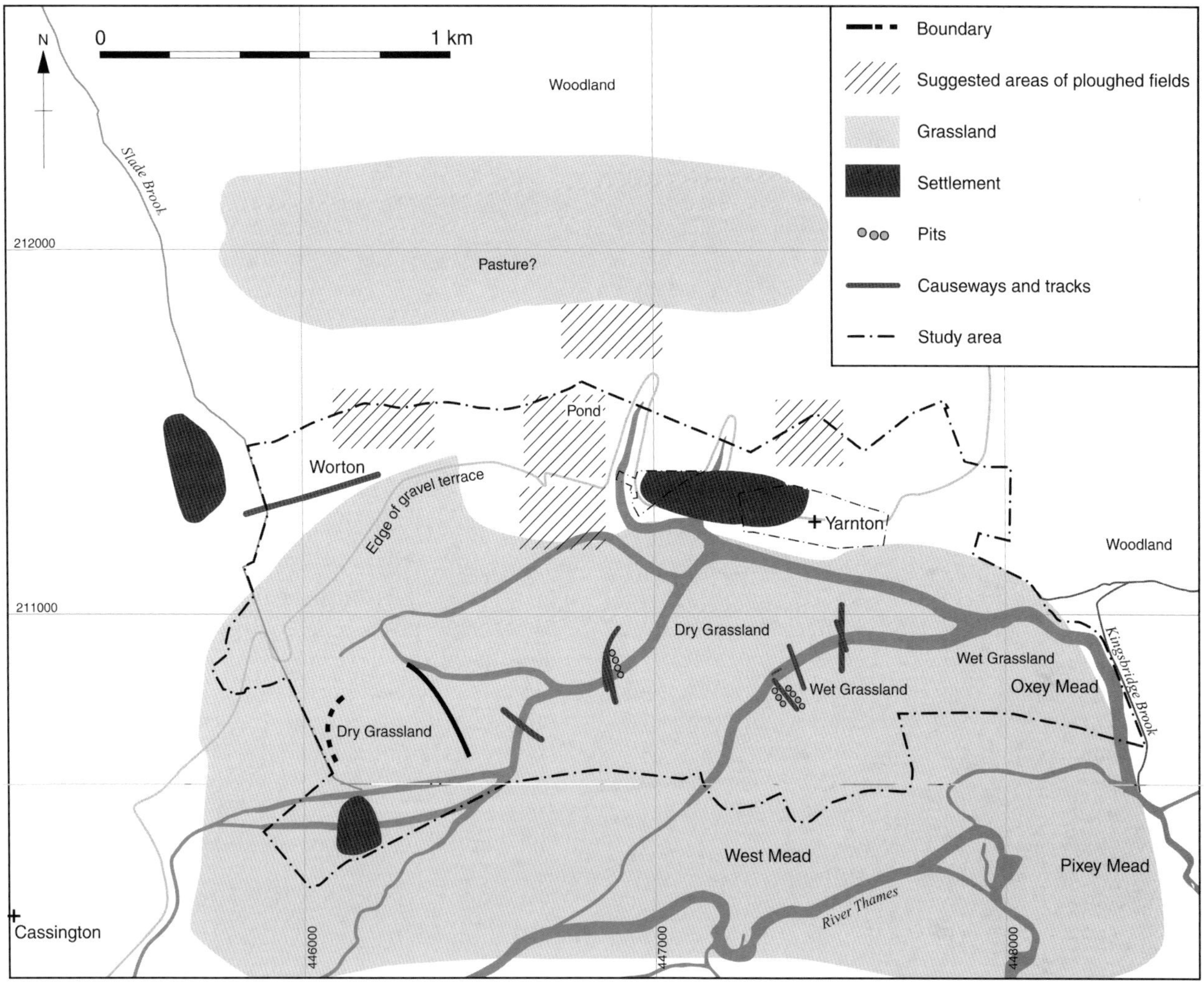

Fig. 7. Iron Age land use at Yarnton.

The Cassington Iron Age gravel terrace site was destroyed by gravel extraction in the 1930s with little record (Leeds 1935) and so its layout and farming strategy is unknown. Air photography and evaluation trenching in 1991, however, show that there were unenclosed farmsteads of Middle and Late Iron Age date on the adjacent floodplain. By contrast, no Iron Age occupation has been found on the Yarnton floodplain and this hints at a difference in settlement and land use patterns between these adjacent areas. There are also differences between the later, Roman settlements: the Yarnton Roman habitation overlay Iron Age features and occupied the same site throughout the Roman period, whereas the late Roman settlement at Cassington and associated track and field system lay on a new site to the north and east of its predecessor, and no earlier Iron Age features were found beneath the Late Iron Age and Roman site.

As in the lower Windrush valley, the sites lay around a spur of gravel, with Middle Iron Age pastoral sites on lower-lying ground, on Port Meadow and at Cassington (Fig. 6 above), but they all seem to have been operating independently. They do not appear to have had a shared strategy for managing the land, the settlement pattern between them differs, and there appears to have been no cleared central core. The Early Iron Age hillfort at Bladon Camp was probably constructed in a woodland clearing, and evidence from the adjacent Eynsham Hall Camp suggests that this lay in oak woodland. In the medieval period this area was part of the forest of Wychwood. In contrast, the focus of agricultural activity was the floodplain. It is interesting, therefore, that Yarnton and Cassington had very different early settlement histories from the Gravelly Guy and Abingdon areas.

There is considerable evidence of Neolithic and Bronze Age activity in the Yarnton–Cassington area, but there is no major ceremonial focus. Ring ditches are found, but they tend to be scattered along the edge of the gravel terrace with a distinct cluster at Cassington Mill. Two Neolithic enclosures have also been uncovered, and flat graves are present, but activity was generally small in scale and, importantly, was mainly domestic in character. Unlike in the lower Windrush valley, this activity is concentrated on the Thames floodplain (Hey *et al.* 2003). The evidence suggests repeated, but not permanent, use of the floodplain from the Early Neolithic, originally in shifting woodland clearings, but by the Later Bronze Age in a widely cleared landscape with small patches of scrub. Small circular houses and associated pits, wells, and other post-built structures show that, by the Bronze Age, there were small pastoral farms, set in grazed grassland with little evidence of cereal cultivation and no field systems. Occupation here may have been seasonal in the first instance but increasingly became permanent, and by the Late Bronze Age there were probably single generation households in the area. This pattern represents a more individualistic settlement pattern.

Habitation on the floodplain seems to have ended as a result of the rising water table, itself largely a factor of widespread forest clearance in the Upper Thames catchment (Robinson and Lambrick 1984), and nucleated settlements were formed on the very edge of the gravel terrace overlooking the floodplain. From then on, boundaries seem to have fossilised; indeed there is remarkable continuity in the location of settlement boundaries into the medieval period. Nevertheless, each habitation site seems to have developed its own strategy to cope with changing environmental circumstances and pressure on land. At Yarnton at least, it is possible to claim that the floodplain remained a critical resource, actively used by this community in the same way to which they were accustomed.

Therefore, the pattern in the Yarnton area does not resemble that in the lower Windrush valley, but it is still very heavily influenced by traditional land use patterns, in a long trajectory that first became established in the Neolithic period. Repeated, recurrent activity became gradually fossilised into permanent, settled ways of life, in which the monuments of past generations would have been visible reference points in the landscape, however interpreted. It was only at the end of the Iron Age, or into the Romano-British period, that the monuments were ploughed flat.

Patterns of discontinuity

The evidence from Dorchester

The areas discussed above all show a gradual intensification of land use from the Neolithic period into the Bronze Age, with field systems being a relatively late introduction. This pattern is not, however, universal. Unlike much of the Upper Thames, field systems are a feature of the Bronze Age landscape of the middle Thames, and are increasingly being found south of Abingdon and in the area around Dorchester-on-Thames (Yates 1999).

It is suggested that these field systems were associated with high-status sites in the middle and lower Thames and are a manifestation of the agricultural intensification linked to the conspicuous consumption that is evident on these sites (Bradley and Yates 2007). It seems probable that field systems south of Abingdon were linked to the rich river island settlement at Wallingford, and the site at Castle Hill, Little Wittenham (Hingley 1983; Lambrick 1992, 86–8). In the Dorchester area, these field systems clearly cut across, rather than respected, the earlier prehistoric monuments which included the major monument complex at Dorchester-on-Thames (Whittle *et al.* 1992, fig. 3), although other fields may have respected Bronze Age barrows (e.g. at Northfield Farm, Long Wittenham; Baker 2002, 21). When the socio-economic system that underpinned these wealthy sites collapsed, the field systems themselves were abandoned and later Iron Age fields were re-orientated and the earlier ditches ploughed over, for example at Mount Farm, Dorchester (Lambrick 1992, 91–3). Nevertheless, well-defined fields are still more common in these areas of the valley than in those which had not been divided in the Bronze Age.

The area around and south of Dorchester not only differs from the Upper Thames valley upstream in terms of its pattern of land division; its settlement pattern is also at variance. Unenclosed habitation sites are present, indeed the Dyke Hills Late Iron Age enclosure probably originated as an open settlement of the Earlier Iron Age, but the gravel terraces are also dotted with small settlement sites lying within enclosures, often sub-rectangular in shape (T. Allen pers. comm.; Baker 2002, 22–4). These occupation sites are comparable with those found on the floodplain further north, suggesting smaller and less long-lived settlement and, perhaps, little formalised land ownership. However, although individual habitations may have operated independently, it is apparent that large numbers of people did collaborate in some way to construct and use the nearby hillfort at Castle Hill, Little Wittenham.

It can be concluded that, in the lower stretches of the Upper Thames valley, a different social and economic history had long-reaching effects, which led to different land-use and settlement patterns.

Lechlade and the Cotswold Water Park

The upper reaches of the Thames appear to have had a more dispersed Iron Age settlement pattern than that

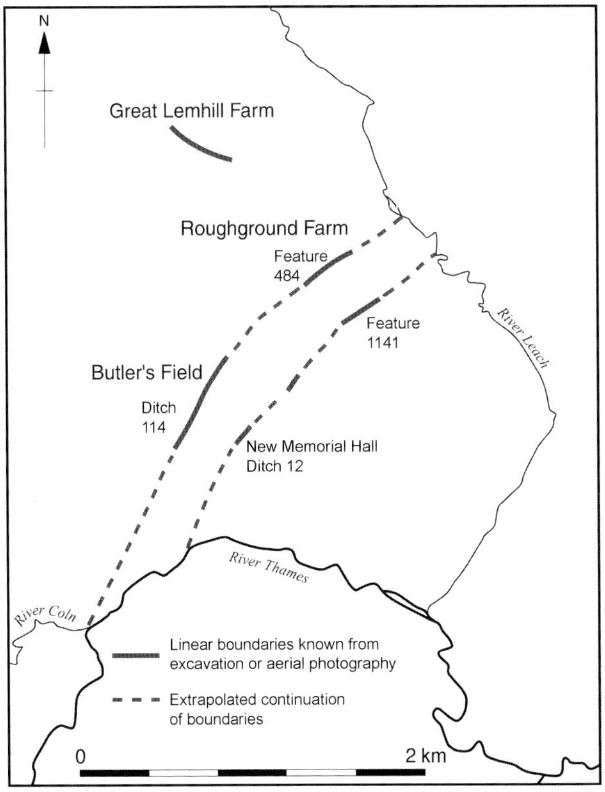

Fig. 8. Iron Age boundaries and field systems at Lechlade.

Fig. 9. The Cotswold Community pit alignment.

found lower down the valley, and this may partly be the result of relatively late woodland clearance. The area does, however, have an important ceremonial complex, with two cursus monuments which lie north and south of the river at Lechlade, near its confluence with the Leach. The Lechlade cursus was constructed within open, grazed grassland (Robinson 2003, 208–9), but that at Buscot, which is associated with a long enclosure and round barrows, was built within a fairly wooded landscape (Robinson and Wilson 1987, 31).

At Lechlade, a co-axial field system was laid out in the Middle Bronze Age respecting the Early Bronze Age barrows, but by the Late Bronze Age/Early Iron Age the situation had changed and newly-built land boundaries sliced through one of the mounds and cut across the cursus (Jennings 1998). There is no known centralising focus for this intensive Bronze Age agricultural activity, and contemporary settlement is poorly understood, but the field pattern resembles that found in the Dorchester area. There is evidence of fairly extensive Iron Age occupation and the substantial linear boundaries and field system in this area appear to be associated with this intensification of settlement (Fig. 8). The linear boundaries originated as pit alignments. Pit alignments are not especially common in the Upper Thames valley, at least in its central section, but do exist in its upper reaches; an impressive alignment is known from air photographs at Long Wittenham near Dorchester (Harding 1972, plates 37–38), highlighting the similarities between these two areas.

A dramatic double pit alignment has recently been exposed close to the source of the Thames near Shorncote. Excavations in 1999 revealed 164 pits in a line 140 m long and further work in 2003 exposed another 280 m of this boundary (Fig. 9). The pit alignment cannot be closely dated, despite extensive excavation, but is of the Late Bronze Age or Early Iron Age.

A considerable area has now been exposed in gravel workings at Shorncote, but the pattern and development of settlement is still being unravelled (Hey and Laws forthcoming). Small-scale occupation activity and clearance from at least the mid Neolithic is indicated by pits with Peterborough ware and polished axe fragments; rich Beaker burials have been found within barrow mounds; and small-scale Bronze Age pastoral farmsteads

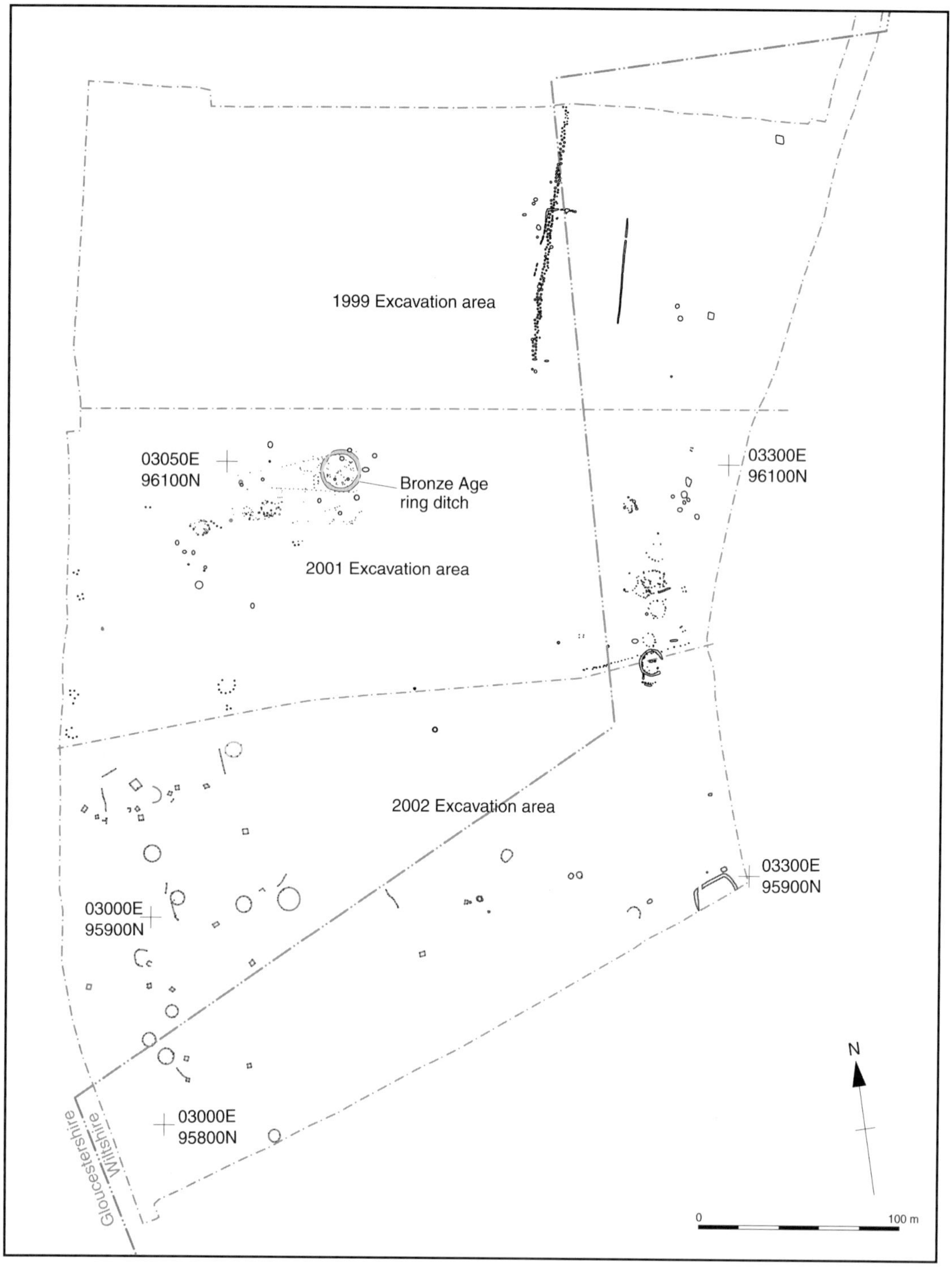

Fig.10. Plan of Bronze Age and Iron Age features excavated at Cotswold Community, Shorncote.

of the type examined on the Yarnton floodplain have been uncovered (Fig. 10). In the Late Bronze Age, however, a substantial nucleated settlement was established to the north (Hearne and Adam 1999), and some field boundaries appear to date to this period, or to the Early Iron Age. Palaeobotanical evidence from a nearby water hole, on the other hand, suggests that at around 1000 BC there was still fairly dense woodland in the vicinity, including some indicators of ancient woodland such as maple (Brossler *et al.* 2002). Iron Age settlement was also diverse in character: one settlement with associated field systems was established to the east of the Late Bronze Age settlement, but other smaller sites dating from the Early to the Late Iron Age lay within an unenclosed landscape further south. The substantial Iron Age settlement at Ashton Keynes was situated to the south of these (Coe *et al.* 1991).

As in other parts of the Upper Thames valley, the Lechlade to Cirencester area witnessed increasing density of settlement and intensity of land use through the Iron Age. Excavations at Claydon Pike and Thornhill Farm revealed little evidence of early activity, but small Middle Iron Age sites were located on drier islands in the first gravel terrace, followed by more substantial late Iron Age settlements (Miles *et al.* forthcoming). The site of Thornhill Farm appears to represent a specialised pastoral settlement showing considerable intensity of use over a relatively short period (Jennings *et al.* 2004).

Conclusions

A justifiable criticism of Iron Age investigations in the Upper Thames valley is that they have mainly been undertaken in the river valley, and have focused too narrowly on one particular topographic zone. This is as true now as it was when Richard Hingley (1984) attempted to understand the relationship between the open settlements of the gravel terraces and the smaller enclosed sites on the Cotswold slopes. If long trajectories ought to tell us anything, it is that people were not confined to local areas; in the Neolithic people may have moved seasonally across a much wider landscape. Undoubtedly Iron Age settlement was more permanent and settled, and people's options may have been more restricted, but this would not necessarily have

Fig. 11. Iron Age settlement below Madmarston hillfort (Crown copyright, NMR).

precluded access to much wider areas than the immediate environs of individual settlements.

In recent years, extensive air photographic coverage has revealed further evidence for Iron Age settlement on the slopes and low hills adjacent to the valley, particularly on the Cotswold slopes (Featherstone and Bewley 2000). Many new banjo enclosures have been found, some of weird and wonderful shape, apparently underlining the differences with the valley sites. There have, however, also been discoveries of open and more dense settlement, for example below the hillfort at Madmarston in north Oxfordshire (Fig. 11), showing that the pattern on these higher topographies is more varied than previously suspected.

The scope of work on hillforts in the region and other major enclosures in the valley and its slopes has been limited, partly as a result of the scale of these sites and their largely protected status. These defended sites, which include valley forts and defences near river tributaries, must have been significant and represent considerable investment of effort, yet we understand little of their relationship with contemporary settlements and their function within the rich pattern of land use. Defended sites are certainly very varied in their date, longevity of use, and the density of activity they contain; unravelling these links will be complex. This is an imbalance that is beginning to be addressed by Chris Gosden and Gary Lock's *Hillforts of the Ridgeway Project* (e.g. Gosden and Lock 2005) and Tim Allen's cumulative work on the Abingdon *oppidum* (Allen 2000), a site which is not protected from urban development. Important religious sites which must have been of regional significance, such as Frilford and Woodeaton, are also poorly understood and are only now receiving the investigation that they merit.

Despite the evident gaps in our knowledge and the uncertainties that still remain, the scale of work undertaken in the Upper Thames valley demonstrates that it is possible to begin to comprehend the detail of how communities developed through time, how they articulated with their neighbours, and how they utilised and/or changed the environment in which they lived. Indeed one may speculate that, in some places, it is possible to understand the mechanisms of change and the level at which decision-making took place at that time without reference to external political forces.

There is considerable value in looking at long time trajectories and individual site histories in order to understand the inherited landscape and appreciate the subtleties of variation in settlement patterns and landscape management. In some parts of the Upper Thames valley, traditional land use patterns running back into the Neolithic seem to have played a crucial role in the development of Iron Age settlement and landscape right up into the Roman period. This is particularly clear in the lower Windrush valley, where shared use of a major ceremonial monument and communal grazing around it appears to have heavily influenced subsequent perceptions and options for land management. Around Abingdon, too, ancestral sites were respected, and, although there is little evidence for communal decision making in the Yarnton–Cassington area (and apparent differences in farming strategies), it is nevertheless possible to see how early activity there strongly influenced later arrangements.

Other parts of the valley demonstrate a different settlement pattern, with clearly defined boundaries and fields from an early date. These are areas where there had been agricultural intensification in the Bronze Age linked to specific political and economic circumstances. South of Abingdon the pattern is associated with high-status sites, although the impetus behind the creation of Bronze Age field systems around Lechlade is uncertain. The collapse of this economic system led to reorganisation of the landscape in the Early Iron Age, associated with substantial boundaries and, probably slightly earlier, with pit alignments. In this context in the Upper Thames valley, it seems plausible to suggest that pit alignments represent a very formal creation of boundaries in a contested landscape, or in areas where past custom did not dictate land use or conform to current practice. Could the interrupted character of the boundary suggest that it was permeable and still open to negotiation? Where land use was agreed on a communal level, or where traditional land use continued to operate, such demarcation may have been unnecessary.

Superficially, the Upper Thames valley has a topographic unity and a broadly similar pattern of settlement and land use, with a standard range of recognised site types. The extent of the excavation that has taken place suggests, however, that these apparent similarities mask a much more complex and diverse settlement history. These investigations demonstrate the potential for shedding light on society and change in the Iron Age, but also the infinite richness and variety of the resource.

Acknowledgements

This paper is largely based on the work of others, principally George Lambrick, Mark Robinson, and Tim Allen; I am very grateful to them for the use of their ideas and for discussions over many years. George was a valuable guide to the Iron Age of the Upper Thames when I first worked in the area and a source of inspiration; Tim continues to provide a helpful sounding board and is a generous source of stimulating ideas. Mark Robinson continues to have an active involvement in environmental work on the Yarnton–Cassington project, as on numerous sites in the Upper Thames; I would particularly like to acknowledge his contribution. I would also like to thank David Miles, Alistair Barclay, and Richard Hingley for helpful discussions; Granville Laws and Chris Bell for their conscientious work in the field; and to acknowledge the help of Susan Lisk at the Oxfordshire Sites and Monuments Record. The drawings are by Ros Smith. An anonymous referee made very useful comments, which have resulted in improvements to this paper; the flaws that remain are my own.

Bibliography

Allen, T. 1990. *An Iron Age and Romano-British Enclosed Settlement at Watkins Farm, Northmoor, Oxon.* Oxford: Thames Valley Landscapes Monograph 1.

Allen, T. 2000. The Iron Age background, in M. Henig and P. Booth, *Roman Oxfordshire*, 1–33. Stroud: Sutton.

Allen, T. and Robinson, M. 1993. *The Prehistoric Landscape and Iron Age Enclosed Settlement at Mingies Ditch, Hardwick-with-Yelford, Oxon.* Oxford: Thames Valley Landscapes Monograph 2.

Baker, S. 2002. Prehistoric and Romano-British Landscapes at Little Wittenham and Long Wittenham, Oxfordshire, *Oxoniensia* 67, 1–28.

Barclay, A., Bradley, R., Hey, G. and Lambrick G. 1996. The earlier prehistory of the Oxford region in the light of recent research, *Oxoniensia* 61, 1–20.

Barclay, A., Gray, M. and Lambrick, G. 1995. *Excavations at the Devil's Quoits, Stanton Harcourt, Oxfordshire 1972–3 and 1988.* Oxford: Thames Valley Landscapes Monograph 3.

Barclay, A. and Halpin, C. 1999. *Excavations at Barrow Hills, Radley, Oxfordshire: the Neolithic and Bronze Age Monument Complex.* Oxford: Thames Valley Landscapes Monograph 11.

Barclay, A. and Hey, G. 1999. Cattle, cursus monuments and the river: the development of ritual and domestic landscapes in the Upper Thames Valley, in A. Barclay and J. Harding (eds), *Pathways and Ceremonies: the Cursus Monuments of Britain and Ireland*, 67–76. Oxford: Neolithic Studies Group Seminar Papers 4.

Barclay, A., Lambrick, G., Moore, J. and Robinson, M. 2003. *Lines in the Landscape: Cursus Monuments in the Upper Thames Valley.* Oxford: Thames Valley Landscapes Monograph 15.

Bonte, P. 1981. Marxist theory and anthropological analysis: the study of nomadic pastoralist societies, in H.S. Kahn and J.R. Llobera (eds), *The Anthropology of Pre-Capitalist Societies*, 22–56. London: Macmillan.

Bradford, J.S.P. 1942. An early Iron Age settlement at Standlake, Oxon., *Oxoniensia* 22, 202–214.

Bradley, R. and Yates, D. 2007. After 'Celtic' fields: the social organisation of Iron Age agriculture, in Haselgrove and Pope 2007, 94–102.

Brossler, A., Gocher, M., Laws, G. and Roberts, M. 2002. Shorncote Quarry: excavation of a late prehistoric landscape in the Upper Thames Valley, *Transactions of the Bristol and Gloucestershire Archaeological Society* 120, 37–87.

Case, H.J. 1982. The Vicarage Field, Stanton Harcourt, in H.J. Case and A.W.R. Whittle (eds), *Settlement Patterns in the Oxford Region: Excavations at the Abingdon Causewayed Enclosure and Other Sites*, 103–117. Oxford: Council for British Archaeology Research Report 44.

Coe, D., Jenkins, V. and Richards, J. 1991. Cleveland Farm, Ashton Keynes: second interim report: Investigations May-August 1989, *Wiltshire Archaeological and Natural History Magazine* 84, 40–50.

Cromarty, A.M., Foreman, S. and Murray, P. 1999. The excavation of a late Iron Age enclosed settlement at Bicester Fields Farm, Bicester, Oxon., *Oxoniensia* 64, 153–233.

Ellis, P., Hughes, G. and Jones, L. 2000. An Iron Age boundary and settlement features at Slade Farm, Bicester, Oxfordshire: a report on excavations, 1996, *Oxoniensia* 65, 211–265.

Evans, M. 1995. The Mollusca from the henge ditch, in Barclay *et al.* 1995, 62–67.

Everett, R.N. and Eeles, B.M.G. 1999. Investigations at Thrupp House Farm, Radley, near Abingdon, *Oxoniensia* 64, 118–152.

Featherstone, R. and Bewley, R. 2000. Recent aerial reconnaissance in North Oxfordshire, *Oxoniensia* 65, 13–27.

Fulford, M. and Nichols, E. (eds) 1992. *Developing Landscapes of Lowland Britain. The Archaeology of the British Gravels: a Review.* London: Society of Antiquaries of London Occasional Paper 14.

Gosden, C. and Lock, G. 2007. The aesthetics of landscape on the Berkshire Downs, in Haselgrove and Pope 2007, 279–292.

Harding, D.W. 1972. *The Iron Age in the Upper Thames Basin.* Oxford: Clarendon Press.

Haselgrove, C. and Pope, R. (eds) 2007. *The Earlier Iron Age in Britain and the Near Continent.* Oxford: Oxbow Books.

Hearne, C.M. 2000. Archaeological evaluation in the Vale of the White Horse, near Abingdon, 1992–99, *Oxoniensia* 65, 7–12.

Hearne, C.M. and Adam, N. 1999. Excavation of an extensive Late Bronze Age settlement at Shorncote Quarry, near Cirencester, 1995–6, *Transactions of the Bristol and Gloucestershire Archaeological Society* 117, 35–73.

Hey, G., Bayliss, A. and Boyle A. 1999. Iron Age inhumation burials at Yarnton, Oxfordshire, *Antiquity* 73, 551–62.

Hey, G., Mulville, J. and Robinson M. 2003. Diet and culture in southern Britain: the evidence from Yarnton, in M. Parker Pearson (ed.), *Food, culture and identity in the Neolithic and early Bronze Age*, 79–88. Oxford: British Archaeological Reports International Series 1117.

Hey, G., *et al.* forthcoming. *Yarnton: Iron Age and Roman Settlement and Landscape.* Oxford: Thames Valley Landscapes Monograph.

Hey, G. and Laws, G., forthcoming. *Excavations at Cotswold Community on the Wiltshire Gloucestershire Border.* Oxford: Thames Valley Landscapes Monograph.

Hingley, R. 1983. Excavations by R.A. Rutland on an Iron Age site at Wittenham Clumps, *Berkshire Archaeological Journal* 70, 21–55.

Hingley, R. 1984. Towards social analysis in archaeology: Celtic society in the Iron Age of the Upper Thames Valley, in B. Cunliffe and D. Miles (eds), *Aspects of the Iron Age in Central Southern Britain*, 52–88. Oxford: University of Oxford Committee for Archaeology Monograph 2.

Hingley, R. 1999. The creation of later prehistoric landscapes and the context of the reuse of Neolithic and earlier Bronze Age monuments in Britain and Ireland, in B. Bevan (ed.), *Northern Exposure: Interpretative Devolution and the Iron Ages in Britain,* 233–251. Leicester: Leicester Archaeology Monograph 4.

Jennings, D. 1998. Prehistoric and Roman activity, in A. Boyle, D. Jennings, D. Miles and S. Palmer, *The Anglo-Saxon Cemetery at Butler's Field, Lechlade, Gloucestershire, Vol. 1. Prehistoric and Roman Activity and Anglo-Saxon Grave Catalogue*, 9–34. Oxford: Thames Valley Landscapes Monograph 10.

Jennings, D., Muir, J., Palmer, S. and Smith, A. 2004. *Thornhill Farm, Fairford, Gloucestershire: an Iron Age and Roman Pastoral Site in the Upper Thames Valley*. Oxford: Thames Valley Landscapes Monograph 23.

Jones, M., with Robinson, M. 1993. The carbonised plant remains, in Allen and Robinson 1993, 120–123.

Lambrick, G. 1992. The development of late prehistoric and Roman farming on the Thames gravels, in Fulford and Nichols 1992, 78–105.

Lambrick, G. 1999. Community and Change in the Iron Age of the Upper Thames. Paper presented to Prehistoric Society Conference.

Lambrick, G. and Allen, T. 2004. *Gravelly Guy, Stanton Harcourt, Oxfordshire: the Development of a Prehistoric and Romano-British Community*. Oxford: Thames Valley Landscapes Monograph 21.

Lambrick, G. and Robinson, M. 1979. *Iron Age and Roman Riverside Settlements at Farmoor, Oxfordshire*. London: Council for British Archaeology Research Report 32.

Leeds, E.T. 1935. Recent Iron Age discoveries in Oxfordshire and North Berkshire, *Antiquaries Journal* 15, 30–41.

Lock, G., Gosden, C. and Daly, P. 2005. *Segsbury Camp: Excavations in 1996 and 1997 at an Iron Age Hillfort on the Oxfordshire Ridgeway*. Oxford: School of Archaeology Monograph 61.

Miles, D. 1986. *Archaeology at Barton Court Farm, Abingdon, Oxon*. Oxford: Council for British Archaeology Research Report 50.

Miles, D., Palmer, S., Lock, G., Gosden, C. and Cromarty, A.M. 2003. *Uffington White Horse and its Landscape. Investigations at White Horse Hill, Uffington, 1989–95 and Tower Hill Ashbury, 1993–4*. Oxford: Thames Valley Landscapes Monograph 18.

Miles, D., Palmer, S., Smith, A. and Jones, G.P. forthcoming. *Iron Age and Roman settlement in the Upper Thames Valley: Excavations at Claydon Pike and Other Sites within the Cotswold Water Park*. Oxford: Thames Valley Landscapes Monograph 26.

Miles, D. 1997. Conflict and complexity: the later prehistory of the Oxford region, *Oxoniensia* 62, 1–19.

Mould, C. 1996. An archaeological excavation at Oxford Road, Bicester, Oxfordshire, *Oxoniensia* 61, 65–108.

Parker, A.G. 1995. *Late Quaternary Environmental Change in the Upper Thames Basin, Central-Southern England*. Unpublished D.Phil. thesis, University of Oxford.

Robinson, M. 1992. Environmental archaeology of the river gravels: past achievements and future directions, in Fulford and Nichols 1992, 47–62.

Robinson, M. 1993. Discussion of the sedimentary and ecological sequence, in Allen and Robinson 1993, 134–139.

Robinson, M. 2003. Molluscs and charred plant remains, in Barclay *et al.* 2003, 208–209.

Robinson, M. and Lambrick, G. 1984. Holocene alluviation and hydrology in the Upper Thames basin, *Nature* 308, 809–814.

Robinson, M. and Wilson, B. 1987. A survey of environmental archaeology in the south midlands, in H.C.M. Keeley (ed.), *Environmental Archaeology: a Regional Review, Vol. 2*, 16–100. London: HBMC(E) Occasional Paper 1.

Stevens, C. forthcoming. The charred plant remains, in Hey *et al.* forthcoming.

Stone, S., 1856–59. Account of certain (supposed) British and Saxon remains, *Proceedings of the Society of Antiquaries of London* (Ser. 1) 4, 92–100.

Whittle, A., Atkinson, R.J.C., Chambers, R. and Thomas, N. 1992. Excavations in the Neolithic and Bronze Age complex at Dorchester-on-Thames, Oxfordshire, 1947–1952 and 1981, *Proceedings of the Prehistoric Society* 58, 143–201.

Yates, D. 1999. Bronze Age field systems in the Thames Valley, *Oxford Journal of Archaeology* 18, 157–170.

Rooted to the spot: the 'smaller enclosures' of the later first millennium BC in the central Welsh Marches

Andy Wigley

Introduction

This paper is concerned with the smaller enclosures, which might also be termed 'non-hillfort' or 'small settlement' enclosures, of the central Welsh Marches (Fig. 1). These can be defined as sites that were originally enclosed by at least one bank and ditch, with a maximum internal area of up to about a hectare. The existence of well-preserved examples of such monuments on higher ground in the western part of the region has long been acknowledged. Because they often have substantial earthworks and are prominently sited in the landscape, these enclosures have traditionally been seen as small hillforts (e.g. Forde-Johnston 1962; Hogg 1965; Stanford 1972a; Jackson 1999). However, aerial photography over the past three decades has now revealed considerable numbers of smaller enclosures across the lower lying parts of the region that have been levelled by the plough. Morphologically, they range from simple single-ditched examples through to complex sites with multiple ditches (Whimster 1989). There has been a tendency to view all of the enclosures on the lower ground as farmsteads, and thus as distinct from the 'small hillforts'.

Because of these distinctions, prehistorians have in the past been slow to appreciate the significance that the smaller enclosures have for our interpretations of the Later Iron Age communities of the central Marches. As elsewhere in Britain, research has often focused upon the larger and more spectacular hillforts, even leading some to argue that the smaller enclosures dated entirely to the Roman period (Stanford 1980). However, a growing number of excavations of smaller enclosures have demonstrated that the tradition of constructing such monuments extended from perhaps the fifth or fourth centuries BC until at least the second century AD,[1] and it now seems certain that a significant proportion of these sites were at least partly contemporary with many of the hillforts. Similarly, the continued construction, use, and reworking of such sites after the mid first century AD has led some to talk of a 'seamless' transition between the later Iron Age and the early Roman period (Carver 1991, 4). Whilst *occupation* of the smaller enclosures that have been investigated was by no means continuous, once established, many of these monuments do appear to have persisted within the later Iron Age landscape for extended periods of time.

This paper will examine two aspects of these monuments – their materiality and their apparent longevity – which provide us with an insight into the nature of the communities who inhabited the central Welsh Marches in the later first millennium BC. In particular, it will investigate how these groups went about constructing and maintaining the boundaries of these monuments, and what this tells us about the structure of social relations at this time. In doing so, I will address how this labour was made possible by – and in turn helped to reproduce – the ways in which people tended both to their land and to each other.

Smaller enclosures in the landscape of the central Welsh Marches

Survival and visibility in the landscape

One of the key characteristics of the landscape of the central Welsh Marches is its topographical diversity. In his seminal book, *The Personality of Britain*, Cyril Fox

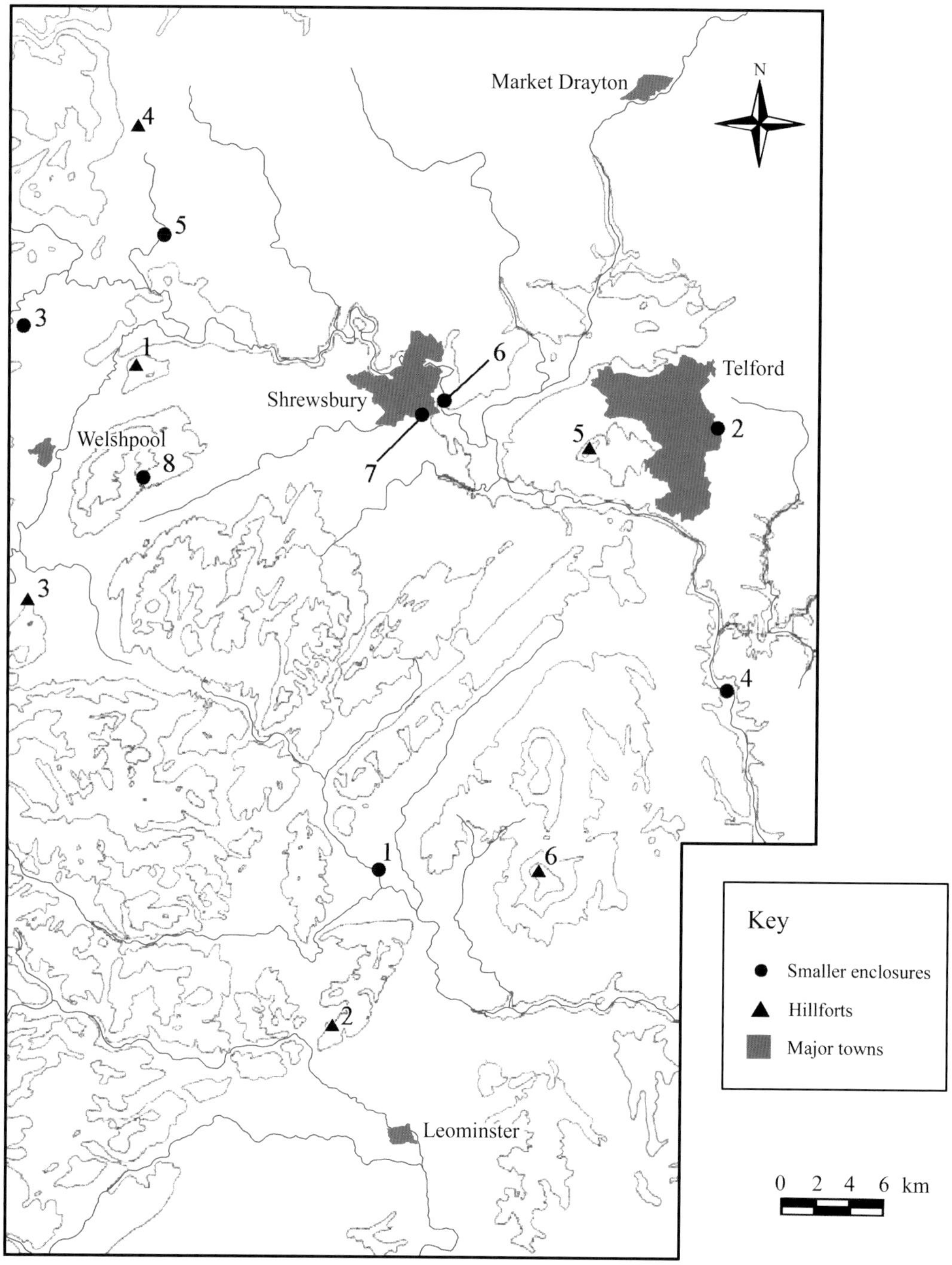

Fig. 1. Map of the central Welsh Marches showing the locations of selected sites mentioned in the text. Hillforts: 1. The Breiddin; 2. Croft Ambrey; 3. Ffridd Faldwyn; 4. Old Oswestry; 5. The Wrekin; 6. Titterstone Clee. Smaller enclosures: 1. Bromfield; 2. Castle Farm; 3. Collfryn; 4. Hay Farm; 5. Osbaston; 6. Preston Farm; 7. Sharpstones Hill Site A.

(1932) attempted to rationalise this variability by drawing the boundary between his Highland and Lowland Zones through its centre. Published at the start of what was to be an important decade in the development of British archaeology, this work effectively formalised the concept of the Welsh Marches as a 'frontier zone' for a new generation of prehistorians. Fox was drawing on a well established antiquarian tradition, which projected the notion of the Marches as a military frontier, derived from the conflation of a series of different monuments from successive historical periods, back into prehistory (e.g. Hartshorne 1843; Anderson 1864; Luff 1888).

Fox's thesis was underpinned by the Invasion Hypothesis and was as influential amongst those working in the emergent field of Iron Age studies as it was with scholars studying earlier periods of prehistory (Barclay 2001). This in part explains why the hillforts, with their as yet unquestioned martial function, were given such primacy in accounts of the period in the Marches. It is this perception of the region as a 'hillfort zone', with all

Fig. 2. Aerial photograph of Walton Camp, Long Mountain, western Shropshire (CPAT©93–MB-0174).

that this implied in terms of the nature of Iron Age society, that dominated interpretations of the Welsh Marches until at least the 1970s (Varley 1948; Hogg 1965; Stanford 1972b; Savory 1976; Cunliffe 1991).

The validity of Fox's distinction was subsequently called into question by Stevenson (1975), and most researchers now accept that it represents a huge overgeneralisation. The simple, bi-partite division fails to capture the subtle and highly complex variations that exist within each of the zones. Stevenson noted that the Lowland Zone mainly consists of agricultural land and thus demonstrates less variability in land use. The Highland Zone, with its extensive tracts of open unimproved land, exhibits a much sharper degree of variation. As a result, he argued that 'the country could be broken down into a large number of small units and not into two large blocks' (*ibid.*, 9). This certainly holds true for the central Welsh Marches. For instance, the hills and high moorland plateaux that exist in the western and the central parts of the region lie in close proximity to verdant river valleys, the most significant of which is that of the River Severn itself. In the north of the region the low-lying, rolling terrain is enriched by a patchwork of meres, mosses and fenland, the extent of which have been significantly reduced by post-medieval agricultural improvement (Leah *et al.* 1998). In the southern and eastern areas the higher hill country of south Shropshire gradually gives way to the gentler contours of sandstone hills and plateaux.

The ways in which successive generations have worked with this diversity over the past two millennia has a number of important implications when it comes to interpreting the Iron Age landscape. Differences in agricultural practices across the central Welsh Marches have resulted in significant variability in the level of preservation of smaller enclosures in the present-day landscape. For instance, medieval cultivation and post-medieval agricultural improvement over much of the lower-lying areas has effectively erased many sites. This process has been compounded since the Second World War by intensive arable agriculture. In these areas, the vast majority of enclosures are now only visible as cropmarks where favourable conditions prevail.

However, smaller enclosures often survive as well preserved earthworks in areas which, until recently, have lain beyond the limits of cultivation, or have traditionally been used for less heavily improved pasture. This inevitably means that monuments of this kind survive in much better condition on the higher ground in western and south-western parts of the region. For example, a survey of 234 small enclosures in the former county of Montgomeryshire (now part of Powys), revealed that 61% of 185 sites located on hilltops survived as earthworks (Silvester and Britnell 1993). However, only 44% of 94 sites in hill-slope settings, and a mere 6% of 55 sites on valley floors, survived as earthworks.

As noted above, these differences in preservation have led to a disparity in the nomenclature that we use in relation to the smaller enclosures, which in turn has had significant consequences for our interpretations of them. Two examples serve to illustrate this point. Walton Camp, located in a prominent hill-slope setting on Long Mountain in western Shropshire (Fig. 2), is a small double-ditched enclosure that until recently was classed

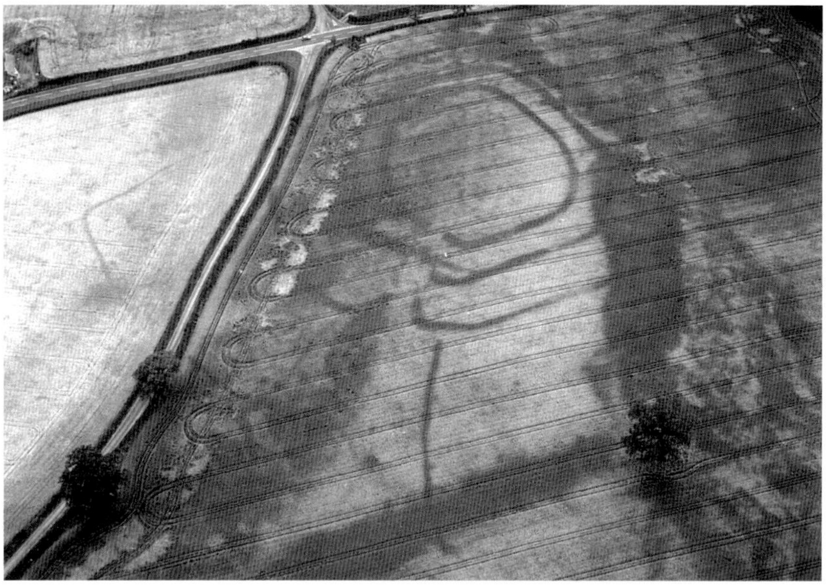

Fig. 3. Aerial photograph of the Osbaston enclosure, north-western Shropshire (CPAT©84–MB-0253).

as a 'small multivallate hillfort'.[2] In contrast, the complex, multi-ditched curvilinear enclosure at Osbaston, in north-western Shropshire, has been entirely levelled by the plough and now survives only as a cropmark (Fig. 3). Despite the fact that the earthworks associated with this site cover a larger area than those at Walton Camp, it has been suggested that this site represents a 'small defended farmstead' (Watson and Musson 1993, 33–4).

Given the primacy that we have traditionally assigned to the hillforts in this region, these distinctions mean that the significance of the cropmark sites has often been downplayed. For example, Jackson (1999) excluded them from his recent analysis of the size distribution of hillforts in the Marches, but used the large number of small hillforts of less than 1.2 hectares on the western side of the region (his Zone 2) to draw a distinction with the areas to the east (his Zone 1), where 'there appears to be an emphasis upon [large hillforts] and [very large hillforts]' (*ibid.*, 202). Analysing these distributions according to the land capability classification used in the 1944 Ordnance Survey map, Jackson noted that there was a greater proportion of poorer quality land in Zone 1 than in Zone 2.

Although elevation is noted as a factor influencing land capability, its effect on the survival of archaeological monuments is *not* discussed. Consequently, Jackson equated the distinctions between his Zones 1 and 2 to differences in the structuring of Iron Age social relations. Thus, Zone 2 was characterised by 'a segmented, competitive society', whereas in Zone 1, 'individual settlements… were strongly integrated into a larger community' focused around the bigger hillforts (*ibid.*, 207–8). Although Jackson acknowledges that there are substantial numbers of non-hillfort settlements (i.e. cropmark enclosures) in Zone 1, their significance for our understandings of Iron Age settlement pattern remained largely unconsidered.

As the examples of Osbaston and Walton Camp illustrate, the distinction between earthwork and cropmark enclosures is to a large degree a false one. If cropmark enclosures had been included in Jackson's analysis, the distinction between Zones 1 and 2 would have begun to dissolve. Instead, one would be left with a pattern of widely distributed smaller enclosures, with the number of larger hillforts gradually diminishing as one moved westward towards the Cambrian Mountains or eastwards onto the Midlands Plain.

Variations in enclosure size and morphology

A number of commentators have drawn attention to the sheer diversity in the size and form of the smaller enclosures in the central Marches. Whimster (1989), for instance, has put forward a typology consisting of nine basic categories (and a series of sub-categories), based upon his survey of cropmark enclosures identified prior to 1981 (Fig. 4). His analysis revealed that the overwhelming majority of these sites were single-ditched enclosures (335 out of a total 449 sites), of which most (201) had a rectilinear form. There were 83 bivallate enclosure, 43 of which were of rectilinear form, whilst the remaining 40 were either of curvilinear or hybrid type. There were only 31 multivallate enclosures within Whimster's study area, the majority (23) of which were curvilinear or hybrid forms.

Attempts to apply Whimster's classification to cropmark and earthwork sites in other parts of the region have met with varying degrees of success. Jones (1994a)

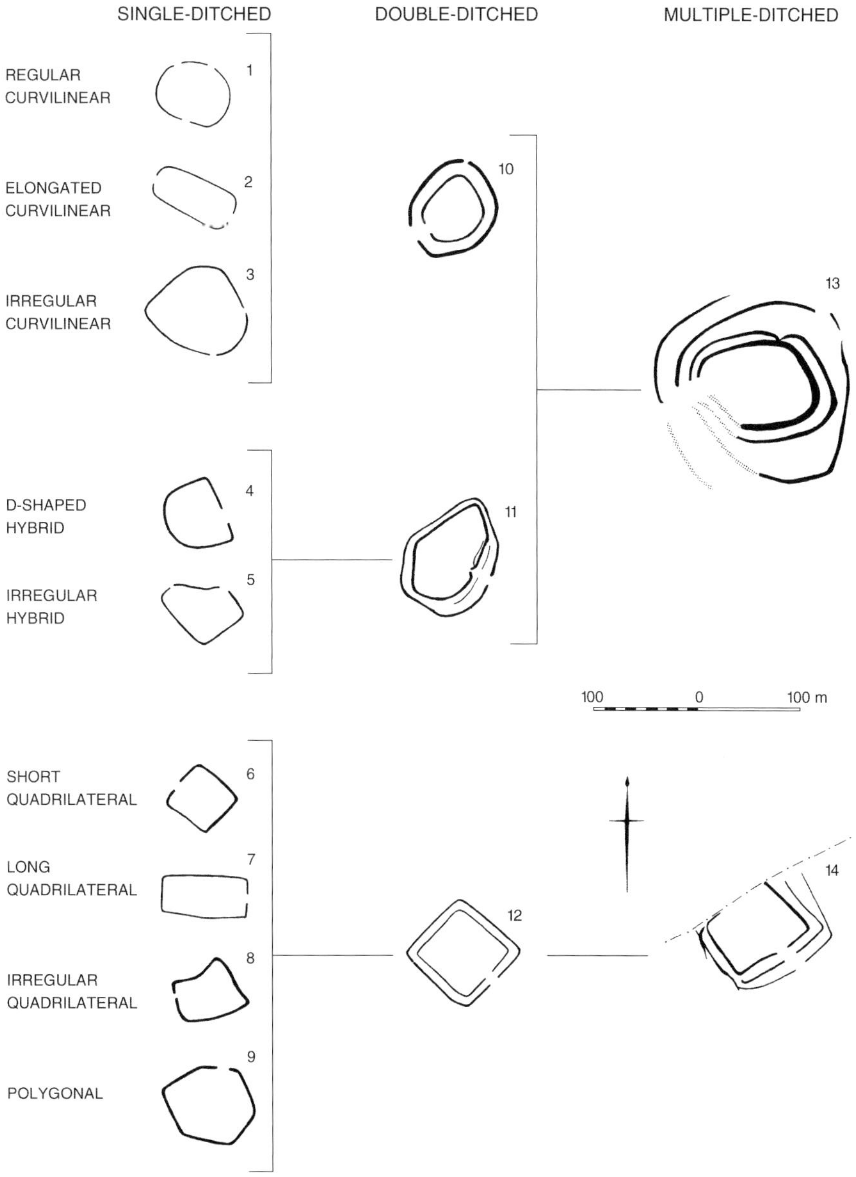

Fig. 4. Whimster's typology of smaller enclosures (source: Whimster 1989, fig. 19). (Crown copyright, NMR).

found that the majority of 187 smaller enclosures (172 of which were cropmarks) identified in the area around Wroxeter, in central Shropshire, could be classified as single-ditched rectilinear enclosures (96 cropmark and 3 earthwork sites). Sites with single curvilinear boundaries, of which there were 40 cropmark and 4 earthwork examples, were also fairly common. The analysis also appears to suggest that bivallate and multivallate sites were less frequent in the Later Iron Age–early Romano-British landscape. With regard to size, Jones found that a significant proportion of sites had an internal area between 0.2–0.4 ha, although he noted that there was a high degree of variability above and beyond this.

Silvester and Britnell (1993) found Whimster's scheme less convincing. They found that seven (10%) of the 68 earthworks examined in the Montgomeryshire Small Enclosures Survey could not be classified using Whimster's typology. Their analysis revealed that, of the 187 sites that could be categorised in this way, the majority (75%) of sites had a curvilinear or hybrid form. This appears to confirm Whimster's and Jones' point that rectilinear enclosures are more common in Shropshire and the eastern part of the region in general. Silvester and Britnell also found that there was a much higher proportion of sites with double (27%, 50 sites) and multiple (12%, 23 sites) ditches in their study area. Further, of the 144 sites discovered in this part of Powys between 1975 and 1991, 37% (54) had double or multiple ditches, nearly half of which survived as earthworks.

Silvester and Britnell drew two conclusions from these findings. Firstly, they suggest that, since a much higher proportion of multi-ditched enclosures survive as earthworks, these sites may originally have had more substantial earthworks than the single-ditched enclosures. Recent reassessment of Iron Age and Romano-British settlements in Shropshire by the Monuments Protection Programme appears to bear this out, allowing a distinction to be drawn between sites with more imposing earthworks on the one hand, and those with less complex boundaries on the other (M. Reid pers. comm.). Secondly, Silvester and Britnell argue that the recent increase in the discovery of multi-ditched enclosures may indicate that sites of this kind are currently under-represented in the archaeological record.

These studies demonstrate that a considerable degree of variability in both enclosure size and form existed across the central Welsh Marches. This suggests that we should avoid being too dogmatic in our classification of these monuments. In emphasising the complexity of the evidence, Carver (1991) has spoken in terms of a 'spectrum' of enclosure sizes in the region, ranging from the simplest single-ditched enclosure at one end up to the largest hillforts at the other. Similarly, Silvester and Britnell point out that:

> 'Whilst a relatively small number of the larger hillforts can probably legitimately be distinguished as a separate phenomenon, the continuous variation in size, shape, complexity, scale of defence and location of the majority of sites have had a tendency to inhibit further attempts to distinguish well defined monuments types' (Silvester and Britnell 1993, 2).

The smaller enclosures thus represent one end of a 'continuum' of enclosure size and form, which extends upwards to include the larger hillforts. Whimster's typology provides us with a useful grammatical framework with which to discuss the smaller enclosures. However, attempting to refine this scheme to any greater degree is unlikely to answer more pressing questions about how these sites were actually inhabited in the later Iron Age.

Differences in the landscape settings of smaller enclosures

Before we examine this point, it is worth considering variations in the topographical settings of the smaller enclosures in the central Marches. As with the differences in size and morphology, this variable has had a significant influence upon the rate of site survival. For example, Whimster (1989) noted that cropmark enclosures generally occur at lower altitudes (although sites have been discovered up to the 390 m contour) and on the steeper hillsides and valley slopes. Again, one must bear in mind that over the past two millennia these factors have also made the land more suitable for cultivation, and that elsewhere in the landscape smaller enclosure sites tend to survive as earthworks.

Nonetheless, more detailed analysis of the cropmarks in the area around Wroxeter has revealed a slight tendency for enclosures with certain forms to be located in particular kinds of locations (Jones 1994a). Thus, univallate rectilinear enclosures are commonly situated on the lower ground, with an increasing bias towards locations along rivers as distance from Wroxeter increases. Single-ditched hybrid enclosures also tend to be located close to rivers. However, Jones found that single-ditched enclosures of curvilinear form are fairly evenly distributed across the landscape, and appear to bear no relation to the rivers. The more complex bivallate and multivallate enclosures also appear to be situated away from rivers, becoming increasingly common as distance from Wroxeter increases.

Silvester and Britnell's (1993) study demonstrates that the small cropmark and earthwork enclosures in Montgomeryshire occupy a wide range of settings, with only wetlands and high moorland seemingly being avoided.[3] Despite this, some trends in the topographical positioning of sites are apparent. For example, 85 of the 235 sites (36%) included in the study occupied prominent locations, such as ridges, hilltops, and knolls, which Silvester and Britnell interpret as concern for display. In contrast, 94 (39%) sites were situated on hillsides or on the end of spurs, 'locations suggestive of a level of natural protection but a greater concern for an unobtrusive existence' (*ibid.*, 17). Arguably, however, whilst such settings may reduce the visibility of an enclosure within its immediate environs, they can make sites more prominent when viewed from a distance. Walton Camp illustrates this point well. Situated at the end of a small spur on the eastern side of Long Mountain, this site sits unobtrusively within its immediate landscape. However, it appears much more prominent when viewed at a distance from neighbouring hills or the floor of the Rea valley.

Silvester and Britnell (1993) also found that a significant number of enclosures (55, 23%) within their study area occupy apparently indefensible positions. Nine of these sites were sited in hollows, cols, or at the heads of valleys, whilst the remaining 46 were located on valley floors or river terraces. Even amongst the latter group, however, there was a propensity toward 'isolated knolls rising above the general ground level' (*ibid.*, 17).

Both Jones' (1994a) and Silvester and Britnell's (1993) studies appear to indicate that univallate rectilinear cropmark enclosures are more common on lower ground. When they appear in groups or clusters they often lie in close proximity to Roman military sites and civil settlements. In the area around Wroxeter, Jones noted a distinct concentration along the line of Watling Street to the south-west of the Roman city. This has led to the tacit assumption that the majority probably date to the Roman period. For example, Silvester and Britnell argue that the lesser extent of Roman influence in their study area may account for the smaller number of single-ditched rectilinear enclosures, compared with the area around Wroxeter.

Whilst future fieldwork may yet prove such assertions to be right, analysis of Whimster's data suggests that several well-known Roman sites[4] acted as 'honey pots' for early flyers (Wigley 2002). An examination of dates of discovery reveals that 75% (52) of the 69 sites discovered between 1945–1959, and 53% (92) of the 174 sites discovered between 1960–1969, lie within 5 km of one of these sites. The proportion falls to 26% (107) for the 418 sites discovered the period 1970–1979, during which Chris Musson began his more systematic programme of aerial survey. Similarly, an examination of Whimster's data relating to the frequency with which sites have been photographed reveals that all 13 sites that had been photographed on more that ten occasions up to 1979, and 25 (76%) of those photographed between 6–10 times, lay with 5 km of one of these Roman sites. These findings may partially account for the larger numbers of single-ditched rectilinear enclosures known in the areas around Roman sites. Similarly, these results suggest that caution is required when we attempt to explain why concentrations of cropmark enclosures occur in certain parts of the region. At the very least, they call into question Jones' (1994a, 108) assertion that large numbers of such sites around Wroxeter indicate that it was a 'favoured area in prehistory' and 'the heartland of the Cornovii'.

Digging in: understanding the smaller enclosures of the central Welsh Marches

The historical and ecological context of the smaller enclosures

Having examined the morphology, survival, and landscape setting of these sites, let us now consider the evidence relating to their inhabitation. We must begin by situating the smaller enclosures in their broader historical and ecological context, since this will enable us to understand how, in the later first millennium BC, the tradition of constructing these monuments emerged out of a pre-existing set of material conditions. Whilst there remain a number of very significant gaps in our knowledge, various lines of evidence are beginning to provide us with a picture of the regional landscape in the Late Bronze Age and Early Iron Age.

Dated pollen sequences from the north Shropshire wetlands (Beales 1980; Twigger and Haslam 1991; Leah *et al.* 1998) and from Buckbean Pond on the Breiddin (Smith *et al.* 1991) indicate that clearance activity gradually increased over the course of the later second millennium BC. Although the relationships between the various landform processes involved were highly complex, this removal of forest cover from the valley sides and floors appears to have promoted hydrological change within the region's river systems. Geoarchaeological evidence from the catchment of the upper Severn suggests that there was also a significant increase in the rate of floodplain alluviation in the last three or four centuries of the second millennium BC (Shotten 1978; Brown 1982, 1988; Brown and Barber 1985; Roseff 1992; Taylor and Lewin 1996; 1997). Thus, by the beginning of the first millennium BC, the landscape appears to have been partially open, and perhaps comprised a patchwork of cultivation plots, hill pasture, managed woodland, and floodplain grazing.

The desire of communities to reproduce their tenure over these newly available areas of open land may have resulted in an important phase of formal land division, which further transformed the structure of the landscape. It seems likely that some areas within the central Welsh Marches were divided up by linear boundary systems, although seemingly not as coherent and extensive as those in southern England. The most distinctive and recognisable of these are the pit alignments, of which numerous examples have now been identified as cropmarks (Owen and Britnell 1989; Wigley 2007). They are poorly dated, but in a number of cases their apparent relationship to round barrows and smaller enclosures suggests a broad Late Bronze Age–Early Iron Age date, as do parallels from better researched areas, such as the Avon valley in Warwickshire (Hingley 1996; Palmer 2001) and the river valleys of the East Midlands (Knight this volume).

It is also possible that the cross-ridge dykes, of which a number survive as earthworks on the higher ground, date to this period. A recent evaluation of the Devil's Mouth cross dyke on the Long Mynd, in south Shropshire, obtained calibrated radiocarbon dates[5] of 1530–1310 cal. BC (3155 ± 45; OxA-5082) and 1500–1210 cal. BC (3105 ± 45; OxA-5083) on a charcoal sample from a pre-bank ground surface (J. Milln and J. Dinn pers. comm.), providing a *terminus post quem* for the earthwork.

Constructing these kinds of boundaries, some of which extend for several hundred metres, would have been a considerable undertaking. Such projects probably brought together the members of different kin groups, and labouring to build them may have created networks of affiliation amongst the participants. It seems likely that their construction also enabled some sections of the community to redefine their tenure over the land, as long-standing rights of access were physically demarcated for the first time, whilst others were cross-cut or curtailed (Giles 2001). The establishment of the linear boundaries not only altered the character of landscape, but may also have transformed the social relations that existed within and between the communities who created them.

As in Wessex and elsewhere, it seems possible –

although it is as yet by no means proven – that the creation of these boundary systems pre-dated the construction of the first hillforts in the early first millennium BC. Excavations at the Breiddin, in north-eastern Powys, have now demonstrated that the earliest phases of the ramparts date to the ninth or eighth centuries BC (Musson 1991). Late Bronze Age pottery with similar forms and fabrics to that from the Breiddin has been recovered from various places within the interior of the hillfort on the Wrekin, in Shropshire (Kenyon 1942; Stanford 1984), suggesting that a settlement of a similar date existed there. It seems likely that this was enclosed, although strictly speaking neither Kenyon's nor Stanford's work provided confirmation of this.

Early phases are also suspected at a number of the other hillforts in the region that were excavated in the 1930s, including Ffridd Faldwyn, Powys (O'Neil 1942), and Old Oswestry (Varley 1948) and possibly Titterstone Clee (O'Neil 1934), in Shropshire. Other key sequences from beyond the region come from Llyn Bryn-dinas, in Powys (Musson *et al.* 1992), and Beeston Castle, in Cheshire (Ellis 1993), where the earliest phases of the ramparts seem to have been broadly contemporary with those at the Breiddin.

These sites appear to fall into two broad categories: hillforts situated on very prominent hills, which often have igneous geologies (e.g. the Breiddin, the Wrekin, Llyn Bryn-dinas), and hillforts situated in less prominent positions in the landscape (e.g. Old Oswestry, Ffridd Faldwyn). The excavated evidence, sparse and problematic though it is, implies that the former group may be the earlier of the two (i.e. ninth–eighth century BC). The occurrence of carinated haematite-coated wares at Old Oswestry – somewhat problematically the only site in the region to have produced pottery of this kind – *might* indicate that the slight univallate hillforts sit marginally later in the sequence, perhaps belonging to the seventh or sixth centuries BC.

It seems possible that the construction of the early hillforts contributed to a further opening up of the landscape, as the pollen sequences from the region suggest that forest clearance accelerated in the early first millennium BC. Evidence for early hillfort ramparts with a substantial timber component has been found at the Breiddin, Ffridd Faldwyn, and Titterstone Clee. At the Breiddin, Musson's (1991) excavations revealed 68 definite and 12 probable post holes within a 48 m section of the Late Bronze Age rampart. The posts appear to have been 12–15 cm in diameter, and charcoal samples from several different post holes all proved to be oak. Presuming that this structure is replicated beneath the entire 1300 m of the inner rampart, in the order of 1820 posts may have been used in the construction of the first earthwork. This figure does not allow for cross-braces or other structural timbers, so that the actual quantity of wood use, might have been far higher. The procurement of these timbers may well have contributed to the creation of ever larger areas of cleared land. Certainly, by the mid first millennium BC, the pollen evidence suggests that we are probably dealing with a largely open landscape.

The construction and reworking of hillforts almost certainly continued through much of the later first millennium BC. Ultimately, this resulted in the creation of an extraordinarily complex suite of monuments, which exhibit considerable diversity in terms of their morphology, topographical setting, and the character of their occupation. At the Breiddin, the evidence suggests that a significant hiatus followed the firing and destruction of the Late Bronze Age rampart towards the end of the eight century BC (Musson 1991). However, in the late fifth or early fourth centuries BC a much larger dry-stone rampart was built over the heat-shattered remains of the earlier timber-framed earthwork. This seems to have been accompanied by a renewal of activity in the interior. Musson argued that the hillfort was probably fairly densely occupied at this time, but a reassessment of insect macrofossils from Buckbean Pond, which lies within the hillfort, implies that habitation was much more localised than he suggested, and was perhaps seasonal or intermittent (Buckland *et al.* 2001).

In contrast, the sequence from Croft Ambrey, in northern Herefordshire, suggests that occupation at this site was more intensive, spanning perhaps the seventh to second centuries BC (Stanford 1974; Jackson 1999). This resulted in the accumulation of deeply stratified deposits, rich in pottery, iron metalwork and animal bones, within the large quarry ditch at the rear of the main rampart. Stanford saw this earthwork as the product of a single phase of construction – albeit one that may have been interrupted on occasions – but the complex stratification revealed within his section drawing, especially when considered alongside the repeated rebuilding and reconfiguration of the entrances, hints at a much more complex structural history.

Although Croft Ambrey and the Breiddin represent two of the most intensively investigated sites in the region, work at other hillforts has provided further evidence of the variability that exists within this class of monument. Excavations of the ramparts at several sites, including Ffridd Faldwyn (O'Neil 1942), Ivington Camp, Herefordshire (Dalwood *et al.* 1997), Old Oswestry (Varley 1948; Hughes 1994), and Titterstone Clee (O'Neil 1934), have all revealed diverse and complex structural histories. Further evidence of morphological variability has been revealed in the recent inspections carried out by the Monuments Protection Programme (M. Reid pers. comm.). This work suggests that at some sites, such as Earl's Hill and the Wrekin, terracing of the steep hillsides in front of the ramparts has created the impression of ditches. At both sites, new rampart circuits appear to have been laid out at some point in the site's history, significantly altering the size of the enclosed area and thus, presumably, the arrangement of the internal space. At a number of hillforts in Shropshire such as Chesterton Walls in the south-east of the county, deep rock-cut ditches have been recognised, providing a dramatic illustration of the large amounts of labour involved in their construction.

The character of hillfort occupation in the region is less clear. Most excavators have focused on the ramparts and, where the interiors have been investigated, the areas examined have generally been fairly small. However, together with the sequences from the Breiddin and Croft Ambrey, the evidence again suggests that there was significant variability between hillforts. Traces of buildings have been found at several sites. The remains of four-post structures that had undergone several phases of construction have been found within the interiors of Caynham Camp (Gelling 1963), Ffridd Faldwyn (O'Neil 1942), and the Wrekin (Stanford 1984), and there is evidence for roundhouses at Burrow Hill (Toller 1978) and possibly Caynham Camp (*pace* Stanford 1991, 56) and Ffridd Faldwyn (O'Neil 1942, fig. 9).

Small-scale excavations at several places within the massive hillfort at Llanymynech, which straddles the Welsh border between Powys and Shropshire, have produced evidence for metalworking (Musson and Northover 1989; Owen 1997; 1999). This site lies over copper-bearing carboniferous limestone and may well have been a significant focus for metalworking in the Middle–Late Iron Age. At Bury Walls, in northern Shropshire, a recent geophysical survey revealed that the interior has been extensively terraced, presumably to provide material for the construction of the ramparts, which on the northern side of the site are built on a massive scale (R. White pers. comm.).

The material culture of the later first millennium BC in the central Welsh Marches, as revealed by excavations of hillforts and smaller enclosures, has always been seen as sparse and impoverished in comparison to that of Wessex. As a result, the Iron Age communities of this region have often been portrayed as the poor cousins of those who dwelt in southern England. However, although usually found in small quantities, pottery has been recovered from most sites dating to the Later Iron Age. Petrological studies suggest that this material originates from a limited number of sources in the vicinity of the Malvern Hills and the Clee Hills (Peacock 1968; Morris 1981; 1982; 1996). By far the most numerous ceramic finds of this period are the fragments of briquetage containers. These probably held salt cakes produced at the inland brine springs at Droitwich, Worcestershire, and the Nantwich/Middlewich area of northern Cheshire (Morris 1985; 1994).

In addition to the pottery and ceramics, important evidence for metalworking has been found at three different types of locations in the north-western part of the region. Aside from Llanymynch, these include the hillforts at the Breiddin (Musson 1991) and Lynn Bryn-dinas (Musson *et al.* 1992); the smaller enclosures at Collfryn (Britnell 1989) and possibly Tycoch Farm (Hannaford 1993); and associated with the remains of Late Neolithic and Early Bronze Age monuments at Four Crosses (Warrillow *et al.* 1986) and Sarn-y-bryn-caled (Gibson 1994). It is also worth bearing in mind that Croft Ambrey has yielded one of the richest assemblages of iron metalwork, in relation to the size of the area investigated, of any British hillfort (N. Sharples pers. comm.). Together, these assemblages suggest that the traditional notions of the material impoverishment of the Iron Age communities in this region are wrong. Instead, it appears that the practices associated with the production, use and deposition of artefacts were significantly different from those that existed in southern England.

The emergence of the smaller enclosures and the definition of tenure in the later first millennium BC

A growing number of smaller enclosures have now been excavated in the central Welsh Marches, enabling us to develop an understanding of how they relate to these broader developments. As outlined above, the evidence suggests that the practice of constructing smaller enclosures emerged after 500 BC, implying that some of these monuments were partly contemporary with the hillforts. They appear to have been 'inserted' into what was already a carefully managed landscape; indeed, some of them were apparently built over pre-existing boundary systems. At Sharpstones Hill Site A, near Shrewsbury, for example, a small univallate rectilinear enclosure seems to have been constructed over the intersection of two linear ditches (Barker *et al.* 1991). These features probably represent earlier field boundaries, dated by pottery found in association with them to the Late Bronze Age–Early Iron Age. The northern and western sides of the enclosure appear to be positioned directly over these features (Fig. 5), implying that the boundaries associated with the linear ditches were still in existence at the time the enclosure was constructed.

Similar evidence has been found at two other small, single-ditched rectilinear enclosures: at Hay Farm, in south-east Shropshire (Hunn 2000); and Bromfield, near Ludlow (Stanford 1995). At Hay Farm, a complex series of ditches was found in the vicinity of the enclosure, three of which appear to pre-date it. Although only a short length was revealed within the excavated area, one of these features was associated with a 'palisade slot', and was overlain by the western side of the enclosure boundary. At Bromfield, two short lengths of ditch appear to pre-date the enclosure, one of which was cut by the southern enclosure boundary.

Smaller enclosures laid out in relation to earlier linear boundaries have also been found along the Warwickshire Avon (Hingley 1996), and in the lower Severn valley (Moore 2007). In the central Marches, their appearance suggests that significant transformations were occurring

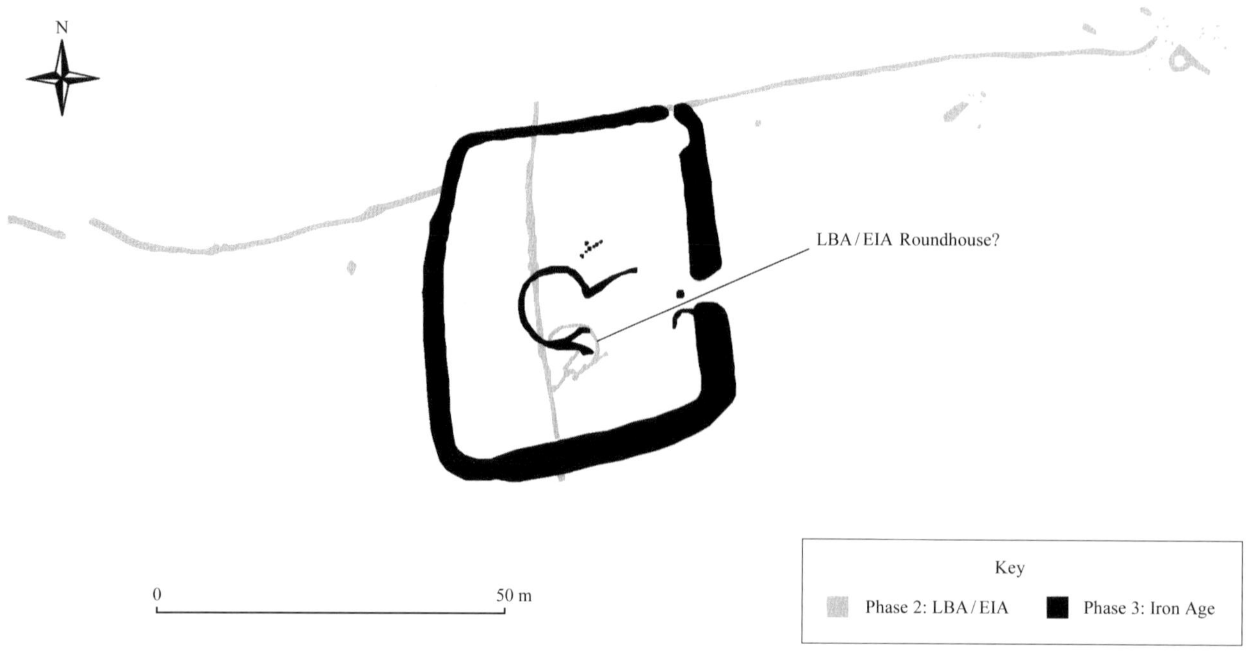

Fig. 5. Sharpstones Hill Site A (after Barker et al. 1991, fig. 7).

in the patterns of land tenure represented by the boundary systems. As noted above, the pit alignments and other linears of the late second–early first millennia BC may have enabled control over the land to be maintained at the level of the local community (Wigley 2007). The nature of the settlement pattern at this period is poorly understood, but a possible roundhouse and other features belonging to an unenclosed settlement were found in association with the linear field boundaries at Sharpstones Hill Site A (Fig. 5; Barker *et al.* 1991).

If this site is in any way representative of the wider picture, then we *may* be dealing with open settlement set amongst linear boundary systems – a situation that again has broad parallels in other parts of the West Midlands, particularly in the Avon valley (Hingley 1996). In contrast, the appearance of the smaller enclosures in the landscape in the later first millennium BC seems to indicate that greater importance was being attached to marking the places where smaller social units dwelt. As a result, these developments may have accompanied a fragmentation and reorientation of the social relations associated with the linear boundaries, with control of the land increasingly focused at the level of the groups that inhabited the enclosures.

The character of these social units may be indicated by the remains of the buildings that have been found within some of the smaller enclosures. Several sites contain evidence of single roundhouse structures, which may represent the dwellings of a household, including Sharpstones Hill Sites A and E (Barker *et al.* 1991); Hay Farm (Hunn 2000); Tycoch Farm, in north-western Shropshire (Hannaford 1993); and possibly Bromfield (G. Guilbert pers. comm.). However, within the hill-slope enclosure at Collfryn, in north-eastern Powys, evidence was found for numerous roundhouses and four-post structures that had been repeatedly rebuilt in much the same positions between the fourth and the first centuries BC (Fig. 6). Britnell (1989, 95) argues that between them the houses represented 15–20 different phases of construction, but that it is unlikely that more than three buildings were standing at any one time. Even so, this implies that some of the more elaborate smaller enclosures were occupied by larger household groups and/or more than one household. Alternatively, some roundhouses may have been used for non-domestic purposes.[6]

Smaller enclosures and the construction of community in the central Welsh Marches

The term 'household' is clearly one that requires qualification when used in relation to later prehistoric societies. Drawing on anthropological evidence from modern non-Western societies, Brück and Goodman (1999, 6) stress that the form of the household and the activities undertaken by it are culturally contingent. They also show how the composition of individual households often varies over the course of their life-cycle, 'as members are born, mature and die', and as various socio-economic

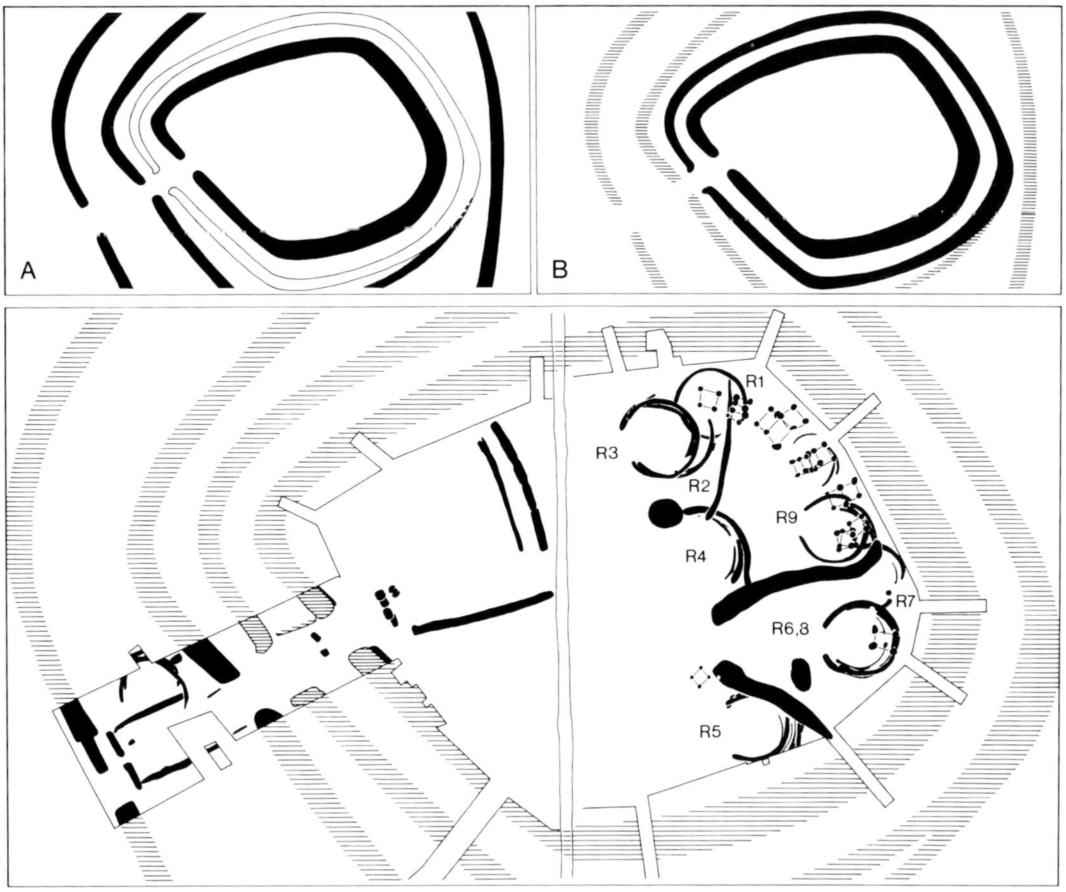

Fig. 6. The Iron Age phases of the Collfryn hill-slope enclosure. A. fourth–second centuries BC; B. first century BC and later (source: Musson 1991, fig. 75).

factors take effect. This suggests that we cannot accurately reconstruct the form of Iron Age households without running the risk of imposing modern norms and values on the past. However, as Brück and Goodman argue (*ibid.*, 7), such categorisations can act as heuristic devices that can be 'defined and redefined as they are employed in different cultural and historical contexts'. In this sense, the smaller enclosures of the Later Iron Age in the central Welsh Marches provide us with a particular set of historically constituted material conditions, which we can use to examine the construction of specific notions of household and community identity.

It is often suggested of the smaller enclosures that existed in southern England at this time that the surrounding banks and ditches signified the desire of the household that dwelt within to isolate itself from the wider community. For instance, in his influential paper on the upper Thames valley, Hingley (1984) drew attention to the differences between the settlement patterns in the Oxford Clay Vale and the Oxfordshire Uplands. Adopting the premise that social relations are symbolised in the organisation of space, he argued that the presence or absence of boundary ditches around settlements could be used to characterise the kinship structures that existed between their inhabitants. For instance, a narrow boundary might have enabled close social ties to be maintained between different groups, whilst a broad boundary may indicate that the opposite was the case. Relating these arguments to the material evidence within his study area, Hingley proposed that the widely dispersed smaller enclosures within the Oxfordshire uplands were indicative of 'social relations of production which involved the control and exploitation of territory by the social group resident within the individual settlement' (*ibid.*, 80).

Consequently, the enclosure boundaries symbolised the independence of these groups from the wider community, whilst the size and scale of these enclosures may have been indicative of their social status. Hingley argued that a different set of conditions prevailed in the Oxford Clay Vale, where large unenclosed settlements existed. He proposed that these were linked into a corporate social system, whereby control of the arable land and grazing resources within the valley rested with the community rather than the individual settlement.

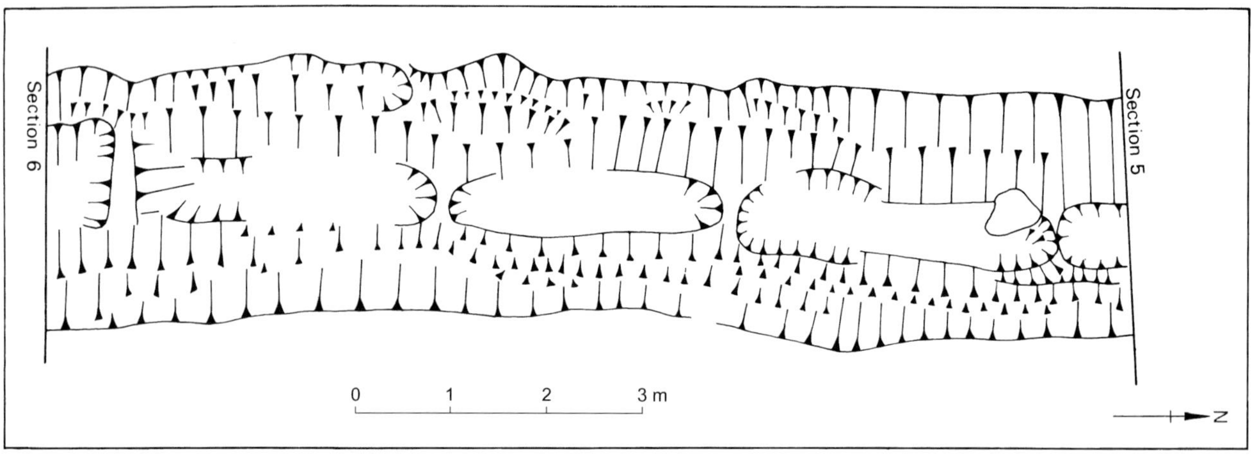

Fig. 7. A section of the inner enclosure ditch at Castle Farm, in eastern Shropshire, showing the lozenge-shaped slots at the base of the ditch (source: Roe 1991, fig. 24).

Subsequent commentators have developed these ideas and applied them to other parts of southern England. Bowden and McOmish (1987, 83) argued that the increasingly elaborate form of the banjo and spectacle enclosures of Later Iron Age Wessex 'owe less to the demands for physical defensive capability than to the desire for increased prestige and isolation'. Hill (1995) has also suggested that the boundaries of the smaller Wessex enclosures were intended to signal the separation of individual households from the wider community, but he maintains that this isolation was more symbolic than real. As the basic social unit, such groups may have controlled their own means of production, tending to their own land and resources. Yet they would also have been linked into wider networks of social relations, through their use of communally controlled resources such as tracts of grazing land and stands of managed woodland. Within this social system, Hill (*ibid.*) argues that ties between different households may have been based upon shared locality, rather than structured through kinship relations. Under these conditions, the status and success of a household would have been hard to maintain over time because of the changes that would have occurred in its composition during the course of its life cycle.

These approaches are extremely useful in illustrating how the boundaries of smaller enclosures may have had a symbolic as well as a practical significance. However, the arguments concerning the ability of such boundaries to isolate the household symbolically from the wider community emphasise their physical *form* over the *process* that resulted in their creation. In other words, these models are based on the assumption that the nature of social relations can be 'read off' from the form of the enclosure. As a result, there is little discussion of the practices associated with the construction of enclosure boundaries; how such activities might affect the symbolism attached to them; or how the labour expended upon these projects articulated with the other tasks that took place across the wider landscape.

The evidence from the central Welsh Marches allows us to begin to address these concerns. To begin with, the enclosure boundaries at a number of sites have produced evidence for gang working. In the excavated section of the ditch of the relatively small rectilinear enclosure at Bromfield, there were eight very slight changes in alignment. Allowing for three further deviations in the unexcavated section, Stanford (1995, 105) argued that the enclosure might have been 'the work of eleven gangs'. At Collfryn, localised deepenings and irregularities in the first phase of the enclosure ditches gave them a distinctly 'cellular' appearance. Britnell (1989, 107) suggested that this was probably the result of gang working, although he was unable to rule out the possibility that it was intended to 'keep the working area free from flooding'. Similar evidence was found at the large bivallate enclosure at Castle Farm, in eastern Shropshire (Roe 1991). A number of discontinuous, lozenge-shaped slots were found in the base of the inner boundary ditch, which were again suggested to be the result of gang working (Fig. 7).

The boundaries of many of these smaller enclosures were also reworked on at least one occasion. At the most basic level, this took the form of a simple clearing out of the enclosure ditches. A pronounced widening of the bases of boundary ditches, variously described as 'cleaning slots' or 'ankle breakers', have been noted at some sites, including Bromfield (Stanford 1995) and Preston Farm, in central Shropshire (Jones 1994b). These probably result from the act of clearing out silts and debris from the ditch.

In many cases, however, enclosure ditches seem to have been allowed quietly to silt up, thus requiring a more concerted effort to redefine the boundaries. Several ditches appear to have been recut at least once. Following the initial cleaning activity, the boundary of the enclosure at Preston Farm was redug at least three times (Jones 1994b). At Sharpstones Hill Site A, Barker *et al.* (1991) noted that the enclosure ditch had been recut on at least one occasion. However at Collfryn the enclosure ditches that were laid out in the fourth century BC do not appear have been reworked until the first century BC (Britnell 1989). Although the earlier boundaries probably survived as earthworks, the ditches that were associated with the second phase of this site enclosed a smaller overall area (see Fig. 6 above).

The labour required to construct and rework the smaller enclosures probably lay beyond that which an individual household could provide. In the case of Collfryn, Britnell (1989, 110) argued that digging the boundaries would have entailed an 'effort disproportionate to the resources of manpower available within the settlement'. Even the small enclosure at Bromfield would have required more labour than the resident group could supply (Stanford 1995). Together with the evidence for gang working, this suggests that smaller enclosures were usually constructed by a labour force comprising members of several different households. The evidence for the re-digging of boundaries also implies that the labour forces necessary to build or rework them may have assembled on a periodic basis. Thus, the evidence relating to the ways in which smaller enclosures were constructed seems to demonstrate just how *interdependent* different household groups would have been.

Taking part in such projects may well have been one of the ways in which networks of debt and obligation were created between the different members of the local community. Sharples (2007) has suggested that in the first millennium BC labour may itself have been seen as a gift, perhaps offered in exchange for objects or agricultural produce. As such, the very ability of a household to procure the labour necessary to construct an enclosure may well have depended upon its position within wider exchange networks. The degree of success in manipulating these networks, to procure items that could be offered as gifts, may well have influenced the size of group they could assemble to build an enclosure. The kinds of objects that were involved in such transactions might have included Malvernian or Clee Hill pottery vessels, or briquetage jars containing salt cakes, which could also have been accompanied by agricultural produce.

Since social authority may have been established by offering such items as gifts, the ability to muster support for such projects may have been both dependent upon and indicative of the social status of a household. In this sense, enclosure boundaries may well have been linked to social status – not because enclosure size simply equalled status, but because enclosure size was dependent upon the size of the labour force that could be assembled to construct it. However, as Hill (1995) has suggested, the social standing of individual households may well have varied over time, as the composition of the group and its agricultural success changed. This may in turn have affected the household's position within the wider exchange networks.

Consequently, as the ability of the household to procure labour varied over time, so would its capacity to rework the enclosure boundaries. This might explain the difference between the earlier and later phases of the Iron Age enclosure at Collfryn (Britnell 1989). When the enclosure was constructed in the fourth century BC, the resident household may have had a high social status, allowing it to assemble the large labour force required to construct the impressive triple-ditch enclosure. By the first century BC, however, the standing of the group may have waned, such that it was unable to gather together sufficient labour to re-dig all the existing ditches. Instead, a new circuit was excavated and the innermost ditch was recut, leaving the remains of the two outer ditches to stand as testimony to the household's former status.

It seems likely that other activities would have taken place alongside the construction work, which may have made these important junctures in the history of a household. Together with the exchange of material objects, agricultural produce and possibly even marriage partners, feasting, and the observance of rites of passage may have accompanied these events. Such gatherings may also have had an important bearing upon a household's right of access to the land. The creation of an enclosure may have been more than a straightforward declaration of a household's tenure over a particular part of the landscape. By coming together to build or rework the boundaries of an enclosure, the broader community may have affirmed the rights of a household to dwell within and husband a particular place. In this sense, the creation of community and household would have been dialectically linked because – amongst other things – the community effectively defined the household, which in turn delineated the nature of the community through its interaction with other households.

For these reasons the biographies of individual households may have become intertwined with those of particular places within the landscape. Tending to, and reworking, enclosure boundaries may have been one way in which people renewed their kin group's ties to particular locales over successive generations. This may also have been marked by the continual rebuilding of structures in the same positions within the interiors of some enclosures. At Collfryn, for example, the architectural plan of this site was remarkably stable, remaining largely unchanged for almost three centuries (Britnell 1989).

Such commitment to certain locales may have fostered in individuals a sense of what we might term *topophilia* – an intense attachment and feeling of belonging to particular places. As the anthropologist Nadia Lovell has argued:

> 'Accounts of how such loyalties are created, perpetuated and modified are of relevance to an understanding of identity at individual and, more importantly, collective levels, since belonging and locality as markers of identity often extend beyond individual experience and nostalgic longing for place. Belonging may thus become seen as a way of remembering… instrumental in the construction of collective memory surrounding place' (Lovell 2000, 1).

The practices involved in constructing and reworking these monuments can, therefore, be seen as a form of memory work, since it involved a remembrance of the genealogical ties that bound people to their land. This may explain why some of the smaller enclosures in the central Welsh Marches appear to have persisted for many generations.

These bonds would have been reinforced by the tasks involved in tending the land around the enclosures. The majority of the population in the later first millennium BC were probably engaged in subsistence agriculture. It is therefore important that we view the labour expended on the construction of the smaller enclosures in relation to the round of activities that made up the agricultural year. In the central Welsh Marches, it seems likely that arable cultivation was largely confined to the lighter, more easily worked soils. At the same time, there was probably frequent movement of people and livestock around the extensive areas of floodplain grasslands and hill pasture, which the environmental sequence suggests existed at this time (e.g. Beales 1980; Twigger and Haslam 1991).

Thus, the nature of the agricultural cycle may have been relatively similar to that proposed for Wessex based on botanical and faunal data from sites excavated during the Danebury Environs Project (Cunliffe 2000, fig 3.10). Nevertheless, the specific patterning of agricultural tasks across the landscape of the central Marches would probably have varied significantly from Wessex, due to the differing availability and distribution of resources. It would have been imperative that the construction and reworking of enclosures was carefully scheduled in relation to important annual events such as the ploughing of the land, the birthing season, or the gathering of the harvest, activities which probably engaged the majority of the community. Cooperation between households during such tasks may have been a further way in which ties of affiliation were created between different kin groups (Barrett 1989). Indeed, together with gift exchange, it seems likely that the labour necessary to build the enclosures was in part procured by making commitments to help other groups with such activities.

Conclusion

The smaller enclosures represent an important, but still under-researched, component of the later first millennium BC landscape of the central Welsh Marches. This paper has attempted to dissolve the distinction between the 'small hillforts' on the higher ground and the cropmark 'farmstead' enclosures that occur at lower elevations. I have suggested that we instead view all these sites as belonging to the same class of monument, but exhibiting differing levels of preservation. Furthermore, they appear to occupy a position at one end of a continuum of enclosures sizes, which extends upwards to include the larger hillforts.

I have also argued that we need to move away from our current focus on the *form* of these monuments, and instead consider the *processes* that were involved in their creation. The appearance of smaller enclosures in the central Welsh Marches in the second half of the first millennium BC probably attended a significant reworking of traditional rights of tenure over the land. This is emphasised by the way in which some of these monuments were set out over earlier linear boundary systems. At the same time, however, this change was both produced by, and a product of, the social processes that resulted in the construction of the smaller enclosures.

As a result, the practices associated with the building and reworking of these sites played an important part in shaping the social relations that existed within and between these communities. This has two further implications. Firstly, it suggests that the activities associated with the construction of the smaller enclosures played an important role in the creation and reproduction of social identity. Secondly, as Hill (1995) has argued, it implies that historical change within these communities was internally driven, rather than externally imposed.

Acknowledgements

The research upon which this paper is based was undertaken with the aid of an AHRB studentship. I owe special thanks to Mark Edmonds and John Barrett who supervised my thesis. Their help in refining the ideas I have presented here was invaluable. I would like to thank Colin Haselgrove and Tom Moore for inviting me to speak at the Durham seminar and patiently awaiting the completion of this paper. I am also grateful for to Malcolm Reid for discussing his important work with the Monuments Protection Programme with me. Finally, I would like to thank the various authors and publishers for granting permission for me to use illustrative materials from their work.

Notes

1. Alex Gibson's ongoing programme of work at Lower Luggy, in Powys, suggests that a small proportion of the single-ditched cropmark enclosures in the region may date to the Neolithic

(Gibson 2003). At the opposite end of the chronological spectrum, recent excavations at New Pieces Camp, in the Breiddin Hills (Arnold and Davies 2000), and at the Arddleen enclosure near Welshpool (Grant 2004) suggests that occupation at some sites may have persisted through the later Roman and into the early medieval periods.

2. Walton Camp has recently been reassessed as part of the Monuments Protection Programme and classified as a 'small enclosed settlement' (M. Reid pers. comm.).
3. Iron Age wetland enclosures are known in Shropshire, including The Berth and the massive 'marsh fort' at Wall Camp, Kynersley.
4. The civilian settlements at Leintwardine and Wroxeter, and the military sites at Bromfield, Brompton, Craven Arms, Eaton Constantine, and Forden Gaer.
5. At 2 sigma.
6. It is by no means certain that a household group resided in every smaller enclosure in the central Marches. For example, very little evidence for settlement was found within the small polygonal enclosure at Calcott Farm, central Shropshire (Jones 1994b). Some sites may well have been used solely for managing or kraaling livestock, and the role of others may have varied over time.

Bibliography

Anderson, J.C. 1864. *Shropshire: its Early History and Antiquities.* London: Willis and Sotheran.

Arnold, C.J. and Davies, J.L. 2000. *Roman and Early Medieval Wales.* Stroud: Sutton.

Barclay, G.J. 2001. 'Metropolitan' and 'parochial'/'core' and 'periphery': a historiography of the Neolithic of Scotland, *Proceedings of the Prehistoric Society* 67, 1–18.

Barker, P.A., Haldon, R. and Jenks, W.E. 1991. Excavations on Sharpstones Hill near Shrewsbury, 1965–71, *Transactions of the Shropshire Archaeological and Historical Society* 67, 15–57.

Barrett, J. 1989. Food, gender and metal: questions of social reproduction, in M.L.S. Sorenson and R. Thomas (eds.), *The Bronze Age–Iron Age Transition in Europe: Aspects of Continuity and Change in European Societies c. 1200 to 500 BC*, 305–20. Oxford: British Archaeological Reports International Series 483.

Beales, P.W. 1980. The late Devensian and Flandrian vegetational history of Crose Mere, Shropshire, *New Phytologist* 85, 133–161.

Bowden, M. and McOmish, D. 1987. The required barrier, *Scottish Archaeological Review* 4, 76–84.

Britnell, W.J. 1989. The Collfryn hillslope enclosure, Llansantffraid, Deuddwr, Powys: excavations 1980–1982, *Proceedings of the Prehistoric Society* 55, 89–133.

Brown, A.G. 1982. Human impact on the former floodplain woodlands of the Severn, in M. Bell and S. Limbrey (eds.), *Archaeological Aspects of Woodland Ecology*, 93–104. Oxford: British Archaeological Report British Series 146.

Brown, A.G. 1988. The palaeoecology of *Alnus* (alder) and the Postglacial history of floodplain vegetation. Pollen percentages and influx data from the West Midlands, United Kingdom, *New Phytologist* 110, 425–436.

Brown, A.G. and Barber, K.E. 1985. Late Holocene palaeoecology and sedimentary history of a small lowland catchment in central England, *Quaternary Research* 24, 87–102.

Brück, J. and Goodman, M. 1999. Introduction: themes for a critical archaeology of prehistoric settlement, in J. Brück and M. Goodman (eds.), *Making Places in the Prehistoric World*, 1–19. London: University College London Press.

Buckland, P.C., Parker Pearson, M., Wigley, A. and Girling, M.A. 2001. Is there anybody out there? A reconsideration of the environmental evidence from the Breiddin hillfort, Powys, Wales, *Antiquaries Journal* 81, 51–76.

Carver, M.O.H. 1991. A strategy for lowland Shropshire, *Transactions of the Shropshire Archaeological and Historical Society* 67, 1–8.

Cunliffe, B. 1991. *Iron Age Communities in Britain* (3rd edn). London: Routledge.

Cunliffe, B. 2000. *The Danebury Environs Programme: The Prehistory of a Wessex Landscape, Vol.1. Introduction.* Oxford: Oxford University Committee for Archaeology Monograph 48.

Dalwood, H., Hurst, D. and Pearson, E. 1997. *Salvage Recording at Ivington Camp, Leominster: Archive Report.* Unpublished Hereford and Worcester County Council Archaeology Service Report 570.

Ellis, P. (ed.) 1993. *Beeston Castle, Cheshire: A Report on the Excavations 1968–85 by Laurence Keen and Peter Hough.* London: English Heritage Archaeological Report 23.

Fox, C. 1932. *The Personality of Britain.* Cardiff: National Museum of Wales.

Forde-Johnston, J. 1962. Earl's Hill, Pontesbury and related hillforts in England and Wales, *Archaeological Journal* 119, 66–91.

Gelling, P. 1963. Excavations at Caynham Camp, near Ludlow: final report, *Transactions of the Shropshire Archaeological and Historical Society* 55, 91–100.

Gibson, A. 1994. Excavations at the Sarn-y-bryn-caled cursus complex, Welshpool, Powys, and the timber circles of Great Britain and Ireland, *Proceedings of the Prehistoric Society* 60, 143–217.

Gibson, A. 2003. A newly discovered Neolithic enclosure at Lower Luggy, Berriew, Powys, *Past* 45, 1–2.

Giles, M. 2001. *Open-weave, Close-knit: Archaeologies of Identity in Later Prehistoric East Yorkshire.* Unpublished Ph.D. thesis, University of Sheffield.

Grant, I. 2004. The excavation of a double-ditched enclosure at Arddleen, Powys, 2002–03, *Montgomeryshire Collections* 92, 1–31.

Hannaford, H. 1993. *Pant/Llanymynech Bypass (Preferred Route): An Archaeological Evaluation.* Unpublished Shropshire County Council Archaeology Unit Report 25.

Hartshorne, C.A. 1841. *Salopia Antiqua.* London: John W. Parker.

Haselgrove, C. and Pope, R. (eds) 2007. *The Earlier Iron Age in Britain and the Near Continent.* Oxford: Oxbow Books.

Hill, J.D. 1995. How should we understand Iron Age societies and hillforts? A contextual study from Southern Britain, in J.D. Hill and C.G. Cumberpatch (eds.), *Different Iron Ages: Studies on the Iron Age in Temperate Europe,* 45–66. Oxford: British Archaeological Reports International Series 602.

Hingley, R. 1984. Towards social analysis in archaeology: Celtic society in the Iron Age of the Upper Thames Valley (400–0 BC), in B. Cunliffe and D. Miles (eds.), *Aspects of the Iron Age in Central Southern* Britain, 72–88. Oxford. Oxford University Committee for Archaeology Monograph 2.

Hingley, R. 1996. Prehistoric Warwickshire: a review of the evidence, *Birmingham and Warwickshire Archaeological Society Transactions* 100, 1–24.

Hogg, A.H.A. 1965. The Early Iron Age in Wales, in I.L. Foster and

G. Daniel (eds), *Prehistoric and Early Wales,* 109–150. London: Routledge and Keegan Paul.

Hughes, G.W. 1994. Old Oswestry Hillfort: excavations by W.J. Varley 1939–1940, *Archaeologia Cambrensis* 144, 46–91.

Hunn, J.R. 2000. Hay Farm, Eardington, Shropshire: an Iron Age and Romano-British Enclosure, in R.J. Zeepat (ed.), *Three Iron Age and Romano-British Rural Settlements on English Gravels: Excavations at Hatford (Oxfordshire), Besthorpe (Nottinghamshire) and Eardington (Shropshire) undertaken by Tempvs Reparatvm between 1991 and 1993,* 119–144. Oxford: British Archaeological Reports British Series 312.

Jackson, D. 1999. Variation in the size distribution of hillforts in the Welsh Marches and its implication for social organisation, in B. Bevan (ed.), *Northern Exposure: Interpretative Devolution and the Iron Ages in Britain,* 197–216. Leicester: Leicester Archaeology Monograph 4.

Jones, A. 1994a. The landscape of the Wroxeter hinterland: the cropmark evidence, *Transactions of the Shropshire Archaeological and Historical Society* 69, 100–108.

Jones, A. 1994b. Two prehistoric enclosures at Preston Farm and Calcott Farm, *Transactions of the Shropshire Archaeological and Historical Society* 69, 15–31.

Kenyon, K.M. 1942. Excavations on the Wrekin, Shropshire, 1939, *Archaeological Journal* 99, 99–109.

Leah, M.D., Wells, C.E., Stamper, P., Huckerby, E. and Welch, C. 1998. *The Wetlands of Shropshire and Staffordshire.* Lancaster: Lancaster University Archaeology Unit.

Lovell, N. 2000. Introduction: Belonging in need of emplacement? in N. Lovell (ed.), *Locality and Belonging,* 1–24. London: Routledge.

Luff, G. 1888. Neolithic man and his remains in Shropshire, *Transactions of the Shropshire Archaeological Society* 11, 211–222.

Moore, T. 2007. The Early to Later Iron Age transition in the Severn–Cotswolds: enclosing the household? in Haselgrove and Pope 2007, 259–278.

Morris, E.L. 1981. Ceramic exchange in western Britain: a preliminary view point, in H. Howard and E.L. Morris (eds.), *Production and Distribution: a Ceramic Viewpoint,* 67–81. Oxford: British Archaeological Reports International Series 120.

Morris, E.L. 1982. Iron Age pottery from western Britain: another petrographic study, in I. Freestone, C. Johns and T. Potter (eds.), *Current Research in Ceramics,* 15–32. London: British Museum.

Morris, E.L. 1985. Prehistoric salt distributions: two case studies from Western Britain, *Bulletin of the Board of Celtic Studies* 32, 336–379.

Morris, E.L. 1994. Production and distribution of pottery and salt in Iron Age Britain: a review, *Proceedings of the Prehistoric Society* 60, 371–393.

Morris, E.L. 1996. Iron Age artefact production and exchange, in T.C. Champion and J.R. Collis (eds.), *The Iron Age in Britain and Ireland: Recent Trends,* 41–65. Sheffield: J.R. Collis Publications.

Musson, C. 1991. *The Breiddin Hillfort: A Later Prehistoric Settlement in the Welsh Marches.* London: Council for British Archaeology Research Report 76.

Musson, C.R., Britnell, W.J., Northover, J.P. and Salter, C.J. 1992. Excavations and metal-working at Llwyn Bryn-dinas Hillfort, Llangedwyn, Clwyd, *Proceedings of the Prehistoric Society* 58, 265–283.

Musson, C.R. and Northover, J.P. 1989. Llanymynech hillfort, Powys and Shropshire: observations on construction work, 1981, *Montgomeryshire Collections* 77, 15–26.

O'Neil, B.H. St J. 1934. Excavations at Titterstone Clee Hill Camp, Shropshire, 1932, *Antiquaries Journal* 14, 13–32.

O'Neil, B.H. St J. 1942. Excavations at Ffridd Faldwyn Camp, Montgomery, 1937–39, *Archaeologia Cambrensis* 97, 1–57.

Owen, G. 1997. *Llanymynech Golf Course: Archaeological Excavation and Watching Brief.* Unpublished CPAT Report 228.

Owen, G. 1999. *13th Green, Llanymynech Golf Club, Powys: Archaeological Assessment.* Unpublished CPAT Report 340.

Owen, G. and Britnell, W.J. 1989. Pit alignments at Four Crosses, Llandysillio, Powys, *Montgomeryshire Collections* 77, 27–40.

Palmer, S.C. 2001. Church Lawford, Ling Hall Quarry, Area Z, *West Midlands Archaeology* 44, 159–160.

Peacock, D.P.S. 1968. A petrographic study of certain Iron Age pottery from western England, *Proceedings of the Prehistoric Society* 34, 414–427.

Roe, A. 1991. Excavations at Castle Farm, Shifnal, 1980, *Transactions of the Shropshire Archaeological and Historical Society* 67, 63–83.

Roseff, R. 1992. *A Study of Alluviation in the River Lugg Catchment, Herefordshire.* Unpublished Ph.D. thesis, University of Birmingham.

Savory, H.N. 1976. Welsh hillforts: a reappraisal of recent research, in D.W. Harding (ed.), *Hillforts: Later Prehistoric Earthworks in Britain and Ireland,* 237–291. London: Academic Press.

Sharples, N. 2007. Building communities and creating identities in the first millenium BC, in Haselgrove and Pope 2007, 174–184.

Shotten, F.W. 1978. Archaeological inferences from the study of alluvium in the lower Severn–Avon valleys, in S. Limbrey and J.G. Evans (eds.), *Man's Effect on the Landscape: The Lowland Zone,* 27–32. London: Council for British Archaeology Research Report 21.

Silvester, R.J. and Britnell, W.J. 1993. *Montgomeryshire Small Enclosures Project: Summary Report.* Unpublished CPAT report.

Smith, A.G., Girling, M.A., Green, C.A., Hillman, G.C. and Limbrey, S. 1991. Buckbean Pond: Environmental Studies, in Musson 1991, 95–112.

Stanford, S.C. 1972a. The function and population of hill-forts in the central Marches, in F. Lynch and C. Burgess (eds.), *Prehistoric Man in Wales and the West: Essays in Honour of Lily F. Chitty,* 307–319. Bath: Adams and Dart.

Stanford, S.C. 1972b. Welsh border hill-forts, in C. Thomas (ed.), *The Iron Age in the Irish Sea Province,* 25–36. London: Council for British Archaeology Research Report 9.

Stanford, S.C. 1974. *Croft Ambrey.* Leominster: Privately published.

Stanford, S.C. 1980. *The Archaeology of the Welsh Marches.* London: Collins.

Stanford, S.C. 1984. The Wrekin hillfort excavations 1973, *Archaeological Journal* 141, 61–90.

Stanford, S.C. 1991. *The Archaeology of the Welsh Marches* (2nd edn). Ludlow: Privately published.

Stanford, S.C. 1995. A Cornovian farm and Saxon cemetery at Bromfield, Shropshire, *Transactions of the Shropshire Archaeological and Historical Society* 70, 95–141.

Stevenson, J.B. 1975. Survival and discovery, in S. Limbrey and H. Cleere (eds), *The Effect of Man on the Landscape: the Highland Zone,* 104–108. London: Council for British Archaeology Research Report 11.

Taylor, M.P. and Lewin, J. 1996. River behaviour and Holocene alluviation: the River Severn at Welshpool, mid-Wales, UK, *Earth Surface Processes and Landforms* 21, 77–91.

Taylor, M.P. and Lewin, J. 1997. Non-synchronous response of adjacent floodplain systems to Holocene environmental change, *Geomorphology* 18, 251–264.

Toller, H. 1978. *Burrow Hill Iron Age Hillfort, Hopesay, Salop. General Report on Excavation and Survey Work Carried Out in 1978.* Unpublished report.

Twigger, S.N. and Haslam, C.J. 1991. Environmental change in Shropshire during the last 13,000 years, *Field Studies* 7, 743–758.

Varley, W.J. 1948. The hill-forts of the Welsh Marches, *Archaeological Journal* 105, 41–68.

Warrilow, W., Owen, G. and Britnell, W.J. 1986. Eight ring-ditches at Four Crosses, Llandysilio, Powys, 1981–85, *Proceedings of the Prehistoric Society* 52, 53–87.

Watson, M. and Musson, C. 1993. *Shropshire From The Air.* Shrewsbury: Shropshire Books.

Whimster, R. 1989. *The Emerging Past.* London: Royal Commission on the Historic Monuments of England.

Wigley, A. 2002. *Building Monuments, Constructing Communities: Landscapes of the First Millennium BC in the Central Welsh Marches.* Unpublished Ph.D. thesis, University of Sheffield.

Wigley, A. 2007. Pitted histories: early first millennium BC pit alignments in the central Welsh Marches, in Haselgrove and Pope 2007, 119–134.

From open to enclosed: Iron Age landscapes of the Trent valley

David Knight

Introduction

Recent excavations in the Trent valley have yielded important evidence for developments in the forms and functions of Iron Age settlements, their spatial interrelationships and the organisation of the agrarian landscape. As a result of this work, the final centuries of the first millennium BC and the opening decades of the first century AD have emerged as periods of significant social and economic change, with the development in some stretches of the valley of landscapes whose salient features – rectilinear enclosures, field systems and major linear boundaries – imply a tightly controlled environment with careful allocation of pasture, arable and other natural resources. This paper reviews the evidence for settlement evolution, the growth of field systems and, more controversially, the progress towards territorial division, with appropriate consideration of the social and economic factors that may underlie these changes.

Attention is focused on the gravel terraces and alluvial floodplain of the Trent, particularly the intensively investigated middle and lower Trent valley between its confluences with the Tame and Idle (Fig. 1). Discussion will concentrate upon the Middle and Late Iron Ages, with consideration of earlier developments where appropriate. Dating remains problematic, depending mainly upon associations with imprecisely dated pottery, rare items of metalwork, glass and other typologically diagnostic finds, plus a handful of radiocarbon dates.[1] The problems of dating have been discussed at length in a recent review of the first millennium BC ceramic sequence of the East Midlands (Knight 2002) and the chronological framework proposed in that study provides the foundation for the present discussion.

Previous research

Images of dense woodland and sparse or transient habitation dominate early reviews of the Iron Age in the Trent valley (Kenyon 1952; Piggott 1958, 13), but over the last forty years our perceptions have changed significantly. Arguably the most important event in forcing a reassessment of Iron Age settlement was the publication in 1960 of *A Matter of Time*. This review of the English river gravels highlighted the dense pattern of cropmarks around Newark (RCHME 1960, 12–15; 37–42; fig. 5; e.g. pl. 4c), and raised the possibility of an unexpectedly high density of Iron Age activity in some stretches of the valley.

Subsequent excavations at such key sites as Willington (Derbyshire), Holme Pierrepont (Nottinghamshire), and Fisherwick (Staffordshire) confirmed this view and provided the foundation for the pioneering syntheses of Iron Age and Romano-British settlement by O'Brien (1978a; 1979a) and Smith (1977; 1978). Later aerial surveys have revealed some remarkable cropmark palimpsests, most notably the elaborate co-axial field systems and enclosures on the gravel terraces near Newark, first described in detail by Whimster (1989; 1992). In addition, further large-scale excavations at sites such as Gamston, Gonalston, and Rampton (Nottinghamshire), Swarkestone Lowes and Barrow-upon-Trent (Derbyshire), and Whitemoor Haye (Staffordshire) have dramatically enhanced the settlement record and have emphasised the potential of the alluvial zone for the survival of well-preserved structural and palaeo-environmental data.

Unfortunately, much of the information obtained in recent years lies buried in archive reports, or is the focus

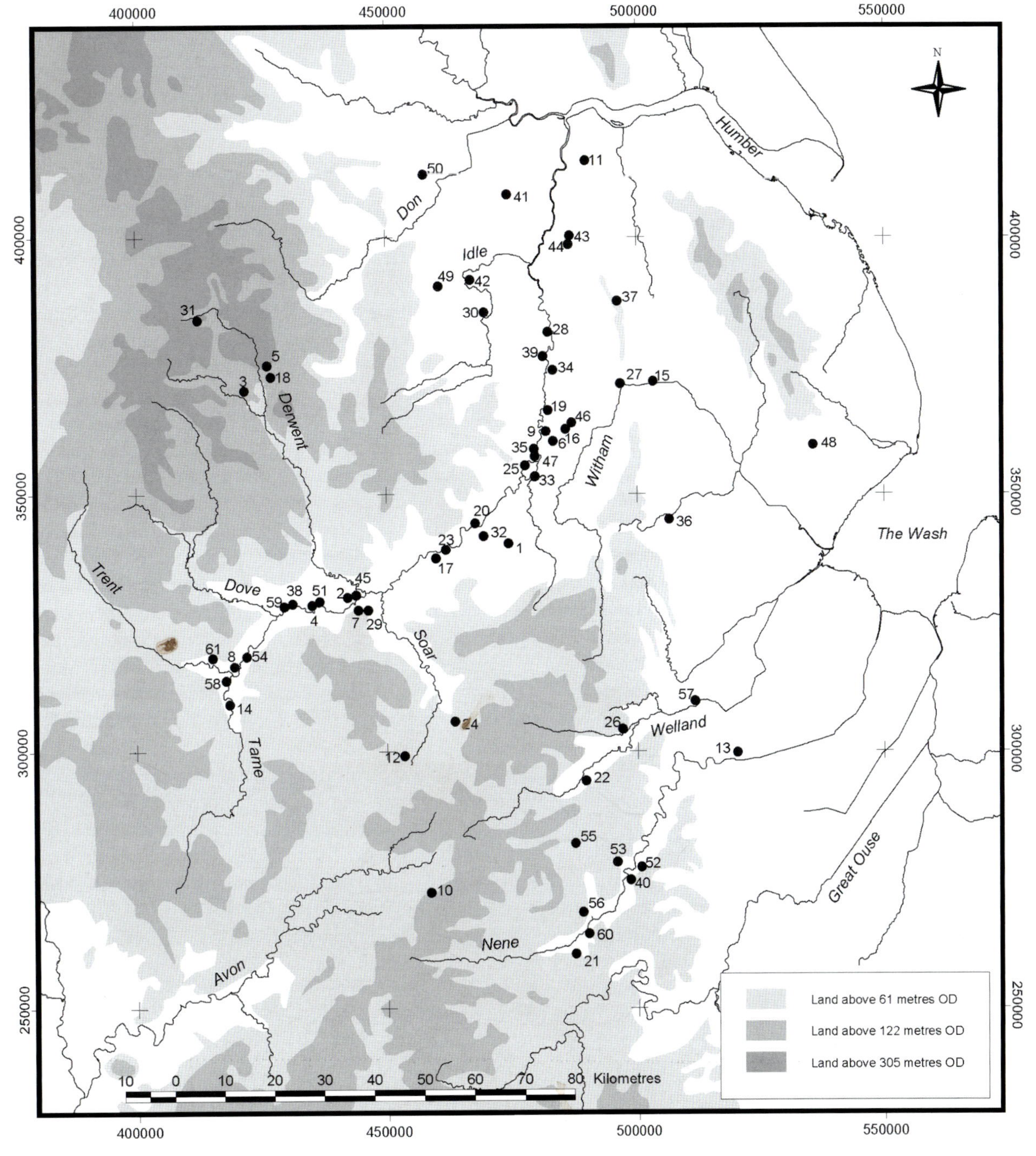

Fig. 1. Location of the study area and sites referred to in the text. 1. Aslockton; 2. Aston-upon-Trent; 3. Ball Cross; 4. Barrow-upon-Trent; 5. Big Moor; 6. Brough-on-Fosse; 7. Castle Donington; 8. Catholme; 9. Collingham; 10. Crick; 11. Dragonby; 12. Enderby; 13. Fengate; 14. Fisherwick; 15. Fiskerton; 16. Gallows Nooking Common; 17. Gamston; 18. Gardom's Edge; 19. Girton; 20. Gonalston; 21. Grendon; 22. Gretton; 23. Holme Pierrepont; 24. Humberstone; 25. Kelham; 26. Ketton; 27. Lincoln; 28. Littleborough; 29. Lockington; 30. Lound; 31. Mam Tor; 32. Margidunum; 33. Newark; 34. Newton-on-Trent; 35. North Muskham; 36. Old Sleaford; 37. Owmby; 38. Potlock; 39. Rampton; 40. Ringstead; 41. Sandtoft; 42. Scaftworth; 43. Scotter; 44. Scotton; 45. Shardlow; 46. Sheep Walk Lodge; 47. South Muskham; 48. Stickford; 49. Styrrup; 50. Sutton Common; 51. Swarkestone Lowes; 52. Thrapston; 53. Twywell; 54. Walton-on-Trent; 55. Weekley Hall Wood; 56. Wellingborough; 57. West Deeping; 58. Whitemoor Haye; 59. Willington; 60. Wollaston; 61. Yoxall.

of continuing post-excavation programmes, and has yet to filter into the published record. In recognition of this, there have been several moves towards regional synthesis – exemplified by surveys of the geoarchaeology of the Trent valley, with particular emphasis upon the relationship of archaeology to alluvium (Knight and Howard 1994; 1995; 2004). The region has also been reviewed as part of the Archaeological Research Framework Projects for the East and West Midlands (Wardle 2003; Wigley 2003; Willis 2006). These studies have emphasised the huge potential of this specialised riverine environment for analyses of first millennium BC settlement and, in particular, the interrelationships between Iron Age communities and their environment.

It seems clear from the substantial body of data now available that the latter centuries of the first millennium BC and the early first century AD saw a fundamental reorganisation of the agrarian landscape. To place these changes in perspective, attention will be focused first upon the evidence for settlement of the Trent valley in the early first millennium. Subsequent sections will consider the key landscape changes of the Later Iron Age and speculate on the social and economic pressures that may have prompted these developments.

Early first millennium BC settlement

The environmental setting

Palaeoenvironmental analyses suggest that by the end of the Iron Age much of the mixed oak woodland that would have blanketed the valley floor in the later Mesolithic had been cleared, creating a predominantly open landscape with stands of regenerated or primeval woodland, a significant proportion of which may have been coppiced or pollarded (Knight and Howard 2004, 83–6). The picture for the earlier first millennium BC, however, is significantly more blurred. Comparatively few palaeoenvironmental samples are from contexts that may definitely be attributed to this period, while even fewer have been fully analysed.

It seems likely, however, that many communities inherited a substantially cleared environment (*ibid.*, 83–4). Analyses of organic deposits from two waterlogged pits at Hoveringham Quarry, Gonalston, identified pollen indicative of a predominantly oak and hazel woodland, with a lower representation of lime/lindens, beech, ash, holly, and alder (Scaife 1999). Hazel twigs from the lower fill of one pit were radiocarbon dated to 970–790 cal. BC (2960 ± 50 BP; Beta-104494), while part of a sharpened hazel post from near the bottom of the other pit provided a *terminus post quem* for the deposit of 1690–1310 cal. BC (3220 ± 80 BP; Beta-104493). Grasses and grassland indicators were also well represented, together with cereal pollen and taxa indicative of disturbed ground. A wood-pasture environment was suggested, with some localised cereal cultivation, recalling the evidence from some other Midlands river valleys for an emphasis in this early period upon pasture (e.g. Lambrick 1992, 86–8; see Hey this volume).

Further samples of pollen, macroscopic plant remains, insects, and molluscs which may elucidate the valley environment at this period have been retrieved from a scatter of sites in the region, notably from auger cores through radiocarbon-dated organic deposits preserved near Girton (Howard *et al.* 1999) and Rampton (Howard and Knight 2001) in Nottinghamshire and at Shardlow (Knight and Malone 1997; 1998) and Hicken's Bridge, near Aston-upon-Trent (Knight and Howard 2004, 52), in Derbyshire. These create an image of great environmental diversity during the later second and earlier first millennia BC, including alder carr with some fen woodland and pasture in the floodplain at Rampton and a largely cleared landscape with little old or mature woodland and some nearby pasture and cultivated land adjacent to abandoned channel wetlands at Girton, Shardlow, and Hicken's Bridge. Interpretation of these and other sites is far from straightforward, but on balance the case for progressive woodland clearance in many parts of the valley in the earlier first millennium seems reasonably well founded (Knight and Howard 2004, 83–4).

It is nevertheless likely that there was significant intra-regional variation, particularly between the middle Trent valley – characterised by a wide floodplain and extensive well-drained gravel terraces with high agricultural potential – and the river's narrower upper reaches. At Yoxall, Staffordshire, for example, pollen, plant macrofossils, and insect fauna from a palaeochannel in the upper Trent valley suggest a well-wooded landscape in the early first millennium BC (Smith *et al.* 2001). Worked hazel from near the base of the channel yielded a date of 1100–800 cal. BC (2780 ± 60 BP; Beta-73350). Associated organics suggest muddy bank sides with dense sedges, rushes, and alder woodland, and away from the channel dense mixed oak, hazel, lime, and birch woodland. These woodland areas eventually succumbed to the demands of agriculture, for the upper part of the sequence provides evidence for significant woodland clearance and cultivation in the later first millennium, with cereal pollen and plants typical of disturbed and bare ground. Associated insects and pollen also suggest the development of dry, acid heathland in the vicinity of the site.

Attention must also be drawn to the growing number of sites in the valley that have yielded evidence for an expansion of floodplain wetlands during the second and first millennia BC, as this has important implications for understanding processes of landscape change. At South Ing Close, Rampton, for example, augering of an area of floodplain enclosed by a meander of the Trent led to the identification of a peat bed some 1–2 m thick, forming a continuous surface across the valley floor beneath *c.* 3 m of alluvium (Howard and Knight 2001). This peat layer dates to between 1530–1210 cal. BC (3130 ± 70 BP; Beta-159224) and 1370–900 cal. BC (2900 ± 70 BP; Beta-159222). Palaeobiological analysis indicated a local alder carr with a small element of old mature woodland, while nearby pastoral activity was deduced from the presence of dung beetles and ribwort plantain.

Wetland areas such as this may well have developed partly due to increasing climatic wetness (Knight and Howard 2004, 80), which could in turn have impacted upon groundwater levels, rates of surface run-off and soil erosion, and the frequency and magnitude of flooding. At the same time, clearance of the protective woodland canopy would have created a progressively open landscape, more vulnerable to soil erosion and flooding. This would have contributed to the redeposition of fine-grained sediments, although on present evidence thick alluvial and colluvial deposits appear to have accumulated in the valley only from the Late Iron Age or early Roman periods. These issues will therefore be discussed in a later section of the paper, where the impact upon soil erosion and flooding of later agriculture is also assessed.

Settlement morphology

Settlements of the earlier first millennium BC are significantly more elusive than those of the Later Iron Age, despite the evidence for progressive woodland clearance. Most have been revealed mainly by chance during excavations of later enclosures such as Gamston (Knight 1992), Gonalston (Elliott and Knight 2002), and Willington (Wheeler 1979). Rare associations are recorded with post-Deverel-Rimbury (PDR) Plainwares, dated currently from the final centuries of the second millennium BC to the tenth or ninth centuries cal. BC (Knight 2002, 123–6), notably at Catholme in Staffordshire, where the discovery of several timber roundhouses suggests an early unenclosed phase of settlement (Losco-Bradley and Kinsley 2002, 15; A.G. Kinsley and G. Guilbert pers. comm.); several four- and six-post structures could also belong to this early phase. In Leicestershire, excavations at Willow Farm, Castle Donington, revealed an extensive open settlement incorporating at least one post-built roundhouse, dated by associated PDR Plainwares (Coward and Ripper 1999; P. Marsden pers. comm.), while at the nearby site of Lockington, a scatter of pits, some yielding plain PDR sherds, was recorded immediately to the west of an earlier Bronze Age barrow (Hughes 2000; Meek 1995).

Associations between domestic structures and pottery of the ninth to fifth/fourth centuries BC are more common, although it should be emphasised that such pottery is still rare in this region by comparison with the ubiquitous Middle and Late Iron Age wares. Many of the settlements yielding Late Bronze Age–Earlier Iron Age pottery also preserve stratigraphic evidence for a progression from an early open settlement to an enclosure phase associated with Earlier or Late La Tène pottery, echoing a trend observed elsewhere in the Midlands and indeed in southern Britain generally (Thomas 1997, 211–13). Notable examples include Gamston, where a Middle to Late Iron Age enclosure ditch cut an earlier semi-circular structure, a palisade trench and several pits (Fig. 2, Phase I; Knight 1992, 23–7); Fleak Close, Barrow-upon-Trent, where the bedding trench, of at least one timber roundhouse and several widely dispersed pits, post holes, and gullies were truncated either by an enclosure ditch or by features cut by this ditch (Knight and Southgate 2001, 201); and Gonalston, where the boundary ditch of a Middle to Late Iron Age rectilinear enclosure cut across a scatter of pits, post holes, and gullies (Elliott and Knight 2002).

The structural elements of these early sites generally form low-density scatters with no discernible spatial patterning, often much truncated by later activity. A particularly extensive spread of features was recorded at Gonalston (Fig. 3), where structural remains associated with PDR Plainwares and Late Bronze Age–Earlier Iron Age pottery – including scattered pits, post holes and possibly the truncated foundations of timber roundhouses – were spread thinly and intermittently over an elongated gravel island monitored prior to quarrying (Elliott and Knight 2002). This pattern of scattered unenclosed features is repeated at other extensively investigated quarries, including Barrow-upon-Trent (Knight and Southgate 2001), Willington (Wheeler 1979, 78–86), and Castle Donington (Coward and Ripper 1999), and raises the possibility of extensive but thinly spread settlement of the river terraces from this early period.

The general absence of archaeologically detectable boundaries, which provides such a striking contrast with settlements of the Middle and Late Iron Ages, could imply a largely unbounded landscape during the early first millennium – and by implication perhaps comparatively unrestricted access to valley resources (compare Pryor 1998, 144–5). This in turn might support the idea that early valley communities were bound into complex cycles of short- and long-distance transhumance (Bishop 2001, 4), conceivably with an emphasis on shifting agriculture rather than the more permanent cultivation implied by the extensive field systems of the Later Iron Age (see Smith 1978, 98). Such widely ranging communities may have had little need for boundaries, which, it is suggested below, might have emerged at a later date as population, livestock and settlement densities increased, especially as access to traditional pastures became more restricted and pressures mounted for the more intensive exploitation of arable resources. More speculatively, contacts

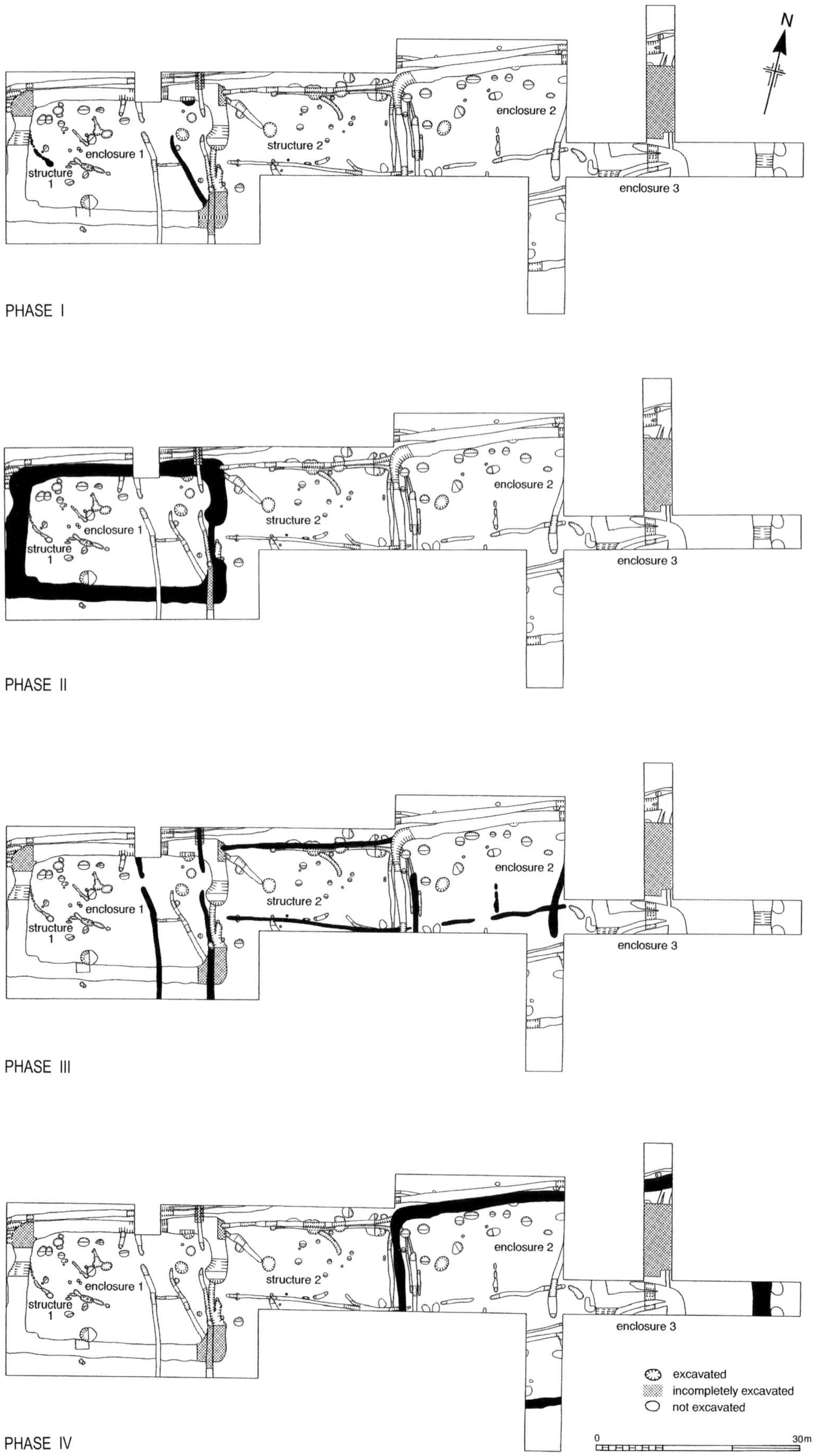

Fig. 2. Iron Age settlement at Gamston, Nottinghamshire (source: Knight 1992; reproduced by permission of the Thoroton Society).

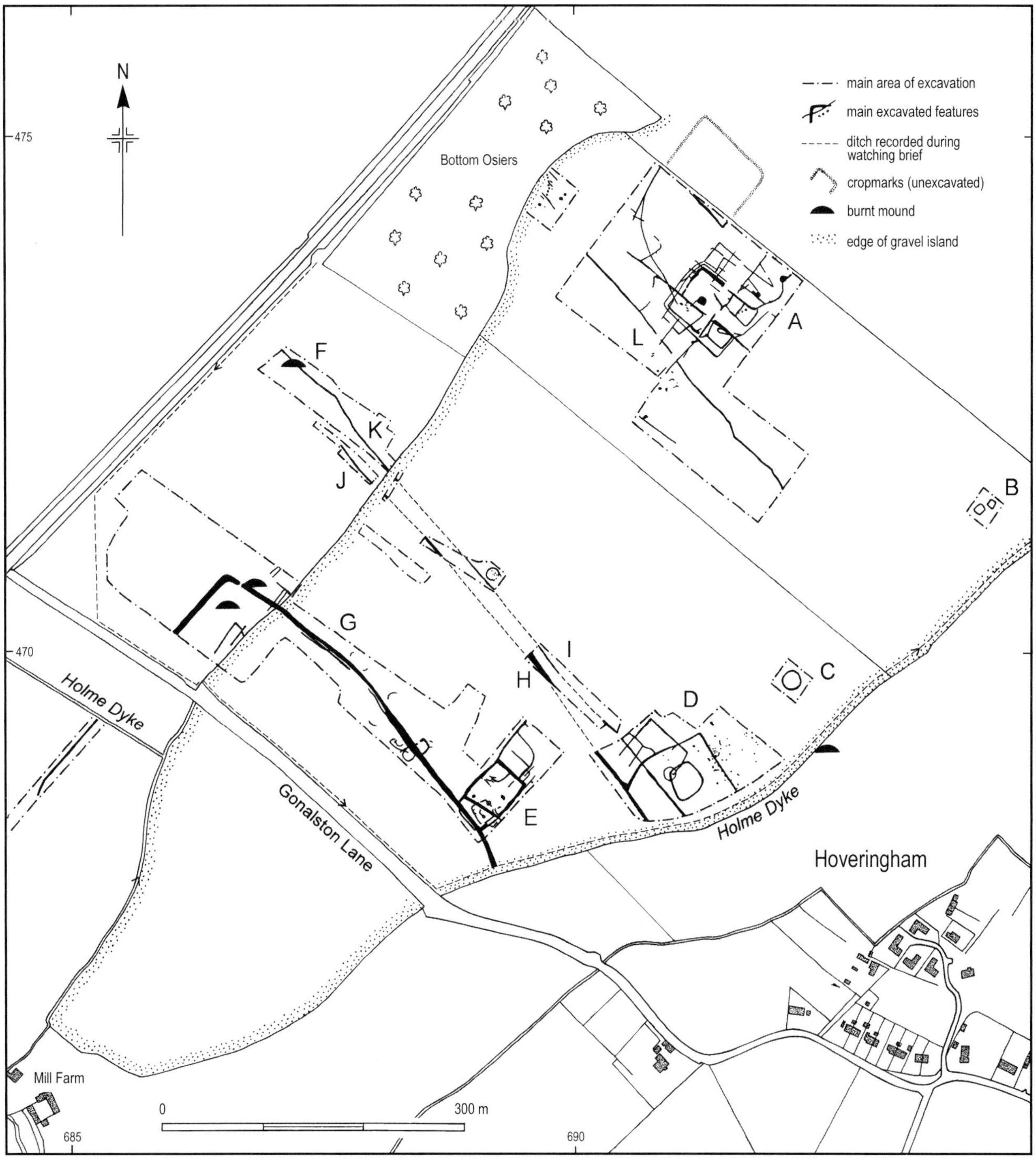

Fig. 3. Prehistoric and Romano-British features revealed during excavations at Hoveringham Quarry, Gonalston, Nottinghamshire (drawing: Jane Goddard).

between widely dispersed communities could have provided a spur to the development of the medium- and long-distance exchange networks in basic commodities such as pottery, salt and querns, or precious items such as glass beads or fine metalwork, which are particularly evident in the Later Iron Age of the Trent valley (e.g. Knight 1992, 85; 2002, 137–41; Knight *et al.* 2003).

Burnt mounds and middens

This model should be adapted to take account of two other monument classes that have recently emerged as significant components of the later prehistoric settlement pattern of the middle Trent valley. The most widespread of these are burnt mounds, first identified adjacent to a palaeochannel of the Trent at Waycar Pasture, Girton (Garton 1993), and now known to be widely distributed along the Trent, Soar, and Idle valleys (e.g. Willington: Beamish and Ripper 2000, 37, fig. 2; Beamish 2001, 13; Holme Dyke, Gonalston: Elliott and Knight 1998, 20).

Current evidence suggests a predominantly later Neolithic to Bronze Age date range, in common with comparable monuments elsewhere in Britain (e.g. Brindley and Lanting 1990), although the possibility should be allowed that some burnt mounds continued in use into the early first millennium BC. Unequivocal evidence for such late dating has yet to be obtained from the region, but there are occasional hints of continuation into the earlier first millennium. At Gonalston, for example, one of several linear ditches forming part of a boundary system that may have originated in the mid first millennium BC (Fig. 3, K) appears to have been deliberately diverted to run into the trough of one of four burnt mounds (Fig. 3, F). This may relate to the final use of a monument designed originally for other purposes and perhaps long decayed, but at the very least it implies that the trough remained a visible feature well into the first millennium BC.

The possible functions of burnt mounds, as cooking sites, saunas, foci for textile production, or locations of other craft or industrial activities, have been widely debated (Buckley 1990; Hodder and Barfield 1991) and the arguments need not be rehearsed again here. More crucial in the present context is the possibility that they performed some specialist role within a system of widely dispersed settlements that continued into the earlier first millennium BC – for example, as communal cooking sites or as foci for specialised craft or industrial activities.

Another indicator of Late Bronze Age–Earlier Iron Age settlement, as yet unparalleled elsewhere within the Trent valley, was located during excavations at Girton to the south of the burnt mound at Waycar Pasture. A remarkable concentration of almost 600 plain and decorated Late Bronze Age–Earlier Iron Age sherds, many in fresh condition, was associated with a thin layer of dark loamy sand incorporating charcoal, fragmentary burnt animal bone and abundant heat-shattered pebbles (Kinsley 1998, 43–7; H. Jones and A.G. Kinsley pers. comm.). This deposit may originally have extended over a roughly circular area at least 7 m in diameter. The dense concentration of burnt stones initially evoked comparisons with burnt mounds, but the association with abundant pottery, bone and other finds would be highly unusual for such monuments.

Comparisons should be sought instead with Late Bronze Age–Earlier Iron Age middens, a class of site that occurs only occasionally in the East Midlands, as at Stickford, Lincolnshire (Lane forthcoming), but is widely distributed in Wessex and neighbouring regions. Notable examples have been recorded at Potterne (Lawson 2000), East Chisenbury (Brown *et al.* 1994), and All Cannings Cross (Cunnington 1923), although all of these extended over far larger areas and preserved a significantly deeper and more complex stratigraphy than the comparatively modest mound at Girton.

All the Wessex midden sites are associated with Late Bronze Age or Early Iron Age pottery, implying a restricted period of use. Whilst evidently a key source of evidence for early first millennium BC domestic activity, the possibility of ritual or ceremonial activities associated with food preparation and consumption should also be considered (e.g. Brown *et al.* 1994). In the case of Girton, evidence for associated settlement may be provided by a scatter of stratigraphically unrelated pits, ditches, and gullies yielding Late Bronze Age–Earlier Iron Age sherds that was recorded adjacent to this deposit.

A wider pattern?

Analysis of site evidence from surrounding regions implies that the proposed model of dispersed open settlement may form part of a broader pattern, extending from the Nene valley northwards to the Humber and southern Pennines, and indeed much further afield (Thomas 1997). There are, however, clear indications that within this physiographically diverse zone the morphology, functions, and spatial organisation of settlement varied significantly. Unenclosed settlements of Later Bronze Age and Earlier Iron Age date are widely distributed, from Northamptonshire – at sites such as Weekley Hall Wood (Jackson 1976), Gretton (Jackson and Knight 1985), and Wellingborough (Enright and Thomas 1998) – northwards to the East Moors of Derbyshire (Rylatt and Bevan this volume). In addition, many excavated enclosures have revealed a similar stratigraphic progression from open to enclosed settlement, notably at Enderby and Humberstone in Leicestershire (Clay 1992; Charles *et al.* 2000); and Crick in Northamptonshire (Hughes 1998).

Few areas, however, display quite such an emphasis upon unenclosed settlement at this period as the Trent valley. In many neighbouring regions, the roots of enclosed settlement may be traced well into the early first millennium BC or earlier. Southwards into Leicestershire and Northamptonshire, for example, a small number of Late Bronze Age and Early Iron Age enclosures may be identified, some apparently with defensive aspirations. They include the hillfort at Rainsborough, Northamptonshire, where abundant pottery and other domestic debris of this date was retrieved from early stratigraphic levels (Avery *et al.* 1967), and the ringwork at Thrapston, Northamptonshire, where the ditch fill yielded a stratified sequence of PDR Plainwares and Late Bronze Age–Earlier Iron Age vessels (Hull 2000–1).

Another contrast between the Nene and Trent valleys, which may indicate significant variations in the pace of landscape development, is provided by the evidence from the Nene for extensive early field and boundary systems, as at Wollaston, Northamptonshire (Meadows 1995). More dramatic contrasts in landscape organisation may be demonstrated eastwards along the Fen margin, within a broad zone extending from Lincolnshire to the lower Welland and Nene valleys. Notable sites in this area include West Deeping, Lincolnshire, and Fengate, Cambridgeshire, where elaborate systems of fields and enclosures, argued by Pryor to have had strong links with sheep raising and flock management, have been shown to span the Bronze Age and Earlier Iron Age (Pryor 1996, 314–19; 1998, 109–23; Yates 2007).

Northwards into upland Derbyshire, additional contrasts in settlement organisation are apparent from excavations on the East Moors, most notably on Big Moor and along Gardom's Edge (Barnatt *et al.* 2002; Rylatt and Bevan this volume). These have revealed extensive prehistoric field systems, linked on Big Moor to an enclosed settlement at Swine Sty (Machin and Beswick 1975) but generally associated with scattered roundhouses and other structures; dating is problematic, but pottery and radiocarbon dates suggest a predominantly Bronze Age to Earlier Iron Age date range. Similar early field systems appear not to have developed in the Trent valley, signifying perhaps that the pressures on land resources which, it is suggested below, impacted upon valley communities in the later first millennium BC, surfaced much earlier in these upland areas – from at least the Earlier Bronze Age, to judge by associated finds and limited radiocarbon dates (Barnatt 1987).

The progress towards enclosure

Significant changes in settlement organisation may be discerned in the Trent valley from the mid first millennium BC, with the progressive enclosure of occupation foci and specialised activity areas by ditches and other barriers to movement, including banks, palisades, and probably hedges. Pottery associations, combined with occasional finds of datable metalwork and radiocarbon dates, suggest an origin for this process no earlier than the fifth or fourth centuries BC, with a rapid gathering of momentum in the Late Iron Age and Romano-British periods. This trend towards enclosure was accompanied in some areas by the development of field systems and the construction of more substantial land boundaries, most notably pit alignments, implying a new concern with the stricter control of land.

The changing environment

The processes of clearance postulated for the earlier first millennium BC appear to have accelerated in the Middle and Late Iron Ages, leading to the development in many areas of a substantially cleared landscape. This is aptly illustrated by the results of analyses of ditch fills from the Middle to Late Iron Age settlement at Fisherwick, in the Tame valley south of its confluence with the Trent (Smith 1979, 93–103). By the Late Iron Age the proportion of arboreal pollen in sampled contexts had plummeted to around 35%, implying extensive clearance of the gravel terraces for grassland and arable farming (*ibid.*, 95).

The arboreal pollen was dominated by species typical of secondary forest or hedges, suggesting that little primeval woodland survived near the site. Alder was particularly well represented, comprising *c.* 41% of the arboreal pollen and 58% of the waterlogged wood retrieved from archaeological contexts, and may have been particularly prevalent on the alluvial floodplain and in other damp environments. Hazel formed around one quarter of the arboreal pollen (24%) and may have been managed as coppice – perhaps even within enclosures designed to prevent browsing by livestock. The floodplain would have provided rich summer pastures as well as hay for winter fodder and a wide range of resources such as reeds for thatch or the raw materials for wattlework, basketry, and hurdles (Smith 1978, 95; 1979, 102).

A comparable landscape has been postulated at Whitemoor Haye, where analyses of insects (Smith 2002), charred and waterlogged plant remains (Ciaraldi 2002; Greig 2002), and charcoal residues (Gale 2002) from Iron Age contexts indicate a mixture of arable and grassland with limited woodland cover (Coates and Woodward 2002, 79). Despite extensive clearance, a fairly wide range of trees and shrubs are attested in the vicinity of the site, including oak, maple, alder, hazel, ash, willow/poplar, and probably birch (Gale 2002, 75). A predominance of oak probably reflects its use as fuel rather than its dominance as a species (Coates and Woodward 2002, 79).

The evidence from Fisherwick and Whitemoor Haye is complemented by palaeoenvironmental analyses of several organic palaeochannel fills radiocarbon dated to the latter half of the first millennium BC, notably at Girton (Howard *et al.* 1999). Pollen, plant macrofossils, and insect fauna from this site indicate reed beds and alder-willow fen woodlands adjacent to a swampy area of shallow sluggishly flowing streams and, farther away, a predominantly cleared floodplain with scattered patches of mixed oak, birch, and hazel woodland.

The full extent of clearance by the end of the first millennium BC remains a vexed issue, along with the problem of determining the ratio of primeval to regenerated woodland. There is persuasive evidence from several sites for woodland regeneration during the first millennium BC. In the Idle marshlands near Scaftworth, Nottinghamshire, fluctuations in the ratio of arboreal to non-arboreal pollen in organic deposits beneath and above the foundations of a Roman road were argued to imply one or possibly two phases of forest regeneration subsequent to Bronze Age clearance (McElearney 1991).

In contrast, excavations within the core of the Romano-British town of *Margidunum*, Nottinghamshire, uncovered a late first-century AD plank-lined well constructed from mature forest oaks (Garton and Salisbury 1995). The trees from which the planks derived were of variable age and displayed signs of slow growth, and were argued to have grown in a competitive environment characteristic of an unmanaged wildwood. The authors speculated whether these might have derived from ancient woodland surviving in the area around *Margidunum* (*ibid.*, 41), although the site's position astride the Fosse Way would have ensured easy access to non-local timber. Such discoveries emphasise the complexity of the relationship between Iron Age farming communities and their landscape, which in many areas may have passed through successive phases of woodland clearance and regeneration.

The retreat of woodland in favour of pasture and arable is implied not only by changes in the proportions of arboreal and non-arboreal pollen but also by increased frequencies of cultivated grains, weeds of cultivation, and pasture indicators in dated assemblages of pollen, plant macrofossils, and charred plants from sites like Gamston (Moffett 1992) and Aslockton (Moffett 1993) in Nottinghamshire, and Fisherwick (Smith 1979) and Whitemoor Haye (Ciaraldi 2002; Greig 2002) in Staffordshire. There was clearly extensive pasture in some stretches of the valley, particularly on the alluvial floodplain, although more detailed assessments of the relationship between crop and animal husbandry must await the completion of ongoing analyses (Monckton 2006). Grazed grasslands may also be deduced from insect remains in waterlogged deposits, as at Fisherwick (Smith 1979, 96; 100) and Whitemoor Haye (Smith 2002, 68), where high proportions of dung beetles imply abundant livestock. More detailed discussion of animal husbandry is frustrated by the poor preservation of faunal remains in the acidic Trent gravels. Although small quantities of cattle, sheep or goat, horse, and pig bone are commonly retrieved, the relative significance of these species, the uses to which they were put, and the extent to which husbandry practices varied over time or space remain far from clear.

Detailed information on crops and crop husbandry practices is also sparse, despite extensive palaeo-environmental sampling of sites located on the river terraces and floodplain. Iron Age charred plant assemblages from the Trent valley regularly yield spelt and emmer wheat and hulled barley, and more rarely legumes such as the bean or pea (Monckton 2006), but the relative significance of these crops and the balance between crop production and processing on individual sites remain uncertain. Arable intensification, demonstrated in other parts of the Midlands and southern England during the Later Iron Age (e.g. Lambrick 1992, 84–5), may be indicated by the increased representation of crops such as spelt, which may be sown in both autumn and spring, and by higher densities of charred cereal remains on some Later Iron Age sites, including Gamston (Monckton 2006). Increases in the density of pits that could have been used to store grain may also be observed at some sites (e.g. Knight 1992, 38), although the significance of this trend is difficult to assess in view of the wide range of other functions that such features might have performed (e.g. Reynolds 1974).

Further, albeit indirect, evidence for the expansion and intensification of arable agriculture is provided by changes in the character and rate of alluviation, and by implication in the levels of soil erosion and flooding. This is particularly apparent in the Trent valley downstream from Newark at such Late Iron Age and Roman sites as Ferry Lane Farm, Collingham (Zeepvat 2000), Rampton (Knight 2000a; 2000b; Ponsford 1992), and Littleborough (Riley *et al.* 1995), all in Nottinghamshire, and at sites like Sandtoft in the Idle marshlands in North Lincolnshire (Samuels and Buckland 1978). Many sites display a stratigraphic progression from anaerobic organically rich silts and clays to oxidised red-brown silty clays. Where datable, as at Rampton and Littleborough, these latter deposits appear to be predominantly Roman or later in date, although earlier origins cannot be ruled out. Comparisons may be drawn with the progressive accumulation of colluvial deposits, which, at sites such as Foxcovert Farm, Aston-upon-Trent (Hughes 1999) and Kelham, Nottinghamshire (Knight and Priest 1998), may be shown to seal Iron Age or Roman features, although the chronology of these deposits is even less certain.

Such changes in the rate and character of alluviation were linked originally to soil erosion caused by Roman agricultural innovations such as deeper ploughing and the cultivation of winter cereals, which would have exposed bare soils to weathering and erosion during the wetter and colder winter months (Buckland and Sadler 1985). It is worth speculating, however, whether the origins of these processes lie in the more intensive farming regimes that seem to have developed in this region during the Later Iron Age. Environmental

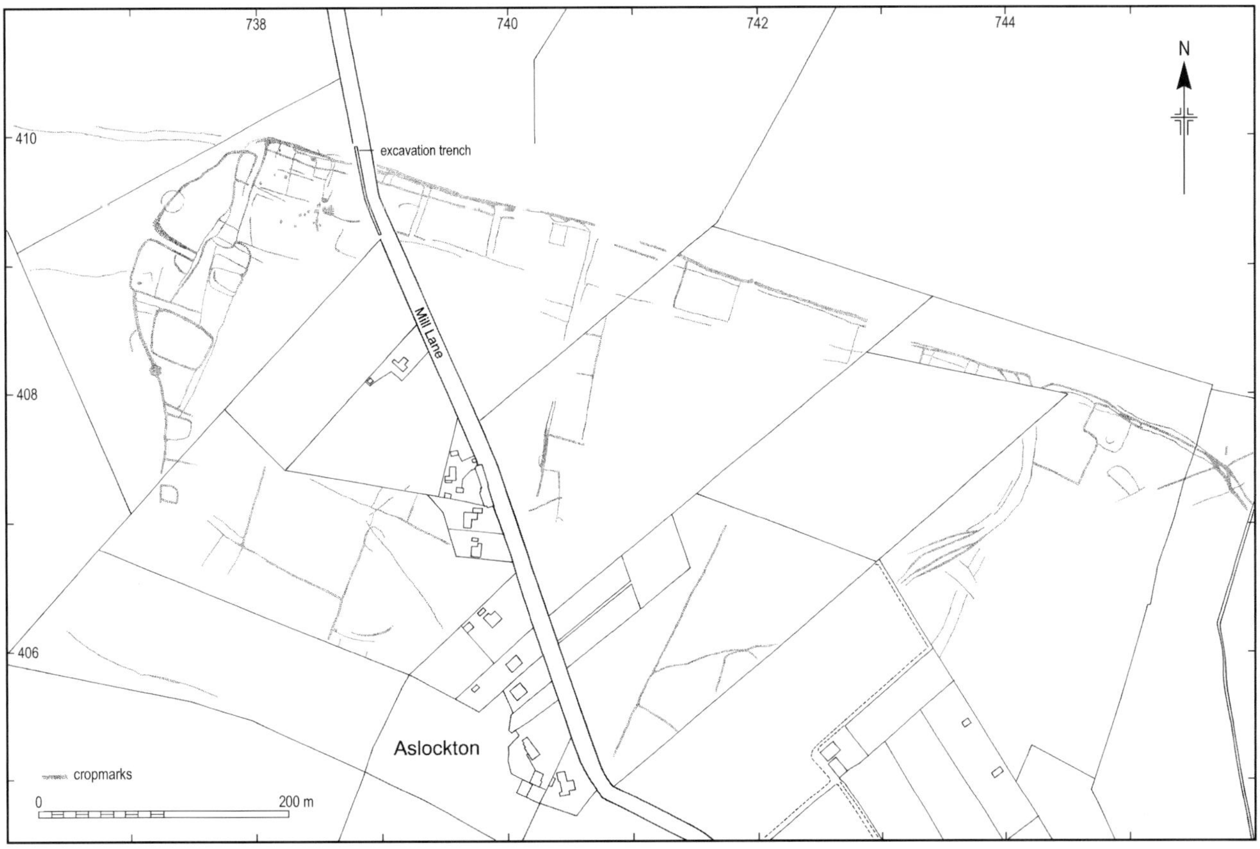

Fig. 4. Cropmark complex at Aslockton, Nottinghamshire (drawing: Jane Goddard, based on cropmark plot by Giles Woodhouse).

degradation may in turn have placed increasing pressures upon land resources and hence may have contributed towards the development of the more tightly managed landscape implied by the evidence discussed below.

Enclosures

The enclosures that dominated much of the Trent valley in the late first millennium BC are morphologically diverse, defined by the presence of one or more continuous or discontinuous circuits of ditch, bank, or palisade (compare Whimster 1989, 28). In contrast to field boundaries, which emerged during the same period as a means of dividing outlying pasture and arable resources, enclosures formed foci for specialised activities associated closely with occupation or, in rare cases, perhaps with burial. Significant variations may be observed in the form, scale, and spatial configuration of their boundaries, the size and shape of the enclosed area, arrangements for access, and the range of associated structural, artefactual, and palaeoenvironmental remains. These in turn indicate a wide range of functions connected not only with the everyday, such as occupation, the sorting and housing of livestock, and the processing and storage of grain, but also perhaps with ceremony, ritual, and burial.

Enclosure morphology

A small number of Iron Age enclosures may have been demarcated wholly or partially by a palisade set in a continuous bedding trench, as at Willington (Wheeler 1979, 103), Gamston (Knight 1992, 28), and Holme Pierrepont (O'Brien 1979b, 1). Most enclosures of this period, however, are represented by a single ditch circuit, commonly preserving evidence of multiple recuts. Very few multiple-ditched enclosures have been recorded, with the striking exception of the elongated curvilinear enclosure postulated at Aslockton (Fig. 4), although the recutting of ditches adjacent to their original alignment has sometimes created complex ground-plans bearing a superficial resemblance to such structures. At Fleak Close, for example, excavations of a postulated double-ditched enclosure revealed a complex sequence of boundary ditches created by progressive recutting of the enclosure along its outer side (Knight and Southgate 2001); at least some of these boundaries may have been defined partly or wholly by a palisade, which would explain the presence of several narrow and vertically sided gullies of variable depth at the eastern and southern entrances.

An internal or external bank may sometimes be postulated from zones of preferential silting within the ditch fill or discontinuities in the distribution of features inside enclosures, or even directly attested by the denuded remains of an earthen bank. At Aslockton, a wide and largely ploughed-out earthwork was observed flanking the north-eastern edge of the outermost of two parallel ditches, visible as cropmarks to the west of Mill Lane and as substantial features in an evaluation trench dug alongside the road (Fig. 4; Palmer-Brown and Knight 1993). At Gonalston, recent excavations revealed a major boundary ditch, which for part of its length was flanked by a sandy clay and gravel spread interpreted as the remains of an associated bank (Elliott and Knight 2003, 201). This spread survived only where the ditch was sealed beneath alluvium, immediately north-west of an elongated 'island' of sand and gravel raised above the floodplain, and was only clearly visible where it was stratified above peat (Fig. 3, G). This boundary may have formed part of a very substantial enclosure traversed by Gonalston Lane, but so far only its north-western and north-eastern sides have been recorded. Further investigations are planned, which it is hoped will clarify the spatial extent and character of this major work.

Some ditches may also have been flanked by hedges set on the ground surface or upon an associated bank, although the case must be argued from indirect evidence such as the discovery in waterlogged ditch fills at Fisherwick of cut twigs from typical hedgerow species such as blackthorn and willow (Smith 1978, 98–9; 1979, 24; 96). Similar problems attend the identification of associated fences. At Fisherwick, these were inferred from the presence of fragments of trimmed and sharpened oak and alder stakes, and the discovery on the inner side of one enclosure ditch of a narrow gully which the excavator interpreted as an associated palisade trench.

A small number of earthwork enclosures within or on the fringes of the valley have been seen by some as Iron Age hillforts, or their lowland equivalents. These include a partially destroyed enclosure of *c.* 3 ha on a gravel terrace at Borough Hill, Walton-on-Trent, Derbyshire, which has been interpreted as a univallate hillfort (Challis and Harding 1975, 47); a sub-rectangular enclosure of *c.* 1.5 ha in the lower Idle valley at Crow Wood, Styrrup, Nottinghamshire, which can be compared to Iron Age 'marsh forts' such as Sutton Common, South Yorkshire (Badcock and Symonds 1994; Parker Pearson and Sydes 1997); and a heterogeneous group of enclosures on the Mercia Mudstone claylands fringing the northern edge of the Trent valley east of Nottingham (O'Brien 1978a, 10–11; Simmons 1963). Serious doubts have, however, been raised regarding the interpretation of Borough Hill as a later prehistoric hillfort (Guilbert 2004), whilst the Crow Wood enclosure cannot yet be closely dated. A recent reassessment of the central Nottinghamshire sites emphasised the likelihood of widely varying origins and functions for these monuments (Bishop 2001, 3).

The internal areas of the enclosures that can confidently be dated to the Iron Age vary dramatically, probably reflecting in part variations in functions. They range from miniscule enclosures of less than 0.01 ha at Gonalston and Brough-on-Fosse, Nottinghamshire (Knight and Howard 2004, 93), to as much as *c.* 20 ha at Aslockton, although doubts remain regarding the full extent of this last site. The emphasis lies firmly upon rectilinear shapes, in sharp contrast to the preference for circularity in domestic architecture, although Iron Age enclosures of curvilinear or polygonal form have occasionally been recorded, as at Chapel Farm, Shardlow, Potlock, Derbyshire (Guilbert and Malone 1994), Fisherwick (SK183098; Smith 1979), and Whitemoor Haye (Coates 2002).

The enclosure circuits were interrupted by one, or more rarely two, entrances, represented either by directly opposing ditch terminals, as with Gamston enclosure 1 (Knight 1992, 28–31), or occasionally by a more elaborate arrangement of inturned terminals or entrance outworks which may have been intended to facilitate the movement of stock, as with the southern entrance to Fleak Close. Post settings for gate structures sometimes survive; at Fisherwick, post hole alignments suggested a gated fenced passage, which might have served to sort livestock entering or leaving the enclosure (Smith 1979). Another link with stock handling may be the occasional provision of corner entrances, which Pryor (1996, 318–9) suggests might have helped funnel stock contained within an enclosure towards the entrance (e.g. Whitemoor Haye Area B; Coates 2002).

Finally, several scholars have drawn attention to the easterly orientation of some enclosure entrances – notably at Fisherwick, Gamston, and Whitemoor Haye – which might signify an orientation upon the rising sun (Willis 1999, 93; Coates and Woodward 2002, 8). A much larger sample of excavated sites would be required, however, to establish whether the preferred easterly orientation of Iron Age enclosure entrances noted in other areas of Britain prevailed in the Trent valley, while doubts must also be expressed regarding the cosmological significance of this observation.

Why enclose?

Many enclosure boundaries would have provided impressive barriers to movement, seemingly well in excess of that required for purely utilitarian purposes such as stock control or drainage. It is worth speculating to what extent such boundaries fulfilled important social as well as economic functions, given that recent Iron Age studies have placed much emphasis on the symbolic role of boundaries, linking their construction and maintenance to strategies designed to emphasise group identity and enhance social cohesion (e.g. Hingley 1990; Bevan 1997; 1999a; Chadwick 1999; Giles this volume).

These strategies could represent reactions to increasing pressures upon land resources, and in their most extreme manifestation could have resulted in the construction of sites such as Aslockton. Here, a trench across part of a cropmark complex reminiscent of some of the elaborate multiple-ditched sites of Lincolnshire (Winton 1998) revealed substantial boundary works

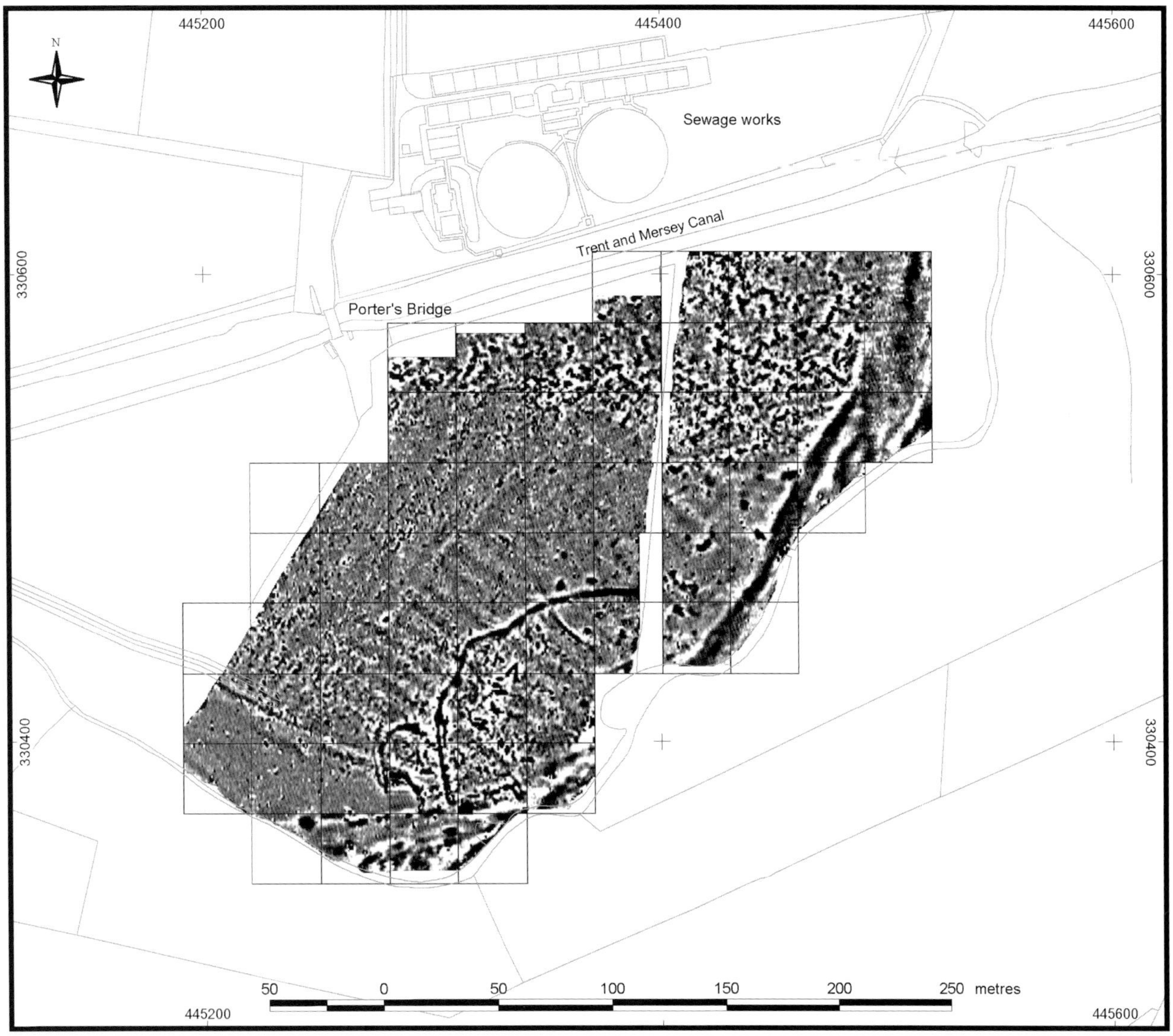

Fig. 5. Gradiometer plot of Late Iron Age/Romano-British curvilinear ditched enclosure near Chapel Farm, Shardlow, Derbyshire (gradiometer plot reproduced by permission of Oxford Archaeotechnics and Lafarge Aggregates Ltd. Base map Crown copyright/database right 2005; an Ordnance Survey/EDINA supplied service).

which may originally have been of defensive proportions (Palmer-Brown and Knight 1993).

Aslockton lies just outside the Trent valley, on the crest of a low drift-covered interfluve separating the River Smite from the Car Dyke, and is defined on its north-east and north-west sides by single or multiple ditches clearly visible as cropmarks. There are suggestions of single or multiple ditches demarcating south-eastern and south-western boundaries to the site, although the cropmarks are intermittent and may not represent originally continuous boundaries. A trench across the north-eastern side of the enclosure revealed two closely spaced and possibly contemporary ditches, up to 6 m wide by 2 m deep, flanked by a levelled bank between the ditches, and a second denuded bank along the outer edge of the external ditch (*ibid.*, 146: Phase 2). A post hole cut through the bank could imply some kind of timber strengthening, but more of the earthwork would need to be excavated to verify this. The site is not in an obviously defensive location, but the scale of the remains implies a formidable barrier to movement, which at the very least would have represented a potent symbol of prestige and display.

Similar arguments can be applied to several other Iron Age enclosures within the region, some on hilltop or promontory locations reminiscent of those favoured by hillfort-builders. These include a substantial curvilinear ditch at Swarkestone Lowes, which may have defined a Middle to Late Iron Age ridge-top enclosure of approximately 8 ha (Elliott and Knight 1999), and Chapel Farm, where a gradiometer survey revealed an irregular curvilinear ditch demarcating a roughly semicircular area of at least 0.5 ha at the end of a low gravel promontory elevated above the Trent floodplain (Fig. 5). Evaluation trenches at Chapel Farm suggested a substantial multi-

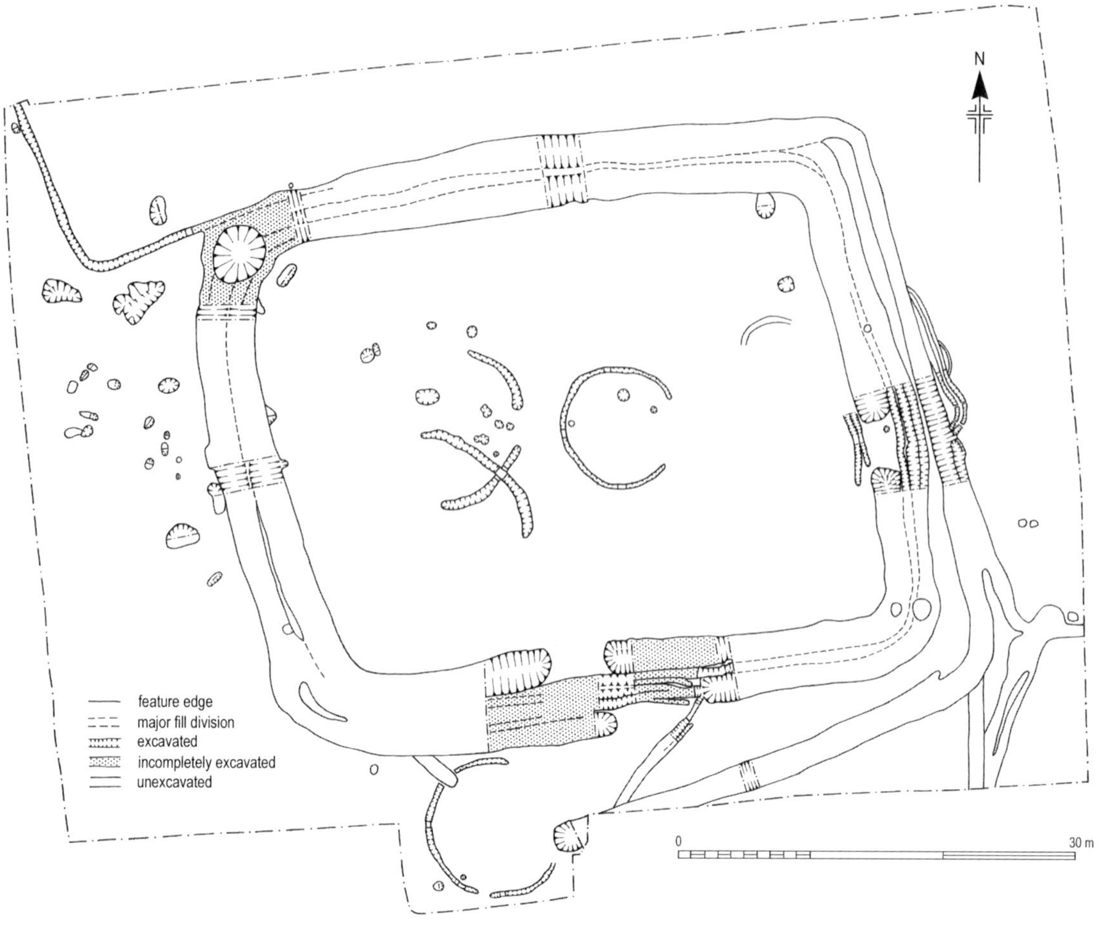

Fig. 6. Iron Age enclosure at Fleak Close, Barrow-upon-Trent, Derbyshire (drawing: Jane Goddard, based on plan by Mark Southgate).

phased ditch, which – on the basis of associated pottery – probably originated towards the end of the Late Iron Age and continued in use into the second century AD. A dense pattern of Late Iron Age/Romano-British gullies, pits and possible post holes was recorded inside the enclosure (Knight and Malone 1997; 1998), but more extensive excavations would be required to clarify the structural sequence and the extent and character of pre-Roman activity.

The above enclosures are distinguished by their large internal areas, well above the average for the period. However, many smaller enclosures display a similar emphasis upon boundary constructions that would seem excessive if they were intended solely for purposes such as stock control. At Brough-on-Fosse, for example, a small sub-oval enclosure was demarcated by an impressive V-shaped ditch, dug originally to a depth of *c.* 1.4 m and almost 2 m wide at the mouth (Knight and Howard 2004, 93; Vyner forthcoming; H. Jones pers. comm.). This seems wholly out of proportion to the internal area of the enclosure (<0.01 ha) and once again prompts consideration of the role of factors such as prestige and display in its construction.

Yet further questions about the social significance of enclosure emerge from the complex and often bewildering sequences of ditch recutting that have emerged during the excavation of many Iron Age sites in the region. At Fleak Close, the boundary ditch had been recut repeatedly along much of its outer edge, causing a gradual but significant expansion of the enclosed area (Fig. 6). The reverse pattern is also found, as at Gonalston, where one of the Romano-British enclosures was repeatedly recut along its inner edge, progressively reducing the internal area (Elliott and Knight 2003, 202).

Such sequences could have a simple functional explanation, reflecting the need for repeated scouring of silted ditches, although it would seem that this could have been achieved far more easily by removing accumulated ditch silts rather than by redigging adjacent to a previous alignment. Some researchers have speculated whether such protracted recutting sequences should be viewed partly as symbolic acts, aimed at emphasising, by means of successive re-inscriptions upon the landscape, the strong links between communities and the lands they farmed (see Hingley 1990; Chadwick 1999, 161–4; Giles this volume). In the context of the Trent valley, with ever-growing pressures during the later first millennium BC upon limited land resources, community activities which reinforced rights of ownership or which served to reinforce group identity and bind individual members more closely together may well have assumed ever-growing significance.

These arguments may be strengthened by the discovery in some enclosure ditches of structured deposits, particularly of animal or human remains, which could imply ceremonial deposition focused upon settlement boundaries (e.g. Hill 1995; Gwilt 1997; Willis 1999, 96–9). Such evidence is extremely rare in the Trent valley, due partly perhaps to poor preservation of bone in the acidic sands and gravels of the river terraces, but there are hints that such practices may have been more common than can be demonstrated at present. At Chainbridge Lane, Lound, in the Idle valley, two virtually complete pig carcasses, at least one of which may have been bound at the feet, were discovered in a Romano-British enclosure ditch (Eccles *et al.* 1988, 17), whilst at Fleak Close, a large assemblage of red deer antler and a pig jaw were deposited in the base of a large pit dug into the fill of an Iron Age enclosure ditch in the exact centre of the north-west corner (Fig. 6; Knight and Southgate 2001). The coincidence is striking and implies a deliberate act of deposition at a time when the corner of the largely infilled enclosure ditch was still remembered and respected, providing perhaps a symbolic link with earlier land divisions (compare Proctor 2001).

Enclosure functions

Whatever the exact reasons for their construction, enclosures probably embraced a wide range of functions. In addition, at occupied sites, the size and status of the population group may have varied significantly. The possibility of differences in community size and status is best illustrated by the sites at Aslockton and Swarkestone Lowes, which stand out from all other Iron Age enclosures in the region on the grounds of their massive internal areas. Both have yielded structural and artefactual remains that could signify contemporary occupation, although as only tiny areas of the interiors have been excavated, any conclusions as to their functions or internal spatial organisation must remain tentative. Major difficulties also arise here and elsewhere due to the loss of structural remains through ploughing and other destructive activities, along with the possible use of constructional techniques that are likely to leave few if any physical traces. Appropriate caution should be exercised, therefore, when interpreting archaeologically blank areas.

At Aslockton, the cropmarks imply that the large elongated curvilinear enclosure may have been divided into two main compounds by ditches constructed on a north-east to south-west alignment, each possibly edged by a series of sub-rectangular ditched enclosures positioned around a central open space (Fig. 4 above). In addition to the parallel ditches already mentioned above, the trench across the north east side of the enclosure revealed dense Middle Iron Age to Romano-British structural and artefactual remains within a zone some 50 m wide adjacent to the enclosure boundary. No other traces of activity were found, conceivably implying that the area away from the edge of the enclosure had been reserved for purposes such as stock grazing. A possible link with stock management is provided by the abundant faunal remains – particularly of cattle and sheep/goat, with a lower representation of pig, horse and dog – although it should be emphasised that soil conditions here were far more conducive to bone preservation than on the river terraces. Further indirect evidence for an association with animal husbandry is provided by fired clay triangular loomweights, bone weaving combs, and other worked bone artefacts (Hamshaw-Thomas 1992). Charred chaff, cereal grains, and seeds included examples of spelt and possibly emmer wheat, hulled barley, and various weeds of cultivation, suggesting crop-processing activities and possibly arable husbandry on site (Moffett 1992, 3).

In contrast perhaps to Aslockton, occupation at Swarkestone Lowes may have been dispersed widely within the area demarcated by the curvilinear ditch (Fig. 7). No evidence of occupation was found over quite extensive areas, raising the possibility that large parts of the interior were reserved for purposes such as stock grazing, with the obvious proviso that certain kinds of structural remains may have eluded discovery. Associated pollen, plant macrofossils, and insect remains support the case for extensive pasture (Elliott and Knight 1999, 139–49), although detailed discussion of the animal husbandry regime is prevented by the poor survival of bone here.

General parallels may be suggested with the pattern of Iron Age land use postulated in the Thames valley at Stanton Harcourt, Oxfordshire, where dispersed terrace-edge communities with juxtaposed arable land may have encircled a zone of communal pasture (Lambrick 1992, 90–3; Hey this volume). This pastoral core was dominated by an extant henge and a Bronze Age barrow cemetery, recalling the demarcation by the curvilinear Iron Age ditch at Swarkestone of a ridge-top barrow cemetery (Fig. 7). Similar monument 'associations' have been observed elsewhere in Britain and Ireland (e.g. Hingley 1999; Armit this volume), and may signify the use of early funerary and ritual sites as foci in the laying out of later agricultural settlements, possibly as a mechanism for defining and reinforcing group identity by reference to ancestry.

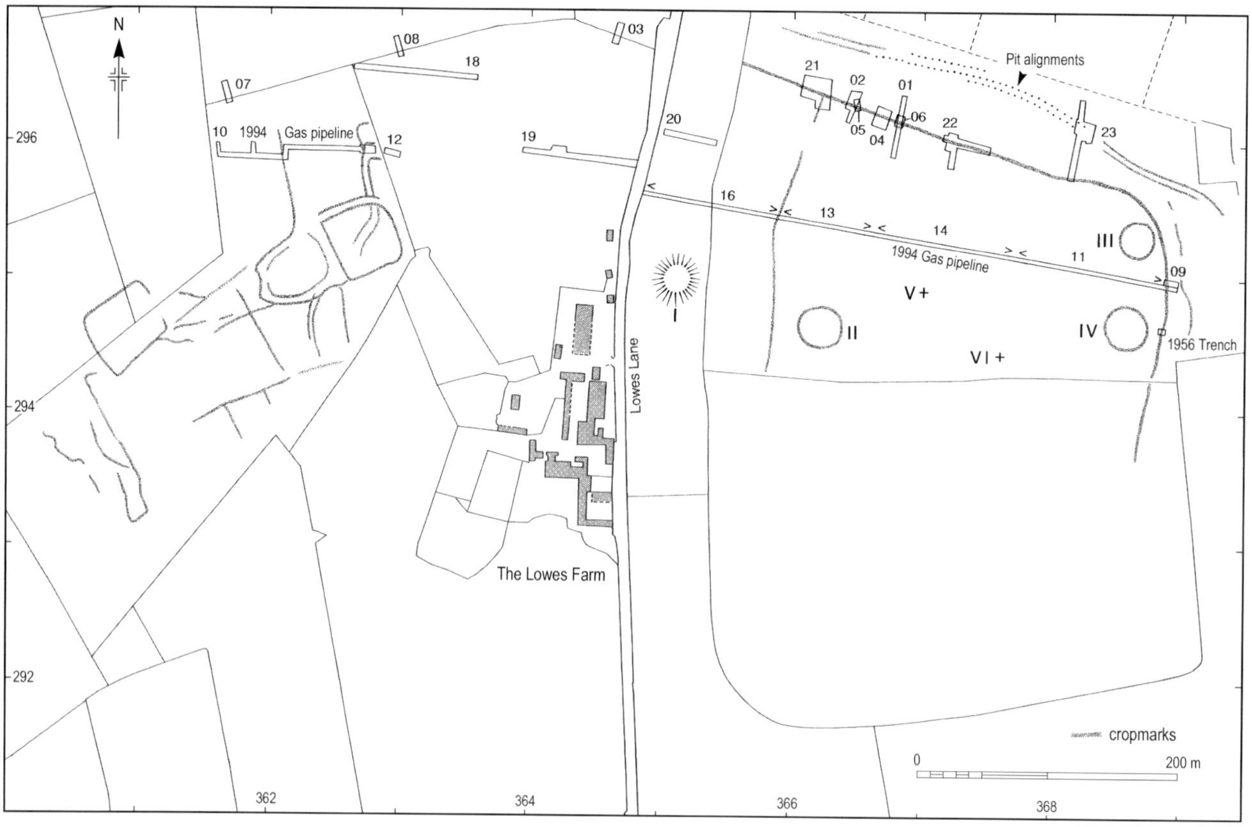

Fig. 7. Bronze Age barrow cemetery, possible Iron Age curvilinear enclosure, and pit alignments at Swarkestone Lowes, Derbyshire (drawing: Jane Goddard, based on plan in Elliott and Knight 1999).

As noted above, most enclosures in the Trent valley fall in the size range *c.* 0.01 to 1.5 ha, the majority enclosing less than 0.5 ha. From the excavated examples, a variety of functions are likely. Many of these smaller enclosures have preserved structural remains in the interior that might signify contemporary occupation, and in view of their size probably served as habitation foci for extended family or kin groups. Associated finds provide little evidence for status variations between these sites, which apart from occasional items of metalwork or objects such as glass beads show little evidence of material wealth. This provides an intriguing contrast with the rich metalwork finds from the River Trent (Knight and Howard 2004, 82–3), which as yet have no counterpart in the contemporary settlements.

The ground plans of most enclosed settlements show a remarkable degree of homogeneity, prompting thoughts of some kind of enclosure template. Time and again evidence has been recovered of rectilinear enclosures up to *c.* 0.3 ha in area with traces of one or more circular structures which may have served as dwellings, scatters of pits for purposes such as grain storage or cooking, and various ancillary structures such as four-post structures, some of which may represent raised granaries. Typical examples include Fisherwick, where the sub-square ditched enclosure contained at least one multi-phased internal roundhouse which was probably contemporary with its use (Fig. 8); Fleak Close, where the ditched sub-rectangular enclosure preserved traces of three centrally placed roundhouses, two of which could have been in contemporary use (Fig. 6 above); and Holme Pierrepont Site 4 (Fig. 9), where a ditched and palisaded enclosure preserved traces in its interior of a cluster of several roundhouses which could have overlapped the period of its use (O'Brien 1978b; 1979b).

Only rarely can a stratigraphic link be demonstrated between the enclosure ditch and internal structures. The case for contemporary occupation generally rests instead upon the less secure grounds of their spatial relationships, warning against over-elaborate interpretations of intra-enclosure spatial patterning. The problem is exemplified by the discovery inside a Middle to Late Iron Age sub-rectangular ditched enclosure at Gonalston of a remarkable roundhouse defined by two phases of bedding trench, 11 m and 12 m in diameter, and by a slightly larger ring of post holes partially cutting the outer bedding trench (Elliott and Knight 2002, 149; Knight and Howard 2004, 98). Its location, towards the

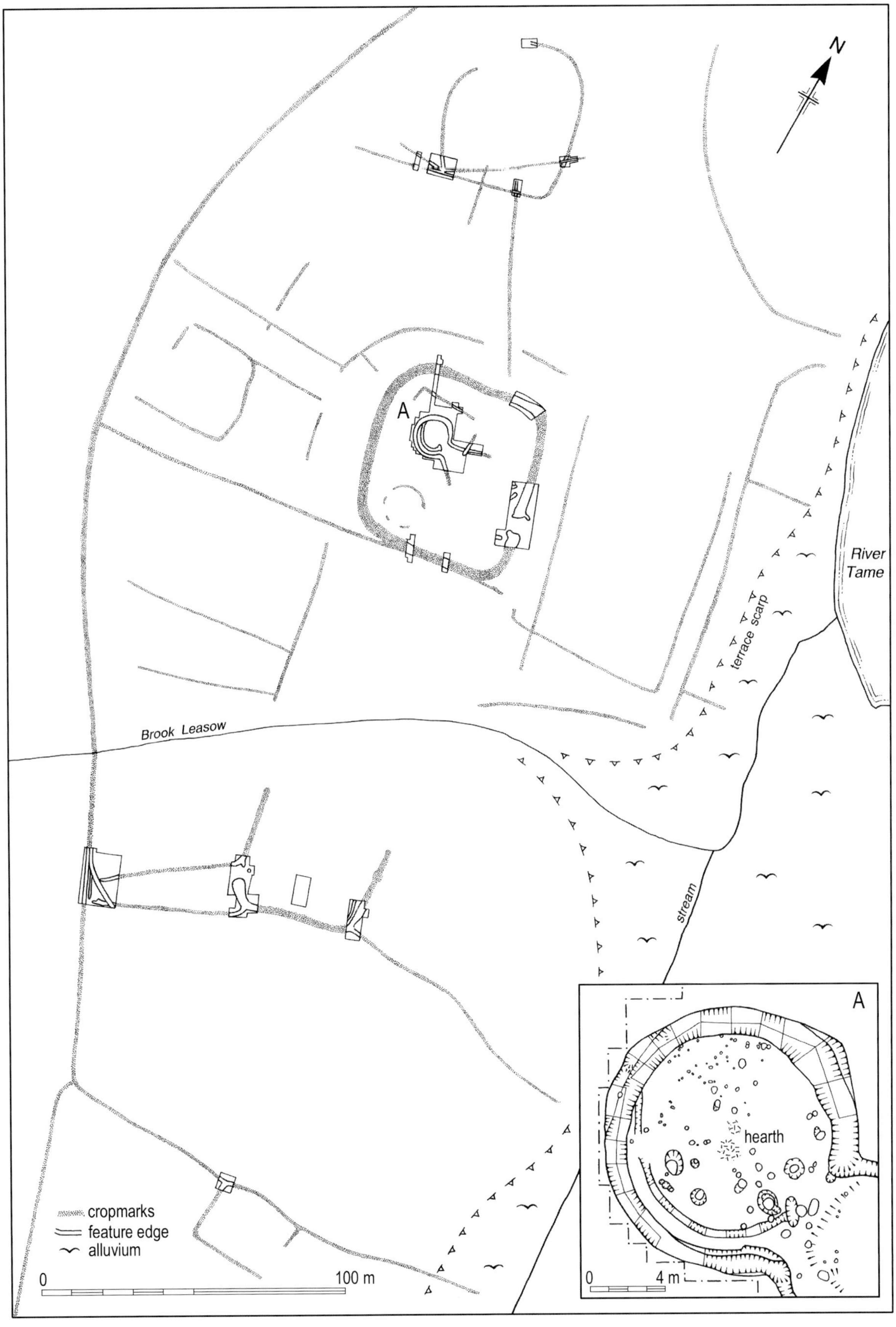

Fig. 8. Iron Age enclosures and associated field system at Fisherwick, Staffordshire (drawing: Jane Goddard, based on plans in Smith 1979).

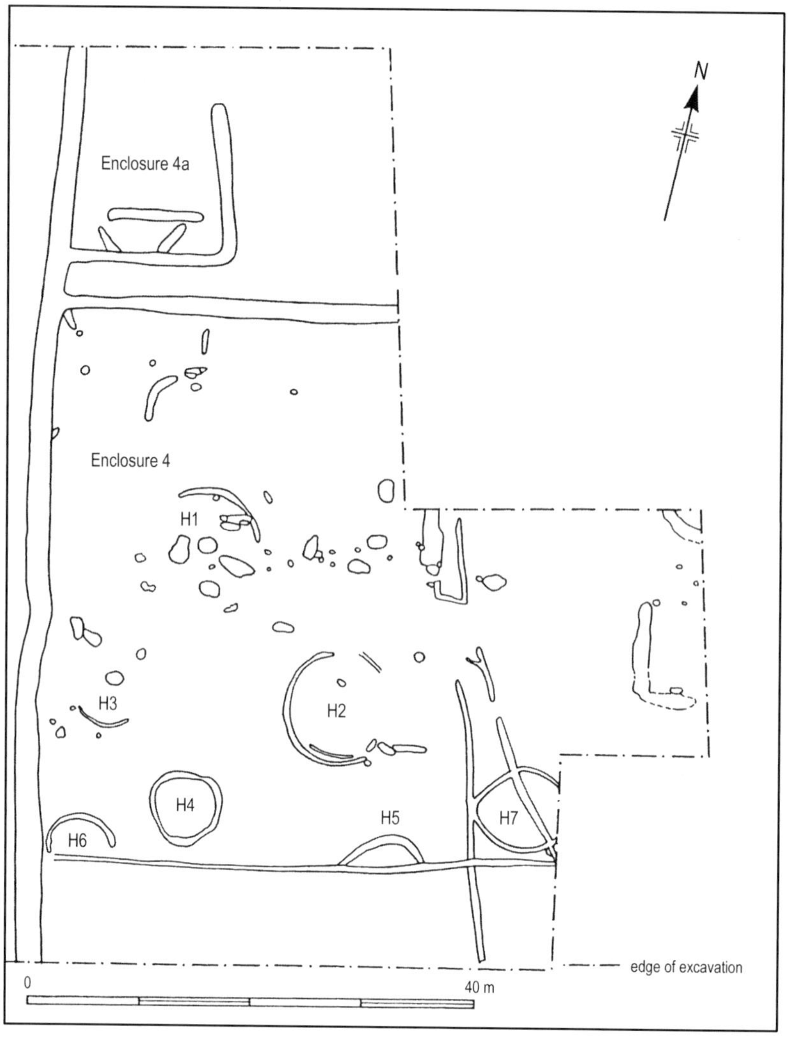

Fig. 9. Iron Age features revealed during excavations at Site 4, Holme Pierrepont, Nottinghamshire (drawing: Jane Goddard, based on plan by Colm O'Brien).

centre of the enclosure and roughly equidistant from the south-western and north-eastern ditches, suggests that it was positioned relative to these boundaries. Nevertheless, the presence of diagnostic sherds of Late Bronze Age–Earlier Iron Age pottery in the recut entrance posts on the south-eastern side of the structure raises the possibility that at least the earlier phases of the roundhouse preceded construction of the enclosure.

Another major problem arises from the difficulty in many cases of establishing whether occupation was permanent or seasonal in nature. Many lower-lying sites, particularly on the edges of gravel terraces, might have been particularly prone to flood. In common, therefore, with sites in other Midlands river valleys, such as Farmoor, Oxfordshire (Lambrick and Robinson 1979), they may have been occupied only during the summer months. Much emphasis has been placed in recent excavations of Trent valley Iron Age sites upon the development of palaeoenvironmental sampling programmes, which it is hoped will eventually permit a more informed assessment of this issue.

The evidence for contemporary occupation, either permanent or seasonal, is rarely unequivocal, and it is likely that some enclosures performed specialised functions connected only indirectly with habitation. Possible functions include paddocks for controlled grazing or for the intensive care of stock during periods of lambing or calving (Lambrick 1992, 100–1; Ciaraldi 2002, 63); fodder and crop stores (Knight 1992, 84); or even coppice enclosures (Smith 1978, 95).

In some cases, there may also be a strong link with ritual. Particular attention may be drawn to a small group of typologically distinct square-ditched enclosures, up to *c.* 10 m across internally (Whimster 1989). Small clusters of these enclosures have been recorded in Nottinghamshire, notably at North Muskham (Fig. 10) and Gonalston (Fig. 3, B above; Woodhouse 1993, 12–13), and examples are known as far upstream as Aston-

Fig. 10. Square-ditched enclosures near North Muskham, Nottinghamshire, showing relationship to the River Trent and palaeochannels (by permission of English Heritage NMR; Riley collection DNR 427/31).

upon-Trent (May 1970) and Barrow-upon-Trent (Derbyshire SMR 16709b) in Derbyshire. They bear a striking resemblance to the square-ditched barrows of eastern Yorkshire, although none of the cropmarks preserves traces of the central pit that is such a distinctive feature of many Arras burials (Stead 1991, figs 5–17).

Three examples in the Trent valley have been excavated, including a *c.* 8 x 8 m enclosure at Acre Lane, Aston-upon-Trent, and two closely spaced *c.* 10 x 10 m enclosures at Gonalston. Small quantities of Iron Age sherds were retrieved from the fills of each of the excavated ditches, supporting the case for a Later Iron Age origin, but none yielded positive evidence of an associated internal mound or burials. Approximately half of the interior of the Aston enclosure was excavated, revealing only a small pit with no associated finds near one corner (May 1970, fig. 2). The absence of a grave pit is not necessarily a problem, as some Arras burials were placed directly on the ground surface (Stead 1991, 179–80). Similarly, inhumations are unlikely to have survived the acidic soil. The Gonalston enclosures were only partially investigated; both were subsequently preserved *in situ,* and remains of associated burials or grave goods could still survive within the areas not examined (Woodhouse 1993).

Although the excavations were inconclusive, a link between these square-ditched enclosures and the barrow burials of the Arras tradition remains likely. The typological parallels are striking, while the tight clustering of enclosures, which is particularly evident at both Aston and North Muskham, strongly suggests cemetery complexes. In addition, the valley locations, close to water, recall the topographical preferences of the barrow-builders in eastern Yorkshire (Bevan 1999a, 137–8). Whatever their functions, their presence in the area emphasises the need to consider ritual as well as everyday processes when contemplating the origins of enclosures. Were an Arras connection to be vindicated, the presence of potentially high-status burials would provide important additional evidence for social ranking, as well as emphasising the role of the Trent as an important artery for the movement of materials (Knight 1992, fig. 30) and the introduction of novel concepts of burial (through the interchange of ideas or, more controversially, movements of population).

Discrete or agglomerated?

Although some enclosures might represent discrete entities, excavations have generally unveiled a complex landscape in which many enclosures formed only one component of a significantly more elaborate settlement plan. These possibilities have been explored for a variety of sites within the region, including the smaller of two sub-rectangular ditched enclosures at Gamston (Enclosure 1; Knight 1992, 28–31). This enclosure contained a variety of features that on stratigraphic grounds mainly pre-dated or followed the period of its use and yielded no convincing evidence for contemporary internal dwellings. With the proviso that houses of turf or other structures lacking deeply dug foundations might have eluded discovery, it was proposed that the enclosure could have served one or more other purposes, perhaps functioning as a stock corral or a protected grain or fodder store, with occupation restricted to the area outside the enclosure. Similar conclusions may be drawn from a host of sites in the Trent valley, suggesting that the concept of the 'agglomerated' settlement, which has been applied to extensive and long-lived sites such as Twywell (Jackson 1975) and Crick (Hughes 1998) in Northamptonshire, should be extended to this region.

Other Later Iron Age sites where occupation had extended beyond the areas enclosed for this or other purposes include Willington, where occupation was represented by scattered roundhouses, pits, hearths, and a curvilinear palisade trench interpreted by the excavator as possibly a 'cattle pound' (Wheeler 1979, 103), and Holme Dyke, Gonalston, where pits and other structural remains yielding Scored ware and other types of pottery extended north-west beyond a Middle to Late Iron Age ditched enclosure (Fig. 3, D above; Elliott and Knight 2002). Interpretation is complicated on all these sites by the difficulty of establishing which features were in contemporary use. However, with this proviso, there are hints that some of these settlements extended over quite large areas, as at Lockington in Leicestershire, where an extensive complex incorporating possible roundhouses, rectilinear enclosures and trackways may indicate a major Iron Age settlement that continued in use into the Roman period (Clay 1985). This in turn raises the possibility of population groupings beyond the level of the extended family unit.

A chronological dimension to this development may perhaps be inferred from the recent excavation of several major Late Iron Age and Roman settlements in the Trent valley and neighbouring areas. Key examples include Ferry Lane Farm, long regarded as exceptional on the grounds of its polyfocal cropmark plan (Fig. 11; Whimster 1989, 77; P. Connolly pers. comm.), and Rampton, where occupation extended over an area of at least 3 ha (Knight 2000a; 2000b). Immediately north of the Roman town at Brough-on-Fosse (*Crococalana*), excavations have unearthed a major Late Iron Age settlement (Jones 2002), which might have overlapped the use of a settlement preceding construction of the Roman town defences (Fig. 12; Vyner forthcoming). There are indications at these sites of sizeable communities engaged in a wide range of agricultural, craft and industrial activities, seemingly beyond the level of the single farmstead and anticipating the major nucleated settlements that developed in the Trent valley in the post-conquest period (Knight and Howard 2004, 139–40).

Comparisons may be suggested between these larger agglomerated sites and the Late Iron Age settlement complexes that have been identified in neighbouring areas such as Lincolnshire, including Dragonby, Old Sleaford, and Owmby (May 1984; 1996; Elsdon 1997). Unlike the Lincolnshire sites, many of which have yielded numerous Iron Age coins, brooches, and other rich artefacts – and in the case of Old Sleaford, a large quantity of clay flan moulds associated with coin production or other kinds of precious metalworking – the agglomerated settlements of the Trent valley have yielded few artefacts indicative of significant status variations. Occasional copper alloy or iron brooches and rare exotic items such as glass beads (e.g. Henderson 1992) imply limited access to high value commodities, but conjure no clear image of material wealth or sharp social stratification.

Field and territorial boundaries

Field systems

A significant number of Later Iron Age enclosures in the Trent valley were closely integrated with systems of predominantly sub-rectangular fields and linear trackways, providing clear evidence for a link between the development of enclosures and field systems. Notable examples include Fisherwick, where Smith (1979, 101) proposed an infield–outfield system centred on a block of annually cultivated arable fields and paddocks adjacent to the habitation focus, and Gonalston (Elliott and Knight 2002; 2003). Dating of these field systems is complicated by the paucity of finds from the accompanying ditches and the likelihood that repeated cleaning may have biased the artefact record towards later periods. With these provisos, however, an origin in the mid first millennium BC, contemporary with the earliest enclosures, may be suggested for some field systems. This is in sharp contrast to many areas of eastern England and the Midlands, where field systems may be traced well into the Bronze Age, if not earlier (e.g. Lambrick 1992; Pryor 1996; Yates 2007).

One of the earliest ceramic associations for the Trent valley systems comes from Gonalston, where an entrance terminal of one of several roughly parallel ditches running from north-west to south-east across an elongated 'island' of gravel (Fig. 3, L above) yielded a deposit of largely unabraded pottery sherds. This included the rim of a pot with a high, everted neck and an internal corrugation, recalling Late Bronze Age–Earlier Iron Age vessels from Gretton in Northamptonshire (Jackson and Knight 1985) and Fiskerton in

Fig. 11. Aerial photograph of part of a Late Iron Age and Romano-British nucleated settlement at Ferry Lane Farm, Collingham, Nottinghamshire (by permission of English Heritage NMR; Pickering collection JAP 1186/7).

Fig. 12. Aerial photograph of north-western side of the Roman town of Crococalana, Brough-on-Fosse, Nottinghamshire, showing the defensive ditches cutting across linear ditches and other features associated with a Late Iron Age/Early Roman settlement; this earlier settlement appears to have focused upon a ditched trackway traversing the defended town core at an oblique angle to the defences and continuing beyond the north-western defensive ditches (by permission of English Heritage NMR; Pickering collection 252/23A).

Lincolnshire (Elsdon and Knight 2003). On this basis, the system may have been in use from at least the mid first millennium BC. Other ditches running parallel to this feature yielded Middle and Late Iron Age pottery, including Scored ware and wheel-made sherds, implying continued use of components of this system throughout the Later Iron Age.

A similarly early origin is possible at Willington, where four linear ditches were attributed to the Iron Age (Wheeler 1979, 86). One ditch with a dark humic fill yielded a substantial group of large Late Bronze Age–Earlier Iron Age sherds and animal bones, mainly towards the bottom of the feature, although it should be noted that very small and abraded Romano-British sherds were retrieved from the upper fills (*ibid.*, 86; 165). In addition, two phases of one of three intersecting ditches some 300 m to the east of this feature disturbed a pit yielding a classic Late Bronze Age–Earlier Iron Age assemblage, while the ditch itself yielded a small collection of pottery of the same period; the values of these associations, however, are much reduced by the protracted sequence of recuts and the likelihood of significant redeposition from earlier features (*ibid.*, 94–6).

Although the origins of such systems may therefore be traced at least to the mid first millennium BC, a significantly later origin is probable for the majority of field boundaries. Yet again, dating is complicated by the likelihood that any associated artefacts register only the latest episodes of activity. In much of Nottinghamshire, large tracts of the Trent valley preserve extensive field systems whose components may be dated from no earlier than the later first century BC or early first century AD, inviting comparison with the well-known brickwork fields which apparently developed from the first century AD on the Sherwood Sandstones of north Nottinghamshire and South Yorkshire (Riley 1980; Garton 1987; Chadwick 1999, 154–5). Traces of one such system were revealed at Gamston, where a rectilinear pattern of ditched boundaries (Phase III; Fig. 2 above) was dated stratigraphically and by associated Late Iron Age pottery to no earlier than the early or mid first century AD (Knight 1992, 31–3).

A similarly late date may be suggested for components of the remarkable co-axial systems which extend along the Trent valley to the north of Newark, notably at Kelham, where excavated field ditches yielded small numbers of Late Iron Age and Romano-British sherds (Knight and Priest 1998), although more extensive excavations may eventually demonstrate a rather earlier origin for these systems. These co-axial field systems extended over large expanses of the Holme Pierrepont terrace downstream from Newark, providing an image of a highly organised landscape in which densely distributed rectilinear enclosures were tied into a well-planned landscape of co-axial fields, trackways and pit alignments (Fig. 13; Whimster 1989, figs 60–1). The limited excavations carried out in this area, combined with the results of systematic fieldwalking (Garton 2002), suggest that some elements of the system may be traced to the Late Iron Age, although it only apparently developed fully in the Roman period.

Significantly more work is required before the contribution of Iron Age farmers to this tightly constrained landscape may be quantified precisely. There seems little doubt, however, given the marked regularities in the spacing of the enclosures and organisation of adjacent field areas, that the fully developed landscape incorporated a dense network of broadly contemporary settlements set within a tightly managed agricultural environment (see also Knight and Howard 2004, 140–4).

Pit alignments

Attention needs also to be drawn to the close relationship between many rectilinear field systems and networks of pit alignments (Whimster 1989; Boutwood 1998). Pit alignments may in some cases represent merely another manifestation of field or trackway boundaries – as perhaps at Lockington, where a trackway which may have formed the focus of an agglomerated Iron Age settlement was demarcated for much of its length by a double line of pits (Clay 1985, 17), and near North Muskham, where the intersection at right angles of a double pit alignment and two widely spaced parallel ditches suggests strongly a crossroads between two corridors of movement (Fig. 14).

Mostly, however, the wide spacing and orientation of pit alignments suggest a division of the landscape into larger blocks, perhaps indicating boundaries between competing groups. This phenomenon is demonstrated particularly clearly by the spatial arrangement of pit alignments within the co-axial field systems round South and North Muskham, where certain striking coincidences with later boundaries – for example, the continuation of the line of a double alignment near North Muskham by the boundary of Cromwell parish (Whimster 1989, fig. 61: SK793603) – raise intriguing questions on the subject of landscape continuity. Similar patterning is apparent at other locations elsewhere in the Trent valley, including Barrow-upon-Trent, immediately upstream of the Trent–Derwent confluence, where extensive excavations revealed lengths of a seemingly rectilinear pattern of pit alignments, possibly defining blocks of land associated with excavated Iron Age enclosures (Knight and Morris 1998; Knight and Southgate 2001).

Most excavated pit alignments in the Trent valley have yielded few if any associated finds – presumably reflecting their location some distance away from contemporary settlement foci generating domestic rubbish – even fewer of which are typologically diagnostic and in primary contexts, so dating is difficult. Origins for this boundary type in the early or mid first millennium BC may, however, be implied by pottery

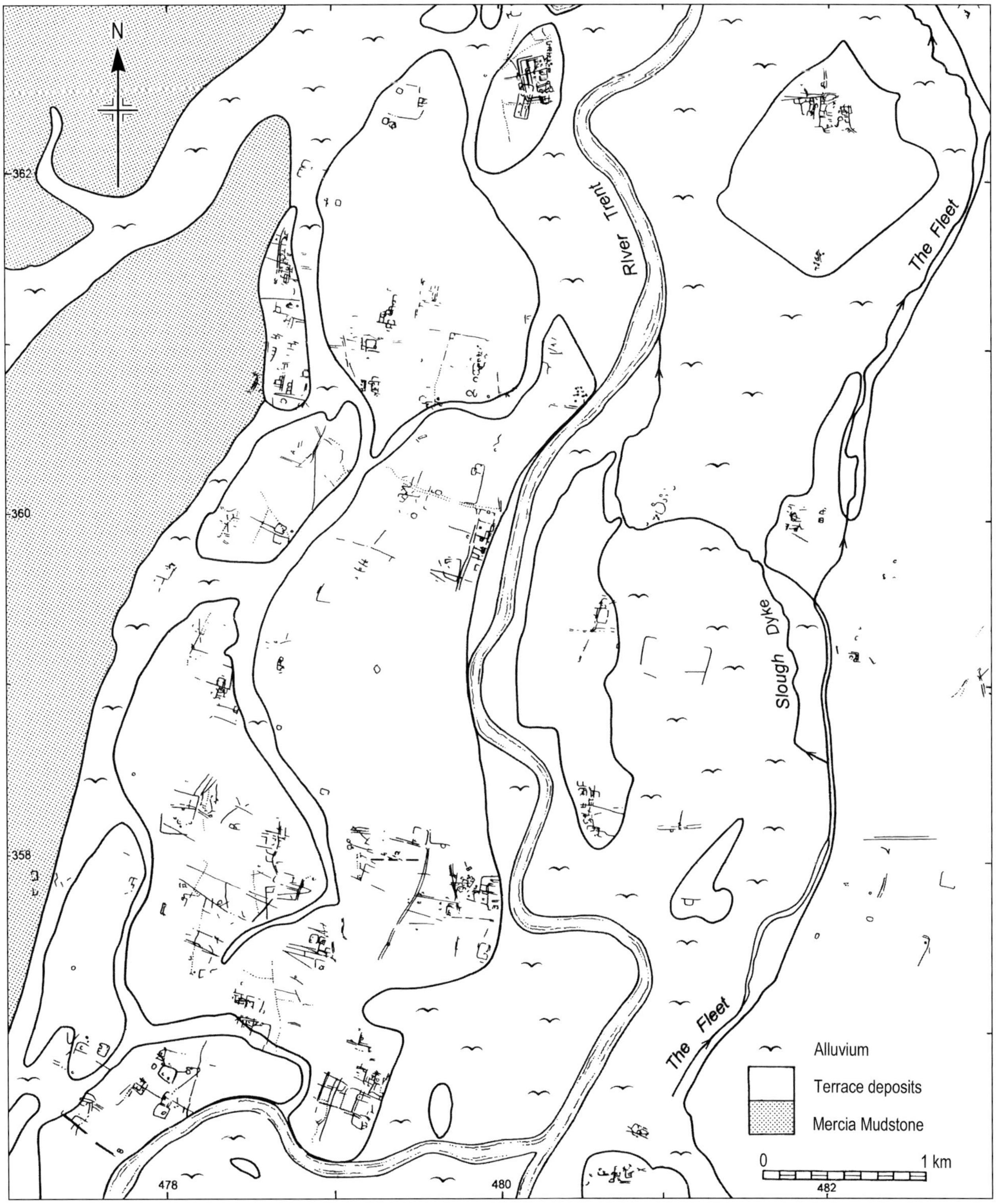

Fig. 13. Cropmarks of co-axial boundary systems and enclosures in the Trent valley to the north of Newark, Nottinghamshire (drawing: Jane Goddard, based on cropmark plots in Whimster 1989).

Fig. 14. Cropmark complex between North Muskham and Cromwell, Nottinghamshire, centred on a double pit alignment leading westwards from the River Trent to beyond the A1 (by permission of English Heritage NMR;Riley collection DNR 847/24).

recovered from an alignment at Aston Hill (Abbott and Garton 1995, 7), although the excavators themselves concluded that the sherds were probably redeposited from earlier activity (Garton and Abbott 1998). Over a hundred coarse quartz-gritted sherds were recovered during surface cleaning of the pits and from various depths within their fills, together with another nine typologically related sherds from a nearby ditch and gully. The sherds – which include fragments of pots with carinated and pronounced rounded girths, sometimes embellished with finger-nail incisions, and thin-walled vessels with finely tapered rims – invite close comparison with typical Late Bronze Age–Earlier Iron Age ceramic assemblages from the region. Their condition varies considerably, providing few clues to the depositional history of the collection, but an origin for this monument within the proposed ninth to fifth/fourth century BC date range of such ceramic assemblages (Knight 2002) cannot be ruled out.

The limited dating evidence from elsewhere in the Trent valley would support a predominantly later origin for pit alignments, broadly contemporary therefore with the proposed shift from open to enclosed settlement in the latter half of the first millennium BC. Several of the most informative ceramic associations come from a double alignment of staggered circular pits at Whitemoor Haye (Coates 2002, 13–15). Most of the pits had been recut at least once, but one feature (F509) yielded parts of the rim and base of two hand-made Iron Age ellipsoid jars in a deposit which had accumulated in the original bowl-shaped cut. Iron Age pottery was also retrieved from three recut pits, together with a granite rubber. The pottery from F526 comprised a group of three ellipsoid or globular vessels represented by large, moderately abraded sherds with many conjoins and, together with the 'large chunks' retrieved from F509, was interpreted as a deliberate placement, recalling structured deposits in Late Bronze Age–Earlier Iron Age pit alignments elsewhere in the Midlands and eastern England (Pollard 1996; Coates and Woodward 2002, 81–2; see also Rylatt and Bevan this volume). All of the pottery may be paralleled in Middle or Late Iron Age assemblages in the East Midlands. Support for a Later Iron Age date was provided by radiocarbon determinations of 400–155 cal. BC from pit F526 (2230 ± 60 BP; Beta-135227) and 410–340 and 320–205 cal. BC (2290 ± 50 BP; Beta-135226) from the primary fill of F537 (Coates 2002, appendix 1).

Important evidence for the late continuation of some pit alignments is provided by the discovery at Rampton of a line of pits forming one side of a large rectilinear enclosure dated firmly to the Roman period (Knight and Howard 2004, 144). A Roman date for the alignment may be postulated on the grounds of its spatial relationship to the ditches forming the remainder of this enclosure and the discovery at various levels in the fills of several pits of small quantities of Romano-British sherds. The discovery is of particular interest in view of the frequent association of pit alignments with the co-axial fields of the Trent valley near Newark, which it has been suggested above developed mainly in the Roman period, and provides useful support for the argument that pit alignments formed an integral element of the Roman boundary system in this area.

The generally late dating for the Trent valley pit alignments stands in sharp contrast to areas such as the Nene valley, where at Wollaston, Grendon, and elsewhere pit alignments – sometimes arranged in a co-axial pattern – were an important component of the early first millennium BC landscape (Meadows 1995). Further excavations may necessitate reappraisal of the chronology of the Trent valley alignments, but until new evidence is obtained a significantly later development may be postulated in this region by comparison with areas such as the Nene or Thames valleys – coinciding perhaps with the general progression from the mid first millennium BC towards an enclosed landscape.

Other linear boundaries

Two enigmatic linear earthworks, lying just beyond the eastern edge of the Trent valley, might support the case for the imposition of territorial boundaries from the Later Iron Age in this and neighbouring regions. Recent investigations along the Fosse Way between Newark and Lincoln identified two linear earthworks which may have been truncated by the Roman road: at Gallows Nooking Common, North Collingham, Nottinghamshire, within an area of predominantly Middle to Late Iron Age settlement; and at Sheep Walk Lodge, near Swinderby in Lincolnshire (Vyner forthcoming). At both sites, later boundaries were found to follow linear earthworks, which might correlate with pre-Roman land divisions.

The work at Gallows Nooking Common revealed a low earthen bank coinciding with the boundary between Nottinghamshire and Lincolnshire and those of North Collingham, Norton Disney, and Swinderby parishes (Knight 1991, 52–3). This somewhat sinuous bank converged towards the south-west with the Fosse Way, but to the north-east it diverged gradually from it before turning abruptly through *c.* 90° to form an alignment perpendicular to the road. This curious arrangement, which isolated a narrow, irregularly-shaped strip of North Collingham from the rest of the parish, suggested that the boundary may have been laid out prior to construction of the Fosse Way, and spurred excavations aimed at investigating the character and date of the bank and its relationship to the Roman road. A trench across the bank revealed a fairly slight construction, much disturbed by burrowing and root activity, flanked on its south-eastern side by a recut ditch yielding fragments of three Late Iron Age wheel-made vessels; in view of the large size and comparatively fresh condition of many of the sherds, these would appear to have been deliberately deposited (Kinsley 1993; Vyner forthcoming).

The close spatial relationship between bank and ditch may indicate that they had formed elements of a contemporary boundary work, although as only a few unstratified Iron Age and later sherds were recovered from the bank it cannot be closely dated. More recent excavations have recovered Late Iron Age sherds from other cuts across the flanking ditch, and have shown the bank to overlie ditches and gullies forming part of a Middle to Late Iron Age system of enclosures aligned obliquely to the bank. It was not possible to investigate the relationship of these sub-bank features to the flanking ditch. If the latter formed an integral component of the boundary, however, both bank and ditch might be argued to relate to a phase of Late Iron Age landscape reorganisation preceding construction of the Roman road (Vyner forthcoming).

The earthwork at Sheep Walk Lodge, some 4 km north-east of Gallows Nooking Common, also raises some difficult questions of interpretation (Knight 1991, 58–9; Vyner forthcoming). A low earthwork, flanked for part of its course by a ditch, may be observed running through woodland for some 370 m along the north-western edge of the Fosse Way, where it forms the boundary between the Lincolnshire parishes of Thurlby and Thorpe-on-the-Hill. A largely infilled ditch, which projects roughly at right angles from this earthwork near its north-eastern end, is also followed by a parish boundary, and creates a tiny triangle of land between the

Fosse Way and the earthwork, which makes little sense except as evidence for truncation by the Roman road of an earlier land boundary. A trench across the earthwork at its northern end, where it turns through a right angle to head north-westwards away from the Fosse, revealed an earthen bank associated with an outer ditch. No evidence of date was obtained, and hence the case for a pre-Roman origin must rest for the present upon its curious spatial relationship to the Fosse Way.

An Iron Age origin has also been suggested for a variety of multiple-ditched boundaries which have been identified from aerial surveys, including examples at Newton-on-Trent, Lincolnshire, and at Scotter and Scotton between the Rivers Eau and Trent (Boutwood 1998, 30–1). An Iron Age or earlier date for some of the boundary systems in the valley may be implied by recent work at Whitemoor Haye, although even here the evidence is equivocal. One of several trenches across an east–west triple-ditch alignment showed that it pre-dated a Romano-British trackway (Coates 2002, 18–20), although none of the relevant features yielded datable finds. More extensive excavations of the triple-ditch system also failed to recover associated artefacts. However, the positioning of these ditches parallel to, and between, a pair of double pit alignments, one argued above to date from the later first millennium BC, would favour the excavator's interpretation of these as part of a contemporary system of land allotment (Coates and Woodward 2002, 81–2).

The case for an Iron Age, or perhaps earlier, origin for at least some major linear boundaries within the region is strengthened by discoveries in neighbouring areas, where single, double, triple or quadruple-ditched boundaries, occasionally associated with earthworks, have been assigned dates from the Later Bronze Age to the Late Iron Age (Boutwood 1998, 37–9; Willis 2006). Notable examples include a triple-ditch system at Ketton, Rutland, which on the basis of associated pottery and metalwork may have experienced a long period of use commencing in the Late Bronze Age or Early Iron Age (Mackie 1993); and a pair of substantial ditches near Gretton, Northamptonshire. The latter yielded a remarkable collection of pottery spanning the transition from the Late Bronze Age–Earlier Iron Age to Earlier La Tène ceramic traditions (Jackson and Knight 1985).

A defensive function seems inappropriate for monuments of this type, which may have been designed instead to control and possibly also to channel movement (Boutwood 1998, 41). The concept of a dual function is particularly attractive in the context of the Gretton ditches. These seem excessively deep to have served only as trackways (Jackson and Knight 1998, fig. 5), and could have served both as a route of movement and as the physical manifestation of a boundary between neighbouring communities, perhaps symbolising and reinforcing group identity.

Conclusions: the mechanisms of change

It has been suggested that enclosures, rectilinear field systems, and networks of pit alignments are interrelated phenomena, indicative of increasing pressures upon finite pasture and arable resources and a growing demand for tighter control of the valley environment. The root causes of these pressures remain uncertain, but there are suggestions of a strong link with population growth and, in particular, demands for increased grazing. It has long been accepted that the population in many areas of lowland Britain increased significantly during the course of the first millennium BC, leading to infilling within established core areas and the colonisation of areas which in the early part of the millennium may not have been favoured for settlement (e.g. Smith 1977; 1978; Lambrick 1992, 80; Haselgrove 1999, 271–2).

These latter areas include the heavy boulder clays of the Nene–Ouse watershed (Knight 1984, 304) and the claylands of Leicestershire (Clay 2002), the exploitation of which may have been facilitated by the introduction of crops more suited to damp and heavy ground (Cunliffe 1991, 372) and changes in agricultural technology following the progressive adoption of iron tools for tillage.

Comparisons of the numbers of pottery collections attributed to successive ceramic phases obtained from sites in the Trent valley appear to support this view (compare Bishop 2001, 2).[2] Pottery attributable to the earlier traditions may have been less widely used, or may survive less often, but the contrasts in the frequencies of sites allotted to each ceramic phase are sufficiently striking to suggest that this is a genuine trend. The well-ordered systems of rectilinear fields and closely spaced enclosures that apparently existed in parts of the valley by the end of the Iron Age, notably in the area north of Newark, contrast strikingly with the thin scatters of seemingly amorphous unenclosed settlements that characterise the earlier first millennium BC.

It would be unwise to speculate on total population levels, but there is little reason to doubt a significant increase in relative population densities. This may have imposed significant strains upon carrying capacity, although in the Trent valley, where pasture may have represented the key agrarian resource, pressure on space may ultimately represent more a function of increasing stock levels and spiralling grazing needs than expansion of the human population (compare Lambrick 1992, 85).

We must also consider the possible impact upon carrying capacity of changes in the valley environment. As shown above, increasing wetness, progressive removal of the protective forest canopy, and the intensification of arable farming may have contributed to significantly higher rates of soil erosion in the river catchment, which in turn may have spurred the accumulation of deep alluvial and colluvial deposits. Although apparently mainly of Roman or later date, these deposits could have begun to accumulate from an earlier period. More research is required, but to Iron Age communities faced with deteriorating land resources, careful demarcation and rationalisation of these may have seemed the most appropriate strategy.

Acknowledgements

An earlier draft of this paper was presented at the Durham seminar and the paper was submitted for publication in 2003. Since that time, the author has published jointly with Andy Howard a geoarchaeological review of the Trent valley (Knight and Howard 2004), which incorporates a revised version of the discussion of settlements and boundary systems that formed the focus of the earlier draft. Thanks are extended to Bill Bevan, Mike Bishop, Andy Howard, Richard Hingley, Jonathan Last, Steve Willis, and Jim Williams for reading and commenting upon one or other of these texts. I am indebted to Bill Bevan, Peter Connolly, Lee Elliott, Daryl Garton, Graeme Guilbert, Andy Howard, Howard Jones, Gavin Kinsley, Patrick Marsden, Colm O'Brien, James Rackham, Blaise Vyner, and Dave Yates for unpublished information and to Dave Barrett and Mike Bishop for providing access to unpublished records in the Derbyshire and Nottinghamshire SMRs. Peter Marshall calibrated the radiocarbon dates. Jane Goddard prepared Figures 3, 4, 6–9, and 13. Steve Baker assisted with Figure 1 and produced Figure 5 from an original plot provided by Tony Johnson of Oxford Archae-otechnics. Figures 10–12 and 14 are reproduced by kind permission of English Heritage (NMR). Thanks finally to Colin Haselgrove and Tom Moore for assistance with editing the text.

Notes

1. The radiocarbon dates cited in this paper have been calibrated using OxCal v.3.5 and are quoted at 2 sigma.
2. Data summarised in www.arch.soton.ac.uk/Projects/default.asp?ProjectID=32.

Bibliography

Abbott, C. and Garton, D. 1995. *Report on the Archaeological Evaluations on the Proposed Site of a Borrow Pit on Aston Hill, Aston-upon-Trent, Derbyshire.* Unpublished report, Trent and Peak Archaeological Trust.

Avery, D.M.E., Sutton, J.E.G. and Banks, J.W. 1967. Rainsborough, Northants: excavations 1961–65, *Proceedings of the Prehistoric Society* 33, 207–306.

Badcock, A. and Symonds, J. 1994. *Archaeological Field Evaluation of Land at Styrrup Hall Farm, Styrrup, Nottinghamshire.* Unpublished ARCUS Report.

Barnatt, J. 1987. Bronze Age settlement on the East Moors of the Peak District of Derbyshire and South Yorkshire, *Proceedings of the Prehistoric Society* 53, 393–418.

Barnatt, J., Bevan, B. and Edmonds, M. 2002. Gardom's Edge: a landscape through time, *Antiquity* 76, 51–56.

Beamish, M. 2001. Excavations at Willington, south Derbyshire. Interim report, *Derbyshire Archaeological Journal* 121, 1–18.

Beamish, M. and Ripper, S. 2000. Burnt mounds in the East Midlands, *Antiquity* 74, 37–38.

Bevan, B. 1997. Bounding the landscape: place and identity during the Yorkshire Wolds Iron Age, in Gwilt and Haselgrove 1997, 181–191.

Bevan, B. 1999a. Land-life-death-regeneration: interpreting a middle Iron Age landscape in eastern Yorkshire, in Bevan 1999b, 123–147.

Bevan, B. (ed.) 1999b. *Northern Exposure: Interpretative Devolution and the Iron Ages in Britain.* Leicester: Leicester Archaeology Monograph 4.

Bewley, R.H. (ed.) 1998. *Lincolnshire's Archaeology from the Air.* Lincoln: Occasional Papers in Lincolnshire History and Archaeology 11.

Bishop, M. 2001. An archaeological resource assessment of the first millennium BC in Nottinghamshire, *East Midlands Archaeological Research Framework Project*, http://www.le.ac.uk/archaeology/east-_midlands_research_framework.htm.

Boutwood, Y. 1998. Prehistoric linear boundaries in Lincolnshire and its fringes, in Bewley 1998, 29–46.

Brindley, A.L. and Lanting, J.N. 1990, The dating of fulachta fiadh, in Buckley 1990, 55–56.

Brown, G., Field, D. and McOmish, D. 1994. East Chisenbury midden complex, in A.P. Fitzpatrick and E.L. Morris (eds), *The Iron Age in Wessex: Recent Work*, 46–49. Salisbury: Trust for Wessex Archaeology.

Buckland, P.C. and Sadler, J. 1985. The nature of Late Flandrian alluviation in the Humberhead Levels, *East Midlands Geographer* 8, 239–251.

Buckley, V.M. (ed.) 1990. *Burnt Offerings: International Contributions to Burnt Mound Archaeology.* Dublin: Wordwell.

Chadwick, A. 1999. Digging ditches, but missing riches? Ways into the Iron Age and Romano-British cropmark landscapes of the north Midlands, in Bevan 1999b, 149–171.

Challis, A.J. and Harding, D.W. 1975. *Later Prehistory from the Trent to the Tyne.* Oxford: British Archaeological Reports British Series 20.

Charles, B.M., Parkinson, A. and Foreman, S. 2000. A Bronze Age ditch and Iron Age settlement at Elms Farm, Humberstone, Leicester, *Transactions of the Leicestershire Archaeological and Historical Society* 74, 113–220.

Ciaraldi, M. 2002. Plant macroremains, in Coates 2002, 62–66.

Clay, P. 1985. A survey of two cropmark sites at Lockington-Hemington, Leicestershire, *Transactions of the Leicestershire Archaeological and Historical Society* 59, 17–26.

Clay, P. 1992. An Iron Age farmstead at Grove Farm, Enderby, Leicestershire, *Transactions of the Leicestershire Archaeological and Historical Society* 66, 1–82.

Clay, P. 2002. *The Prehistory of the East Midlands Claylands.* Leicester: Leicester Archaeology Monograph 9.

Coates, G. 2002. *A Prehistoric and Romano-British Landscape. Excavations at Whitemoor Haye Quarry, Staffordshire, 1997–1999.* Oxford: British Archaeological Reports British Series 340.

Coates, G. and Woodward, A. 2002. Discussion, in Coates 2002, 79–90.

Cooper, N. (ed.) 2006. *East Midlands Archaeology: An Archaeological Resource Assessment and Research Agenda*. Leicester: Leicester Archaeology Monograph 13.

Coward, J. and Ripper, S. 1999. Castle Donington. Willow Farm (SK 445 288), *Transactions of the Leicestershire Archaeological and Historical Society* 73, 87–91.

Cunliffe, B. 1991. *Iron Age Communities in Britain* (3rd edn). London: Routledge.

Cunnington, M.E. 1923. *The Early Iron Age Inhabited Site at All Cannings Cross Farm, Wiltshire*. Devizes: George Simpson and Co. Ltd.

Eccles, J., Caldwell, P. and Mincher, R. 1988. Salvage excavation at a Romano-British site at Chainbridge Lane, Lound, Nottinghamshire, 1985, *Transactions of the Thoroton Society* 92, 15–21.

Elliott, L. and Knight, D. 1997. Further excavations of an Iron Age and Romano-British settlement near Gonalston, Nottinghamshire, *Transactions of the Thoroton Society* 101, 65–72.

Elliott, L. and Knight, D. 1998. A burnt mound at Holme Dyke, Gonalston, Nottinghamshire, *Transactions of the Thoroton Society* 102, 15–22.

Elliott, L. and Knight, D. 1999. An early Mesolithic site and first millennium BC settlement and pit alignments at Swarkestone Lowes, Derbyshire, *Derbyshire Archaeological Journal* 119, 79–153.

Elliott, L. and Knight, D. 2002. Gonalston Holme Dyke, *Transactions of the Thoroton Society* 106, 14–89.

Elliott, L. and Knight, D. 2003. Hoveringham Gonalston Lane, *Transactions of the Thoroton Society* 107, 20–22.

Elsdon, S. 1997. *Old Sleaford Revealed*. Oxford: Oxbow Monograph 78.

Elsdon, S. and Knight, D. 2003. The Iron Age pottery, in N. Field and M. Parker Pearson 2003, *Fiskerton. An Iron Age Timber Causeway with Iron Age and Roman Votive Offerings*, 87–92. Oxford: Oxbow Books.

Enright, D. and Thomas, A. 1998. Wellingborough, land off Wilby Way, *South Midlands Archaeology* 28, 31–32.

Fulford, M. and Nichols, E. (eds) 1992. *Developing Landscapes of Lowland Britain. The Archaeology of the British Gravels: a Review*. London: Society of Antiquaries of London Occasional Paper 14.

Gale, R. 2002. Charcoal, in Coates 2002, 74–78.

Garton, D. 1987. Dunston's Clump and the brickwork plan field systems at Babworth, Nottinghamshire: excavations 1981, *Transactions of the Thoroton Society* 91, 16–73.

Garton, D. 1993. A burnt mound at Waycar Pasture, Girton, Nottinghamshire: an interim report, *Transactions of the Thoroton Society* 97, 148–149.

Garton, D. 2002. Walking the fields: the results of the South Muskham field walking survey 1992–7 and some implications for the interpretation of Romano-British cropmark landscapes in Nottinghamshire, *Transactions of the Thoroton Society* 106, 17–39.

Garton, D. and Abbott, C. 1998. Aston Hill, *Derbyshire Archaeological Journal* 118, 150.

Garton, D. and Salisbury, C.R. 1995. A Romano-British wood-lined well at Wild Goose Cottage, Lound, Nottinghamshire, *Transactions of the Thoroton Society* 99, 15–43.

Greig, J. 2002. Waterlogged seeds, in Coates 2002, 72–74.

Guilbert, G. 2004. Borough Hill, Walton-upon-Trent – if not a hill fort, then what? *Derbyshire Archaeological Journal* 124, 248–257.

Guilbert, G. and Malone, S. 1994. Potlock cursus, in D. Knight (ed.), *A564 Derby Southern Bypass. Summary of Rescue Archaeological Works at Aston Cursus, Potlock Cursus and Swarkestone Lowes*, 13–18. Unpublished report, Trent and Peak Archaeological Trust.

Gwilt, A. 1997. Popular practices from material culture: a case study of the Iron Age settlement at Wakerley, in Gwilt and Haselgrove 1997, 153–166.

Gwilt, A. and Haselgrove, C. (eds) 1997. *Reconstructing Iron Age Societies*. Oxford: Oxbow Monograph 71.

Hampton, J. 1975. The organization of aerial photography in Britain, in D.R.Wilson (ed.), *Aerial Reconnaissance for Archaeology*, 118–125. London: Council for British Archaeology Research Report 12.

Hamshaw-Thomas, J. 1992. *Aslockton, Nottinghamshire: Faunal Analysis*. Unpublished report, Trent and Peak Archaeological Trust.

Haselgrove, C. 1999. Iron Age societies in central Britain: retrospect and prospect, in Bevan 1999b, 253–275.

Henderson, J. 1992. Glass bead, in Knight 1992, 68–70.

Hill, J.D. 1995. *Ritual and Rubbish in the Iron Age of Wessex*. Oxford: British Archaeological Reports British Series 242.

Hingley, R. 1990. Boundaries surrounding Iron Age and Romano-British settlements, *Scottish Archaeological Review* 7, 96–103.

Hingley, R. 1999. The creation of later prehistoric landscapes and the context of reuse of Neolithic and earlier Bronze Age monuments in Britain and Ireland, in Bevan 1999b, 233–251.

Hodder, M.A. and Barfield, L.H. (eds) 1991. *Burnt Mounds and Hot Stone Technology*. West Bromwich: Sandwell Metropolitan Borough Council.

Howard, A.J. and Knight, D. 2001. *South Ing Close, Rampton, Nottinghamshire. Auger Survey of the Floodplain Deposits*. Unpublished report, Trent and Peak Archaeological Unit.

Howard, A.J., Hunt, C.O., Rushworth, G., Smith, D. and Smith, W. 1999. *Girton Quarry Northern Extension: Palaeobiological and Dating Assessment of Organic Samples collected during Stage 1 Geoarchaeological Evaluations*. Unpublished report, Trent and Peak Archaeological Unit.

Hughes, G. 1998. *The Excavation of an Iron Age Settlement at Covert Farm (DIRFT East), Crick, Northamptonshire. Post-excavation Assessment and Updated Research Design*. Unpublished report, Birmingham University Field Archaeology Unit.

Hughes, G. 1999. The excavation of an Iron Age cropmark site at Foxcovert Farm, Aston-on-Trent 1994, *Derbyshire Archaeological Journal* 119, 176–188.

Hughes, G. 2000. *The Lockington Gold Hoard. An Early Bronze Age Barrow Cemetery at Lockington, Leicestershire*. Oxford: Oxbow Books.

Hull, G. 2000–1. A Late Bronze Age ringwork, pits and later features at Thrapston, Northamptonshire, *Northamptonshire Archaeology* 29, 73–92.

Jackson, D.A. 1975. An Iron Age site at Twywell, Northamptonshire, *Northamptonshire Archaeology* 10, 31–93.

Jackson, D.A. 1976. Two Iron Age sites north of Kettering, Northamptonshire, *Northamptonshire Archaeology* 11, 71–88.

Jackson, D.A. and Knight, D. 1985. An early Iron Age and Beaker site near Gretton, Northants, *Northamptonshire Archaeology* 20, 67–85.

Jones, H. 2002. Brough, Glebe Farm, *Transactions of the Thoroton Society* 106, 147–148.

Kenyon, K.M. 1952. A survey of the evidence concerning the chronology and origins of Iron Age 'A' in southern and midland Britain, *Bulletin of the Institute of Archaeology University of London* 8, 29–78.

Kinsley, G. 1993. *Evaluation Excavations at Gallows Nooking Common, Nottinghamshire: Summary Report*. Unpublished report, Trent and Peak Archaeological Trust.

Kinsley G. 1998. Interim report on archaeological watching briefs and excavations at Girton Quarry Extension, Newark, *Tarmac Papers* 2, 41–49.

Knight, D. 1984. *Late Bronze Age and Iron Age Settlement in the Nene and Great Ouse Basins*. Oxford: British Archaeological Reports British Series 130.

Knight, D. 1991. *Archaeology of the Fosse Way. Implications of the Proposed Dualling of the A46 between Newark and Lincoln*. Unpublished report, Trent and Peak Archaeological Trust.

Knight, D. 1992. Excavations of an Iron Age settlement at Gamston, Nottinghamshire, *Transactions of the Thoroton Society* 96, 16–90.

Knight, D. 2000a. *An Iron Age and Romano-British Settlement at Moor Pool Close, Rampton, Nottinghamshire*. Unpublished report, Trent and Peak Archaeological Trust.

Knight, D. 2000b. Rampton, Moor Pool Close, *Transactions of the Thoroton Society* 104,159–160.

Knight, D. 2002. A regional ceramic sequence: pottery of the first millennium BC between the Humber and the Nene, in Woodward and Hill 2002, 119–142.

Knight, D. and Howard, A.J. 1994. The Trent valley Survey, *Transactions of the Thoroton Society* 98, 126–129.

Knight, D. and Howard, A.J. 1995. *Archaeology and Alluvium in the Trent Valley: an Archaeological Assessment of the Floodplain and Gravel Terraces*. Nottingham: Trent and Peak Archaeological Trust.

Knight, D. and Howard, A.J. 2004. *Trent Valley Landscapes*. Kings Lynn: Heritage Marketing and Publications Ltd.

Knight, D. and Malone, S. 1997. *Evaluation of a Late Iron Age and Romano-British Settlement and Palaeochannels of the Trent at Chapel Farm, Shardlow and Great Wilne, Derbyshire*. Unpublished report, Trent and Peak Archaeological Trust.

Knight, D. and Malone, S. 1998. *Further Evaluations of an Iron Age and Romano-British Settlement and Fluvial Features at Chapel Farm, Shardlow and Great Wilne, Derbyshire*. Unpublished report, Trent and Peak Archaeological Trust.

Knight, D. and Morris, T. 1998. Fernello Sitch, *Derbyshire Archaeological Journal* 118, 156–157.

Knight, D. and Priest, V. 1998. Excavations of a Romano-British field system at Lamb's Close, Kelham, Nottinghamshire, *Transactions of the Thoroton Society* 102, 27–37.

Knight, D. and Southgate, M. 2001. Barrow-upon-Trent: Fleak Close and Captain's Pingle, *Derbyshire Archaeological Journal* 121, 201–202.

Knight, D., Marsden, P. and Carney, J. 2003. Local or non-local? Prehistoric granodiorite-tempered pottery in the East Midlands, in A. Gibson (ed.), *Prehistoric Pottery. People, Pattern and Purpose*, 111–125. Oxford: British Archaeological Reports International Series 1156.

Lambrick, G. 1992. The development of late prehistoric and Roman farming on the Thames gravels, in Fulford and Nichols 1992, 78–105.

Lambrick, G. and Robinson, M. 1979. *Iron Age and Roman Riverside Settlements at Farmoor, Oxfordshire*. London: Council for British Archaeology Research Report 32.

Lane, T. forthcoming. *Prehistoric Sites from the Fenland Management Project in Lincolnshire*. Lincoln: Lincolnshire Archaeology Heritage Report Series.

Lawson, A.J. 2000. *Potterne 1982–5: Animal Husbandry in Later Prehistoric Wiltshire*. Salisbury: Wessex Archaeology Report 17.

Losco-Bradley, S. and Kinsley, G. 2002. *Catholme. An Anglo-Saxon settlement on the Trent Gravels in Staffordshire*. Nottingham: Department of Archaeology, University of Nottingham.

Machin, M.L. and Beswick P. 1975. Further excavations of the enclosure at Swine Sty, Big Moor, Baslow, and a report on the shale industry at Swine Sty, *Transactions of the Hunter Archaeological Society* 10, 204–211.

Mackie, D. 1993. Prehistoric ditch systems at Ketton and Tixover, Rutland, *Transactions of the Leicestershire Archaeological and Historical Society* 67, 1–14.

May, J. 1970. An Iron Age square enclosure at Aston-upon-Trent, Derbyshire: a report on excavations in 1967, *Derbyshire Archaeological Journal* 90, 10–21.

May, J. 1984. The major settlements of the later Iron Age in Lincolnshire, in N. Field and A.J. White (eds), *A Prospect of Lincolnshire*, 18–22. Lincoln: N. Field and A.J. White.

May, J. 1996. *Dragonby. Report on Excavations at an Iron Age and Romano-British Settlement in North Lincolnshire*. Oxford: Oxbow Monograph 61.

McElearney, G. 1991. *Pollen Analysis from Scaftworth Roman Road Excavations, 1991*. Unpublished report, University of Sheffield Archaeological Services.

Meadows, I. 1995. Wollaston, *South Midlands Archaeology* 25, 41–45.

Meek, J. 1995. *The Excavation of a Pit Complex at Lockington-Hemington, Leicestershire*. University of Leicester Archaeological Services Report 95/981.

Moffett, L. 1992. *Charred plant remains*, in Knight 1992, 79–82.

Moffett, L. 1993. *Plant Remains from Aslockton*. Unpublished report, Trent and Peak Archaeological Trust.

Monckton, A. 2006. Environmental archaeology in the East Midlands, in Cooper 2006, 259–286.

O'Brien, C. 1978a. Land and settlement in Nottinghamshire and Lowland Derbyshire. An archaeological review, *East Midlands Archaeological Bulletin* 12, Supplement.

O'Brien, C. 1978b. Excavations at Holme Pierrepont, *Transactions of the Thoroton Society* 82, 76.

O'Brien, C. 1979a. Iron Age and Romano-British settlement in the Trent basin, in B.C. Burnham and H.B. Johnson (eds), *Invasion and Response. The Case of Roman Britain*, 299–313. Oxford: British Archaeological Reports British Series 73.

O'Brien, C. 1979b. *Excavations at Holme Pierrepont Site 4*. Unpublished report, Trent Valley Archaeological Research Committee.

Palmer-Brown, C. and Knight, D. 1993. Excavations of an Iron Age and Romano-British settlement at Aslockton, Nottinghamshire: interim report, *Transactions of the Thoroton Society* 97, 146–147.

Parker Pearson, M. and Sydes, R.E. 1997. The Iron Age enclosures and prehistoric landscape of Sutton Common, South Yorkshire, *Proceedings of the Prehistoric Society* 63, 221–259.

Piggott, S. 1958. Native economies and the Roman occupation of north Britain, in I.A. Richmond (ed.), *Roman and Native in North Britain*, 1–27. London: Nelson.

Pollard, J. 1996. Iron Age riverside pit alignments at St Ives, Cambridgeshire, *Proceedings of the Prehistoric Society* 62, 93–115.

Ponsford, M.W. 1992. A late Iron Age and Romano-British settlement at Rampton, Nottinghamshire, *Transactions of the Thoroton Society* 96, 91–122.

Proctor, J. 2001. Late Bronze Age/Early Iron Age placed deposits from Westcroft Road, Carshalton: their meaning and interpretation, *Surrey Archaeological Collections* 89, 65–103.

Pryor, F. 1996. Sheep stockyards and field systems: Bronze Age livestock populations in the Fenlands of eastern England, *Antiquity* 70, 313–324.

Pryor, F. 1998. *Farmers in Prehistoric Britain*. Stroud: Tempus.

Reynolds, P.J. 1974. Experimental Iron Age storage pits: an interim report, *Proceedings of the Prehistoric Society* 40, 118–131.

Riley, D.N. 1980. *Early Landscape from the Air: Studies of Cropmarks in South Yorkshire and North Nottinghamshire*. Sheffield: Department of Archaeology and Prehistory, University of Sheffield.

Riley, D.N., Buckland, P.C. and Wade, J.S. 1995. Aerial reconnaissance and excavation at Littleborough-on-Trent, Notts, *Britannia* 26, 253–284.

RCHME. 1960. *A Matter of Time. An Archaeological Survey of the River Gravels of England*. London: HMSO.

Samuels, J. and Buckland, P.C. 1978. A Romano-British settlement at Sandtoft, South Humberside, *Yorkshire Archaeological Journal* 50, 65–75.

Scaife, R. 1999, *Gonalston: Pollen Analysis of the Bronze Age and Romano-British Features*. Unpublished report, Trent and Peak Archaeological Unit.

Simmons, B.B. 1963. Iron Age hill forts in Nottinghamshire, *Transactions of the Thoroton Society* 67, 9–20.

Smith, C.A. 1977. The valleys of the Tame and middle Trent – their populations and ecology during the late first millennium BC, in J.R. Collis (ed.) 1977, *The Iron Age in Britain: a Review*, 51–61. Sheffield: J.R. Collis Publications.

Smith, C.A. 1978. The landscape and natural history of Iron Age settlement on the Trent gravels, in B. Cunliffe and T. Rowley (eds) 1978, *Lowland Iron Age Communities in Europe*, 91–101. Oxford: British Archaeological Reports International Series 48.

Smith, C.A (ed.) 1979. *Fisherwick. The Reconstruction of an Iron Age Landscape*. Oxford: British Archaeological Reports British Series 61.

Smith, D. 2002. Insect remains, in Coates 2002, 67–72.

Smith, D., Roseff, R. and Butler, S. 2001. The sediments, pollen, plant macrofossils and insects from a Bronze Age channel fill at Yoxall Bridge, Staffordshire, *Environmental Archaeology* 6, 1–12.

Stead, I.M. 1991. *Iron Age Cemeteries in East Yorkshire*. London: English Heritage Archaeological Report 22.

Thomas, R. 1997. Land, kinship relations and the rise of enclosed settlement in first millennium BC Britain, *Oxford Journal of Archaeology* 16, 211–217.

Vyner, B. (ed.) forthcoming. *Archaeology on the A46 Fosse Way: Newark–Lincoln*. York: Council for British Archaeology Research Report.

Wardle, C. 2003. The Late Bronze Age and Iron Age in Staffordshire: the torc of the Midlands? *West Midlands Regional Research Framework for Archaeology*. http://www.arch-ant.bham.ac.uk/wmrrfa/sem2.htm.

Wheeler, H. 1979. Excavations at Willington, Derbyshire, 1970–2, *Derbyshire Archaeological Journal* 99, 58–220.

Whimster, R. 1989. *The Emerging Past. Air Photography and the Buried Landscape*. London: RCHME.

Whimster, R. 1992. Aerial photography and the British gravels: an agenda for the 1990s, in Fulford and Nichols 1992, 1–14.

Wigley, A. 2003. Touching the void: Iron Age landscapes and settlement in the West Midlands, *West Midlands Regional Research Framework for Archaeology*. http://www.arch-ant.bham.ac.uk/wmrrfa/sem2.htm.

Willis, S.H. 1999. Without and within: aspects of culture and community in the Iron Age of north-eastern England, in Bevan 1999b, 81–110.

Willis, S.H. 2006. The Later Bronze Age and Iron Age, in Cooper 2006, 89–136.

Winton, H. 1998. The cropmark evidence for prehistoric and Roman settlement in west Lincolnshire, in Bewley 1998, 47–68.

Woodhouse, G. 1993. *Tarmac Hoveringham: Archive Report*. Unpublished report, Trent and Peak Archaeological Trust.

Woodward, A. and Hill, J.D. (eds) 2002. *Prehistoric Britain: the Ceramic Basis*. Oxford: Oxbow Books.

Yates, D. 2007. *Land, Power and Prestige. Bronze Age Field Systems in Southern England*. Oxford: Oxbow Books.

Zeepvat, R.J. (ed.) 2000. *Three Iron Age and Romano-British Rural Settlements on English Gravels: Excavations at Hatford (Oxfordshire), Besthorpe (Nottinghamshire) and Eardington (Shropshire) undertaken by Tempvs Reparatvm between 1991 and 1993*. Oxford: British Archaeological Reports 312.

Realigning the world: pit alignments and their landscape context

Jim Rylatt and Bill Bevan

In this paper we discuss Later Iron Age pit alignments with reference to two examples situated in upland and lowland landscapes in the East Midlands, which the authors were recently involved in excavating (Fig. 1). Pit alignments are enigmatic because their form does not immediately betray their function. Unlike ditches, they do not appear to create effective barriers dividing the land surface; equally they do not facilitate drainage of surface and groundwater, nor can they be easily categorised as storage or rubbish pits. This ambiguity has led to two common approaches to their interpretation. One tack has been to countenance a functional explanation, and by ignoring the above *caveats* it has been proposed that they facilitated stock control, were Neolithic tree planting pits, or that they comprised an initial phase of ditch digging and/or bank construction (Halliday *et al.* 1981; Halliday 1982; Barber 1985; Pickering 1992). The other approach has been to set aside notions of pure functionality and refer to symbolic and ritual properties, although the ritual is left largely undefined (J. Pollard 1996; Waddington 1997). However, both approaches are somewhat unsatisfactory and have left pit alignments largely in limbo as a strange category of monument, which is not satisfactorily integrated into a site or landscape interpretation.

When alignments are placed in the context of their

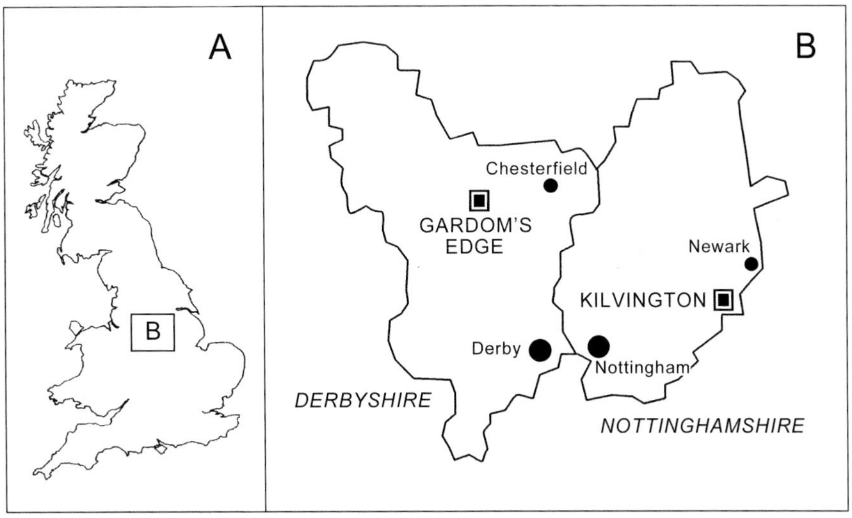

Fig. 1. Location of Kilvington and Gardom's Edge (drawing: Jim Rylatt)

surrounding landscape more informed interpretations seem possible. A later Bronze Age pit alignment at Heslerton, North Yorkshire, served as a significant landscape division and a focus for open settlement (Powlesland 1986). It was later redefined by a ditch that formed part of the major boundary system characterising the heavily enclosed late prehistoric landscape of the region, and Powlesland has suggested that much of the Yorkshire Wolds dyke system was initially laid out as a series of pit alignments. This view is mirrored by Pryor (1993) for the 'enclosure' of the Fenland basin, and by Boutwood (1998) for the creation of the multiple ditch systems of western Lincolnshire. These alignments may be thought of as social boundaries, dug by local communities to define relationships with the land, with each other and with water.

As with all types of features that archaeologists need to classify to aid understanding, we must see beyond our own broad categories and at the same time avoid blanket interpretations that treat the whole distribution as a unit of study. In comparison to the prehistoric communities we study, archaeologists benefit from an over-arching view of material culture with the advantage of being able to see national distributions on a single plan, and the hindsight of long-term time frames. An individual living in the Iron Age would not benefit from these privileged viewpoints, perspectives that nevertheless tend to over-simplify the past and, crucially, lose an understanding of how a community may choose to build and maintain their own pit alignment within the context of their landscape of experienced inhabitation.

To gain some insight into the purpose of Later Iron Age alignments it is necessary to review their distribution, date, form and their locally constituted landscape relationships. Although this paper is primarily concerned with monuments created toward the end of the Iron Age, only a relatively small number of pit alignments have been excavated, and even fewer are securely dated. As a consequence, data obtained from comparable features that were created prior to the Late Iron Age have been incorporated into the next two sections in order to obtain a meaningful overview.

Distribution and dating

Pit alignments are a common component of later prehistoric landscapes in the Midlands and the Yorkshire Wolds, with further examples in the Welsh Borders and eastern Scotland (Wilson 1978). In contrast, they are largely absent from East Anglia, Kent, much of Wessex, and Cumbria. This uneven distribution suggests that this architectural form had an intrinsic meaning that was actively employed or avoided by different social groups.

Examination of excavation reports suggests that pit alignments were first created in the Late Neolithic (e.g. Burgess 1976; Harding 1981), with the tradition continuing into the Anglo-Saxon period (Powlesland 1986). It is, however, apparent that the term 'pit alignment' is, at present, too inclusive, as it embraces two types of feature with contrasting forms. While the individual components of Neolithic 'pit alignments' are broadly comparable in size, shape and inter-relationships to those constituting later examples, their fills are distinctly different. The Neolithic pits appear to have been deliberately backfilled to consolidate and support a series of posts, possibly to create avenues linking ritual monuments (Harding 1981; Miket 1981; Waddington 1997; see also Holm, Dumfriesshire: Thomas 1998). In contrast, the rows of pits created from the Late Bronze Age onwards contain deposits that are indicative of gradual accumulation in pits that were left open to fill naturally. It therefore seems that there is a specific class of Later Neolithic monument that would be less ambiguously described as a 'post alignment' and so we will have no more to do with them here.

The majority of the 'open' pit alignments appear to have been created between the Late Bronze Age and the consolidation of Roman control in lowland Britain. Nevertheless, dating is often difficult due to the paucity of finds within the pit fills. This dearth may partly be a consequence of location, as pit alignments are often sited away from the immediate environs of contemporary settlement, but is it also likely to reflect considered and deliberate depositional practices. At Heslerton, the stratigraphic relationships and artefactual material associated with the earliest alignment on the site indicated a construction date between the ninth and seventh centuries BC (Powlesland 1986). Similarly, at Tallington, Lincolnshire, the relationships between a pit alignment and earlier or later features were indicative of a Late Bronze Age to Early Iron Age date (French *et. al.* 1993). At St Ives, Cambridgeshire, radiocarbon dates ranging from the eighth to mid second centuries BC were obtained from waterlogged organic materials in the basal fills of the pits (J. Pollard 1996).[1] The impressive double pit alignment excavated near Shorncote, Gloucestershire, is also of Late Bronze Age or Early Iron Age date (see Hey this volume).

There is also substantial evidence for Later Iron Age to early Romano-British activity, indicating either the original creation, or the later recutting and reworking, of alignments. Dates obtained from secondary fills are more common, and tend to be somewhat later than those mentioned above. For example, a charcoal-rich deposit in pit 7 at Eskbank Nurseries, Dalkeith, was radiocarbon dated to the mid fourth century BC–later first century AD (Barber 1985).[2] At Plant's Farm, Maxey, Cambridgeshire, a Middle Iron Age vessel was recovered from pit 13, suggesting a fourth- to late second-century BC date for deposition (Gurney *et al.* 1993). Frequently, the dating is even more general, as late prehistoric pottery typologies are often imprecise. For example, 'Iron Age' pottery was recovered from the upper fills of five pits in a double alignment at Swarkestone Lowes, Derbyshire (Elliott and Knight 1999). The secondary fills of a pit alignment at Cat Babbleton Farm, North Yorkshire, contained pottery spanning the Late Iron Age and Romano-British periods, the assemblage being biased toward the second–fourth centuries AD (Cardwell 1989).

More recently, a clay-lined pit alignment on Gardom's Edge, Derbyshire, has been radiocarbon dated and placed firmly in the Later Iron Age. Determinations were taken from two samples, one being a peaty basal fill within one of the pits, the second being the old ground surface lying immediately below the bank of upcast material excavated from the same pit. Both samples produced the same date of 350 cal. BC–cal. AD 10 (2 sigma).

Form, function and the possible significance of water

Although pit alignments exhibit a degree of variability, both within and between individual monuments, they share a series of traits that allow a generalised characterisation. The pits are generally circular, sub-oval or sub-rectangular in plan, and usually around 1.0–2.0 m across. Their profiles are more inconsistent, and range from examples with steep sides and flat bases, to others having bowl-shaped cross-sections. The pits have a distinct and clear linear arrangement, with each example being separated from its neighbours by causeways that were usually between 1.0 and 2.0 m in width. The very presence of these gaps lies behind the difficulties in interpretation and determination of the purpose of pit alignments.

There is a general lack of evidence for associated hedges or fences. Combined with the frequency and width of causeways, this implies that the alignment would not have functioned as an effective stock-proof boundary. Consequently, the idea that the pits were merely quarries used to create adjacent banks has been readily accepted (Halliday *et al.* 1981; Barber 1985; French *et al.* 1993). This hypothesis attempts to make sense in functional terms of the explicitly unfunctional behaviour exhibited by an unambiguously discontinuous linear feature – i.e. the idea that, as the causeways provided multiple routes of passage across the alignment, the banks must have formed the barrier (Pryor 1993).

The few pit alignments that survive as earthworks do not support the proposal that the pits were incidental to the creation of a bank. The banks flanking alignments at Marygoldhill Plantation, Berwick (Halliday 1982), Easington High Moor, North Yorkshire (Lofthouse 1993; Vyner 1994), and Gardom's Edge (Rylatt 1999) are all insubstantial, and probably always have been. Additionally, there is relatively little evidence from excavated sites for bank deposits eroding back into the pits. This again suggests that banks were never particularly high or steep sided, as at Long Bennington, Lincolnshire (Fearn 1993) or Swarkestone Lowes (Elliott and Knight 1999). It is also significant that where pit alignments meet at right angles, the pits remain evenly spaced; there is no break in either row that would allow flanking banks to meet and form an effective barrier (e.g. Boutwood 1998). Finally, as many archaeologists can personally attest, the digging of a series of pits is usually more labour-intensive than extracting material from a continuous ditch. Using this method purely to generate bank material again confounds notions of pure functionality.

The rows of pits are a consciously implemented design feature chosen from a range of possibilities (Pryor 1993). If the design is functionally inefficient, in that it allows relative ease of movement across the boundary, then it is necessary to look to other attributes of the monument to explain its purpose. A pit alignment would have been a man-made, linear feature that could be easily distinguished from a ditch or hedge, even with the most cursory of visual inspections. This implies that the distinctive physical appearance would have signified a particular class of landscape division. The fact that these monuments were constructed over large areas of Britain and for an extended period of time implies that they were imprinted with a series of inherent properties that were almost universally understood. However, it is probable that individual communities manipulated different aspects of this embedded social meaning to serve specific interests and objectives.

The deliberate clay lining identified in pits at Gardom's Edge provides a starting point for an exploration of the possible social attributes of pit alignments. The presence of an impermeable membrane appears to indicate intent to contain water, a purpose for which pits are better suited than a ditch, as the latter would tend to channel water away. The alignment on Gardom's Edge crosses clays and sands, which have varying potentials to collect or drain water downwards. On days of high rainfall the excavated pits became full of water, which did not readily drain. Unexcavated pits, preserved as shallow depressions, also collected water on their surface (Fig. 2). The result in both cases was to create reflective watery pools.

A layer of puddled clay also coated the walls of two pits at Kilvington, Nottinghamshire, which had been cut into a localised deposit of sandy drift (Rylatt 2001). Clay linings do not appear to be paralleled in other excavated pit alignments, but in some instances, naturally occurring heavy subsoils and drift deposits would have operated in the same way; this was certainly apparent along the rest of the Kilvington alignment, where the clay substrate retained rainfall in any excavated pits. Furthermore, pollen extracted from the fills of four of these pits indicated that they contained water for extended periods of time, as aquatic and marsh taxa constituted a large proportion of each sample (*ibid.*). Elsewhere, the black organic fills and preserved wood found in pits at Messingham, Lincolnshire, provide more conclusive evidence of waterlogging (Laskey 1979).

The link with water is strengthened by the direct spatial relationships between a number of pit alignments and contemporary watercourses. Such an association is most

Fig. 2. Bringing the deities down to ground! The rain collecting capabilities of the pits on Gardom's Edge are still obvious today, making them distinctive landscape features (photo: Bill Bevan).

explicit where the channel bisects the row of pits. This occurs at Gardom's Edge, where the pit alignment crosses a marshy former stream bed toward its eastern end. The same interplay was identified at Heslerton, where the Late Bronze Age pit alignment crossed a stream channel near the western edge of the excavated area (Powlesland 1986).

Other alignments respect the edge of watercourses. At St Ives, two successive pit alignments were constructed along the edge of an active channel of the River Great Ouse; each row contained stagnant, sulphidic water for much of its existence (J. Pollard 1996). In a variation to this relationship, the pit alignment at Plant's Farm, Maxey, Cambridgeshire, ran from north to south across the full width of a large island situated within the River Welland; each end of the alignment terminated near the water's edge (Gurney *et al.* 1993). A comparable system of landscape division was created at Castlesteads and Newton, Midlothian, where over 130 ha was divided into smaller units by a rectilinear grid of pit alignments that appear to have been laid out with reference to an adjacent river (Halliday 1982). Comparable relationships have been noted in the Welsh Borders (Whimster 1989). The pit alignment at Kilvington can also be understood through its relationship to water, as the row of pits run along the edge of the floodplain of the River Devon and the River Smite, thereby dividing an area subject to frequent flooding from a slope that was always 'dry land'.

It has long been recognised that Iron Age communities had a particular interest in water. There is a well-established relationship between watery places and objects of high status, or unusual form, which in many contexts suggests that items were intentionally deposited during certain ritual or religious acts (Fitzpatrick 1984; Bradley 1990; Field and Parker Pearson 2004). The origins of such practices lie in the Neolithic, or possibly even earlier, when the only physical barriers were cliffs, watery contexts and other natural features. The deposition of prestige goods within rivers, streams, springs, lakes, and bogs suggests that these primeval boundaries were regarded as portals to alternative, supernatural dimensions, or as sentient deities in their own right. More recently, one of the authors has demonstrated a relationship between square barrow burials, boundaries, and seasonal watercourses in East Yorkshire, which he has interpreted as a complex and active expression of ideals about community identity, land occupation, and fertility (Bevan 1999a).

The form and composition of votive deposits became increasingly complex throughout later prehistory, culminating in the structured multi-component offerings of the Late Bronze Age and Iron Age (Bradley 1990; Hingley 2005). The evolution of this form of ritual practice appears to be coincident with the widespread adoption and expansion of artificial boundaries and field systems as a means of physically alienating tracts of the landscape. That man-made boundaries also became foci for structured deposition suggests that ditches, pit alignments, and natural bodies of water were believed to have a number of directly comparable intrinsic properties.

Excavations of some pit alignments have indicated that a small number of pits were selected as receptacles for artefacts that are likely to have been deliberately introduced during ritual acts. These offerings included whole or nearly complete pottery jars placed in pits at Plant's Farm, Maxey (Gurney *et al.* 1993), Ringstead, Northamptonshire (Jackson 1978), and at Gretton, Northamptonshire, where a textile bundle with a bronze-headed pin and a hoard of iron currency bars were also successively deposited in the terminal pit (Jackson 1974).[3] Skeletal material was also utilised: the shaft of a horse bone was inserted vertically into the fill of a pit at Long Bennington (Fearn 1993) and the skull of a small horse, the right limb bones of several cattle, and human skull fragments were found in pits at Tallington (French *et al.* 1993). A number of the pits forming two interrelated alignments at Ferrybridge, West Yorkshire, contained complete human burials (Roberts 2005);

radiocarbon dates obtained from these human remains indicate that this practice began in the Late Iron Age, but was perpetuated throughout the period of Roman dominion and, surprisingly, at least one interment occurred during the medieval period.

Acts of boundary construction and maintenance would have been of immense social significance. They were material manifestations of the desires of their constructors, creating bounded spaces that structured movement, activity and communication (Hingley 1990; Bevan 1997; Taylor 1997; Chadwick 1999). The boundary would have increased social isolation and thus would define the composition of the group that created it (Bowden and McOmish 1987). Boundaries were also foci for interaction, places where different communities saw their group identities, as defined through their association with geographical space, meeting with the potential for confirmation or conflict over the demarcating of those identities.

The work involved in building and maintaining boundaries would regularly bring people to the edges of their own lands. The scale of pit alignments indicates that they required the investment of substantial amounts of human labour. The example on Gardom's Edge parallels others, by extending beyond individual field systems (RCHME and PPJPB 1993). This implies that labour was drawn from a corporate social group, which probably comprised several family units linked by common ancestry. Participation in periodic maintenance would reiterate claims to the enclosed land and re-emphasise membership of the larger group. Although the evidence is equivocal, morphological variation along the length of several alignments may be an indicator of such collective activities. The alignments on Gardom's Edge and at St Ives (J. Pollard 1996) are composed of short sections of pits of a uniform size or shape. While internally coherent, each segment is dissimilar to those adjoining either end. This variation possibly signifies 'gang-digging', with each section being created by a different residential group. Subtle changes in form could be used to imprint a section of the communal boundary with a 'signature' indicating the involvement of a particular family.

The creation of new boundaries altered existing human relationships with the land. Consequently, these transformations may have been vulnerable to challenges from disaffected groups or individuals. The morphological characteristics of pit alignments may have been utilised to counteract such opposition. If some of the pits contained water for some of the time, it is possible that they were perceived as extending the domain of the supernatural entities associated with rivers and bogs. The water may have signified the presence of a divinity or ancestral being, thereby investing each such boundary with powerful properties that would help legitimise it:

> 'New developments are more secure where they are invested with the authority of the past' (Bradley 1993, 116).

The potency and significance of these forces would be universally comprehended, as they were already the focus of ritual activity throughout later prehistoric Britain and much of western and central Europe.

Kilvington, Nottinghamshire

A pit alignment was discovered during the investigation of an area of 16 ha earmarked for the expansion of an opencast mine belonging to British Gypsum Ltd situated to the west of the village of Kilvington. The alignment ran from north-east to south-west and was traced for over 250 m (Fig. 3). In all, 80 pits were identified, but several gaps in the alignment suggested that further pits had been lost to ploughing, or had been obliterated by the heavy machinery used to strip the topsoil and subsoil (Rylatt 2001). The pits were sub-circular to sub-oval in plan, and were around 1.0–1.4 m in diameter, while the associated causeways were approximately 1.0 m wide. Thirty-one pits were half-sectioned, a process which demonstrated that there was a degree of variation in the form of the different elements of this monument (Fig. 4). Some of the pits had almost vertical sides and flat bases, while others had sides that sloped gently toward rounded bases.

The pit alignment ran along the base of a north-west facing slope, thereby defining the edge of the flood plain of the River Smite and the River Devon. All of the pits forming the south-western half of the alignment contained two fills, the upper being a dark grey-brown clay, while the lower was an orangey-brown clayey sandy silt. This basal fill was identical to a layer of material that had been deposited on the floodplain to the north-west of the alignment, and is likely to be an alluvial deposit, floodwater being the most likely agent.

There was much greater variability in the number and composition of the fills contained by the pits forming the north-eastern half of the alignment. Seven pits contained only one fill. In two instances this directly reflected truncation by later features, while the other five examples probably represented a single deposit situated within recuts of earlier pits. Eight pits contained two fills, but this latter group can be divided into three subsets with differing depositional histories. The spatial distribution of these different fill sequences was not random, as comparable fills occupied clusters of around four to six adjacent pits. This suggests that the landscape division was periodically redefined by the re-excavation of a small group of pits forming a contiguous section of the boundary. Such localised events may have represented a symbolic re-emphasis of the whole monument.

The fills of several of the pits were analysed for the presence of relict pollen. The samples indicated that the alignment was set within an environment where grasses were predominant; associated vegetation

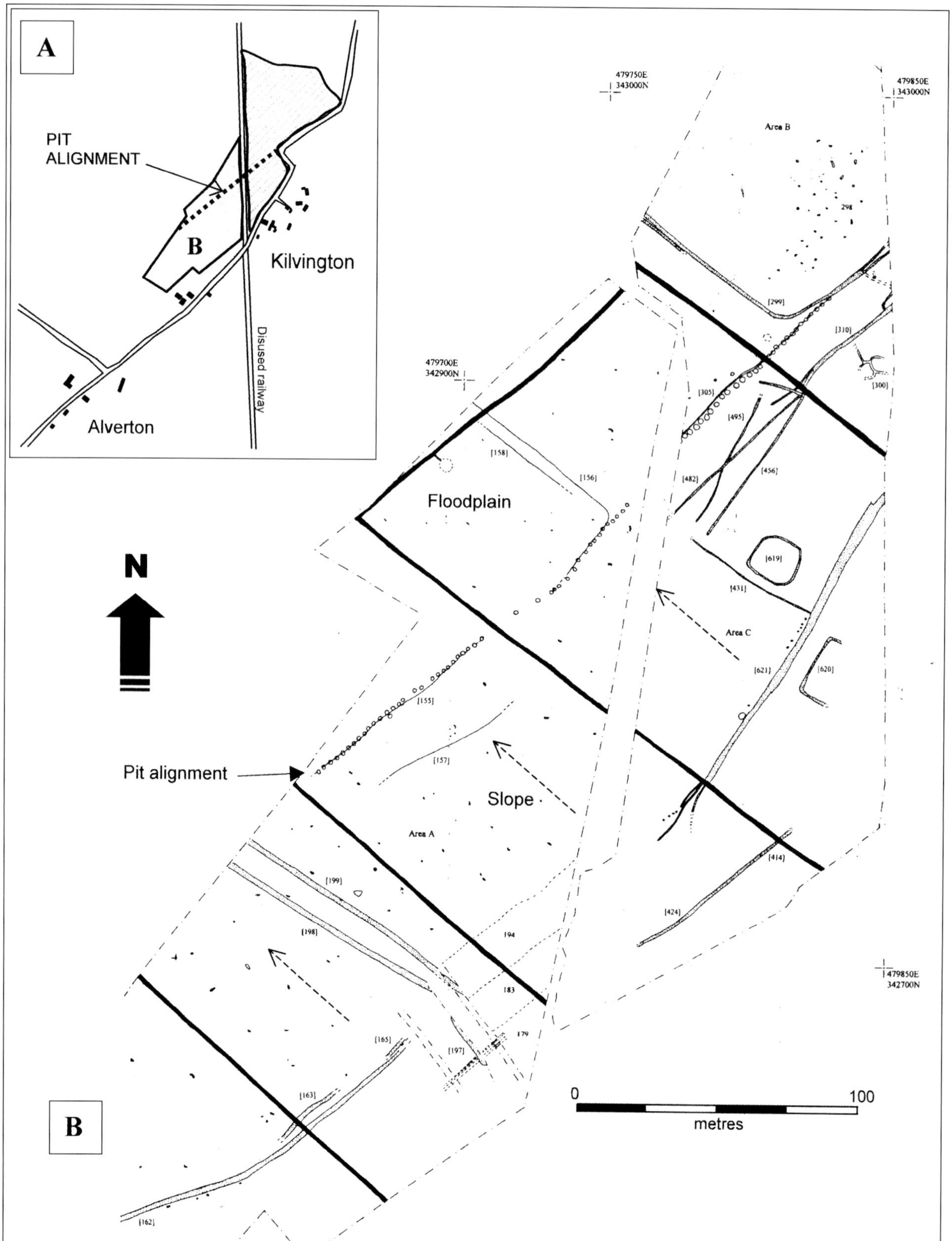

Fig. 3. Plan of Kilvington Opencast Mine sites, showing location and orientation of the pit alignment (drawing: Jim Rylatt and Simon Savage)

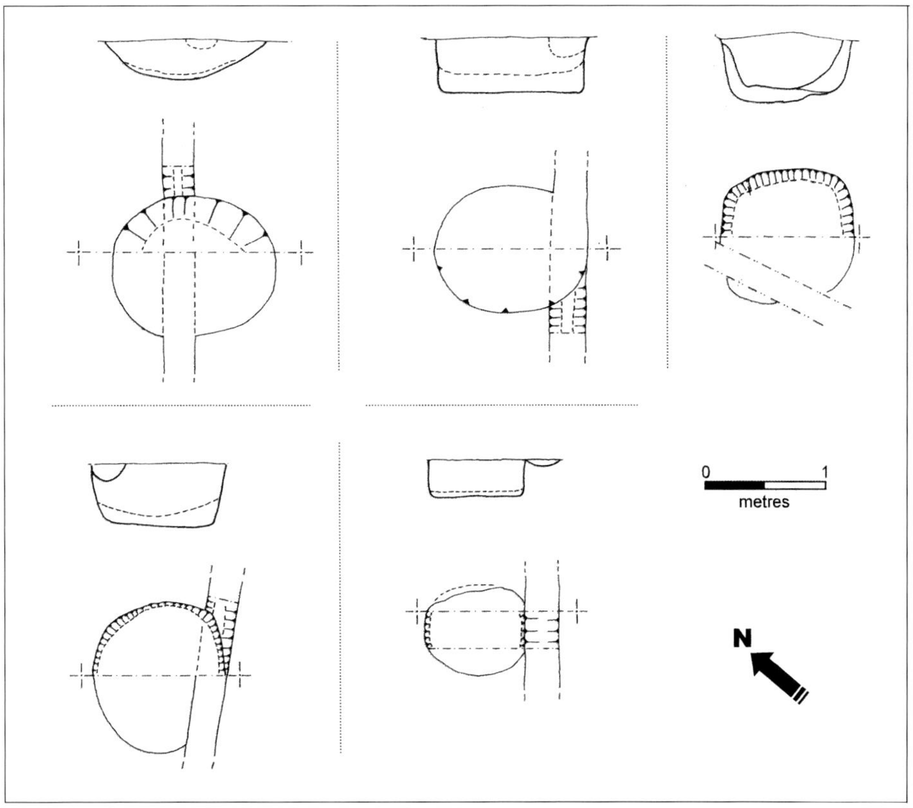

Fig. 4. Plans and sections of a sample of the excavated pits that formed the pit alignment at Kilvington. This demonstrates the variation in size and form, along with their spatial relationship to the gully that replaced them (drawing: Simon Savage and Jim Rylatt).

included dandelions, ferns and bracken. Pollen derived from a range of marginal-aquatic species was also identified, indicating that the pits periodically contained standing water. Trees formed a very small part of the sample, but species noted included oak, elm, lime, ash, alder, and hazel. These may have been situated within woodland in the wider environs of the site or dotted about it in small stands. Cereal pollen was present in pits situated toward the north-eastern end of the alignment, but not in pits further to the south-west. This may indicate that some arable cultivation was undertaken on, or adjacent to parts of the site, but it is equally possible that this pollen was introduced in crop processing residues, or faecal matter. The pollen therefore suggests that the pit alignment ran through an expanse of open grassland, which is likely to have been utilised as rough pasture. The low incidence of tree pollen indicates that woodland regeneration was effectively prevented, most likely by regular grazing of flocks of domesticates. Associated macroscopic remains included small quantities of charcoal, a few charred grains of barley and wheat, some calcined bone, and snail shells indicative of open grassland.

Eventually the pits were allowed to fill without being recut, at which point shallow gullies were created to redefine the alignment. These features closely followed the pit alignment along most of its length, and mirrored slight curves in the earlier monument. This indicates that the pits were still visible as depressions in the ground surface when the gullies were dug. These initial continuous linear features were then supplemented by further gullies and ditches, which subdivided the hill slope into a series of elongated sub-rectangular fields, this system becoming increasingly complex with the passage of time.

Unfortunately, none of the excavated pits contained any material that would facilitate direct dating of the monument. However, stratigraphic relationships with other archaeological features indicate that the pit alignment was the earliest element of this system of landscape division. Some of the first gullies and ditches to be created were found to contain sherds of Late Iron Age to early Roman pottery. The propensity for waterborne sediment to be deposited across the area traversed by the pit alignment indicates that it would have required frequent maintenance to prevent it from 'disappearing'. It is therefore probable that the transformation to continuous boundaries occurred long after the alignment had ceased to be a novel element of the landscape. These factors, albeit somewhat conjectural, suggest that the pit alignment was constructed during the Later Iron Age.

The majority of the pits examined were cut into a layer of impermeable clay representing the degraded upper surface of the underlying Mercia Mudstone. The exceptions were the two pits situated closest to the north-eastern edge of the area of investigation, which had been cut into relatively free-draining fluvioglacial sands and gravels. Both of these sub-oval pits had subsequently been redefined on a slightly different alignment, which meant that each pair resembled a figure '8' in plan. Their edges had been plastered with clay that created a lining up to 0.08 m thick. The homogenous nature and purity of this material suggested that it had been deliberately prepared by levigation. The presence of such a lining implies that there was an intention to ensure that the pits retained water, the geological deposits adequately performing this function along the rest of the alignment.

The location of the Kilvington pit alignment can be understood through its relationship to water. The River Devon runs from east to west, approximately 1 km to the north of the alignment, while the River Smite is located some 2 km to the north-west, the intervening area constituting part of a broad floodplain. A map of 1842 depicts the land in Kilvington and the surrounding parishes that was subject to inundation by floodwater from these rivers.[4] There is a remarkable correspondence between the location and orientation of the pit alignment, and the level attained by the highest floodwaters at this time. This reflects the fact that the pit alignment runs along the base of a slight incline, which forms the tail of a more pronounced north-west facing slope that was the focus of Later Iron Age and Romano-British settlement in the area. This precise positioning indicates that the constructors of the pit alignment had an intimate knowledge of their environment. To locate it so close to the flood maximum is likely to have involved years of observation prior to the physical act of definition. There is evidence for the utilisation of similar fine-grained knowledge at nearby Long Bennington, where one section of a later prehistoric multiple-ditched boundary runs along the junction between two different types of soil (Boutwood 1998).

These relationships are unlikely to be fortuitous. The location of the Kilvington alignment is an excellent example of the structuring properties of the natural topography (cf. Tilley 1994), as it is positioned at the level reached by the most severe floods. Thus at Kilvington, it appears likely that the pits were used to distinguish between two areas of the landscape that were considered to be fundamentally different in nature. While the area to the south-east of the alignment was always land, it is possible that the area to the north-west was not perceived as being either land or water, much like a beach or other inter-tidal zone (cf. Bradley 1990; T. Pollard 1996; Willis this volume). As such, the area between the pits and the rivers may have been conceptualised as a liminal zone. Ethnographic evidence suggests that such places did not conform to normal classificatory structures and were subject to proscriptions imposed to minimise the potential danger presented by any supernatural agencies considered to inhabit, or 'manage' the area (Tilley 1994; Bradley 2000).

It is also important to note that the area to the north-west of the pit alignment would have been largely unsuitable for cultivation due to its propensity for flooding. Inundation by the nearby rivers will have been most likely during the autumn, winter, and the early part of spring, at which times the floodplain would also have been unsuitable for use as pasture. However, in summer it would have been transformed into rich meadows fertilised by water-borne organic material and silts. The appearance of lush summer pasture would have been essential to the continued prosperity of the adjacent communities. The waning of the floodwaters during spring may have been perceived as a divine gift of dry land by a society that appears to have deified the natural world it inhabited (Green 1995). Such an important difference in the perceived status or ownership of the land may have motivated the creation of a boundary along the edge of the floodplain in order to clearly demarcate its full extent.

Evidence of a similar pattern of seasonally differentiated landscape utilisation has been identified in the upper Thames valley, where there are indications that pastoral production was significantly increased during the Middle Iron Age (Lambrick 1992; Hey this volume). This intensification was partially facilitated by the creation of specialised farms located on the floodplain or on the lower gravel terraces at its margins. The smallest of these settlements were single phase farmsteads, such as Farmoor (Lambrick and Robinson 1979), which were constructed on low-lying areas of the valley floor and were thus subject to seasonal flooding. They could only have been seasonally occupied and would have facilitated the exploitation of the verdant pasture during the late spring and summer. The transitory nature of activity at these sites indicates that the occupants and their livestock spent a large proportion of the year elsewhere. Hingley (1984) has proposed that the cattle spent the autumn and winter in fields surrounding larger mixed farms on the higher gravel terraces. In late spring the livestock would have been driven onto the floodplain, thus preventing them from damaging the newly sown crops, and would only return after the latter had been harvested. Consequently, it would appear that these different types of settlement operated synchronously and represented distinct elements of the same social system (Lambrick 1992). Documentary evidence attests to the operation of a comparable bi-partite, transhumant system in medieval Ireland (Hingley 1984).

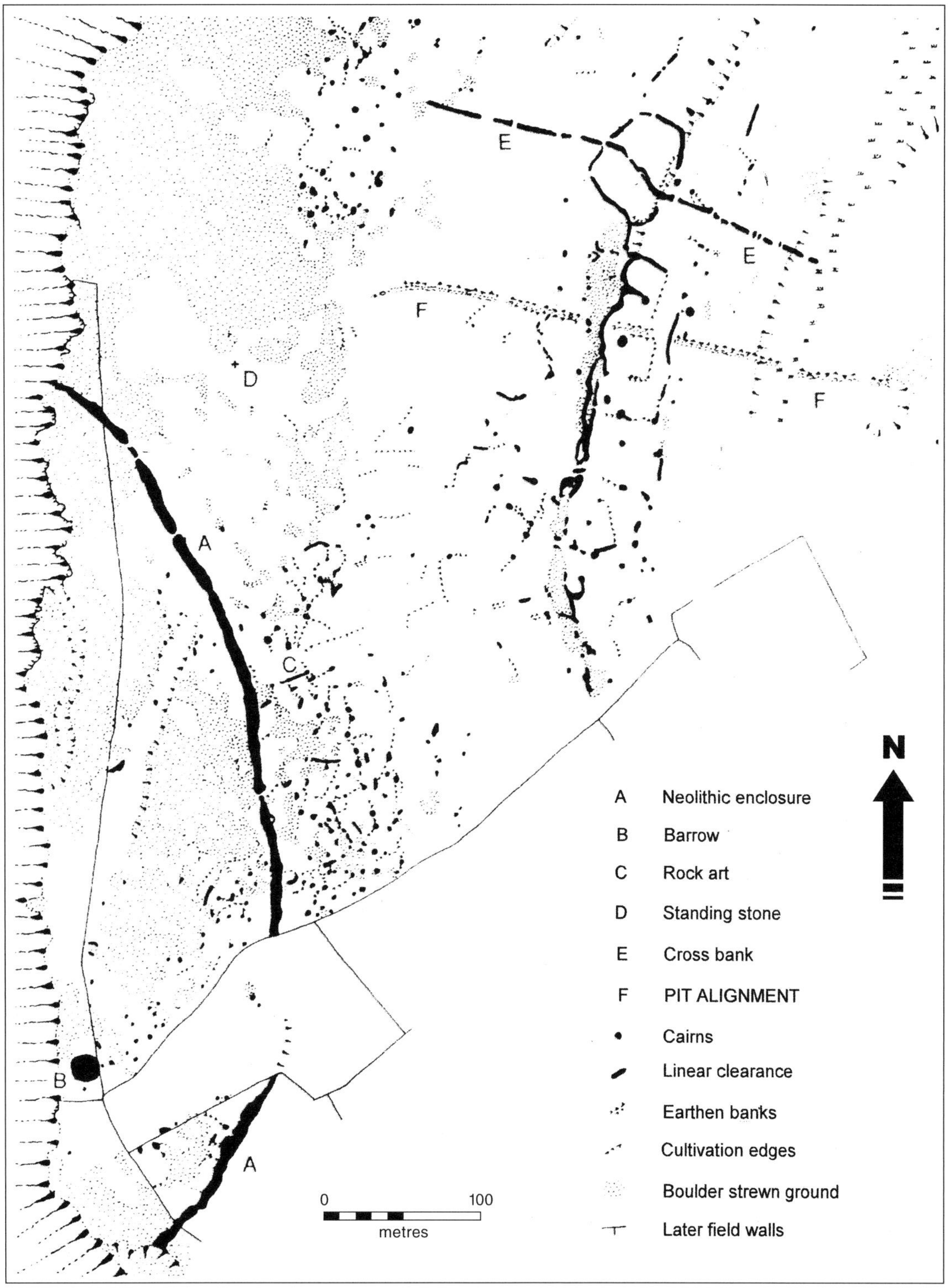

Fig. 5. The central area of Gardom's Edge, showing the relationship of the pit alignment (F) to other prehistoric features (drawing: Stuart Ainsworth and John Barnatt).

Gardom's Edge, Derbyshire

As stated above, the Gardom's Edge pit alignment (Fig. 5) dates to the last four centuries of the first millennium BC, comprises a series of clay-lined pits flanked by insubstantial banks, provides some evidence for gang-digging, and is related to later prehistoric settlements and fields (Barnatt *et al.* 2002). The excavated pits were

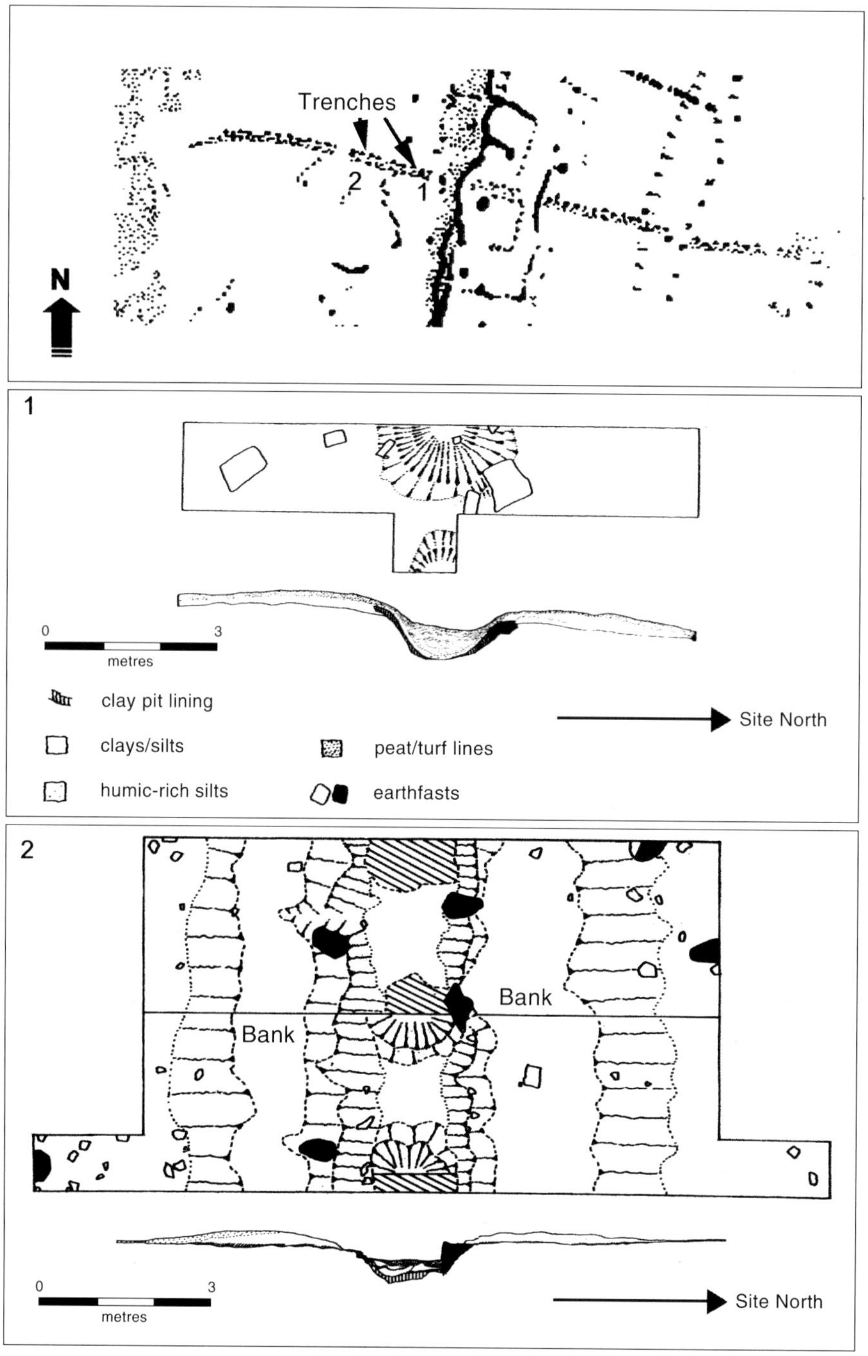

Fig. 6. Gardom's Edge, showing locations of trenches with plans and simplified sections across excavated pits indicating the location and thickness of the clay lining (drawing: John Barnatt).

sub-circular, between 0.9 m and 1.6 m across, from 0.48–0.70 m deep and were separated by causeways approximately 1.2 m wide (Figs 6 and 7; Barnatt *et al.* 1998; 1999). The alignment is located on a shelf of land lying at approximately 270 m OD, which forms part of the Eastern Moors of the Peak District and, like many favourable locations on these moors, contains evidence for extensive later prehistoric occupation (Barnatt 1987; 2000).

The shelf is bounded to the east by Birchen Edge, which rises to higher moorland, and to the west by the scarp of Gardom's Edge, which drops away toward the confluence of two tributaries of the River Derwent. The shelf itself consists of two gentle slopes, which descend northwards and southwards towards each of the streams. The alignment effectively divides the shelf into southern and northern halves, and runs along the broad watershed between the two dip-slopes. However, an outcropping ridge of solid rock divides the pit alignment into distinct eastern and western sections. The alignment runs across

Fig. 7. Gardom's Edge pit alignment before and during excavation, looking west-south-west (photos: Bill Bevan).

and appears to overlie elements of a prehistoric field system that occupies the centre of the shelf.

It tended to rain more often than not during our fieldwork, and the pits would quickly fill with water that they then retained. Sunlight would reflect off the water held in the pits once the clouds had dispersed. These shimmering reflections were extremely conspicuous from areas of surrounding land with sufficient elevation to look down onto the water's surface. In contrast, the pits were generally not visible from lower lying land unless the observer approached to within 30 m of the alignment. A simple walk-over survey demonstrated that there were only a small number of places on the shelf high enough to see onto the pits, whereas they were clearly visible from the neighbouring high ground to the east.

Both ends of the eastern section of the alignment are associated with other elements of the prehistoric landscape. The western terminal lies immediately to the north of a large cairn that contained a gritstone slab decorated with cup marks; the presence of rock-art suggests that this cairn was a funerary monument. The other end is defined by a small standing stone and is aligned upon a prominent rock-stack projecting from Birchen's Edge. Tilley (1994) has argued that certain topographical and geological formations were important structuring agents in the creation and maintenance of prehistoric domains. Both the rock-stack and cairn are 'landmarks', having clear form, prominence of location, and an element of 'bigness' (Higuchi 1983). As such they may have acted as significant nodal points in the socialisation of the landscape. Any conceptual partition of the landscape could have been made in reference to these foci, which would have acted as mnemonic devices to recall specific aspects of the oral tradition that governed social action. Thus, the creation of a physical boundary running between the cairn and rock-stack may have given material form to a pre-existing cognitive division. The creation of bounded spaces results in notions of 'inside' and 'outside'. The relationship between the bank running along one side of the pit alignment and several slight lynchets suggests that the south side was the 'inside' at Gardom's Edge.

The alignment runs roughly parallel to a linear stone bank lying some 70–100 m to the north (RCHME and PPJPB 1993). This boundary runs from the edge of a field system near the north-western edge of the shelf to a relict watercourse at its north-eastern corner. Sections were excavated through the bank in 1997 to examine its structure. These investigations identified a complex relationship with one of the field systems. The linear bank overlay a sub-circular enclosure and was itself overlain by clearance cairns associated with sub-rectangular field plots (Barnatt *et al.* 1997). This reave-like bank and the pit alignment are the only land divisions to extend beyond any of the individual field systems thus far identified in the Peak District. This implies that they represent some form of territorial division or differentiation of the northern and southern areas of Gardom's Edge and, as such, would have necessitated the collective labour and acceptance of the various family groups occupying the surrounding settlements.

The linear bank was built when at least some of these settlements were still occupied and actively cultivating land. In contrast, the pit alignment appears to have been constructed at, or close to, the time that the adjacent settlements were being abandoned. Abandonment of later prehistoric settlements on Eastern Moors was not a simple process of wholesale settlement relocation, but part of a complex pattern of shifting occupation that was conditioned by very local variations in soils and topography. For example, elements of some later prehistoric fields survive on rocky outcrops, which are encompassed by more productive land belonging to farms that have been occupied from the medieval period onwards (Barnatt 2000; Bevan forthcoming). It is likely that favourable areas of the Eastern Moors have been settled and farmed continuously throughout later prehistory and the historic period, while less favourable areas were occupied on a much more intermittent basis. There is an existing farmstead on the lower southern slope of Gardom's Edge and another, which has now been abandoned. The fields associated with these farms extend part of the way up the slope without reaching the highest point where the pit alignment is located, this area now being too marginal.

Given these factors, it is possible that, like Kilvington, the Gardom's Edge alignment was constructed to define distinct hydrological zones, in this instance the water being manifest as greater levels of soil saturation. Peat formed across the shelf during the Later Iron Age or early Roman period, possibly as a result of overworking of soils and extended maintenance of cleared woodland (Long 1994; Long *et al.* 1998). The higher parts of the Gardom's shelf may have progressively become less suitable for agriculture as the soils were gradually waterlogged and peat spread from Leash Fen and the associated peat-filled stream (the same brook that bisects the alignment). This environmental change occurred over a number of generations and it is unlikely that any one individual would have seen a dramatic alteration to their landscape. Land may, however, have become more difficult to work from one generation to the next and at some point people may have decided to take action to halt the decline and return the fertility to the soil, a fertility they were aware of through communal traditions and stories.

The Gardom's Edge pit alignment may therefore have been a device created to facilitate this transformation, serving explicitly to bring the supernatural powers associated with water into the landscape as a response to the increased saturation of the ground. It may have been intended to demarcate the limit of soil degradation and thus halt the progressive worsening of the land's fertility.

As such, it may show how later prehistoric communities incorporated changes in conditions into their social understanding of the world. Furthermore, it may provide an indication that mechanisms other than reactive abandonment were also available to deal with such environmental alterations.

Discussion

The 'problem' with pit alignments is that their purpose is not explicitly manifest in their form and construction. While historical and ethnographic parallels have provided a basis, rightly or wrongly, for interpreting the function of 'hillforts' and multiple ditched boundaries, analogues for this form of discontinuous or permeable land division have yet to be established. As a result, much of the existing literature relating to pit alignments has either tended to be purely descriptive, or has attempted to formulate highly generalised explanations to which all such designated monuments largely conform (e.g. Waddington 1997). Broad variations in the morphology, chronology and nature of the material culture associated with these features have hindered the process of devising such universal interpretations.

However, these same differences provide a basis for developing a clearer understanding of pit alignments. The existing data suggest that the current classification incorporates, and to some extent homogenises, two different types of alignment: the Late Neolithic monuments found in southern Scotland and northern England clearly represent a different class of monument from the open pits of Late Bronze to Romano-British date. It is therefore suggested that a reclassification to differentiate between rows of holes dug to support posts (*'post alignments'*) and those created as open pits would provide a basis for more focussed questioning of the whole dataset.

The pit alignments at Kilvington and Gardom's Edge both define boundaries between different topographical zones. The former follows the edge of a lowland flood-plain, the latter runs along the watershed dividing two dip-slopes that are framed by scarp edges. Not only were both alignments deliberately built to hold water, but they were also positioned to demarcate different hydrological domains. They were thus important structural elements of settled agricultural landscapes that were subdivided by more localised field boundaries. At Kilvington, the alignment appears to be early in the sequence of archaeologically visible enclosure, while the example at Gardom's Edge was constructed towards or at the end of a sustained period of occupation of the shelf.

Crossing boundaries defined by pit alignments may have been a part of the everyday routines of agricultural activity. The very nature of the alignments does not greatly inhibit the movement of individuals, while at the same time they define a line in the ground as a form of boundary. The narrow causeways ensure that a degree of care is required when passing between pits, a care that might bring with it thoughts about the importance of the boundary, the significance of water, and the implication of movement from one side to the other. At Kilvington there may have been important times of the year when this passage was significant because it related to the movement of livestock onto and away from the summer water meadows, whilst at Gardom's Edge it may have been the progressive degradation of soils that was perceived.

This paper has sought to emphasise the conceptual properties of pit alignments, suggesting that interaction with the supernatural is implicit in their design and construction. While it is impossible to determine the mindset and motivations of the constructors, analysis of these monuments suggests some intriguing possibilities that could act as a basis for future investigations. What follows is a short detour into more conjectural reasoning.

Boundaries partition the land to create areas of differing function, with differential access. Implicit in this process is recognition of the purpose and meaning manifest in the boundary:

> 'no feature of the landscape is, of itself, a boundary. It can only become a boundary, or the indicator of a boundary, in relation to the activities of the people (or animals) for whom it is recognised or experienced as such' (Ingold 1993, 156).

We have suggested that pit alignments were constructed specifically to contain water at certain times of the year, and that the purpose of this was to seek the approval and assistance of supernatural forces associated with natural phenomena. As such, it is reasonable to conclude that these ethereal entities must also have been asked to 'experience and recognise' the boundary. The pit alignment would therefore not only divide the familiar world of the constructors, but it could also act as a metaphor for a contract between people and their deities. The initial construction of the alignment would have involved the labour of many people, potentially bringing together the whole of the wider community. Through this process all of these individuals would have become aware of the intended purpose of the boundary and would have observed some of the concomitant rituals. As a consequence, the meaning implicit in the monument would have become unambiguous both to the general population and to the gods they had invoked.

At Kilvington and Gardom's Edge alike, the alignments separate areas of land with different physical and conceptual properties. In this respect they could potentially be perceived as separating land belonging to the people, in which a deity has a presence, from land belonging to a deity, where people have a presence. Furthermore, it seems likely that the supernatural being would have performed the role of a 'gatekeeper' managing movement between the two areas:

> 'The perception of spirits in the landscape is amply demonstrated by the names of gods on epigraphic dedications of the Romano-Celtic period, which betray their topographic character, as perceptions of places' (Green 1995, 466).

As with all boundaries, there was a risk that one or more of the interested parties would not accept the new arrangement imposed by the pit alignment. It is possible that such a conflict is represented by the sequence of events surrounding the construction and abandonment of the Gardom's Edge pit alignment. The community was losing farmland due to deteriorating soil conditions. In response they constructed the pit alignment, a physical expression of their recognition that the land to the north was lost to them. It was surrendered to the attendant supernatural entity in the hope that this would prevent the loss of further productive land. However, it appears that this 'contract' was not acceptable to the deity, as the moor continued its southerly expansion across the shelf. In the face of such intractable opposition, the Late Iron Age community had to retreat. Consequently, the pit alignment is one of the last prehistoric features created on Gardom's Edge and marks the termination of more than 1500 years of activity.

In contrast, the outcome at Kilvington appears to have been successful, as the floodwaters of the River Devon and River Smite remained within the area defined by the pit alignment. Although the reasons for this are a direct function of the topography, it is possible that the Iron Age community would have perceived this as an acceptance of the new order by the forces that they had summoned. This approval may have provided these people with a mandate to create continuous land divisions that divided the hillside into a series of sub-rectangular fields.

Greater appreciation of the intended purpose of pit alignments can only be achieved through the consideration of individual monuments in relation to their specific landscape settings. This also requires placing them in the local chronological sequence to identify how they relate in time and space to settlements, fields, enclosures, monuments, funerary sites, hoards or whatever other features are present. Only then can we bring pit alignments in from the periphery of archaeological interpretation and place them firmly within local and regional histories.

Acknowledgements

The authors would like to thank British Gypsum for the opportunity to investigate a substantial proportion of the pit alignment at Kilvington. Thanks are also extended to Pre-Construct Archaeology (Lincoln) for allowing reproduction of plans of the site, most of which were produced by Simon Savage. Thanks are due to the Peak District National Park Authority for permission to conduct fieldwork on Gardom's Edge, and to John Barnatt, Mark Edmonds, Talya Bagwell, Olaf Bayer, and Sarah 'Mutley' Massey for the discussions and advice offered during fieldwork. Finally, we would like to express our gratitude to Jane Richardson and Ian Roberts of Archaeological Services WYAS, for providing unpublished data relating to the Ferrybridge excavations.

Notes

1. Samples from pit F76, dating at 2 sigma to 780–400 cal. BC (Beta-77757), and from pit F78 dating to 800–650 or 550–150 cal. BC (Beta-77756).
2. Dated at 2 sigma to 350 cal. BC–cal. AD 79 (GU-1632: 2060 ± 70 BP).
3. It is also possible that organic materials were commonly utilised as deposits, but no longer survive in the archaeological record. Quantities of waterlogged roundwood and twigs were found in a number of the pits at St Ives (J. Pollard 1996). Although it appeared to be the by-product of hedge cutting, some of the wood was partially burnt or worked, and many of the pieces had a consistent orientation, implying that they had been placed in position.
4. 'Lands within the parishes or townships of Alverton, Bottesford, Cotham, Elston, Farndon, Flawborough, Flintham, Hawton, Kilvington, Normanton, Shelton, Sibthorpe, Staunton, Stoke, Syerston, and Thorpe, in the Counties of Nottingham and Leicester, which are inundated by floods from the Rivers Devon and Smite' (Notts. Archives ref. XW 3L).

Bibliography

Barber, J. 1985. The pit alignment at Eskbank Nurseries, *Proceedings of the Prehistoric Society* 51, 149–166.

Barnatt, J. 1987. Bronze Age settlement on the gritstone East Moors of the Peak District of Derbyshire and South Yorkshire, *Proceedings of the Prehistoric Society* 53, 393–418.

Barnatt, J. 2000. To each their own: later prehistoric farming communities and their monuments in the Peak, *Derbyshire Archaeological Journal* 120, 1–86.

Barnatt, J., Bevan, B. and Edmonds, M. 1997. *A Prehistoric Landscape at Gardom's Edge, Baslow, Derbyshire: Excavations 1997. 3rd Interim Report.* Unpublished report, Peak District National Park Authority.

Barnatt, J., Bevan, B. and Edmonds, M. 1998. *A Prehistoric Landscape at Gardom's Edge, Baslow, Derbyshire: Excavations 1998. 4th Interim Report.* Unpublished report, Peak District National Park Authority.

Barnatt, J., Bevan, B. and Edmonds, M. 1999. *A Prehistoric Landscape at Gardom's Edge, Baslow, Derbyshire: Excavations 1999. 5th Interim Report.* Unpublished report, Peak District National Park Authority.

Barnatt, J., Bevan, B. and Edmonds, M. 2002. Gardom's Edge: a landscape through time, *Antiquity* 76, 50–56.

Bevan, B. 1997. Bounding the landscape: place and identity during the Yorkshire Wolds Iron Age, in Gwilt and Haselgrove 1997, 181–191.

Bevan, B. 1999a. Land–Life–Death–Regeneration: interpreting a middle Iron Age landscape in Eastern Yorkshire, in Bevan 1999b, 123–148.

Bevan, B. (ed) 1999b. *Northern Exposure: Interpretative Devolution and the Iron Ages in Britain*. Leicester: Leicester Archaeology Monograph 4.

Bevan, B. 2007. The early Iron Age of the Peak District: re-reading the evidence, in C. Haselgrove and R. Pope (eds), *The Early Iron Age in Britain and the Near Continent*, 248–258. Oxford: Oxbow Books.

Boutwood, Y. 1998. Prehistoric linear boundaries in Lincolnshire and its fringes, in R.H. Bewley (ed.), *Lincolnshire's Archaeology from the Air*, 29–46. Lincoln: Occasional Papers in Lincolnshire History and Archaeology 11.

Bowden, M. and McOmish, D. 1987. The required barrier, *Scottish Archaeological Review* 14, 76–84.

Bradley, R. 1990. *The Passage of Arms: An Archaeological Analysis of Prehistoric Hoards and Votive Deposits*. Cambridge: Cambridge University Press.

Bradley, R. 1993. *Altering the Earth*. Edinburgh: Society of Antiquaries of Scotland Monograph 8.

Bradley, R. 2000. *An Archaeology of Natural Places*. London: Routledge.

Burgess, C. 1976. Meldon Bridge: a Neolithic defended promontory complex near Peebles, in C. Burgess and R. Miket (eds), *Settlement and Economy in the Second and Third Millennia BC*, 151–180. Oxford: British Archaeological Reports British Series 33.

Cardwell, P. 1989. Excavations at Cat Babbleton Farm, Ganton, North Yorkshire, *Yorkshire Archaeological Journal* 61, 15–27.

Chadwick, A. 1999. Digging Ditches, but Missing Riches? Ways into the Iron Age and Romano-British cropmark landscapes of the north Midlands, in Bevan 1999b, 149–172.

Cunliffe, B. and Miles, D. (eds) 1984. *Aspects of the Iron Age in Central Southern Britain*. Oxford: Oxford University Committee for Archaeology Monograph 2.

Elliott, L. and Knight, D. 1999. An early Mesolithic site and first millennium BC settlement and pit alignments at Swarkestone Lowes, Derbyshire, *Derbyshire Archaeological Journal* 119, 79–153.

Fearn, K. 1993. Excavations of two pits of an alignment at Moor Lane, Long Bennington, *Lincolnshire History and Archaeology* 28, 5–8.

Field, N. and Parker Pearson, M. 2004. *Fiskerton: An Iron Age Timber Causeway with Iron Age and Roman Votive Offerings*. Oxford: Oxbow Books.

Fitzpatrick, A.P. 1984. The deposition of La Tène Iron Age metalwork in watery contexts in Southern England, in Cunliffe and Miles 1984, 178–190.

French, C.A.I., Gurney, D.A., Pryor, F.M.M. and Simpson, W.G. 1993. A double pit alignment and other features at Field OS 29, Tallington, Lincolnshire, in Simpson *et al.* 1993, 29–68.

Green, M.J. 1995. The gods and the supernatural, in M.J. Green (ed.), *The Celtic World*, 465–488. London: Routledge.

Gurney, D.A., Neve, J. and Pryor, F.M.M. 1993. Excavations at Plant's Farm, Maxey, Cambridgeshire, in Simpson *et al.* 1993, 69–101.

Gwilt, A. and Haselgrove, C. (eds) 1997. *Reconstructing Iron Age Societies*. Oxford: Oxbow Monograph 71.

Halliday, S.P. 1982. Later prehistoric farming in south-east Scotland, in D.W. Harding (ed.), *Later Prehistoric Settlement in South-East Scotland*, 75–91. Edinburgh: University of Edinburgh, Department of Archaeology Occasional Paper 8.

Halliday, S.P., Hill, P.J. and Stevenson, J.B. 1981. Early agriculture in Scotland, in R. Mercer (ed.), *Farming Practice in British Prehistory*, 55–65. Edinburgh: Edinburgh University Press.

Harding, A.F. 1981. Excavations in the prehistoric ritual complex near Milfield, Northumberland, *Proceedings of the Prehistoric Society* 47, 87–135.

Higuchi, T. 1983. *The Visual and Spatial Structure of Landscapes*. London: MIT Press.

Hingley, R. 1984. Towards social analysis in archaeology: Celtic society in the Iron Age of the Upper Thames Valley (400–0 BC), in Cunliffe and Miles 1984, 72–88.

Hingley, R. 1990. Boundaries surrounding Iron Age and Romano-British settlements, *Scottish Archaeological Review* 7, 96–103.

Hingley, R. 2005. Iron Age 'currency bars' in Britain: items of exchange in liminal contexts? in C. Haselgrove and D. Wigg-Wolf (eds), *Iron Age Coinage and Ritual Practices*, 183-205. Mainz: Studien zu Fundmünzen der Antike 20.

Ingold, T. 1993. The temporality of the landscape, *World Archaeology* 25, 152–174.

Jackson, D.A. 1974. Two new pit alignments and a hoard of currency bars from Northamptonshire, *Northamptonshire Archaeology* 9, 13–45.

Jackson, D.A. 1978. A Late Bronze–Early Iron Age vessel from a pit alignment at Ringstead, Northants., *Northamptonshire Archaeology* 13, 168–169.

Lambrick, G. 1992. The development of late prehistoric and Roman farming on the Thames gravels, in M. Fulford and E. Nichols (eds), *Developing Landscapes of Lowland Britain: the Archaeology of the British Gravels – a Review*. London: Society of Antiquaries of London Occasional Paper 14.

Lambrick, G. and Robinson, M. 1979. *Iron Age and Roman Riverside Settlements at Farmoor, Oxfordshire*. London: Council for British Archaeology Research Report 32

Laskey, J. 1979. Messingham, pit alignments, *Lincolnshire History and Archaeology* 14, 73–74.

Lofthouse, C.A. 1993. Segmented embanked pit-alignments in the North York Moors: a survey by the Royal Commission on the Historical Monuments of England, *Proceedings of the Prehistoric Society* 59, 383–392.

Long, D.J. 1994. *Prehistoric Field Systems and the Vegetation Development of the Gritstone Uplands of the Peak District*. Unpublished Ph.D. thesis, Keele University.

Long, D., Chambers, F. and Barnatt, J. 1998. The palaeoenvironment and the vegetation history of a later prehistoric field system at Stoke Flat on the Gritstone uplands of the Peak District, *Journal of Archaeological Science* 25, 505–519.

Miket, R. 1981. Pit alignments in the Milfield Basin, and the excavation of Ewart 1, *Proceedings of the Prehistoric Society* 47, 137–146.

Pickering, J. 1992. Pit alignments, *Current Archaeology* 130, 417–419.

Pollard, J. 1996. Iron Age riverside pit alignments at St Ives, Cambridgeshire, *Proceedings of the Prehistoric Society* 62, 93–115.

Pollard, T. 1996. Time and tide: coastal environments, cosmology and ritual in early prehistoric Scotland, in T. Pollard and A. Morrison (eds), *The Early Prehistory of Scotland*, 198–210. Edinburgh: Dalrymple Monograph 3.

Powlesland, D. 1986. Excavations at Heslerton, North Yorkshire 1978–82, *Archaeological Journal* 143, 53–173.

Pryor, F.M.M. 1993. Concluding remarks: III. Pit-alignments in the Welland Valley: a possible explanation, in Simpson *et al.* 1993, 141–142.

RCHME and PPJPB 1993. *An Archaeological Survey of the Northern Halves of Gardom's and Birchen's Edges, Baslow, Derbyshire.* Unpublished report, National Monuments Record, NMR No. SK 27 SE 98.

Roberts, I. (ed.) 2005. *Ferrybridge Henge: the Ritual Landscape.* Wakefield: Yorkshire Archaeology 10.

Rylatt, J.D. 1999. *A Survey of the Pit Alignment on Gardom's Edge (North), Baslow, Derbyshire.* Unpublished report, Department of Archaeology and Prehistory, University of Sheffield.

Rylatt, J.D. 2001. *Report on a Programme of Archaeological Fieldwork Undertaken at Kilvington Opencast Mine, Kilvington, Nottinghamshire.* Unpublished Report, Pre-Construct Archaeology, Lincoln.

Simpson, W.G., Gurney, D.A., Neve, J. and Pryor, F.M.M. (eds) 1993. *The Fenland Project, No. 7: Excavations in Peterborough and the Lower Welland Valley 1960–69.* Peterborough: East Anglian Archaeology Report 61.

Taylor, J. 1997. Space and place: some thoughts on Iron Age and Romano-British landscapes, in Gwilt and Haselgrove 1997, 192–204.

Thomas, J. 1998. Pict's Knowe, Holywood, and Holm: prehistoric sites in the Dumfries area, *Current Archaeology* 160, 149–154.

Tilley, C. 1994. *A Phenomenology of Landscape: Places, Paths and Monuments.* Oxford: Berg.

Vyner, B.E. 1994. The territory of ritual: cross-ridge boundaries and the prehistoric landscape of the Cleveland Hills, northeast England, *Antiquity* 68, 27–38.

Waddington, C. 1997. A review of 'pit alignments' and a tentative interpretation of the Milfield complex, *Durham Archaeological Journal* 13, 21–33.

Whimster, R. 1989. *The Emerging Past: Air Photography and the Buried Landscape.* London: RCHME.

Wilson, D.R. 1978. Pit alignments: distribution and function, in H.C. Bowen and P.J. Fowler (eds), *Early Land Allotment*, 3–6. Oxford: British Archaeological Reports British Series 48.

Good fences make good neighbours? Exploring the ladder enclosures of Late Iron Age East Yorkshire

Melanie Giles

Introduction

Between 1967 and 1969, quarrying for chalk gravel in the valley of Garton Slack brought to light a clutch of chalk figurines (Fig. 1), which were rescued by a pair of assiduous amateur archaeologists from Driffield, C. and E. Grantham (Stead 1988). These artefacts had apparently been deposited in ditches that formed part of a larger series of rectilinear enclosures to the east and south of T.C.M. Brewster's Garton Slack Site 5 (Brewster 1980, 198). Once the site had been scheduled and

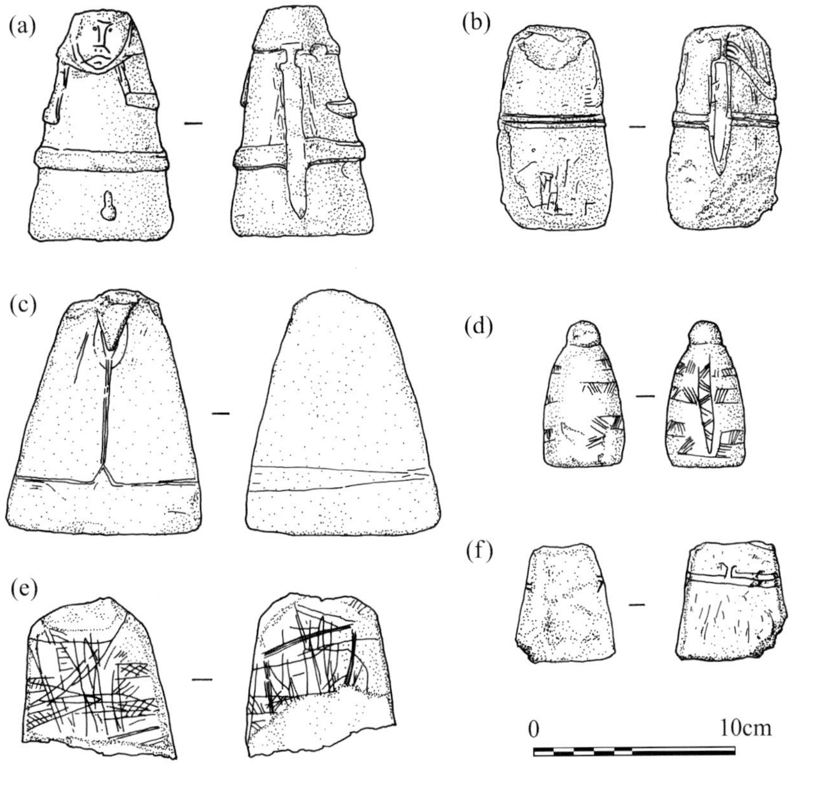

Fig. 1. Chalk figurines from rectilinear enclosures, Yorkshire Wolds: a. Withernsea; b. Garton Slack; c. Fimber; d. Malton; e. Garton Slack; f. Wharram Grange Crossroads (after Stead 1988, figs. 1, 4, and 9, and Brewster 1980, fig. 76).

excavation progressed, further figurines were recovered by both Brewster and John Dent between the parishes of Garton and Wetwang Slack. They are part of a phenomenon usually associated with the so-called ladder enclosures or droveway settlements found in the Yorkshire Wolds, as in the case of the fragment found at Blealand's Nook, Fimber (Mortimer 1905, fig. 9). Other figurines have been recovered from early structures at Roman villa sites such as Rudston and Harpham, and from late third- to fourth-century AD deposits at the vicus in Malton. Sound contextual information is, however, rare: the well-worn and damaged appearance of many figurines suggests that they are residual, and an outlier from the main distribution at Withernsea may well have been 'exported' with chalk gravel to this site (Stead 1988). Stead has therefore suggested that they probably date to the first centuries BC and AD (*ibid.*, 23).

More than half of the near complete figurines appear to depict armed figures, with a sword, blade or hilt generally represented running along the back. Unusual as this may seem, Stead's excavations of square barrow burials dating from the fourth to first centuries BC have frequently revealed swords lying in this position, and the central suspension loop on the sword from Kirkburn suggests that this may be a faithful representation of how they were worn in the region during the Late Iron Age (Stead 1991, 183). Most of the figures are incised with fine lines or scratches, some of which clearly depict elements of dress: patterned or textured clothing, belts, hems and collars. The Withernsea figurine is depicted with beard and genitals, as are a couple of other examples, but explicit indications of gender are rare. Many of the figurines have lost their heads in what may be a tradition of decapitation at the end of their 'lives', although the neck represents a line of weakness in the carving which might be expected to fracture with rough or repeated handling. Others are scratched and scarred by deep incisions. What is common to many of those figurines that have arms and hands depicted, is the gesture that they embody: the left arm folded across the chest, open to view, whilst the right arm twists or turns backwards to touch the sword (Stead 1988, 13). Whilst it is perhaps dangerous to infer the meaning of such body language, they seem to embody a stance of openness and hospitality on the one hand, whilst being ready to defend with the other.

This article is interested in the kind of world inhabited by the makers of these figurines. Focusing on the period from the first century BC to the first century AD, I shall seek to understand the character of the landscape in which these communities lived, through an analysis of the architecture by which this was becoming increasingly divided and defined. Challenging previous interpretations of droveway, rectilinear or ladder enclosures, the paper suggests that these complexes were part of the media through which changing perceptions of land and relationships with place were negotiated. I shall also consider the consequences of these historical transformations in terms of the social relationships through which they were reproduced, placing this within the context of contact with the Roman empire. Returning to the figurines, I will discuss the particular nature of violence that may have been endemic during the period and will conclude by calling for a research agenda and appropriate methodology to address the issues raised here.

The Later Iron Age–Roman landscape

During the course of the first millennium BC, the Yorkshire Wolds were increasingly divided and enclosed by a series of linear earthworks (Fig. 2; Dent 1982; Stoertz 1997). Although some of the larger, long-range dykes have an origin in the Late Bronze Age, many of the smaller subdivisions appear to have been raised during the Middle and Late Iron Age, and continued to be modified into the Roman era, as at Wetwang Slack (Dent 1982; 1984). The earthworks were related to, and formed part of, a network of trackways across the Wolds, which presumably connected the many open settlements of the period that have so far proved very difficult to find and date. Wetwang and Garton Slack is currently the only example of an extensive open settlement that has proved to be contemporary with the square barrow cemetery that exists alongside (Brewster 1980; Dent forthcoming). It consists of circular buildings, four-post structures, and storage pits spread out along the lower side of the dry valley, adjacent to a major road (Fig. 3A; Dent 1983a, 36). From the third to second century BC, however, Dent detected increasing nucleation in both the settlement and cemetery, culminating in a collection of independent units defined by small fields or animal enclosures, which cluster along the roadside. By the first century BC to first century AD, these so-called droveway or ladder enclosures (named after the aerial appearance of their contiguous adjacent plots) appear to have replaced earlier open settlement (Fig. 3B).

Archaeologists such as Ramm noted that many of these enclosures overlie and obliterate earlier monuments such as square barrows, as at Bell Slack, Burton Fleming, and Wetwang Slack (Ramm 1978; Dent 1984). Not only did the burial rite cease to be practised, it seemed to be defamed by this new architecture. Prior to the systematic excavation of any of these enclosures, fieldwalking over the surface had picked up Roman coins and wheel-made pottery. This evidence, coupled with the appearance of the plots (which were often of half a hectare or less in size) led Ramm (1978, 77) to believe that they were the work of colonisers dividing up the landscape with 'military type ditches'. He interpreted

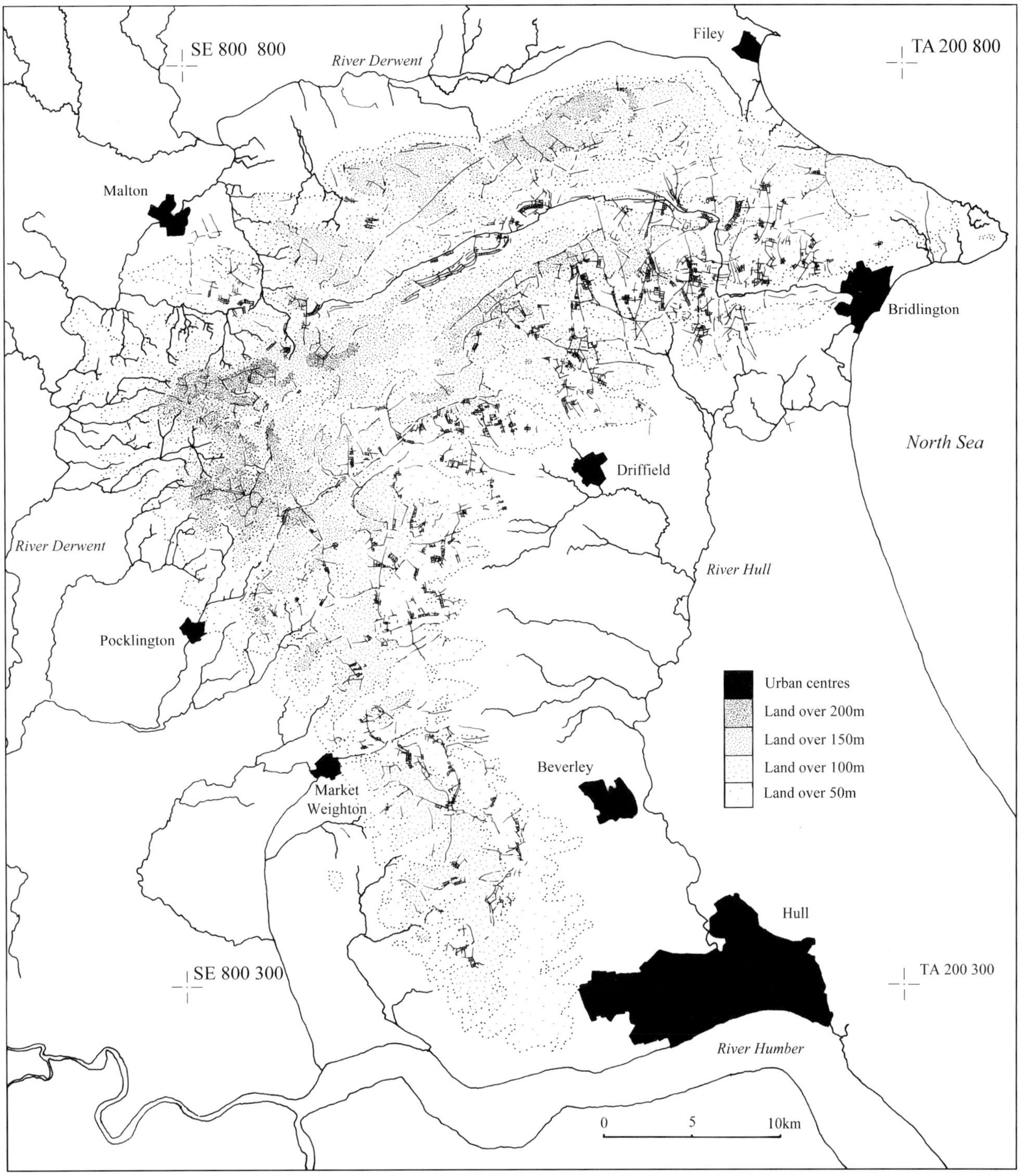

Fig. 2. Rectilinear enclosures and linear features, Yorkshire Wolds (after Stoertz 1997, fig. 34).

them as the rural residences of veterans, seizing the land from its previous inhabitants and settling in districts close to their forts at Malton, Brough, and York. The regularity of the enclosures in plan view seemed to fit the model of intensified land use and stock regimes associated with Romanisation. Certainly the close relationship between droveways and enclosures may indicate an increasing concern with the movement and stabling or corralling of stock. However, there were a number of problems with Ramm's interpretation.

First and foremost, it was the product of an aerial view. By prioritising the plan, it produced an illusion of coherence and regularity which suited the meta-narrative of colonisation. The photographs analysed by Ramm

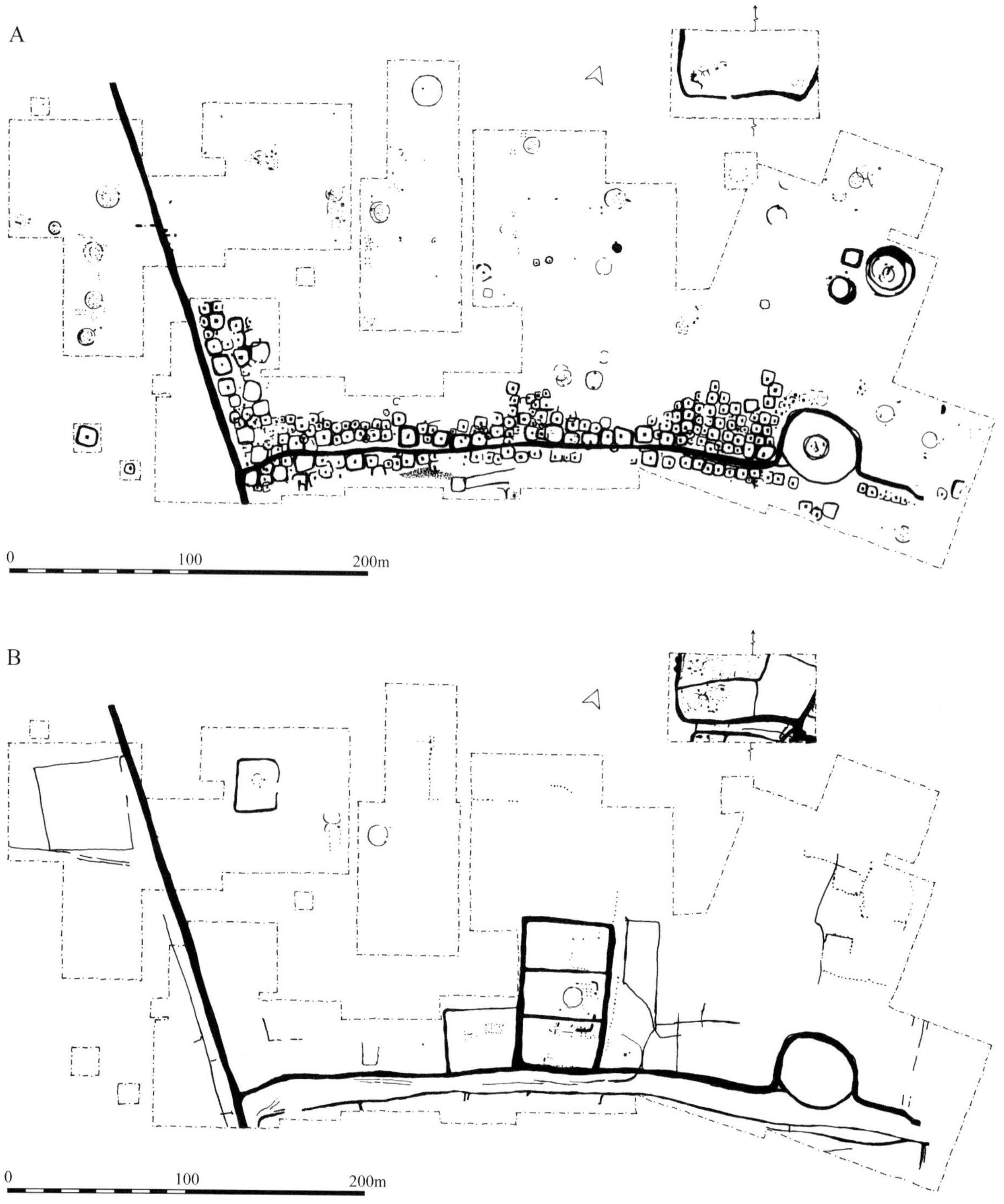

Fig. 3. Wetwang Slack cemetery and settlement, including round barrows, square barrows, roundhouses, pits, and post holes, replaced by rectilinear ditched enclosures and associated features. A. Late Bronze Age–Late Iron Age; B. Late Iron Age–Romano-British (after Dent 1982, fig. 3).

conflated a palimpsest of features into an ordered whole. They could not reveal the time-depth of these enclosures, nor the character of occupation that occurred within them. The dating evidence was also misleading; robust, wheel-made or kiln-fired ceramics and coins survived better than the friable, hand-made ceramics of the Later Iron Age (Hayfield 1987). A reliance on ploughsoil material inevitably failed to pick up this earlier occupation.

Excavations of ditch deposits, as well as structures

contained within the enclosures, began to erode confidence in this model. Mortimer's investigations at Blealand's Nook had revealed unaccompanied inhumations, animal burials, coarse-tempered calcite wares, and a small figurine fragment (Mortimer 1905, 194), which, in Dent's opinion, suggested a Late Iron Age date in origin. More recent work on the same site recovered Colchester, Hod Hill, and Nauheim derivative brooches associated with the enclosures, again suggesting a pre-conquest date (Dent 1983a, note 18). Similar brooch types were recovered from Wetwang and Garton Slack, as well as at Rudston, Wharram Percy, and Wharram Grange Crossroads. The period of transition between Iron Age and Romano-British East Yorkshire has been investigated at Driffield (Philips 1960), North Cave (Dent 1989), Foxholes (Lang 1984), Malton (Wenham and Heywood 1997), and Welton (Mackey 1998), whilst more recent contract work on and off the Wolds has occurred at sites such as Beeford, Leven, Sewerby, Saltshouse Road and Creyke Beck, Cottingham (see summaries in Evans and Steedman 1997; 2001). Other sites which have been more fully published include Caythorpe (Abramson 1996), Melton (Bishop 1999), and Swaythorpe (Mackey 2001). In the Vale of Pickering, the long-term research project at Heslerton has resulted in the first landscape-scale geophysical survey of a droveway settlement, with magnificent results (Powlesland 2003).

This explosion of developer-led work has enabled Pete Didsbury of the Humber Archaeological Partnership to build up an extensive typology of Late Iron Age ceramics (pers. comm.). They are distinguished from their Middle Iron Age antecedents by a proliferation of rim forms (including externally thickened rims); greater diversity in capacity and form; finger-tipped or slashed rim decoration; and rare examples of cordoned vessels and finewares, as for example at Wetwang Slack; Brantingham villa: Rudston; and Creyke Beck, Cottingham Dent 1989; Dent forthcoming; Stead 1980; Evans and Steedman 2001).

Many of the excavations on such enclosures reveal early phases of settlement represented by these latter types of ceramics, within deposits of entirely pre-conquest material. Caution is needed as Romanised material culture generally reached enclosures on the northern Wolds rather late, despite an evident trade in exotic wares on the banks of the Humber, at Redcliff and Ferriby, during the first century BC (Challis and Harding 1975; Evans 1988; Crowther *et al.* 1989). Contrary to other regions during this period, eastern Yorkshire may not therefore have seen the consolidation of Roman power through the rapid 'Romanisation' of a local elite who identified their interests with those of the empire (Whyman 2001, 198).

The piecemeal way in which these enclosures grew also belies the idea that they were a synchronic phenomenon, representing a coherent system of land management. Where junctions of enclosures have been investigated, they often reveal a history of successive additions, or the subdivision of a once open compound. Ditch 4 of Area 3b at Garton Slack, for example, dated to the late first century BC–first century AD, was elaborated by a set of slighter subsidiary enclosures (Ditches 2 and 3) in the second–third century AD. Enclosures were added to the Iron Age Main Ditch 1 in Areas 6 and 9, and in Area 5 a series of enclosures were built in four distinct phases (Brewster 1980, fig. 33). Similar additions and subdivisions occur at Welton and Melton (Mackey 1998; Bishop 1999). At Wetwang Slack, enclosures were dug and recut in Areas 11 and 8a, amongst the old square barrow cemetery (Dent forthcoming), and at Rudston, an enclosure was built over roundhouses dating to the first century BC (Stead 1980, fig. 13). Ladder settlements therefore came into existence through the changing projects and accretive acts of *many* generations.

The enclosures continued to be occupied throughout the Roman period, but third–fourth century AD ceramics in the upper fills of these ditches suggest that they were being allowed to silt up by this date, indicating that their original purpose may have changed. Some may even have been levelled by this time (Dent 1983a, 41). A substantial reorganisation of the ladder settlements therefore seems to have occurred during the late Roman period. Stoertz (1997, 53) notes that several rectilinear complexes see the construction of a single, large, broad-ditched enclosure within their midst, apparently late in their occupation. This is complemented by the increasing subdivision of enclosed plots into smaller and smaller units (M. Atha pers. comm.). Other sites develop into villa-style complexes, including structures with stone foundations, tiled roofs and mosaic floors, as for instance at Rudston and Wharram Grange (Stead 1980; Rahtz *et al.* 1986).

Whyman (2001) has therefore suggested that we should not see the enclosed and subdivided landscape presented by Stoertz (1997, fig. 34) as essentially Late Iron Age in character. The changeover to villa estates with opulent architecture, enclosure of Wold tops, extensive manuring, and increased control over craft and domestic production may all actually date to the third–fourth century AD. Whyman interprets this as the result of a late Roman urban aristocracy maximising the agricultural surplus from their villa estates, in order to reproduce the social standing and lifestyle of their class, rather than simply feeding the demands of the state. However, once the demands of taxation exceeded the surplus needed to maintain this position during the fifth century AD, the aristocracy's affiliation to Rome became untenable, contributing to the eventual collapse of provincial Roman power and the disappearance of ladder settlements (Whyman 2001).

Three points can be made following this review. First, even if their final appearance is a product of the late Roman period, many of the ladder or droveway enclosures began to be constructed in the Late Iron Age. Their origin must be situated within the historical context of this period, instead of attributing it to external factors. Second, if we are to understand the social transformations these enclosures embodied, we must approach them at the scale at which they were *inhabited:* through the architecture and material activities through which people gained a sense of self and place within this landscape. The plan view will not suffice. Third, this requires us to adopt a theoretical position that sees space as *generative* of relations (Lefebvre 1991). By seeing space as both medium and outcome of human practice, we avoid fetishising it. Instead, we can begin to explore how certain kinds of people – certain possibilities of social being – are made through the inhabitation of certain kinds of places (Barrett 1994).

Genealogies in the landscape

The changes identified by Dent (1984; 1995) in the settlement and cemetery at Wetwang Slack provide a context in which to understand the appearance of enclosure. In the latter stages of the square barrow burial rite, barrows were pressed into the interstices of earlier monuments. They also became smaller, with deeper grave pits. Dent interprets this as the result of population growth and a concomitant pressure upon available land. Alternatively, this phenomenon could be interpreted as an obsession with the position in which one was buried: a desire to be associated with *particular* founder monuments.

Dent's stratigraphic analysis of the barrows reveals a gradual growth of the cemetery northwards, clustering in three main groups: up against an earthwork to the west, around an ancient Bronze Age barrow to the east, with a central group in the middle (Dent 1984). Similarities in details of the burial rites and grave goods, as well as the sharing of non-metric traits between adjacent burials at both Wetwang Slack and amongst the cemeteries in the Great Wolds valley excavated by Stead, suggest that we may be seeing members of the same extended family, buried close to each other (Giles 2000). In other words, contrary to the overall symbolism of a communal cemetery, it appears to be vertically divided by kinship affiliations. The architecture of the barrows therefore had a mnemonic role, enabling people to trace the genealogy of their relationships in these valleys across several generations.

At Wetwang Slack, it is assumed that the individuals buried in the cemetery were residents of the parallel settlement, perched on the slopes of the valley. However, even within the domestic sphere, similar tensions were visible. By the third to second century BC, roundhouses tend to cluster in groups of three to four buildings. Many of them were repeatedly rebuilt on the same foundations; a reiterative act which served to remind people of the household's association with a particular place. Ancillary structures such as storehouses and pits also begin to cluster around particular houses, and towards the end of the period, a series of small fences create yards and compounds which further break up the supposedly 'open' settlement.

Through their inhabitation of this architecture, people would have begun to experience a growing solidarity between members of their households. The latter term can only be used heuristically, as we know little about the social composition of these units. The physical structure of a roundhouse is unlikely to have been coterminous with an extended family or kin group (Brück and Goodman 1999, 6). It is, however, evident that the material conditions through which people encountered and worked with others were changing. One implication is that these households may increasingly have withdrawn their produce and labour from use by the broader community. This may have ruptured the traditional means by which particular individuals established their authority over a number of different kin groups, as they were no longer able to harness the agricultural labour, produce, and craftwork of the community. It may be no coincidence that the lavish ceremonies of cart burials began to disappear at this time.

By the end of the first century BC, various aspects of funeral and domestic practices suggest that the broader skein of the community was gradually being pulled apart by the closer-knit relations of smaller communities, perhaps defined by common relations of kinship. Incidences of violence begin to increase in burials of this period (often distinguished by an east–west orientation, sometimes under a round mound); the inclusion of weapons with the dead becomes more common; and armed chalk figurines begin to be carved by the inhabitants of these settlements (Dent 1983b; Stead 1991). It is in the context of these long-term transformations in social relations that we should understand the rejection of communal ceremonies which no longer expressed the interests of its members, and the abandonment of cemeteries in which people could no longer recognise their sense of identity.

Droveway enclosures

By the first century AD, the landscape in which people lived and worked was *qualitatively* different from the places inhabited by their grandparents (Fig. 4). Most rectilinear enclosures occur within a linear complex or 'ladder' of contiguous compounds, laid out from a trackway or earlier earthwork ditch (Stoertz 1997, 51). Aerial photographs suggest these many of these features are double-ditched droveways, such as the one excavated at Wharram Grange Crossroads. Here, the frequent passage of feet and hooves had compacted and crushed the chalk bedrock into an almost 'metalled' surface, 0.3 m

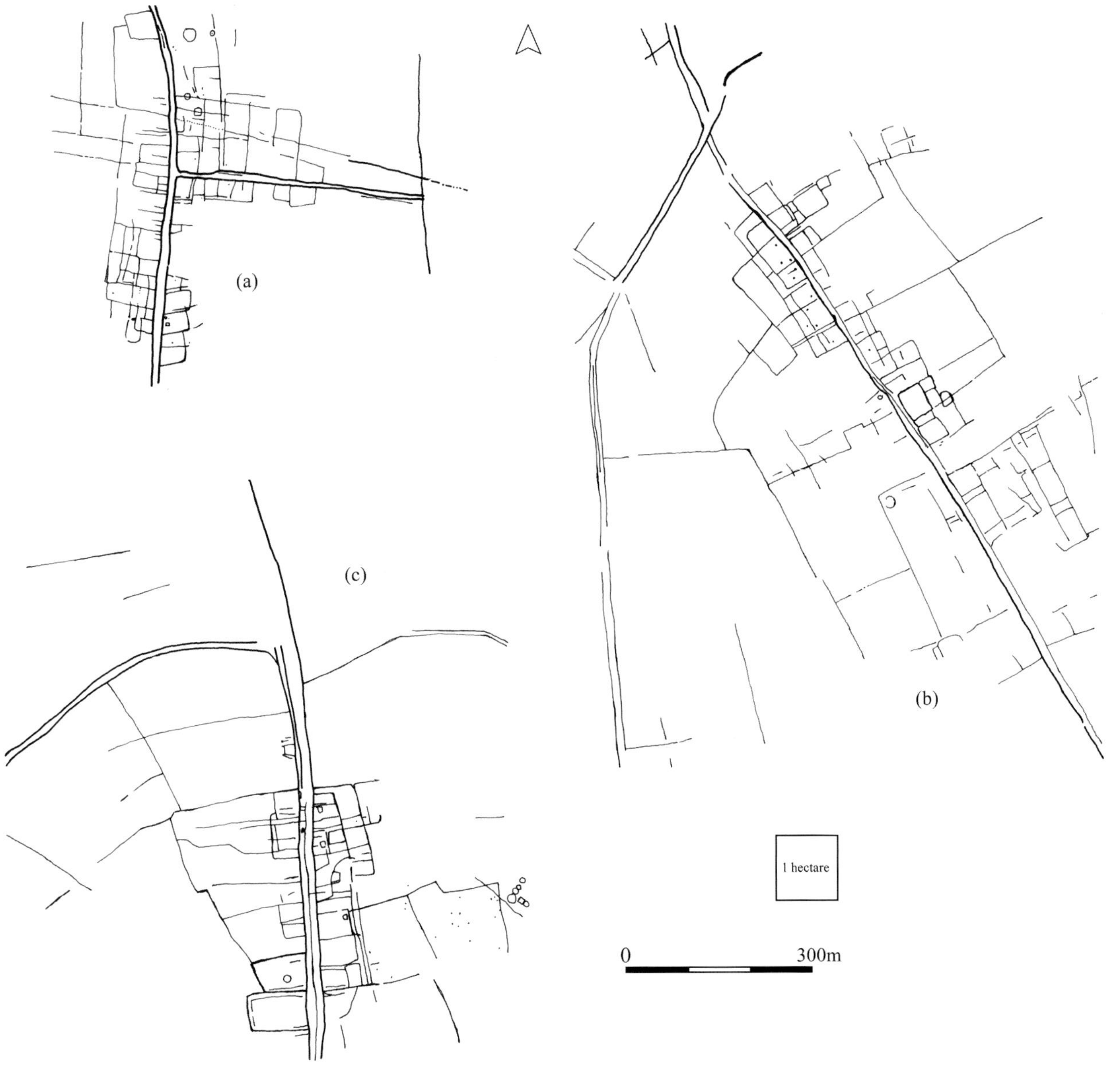

Fig. 4. Examples of rectilinear enclosure complexes: a. Kilham parish (TA 046 672); b. Langtoft parish (TA 020 685); c. Rudston parish (TA 080 695) (after Stoertz 1997, fig. 26 and fig. 38).

below the surface of the bedrock (Giles 1998). Interestingly, it was also slightly rutted, suggesting that wheeled traffic had also made use of the track. At Heslerton, the geophysical survey suggests that small farmsteads were strung out along such a routeway, at intervals of approximately 250 m (Powlesland 2003). This repeated association between droveway and enclosures suggests they should be thought of as an architectural whole rather than as discrete elements. They relate to movement: the flow of people, objects, and especially stock, into and out from the settlement. Such pathways may have been perceived as liminal channels, through which the outside world might pass, separated from the internal world of the settlements.

The increasing prescription of paths of movement and their monumentalisation through banks and ditches would have changed people's perception of the landscape. At a phenomenological level, they and their stock would have been enclosed and restricted, driven through a series of embanked enclosures, from which their movements could have been scrutinised or monitored. Enclosure banks may have been flanked or finished by fences, hurdles, or hedges, as suggested by a series of stake holes spaced at 2 m intervals along the eastern edge of an enclosure ditch at Skipwith (Wagner 1989), or by molluscan species associated with shady habitats on banks at Heslerton (Powlesland *et al.* 1986). For those on foot, sound would have been channelled, views into the compounds concealed. The narrowness of these droveways also meant that they could have been blocked or obstructed, if people chose to do so.

Where one was defined *who* one was. To be inside a compound, or returning to it, was to belong, but to be passing through was to be marked as an outsider. Access into the enclosures occurred through small gaps, as in the two eastern entrances detected in enclosure 12b at Wetwang Slack, which could have been closed with the aid of a simple gate. However, other enclosures have continuous ditch profiles (e.g. Wetwang Slack 8a, 7a–c) that would have had to be bridged by planks or boards. Such an architecture would have further facilitated control of where, and how, people gained access to the enclosure, marking arrivals either by a refusal of entry, or the dramatic throwing open of gates and hurdles.

In summary, by the Late Iron Age, people met across a series of boundaries that heightened the drama of these face-to-face encounters. Boundaries are never only physical, but also social and political (Barth 1994); they change space in that they formalise thresholds, which one must have sanction to cross. As Barth notes, boundaries seldom concern strangers but instead relate to adjacent and familiar 'others': co-residents in the landscape from which one is trying to establish difference and distinctiveness. This sense of independence may be illusory: groups work hard at maintaining their 'imagined communities' through highly symbolic performances, despite flows of people and things across them (Connerton 1989). These groups probably shared similar concerns and habits: the 'cultural stuff' that boundaries enclose may therefore differ little (Barth 1969), but their *interests* in the landscape differed. That is to say, by enclosing space they laid claim to a particular place and the productivity of its soil, to be used to their own ends. As social scientists, our main interest is to understand how these rights were reproduced, and so this article now turns to an analysis of the character of inhabitation within the enclosures themselves.

Living with divisions

The interior space of each compound was defined by a series of subdivisions, using gullies, posts, and stake holes, further separating or regionalising activities. At Wetwang Slack, fences were erected in Area 8d/7d (structure B8:6) and Area 6f (fence line 3.32). These were often attached to the pre-existing ditches, as in Area 6c (Dent forthcoming). At Garton Slack, a long fence line crosses from WS3, through GS29 and into GS27 (Brewster 1980). Small gullies are often crossed by shallow features that could represent lockspits (e.g. WS12a [340]; Dent forthcoming). At Foxholes, a series of internal partitions were used to subdivide Site 1a (Lang 1984). To move within these spaces was to negotiate an intricate architecture of barriers and boundaries, drawing attention to an agent's knowledge of place: their embodied, unconscious disposition to turn right or left, to carry out certain tasks in particular places.

Aerial photographs reveal ring ditches in some enclosures (Stoertz 1997), and excavated examples of post-built roundhouses dating to the first centuries BC to AD include huts 801 and 802, trench F at Melton (Bishop 1999), and Bell Slack at Burton Fleming (Stead 1991, 17). Particular compounds, such as the central bay of the tripartite enclosure at WS7 (Dent 1984), the main enclosure in GS10 (Brewster 1980), or the southern enclosure at Sewerby (Steedman 1991), may therefore have been used for residential activities. Rebuilding over the same foundations is common: at Sewerby, two roundhouses were replaced by a third (*ibid.*), and on the East Site at Rudston, a close cluster of roundhouses included one with at least five phases of reconstruction (Stead 1980, fig. 13). This pattern of rebuilding was also found in the Late Iron Age roundhouses excavated at Argam Lane, Burton Fleming (Stead 2003). At Wetwang and Garton Slack, many roundhouses date to this period (Brewster 1980; Dent forthcoming). Roundhouse B7:4 replaced two earlier dwellings, and was superseded in turn by B7:6 and B7:5. House 2 replaced House 1 in WS1 and a third structure in alignment with these two buildings suggests that the habit of arranging houses in rows noted from the preceding period was still being followed.

Such rebuilding consolidated the identity of the household and its attachment to particular places (Brück and Goodman 1999). By setting the roundhouse within the confines of an enclosure, people drew attention to the significance of the boundary between themselves and the outside world. By forcing visitors to cross both the enclosure ditch with its gates or fences, and the threshold of the house itself, they could elaborate the performance associated with arrivals and departures. More formal codes of hospitality may have accompanied these transformations. As has been noted, changes in ceramics during the period seem to indicate a more diverse range of forms associated with feasting: large cooking and storage jars, smaller drinking vessels or cups, and some finewares (Fig. 5). However, these were not adopted from Rome: they were locally made, idiosyncratic in design, and decorated by the hands and fingers of their makers. They would have reminded both hosts and guests of their distinctiveness and difference, reproducing the local identity of the household in the face of larger gatherings.

The votive deposition of well-worn domestic artefacts within the roundhouse itself, inscribed its history into the foundations. Truncation and erosion have removed floor deposits at most sites, but at Garton Slack, several survived, sealed by later episodes of

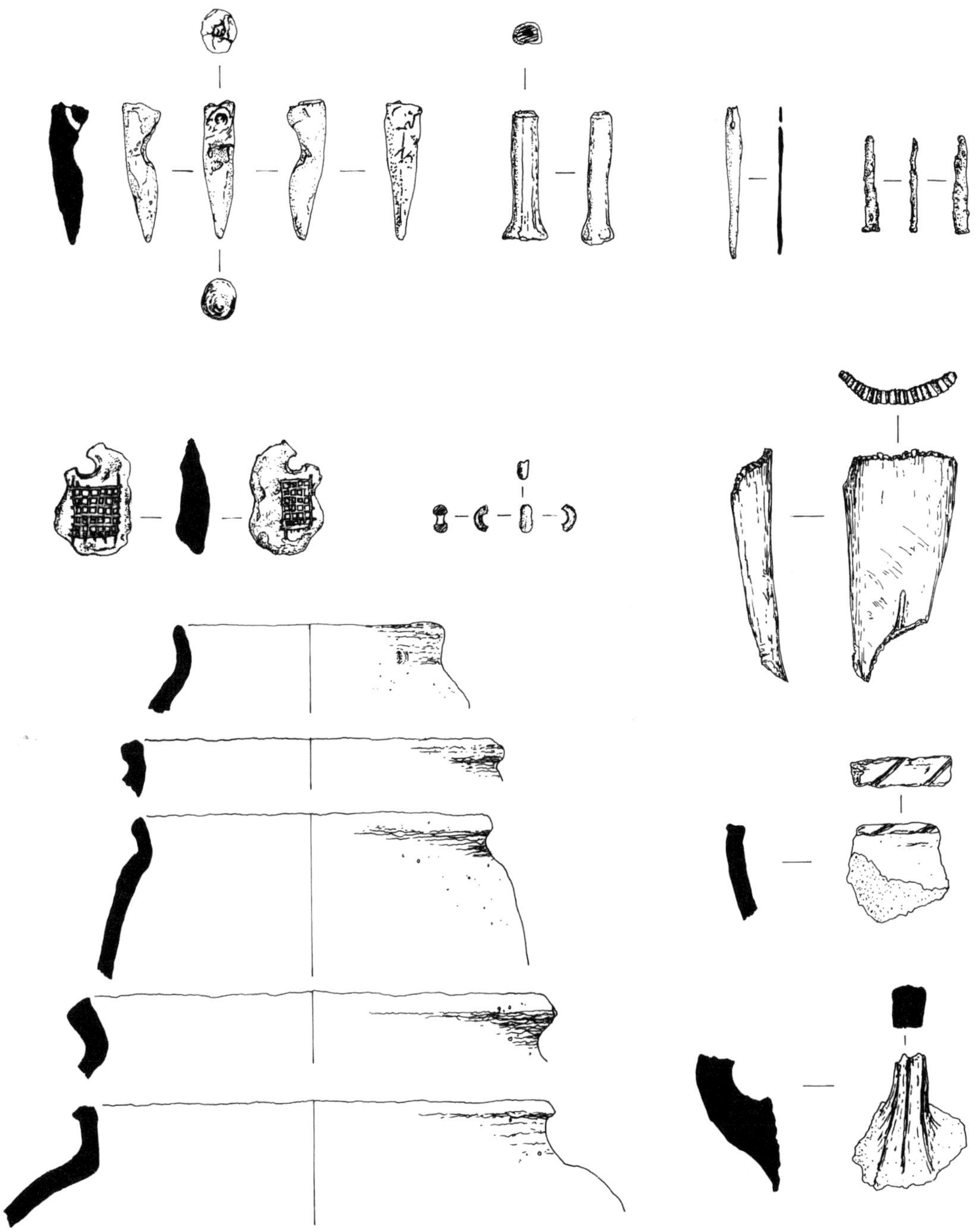

Fig. 5. Material culture from enclosure ditches at Wharram Grange Crossroads: worked bone toggle, handle, needle, and comb, inscribed chalk pendant, blue glass bead, and selection of decorated and plain ceramic rim forms and handle (source: author).

reflooring with fresh chalk rubble (e.g. WS1 Houses 2 and 3). A central hearth seems to be indicated by burnt stone in section Z3 of GS10 House 1, but other material appears to be integral to the packed surface of the floor rather than representing actual activity areas. Artefacts associated with weaving are common, such as the loomweights found in WS1 House 2, along with small metalwork fragments, pottery sherds and animal bone. Pits within houses are rare, but one in the east side of GS11's 'circular stain' house contained three bone combs, two cylindrical slides, a chalk loomweight, and a pig's jaw. The re-use or deposition of weaving paraphernalia within roundhouses is particularly interesting, given the attention paid to clothing on the chalk figurines. By the Late Iron Age, weavers were capable of producing impressive patterned textiles, such as the one preserved in mineralised impressions at Burton Fleming (Stead 1991, figs 79–80). During this era, the cut, colour, and design of garments may well have been a further way in which people implicitly signalled their identity and affiliations to others.

The enclosures appear to have been used spatially to segregate tasks such as food production and consumption, sleeping, storage, and certain kinds of craft activity, from other arenas of work. For example, metalworking appears to been concentrated in WS11 and WS7 at Wetwang Slack, and in Site 1a at Foxholes (Lang 1984). Bronze and iron smelting debris, including fragments of crucibles, moulds, and slag were concentrated in the northerly enclosure at Wharram Grange Crossroads (Wagner 1995). A pit within this enclosure also contained roundels of blue-grey clay (3–5 kg in weight) whose low iron content may also indicate a role in the making of ceramics for melting and casting metal (*ibid.*).

Other enclosures may have been used for storing agricultural produce. Pits, and six- or four-post structures usually interpreted as raised granaries or storehouses, were gradually replaced by rectangular timber structures. By the later Roman period, these were quite substantial: B8:1 in WS8a, B7:9 in WS7B and B6:5 (built over an older area of settlement in WS6d) may have been barns, byres or stores. A rectangular building in GS12 (Brewster 1980) and post settings in Trench E at Birdsall High Barn may also represent barns (Hayfield 1987, 46, fig. 20). The enclosure of storage facilities again suggests a growing concern to restrict access to the produce of these settlements. Whilst it has been suggested that the acreage of these plots is ideal for a self-sustaining household garden, other plots may have been used as fields. However, cultivation may also have occurred in open fields, as represented by an area of middening south of Wetwang Slack WS7 (Dent 1984). The enclosures may therefore have been more commonly to corral stock at key times in the agricultural year, to prevent them from damaging crops.

Enclosures that are devoid of features, such as the one surveyed and sampled at Wharram-le-Street, might therefore represent such yards or paddocks (Northern Archaeological Associates 1996). Many of the droveways have funnel-shaped mouths to facilitate the movement of animals from compounds within the enclosure, out to open areas of pasture. Their size and architectural form may indicate a particular concern with cattle rather than sheep. Lang discovered a series of phosphate-rich, clay-filled and trampled hollows at Site 1a, Foxholes, which he interpreted as cattle stalls (Lang 1984, 6). Mackey (2001, 33) also interpreted two semi-circular depressions at Swaythorpe as cattle shelters or screens, although these are probably Roman in date. Stock management on a large scale is suggested by massive crescent-shaped enclosures at Dykes Fields, above the villages of Weaverthorpe, Helperthorpe, and the Luttons, which probably have their origin in this period. However, these are separated at spaced intervals by droveways, each linked to a ladder settlement in the valley below. This architecture suggests a desire to separate herds that may have routinely grazed together in open pasture, giving them discrete access to shelter and – most importantly – water, the management of which was essential to cattle rearing in this landscape. The architecture of enclosures therefore allowed people to bring stock in close to the settlement, for tending or over-wintering. It also helped people to protect stock from theft or raiding, making the ownership of them explicit in an era where they appear to be an increasing source of wealth and prestige.

As wealth on the hoof, animals may have been displayed and paraded, driven through the settlements of others or gathered together with other herds at key times of the year. Not only was this necessary to count heads, inspect stock, sort them for culling, and ensure successful breeding, but these shows may have been an important source of prestige for the community, as the herd may well have provided a broader metaphor for the lineage and fortunes of the kin group (cf. Edmonds 1999). The phenomenon of animal burial that appears at this time, sometimes within formal cemeteries and frequently associated with human infants and neonates, might be understood in this light (Fig. 6). At Wetwang Slack, 20 complete animal burials were found, dating to this period, including a horse burial to the east of the enclosure in Area 7. At Garton Slack, three animal burials and 14 partial burials (some of which had been cremated) were included within an infant cemetery. The formal burial of two horses at Kirkburn Site 2 at the end of the first century AD need no longer seem anomalous (cf. Stead 1991, 27). Similar burials have been found at Blealand's Nook (Mortimer 1905) and animals were interred under roundhouses at Wetwang Slack and Rudston (Stead 1980).

Each animal is buried with formal care and attention, and as the whole carcass is interred, it suggests they may have died accidentally, through disease, or else have been sacrificed. The infants and neonates who also died preternaturally appear to be have been deliberately paired with these members of the herd, stable and flock. Where pastoralism characterises the relationship between people and animal, this equivalence between young children and stock is common: both are seen as dependents of the household, jural minors who are subject to the authority of its elders (Ingold 2000). The troubling circumstances of their death may have threatened its vitality and security: they were literally brought back into the fold from death, perhaps to regenerate the household's fertility. The presence of these cemeteries in the heart of the enclosures also suggests that these burials were an important part of the way in which its inhabitants thought through and remembered their long-term attachments to place.

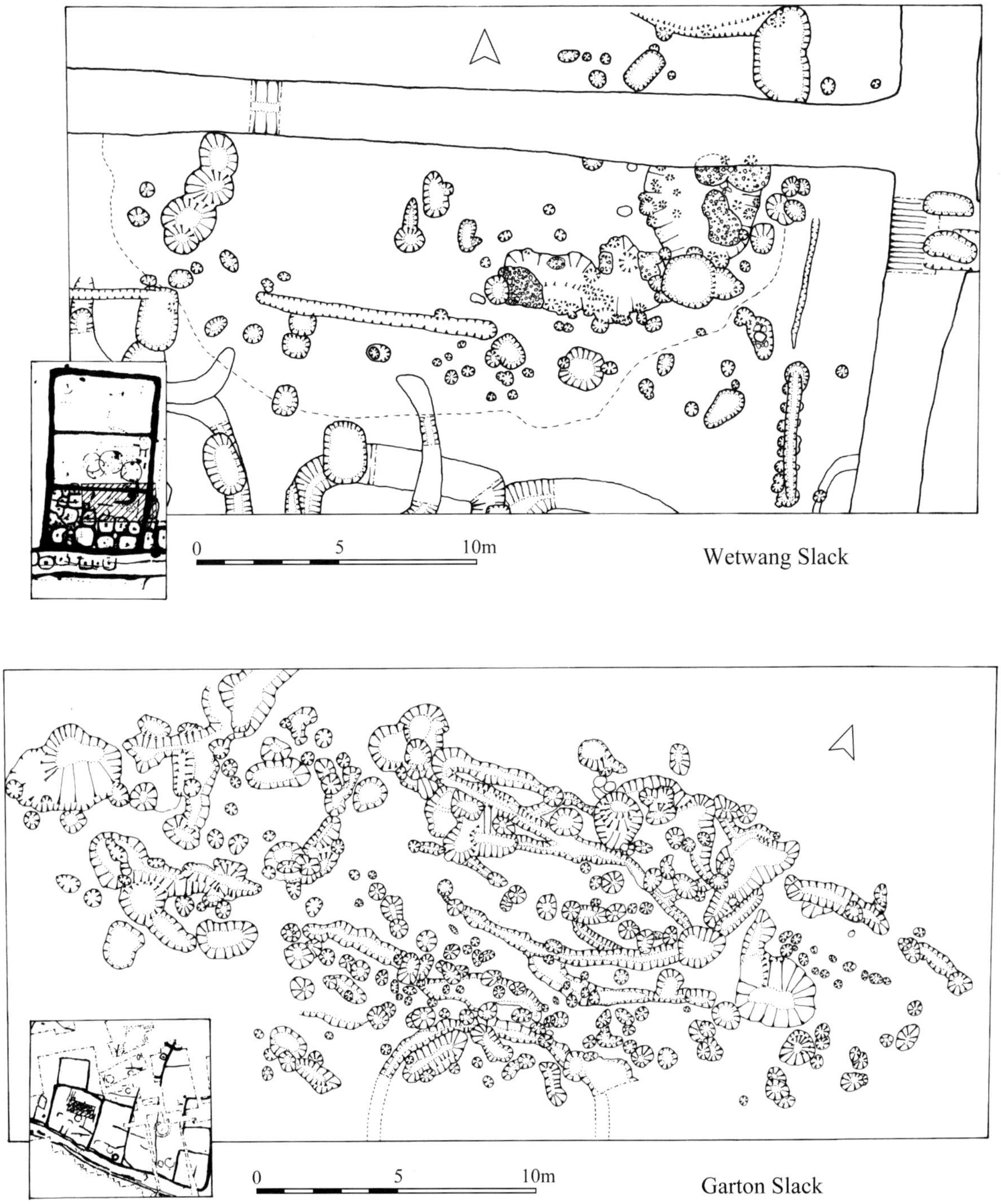

Fig. 6. Animal and infant 'cemeteries' – burials in pits, post holes and gullies (location shown by hatched area on inset plan): a. Wetwang Slack (source: Dent 1984 and archive plans) and b. Garton Slack (after Brewster 1980, fig. 169).

In summary, the architecture of the enclosures separated the community's members according to the task in which they were engaged. Its banks and ditches, gates and latches choreographed movements from task to task, drawing attention at each step to the group one worked with. Their sense of time was therefore composed of serial encounters with others: punctuated episodes of work, carried out in particular enclosures. This would have highlighted aspects of identity by which that labour was organised – age, gender, skill, or position within the family – helping to reproduce these categories. This would have been important in a small-scale community held together by common bonds of kinship, in which authority would have been increasingly defined and ascribed along such horizontal distinctions. The pattern of people's movements during their day-to-day labours embodied and performed these relations of power, within the enclosed spaces of the settlement.

Making places, making histories

The above analysis suggests that the pattern, tempo, and composition of work within these small-scale communities may have given rise to a particular concept of tenure. It has been argued that some of the ladder enclosures may well have been used as paddocks for stalling stock, grazing, and cropping winter fodder. Stoertz (1997, 69) also notes that many of these settlements are flanked by corridors or blocks of enclosed land that may have been areas of arable. Environmental analysis in the landscape surrounding Heslerton may reinforce this model, as it suggests that the heavier soils on the slopes of the Wolds were beginning to be farmed at this time (Powlesland 2003). All of these strands of evidence suggest that communities were practising short-fallow agriculture (Boserup 1965), characterised by the intensive and repeated use of particular plots of land, including periods of grass-fallow and a degree of multi-cropping (Harding 1989). This does not mean that the landscape was divided into mutually exclusive territories; summer pasturing, watering of stock, hunting, gathering of seasonal foodstuffs, and working of woodland would all have taken people out of their enclosed landscapes into more open regions where they had to negotiate their rights with other groups. What is important, however, is that the short-fallow system depends upon a particular sense of tenure invested in a tightly drawn group, rather than through membership of a broader community who assume mutual responsibility for the care and condition of the landscape (Barrett 1994). This involves closing down access to land and withdrawing co-operation from larger projects, in order to turn the resources of each community inwards towards its own purposes. Crucially, this group must be able to sustain its tenurial claims over particular plots of land from one generation to the next (Goody 1976).

In the ladder settlements of East Yorkshire, tenurial rights were reproduced in several ways. Claims to place were inscribed into the landscape through the architecture of banks and ditches, as well as repeated acts of care and maintenance, such as repairing or rebuilding structures, manuring and tilling soil, sowing and weeding crops, or cutting and gathering produce. In anthropological studies of small-scale cultivators, this work is seen as a moral, even sacred duty (Strathern 1988; Ballard 1994). Their appearance is important: well-tended plots, renewed dwellings, and well-fed stock in the yard would have been read as a symbol of success and fertility, in comparison with less fortunate signs of dereliction and decay (Moore 1986). Different perceptions of the landscape would therefore have arisen between communities as their fortunes changed.

As the network of enclosures grew, they could have been traced through talk as histories of the households that occupied them. In the Tari Basin of the southern Highlands of Papua New Guinea, such field systems and drainage ditches stand as mnemonics for the names of inhabitants who have cultivated them (Ballard 1994): a history of inhabitants stretching back beyond normal living memory. The intersecting network of drains is also used to trace the bonds of kinship through which families were related. In East Yorkshire, work on the ditches – weeding, clearing, cutting, and shovelling – may well have helped engrain such lineages into people's bodies. Notably, ditches within the ladder enclosures of East Yorkshire are frequently recut: at Garton Slack Area 5, the western ditch was recut four times, and at Wharram Grange Crossroads, three phases of recutting were recorded in a length of enclosure ditch, all within the first century BC or first century AD. This reworking of the enclosures provided an occasion for the inhabitants to speak of – and perhaps communicate with – forebears; acknowledging the gifts they had inherited, whilst being reminded of their obligations towards descendents. Rather than seeing these ditches simply as boundaries defining physical territories, they were the medium through which people transmitted rights of tenure and customs of use across time: a grid of inheritances (Thompson 1994).

Conversations that once took place amongst the low mounds of the cemeteries would now have taken place amongst the enclosures. The unintended consequence of the square barrow rite was to promote the vertical interests of each kin group and its particular history of inheritance, at the expense of horizontal relations between lineages. By dwelling within such a tightly framed landscape, the biographies of households were bound to the biography of particular places. Importantly, these histories were not only constituted through the inscriptive practices of ditch digging, but through acts of deposition within them (cf. Chadwick 1996; 1999). Concentrations of pottery, animal bone waste from cooking and craftwork, broken tools, knives and weapons, items of dress, and artefacts such as figurines, are often found in enclosure ditches (cf. Fig. 5 above), as in the 'dark soil' described by Mortimer (1905, 198) at Blealand's Nook. Similar dumps of organic-rich material were also found at Wetwang and Garton Slack, Foxholes, Welton, and Wharram Grange Crossroads. Such midden material was valuable as manure and therefore an important symbol of productivity and fertility (Parker Pearson and Sharples 1999). As people recut their ditches and worked amongst these rotting deposits, they excavated and encountered a history of the household through its material remains. Through these fragments, they would have remembered the stories, seasons, and events that wedded them to this place.

The deposition of human remains reiterated these bonds. Adult burials are rare until the later Roman period, but fragments of bone, limbs, and skulls are frequently found incorporated into ditches or pits. Instead of seeing these as the result of massacres (cf. Dent 1983a), they probably represent the excarnation and selective deposition of human remains within the setting of the enclosure. In death, individuals were dissipated into a generic body of ancestors, immanent in the settlement. This promoted the identity of the tightly-knit community – possibly an extended kin group – over the interests of any one family. Why was this important? One of the fundamental aspects of the short-fallow system is its system of inheritance (Goody 1976): land must remain within a narrowly defined community. Occasions such as marriage and death may have necessitated gifts of land, but this risked partitioning or subdividing it into unproductive units. Amongst the Fijian Kasuan, where inheritance operates through such a principle of land division, there is a great risk that the land will 'grow small' through such acts (Riles 1998, 413), leading to 'divisions amongst the lines'. In reality these plots tend to re-aggregate through a strong preference for inter-clan marriage, expressed in the idea that 'blood looks for its own' to 'close the circle... renew the link' (*ibid.*). Families therefore perceive of themselves as members of a 'shared geometry, dictated by a series of divided parcels acquired by their ancestor'. Genealogical talk is therefore talk about divisions in the land.

Do good fences make good neighbours? Transgression and trespass in Late Iron Age East Yorkshire

'Something there is that does not love a wall' begins Robert Frost, in his poem *Mending Wall*, from which the title of this article is taken: gaps appear so that the line must be set again between his neighbour and himself. Frost questions why boundaries are necessary, touching on their symbolic role, but several authors have seen enclosure in later prehistoric East Yorkshire as a practical response to escalating warfare, caused by population growth and pressure upon resources (Brewster 1980; Dent 1983a; 1983b). However, this article has suggested that the division and demarcation of land must be understood within the context of long-term social transformations in concepts of community, tenure, and inheritance. More radically then, it could be argued that acts of enclosure precipitated, prompted or drew attention to particular *kinds* of violence in this landscape.

By monumentalising thresholds, creating barriers and impeding movement, the idea of trespass became possible. Crossing boundaries without appropriate permission or sanction would have become a way in which people demonstrated their contempt for others. Entering and occupying compounds and buildings, despoiling crops or befouling water, backfilling and levelling ditches, thieving and raiding people, stock, and belongings; these acts of transgression came to have an exaggerated importance because of the very *existence* of boundaries which defined an inside from an outside world. Their digging and excavation were political acts, with consequences for the interests and resources of others. Such acts of construction may also have been caught up in internal disputes over inheritance or contested alliances.

What do the chalk figurines tell us about such a world, and their role in it? Their size, averaging 125 mm (Stead 1988), suggests they were designed to fit the hand, and many are indeed worn or damaged from use. They may have been dolls or toys for children, gaming pieces, or even models for spirits who might temporarily inhabit them, during ceremonies of invocation (Stead 1988). Given their association with warfare, some may have been used as surrogates for enemies in rituals of sympathetic magic, to ensure their capture or execution. The scratched damage on their bodies may have mimicked the intended stabbing, scarification, or mutilation of a corpse. However, many of them are pierced on the base by a small dot or hole used to steady them, suggesting that they spent their lives as figures in a niche or shrine. Their appearance, including the cut and design of their clothing, facial hair, and sometimes gender, is clearly important. As such, they may embody a mythical founder figure, an archetypal warrior or ancestor possessed with magical or supernatural powers, perhaps drawn from stories of the cart burials, a century earlier.

Most persuasively then, they might be seen as household gods or ancestral figures (Stead 1988), kept within a structure in the enclosure. Their association with the life of a household may have led to their ceremonial 'death' through decapitation, alongside the demise of a significant figure, or upon the occasion of rebuilding the roundhouse itself. This may explain the context of their deposition, within other midden material and structural debris. Until future examples are excavated from secure contexts, they will remain something of a mystery. For now, the figurines leave us with a powerful metaphor for these people, who were open-handed but ever watchful: a landscape in which the sword had become the backbone of the community.

Conclusion

This article began by seeking to return the chalk figurines to the social context of the world in which they were made. Through an analysis of the way in which people inhabited the landscape, this article has suggested that by the end of the first century AD, fundamental changes had taken place in the way in which people defined themselves and their sense of community, and conceived of their relationship with place. It has argued that this process cannot be attributed to Romanisation, but must instead be understood as the long-term consequences of historical transformations originating in the Iron Age. The apparent reluctance of this region to become involved in pre-conquest exchanges and political alliances with the Roman empire might therefore be understood as a product of an inwardly turned and circumscribed world, concerned with very local political issues.

This review has by no means been exhaustive; many of the sites discussed here have yet to be fully published, and a coherent synthesis of developer-funded contract work has yet to be produced (see Atha 2003). There is also a need for a strong research agenda that makes use of our existing knowledge of settlement character and depositional practice, to drive future investigations. The potential of large-scale geophysics analysis on rectilinear complexes has already been revealed by Powlesland (2003). This could be used to target areas of differential activity, for sampling and open-area excavation. As chemical and micro-morphological techniques would further enhance this analysis, we need to identify sites where soils and land surfaces have been preserved. Finally, sealed ditch deposits provide an opportunity to use environmental and material culture analysis, to examine how the inhabitation of these enclosures changed over time. To conclude, research-driven future investigations are essential, if we are to be able to explore – and hopefully challenge! – many of the ideas presented in this article.

Acknowledgements

The research for this article was undertaken whilst the author was in receipt of a three-year AHRB doctoral award based at the University of Sheffield, under the supervision of John Barrett and Mike Parker Pearson. The article itself was written during a one-year post-doctoral fellowship, funded by the IRCHSS, at University College Dublin, under the mentorship of Joanna Brück. I would like to thank the funding bodies for their financial assistance and the members of these academic institutions for the creative, scholarly environment they sought to facilitate, in which this work developed. Thanks are also due to Ian Stead, John Dent, Dominic Powlesland, Pete Didsbury, Colin Hayfield, Pat Wagner, Steve Roskams, Mark Whyman, and Mick Atha, who gave me access to unpublished material and shared their own ideas. On an individual note, this work was developed through conversations with Bill Bevan, Mark Edmonds, Adrian Chadwick, Graham Robbins, and Danny Hind, who have been generous with both their time and their support. Responsibility for the views expressed herein, of course, remains solely with the author.

Bibliography

Abramson, P. 1996. Excavations along the Caythorpe Gas Pipeline, North Humberside, *Yorkshire Archaeological Journal* 68, 1–88.

Atha, M. 2003. *Iron Age and Romano-British Ladder Settlements in Eastern Yorkshire: A Review of Previous Research and a Reassessment of the Distribution of such Features Relative to the Physical Environment of the Region.* Unpublished M.A. dissertation, University of York.

Ballard, C. 1994. The centre cannot hold: trade networks and sacred geography in the Papua New Guinea Highlands, in L. Head, C. Gosden and J.P. White (eds.), Social Landscapes, *Archaeology in Oceania* 29, 130–148.

Barrett, J. 1994. *Fragments From Antiquity.* Oxford: Blackwell.

Barth, F. (ed.) 1969. *Ethnic Groups and Boundaries. The Social Organisation of Cultural Difference.* London: Allen and Unwin.

Barth, F. 1994. Enduring and emerging issues in the analysis of ethnicity, in H. Vermeulen and C. Govers (eds.), *The Anthropology of Ethnicity. Beyond 'Ethnic Groups and Boundaries',* 11–32. Amsterdam: Het Spinhuis.

Bishop, M. 1999. An Iron Age and Romano-British 'Ladder' settlement at Melton, East Yorkshire, *Yorkshire Archaeological Journal* 71, 23–64.

Boserup, E. 1965. *The Conditions of Agricultural Growth: the Economics of Agrarian Change under Population Pressure.* New York: Aldine Publishing Company.

Brewster, T.C.M. 1963. *The Excavation of Staple Howe.* Malton: East Riding Archaeological Research Committee.

Brewster, T.C.M. 1980. *The Excavation of Garton and Wetwang Slacks.* Malton: East Riding Archaeological Research Committee Prehistoric Excavation Report 2.

Brück, J. and Goodman, M. (eds) 1999. *Making Places in the Prehistoric World: Essays in Settlement Archaeology.* London: UCL Press.

Chadwick, A. 1996. Towards a social archaeology of later prehistoric and romano-british field systems in South Yorkshire, West Yorkshire and Nottinghamshire. http://www.shef.ac.u/~asse,/2/2chad.html

Chadwick, A. 1999. Digging Ditches but Missing Riches? Ways into the Iron Age and Romano-British cropmark landscapes of the north midlands, in B. Bevan (ed.), *Northern Exposure: Interpretative Devolution and the Iron Ages in Briatin*, 149–172. Leicester: Leicester Archaeology Monograph 4.

Challis, A.J. and Harding, D.W. 1975. *Later Prehistory from the Trent to the Tyne.* Oxford: British Archaeological Reports British Series 20.

Connerton, P. 1989. *How Societies Remember.* Cambridge: Cambridge University Press.

Crowther, D., Willis, S. and Creighton, J. 1989. Excavations at Redcliff, in Halkon 1989, 6–9.

Dent, J.S. 1982. Cemeteries and settlement patterns of the Iron Age on the Yorkshire Wolds, *Proceedings of the Prehistoric Society* 48, 437–457.

Dent, J.S. 1983a. The impact of Roman rule on native society in the territory of the Parisi, *Britannia* 14, 35–44.

Dent, J.S. 1983b. Weapons, wounds and warfare in the Iron Age, *Archaeological Journal* 140, 120–128.

Dent, J.S. 1984. *Wetwang Slack: an Iron Age Cemetery on the Yorkshire Wolds.* Unpublished M.Phil. thesis, University of Sheffield.

Dent, J.S. 1989. Settlements at North Cave and Brantingham, in Halkon 1989, 26–31.

Dent, J.S. 1995. *Aspects of Iron Age Settlement in Yorkshire*. Unpublished Ph.D. thesis, University of Sheffield.

Dent, J.S. forthcoming. *Excavations at Wetwang Slack*.

Edmonds, M. 1999. *Ancestral Geographies*. London: Routledge.

Evans, D.H. and Steedman, K. 1997. Recent Archaeological work in the East Riding, *East Riding Archaeologist* 9, 116–166.

Evans, D.H. and Steedman, K. 2001. Recent Archaeological work in the East Riding, *East Riding Archaeologist* 10, 67–94.

Evans, J. 1988. All Yorkshire is divided into three parts: social aspects of later Roman pottery distribution in Yorkshire, in J. Price and P.R. Wilson (eds), *Recent Research in Roman Yorkshire*, 323–337. Oxford: British Archaeological Reports British Series 193.

Giles, M. 1998. *Excavations at Wharram Grange Crossroads*. Unpublished interim report.

Giles, M. 2000. *Open-weave, Close-knit: Archaeologies of Identity in the Later Prehistoric Landscape of East Yorkshire*. Unpublished Ph.D. thesis, University of Sheffield.

Goody, J. 1976. *Production and Reproduction: A Comparative Study of the Domestic Domain*. Cambridge: Cambridge University Press.

Halkon, P. (ed.) 1989. *New Light on the Parisi. Recent Discoveries in Iron Age and Roman East Yorkshire*. Hull: East Riding Archaeological Society.

Harding, A.F. 1989. Interpreting the evidence for agricultural change in the late bronze age in northern Europe, in H.A. Nordstrom and A. Knape (eds), *Bronze Age Studies*, 173–314. Stockholm: Statens Historika Museum.

Hayfield, C. 1987. *An Archaeological Survey of the Parish of Wharram Percy, East Yorkshire. 1. The Evolution of the Roman Landscape. (Wharram: A Study of Settlement on the Yorkshire Wolds, Vol. V)*. Oxford: British Archaeological Reports British Series 172.

Ingold, T. 2000. From trust to domination: an alternative history of human-animal relations, in T. Ingold, *The Perception of the Environment. Essays in Livelihood, Dwelling and Skill*, 61–76. London: Routledge.

Lefebvre, H. 1991. *The Production of Space*. Oxford: Blackwell.

Lang, N. 1984. *The Foxholes Project, North Yorkshire*. Unpublished interim report.

Mackey, R. 1998. The Welton villa – a view of social and economic change during the Roman period in East Yorkshire, in P. Halkon (ed.), *Further Light on the Parisi*, 23–35. Hull: East Riding Archaeological Society.

Mackey, R. 2001. An investigation of Romano-British enclosures at Swaythorpe Farm, Kilham, *East Riding Archaeologist* 20, 29–41.

Moore, H. 1986. *Space, Text and Gender: An Anthropological Study of the Marakwet of Kenya*. Cambridge: Cambridge University Press.

Mortimer, J.R. 1905. *Forty Years Researches in British and Saxon Burial Mounds of East Yorkshire*. London: A. Brown and Sons.

Northern Archaeological Associates. 1996. *Wharram-le-Street, North Yorkshire. An Archaeological Watching Brief of a Pipe Trench Excavation for Yorkshire Pipeline Services*. Barnard Castle: Northern Archaeological Associates Report 96/52.

Parker Pearson, M. and Sharples, N. 1999. *Between Land and Sea: Excavations at Dun Vulan*. Sheffield: Sheffield Academic Press.

Philips, J. 1960. An Iron Age Site at Driffield, *Yorkshire Archaeological Journal* 40, 183–191.

Powlesland, D. 2003. *25 Years of Archaeological Research on the Sands and Gravels of Heslerton*. Colchester: The Landscape Research Centre/ English Heritage.

Powlesland, D., Haughton, C.A. and Hanson, J.H. 1986. Excavations at Heslerton, North Yorkshire 1978–1982, *Archaeological Journal* 143, 53–173.

Rahtz, P., Hayfield, C. and Bateman, J. 1986. *Two Roman Villas at Wharram Le Street*. York: York University Archaeological Publications 2.

Ramm, H. 1978. *The Parisi*. London: Duckworth.

Riles, G. 1998. Division within the boundaries, *Journal of the Royal Anthropological Institute* (N.S.) 4, 409–424.

Stead, I.M. 1980. *Rudston Roman Villa*. Leeds: Yorkshire Archaeological Society.

Stead, I.M. 1988. Chalk figurines of the Parisi, *Antiquaries Journal* 68, 9–29.

Stead, I.M. 1991. *Iron Age Cemeteries in East Yorkshire*. London: English Heritage Archaeological Report 22.

Stead, I.M. 2003. *Argam Lane, Burton Fleming*. Unpublished Interim Report.

Steedman, K. 1991. *An Archaeological Evaluation at Home Farm, Sewerby*. Hull: Humberside Archaeology Unit.

Stoertz, C. 1997. *Ancient Landscapes of the Yorkshire Wolds*. Swindon: RCHME.

Strathern, M. 1988. *The Gender of the Gift*. Berkley: University of California Press.

Thompson, E.P. 1994. *Persons and Polemics. Historical Essays: the Grid of Inheritance*. London: Merlin.

Wagner, P. 1989. *Excavations at Skipwith*. Unpublished interim report.

Wagner, 1995. *Excavations at Wharram Grange Crossroads*. Unpublished interim report.

Wenham, L.P. and Heywood, B. 1997. *The 1968 to 1970 Excavations at the Vicus at Malton, North Yorkshire*. Leeds: Yorkshire Archaeological Report 3.

Whyman, M. 2001. *Late Roman Britain in Transition AD 300–500. A Ceramic Perspective from East Yorkshire*. Unpublished Ph.D. thesis, University of York.

Putting the neighbours in their place? Displays of position and possession in northern Cheviot 'hillfort' design

Paul Frodsham, Iain Hedley and Rob Young

Introduction

To start by quoting J.D. Hill (1996, 95) 'This is yet another paper about hillforts, about Iron Age social organisation.' But this paper is about Northumberland, not Wessex, and about one area – the Cheviot Hills – in particular. In this contribution we present some results from the Northumberland National Park Authority's *Discovering our Hillfort Heritage* project to offer what, we freely admit, is a highly regionalised insight into Iron Age social relations in one part of north-east England. We hope that it will serve as a corrective to any (we believe) misguided attempts to impose models of hillfort function and development from southern Britain onto the 'distant borderlands' of the north. Indeed, we would like to stress that these 'distant borderlands' actually represent the centre of Britain (cf. Haselgrove 1999, 253), and that the concentration of 'hillforts' in this area is of no less importance to the understanding of Iron Age Britain than the much studied monuments of Wessex. As long as accounts of later prehistoric societies persist in ignoring northern England and southern Scotland – Bevan (1999) is an all too rare exception – they will fail to provide a meaningful overview of British prehistory.

In this paper we make no attempt to define the term 'hillfort', although we would note in passing that the sites considered here are a world removed from the giants of Wessex. Indeed, to lump all these sites together as 'hillforts' could be likened to classifying Buckingham Palace and an average two-up/two-down terrace in a north-east mining village as 'houses', or Westminster Abbey and a Wesleyan meeting house as 'churches'. The hillforts of Wessex and the Cheviots are hundreds of miles, and (in origin) quite possibly hundreds of years, apart, even though their occupation may have overlapped just like that of the aforementioned 'houses' and 'churches' in today's landscape. That said, the Wessex sites remain much better studied than those of central Britain, and we will consider below some recent thinking about them where this might be relevant to the understanding of our Cheviot sites.

Discovering Our Hillfort Heritage

The Northumberland National Park Authority's *Discovering our Hillfort Heritage* project represents the first large-scale initiative aimed at the study, conservation, and interpretation of the archaeology of the Cheviot Hills and Upper Coquetdale: some of the most spectacular, yet least recognised, archaeological landscapes in Britain. Over a five-year period (1999–2004), in conjunction with many partners, this project completed programmes of survey and excavation, conservation, and public interpretation (Hedley 2001). As an essential element of the project, English Heritage undertook detailed surveys of a dozen hillforts in their landscape settings. These should prove invaluable to future research, and have already been used to inform conservation and interpretation work by the National Park Authority.

Four of the English Heritage surveys, West Hill, St Gregory's Hill, Mid Hill, and Staw Hill, are examined in detail here for the light that they might shed on hillfort function and, by extrapolation, on Iron Age social relations.[1] Many other examples could be presented, and similar conclusions perhaps reached, but these four were

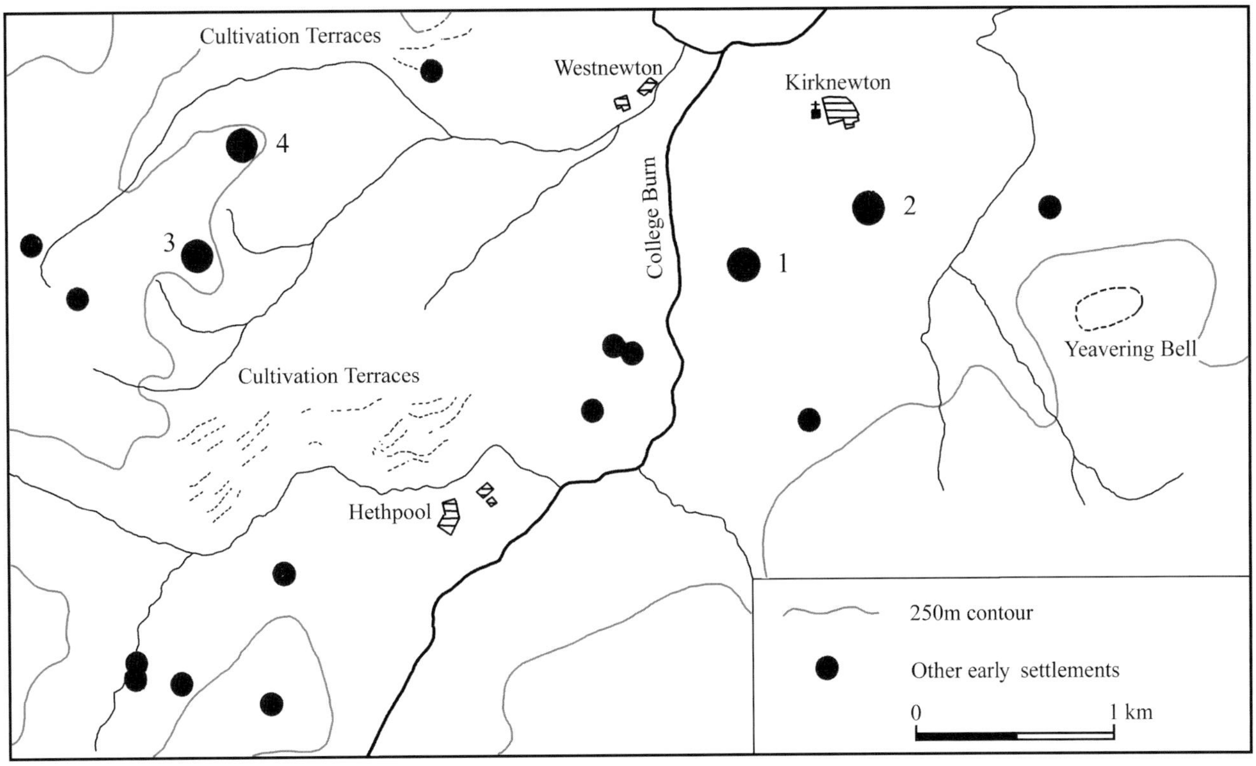

Fig. 1. Map of part of the northern Cheviots showing the locations of the site surveys discussed in this paper. Key: 1. West Hill; 2. St Gregory's Hill; 3. Mid Hill; 4. Staw Hill. Note the concentration of other possibly contemporary settlement sites within this area, including the great hillfort on Yeavering Bell.

chosen by virtue of their close proximity to one another (Fig. 1). They lie in the northern Cheviots, in the shadow of the great hillfort on Yeavering Bell (Pearson 1998; Frodsham and O'Brien 2005), which became the focus for the Anglian 'palace', *Ad Gefrin,* in post-Roman times. Yeavering Bell is by far the largest hillfort in Northumberland, and we did consider attempting to incorporate a discussion of the relationship between it and the smaller forts discussed in this account. However, this is a complex subject, and would necessitate the inclusion of many other small and medium sized hillforts throughout the region. For now, we merely offer the suggestion that the Yeavering fort is probably of far greater age than the sites under discussion here and should perhaps be considered as a separate class of monument, alongside southern Scottish sites like Hownam Law (RCAHMS 1956, 157–9), Traprain Law (Armit *et al.* 2002), Eildon Hill North (Owen 1992) and Burnswark (RCAHMS 1997, 129–30). It is possible that the summit of Yeavering was not actually occupied for much of the Iron Age, and its relationship to surrounding sites both then and in the Romano-British period remains to be explored.

West Hill

The site of West Hill (Fig. 2) lies 1 km south-west of Kirknewton (NT 90962951) at a height of 215 m OD. Although overlooked by Yeavering Bell and the Newton Tors, it commands exceptional all round views, over the Milfield Plain to the north-east, the confluence of the river Bowmont and the College Burn (which then becomes the Glen) to the north, and the College valley to the west. The hillfort is intervisible with the enclosures on St Gregory's Hill (below) and Yeavering to the east, and Hethpool Bell to the south-west. Of all the sites surveyed by English Heritage during the recent project, this is the most fascinating, covering as it does an extensive and generally very well-preserved multi-period archaeological landscape centred on the hillfort (Oswald *et al.* 2000; Oswald 2004).

The principal monuments on the summit of West Hill are the stone-built Iron Age hillfort itself; an arc of bank and ditch, which possibly represent part of an earlier enclosure; an outer enclosure surrounding the hillfort, which may be a Romano-British addition; and a small enclosed settlement, built over the bank of the

Fig. 2. Air photograph looking south over West Hill (photo: Tim Gates).

outer enclosure. This last enclosure is of a type generally agreed to be of Romano-British date…' (Oswald *et al.* 2000, 2). Thirteen structures were identified inside the rampart and it is suggested by the surveyors that all but one are of Romano-British date or later and post-date the collapse of the hillfort rampart.

The survey evidence suggested that the possible earlier enclosure, consisting of a ditch with a surrounding bank, could be of Neolithic or Bronze Age date, but on balance it seems more likely to be a fore-runner of the stone-built fort (*ibid.,* 51). It is the main rampart of the hillfort that concerns us here. This encloses an area of some 0.28 ha and has one original east-facing entrance. 'Its course follows natural crests in places, but the circuit as a whole is remarkable for its pronounced 'tilt' across the contours, sloping downhill to the north so that the actual summit is only just enclosed' (*ibid.,* 10).

This curious 'tilt' has the effect of making the site visible from the river valley to the north-west 'by counteracting the convex slope on that side of the hill' (*ibid.,* 53). The fact that the summit is only just enclosed raises the question of whether the rampart was intended primarily for defence, or whether architectural display was more important. Oswald *et al.* acknowledge this fact when they say, 'If the placement of the defences was intended to signify the power or wealth of the inhabitants, it is interesting that the display was apparently directed towards the floor of the College Valley to the north' (*ibid.,* 53), meaning that the hillfort effectively dominates, in a visual sense, the approach to the valley. It also faces towards the hillfort on St Gregory's Hill to the north-east, the most impressive ramparts of which face back towards West Hill. It is also significant that the gateway into the hillfort occupies what was probably the most visually impressive section of the perimeter bank.

The surveyors observe that the east-facing gateway may have a symbolic importance (cf. Hill 1993, 66 and fig. 3; 1995, fig. 7; Oswald 1997), also suggesting that the almost circular plan of the rampart may replicate the design of Iron Age houses (Oswald *et al.* 2000, 53–4), providing an insight into the ideology of its builders. If relevant, this tantalising observation inevitably leads us to ask why all forts were not circular in plan. Several other Cheviot forts are indeed circular or roughly circular in outline, but many are not. In some cases, the form of a site is clearly related to the local topography, and it could be argued that circular sites are so shaped because they sit on top of dome-shaped hills. The extent to which cosmology is built into hillfort architecture is a subject worthy of further study, but is beyond the confines of this account.

In short, the spectacular West Hill site is far more than a few roundhouses clustering within a simple defensive earthwork. Rather, its architecture is complex, multi-period, and possibly highly symbolic. While its ramparts may, on occasion, have offered refuge, this site's primary function was surely not one of simple defence.

St Gregory's Hill

This site lies on an adjacent summit to West Hill, at NT 91612979 some 500 m south of Kirknewton, at a height of 180 m OD (Fig. 3). It commands broad views across the Glen valley and the Milfield plain. A significant observation in the light of our discussion below is that

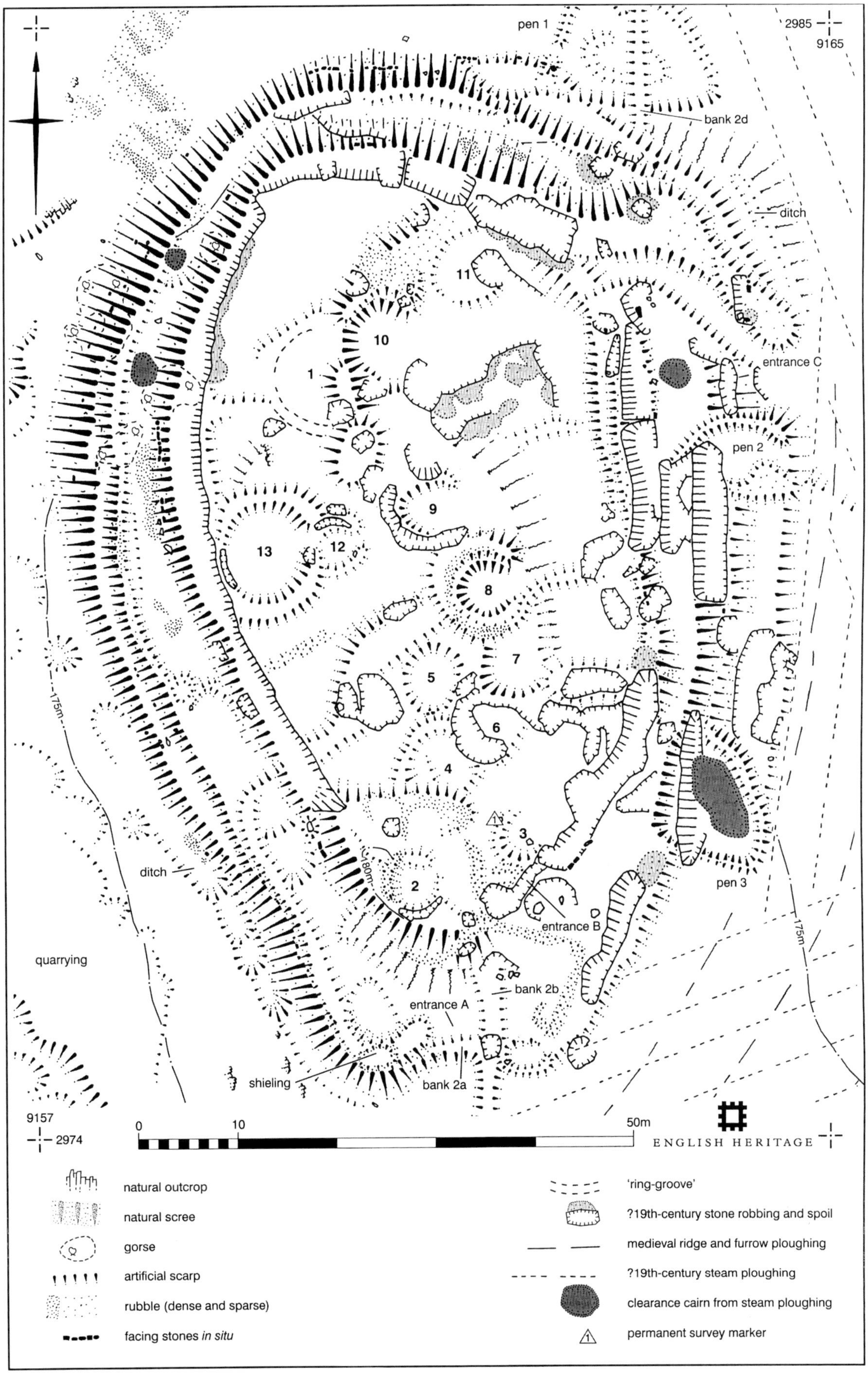

Fig. 3. Plan of St Gregory's Hill produced by the Discovering our Hillfort Heritage project (© English Heritage).

the hillfort is itself overlooked by a hillock, some 5 m higher, only 80 m south of the southern rampart. The site itself comprises 'the remains of two circuits of stone-built rampart, overlain by two enclosed settlements of a type usually thought to be of Romano-British or possibly late Iron Age date. Traces of as many as thirteen buildings are identifiable in the interior, of which all but one are probably Romano-British' (Oswald and McOmish 2002a, 2). The site was subjected to systematic stone robbing in the nineteenth century.

As Oswald and McOmish highlight, one of the most striking features of the hillfort is the angular plan of the ramparts. The outer circuit is virtually oval, enclosing an area of 0.4 ha and follows the hill's contours 'except for the southern tip, which is squared off to form a straight frontage facing the level approach where what can probably be interpreted as the original gateway was sited' (entrance 'A'; *ibid.,* 10). The inner circuit is almost pentangular in plan with a probable original entrance on its south-east side, slightly offset from entrance 'A'. From this set of observations Oswald and McOmish conclude that the outer circuit might have been constructed first. They also observe that sections of both circuits were certainly rebuilt in the Romano-British period.

The defences of the outer circuit follow the natural contour, and on the western and northern sides of the hill they are located along the edge of a steep escarpment. On the eastern side the slope is gentler, but still fairly pronounced. 'On the south, however, where the original entrance (A) seems to have been located, the ground is level for some distance before rising gently to an eminence some 5 m higher. The potential defensive weakness does not seem to have been reflected in the size of the defences, which were apparently higher where the natural slope is steepest' *(ibid.,* 10).

At St Gregory's Hill then, as at neighbouring West Hill, the so-called 'defences' may have been more for show than actual defence. As Oswald and McOmish observe (*ibid.,* 30), 'Around the northern and western perimeter of the hillfort, the steep natural slope has evidently been deliberately used to lend the defences on that side the illusion of great strength. This contrasts with the less impressive size of even the well-preserved earthworks on the south, although that sector, where the original gateway was probably sited on a stretch of level ground which offers little natural protection, would arguably have been far more vulnerable to attack.'

Oswald and McOmish discuss the factors that may have conditioned this situation and conclude that all of this was intentional because the entrance at A was consciously sited at the tip of the perimeter to create a striking architectural effect when seen by anyone approaching from the relatively gentle route from the south (*ibid.,* 30). In this context, we might note that a similarly sited entrance exists at the enigmatic site of Hethpool Bell, some 2 km south-west of St Gregory's Hill – a site which the English Heritage survey concludes had a symbolic or ritual purpose rather than a practical role as a settlement (Pearson and Ainsworth 2000). If this observation is correct, the display may have been intended to convey the wealth and social status of the occupants rather than any military dominance. Oswald and McOmish are certainly correct in pointing out that the existence of ramparts does not prove that warfare was endemic throughout Iron Age society, or even that the function of hillforts was primarily military.

Mid Hill

This hillfort lies very close to the northern edge of the Cheviots, some 2 km north-west of the hamlet of Hethpool (NT 88122958) at a height of 290 m OD (Oswald and McOmish 2002b). The site is well preserved and comprises the remains of a rampart described as a 'massive stone wall', with as many as eleven circular buildings in the interior. Of these buildings, 'ring grooves', potentially indicating timber structures contemporary with the building of the Iron Age defences, are most dominant. The site is oval in plan, and encloses some 0.24 ha. The original entrance probably lies at the northern end of the south-western side of the perimeter (Fig. 4). The site commands superb views to the south-east, but is clearly overlooked by land some 30 m higher to the south-west. The hillfort is intervisible with prehistoric enclosures on Staw Hill, East Laddies Knowe, Little Hetha, Great Hetha, West Hill, and St Gregory's Hill, the furthest of which lies less than 4 km away.

One of the most important conclusions of the survey is that the site is not the product of a single constructional episode. The investigators suggest that it evolved through two, if not three, phases of construction and re-modelling, at least one of them within the Romano-British period. A timber palisade with internal circular timber structures seemingly preceded the stone ramparts, and the timber buildings may already have been in existence when the stone ramparts were constructed (Oswald and McOmish 2002b, 22).

The interior would certainly have been visible from higher ground to the south-west and the siting of the stone-built circuit does not make best 'defensive' use of the natural topography. The approach from the south-east, via the tip of a spur, is essentially a blind spot in terms of defence. Given this observation, it is even more remarkable that the rampart on this seemingly weaker south-east sector is 'of negligible height, with little sign that it could ever have stood to truly defensible proportions' (*ibid.*, 23). This contrasts with the massive size of the ramparts on the north-west side of the site, the direction that offers the easiest natural approach to the hillfort and its entrance. As the investigators say, 'the inescapable conclusion is that the function of the rampart was more about impressing the approaching visitor than about defending against a well-planned or prolonged attack'.

Fig. 4. Air photograph looking north-west over Mid Hill and Staw Hill (photo: Tim Gates).

Staw Hill

Staw Hill lies only 500 m north-east of Mid Hill (NT 88453010), at a height of 277 m OD (Figs. 4–5). The site is well preserved (Ainsworth *et al.*, 2002, 2) and comprises an enclosure with a single stone-built rampart, with an additional rampart around the south and west sides only. It is oval in plan, with an entrance facing south-east. The enclosure measures only some 50 m by 33 m overall, giving an internal area of only 0.16 ha. Traces of four circular buildings (two of which are thought to be of Romano-British date) are visible within the main enclosure.

Staw Hill does not sit on the highest part of the ridge, 'but is located on a natural shelf on the ridge top, separated from rising higher ground on the south-west by a natural depression which crosses the ridge' (*ibid.*, 3). Most of the interior would have been visible from the higher ground to the south-west. Assuming they were in existence at roughly the same time, the site was intervisible with Little Hetha, Great Hetha, Mid Hill, West Hill, and St Gregory's Hill, the furthest of which lies only 3.5 km away.

The internal arrangements at Staw Hill contrast markedly with Mid Hill. There is no obvious evidence for an earlier palisaded phase and no ring-groove buildings have been identified. Indeed only two platforms for buildings that might be contemporary with the ramparts have been identified. The secondary rampart defies any attempts at 'functional' interpretation, and it is hard to see it as anything other than architectural embellishment intended to enhance the prestige of those responsible for it.

The Staw Hill site is on an altogether smaller scale than Mid Hill, and perhaps relates more closely to the many small and as yet undated settlements which clutter the surrounding hills. Given the difference in their size and apparent populations, the nature of the possible relationship between the two sites is intriguing, although it is not something that we have yet considered in any detail. Interestingly, the elaborate nature of the Staw Hill ramparts is best appreciated from Mid Hill, and the same could be argued in reverse. Perhaps the two sites were closely interdependent, with each playing a different but complementary role. It is hard to envisage sites of such contrasting scales existing in such close proximity to each other for any length of time if the relationship between them was in any way 'competitive'.

Regardless of the relationship between the two sites, we can apparently see at Staw Hill a situation where the impression of defensive strength may have been at least as important as defensive strength itself. As Ainsworth *et al.* note, if Staw Hill is approached from the south-west along the ridge top, 'when viewed from a distance it actually disappears from view below some locally higher ground beyond what may be a cross-ridge dyke' (*ibid.,* 24). However, once anyone approaching the site from this direction gets beyond the dyke, the natural route to the hillfort is through a saddle in this higher ground and 'once this has been reached the hillfort re-emerges and is framed perfectly by the gap between the higher ground either side of the saddle' (*ibid.,* 24).

Ainsworth *et al.*'s further observations are worth quoting in detail here:

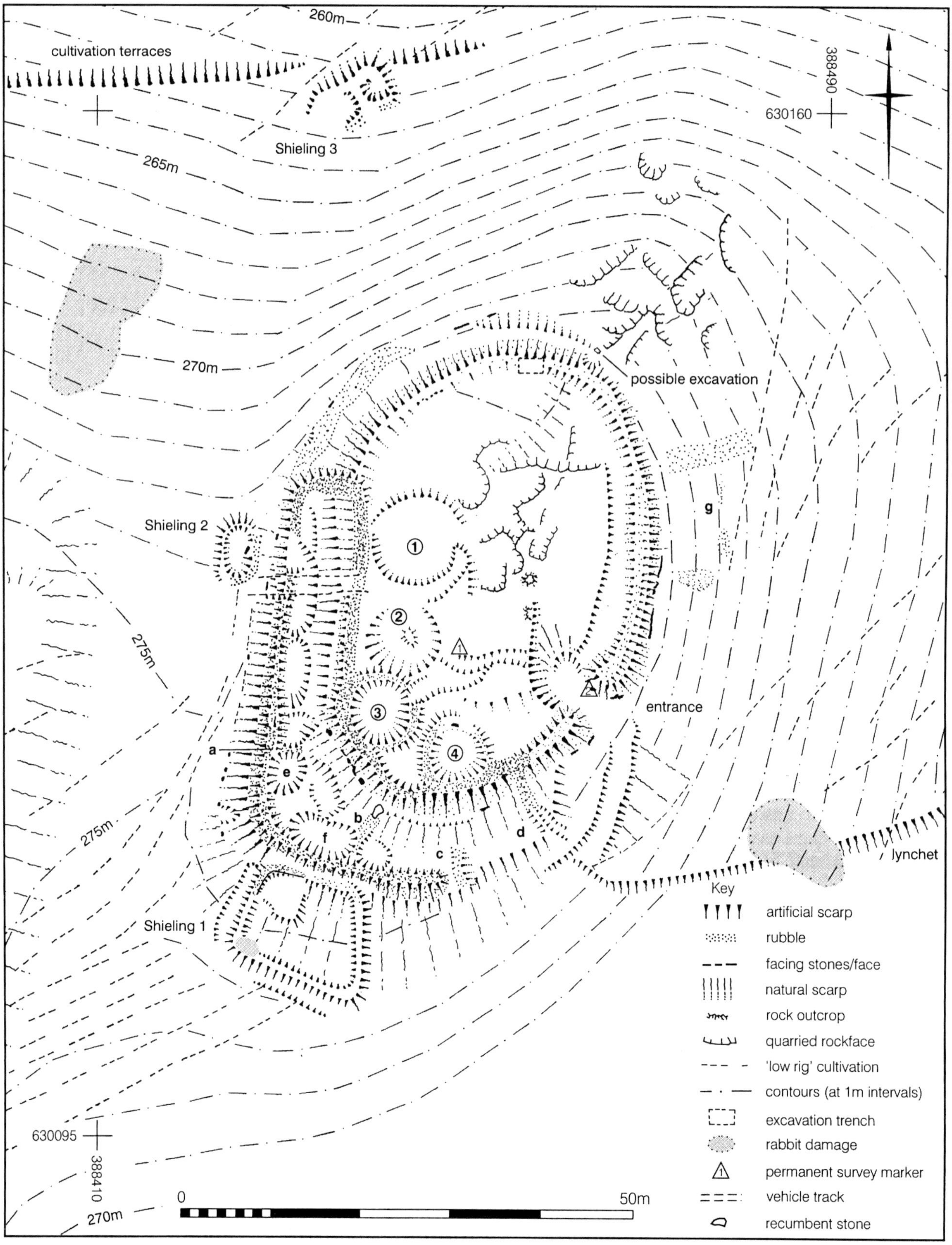

Fig. 5. Plan of Staw Hill produced by the Discovering our Hillfort Heritage project (© English Heritage).

'This factor may provide the context for the addition of the outer rampart. From this view, and with the addition of an outer rampart on only the south and west sides, the hillfort would appear to have double ramparts and the visitor be unaware that these did not continue around the rest of the perimeter as the east and north sides cannot be seen. Similarly as visitors got closer to the hillfort they would be below the natural summit on which the hillfort is located, thus the double rampart would look even more intimidating when combined with the deliberate enhancement of the natural slopes. The addition of an outer rampart along this side would have had the cumulative effect of not only looking very impressive as the site was approached... but also would have functioned as a defence commanding the approach to the entrance. That no additional rampart was taken around the east and north side implies that defence cannot have been its sole function as these sides would have been vulnerable without additional outworks. Even when directly approaching the entrance visitors would not be able to perceive the lack of a double defence around the other sides.' (Ainsworth *et al.* 2002, 25)

What were hillforts? The ongoing debate

If we are to interpret the observations made in the course of the field survey documented above, it is important to have an insight into current thinking on the economic and social roles of hillforts generally in Britain. As noted above, the situation in Wessex may be largely irrelevant to our understanding of the Cheviots. The Cheviot sites are clearly part of a tradition that extends throughout much of north Northumberland and southern Scotland, where hundreds of small and medium sized hillforts are known, and indeed still being discovered, in the lowlands as cropmarks, as for example in the Tweed valley (C. Waddington pers. comm.). Consequently, we should probably be looking north to Scotland rather than south to Wessex in seeking to interpret the Cheviot sites. Nevertheless, we must consider the potential relevance of recent thinking about hillforts in southern Britain.

In the last two decades, Iron Age archaeologists have seriously 're-thought' the hillforts of southern Britain. The almost traditional interpretation of them as the central places of farming communities, dominated by societal elites – based mainly on Cunliffe's work at Danebury (Cunliffe 1983; 1984a; 1984b; 1990; 1995) – has been challenged and largely rejected in some quarters (e.g. Hingley 1984; 1989; Barrett 1986; Haselgrove 1986; Sharples 1991a; 1991b; Hill 1995). Ironically, Cunliffe's own subsequent fieldwork in the Danebury environs has done much to validate these objections, by showing that during the Middle Iron Age, when the hillfort was supposedly at its most important as a central place, the lesser settlements in its immediate territory were apparently almost all abandoned (Cunliffe 2000). A similar phenomenon is apparent in the area around Maiden Castle (Sharples 1991a).

The complex and regionally varied nature of southern British Iron Age social organisation, something that no researcher in the field would now deny, is an important point to bear in mind when we come to consider the northern evidence in more detail. As Hill (1996, 101) has shown, large areas of southern England were quite happy to do without hillforts throughout the Iron Age and other forms of settlement could be dominant. Much has been made of a 'new (tribal, egalitarian and boundary obsessed) Wessex' (*ibid.*, 104) and, whilst Sharples (1991b) has suggested that hillforts may reflect warfare between large communities for control of land, there is a growing tendency to challenge such traditionally dominant military explanations (e.g. Bowden and McOmish 1987; 1989; Hill 1996).

Bowden and McOmish's (1987) work is particularly relevant here. They argued that hillfort 'defences' fulfilled non-utilitarian roles alongside purely defensive functions – in other words they may have been as much symbolic as practical. Elaborate hillfort boundaries may have served to enhance the prestige of the settlements and increase notions of their social isolation, and elaboration of the entrances may have been carried out for similar reasons (*ibid.*, 77). However, much of Bowden and McOmish's re-interpretation of hillforts, and boundaries in general, is still predicated upon the idea that discrete settlement and social hierarchies were in existence in Wessex.

In a Wessex context at least, it is easier to say what hillforts were *not*, rather than what they were. Hill (1995; 1996) rejects entirely the idea of them as a uniform class of Iron Age monument, noting that:

'we need to view hillforts not as a coherent entity but foremost as a class of monument whose internal variability is united in their difference as *not farmsteads*. What we are visualising in the proscription of these sites is the definition of a place considered as different from the outside. Hillforts do not represent a separate, recognisable class of field monuments with a distinct form and corresponding function; rather we need to see them in terms of the specific manifestation of a long tradition of making special places by enclosure, with origins in the Neolithic.' (Hill 1996, 109).

Hill goes on to suggest that in Early and Middle Iron Age Wessex, individual, independent households formed the basic economic/social/cultural unit, constituting what he terms a heterarchical, rather than a hierarchical, society. In this scenario, hillforts cease to be elite residences and become phenomena to be understood in terms of a deep rooted tradition of using earthworks and enclosures to mark significant social discontinuities in space (Hill 1996, 112).

We have already noted that Scottish hillforts should be of greater relevance to an understanding of our Cheviot sites than those of Wessex can realistically hope to be. This should be clear from a glance at Figure 6 (a and b). There are several hundred monuments classified as 'hillforts' throughout Scotland, and it might reasonably be thought that an analysis of the southern Scottish sites in particular would do much to help our understanding of the Iron Age in Northumberland. Unfortunately, while there have been several informative excavations north of the border, it is very difficult to isolate clear trends in the origins and development of hillforts. Indeed, a review of the available evidence in the early 1990s was forced to conclude that 'we have yet to come to grips with the complexity, scale, date and duration of the several periods of settlement represented in southern Scottish hillforts' (Rideout *et al.* 1992, 143).

In a more recent discussion, Armit (1997, 46–65) succinctly summarised current thinking with regard to Scottish hillforts. He notes that the name 'hillfort' implies that these sites were 'military structures built by strutting conquerors or nervous natives in times of unrest or change', but that for many sites 'there are reasons to believe that defence may not have been the sole or even the principal consideration'. Armit also makes the important observation that the 'defences' of many smaller hillforts are out of all proportion to the size of the 'defended' interiors, and suggests that many more people must have been involved in the construction of these sites than could ever have lived within them.

There is, however, much regional variation in the distribution of hillforts throughout Scotland. North of the Tay, a few hillforts occupy commanding positions overlooking a landscape of undefended, open settlements, in a situation clearly not analogous to that in the Cheviots. Throughout much of southern Scotland, however, the Iron Age landscape appears very similar to that of north Northumberland. In East Lothian and Tweeddale, there are so many enclosures of probable Iron Age date 'that it is hard to believe that they could all have been home to high-ranking families: indeed, it is possible that the majority of the rural population may have occupied such settlements' (Armit 1997, 61). Given that the 'rural population' at this time must have represented virtually the entire population, the suggestion here is that everyone may have been living within 'defended' enclosures of one kind or another.

The concentration of small hillforts (however defined) to the immediate north of the Border is certainly striking, as a glance at the Scottish Royal Commission's volumes on East Dumfriesshire (RCAHMS 1997) and Roxburghshire (RCAHMS 1956) will testify. Indeed, the latter publication states unambiguously that 'the dominant feature of Roxburghshire field archaeology is the abundance of hillforts' (*ibid.*, 16). The same could reasonably be said of the Northumberland Cheviots, demonstrating the irrelevance of the Anglo-Scottish Border to Iron Age studies (cf. Haselgrove 1989, 2; Frodsham 2000).

Back to the Cheviots

Our discussion of Scottish sites has brought us back to north Northumberland. We have already touched upon the problem of defining hillforts, as distinct from other earthwork enclosures. Any attempt to draw a clear distinction between the two is perhaps misguided, as the enclosures of presumed Iron Age date throughout Northumberland display a whole range of characteristics and defy ready classification into meaningful typological or chronological groups. Back in 1965, George Jobey catalogued 141 such sites in Northumberland, noting that only seven of these were greater than three acres (1.2 ha) in area, with the vast majority (113) occupying less than a single acre (0.4 ha). Jobey (1965, 22) observes that 'the distinction between a fort and a settlement is often slight; both can be used for permanent habitation and the so-called 'hill-forts' of the area are not always in positions of outstanding natural defence, nor do they normally excel in internal area.' More recently, the Scottish Royal Commission reached an analogous conclusion with regard to essentially similar sites in Dumfriesshire, noting that problems of classification are 'particularly acute with respect to any division between fortified sites on the one hand, and more lightly enclosed settlements on the other. The identification of a fort involves a qualitative judgement of its defensive strength, in terms of both the perimeter itself and the natural feature upon which it is located. In short, it is subjective, perhaps telling more of the preconceptions of the visitor than of the original function of the site.' (RCAHMS 1997).

Before moving on to consider some theoretical ideas that might be of relevance to Cheviot hillforts, we must highlight the dearth of hard evidence relating to their chronology. It is important to stress that the circumstances that gave rise to a particular hillfort's construction may only have been relevant to a few generations, although the spectacular nature of these sites in today's landscape suggests to us that they were of great importance over a long period of time. What little evidence there is suggests that hillfort ramparts of stone and earth were being constructed in Northumberland by the third century BC (Frodsham 2004, chapter 4). However, as we saw above, surface evidence shows that many, if not most, hillfort sites have both earlier and later phases.

Regardless of the general relevance of the traditional Hownam sequence (cf. Armit 1999), it is clear that some of our hillforts were preceded by unenclosed settlements and/or palisaded enclosures. These could date from a few decades prior to the overlying hillforts, or much earlier during the first half of the first millennium BC. At Wether Hill, for example, recent excavations demonstrate that an unenclosed settlement of timber roundhouses was superseded by a palisaded enclosure, before the impressive hillfort ramparts were constructed,

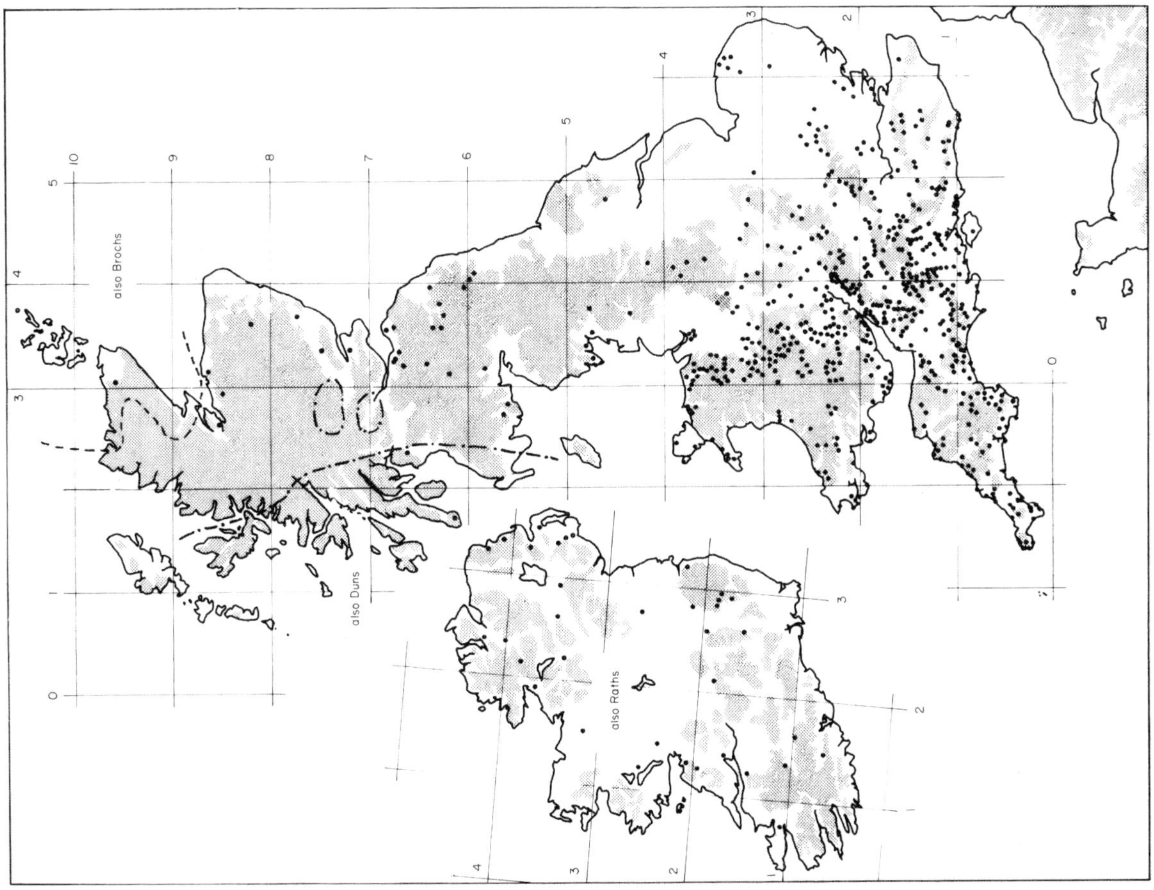

Fig. 6a. Distribution of hillforts in Britain. Sites greater than 1.2 ha in extent (after Harding 1976).

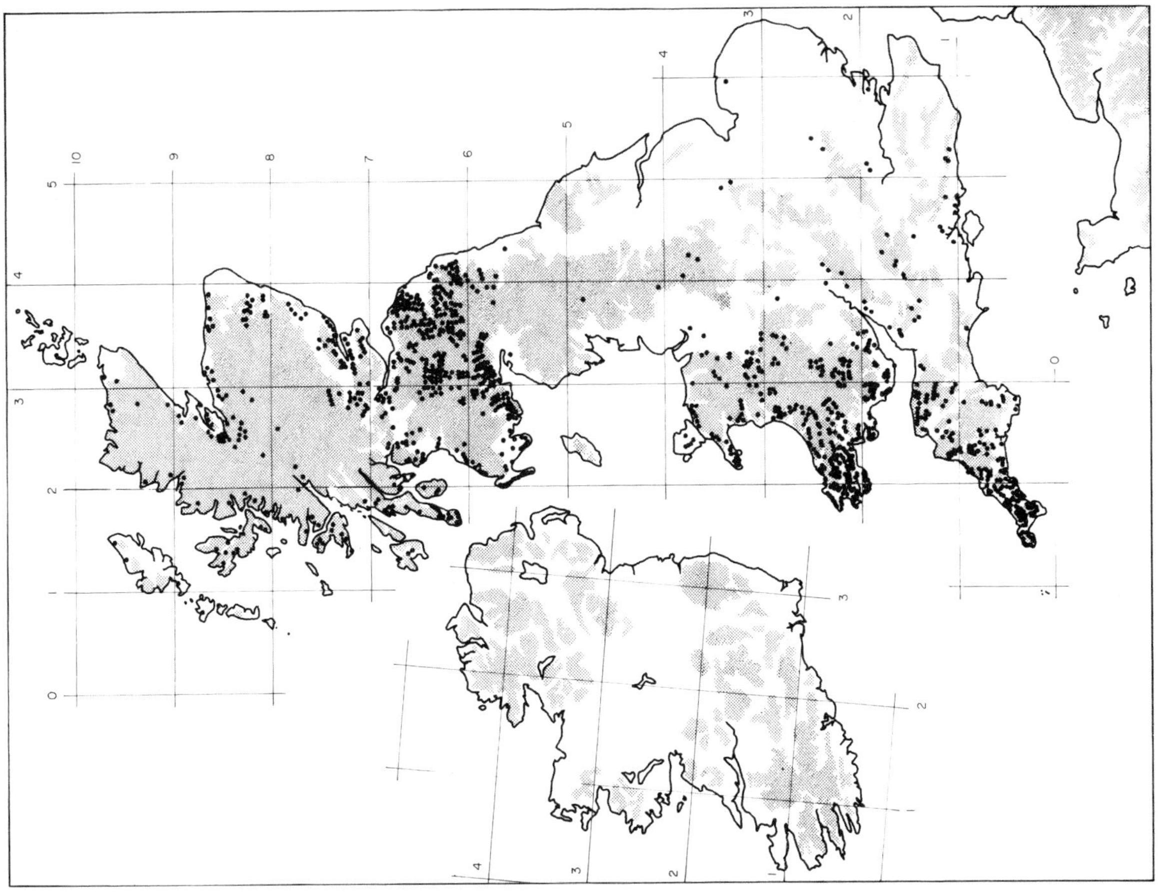

Fig. 6b. Distribution of hillforts in Britain. Sites extending over less than 1.2 ha (after Harding 1976).

probably in the third century BC (Topping 2004). In such cases, the location of the hillfort was effectively dictated by decisions taken several centuries earlier, when the original unenclosed settlement was founded. Therefore, while today's field evidence might suggest that a particular site was chosen so that its ramparts would appear impressive when viewed from a particular angle, it may be that the location of the site was fixed several generations before anyone thought of constructing the ramparts.

We must consider issues such as this when trying to account for the location of hillforts. As timber-built sites can be completely hidden by later activity, we will need to excavate a carefully chosen sample of sites before stating with any confidence how many hillforts were built on 'green-field' sites and how many were constructed on sites that had been previously (or were perhaps still) occupied. It is also worth noting that a large number of hillforts incorporate presumably much earlier burial cairns within their interiors. While it is possible to argue that this is no more than coincidence, as both cairns and hillforts demanded impressive locations, the presence of such cairns would not have been without significance to Iron Age people, and may conceivably have influenced the location and design of some hillforts.

Another key issue is the apparent distinction between 'Iron Age' and 'Romano-British' architecture. The recent English Heritage surveys interpret ring-groove houses as Iron Age, which is almost certainly correct, but assume all stone-founded round buildings to be of later, Romano-British date, which may not be. Whilst the new surveys have reinforced the fact that many hillforts were superseded by apparently 'undefended' settlements of stone roundhouses, exactly when this change occurred remains unclear in virtually all cases. The recent excavation of overlapping enclosures at Fawdon Dean, Ingram (Frodsham and Waddington 2004), strongly suggests that substantial stone roundhouses were being built by the first century BC. Consequently, the distinction between pre-Roman and Roman period phases on the basis of the presence or absence of stone-built houses must be questioned.

The chronology of the various forms of field systems (including cord rig and terraces) found adjacent to the hillforts is also poorly understood. Agricultural production was clearly critical to life within the hillforts, and more evidence for contemporary farming practice is sorely needed. Indeed, these field systems, details of which are included on several of the new English Heritage surveys, would offer an intriguing avenue of enquiry into the lives of the hillfort dwellers if the chronological relationships between fields and forts could be unravelled. Better comprehension of the fields might, for example, enable us to speculate about the extent to which discrete communities may have cooperated during the different stages of the agricultural calendar. The relationship between the hillforts and the hundreds of 'undefended' settlements scattered throughout the Cheviots, normally thought to be Romano-British but quite possibly earlier in many cases, is also essential to our understanding of the hillforts. As with so many other aspects of Cheviot prehistory, the resolution of these problems can only be sought through new fieldwork.

In an important contribution in the 1990s, Gill Ferrell analysed the available field evidence from north-east England (1992; 1997), noting that despite the wealth of settlement data, many basic questions about life in the Iron Age remained unanswered. Chief amongst the underlying reasons for this, she believes, is the way that archaeologists have appraised the data. 'The Iron Age of the north-east of England has an extensive but dull domestic settlement record. It lacks obvious 'type sites', a distinctive funerary tradition or a distinctive material culture on which to hang (and then endlessly refine) chronologies. Most seriously of all it lacks research projects attempting to surmount these imagined obstacles' (Ferrell 1997, 228). While we would dispute her claim that the settlement record of the region is 'dull', we would be forced to agree with the rest of her observation, particularly the last element. Even in recent work dealing specifically with central Britain (see Bevan 1999), there often seems to be a relative lack of interest in the physical remains of settlement compared to other aspects of the archaeology.

Ferrell considered that the Iron Age past should be viewed not simply in terms of settlement or artefact typologies, but in terms of social organisation. Her conviction is that social meaning and spatial order are inextricably linked and that the technique of rank size analysis, first developed in human geographical research, can be used to investigate the social processes and structures underlying different forms of settlement pattern (Ferrell 1992; 1997). Accordingly, she applied rank size analysis to settlement data from four study areas, one in Durham, the other three in Northumberland – in the Breamish valley (her Area 1); south of Rothbury (Area 2); and around Yeavering (Area 3) – and thus directly relevant to the current discussion.

In her analysis, Ferrell drew heavily on the concepts of 'closure' and 'interdependence' first introduced into human geography by Vapnarsky (1969). Closure measures the proportion of interactions beginning or ending within a particular settlement system that are completed within that system (Ferrell 1997, 229). It is thus at its highest if no obvious interactions occurred between the system and the outside world, and lowest if all interactions are initiated or completed outside the system. Interdependence is gauged by the amount of interaction that takes place within units belonging to the system. A low value indicates relative isolation of the units. High interdependence is necessary, however, for a pattern of settlements approximating to the rank size rule to emerge, since, as Ferrell (*ibid.*, 229) points out, 'a high level of interaction between units is required for a well-developed settlement hierarchy'.

In the Breamish valley (Area 1), which has been subjected to detailed survey by RCHME and subsequently to continued research by the National Park Authority in association with Durham University and the Northumberland Archaeological Group, Ferrell's work suggested no discernible hierarchy of settlement. In Vapnarsky's terms, this is an area of high closure and low interdependence, 'isolated from the external world with no settlements of appreciable size and no well-defined hierarchy' (Ferrell 1997, 229). This pattern appears to be replicated in Area 2, and, if we exclude Yeavering itself from her calculations, in Area 3. For Ferrell then, the overarching picture in the Cheviots is seemingly 'one of highly autonomous, isolated groups with a low level of interdependence and integration' with 'little differentiation in site size and no evidence for any form of settlement hierarchy' (*ibid.*, 233).

As a result, Ferrell argued that we need to reappraise the traditional notion of hillforts as 'relating to the centralisation of authority and the control of territory'. She believes that these sites represent the residences of extended family groups and that any display of status or small-scale raiding took place between peers without altering the balance of power. This notion may be supported by the fact that there is no obvious difference in house size within any of the hillforts surveyed by English Heritage: there is no hint of the kind of internal architectural elaboration that might be expected if these sites did contain the elite residences of local 'chiefs'. We believe that Ferrell's observations have important ramifications for the social analysis of hillforts and related settlements in the Cheviot uplands in the light of the detailed field evidence discussed in the first part of this paper.

Two other contributions should be highlighted. In discussing the results of the Northumberland Archaeological Group excavations at Wether Hill, David McOmish (1999) made several observations that in essence complement Ferrell's approach. He notes the effects of having outsized defences around a small settlement area, which 'not only creates a strong focus on the social group which occupies it but also affords these individuals the opportunity for public display' (*ibid.*, 116). Some sites, moreover, are located so that their interiors can clearly be seen from outside, and could have been attacked with missiles thrown from higher ground. Lastly, 'defences' can also serve to reinforce notions of social isolation and help differentiate the inhabitants from outsiders, thus enhancing their 'sense of place' and attachment to the particular site and its environs (*ibid.*, 118). Meanwhile, Welfare (2002, 74) has remarked on the prestige that may have attached to particularly prominent topographical positions or to the choice of specific building materials. He also draws attention to the fact that current debate on the function of hillforts places a greater emphasis on understanding the activities that went on inside the enclosures.

Cheviot 'hillforts': towards an alternative model

We have attempted to set the scene in terms of some recent thinking about hillforts in Wessex, Scotland, and Northumberland. Armed with a range of ideas derived from this contextualisation of current research, let us now further consider the four sites that represent the main focus of this contribution.

It should be fairly obvious that the four sites under detailed study here are fortified homesteads, arguably housing one family unit, with minimal surviving evidence for internal spatial divisions and for internal structures generally. None are in good defensive locations. Indeed, all four are in places where their interiors could be easily observed (or attacked). Why was this? Was it an Iron Age equivalent of the modern practice among some people of leaving the lights on and the curtains open at night to show off their best room? We think that we can safely conclude, along with other observers, that defence was not the overriding priority in the construction and siting of these enclosures. Perhaps the very term 'hillfort' is now of questionable value for such sites, given the historical baggage and connotations associated with it.

The recent surveys suggest that the occupants of these four Cheviot sites may well have been engaged in an almost proxy conflict with their neighbours: a kind of style war in which the aim was to out-do the neighbouring site/group by means of architectural expression and activity. As a result, what we see in the 'hillforts' are complex and multi-layered statements about social position and possession. Central to all of this seems to have been an overt desire to impress visitors.[2] Thus, at West Hill we have an impressive gateway linked to the most imposing section of bank, at a site so strangely skewed in its general location that anyone could see into it, whilst the top of the hill on which it sits was only just enclosed. Similarly, anyone could have seen into St Gregory's Hill, where the scale of the ramparts bears no relation to their defensive capabilities. At Mid Hill, the so-called defences were probably weakest where the obvious defensive blind spot was, and most impressive facing the easiest approach to the site.

These observations accord well with, and indeed enhance, Ferrell's arguments about the social relations that existed in the Iron Age in this region. The evidence we have would seem to support the notion of locally autonomous groups, keen to 'do their own thing', who seem, on the surface, to be socially isolated and in competition with each other. But does this really only tell one part of the social story? Rank size analysis and the application of Vapnarsky's concepts do seem to have some explanatory power when applied to Iron Age settlement in the Cheviots, as Ferrell has shown, but is the binary opposition of 'closed' and 'interdependent' social groups too mechanistic and functionalist to get below the complexities of regional social relations?

An alternative approach, which might still allow us to integrate all of our field observations and most of the theoretical shifts that we have documented, might be to start from the premise that cultural and social relations were much more fluid than has previously been argued from a twenty-first-century perspective. We would argue that spatial organisation, and social interaction, are reflections of attitudes towards, and perceptions of, environment and other people, rather than the simple results of population pressure, resource distribution, or core–periphery relationships as might be measured by techniques like rank size analysis of settlement units. As such, conceptions of spatial and social organisation might be much more culturally embedded, and the rules of activity much more socially prescribed, than previously thought. They may be intimately related to, and bound up with, types of production rather than scales of difference.

Andrew Fleming has discussed the types of social organisation that we may envisage in later prehistory in different parts of Britain, relating settlement evidence to land tenure and patterns of collective organisation. His fieldwork on Dartmoor has identified scattered houses, small hamlets, and field systems dating to the second millennium BC (Fleming 1985). He suggests a socio-economic model for these communities in which the 'household' is the main unit of labour. A 'household' is defined as a nuclear or small extended family occupying one or two houses set within the fields farmed by the family. Kinship structures link these households into wider groups. Thus, what appears at first glance to be a dispersed settlement pattern of isolated units, possibly reflecting the physical isolation of families within the landscape, may in fact be a closely linked society made up of localised groupings (*ibid.*, 131). Significantly, the settlement pattern will still appear dispersed in terms of its distribution over the land, but social relationships within the system promote a much closer association of individuals in terms of action.

Fleming draws on the rural sociological models of Rees (1968) and of Arensberg and Kimball (1948). These researchers have argued that a farmstead is not simply an outlier of a nucleated community, but forms a focus in its own right. The integration of farmsteads into interdependent social networks does not require the existence of a dominant centre with managerial functions, but results from the nature of the relationships between the farmsteads themselves. Fleming (1985, 132) examines the processes through which distinct, behaviourally linked social groupings are formed within this network of kinship and affinal ties. For a variety of reasons, individuals may command sufficient respect to form wider relationships because people related to them perceive that an 'advantage' may be gained through the reciprocal arrangements on which the system functions.

If the household is seen as the primary level of social organisation, Fleming suggests that secondary levels of organisation are represented by economic co-operation between households located in the neighbourhood, or groups of households from different neighbourhoods (*ibid.*, 132). Activities such as harvesting requiring a more substantial labour force could be carried out by groups from different farms working together. Rees (1968, 59), Emmett (1964), and Arensberg and Kimball (1948) all attest to this form of co-operation among rural communities, even with the advent of mechanisation. Fleming (1985, 133) is at pains to point out that this form of reciprocity may well have been even more pronounced in prehistory.

Local historical sources may also be of some relevance to our study of Iron Age society in the Cheviots. Documentary evidence demonstrates that sixteenth-century society on both sides of the Anglo-Scottish Border was based on extended kinship groups known as 'families', 'surnames' or 'graynes'. This period is sometimes referred to rather grandly as the era of the 'Border Reivers' (Fraser 1971; Frodsham 2004, 98–106), but its study is actually rather muddled through the confusion of myth and historical fact. In reality it is debatable whether the glorified 'Border Reivers' of local tradition, engaged in more-or-less constant raiding and fighting to uphold the honour of their grayne, actually existed at all. Most people were not constantly engaged in raiding even if they did belong to a grayne, and there were gangs of common thieves and outlaws who chose a violent life but belonged to no grayne.

A common mistake is made here by conflating different groups of people and referring to them collectively as Border Reivers (a term that was certainly not used by local people to describe themselves). We should bear such problems in mind when seeking to generalise about earlier societies. However, while debate about the historical authenticity of the term will continue to rage, there is no doubt that the structure of society at the time was based to a large extent on the graynes, which could subdivide and coalesce at different times for different reasons, paying scant regard to the Anglo-Scottish Border and associated Border law (Meikle 2005).

The graynes were 'true kinship units; they were united groups acting together in all things, seeking vengeance together when one of their number was harmed and often accepting joint responsibility when an individual was in trouble.' (Rae 1966, 6). Although each surname had a leader, or head man, chosen from within the grayne, no principle of primogeniture existed. The efficiency of leaders to provide for their followers enough land to till or graze, a fair share of the proceeds of raids, protection, and justice, was the main factor in maintaining their position (*ibid.*, 7). Perhaps things were not so very different during the Iron Age.

A further important factor raised by mention of sixteenth-century borderland society is that of mobility. Large numbers of people moved 'en masse' with their livestock from lowland winter steadings to occupy upland shielings during the summer months, the shieling grounds belonging to individual graynes as customary tenants by right of inheritance. Back in the Mesolithic and Neolithic, and historically through into post-medieval times, such mobility, or transhumance, was a key element in the annual cycle of life in and around the Cheviot Hills. It is usually thought that Bronze Age and Iron Age settlement patterns were more static, but the possibility remains that hillforts were occupied seasonally rather than permanently throughout the year. While it may never be feasible to reach firm conclusions, the possibility of seasonal occupation by part, if not all, of a hillfort's inhabitants should be considered when discussing Iron Age social organisation in the Cheviots and elsewhere.

Although Fleming's ideas were developed in a Bronze Age context and for the uplands of south-west England, they may well be relevant to an understanding of the way in which our Cheviot 'hillforts' functioned. Individual farmsteads may well have been 'isolated' in terms of their being bounded by banks and ditches, as McOmish suggests, and their rank size similarities may well support Ferrell's idea that the groups who lived in them were autonomous. Equally, an element of inter-site 'competition' is clearly apparent in the way that their defences were constructed and gateways located, whilst the fact that many sites could be so easily looked into may well have provided further opportunities to 'show off' to anyone who happened to see. While all of this may be taken at one level to indicate the differences that might have existed between groups, beneath this veneer of apparent competition and differences, similar forces may have been at work.

If all of these sites were broadly contemporary, it seems inconceivable that there would have been no interaction between their occupants. What we probably have in the Cheviot Iron Age is a situation not unlike that which exists today. There may be an outward show of indifference to neighbours, and an element of inter-farm competition represented, for example, by who can buy the most expensive rams at the local agricultural show, or drive the most up-to-date 4x4 vehicle. However, when certain situations arise and tasks demand it, all such differences are cast aside, labour is pooled, and co-operation becomes almost second nature.

It may have been the tensions between competition and co-operation that gave form to the hillforts we have included here in our North Cheviot case studies. The structures themselves may have been but one outward physical manifestation and embodiment of a complex social system, the very glue of which consisted of kinship ties, reciprocal labour exchanges, and a range of other social phenomena that existed against this background but which have left no direct physical trace in the archaeological record. The competitive element may well have served to ensure that no one group over-reached itself. The very fact that their ramparts and related features are so well preserved has led us to assume that our hillforts must have had a primarily 'defensive' function, but this need not have been the case. Hillfort ramparts, just like the many splendid swords and other 'offensive' weapons of the Iron Age, may have had practical uses on occasions while being of constant symbolic value.

Conclusions

To sum up, having considered some relevant theory and highly detailed topographic surveys, we believe that the model presented here is relevant to an understanding of the many small 'hillforts' scattered throughout the Cheviots. Although their architecture seems to indicate, at one level, a degree of inter-site competition, these sites are best viewed not primarily as defensive and hierarchical but as the residences of extended family groups that co-operated effectively with one another. Different sites may well have been linked by kinship, and groups of individuals would probably have co-operated in different ways, perhaps on a regular basis at certain key points in the agricultural calendar, to achieve particular objectives. At other times they would have gone their own way, being largely self-sufficient.

We certainly do not wish to imply at this stage that our model is relevant to all the hillforts in the Cheviots. These come in a wide range of shapes and sizes, and were almost certainly constructed, and often modified, at different times throughout the first millennium BC. The extent of our model's relevance throughout the region and elsewhere will only become clear as further fieldwork is completed. We hope that the recent English Heritage surveys, completed as part of the *Discovering our Hillfort Heritage* project, will now provide a stimulus for such work.

Acknowledgements

The writers are grateful to the English Heritage DoHH survey team, especially Al Oswald, Trevor Pearson, and Stewart Ainsworth, without whose work this paper could not have been written. We are also greatly indebted to Tim Gates for his contribution to the DoHH project in general, and in particular for his consent to reproduce Figures 2 and 4. We are also grateful to Colin Haselgrove for inviting this contribution, which we hope will go some way towards putting the Cheviots where they belong, literally at the centre of Iron Age Britain.

Notes

1. The other hillforts surveyed by English Heritage as part of *Discovering our Hillfort Heritage* are Castle Hill, Alnham (Pearson *et al.* 2001); Fawcett Shank (Oswald 2000); Glead's Cleugh (Pearson and Ainsworth 2001); Great Hetha (Pearson and Lax 2001); Hethpool Bell (Pearson and Ainsworth 2000); Middleton Dean (Ainsworth and Hunt 2004); Ring Chesters (Oswald *et al.* 2002); and South Heddon (Pearson and Hunt 2004). In addition, Yeavering Bell (Pearson 1998) was surveyed as part of a trial project for the DoHH initiative, and surveys of Humbleton Hill, Harehaugh Camp, and Lordenshaws were completed by RCHME in the 1980s and 1990s. Further information about these sites is available from the Northumberland Sites and Monuments Record, or from the National Monuments Record in Swindon.
2. Similar things appear to be going on today. Until recently, the view from the back of my house was of a pleasant green hill. It is now dominated by a very large new house (draped, at the time of writing, with the most garish Christmas lights imaginable) with a grand entrance framed by an imposing stone staircase. The house is fronted by the most neatly manicured lawn in the village, together with an extensive gravel area on which to park the glossy black BMW. My neighbours obviously feel superior and in terms of wealth they undoubtedly are. Perhaps their desire to display this 'superiority' bears a distant echo of the thinking behind the location and design of at least some of our Iron Age 'hillforts'. (PF).

Bibliography

Ainsworth, S. and Hunt, A. 2004. *An Iron Age Hillfort at Middleton Dean, Northumberland.* York: English Heritage Survey Report AI/4/2004.

Ainsworth, S., Oswald, A. and Pearson, T. 2002. *An Iron Age Hillfort on Staw Hill, Northumberland.* York: English Heritage Survey Report AI/17/2002.

Arensberg, C.M. and Kimball, S.T. 1948. *Family and Community in Ireland.* Cambridge (MA): Harvard University Press.

Armit, I., Dunwell, A. and Hunter, F. 2002. The Hill at the Empire's Edge: Recent work on Traprain Law, *Transactions of the East Lothian Antiquarian and Field Naturalists' Society* 25, 1–11.

Armit, I. 1997. *Celtic Scotland.* London: Batsford.

Armit, I. 1999. Life after Hownam: the Iron Age in south-east Scotland, in Bevan 1999, 65–79.

Barrett, J. 1986. Hillforts as centralised foodstores: an unlikely explanation. Paper presented to World Archaeology Congress, Southampton.

Bevan, B. (ed.) 1999. *Northern Exposure: Interpretative Devolution and the Iron Ages in Britain.* Leicester: Leicester Archaeology Monograph 4.

Bowden, M. and McOmish, D. 1987. The required barrier, *Scottish Archaeological Review* 4, 77–84.

Bowden M. and McOmish, D. 1989. Little boxes: more about hillforts. *Scottish Archaeological Review* 6, 12–16.

Cunliffe, B. 1983. *Danebury: Anatomy of an Iron Age Hillfort.* London: Batsford

Cunliffe, B. 1984a. *Danebury: An Iron Age Hillfort in Hampshire. The Excavations 1969–1978.* London: Council for British Archaeology Research Report 52.

Cunliffe, B. 1984b. Iron Age Wessex: continuity and change, in Cunliffe and Miles 1984, 12–24.

Cunliffe, B. 1990. Before hillforts, *Oxford Journal of Archaeology* 9, 323–336.

Cunliffe, B. 1995. *Danebury: An Iron Age Hillfort in Hampshire, Vol. 6. A Hillfort Community in Perspective.* London: Council for British Archaeology Research Report 102.

Cunliffe, B. 2000. *The Danebury Environs Programme: The Prehistory of a Wessex Landscape, Vol. 1. Introduction.* Oxford: Oxford University Committee for Archaeology Monograph 48.

Cunliffe, B. and Miles, D. (eds) 1984. *Aspects of the Iron Age in Central Southern Britain.* Oxford: Oxford University Committee for Archaeology Monograph 2.

Emmett, I. 1964. *A North Wales Village: A Social Anthropological Study.* London: Routledge and Kegan Paul.

Ferrell, G. 1992. *Settlement and Society in the Later Prehistory of North-East England.* Unpublished Ph.D. thesis, University of Durham.

Ferrell, G. 1997. Space and society in the Iron Age of north-east England, in Gwilt and Haselgrove 1997, 228–238.

Fleming, A. 1985. Land tenure, productivity and field systems, in G. Barker and C. Gamble (eds), *Beyond Domestication in Prehistoric Europe*, 129–146. London: Academic Press.

Fraser, G.M. 1971. *The Steel Bonnets. The Story of the Anglo-Scottish Border Reivers.* London: Barrie and Jenkins.

Frodsham, P. 2000. Worlds without ends: towards a new prehistory for central Britain, in J. Harding and R. Johnson (eds), *Northern Pasts. Interpretations of the Later Prehistory of Northern England and Southern Scotland.* Oxford: British Archaeological Reports British Series 302.

Frodsham, P. 2004. *Archaeology in Northumberland National Park.* York: Council for British Archaeology Research Report 136.

Frodsham, P. and Waddington, C. 2004. The Breamish Valley Archaeology Project, 1994–2002, in Frodsham 2004, 171–189.

Frodsham, P. and O'Brien, C. (eds) 2005. *Yeavering. People, Power and Place.* Stroud: Tempus.

Gwilt, A. and Haselgrove, C. (eds) 1997. *Reconstructing Iron Age Societies.* Oxford: Oxbow Monograph 71.

Harding, D.W. 1976. *Hillforts. Later Prehistoric Earthworks in Britain and Ireland.* London: Academic Press.

Haselgrove, C. 1986. Central places in British Iron Age studies: a review and some problems, in E. Grant (ed.), *Central Places, Archaeology and History*, 3–12. Sheffield: J.R. Collis Publications.

Haselgrove, C. 1989. The later Iron Age in southern Britain and beyond, in M. Todd (ed.), *Research on Roman Britain, 1960–1989*, 1–18. London: Britannia Monograph 11.

Haselgrove, C. 1999. Iron Age societies in central Britain: retrospect and prospect, in Bevan 1999, 253–278.

Hedley, I. 2001. The Discovering Our Hillfort Heritage Project, *Archaeology North* 18, 2001, 14–15.

Hill. J.D. 1993. Can we recognise a different European past? A contrastive archaeology of later prehistoric settlements in southern England, *Journal of European Archaeology* 1, 57–75.

Hill, J.D. 1995. How should we understand Iron Age hillforts: a contextual study, in C.G. Cumberpatch and J.D. Hill (eds), *Different Iron Ages*, 45–66. Oxford: British Archaeological Reports International Series 602.

Hill, J.D. 1996. Hillforts in the Iron Age of Wessex, in T.C. Champion and J.R. Collis (eds), *The Iron Age in Britain and Ireland: Recent Trends*, 95–116. Sheffield: J.R. Collis Publications.

Hingley, R. 1984. Towards social analysis in archaeology: Celtic society in the Iron Age of the Upper Thames Valley, in Cunliffe and Miles 1984, 72–88.

Hingley, R. 1989. Iron Age settlement and society in central and southern Warwickshire, in A. Gibson (ed.), *Midlands Prehistory*, 122–157. Oxford: British Archaeological Reports British Series 204.

Jobey, G. 1965. Hillforts and settlements in Northumberland, *Archaeologia Aeliana* (Ser. 4) 43, 21–64.

McOmish, D. 1999. Wether Hill and Cheviots Hillforts, in P. Frodsham, P. Topping and D. Cowley (eds), '*We Were Always Chasing Time.' Papers Presented To Keith Blood* (*Northern Archaeology* 17/18), 113–121.

Meikle, M.M. 2005. *A British Frontier? Lairds and Gentlemen in the Eastern Borders, 1540–1603.* East Linton: Tuckwell Press.

Oswald, A. 1997. A doorway on the past: practical and mystic concerns in the orientation of roundhouse doorways, in Gwilt and Haselgrove 1997, 87–95.

Oswald, A. 2000. *An Iron Age Hillfort on Fawcett Shank, Northumberland.* York: English Heritage Survey Report AI/13/2000.

Oswald, A. 2004. An Iron Age hillfort in an evolving landscape. Analytical field survey on West Hill, Kirknewton, in Frodsham 2004, 202–212.

Oswald, A. and McOmish, D. 2002a. *An Iron Age Hillfort and its Environs on St Gregory's Hill, Northumberland.* York: English Heritage Survey Report AI/1/2002.

Oswald, A. and McOmish, D. 2002b. *An Iron Age Hillfort on Mid Hill, Northumberland.* York: English Heritage Survey Report AI/2/2002.

Oswald, A., Jecock, M. and Ainsworth, S. 2000. *An Iron Age Hillfort and its Environs on West Hill, Northumberland.* York: English Heritage Survey Report AI/12/2000.

Oswald, A., Pearson, T. and Ainsworth, S. 2002. *Ring Chesters, Northumberland: an Iron Age Hillfort and its Environs.* York: English Heritage Survey Report AI/3/2002.

Owen, O.A. 1992. Eildon Hill North, Roxburgh, Borders, in Rideout *et al.* 1992, 21–71.

Pearson, T. 1998. *Yeavering Bell Hillfort, Northumberland.* York: English Heritage Survey Report AI/24/1998.

Pearson, T. and Ainsworth, S. 2000. *A Prehistoric Enclosure on Hethpool Bell, Northumberland.* York: English Heritage Survey Report AI/11/2000.

Pearson, T. and Ainsworth, S. 2001. *An Iron Age Hillfort at Glead's Cleugh, Northumberland.* York: English Heritage Survey Report AI/9/2001.

Pearson, T. and Hunt, A. 2004. *An Iron Age or Romano-British Enclosure at South Heddon, Northumberland.* York: English Heritage Survey Report AI/5/2004.

Pearson, T. and Lax, A. 2001. *An Iron Age Hillfort at Great Hetha, Northumberland.* York: English Heritage Survey Report AI/3/2001.

Pearson, T., Lax, A. and Ainsworth, S. 2001. *An Iron Age Hillfort and its Environs on Castle Hill, Alnham, Northumberland.* York: English Heritage Survey Report AI/2/2001.

Rae, T.I., 1966. *The Administration of the Scottish Frontier 1513–1603.* Edinburgh: Edinburgh University Press.

RCAHMS 1956. *An Inventory of the Ancient and Historical Monuments of Roxburghshire.* Edinburgh: HMSO.

RCAHMS 1997. *Eastern Dumfriesshire: An Archaeological Survey.* Edinburgh: The Stationery Office.

Rees, A.D. 1968. *Life in the Welsh Countryside.* Cardiff: University of Wales Press.

Rideout, J.S., Owen O.A. and Halpin, E. 1992. *Hillforts of Southern Scotland.* Edinburgh: AOC Scotland Monograph 1.

Sharples, N. 1991a. *Maiden Castle.* London: English Heritage.

Sharples, N. 1991b. Warfare in Iron Age Wessex, *Scottish Archaeological Review* 4, 70–75.

Stopford, J. 1987. Danebury: An alternative view, *Scottish Archaeological Review* 4, 70–75.

Topping, P. 2004. Hillforts, farms and fields. Excavations on Wether Hill, Ingram, 1993–2002, in Frodsham 2004, 190–201.

Vapnarsky, C.A. 1969. On rank size distributions of cities: an ecological approach, *Economic Development and Cultural Change* 17, 584–595.

Welfare, H. 2002. The uplands of the northern counties in the first millennium BC, in C. Brooks, R. Daniels and A. Harding (eds.) *Past, Present and Future: The Archaeology of Northern England*, 71–78. Durham: Architectural and Archaeological Society of Durham and Northumberland Research Report 5.

Dominated by unenclosed settlement? The Later Iron Age in eastern Scotland north of the Forth

Mairi H. Davies

Introduction

This paper focuses on evidence for Later Iron Age settlement in the former counties of Stirlingshire, Perthshire and Angus (Fig. 1). The study area straddles the Highland and Lowland zones of Scotland, permitting comparison of both areas, and allowing examination of the idea that the Forth was a significant cultural boundary. The effect of the history of Iron Age research is discussed, and the oft-reiterated model, wherein open settlement dominates in the Iron Age north of the Forth, is examined and its origin traced. Previous perceptions are shown to be misleading, as there is in fact considerable evidence for enclosed settlement at this period.

In order to characterise the Later Iron Age of the study area, cropmark sites in particular are considered, including multivallate enclosures and palisades. A more complex model is proposed, based on reassessment of old material and synthesis of evidence from more recent excavations. Armit's (1999) 'souterrain abandonment horizon' hypothesis is also challenged and suggestions are made as to where we might find the 'missing' dead of this period, with long, un-urned short and oval cists, square barrows, and cremation burials all considered. Whilst a comprehensive synthesis of the Later Iron Age in the area is beyond the scope of this paper, I endeavour to show how data gathered over the past thirty years can generate a model of settlement and society that differs significantly from those previously proposed.

The history of research

A recent assessment of existing knowledge of the Iron Age throughout Britain categorises Perthshire and Angus as 'unsorted' and Stirlingshire as a 'black hole' (Haselgrove *et al.* 2001, 25). This is despite a history of archaeological investigation and excavation in the area stretching back to the mid eighteenth century. The first recorded hillfort excavation, for instance, took place in 1799 at Dunsinane (Christison 1899–1900, 86; Playfair 1819; Robertson 1799) and souterrains were being 'cleared out' by enthusiastic amateurs as early as 1748 (Wainwright 1963, 189). One of the first people to write extensively on the area's prehistoric remains was also one of the first female antiquarians, Christian Maclagan, who published several books and articles, including accounts of the upstanding monuments of the Forth valley (Maclagan 1870–1; 1884) and north-east Scotland (Maclagan 1875; 1881). Despite some idiosyncratic interpretations, she was an accurate observer of archaeological remains (Elsdon 2004) and little deserves the label of 'poor scholar' given her by Matthew in an updated entry in the *Dictionary of National Biography* (Millar and Matthew 2004).

In the late nineteenth century, the pioneers of modern excavation methods in Scotland, John Abercromby, Joseph Anderson, and David Christison, excavated three multivallate enclosures in the region: at Orchill, near Kaims Castle (Christison 1900–1); Castle Law, Abernethy (Christison 1898–9); and a third adjacent to the Inchtuthil legionary fortress (Abercromby *et al.* 1901–2, 230–4). Christison also produced a monumental synthesis of Scottish forts, including many in this area, which he presented as the Society of Antiquaries of Scotland's

Fig. 1. The study area, showing the old counties of Stirlingshire, Perthshire, and Angus and the modern cities of Perth, Edinburgh, and Glasgow.

1894 Rhind Lectures (Christison 1898), and followed with a paper detailing sites in Perthshire and Angus (Christison 1900–1).

The death of Christison and Anderson's retirement marked a distinct downturn in field research in the area, no doubt exacerbated by the two World Wars. The only significant fieldwork at this period was by W.J. Watson (1912–13; 1914–15) and Wallace Thorneycroft (1932–3; 1945–6), who both excavated stone roundhouses, and by V.G. Childe, at Finavon fort, Angus (Childe 1934–5; 1935–6). The subsequent dramatic increase in *recorded* excavations on later prehistoric sites seen in Figure 2 coincides with the founding of the Archaeological Section of the Perthshire Society of Natural Science (PSNS) in 1948 and the launch of *Discovery and Excavation in Scotland*, but is likely to be a real trend, since it also coincided with Margaret Stewart's relocation to Perthshire. Stewart, who gained her doctorate under Childe at Edinburgh University, was the first President of the Archaeological Section of the PSNS, and the strong tradition of amateur involvement in the field that she fostered (Fig. 3), along with D.B. Taylor and F.T. Wainwright in his important work on souterrains (e.g. Wainwright 1953a; 1963), sustained interest until the growth of rescue archaeology in the 1970s (Sherriff 2000).

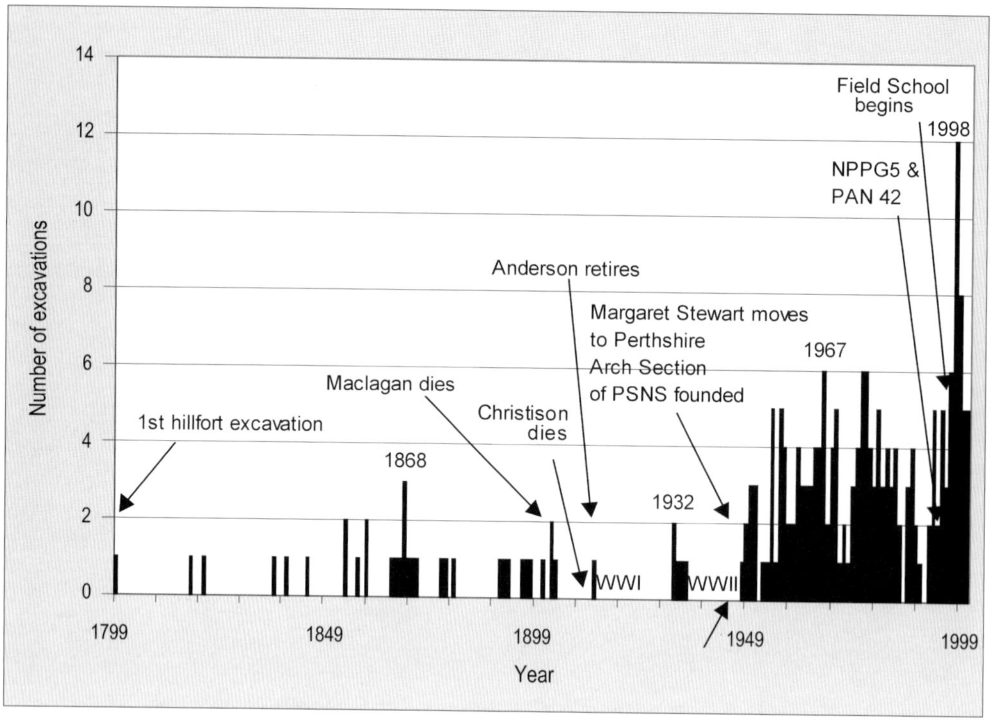

Fig. 2. Recorded excavations of later prehistoric sites in Stirlingshire, Perthshire, and Angus 1799–2001, indicating events that may have affected either the number of excavations that took place, or the number reported. Some excavations have been omitted because the date is not recorded. Others, particularly in the eighteenth and nineteenth centuries, may have gone entirely unrecorded. The upsurge in reported excavations and events in the late 1940s and early 1950s are inextricably linked to the renaissance in amateur archaeological fieldwork triggered by Margaret Stewart's move to Perthshire. Stewart was also involved in the Scottish Branch of the Council for British Archaeology (which evolved into the Council for Scottish Archaeology), the foundation of Discovery and Excavation in Scotland, and many rescue excavations.

Fig. 3. Margaret Stewart's excavation of a stone roundhouse on Law Hill, Arnbathie, 1950; the diggers were volunteers from the Perthshire Society of Natural Science (Perth Museum and Art Gallery, reproduced by kind permission of The Perthshire Advertiser).

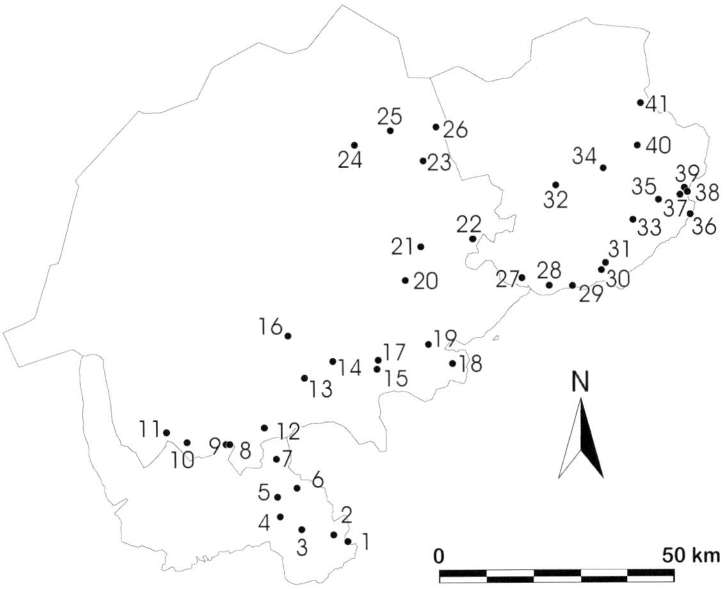

Fig. 4. The study area, showing sites mentioned in the text: 1. Avonglen Quarry; 2. Bowhouse; 3. Camelon; 4. Denovan Mains; 5. West Plean; 6. Easter Moss; 7. Abbey Craig; 8. East Coldoch; 9. Mains of Burnbank; 10. Flanders Hill; 11. Portend; 12. Barbush; 13. Orchill; 14. North Mains; 15. Dun Knock, Dunning; 16. Lochlane; 17. Inverdunning House; 18. Castle Law, Abernethy; 19. Moncrieffe House; 20. Newmill, Bankfoot; 21. Inchtuthil; 22. Wester Denhead; 23. Dalrulzion; 24. Carn Dubh; 25. Tulloch Field; 26. Dalnaglar; 27. Hurly Hawkin; 28. Dundee Law; 29. Craigie; 30. Ardestie; 31. Carlungie; 32. Fletcherfield; 33. West Grange of Conon; 34. Finavon; 35. Boysack Mills; 36. West Mains of Ethie; 37. Ironshill; 38. Red Castle; 39. Hawkhill; 40. Dubton; 41. Mains of Edzell.

Several important later prehistoric sites were excavated in the 1970s and 1980s, although many were not published until the 1990s (e.g. Kendrick 1995; Rideout 1996; Hingley *et al.* 1997; Murray and Ralston 1997; Pollock 1997). The inception of National Planning Policy Guideline 5 (Scottish Office 1994), equivalent to PPG16 in England and Wales, has ensured that the *floruit* of excavation in the 1970s has been sustained. Over the last ten years, most excavations of later prehistoric sites have been undertaken by commercial units, although Angus and south Aberdeenshire were the focus of a long-term project by Edinburgh University's Archaeology Department, investigating management issues but largely targeting Iron Age sites (Finlayson *et al.* 1999).

There has, however, been little modern synthesis aside from brief popular accounts (Stevenson 1999, 28–33; MacGregor and Oram 2000; Main 2002). Although the last comprehensive inventory of monuments in Stirling by the Royal Commission on the Ancient and Historical Monuments of Scotland (RCAHMS 1963) was later updated (RCAHMS 1979), these volumes contain information on just a handful of later prehistoric sites and provide little interpretation or discussion. They were followed by the landmark volumes on the 'archaeological landscapes' of north-east Perth (RCAHMS 1990) and south-east Perth (RCAHMS 1994a) and a new survey in the Braes of Doune (RCAHMS 1994b), but again these offer a minimalist interpretation, grouping sites by supposed function, rather than period. Although of high quality and undoubted worth as a resource, one is left with the feeling that the full potential of the new data has not yet been realised (Haselgrove *et al.* 2001). Major strides were made by Lesley Macinnes (1983) in her comparative survey of later prehistoric settlement north and south of the Forth, but much of her work has never been followed up, although simplified generalisations of her models for Angus and north-east Fife (*ibid.*) were adopted and applied to the whole of eastern Scotland 'north of the Forth'. The most recent overviews of Iron Age Scotland (Hingley 1992; Armit 1997) have necessarily relied on models produced for adjacent counties in providing syntheses of north-eastern Scotland.

Of the three former counties on which this paper focuses (Fig. 4), Macinnes only directly addressed Angus. They straddle the Highland Boundary Fault and, in the case of Stirlingshire, areas to both the west and east, providing an opportunity to examine settlement in both Highland and Lowland zones. Most of the study area is in Stuart Piggott's North-Eastern Province, but Stirlingshire is bisected by the River Forth and strays into the Tyne–Forth province (Piggott 1966). This division, however, was effectively broken down in the early 1980s

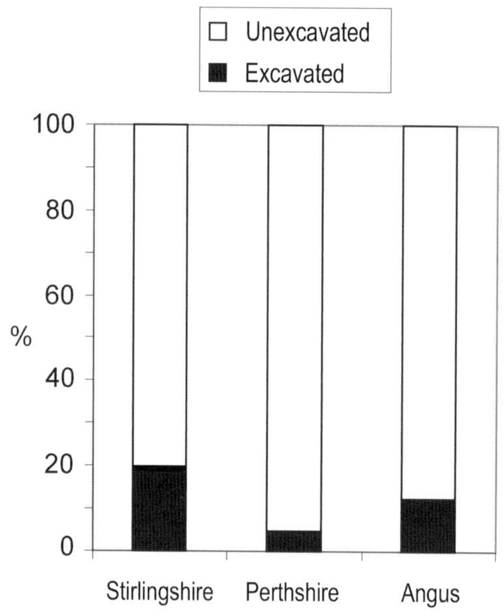

Fig. 5. Relative proportions of later prehistoric sites excavated in the study area.

when Angus was included in a reappraisal of the later prehistory of south-east Scotland (Harding 1982).

This paper examines the implications of the data collected over the past thirty years for our understanding of late prehistoric settlement and society in the study area. Owing to the apparent longevity of many settlement types and the lack of tight chronological control, evidence from around 500 cal. BC to cal. AD 400 is discussed.[1] The terminal date is dictated by the changes which occur in the settlement record of Perthshire from the fifth century AD onward, for example at Pitcarmick (Barrett and Downes 1996), significantly later than the first historical reference to the 'Picts' (AD 297).[2] As Figure 5 shows, proportionally more late prehistoric sites have been excavated in Stirlingshire than in the other two counties, with Perthshire having the lowest proportion of all.

The origins of the prevalent model of settlement

It is useful to begin by examining the origins of the assumption that open settlement predominated north of the Forth in later prehistory. The concept of a cultural cleavage between the North-Eastern and Tyne–Forth provinces has a long history, of course, going back to Tacitus' *Agricola*, and most explicitly articulated in Piggott's (1966) scheme, but it was in the early 1980s, when the first results of extensive aerial survey by RCAHMS became available, that we find the first suggestion that this divide was manifested in the predominant settlement types (Maxwell 1983a; 1983b).

Macinnes' doctoral study, which was based on the aerial photographs amassed by RCAHMS up to 1978, aimed to test the hypothesis that the River Forth acted as a cultural boundary throughout later prehistory. For her analysis, she selected the three areas that had produced the densest concentrations of cropmarks: East Lothian, north-east Fife, and Angus. These are not, of course, necessarily representative of regional patterns in the later prehistoric period. She found that south of the Forth in the later second and early first millennium BC, discrete, isolated homesteads or small settlements well separated from their neighbours, whereas in Angus less distinct agglomerations of small enclosures or unenclosed sites predominated (Macinnes 1983). In north Fife, however, she noted that 'settlement has affinities both with north of the Tay and south of the Forth, for in the Mottray region agglomerations of settlement were evident, but elsewhere discrete homesteads prevailed' (*ibid.*, 377). Notably, Macinnes did not say that unenclosed sites alone predominate in Angus: rather, small enclosed sites predominated with them. In north Fife, she argued that there are complementary distributions of enclosed and unenclosed settlements.

For the later first millennium BC, Macinnes (1983) described a different picture, arguing that contrasts between north and south of the Forth were now more marked. In East Lothian, emphasis on enclosure and defence increased, whereas in Angus unenclosed settlements predominated. Defended enclosures did nevertheless exist in Angus, although confined largely to the upland zone, leading her to conclude that whilst hillforts dominated the settlement pattern south of the Forth, north of it, they were an integral part of a complex settlement system. Her interpretation was that Later Iron Age society in East Lothian was highly organised and stratified, possibly with an emphasis on land and/or stock ownership, whereas in Angus it was made up of largely autonomous settlements with no central authority. This need not imply an egalitarian society, however, since a local chief could for instance have controlled each souterrain, which she argued was a centralised storage unit. Macinnes also suggested that the development of north Fife in the later part of the Iron Age paralleled that of the area to the south, which she hints was linked to the construction of the Roman Gask frontier (*ibid.*, 382–5). Consequently, she concluded that the 'cultural boundary thought to exist at the Forth–Clyde isthmus should therefore, properly be seen as a fluctuating boundary between the Forth and the Tay, with the affinities of the intermediate zone oscillating one way or the other' (*ibid.*, 398).

Maxwell (1987) injected a further note of caution in his synthesis of Roman Iron Age settlement in Scotland, suggesting that while the Firth of Forth might mark a cultural boundary, the same could not be said of the rest of the River Forth. At least for the Roman period, the southern boundary of Caledonian territory might, he argued, run from the Tay valley to the Tay–Earn confluence and thence south-east across the Fife peninsula. This model was based on what Maxwell saw as a complementary distribution of, on the one hand, brochs, duns, homesteads, and 'palisaded works' in the Teith and Forth valleys and on the other, open settlements and souterrains north of the Tay. As we will see, this model does not fit the evidence that we have now: palisades similar to those in Stirlingshire have now also been detected in Perthshire and Angus.

Richard Hingley (1992, 33) argued that open settlements predominated north of the Forth, in Fife and Tayside, apparently following Macinnes (1982; 1984), Maxwell (1983b; 1985), and Halliday (1985). This was seen to contrast sharply with the prevalence of enclosed settlements south of the Forth. This impression is repeated by Ian Armit (1997, 61), in the first book to synthesise the Scottish Iron Age for 104 years. However, the data that have accumulated since significantly modify the general picture, which is hardly surprising given that Macinnes' research only took account of material gathered up to 1978 and was focused on three areas. In particular, subsequent researchers have invariably played down the abundant evidence for enclosed settlement north of the Forth. In order to assess to what extent these models are still relevant, the later prehistoric settlement evidence is re-examined here in the light both of my own doctoral research on Stirlingshire, Perthshire, and Angus (Davies 2006), and of clearer understanding of the limitations of the available radiocarbon dates (Ashmore 1999; Ashmore *et al.* 2001; Rees 1998). My intention is not to question the value of Macinnes' work, but rather to do justice to the new data available from survey and excavation, and to highlight the misunderstandings which have arisen as a result of summarising and over-generalising her results elsewhere.

Multivallate enclosures

What has not so far been appreciated, despite the admirable publication by RCAHMS (1994a) on south-east Perth, is the number of cropmark enclosures recorded in this part of lowland Scotland over the past thirty years. Numerous ditched, often multivallate, enclosures are now known in lowland contexts (Fig. 6), sometimes side-by-side with open settlements. In the

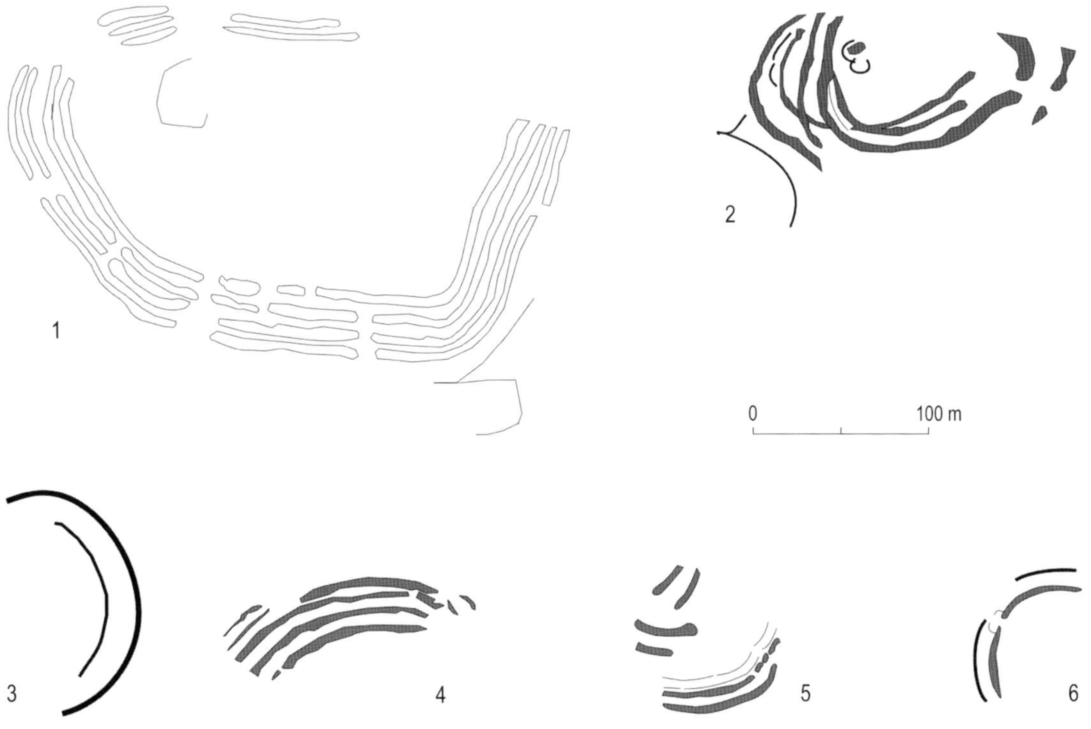

Fig. 6. Examples of multivallate enclosures, transcribed by the author at a common scale from RCAHMS aerial photographs. 1. Auchray (NO33SE55); 2. Wester Carmuirs – note adjacent palisade (NS88SW27&50); 3. Craig Shot (NN91NW13); 4. Dun Knock (NO01SW18); 5. Haughbrae of Grandtully (NN95SW66); 6. South Mains, Innerpeffrey (NN91NW20). Modern field boundaries have been omitted for clarity; in many cases, only part of the site has shown as a cropmark.

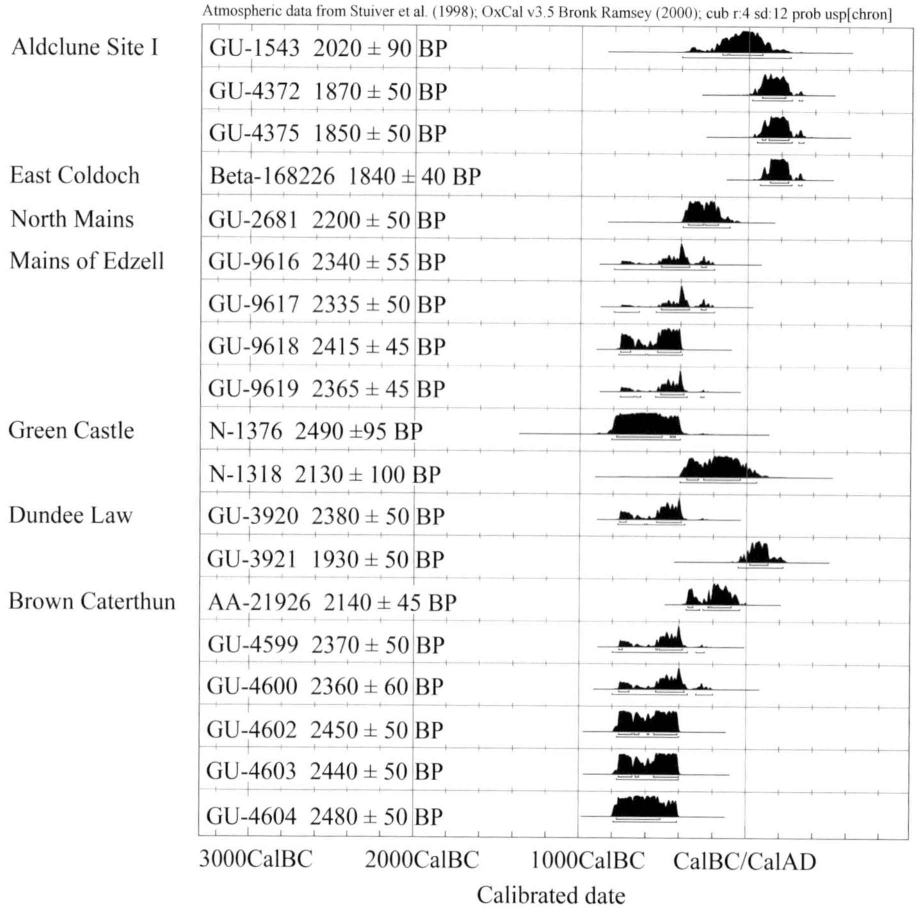

Fig. 7. Radiocarbon dates for multivallate enclosures in Perthshire and Angus.

south of the study area, there seems to have been a localised tradition of small circular ditched homesteads, typified by the excavated site at West Plean (Steer 1955–6), south of the Forth. They are of comparable size to the brochs and duns of the area and may have served a similar purpose, as rather ostentatious dwellings, in the later pre-Roman and Roman Iron Age (cf. Macinnes 1984). West Plean did not produce any closely dateable artefacts, but a similar site at East Coldoch north of the Forth, which is the subject of ongoing excavation, yielded some Roman glass from a roundhouse floor deposit and a radiocarbon date in the early first millennium AD for charcoal from a roundhouse destruction deposit (Woolliscroft and Hoffmann 2003). There is a difficulty in identifying parallels to these ditched homesteads owing to their superficial similarity to mini-henges (Harding and Lee 1987; RCAHMS 1994a, 30), but cropmark enclosures at Inverdunning House, Perthshire (NMRS No. NO01NW19) and Bowhouse, Stirlingshire (NMRS No. NS97NW2: RCAHMS 1963, 91–2) may be analogous.

Although the radiocarbon revolution has, in general allowed us to push back the dating of hillforts, sometimes even into the Bronze Age, most multivallate enclosures excavated in this area since 1978 have yielded dates between 800–400 cal. BC. There are hints, however, that some of the sites may have continued in use – or been reoccupied – in the later first millennium BC, although the relevant radiocarbon dates (Fig. 7) were mostly obtained before it became possible to date small samples such as burnt seeds, and so must be treated with appropriate caution. AMS dating should in the future enable us to obtain extensive series of dates from these sites with a minimum of taphonomic complications associated with their interpretation.

At the multivallate terrace-edge enclosure of North Mains, Strathallan, an oak post, apparently burnt *in situ*, was radiocarbon dated to 390–110 cal. BC (GU-2681). No other radiometric dates are yet available from excavated cropmark 'forts' in Perthshire, but similar enclosures in Angus provide useful comparative data. At Mains of Edzell, recent excavations on a trivallate enclosure yielded a series of radiocarbon dates falling mainly between 800–400 cal. BC, but these are from material in secondary ditch fills, and thus not entirely helpful in determining when the site was constructed,

Fig. 8. Dun Knock multivallate enclosure cropmark, which has been interpreted variously as later prehistoric or Pictish (Crown copyright, RCAHMS).

although the excavator argues that it was before 400 BC (Strachan *et al.* 2003). A bivallate enclosure at Hawkhill, also excavated by the Field School, yielded no material suitable for radiocarbon dating (*ibid.*). The dates from the large multivallate enclosure at Brown Caterthun, Angus, are mostly between 800–400 cal. BC, but indicate some occupation later in the millennium (Dunwell and Strachan forthcoming). The lowland multivallate enclosure at Cairnton of Belbegno (just over the Aberdeenshire border), first excavated by Sir Walter Scott in 1796, and again by L.M.M. Wedderburn in 1973, has dates of 810–400 cal. BC (N-1376) for a timber beam resting on the rampart foundation, and 400 cal. BC–cal. AD 60 (N-1318) for twigs from a destruction deposit at the same location (Wedderburn 1973). The implication is that the excavated 'forts' were primarily in use in the period covered by the radiocarbon plateau, but there is no statistical reason why they should all be placed in the earlier part of this range, and a sufficient minority of later dates to suggest some activity in the later first millennium BC.

Indeed, the radiocarbon dates from Dundee Law (Driscoll 1995) and Aldclune (Hingley *et al.* 1997) and the Roman period finds from the trivallate promontory fort at West Mains of Ethie (Wilson 1980) imply that some multivallate enclosures could have continued in use into, or been reoccupied in, the Roman period, whilst the so-called 'nuclear' forts (Stevenson 1948–9), such as Dundurn (Alcock *et al.* 1989), may have been constructed and used only in the first millennium AD (Alcock 2003, 179–80). Samples obtained from the inner rampart[3] at Abbey Craig, an upstanding (although badly damaged) fort in Stirling, indicate a date in the sixth to eighth centuries AD (Glendinning and Hall 2003). Some of the cropmark forts of Strathearn may also be Pictish (Driscoll 1987). Dun Knock (Fig. 8), a multivallate enclosure at Newton of Pitcairn (immediately south of Dunning) with some evidence of vitrification (Donaldson *et al.* 2004) has been interpreted as the Early Historic *caput* of Dunning on the basis of place-name evidence and early historical sources (Driscoll 1991, 104–6). Some of the sites may span the 'long Iron Age' of Scotland, being used in both the Iron Age and Early Historic periods, and further archaeological investigation might enhance our understanding of the notional transition period.

Palisades

One of the major site types in the study area is the circular or oval palisaded enclosure, largely known from the cropmark record. These are referred to here simply as palisades, in order to avoid confusion with the classification devised by RCAHMS for upstanding sites in the Scottish Borders (RCAHMS 1956, 19–20; 1967, 23–4; see Davies 2006 for justification of this approach). Due to their ephemeral nature, it is likely that many palisades are as yet undetected. As Table 1 shows, it is also evident from excavation that, in several cases, a small palisade (i.e. some 20–30 m in diameter) preceded a more elaborate house or homestead, implying that still more examples are likely to be masked by later structures or cropmarks. Of course, palisades are no more chronologically diagnostic than ditches; they have been used from the Neolithic to the present day. However, the aerial evidence indicates that many of the palisaded enclosures apparent in the region share morphological similarities (Davies 2006). They are circular or oval, ranging in diameter from 20–55 m. Some have cropmarks indicating internal features or structures, as at Flanders Hill (Fig. 9) and Lochlane (Fig. 10), and four of the nine excavated sites in the study area have coherent evidence for a central circular timber building. Many have entrance terminals that have been elaborated or exaggerated, suggesting that there may have been a gateway or entrance structure, including Portend, Mains of Burnbank, and East Coldoch.

There is no reason to think that these palisades, with their central circular buildings, were not domestic establishments. This does not, of course, preclude a parallel ritual or religious function; ritual is inherent in the everyday (Hill 1989). All the artefacts thus far recovered from palisades have been prosaic: coarse pottery, spindle whorls, cobble tools and a bone pin. In the one instance where Roman pottery was present, it was coarseware, rather than samian, which predominates on other Iron Age sites (Hunter 2001a, 299). That said, we probably have a biased picture; the apparent cleanliness of these sites may simply be a function of their situation on high quality land, which has been heavily ploughed, particularly in the past fifty years. In the case of sites beneath upstanding monuments, much may have been removed in preparation for the new structure. Many of the features are relatively shallow and fragile, and would not act as reservoirs for material in the way that brochs, for instance, do (Hunter 1998).

Then again, the people who lived and worked on these sites may not have been in the habit of depositing objects in such a way that they would be recovered during excavation, even where the site was unploughed. Support for this view comes from sites in the Borders and Northumberland, where traces of surfaces survived. Glenachan Rig in Peebleshire, produced only a flint flake, two utilised pebbles, and a fire-cracked stone, despite a substantial area being investigated (Feachem 1958–9, 22). High Knowes A, Northumberland, produced no small finds at all, 'despite the fact that all areas were trowelled down to rock level and all post-holes and construction trenches emptied' (Jobey and Tait 1966, 16). At High Knowes B, a bi-palisaded enclosure, finds were restricted to some 26 sherds of later prehistoric pottery (*ibid.*, 18–20). Another possible hypothesis has been advanced by Willis (1999, 90) in a consideration of Iron Age communities in north-east England; he suggests that the small quantities of pottery habitually found there indicate a social awareness of pottery – a 'ceramic consciousness' – but not a habit of everyday use. This could imply that pottery had special, occasional uses and thus was only manufactured on an infrequent basis. If vessels made of organic materials such as wood were the norm,[4] the low quantities of pottery might, after all, be representative of the quantity that was used.

The prevailing assumption that palisades north of the Forth were of Late Bronze Age or Early Iron Age date derives ultimately from the Hownam sequence (Piggott 1947–8) and the early radiocarbon dates obtained for palisaded phases at sites such as Huckhoe, Northumberland (Jobey 1959; 1968), seemingly supported by more recent excavations in East Lothian, the Borders, Dumfriesshire and Renfrewshire, as at Dryburn Bridge (Triscott 1982). This, however, reflects a failure in the past rigorously to distinguish between palisaded phases or elements of ditched enclosures, and the free-standing oval or circular enclosures discussed here. These can now be seen to form a separate class, whilst it has become clear that palisades in general are not culturally or chronologically diagnostic.

As Figure 11 and Table 1 show, there is little evidence to suggest the construction or use of this class of site in the study area earlier than the fifth or fourth centuries BC. Only three – Fairy Knowe, Ironshill East, and Lower Greenyards 2 – have relevant radiocarbon dates, all of which point firmly to the Later Iron Age. There is nothing from any of the other excavated palisades to require their occupation before the second half of the first millennium BC. Whilst it is obviously possible that some of the unexcavated palisades do belong to the Late Bronze Age or Early Iron Age, it would seem unwise to assume this either from the material so far amassed in the study area, or on the basis of excavated parallels such as Dryburn Bridge in neighbouring areas like East Lothian. On the other hand, there are grounds for thinking that the geographical and chronological distribution of this type of settlement may be much wider than has previously been suspected, since the earlier dates from similar sites excavated elsewhere, such as Aird Quarry, Dumfries and Galloway (Cook 2002; 2004), indicate that some of them may indeed be Bronze Age in date.

Souterrains and open settlements

Souterrains and their associated open settlements seem to dominate our understanding of the Later Iron Age in eastern Scotland north of the Forth, their distribution

Site Name NMRS Number	*County*	*Reference*	*Date claimed by author*	*Direct dating evidence*	*Indirect dating evidence*	*Diameter (approx.)*	*Diam of central structure*
West Plean (possible)	Stirling	Steer 1956	Early Iron Age or earlier	None	Earlier than ditched homestead which had no Roman material	28 m	6.1 m
Easterton of Argaty	Perth	Main 1992	Late Bronze Age/Early Iron Age	None	None	48 m	?
Myrehead	Stirling	Barclay 1983a	mid/late first millennium bc	None	Post-dates early/mid first millennium bc phase; pre-dates late first millennium bc/early first millennium ad phase	40 m	?Ring-groove in S: 8–8.5 m
Methven Wood (possible)	Perth	Sherriff 1986	None	None	None	?	?
East Coldoch (2, possibly 3)	Perth	Woolliscroft and Hoffmann 2003	Late Bronze Age/ Early Iron Age	None	Pre-date context with charcoal dated AD 70–AD 320	Feature B: 43 m x 36 m Feature D: ? Enclosure under Feature A: 22.5 m	Feature A: 12 m
Lower Greenyards (Homestead 1)	Stirling	Rideout 1996	Iron Age	'Iron Age' pottery from palisade slot and pit cutting house wall; spindle whorl		46 m	14.5–18.6 m
Lower Greenyards (Homestead 2, under fort)	Stirling	Rideout 1996	fifth/sixth centuries BC	C14 dating, IA pottery, similarities to Homestead 1, Hownam paradigm	Pre-dates late first millennium BC fort	?	14.4 m
Fairy Knowe	Stirling	Main 1998	first century BC to first century AD	Charcoal (*Quercus*) from post hole F93 in rh interior 2 400 BC–AD 250	Pre-dates broch; close relationship between ground plans of timber roundhouse and broch implies remains visible when broch built.	21 m	8–9.5 m
Ironshill East	Angus	McGill 2003	second half of first millennium BC	C14 dates from material in pits; later prehistoric pottery		55 m	17–18 m

Table 1. Details of excavated palisaded enclosures.

Fig. 9. Flanders Hill palisade (NS69NW10) photographed in 1977 (Crown copyright, RCAHMS).

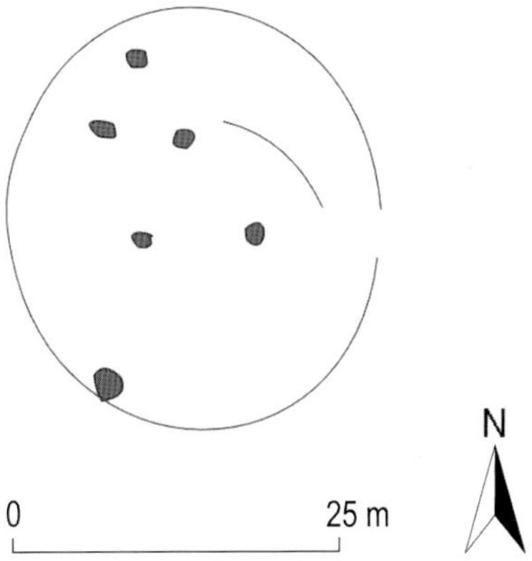

Fig. 10. Lochlane palisade (NN82SW2), transcribed by the author from RCAHMS aerial photograph. As at Flanders Hill, a curvilinear feature, which may represent the foundation of a circular building, is clearly visible within the enclosure.

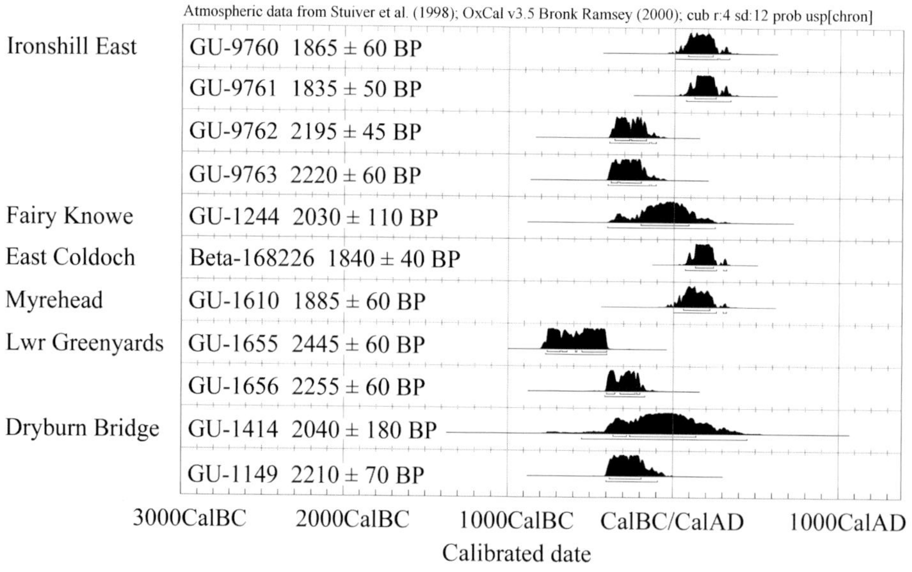

Fig. 11. Radiocarbon dates for palisades. The East Coldoch date is from a later phase on the site.

extending from a core in Angus into Perthshire and now even as far as Stirlingshire, with the confirmation of a timber-lined example at Easter Moss, Cowie (Strachan 1998; 1999). Armit (1999) provides the most recent review of souterrains, but reinforces some of the misconceptions concerning them, which are challenged here.

Given the impressive size of the souterrains in the 'southern Pictland' core area, it is undeniably tempting to see them as providing centralised storage for a community and/or storage of an agricultural surplus, which could eventually be traded with neighbouring communities (Macinnes 1983) or even the Roman army (Armit 1999, 593). As Watkins (1980, 199) noted, souterrains such as Newmill could have stored far more food than was necessary for a family living in the associated roundhouse. The attraction of this hypothesis is further enhanced when one notes that the souterrains in the Northern Isles are far smaller, arguably reflecting the smaller communities and the lower agricultural potential there compared to the fertile lowlands of Scotland.

It was first suggested by Munro (1899, 349) and reiterated by Wainwright (1963, 6–7) that souterrains were part of unenclosed settlements. This view was repeated by Maxwell (1983b; 1987), who argued that the majority of souterrains discovered aerially were associated with open settlements, and is now the working assumption, with Armit (1999, 581) suggesting that souterrains are to be found at many, if not most, farming settlements throughout the fertile lowlands, acting as centralised storage facilities. Armit argued that a contemporary building was uncovered during Jervise's excavation of a souterrain at West Grange of Conon (Jervise 1861–2), although recent re-excavation has cast doubt on this theory, showing that the apparent paving noted by Jervise was actually a sub-circular area of bedrock (Cameron 2003). At Redcastle, a large timber-lined souterrain, there was no evidence for an associated roundhouse (Alexander 2005), although Armit (1999, 581) argues, not unreasonably given the sandy subsoil and erosion evident elsewhere on the site, that ploughing obliterated it.

West Grange of Conon and Redcastle were both later used as burial grounds. 'Stone coffins' were also reported on the same land as a souterrain at Fowlis Easter (Stuart 1865) and a similar juxtaposition may have occurred at Carlungie I, where there were short cists and possibly also long cists nearby (Wainwright 1963, 121). These 'isolated' souterrains may in fact hold the key to identifying the function(s) of souterrains in general; it is tempting to see the long cist burials as a later re-use of sacred ground, although it could also be coincidence, perhaps owing to the favouring of free-draining soils. The key point, however, is that there are more excavated souterrains juxtaposed with cist burials than there are those proven to be associated with roundhouses, even allowing for the antiquity of some of the excavations. It may not be wise therefore to assume the presence of dwellings at souterrain sites, particularly when this may then lead to a further assumption of domestic function. At Carlungie I, the buildings uncovered were actually later than the souterrain (Wainwright 1963).

The prevailing view, following Wainwright's (1963) excavations at Ardestie and Carlungie I and Watkins'

Fig. 12. Newmill stone-lined souterrain during excavation by Trevor Watkins; note the remains of post-built roundhouses behind (Crown copyright, RCAHMS).

(1980) at Newmill (Fig. 12), is that souterrains were backfilled in a single episode. Armit (1999) used this to argue for the existence of a 'souterrain abandonment horizon' in the second century AD. The evidence for deliberate backfilling at Newmill is quite convincing, but the radiocarbon date from the bonfire – which Armit argues dates the destruction – does not necessarily indicate a second or third century date, as he suggests. The full date range is cal. AD 130–410 (GU-1019), and even at one sigma, it is cal. AD 220–390, i.e. third to fourth centuries AD. Thus, the argument that the radiocarbon date agrees with the Roman finds in suggesting that the backfill were deposited during, or very soon after, the Roman occupation of Scotland, falls down. The wood in the bonfire was most likely felled between AD 220 and AD 390 and possibly as late as AD 410. This is not a sound basis on which to deduce the date of the abandonment episode between two historical events in the second and third centuries.

Nor does evidence from recently excavated souterrains fit Armit's hypothesis. At Shanzie, for instance, there was no evidence for deliberate backfilling; rather, the excavators argued that the souterrain gradually silted up over a period of 700–800 years before it was reused, with a cobbled surface being laid on top of the primary silt (Coleman and Hunter 2002). When it fell out of use once more, it again silted up naturally. At Fletcherfield, the first 0.45 m of fill was clearly the result of natural silting, although the next 0.65 m was more homogenous and could have been the result of deliberate backfilling (Dick 2002). This suggests that any backfilling took place long after the souterrain had fallen out of use, and certainly not in the narrow window in the Roman Iron Age that Armit suggested. And whilst McGill (2003) tentatively suggests that the timber-lined souterrain at Ironshill was backfilled in a single episode, the evidence implies that it had lain open for some time before it was backfilled, as 0.6 m of primary silting was evident below the homogenous fill. At West Mains, Lunan Bay, a possible souterrain yielded only evidence of natural silting; unfortunately it produced no artefacts or other dating evidence (Alexander 2000). At Hurly Hawkin, there was a layer of silt 0.2 m deep in the bottom of the souterrain, again suggesting that it had fallen out of use some time before the collapse or dismantling of the roof (Taylor 1982, 220–1).

Coupled with Coleman and Hunter's (2002, 97) observation that the Roman artefacts found in souterrain fills cannot be assigned to such a narrow a chronological range as Armit argued, there seems little merit in retaining the idea of a specific souterrain abandonment horizon. While some souterrains, including Ardestie (Wainwright 1963), Carlungie I and II (Wainwright

1953b; 1963), Dubton (Cameron 2002) and Newmill do indeed seem to have been backfilled and partially dismantled in a single episode, many others definitely were not. Hawkhill was deliberately backfilled, but in two separate episodes, and with no other finds than a broken saddle quern and a broken rotary quern,[5] not the Roman artefacts which Armit stresses (Rees forthcoming). Moreover, there is little to support the contemporaneity of these backfilling episodes. We could perhaps envisage an alternative scenario, where souterrains were backfilled when people felt it necessary, for whatever reason: to reclaim the site for cultivation or to ensure that domestic animals or children did not fall in. Sometimes the decision to do so was made immediately the structure went out of use, as at Carlungie I where the site was subsequently used for settlement; at other sites it might have been centuries later. This model is not as neat as Armit's, but it does appear to fit the available evidence better.

Although the emphasis in the Later Iron Age in this area is on lowland unenclosed settlement, there are hints that open settlement may also have continued in the uplands. The principal occupation at sites like Carn Dubh, Dalnaglar, and Dalrulzion was of Late Bronze Age date, but occasional radiocarbon dates suggest some occupation in the Later Iron Age. At Tulloch Field Site B, in Perthshire, a pit full of burnt material in the centre of the roundhouse, which Thoms interpreted as a hearth pit, yielded charcoal dated to 420–160 cal. BC (GU-1489; L. Thoms pers. comm.); the radiocarbon dates from Site A, however, were all firmly in the Late Bronze Age. At Carn Dubh, too, there was evidence of continued occupation of the roundhouses into the final centuries of the first millennium BC (Rideout 1995). This evidence cannot, however, be used conclusively to demonstrate continuity and the Iron Age remains may be little more than the debris of transhumant activity. Further north, evidence of upland settlement continuing into the Late Iron Age is more plentiful, as at Lairg, House 6 (McCullagh and Tipping 1998, 52–6), but in the study area no definite conclusions can be reached at the moment, since so few upland settlements have been excavated and even fewer are dated, at which point we may turn to the burial evidence.

Burial

Recent syntheses have noted the paucity of Iron Age burials in Angus, Perthshire, and Stirlingshire (Hingley 1992, 38; Armit 1997); indeed, evidence has been so far from forthcoming, that many have been tempted to argue that Iron Age bodies were disposed of in archaeologically invisible ways (e.g. Armit 1997, 96). However, a review of the accumulated evidence implies that many burials may simply not have been recognised as Iron Age, largely because erroneous assumptions were made, mostly obviously by attributing burials without grave goods and orientated west–east to the Early Christian period. Dating burials by orientation is a crude device and ignores the possibility that prehistoric communities may also have had reasons for orientating their dead towards the rising sun. For instance, it may have been considered appropriate to orientate bodies towards the equinox, as is the case with many Iron Age roundhouses and enclosure entrances (Hill 1993; Oswald 1997).[6] Equally, without knowing what the normative burial rite was, we cannot assume that the absence of grave goods was unusual. The general rule of thumb is that crouched inhumations are Bronze Age and that extended inhumations date to the first millennium AD or later, but as we will see below, there are informative exceptions to this rule. In an area where human remains often do not survive due to the acidity of the soil, it must also be borne in mind that organic grave goods (and even small metal objects) might leave no trace.

Several long cist burials have been excavated in the study area. At Avonglen, seven long cists were discovered during quarrying, of which two were excavated (Close-Brooks 1973; Walker 1974; 1976; Main and Murray 1980). Of these, Cist 2 was orientated south-west–north-east and Cist 3 slightly off west–east. There were no grave goods, although a pebble was found between two stone slabs at the eastern end of Cist 2. Young was only able tentatively to identify the individual in Cist 3 as male (Young 1973). One of the cists not excavated was that of a child (Walker 1974). Long cists were found here in the nineteenth century, so it could represent a larger cemetery. Similar long cists were found at Denovan, on the same site as two short cists of Bronze Age date. The excavator believed these to be Iron Age, rather than early Christian, based on the fact that they were orientated north-east–south-west rather than west–east (Hunter 1971, 31). The long cists had been badly damaged by ploughing and presumably chemical action; no bones were evident.

Hunter (*ibid.*) argued against continued sanctity of the Denovan site, suggesting instead that it was chosen for burial in the Iron Age, as in the Bronze Age, because it was on sandy ground overlooking a river. However, a break in use need not preclude an Iron Age community from deliberately choosing the site as one associated with the 'ancestors'. Hingley (1999) has recently argued for a sense of the past in the Iron Age, as manifested in the reuse of Neolithic and Bronze Age monuments. The juxtaposition of Bronze Age and Iron Age cemeteries is therefore potentially highly significant. However, there is also an implicit and unsubstantiated assumption in Hingley's argument: that later prehistoric people had a linear view of the past. Later prehistoric activity on earlier sites does not prove that people saw the monuments as part of *their* past (Whitley 2002). In more modern times, prehistoric monuments have been associated with a variety of mythical creatures (*ibid.*),[7] and MacRitchie (1916–17) suggested that the souterrains of southern Pictland, traditionally known as *eirde hooses* (earth houses) might be the origin of local myths about the 'little people'. We must remain open to various possible motivations behind the reuse of old sites or burial grounds.

Moncrieffe, a stone circle in Perthshire, reused as a metalworking area in the Iron Age (Stewart 1985), is cited by Hingley (1999) as an example of conscious use by later prehistoric people of a site associated with the ancestors, but pragmatic reuse should also be considered: the circle could have provided a sheltered spot with good light, away from any settlement. Even if metalworking was not, as some have argued, a 'magical task', the poisonous nature of the fumes may have been recognised. If future excavations and radiocarbon dates were to indicate that the Iron Age inhabitants living in Angus, Stirlingshire, and Perthshire were consistently choosing older burial grounds in which to bury their dead, this might provide further support for Hingley's argument, but this is not likely to happen until there is a regional research design which specifically addresses burials and the fact that they are not usually found on sites targeted for excavation, perhaps combined with retrospective AMS dating of human remains surviving in archives.

Close-Brooks (1984) has argued that long cists are a tradition of the first few centuries AD, but this is based on the dating of grave goods in the Tyne–Forth province, and some of the cists which do not include Roman period objects might well be earlier. There are occasional antiquarian accounts of long cists being found in the study area, as at Craigie near Dundee, where one containing an inhumation with an iron penannular brooch was found (Hutcheson 1902–3). The inhumation has recently been radiocarbon dated to cal. AD 130–250 (Sheridan 2004, 176). We should, however, be wary of allowing the presence of Roman goods in some long cists to skew the dating of potentially earlier graves. At East Coldoch, a child's long cist, orientated south-north was uncovered at the entrance to a roundhouse dated to the Later Iron Age, at least in its later phases. Although the cist was empty and the exact chronological relationship to the roundhouse has not been established (Woolliscroft and Hoffmann 2003), its position is unlikely to be coincidental. It seems reasonable, therefore, to accept a Later Iron Age date for the grave.

In Stirlingshire, there appears to be a local concentration of 'warrior' burials. Those at Camelon were originally interpreted as being those of Roman soldiers, or at least local people recruited to serve as auxiliaries (Breeze *et al.* 1976), but Hunter has argued more recently that they are of Iron Age date (Hunter 2001b). The sword is a late pre-Roman Iron Age type, the mode of burial is not Roman, and the double burials and weapon burials are far more common in an Iron Age (albeit southern) context (*ibid.*, 121). Until recently, the one Scottish parallel was from Merlsford, Fife (Hunter 1996),[8] but another 'warrior' burial belonging to this central Scottish group has now been found at Marshill, Alloa, Clackmannanshire, comprising an extended male inhumation placed in a corbelled cist with a sword, scabbard suspension rings, a spear, a pin, toe rings, and a glass bead (Mills 2004; Hunter 2005).

An Early Bronze Age date was assumed for three oval cists from Barbush, until the bone from Cist 3 (which had no grave goods) yielded a date of 1190–840 cal. BC (AA-36507; Holden and Sheridan 2001). One could probably explain this away, were it not for the still later dates (Fig. 13), running into the Iron Age, for burials in oval pits or cists from East Lothian, at Dryburn Bridge (Triscott 1982, 122; Dunwell forthcoming), Dunbar Golf Course (Baker 2002), and Broxmouth (Hill 1982). Another oval cist has been excavated at East Coldoch (Fig. 14), apparently within a round barrow (Woolliscroft and Hoffmann 2003). Its position in the site sequence suggests that it dates to the first millennium BC or earlier. Round barrows in this area are assumed mainly to be Early Bronze Age (RCAHMS 1994a),[9] but recent excavations at Redcastle in Angus show that they were also used, along with square barrows, in the Early Historic period (Alexander 2005); indeed, one of the round barrows at Inchtuthil overlay the remains of the legionary fortress (Abercromby *et al.* 1901–2, 201–2). We should not therefore rule out the idea that round barrows and oval cists were used in the Iron Age. It is equally possible that some rectilinear short cists identified as Bronze Age are in fact later, since a femur from a short cist at Kingsbarns, Fife, was recently dated to 460–160 cal. BC (GU-8219; James 2001). We should be wary of assuming an Early Bronze Age date for what Coutts (1971, 14 and 18) termed 'un-urned' short cists.

Square barrows are another possible candidate to fill the apparent gap in the burial record. Like souterrains, Scottish square barrows are concentrated in Angus, but the distribution strays into eastern Perthshire and Fife. Although the Redcastle examples proved to be Early Historic (Alexander 2005), the rather larger one at Wester Denhead produced a sherd of Roman pottery (RCAHMS 1994, 18), and Boysack Mills, a first century BC/AD ring-headed pin (Murray and Ralston 1997). There are also apparently stylistically related square cairns in Fife, at Lundin Links (Greig *et al.* 2000), and further north, such as Garbeg and Whitebridge (Wedderburn and Grime 1984). Although none of the Scottish square barrows uncovered so far have been cart/chariot burials, the Iron Age chariot/cart burial found at Newbridge, Edinburgh (Carter and Hunter 2003), raises the possibility that contacts between eastern Scotland and the Continent influenced Scottish Iron Age burial practices. Certainly, the late first millennium BC to early first millennium AD

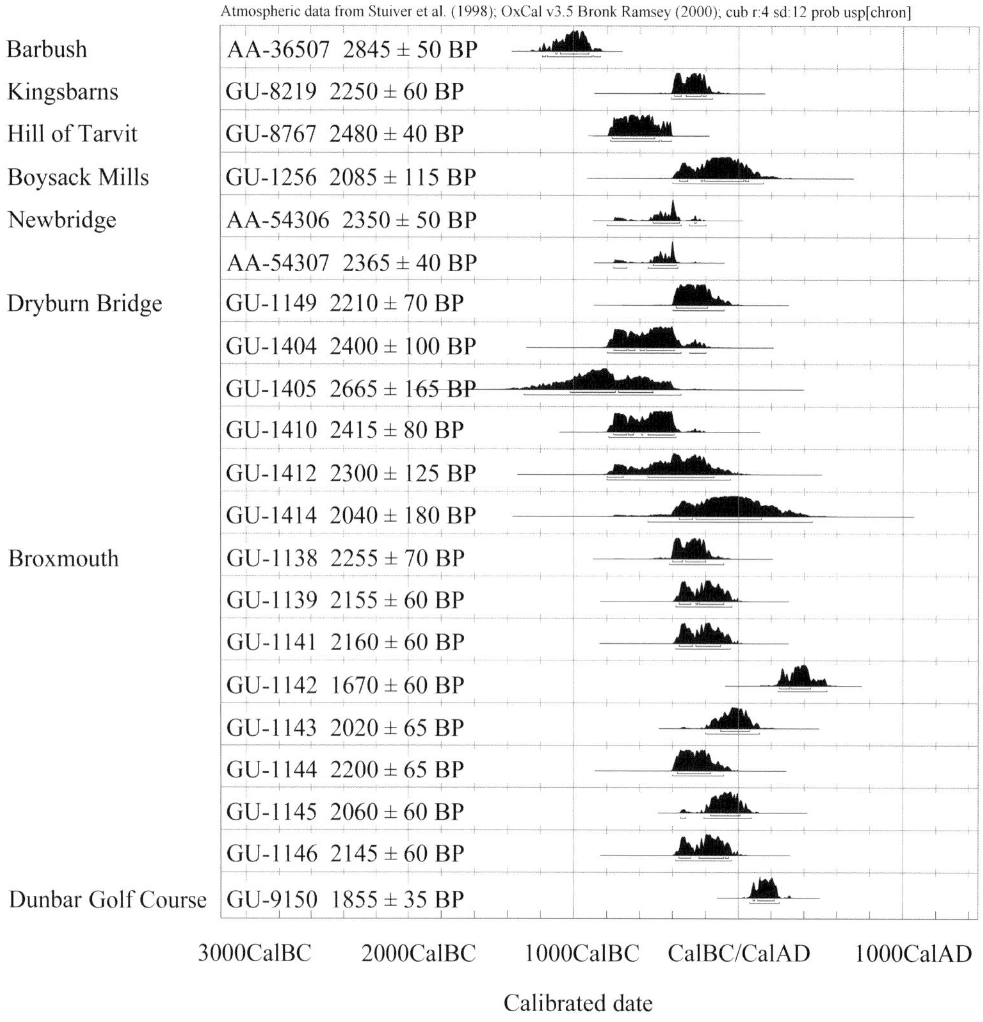

Fig. 13. Radiocarbon dated burials.

Fig. 14. Oval cist at East Coldoch. Some oval cists may be Iron Age rather than Bronze Age (by kind permission of the Roman Gask Project).

radiocarbon date and first century BC/AD ring-headed pin from a square barrow burial at Boysack Mills (Murray and Ralston 1997) should not be too readily dismissed.

It is also possible that some cremation burials in the area are of Iron Age date and that some of the missing dead were scattered and rendered archaeologically invisible. A cremation from Hill of Tarvit, Fife, was recently interpreted as Bronze Age despite containing charcoal dated to 780–410 cal. BC (GU-8767) and no other evidence (James 2001). Whilst the only other feature on site contained Bronze Age pottery, this does not seem to be sufficient grounds to dismiss an Early Iron Age date for the burial. Indeed, it raises the possibility that at least some of the 'missing' burials were cremations, although so far, the radiocarbon dates for cremations in the study area all fall in the third or second millennia BC.[10]

Conclusion

In the light of evidence collected over the past 25 years, particularly since the inception of NPPG5 and the Angus and South Aberdeenshire Field School (Finlayson *et al.* 1999), the current model of later prehistoric settlement in eastern Scotland requires revision. In Perthshire, Stirlingshire, and Angus the Later Iron Age is characterised by a suite of settlement evidence, comprising both unenclosed and enclosed settlement, the latter including palisades and probably some multivallate enclosures. Substantial stone roundhouses (not only lowland brochs, but also the less well-known duns and circular homesteads), although not discussed here, also had a place in this settlement pattern. It is becoming clear that souterrains are not as certainly associated with open settlements as has been thought. Interpretation of all these sites is hampered by a lack of appropriate radiocarbon dates, but there are enough data to reject the concept of a specific souterrain abandonment horizon as proposed by Armit (1999). Coupled to the recognition of some burials belonging to the first millennium BC and early centuries AD, further progress is finally being made towards a better understanding of the Iron Age communities of Stirlingshire, Perthshire, and Angus.

Acknowledgements

This paper is based on doctoral research (Davies 2006) funded by the University of Durham. Elements of it were presented at the Iron Age Research Student Seminar in Durham (2001) and the Aerial Archaeology Research Group conference in Winchester (2003) and I am grateful to the audiences on those occasions for their comments. I am grateful to Lorna Main, Archaeologist for Stirling Council, and Lisbeth Thoms for providing additional information on Easterton of Argaty and Tulloch Field respectively. Thanks are also due to Fraser Hunter for discussing the 'warrior' burial evidence with me. Earlier versions of this paper were read and commented on by D.C. Cowley, Prof. W.S. Hanson, Prof. C.C. Haselgrove, Dr R. Hingley, Dr L. Macinnes, Dr T.H. Moore and Prof. I.B.M. Ralston, who provided many valuable suggestions for improvement. Responsibility for any remaining errors remains, of course, with the author.

Notes

1. Radiocarbon dates cited in the paper were calibrated by the author using OxCal v.3.5 and are quoted at 2 sigma.
2. See Harding (2004, 3–5) for a discussion of the chronological framework for the Scottish Iron Age.
3. Although only one rampart was noted by RCAHMS (1963) in its Stirlingshire Inventory, Maclagan (1870–1, 24; 1875, 55 & pl. 35; 1884, 39) described two and the second was rediscovered by Aitchison (1981).
4. Wooden vessels have been found at Leckie broch, Stirlingshire, and Oakbank crannog, Perthshire.
5. There is some evidence that quernstones were deliberately placed in souterrain entrances, including Carlungie I (Wainwright 1963), Hawkhill (Rees forthcoming), and Newmill (Watkins 1980), as part of ritual 'closure' deposits, and Hingley (1992) argues that there may be a conceptual link between the use of souterrains for storing grain and the disposal of the tools used for grinding it. However, this pattern of deposition does not in itself prove that there was a single backfilling episode at these sites, nor indicate contemporaneity.
6. Although the cosmological interpretation of the roundhouse evidence has been convincingly challenged by Pope (2007).
7. There are at least nine instances of site names in the study area that include the word 'fairy', including seven 'Fairy Knowes'.
8. This was not a long-cist burial.
9. Excavations at Pitnacree (Coles and Simpson 1965) and North Mains, Strathallan (Barclay 1983b), indicated that some are Neolithic (Barclay and Maxwell 1998, 115–16).
10. Apart from a cremation deposit in an urn at Sandy Road stone circle, New Scone, which produced a medieval date (Stewart 1965), which has since been shown to have been unreliable.

Bibliography

Abercromby, J., Ross, T. and Anderson J. 1901–2. Account of the Excavation of the Roman Station at Inchtuthil, Perthshire, undertaken by the Society of Antiquaries of Scotland in 1901, *Proceedings of the Society of Antiquaries of Scotland* 36, 182–242.

Aitchison, N.B. 1981. Abbey Craig (Logie p): Rampart, *Discovery and Excavation in Scotland 1981*, 7.

Alcock, L. 2003. *Kings and Warriors, Craftsmen and Priests in Northern Britain AD 550–850.* Edinburgh: Society of Antiquaries of Scotland Monograph 24.

Alcock, L., Alcock, E.A. and Driscoll, S.T. 1989. Reconnaissance excavations on early historic fortifications and other royal sites in Scotland, 1974–84, 3: Excavations at Dundurn, Strathearn, Perthshire, 1976–77, *Proceedings of the Society of Antiquaries of Scotland* 119, 189–226; fiche 2, A2–3: E11.

Alexander, D. 2000. Investigation of a cropmark enclosure at West Mains, Lunan Bay, Angus, *Tayside and Fife Archaeological Journal* 6, 18–25.

Alexander, D. 2005. Redcastle, Lunan Bay, Angus: the excavation of an Iron Age timber-lined souterrain and a Pictish barrow cemetery, *Proceedings of the Society of Antiquaries of Scotland* 135, 41–118.

Armit, I. 1997. *Celtic Scotland.* London: Batsford.

Armit, I. 1999. The abandonment of souterrains: evolution, catastrophe or dislocation? *Proceedings of the Society of Antiquaries of Scotland* 129, 577–596.

Ashmore, P. 1999. Radiocarbon dating: avoiding errors by avoiding mixed samples, *Antiquity* 73, 124–130.

Ashmore, P., Cook, G.T. and Harkness, D.D. 2001. *Carbon Dating Database: Radiocarbon Dates for Archaeological Sites in Scotland Issued Before June 1996*, http://www.historic-scotland.gov.uk/scripts/carbon-dating.asp

Baker, L. 2002. An Iron Age child burial at Dunbar Golf Course, East Lothian, *Proceedings of the Society of Antiquaries of Scotland* 132, 205–212.

Barclay, G.J. 1983a. The Excavation of a Settlement of the Later Bronze Age and Iron Age at Myrehead, Falkirk District, *Glasgow Archaeological Journal* 10, 41–72.

Barclay, G.J. 1983b. Sites of the third millennium bc to the first millennium ad at North Mains, Strathallan, Perthshire, *Proceedings of the Society of Antiquaries of Scotland* 113, 122–281.

Barclay, G.J. and Maxwell, G. 1998. *The Cleaven Dyke and Littleour: Monuments in the Neolithic of Tayside*. Edinburgh: Society of Antiquaries of Scotland Monograph 13.

Barrett, J. and Downes, J.M. 1996. Pitcarmick, *Discovery and Excavation in Scotland 1996*, 141.

Bevan B. 1999. *Northern Exposure: Interpretative Devolution and the Iron Ages in Britain*. Leicester: Leicester Archaeology Monograph 4.

Breeze, D.J., Close-Brooks, J. and Ritchie J.N.G. 1976. Soldiers' burials at Camelon, Stirlingshire, *Britannia* 7, 73–95.

Cameron, K. 2002. The excavation of Neolithic pits and Iron Age souterrains at Dubton Farm, Brechin, Angus, *Tayside and Fife Archaeological Journal* 8, 19–76.

Cameron, K. 2003. A new investigation at West Grange of Conon Souterrain, *Tayside and Fife Archaeological Journal* 9, 65–73.

Carter, S.P. and Hunter, F. 2003. An Iron Age chariot burial from Scotland, *Antiquity* 77, 531–535.

Childe, V.G. 1934–5. Excavation of the vitrified fort of Finavon, Angus, *Proceedings of the Society of Antiquaries of Scotland* 69, 49–80.

Childe, V.G. 1935–6. Supplementary excavations at the vitrified fort at Finavon, Angus, *Proceedings of the Society of Antiquaries of Scotland* 70, 347–352.

Christison, D. 1898. *The Rhind Lectures in Archaeology 1894 – Early Fortifications in Scotland: Motes, Camps, and Forts*. Edinburgh: William Blackwood and Sons.

Christison, D. 1898–9. On the recently excavated fort on Castle Law, Abernethy, Perthshire, *Proceedings of the Society of Antiquaries of Scotland* 33, 13–33.

Christison, D. 1899–1900. The forts, 'camps' and other field-works of Perth, Forfar and Kincardineshire, *Proceedings of the Society of Antiquaries of Scotland* 34, 43–120.

Christison, D. 1900–1. Excavations undertaken by the Society of Antiquaries of Scotland of earthworks adjoining the 'Roman Road' between Ardoch and Dupplin, Perthshire, *Proceedings of the Society of Antiquaries of Scotland* 35, 15–43.

Close-Brooks, J. 1973. Polmont: Avonglen Quarry, long cist, *Discovery and Excavation in Scotland 1973*, 53.

Close-Brooks, J. 1984. Pictish and other burials, in Friell and Watson 1984, 87–114.

Coleman, R. and Hunter, F. 2002. The excavation of a souterrain at Shanzie Farm, Alyth, Perthshire, *Tayside and Fife Archaeological Journal* 8, 77–101.

Coles, J.M. and Simpson, D.S. 1965. The excavation of a Neolithic round barrow at Pitnacree, Perthshire, *Proceedings of the Prehistoric Society* 31, 34–57.

Cook, M. 2002. Aird Quarry, Stranraer (Inch parish): palisade enclosure; roundhouse, *Discovery and Excavation in Scotland 2002*, 29.

Cook, M. 2004. Aird Quarry, *Discovery and Excavation in Scotland 2004*, 160.

Coutts, H. 1971. *Tayside Before History: a Guide-Catalogue of the Collection of Antiquities in Dundee Museum*. Dundee: Dundee Museum and Art Gallery Catalogue 1.

Davies, M.H. 2006. *An Archaeological Analysis of Later Prehistoric Settlement and Society in Perthshire and Stirlingshire*. Unpublished Ph.D. thesis, University of Durham.

Dick, A.M. 2002. Trial excavation of a souterrain at Fletcherfield, Angus, *Tayside and Fife Archaeological Journal* 8, 102–109.

Donaldson, C.H., Allison, S. and Hall, M.A. 2004. Vitrified rocks from Dun Knock hillfort, Dunning, Perthshire, *Tayside and Fife Archaeological Journal* 10, 64–72.

Driscoll, S.T. 1987. *The Early Historic Landscape of Strathearn: the Archaeology of a Pictish Kingdom*. Unpublished Ph.D. thesis, University of Glasgow.

Driscoll, S.T. 1991. The archaeology of state formation in Scotland, in W.S. Hanson and E.A. Slater, *Scottish Archaeology: New Perceptions*, 81–111. Aberdeen: Aberdeen University Press.

Driscoll, S.T. 1995. Excavations on Dundee Law, 1993, *Proceedings of the Society of Antiquaries of Scotland* 125, 1091–1108.

Dunwell, A. forthcoming. Cist burials and an Iron Age settlement at Dryburn Bridge, Innerwick, East Lothian, *Scottish Archaeological Internet Reports*.

Dunwell, A. and Strachan, R.J. forthcoming. *Excavations at the Caterthun Forts, Angus*. Perth: Tayside and Fife Archaeology Committee Monograph.

Elsdon, S.M. 2004. *Christian Maclagan: Stirling's Formidable Lady Antiquary*. Forfar: The Pinkfoot Press.

Feachem, R.W. 1958–9. Glenachan Rig homestead, Cardon, Peebleshire, *Proceedings of the Society of Antiquaries of Scotland* 92, 15–24.

Finlayson, B., Coles, G., Dunwell, A. and Ralston, I. 1999. The Angus and South Aberdeenshire Field School of the Department of Archaeology, University of Edinburgh: research design, *Tayside and Fife Archaeological Journal* 5, 28–35.

Friell, J.G.P. and Watson, W.G. 1984. *Pictish Studies: Settlement, Burial and Art in Dark Age Northern Britain*. Oxford: British Archaeological Reports British Series 125.

Glendinning, B. and Hall, D. 2003. Wallace monument, *Discovery and Excavation in Scotland* 4, 166.

Greig, C., Greig, M. and Ashmore, P. 2000. Excavation of a cairn cemetery at Lundin Links, Fife, in 1965–6, *Proceedings of the Society of Antiquaries of Scotland* 130, 585–636.

Halliday, S.P. 1985. Unenclosed upland settlement in the east and south-east of Scotland, in D. Spratt and C. Burgess, *Upland Settlement in Britain: the Second Millennium BC and After*, 231–251. Oxford: British Archaeological Reports British Series 143.

Harding, A.F. and Lee, G.E. 1987. *Henge Monuments and Related Sites of Great Britain: Air Photographic Evidence and Catalogue*. Oxford: British Archaeological Reports British Series 175.

Harding, D.W. (ed.) 1982. *Later Prehistoric Settlement in South-East Scotland*. Edinburgh: Department of Archaeology, University of Edinburgh Occasional Paper 8.

Harding, D.W. 2004. *The Iron Age in Northern Britain: Celts and Romans, Natives and Invaders*. Abingdon: Routledge.

Haselgrove, C., Armit, I., Champion, T., Creighton, J., Gwilt, A., Hill, J.D., Hunter, F. and Woodward, A. (eds). 2001. *Understanding the British Iron Age: An Agenda for Action*. Salisbury: Wessex Archaeology.

Hill, J.D. 1989. Re-thinking the Iron Age, *Scottish Archaeological Review* 6, 16–24.

Hill. J.D. 1993. Can we recognise a different European past? A contrastive archaeology of later prehistoric settlements in southern England, *Journal of European Archaeology* 1, 57–75.

Hill, P.H. 1982. Broxmouth hill-fort excavations, 1977–78: an interim report, in Harding 1982, 141–188.

Hingley, R. 1992. Society in Scotland from 700 BC to AD 200, *Proceedings of the Society of Antiquaries of Scotland* 122, 7–53.

Hingley, R. 1999. The creation of later prehistoric landscapes and the context of the reuse of Neolithic and earlier Bronze Age monuments in Britain and Ireland, in Bevan 1999, 233–251.

Hingley, R., Moore, H.L., Triscott, J.E. and Wilson, G. 1997. The excavation of two later Iron Age fortified homesteads at Aldclune, Blair Atholl, Perth and Kinross, *Proceedings of the Society of Antiquaries of Scotland* 127, 407–466.

Holden, T.G. and Sheridan, A. 2001 Three cists and a possible Roman Road at Barbush Quarry, Dunblane, *Proceedings of the Society of Antiquaries of Scotland* 131, 87–100.

Hunter, D.M. 1971. Two groups of cists at Denovan, near Dunipace, Stirlingshire, *Glasgow Archaeological Journal* 2, 31–38.

Hunter, F. 1996. Recent Roman Iron Age metalwork finds from Fife and Tayside, *Tayside and Fife Archaeological Journal* 2, 113–125.

Hunter, F. 1998. Discussion of the artefact assemblage, in L. Main, Excavation of a timber round-house and broch at the Fairy Knowe, Buchlyvie, Stirlingshire, 1975–8, *Proceedings of the Society of Antiquaries of Scotland* 128, 393–401 (293–417).

Hunter, F. 2001a. Roman and native in Scotland: new approaches, *Journal of Roman Archaeology* 14, 289–309.

Hunter, F. 2001b. Unpublished Roman finds from the Falkirk area, *Calatria: The Journal of the Falkirk Local History Society* 15, 111–123.

Hunter, F. 2005. The image of the warrior in the British Iron Age – coin iconography in context, in C. Haselgrove and D. Wigg-Wolf (eds), *Iron Age Coinage and Ritual Practices*, 43–68. Mainz: Studien zu Fundmünzen der Antike 20.

Hutcheson, A.A. 1902–3. Discovery of a full-length stone cist containing human remains and a penannular brooch at Craigie, near Dundee, *Proceedings of the Society of Antiquaries of Scotland* 37, 233–240.

James, H.F. 2001. Excavations at Kingsbarns, Fife, in 1997–8: an Iron Age short cist burial, prehistoric pits and a buried eighteenth century bridge within the designed landscape of Cambo, *Tayside and Fife Archaeological Journal* 7, 16–26.

Jervise, A. 1861–2. An account of the excavation of the round or 'bee-hive' shaped house, and other underground chambers, at West Grange of Conon, Forfarshire, *Proceedings of the Society of Antiquaries of Scotland* 4, 492–499.

Jobey, G. 1959. Excavations at the native settlement at Huckhoe, Northumberland, 1955–7, *Archaeologia Aeliana* (Ser. 4) 37, 217–278.

Jobey, G. 1968. A radiocarbon date for the palisaded settlement at Huckhoe, *Archaeologia Aeliana* (Ser. 4) 46, 293–295.

Jobey, G. and Tait, J. 1966. Excavations on palisaded settlements and cairnfields at Alnham, Northumberland, *Archaeologia Aeliana* (Ser. 4) 44, 5–48.

Kendrick, J. 1995. Excavation of a Neolithic enclosure and an Iron Age settlement at Douglasmuir, Angus, *Proceedings of the Society of Antiquaries of Scotland* 125, 29–67.

MacGregor, L.J. and Oram, R. 2000. *Atholl and Gowrie, North Perthshire: A Historical Guide*. Edinburgh: Birlinn Limited.

Macinnes, L. 1982. Pattern and purpose: the settlement evidence, in Harding 1982, 57–73.

Macinnes, L. 1983. *Later Prehistoric and Romano-British Settlement North and South of the Forth – a Comparative Survey*. Unpublished Ph.D. thesis, University of Newcastle.

Macinnes, L. 1984. Brochs and the Roman occupation of lowland Scotland, *Proceedings of the Society of Antiquaries of Scotland* 114, 235–249.

Maclagan, C. 1870–1. On the round castles and ancient dwellings of the valley of the Forth, and its tributary the Teith, *Proceedings of the Society of Antiquaries of Scotland* 9, 29–44.

Maclagan, C. 1875. *The Hill Forts, Stone Circles and Other Structural Remains of Ancient Scotland*. Edinburgh: Edmonston and Douglas.

Maclagan, C. 1881. *Chips from Old Stones*. Edinburgh: privately published.

Maclagan, C. 1884. Notices of the fortresses and dwellings of the ancient peoples who inhabited the valley of the Forth and its tributary the Teith, *Transactions of the Stirling Natural History and Antiquarian Society* 5, 13–25.

MacRitchie, D. 1916–17. Earth-houses and their occupants, *Proceedings of the Society of Antiquaries of Scotland* 51, 178–197.

Main, L. 1992 Palisaded enclosure, Easterton of Argaty, *Glasgow Archaeological Society Bulletin* 28, 2–5.

Main, L. 1998 Excavation of a timber round-house and broch at Fairy Knowe, Buchlyvie, Stirlingshire, 1975–8, *Proceedings of the Society of Antiquaries of Scotland* 128, 293–417.

Main, L. 2002. *First Generations: The Stirling Area from Mesolithic to Roman Times*. Stirling: Stirling Council.

Main, L. and Murray J.F. 1980. Avonglen Quarry, Polmont (Muiravonside p): long cist, *Discovery and Excavation in Scotland 1980*, 3.

Maxwell, G.S. 1985. 'Roman' settlement in Scotland, in J.C. Chapman and H.C. Mytum, *Settlement in Northern Britain 1000 BC–AD 1000*, 233–261. Oxford: British Archaeological Reports British Series 118.

Maxwell, G.S. 1983a. Cropmark categories observed in recent aerial reconnaissance in Scotland, *Scottish Archaeological Review* 2 (1), 45–52.

Maxwell, G.S. 1983b. Recent aerial survey in Scotland, in G.S. Maxwell, *The Impact of Aerial Reconnaissance on Archaeology*, 27–40. London: Council For British Archaeology Research Report 49.

Maxwell, G.S. 1987. Settlement in southern Pictland: a new overview, in A. Small (ed.), *The Picts: a New Look at Old Problems*, 31–44. Dundee: privately published.

McCullagh, R. and Tipping, R. 1998. *The Lairg Project 1988–96: The Evolution of an Archaeological Landscape in Northern Scotland*. Edinburgh: Scottish Trust for Archaeological Research Monograph 3.

McGill, C. 2003. The excavation of a palisaded enclosure and associated structures at Ironshill East, near Inverkeilor, Angus, *Tayside and Fife Archaeological Journal* 9, 14–33.

Millar, A.H. and Matthew, H.C.G. 2004. *Maclagan, Christian (1811–1901)*, http://www.oxforddnb.com/view/article/34771

Mills, S. 2004. Alloa: a Bronze Age woman and an Iron Age warrior, *Current Archaeology* 191, 486–489.

Munro, R. 1899. *Prehistoric Scotland and its Place in European Civilisation*. Edinburgh: Blackwood.

Murray, D. and Ralston, I. 1997. The excavation of a square-ditched barrow and other cropmarks at Boysack Mills, Inverkeilor, Angus, *Proceedings of the Society of Antiquaries of Scotland* 127, 359–386.

Oswald, A. 1997. A doorway on the past: practical and mystic concerns in the orientation of roundhouse doorways, in A. Gwilt and C. Haselgrove (eds), *Reconstructing Iron Age Societies*, 87–95. Oxford: Oxbow Monograph 71.

Piggott, C.M. 1947–8. Excavations at Hownam Rings, Roxburghshire, 1948, *Proceedings of the Society of Antiquaries of Scotland* 82, 193–225.

Piggott, S. 1966. A scheme for the Scottish Iron Age, in A.L.F. Rivet, *The Iron Age in Northern Britain*, 1–15. Edinburgh: Edinburgh University Press.

Playfair, J. 1819. *A Geographical and Statistical Description of Scotland.* Edinburgh: A. Constable.

Pollock, D. 1997. The excavation of Iron Age buildings at Ironshill, Inverkeilor, Angus, *Proceedings of the Society of Antiquaries of Scotland* 127, 339–358.

Pope, R.E. 2007. Ritual and the roundhouse: a critique of recent ideas on the use of domestic space in later British prehistory, in C. Haselgrove and R. Pope (eds), *The Earlier Iron Age in Britain and the Near Continent*, 204–228. Oxford: Oxbow Books.

RCAHMS 1963. *Stirlingshire: An Inventory of the Ancient Monuments.* Edinburgh: HMSO.

RCAHMS 1967. *Peeblesshire: An Inventory of the Ancient Monuments, Vol. I.* Edinburgh: HMSO.

RCAHMS 1979. *The Archaeological Sites and Monuments of Stirling District, Central Region.* Edinburgh: RCAHMS.

RCAHMS 1990. *North-East Perth: An Archaeological Landscape.* Edinburgh: HMSO.

RCAHMS 1994a. *South-East Perth: An Archaeological Landscape.* Edinburgh: HMSO.

RCAHMS 1994b. *Braes of Doune: An Archaeological Survey.* Edinburgh: HMSO.

RCAMS 1956. *An Inventory of the Ancient and Historical Monuments of Roxburghshire, Vol. I, with the Fourteenth Report of the Commission.* Edinburgh: HMSO.

Rees, A.R. forthcoming. The excavation of an Iron Age unenclosed settlement, souterrain, Early Historic punishment burial and metalworking area, at Hawkhill, Lunan Bay, Angus, *Tayside and Fife Archaeological Journal.*

Rees, T. 1998. Excavation of Culhawk Hill ring ditch house, Kirriemuir, Angus, *Tayside and Fife Archaeological Journal* 4, 106–128.

Rideout, J. 1995. Carn Dubh, Moulin, Perthshire: survey and excavation of an archaeological landscape 1987–1980, *Proceedings of the Society of Antiquaries of Scotland* 125, 139–195; fiche 2 A4–C5.

Rideout, J. 1996. Excavation of a promontory fort and a palisaded homestead at Lower Greenyards, Bannockburn, Stirling, 1982–5, *Proceedings of the Society of Antiquaries of Scotland* 126, 199–269.

Robertson, J. 1799. *General View of the Agriculture of the County of Perth.* Perth: James Morrison.

Scottish Office 1994. *National Planning Policy Guideline 5: Archaeology and Planning.* Edinburgh: The Scottish Office Environment Department Planning Series.

Sheridan, A. 2004. The National Museums of Scotland radiocarbon dating programmes: results obtained during 2003/4, *Discovery and Excavation in Scotland* 5, 174–176.

Sherriff, J.R. 1986 The Excavation of a Palisaded Enclosure at Methven Wood, Almondbank, Perthshire, 1979, *Proceedings of the Society of Antiquaries of Scotland* 116, 93–99.

Sherriff, J.R. 2000. Excavation in Perthshire: 1948–1998, in M.L. Stavert, *Dirt, Dust and Development: 50 Years of Perthshire Archaeology*, 26–45. Perth: Perthshire Society of Natural Science Archaeological and Historical Section.

Steer, K.A. 1955–6. An early Iron Age homestead at West Plean, Stirlingshire, *Proceedings of the Society of Antiquaries of Scotland* 89, 227–251.

Stevenson, J. 1999. Prehistory, in D. Omand, *The Perthshire Book*, 19–33. Edinburgh: Birlinn Ltd.

Stevenson, R.B.K. 1948–9. The nuclear fort of Dalmahoy, Midlothian, and other Dark Age capitals, *Proceedings of the Society of Antiquaries of Scotland* 83, 186–198.

Stewart, M.E.C. 1965. Excavation of a circle of standing stones at Sandy Road, Scone, Perthshire, *Transactions and Proceedings of the Perthshire Society of Natural Science* 11, 7–23.

Stewart, M.E.C. 1985. The excavation of a henge, stone circles and metal-working area at Moncrieffe, Perthshire, *Proceedings of the Society of Antiquaries of Scotland* 115, 125–150.

Strachan, R.J. 1998. *Archaeological Evaluation at Cowiehall Quarry, Easter Moss, Stirling.* Unpublished Centre for Field Archaeology Data Structure Report 448.

Strachan, R.J. 1999. Easter Moss, Cowie (St Ninian's parish): evaluation: souterrain, *Discovery and Excavation in Scotland 1999*, 88.

Strachan, R.J., Hamilton J.E. and Dunwell A.J. 2003. Excavations of cropmark enclosures in Angus at Mains of Edzell, Edzell and Hawkhill, Lunan, *Tayside and Fife Archaeological Journal* 9, 34–64.

Stuart, J. 1865. *Historical Sketches of the Church and Parish of Fowlis Easter.* Dundee: J Middleton.

Taylor, D.B. 1982. Excavation of a promontory fort, broch and souterrain at Hurly Hawkin, *Proceedings of the Society of Antiquaries of Scotland* 112, 215–253.

Thorneycroft, W. 1932–3. Observations on hut-circles near the eastern Border of Perthshire, North of Blairgowrie, *Proceedings of the Society of Antiquaries of Scotland* 67, 187–203.

Thorneycroft, W. 1945–6. Further observations on hut-circles, *Proceedings of the Society of Antiquaries of Scotland* 80, 131–135.

Triscott, J. 1982. Excavations at Dryburn Bridge, East Lothian, 1978–1979, in Harding 1982, 117–124.

Wainwright, F.T. 1953a. Souterrains in Scotland, *Antiquity* 27, 219–232.

Wainwright, F.T. 1953b. A souterrain identified in Angus, *Antiquaries Journal* 33, 65–71.

Wainwright, F.T. 1963. *The Souterrains of Southern Pictland.* London: Routledge and Kegan Paul.

Walker, J.J. 1974. Avonglen Quarry: long cist, *Discovery and Excavation in Scotland 1974*, 66.

Walker, J.J. 1976. Polmont/Avonglen Quarry: long cist, *Discovery and Excavation in Scotland 1976*, 63.

Watkins, T. 1980. Excavation of a settlement and souterrain at Newmill, near Bankfoot, Perthshire, *Proceedings of the Society of Antiquaries of Scotland* 110, 165–208.

Watson, W.J. 1912–13. The circular forts of North Perthshire, *Proceedings of the Society of Antiquaries of Scotland* 47, 30–60.

Watson, W.J. 1914–15. Circular forts in Lorn and North Perthshire: with a note on the excavation of one at Borenich, Loch Tummel,

Proceedings of the Society of Antiquaries of Scotland 49, 17–32.

Wedderburn, L.M.M. 1973. *Excavations at Greencairn Cairnton of Balbegno, Fettercairn, Angus: A Preliminary Report.* Dundee: Dundee Museum and Art Gallery Occasional Papers in Archaeology 1.

Wedderburn, L.M.M. and Grime, D.M. 1984. The cairn cemetery at Garbeg, Drumnadrochit, in Friell and Watson 1984, 151–168.

Whitley, J. 2002. Too many ancestors, *Antiquity* 76, 119–126.

Willis, S.H. 1999. Without and within: aspects of culture and community in the Iron Age of north-eastern England, in Bevan 1999, 81–110.

Wilson, E.M. 1980. Excavations at West Mains of Ethie, Angus, *Proceedings of the Society of Antiquaries of Scotland* 110, 114–122.

Woolliscroft, D.J. and Hoffmann, B. 2003. *Iron Age and Roman Period Native Sites at East Coldoch, Stirling: An Interim Report for Work up to 2002*, http://www.romangask.org.uk/Pages/Papers/Coldoch2.html

Young, A. 1973. *Avonglen Quarry, Polmont: Appendix 1: The Human Bones.* Unpublished Manuscript MS/37/1, National Monuments Record of Scotland, Edinburgh.

Artefacts, regions, and identities in the northern British Iron Age

Fraser Hunter

Introduction

Regionality and identity have been key issues in recent studies of the Iron Age. This paper will explore how regions have been constructed in previous approaches to the period in Scotland, and look at some of the problems and prospects for using material culture to understand regional and other identities. I will then consider the appearance of decorative metalwork as a case study in the expression of regional and social identities, comparing the pre-Roman to the Roman Iron Age and considering the reasons behind the development of regional metalwork styles in the latter.

Regions

The four provinces of the Scottish Iron Age defined by Piggott remain influential today (Fig. 1; Piggott 1966; RCAHMS 1956, 15–16). These were an expansion of Hawkes' (1959) scheme northwards, the provinces each having regional subdivisions supported by Feachem's (1966) analysis of the field monuments. There has however been little consideration of the validity or theoretical basis of these divisions, or of what they meant in human terms. The provinces in particular are so large (substantially bigger even than Ptolemy's tribal areas) that how they could have articulated in social terms is a key question. The system is also chronologically static, although it must be admitted that our understanding of change through time is little better than it was in Piggott's day. These provinces were seen not simply as geographical entities but cultural zones – 'Atlantic Second B' or 'Tyne Forth Third C' in a further extension of Hawkes' scheme. This built on Childe's ground-breaking analysis of the major 'cultural groupings' of the Iron Age, which he saw as a fusion of indigenous Late Bronze Age cultures with regular influxes of migrants to stimulate development (Childe 1935, 236–57). In turn these models were refined and developed in detail by Euan MacKie (e.g. 1969; 1971).

Much of this work was rightly critiqued as archaeologists became more aware of the complexities of their material. The straightforward equation of 'type fossils' of sites and finds with cultures was discredited, and the various building blocks were assailed (e.g. Clarke 1970; 1971; Lane 1987). There has however been little attempt to replace these broad narratives. In particular, the artefacts which were crucial to early attempts at cultural definition fell from favour, seen as fit only for dating and a little local colour rather than any serious interpretation. Even in the Atlantic zone, with its enviable wealth of material culture, extensive reappraisals have made little use of the finds, focussing primarily on debates over structural sequences and their interpretation (e.g. Armit 1990; 1992; 1997; Sharples and Parker Pearson 1997). Here the report on Scalloway stands out as a notable exception (Sharples 1998), although there are problems with the approach. This failure to address material culture has been a major weakness in recent scholarship.

Yet while the critique of culture-historical approaches was valid, this did not invalidate the patterns which gave rise to these theories. There are indeed regional differences among the sites and artefacts of northern Britain, but they require more subtle approaches. In particular, we need to make more use of our theoretical understandings concerning the active use of material culture to create and express identity, and the existence

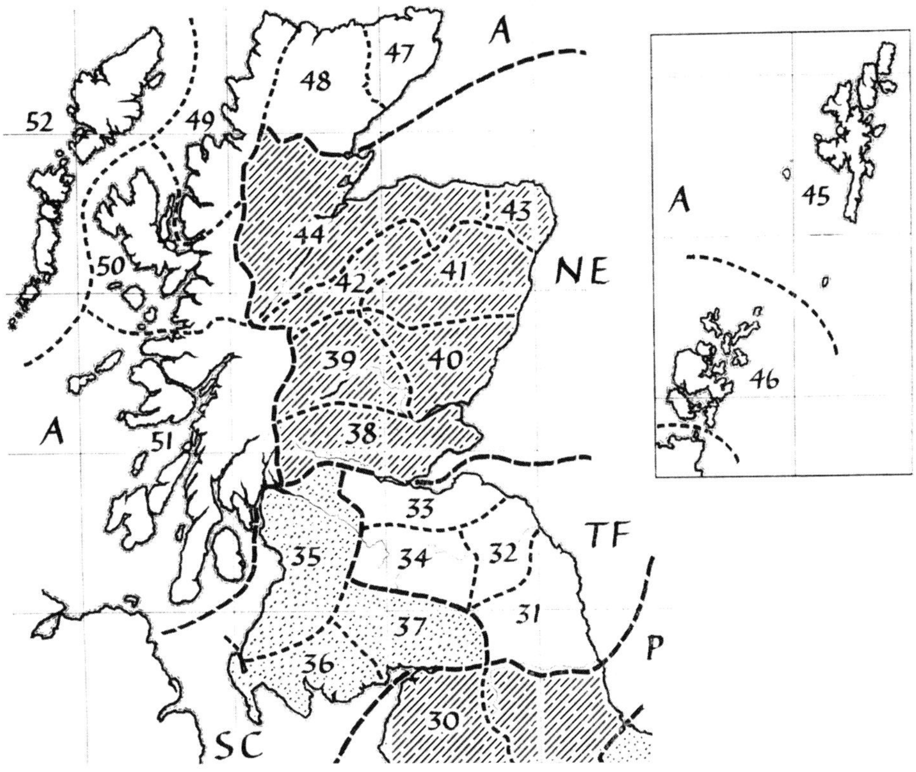

Fig. 1. The provinces of the north British Iron Age defined by Piggott (1966).

of different identities at different scales. What we can see are traces of a complex interlocking series of connections and identities partly reflected in the varying distributions and contexts of different kinds of artefacts. This is of course a complex topic, and I would not pretend to be unveiling a polished final analysis. My aim is to illustrate the issues with a few examples before turning to a more extensive case study of decorative metalwork.

Artefacts as identifiers

There is a tendency in artefact studies to value the large scale over the small scale: big regional differences are seen as more significant than small local ones. In fact what the record shows is a wide diversity of distributions and variations, from site-specific to national. Differences in taphonomy and excavation strategy complicate matters, but there are underlying patterns. These variations at different scales reflect different perceptions and uses of material culture, which in turn should tell us about the cultural practices involved.

To take the example of Scottish Iron Age pottery, at a broad scale there is a basic difference between a pot-rich Atlantic zone and a pot-poor remainder. This can then be analysed at different levels: the occurrence of decorated pottery, for instance, is highly regional, and its frequency varies from site to site; the pottery sequence from Orkney does not match that of Shetland; while within the Western Isles there is considerable variation from one site to the next within a broadly equivalent sequence (e.g. Lane 1990; Campbell 2002, esp. 143–4; MacSween 2002, 149–52). This very diversity, the bane of would-be typologists, is itself of interest. Analysis of fabrics points to localised manufacture (Topping 1986; Hingley 1992, 20–1), and this is surely what these diverse site sequences indicate – broad regional trends defining some form of shared regional or island-group identity, with localised, even site-specific variations at a more everyday level of interaction. Rather than frustrating our typochronological endeavours, these are intrinsically interesting examples of local self-expression which merit more attention. Such use of pot-styles to indicate identity has been better addressed elsewhere in Britain (e.g. Blackmore *et al.* 1979): the data exist for similar studies in the Atlantic zone, were someone to take up the challenge.

There are similar local and regional variations in other object types. For instance whalebone ard-shares are almost exclusively a Western Isles phenomenon (Hallén 1994, 202), while rare surviving bone assemblages from southern Scotland reveal types unknown among the more plentiful Atlantic material (e.g. pins from Broxmouth, East Lothian; Hill 1982, fig. 10). Some of the variety arises from raw material availability – in the Atlantic province bone was often used as a substitute for metal or wood (e.g. Rynne 1983) – but this in itself created a regional cultural practice. In coarse stone, some tool types are site-specific (Clarke 1998, 389), while others show regional distributions, such as the miniature querns of Fife and Angus.[1] Other artefacts show broader distributions: for instance, certain glass beads concentrate strongly in north-east Scotland, while glass bangles, commonplace in southern Scotland and northern England, are exceedingly rare north of the Forth (Stevenson 1976; Guido 1978, 85–9). The Forth is in fact a persistent north–south boundary, with items such as stone lamps and discs rare to the south (Stevenson 1966). Quern types also differ: to the north, bun and beehive querns are markedly rarer, with the disc quern predominating. Euan MacKie has long emphasised this major difference, which is not just a typological issue but represents a different way of grinding grain (MacKie 1971, 5; 1989, 5–11). However, explanations for such a basic difference in daily practice remain elusive. Other types show even broader distributions, across much of Scotland (e.g. projecting ring-headed pins; Clarke 1971, fig. 4), or Britain (e.g. bone weaving combs, albeit in various regional guises; Hodder and Hedges 1977).

At one level, localised variation doubtless reflects local resources and specific needs, but the use and persistence of such types points to the maintenance of a local level of cultural tradition which we rarely consider. For example, coarse stone tools bulk large in northern Iron Age assemblages, but because of their very mundanity tend to be overlooked. Yet they are key sources for reconstructing the daily lives of the inhabitants: their comparative study should allow insights into habits and differences in the routines of life at site, local and regional levels. This ought to be crucial to current theoretical concerns about the practices of everyday life (e.g. Fitzpatrick 1997); but sadly there has been more theory than practice in this area. This prosaic domestic material has not received the attention it merits, and we flounder in the dark with an absence of agreed methodologies for studying coarse stone tools or understanding their functions.

The larger-scale distributions sometimes reinforce and sometimes cross-cut Piggott's boundaries – as we should expect when material culture was used in a variety of social situations rather than restricted to a monolithic 'culture group'. However interpretation is not straightforward, as we lack developed social models to explain patterns of variation. We do not suffer solely from a lack of data, however much we may bemoan their quality – we suffer from a lack of interpretation. What scales of interaction should we be looking for? How and why were people interacting? Why were certain pots decorated, querns used, or pins worn? Why did things change? And can we link our evidence with historical models such as the tribes of the Roman period recorded by Ptolemy? Many of the patterns are on such a scale (e.g. traditions of hoard deposition; Hunter 1997a) that they must reflect broader regional or specific social identities. Of course topography is a major factor behind distributions: the nature of the landscape had a key influence on interaction and identity, and it is such large-scale land-blocks which are reflected in Piggott's provinces. But geography alone does not define the personality of north Britain (to adapt Fox's (1952) term). Alternative, complementary or contrasting social identities and practices lie behind these different finds and their different distributions, as yet barely examined.

Metalwork and identity

To explore this question of expressing and creating identity through material culture I would like to look at the development of regional decorative metalwork traditions in northern Britain. Given the restricted nature of this material, it seems likely that we are looking here at the expressions of only certain high-status groups within society.

We can identify clear change through time, with the BC/AD turning point as an approximate boundary. There is an explosion of metalwork after this broad date, and what went before is of a different character. Decorative metalwork is rare prior to the first century AD, and much of what survives was imported, such as the north French torc from Dungyle, Kirkcudbrightshire, or the Snettisham-style torc terminal from Netherurd, Peeblesshire (MacGregor 1976, nos 191, 95; J.V.S. Megaw, pers. comm.). To these more dramatic items may be added a few finds of Iron Age coins in southern Scotland, while a thin but widespread scatter of brooches shows that the Atlantic zones also had access to decorative metalwork, although the lack of a hoarding tradition makes it less obvious (Hull and Hawkes 1987, 131, 150–1, 177–8, 196; Ballin Smith 1994, 223–4; Hunter 1997b).

External contacts did not just supply exotica, however; they could provide habits used to mark affiliation to a wider world. This is seen in the fifth-century BC chariot burial from Newbridge, Midlothian, which mirrors funerary practices from northern France and the Belgian Ardennes, but the vehicle itself was a local one, not an import (Carter and Hunter 2003). Strong continental contacts are also seen in some British-made metalwork, notably the Torrs 'chamfrein' (Atkinson and Piggott 1955, 227–34), an example of a widespread British tradition which drew closely on continental styles. The clear and strong connection to European traditions indicates a desire to mark contacts to a wider world, rather than develop distinctively regional or local styles.

By contrast, identifying indigenous regional metalwork styles in north Britain in the last few centuries BC is tricky. The only good candidates are gold ribbon torcs, whose dating has been extensively discussed (Eogan

1983; Raftery 1984, 178–81; Warner 1993, 111–12), with the balance swinging away from a previous middle Bronze Age orthodoxy towards a middle to late pre-Roman Iron Age date, perhaps fourth–first century BC. While best known as an Irish type, some can be argued as Scottish products from differences in terminal design (Coles 1968, 170–1). Their distribution is broad but concentrates in north-east Scotland and they may be a product of this region (which regularly shows contacts to Ireland throughout prehistory; Cowie 1988, 7, 11).

From this we can characterise the last few centuries BC in north Britain as showing extensive but intermittent contacts, with no development of regional metalwork styles except arguably the gold ribbon torcs of the north-east. There was a concern with exotica throughout the area, presumably as markers of wider affiliations as well as valued status goods; but there was no recurrent or systematic use of locally-made metalwork to transmit more regional affiliations. This contrasts with much of southern England, where the last two centuries BC in particular saw markedly more decorative metalwork and the development of distinctive regional styles (e.g. Cunliffe 1995, 33–7; Stead 1996, 32–5).

Regional metalworking traditions in the late pre-Roman and Roman Iron Age

Things changed markedly around the start of the first century AD, with an explosion of metalwork in different regional traditions. In north Britain there were two such traditions: 'massive' metalwork in north-east Scotland, between the firths of Moray and Forth; and a central British style zone from the Forth to the Humber. These are part of a broadly simultaneous development of large-scale regional Celtic art styles across much of Britain (e.g. Jope 2000, 152, map 8). Precisely when remains a problem: tight dating is difficult, and the nature of the evidence means we can realistically say only that change is 'peri-Roman'. There has been a tendency to assume that the art in the south is earlier than that in the north, but since this is the inherent pattern of datable associations (following the progress of Roman contact and invasion) it need not reflect reality. Equally it is clear that much 'Celtic' art was created after the conquest. In southern Britain many major hoards of Iron Age metalwork include Roman material (e.g. Polden Hill, Somerset; Westhall, Suffolk; Seven Sisters, Glamorgan; Brailsford 1975; Clarke 1939, 68–9; Davies and Spratling 1976), and on settlement sites Iron Age-style metalwork often occurs in early Roman contexts (as the listings in MacGregor 1976 demonstrate). In the north at least, contextual associations go well into the second century (e.g. bridle bit moulds from Prestatyn, AD 120–140; boss-and-petal ornaments to at least Antonine; Blockley 1989, 187–8; Bishop 1998, 63–4). Dungworth's (1996, 407–11) analytical work confirms this, showing much of the central British 'Celtic' material re-uses Roman metal. Rather than worry about precise dating and its connection to conquest (since we can rarely attain such chronological certainty) we should consider why it evolves at this time.

While the detailed reasons were undoubtedly varied and complex, an obvious stimulus was the proximity of Rome (e.g. MacGregor 1976, 177–8), which can be seen as a threat to local society and its identity. There is the danger that we make a known historical event 'suck in' unrelated processes around it, but it is clear both from southern England and the Continent that Rome could have a significant impact from proximity as well as conquest. This is not to see the development of these art styles as necessarily reflecting resistance to Rome – the enthusiasm with which Roman artefacts were adopted in many areas suggests quite the contrary. However in this uncertain situation, conditions were ripe for the development of art styles drawing on past traditions but also being new, distinctive and local. The art is lavished on exactly the kinds of objects which Celtic art traditionally graced – the elite playthings of jewellery, weapons, feasting equipment, horse and chariot gear – but the styles now mark out regional identities. Such a trend of expressing identity at times of stress can be paralleled more generally (e.g. Hodder 1982, 186–7; Jones 1997, 113–15, 123–4).

While the presence or proximity of Rome played a pivotal role in these developments, it cannot take full responsibility. Across Britain, site assemblages show an increasing materiality in the course of the Iron Age, suggesting by the late pre-Roman period a changed concept of the individual with more marking of individual and group identities through material culture. This is best demonstrated in case-studies from southern England, where both increased quantities and changes in the nature of material culture have been identified in ornaments, other personal items, and cooking and eating styles (e.g. Hill 1997; Rigby and Freestone 1997).

The northern evidence has not been synthesised, but there are clear signs of similar patterns with an increase in the quantity of personal ornaments recovered, whether it be glass beads and bangles, penannular brooches or projecting ring-headed pins. The dating evidence is rarely strong, but the trends appear to start before the Roman Iron Age[2] and are found across north Britain. This runs against the arguments of Armit (1997, 252–3) and Sharples (2003), who see material culture in the Atlantic as essentially prosaic at this time with an upsurge of personal ornaments only in the Early Historic period. While the trend they identify is correct – there is a much more diverse range of artefacts, especially personal artefacts, in the later period – their dichotomy is a false one, as the origins of the trend lie earlier. Already in the second century BC–second century AD there was a range of pins, beads and brooches which was absent in Early Iron Age contexts.[3]

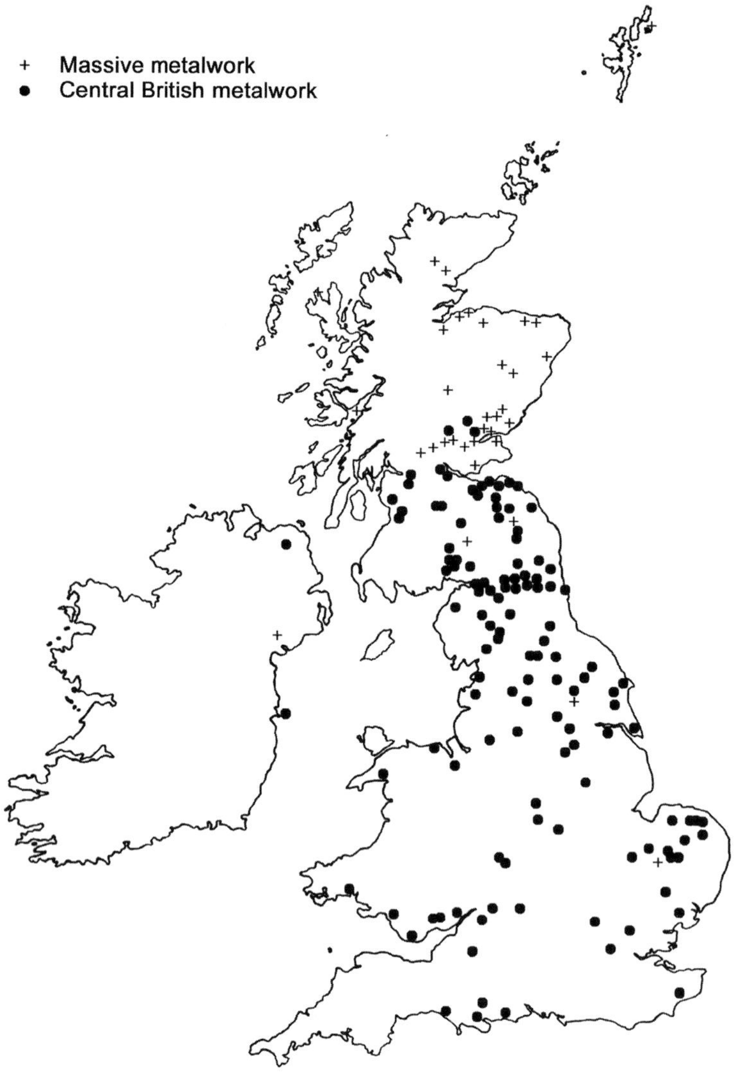

Fig. 2. Distribution of metalwork in massive and central British styles (after MacGregor 1976, with additions). For Scotland it covers both published and unpublished material, but it will be incomplete for England as it relies on published data, and metal-detecting finds are rarely published.

Thus the development of regional art styles can be seen as a key stage in a longer process. There was an increasing interest in signalling inter-personal and inter-group identities with ornaments; and in the north-east of Scotland, the Forth–Humber area and parts of southern England and Wales, this was taken a stage further in the first two centuries AD with the development of much more elaborate and visible forms of display metalwork. While the specific stimulus can be connected to social changes set in motion by Rome, the origins lie earlier, in existing developments.

Having suggested stimuli, what of scale? Defining this is not straightforward: there are sub-styles, individual traditions within wider ones, hybridisation and so on, all as yet barely understood. However the regions covered by these metalworking traditions are substantial (Fig. 2); this and the material involved suggests we are seeing a pattern of wider elite contacts. It is also important to note that the areas were not new – they were prefigured by history. The north-east Scottish group fills the area from the firths of Forth to Moray which was a persistent (if often bipartite) cultural zone throughout prehistory (e.g. Maxwell 1990, 45–6; Stevenson 1966, 37), while the southern edge of the central British group reflects the boundary between coin-using and non-coin-using areas in the later Iron Age. This same boundary has been followed in splitting the Iron Age in three, with 'core' and 'periphery' to the south and 'beyond' to the north (Haselgrove 1982; Cunliffe 1991, 130). Such core–periphery theories now seem dubious, but they were responding to patterns observed in the data, and the patterns remain as a cultural scar on the landscape which is broadly reflected in the metalwork.

Massive metalwork

The massive tradition (Fig. 3) is dominated by large armlets and zoomorphic spiral bracelets, but also includes finger rings, arguably a small group of strap junctions, and individual items such as the Deskford carnyx (Piggott 1959; Simpson 1968; 1969–70; MacGregor 1976; Ralston 1979, 482–3; Hunter 2001a). Two regional sub-groups can be defined, with the area south of the Mounth producing spiral bracelets and folded-type armlets, and the northern area producing oval-type armlets (MacGregor 1976, 107–8; Kilbride-Jones 1980, 154). It was a highly individual tradition in both decoration and form, but drew on wider influences. The decorative repertoire is typical of north British metalwork, albeit using more pronounced, higher-relief forms (MacGregor 1976), while the finger rings show rapid adoption of Roman types and the carnyx draws on a widespread European tradition (*ibid.*, 105, 116; Hunter 2001a).

The interpretation of these influences is, however, distinctively local, while the most striking products of all, the massive armlets, have no convincing prototypes and are best seen as an entirely local invention. The relationship with Rome is ambivalent: Roman metal was extensively re-used as raw material and the finger rings show Roman stylistic influence. But unlike the central British tradition there is a marked avoidance of Roman associations: within its home area, material belonging to the massive tradition is never hoarded with Roman items, and it is very rare on Roman sites (with only two examples).

Central British metalwork

The central British material is more diverse. MacGregor (1976) defined three separate 'schools' in the area from Humber to Forth, but this was rooted in diffusionism and art-historical assumption; much of the material is stylistically closely related and can be treated as a unit. The range is much broader than the massive tradition, covering horse harness, personal ornaments and weaponry, much falling into what Leeds (1933, 110–11) termed 'boss style' (e.g. Fig. 4). The whole group is less

Fig. 3. Selection of massive metalwork. Back: massive armlets from Auchenbadie and Bunrannoch; centre: spiral bracelets from West Grange of Conan, Culbin Sands, and Hurly Hawkin; front: finger rings from Forfar and Tarnavie (© National Museums of Scotland).

Fig. 4. Hoard of horse and chariot fittings in boss style from Middlebie, Dumfriesshire (© National Museums of Scotland).

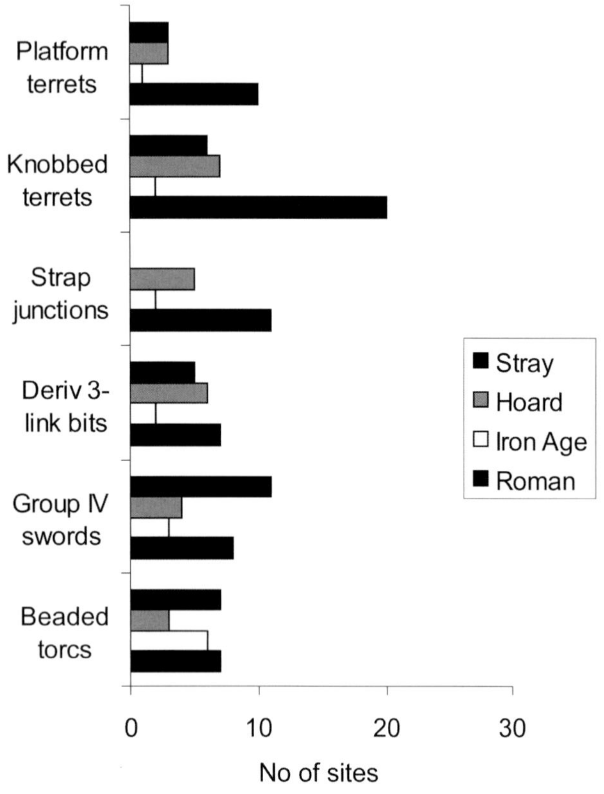

Fig. 5. The contexts of a range of central British metalwork.

tightly defined – unsurprisingly, given the area covered – and the variety and degree of style-sharing, hybridisation and experimentation indicates a vibrant tradition with a number of centres.[4] A good example is the Dinnington torc (Beswick *et al.* 1990), which is a hybrid between a beaded and a hinged torc. The distribution of this central British style is mapped in Figure 2 (above). While the northern boundary with the massive tradition is quite sharp, the southern one is less well defined, and considerable quantities of metalwork were moving south. However a diffuse boundary around the Humber is reasonably clear.

This central British tradition raises some critical questions, especially in its relation to Rome. Much, at times all, of the area lay within the Roman province, and the relationship with Rome is crucial. Indeed a high proportion of the relevant material comes from Roman sites, notably forts: as Figure 5 indicates, between 30 and 60% is from Roman contexts, with most of the rest from hoards. Manufacturing evidence too comes from both Roman and Iron Age sites.[5]

Clearly this metalwork was intimately linked to Rome's presence in the north. Further work may reveal subtle differences in style or decoration, and some hybridisation with Roman forms (e.g. Spratling 1971; MacGregor 1976, no. 35; Davies 2000, 226, no. 5), but essentially the same range of material was in use in both Iron Age and Roman contexts. We cannot of course draw a simple Iron Age : Roman opposition, especially in northern England, but Roman forts and their associated annexes and *vici* are taken here as different in character from the bulk of rural settlements with more of an indigenous air in the first and second centuries AD. Yet the occupants of both were making and using the same 'Celtic' art objects.

Past interpretations of this metalwork have been rather straightforward and simplistic. It was put down to the recruitment of local auxiliaries and thus the adoption of local styles, or to the conversion of craft workers to new patrons with corresponding debasement of noble Celtic art from torcs to trinkets (e.g. Megaw and Megaw 1989, 228, 230; Henig 1995, 103). In part this latter view comes from the incorporation of Celtic-style motifs in the decorative repertoire of small Roman objects, especially brooches (Johns 1996, 182–5) and less frequently other items (e.g. seal boxes; Megaw and Megaw 1989, ill. 392). Yet the material under review here cannot so easily be dismissed as trinkets. In an Iron Age context they would be classed as significant objects, and there is no reason to devalue them in a Roman one – especially given the occurrence of torcs and swords. Neither is the local recruitment argument so straightforward: we cannot easily assume who was using 'Celtic' material in and around Roman forts. It is uncertain how far the inhabitants of a *vicus* were locals rather than incomers following the troops, while whatever the origins of a unit, the (rather limited) epigraphic evidence for subsequent recruitment in the late first and second century shows recruits from Belgic Gaul predominating over Britons (Holder 1982, 51–3). Indeed Webster (1985, 145) argues the evidence could even suggest most Britons served overseas, although the case of Nectovelius, the Brigantian who served with a Thracian cohort at Mumrills on the Antonine Wall, shows there was more localised recruiting (Collingwood and Wright 1965, no. 2142). Clearly we cannot simply say that local styles were adopted because local recruits were dragooned into the army. However there are wider considerations of background and artistic tradition: much of Britannia's garrison was from the north-west provinces and were arguably sympathetic in taste. This is reflected in the popularity of enamelling and *Trompetenmuster* ornament in the frontier zones of the north-west provinces; the latter, a style introduced from central Europe, became intermingled with northern 'Celtic' designs (Megaw and Megaw 1989, 238).

How then should we interpret this material which was at home in both Iron Age and Roman contexts? I suggest the problem is of our own making. We lump these objects together as 'Celtic art', but how you viewed them at the time would depend on who you were. On an Iron Age settlement, a beaded torc or a knobbed terret meant 'local': when consigned to the earth in a hoard it was a statement of local identity. On a Roman fort, it also meant 'local', but a different kind of local: here local was Roman frontier culture. Thus in the south of the province, it may well have been seen as 'soldier' or 'frontier', not 'Celt' or 'barbarian'. The same material could be perceived differently by different users and read differently by different observers.

Theoretically this point is well established (e.g. Jones 1997, 118), and finds further support in Romano-British brooches. Distinctive British types developed (particularly in central Britain), such as the trumpet, the headstud, and the dragonesque, which drew on indigenous styles or technologies. These would be seen as Roman (perhaps specifically from the frontier) within the province; elsewhere in the Empire they would mark the wearer as someone with British connections; but beyond the frontier they were preferentially selected over other Roman brooches because they resonated with local taste (Hunter 1996, 122–3; 2001b, 300–1). While 'Roman' in some contexts, they were also seen as 'local', or at least appropriate, in others (see also Jundi and Hill 1998).

Conclusions

The decorative metalwork of northern Britain shows marked chronological variation (summarised in Table 1), which indicates changing concerns with definitions of identities. There was a lack of regional decorative metalwork traditions until the first century AD, stemming from a lack of any perceived need to express regional identities. In the early Iron Age the scale of interaction was quite limited, and there is no evidence of substantial contacts with other areas of Britain, Ireland or the Continent. From *c.* 450 BC to the Roman Iron Age, all areas (except perhaps the north-east of Scotland) developed an interest in exotica as a marker of the wider affiliations of part of the population. It appears that this segment wanted to identify with wider rather than local trends.

The ultimate uses of this material varied regionally: only in the south was it routinely hoarded, making it more visible to us, but finds such as La Tène brooches (see above) and Irish-style ring-headed pins (Simpson and Simpson 1968; MacGregor 1976, 138–9; Ballin Smith 1994, 232, no. 4932) provide evidence of other areas' wider connections. It seems these exotica fulfilled social needs for display without the desire to develop local artistic traditions. This differs from developments in southern Britain. The north-east was arguably an exception; there is no evidence at present of imports north of the Tay until the later first century BC but it did develop a local (Irish-influenced) tradition of gold jewellery.

This interest in exotica continued into the late pre-Roman to Roman Iron Age, along with a general increase in the use of personal ornaments, both local and imported, at all levels from beads to torcs. Again hoarding biases the evidence, with the south of Scotland having a continuing tradition of hoarding exotica which was not reflected in other areas (Hunter 1997a). However, a few more far-flung examples and the evidence of skeuomorphs indicate their wider circulation.[6] This existing openness to exotica also explains the readiness with which (selected) Roman material was taken up across Scotland (Hunter 2001b).

The genesis of a strong local tradition of Celtic art lay in this later period, during the first century AD, when there was a need to signal local or regional identities as well as wider affiliations. This need can be linked to both longer-term social trends towards increasing materiality, and more immediate turmoil and threat at the time of contact with Rome. However, the two main regional styles in north Britain have very different trajectories. The north-east material, while drawing on wider trends in its style, remained distinctively local, an opposition to

Period	*Region*	*Exotica*	*Local decorative metalwork*	*General material culture*
c. 700–450 BC	All	Almost none	None	Prosaic
c. 450–1 BC	Atlantic	Yes (settlement finds of La Tène brooches etc)	None	Increasing ornamental material
	NE	V limited (Irish link?)	Ribbon torcs	Increasing ornamental material
	S	Yes (S English and Continental m/w)	None	Increasing ornamental material
c. AD 1–200	Atlantic	- Access to central & southern LIA m/w (seen in skeuomorphs) & NE m/w - Roman material	None (but some decorated pottery)	Peak in ornamental material
	NE	- Limited central & southern LIA m/w - Roman material	Massive m/w (also glass beads)	Peak in ornamental material
	S	- Southern and NE LIA m/w - Roman material	Central British m/w	Peak in ornamental material

Table 1. Trends in decorative metalwork and other items during the Scottish Iron Age. "m/w" = metalwork.

external forces. In contrast, the central British material had a more complex history, starting as an expression of local identity which was adopted within a Romano-British frontier milieu and interpreted in different ways by people of different backgrounds.

Much of this is speculative, and it is clearly a major task to develop these ideas in detail. This paper has concentrated on one particular class of evidence to look at how it was used in the construction of regional and social identities; for a better-rounded picture other artefact categories must be drawn into the frame and a broader social narrative developed. I hope, however, that this study has served as an example of the active role of artefacts in expressing and changing identity at a range of levels, and given some initial insights into the complexities of identity and its negotiation in the Roman frontier zone.

Acknowledgements

I am grateful to the editors for the chance to present these ideas at a stimulating conference and to develop them for publication, to David Clarke, Andrew Heald, Rick Jones, and Rachel Pope for invaluable discussion and comments, and to Craig Angus for producing Figure 2.

Notes

1. The type has only recently been recognised, with examples from Easter Kinnear, Fife, and Hawkhill and West Grange of Conan, Angus (Driscoll 1997, 100–1; A. Rees, pers. comm.; Anon 1892, 245, nos HD 40–41).
2. For instance, the projecting ring-headed pin from the third-century BC roundhouse at South Shields (Tyne and Wear) has finally confirmed the much-debated early origins of the type (Croom 2001, 141–3). Another from Howe, Orkney (Ballin Smith 1994, 221–2, no. 7101), from phase 5/6, has a broader fourth–first century BC date range.
3. The distribution of types such as projecting ring-headed pins and spiral finger rings (Clarke 1971, figs 3–4) serve to show an increasing interest in ornament throughout north Britain. The types are poorly dated, and Sharples (2003) argues that such decorative items do not pre-date the second century AD. However this position is unsustainable; note for instance the dates for pins and beads from Howe (Ballin Smith 1994, 221–2; Henderson 1994). Typologically 'early' items do occur in later contexts, as Sharples notes; this may be because the artefactual dating is wrong (or needs broadening) as he argues, but may equally stem from problems of residuality on complex sites. Note, for instance, the La Tène I brooch from Howe found in abandonment contexts of the seventh–ninth centuries AD (Ballin Smith 1994, 223–4). It seems unwise to put too much weight on the few finds from well-dated contexts without more dates; are we sure the contexts do actually date the finds?
4. Included in this group for the current study are: derivative three-link bridle bits; boss-and-petal strap junctions and mounts; knobbed and platform terrets; beaded torcs; hinged strap bracelets; group IV ('Brigantian') swords and scabbards; ovoid scabbard fastenings (previously seen as harness mounts, but note the association with a sword at Asby Scar; Richardson 1999, 6–7). Button-and-loop fasteners of Wild (1970) classes III, IV, Va, VIa and b also fall within this tradition, but they are not considered in detail as recent finds have not been readily synthesised.
5. From Iron Age contexts, there are button-and-loop fastener moulds from Traprain, East Lothian (Burley 1955–6, 220). In Roman contexts, there is an unfinished type III button-and-loop fastener from Newstead, Roxburghshire (Curle 1911, pl. LXXV, 7); a lead knobbed terret, probably a pattern for castings, from Castledykes, Lanarkshire (MacGregor 1976, no. 80); and moulds for (*inter alia*) derivative three-link bits from Prestatyn, Denbighshire (Blockley 1989, 187–8).
6. Skeuomorphs are known from the Atlantic area, notably ceramic copies of metal vessels (e.g. Ross 1994, 247–8, no. 7114, cf. MacGregor 1976, no. 292), bone mirror handles (*ibid.*, no. 271), and bone sword fittings (Rynne 1983).

Bibliography

Anon. 1892. *Catalogue of the National Museum of Antiquities of Scotland.* Edinburgh: Society of Antiquaries of Scotland.

Armit, I. (ed.) 1990. *Beyond the Brochs: Changing Perspectives on the Later Iron Age in Atlantic Scotland.* Edinburgh: Edinburgh University Press.

Armit, I. 1992. *The Later Prehistory of the Western Isles of Scotland.* Oxford: British Archaeological Reports British Series 221.

Armit, I. 1997. Cultural landscapes and identities: a case study in the Scottish Iron Age, in Gwilt and Haselgrove 1997, 248–253.

Atkinson, R.J.C. and Piggott, S. 1955. The Torrs chamfrein, *Archaeologia* 96, 197–235.

Ballin Smith, B. 1994. *Howe: Four Millennia of Orkney Prehistory.* Edinburgh: Society of Antiquaries of Scotland Monograph 9.

Ballin Smith, B. and Banks, I. (eds) 2002. *In the Shadow of the Brochs: the Iron Age in Scotland.* Stroud: Tempus.

Beswick, P., Megaw, M.R., Megaw, J.V.S. and Northover, P. 1990. A decorated late Iron Age torc from Dinnington, South Yorkshire, *Antiquaries Journal* 70, 16–33.

Bishop, M.C. 1998. Military equipment, in H.E.M. Cool and C. Philo (eds), *Roman Castleford, Excavations 1974–85. Volume I: the Small Finds*, 61–81. Wakefield: West Yorkshire Archaeology Service.

Blackmore, C., Braithwaite, M. and Hodder, I. 1979. Social and cultural patterning in the late Iron Age in southern England, in B.C. Burnham and J. Kingsbury (eds), *Space, Hierarchy and Society*, 93–111. Oxford: British Archaeological Reports British Series 59.

Blockley, K. 1989. *Prestatyn 1984–5.* Oxford: British Archaeological Reports British Series 210.

Brailsford, J.W. 1975. The Polden Hill hoard, *Proceedings of the Prehistoric Society* 41, 222–234.

Burley, E. 1955–56. A catalogue and survey of the metal-work from Traprain Law, *Proceedings of the Society of Antiquaries of Scotland* 89, 118–226.

Campbell, E. 2002. The Western Isles pottery sequence, in Ballin Smith and Banks 2002, 139–144.

Carter, S. and Hunter, F. 2003. An Iron Age chariot burial from Scotland, *Antiquity* 77, 531–535.

Childe, V.G. 1935. *The Prehistory of Scotland.* London: Kegan Paul.

Clarke, A. 1998. Stone, in L. Main, Excavation of a timber roundhouse and broch at the Fairy Knowe, Buchlyvie, Stirlingshire, 1975–8, *Proceedings of the Society of Antiquaries of Scotland* 128, 377–390 (293–417).

Clarke, D.V. 1970. Bone dice and the Scottish Iron Age, *Proceedings of the Prehistoric Society* 36, 214–232.

Clarke, D.V. 1971. Small finds in the Atlantic province: problems of approach, *Scottish Archaeological Forum* 3, 22–54.

Clarke, R.R. 1939. The Iron Age in Norfolk and Suffolk, *Archaeological Journal* 96, 1–113.

Coles, J.M. 1968. The 1857 Law Farm hoard, *Antiquaries Journal* 48, 163–174.

Collingwood, R.G. and Wright, R.P. 1965. *The Roman Inscriptions of Britain I. Inscriptions on Stone*. Oxford: Oxford University Press.

Cowie, T.G. 1988. *Magic Metal: Early Metalworkers in the North-East*. Aberdeen: Anthropological Museum, University of Aberdeen.

Croom, A.T. 2001. The Iron-Age finds, in N. Hodgson, G.C. Stobbs and M. van der Veen, An Iron-Age settlement and remains of earlier prehistoric date beneath South Shields Roman fort, Tyne and Wear, *Archaeological Journal* 158, 141–146 (62–160).

Cunliffe, B. 1991. *Iron Age Communities in Britain* (3rd edn). London: Routledge.

Cunliffe, B. 1995. The Celtic chariot: a footnote, in B. Raftery (ed.), *Sites and Sights of the Iron Age. Essays on Fieldwork and Museum Research Presented to Ian Mathieson Stead*, 31–39. Oxford: Oxbow Monograph 56.

Curle, J. 1911. *A Roman Frontier Post and its People: the Fort of Newstead in the Parish of Melrose*. Glasgow: Maclehose.

Davies, J.A. 2000. The metal finds, in S. Bates, Excavations at Quidney Farm, Saham Toney, Norfolk 1995, *Britannia* 31, 226–231 (201–237).

Davies, J.L. and Spratling, M.G. 1976. The Seven Sisters hoard: a centenary study, in G.C. Boon and J.M. Lewis (eds), *Welsh Antiquity*, 121–147. Cardiff: National Museum of Wales.

Driscoll, S.T. 1997. A Pictish settlement in north-east Fife: the Scottish Field School of Archaeology excavations at Easter Kinnear, *Tayside and Fife Archaeological Journal* 3, 74–118.

Dungworth, D.B. 1996. The production of copper alloys in Iron Age Britain, *Proceedings of the Prehistoric Society* 62, 399–421.

Eogan, G. 1983. Ribbon torcs in Britain and Ireland, in O'Connor and Clarke 1983, 87–126.

Feachem, R.W. 1966. The hill-forts of northern Britain, in Rivet 1966, 59–87.

Fitzpatrick, A. 1997. Everyday life in Iron Age Wessex, in Gwilt and Haselgrove 1997, 73–86.

Fox, C. 1952. *The Personality of Britain* (4th edn). Cardiff: National Museum of Wales.

Guido, M. 1978. *The Glass Beads of the Prehistoric and Roman Periods in Britain and Ireland*. London: Reports of the Research Committee of the Society of Antiquaries of London 35.

Gwilt, A. and Haselgrove, C. (eds). *Reconstructing Iron Age Societies*. Oxford: Oxbow Monograph 71.

Hallén, Y. 1994. The use of bone and antler at Foshigarry and Bac Mhic Connain, two Iron Age sites on North Uist, Western Isles, *Proceedings of the Society of Antiquaries of Scotland* 124, 189–231.

Haselgrove, C. 1982. Wealth, prestige and power; the dynamics of late Iron Age political centralization in south-east England, in C. Renfrew and S. Shennan (eds.), *Ranking, Resource and Exchange: Aspects of the Archaeology of Early European Society*, 79–88. Cambridge: Cambridge University Press.

Hawkes, C.F.C. 1959. The ABC of the British Iron Age, *Antiquity* 33, 170–182.

Henderson, J. 1994. The glass, in Ballin Smith 1994, 234–236.

Henig, M. 1995. *The Art of Roman Britain*. London: Batsford.

Hill, J.D. 1997. 'The end of one kind of body and the beginning of another kind of body'? Toilet instruments and 'Romanisation' in southern England during the first century AD, in Gwilt and Haselgrove 1997, 96–107.

Hill, P.H. 1982. Broxmouth hillfort excavations, 1977–1978: an interim report, in D.W. Harding (ed.), *Later Prehistoric Settlement in South-East Scotland*, 141–188. Edinburgh: Department of Archaeology, University of Edinburgh.

Hingley, R. 1992. Settlement in Scotland from 700 BC to AD 200, *Proceedings of the Society of Antiquaries of Scotland* 122, 7–53.

Hodder, I. 1982. *Symbols in Action*. Cambridge: Cambridge University Press.

Hodder, I. and Hedges, J.W. 1977. 'Weaving combs': their typology and distribution with some introductory remarks on date and function, in J.R. Collis (ed.), *The Iron Age in Britain: a Review*, 17–28. Sheffield: Department of Prehistory and Archaeology, University of Sheffield.

Holder, P.A. 1982. *The Roman Army in Britain*. London: Batsford.

Hull, M.R. and Hawkes, C.F.C. 1987. *Corpus of Ancient Brooches in Britain: Pre-Roman Bow Brooches*. Oxford: British Archaeological Reports British Series 168.

Hunter, F. 1996. Recent Roman Iron Age metalwork finds from Fife and Tayside, *Tayside and Fife Archaeological Journal* 2, 113–125.

Hunter, F. 1997a. Iron Age hoarding in Scotland and northern England, in Gwilt and Haselgrove 1997, 108–133.

Hunter, F. 1997b. Iron Age coins in Scotland, *Proceedings of the Society of Antiquaries of Scotland* 127, 513–525.

Hunter, F. 2001a. The carnyx in Iron Age Europe, *Antiquaries Journal* 81, 77–108.

Hunter, F. 2001b. Roman and native in Scotland: new approaches, *Journal of Roman Archaeology* 14, 289–309.

Johns, C. 1996. *The Jewellery of Roman Britain: Celtic and Classical Traditions*. London: University College London Press.

Jones, S. 1997. *The Archaeology of Ethnicity*. London: Routledge.

Jope, E.M. 2000. *Early Celtic Art in the British Isles*. Oxford: Clarendon Press.

Jundi, S. and Hill, J.D. 1998. Brooches and identity in first century AD Britain: more than meets the eye?, in C. Forcey, J. Hawthorne and R. Witcher (eds), *TRAC 97. Proceedings of the Seventh Annual Theoretical Roman Archaeology Conference, Nottingham 1997*, 125–137. Oxford: Oxbow Books.

Kilbride-Jones, H.E. 1980. *Celtic Craftsmanship in Bronze*. London: Croom Helm.

Lane, A. 1987. English migrants in the Hebrides: 'Atlantic Second B' revisited, *Proceedings of the Society of Antiquaries of Scotland* 117, 47–66.

Lane, A. 1990. Hebridean pottery: problems of definition, chronology, presence and absence, in Armit 1990, 108–130.

Leeds, E.T. 1933. *Celtic Ornament in the British Isles down to AD 700*. Oxford: Clarendon Press.

MacGregor, M. 1976. *Early Celtic Art in North Britain*. Leicester: Leicester University Press.

MacKie, E. 1969. Radiocarbon dates and the Scottish Iron Age, *Antiquity* 43, 15–26.

MacKie, E. 1971. English migrants and Scottish brochs, *Glasgow Archaeological Journal* 2, 39–71.

MacKie, E. 1989. Impact on the Scottish Iron Age of the discoveries at Leckie broch, *Glasgow Archaeological Journal* 14, 1–18.

MacSween, A. 2002. Dun Beag and the role of pottery in interpretations of the Hebridean Iron Age, in Ballin Smith and Banks 2002, 145–152.

Maxwell, G. 1990. *A Battle Lost: Romans and Caledonians at Mons Graupius*. Edinburgh: Edinburgh University Press.

Megaw, M.R. and Megaw, J.V.S. 1989. *Celtic Art: From its Beginnings to the Book of Kells*. London: Thames and Hudson.

O'Connor, A. and Clarke, D.V. (eds) 1983. *From the Stone Age to the 'Forty-Five*. Edinburgh: John Donald.

Piggott, S. 1959. The *Carnyx* in Early Iron Age Britain, *Antiquaries Journal* 39, 19–32.

Piggott, S. 1966. A scheme for the Scottish Iron Age, in Rivet 1966, 1–15.

Raftery, B. 1984. *La Tène in Ireland: Problems of Origin and Chronology*. Marburg: Veröffentlichung des Vorgeschichtlichen Seminars Marburg Sonderband 2.

Ralston, I.B.M. 1979. The Iron Age: Northern Britain, in J.V.S. Megaw and D.D.A. Simpson (eds), *Introduction to British Prehistory*, 446–501. Leicester: Leicester University Press.

RCAHMS 1956. *Roxburghshire, Vol 1*. Edinburgh: HMSO.

Richardson, C. 1999. A catalogue of recent acquisitions to Tullie House Museum and reported finds from the Cumbrian area 1990–1996. Part II: Reported finds, *Transactions of the Cumberland and Westmorland Antiquarian and Archaeological Society* 99, 1–51.

Rigby, V. and Freestone, I. 1997. Ceramic changes in late Iron Age Britain, in I. Freestone and D. Gaimster (ed.), *Pottery in the Making*, 56–61. London: British Museum.

Rivet, A.L.F. (ed.) 1966. *The Iron Age in Northern Britain*. Edinburgh: Edinburgh University Press.

Ross, A. 1994. Pottery report, in Ballin Smith 1994, 236–257.

Rynne, E. 1983. Some early Iron Age sword-hilts from Ireland and Scotland, in O'Connor and Clarke 1983, 188–196.

Sharples, N. 1998. *Scalloway: A Broch, Late Iron Age Settlement and Medieval Cemetery in Shetland*. Oxford: Oxbow Books.

Sharples, N. 2003. From monuments to artefacts: changing social relationships in the later Iron Age, in J. Downes and A. Ritchie (eds), *Sea Change: Orkney and Northern Europe in the Later Iron Age AD 300–800*, 151–165. Balgavies: Pinkfoot Press.

Sharples, N. and Parker Pearson, M. 1997. Why were brochs built? Recent studies in the Iron Age of Atlantic Scotland, in Gwilt and Haselgrove 1997, 254–265.

Simpson, D.D.A. and Simpson, M. 1968. Decorative ring-headed pins in Scotland, *Transactions of the Dumfriesshire and Galloway Natural History and Antiquarian Society* 45, 141–146.

Simpson, M. 1968. Massive armlets in the North British Iron Age, in J.M. Coles and D.D.A. Simpson (eds), *Studies in Ancient Europe*, 233–254. Leicester: Leicester University Press.

Simpson, M. 1969–70. Some Roman-Iron Age finger rings, *Proceedings of the Society of Antiquaries of Scotland* 102, 105–108.

Spratling, M.G. 1971. Bronze terret, in P.V. Webster, Melandra Castle Roman fort: excavations in the civil settlement 1966–1969, *Derbyshire Archaeological Journal* 91, 113–5 (58–118).

Stead, I.M. 1996. *Celtic Art in Britain Before the Roman Conquest*. London: British Museum.

Stevenson, R.B.K. 1966. Metal-work and some other objects in Scotland and their cultural affinities, in Rivet 1966, 17–44.

Stevenson, R.B.K. 1976. Romano-British glass bangles, *Glasgow Archaeological Journal* 4, 45–54.

Topping, P.G. 1986. Neutron activation analysis of later prehistoric pottery from the Western Isles of Scotland, *Proceedings of the Prehistoric Society* 52, 105–129.

Warner, R.B. 1993. Irish prehistoric goldwork: a provisional analysis, *Archeomaterials* 7, 101–113.

Webster, G. 1985. *The Roman Imperial Army of the First and Second Centuries A.D.* (3rd edn). London: A. and C. Black.

Wild, J.P. 1970. Button-and-loop fasteners in the Roman provinces, *Britannia* 1, 137–155.

Silent Silures? Locating people and places in the Iron Age of south Wales

Adam Gwilt

> 'The march then proceeded against the Silurians, whose native boldness was heightened by their confidence in the prowess of Caratacus; whose many successes, partial or complete, had raised him to a pinnacle above the other British leaders' (Tacitus, *Annals* XII, 33).

> 'Particularly marked was the obstinacy of the Silures, who were infuriated by a widely repeated remark of the Roman commander, that, as once the Sugambri had been exterminated or transferred to the Gallic provinces, so the Silurian name ought once for all to be extinguished. They accordingly cut off two auxiliary cohorts which, through the cupidity of their officers, were ravaging the country too incautiously; and by presents of spoils and captives they were drawing into revolt the remaining tribes also, when Ostorius – broken by the weary load of anxiety – paid the debt of nature; to the delight of the enemy, who considered that, perhaps not a battle, but certainly a campaign had disposed of a general whom it was impossible to despise' (*ibid.*, 39).

The inspiration for this paper is drawn from the prolonged and distinctive 'noise' generated by the Silures during the first century AD. The quoted sections and others recorded in the *Annals* and *Agricola* confirm their identity and power at the time of the Roman invasion and illuminate their persistent struggle against conquest (Manning 2002, 38). In stark contrast, the material remains of these people, who occupied south Wales and possibly parts of Gloucestershire (Jarrett and Mann 1968–9; Manning 1981a, 14–23; 2004, 178), are only able to generate a distant and anonymous 'whisper', barely audible within wider debate about the Later Iron Age. This is manifested through a dearth of articles, monographs and syntheses about, or including reference to, discoveries in south Wales over the past twenty years. It is this contradiction – the recorded hubbub set against the apparent silence of the archaeological record – which this paper sets out to examine.

That this state of affairs is partly a symptom of the paucity of survey, excavation, and research is an explanation not entirely devoid of merit (see below). Nevertheless, there is a pressing need to challenge the stereotypical and long-held expectation of a dearth of cultural material in this region. A range of evidence from south-east Wales will be presented, in an attempt to shift this now unhelpful and inaccurate view (cf. Martin 2003), which does little to aid the development of innovative new research here. In no way does this paper constitute a coherent synthesis about the Silures or of the archaeology of the period from the fifth century BC to the first century AD. Nor is it a polished exploration of a new idea or theory. It is rather an attempt to re-invigorate a regional archaeology and communicate some interesting and little known discoveries to a wider audience. Emerging from these are some themes of wider relevance, which it is hoped will help both integrate and differentiate this region, with and from other parts of Later Iron Age Britain.

Glamorgan has been the subject of a survey by the Royal Commission on Ancient and Historic Monuments in Wales (RCAHMW 1976a) and County History volumes (Savory 1984), each including Iron Age coverage. In contrast, Gwent has largely been overlooked by RCAHMW (T. Driver pers. comm.) and a County History volume was only very recently published (Aldhouse-Green and Howell 2004). This paper aims to balance up this unevenness by giving prominence to the archaeology and material culture of Gwent.

Hillfort and settlement diversity

South-east Wales sits on the western margins of the 'hillfort dominated zone' of central southern England and the Welsh Marches during the Middle and Late Iron Age (Cunliffe 1991, fig. 14.38). Whilst there is ample scope to argue over the often fine distinction between hillforts and defended settlements, in broad terms over 130 hillforts have been identified (Hogg 1979; RCAHMW 1976a). This abundant resource exhibits a diversity of morphology, within which complex sequences of development can be inferred, but is still largely unexplored, only 23 sites (18%) having received any kind of investigation through excavation.

Strong regional variations in hillfort size have long been recognised in Wales and the Marches (e.g. Hogg 1972; Stanford 1974). Hogg's distribution maps showed the preponderance of small hillforts and defended enclosures in west Wales, contrasting with the largest hillforts extending along the Welsh Marches. South-east Wales has a mix of small (<1.2 ha) and medium to large (1.2–6 ha) examples, only two exceeding 6 ha in area (Dunraven and Gaer Hill Camp, Penterry). In Gwent, 18 hillforts are medium to large in size (*c.* 40%), compared with only 14 in Glamorgan (*c.* 15%). Most of these have bi-vallate or multivallate defences. Recently, Jackson (1999) has contrasted the size distributions of the hillforts from Gwent and Clwyd with those of Powys, the English Marches, and Wessex. He interpreted the regionally distinctive hillfort size patterns in relation to topography and land capability, and in turn, to social organisation. The varied topography and land capability of Gwent is highlighted and a combination of competitive and community-based forms of social organisation suggested (*ibid.*; see also Wigley this volume).

The regional character of hillforts in south-east Wales is also captured in their morphological diversity (Fig. 1). There are medium and small sized univallate forts, the latter in both defensive and non-defensible situations, and there are small and medium to large sized multivallate forts with close-set defences (RCAHMW 1976a, 11–16; Howell and Pollard 2004). Coastal promontory forts, while rare in Gwent, occur with increasing frequency westwards around the Glamorgan coastline, and may have wide- or close-set ramparts. These are typical along the western coasts of Britain, finding parallel with the promontory forts of Pembrokeshire and the cliff castles of Cornwall (Cripps this volume), also sharing similarities with the promontory forts of Ireland and Brittany (Cunliffe 2001, 349–50). Forming another distinctive class are the ten hillforts with wide-spaced and concentric ramparts in south-east Wales, also common in south-west England, and first discussed in detail by Fox (1952). The outer enclosures may have acted to control cattle, rather than being defensive (*ibid.*, 18–19; Savory 1984). Possibly related in function (Savory 1976a), are the seven hillforts with annexes, including Llanmelin Wood, Gaer Fawr, Llancayo Camp, and Twyn-y-Gaer in Gwent. Taken in conjunction with the seasonally occupied cattle byres along the Gwent Levels (discussed below), these wide-spaced enclosures and annexes may be interpreted as potential evidence for a pastoral emphasis to the farming regime of this region.

It is one thing to be able to locate hillforts and describe them on morphological grounds, but quite another to fix their construction, development, and occupation through time. Too few have been excavated to support a credible picture for the region. Only Twyn-y-Gaer (Probert 1976), Cae Summerhouse, a multivallate hillfort with wide-spaced concentric ramparts (Davies 1966; 1967a; 1973a; Robinson 1988, xvi–xvii), and Coed-y-Cymdda hill-slope enclosure (Owen-John 1988a) have seen large area excavations of defences and interior spaces, the former two remaining unpublished. The only other defended enclosure with a coherent interior plan is Mynydd Bychan (Savory 1954a; 1955) in the Vale of Glamorgan. In the last five years, small-scale excavations have been undertaken at Lodge Wood Camp, Newport (Howell and Pollard 2004, 154–6), and Sudbrook fort, Monmouthshire (Sell 2001). A mere eight radiocarbon dates from only three hillforts exist in the literature, leaving a weak chronological framework, dependent upon localised sequence, comparative hillfort architecture, and associated material culture.

This is not the place to rehearse the detailed structural sequences for the region's hillforts, although some general observations will help to illustrate their character and complexity. Previous accounts have tended to see hillforts as late arrivals (e.g. Davies and Lynch 2000; Savory 1976a; 1984), in contrast with Late Bronze Age beginnings in north-east and west Wales. However, early architectural features such as palisades, timber-laced or framed ramparts, and stone-walled ramparts are increasingly represented in south-east Wales (Nash-Williams 1933; Hogg 1976; Babbidge 1977; Probert 1982; Owen-John 1988a; Howell and Pollard 2004, 154–6). Dump ramparts of soil and rubble construction, often with front or rear stone revetments are the commonest form (Nash-Williams 1933; 1939; Williams 1939a; 1940; 1941; Savory 1954a; Alcock 1963; Davies 1967a; 1967b; Hogg 1973; 1976). Traditionally, these ramparts are dated between the second century BC and the first century AD, although it remains possible that some were constructed in the fourth and third centuries BC. Gateways and entrance architecture range from simple rampart terminals – some with three- or four-post gate structures (e.g. Hogg 1973; 1976) – to inturned entrances with funnelled gate passages and hornworks (Nash-Williams 1933; Davies 1973a; Probert 1976; 1982; Robinson 1988), bastions (Savory 1954a), and recessed guard chambers (Howell and Pollard 2004, 154–6).

Iron Age timber roundhouses have been excavated in

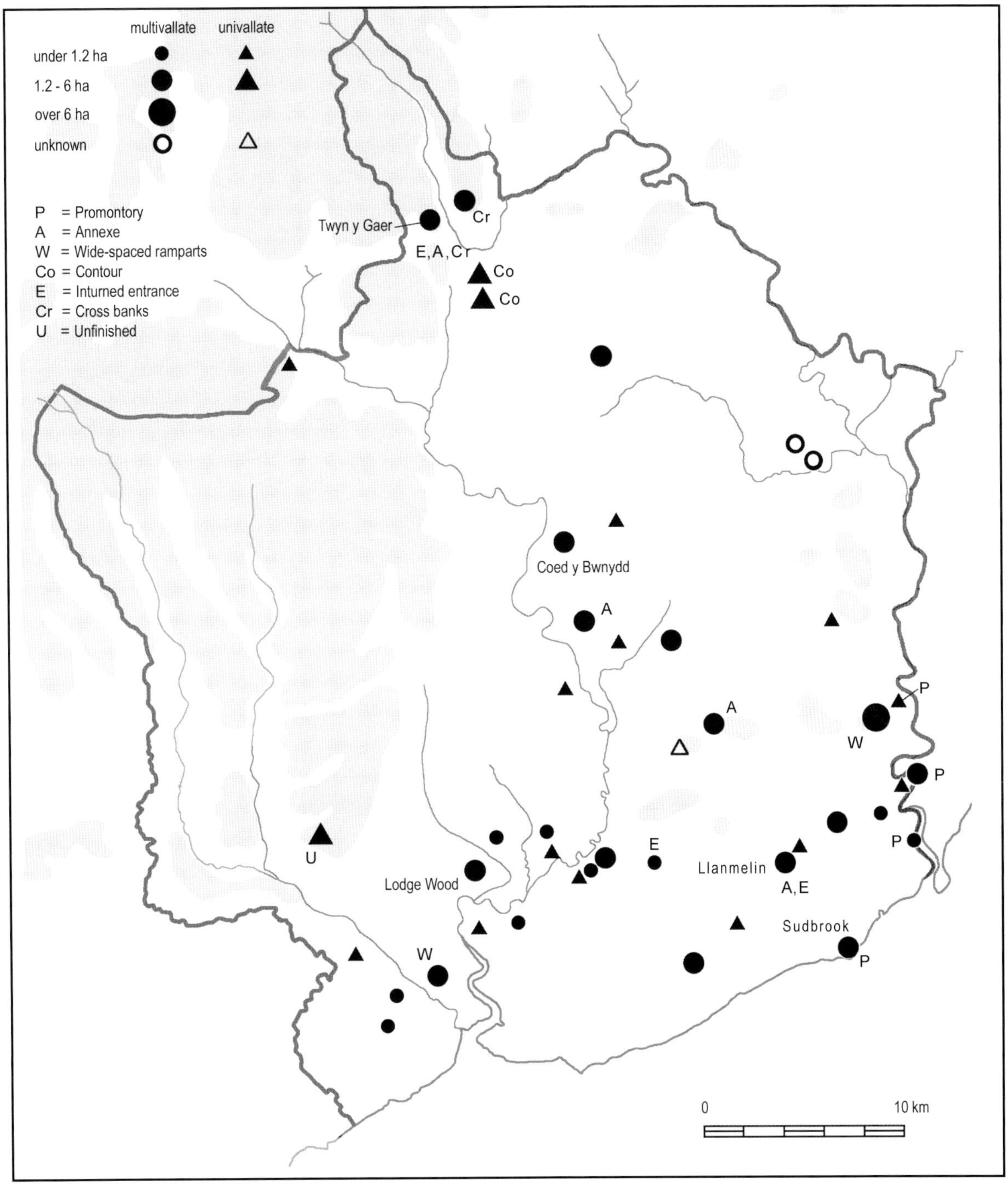

Fig. 1 Hillforts of Gwent (excavated examples named).

seven hillforts (Savory 1954a; Davies 1973b; Hogg 1973; 1976; Probert 1976; 1982; Owen-John 1988a; Howell and Pollard 2004, 154–6). Oval buildings utilising a timber frontage and rampart back wall have been located on three occasions (Williams 1940; 1941; Hogg 1973), whilst floors, occupation surfaces and deposits containing material culture have been identified within seven hillforts (H. Williams 1902; Nash-Williams 1933; 1939; A. Williams 1939a; 1940; 1941; Davies 1964). Recently, a Late Iron Age or early Roman timber roundhouse was excavated outside the promontory fort at Burry Holms, Rhossili (Walker 2001). Storage pits are absent in the region, although small rectangular post and slot structures have been located during three excavations (Davies 1966; 1967a; Owen-John 1988a; Howell and Pollard 2004, 154–6).

Thirteen of the 23 excavated hillforts have provided some evidence for Romano-British occupation (e.g.

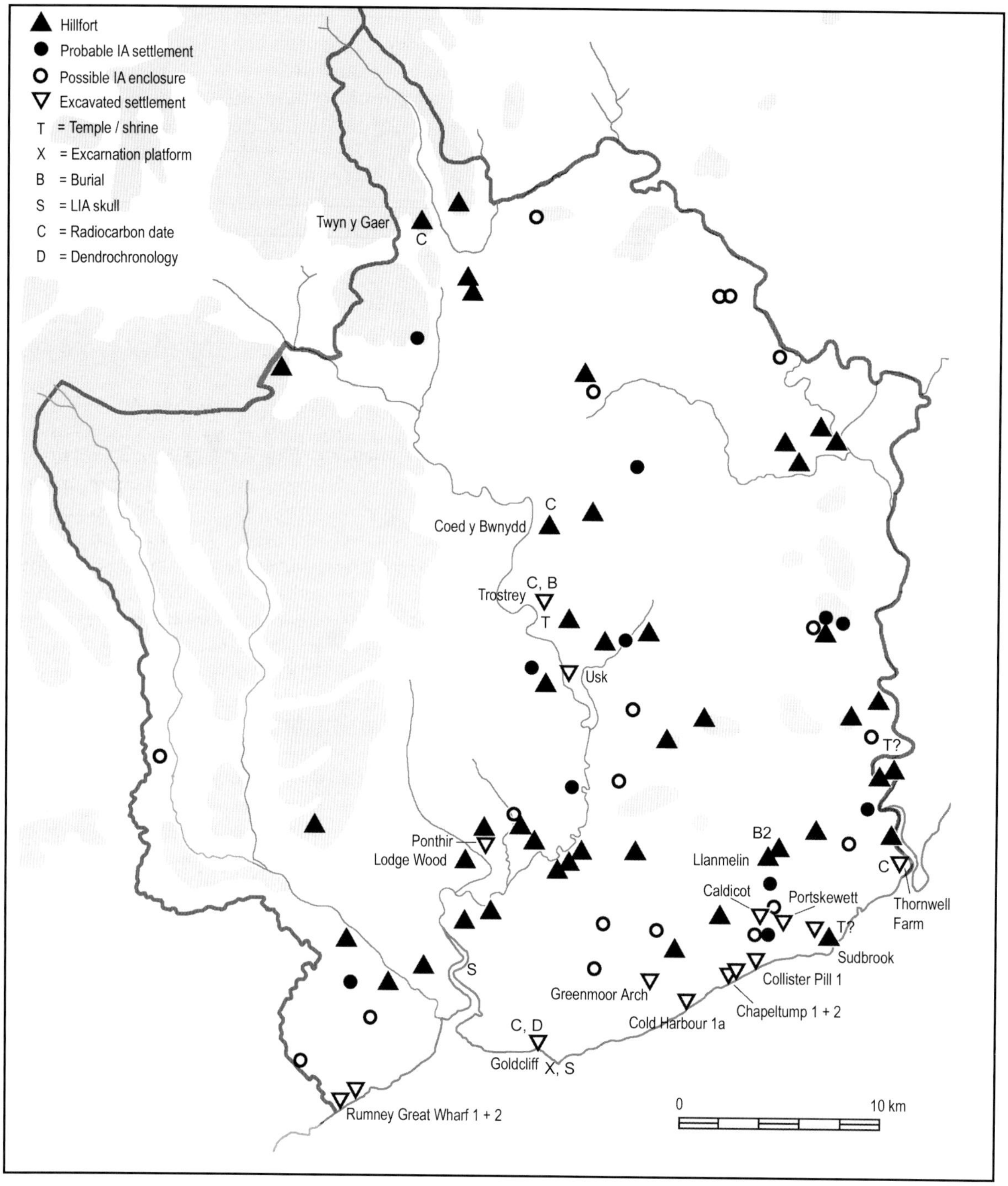

Fig. 2. Iron Age settlements and hillforts in Gwent (excavated sites named).

Savory 1954a; Davies 1973b; Sell 2001). In some instances this may indicate episodic activity, rather than continuity of settlement. Nevertheless some hillforts appear to have been continuously occupied from the Late Iron Age into the early Roman period (Robinson 1988, xi; Arnold and Davies 2000, 76–80, 87–9), raising interesting questions about power relations, Roman control and native–Roman acculturation during the first century AD.

Over many parts of Britain, the last 30 years of aerial survey and excavation have revealed densely settled, well-organised and often bounded farming landscapes of Later Iron Age date. Non-hillfort farmsteads are now regarded as more typical and abundant settlement forms than hillforts (Hill 1995; Haselgrove 1999). In Wales, surveys of the upland open stone settlements and landscape features of Gwynedd and southern Powys, and the cropmark enclosures revealed in the Vale of

Clwyd and northern Powys are reinforcing this picture (Davies and Lynch 2000, 162–72). By contrast, in parts of south-east Wales, work to locate non-hillfort settlement has only just begun (Haselgrove *et al.* 2001, 25; Gwilt 2003; Gwilt *et al.* 2003). A recent audit of Glamorgan and Gwent revealed only 60 non-hillfort settlements of Iron Age date, less than half the known number of hillforts (Evans 2002). No certain Iron Age field boundaries or field systems were identified, whilst only nine landscape boundary features of either prehistoric or Roman date were recorded.

Following a trawl of SMR records, published literature, and some of the unplotted cropmark evidence held by RCAHMW, a working map of hillfort and non-hillfort settlement in Gwent is presented, with the assistance of Toby Driver (Fig. 2). This is far from a systematic survey, yet it does for the first time provide grounds for suggesting that central and northern Monmouthshire, especially the Usk valley, were densely settled and farmed landscapes during the Later Iron Age. Some 40 definite or possible Iron Age settlements and enclosures in Gwent can now be suggested, compared with 17 before this study. These include a range of circular, oval, polygonal, and sub-rectangular enclosures. The picture is similar in the Vale of Glamorgan, where univallate and multivallate defended rectilinear and curvilinear enclosures have also been identified (Driver 1995; Evans and Driver 2000; Howell 2001). In addition, two or possibly three previously unknown multivallate hillforts or enclosures have recently been identified in Gwent – at the Grondra, Lower White Castle, and Taloches Farm (T. Driver pers. comm.) – whilst a recent survey in lowland south-east Wales has identified possible Iron Age enclosures beneath a number of Romano-British settlements (Evans 2001). At one level, this merely confirms our general expectations about Later Iron Age site densities in southern Britain, but is nevertheless new and unexplored evidence, worthy of independent study.

The apparent virtual absence of visible settlement in many upland areas of Gwent and Glamorgan is a continuing problem, contrasting with the extensively occupied upland landscapes of Gwynedd and southern Powys. A small number of settlements, comprising groups of stone roundhouses next to small curvilinear enclosures of stone, are known in upland Glamorgan, but none are convincingly dated to the Iron Age (RCAHMW 1976a, 72–9). Other recent surveys of upland areas in south-east Wales have singularly failed to identify Iron Age settlement and landscape features (Locock 2000). The possibility that some areas were little inhabited in the Iron Age should not now be dismissed. On the other hand, regions with timber roundhouse traditions may simply remain invisible unless excavated. Alternative strategies need to be devised to investigate this. Also, most of the lower slopes and bases of the steep-sided river valleys of south-east Wales have been heavily settled and altered over the past 250 years. Prehistoric settlement here may therefore have been destroyed or built over.

Owing to their poor visibility, open settlements tend to be under-represented, contributing to a scarcity of Late Bronze Age and Early Iron Age evidence (but see Alcock 1963, 16–19; Savory 1952–3; Whittle 1989; Mein 1996; 2001; Bell *et al.* 2000, 300–3). An exception is Thornwell Farm, near Chepstow, where a large Late Bronze Age to Early Iron Age roundhouse, 12.4 m in diameter and with a south-east facing entrance, was discovered; another roundhouse, 9 m in diameter, was occupied on this small open settlement during the Early Iron Age (Hughes 1996).

The most important Iron Age discoveries during the 1990s were those made along the Severn estuary (e.g. Bell 2000; Bell *et al.* 2000; Locock *et al.* 2000), notably on the foreshore at Goldcliff where eight unenclosed rectangular timber buildings of Early Iron Age to early Roman date were revealed. They are of an architectural tradition so far unparalleled elsewhere in Britain. Combined dendrochronology and radiocarbon dating shows that these and a series of associated timber trackways were mostly used in the fourth and third centuries BC. Building 6 comprised timbers which were felled in spring 273 BC and Trackway 1108 was made with timbers felled between 336–318 BC (Bell *et al.* 2000). This architectural tradition may have its origins locally in the Middle Bronze Age, since at nearby Redwick, five similar rectangular buildings of Middle to Late Bronze Age date have recently been investigated (Bell and Neumann 1999; Bell 2001).

Environmental analysis of floor layers in the Goldcliff buildings (notably beetle studies), combined with research on their internal layout and the recording of hoof prints surviving around them, indicates their use as cattle byres. Excellent preservation, research, and precision dating, have thus located the seasonal movements of cattle to coastal pasture, one distinctive strand of the Iron Age farming regime in the region. Integrated study has enabled the reconstruction of this coastal wetland landscape during the later first millennium BC: an unenclosed landscape reached by trackways and by boat. More recently, three further Middle Iron Age rectangular buildings have been partially excavated at Greenmoor Arch, Bishton (Locock 1999; Locock and Yates 1999). Further investigation of the hillforts, settlements, and landscapes on the dry land margin is now required, to understand how these seasonal elements were organised and articulated within these farming societies (Bell 2001; Gwilt *et al.* 2003).

Other potentially seasonally occupied sites exist on Merthyr Mawr Warren (Bridgend) and at Radyr (Cardiff). At the former, a large coastal sand dune system has buried Iron Age settlements and activity areas, which have periodically been uncovered and investigated in piecemeal fashion. Fox (1927a) examined three exposed mounds near Candleston Castle, finding multi-period hearths and evidence for the working of bronze and iron. These were interpreted as used seasonally during the Early to Middle Iron Age, a date supported by the discovery of two La Tène I brooches and an iron ring-headed pin in or near one of these mounds (Fox 1927a; 1929). Over subsequent decades, more artefacts and metalworking evidence (pins, brooches, crucibles, and pottery) were discovered in the surrounding dunes (Savory 1951; 1954b; 1976b). At Radyr, a 'cooking mound' containing pot-boilers, much burnt charcoal, and sherds of Middle to Late Iron Age pottery was excavated in 1916 (Grimes and Hyde 1935).

Unenclosed sites continue to form an element of the lowland settlement pattern in the Late Iron Age. At Biglis, in the Vale of Glamorgan, and Caldicot in Monmouthshire, ephemeral open settlements comprising dense post hole scatters, from which timber roundhouses could be identified, were discovered through area excavation (Parkhouse 1988; Vyner and Allen 1988). Both were enclosed by palisades and banks in the Romano-British period, with roundhouse occupation continuing at Caldicot into the second century AD. These open settlements are dated to the early first century AD by finds of hand-made calcite-gritted pottery, including decorated Glastonbury ware (Spencer 1988; Webster 1988a), and at Caldicot by two brooches and an Iron Age silver coin (Robinson 1988, 91–9).

During the Late Iron Age, the construction of rectilinear settlement enclosures became increasingly frequent. The best known is the bank and ditched enclosure at Whitton in the Vale of Glamorgan (Jarrett and Wrathmell 1981). This had a prominent gate, modified on a number of occasions and with a possible flanking tower structure, and contained a complex sequence of roundhouses of early first- to mid second-century AD date, of which three or four were occupied at any time; these were succeeded by a villa in the later second century AD. Recently, another rectilinear enclosure with a simple two-post gate structure was excavated at St Athan (Barber *et al.* forthcoming). Late Iron Age pottery and large quantities of animal bone were found in the enclosure ditch primary fills, whilst in the interior were three roundhouses. Moreover, recent geophysical survey of the Roman villa at Ely, Cardiff, indicates the presence of an imposing rectilinear multivallate ditched enclosure beneath the later buildings, which could be another enclosure of Late Iron Age or early Roman date (Young 2001). These sites hint at the emergence of a class of rectilinear defended enclosure during the Late Iron Age, at a time when at least some hillforts continued to be used and elaborated. Traditionally in Wales, rectangular enclosures found through aerial survey have been interpreted as Romano-British and often military in function (e.g. Jarrett 1969), but this assumption needs to be challenged. Many could belong to the Late Iron Age (Evans 2001, 11; Manning 2004, 201).

Yet another group of Late Iron Age settlements were enclosed by banks or palisades, whose function appears not to have been defensive (e.g. Savory 1952–3). At Church Farm, Caldicot, the corner of a rectangular enclosure, possibly constructed during the Late Iron Age, yet occupied throughout the Romano-British period, was recently revealed (Insole 2000). During the Late Iron Age and early Roman phases at Thornwell Farm, Chepstow, a low discontinuous D-shaped stone bank enclosed a small settlement of two or three small roundhouses (Hughes 1996), whilst a palisaded enclosure containing a roundhouse gully underlay the villa at Llandough (Owen-John 1988b).

As implied above, south-east Wales provides strong evidence for settlement continuity between the Late Iron Age and early Romano-British periods. Some *enclosed* settlements became villas, as at Whitton, Llandough, and possibly Ely, whilst others like St Athan, Thornwell Farm and Church Farm did not. It is interesting, however, that the *open* Late Iron Age settlements of Biglis and Caldicot were not superseded by villas. In this context, the ill-defined Iron Age occupation evidence from beneath the Roman small town at Cowbridge (Valentin and Robinson 2001) and the villas at Dan-y-Graig (Newman 1990), Llantwit Major (Hogg 1974), and Moulton (RCAHMW 1976a, 114) must be noted. In each case, insufficient evidence exists to define whether they were enclosed. Six roundhouses, possibly belonging to an open Iron Age settlement were also discovered beneath the Roman fortress at Usk (Marvell 1988).

Datable material culture: an under-utilised resource

Appendix 1 lists Iron Age brooches and ring-headed pins from south-east Wales. When the scattered sources are drawn together, a total of 47 La Tène I or later bow brooches from 12 Iron Age hillforts or settlements are known, with a further 22 from Roman military or town sites. To these can be added two brooches of Hallstatt date, 11 swan's neck pins of Late Bronze Age to Middle Iron Age date and 22 penannular brooches of Middle Iron Age to Romano-British date (Fowler 1960, Types A–D), the latter excluding all examples from Romano-British military sites. This challenges the pre-conceived notion of a dearth of datable Iron Age material culture in the region.

Five examples of La Tène I brooches of Types 1A and 1B can be added to the three recorded in Hull and Hawkes (1987): two from excavations (Lodge Wood Camp and Portskewett) and three metal-detector finds (Newton Moor, Penllyn, and Penllyn Moor). By far the most important brooch assemblage comes from Twyn-y-Gaer hillfort, where 19 iron brooches or fragments are known. The assemblage is characterised by long flat bow brooches and involuted brooches (Hull and Hawkes Types 1C–3) spanning the Middle Iron Age (Probert 1976). Parallels have naturally been made with a similar Middle Iron Age assemblage from Croft Ambrey in Herefordshire (Stanford 1974; Probert 1976), but it would be incorrect to see the presence of brooches as a defining feature of the Welsh Marches, with the record becoming progressively more impoverished further west into Wales, since the long-running excavations at Castell Henllys hillfort in Pembrokeshire (Mytum 1989; 1999) have so far yielded an assemblage of at least 12 La Tène brooches, including arched bow, long flat bow, and involuted forms, and four iron penannular brooches.[1] These assemblages may be viewed, with some justification, as two of the most important Middle Iron Age hillfort groups in Britain. Two iron La Tène II brooches (Type 2Ab and 2Cb) and an iron ring-headed pin were found at Coygan Camp in Carmarthenshire (Wainwright 1967; Savory 1976b; J. Deacon pers. comm.), whilst most excavated settlements across the coastal fringes of south-east Wales have produced examples of Late Iron Age or penannular brooches (Appendix 1).

A preference for *iron* brooches during the Middle Iron Age and continuing until the conquest period seems to be emerging in south-east Wales, with 32 of the 47 brooches from Iron Age sites made of iron (68.1%). To these can be added ten iron brooches from Castell Henllys and the two from Coygan Camp. This hints at more frequent deposition of brooches during the Later Iron Age than previously anticipated. Hill (1997) has termed an apparent explosion in brooch styles and deposition in southern and eastern England in the first centuries BC and AD the 'fibula event' horizon and linked this to social changes. In south Wales, a proliferation of brooch assemblages can be seen slightly later, during the decades of Roman conflict and eventual conquest. Nevertheless, one begins to wonder whether, here at least, this phenomenon is partially a 'brass or bronze event horizon', explained by a changing preference for copper alloys over the pre-existing iron traditions. Poor survival and visibility of iron in soils, the lack of routine X-radiography and conservation of ironwork assemblages, and the low priority given by archaeologists to small pieces of corroded ironwork, compared to copper alloy artefacts, have served to hinder the discovery and reporting of iron brooches.

Pottery, whilst never abundant, is a persistent presence in the region. Appendix 2 lists at least 70 discrete places where Late Bronze Age and Iron Age ceramics have been found (*c.* 1150 BC–AD 75). It is rarely possible accurately to quantify the assemblages from published sources, but at least a dozen contain over 100 sherds. The largest, from Thornwell Farm, Chepstow, comprising over 2000 sherds (Woodward 1996), compares broadly with the size of assemblage expected from a small settlement in southern or eastern England. Excavations at Llanmelin, Sudbrook, and Mynydd Bychan yielded assemblages of between 500–1500 sherds, whilst 100–500 sherds came from Caldicot, St Athan, Portskewett, Greenmoor Arch, Chapeltump II, Magor Pill, Culver Hole, and Merthyr Mawr. Many other excavations have produced up to 100 sherds, typically with between 3–20 diagnostic sherds being illustrated. Viewed against this trend, it is perhaps appropriate to see those few excavations which have yielded no Iron Age pottery, such as Coed-y-Bwnydd or High Pennard, as exceptional, rather than typical.

No regional ceramic synthesis for the first millennium BC has been attempted for south-east Wales, hindering a clear understanding of chronological sequence and diagnostic traits. The generally held perception – that ceramic production virtually ceased in Wales during the Late Bronze Age and until the Late Iron Age – has tended to be a self-fulfilling prophesy, with a reticence to use multiple radiocarbon dates to fix excavated Iron Age sequences and pottery. Ceramic researchers have accordingly tended to rely upon secure benchmarks within the Bronze Age and Romano-British periods, in a conservative manner. Too little thought has been given to the possibility, firstly, of ceramic traditions continuing into the Early Iron Age and secondly, earlier Middle Iron Age origins of assumed Late Iron Age styles (see also Moore this volume).

For all this, recently excavated assemblages are now throwing light upon the regional sequence of vessel forms. The Late Bronze Age assemblage at Thornwell Farm is characterised by hook-rim and straight-necked jars, and rims with internal bevelling or cable effect decoration. They were succeeded in the Early Iron Age by vessels with sharp and finger-impressed shoulders (Woodward 1996, 44). The Early Iron Age occupation has radiocarbon dates of 800–200 and 770–380 cal. BC (Hughes 1996, 88). At Chapeltump II on the Gwent Levels, an occupation surface produced an important ceramic assemblage apparently with Middle and Late Bronze Age characteristics, but the associated radiocarbon dates allow for possible continuity into the Early Iron Age (Locock *et al.* 2000; Woodward 2000a). Three Early Iron Age straight-necked and thin-walled jars from a palaeochannel at Collister Pill 3 (with parallels at Cadbury Castle, Ham Hill, and Danebury) were associated with a timber post radiocarbon dated to 770–380 cal. BC (Bell *et al.* 2000, 310; Woodward 2000b).

There is growing evidence for Middle Iron Age pottery in the region. A barrel jar with chevron decoration from Coed-y-Cymdda enclosure, associated with a radiocarbon date of 410–90 cal. BC, has been known for some time (Owen-John 1988, 95). At Greenmoor Arch, Bishton, undecorated Iron Age pottery was discovered on the surface of a peat layer radiocarbon dated 550–150 cal. BC at 89.0%, associated with rectangular Iron Age buildings (Locock 1999). At Twyn-y-Gaer, a stamped Malvernian ware vessel was found in a fourth- to early third-century BC structural phase. Plain vessels of the Lydney–Llanmelin style were only deposited on the site during later phases, probably spanning the later third to first centuries BC (Probert 1976, 116–18). Undecorated jars with simple, incipient and bead rims have also been discovered in Middle Iron Age phases at Lodge Wood hillfort in direct association with an iron La Tène I brooch of Type 1B (Howell and Pollard 2004, 154–6). At Portskewett, a Type 1A brooch was discovered in an enclosure ditch, associated with hand-made bead-rimmed jars (Clarke 1999). Taken together, these assemblages suggest that the regional expression of the so called 'saucepan pot continuum' had its origins in the Middle Iron Age, in line with other parts of central and southern England (Brown 2000, 122–4; Cunliffe 1991).

Decorated Later Iron Age pottery is known from at least 16 sites, either comprising chevrons and curved 'eyebrow' decoration, or with filled-in geometric and curvilinear decoration most characteristic of 'Glastonbury ware' (e.g. Nash-Williams 1933; Spencer 1983; Webster 1988a). Whether these constitute a regional style – tentatively identified by Cunliffe (1991, 81) as the Lydney–Llanmelin style – distinct from ceramic traditions in Somerset and Gloucestershire, remains unclear. Building upon Peacock's research (1969), Allen (1998) has recently situated many of the decorated vessels within a wider plain vessel tradition using calcite temper and straddling both sides of the Bristol Channel–Severn estuary. Whilst it is possible that this pottery was made in the Bristol–Mendip area, where good Carboniferous Limestone outcrops containing calcite occur, production in south Wales cannot be discounted. Thin-section analysis, now underway, of undecorated calcite-gritted vessels from an Iron Age enclosure at St Athan, together with a study of calcite from outcrops in south Wales, will explore this possibility (J. Horak pers. comm.). Moreover, much of the Iron Age pottery from south-east Wales is made with limestone rather than calcite temper, sources of which could easily be local.

At present, the introduction and chronological development of decorated pottery is not clearly understood: the chevron-decorated vessel from Coed-y-Cymdda and its associated radiocarbon date hints at Middle Iron Age origins, possibly as early as the third century BC, whilst the cumulative evidence of decorated pottery from Late Iron Age settlements suggests that they continued in use until the conquest period. Woodward (1996) has suggested that proto-bead-rimmed jars and decorated pottery spanned the whole of the Later Iron Age at Thornwell Farm, whilst the bead- and everted-rimmed jars were introduced later in the period, but it remains to be seen whether this reflects a wider regional trend. It is difficult to view the introduction of new wheel-made pottery forms during the Late Iron Age as anything other than very late and unusual. The assemblages, previously termed 'Belgic', identified at Mynydd Bychan, Sudbrook, and Llanmelin hillforts probably span the middle decades of the first century AD, their continuation into the conquest period being confirmed by their presence in the Roman fortresses at Usk (Greene 1993, 59–62) and Caerleon (P. Webster 1981, 111).

Contrary to widespread opinion, the Iron Age communities of south-east Wales did use and deposit datable portable material culture. Diagnostic brooches and pins are surprisingly frequent, whilst research on newly discovered ceramic assemblages is beginning to reveal a sequence of changing forms and decorative techniques through the first millennium BC. Insufficient research, patchy publication, and infrequent multiple radiocarbon dating of excavated sequences with associated material culture have so far hindered the generation of a coherent chronological framework. Yet this existing body of material culture has huge potential, through further synthesis, targeted dating programmes, and innovative question-oriented fieldwork and research projects over coming years.

Material exchanges and maritime contacts

Iron Age coin finds from Wales were last listed over 15 years ago (Boon 1988, 92). Since then, 12 new finds have been made, all through metal detecting. Whilst none of the Iron Age peoples of Wales minted their own coins, 32 coins from other parts of Britain or Gaul, and 12 Greek coins have come to be deposited here. Most come from south-east Wales, but it is felt appropriate to discuss all the Welsh finds here. Along with a number of other artefacts of disparate origins, the coins indicate something of the social and political relations existing between communities on either side of the Severn estuary in the Late Iron Age. Secondly, they hint at the significance of short- and long-distance relationships between the coastal communities of south-east Wales, south-west England, Armorica, and the Mediterranean. Mindful of various publications which have developed ideas about Atlantic and Irish seaways, ports and maritime contacts (e.g. Cunliffe 1982; 1987; 1988; 2001; Cunliffe and de Jersey 1997; Matthews 1999; Taylor 2001), this paper aspires to add to the discussion, as it relates to the western coastlines of Wales. An updated listing of Iron Age and Greek coins discovered in Wales is contained in Appendix 3.

Sixteen coins originating in the Severn–Cotswold region have been discovered in south-east Wales (Fig. 3), both along the coastal areas of the Vale of Glamorgan and Monmouthshire, and inland west of the River Wye and along the eastern borders of Monmouthshire. In part, the new finds confirm the tail-off of gold staters at the north-western edge of the 'Dobunnic' circulation zone noted by Sellwood (1984) and termed a 'gateway'

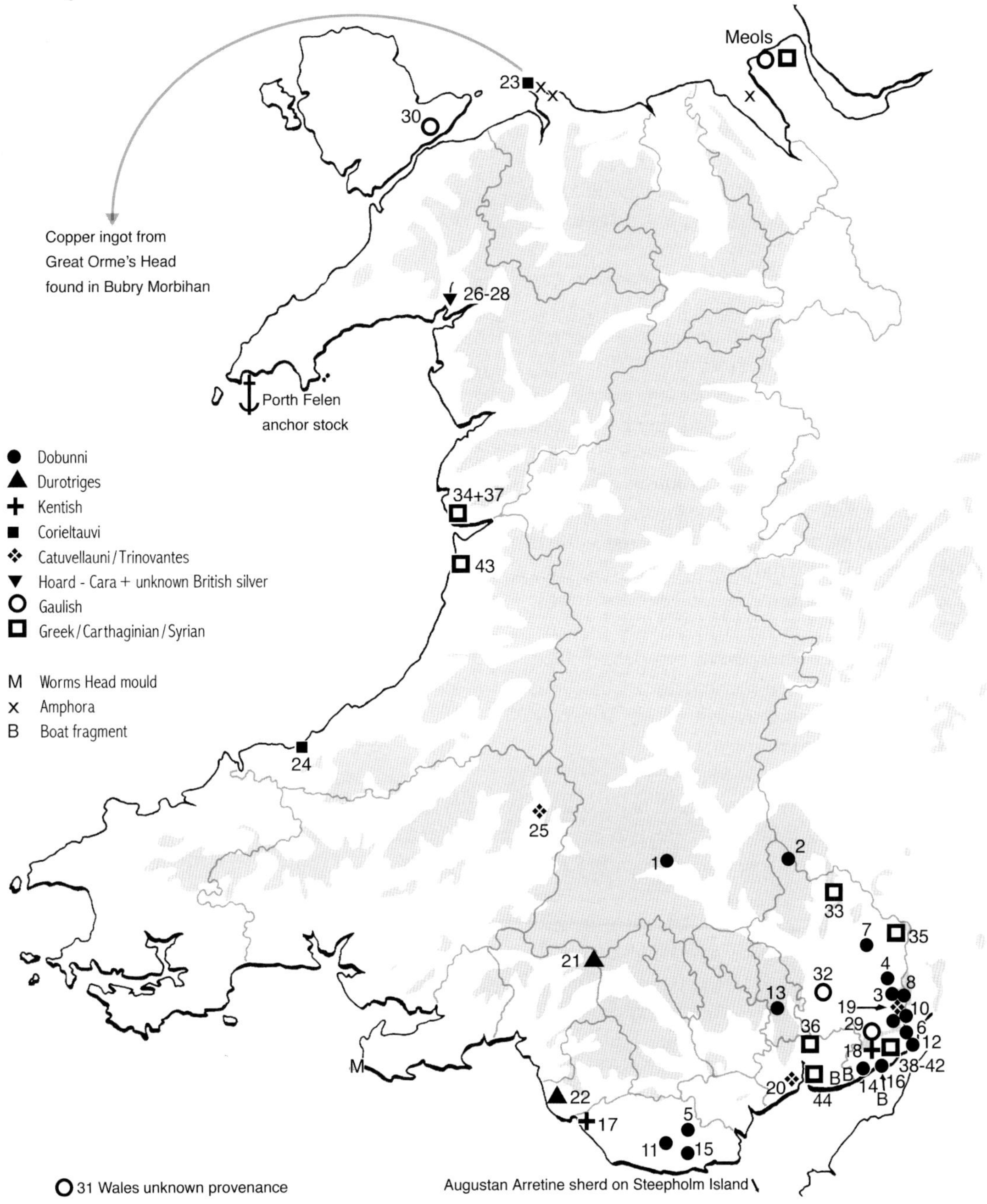

Fig. 3. Iron Age and Greek coins from Wales (with selected artefacts suggesting maritime contacts).

by Van Arsdell (1994); the high frequency of gold (13) over silver (3) finds around this periphery has also been maintained. Manning (1981a, 20–3) has suggested that the scarcity of silver coinage west of the Severn, including parts of Gloucestershire and Herefordshire, indicates that this area was outside Dobunnic territory, but it remains a strong possibility that it formed part of an overlap zone towards the edges of the Silurian and Dobunnic territories, implicit in Van Arsdell's use of the terms 'gateway' and 'no man's land', and Sellwood's 'border zone'. Since the Silures did not issue coins, a reciprocal overlap into Dobunnic territory is absent, serving to complicate boundary discussions. Discoveries from Whitton, Penllyn, and St Nicholas in the Vale of Glamorgan (Appendix 3, nos 5, 11, 15), extend the circulation further west than previously presumed, hinting at coastal interaction across the Severn estuary. These Dobunnic coins most likely represent interaction between the two peoples, yet within Silurian territory.

Less predicted was the mix of regional coinages

represented in Wales. In south-east Wales, there are coins from south-east England and from Dorset, as well as a central Gaulish potin coin and an unidentified Gaulish coin (*ibid.*, nos 29, 32). Types originating in eastern and southern England are present in north and west Wales, as well as a Gaulish coin attributed to the Carnutes. Another Gaulish coin, this time of the Aedui, was apparently found in Wales (*ibid.*, no. 31), but the precise provenance is unknown. The spread of coins seems chronologically early; Kentish Primary potins (*ibid.*, no. 17–18) are dated to the second century BC (Haselgrove 2006), as is the Gaulish potin, whilst more than half the remainder are probably of first-century BC date. Unfortunately, little is known about the archaeological contexts: the only coin retrieved during excavation, at Whitton, was unstratified. Of the rest, 16 were casual discoveries and 14 were found metal detecting, although the discovery of a coin of Eisv at Caldicot subsequent led to excavation of the settlement (Vyner and Allen 1988, 67). A small coin hoard found in the mid nineteenth century at Minffordd, near Penrhyndeudraeth, included a silver coin of Cara (Appendix 3, no. 26), generally attributed to Caratacus, the war leader who led the Silures and Ordovices in the battle against the Romans. The coin was probably minted in Atrebatic territory during the 40s AD.

Great caution must be exercised when discussing Greek coin finds in the context of Iron Age Britain, since many may have been lost in the Roman period or in modern times (Milne 1948; Laing 1968; Collis 1975; Boon 1991). Nevertheless, the possibility that some were the result of tin trading with the Mediterranean world has not been entirely discounted (e.g. Hawkes 1984; Cunliffe 1997; Matthews 1999). Accordingly, the 12 Greek, Carthaginian, and Syrian coins from seven locations in Wales are included in Appendix 3, although information concerning their discovery is poor, and it may be significant that no new finds have been added by metal detecting over the last 20 years.

Nevertheless, when their location is compared to the Iron Age coins, it is clear that they share a strong tendency for coastal and river mouth findspots, not incompatible with the idea that sea transport was involved in their circulation (although this might instead relate to the Roman period). The Caerleon, Monmouth, Newport, and Aberdyfi coins (Appendix 3, nos 34–37, 44) were associated with rivers, whilst those from Borth and Caerwent (*ibid.*, nos 38–43) are from coastal locations. So too are the Iron Age finds from Caerwent, Porthcasseg, Merthyr Mawr, Penbryn, Llanfaes, and Great Orme's Head (*ibid.*, nos 17–19, 23–24 and 30), whilst both Bassaleg and Minffordd are at river mouths (*ibid.*, nos 20, 26–28). This tendency is echoed in the recent find of a Carthaginian coin with two coins of Pyrrhus recovered from the bed of the River Irk at Cheetham Hill, Manchester (Matthews 1999, 183). The distribution of early, high value Roman coins from non-military sites in Wales, such as the *denarius* of Claudius reported from the River Tywi, near Carmarthen (E. Besly pers. comm.), could further add to the pattern.

The mix of distant British and central Gaulish coinages might lend support to the theory of circulation via the sea. The current absence of Armorican coins from Wales should, however, be mentioned, although examples are known from Meols on the Wirral and Scowles near Lydney (De Jersey 1997, 97–8). The east Kentish potin from Merthyr Mawr and the Carnutes bronze coin from Llanfaes, Anglesey, have some resonance with possible landing points discussed by previous researchers. Cunliffe (1997, 40) has speculated on the involvement of Merthyr Mawr in long-distance trade, whilst Matthews (1999, 186) hypothesised a possible landing point on Anglesey, one day's sailing from both St David's Head and Meols. We should also, however, note that non-local Iron Age coin types occur in the Severn–Cotswold region (C. Haselgrove pers. comm.), which might therefore be the immediate source of some of the Welsh imports, particularly as – like the Dobunnic issues – they, too, tend to cluster in south-east Wales.

Building a plausible context for sea contact and exchange is inevitably difficult, based upon piecemeal evidence often distant in space and time. The coastal dune location, metalworking evidence and unusual artefact discoveries, together with possible parallels at Mount Batten and Hengistbury Head, contribute to the view that Merthyr Mawr could have been an important coastal trading site or port in south-east Wales. The existing assemblage requires re-appraisal, whilst re-investigation of the site could add much to our understanding of its character and longevity. We may also note the triangular crucible base of Late Iron Age form associated with a charcoal scatter found in dunes at Morfa Harlech in Gwynedd, not far away from the Minffordd coin hoard (Crew 1985). Sudbrook coastal fort has been interpreted as becoming a Roman sea-landing base during the first century AD (Manning 1981a, 42), perhaps guarding a crossing over the Severn estuary. The probable Roman coin offerings found at Black Rock, Portskewett (Hudson 1977) may provide evidence for this crossing having continued during the Roman period

The thinking behind these views is, however, anachronstic, seeing the existence of the primate 'place' or single crossing point as an efficient way of satisfying operational needs or demands within a region. I remain unconvinced that sea travel and contacts operated in this manner, certainly during the Iron Age and probably also in the Roman period. Recent research in the Gwent Levels suggests a continuously utilised coastal landscape with boat landing points and trackways leading inland (Rippon 1997, 54; Bell *et al.* 2000, 322–50; Marvell 2004, 103–4). This supports the view that there were many landing and contact points, at least for smaller vessels, along the south Wales coastline. Some of the Roman harbours identified in Wales (e.g. Jones and Mattingly 1990, map 6:19) could also have had pre-Roman origins, even if the evidence barely yet exists to demonstrate this.

Early Bronze Age sewn plank boat fragments have been found at Caldicot (McGrail 1997), yet in a boatbuilding tradition that spanned the Bronze and Iron Ages, whilst Middle Bronze Age boat planks were incorporated into a later trackway at Goldcliff (Bell *et. al* 2000, 77). The boat from Barland's Farm, Magor (Nayling and McGrail 2004) also merits a mention: it was placed to stabilise the river edge next to a bridge or jetty in the early fourth century AD, but belongs to a tradition of boat building spanning the first to fourth centuries AD. Although not strictly contemporary with the Iron Age, such boats provide some context for seafaring around the coastal waters of western Britain, longer journeys perhaps being made by coastal hopping.

Evidence that Mediterranean ships sometimes travelled past the Welsh coast in the Iron Age is provided by the Porth Felen anchor-stock, discovered by divers off the Llŷn peninsula, Gwynedd (Boon 1977). This dates to the second century BC, if not earlier, and probably belonged to a small Greco-Italic ship, wrecked in the treacherous waters of Bardsey Sound. If so, we can only speculate about the purpose of her voyage: we know of the voyage of Pytheas around Britain during the fourth century BC and we have Diodorus Siculus' reference (V, 22) to a tin trade with south-west England.[2] Her crew may have been exploring the potential for obtaining metals from Wales, for example gold at Pumsaint, Dolaucothi; copper deposits on Anglesey and the Great Orme's Head; lead from Halkyn Mountain, Flintshire; or iron from Gwynedd or the Forest of Dean (e.g. Jones and Mattingly 1990, 179–96; Arnold and Davies 2000, 95–105). They may also have been interacting with Iron Age communities and exchanging a wider range of goods and materials, including salt (Matthews 1999), wherever they set anchor.

Matthews (*ibid.*, 177) suggests that a Massaliote amphora dating to the fifth century BC, dredged out of the River Dee around 1900, could have been deposited during the Iron Age. To this, we may add two further discoveries of amphorae from Rhos-on-Sea, Conwy (Manley and Grenter 1987); one is of the Dressel 2–4 type, dating between the mid first century BC and the second century AD; the other has not been identified, although it was allegedly found half full of Roman coins. A number of Roman coin hoards and copper ingots have been found nearby on the Great Orme and near to the Iron Age gold coin mentioned above. The discovery of a round stamped copper ingot at Bubry, Morbihan, closely matching the size and weight of those from the Great Orme, is symptomatic (André 1976); although precise dating of this artefact is not yet possible, it hints at an established trade route between north Wales and Armorica during the Roman period. Much earlier exchange relations between south-east Wales, south-west England and north-west France are implied in the deposition of Armorican axes belonging to the Bronze–Iron Age transition (Savory 1980; Cunliffe 1982; Lodwick and Gwilt 2004). Finally, an Arretine sherd of Augustan date has been found on Steepholm, a small island in the Bristol Channel (Boon 1987). When viewed together, these fragments of evidence begin to make the notion of long-distance sea contacts during the Iron Age seem plausible.

The Later Iron Age metalworking evidence at Merthyr Mawr need not be viewed as entirely alien, restricted, or stimulated by or for external communities. The discovery of other early La Tène brooches in the region cast the two from this site in a slightly different light.[3] Crucibles for copper alloy have been found at Llanmelin and Castle Ditches, Llancarfan, and further west at Walesland Rath in Pembrokeshire (Nash-Williams 1933; Wainwright 1971; Hogg 1976). These finds hint at a vigorous south Wales tradition in the Later Iron Age, metalworking being undertaken at a variety of places and capable of producing finished artefacts to suit regional tastes. The casting jets, ingots, and billets of bronze in the mid first century AD Seven Sisters hoard support this view (Davies and Spratling 1976; Savory 1976b).

Instructive here is the quite exceptional stone mould pair from Worm's Head, Gower, with cut-out patterns for a decorated disc and three ring beads (Cunnington 1920). This may have been associated with the stone-walled fort known on this headland (RCAHMW 1976a, 23). Savory (1974) has argued their early to middle La Tène character, citing continental parallels. Whilst the stone may have come from Old Red Sandstone outcrops north of Carmarthen Bay, allowing for local manufacture, the styles suggest Armorican influence. The Stage I motifs on the Cerrig-y-Drudion crown from north Wales are similarly influenced by Gaulish metalwork, showing a resemblance to Armorican decorated ceramic styles, yet exhibiting evidence for British origin and inspiration (Stead 1982; 1995; Cunliffe 1997, 39–40; Jope 2000, 23–5). We may note that the stamped decorated sherd from Merthyr Mawr has been compared with early to middle La Tène ceramics in Armorica (Savory 1976b) and needs to be re-examined in the light of recent discoveries in southern England and north-west France.

Associated with the Worm's Head mould, and largely overlooked by Savory, were two further mould pieces (Cunnington 1920, 255–6). One, now lost, was a complete disc, about 20 cm in diameter, with a projecting mouth, made of volcanic tuff. Its face was flat and smoothed, whilst the reverse had a pronounced groove from mouth to opposite side, bisecting the stone. Another, still surviving, disc fragment is 18 cm in diameter and has a negative circular disc template cut into each face. It is carefully smoothed on the faces and rim edges. Cunnington quite reasonably suggested that both moulds were for casting flat circular objects, perhaps mirrors.

These discs are closely paralleled by three other finds in Wales: from Braich-y-Dinas and Dinorben hillforts, and an unknown location on Anglesey (Guilbert 1979; Jones 1985; Lynch 1986). The Braich-y-Dinas disc has a diameter of 18.3 cm, with a mouth, whilst its reverse has a groove exactly like the reverse of the complete stone from Worm's Head, probably for clamping the mould pair together before casting. The complete circular stone mould pair from Dinorben, in north-east Wales, came from a four-poster in the interior. They were deposited in a post pit when the structure was removed, probably during the Romano-British occupation of the site. Both have projecting mouths and are approximately 42 cm in diameter. One has a circular disc groove 38–39 cm in diameter cut into it, the other is flat. The Anglesey piece has small disc sinkings of 5.5, 6.5 and 7.5 cm, two on a single face, the other on the reverse.

Given that all these disc templates are 5–7 mm deep, we might speculate that they were used to cast blanks for beaten cauldrons or bowls rather than mirrors, since when hammered out the discs would make circular sheets too large for mirrors. If such an interpretation is accepted, these moulds must be seen as relatively abundant evidence for sheet vessel manufacture across Wales during the Later Iron Age and Romano-British periods. This lends weight to Hawkes' (1951, 177) comments about the importance of a continuing native tradition of sheet metalworking, for bowls, cauldrons, buckets, and tankards, in western Britain

Mention must also be made of the range of material culture exchanges between the Silurian, Dobunnic, and Durotrigian communities, supporting the inference gained via the coin circulation patterns. As noted above, some of the decorated, calcite-tempered, Middle to Late Iron Age pottery from south-east Wales may have been made in the Mendip area. On settlements where pottery is uncommon, we may speculate about perhaps specific roles and uses of these vessels, if not for everyday food storage and cooking. Glass beads of Iron Age and Iron Age or Roman type are now known from at least 20 sites in the region (e.g. Guido 1978; Standley 2005). Henderson (1987a; 1987b; 1991) has confirmed the existence of a glass making centre at Meare in Somerset, producing small opaque yellow annular 'Meare spiral' beads and 'Meare variant' beads (Guido Classes 8, 10, 11). These types are found at Twyn-y-Gaer and Caerwent (*Venta Silurum*), the Roman *civitas* capital, as well as Coygan Camp in Carmarthenshire (Charlesworth 1967) and Gwernvale chambered tomb in Powys. South and west Wales therefore forms one important area of their westerly British distribution. The distribution patterns of other bead types (e.g. Classes 1, 3, 9, and Groups 6–7), also show a common circulation in south Wales, Somerset, Dorset, and Gloucestershire, hinting at their manufacture within this area, possibly at Meare or Hengistbury Head (Henderson 1987c).

The potential significance of shale armlets or bracelets in the region has generally been underplayed. A rapid survey shows their presence at Caerleon, Caerwent, Caldicot, Cowbridge, Dinas Powys, Llanmaes, Loughor, Usk, and Whitton, giving a strong early Roman showing, but also including possible Late Iron Age examples (e.g. Alcock 1963; Lawson 1981; Zienkiewicz 1986; Robinson 1988; Greep 2000). Most are made of Kimmeridge shale from Dorset, where an industry thrived throughout the Iron Age and Roman periods (Cunliffe 1991, 463–5). The possible evidence for shale working at Dinas Powys, as indicated by an armlet disc core with square chuck holes is noteworthy. This technology is thought to have been introduced into Britain in the first century BC (Cunliffe 1987, 176–7). Associated with this core is a flint lathe tool and a possible rim from a shale vessel, now paralleled in the region by a sizeable shale vessel assemblage at Caerleon (Zienkiewicz 1986, 213–14).

The glass and shale finds suggest that the Silures shared certain tastes in personal adornment with the Dobunni and Durotriges. We may also note that distinctly south-westerly native styles of brooches are frequent during the first and early second centuries AD, including light Polden, Dolphin, penannular, certain trumpet, and T-shape varieties (Hull types 103–111). Discussions of artefact distributions can tend to promote a passive and flat view of the past, but we must remember that they were actively and selectively exchanged, with significances that were played upon and used in the daily renegotiation of social and power relations (see also Moore this volume). It remains frustratingly difficult to identify items made in south-east Wales and found in neighbouring regions, thereby acknowledging that exchanges constitute two-way relationships, but these must have existed; candidates include bronze metalwork and enamelling, iron (in raw or finished form), cattle, horses, boats, a range of organic foodstuffs, and artefacts and labour commitments.

It is thus becoming possible to construct an archaeological context for the Later Iron Age in south-east Wales, within which sea transport performed a significant role. Maritime contacts offer one plausible interpretation of the Iron Age and Greek coin distribution in Wales, whilst the Bristol Channel and Severn estuary are perhaps better seen as a stretch of water connecting – not dividing – the societies of south-western Britain. Certainly, the common circulation zones of a number of artefact types support the idea that the Silures, the Dobunni, and perhaps the Durotriges enjoyed close exchange (and possibly social and political) relations. Some direct sea contact between south-east Wales, south-west England, and Armorica is implied, while occasional early contact with the Classical world, either direct or indirect, can be inferred.

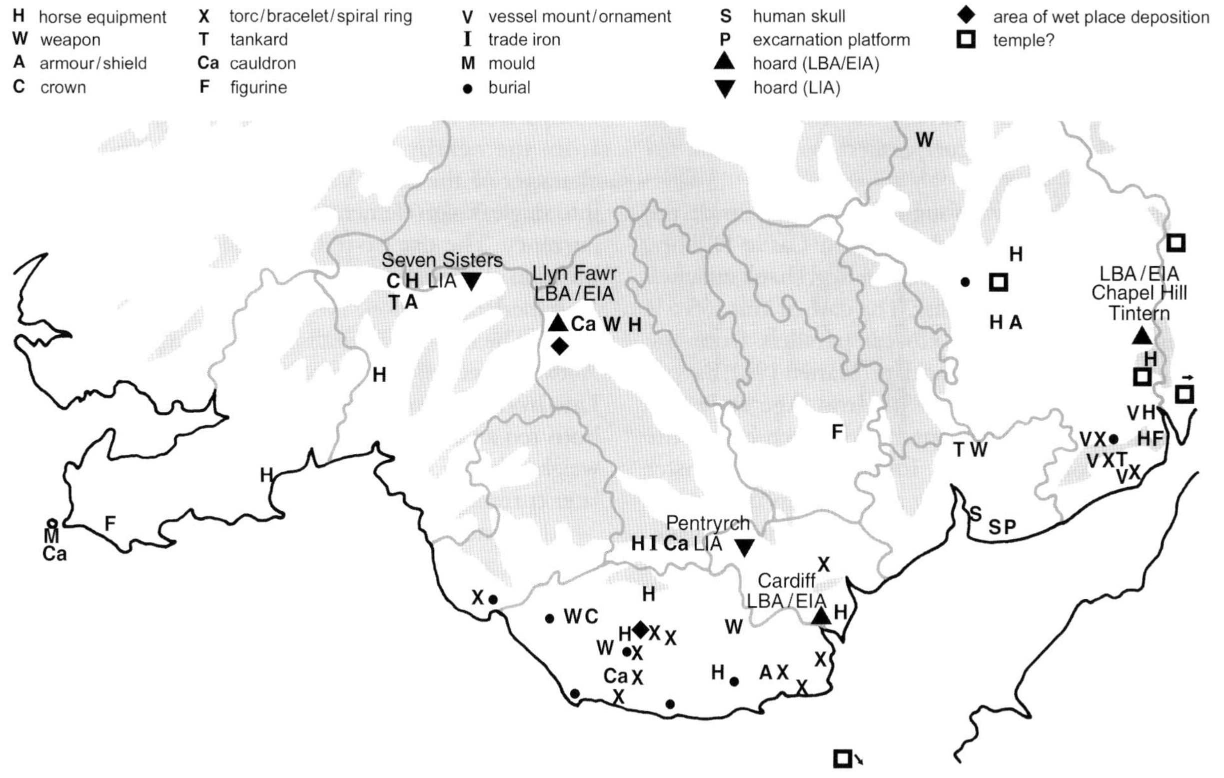

Fig. 4. Artefact deposition and burial practices in south-east Wales.

Arenas of consumption and personal display

The second half of the paper sketches out some themes relevant to developing a more detailed understanding of the Later Iron Age in this region. They can be grouped together under the umbrella term 'arenas for consumption and personal display', whilst the artefactual evidence discussed often exhibits late La Tène decoration (Fig. 4). Some general contrasts can also be made with Late Iron Age innovations in parts of southern and eastern England, such as the appearance of lowland nucleated settlements and temples – and a trend towards the abandonment of hillforts – and the adoption cremation burial, wheel-made pottery and coinage. Evidence for these developments is sparse in Wales, although the apparent increasing frequency of rectilinear enclosures at this time has already been noted. Instead, it would appear that an emergent Silurian elite was selectively interested in horses and chariots, forms of personal ornament, and displays of consumption during the first centuries BC and AD.

Discoveries by detectorists have considerably augmented the examples of horse-related equipment in south-east Wales. It will be argued that a martial ideology developed amongst the Silurian elite during the late first century BC and first century AD, most prominently expressed through the decoration and display of horse harnesses and chariots, a trend that may also extend to other regions such as the West Midlands (see Worrell this volume). As in northern Britain, 'native' or 'Celtic' horse-related metalwork was also deposited on early Roman military sites in Wales. Accepting the frequently complex histories of artefacts between manufacture and deposition, and admitting the possibility of simultaneous 'native elite' and 'cavalry' identities developing during the period AD 50–150 (Hunter this volume), these items are included within the following discussion. This 'borrowing back' of certain artefacts with Iron Age attributes from Roman military sites seems apt, given the successful and long-lived tradition of cultural and technological appropriation adopted by the Roman army.

A range of terret and strap union forms may be identified in the region: enamelled and knobbed terrets are known from two Late Iron Age hoards, Lesser Garth, Pentyrch and Seven Sisters (Davies and Spratling 1976; Savory 1966; 1976b; Palk 1988). The exceptional Pentyrch terret is inlaid with red enamel, set into Stage V motifs on a flat ring and into its three domed bosses.[4] Lines of small punched pointils define the borders. It was once the large central terret within a five terret chariot set. A date between 50 BC–AD 50 is likely, although anywhere in the first centuries BC or AD is possible. The two Iron Age terrets in the Seven Sisters hoard are

the invasion. Equally, it cannot be denied that certain artefacts and decorative traits were widely distributed (e.g. MacGregor 1976, maps 5, 12; Cunliffe 1995, fig. 17; Jope 2000, maps 8A, 10A, 11B). For the moment, it is enough to say that the Silures were concerned with horse and chariot display, a concern which may have continued into the early Roman period.

The existence of a high-status warrior or religious elite during the Late Iron Age is difficult to demonstrate convincingly, although a number of lines of evidence support this inference. Noteworthy is the recent relocation of the findspot of the 'Ogmore' helmets, originally found with burials and weapons in 1818. A combination of archive research and recent reporting of probably associated artefacts from the locality have traced them to Old Castle Down in the Vale of Glamorgan (Toft 1998; 2000; Macdonald 1999a; 2000a; Macdonald and Davis 2002). A number of inhumations were found associated with barbed iron daggers and spearheads, between two and four bronze helmets or headpieces, one or two decorated with enamel, gold, silver wire, and with a silver crest piece. These artefacts were lost on the way to London, where they were to be shown at the Society of Antiquaries, so we are reliant upon an account and drawings published later by Francis (1871–2). In the light of the crowned warrior burial at Deal in Kent, Stead (1995, 82–6) brought together the evidence for crown and helmet discoveries in Britain, spanning a period from the Middle Iron Age to late Roman times, discussing the Ogmore crowns alongside those from Cerrig-y-Drudion and Lydney, Gloucestershire. A first-century BC or AD date for the Old Castle Down burials is supported by the recent identification of two Oldbury-type glass beads and a cannel coal ring from the locality, suggesting the existence of contemporary burials within a cemetery (Macdonald and Davis 2002, 29).

In the light of this research, the helmet crest knob with tricorne motif in the Seven Sisters hoard (Davies and Spratling 1976) and the boar figurine crest from Gaer Fawr, Powys (Foster 1977), provide further evidence for ceremonial crowns or helmets between the Middle Iron Age and conquest period in Wales. Also from Seven Sisters, a pair of red-enamelled pendant hooks can now be plausibly interpreted as hooks to secure the shoulder flaps of a mail tunic or warrior's cloak (Davies and Spratling 1976; cf. Stead 1991, 55). Similar in form are a pair described as trace-hooks in the Polden Hill hoard (Brailsford 1975), which may be a variant of the pairs of S-shaped cuirass hooks present in the Polden Hill and Melsonby/Stanwick hoards (MacGregor 1962; Brailsford 1975); their interpretation as chariot or cart fittings now seems unlikely. A single example was found in a pre-Flavian context at Usk, decorated in a Celtic rendering of a ram's headed serpent (Webster 1995b). A similar duck-headed form was also found at Camerton in Somerset (Jackson 1990). Warrior or ceremonial, elite attributes may therefore be identified within the Seven Sisters hoard, in common with the finds from Polden Hill and Melsonby/Stanwick (Fitts *et al.* 1999). Its composition, with Iron Age and Roman military, ceremonial and horse related aspects is echoed by the grave goods associated with the contemporary Folly Lane burial, dated to *c.* AD 55 (Foster 1999).[6]

On the border of the region, mention should be made of the warrior burial discovered during building work at High Nash, Coleford, in the Forest of Dean (Webster 1990; Walters 1992, 55–6). This inhumation was accompanied by a late La Tène sword, bent double, an iron shield boss, an enamelled button-and-loop suspension fitting and two scabbard rings. The use of both red and yellow enamelling with a simple double petal motif on the suspension fitting, suggests a date in the mid to later first century AD. Other warrior or high-status burials in Wales are the sword burial from Gelliniog Wen, Anglesey, the possible mirror burial from Llechwedd-du-Bach, Gwynedd, and the probable cremation burial from Welshpool (Boon 1961; Fox 1925; Hughes 1909).

Bladed weapons are infrequent discoveries in the region, although the existing evidence is worth mentioning. The unpublished excavations at Twyn-y-Gaer yielded a sword, a sword hilt-guard and a spearhead, all of iron. The sword is largely complete, but missing its hilt guard, and has a bone pommel. Its short length (total 47 cm; blade length 37 cm) is unusual for an Iron Age sword (Stead 1995, 63), although a parallel comes from a square barrow grave at Rudston (R154) in East Yorkshire (Stead 1991, 205–6; J. Deacon pers. comm.). This suggests a date in the third or second centuries BC, consistent with the large brooch assemblage from the hillfort. A 'Worton' type sword hilt belonging to Piggott's (1950) Group IV was found in the vicinity of the Roman fortress at Caerleon, although nothing is known of its archaeological context (Boon 1974). Recently discovered by a metal detectorist at Llysworney, in the Vale of Glamorgan, is the first Welsh example of a crown-hilt of Piggott's Group IVB (Chapman 2003), extending their known distribution beyond Dorset (Jope 2000, map 7B). These two swords probably date to the first century AD (Piggott 1950; Dungworth 1996, 407–10).

A sword belt fitting has recently been reported from St Nicholas in the Vale of Glamorgan (Lodwick 2003b), apparently similar in form to the button ring found within warrior burial 39 at Owslebury (Collis 1994), though this example has a knop lying flat rather than at right angles to the ring. A similar buttoned sword belt ring was found in recent excavations of a spring at Glyn, Llanbedrgoch, in Anglesey (M. Redknap pers. comm.). A red enamelled domed boss with central rivet hole was discovered at Whitton, which Spratling (1981) suggested was from a shield, possible parallels being found on the Battersea shield (Stead 1985). The presence of U-sectioned bronze binding in the Whitton assemblage might lend support to this interpretation. Further examples of riveted and enamelled bosses are illustrated by Jope (2000).

Button-and-loop fasteners, harness rings, belt fittings and strap junctions occur in early Roman forts in the region, often displaying styles and enamelling in a native tradition (e.g. Fox 1941; Brewer 1986; Webster 1992; Lloyd-Morgan 1997; 2000a). Given the dearth of similar finds from native sites, it remains unclear how much they were used by the Silures, although the enamelled sword belt ring in the Coleford warrior burial is certainly relevant. They form part of a wider distribution across south-west England, north Wales, northern England and southern Scotland (e.g. MacGregor 1976). To these military pieces may be added a range of decorative and enamelled personal items, for example, knife handles (Fox 1993), vessel handles, brooches, and seal boxes, strengthening the impression of a continuing enamelling tradition here during the early Roman period.

Few Iron Age precious metal artefacts are known from south-east Wales. The electrum bracelet or torc fragment from Merthyr Mawr has already been mentioned; to this we can add a tantalising account of a gold torc or bracelet discovered in 1861 in the Vale of Glamorgan near Llantwit Major (Savory 1984, 267; 432). It was formed by a combination of six linking pieces, looking like rope, recalling the Clevedon, Somerset; Glascote and Needwood, Staffordshire; and Hengistbury Head torcs of the second and first centuries BC (Cunliffe 1987; Jope 2000). However the account also mentions that the ends were finished off with snake heads, which on current knowledge would better suit an early Romano-British date (Johns 1996), the snake terminals on two gold bracelets from Dolaucothi affording possible Welsh parallels (Nash-Williams 1950). Nevertheless, coins of 'very early date' were supposedly found at the same time, hinting at a first century AD context. A gold spiral finger or toe ring from Whitchurch, Cardiff, has been argued to be Iron Age (Savory 1961), but might also be Bronze Age date.

Beaded bronze torc fragments have been reported from Sully, Caerwent, and Stalling Down (Brassil 1990; Macdonald 1999b; 1999c). They may be dated to the first century AD, and these examples extend their westerly distribution (MacGregor 1976). The lack of archaeological context is frustrating, though the discovery of an example in a field immediately outside the town walls at Caerwent is interesting. To these may be added bronze spiral finger or toe rings from Mynydd Bychan (Savory 1955) and Newton (Gwilt 1997). The ribbed bracelet pair from Llanmelin (Nash-Williams 1933) is also noteworthy, although their dating within the Iron Age remains problematic (Cunliffe 1987, 153–6). In sum, there is now considerable potential for research on Later Iron Age personal adornment and identities in this region, and further significant discoveries can be anticipated.

The dearth of available plant macrofossil and faunal assemblages from south-east Wales severely hinders our understanding of diet and feasting practice (cf. Caseldine 1990; Hambleton 1999), although the marked scarcity of querns from excavated hillforts and settlements perhaps suggests a pastoral emphasis. However, tankard handles and cauldrons provide some insight into feasting and drinking during the Iron Age. Tankards were first made in the Late Iron Age, although they continued to be used and buried throughout the Romano-British period (Corcoran 1952; Earwood 1993). The five tankard handles in the Seven Sisters hoard are the largest group (Davies and Spratling 1976), matched only by the three handles and one fitting from Camerton (Jackson 1990). Four of the Seven Sisters examples are decorated in a typically Late Iron Age style, one with cross-scored domes for enamel decoration; they are closely paralleled by two examples from Hod Hill (Corcoran 1952) and one from Camerton.

Two tankard handles have been found at Caerleon in first to early third century AD contexts (Webster 1992; 1995d). The first closely resembles an example from Okstrow, Orkney (Corcoran 1952); the second, in the form of two confronting dolphins, appears unparalleled. A decorated Stage V tankard handle fragment from an unstratified context at Caerwent probably dates between AD 50–75 (Fig. 6.1; Simpson 1972), whilst another half fragment of a tankard handle decorated in the Stage V style with a circular inset of red enamel decoration was recently reported from an area of boggy land next to the Roman fort at Coelbren. The head of the mount comprises an openwork design resembling the eyes and face of an owl, whilst the handle is characterised by motifs moulded in deep relief, making it one of the most strikingly decorated tankard handles known (M. Lodwick pers. comm.). It was found only 4–5 km away from the Seven Sisters hoard, and is best dated to the first century AD.

Other tankards from Wales comprise the complete example from Trawsfynydd, Gwynedd; the handle from Porth Dafarch, Anglesey; the mount from Braich-y-Dinas hillfort, Conwy; and handle fragments from Castell Henllys and the Roman military sites at Brithdir and Caernarfon, Gwynedd (Hughes 1934; Boon 1978, 47–8; Lynch 1986; Allason-Jones 1993). Given that only 35 or so published tankards are known from Britain (e.g. Corcoran 1952; Jope 2000; Spratling 1972), the nine from south-east Wales represent a strong showing. Combined with the eleven finds from south-west England this provides a strong westerly British focus. This pattern is complemented by a contemporary popularity, during the first and second centuries AD, of ceramic tankard forms: the Durotrigian examples in Dorset and the Romano-British Severn Valley distribution in Somerset, south-east Wales, Gloucestershire, and the Welsh Marches (Webster 1975). Perhaps we should view the popularity of this form of drinking vessel as indicative of a continued preference for beer over wine, a view with

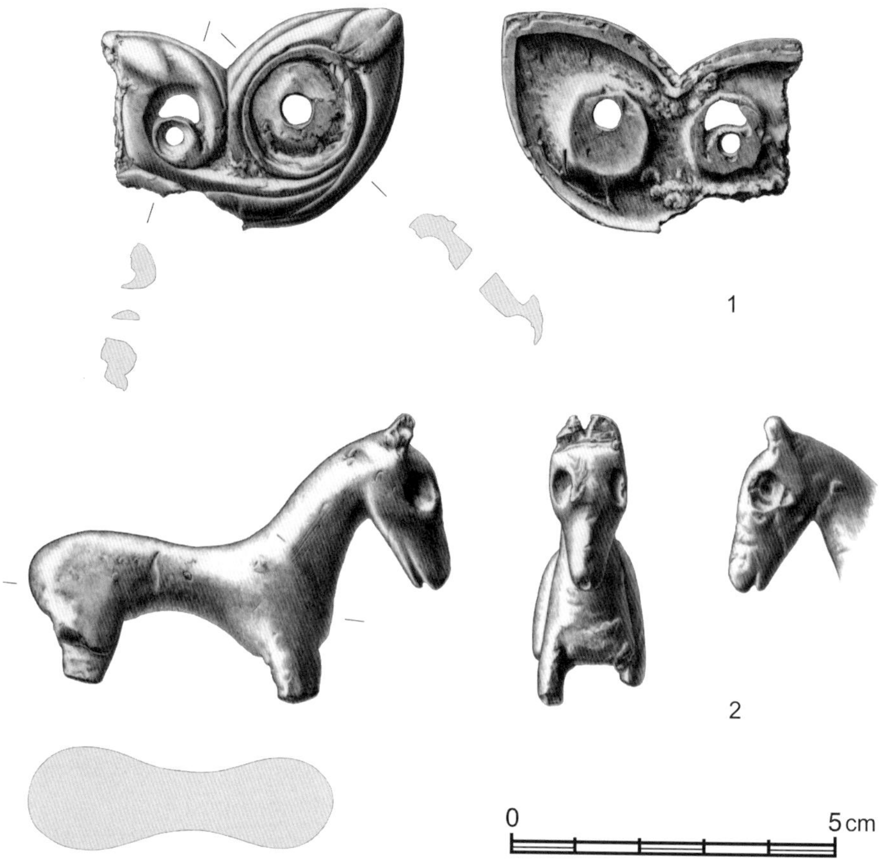

Fig. 6. 1. Caerwent tankard handle fragment; 2. Abercarn horse figurine.

which the scarcity of early Roman samian and amphora in Wales is not inconsistent. The large tankard may have been a vessel to be passed around the drinking group in a less individualised way than in Romanised drinking practice, where cups were seemingly more tailored to personal needs.

The evidence for communal eating during the Later Iron Age, in the form of cauldrons and associated equipment, is slight and inevitably coloured by the Early Iron Age evidence from the region, comprising the two complete bronze cauldrons from Llyn Fawr (Crawford and Wheeler 1920–1; Fox and Hyde 1939), and fragments of at least nine cauldrons and ring-handled bowls recently discovered at Llanmaes (Lodwick and Gwilt 2004). The other two metalwork hoards from the region, from Cardiff and Chapel Hill, Tintern, both also belong to the Llyn Fawr period (Savory 1980). After this there are none until the first century AD, when the Seven Sisters and Lesser Garth hoards were deposited. Prominent within the latter were a cauldron ring and staple, a cauldron hanger, and cauldron chain all of iron, together with two large spiral tanged knives, possibly for the preparation of food (Savory 1966). Whilst cauldrons seem to become visible at times when hoarding was a social practice, it is probable that they were used equally during the intervening period. If a Middle Iron Age date is accepted, the Worm's Head moulds certainly hint at this. The exquisitely worked iron flesh-hook from Castell Henllys Iron Age hillfort in Pembrokeshire, and the cauldron, firedog, and ewer in the rich early Roman cremation burial from Welshpool in Powys (Boon 1961) are relevant discoveries from neighbouring regions.

Ability to control the production and consumption of iron is also suggested by the selection of items in the Lesser Garth hoard. This includes trade iron in the form of a large chisel-shaped bar and a tapering billet, deposited beside a range of mainly iron artefacts. This may be viewed within a wider context of ironwork hoarding in Britain between the Middle Iron Age and Roman periods (Manning 1972; Hingley 1997; 2005). Trade iron is surprisingly rare in Wales, considering the abundance of ore sources and numerous Iron Age smelting sites now revealed in north-east Wales (Crew 1986; 1989; 1990; 1995). Convincing evidence for Iron Age iron smelting has yet to be found in south-east Wales, but some may well prove to be located beneath the

Roman smelting sites now being identified in the region (T. Young pers. comm.).

Similar control of copper alloy production and consumption is implied by the contents of the Seven Sisters hoard, where billets and jets of bronze are found alongside artefacts of bronze and brass. The Worm's Head moulds could equally be viewed as a structured deposit echoing this theme. The juxtaposed social control of food and metals in these hoards, possibly relating to reproducing the cycles of production and consumption, may have echoed themes further played out during the Late Iron Age in this region, otherwise remaining invisible to us. Lead mining was potentially another important activity, although at present possible traces of pre-Roman mining are restricted to a few sites such as Draethen, near Lower Machen (Tuck and Tuck 1971; Timberlake 2003).

In common with parts of southern Scotland, north Wales, Ireland and many of the major river basins of eastern England (e.g. Fitzpatrick 1984; Wait 1985; Hunter 1997; Bourke 2001;), a long-lived tradition of depositing metalwork in rivers, lakes, and bogs existed in south-east Wales. The Llyn Fawr hoard was deposited in the side of a lake, whilst at Caldicot, Late Bronze Age metalwork and animal bones were deposited in palaeochannels next to a timber structure (Nayling and Caseldine 1997). Associated were a group of wooden vessels – bowl, trough, stave-built bucket, and ladle – and four sword-shaped objects, which could have been ritual substitutes for metal swords (Earwood 1997, 205). A later parallel for this practice in Wales is the wooden sword and associated wooden vessels found in a water cistern within the Breiddin hillfort in Powys (Musson 1991).

In an area of boggy land, comprising meandering stream channels at the headwaters of the River Thaw, north of Cowbridge, weapons and tools were deposited from the Early Bronze Age until the Late Iron Age (Graves-Brown 1997). Three iron socketed axes are probably of Early Iron Age date, whilst three La Tène I brooches (Appendix 1, nos 6–7), a shaft hole axe, and a Dobunnic stater (Appendix 3, no. 11) indicate a continuing practice during the Later Iron Age.[7] Such long-lived practice, often in the vicinity of causeway or bridge structures, is paralleled at Flag Fen, Fengate (Pryor 2001), whilst other Later Iron Age assemblages such as Llyn Cerrig Bach and Fiskerton are also relevant (Fox 1946; Macdonald and Young 1995; Field and Parker Pearson 2003). In this context, the discovery of a Durotrigian stater at Llyn-fach (Appendix 3, no. 21), a lake neighbouring Llyn Fawr, and a Dobunnic stater on a mountain top at Mynydd-Twyn-glas (*ibid.*, no. 13) may be indicative of votive intent. Here, watery and isolated places would appear to be selected over more formalised temple or shrine sites.

Like most parts of Britain, the region lacked a visible normative burial rite. The known Iron Age burial evidence from Wales has been summarised by Murphy and Williams (1992) and we may add a cremation deposit placed into the bottom of a rock-cut hole on an Iron Age settlement at Trostrey, Monmouthshire. This was radiocarbon dated to 550–200 cal. BC at 88.3% (Mein 1996). The Old Castle Down burials discussed above were accompanied by a range of grave goods, whilst two inhumation burials from Mynydd Bychan and one from Merthyr Mawr Warren were apparently associated with Late Iron Age iron brooches (Savory 1954a, 98; 1954b; 1955). Crouched inhumations without goods have been located adjacent to the Late Iron Age enclosure at St Athan, but have yet to be radiocarbon dated (S. Cox pers. comm.).

The potential significance of Late Iron Age and early Roman vessel ornaments should not be overlooked. They often depict animals, providing some insight into species particularly valued and imbued with symbolic significance. Secondly, the usage of such decorated vessels, including buckets and caskets, deserves interpretation. The stylised bovine head, probably from the Gaer hillfort near Chepstow (Megaw *et al.* 1992), is closely paralleled by the mount from Ham Hill, Somerset, and the knife handle in the Birdlip burial, both depicting cows or bulls. It was apparently attached to the corner of a rectangular container. A sizeable number of ox-head escutcheons are now known from Wales (*ibid.*, 65–72), ranging from the one reported recently from Kemmeys in Monmouthshire (Lodwick 2002) to the elaborate example found with fragments of a stave-built bucket in the rich cremation from Welshpool (Boon 1961). Nor should we overlook the Late Iron Age iron bowl and early Roman enamelled bronze mount from Lydney, depicting bull's heads in La Tène style (Wheeler and Wheeler 1932).

The frequent depiction of bovine heads hints at their importance, possibly as a means of displaying wealth. To these, we may add a bronze boar's head escutcheon from near Caerwent (Lodwick 2003c). The form is discussed by Foster (1977), who argued, largely on stylistic grounds, for a Romano-British date. Only three parallels from Britain are known, none of them adequately dated. This example, with raised crest and ears, prominent tusks, and snarling snout, may perhaps be regarded as either first or second century AD in date (see also Jackson 1990, 26). A boar figurine from Gower (see below), also hints at the importance of pigs to the Silures.

In the context of increasingly observed animal depiction in regional La Tène art, renewed attention may be given to the bronze horse figurine from Abercarn, Monmouthshire (Fig. 6.2; Savory 1952). The figure is gracefully styled with enlarged eye sockets, once probably containing enamel (also the case with the eye voids on the Chepstow bovine mount). The apparent lack of a tail, which adds to the impression of its symbolic significance and possible religious use, is also noteworthy. Both Jacobsthal and Savory had doubts about its Iron Age date (*ibid.*) – partly because of a reluctance to accept an early discovery in this region – but in the light of more recent finds, a Late Iron Age to early Roman date seems increasingly plausible. A second bronze horse figurine was recently reported from Clydach, Swansea (M. Lodwick pers. comm.), increasing the frequency of horse-associated metalwork found in the western part of the Silurian territory. The lower legs, head and tail are missing, but the form is three-dimensional and elongate, with a graceful curving and fine moulding of the neck. The figurine is decorated with red sealing-wax enamel, forming a linear strip along the mid line of the back and with a small circular inset at the centre of the chest, suggesting a date between 50 BC–AD 50. The exaggerated curved form of the neck is echoed on the Silchester horse, the Uffington White Horse, and depictions of horses on Iron Age coins (Jope 2000), perhaps heightening the sense of movement yet also possibly drawing attention to the symbolic importance of the horse's neck and head.

A Late Iron Age human-head vessel mount was recently recorded from near Llanmelin hillfort (Macdonald 1999d). The form is paralleled by escutcheons from Aylesford and Welwyn, being shield-shaped and having a fixing hole at the top of the mount, possibly to accommodate a handle. The male face has side whiskers, strong eyebrows and triangular-shaped eyes with central dots and a wide flaring nose. A small bronze head, crudely shaped though with Iron Age affinities, was found during excavations at Thornwell Farm, Chepstow, although its function is not entirely clear (Henig 1996). Finally, a fragment of decorated casket ornament, with repoussé decoration, including a rosette with berried cluster motif linked by curvilinear double leaf pattern was found during the excavation of the settlement at Caldicot (Robinson 1988, 95). A first century AD date is not unreasonable for this. Elsewhere, buckets and casket ornaments are frequently found as grave goods in rich Late Iron Age cremation burials and hoards (e.g. Foster 1986; 1999; Stead and Rigby 1986; Fitts *et al.* 1999). Whether or not such objects had a funerary connotation in south Wales, they could well have been the possessions of a Late Iron Age elite. In this context, it is worth noting that one of the Oldbury type glass beads from Old Castle Down and the Alltwen quadrilobed harness mount had been burnt prior to their deposition (Gwilt 2003; Macdonald and Davis 2002, 29). Whether they were associated with cremations or represent a practice of burning before depositing votive offerings remains unclear.

There is some tentative evidence from the region to support the view that excarnation was the commonest way of disposing of the dead. At Goldcliff, a cluster of 12 posts was revealed on the foreshore, one of which was radiocarbon dated to 910–510 cal. BC at 93.4% (Bell *et al.* 2000, 67–8). Within metres, were found two human and one dog crania, radiocarbon dated to 830–540, 1440–1250 (94.3%) and 920–790 cal. BC respectively (*ibid.*, 64–8, 379). Six species of wood were represented within the post cluster, suggesting careful selection, whilst the platform was placed next to an ancient island within an area of coastal peat bog, echoing the tendency for liminal locations to be selected for votive deposition and religious expression. Bell suggests that the structure was a either a platform from which skulls were hung, or an excarnation platform (*ibid.*, 72).

A wider and long-lived tradition of skull deposition, from the Neolithic onwards, has now been identified in rivers and along the coastline either side of the Severn. One of these skulls, from the Orbs steelworks at Newport, in the Usk river mouth, has been radiocarbon dated to cal. AD 1–180 at 90.8% (Bell *et al.* 2000, 69), whilst at Chapeltump II, long-term curation of human bone could be implied. A human femur and small long-bone fragments were found with a timber post in the area of a coastal occupation scatter, comprising pottery, charcoal, and burnt stone (Locock *et al.* 2000). Radiocarbon dating indicated the bone and the timber to be of Middle Bronze Age date, whilst the charcoal and pottery belonged within the second half of the Late Bronze Age, making it plausible that human bone was used within ancestor-linked rites spanning the Later Bronze and Iron Ages. The discovery of human skulls at Glastonbury Lake Village, beyond the palisade boundary of the settlement (Coles and Minnitt 1995, 203), provides further evidence not so far away, of disarticulated human bone being deposited in wetland contexts.

A number of caves, mostly on Gower, were apparently regarded as appropriate places for periodic human burial, with grave goods and probable votive deposits, between the Middle Bronze Age and the Early Medieval periods (Rutter 1948; Hussey 1964–6; RCAHMW 1976b, 10–21; Branigan and Dearne 1992). Whilst the human bone from Gower remains largely undated either by stratigraphic evidence or by radiocarbon dating, a human mandible from Priory Farm Cave, Pembrokeshire has been radiocarbon dated to the Middle Iron Age (R. Schulting pers. comm.), whilst human and associated dog bones from a sink-hole cave at Alveston, near Bristol, are dated to the Late Iron Age (Aldhouse-Green 2001, 59).

Amongst the more unusual artefacts from caves are a bronze boar figurine from one of the Gower caves (Foster 1977) and a small bronze female figurine from Culver Hole, probably Roman, although 'Celtic' in style (Taylor 1935). The vessel in the All Cannings Cross style from Bacon Hole is exceptional for the region (Appendix 2, no. 7), whilst the penannular brooches and a ring-headed pin from Minchin Hole and Culver Hole (Appendix 1, nos 87, 92, 96) are worthy of note. From the Lesser Garth Cave, Cardiff, a necked jar or flask, derived from Gallo-Belgic butt beakers, probably dates to the mid first century AD (Boon 1964–6). At Ogof-yr-Esgyrn cave, just into Powys, a votive metalwork assemblage in 'Celtic' style of first or second century AD date was deposited in the vicinity of a disturbed area of human bones. These remain undated, but to judge from the artefact discoveries in the cave could be anywhere between Middle Bronze Age and Roman in date (Mason 1968).

No Late Iron Age temples are known from this region, suggesting continued religious practice at non-formalised, naturally significant places. However, we may note a possible cluster of possible Romano-Celtic temples in eastern Monmouthshire and western Gloucestershire at High Nash Coleford, Gwehelog, and Wyndcliff (Walters 1992; Arnold and Davies 2000; Evans 2001, 11), together with the late temple at Lydney. It is possible that early temples may underlie the visible later phases. The tendency for temples to be situated at the borders of territories is now well known (e.g. Stevens 1940; Haselgrove 1987, 137; Brunaux 1988, 3; Bradley 1990, 179–80), so that this distribution may delineate a border zone between the Silures and the Dobunni. On Steepholm Island, an oval-shaped stone-built enclosure with a west-facing entrance has been identified as a possible Roman signal station (Rendell and Rendell 1993), but given the discovery of Late Iron Age brooches, Arretine ware, fragments of Dressel 20 amphora, and a carved stone head of Celtic style (Appendix 1, nos 49–50; Boon 1987; Green 1993), together with its location in a possibly liminal stretch of water between tribal areas, we may speculate upon the presence of a Late Iron Age temple or shrine on the island.

Conclusions

This paper, like many gathering and sorting exercises, is neither elegant nor succinct. In a sense, its length is material witness to the diverse Iron Age evidence now known from south-east Wales, combined with the author's desire to relate new ideas to as near a comprehensive update of these material evidences as possible. Without a commitment to synthesis, based upon periodically reviewed corpora, it is too easy for the significance of short accounts of single discoveries to become dissipated within the mass of archaeological data held within regional journals and small-finds catalogues. So too, records of recent discoveries, now increasingly accessible via the web and significant in number, must be researched by archaeologists, if they wish to write accurate and up-to-date regional archaeologies.

I have sought to make the description and listing of finds the means towards answering questions, rather than an end in itself. In places, there are interpretative weaknesses in the text, whilst undoubtedly some errors in dating and emphasis may have crept in. Despite these, it should be apparent that, far from being a pale and peripheral reflection of events more keenly felt elsewhere, the Iron Age of the region has its own distinctive character, challenges, strengths and potentials. This is true of settlements and hillforts, material culture, exchange, and burial practices.

To return to my title, a recurring concern has been to locate people and material culture through space and time within the Iron Age of south-east Wales. This is groundwork, a necessary amassing of data from which plausible prehistories can be written, and where new ideas may be trialled. It is to be hoped that researchers will take up this challenge and make this region more a focus for informed debate, and less a faint echo or occasional report[8] from the margins.

Acknowledgements

I am particularly grateful to Toby Driver for identifying a number of hillfort and enclosure cropmarks in Monmouthshire from unplotted aerial photographs held by RCHAMW at Aberystwyth. Edward Besly has been generous with his time and in sharing information about the Iron Age coins he has recorded from Wales over recent years. Thanks to Jackie Chadwick and Tony Daly for generating the illustrations. Victoria Newton-Davies, formerly at Newport Museum and Art Gallery, has been generous in allowing me to borrow artefacts for study and illustration. My colleagues, Mark Lodwick, Evan Chapman, and Jody Deacon have allowed me to pester them about recently recorded artefacts, whilst conversations with Caroline Martin have helped me to clarify my own ideas. Finally, I am most grateful to Diane, Sophie, and Erin, for allowing me to spend weekends and evenings getting this research finished!

Notes

1. Identified in the course of X-radiography and curation at NMGW.
2. Interestingly, the shape of the four apotropaic astragali (so called knuckle-bones) on this stock, and others of its kind, is echoed in the tin ingots of knuckle-bone shape found on an undated wreck in Bigbury Bay, south Devon.
3. The discovery here of an electrum bracelet or torc fragment remains remarkable for Wales, perhaps inviting comparison with the precious metalworking evidence from Hengistbury Head (Northover 1987).
4. For a critique of the chronological validity of La Tène art styles in Britain, see Macdonald this volume.
5. But see also Palk (1988, cats 442–5), Spratling (1972, 116–8) and Taylor and Brailsford (1985, cats 43–54).
6. Fitts *et al.* (1999, 48) suggest that the Stanwick/Melsonby deposit may in fact be the remains of a lavish cremation burial akin to that at Folly Lane.
7. As noted above, the Penllyn disc may also form part of this series of deposits, as might the Aberthin strap union.
8. Whether by classical author, or from contemporary archaeologist.

Appendix 1: Iron Age brooches and pins from south-east Wales

Hallstatt brooches

1. Hull and Hawkes Type B; 'Caerleon' (CuA) (NMGW Acc. No. 31.78/116)
2. Hull and Hawkes Type F; 'Tregate Castle' (just into Glos.) (CuA) (Mackreth 1982; Walters 1992, fig. 51)

La Tène (Hull and Hawkes Types 1A–1B)

3–4. Candleston Castle, Merthyr Mawr Warren (2 CuA), 1 Type 1Ab; 1 Type 1Bb (Hull and Hawkes 1987, 84, 104)

5. New School Site, Portskewett (CuA), Type 1Ab (Clarke 1999)

6. Penllyn (CuA), Type 1Aa (M. Lodwick pers. comm.; NMGWPA 2004.143)

7. Newton Moor (CuA), Type 1Ba (Macdonald 2000b)

8. Penllyn Moor (CuA), Type 1B (NMGWPA 2002.4.1)

9. Lodge Wood Camp (Fe), Type 1B (Howell and Pollard 2000, 82; P. Macdonald pers. comm.)

10. Sudbrook (Fe), Type 1B? (Hull and Hawkes 1987, 106)

La Tène I–II (Hull and Hawkes Types 1C, 2Ca–2Cb, 3)

11–29. Twyn y Gaer (19 Fe), 3 Type 1C (B–D); 1 Type 1Cb (C); 3 Type 1C/2A (B-D); 4 Type 1Cb/2A (C-D); 1 Type 2Ca (D); 2 Type 2Cb (F); 5 unidentifiable brooch pins or fragments (Probert 1976; author's identifications)

30. Caerleon Canabae (RB military), (CuA), Type 3B or 3C (Lloyd-Morgan 2000b, cat. 1)

31. Usk (RB military), (CuA), Type 1Ca? (J. Webster 1989, cat. 1)

Late Iron Age (excludes most Conquest and all post-Conquest types)

32–33. Sudbrook (2 CuA) (Nash-Williams 1939, cats 1 & 2)

34. Dinas Powys (CuA), Nauheim (Alcock 1963, cat. 13)

35–36. Thornwell Farm (2 CuA), 1 Drahtfibel/derivative; 1 Nauheim/Drahtfibel derivative (Mackreth 1996, cat. 4, p. 71)

37–38. Caldicot (1 CuA, 1 Fe), 1 Hawkes and Hull Type 6 (Boon in Robinson 1988, cats 1 and 30)

39–44. Mynydd Bychan (6–8 Fe) (Savory 1955, cats 2–7)

45–48. Merthyr Mawr Warren (3 Fe, 1 CuA), 1 Hull and Hawkes Type 6 (author's identification)

49–50. Steep Holm Island (2 CuA) (Boon 1987; Rendell and Rendell 1993)

51. Whitton (Fe), long brooch pin – unknown type (Manning 1981b, cat. 26)

52–61. Usk (RB military), (9 CuA, 1 Fe), 7 one-piece Nauheim derivatives; 1 Colchester A; 1 Kräftig Profilierte; 1 hinged-strip bow brooch (Webster 1995c, cats 1–9, p. 80)

62–63. Caerwent (RB town), (2 CuA), 2 Colchester A (Webster 1995c, 65; 2003, 218)

64–65. Caerleon (RB military, extra mural), (2 CuA) 2 Nauheim derivatives (Lee 1850, pl. 4.7; 1862, pl. 31.6)

66. Caerleon (RB military, amphitheatre), (CuA), Nauheim derivative (Wheeler and Wheeler 1928, cat. 1)

67–68. Loughor (RB military), (2CuA), 2 Nauheim derivatives (Lloyd-Morgan 1997, cats 20 & 23)

69. Cowbridge (RB military/town), (Fe) hinged bow brooch (Scott 1996, cat. 70)

70–71. Abergavenny, Orchard Site (RB military) (2 CuA) 1 Nauheim Derivative, 1 Bagendon C (Webster 1993, cats 1 & 6)

Penannular brooches (Fowler Types A–D; selective, excludes RB military sites)

72. Llanmelin (CuA), Type B (Nash-Williams 1933, 306–7)

73. Thornwell Farm (CuA), Type D5 (Mackreth 1996, cat. 10)

74–75. Biglis (2 CuA), 1 Type D; 1 Type D1 (J. Webster 1988, cats 5 & 6)

76–77. Caldicot (1 Fe, 1 CuA), 1 Type B; 1 Type D6 (Boon in Robinson 1988, cats 8 & 31)

78. Mynydd Bychan (CuA), Type D1 (Savory 1955, cat. 1)

79–83. Whitton (1 Fe, 3 CuA), 1 Type A1; 1 Type D1; 1 Type D1/D4; 1 Type D1/D2, 1 penannular brooch pin (J. Webster 1981, cats 29–31 & p. 178; Manning 1981b, cat. 25)

84. Sudbrook (CuA), Type A1 (Nash-Williams 1939, cat. 14)

85. Bishopston Valley (CuA), Type Aa (Williams 1940, cat. 1)

86. Portskewett (CuA), Type Aa (Clarke 1999)

87. Culver Hole (CuA), Type D5 (Rutter 1948, 75; author's identification)

88–91. Merthyr Mawr Warren (3 CuA, 1 unknown), 1 Type A; 1 Type D1; 1 Type D5; 1 unknown (author's identification)

92. Minchin Hole (CuA), Type D2 (Nash-Williams 1946)

93. Cae Summerhouse (Fe), unknown type (Davies 1967a)

Swan's-neck/ring-headed pins

94–95. Candleston Castle, Merthyr Mawr Warren (1 Fe, 1 CuA) (Savory 1976b, cat. 62.) N.B. There is also a CuA pin with expanded head and curved neck from Merthyr Mawr – a disc-headed pin (?) without the disc.

96. Minchin Hole Cave (CuA) (Savory 1976b, cat. 78)

97. Gower (CuA) (Savory 1984, 244)

98. Margam Beach (CuA) (NMGW 88.48H/1)

99. Whitton (Fe) (Manning 1981b, cat. 63)

100–104. Llanmaes (5 CuA) (Lodwick and Gwilt 2004)

Appendix 2: Ceramic discoveries from south-east Wales (*c.* 1150 BC–AD 75)

1. Abergavenny, Flannel Street (Savory 1968–9) 2 plain MIA/LIA vessels (illus.).
2. Abergavenny, Castle Street (Savory 1968–9) 1 plain MIA/LIA sherd (illus.).
3. Abergavenny, Dump Site (Savory 1968–9) 1 plain MIA/LIA sherd.
4. Abergavenny, Cross Street (Evans 1995, 15–16) 1 Malvernian fabric jar, 3 native ware jars, LIA/conquest.
5. Abernant Farm (Mein 1997) 1 decorated MIA/LIA sherd.
6. Atlantic Trading Estate, Barry (Gibson 1998) 2 MBA/LBA vessels and undiagnostic sherds.
7. Bacon Hole Cave (Williams 1939b; Savory 1946) EIA vessel (All Cannings Cross style) and MIA/LIA sherds.
8. Biglis (Webster 1988a) 21 decorated MIA/LIA sherds (illus.), 20 plain MIA/LIA sherds (illus.).
9. Bishopston Valley (Williams 1940) single sherd of indeterminate form.
10. Cae Summerhouse (Davies 1966; 1967a) 1 decorated MIA/LIA vessel, plain MIA/LIA sherds.
11. Caerau, Pontir (Wardle 1987) 4 IA sherds.
12. Caerau-super-Ely (Jarvis 1965) 2 IA sherds.
13. Caer Dynnaf (Davies 1967b) sherds MIA/LIA plain vessels, sherds 'Belgic' pottery.
14. Caerleon (Spencer 1983).
15. Caerwent Quarry Site (Figgis 1999, 50) 2 MIA/LIA sherds.
16. Caldicot, Church Farm (Insole 2000) 4 sherds from plain MIA/LIA jar.
17. Caldicot (Spencer 1988) MIA/LIA plain sherds (100 sherds, 2 rims).
18. Caldicot, Castle Lake (Woodward 1997) 6 MBA/LBA illustrated vessels (dendro dates 998/997 BC and 990/989 BC).
19. Castle Ditches, Llancarfan (Hogg 1976) 1 decorated MIA/LIA vessel, 11 illustrated MIA/LIA vessels, 380 sherds.
20. Chapeltump 1 (Whittle 1989) 9 MBA/LBA sherds (C14 date 1330–910 cal. BC).
21. Chapeltump 2 (Woodward 2000a) MBA/LBA sherds (C14 date 1220–820 cal. BC).
22. Coed-y-Cymdda (Savory 1988) 1 illus LBA vessel, 1 decorated MIA vessel (C14 date 410–90 cal. BC).
23. Cold Harbour 1 (Whittle 1989) MBA/LBA sherds (C14 date 1290–910 cal. BC).
24. Collister Pill (Woodward 2000b) 14 sherds ?MBA pottery (C14 date 800–410 cal. BC).
25. Collister Pill Palaeochannel 3 (Woodward 2000b) 3 LBA/EIA illustrated vessels (C14 date 770–380 cal. BC).
26. Crawley Rocks Fort (RCAHMW 1976a, 44–6) single sherd IA pottery.
27. Culver Hole Cave (RCAHMW 1976b, 17) MBA and IA pottery, 165 sherds.
28. Dinas Powys (Alcock 1963) 7 illustrated EIA vessels.
29. Ewenny, Beech Court Farm (Yates 2000a) MIA/LIA sherds.
30. Goldcliff (Allen in Bell *et al.* 2000, 113–7) 1 sherds plain MIA/LIA pottery.
31. Gower Caves (Williams 1939b) 2 MIA/LIA vessels (illus.).
32. Great Pencarn Farm (Sell 2000) 5 undiagnostic IA sherds.
33. Greenmoor Arch, Bishton (Locock and Yates 1999; Locock 1999) MIA sherds (C14 date 550–150 cal. BC at 89.0%).
34. Harding's Down West (Hogg 1973) 3 MIA/LIA vessels, 30 sherds.
35. Lesser Garth Cave (Boon 1964–6) 1 LIA/Conquest 'Belgic' necked jar.
36. Llandough (Webster 1988b) 1 decorated MIA/LIA vessel, 2 plain MIA/LIA vessels.
37. Llanmaes (Lodwick and Gwilt 2004) LBA/EIA vessels, decorated MIA/LIA sherd, plain IA sherds, 50–100 sherds.
38. Llanmelin (Nash-Williams 1933) decorated MIA /LIA vessels, plain MIA/LIA vessels, 'Belgic' forms, 75 catalogued vessels, 500–1000 sherds.
39. Llanmelin Outpost (Nash-Williams 1933) 1 MIA/LIA plain vessel.
40. Llantrithyd (Savory 1977) MBA/LBA sherds.
41. Lodge Wood Camp (Howell and Pollard 2000; 2004, 154–6 & fig. 6.5) MIA plain vessels (La Tène I/A brooch).
42. Maendy Camp (Williams 1902) plain hand-made pottery.
43. Magor, Plot 2, West End (Clarke and Bray 2001) 2 sherds MIA/LIA pottery.

Appendix 3: Iron Age and Greek coins from Wales

Coin references are as follows: BM = Hobbs 1996; BMC II = Allen 1990; BMC III = Allen 1995; CCI = Celtic Coin Index, Oxford. Not included here are 'three early British coins of gold, said to have been found in Glamorganshire' exhibited at the Fourth Annual Meeting of the Cambrian Archaeological Association (Anon. 1850), and a reported find of gold coins of Anted in dredged river silts at The Ham, Monmouthshire, subsequently dismissed by Boon (1970–1) as false.

Western region (Dobunni) gold		
British RA stater, BM 2937		
1. Dinas, nr. Brecon (Powys)	SO1730	Boon 1988, no. 6; De Jersey 1994, 69
Corio stater, BM 3064		
2. Llanthony Abbey (Monmouthshire)	SO 288278	Boon 1988, no. 11; De Jersey 1994, 70; CCI 69.0099; SMR PRN 01741g. British Museum 1919.2.13.
3. Trellech Grange (Monmouthshire) (m/d)	SO 4901	Bray 1998. In private possession.
4. Trellech (Monmouthshire) (m/d)	SO 4903	Bray 1999. In private possession.
Corio quarter stater, BM 3134		
5. St Nicholas (Vale of Glamorgan) (m/d)	ST 0974	NMGWPA 2003.109; CCI 03.0458. In private possession.
Anted stater, BM 3023		
6. Chepstow (Monmouthshire)	ST 533940	Boon 1988, no. 7; De Jersey 1994, 71. Now lost.
7. Dingestow (Monmouthshire)	SO 447110	Boon 1988, no. 8; De Jersey 1994, 71; SMR PRN01546g. In private possession.
8. Tintern (Monmouthshire)	SO 5300	Boon 1988, no. 9; De Jersey 1994, 71; CCI 70.0006. NMGW 70.21H.
9. Itton (Monmouthshire) (m/d)	ST 4995	De Jersey 1994, 71; CCI 91.0463. In private possession.
10. St Arvans (Monmouthshire) (m/d)	ST 513968	Hudson 1994, 50. Newport Museum 94.150
11. Penllyn (Vale of Glamorgan) (m/d)	SS 9975	NMGW unpublished record. NMGW 91.44H.
Catti stater, BM 3057(this coin)		
12. near Chepstow (Monmouthshire)	(ST 5393)	Boon 1988, no. 10; De Jersey 1994, 72; CCI 69.0086; SMR PRN 01177g. British Museum 1851.9.4.1.
13. Mynydd Twyn-glas (Torfaen) (m/d)	ST 2697	De Jersey 1994, 72; CCI 91.0462. NMGW 90.74H
Western region (Dobunni) silver		
Dobunnic B, BM 2953		
14. Magor (Monmouthshire) (m/d)	ST 4387	NMGW unpublished record. In private possession
Eisv, BM 3043		
15. Whitton (Vale of Glamorgan) (excavations)	ST 081713	Boon 1988, no. 13. NMGW 77.40H/1.
16. Caldicot (Monmouthshire) (m/d)	ST474797	Boon 1988, no. 12. NMGW 77.35H.
Kentish		
Kentish Primary potin, BM 660		
17. Merthyr Mawr Warren (Bridgend)	SS 8676	Boon 1988, no. 14; M. Mays pers. comm.
Kentish Primary potin – or Gaulish? BMC III S343 (this coin)		
18. Caerwent, Pound Lane (Monmouthshire)	ST 4790	Boon 1988, no. 15; De Jersey 1999, 213; CCI 89.0215. NMGW 50.190
Eastern region (Trinovantes)		
British LB gold plated stater, BM 338		
19. Porthcasseg (Monmouthshire) (m/d)	ST 5297	NMGW unpublished record. In private possession.
Tasciovanus gold stater, BM 1620		
20. Bassaleg (Newport)	ST 268863	Hudson 1994, 50. Newport Museum 94.94
South-Western (Durotriges)		
Uninscribed silver plated stater, BM 2525		
21. Llyn-fach, Hirwaun(Neath-Port Talbot)	SN 9003	Boon 1988, no. 4. NMGW 87.45.
Uninscribed bronze stater, BM 2790		
22. Pyle (Bridgend)	SS 8282	Boon 1988, no. 5. NMGW 87.46.

North-Eastern region (Corieltauvi)		
British HA gold stater, BM 182		
23. Dinas, Great Orme's Head	SH 7882	Boon 1988, no. 1. Rapallo House Museum Llandudno.
24. Penbryn (Ceredigion)	SN 2952	Boon 1988, no. 2. Now lost
Eastern region (Catuvellauni)		
Cunobelin, silver, possibly BM 1902		
25. Llandovery Roman Fort (Carmarthenshire)	SN 7735	Boon 1988, no. 3
Southern region (Atrebates)		
Caratacus silver, probably BM 2376		
26. Minffordd, nr. Penrhyndeudraeth (Gwynedd)	SH 5937	Boon 1988, 92. Now lost. Hoard association with nos. 27–28.
Unknown		
Silver, unknown types		
27–28. Minffordd, nr. Penrhyndeudreath (Gwynedd)	SH 5937	Anon. 1850; Boon 1988, 92. Now lost. Hoard association with no. 26.
Central Gaulish		
Tête diabolique potin, BMC III, 287		
29. Llanmelin (Monmouthshire)	ST 4591	Besly and Macdonald 2000; NMGWPA 2000.17.1. In private possession.
Carnutes bronze, BMC III, 128 or 140		
30. Llanfaes (Anglesey)	SH 6078	NMGW 92.244H
Aedui silver, BMC II, 472		
31. Wales (unknown provenance)		De Jersey 1999, 206 (CCI 93.0630)
Unidentified		
32. Usk (Monmouthshire) Private possession	SO 3700	NMGWPA 99.103.1; P. de Jersey pers. comm.
Greek and Carthaginian		
Carmo		
33. Dan-y-Graig, nr. Cross Ash (Monmouthshire)	SO 3820	Milne 1948, 39; SMR PRN 01657g
Poseidonia		
34. Aberdyfi (Gwynedd)	SN 6196	Milne 1948, 39
Carthage		
35. Goldwire Lane, Monmouth (Monmouthshire)	SO 5012	Laing and Laing 1983; SMR PRN 01260g; NMGW 49.468
36. Caerleon (Newport)	ST 3490	Laing and Laing 1983
37. Aberdyfi (Gwynedd)	SN 6196	Milne 1948, 39
Acragas		
38. Caerwent (Monmouthshire)	ST 4790	Milne 1948, 39
Centuripae		
39. Caerwent (Monmouthshire)	ST 4790	Milne 1948, 39
Mamertini		
40. Caerwent (Monmouthshire)	ST 4790	Milne 1948, 39
Syracuse		
41. Caerwent (Monmouthshire)	ST 4790	Milne 1948, 39
Tauromenium		
42. Caerwent (Monmouthshire)	ST 4790	Milne 1948, 39
Alexandria, Augustus		
43. Borth (Ceredigion)	SN 9060	Milne 1948, 41
Syria, tetradrachm of Demetrius		
44. River Usk bed, Newport (Newport)	ST 3286	SMR PRN 00229g

Bibliography

Alcock, L. 1963. *Dinas Powys: An Iron Age, Dark Age and Early Medieval Settlement in Glamorgan*. Cardiff: University of Wales Press.

Aldhouse-Green, M. 2001. *Dying for the Gods: Human Sacrifice in Iron Age and Roman Europe*. Stroud: Tempus Publishing.

Aldhouse-Green, M. and Howell, R. (eds) 2004. *The Gwent County History, Vol. I. Gwent in Prehistory and Early History*. Cardiff: University of Wales Press.

Allason-Jones, L. 1993. Small Finds, in P.J. Casey and J.L. Davies, *Excavations at Segontium (Caernarfon) Roman Fort, 1975–1979*, 165–210. London: Council for British Archaeology Research Report 90.

Allen, D.F. 1990. *Catalogue of the Celtic Coins in the British Museum, Vol. 2. Silver coins of North Italy, South and Central France, Switzerland and South Germany*. London: British Museum Press.

Allen, D.F. 1995. *Catalogue of the Celtic Coins in The British Museum, Vol. 3. Bronze Coins of Gaul*. London: British Museum Press.

Allen, J.R. 1905. Finds of Late-Celtic bronze objects at Seven Sisters, near Neath, Glamorganshire, *Archaeologia Cambrensis* 5 (Ser. 6), 127–146.

Allen, J.R.L. 1996. Three final Bronze Age occupations at Rumney Great Wharf on the Wentlooge Level, *Studia Celtica* 30, 1–16.

Allen, J.R.L. 1998. Late Iron Age and earliest Roman calcite-tempered ware from sites on the Severn Estuary Levels: character and distribution, *Studia Celtica* 32, 27–42.

André, P. 1976. Un lingot de cuivre en Bretagne, *Bulletin of the Board of Celtic Studies* 27 (1), 148–153.

Anon. 1850. Coins, in The Cambrian Archaeological Association, Fourth Annual Meeting, Dolgellau, *Archaeologia Cambrensis* 1 (Ser. 2), 334.

Arnold, C. and Davies, J.L. 2000. *Roman and Early Medieval Wales*. Stroud: Sutton.

Babbidge, A. 1977. Reconnaissance excavations at Coed y Bwnydd, Bettws Newydd, 1969–1971, *The Monmouthshire Antiquary* 3 (3/4), 159–178.

Barber, A., Cox., S. and Hancocks, A. forthcoming. A later Iron Age and Roman farmstead at RAF St Athan, Vale of Glamorgan, Evaluation an excavation 2002–3, *Archaeologia Cambrensis*.

Bell, M. 2000. Environmental Archaeology in the Severn Estuary: Progress and Prospects, in S. Rippon (ed.), *Estuarine Archaeology: The Severn and Beyond; Archaeology in the Severn Estuary* 11, 69–103.

Bell, M. 2001. Interim report on the excavation of a middle Bronze Age settlement at Redwick 2000–1, *Archaeology in the Severn Estuary* 12, 99–117.

Bell, M., Caseldine, A. and Neumann, H. 2000. *Prehistoric Intertidal Archaeology in the Welsh Severn Estuary*. York: Council for British Archaeology Research Report 120.

Bell, M. and Neumann, H. 1999. Intertidal survey, assessment and excavation of a Bronze Age site at Redwick, Gwent 1999, *Archaeology in the Severn Estuary* 10, 25–37.

Besly, E. and Macdonald, P. 2000. Lower Llanmelin, Caerwent (ST 4591), *Archaeology in Wales* 40, 77.

Bevan, B. (ed.) 1999. *Northern Exposure: Interpretative Devolution and the Iron Ages in Britain*. Leicester: Leicester Archaeology Monograph 4.

Bevan, L. 1996. The iron objects, in Hughes 1996, 73–76.

Blockley, K. 1993. Excavations on the Roman Fort at Abergavenny, Orchard Site, 1972–73, *Archaeological Journal* 150, 169–242.

Boon, G.C. 1961. Roman Antiquities at Welshpool, *Antiquaries Journal* 41, 13–31.

Boon, G.C. 1964–6. Roman pottery, in Hussey, 1964–6, 28.

Boon, G.C. 1970–1. A gold stater of Antedrig from Tintern, *The Monmouthshire Antiquary* 3 (2), 62–63.

Boon, G.C. 1974. A 'Worton'-type bronze sword-hilt at Caerleon, *Proceedings of the Prehistoric Society* 40, 205–206.

Boon, G.C. 1977. A Greco-Roman anchor-stock from North Wales, *Antiquaries Journal* 57, 10–30.

Boon, G.C. (ed.) 1978. *Monographs and Collections Relating to Excavations Financed by H.M. Department of the Environment in Wales*. Cardiff: Cambrian Archaeological Association.

Boon, G.C. 1987. Exhibit at ballots: a decorated Arretine sherd from Steepholm, Bristol Channel, *Antiquaries Journal* 67, 375–376.

Boon, G.C. 1988. The coins, in Robinson 1988, 91–92.

Boon, G.C. 1991. Byzantine and other exotic ancient bronze coins from Exeter, in N. Holbrook and P.T. Bidwell, *Roman Finds from Exeter*, 38–45. Exeter: Exeter Archaeological Reports 4.

Boon, G.C. and Lewis, J.M. (eds) 1976. *Welsh Antiquity: Essays mainly on Prehistoric Topics Presented to H.N. Savory*. Cardiff: National Museum of Wales.

Bourke, L. 2001. *Crossing the Rubicon: Bronze Age Metalwork from Irish Rivers*. Galway: Bronze Age Studies 5.

Bradley, R. 1990. *The Passage of Arms: An Archaeological Analysis of Prehistoric Hoards and Votive Deposits*. Cambridge: Cambridge University Press.

Brailsford, J.W. 1975. The Polden Hill Hoard, Somerset, *Proceedings of the Prehistoric Society* 41, 222–234.

Branigan, K. and Dearne, M.J. 1992. *Romano-British Cavemen: Cave Use in Roman Britain*. Oxford: Oxbow Monograph 19.

Brassil, K.S. 1990. A beaded torc fragment from Stalling Down. Unpublished record IA 90.7.

Bray, J. 1998. Trelech area (SO 4804), *Archaeology in Wales* 38, 100.

Bray, J. 1999. Trelech area (SO 4804), *Archaeology in Wales* 39, 86.

Brewer, R.J. 1986. Other objects of bronze, in Zienkiewicz 1986, 172–189.

Britnell, W. 1989. The Collfryn hillslope enclosure, Llansantffraid Deuddwr, Powys: excavations 1980–1982, *Proceedings of the Prehistoric Society* 55, 89–133.

Brown, L. 2000. The regional ceramic sequence, in B. Cunliffe, *The Danebury Environs Programme. The Prehistory of a Wessex Landscape, Vol. 1. Introduction*, 79–127. Oxford: Oxford University Committee for Archaeology Monograph 48.

Brunaux, J.-L. 1988. *The Celtic Gauls: Gods, Rites and Sanctuaries*. London: Seaby.

Burnham, B.C. 1997. Roman mining at Dolaucothi: the implications of the 1991–3 excavations near the Carreg Pumsaint, *Britannia* 28, 325–336.

Caseldine, A. 1990. *Environmental Archaeology in Wales*. Lampeter: Saint David's University College.

Chapman, E. McC. 2003. Portable Antiquities Scheme record NMGW-9D6CA5, www.find.org.uk.

Charlesworth, D. 1967. Glass, in Wainwright 1967, 186–187.

Clarke, S. 1999. *Proposed School Development at Portskewett, Monmouthshire: Archaeological Evaluation*. Unpublished report by Monmouth Archaeology.

Clarke, S. and Bray, J. 2001. Magor, Plot 2, West End (ST 4202 8696), *Archaeology in Wales* 41, 120–121.

Coles, J. and Minnitt, S. 1995. *Industrious and Fairly Civilised. The Glastonbury Lake Village.* Taunton: Somerset Levels Project and Somerset County Council Museums Service.

Collis, J.R. 1975. The coin of Ptolemy V from Winchester, *Antiquity* 49, 47–48.

Collis, J.R. 1994. An Iron Age and Roman cemetery at Owslebury, Hampshire, in A.P. Fitzpatrick and E.L. Morris (eds), *The Iron Age in Wessex: Recent Work*, 106–108. Salisbury: Trust for Wessex Archaeology.

Corcoran, J.X.W.P. 1952. Tankards and tankard handles of the British Early Iron Age, *Proceedings of the Prehistoric Society* 18, 85–102.

Crawford, O.G.S. and Wheeler, R.E.M. 1920–1. The Llynfawr and other hoards of the Bronze Age, *Archaeologia* 71, 133–140.

Crew, P. 1985. Morfa Harlech, Llandanwg (SH 57 32), *Archaeology in Wales* 25, 49.

Crew, P. 1986. Bryn y Castell hillfort – a late prehistoric iron working settlement in north-west Wales, in B.G. Scott and H. Cleere (eds), *The Crafts of the Blacksmith*, 91–100. Belfast: UISPP Comité pour la sidérurgie ancienne.

Crew, P. 1989. Excavations at Crawcwellt West, Merioneth, 1986–1989. A late prehistoric upland iron-working settlement, *Archaeology in Wales* 29, 11–16.

Crew, P. 1990. Late Iron-Age and Roman iron production in north-west Wales, in B.C. Burnham and J.L. Davies (eds), *Conquest, Co-existence and Change; Recent Work in Roman Wales*, 150–160. Lampeter: Trivium 25.

Crew, P. 1995. Aspects of the iron supply, in B. Cunliffe, *Danebury: an Iron Age hillfort in Hampshire, Vol. 6. A Hillfort Community in Perspective*, 276–284. York: Council for British Archaeology Research Report 102.

Cunliffe, B. 1982. Britain, the Veneti and beyond, *Oxford Journal of Archaeology* 1, 39–68.

Cunliffe, B. 1987. *Hengistbury Head, Dorset, Vol. 1. The Prehistoric and Roman Settlement, 3500 BC–AD 500.* Oxford: Oxford University Committee for Archaeology Monograph 13.

Cunliffe, B. 1988. *Mount Batten, Plymouth: A Prehistoric and Roman Port.* Oxford: Oxford University Committee for Archaeology Monograph 26.

Cunliffe, B. 1991. *Iron Age Communities in Britain* (3rd edn). London: Routledge.

Cunliffe, B. 1995. The Celtic chariot: a footnote, in B. Raftery (ed.), *Sites and Sights of the Iron Age. Essays on Fieldwork and Museum Research Presented to Ian Mathieson Stead*, 31–39. Oxford: Oxbow Monograph 56.

Cunliffe, B. 1997. Armorica and Britain: the ceramic evidence, in Cunliffe and De Jersey 1997, 2–71.

Cunliffe, B. 2001. *Facing the Ocean: The Atlantic and its Peoples 8000 BC–AD 1500.* Oxford: Oxford University Press.

Cunliffe, B. and De Jersey, P. 1997. *Armorica and Britain: Cross-Channel Relationships in the Late First Millennium BC.* Oxford: Oxford University Committee for Archaeology Monograph 45.

Cunliffe, B. and Miles, D. (eds) 1984. *Aspects of the Iron Age in Central Southern Britain.* Oxford: Oxford University Committee for Archaeology Monograph 2.

Cunliffe, B. and Poole, C. 2000. *The Danebury Environs Programme. The Prehistory of a Wessex Landscape, Vol. 2 – Part 2. Bury Hill, Upper Clatford, Hants, 1990.* Oxford: Oxford University Committee for Archaeology Monograph 49.

Cunnington, M.E. 1920. Notes on objects from an inhabited site on the Worms Head, Glamorgan, *Archaeologia Cambrensis* 20 (Ser. 6), 251–256.

Davies, A.G. 1964. The Excavations at The Bulwark, Llanmadoc (Glam.), September 1957, *Bulletin of the Board of Celtic Studies* 21 (1), 100–104.

Davies, J.L. 1966. Excavations at Cae Summerhouse, Tythegston, Glam. 1966, *Morgannwg, Transactions of the Glamorgan History Society* 10, 54–59.

Davies, J.L. 1967a. Excavations at Cae Summerhouse, Tythegston, Glam.: Second Interim Report, *Morgannwg, Transactions of the Glamorgan History Society* 11, 75–77.

Davies, J.L. 1967b. Excavations at Caer Dynnaf, Llanblethian, Glam. 1965–1967, *Morgannwg, Transactions of the Glamorgan History Society* 11, 77–78.

Davies, J.L. 1973a. Cae Summerhouse, Tythegston, *Archaeology in Wales* 13, 24–25.

Davies, J.L. 1973b. An excavation at the Bulwarks, Porthkerry, Glamorgan, 1968, *Archaeologia Cambrensis* 122, 85–98.

Davies, J.L. and Lynch, F. 2000. The Late Bronze Age and Iron Age, in F. Lynch, S. Aldhouse-Green and J.L. Davies (eds), *Prehistoric Wales*, 139–219. Stroud: Sutton.

Davies, J.L. and Spratling, M.G. 1976. The Seven Sisters hoard: a centenary study, in Boon and Lewis 1976, 121–147.

Deacon, J. 2003. Portable Antiquities Scheme Record NMGW-3F88F4, www.finds.org.uk.

De Jersey, P. 1994. Gazetteer of findspots of Dobunnic coins, in Van Arsdell 1994, 67–84.

De Jersey, P. 1997. Armorica and Britain: the numismatic evidence, in Cunliffe and De Jersey 1997, 72–108.

De Jersey, P. 1999. Exotic Celtic Coinage in Britain, *Oxford Journal of Archaeology* 18, 189–216.

Driver, T. 1995. New crop mark site at Aberthaw, South Glamorgan, *Archaeology in Wales* 35, 3–9.

Dungworth, D.B. 1996. The production of copper alloys in Iron Age Britain, *Proceedings of the Prehistoric Society* 62, 399–421.

Earwood, C. 1993. *Domestic Wooden Artefacts in Britain and Ireland from Neolithic to Viking times.* Exeter: University of Exeter Press.

Earwood, C. 1997. The wooden artefacts, in Nayling and Caseldine 1997, 204–209.

Evans, D.R. 1995. Excavations at 19 Cross Street Abergavenny 1986, *The Monmouthshire Antiquary* 11, 5–53.

Evans D.R. and Metcalf V.M. 1992. *Roman Gates Caerleon: The 'Roman Gates' Site in the Fortress of the Second Augustan Legion at Caerleon, Gwent.* Oxford: Oxbow Books.

Evans, E. 2000. *The Caerleon Canabae: Excavations in the Civil Settlement 1984–90.* London: Britannia Monograph 16.

Evans, E. 2001. *Romano-British South East Wales Settlement Survey: Final Report, March 2001.* Unpublished GGAT Report 2001/023.

Evans, E. 2002. *A Research Agenda for Wales: Resource Audit, Southeast Wales.* Unpublished GGAT Report 2002/045

Evans, E. and Driver, T. 2000. Fonmon Castle Wood, Rhoose (ST 0445 6822), *Archaeology in Wales* 40, 90.

Feachem, R. 1991. Two quadrilobed harness-mounts from Hambleden, Buckinghamshire, *Antiquaries Journal* 71, 216–220.

Field, N. and Parker Pearson, M. 2003. *Fiskerton: An Iron Age Timber Causeway with Iron Age and Roman Votive Offerings.* Oxford: Oxbow Books.

Figgis, N.P. 1999. *Welsh Prehistory. Catalogue of Accessions in the County and Local Museums of Wales and other Collections*. Machynlleth: Atelier Productions.

Fitts, R.L., Haselgrove, C.C., Lowther, P.C. and Willis, S.H. 1999. Melsonby revisited: survey and excavation 1992–95 at the site of discovery of the "Stanwick", North Yorkshire, hoard of 1843, *Durham Archaeological Journal*, 1–52.

Fitzpatrick, A.P. 1984. The deposition of La Tène Iron Age metalwork in watery contexts in southern England, in Cunliffe and Miles 1984, 178–190.

Foster, J. 1977. *Bronze Boar Figurines in Iron Age and Roman Britain*. Oxford: British Archaeological Reports British Series 39.

Foster, J. 1986. *The Lexden Tumulus: A Re-approaisal of an Iron Age Burial from Colchester, Essex*. Oxford: British Archaeological Reports British Series 156.

Foster, J. 1999. The metal finds, in R. Niblett, *The Excavation of a Ceremonial Site at Folly Lane, Verulamium*, 133–171. London: Britannia Monograph 14.

Fowler, E. 1960. The origins and development of the penannular brooch in Europe, *Proceedings of the Prehistoric Society* 26, 149–177.

Fox, A. 1941. *The Roman Legionary Fortress at Caerleon in Monmouthshire; Report on the Excavations carried out in Myrtle Cottage Orchard in 1939*. Cardiff: National Museum of Wales.

Fox, A. 1952. Hill-slope forts and related earthworks in south-west England and south Wales, *Archaeological Journal* 109, 1–22.

Fox, C. 1925. A 'Late Celtic' bronze mirror from Wales, *Archaeologia Cambrensis* 80, 190–196.

Fox, C. 1927a. A settlement of the Early Iron Age (La Tène I sub-period) on Merthyr Mawr Warren, Glamorgan, *Archaeologia Cambrensis* 82, 44–66.

Fox, C. 1927b. A La Tène I brooch from Wales: with notes on the typology and distribution of these brooches in Britain, *Archaeologia Cambrensis* 82, 67–112.

Fox, C. 1929. La Tène I brooch from Merthyr Mawr, Glamorgan, *Archaeologia Cambrensis* 84, 146–147.

Fox, C. 1946. *A Find of the Early Iron Age from Llyn Cerrig Bach, Anglesey*. Cardiff: National Museum of Wales.

Fox, C. and Hyde, H.A. 1939. A second cauldron and an iron sword from the Llyn Fawr hoard, Rhigos, Glamorganshire, *Antiquaries Journal* 19, 369–404.

Fox, S. 1993. Objects of copper alloy, in J.D. Zienkiewicz, Excavations in the *Scamnum Tribunorum* at Caerleon: The Legionary Museum Site 1983–5, *Britannia* 24, 106–114 (27–140).

Francis, G.G. 1871–2. Appendix: On ancient bronze helmets found in 1818 at Ogmore Down, Glamorganshire, *Archaeologia* 43, 553–536

Gibson, A. 1998. The prehistoric pottery, in S.H. Sell, Excavations of a Bronze Age settlement at the Atlantic Trading Estate, Barry, South Glamorgan, *Studia Celtica* 32, 12–20.

Graves-Brown, P. 1997. *River Thaw Valley Project*. Unpublished GGAT Report Cur. 6.

Green, M. 1993. A carved stone head from Steep Holm, *Britannia* 24, 241–242.

Greene, K. 1993. Part I; The Fortress coarse ware, in W.H. Manning (ed.), *Report on the Excavations at Usk 1965–1976: The Roman Pottery*, 3–124. Cardiff: University of Wales Press.

Greep, S. 2000. Objects of shale, in Evans 2000, 444–448.

Griffith, Rev. J. 1906. Hen Dre'r Gelli: A buried prehistoric town in the Rhondda valley, *Archaeologia Cambrensis* 6 (Ser. 6), 281–307.

Grimes, W.F. and Hyde, H.A. 1935. A prehistoric hearth at Radyr, Glamorgan, and its bearing on the nativity of beech (*Fagus sylvatica l.*) in Britain, *Transactions of the Cardiff Naturalists' Society* 68, 46–54.

Guido, M. 1978. *The Glass Beads of the Prehistoric and Roman Periods in Britain and Ireland*. London: Reports of the Research Committee of the Society of Antiquaries of London 35.

Guilbert, G. 1979. Dinorben 1977–8, *Current Archaeology* 65, 182–188.

Gwilt, A. 1997. Spiral ring from Newton, near Cowbridge. Unpublished record IA 97.1.

Gwilt, A. 2003. Understanding the Iron Age: towards an agenda for Wales, in C.S. Briggs (ed.), *Towards a Research Agenda for Welsh Archaeology. Proceedings of the IFA Wales/Cymru Conference, Aberystwyth 2001*, 105–122. Oxford: British Archaeological Reports British Series 343.

Gwilt, A. and Haselgrove, C. (eds) 1997. *Reconstructing Iron Age Societies*. Oxford: Oxbow Monograph 71.

Gwilt, A. and Webster, P.V. 2001. The pottery, in Sell 2001, 128–134.

Gwilt, A., Bell, M., Cardy, B., Davis, M., Lodwick, M., Makepeace, G., Northover, P., Olding, F., Sharples, N. and Yates, A. 2003. *A Research Framework for the Archaeology of Wales; south-east Wales – later prehistory*, http://www.cpat.org.uk/research/selpre.htm.

Hambleton, E. 1999. *Animal Husbandry Regimes in Iron Age Britain: A Comparative Study of Faunal Assemblages from British Iron Age Sites*. Oxford: British Archaeological Reports British Series 282.

Haselgrove, C. 1987. *Iron Age Coinage in South-East England: The Archaeological Context*. Oxford: British Archaeological Reports British Series 174.

Haselgrove, C. 1999. The Iron Age, in J. Hunter and I. Ralston (eds), *The Archaeology of Britain: An Introduction from the Upper Palaeolithic to the Industrial Revolution*, 113–134. London: Routledge.

Haselgrove, C. 2006. Early potin coinage in Britain: an update, in P. de Jersey (ed.), *Celtic Coinage: New Discoveries, New Discussion*, 17–27. Oxford: British Archaeological Reports International Series 1532.

Haselgrove, C., Armit, I., Champion, T., Creighton, J., Gwilt, A., Hill, J.D., Hunter, F. and Woodward. A. 2001. *Understanding the British Iron Age: An Agenda for Action*. Salisbury: Wessex Archaeology.

Hawkes, C.F.C. 1951. Bronze-workers, cauldrons and bucket-animals in Iron Age and Roman Britain, in W.F. Grimes (ed.), *Aspects of Archaeology in Britain and Beyond: Essays presented to O.G.S. Crawford*, 172–199. London: H.W. Edwards.

Hawkes, C.F.C. 1984. Ictis disentangled, and the British tin trade, *Oxford Journal of Archaeology* 3, 211–233.

Henderson, J. 1987a. The Iron Age of 'Loughey' and Meare: some inferences from glass analysis, *Antiquaries Journal* 67, 29–42.

Henderson, J. 1987b. The archaeology and technology of glass from Meare Village East, in J.M. Coles, *Meare Village East: The Excavations of A. Bulleid and H. St George Gray 1932–1956*, 170–182. Exeter: Somerset Levels Papers 13.

Henderson, J. 1987c. Glass working, in Cunliffe 1987, 180–186.

Henderson, J. 1991. Industrial specialisation in late Iron Age Britain and Europe, *Archaeological Journal* 148, 104–148.

Henig, M. 1996. The bronze head, in Hughes 1996, 71.

Hill, J.D. 1995. The pre-Roman Iron Age in Britain and Ireland (*c.* 800 BC to AD 100): an overview, *Journal of World Prehistory* 9, 47–98.

Hill, J.D. 1997. 'The end of one kind of body and the beginning of another kind of body'? Toilet instruments and Romanization, in Gwilt and Haselgrove 1997, 96–107.

Hingley, R. 1997. Iron, ironworking and regeneration: a study of the symbolic meaning of metalworking in Iron Age Britain, in Gwilt and Haselgrove 1997, 9–18.

Hingley, R. 2005. Iron Age 'currency bars' in Britain: items of exchange in liminal contexts, in C. Haselgrove and D. Wigg-Wolf (eds), *Iron Age Coinage and Ritual Practices*, 183–205. Mainz: Studien zu Fundmünzen der Antike 20.

Hobbs, R. 1996. *British Iron Age Coins in the British Museum*. London: British Museum Press.

Hogg, A.H.A. 1972. The size-distribution of hill-forts in Wales and the Marches, in F. Lynch and C. Burgess (eds), *Prehistoric Man in Wales and the West: Essays in Honour of Lily F. Chitty*, 293–305. Bath: Adams and Dart.

Hogg, A.H.A. 1973. Excavations at Harding's Down West fort, Gower, *Archaeologia Cambrensis* 122, 55–68.

Hogg, A.H.A. 1974. The Llantwit Major Villa: a reconsideration of the evidence, *Britannia* 5, 225–250.

Hogg, A.H.A. 1976. Castle Ditches, Llancarfan, Glamorgan, *Archaeologia Cambrensis* 125, 13–39.

Hogg, A.H.A. 1979. *British Hill-Forts: An Index, Occasional Papers of the Hill-Fort Study Group No. 1*. Oxford: British Archaeological Reports British Series 62.

Howell, J.K. 2001. Rhoose, 'Bronze Site' carpark, Cardiff International Airport (ST 068 680), *Archaeology in Wales* 41, 127–129.

Howell, R. and Pollard, J. 2000. Caerleon, Lodge Wood Camp (ST 323 914), *Archaeology in Wales* 40, 81–83.

Howell, R. and Pollard, J. 2004. The Iron Age: settlement and material culture, in Aldhouse-Green and Howell 2004, 140–159.

Hudson, R. 1977. Roman coins from the Severn estuary at Portskewett, *The Monmouthshire Antiquary* 3 (3/4), 179–185.

Hudson, R. 1994. Newport Museum, recent acquisitions, *Archaeology in Wales* 34, 50.

Hughes, G. 1996. *The Excavation of a Late Prehistoric and Romano-British Settlement at Thornwell Farm, Chepstow, Gwent, 1992*. Oxford: British Archaeological Reports British Series 244.

Hughes, H. 1909. Note: Sword found at Gelliniog Wen, Anglesey, *Archaeologia Cambrensis* 9 (Ser. 6), 256–257.

Hughes, H.H. 1934. A Bronze Mount from Braich-y-Dinas, Penmaenmawr, *Archaeologia Cambrensis* 89, 174–176.

Hull, M.R. and Hawkes, C.F.C. 1987. *Corpus of Ancient Brooches in Britain*. Oxford: British Archaeological Reports British Series 168.

Hunter, F. 1997. Iron Age hoarding in Scotland and northern England, in Gwilt and Haselgrove 1997, 108–133.

Hussey, M.S. 1964–6. Final excavations at the Lesser Garth Cave, Pentyrch, *Transactions of the Cardiff Naturalists' Society* 93, 18–36.

Insole, P. 2000. The archaeological excavation of a Romano-British farmstead at Church Farm, Church Road, Caldicot, Monmouthshire, *Archaeology in Wales* 40, 20–33.

Jackson, D. 1999. Variation in the size distribution of hillforts in the Welsh Marches and its implication for social organisation, in Bevan 1999, 197–216.

Jackson, R. 1990. *Camerton: The Late Iron Age and Early Roman Metalwork*. London: British Museum Publications.

Jarrett, M.G. 1969. *The Roman Frontier in Wales* (2nd edn). Cardiff: University of Wales Press.

Jarrett, M.G. and Mann, J.C. 1968–9. The tribes of Wales, *Welsh History Review* 4 (2), 161–174.

Jarrett, M.G. and Wrathmell, S. 1981. *Whitton: An Iron Age and Roman Farmstead in South Glamorgan*. Cardiff: University of Wales Press.

Jarvis, P.H. 1965. Caerau-super-Ely, *Archaeology in Wales* 5, 17.

Johns, C. 1996. *The Jewellery of Roman Britain: Celtic and Classical Traditions*. London: University College London Press.

Jones, J.E. 1985. Museum of Welsh Antiquities, Bangor: Work on the collections and exhibitions, an archaeological catalogue and recent archaeological accessions, *Archaeology in Wales* 25, 5–7.

Jones, B. and Mattingly, D. 1990. *An Atlas of Roman Britain*. Oxford: Blackwell.

Jope, E.M. 2000. *Early Celtic Art in the British Isles* . Oxford: Clarendon Press.

Laing, L.R. 1968. A Greek tin trade with Cornwall?, *Cornish Archaeology* 7, 15–23.

Laing, J. and Laing, L. 1983. A mediterranean trade with Wirral in the Iron Age, *Cheshire Archaeological Bulletin* 9, 6–8.

Lawson, A.J. 1981. Shale objects, in Jarrett and Wrathmell 1981, 225–226.

Lee, J.E. 1850. *Description of a Roman Building and Other Remains Lately Discovered at Caerleon*. London: J.R. Smith.

Lee, J.E. 1862. *Isca Silurum: Or an Illustrated Catalogue of the Museum of Antiquities at Caerleon*. London: Lonman, Green and Roberts.

Lloyd-Morgan, G. 1995. Items of copper alloy, in Evans 1995, 37–43.

Lloyd-Morgan, G. 1997. Objects of copper alloy and silver, in A.G. Marvell and H.S. Owen-John, *Leucarum: Excavations at the Roman Auxiliary Fort at Loughor, West Glamorgan 1982–84 and 1987–88*, 234–273. London: Britannia Monograph 12.

Lloyd-Morgan, G. 2000a. Other objects of copper alloy, in Evans 2000, 344–386.

Lloyd-Morgan, G. 2000b. Other jewellery and dress accessories in gold, silver and copper alloy, in Evans 2000, 328–344.

Locock, M. 1999. Iron Age and later features at Greenmoor Arch (Gwent Europark), Newport, *Archaeology in the Severn Estuary* 10, 128–130.

Locock, M. 2000. *Uplands archaeology in Glamorgan and Gwent: a review of progress, 1989–1999*. Unpublished GGAT Report 2000/04.

Locock, M., Trett, R. and Lawler, M. 2000. Further Late Prehistoric Features on the Foreshore at Chapeltump, Magor, Monmouthshire: Chapeltump II and the Upton Trackway, *Studia Celtica* 34, 17–48.

Locock, M. and Yates, A. 1999. Greenmoor Arch, Bishton (ST 400 866), *Archaeology in Wales* 39, 88.

Lodwick, M. 2002. Portable Antiquities Scheme record number NMGWPA 2002.68.2, www.finds.org.uk.

Lodwick, M. 2003a. Portable Antiquities Scheme record number NMGW-FD38C2, www.finds.org.uk.

Lodwick, M. 2003b. Portable Antiquities Scheme record number NMGW-DA9283, www.finds.org.uk.

Lodwick, M. 2003c. Portable Antiquities Scheme record number NMGW-2FC205, www.finds.org.uk.

Lodwick, M. and Gwilt, A. 2004. Cauldrons and consumption: Llanmaes and Llyn Fawr, *Archaeology in Wales* 44, 77–81.

Lynch, F. 1986. *Museum of Welsh Antiquities, Bangor: Catalogue of Archaeological Material*. Bangor: University College of North Wales.

Macdonald, P. 1999a. St Brides Major (SS 90 75), *Archaeology in Wales* 39, 94.

Macdonald, P. 1999b. Portable Antiquities Scheme record NMGW-99.34.6, www.finds.org.uk.

Macdonald, P. 1999c. Portable Antiquities Scheme record NMGW-99.96.1, www.finds.org.uk.

Macdonald, P. 1999d. Portable Antiquities Scheme record NMGW-99.79.1, www.finds.org.uk.

Macdonald, P. 2000a. St Brides Major (SS 90 75), *Archaeology in Wales* 40, 93–94.

Macdonald, P. 2000b. Newton Moor, Penllyn (SS 98 75), *Archaeology in Wales* 40, 91–92.

Macdonald, P. 2001. Aberthin, Cowbridge (ST 00 75), *Archaeology in Wales* 41, 127.

Macdonald, P. and Davis, M. 2002. Old Castle Down revisited: some recent finds from the Vale of Glamorgan, in M. Aldhouse-Green and P. Webster (eds), *Artefacts and Archaeology: Aspects of the Celtic and Roman World*, 20–32. Cardiff: University of Wales Press.

Macdonald, P. and Young, T. 1995. Llyn Cerrig Bach: Field Survey 1995, *Archaeology in Wales* 35, 20–24.

MacGregor, M. 1962. The early Iron Age metalwork hoard from Stanwick, N.R. Yorks., *Proceedings of the Prehistoric Society* 28, 17–57.

MacGregor, M. 1976. *Early Celtic Art in North Britain: a Study of Decorative Metalwork from the Third Century BC to the Third Century AD*. Leicester: Leicester University Press.

Mackreth, D. 1982. Tregate Castle Mystery, *Monmouth Archaeology* 9, 1–2.

Mackreth, D. 1996. The copper alloy brooches, in Hughes 1996, 67–73.

Manley, J. and Grenter, S. 1987. An amphora from Rhos-on-Sea, Clwyd, *Britannia* 18, 284–285.

Manning, W.H. 1972. Ironwork hoards in Iron Age and Roman Britain, *Britannia* 3, 224–250.

Manning, W.H. 1981a. *Report on the excavations at Usk 1965–1976: The Fortress Excavations 1968–1971*. Cardiff: University of Wales Press.

Manning, W.H. 1981b. Ironwork, in Jarrett and Wrathmell 1981, 188–201.

Manning, W.H. 1995. *Report on the Excavations at Usk 1965–1976: The Roman Small Finds*. Cardiff: University of Wales Press.

Manning, W.H. 2002. Early Roman campaigns in the south-west of Britain, in R.J. Brewer (ed.), *The Second Augustan Legion and the Roman Military Machine*, 27–44. Cardiff: National Museums and Galleries of Wales.

Manning, W.H. 2004. The Romans: conquest and the army, in Aldhouse-Green and Howell 2004, 178–204.

Mariën, M.E. 1961. *La Période de la Tène en Belgique: Le Groupe de la Haine*. Brussels: Monographies d'Archéologie Nationale 2.

Martin, C. 2003. *Iron Age Artefacts in Wales: An Investigation into the Material Culture of South-East Wales during the Pre-Roman Iron Age*. Oxford: British Archaeological Reports British Series 353.

Marvell, A. 1988. Usk (ST 3770 0062), *Archaeology in Wales* 28, 55.

Marvell, A. 2004. Roman Settlement and Economy, in Nayling and McGrail 2004, 91–110.

Mason, E.J. 1968. Ogof-yr-Esgyrn, Dan-yr-Ogof caves, Brecknock, excavations 1938–50, *Archaeologia Cambrensis* 117, 18–71.

Matthews, K.J. 1999. The Iron Age of north-west England and Irish Sea trade, in Bevan 1999, 173–195.

McGrail, S. 1997. The boat fragments, in Nayling and Caseldine 1997, 210–214.

Megaw, J.V.S., Megaw, M.R. and Trett, R. 1992. A Late Iron Age cast bronze head probably from Chepstow, *Antiquaries Journal* 72, 54–75.

Mein, A.G. 1992. Excavations at Trostrey Castle, Usk, Gwent, *Archaeology in Wales* 32, 11–14.

Mein, A.G. 1994. Trostrey, Trostrey Castle (SO 3605 0435), *Archaeology in Wales* 34, 48–50.

Mein, A.G. 1996. Trostrey Castle, Trostrey (SO 3595 0435), *Archaeology in Wales* 36, 64–66.

Mein, A.G. 1997. Abernant Farm, Kemeys Inferior (ST 3710 9175), *Archaeology in Wales* 37, 71.

Mein, A.G. 2001. Trostrey Castle, Trostrey (SO 3605 0435), *Archaeology in Wales* 41, 121–123.

Milne, J.G. 1948. *Finds of Greek Coins in the British Isles: The Evidence Reconsidered in the Light of the Rackett Collection from Dorset*. London: Oxford University Press.

Morris, E.L. 1996. Iron Age artefact production and exchange, in T.C. Champion and J.R. Collis (eds), *The Iron Age in Britain and Ireland: Recent Trends*, 41–65. Sheffield: J.R. Collis Publications.

Murphy, K. and Williams, G. 1992. Appendix: Gazetteer of Iron Age burials in Wales, in K. Murphy, Plas Gogerddan, Dyfed: A multi-period burial and ritual site, *Archaeological Journal* 149, 30–35 (1–38).

Musson, C.R. 1991. *The Breiddin Hillfort: A Later Prehistoric Settlement in the Welsh Marches*. London: Council for British Archaeology Research Report 76.

Mytum, H. 1989. Excavation at Castell Henllys, 1981–89: The Iron Age fort, *Archaeology in Wales* 29, 6–10.

Mytum, H. 1999. Castell Henllys, *Current Archaeology* 161, 164–172.

Nash-Williams, V.E. 1932. Harness-trapping from Chepstow, Monmouthshire, *Archaeologia Cambrensis* 87, 393–394.

Nash-Williams, V.E. 1933. An Early Iron Age hill-fort at Llanmelin, near Caerwent, Monmouthshire, *Archaeologia Cambrensis* 88, 237–346.

Nash-Williams, V.E. 1939. An Early Iron Age coastal camp at Sudbrook, near the Severn Tunnel, Monmouthshire, *Archaeologia Cambrensis* 94, 42–79.

Nash-Williams, V.E. 1946. Early Iron Age and Roman pottery and other objects from Minchin Hole, Gower, *Bulletin of the Board of Celtic Studies* 12, 62–63.

Nash-Williams, V.E. 1950. The Roman gold-mines at Dolaucothi (Carm.), *Bulletin of the Board of Celtic Studies* 14 (1), 79–84.

Nayling, N. and Caseldine, A. 1997. *Excavations at Caldicot, Gwent: Bronze Age Palaeochannels in the Lower Nedern Valley*. York: Council for British Archaeology Research Report 108.

Nayling, N. and McGrail, S. 2004. *The Barland's Farm Romano-Celtic Boat*. York: Council for British Archaeology Research Report 138.

Newman, R. 1990. Excavations of a Romano-British building at Dan-y-Graig, Porthcawl, Mid Glamorgan (SS 8407 7805), *Bulletin of the Board of Celtic Studies* 37 (3), 247–280.

Northover, J.P. 1987. Non-ferrous metallurgy, in Cunliffe 1987, 186–196.

Northover, J.P. 1997. The metalwork, in Nayling and Caseldine 1997, 249–253.

Northover, J.P. 1998. Analysis of a simple terret. Unpublished report R861.

Owen-John, H. 1988a. A hill-slope enclosure in Coed y Cymdda, near Wenvoe, South Glamorgan, *Archaeologia Cambrensis* 137, 43–98.

Owen-John, H. 1988b. Llandough: The rescue excavation of a multi-period site near Cardiff, South Glamorgan, in Robinson 1988, 125–177.

Palk, N.A. 1988. *Metal Horse Harness of the British and Irish Iron Ages*. Unpublished D.Phil. thesis, University of Oxford.

Parkhouse, J. 1988. Excavations at Biglis, South Glamorgan, in

Robinson 1988, 3–64.

Peacock, D.P.S. 1969. A contribution to the study of Glastonbury ware from south-western Britain, *Antiquaries Journal* 49, 41–61.

Piggott, S. 1950. Swords and scabbards of the British Early Iron Age, *Proceedings of the Prehistoric Society* 16, 1–28.

Probert, L.A. 1976. Twyn-y-Gaer hill-fort, Gwent: an interim assessment, in Boon and Lewis 1976, 105–119.

Probert, L.A. 1982. *Twyn-y-Gaer hill-fort.* Unpublished typescript.

Probert, L.A., Davies, J.L., Savory, H.N., Boon, G.C., Greene, K.T. and Spratling, M.G. 1968–9. Excavations at Abergavenny 1962–1969; I. Prehistoric and Roman finds, *The Monmouthshire Antiquary* 2 (4), 163–198.

Pryor, F. 2001. *The Flag Fen Basin: Archaeology and Environment of a Fenland Landscape.* Swindon: English Heritage Archaeological Reports.

Rendell, S. and Rendell, J. 1993. Steep Holm – A brief summary of archaeological research, *Archaeology in the Severn Estuary* 3, 47–54.

Roberts, R. 1998. Rogiet, Manor House Farm (ST 456 876), *Archaeology in Wales* 38, 121.

Rippon, S. 1997. *The Severn Estuary: Landscape Evolution and Wetland Reclamation.* Leicester: Leicester University Press.

Robinson, D.M. (ed.). 1988. *Biglis, Caldicot and Llandough: Three Late Iron Age and Romano-British Sites in South-East Wales.* Oxford: British Archaeological Reports British Series 188.

RCAHMW 1976a. *An Inventory of the Ancient Monuments in Glamorgan, Vol. I. Pre-Norman. Part II The Iron Age and the Roman Occupation.* Cardiff: HMSO.

RCAHMW 1976b. *An Inventory of the Ancient Monuments in Glamorgan, Vol. I. Pre-Norman. Part I The Stone and Bronze Ages.* Cardiff: HMSO.

Rutter, J.G. 1948. *Prehistoric Gower.* Swansea: Welsh Guides.

Savory, H.N. 1946. Early Iron Age pottery from the Bacon Hole Cave, Gower, *Bulletin of the Board of Celtic Studies* 12 (1–3), 61.

Savory, H.N. 1951. Discoveries on Merthyr Mawr Warren (Glam.), *Bulletin of the Board of Celtic Studies* 14 (2), 170–171.

Savory, H.N. 1952. Bronze figurine from Abercarn (Mon.), *Bulletin of the Board of Celtic Studies* 15 (1), 72–73.

Savory, H.N. 1952–53. An ancient settlement on Merthyr Mawr Warren (Glam.), *Transactions of the Cardiff Naturalists' Society* 82, 42–43.

Savory, H.N. 1954a. The excavation of an Early Iron Age fortified settlement on Mynydd Bychan, Llysworney (Glam.), 1949–50: Part I, *Archaeologia Cambrensis* 103, 85–108.

Savory, H.N. 1954b. Early Iron Age discoveries on Merthyr Mawr Warren (Glam.), *Bulletin of the Board of Celtic Studies* 16 (1), 53–54.

Savory, H.N. 1955. The excavation of an Early Iron Age fortified settlement on Mynydd Bychan, Llysworney (Glam.), 1949–50: Part II, *Archaeologia Cambrensis* 104, 14–51.

Savory, H.N. 1961. Gold spiral ring from Whitchurch (Glam.), *Bulletin of the Board of Celtic Studies* 19 (2), 173

Savory, H.N. 1966. A find of Early Iron Age metalwork from the Lesser Garth, Pentyrch (Glam.), *Archaeologia Cambrensis* 115, 27–44.

Savory, H.N. 1968–9. The prehistoric material, in Probert *et al.* 1968–9, 170–173.

Savory, H.N. 1969. The excavation of the Marlborough Grange Barrow, Llanblethian (Glam.), 1967, *Archaeologia Cambrensis* 118, 49–72.

Savory, H.N. 1974. An Early Iron Age metalworker's mould from Worms Head, *Archaeologia Cambrensis* 123, 170–174.

Savory, H.N. 1976a. Welsh hillforts: A reappraisal of recent research, in D.W. Harding (ed.), *Hillforts, Later Prehistoric Earthworks in Britain and Ireland*, 237–291. London: Academic Press.

Savory, H.N. 1976b. *Guide Catalogue of the Early Iron Age Collections.* Cardiff: National Museum of Wales.

Savory, H.N. 1976c. The harness ring, in Hogg 1976, 30–31.

Savory, H.N. 1977. The prehistoric finds, in P. Charlton, J. Roberts and V. Vale (eds), *Llantrithyd: A Ringwork in South Glamorgan*, 57–60. Cardiff: Cardiff Archaeological Society.

Savory, H.N. 1980. *Guide Catalogue of the Bronze Age Collections.* Cardiff: National Museum of Wales.

Savory, H.N. (ed.) 1984., *Glamorgan County History, Vol. 2. Early Glamorgan, Pre-History and Early History*, Cardiff: University of Wales Press.

Savory, H.N. 1988. Prehistoric pottery, in Owen-John 1988a, 87–93.

Savory, H.N. 1993. Strap hook, in Blockley 1993, 211–214.

Scott, I. 1992. The objects of iron, in Evans and Metcalf 1992, 164–174.

Scott, I. 1996. Other objects of iron, in J. Parkhouse and E. Evans (eds), *Excavations at Cowbridge, South Glamorgan, 1977–88*, 198–205. Oxford: British Archaeological Reports British Series 245.

Scott, I. 2000. Objects of iron, in Evans 2000, 386–407.

Sell, S.H. 2000. Pre-Roman pottery, in A.M. Yates, Excavations of a Roman Site South of Great Pencarn Farm, 1997: Coedkernew, Newport, *Studia Celtica* 34, 60 (49–80).

Sell, S.H. 2001. Recent excavation and survey work at Sudbrook Camp, Portskewett, Monmouthshire (ST 507873), *Studia Celtica* 35, 109–141.

Sellwood, L. 1984. Tribal boundaries viewed from the perspective of numismatic evidence, in Cunliffe and Miles 1984, 191–204.

Simpson, M. 1972. An Iron Age tankard fragment from Caerwent, *Antiquaries Journal* 52, 330–331.

Spencer, B. 1983. Limestone-tempered pottery from south Wales in the Late Iron Age and early Roman period, *Bulletin of the Board of Celtic Studies* 30 (3/4), 405–419.

Spencer, B. 1988. The coarse pottery, in Robinson 1988, 102–118.

Spratling, M.G. 1968–69. A bronze loop-shanked triskele pendant from Flannel Street, in Probert *et al.* 1968–9, 196–198.

Spratling, M.G. 1972. *Southern British Decorated Bronzes of the Late Pre-Roman Iron Age.* Unpublished Ph.D. thesis, Institute of Archaeology, University of London.

Spratling, M.G. 1981. Enamelled bronze boss, in Jarrett and Wrathmell, 1981, 180–182.

Spratling, M.G. 1989. Report on the bronze linchpin, in Britnell 1989, microfiche 2.9.

Standley, E. 2005. *Iron Age Glass Beads from South-East Wales: Iron Age Glass Beads from Glamorgan and Gwent Described, Catalogued and Interpreted.* Unpublished B.A. dissertation, University of Durham.

Stanford, S.C. 1974. *Croft Ambrey.* Leominster: privately published.

Stead, I.M. 1982. The Cerrig-y-Drudion 'Hanging Bowl', *Antiquaries Journal* 62, 221–234.

Stead, I.M. 1985. *The Battersea Shield*, London: British Museum Publications.

Stead, I.M. 1991. *Iron Age Cemeteries in East Yorkshire.* London: English Heritage Archaeological Report 22.

Stead, I.M. 1995. The metalwork, in K. Parfitt, *Iron Age Burials from Mill Hill, Deal*, 58–111. London: British Museum Press.

Stead, I.M. and Rigby, V. 1986. *Baldock; The Excavation of a Roman and Pre-Roman Settlement, 1968–72*. London: Britannia Monograph 7.

Stevens, C.E. 1940. The Frilford site – a postscript, *Oxoniensia* 5, 166–167.

Taylor, J. 2001. The Isle of Portland: an Iron Age port-of-trade, *Oxford Journal of Archaeology* 20, 187–205.

Taylor, M.V. 1935. Sites explored: Wales, *Journal of Roman Studies* 25, 201–202.

Taylor, R.J. and Brailsford, J.W. 1985. British Iron Age strap-unions, *Proceedings of the Prehistoric Society* 51, 247–272.

Thomas, H. 1958. Moulton ST 074696/7, *Bulletin of the Board of Celtic Studies* 17 (4), 294.

Timberlake, S. 2003. Early mining research in Britain: the developments of the last ten years, in P. Craddock and J. Lang (eds), *Mining and Metal Production Through the Ages*, 21–42. London: British Museum Press.

Toft, L. 1998. The nineteenth-century discovery and loss of the 'Ogmore Helmets', *Archaeologia Cambrensis* 147, 68–79.

Toft, L. 2000. The Ogmore Helmets: Theophilus Redwood's memories of the find-spot, *Archaeologia Cambrensis* 149, 166–169.

Trett, B. and Hudson, R. 1988. Newport Museum, recent acquisitions, *Archaeology in Wales* 28, 56.

Tuck, N.W. and Tuck, J.P. 1971. *Roman Mine, Draethen, Glamorganshire*. Bristol: Bristol Exploration Club Caving Report 15.

Valentin, J. and Robinson, S. 2001. *11A Westgate Street, Cowbridge, Vale of Glamorgan*. Unpublished AC Archaeology Assessment Report 3200/2/0.

Van Arsdell, R.D. 1994. *The Coinage of the Dobunni*. Oxford: Oxford University Committee for Archaeology Monograph 38.

Vyner, B.E. and Allen, D.W.H. 1988. A Romano-British settlement at Caldicot, Gwent, in Robinson 1988, 65–122.

Wainwright, G.J. 1967. *Coygan Camp: A Prehistoric, Romano-British and Dark Age Settlement in Carmarthenshire*. Cardiff: Cambrian Archaeological Association.

Wainwright, G.J. 1971. The Excavation of a Fortified Settlement at Walesland Rath, Pembrokeshire, *Britannia* 2, 48–108.

Wait, G.A. 1985. *Ritual and Religion in Iron Age Britain*. Oxford: British Archaeological Reports British Series 149.

Walker, E.A. 2001. Burry Holms (SS 4001 9247), *Archaeology in Wales* 41, 126.

Walters, B. 1992. *The Archaeology and History of Ancient Dean and the Wye Valley*. Cheltenham: Thornhill Press.

Wardle, P. 1987. Caerau Hillfort, Pontir (SS 329 925), *Archaeology in Wales* 27, 41.

Ward-Perkins, J.B. 1940. Two early linch-pins, from Kings Langley, Herts., and from Tiddington, Stratford-on-Avon, *Antiquaries Journal* 20, 358–367.

Webster, G. 1990. A Late Celtic sword-belt with a ring and button found at Coleford, Gloucestershire, *Britannia* 21, 294–295.

Webster, J. 1981. The brooches, in Jarrett and Wrathmell 1981, 165–178.

Webster, J. 1988. Bronze and silver objects, in Robinson 1988, 53–56.

Webster, J. 1989. The bronzes, in D.R. Evans and V.M. Metcalf, Excavations at 10 Old Market Street, Usk, *Britannia* 20, 52–56.

Webster, J. 1992. The objects of bronze, in Evans and Metcalf 1992, 103–163.

Webster, J. 1993. Objects of copper alloy, in Blockley 1993, 201–210.

Webster, J. 1995a. Harness Fittings, in Manning 1995, 36–41.

Webster, J. 1995b. Cuirass Hook, in Manning 1995, 16–18.

Webster, J. 1995c. The brooches, in Manning 1995, 60–96.

Webster, P.V. 1975. Roman and Iron Age tankards in western Britain, *Bulletin of the Board of Celtic Studies* 26 (2), 231–236.

Webster, P.V. 1981. The pottery, in Jarrett and Wrathmell 1981, 102–145.

Webster, P.V. 1988a. Coarse pottery, in Robinson 1988, 33–47.

Webster, P.V. 1988b. Coarse pottery, in Robinson 1988, 161–171.

Webster, P.V. 1989. Pottery, in Whittle 1989, 219–221.

Webster, P.V. 2003. An early fort at Caerwent? A review of the evidence, in P. Wilson (ed.), *The Archaeology of Roman Towns; Studies in honour of John S. Wacher*, 214–220. Oxford: Oxbow Books.

Wheeler, R.E.M. and Wheeler, T.V. 1928. The Roman amphitheatre at Caerleon, Monmouthshire, *Archaeologia* 128, 111–218.

Wheeler, R.E.M. and Wheeler, T.V. 1932. *Report on the Excavation of the Prehistoric, Roman, and Post-Roman Site in Lydney Park, Gloucestershire*. London: Reports of the Research Committee of the Society of Antiquaries of London 9.

Whittle, A.W.R. 1989. Two Later Bronze Age occupations and an Iron Age channel on the Gwent foreshore, *Bulletin of the Board of Celtic Studies* 36 (3), 200–223.

Williams, A. 1939a. Excavations at The Knave promontory fort, Rhossili, Glamorgan, *Archaeologia Cambrensis* 94, 210–219.

Williams, A. 1939b. Prehistoric and Roman pottery in the museum of the Royal Institution of South Wales, Swansea, *Archaeologia Cambrensis* 94, 21–29.

Williams, A. 1940. The excavation of Bishopston valley promontory fort, Glamorgan, *Archaeologia Cambrensis* 95, 9–19.

Williams, A. 1941. The excavation of High Pennard promontory fort, Glamorgan, *Archaeologia Cambrensis* 96, 23–30.

Williams, H.W. 1902. The exploration of a prehistoric camp in Glamorganshire, *Archaeologia Cambrensis* 2 (Ser. 6), 252–260.

Woodward, A. 1996. The prehistoric and native pottery, in Hughes 1996, 36–45.

Woodward, A. 1997. The Bronze Age pottery, in Nayling and Caseldine 1997, 243–245.

Woodward, A. 2000a. The pottery, in Locock *et al.* 2000, 24–31.

Woodward, A. 2000b. Bronze Age pottery from Collister Pill 3, Peterstone Palaeochannel 2 and Collister Pill Roundhouse, in Bell *et al.* 2000, 311–334.

Yates, A. 2000a. Ewenny, Beech Court Farm prehistoric enclosure, *Archaeology in Wales* 40, 89.

Yates, A. 2000b. Western Valley Trunk Sewer, St Brides (ST 2855 8306 to ST 2895 8153), *Archaeology in Wales* 40, 84.

Young, T. 2001. Ely Roman villa (ST 147 761), *Archaeology in Wales* 41, 130–132.

Zienkiewicz, J.D. 1986. *The Legionary Fortress Baths at Caerleon, II: The Finds*. Cardiff: National Museum of Wales.

Perspectives on insular La Tène art

Philip Macdonald

Two textual or linguistic analogies are in vogue in British archaeology. The first is that archaeology is a textual practice, whilst the second is that material culture can be read as text. The first analogy informs the initial part of this paper, whilst the latter is considered in the final section.

As discourse, archaeology is inescapably situated in the socio-political present and it is impossible to write archaeology without being influenced by the past work of earlier archaeologists. At an interpretative level this leads to contemporary archaeology being unduly influenced by the political outlook and assumptions of past generations. It also has a more prosaic influence, on the typological and stylistic schemes used to classify artefacts and art styles, which manifests itself in a tendency toward conservatism. For example, a museum archaeologist presented with a recently discovered artefact with unusual traits, will, almost invariably, attempt to fit it into a pre-existing scheme rather than add the newly acquired evidence to the pre-existing data and construct a new typology from scratch.

Consequently, classifications develop a stubborn inertia and hold currency and influence long after the point in time when a sober review of the primary evidence would discredit them. This paper argues that the way insular La Tène art is classified and stylistically dated is an example of just such a tendency, which even a brief survey of the evidence suggests can no longer be supported.

Survey of past classifications

Traditionally, the insular La Tène art sequence is classified into an early period of imported and locally produced material decorated along continental lines, which is only represented by a small number of known examples, followed by a peculiarly insular phase divided into two parts and represented by a relatively large and diverse range of artefacts.

This traditional classification has its beginnings in the work of Arthur Evans, who gave the Society of Antiquaries of Scotland's 1895 Rhind Lectures on 'The origins of Celtic art'. These lectures form a landmark in both British and continental Hallstatt and La Tène studies, representing the first time that the British term 'Late Celtic' was equated with the Continental La Tène terminology. Although Evans' lectures were never published, presumably owing to the demands of his growing interest in Aegean archaeology, well-written summaries of each lecture were published in *The Scotsman*.[1] The lectures were well attended and influential; both Romilly Allen and E.T. Leeds referred to them in their later work.

The earlier lectures covered a variety of subjects including the spread of iron technology, the influence of the Graeco-Roman world on Celtic culture, and continental La Tène typologies. In the final lecture, entitled 'Late Celtic art in Britain', Evans considered insular La Tène art and outlined the classificatory scheme that has remained in vogue until today. Evans identified two sequential classes or phases of British Late Celtic remains, both of which he equated with invasions of Brythonic Celts. The beginnings of the first phase, represented by discoveries from East Yorkshire, he dated to the fourth century BC and equated with an initial Belgic colonisation. The second phase, dated to the last two centuries BC, he represented by finds from the Aylesford cemetery and the Glastonbury Lake Village and he equated its introduction with a secondary Belgic invasion.

Evans illustrated his lecture with a wide range of

insular artefacts, although it is not known into which phase he placed the majority of them. Although in an earlier lecture Evans had discussed Hallstatt imports, in his final lecture he did not cite any examples of imported continental La Tène material that may have influenced or prompted the genesis of the insular sequence. However, in a paper on the Broighter hoard, Evans did imply that some early examples of continental style La Tène art were known from the British Isles (Evans 1894–7, 404).

The next significant work on insular La Tène art was Romilly Allen's *Celtic Art in Pagan and Christian Times* (1904), which was largely compiled from articles previously published in *Archaeologia Cambrensis*. The book is disappointingly confused and is especially weak on the stylistic development of what Allen consistently calls Late Celtic art. Allen separates his discussion of the dating of British art from that of its stylistic development and makes no attempt to integrate the two themes. He follows Evans in recognising two main chronological divisions, as represented by the East Yorkshire and Aylesford burial traditions, but in his analysis of the style of Late Celtic art he hardly considers the possibility of change through time.

In a passage influenced by Evans, he does, however, note a tendency to move from the more naturalistic representation of motifs towards a curvilinear geometrical form of ornament, as witnessed by the contrast of the Lisnacrogher sheaths and the designs on the reverse of the southern British mirror series. Allen (*ibid.*, 148–59) unconvincingly parallels this tendency with a hypothetical trend from engraved designs made on a flat surface to designs in relief being made on a flat background and designs executed in the round. Again, albeit weakly stated, the idea of the two-part division of the peculiarly insular La Tène material is repeated.

The idea hinted at by Evans (1894–7, 404), that there was a phase pre-dating the advent of the insular sequence proper, in which a small number of imports or local productions along continental lines circulated and were deposited in the British Isles, was also implied by R.A. Smith (1925, 29; 100), but it was first fully articulated by E.T. Leeds in his *Celtic Ornament in the British Isles down to AD 700* (1933). In this remarkable book, Leeds proposed that there was an initial phase of imports or local productions along continental lines that was associated with the wave of migrants represented by the East Yorkshire burials, and that it inspired and was succeeded by a peculiarly insular phase of art that could be divided into earlier and later stages.

Leeds suggested some defining characteristics for these two insular phases; for the earlier phase, these included motifs recognisably derived from the enclosed palmette, key patterns, tenuous scroll work and faint basketry hatching in small fields (Leeds 1933, 16–40); for the later phase, they included a predilection for 'flamboyant' scrolled decoration frequently filled with hatching, a full realisation of graceful mouldings, *champlevé* and later polychrome enamelwork, and curvilinear motifs with broken-backed curves (*ibid.*, 40–62).

Although few would now support the relative dating of all the artefacts that Leeds discussed within his stylistic scheme, the basic framework that he derived from Evans' work and proposed for classifying the insular La Tène art sequence has remained unchanged ever since. Although subsequent commentators on insular art have varied their approaches to the material, they all employ the same underlying tripartite structure of an early period of imported or home-produced material with only few known artefacts, followed by a peculiarly insular phase divided into two parts.

The next important development was Jacobsthal's (1944) detailed study of the continental sequence up to the end of La Tène II. Jacobsthal's approach, concerned as it was with identifying workshops and styles, was greatly influenced by the Classical art tradition. He defined three styles: the 'Early style', which was principally influenced by Classical art and, to a lesser degree, by native Hallstatt and 'Oriental' sources; the 'Waldalgesheim style' a more mature development of the 'Early style'; and finally two contemporary sub-styles, the 'Sword style' and the 'Plastic style', which overlapped chronologically with the 'Waldalgesheim' style. Despite minor revisions, Jacobsthal's scheme remains fundamental to our appreciation of the continental material and has also been influential in the study of insular La Tène art. In particular, the post-War fixation with defining regional schools and style groups and recognising the products of individual workshops, masters, and pupils is largely due to Jacobsthal's influence.

Sadly, Jacobsthal published little on the subject of insular La Tène art. From De Navarro's summary of La Tène chronology, it seems that Jacobsthal recognised four insular styles: Style I corresponding to the Early style, Style II corresponding to Waldalgesheim, Style III corresponding to both Sword and Plastic styles, and Style IV which, at that time, was related to the initial phase of insular items that were influenced by the continental material previously discussed by Leeds (De Navarro 1943). Stead has suggested that Jacobsthal himself did not approve of the term Style IV (1985a, 19; 1985b, 27), although his objections appear to have been over nomenclature rather than the stylistic uniformity of the material so grouped (Jope 1986, 166).

In a subsequent, popular account, De Navarro (1952) elaborated on the insular scheme by reviewing the evidence and significance of Styles I to III within the insular sequence and detailing a dozen or so examples of the insular Style IV art. Although De Navarro did not specifically define Style IV ornament, he did note some common characteristics, including the execution of motifs in both linear and plastic form; the frequent embellishment of raised ornament with further linear ornament; the prominent use of palmette and tendril or scroll motifs; the occurrence of bird-headed finials on tendril motifs; and the circular rhythm of some designs (*ibid.*, 75). De Navarro also recognised a later insular style of La Tène art, which incorporated the 'Mirror style', and a late Belgic influence manifested in both *champlevé* enamel and naturalistic figural work (*ibid.*, 79–80). Again, although the place of some individual artefacts within the scheme changes, the same basic tripartite structure as before is employed.

In their analysis of the Torrs chamfrein, Atkinson and Piggott (1955) expanded the Jacobsthal/De Navarro Style IV and re-grouped the British pieces into an 'Early School' (or Torrs–Wandsworth style, broadly equivalent to Style IV), which was subdivided into an early phase (Newnham–Torrs) and a later phase (Witham–Wandsworth; *ibid.*, 228–30). They also recognised a separate, and earlier, Cerrig-y-Drudion–Wisbech–Standlake group (*ibid.*, 230–1) which equates with De Navarro's Styles I and II. Although Atkinson and Piggott's scheme was not a full analysis of the insular sequence it was firmly centred on the traditional model employed in defining it.

Subsequent studies of insular La Tène art have also maintained the basic form of this classification. Thus, although Cyril Fox's main concern in *Pattern and Purpose* (1958) was to identify regional schools and workshops, underlying this overly elaborate approach was a broader division of insular art separated into a primary and secondary phase, which largely equated with De Navarro's Style IV and his later insular material (Fox 1958, 22–57). These phases were preceded by a phase of early imported and 'Marnian' material which broadly correlated with those objects we would identify with Jacobsthal's earlier continental styles (*ibid.*, 1–21).

The main text of Martyn Jope's *Early Celtic Art in the British Isles* (2000) was completed by 1972. Although not published at the time, it is within an early 1970s context that the text and its influence on subsequent authors should be assessed (Stead 2000, v). Whilst emphasising a unifying integrity and continuity within the insular La Tène art sequence, Jope's survey follows the conventional pattern of recognising an initial period of continental influence, where foreign ideas were absorbed into insular practice, followed by a truly insular sequence divisible into two broad phases.

The initial phase, which is variously described as 'formative' and the first 'full flowering of distinctive insular styles in early Celtic art', appears in the fourth century BC with a growing sensitivity to the flow of curves and develops by the third century BC with the full spatial shaping of curved surfaces (Jope 2000, 53; 221). Jope largely illustrates the development of this phase with reference to insular La Tène shields (*ibid.*, 53–72).

From the first century BC, this initial phase is succeeded by an 'increasingly vigorous' art, which although regionally varied, still forms a cohesive set of styles interrelated through 'their use of a common basic stock of design and thematic materials' (*ibid.*, 222). Jope illustrates the diversity and character of this second phase with reference to gold work, imagery on the Aylesford and Marlborough buckets, as well as a diversity of insular La Tène metalwork types including swords, mirrors, personal ornament, and coins (*ibid.*, 80–175).

Ian Finlay, whilst influenced by Fox's concern with identifying regional schools, also recognised two main phases of insular La Tène art, preceded by a period of continental imports (Finlay 1973, 79). The pattern is again repeated in the work of the Megaws. Vincent Megaw included a discussion of the British Isles in *Art of the European Iron Age* (Megaw 1970), in which Jacobsthal's Waldagesheim Style is identified, along with a few imported objects, as the foundation of the peculiarly British La Tène art (*ibid.*, 34–5). British art is divided into a 'first step' (equivalent to De Navarro's Style IV), which was succeeded by an 'incised tradition' of 'asymmetrical engraved matting or basketry patterns' that was incorporated within a 'last phase of mainstream British Iron Age art' (*ibid.*, 35–7).

The Megaws' subsequent survey (1989) followed this same structure for the insular sequence. They have a Vegetal style (equated with the Waldalgesheim style), and a number of Sword style and Plastic style elements, which they recognise as forming an early, continental phase of the insular sequence (*ibid.*, 192–3). Their classification of the distinctively insular art begins with what they termed the 'Early La Tène art style of the British Isles' (*ibid.*, 193–202) and it was followed by a 'late insular art' (*ibid.*, 206–28).

The most important recent study of insular La Tène art is Stead's explicit revival and expansion of the Jacobsthal/De Navarro scheme in his books on *Celtic Art in Britain before the Roman Conquest* (Stead 1985a, 15–23) and the *Battersea Shield* (Stead 1985b, 27–36). Stead made little or no revision to the definition of the first three continental style groupings, although the identification of the Cerrig-y-Drudion, Denbighshire, decorated bronze fragments, and the bronze sheath or scabbard plate from the collection of 'Philosopher' Smith of Wisbech, Cambridgeshire, as examples of Style I (1985a, 16) is contrary to the opinion of those commentators who maintain that Jacobsthal's Early Style is not represented in the British Isles (e.g. De Navarro 1952, 73; Megaw 1970, 34; 37; Megaw and Megaw 1989, 192). Stead's understanding of Style IV follows that of De Navarro; although he offered no specific definition he did expand on De Navarro's list of its most notable features and characteristics by recognising the influence of the 'Waldalgesheim' tendril and the importance of the half-palmette to the style (Stead 1985a, 19–21).

Stead's Style V was presented as a continuation of the insular sequence into the first century BC and beyond. Again, no specific all-encompassing definition was offered although a number of typical features were cited, including: tendril designs in elongated fields; fragments

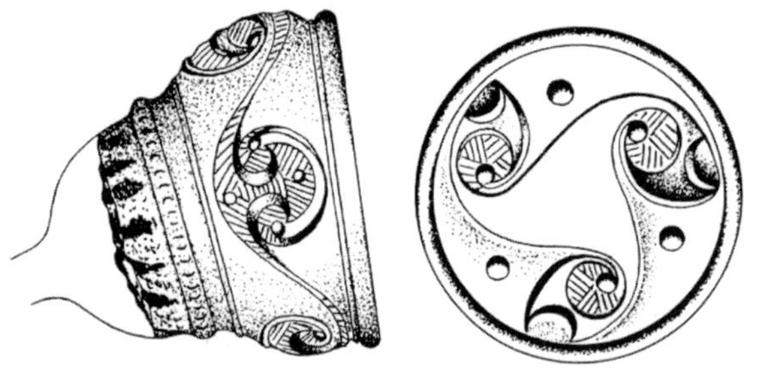

Fig. 1. Torc fragment from Clevedon, Somerset (courtesy of the Trustees of the British Museum).

of tendrils in minor panels; ambitious designs in both circular and rectangular frames; the use of hatching as background; the frequent interruption of hatching with circles; the use of trumpet motifs to terminate tendrils giving the impression of a 'bird's head'; and the importance of voids (especially the so-called Llyn Cerrig Bach or trumpet void composed of a triangle made up of three curves, one convex, one concave and one compound; *ibid.*, 22).

Stead noted that Style V was also typified by the popular use of *repoussé* and lost-wax techniques and a willingness to sometimes employ a number of different techniques on the same piece (*ibid.*, 22–3). Thus Stead's classification subscribes to the same underlying structure as the other schemes reviewed above; an early period of imported and home produced material decorated along continental lines (his Styles I–III), followed by a insular phase divided into two sequential parts (his Styles IV–V).

Critique of the existing classification

Although the frameworks of the different schemes outlined above are essentially the same, and there is a broad concordance of opinion in the allocation of individual pieces to various points within them, each reworking of the insular La Tène art sequence has also added its own refinements. Despite all these alterations and improvements, however, an innate conservatism runs through the classifications, which is problematic. Although it might be suggested that the longevity of the classification is a reflection of its accuracy and value, this is not in fact so. There have always been problems with the sequential character of the scheme, and work undertaken in the last 15 years has highlighted some fundamental problems. In fairness to previous scholars, the failings and weaknesses of their schemes have always been fully admitted. It is widely acknowledged that a precise absolute chronology for insular La Tène art is unobtainable, and that the generalising nature of the various classifications resulted in a simplification of the real diversity of insular art.

The principal drawback of the classification is that the chronological significance of the style sequence is itself suspect. Using independent brooch and scabbard typologies, Stead attempted to validate the integrity of the scheme (1985b, 27–32), but this was only a partial success. Although the scabbard typology corresponded closely with the sequence of insular art styles, the brooch typology, especially the La Tène II brooches, provided less of a close fit. Stead conceded that if the brooch typology is considered valid then, at least in some areas, the use of Style II ornament was concurrent with that of Style IV (*ibid.*, 32).

Faith in the chronological significance and integrity of the stylistic sequence has long been undermined by pieces such as the Clevedon torc from Somerset, which juxtaposes both early and late art styles (Savory 1990, 85). The terminal of the torc is decorated with a Style V design reminiscent of the Tal-y-Llyn triskele (Savory 1976, 56; 82, fig. 12.1), while the collar of the terminal is decorated with a vegetal scroll pattern similar to that on the Cerrig-y-Drudion decorated bronze fragments which most commentators identify as Style II, and which some might even consider Style I (Fig. 1). Thus two styles at opposite ends of the insular art sequence can occur on the same piece.

Since he published his revision and expansion of the Jacobsthal/De Navarro scheme, Stead's own studies of excavated finds from East Yorkshire (1991) and Deal in Kent (1995) have further undermined the integrity of the sequence. The Kirkburn, East Yorkshire, sword has a La Tène I chape-end and a scabbard decorated with Style V motifs, in particular the so-called Llyn Cerrig Bach or trumpet void (Stead 1991, 66–70; 180–1). Stead has plausibly argued that the decoration on the Kirkburn sword and scabbard is closely related to that on grave goods from other East Yorkshire burials that collectively form a 'Yorkshire Scabbard Style' which cannot be dated later than the third century BC (*ibid.*, 181–3).

The East Yorkshire evidence of an early date for Style V is mirrored at the Mill Hill cemetery, Deal, where the warrior burial contained a La Tène I sword and an openwork shield boss mount, both decorated with the so-called Llyn Cerrig Bach or trumpet void motif, which in the case of the sword is also associated with Style IV motifs (Stead 1995, 58–72). Stead dated the burial to the early second century BC on the basis of the sword's chape-end and an associated hinged plate-brooch (*ibid.*, 64; 86). However, the form of these two items is neither typical, nor easily paralleled with early La Tène II material, and a third century BC date, on the basis of the La Tène I sword, is not unreasonable.

The burial evidence from East Yorkshire and Deal is important, because it includes early, datable assemblages of decorative metalwork. The perennial problem of the study of insular La Tène art is the lack of associated and independently dated material. Prior to these finds, the only fixed dates for insular metalwork assemblages were all relatively late, such as those provided by the mirror burials of southern England. This bias towards late datable assemblages led Spratling, in an unpublished but highly influential study (Spratling 1972), to construct typological sequences for Iron Age metalwork, which were largely confined to the first century BC simply because the only datable material was late (Stead 1991, 183). Although such low chronologies have always had their critics (e.g. Savory 1971, 70; 1990), they probably influenced Stead to view Style V as a relatively late development in insular La Tène art. As Stead's own recent work has shown, both Style V – if it is to be defined by the so-called Llyn Cerrig Bach or trumpet void – and at least some of the insular La Tène metalwork types which Spratling also viewed as late developments, have much earlier origins than was previously thought.

The recognition that the inception of Style V goes back to at least the third century BC, combined with the identification of Style IV and V motifs on items decorated in 'earlier' La Tène Styles, implies that the sequential character of the insular art classification may be largely invalid. Recognising the problem, Stead (1996) conceded that the so-called Llyn Cerrig Bach void was a motif used in the 'Yorkshire Scabbard Style' (part of his Style IV), but sought to justify the sequential relationship between Styles IV and V by renaming the 'Styles' as 'Stages' and speculatively illustrating how a lobe and cusp design derived from a half-palmette motif could develop into a Llyn Cerrig Bach void (*ibid.*, 34, fig. 34).

The arguments outlined above are not intended to suggest that Style IV and Style V do not form meaningful, distinct and largely separate groups of decorative motifs on insular metalwork. However, they do prompt the question: what does each represent if they are not successive stages in the development of insular La Tène art? That the vogue of different styles of insular art overlap, at least partly, is demonstrated by the examples cited above, but why are there not more examples of individual items of Iron Age metalwork containing decorative motifs of more than one style? A related question is why do the majority of insular La Tène metalwork assemblages arguably accumulated over a considerable period of time, such as Llyn Cerrig Bach (Fox 1947; Macdonald 2000), contain only objects decorated in a single style? Although some still favour a chronological answer to these questions (e.g. Stead 1996, 29–35; Stead and Hughes 1997, 15–18), the possibility that other factors, such as localised variations in depositional practice and in the cultural significance attached to individual motifs and patterns, caused the largely separate occurrence of these insular La Tène art styles should not be dismissed.

Discussion

Whilst the flaws in the existing schemes for classifying insular La Tène art are now appreciated, what is less obvious is the best way for scholarship to proceed. In many respects a fresh analysis of the insular material is desirable: one that is deliberately free from the influence of the traditional classification and which accounts for a wider range of aspects and motifs than has hitherto usually been considered.

It is difficult to foresee how any new scheme would escape the problem of the limited scope for independent dating of the relevant material. A related issue is the difficulty in reconciling the differences in date between an object's manufacture and its deposition, which is highlighted by contrasting stylistic and conventional archaeological dating techniques. Despite these problems, the importance of the chronological dynamic cannot be conveniently forgotten and it would be a mistake to adopt an overly reductive approach to insular La Tène chronology.

Three related approaches to the problem of insular La Tène art chronology are recommended. Firstly, the dating evidence for the vogue of individual motifs and designs, rather than stylistic groups, should be considered. Jope's study of formal ornament (2000, 176–207) forms a useful point of departure for such a venture. Secondly, an attempt should be made to identify, excavate, and comprehensively study new foundry deposits. Even a small number of closely datable assemblages of mould fragments, comparable to those recovered from Gussage All Saints, Dorset (Spratling 1979; Foster 1980), and Weelsby Avenue, Lincolnshire (Foster 1995), if studied to their full potential, would result in significant advances in insular La Tène chronology. Thirdly, a comprehensive programme, comparable to that undertaken for Bronze Age metalwork (Needham *et al.* 1997), of radiocarbon dating organic material directly associated with existing examples of insular La Tène art should be undertaken (cf. Haselgrove *et al.* 2001, 6). It should be remembered that although classification and stylistic analysis are important tools for the study of insular La Tène art, they are a means to an end and not an end in themselves.

One of the challenges of studying insular La Tène art is that the material is so frequently divorced from the rest of the archaeological record. Practically, this manifests itself in the lack of finds that are independently datable through association. This physical separation in the archaeological record has also resulted in a significant methodological split between the way that we study the art and how we interrogate the rest of the record. Whilst students of the art have largely concerned themselves with establishing evolutionary sequences and identifying the origins and influences of certain motifs, archaeologists have been tackling, with the aid of a range of theoretical models, more

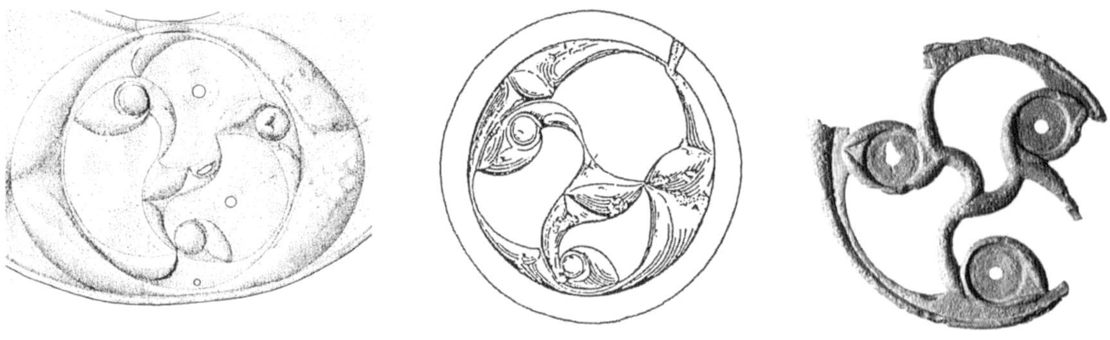

Fig. 2. Details of the same design replicated on the crescentic plaque from Llyn Cerrig Bach, Anglesey (left), the so-called horn-cap from Saxthorpe, Norfolk (centre), and an unprovenanced openwork mount from the Ashmolean Museum (right). Not to scale. For purposes of clarity and to aid comparison the image of the Saxthorpe decoration has been reversed (by permission of the National Museums & Galleries of Wales and courtesy of the Trustees of the British Museum and the Ashmolean Museum, Oxford).

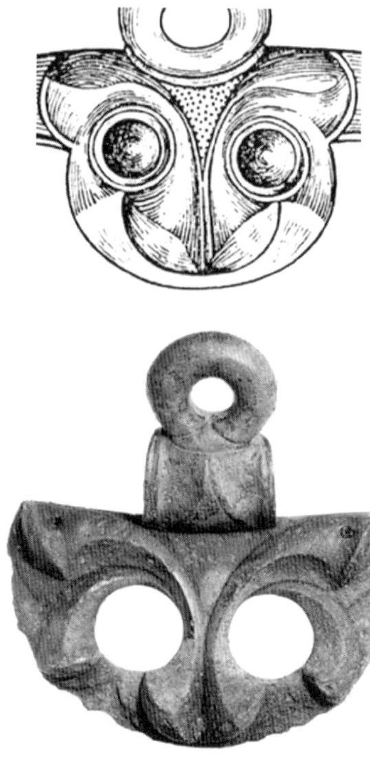

Fig. 3. Details of the same design replicated on the mirror from Holcombe, Devon (above) and the vessel handle mount from near Whitchurch, Shropshire (below). Not to scale (by permission of the National Museums & Galleries of Wales and courtesy of the Trustees of the British Museum).

engaging topics such as agency, gender, identity, cosmology, and belief.

This split in approaches has resulted in a situation where it is the norm for archaeological accounts of the Iron Age to fail to integrate discussions of art into their narratives, and rare for books on Celtic art meaningfully to address the contemporary concerns of mainstream archaeology. Study of insular La Tène art is too often a separate and isolated study which contributes little to our construction of the Iron Age and fails to stretch the evidence to address some of the more interesting questions that could be asked of this material.

The 'art historical' approach, as applied to La Tène art, is bound up with a number of concepts that have proved problematic to apply. Although the essentially modernist social constructs of aesthetics and connoisseurship should be valued for their own sake, it is not obvious that identifying the design of the Llyn Cerrig Bach crescentic plaque as a glimpse of an assembly of wise and sedate puffins (Jope 2000, 115) tells us anything of interest about the Iron Age.

As Coote and Shelton note in discussing the art of so-called primitive societies, although the intrinsic value of applying Western art historical scholarship to non-Western material culture is not in question – it is clearly useful for collectors, dealers, and museum curators – it is reasonable to ask what is its significance to the anthropological study of art (Coote and Shelton 1992a, 2). It may become necessary to disassociate ourselves from projects of aesthetic appreciation and develop into methodological Philistines (see Gell 1992, 40–3), because there are more interesting questions we could be asking about this material.

For example, why is the design on the Llyn Cerrig Bach crescentic plaque repeated on the diaphragm of the so-called horn-cap from Saxthorpe, Norfolk, and the unprovenanced openwork mount from the Ashmolean (Fig. 2)? Why is the design of the vessel handle mount from Whitchurch, Shropshire, repeated on the handle attachment plate of the copper alloy mirror from Holcombe, Devon (Fig. 3; Fox and Pollard 1973)? What is the significance of different types of artefacts being found on opposite sides of Britain bearing the same design, albeit executed by different methods? And what is the role of the individual artist's creativity, his patron's expectations, their audience's reactions, and even the art itself, within Iron Age social relations?

One reason why La Tène art is so difficult to study from a traditional, art historical approach is that it lies outside the conceptual framework of the subject (Price 1989). This paradigm has its origins in the Classical world and sees Western art as part of a continuous tradition from antiquity to the present. Four main chronological periods of Western art are recognised by art historians: Classical, medieval, Renaissance, and modern. Finer divisions are also recognised which fit within these four main categories, such as late antiquity and early medieval, but they do not invalidate the sequential integrity of the four-part scheme (Scharf and Bayley 1978, 47).

European Iron Age art, however, lies outside this essentially linear, if not evolutionary, conceptual scheme, despite being contemporary with, and partly informed by, the art of the Graeco-Roman world and also being a minor influence on early medieval art (Roth 1987, 23). It is this alien quality of Iron Age art which makes its recognition, appreciation, and analysis as art from a modern perspective so problematic and justifies an interest with anthropological approaches to non-Western art. It would be inappropriate to employ the criteria, which have come about for studying the Classical and Western traditions of art, to review an all but unrelated style of art.

A mystique has built up around the importance of connoisseurship in the study of insular La Tène art, which simultaneously justifies the attribution of dates and provenances to individual pieces, validates implicit assumptions about artistic evolution, rhetorically legitimates arbitrary aesthetic judgements, and discourages most archaeologists from engaging with the evidence. By their failure, until relatively recently, to engage critically with the problematic topics of material culture and art, Iron Age archaeologists have failed to dispel this mystique. Ironically, it is unlikely that insular La Tène art was intended to elicit an aesthetic response or appreciation in the sense that we understand it today. Even if it were possible to reconstruct a descriptive account of Iron Age aesthetics this would still not account for the production, circulation, and deposition of art works in the context of social relations during the Iron Age.

There are other potential ways of approaching and thinking about insular La Tène art. Since the Iron Age inhabitants of Britain and Ireland did not subscribe to our modern view of Western art, it is not obvious why archaeologists should prioritise a narrow art historical approach to this material, which needs to be opened up to a multitude of perspectives. The real challenge is to integrate accounts of insular La Tène art with the concerns and narratives of archaeologists studying all of the other aspects of the Iron Age, as is now beginning to happen (e.g. Fitzpatrick 1996; this volume).

One way of bridging the gap between the study of insular La Tène art and the rest of the archaeological record is to exploit some of the recent work on the anthropology of art. At the start of the paper, I noted that two textual analogies are currently in vogue in British archaeology. The first of these, that archaeology is textual practice, is one that the above review of past and present classifications of insular La Tène art has hopefully demonstrated to be of value. The second analogy, that material culture can be read as text and somehow contains meaning in a way comparable with language, is arguably less valuable when applied to the study of non-Western art.

Analyses of insular La Tène art have long adopted linguistic analogies, such as the grammars of Celtic ornament constructed by Fox (1958, 147–51) and MacGregor (1976, xvii–xix). A linguistic metaphor has also been used to justify the identification of insular La Tène art as 'art'. The Megaws argue that the examples of La Tène material culture, which they discuss, should be considered art because they encompass elements of decoration beyond those necessary for functional utility. Furthermore these motifs are a form of symbolic visual communication, which is now only partially accessible (Megaw and Megaw 1989, 19). This is a position that has been, usually implicitly and occasionally explicitly, adopted by most other commentators (e.g. Piggott 1970; Finlay 1973, 20; Laing and Laing 1992, 14–18). It has been maintained and reiterated by the Megaws (1994, 296) subsequent to criticism (Taylor 1991). In more recent years the influence of contextual archaeology has prompted far from convincing attempts to read the messages of 'Celtic art', or reconstruct the biographies of individual artefacts.

The argument that La Tène art motifs are visual metaphors, which had a specific conceptual or symbolic meaning, and that therefore their application is more than just embellished decoration is, at one level, attractive. It could be argued that at least some insular motifs were more than just decorative embellishments with reference to examples like the so-called armourer's mark stamped on one of the swords in the Llyn Cerrig Bach assemblage (Savory 1966). This pelta-shaped mark is arguably too small, and – being set on a blade which presumably was almost permanently sheathed – would not normally be visible enough to be considered purely decorative. What the mark's actual significance was, however, remains unknown. By analogy with Roman examples it could be speculated that it identified the product of an individual swordsmith or workshop, or had a protective or apotropaic function (Savory 1966, 376; Green 1991, 609).

It is difficult to envisage a methodology that would enable us to recover the symbolic meanings of La Tène art motifs, even if the available contextual information concerning their use and deposition was greatly improved.[2] Even where the Classical roots of a La Tène motif are identifiable with reasonable confidence, such as the probable Etruscan origins of the swastika, it does not follow that the Classical meaning of the symbol was maintained by the La Tène communities which adopted it. The view that insular La Tène art motifs possessed a significance over and beyond the decorative is not ostensibly unreasonable; what however those meanings were is – at least at present – unreconstructable.

One clue may lie in the non-representational character of many of the motifs; as Appignanesi and Garratt (1995, 22) argue for modern art, the only way to present what is conceivable but not representable naturalistically is by abstraction. The general absence of a clearly naturalistic element in insular La Tène art is noteworthy and requires explanation. Scharf and Bayley (1978, 20) have noted the problems of interpretation that occur within any particular art form, or set of conventional graphic expectations, when unfamiliar forms are introduced. Perhaps the reconciliation of problematic Classical motifs, to which European Iron Age communities were exposed through trade and other contacts with the Graeco-Roman world was the motive for their adoption and transformation into forms compatible with Iron Age art traditions.

Attempts to develop a visual literacy in order to elucidate the meaning of insular La Tène art ultimately fail to satisfy. In addition to the methodological problems discussed above, this approach reductively treats art as a form of writing and fails to account for the individual work of art as a whole, and engage with its specificity and efficacy (Gell 1992, 43). One potential approach, which overcomes this obstacle, is that outlined by Gell in his work towards an anthropological theory of art (1998). Gell's rejection of linguistic analogies mobilised by semiotic and symbolic theories of art is appealing. In its place, Gell makes the radical suggestion that it would be profitable to study individual art objects as if they acted as 'secondary' agents within social relations; that is as sources of, and targets for, social agency. If successfully adopted, such an approach would help overcome the problem of the study of insular La Tène art being peripheral to archaeological accounts of the Iron Age.

Gell suggests that art should be considered a special form of technology 'for securing the acquiescence of individuals in the network of intentionalities in which they are enmeshed' (1992, 43). This technology works because it is both enchanted and enchanting. The production of art is perceived as the outcome of a barely comprehensible virtuosity, which – within the field of expectations and understandings – envelops artefacts with a magical prowess.

Gell illustrates this argument with reference to the ornately carved canoe prows of the Trobriand Islands. These, he suggests, are used to their owners' advantage in ceremonial exchanges of valuables. It is not the complexity of the designs, or the mild disturbances to normal cognitive functions that observing them produces, which causes the advantage. Rather, the mild visual effects are interpreted as evidence of the magical power emanating from the carved prows, which are perceived as physical tokens of the magical prowess of their owners and of their access to the services of a carver whose artistic prowess is the result of their access to superior carving magic. The power of the canoe prow is not that it is a dazzling object physically, but that it is a display of artistry which could only be produced by magical means (*ibid.*, 44–6).

Such an idea, if extended to Iron Age Britain, might for example result in the often complex and ambiguous designs applied to shields (see Fitzpatrick this volume) being interpreted as beguiling, confusing and entrapping those who viewed the shields, providing the shield owners with an advantage in whatever social arena (be it warfare, trade, diplomacy or whatever) that they and the shield's audience are engaged in.

Gell proposes considering art objects in terms of a nexus defining and formulaically expressing the nature of their social relationships to artists, recipients, and their prototypes (Gell 1998, 12–65). Such nexuses express the fields of expectations and understandings which surround art objects and define whether the participants act as agents or are acted upon as patients. They are attempts to order and classify empirical evidence rather than models for producing law-like generalisations or predictions.

With reference to the previous example, the original form of the shield recovered from the River Witham (Brailsford 1975, 10–13) might be seen as one in which a powerful individual (recipient-agent) commissioned a metalworker (artist-agent) to manufacture a shield with a design derived from a boar (prototype-agent), which the owner could use (index-agent) to beguile an audience (recipient-patient) to their advantage. Gell would express the nexus for this arrangement as:

[[[[Patron/Recipient-A] →Boar/Prototype-A] → Artist-A] →Index-A] →Audience/Recipient-P.

Exploring the potential artistic nexus provides a useful way of thinking about the possible roles of art within the social relations of Iron Age societies.

Gell also suggests that we should view art objects not as simple products or the end point of an action, but rather as a distributed extension of an agent. Gell famously cites the chilling example of a soldier distributing elements of his efficacy in the form of landmines (1998, 20–1); however, it is not just artists and recipients who can be considered distributed persons. With reference to a discussion of volt sorcery, Gell demonstrates that indexes can also be detached parts of their prototypes (*ibid.*, 102–4).

This concept of artwork being a distributed extension of an agent provides a mechanism for addressing the questions, posed above, concerning the interpretation of La Tène objects with the same design found in geographically distant areas. Whether these finds reflect the distributed elements of a single artist, patron, or even prototype, is not, as yet, clear; however, Gell's theory demonstrably provides a means for exploring, through the study of insular La Tène art, the agency of individuals within Iron Age societies.

Although far from being full analyses, the hypothetical sketches of how Gell's anthropological theory of art might be applied to the study of insular La Tène art hopefully demonstrate that there are other potential approaches to the study and interpretation of this material. One attraction of the approach is that it provides a mechanism to overcome the methodological split which isolates the study of insular art from other aspects of Iron Age archaeology. It is the author's intention further to explore the archaeological viability of Gell's anthropological theory of art and apply his ideas to the study of insular La Tène art.

Acknowledgements

A version of the critique of existing classifications of insular La Tène art formed part of the author's Ph.D. thesis (Macdonald 2000) and benefited greatly from the comments of Professor William Manning. Other ideas raised in this paper have profited from conversations with a number of individuals; in particular, the criticisms and support of Ian Armit, Mary Davis, Andrew Fitzpatrick, Colin Haselgrove, Richard Hingley, Fraser Hunter, John Ó Néill, Niall Sharples, and Siobhan Stevenson are gratefully acknowledged. The paper was originally presented at the conference *Approaches to Iron Age 'Celtic' Art* held at the School of World Art Studies and Museology, University of East Anglia, in 2001. The author is grateful to the conference organisers, Natasha Hutcheson and J.D. Hill, for their encouragement to present the paper. Copies of the summaries of Arthur Evans' Rhind Lectures published in *The Scotsman* were kindly supplied by the National Library of Scotland.

Notes

1. The first lecture 'Hallstatt and the Early Iron Age Culture of the East Mediterranean Countries' was summarised in *The Scotsman* on Wednesday 11th December 1895; 'Hallstatt the beginnings of the Iron Age Culture in the British Isles' on Thursday 12th December; 'The ancient Venetian Art Province, and its influence on the Celtic Races' on Saturday 14th December; 'The rise of Late Celtic Culture on the Continent, and its Mix-Hellenic character' on Tuesday 17th December; 'The Gauls of the Heroic Age–La Tène and Mons Beuvray' on Thursday 19th December; and 'Late Celtic Art in Britain' on Saturday 21st December.
2. The theoretical argument that La Tène art should be considered 'art' because its motifs are a form of symbolic visual communication is itself problematic. Some would argue that language is a unique institution and art is not like language; therefore we cannot infer from it, by following semiotic conventions, linguistic-like meanings (see e.g. Gell 1998, 6).

Bibliography

Allen, J.R. 1904. *Celtic Art in Pagan and Christian Times*. London: Methuen & Co..

Appignanesi, R. and Garratt, C. 1995. *Postmodernism for Beginners*. Cambridge: Icon.

Atkinson, R.J.C. and Piggott, S. 1955. The Torrs chamfrein, *Archaeologia* 96, 197–235.

Brailsford, J. 1975. *Early Celtic Masterpieces from Britain in the British Museum*. London: British Museum Publications.

Coote, J. and Shelton, A. 1992a. Introduction, in Coote and Shelton 1992b, 1–11.

Coote, J. and Shelton, A. (eds) 1992b. *Anthropology, Art, and Aesthetics*. Oxford: Clarendon Press.

De Navarro, J.M. 1943. A note on the chronology of the La Tène period, in R.E.M.Wheeler, *Maiden Castle, Dorset*, 388–394. Oxford: Reports of the Research Committee of the Society of Antiquaries of London 12.

De Navarro, J.M. 1952. The Celts in Britain and their art, in M.P. Charlesworth and M.D. Knowles (eds), *The Heritage of Early Britain*, 56–82. London: G. Bell and Sons Ltd.

Evans, A.J. 1894–7. On a votive deposit of gold objects found on the north-west coast of Ireland, *Archaeologia* 55, 391–408.

Finlay, I. 1973. *Celtic Art. An Introduction*. London: Faber and Faber.

Fitzpatrick, A.P. 1996. Night and day: the symbolism of astral signs on later Iron Age anthropomorphic short swords, *Proceedings of the Prehistoric Society* 62, 373–398.

Foster, J. 1980. *The Iron Age Moulds from Gussage All Saints*. London: British Museum Occasional Paper 12.

Foster, J. 1995. Metalworking in the British Iron Age: the evidence from Weelsby Avenue, Grimsby, in B. Raftery (ed.), *Sites and Sights of the Iron Age. Essays on Fieldwork and Museum Research Presented to Ian Mathieson Stead*, 49–60. Oxford: Oxbow Monograph 56.

Fox, A. and Pollard, S. 1973. A decorated bronze mirror from an Iron Age settlement at Holcombe, near Uplyme, Devon, *Antiquaries Journal* 53, 16–41.

Fox, C. 1947. *A Find of the Early Iron Age from Llyn Cerrig Bach, Anglesey*. Cardiff: National Museum of Wales.

Fox, C. 1958. *Pattern and Purpose. A Survey of Early Celtic Art in Britain*. Cardiff: National Museum of Wales.

Gell, A. 1992. The technology of enchantment and the enchantment of technology, in Coote and Shelton 1992b, 40–63.

Gell, A. 1998. *Art and Agency. An Anthropological Theory*. Oxford: Oxford University Press.

Green, S. 1991. Metalwork from Llyn Cerrig Bach, in V. Kruta, O.-H. Frey, B. Raftery and M. Szabó (eds), *The Celts*, 609. London: Thames and Hudson.

Haselgrove, C., Armit, I., Champion, T., Creighton, J., Gwilt, A., Hill, J.D., Hunter, F. and Woodward, A. 2001. *Understanding the British Iron Age: An Agenda for Action*. Salisbury: Wessex Archaeology.

Jacobsthal, P. 1944. *Early Celtic Art*. Oxford: Clarendon Press.

Jope, E.M. 1986. 'The Battersea shield' by I.M. Stead, *Antiquaries Journal* 66, 165–166.

Jope, E.M. 2000. *Early Celtic Art in the British Isles*. Oxford: Clarendon Press.

Leeds, E.T. 1933. *Celtic Ornament in the British Isles down to AD 700*. Oxford: Clarendon Press.

Laing, L. and Laing, J. 1992. *Art of the Celts*. London: Thames and Hudson.

Macdonald, P. 2000. *A Reassessment of the Copper Alloy Artefacts from the Llyn Cerrig Bach Assemblage*. Unpublished Ph.D. thesis, University of Wales Cardiff.

MacGregor, M. 1976. *Early Celtic Art in North Britain: a Study of Decorative Metalwork from the Third Century BC to the Third Century AD.* Leicester: Leicester University Press.

Megaw, J.V.S. 1970. *Art of the European Iron Age. A Study of the Elusive Image*. Bath: Adams and Dart.

Megaw, M.R. and Megaw, J.V.S. 1989. *Celtic Art from its Beginnings to the Book of Kells*. London: Thames and Hudson.

Megaw, M.R. and Megaw, J.V.S. 1994. Through a window on the European Iron Age darkly: fifty years of reading early Celtic art, *World Archaeology* 25, 287–303.

Needham, S., Bronk Ramsey, C., Coombs, D., Cartwright, C. and Pettitt, P. 1997. An independent chronology for British Bronze Age metalwork: the results of the Oxford Radiocarbon Accelerator Programme, *Archaeological Journal* 154, 55–107.

Piggott, S. 1970. *Early Celtic Art*. Edinburgh: Edinburgh University Press.

Price, S. 1989. *Primitive Art in Civilized Places*. Chicago: University of Chicago Press.

Roth, U. 1987. Early insular manuscripts: ornament and archaeology, with special reference to the dating of the Book of Durrow, in M. Ryan (ed.), *Ireland and Insular Art AD 500–1200*, 23–29. Dublin: Royal Irish Academy.

Savory, H.N. 1966. Armourer's mark from Llyn Cerrig Bach (Ang.), *Bulletin of the Board of Celtic Studies* 22, 374–376.

Savory, H.N. 1971. *Excavations at Dinorben 1965–9*. Cardiff: National Museum of Wales.

Savory, H.N. 1976. *Guide Catalogue of the Early Iron Age Collections*. Cardiff: National Museum of Wales.

Savory, H.N. 1990. 'Celtic art from its beginnings to the Book of Kells' by Ruth and Vincent Megaw, *Archaeologia Cambrensis* 139, 83–85.

Scharf, A. and Bayley, S. 1978. *Introduction to Art*. Milton Keynes: Open University Press.

Smith, R.A. 1925. *Guide to Early Iron Age Antiquities* (2nd edn). Oxford: Oxford University Press.

Spratling, M.G. 1972. *Southern British Decorated Bronzes of the Late Pre-Roman Iron Age*. Unpublished Ph.D. thesis, University of London.

Spratling, M.G. 1979. The debris of metalworking, in G.J. Wainwright, *Gussage All Saints: an Iron Age Settlement in Dorset*, 125–149. London: Department of the Environment Archaeological Report 10.

Stead, I.M. 1985a. *Celtic Art in Britain before the Roman Conquest*. London: British Museum Press.

Stead, I.M. 1985b. *The Battersea Shield*. London: British Museum Publications.

Stead, I.M. 1991. *Iron Age Cemeteries in East Yorkshire*. London: English Heritage Archaeological Report 22.

Stead, I.M. 1995. The metalwork, in K. Parfitt, *Iron Age Burials from Mill Hill, Deal*, 58–111. London: British Museum Press.

Stead, I.M. 1996. *Celtic Art in Britain before the Roman Conquest* (2nd edn). London: British Museum Press.

Stead, I.M. 2000. Preface, in Jope 2000, v.

Stead, I.M. and Hughes, K. 1997. *Early Celtic Designs*. London: British Museum Press.

Taylor, T. 1991. Celtic Art, *Scottish Archaeological Review* 8, 129–132.

Dancing with dragons: fantastic animals in the earlier Celtic art of Iron Age Britain

A.P. Fitzpatrick

For Otto-Hermann Frey

Introduction: a mute icon

Some of the finest pieces of Celtic art in Europe come from Britain. It is an art that is displayed prominently in the modern iconography used in presentations and interpretations of the Iron Age peoples of Britain and the ancient Celts. Yet the same art has been passed over almost silently in most recent discussions of the Iron Age in Britain. It is a curious contradiction.

Several factors may, in part, explain this disjunction. One is undoubtedly the direct association that is often made between an art style – Celtic art – and a people – the Celts. A second factor is the intertwining of the study of Celtic art with that of the classical world and traditional art history in the middle of the twentieth century. The increasingly independent investigation of the prehistoric and protohistoric archaeology of Europe has diverged from both disciplines. And a third factor is that research on Iron Age art, usually seen as abstract and decorative, has been largely conducted in isolation from other studies of the archaeology of the period.

The construction of Celtic art

Celtic art is one of the building blocks of most modern constructions of the ancient Celts (Fitzpatrick 1996a; Collis 2003). In continental Europe, their study was, and remains, inextricably linked (Megaw and Megaw 1989). In Britain this intertwining is deeply rooted and the association – along with the assumption that the makers of Celtic art spoke a Celtic language – was flowering as early as 1863, with the publication of *Horae Ferales* (Kemble 1863). At that time, the identification of a material culture with the historically attested Celts was beginning to be systematically formulated across continental Europe by scholars such as Gabrielle de Mortillet. This identification was rapidly integrated with the emerging Three Age system, and in 1872 Hans Hildebrand divided the pre-Roman Iron Age into the Hallstatt and La Tène periods. When Joseph Déchelette linked the British conception of Celtic art and language to the continental European material associated with the historically attested Celts, the circle of what is considered today to be the Celtic art of the European Iron Age was closed.

The distribution of Celtic art became a *Leitmotif* for the historically attested migrations and expansion of Celtic groups, as well as evidence of migrations not recorded by surviving written histories (Collis 2003). This art was often seen as an abstract and decorative art that in some way reflected an elusive Celtic spirit (Merriman 1987). The nature of that spirit was often characterised using a particular reading of the ancient historical sources. In this, the art was made for, and used by, brave, sometimes reckless Celtic warriors: the barbarian Celts.

The 1980s and 1990s saw a sustained critique – a second 'Celtomania' according to John Collis (2003, 10) – of the unqualified association of the Iron Age archaeology of central and western Europe with the ancient Celts. In that critique some of the distinctions between the art of early medieval Christian Britain, also called Celtic, and the art of the ancient Celts became better appreciated, but relatively little attention was given to nature of Celtic art in Britain or continental Europe or to the study of it. In this curious contradiction, the widespread perception of the art as largely decorative and abstract remained largely unchallenged. An art that nonetheless remained, sometimes uncomfortably so, clearly related to material elsewhere in Europe.

Other readings of the art followed those of continental European scholars, seeing it as an essentially religious art (e.g. Pauli 1985), but maintaining the fundamental association of Celtic and Art (Taylor 1991). The position could, *in extremis*, be reduced to 'the "Celts" were indeed those who produced "Celtic" or "La Tène" art' (Megaw and Megaw 1993, 221). The essentially symbolic nature of the art, implied by the view that the art was religious in nature, has rarely been explored in English.

The legacy of Paul Jacobstahl

If the significance of Celtic art – and the association of it with Celtic languages and the historically attested Celts – is rooted in the nineteenth century, the intellectual framework within which it has largely been approached to this day lies in the earlier twentieth century. And it lies in precise circumstances.

Paul Jacobstahl, author of the magisterial *Early Celtic Art* (1944) that collated material from much of western Europe, was Professor of Classical Archaeology at Marburg from 1912 until 1935, when he left Nazi Germany and came to Britain. Those historical circumstances led to an emphasis in the book on western Europe, as much material in central and eastern Europe was not available for study (Hawkes 1947; Evans 1989). *Early Celtic Art* was preceded by Jacobstahl's studies of classical goods imported into Iron Age Europe and on the hellenisation of Provence. It covered the period up to Middle La Tène, between the third and second centuries BC. Its successor, *Early Celtic Art in the British Isles* (Jope 2000), was not completed or published either in his lifetime, or that of his intended co-author, Martyn Jope.

Perhaps more important to the future study of Celtic art than either the chronological parameters of *Early Celtic Art* or the distinctive stamp of one tradition of Germanic scholarship, was Jacobstahl's training and early work in classical art. That art was, and is, often construed as one of civilisation in which the creative and representational arts form one of the higher classical arts. In Jacobstahl's work on Celtic art there is an emphasis on the ornamental and decorative, on shape and pattern, that derives from the study of classical art (Hawkes 1947). An important consequence of this was that barbarian Celtic art – the art of those who spoke a different tongue – was seen as almost exclusively concerned with shape and pattern. Conceptually it was separated from the higher arts.

These origins in classical archaeology and art history are reflected in studies of Celtic art in the emphases placed by Jacobstahl on (1) origins, both chronologically and geographically; (2) affinities, both in the form of stylistic links, and for the British Isles, whether objects bearing Celtic art have been imported; and (3) typologies, in the sense of formal styles and morphologies, and pattern making. The frequent use of the language of connoisseurs, for example 'a masterpiece' and an emphasis on the craftsmen and their artistic sensitivities and influences (Jope 1971a) and their perceived role as proxy for their clients, presumed to be an elite, is also heavily indebted to studies of the classical arts (see also Macdonald this volume). Very often there is a presumption that the modern and ancient viewers have a shared understanding of the art and read the visual languages in the same ways.

One result of the increasingly independent study of prehistoric and protohistoric archaeology in temperate Europe has been a growing distance from the study of classical art. One consequence is that in relation to the mainstreams of Iron Age studies, the study of Celtic art is seen as highly specialised, often inaccessible – as it is conducted in a specialist language – and, sometimes, arcane. In consequence, the analysis of Celtic art – an art, moreover, seen as largely concerned with pattern – has become divorced from the mainstream of Iron Age archaeology, and the undoubted difficulties of dealing with this complex, diverse and often beautiful material, can appear daunting:

> 'Most celtic art takes the form of abstract decoration on functional objects, which would have appealed to the Celt because of its meaning or usefulness but which is also in tune with current taste. Sensitive and appreciative modern writers have made valiant efforts to interpret its meaning. But the imagination of modern people is an unreliable guide to the aims, beliefs and feelings of their primitive forebears. Only the Celtic artists and their patrons could explain Celtic art, and as they never set pen to paper, their knowledge died with them.' (Stead 1996, 7).

Even for the more optimistic, the outlook is uncertain:

> '[Celtic art] encompasses elements of decoration beyond those necessary for functional utility, though these elements represent a form of symbolic visual communication which is only partly accessible to us' (Megaw and Megaw 1989, 19).

This paper attempts to attract a little more attention to the study of the Celtic art of the British Iron Age. It follows Robert Layton's approach to visual art, namely that is 'treated as a "focus" of cultural activity rather than a precisely delimited area of study' (Layton 1991, 40). The existing underlying framework for the study of the British material has been adopted, but this is not the place for a detailed exposition of the British material, its character, typology or chronology, to define styles, or to reconcile the precise versions of those matters that have

Date	*Reinecke*	*Déchelette*	*Jacobstahl*	*Stead*
500 BC	La Tène A 475–400 BC	La Tène I 475–250 BC	Early Style Waldalgesheim	Style I Style II
350 BC	La Tène B 400–250 BC		Sword Style/Plastic Style	Style III
250 BC	La Tène C 250–150 BC	La Tène II 250–120 BC		Style IV
125 BC	La Tène D 150–20 BC	La Tène III 120–20 BC		Style V

Table 1. Art styles and La Tène chronology.

been set out by Vincent and Ruth Megaw (1986; 1989), Ian Stead (1996), and Martyn Jope (2000), and which are discussed in more detail by Philip Macdonald elsewhere in this volume. It is still helpful to call the art styles 'Celtic art.' But this need not be read as an uncritical association (Taylor 1991).

Instead, this paper concentrates on one small group of famous objects, shields, and in particular just five of the early metal-faced shields. These shields are not adorned with an abstract, decorative, art. They bear fantastic animals, *animaux fantastique*, whose origins and something of their meanings are, it will be argued, to be found far away in continental Europe, in an age of migrations and mercenaries. The subsequent story of these fantastic animals, and how they came to be portrayed on other objects – most notably the decorated scabbards of swords, but also on later shields – has no place in the space available here. Descriptions of the shields, along with the details of the readings deployed here, are given in the Appendix.

Celtic art and shields in Iron Age Britain

In broad outline, the art of Iron Age Britain develops in a similar way to that of continental Europe. In this regard it is no different from other regional variations across the rest of Europe, being both similar, and different. However, a great deal of emphasis has been placed on the origins of the British material and the groupings used to study it reflect this.

Most attempts to order the British material follow the groupings proposed by Jacobstahl, often with numbered styles, which were used by De Navarro (1952), or stages (Stead 1996). Table 1 sets out the correlation between the two systems, together with the sub-divisions of the La Tène period employed by Reinecke and Déchelette.

The first distinctive British pieces, of fifth and early fourth century BC date, are a small number of metal objects decorated in a symmetrical style: Jacobstahl's 'Early Style' (Stage 1). These include the head dress from Cerrig-y-Druidon, Clwyd, several scabbards of La Tène I short swords from the River Thames, and an openwork fitting, perhaps a harness mount, from Danebury, Hampshire (Megaw and Megaw 1991). Shortly afterwards in the fourth century BC, pieces decorated in a curvilinear style that it ultimately based on plant or vegetal motifs appears, and named after the very well-furnished burial of a woman found at Waldalgesheim, Kr. Mainz-Bingen, in Germany. Examples of the Waldalgesheim style from Britain include the decorated metal fittings of a scabbard on a sword from the River Thames at Standlake (Fig. 1).

On typological grounds the Standlake sword would be dated to the fifth century BC, but a much later date has often been proposed for the decoration, either on the basis of a supposed delay in the appearance of a new style in Britain, or by suggesting that the decorated fittings are later additions (e.g. Jope 2000, 26–8; Harding 2002, 196–7). While some repairs to scabbards are known (e.g. Stead 1991a, 68), André Rapin has swept these arguments aside:

> 'Malgré l'appartenance évidente des images au style de Waldalgesheim, un retard théorique imputable à une perception idéologique de l'art celtique insulaire induit depuis longtemps le rajeunissement d'un à deux siècles du material britannique et de son iconographie en regard de leurs equivalents continentaux.' (Rapin 2003, 56).

Other finds from Britain that are either decorated in Waldalgesheim style or clearly related to it, include metal objects from the third-century BC inhumation burials at Deal, Kent (grave 112) and Newnham Croft, Cambridgeshire. Well-furnished burials are rare in southern England at this date and both these graves contained ritual head-dresses (Stead 1995), perhaps indicating a status that was based on sacred as well as secular authority.

What followed has been less well understood. Jacobstahl's next Style (Stage III) was sub-divided into

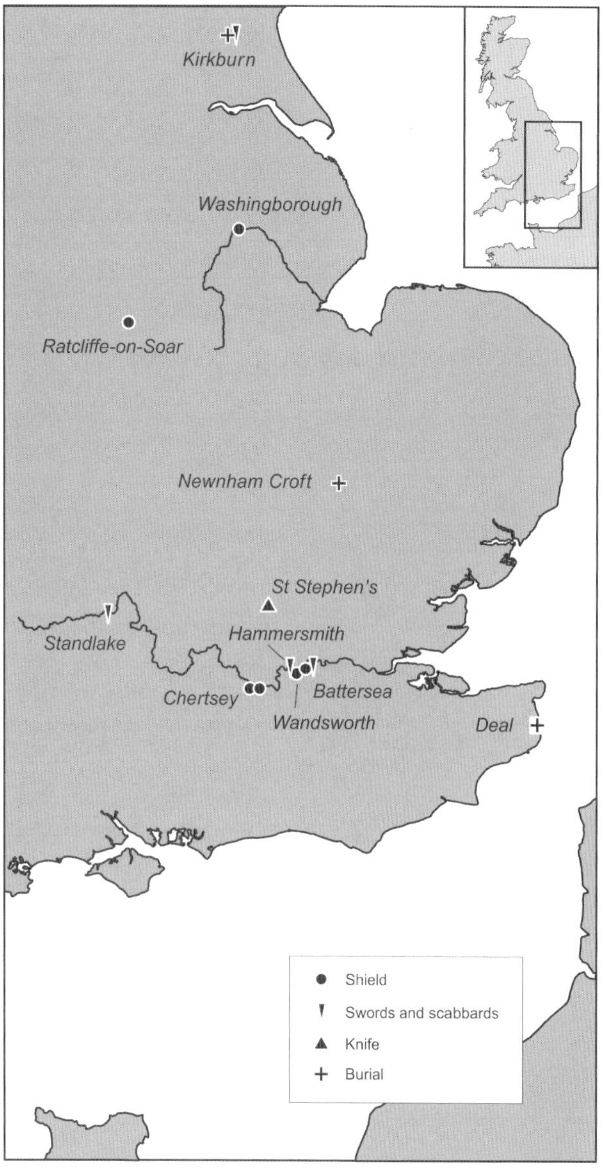

Fig. 1. Location of sites and finds.

'Plastic' and 'Sword' sub-styles, which, despite their names, can now be seen to reflect geographical differences in the distributions of the material as then known. These sub-styles were seen by Jacobstahl and De Navarro as the source of the first British Celtic art, which Jacobstahl termed Style IV (De Navarro 1952, 75), and which included some of the metal-faced shields. The group of material had already been identified as forming an 'Early School' by Leeds (1933), and Atkinson and Piggott (1955) subsequently termed this the Wandsworth–Witham–Torrs style. They recognised, however, that some elements in the designs of this group derived not from Stage III, but from the earlier Stage II Waldalgesheim style (*ibid.*). On one recently identified find, the Ratcliffe-on-Soar shield, different motifs within the same design can be classified as Stage II and III motifs.

It is plain, then, that these Styles or Stages did not follow an absolute sequence (see also Macdonald this volume). It seems likely that material that is distinctively British in style (Stage IV) originated at the time that Waldalgesheim (Stage II) designs were current, and that the British Stage IV material is a regional variant contemporary with the Plastic and Sword sub-styles of Jacobstahl's Stage III, which is likely to have emerged during the fourth–third centuries BC. It also appears clear that elements of the distinctive Style V, which is found only in Britain, are likely to have emerged by the third century BC (Stead 1995, 95; 1996, 34).

There is a consensus that many of the objects decorated with this art were used by an elite (e.g. Fox 1958; Parker Pearson 1999, 54–7; Harding 2002).

Shields

Amongst these objects are the sheet metal coverings and bosses of oval-shaped wooden shields. One shield, from an old course of the River Thames at Chertsey, Surrey, was made entirely of metal. These objects, which include the Witham shield, are regarded as some of the finest examples of Celtic art in Britain, and in Europe. The wafer thin metal facings, sometimes with delicate and elaborately decorated bosses, would not have survived physical combat engagement. They were display or parade items (Jope 1978). Like so many other pieces of weaponry from Iron Age Britain, the shields were ritually deposited, complete and apparently undamaged, in east-flowing rivers.

In the main, the objects were found in the nineteenth century in the course of dredging or building works, and entered museum collections from private collections, unaccompanied by the exact details of their discovery, or of their subsequent history. Some have had chequered histories. The shield spine from the River Trent near Ratcliffe-on-Soar was discovered in 1895, accessioned to a museum in 1928, but only identified as an Iron Age shield – rather than a piece of horse armour – in 1994, almost a century after its discovery (Watkins *et al.* 1996).

The Chertsey and Witham shields are almost complete. The former is oval in shape (Fig. 2), the latter more rectangular. The two shields from the River Thames at Wandsworth and the one from Ratcliffe-on-Soar are incomplete. They are represented only by the bosses that in combat would notionally have protected the hand that held the shield, and by all, or some, of the decorative spine that ran up the vertical axis of the shield. It is thought likely here that the Wandsworth round boss came from a sub-rectangular shield as the other shields are of this or a similar shape, but this is not certain. These pieces of weaponry are amongst the earliest Iron Age shields in Britain.

In contrast to these rectangular shields, most of the

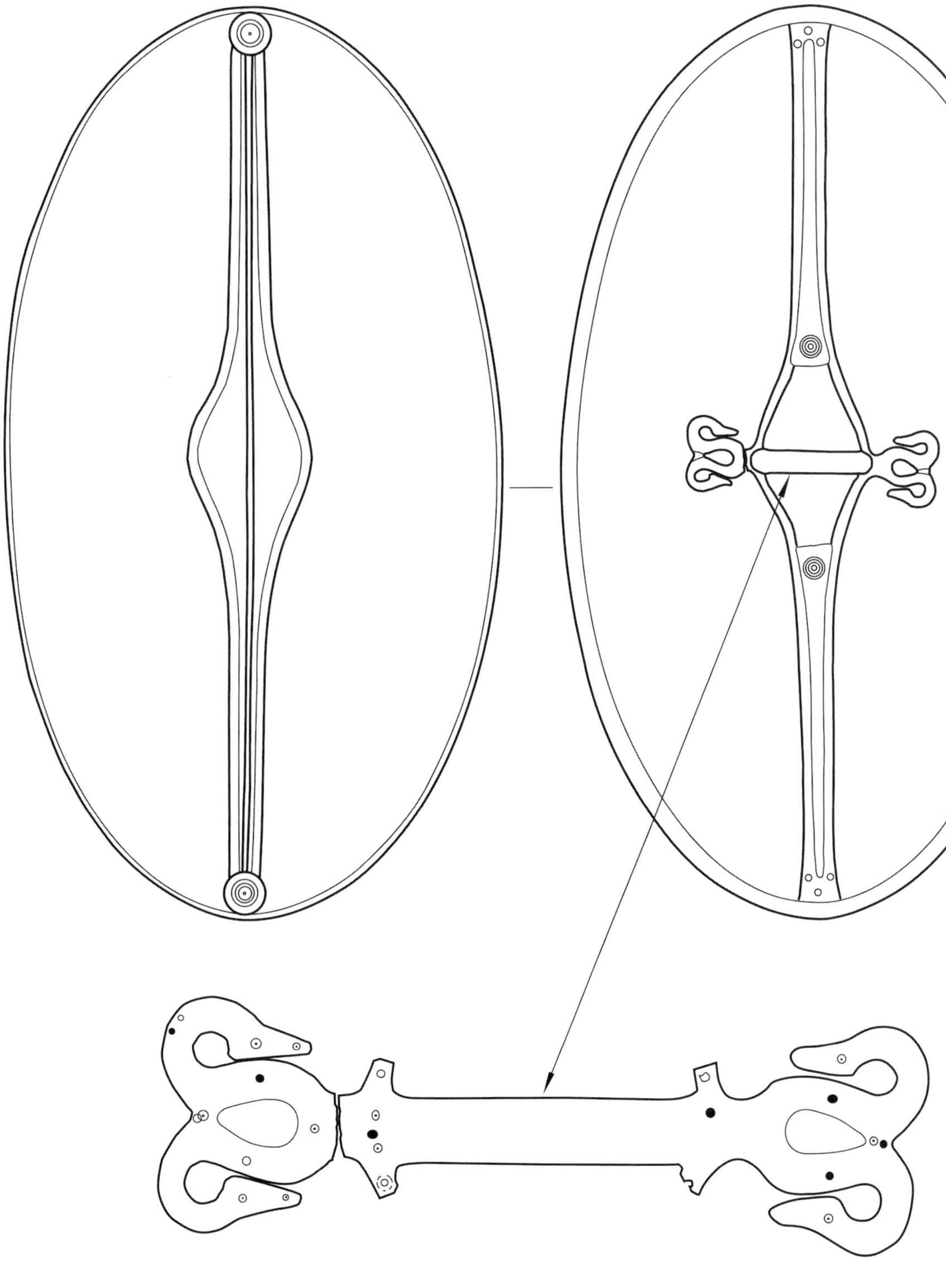

Fig. 2. The Chertsey shield (scale 1:6), with detail of handle (after Stead 1991b, figs 1–2 and 8).

shields known from Iron Age Britain represent the shape of an animal hide with four legs. They are best known from the distinctively shaped copper alloy bindings that protected and emphasised the 'corners' (or legs) of these shields. Although many of the finds are of second and first century BC date, an example was placed in the Deal burial, which may well be third century BC, suggesting some overlap in date with the oval and sub-rectangular shields. The shape of the many organic shields represented only by their metal bosses or spines, binding clamps, decorative fittings or fragments of facing, or simply by their mineral replaced remains, is not known

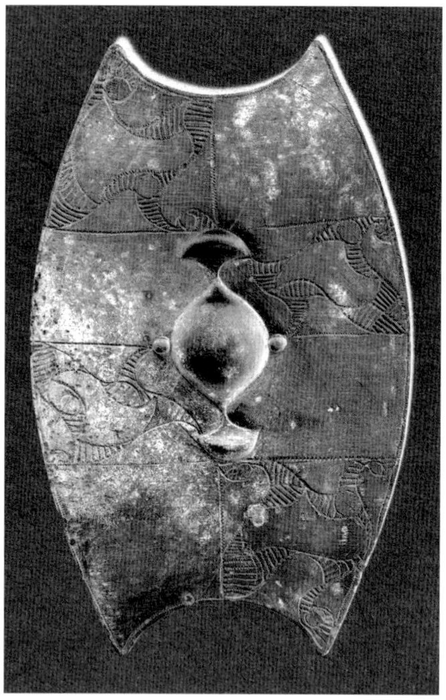

Fig. 3. Miniature shield from the Salisbury, Wiltshire, hoard. Scale 1:1 (photograph courtesy of the Trustees of the British Museum).

(Stead 1967; 1979; 1991a, 63–4; Ritchie 1969; Spratling 1970; 1972; Fitzpatrick 1996b; Barrett *et al.* 2000). The faces of a number of shields were decorated with metal mounts, and the faces of some of the miniature hide-shaped shields from the Salisbury, Wiltshire hoard, have incised curvilinear decoration in panels (Fig. 3), usually on one side only (Stead 1991b; 1998).

One of the most striking features of the decoration on these metal shield faces and bosses is that, in contrast to the perceived orthodoxy that Celtic art is abstract and decorative, they contain clear figural representations. Some of the shields – Witham and the Wandsworth long boss – also contain elusive images of faces, which have attracted considerable attention (e.g. Jope 1971b; 1976; 2000, 54–65). Much less attention has been devoted to the figural representations at the heart of the shields. Adorning the bosses are what appear to be birds or bird-like beasts.

To a modern eye, these fantastic animals are seen most easily on the round boss from Wandsworth (Fig. 4): what appear to be winged birds, perhaps swans (Jope 2000, 68–9, pl. 86b), are raised in relief and sweep round the large flat flange of the boss in a symmetrical arrangement. The design may be rotated, but still remains symmetrical. Smaller incised renditions of the fantastic animals infill some of the decoration of the flange, and they appear in relief on the hemispherical boss (Brailsford 1975, 14–19). The long Wandsworth boss (Fig. 5) has symmetrical relief decoration of opposed heads with large beaks (*ibid.*, 21–23). The arrangement of the decoration on the boss of the Witham shield is very similar to that of the Wandsworth long boss, and although the representation is less naturalistic (*ibid.*, 10–13; Jope 1971b; 2000, 55–60), there can be little doubt that it is essentially similar. The boss and spine of the Witham shield overlay a representation of a boar (Fig. 6). The boar was in a material that was either removed or has perished, but its shape is picked out by both the differential corrosion of the metal face behind it, and by the rivet holes by which it was attached.

Opposed fantastic animals also occur on the handle on the back of the Chertsey shield (Fig. 2, above), where they might be read as serpents (Stead 1991b), and, in a fantastic overlapping and swirling arrangement, on the spine and boss of the find from Ratcliffe-on-Soar (Watkins *et al.* 1996). On this find the winged and clawed animals run the whole length of the spine with their body and wings at one end of the shield and their tails at the other (Fig. 7). When a warrior gripped the handle of the shield, he was placing his hand right behind the fantastic animals on the boss. On the Chertsey shield, where the fantastic animals are on the rear of the shield, his hand would have been between the fantastic animals.

Colour

The original colour of many of the shields was likely to have been a bright, shining, and perhaps deeply polished, golden yellow, although the Chertsey shield may have had a deliberately applied finish that used tin (Stead 1991b, 10, 28). The representations of the fantastic animals are physically raised above the face of the shields and the contrasting textures of their relief and shadow and light would have picked out the incised images. Red coral, or glass studs in a brilliant sealing-wax red, ornamented many of the bosses. Either the original settings, the rivets that retained them, or the openwork or reserved settings for the studs show that the Ratcliffe-on-Soar, Witham, Wandsworth round, and perhaps Wandsworth long shields were decorated in this way. Coral was also used in the decoration of the terminals of the boss of the Witham shield. The use of the colour red (as perceived and defined today) to adorn the shield was precise. Coral and red glass were used not only to decorate shields and sword scabbards, but also pieces of costume jewellery such as brooches (Champion 1976).

In Britain, only the Arras burials of East Yorkshire provide a sufficient sample to assess the choice of colours and this is almost entirely based on objects selected for placement with the dead. Here, many red materials and colorants were used to decorate brooches and pendants placed in the graves of both females and males. The objects are relatively infrequent, suggesting that the colour helped symbolise some status. The only instance yet known in which the colour was used extensively is on

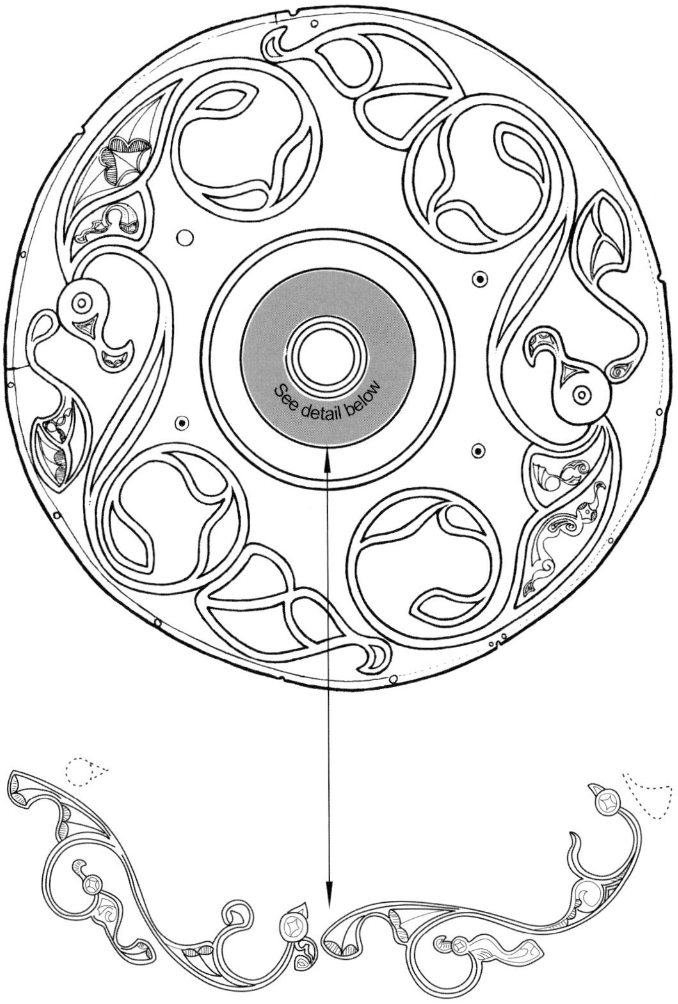

Fig. 4. The Wandsworth 'round' shield boss. Scale 1:4 (after Brailsford 1975, figs 7 and 14).

weaponry, on the lavishly decorated handle of the Kirkburn sword (Stead 1991a; 1996, 66, fig. 73). In this context, the colour red might be associated with aggression and blood. In contrast the colour blue was widely used for beads, and necklaces made from them seem to have been worn only by females.[1]

These pieces of jewellery and the contrasting colours and textures of swords and their scabbards, and perhaps helmets also, were only one part of a visual language of appearance. Finds of mineral-replaced textiles from Burton Fleming are decorated in a chevron or broken diamond border with stripes, implying that some garments worn by – or placed with – the dead were decorated in at least two distinct colours (Stead 1991a, 119–22). The body itself may have been coloured or otherwise adorned (Pyatt *et al.* 1991; Van der Veen *et al.* 1993). The colours, textures, and the fantastic animals of the parade shields all spoke a visual language. The fragility of the shields suggests that the language was only spoken, and read, at certain times.

Dating

Although the five shields were all recovered without associated finds from watery contexts, they are relatively well dated in relation to British Early to Middle Iron Age chronologies, with a date range of no more than one or two centuries. The date ranges set out by Stead (1985; 1991b; 1996; Watkins *et al.* 1996) are based on careful stylistic analyses and comparison with contemporary, but better dated, continental European finds, and are followed here. In general, the ranges are earlier than those suggested by, for example, Jope (2000). As a consequence, the dates chart a different development from that proposed by Jope (1976; 1978), who looked to Italy for the inspiration behind the British typological sequence.

While the wooden handle of the Chertsey shield yielded a radiocarbon date, at two sigma this spans the eighth to third centuries cal. BC (see Appendix). Oval shields are frequently shown in depictions of Celts, Gauls and related peoples in Greek and Roman art, for example in the sculpted freezes that decorated the great sanctuary

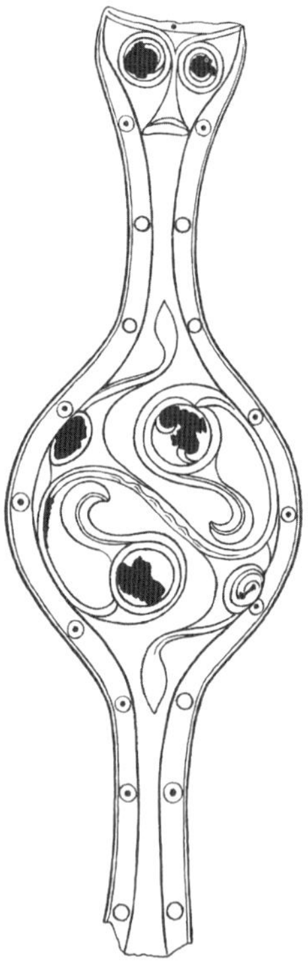

Fig. 5. The Wandsworth 'long' shield boss. Scale 1:4 (after Brailsford 1975, fig. 16).

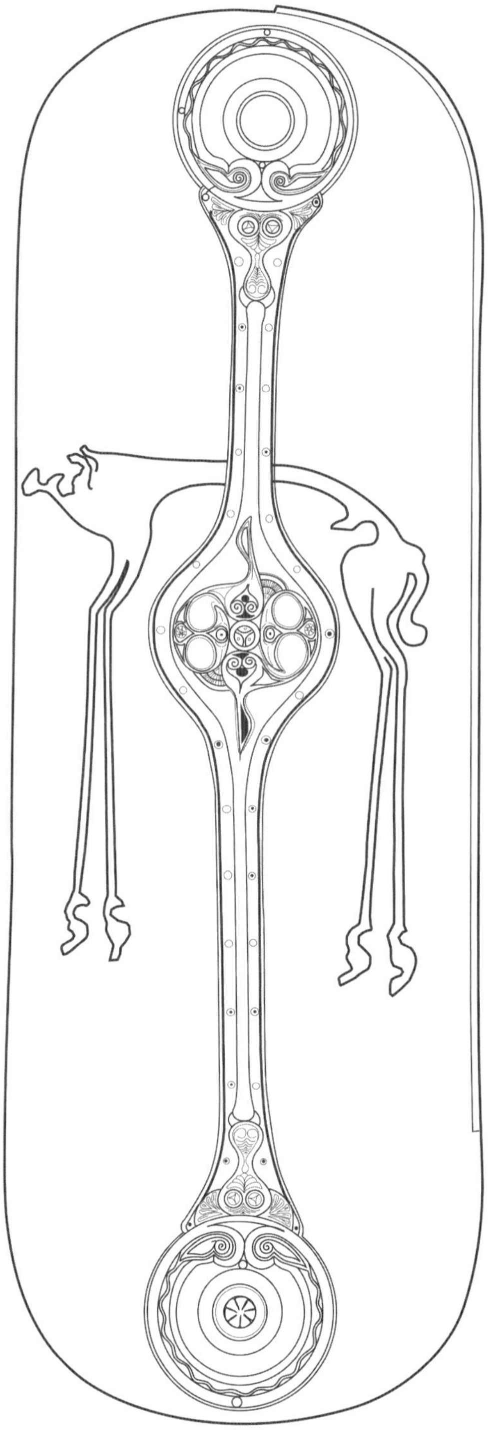

Fig. 6. The Witham, Lincolnshire, shield. Scale 1:6 (after Brailsford 1975, figs 1 and 2).

of Pergamon in Turkey. But these warriors were not the only ones to use oval shields (Szabó 1995), nor was it the only shape of shield that they used (Gunby 2000). However, in continental Europe oval-shaped shields can be seen to date into the fifth century BC (Stary 1981, 300; 1986–7; Szabó 1995) and, as Jope argued, the ultimate inspiration seems likely to have been in Italy (Stary 1981). For these reasons, the simply decorated Chertsey shield seems likely to be the earliest of the British metal-faced shields, and to be of fourth century BC date (Stary 1981, 300; Stead 1991b; Rapin 2001).

If the Chertsey shield is decorated simply, the elaborate decoration of the other shields allows a more accurate estimate of the date of manufacture. The Ratcliffe-on-Soar shield is the closest of any British find to the continental European Waldalgesheim style. The types of motif used in this style have been grouped and dated (Verger 1987) and the vegetal style decoration on the shield spine belongs to the Waldalgesheim A1 motif. This has been dated to the later fourth or earlier third centuries BC, implying a similar date for the shield. The other three shields considered here seem likely to date to the third century BC.

The origins of the fantastic animals on the Ratcliffe-on-Soar shield also provide comparative dating. If, as Stead suggested (in Watkins *et al.* 1996, 27) – and is discussed below – the fantastic animals derive from the dragon pairs, fantastic animals that decorated the mouth of sword scabbards, they could date from the fourth century BC onwards. The best known of the continental European scabbards with Waldalgesheim style decoration and dragon pairs is the example from Litér, Veszprém, Hungary. Here, the front of the scabbard

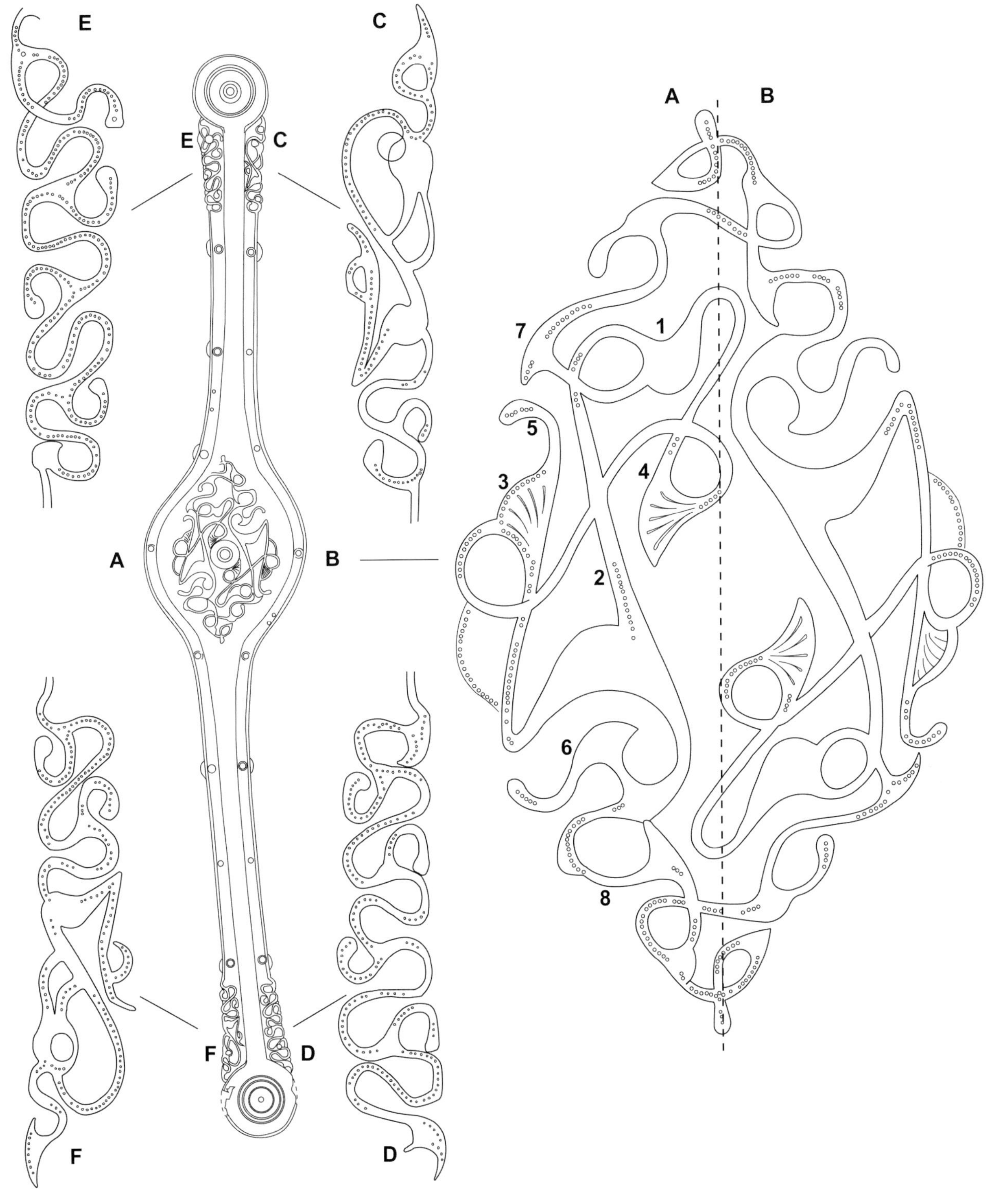

Fig. 7. The Ratcliffe-on-Soar, Nottinghamshire, shield (scale 1:5), with details of the motifs described (after Watkin et al. 1996, figs 1, 3 and 5).

bears a Type 1 dragon pair and the reverse is decorated with diagonal bands of type A1 Waldalgesheim tendrils, an arrangement which is typical of the Hungarian sword style (Szabó 1977; Rapin *et al.* 1992; Szabó and Petres 1992, no. 39, pl. 43–4).

The Ratcliffe-on-Soar shield spine (Fig. 7) also has parallels with a number of other pieces at the level of the individual motif. With British finds, it is rare for the flowing line of the design to cross over itself. Asymmetrical crossovers occur in the Ratcliffe-on-Soar

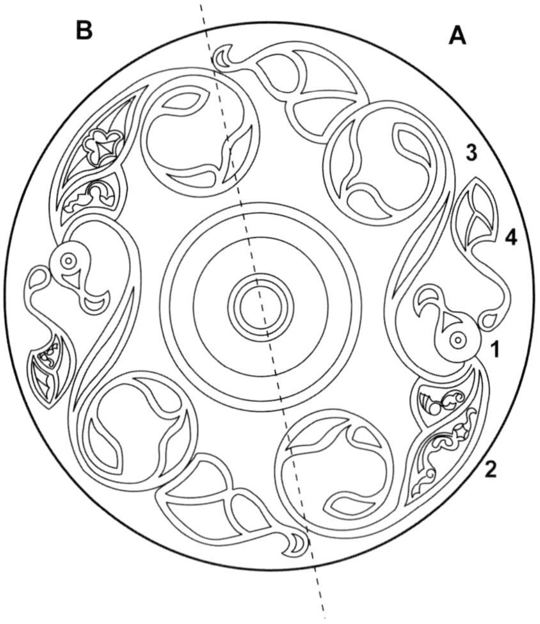

Fig. 8. Bird motifs on the Wandsworth round shield boss. Scale 1:5 (after Stead 1985).

design; this seemingly minor detail is chronologically significant as similar crossovers occur on the relatively well-dated French sword scabbards from Cernon-sur-Coole (Marne; Duval and Kruta 1986), Montbellet (Saône-et-Loire; Bonnamour and Bulard 1976) and Gournay-sur-Aronde (Oise). These finds date to the later fourth or earlier third centuries BC (Lejars 1994, 43–4; Watkins *et al.* 1996). Numerous scabbards decorated with asymmetrical crossovers are known to the east, where they are a typical element of the Hungarian sword style (Szabó and Petres 1992). On the Ratcliffe-on-Soar spine there are several asymmetrical crossovers on the boss and one on the terminal panel (panel C). Again this is consistent with a date in the late fourth or early third century BC.

Two of the other shields have crossovers: the Wandsworth round boss, in the panel on the wing of animal A (Fig. 8), and the Witham shield, on the upper roundel (Stead 1996, 26–9, fig. 28, a–b; Watkins *et al.* 1996). Symmetrical figure-of-eight crossovers occur on the finds from the Waldalgesheim burial itself (Joachim 1995). The change from the chased decoration on Ratcliffe-on-Soar to the higher relief repouseé decoration on the Wandsworth round boss and Witham shield is also chronologically significant. This reflects the change from Jacobstahl's Waldalgesheim style to his Plastic or relief style.

On the basis of an admittedly simple typological progression, as both the Wandsworth round and Wandsworth long bosses have readily recognisable representations of birds' heads, it seems likely that they stand between the intricate but recognisable animals on the Ratcliffe-on-Soar boss, and the more abstracted representations on the Witham shield (Fig. 9). A small ritual knife from St Stephen's, St Albans, Hertfordshire, which is bird-shaped, is closely related to the Wandsworth round shield boss (Fig. 10); it may be a split representation of a dragon or bird, with the different form of decoration incised on its wings representing different characteristics (Megaw *et al.* 1999). The elements that support the roundels on the Witham shield, often taken as a representation of an animal (e.g. Kilbride-Jones 1994, 3; Stead 1996, 72), also bear a striking resemblance to the dragon pair on a scabbard from Köröshegy, Hungary (Fig. 11; Ginoux 2002, 75, fig. 5, 4).

Although it cannot be considered fully here, it is likely that the Battersea shield – on which the animal decoration has become more abstracted – is slightly later in date. The overall composition is similar to the Witham shield, and the opposed motifs on the central boss, and the animals' heads that support it, are also clearly related. On typological grounds it is likely that that the Battersea shield dates to the late third/early second century BC (Stead 1985) and this is supported by the chemical composition of the glass studs, which suggest a second century BC or earlier date (Jope 2000, 351).

Dragon pairs

Dragon pairs have already been mentioned in relation to the Ratcliffe-on-Soar shield. These opposed fantastic animals are one of the most well-known motifs in Celtic art. They decorate equipment associated with weaponry, above all sword scabbards, where they adorn the outer face of the scabbard mouth. As the warrior gripped the hilt of the sword to unsheathe the blade, he placed his hand next to the dragon pair. He did the same when the sword was sheathed. Both actions would have created distinctive sounds.

Almost uniquely in Celtic art, opposed fantastic animals, called dragon pairs, are an exceptionally widely distributed and long-lived motif. Scabbards with these dragon pairs are found across western, central and eastern Europe (De Navarro 1959; Bulard 1979; Petres 1982; Stead 1984, 273–8, fig. 3; Szabó 1989; Megaw and Megaw 1990, 65–71, fig. 5; Frey 1995a, fig. 81; Ginoux 1995; 2002). Hundreds of finds are known, including two from the River Thames, at Battersea and Hammersmith (Stead 1984). Ginoux (2002) has distinguished two main types of dragon pair, a division that supersedes the threefold grouping set out by De Navarro (1972). While there is considerable variety within each individual type, and there are occasional representations of other types of animal such as horses (Schwappach 1974), the longevity of this motif over several centuries is most unusual in Celtic art (Frey 1995a). Nearly all representations are of what have been interpreted as serpents and griffins. Distinguishing between the two can be

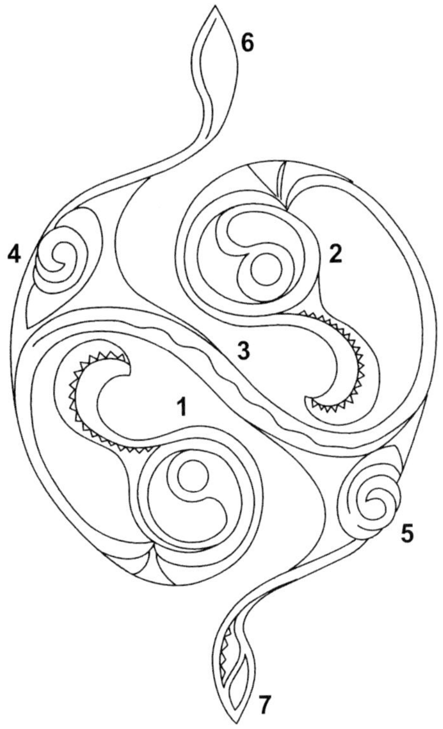

Fig. 9. Bird motifs on the Wandsworth long shield boss (left) and (right) the Witham shield (after Stead 1985).

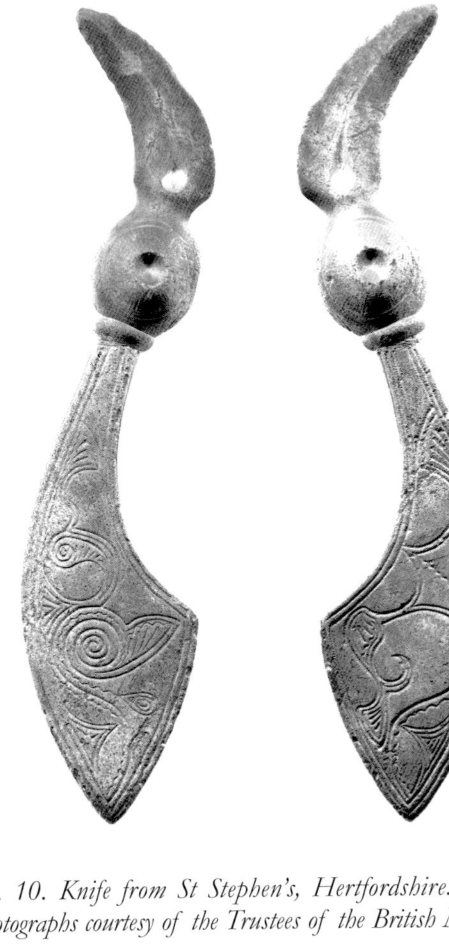

Fig. 10. Knife from St Stephen's, Hertfordshire. Scale 1:1 (photographs courtesy of the Trustees of the British Museum).

Fig. 11. Motifs from the Witham shield (left, scale 1:3; after Brailsford 1975, fig. 1) and on a sword scabbard from Köröshegy, Hungary (right, scale 1:2; after Ginoux 2002, fig. 5, 4).

difficult, as will be shown below, and for simplicity all will simply be called dragon pairs here.

The earliest type of dragon pair, Ginoux's Type 1 (equivalent to De Navarro Type II), is in the form of a lyre in which opposed S shapes face the central rib of the scabbard. The head has a gaping mouth – as on the Ratcliffe-on-Soar fantastic animals – and the tail curls away from the body. The field between and around the fantastic animals is often stippled. Dragon pairs apparently first appeared after the turn of the fifth and fourth centuries BC (Rapin 2002, 58); the earliest example comes from Ensérune (Hérault, France; Rapin and Schwaller 1987), whilst a number of Ginoux Type I dragon pairs occur on finds from the Italian cemetery at Monte Bibele (Emilia-Romagna), dating from just after the mid-fourth century BC to the mid-third century (Vitali 1984; 1987a; Rapin *et al.* 1992).

Ginoux's Type 2 encompasses De Navarro's Types I and III and represents wingless, beaked griffins. The distinctive form is a deliberate rendition of the griffins represented in classical art and is found on Iron Age metalwork of fifth and fourth century BC date (Duceppe-Lamarre 2002). The earlier renditions on scabbards (broadly equivalent to De Navarro Type I) have horizontal legs and what are conventionally described as forelegs, but may be phalli, that reach up towards the beaks of the fantastic animals. These examples date to the mid-fourth to mid-third centuries BC. The dragons (griffins) become increasingly geometric in their form, so that the foreleg and jaw join together forming a circle. These varieties (De Navarro Type III) date from the mid-third to the later second centuries BC.

The fantastic animals on the scabbard of the anthropomorphic hilted short sword from Baron-sur-Odon (Calvados, France) are inlaid with gold (Bertin 1974). The animals on the short sword from grave 15 Radosevice, Okr Teplice (Czech Republic), may also have been intended to be inlaid with gold like the vertical line on the blade (Sankot 2000; Rapin 2002). This form of decoration is otherwise seen almost exclusively in the lunar symbols found on these short swords, in which two or more inlaid symbols are separated by a vertical line of inlay (Fitzpatrick 1996c). A clear link with this astral symbolism is shown by the Radosevice sword, where the animals face the vertical gold inlay. A variation on this theme is seen in the copper inlay on the dragons on the scabbard of the anthropomorphic hilted sword from Châtenay-sur-Seine (Seine-et-Marne, France). Base metals were sometimes used in the inlays of the astral symbols on the blades (Fitzpatrick 1996c, 381; Craddock *et al.* 2004, 343), whilst the dragons on the sword from Ensérune grave 163 are inlaid with coral (Rapin and Schwaller 1987). These inlays, especially those from Baron-sur-Odon and Radosevice, suggest that the dragon pairs echoed some of the astral symbolism of the short swords.

Only two scabbards with dragon pairs are known from Britain; although both were found in the River Thames in the mid nineteenth century, their decoration was not identified until the later twentieth century (Stead 1984). The dragon pair on the scabbard from the river at Battersea is of Ginoux's Type 1; that on the scabbard from the river at Hammersmith (Fig. 12) may also be related to Type 1 dragon pairs.

The origin of dragon pairs has been much discussed, and represents a microcosm of many of the debates which have characterised the study of Celtic art, and/or Celtic origins, as a whole. Were they introduced to Celtic art from the east, from Greek Orientalising and Archaic Art, or were they adopted from the Etruscan renditions of these motifs that were used in northern Italy? Or were dragon pairs created in the west? And is their widespread distribution due to the migrations and the movement of mercenaries at this time, which are widely documented in the surviving historical sources (De Navarro 1959; 1972; Bulard 1982; Kruta 1982; Szabó 1989; Megaw and Megaw 1990; Ginoux 1995, 405, fig. 1). Much of the earlier debate on origins was based on a handful of finds, but with hundreds now known, there is a general agreement that the opposed fantastic animals were copied from elaborately decorated belt hooks that have been found mainly in northern Italy and the Alpine region (see Fig. 12).

Belt hooks

These triangular belt plates served as fasteners, like buckles, for the belts from which swords were carried in La Tène A–B1 (475–325 BC). As the style of carrying the sword changed (Brunaux and Lambot 1987), and this sort of belt hook passed from fashion, the motif was transferred from the belt to the scabbard. Several of these triangular plates have openwork decoration that would have been reserved against the leather of the belt. Of particular relevance here are those that have opposed griffins or bird-headed volutes (S-shapes) that may face a plant, usually interpreted as a tree of life; they are sometimes supported by a small human figure, known as 'the master of the beasts'.

Debates about the meaning of the belt hooks have echoed those over dragon pairs. Did the belt hooks originate north of the Alps (Bulard 1982), or to the south of them (Kruta 1986)? If they were brought from beyond the Alps, were they brought to northern Italy by trade and exchange, or by Celtic settlers? If brought by settlers, were they the peoples whom later sources record as sacking Rome in 387–386 BC? Or did earlier groups, whose arrival was not recorded by history, bring them? (Kruta 1983; Frey 1987; 1991). And where were the homelands of these groups? (Kruta 1986). Or did they move repeatedly, perhaps serving as mercenaries? (Frey 1991; 1995b). Whatever the exact reason or reasons, there is now a consensus that – as with the distribution of dragon pairs – the long distance movement of people and/or ideas was involved. The motif became, when transferred to sword scabbards, one of the most enduring and widespread symbols in Celtic art.

Although simple opposed volutes, or a lyre, may require little more than the addition of eyes to turn them into a dragon, and such opposed volutes are known in Britain on the La Tène A 'Wisbech', Cambridgeshire, scabbard (Piggott 1950, 4–5, fig. 1; Stead 1996, 22, fig. 23; Jope 2000, 22–3), it seems highly likely that the idea of opposed animals was introduced to Britain from continental Europe in the shape of dragon pairs.

As scabbards decorated with dragon pairs have been found in Britain, whilst the slightly earlier belt hooks have not, it seems likely that the fantastic animals on the British shields derive from dragon pairs on sword scabbards. In the same way that it has been argued that dragon pairs were transferred to sword scabbards from the fantastic animals that decorated the belt used to suspend the sword, the fantastic animals on the British shields may very well have been transferred from scabbard to shield. The simple motifs on the reverse of the Chertsey shield, likely to be the earliest of the British finds, would represent an intermediate stage, before the fantastic animals were transposed again to decorate the face of the shield from Ratcliffe-on-Soar.

The meaning of dragon pairs and fantastic animals

The fantastic animals on the metal-faced shields appear as birds. On the Wandsworth round boss, the representations of what were swirling fantastic animals on the Ratcliffe-on-Soar shield, have become naturalistic enough for it to be suggested that swans are represented (e.g. Jope 2000). It might be tempting to emphasise some of the characteristics ascribed to these brilliant white and aggressive birds, some of which are migratory (Megaw 1981; Megaw and Megaw 1993). But the representations were soon abstracted, which may suggest that the opposition of the fantastic animals and the ideas that they symbolised was more important than clear figural representation. This might seem to be borne out by the occasional representation of other types of beast in an opposed pair on the scabbard.

In contrast the boar applied to the surface of the Witham shield is, superficially at least, more readily understood. Boars appear on standards such as Soulac-sur-Mer (Gironde, France; Moreau *et al.* 1995), on carnyces (Hunter 2001), as miniatures, and on coins (Green 1992); and portions of the animals were frequently selected as offerings of meat to be placed in burials and are thought to be associated with funerary feasts.

Jose de Navarro famously described dragon pairs as 'an inter-Celtic currency' (1972, 237). In view of the likely origins of the dragon pair in the ornament of belt

Fig. 12. Sword and scabbard from the River Thames at Hammersmith. Scale 1:4 (after Stead 1984, fig. 1, 2). Details: 1. Belt hook from Tomba Benevenulti 116, Este, Italy (after Frey 1991, Abb. 9, 7); 2. Scabbard mouth from Taliandgöröd, Hungary (after Szabó 1989, Abb. 1, 1); 3. Fantastic animals on Hammersmith scabbard (after Stead 1984, fig. 2.4). All scale 2:3.

hooks, which are found mainly in northern Italy, it is possible that the motif acquired a special significance in the course of the Celtic settlement of that region. In addition to the widespread distribution of the motif, in the context of Celtic art its exceptional durability is remarkable. It seems very unlikely that the dragon pairs were mere ornaments:

> 'It is particularly noticeable that, despite certain variations and, in time, stylistic degeneration, it is, in general produced in a rigid, almost formula-like manner. It thus contrasts with other representations in Early La Tène art. There is no subsequent development, rather it represents a particular stage of consciousness. It has become a "symbol" within a narrow time frame. The "dragon symbol" may thus be regarded as a Heilszeichen [a heavenly or sacred symbol] of the Celtic warrior class – doubtless linked with death' (Frey 1995a, 165).

By warrior class, Frey means an elite. An elite for whom the practice and display of martial prowess was important. An elite that was bound by shared values, perhaps of valour and of loyalty, some of which were symbolised by the art, which incorporated heavenly symbols, that was used to adorn the very weaponry that helped define their status (Frey 2000). As the Megaws have suggested, it is also possible that the art 'later came to be a symbol of rank and achievement in battle. It most probably also had the apotropaic intention of warding off harm' (Megaw and Megaw 1990, 72).

The link with death that Frey talks of is a belief in the fate of the spirit. It is no coincidence that representations either side of the head on the Unterradlberg, St Pölten, Austria, lynch pin are S-shaped serpents (Megaw *et al.* 1989, 506–19, Abb. 14). It is in the context of such fundamental concepts and beliefs as death that the opposition – or perhaps split representation of a single creature – of the dragon pairs is best understood (Ginoux 2002). This may be an opposition between good and evil; between courage and fear; between lucky and unlucky; between light and dark. Alternatively the opposition could represent shape changing, from animal to human, or it could represent a particular group, such as a warrior class or descent group.

The display nature of the shields suggests that they may only have been used at certain times, whilst the quality of the craftsmanship means that few will have had the skills to make such pieces. The watery contexts in which these shields were gifted to the gods, along with many pieces of weaponry were also chosen precisely (Fitzpatrick 1984; Hunter 1997; Field and Parker Pearson 2003).

Conclusion

Often regarded as an abstract and decorative art, yet still inextricably linked with the identification and representation of the Celts, the study of Iron Age art has become abstracted from Iron Age studies. It is time to look anew at the curious contradiction that the Celtic art of Britain has become.

Some of the finest pieces of Celtic art in all Europe come from Iron Age Britain. Aspects of the ways in which colour, texture, and light were used can still be discerned. At the heart of some of these display objects were fantastic animals. These beasts had made a long journey, changing their shape during it. As griffins they came from the east. In the heart of Europe, they were transformed into dragons, pairs of serpents, and griffins. On the islands of Britain they became birds in societies where everyday life was lived amongst roundhouses, hillforts, and where the remains of ancestors were buried in grain storage pits in settlements.

Yet despite changes through time, place and peoples, elites and mercenaries, the pairing or opposition of these fantastic animals endured. It seems likely that they symbolised fundamental ideas such as death, and that they had heavenly associations. When the bearer grasped the weapon, they placed their hands next to these fantastic animals, transferring something of their essence to mortal men.

Acknowledgments

This paper could not have been attempted without Ian Stead's meticulous research on some of the key British finds and Otto-Hermann Frey's inspirational studies of the continental European material. I am grateful to both of them for all their help, and to Nathalie Ginoux, Vincent Megaw, Felix Müller, and Pavel Sankot, without whose assistance this paper could not have been completed. But for Colin Haselgrove's forbearance over my temporary diversion to Copper Age studies, this paper would not have been published here. The illustrations are by Linda Coleman, Wessex Archaeology.

Note

1. As well as coral and red glass/enamel, four, perhaps six, other materials were employed, either stones or shell, sometimes with red haematite colorants (Stead 1979; 1991a). Over 80% of the glass beads on necklaces are plain blue; most of the remainder incorporate blue in their design. Only about 6% do not incorporate the colour blue (Dent 1982; Stead 1979; 1991a).

Appendix: Descriptions of shields

River Abbey, Chertsey, Surrey (Fig. 2)

Oval shield. Found 1985 in gravel extraction, probably disturbed from an old course of the Abbey river, a backwater of the Thames. Length 836 mm and on average 1–16 mm thick. Unlike Ratcliffe-on-Soar, Witham, or Battersea, which are the metal faces to shields of wood or leather, the Chertsey shield is entirely of metal. The face has a darkened appearance that may be the remains of a deliberately applied finish using tin.

The terminal roundels are – in relation to later examples – small and plain, comprising a boss surrounded by two raised concentric circles, the inner rope-decorated. The face of the spindle-shaped boss and spine are made in a single piece that runs the length of the shield and are decorated with a central ridge. There is a hole in the ridge at the centre of the boss for some form of decoration that does not survive. A narrow strip ornamented with simple punched marks embellishes the junctions of the spine with the shield face. Large domed rivet covers protect the rivets attaching the handle, three on each side of the boss (not all the covers survive).

On the reverse of the shield, the one-piece handle has omega or 'm'-shaped terminals, the ends of which taper slightly and are decorated with ring and dot punch decoration giving the impression of an eye. The appearance is of a swan or serpent. The left terminal also has punch marks by the nose or snout that may be original, but could also be associated with a repair to this side of the handle. A hand could only be inserted into the shield from one side. The beasts on the handle face inwards towards each other like dragon pairs on the outside of scabbards.

A radiocarbon date of 760–390 cal. BC at 1 sigma or 800–200 cal. BC at 2 sigma (OxA-993; 2390 ± 80 BP; calibrated using OxCal v.3.8) was obtained from mineralised ash wood in the handle.

Stead 1991; 1996, 71–2, fig. 78; Jope 2000, 247–8.

River Trent near Ratcliffe-on-Soar, Nottinghamshire (Fig. 7)

The spine, boss, and terminals are all made from a single sheet of copper alloy. Found 1895. Length *c.* 892 mm (the spine is slightly distorted). The shield was of wood faced with copper alloy and was probably oval, like Chertsey, Witham, and Battersea, accepting Stead's (1985) early date for the latter. The two sections of the spine are of different lengths and it is assumed that as on the Witham shield, the shorter one was the uppermost.

The spine, boss, and terminals are bordered by a flat flange, which has a slight groove at its edge. The oval boss and areas on the spine either side of the terminals are ornamented with shallow relief decoration made by removing the metal from around the designs. The decoration on the spine is formed of two opposing beasts, each made up of a panel with the beast and a panel of wave patterns at the other end of the spine.

The shield is described here from the perspective of the man carrying it, although it is viewed and illustrated the other way round. Thus what was top left to the bearer (panel B) is seen by the viewer as top right.

The boss has an opposed and reversed pair of intertwining beasts (A on the left, and B on the right; Fig. 7). A large concave washer in the centre of the boss presumably originally contained either coral or red glass. The two beasts are very similar but by no means symmetrical. Strands link all the elements of the beasts and it is suggested here that the individual elements of the beasts may be identified as follows. A head (1), a body and neck (2), two wings (3 and 4), and two legs (5 and 6). A tongue or other projection issues from the mouth (7), while a tail (8) runs from the rear leg. The tails and tongues of the beasts overlap, each becoming the other of the opposing beast. Leg 5, with a sharp angle and a claw, and wing 3 also overlap. Incised lines mark the wings.

On the spine, the bodies of the beasts – which are closely related to those on the boss – are in panels C and F with corresponding tails in the form of wave patterns at the other end of the spine in panels D and E. The pairs are, on the left, panels C and D; and on the right, panels E and F.

The areas either side of the terminals have panels of sinuous decoration. The uppermost panel on the left-hand side (C) is decorated with a beast that is seen here as a backward-facing bird or dragon with a small wing extended in front of it, an open beak that could also represent the other wing, and a strong body that runs into an angled leg that has a claw. A domed rivet that could have formed the eye is placed off-centre of the head, but on the beast on the right-hand side (panel F) the rivet/eye is placed within the head. The other leg or tail forms a single, typically Waldalgesheim style wave, before running on to become the groove that borders the flange that runs around the whole spine and its terminals.

At the bottom of the spine the groove runs into a panel (D) of wave decoration of Verger's (1987) type AI. There are five waves and the tendrils that spring from them share the same direction as those in panel A. The final tendril in panel D terminates in a crescent shape that recalls the claws of the beasts in panels C and F.

The beast in panel F at the bottom right of the spine is similar to that in C, although the extended wing and one of the talons of the claw are separate from the main pattern and the rivet that could have acted as the eye is well placed. There are two waves behind the beast in panel F, but the direction of the tendrils on the four waves in panel E are reversed from those in F.

The top right panel (E) is a typical Waldalgesheim

pattern, again with tendrils of Verger's type AI. The top of the last wave nearest to the top of the shield flows into (i) a simple terminal that crosses back over the last wave, and which echoes the tongue/tail of the beasts on the boss, and (ii) a plain tendril that runs into the flange at the terminal. This plain tendril could be seen as joining together the two halves of the spine in the way of the tongues/tails on the boss. The last wave at the bottom of the panel runs into the groove that forms the edge of the flange and runs all around the spine and terminals. At the bottom of the spine this wave forms the beginning of a very similar pattern (panel F), but the direction of the waves are reversed and they become the tail of a beast. The beast is seen here as a backward-facing bird or dragon with a small wing extended in front of it, an open beak that could also represent the other wing, and a strong body that runs into an angled leg that has a claw. A domed rivet would have formed the eye.

Both sides of the spine have an equal number of waves (six), although the pattern between those on panels C and D is reversed.

There are two main differences between the reading given here and that given by Ian Stead. The first is that the beasts are seen the other way up, i.e. with their feet down and so resting on the spine. From this perspective what was taken to be 'a curling horn or plume terminating in a fan' (Watkins *et al.* 1996, 25) becomes a wing in an arrangement not dissimilar to that on the Wandsworth round boss. The second difference is that instead of viewing the decoration on the spine as four separate panels, it is seen here as forming two opposed beasts each made up of a panel with the beast and a panel of wave patterns at the other end of the spine. The tail/leg of the beasts are seen here as turning into a wave pattern which is continued along the groove that borders the flange and then joins with wave pattern at the other end of the spine.

Watkins *et al.* 1996; Jope 2000, 247.

River Thames at Wandsworth: Wandsworth round boss (Figs 4, 8)

The central boss of a shield, presented to the British Museum in 1858 by the Royal Archaeological Institute. Diameter 365 mm. Found at the same time as the Wandsworth long or 'mask' boss, but not necessarily related.

The wide flange of the boss has two opposed, and reversed, beasts in relief. The beasts, probably birds, are similar, but not identical. Elements of both beasts bear incised decoration. There are also two opposed beasts incised on the raised part of the boss.

The eye of the upper (?) bird (A) has a rivet that indicates that the head (1) was once decorated with coral or red glass (Fig. 8). To its left, part of the wing (2) is marked by two panels that bear incised decoration. The wing continues as a raised line, turning into a circle. The three areas that spring from or are formed by the circle do not have incised decoration. Sweeping below the head of the beast is either its body or the other wing (3). This also flows into a circle. The line continues beyond the circle, forming three areas, the last of which has a hooked terminal that echoes the beak of the bird. Joined to the head of the beast is either the other wing, or the body or tail (4), or what may be a separate object. In the upper wing (2), one panel is decorated with a bird. The lower (?) bird (B) is very similar to bird A. One panel in the upper wing has palmette-based decoration.

Around the centre of the boss are two opposed and reversed birds (Fig. 4 detail) that are similar to the one within the wing of bird A on the flange. These could also be read as representing larger heads. The two heads are directly between the heads on the flange. A line leads from the bird/head before sweeping as a wing in front of the beak and then behind it either as another wing or as the body of the bird. The latter wing/body ends with a circle that has a star within it, as in the bird's head, and a triangle recalls the beak.

A hole in the centre of the boss presumably once held a rivet that retained a disc of coral or red glass. The ridge that surrounds the central raised boss which has been punched alternately from different sides giving a crimped appearance.

Brailsford 1975, 14–20; Jope 2000, 68–9, 248–9.

River Thames at Wandsworth: Wandsworth long or 'mask' boss (Figs 5, 9)

Found before 1849 and presented to the British Museum in 1858 by the Royal Archaeological Institute. Surviving length *c.* 380 mm. Found at the same time as the Wandsworth round boss, but not necessarily related.

The central boss and – on the assumption that the shorter length of the spine was the upper one, as on the Witham shield – the upper spine of a metal-faced shield. The uppermost roundel and part of lower part of the spine and the corresponding roundel are missing.

The central boss is oval and was decorated in repoussé with two birds' heads (Fig. 9, 1–2). Some of the high relief parts of the wafer-thin sheet metal have been damaged but it is clear that the decoration on the central boss consists of two opposed, reversed, and perhaps symmetrical birds' heads, with hooked beaks. The ridges of the beaks are punch decorated giving a slightly crenulated appearance.

The necks of both birds sweep round into a ridge (3) that they share and which has been punched to create a crimped appearance (similar to that on the Wandsworth round boss). Below this ridge on either side are relief trisceles (4 and 5) set in a panel. These panels sweep back past the back of the birds' heads and end in small oval shaped panels (6 and 7), considered here to be wings.

The arrangement on the boss can be read as two birds sharing a single body and perhaps a pair of wings, only one of which immediately appears to belong to a head.

The 'wings' are divided into two panels, one of which has three spirals left in relief in it, the opposite side of the other panel is punch decorated in the same way as the beaks of the birds. Three spirals are also incised onto the panels just below the heads (8–9), and quite possibly on a triangular panel within the heads. Due to the damage it is uncertain whether the eyes of the birds were decorated with coral or red glass, but it may be that they were represented by relief trisceles next to the decorated triangular panels.

The form of the eyes on the human head or mask at the top of the spine is also unknown, but the nose and mouth bear similar incised decoration to that on the birds: three spirals on the nose, and punch impression along the mouth.

Brailsford 1975, 14–20; Jope 2000, 62–5; 248.

River Witham near Washingborough, Lincolnshire (Figs 6, 8–9)

Found *c.* 1826 and presented to the British Museum in 1872 by A.W. Franks from the Meyrick Collection. Length 1 m.

The copper alloy facing, boss and spine of a wooden shield. The 0.2–0.3 mm thick facing is made from two parts, the join between them covered by the spine. The spine, boss and roundels appear to be raised from a single piece of metal. There are two terminal roundels, which, like the boss, are elaborately decorated in repoussé. The face of the shield was also decorated with an appliqué in the form of a boar. This is now only represented by differential patination and the rivet holes that were used to attach it. The central motif for the upper roundel and much of the edge binding are missing.

The roundels each had a central petalled boss – only one of which survives – ringed by engraved decoration based on half palmettes, some of which may be read as birds' heads (Megaw *et al.* 1999, 381, pl. 3a). This in turn is surrounded by an open circle in relief with wavy or crimped decoration, which terminates above the spine in two half palmettes. Between and just below the junction of the half-palmettes are three perforations that presumably once held an inlay of glass or coral.

The roundels rest on the top of the heads of beasts at the ends of the spine (Fig. 11). The beasts have been identified variously, often as horses (e.g. Jope 2000, 58), but while the palmette derived decoration either side of the head has been interpreted as ears, this style is seen on what have been interpreted as bird wings on the Ratcliffe on Soar boss. Zigzag decoration runs from the edge of the ears/wings all the way round the edge of the spine and boss. The upper parts of the spine are decorated with incised decoration based on half palmettes similar to that on the roundels. This decoration ends in tear-shaped lobes that echo the ends of the decoration on the boss.

The elaborate repoussé decoration on the boss is almost symmetrical across a diagonal line and may be based on half palmettes. The design is made of a swirling pattern that flows from paired scrolls that flank the central boss, which is decorated with three coral studs. The scrolls lead in one direction onto the spine where they terminate in teardrops. In the other direction they lead into a swirling pattern that encloses almost circular shapes. A similar motif is seen on the edge of the central roundel of the Battersea shield (Stead 1985). At the top of this pattern, adjacent to the top of the boss, there are circular coral studs. It is likely that circular and triangular perforations to either side of the scrolls also held glass or coral. The area between the teardrop extension and the design on the boss is filled with incised ornament recalling the decoration next to the heads at the end of the spine.

Although not immediately obvious as representation of animals, the symmetry of the design and overall arrangement strongly recalls the beasts on the Ratcliffe on Soar and Wandsworth mask bosses, suggesting that the Witham design also represents opposed beasts.

Jope 1971b; 2000, 54–62, 246–7.

Bibliography

Atkinson, R.J.C. and Piggott, S. 1955. The Torrs chamfrein, *Archaeologia* 96, 197–235.

Barrett, J.C., Freeman, P.W.M. and Woodward, A., 2000. *Cadbury Castle, Somerset. The Later Prehistoric and Early Historic Archaeology.* London: English Heritage Archaeological Report 20.

Bertin, D. 1974. Le fourreau d'épée celtique décoré de Baron-sur-Odon (Calvados), *Gallia* 32, 243–248.

Bonnamour, L. and Bullard, A. 1976. Une épée celtique à fourreau décoré, découverte à Montbellet (Saône-et-Loire), *Gallia* 34, 279–284.

Brailsford, J.W. 1975. *Early Masterpieces from Britain in the British Museum.* London: British Museum Press.

Brunaux, J.-L. and Lambot, B. 1987. *Guerre et armement chez les gaulois, 450–52 av. J.-C.* Paris: Errance.

Bulard, A. 1979. Fourreaux ornés d'animaux fantastiques affrontés découvertes en France, *Études Celtiques* 16, 27–52.

Bulard, A. 1982. A propos des origines de la paire d'animaux fantastiques sur les fourreaux d'epée laténiens, in Duval and Kruta 1982, 149–160.

Champion, S. 1976. Coral in Europe: commerce and celtic ornament, in Duval and Hawkes 1976, 29–40.

Collis, J.R. 2003. *The Celts. Origins, Myths and Inventions.* Stroud: Tempus.

Craddock, P., Cowell, M. and Stead, I.M. 2004. 'Britain's first brass', *Antiquaries Journal* 84, 346–352.

De Navarro, J.-M. 1952. The Celts in Britain and their art, in M.P. Charlesworth and M. Knowles (eds), *The Heritage of Early Britain,* 56–82. London: Bell.

De Navarro, J.-M. 1959. Zu einigen Schwertscheiden aus La Tène, *Bericht der Römisch-Germanischen Kommission* 40, 79–119.

De Navarro, J.-M. 1972. *The Finds from the Site of La Tène, I. Scabbards and the Swords found in them.* London: British Academy.

Duceppe-Lamarre, A. 2002. De la figuration ou de l'abstraction des monsters dans l'art laténien: l'exemple du griffon, *Sborník Národního*

Muzea v Praze. Řada A – Historie 56 (1–4), 65–70.

Duval P.-M. and Hawkes C.F.C. (eds) 1976. *Celtic Art in Ancient Europe: Five Protohistoric Centuries.* London: Academic Press.

Duval, P.-M. and Kruta, V. 1986. Le fourreau celtique de Cernon-sur-Coole (Marne), *Gallia* 44, 1–27.

Duval, P.-M. and Kruta, V. (eds), 1982, *L'Art celtique de la période de l'expansion, IVe et IIIe siècles avant notre ère.* Paris: Librairie Droz.

Evans, C. 1989. Archaeology and modern times: Bersu's Woodbury 1938 & 1939, *Antiquity* 63, 436–450.

Field, N. and Parker Pearson, M. 2003. *Fiskerton. An Iron Age Timber Causeway with Iron Age and Roman Votive Offerings.* Oxford: Oxbow Books.

Fitzpatrick, A.P. 1984. The deposition of La Tène Iron Age metalwork in watery contexts in southern England, in B. Cunliffe and D. Miles (eds), *Aspects of the Iron Age in Central Southern England*, 178–190. Oxford: Oxford University Committee for Archaeology Monograph 2.

Fitzpatrick, A.P. 1996a. 'Celtic' Iron Age Europe: the theoretical basis, in P. Graves-Brown, S. Jones and C. Gamble (eds), *Cultural Identity and Archaeology: The Construction of European Communities*, 238–255. London: Routledge.

Fitzpatrick, A.P. 1996b. An Iron Age shield mount from Meare Village East 'lake village', Somerset, *Somerset Archaeology and Natural History* 141, 69–72.

Fitzpatrick, A.P. 1996c. Night and Day: the symbolism of astral signs on later Iron Age anthropomorphic hilted short swords, *Proceedings of the Prehistoric Society* 62, 373–398.

Fox, C. 1958. *Pattern and Purpose: A Survey of Early Celtic Art in Britain.* Cardiff: National Museum of Wales.

Frey, O.-H. 1987. Sui gancu di cintura celtici e sulla prima fase de La Tène nell'Italia del Nord, in Vitali 1987b, 9–22.

Frey, O.-H. 1991. Einige Bemerkungen zu den durchbrochenen Frühlatènegürtelhaken, in A. Haffner and A. Miron (eds), *Studien zur Eisenzeit im Hunsrück-Nahe-Raum. Symposium Birkenfeld 1987*, 101–111. Trier: Trierer Zeitschrift Beiheft 13.

Frey, O.-H. 1995a. Some comments on swords with dragon pairs, in Raftery 1995, 163–175.

Frey, O.-H. 1995b. The Celts in Italy, in M.J. Green (ed.), *The Celtic World*, 515–532. London: Routledge.

Frey, O.-H. 2000. Book review essay: ethnicity and identity in archaeology, *European Journal of Archaeology* 3 (1), 115–122.

Ginoux, N. 1995. Lyres et dragons, nouvelles données pour l'analyse d'un des principaux thèmes ornementaux des fourreaux laténiens, *L'Europe celtique du Ve au IIIe siècle avant J.-C. Contacts, échanges et mouvements de population (Actes du 2e symposium international d'Hautvillers, 8–10 octobre 1992)*, 405–413. Reims: Mémoire de la Société Archéologique Champenoise 9.

Ginoux, N. 2002. La figuration et sa déconstruction: l'exemple du motif de la paire d'animaux fantastique affrontés sur les fourreaux d'épée laténiens, *Sborník Národního Muzea v Praze. Řada A – Historie* 56 (1–4), 71–82.

Green, M. 1992. *Animals in Celtic Art and Myth.* London: Routledge.

Gunby, J. 2000. Oval shield representations on the Black Sea littoral, *Oxford Journal of Archaeology* 19, 359–365.

Harding, D.W. 2002. Torrs and the early La Tène ornamental style in Britain and Ireland, in B. Ballin Smith and I. Banks (eds), *In the Shadow of the Brochs. The Iron Age in Scotland*, 191–204. Stroud: Tempus.

Hawkes, C.F.C. 1947. Review of Jacobstahl 1944, *Journal of Roman Studies* 37, 191–198.

Hunter, F. 1997 Iron Age hoarding in Scotland and northern England, in A. Gwilt and C. Haselgrove (eds), *Reconstructing Iron Age Societies*, 108–133. Oxford: Oxbow Monograph 71.

Hunter, F. 2001. The carnyx in Iron Age Europe, *Antiquaries Journal* 81, 77–108.

Jacobstahl, P. 1939. The Witham sword, *Burlington Magazine* 75 (no. 436, July 1939), 28–31.

Jacobstahl, P. 1944. *Early Celtic Art.* Oxford: Clarendon Press.

Joachim, H.-E., 1995. *Waldalgesheim. Das Grab einer Fürstin.* Bonn: Katalog des Rheinischen Landesmuseums Bonn 3.

Jope, E.M. 1971a. The Witham shield, in G. de G. Sieveking (ed.), *Prehistoric and Roman Studies*, 61–90. London: British Museum Quarterly 35.

Jope, E.M. 1971b. The Waldalgesheim master, in J. Boardman, M.A. Brown and T.G.E. Powell (eds), *The European Community in Later Prehistory*, 167–180. London: Routledge and Kegan Paul.

Jope, E.M. 1976. The Wandsworth mask shield and its European stylistic sources of inspiration, in Duval and Hawkes 1976, 167–184.

Jope, E.M. 1978. The southward face of Celtic Britain; 300 BC–AD 50: four British parade shields, *Academia Nazionale dei Lincei* 375, 27–36.

Jope, E.M. 2000. *Early Celtic Art in the British Isles.* Oxford: Oxford University Press.

Kemble, J.M. 1863. *Horae Ferales: Studies in the Archaeology of the Northern Nations* (ed. R.G. Latham and A.W. Franks). London: Lovell Reeve.

Kildbride Jones, H.E. 1994. A note on the date of the Battersea shield, *Studia Celtica* 28, 1–9.

Kruta, V. 1982. Aspects unitaires et faciès dans l'art celtique du IVe et IIIe siècles av. notre ère, in Duval and Kruta 1982, 35–75.

Kruta, V. 1983. Faciès celtiques de la Cisalpine aux IVe et IIIe siècles av. notre ère, in *Popoli e facies culturali celtiche a nord e a sud dell'Alpi dal V al I secolo a.c. Atti del Colloquio Internazionale*, 1–15. Milan: Civico Museo Archeologico.

Kruta, V. 1986. Le corail, le vin et l'arbre de vie: observations sur l'art et la religion des Celtes du Ve au Ier siècle avant J.-C., *Études Celtiques* 23, 7–32.

Layton, R. 1991. *The Anthropology of Art* (2nd edn). Cambridge: Cambridge University Press.

Leeds, E.T. 1933. *Celtic Ornament in the British Isles down to AD 700.* Oxford: Oxford University Press.

Lejars, T. 1994. *Gournay III. Les fourreaux d'épée. Le sanctuaire de Gournay-sur-Aronde et l'armement des Celtes de La Tène moyenne.* Paris: Errance.

Megaw, J.V.S. 1981. Une volière celtique: quelques notes sur l'identification des oiseaux dans l'art celtique ancienne, *Revue Archéologique de l'Est et du Centre-Est* 32, 137–143.

Megaw, J.V.S. and Megaw, M.R. 1990. "Semper aliquid novum…" – Celtic dragon pairs re-reviewed, *Acta Archaeologica Hungaricae* 42, 55–72.

Megaw, J.V.S. and Megaw, M.R. 1991. The earliest insular Celtic Art: some unanswered questions, *Études Celtiques* 28, 283–307.

Megaw, J.V.S., Megaw, R.M. and Neugebauer, J.-W. 1989. Zeugnisse frühlatènezeitlichen Kunsthandwerks aus dem Raum Herzogenberg, Niederösterreich, *Germania* 67, 477–451.

Megaw, M.R. and Megaw, J.V.S. 1986. *Early Celtic Art in Britain and*

Ireland. Princes Risborough: Shire Publications.

Megaw, M.R. and Megaw, J.V.S. 1989. *Celtic Art from its Beginnings to the Book of Kells.* London: Thames and Hudson.

Megaw, M.R. and Megaw, J.V.S. 1993. The swans of Radosevice reviewed, in J. Waldhauser *et multi alii, Die Hallstatt- und Latènezeitliche Siedlung mit Gräberfeld von Radosevice in Böhmen*, 227–234. Prague: Archeologický Výzkum v Severních Čechách 21.

Megaw, M.R., Megaw, J.V.S. and Niblett, R. 1999. A decorated Iron Age copper alloy knife from Hertfordshire, *Antiquaries Journal* 79, 379–387.

Merriman, N.J. 1987. Value and motivation in prehistory: the evidence for 'Celtic spirit,' in I. Hodder (ed.), *The Archaeology of Contextual Meanings*, 111–116. Cambridge: Cambridge University Press.

Moreau, J., Ankner, D., Boudet, R., Dhénin, M. and Fecht, M. 1995. *Le sanglier-enseigne gaulois à Soulac-sur-Mer (Gironde).* Soulac-sur-Mer: Musée Archéologique de Soulac-sur-Mer

Parker Pearson, M. 1999. Food, sex and death: cosmologies in the British Iron Age with particular reference to East Yorkshire, *Cambridge Archaeological Journal* 9, 43–69.

Pauli, L. 1985. Early Celtic society: two centuries of wealth and turmoil in central Europe, in T.C. Champion and J.V.S. Megaw (eds), *Settlement and Society: Aspects of West European Prehistory in the First Millennium BC*, 23–43. Leicester: Leicester University Press.

Petres, E. 1982. Notes on scabbards decorated with dragons and bird-pairs, in Duval and Kruta 1982, 161–174.

Piggott, S. 1950. Swords and scabbards of the British Iron Age, *Proceedings of the Prehistoric Society* 16, 1–28.

Pyatt, F.B., Beaumont, E.H., Lacy, D., Magilton, J.R. and Buckland, P.C. 1991, Non Isatis sed Vitrum, or, the colour of Lindow Man, *Oxford Journal of Archaeology* 10, 61–73.

Raftery, B. (ed.) 1995. *Sites and Sights of the Iron Age. Essays on Fieldwork and Museum Research Presented to Ian Mathieson Stead.* Oxford: Oxbow Monograph 56.

Rapin, A. 2001. Un bouclier celtique dans la colonie grecque de Camarina (Sicile), *Germania* 79, 273–296.

Rapin, A. 2002. Une épée celtique demasquinée d'or du Ve s. av. J.-C. au Musée des Antiquités Nationales, *Antiquités Nationales* 34, 155–171.

Rapin, A. 2003. Les analyses semiologique de l'image: l'iconographie du deuxième âge du Fer, in O. Büchsenschütz, A. Bulard, M.-B. Chardenoux and N. Ginoux (eds), *Décors, images, signes de l'âge du Fer européen (Actes du XXVIe Colloque AFEAF à Paris et Saint Denis 2002)*, 49–62. Tours: Revue Archéologique du Centre de la France supplément 24.

Rapin, A. and Schwaller, M. 1987. Contribution à l'étude de l'armement celtique: la tombe 163 d'Ensérune (Hérault), *Revue Archéologique Narbonnaise* 20, 155–183.

Rapin, A., Szabó, M. and Vitali, D. 1992. Monte Bibele, Litér, Rezi, Pişcolt. Contributions à l'origine du style des épées hongroises, *Communicationes Archaeologicae Hungariae* 1992, 23–54.

Ritchie, J.N.G. 1969. Shields in north Britain in the Iron Age, *Scottish Archaeological Forum* 1, 31–40.

Sankot, P. 2000. Aktueller Stand der Konservierung latènezeitlicher Schwerter aus dem Gräbern Radosevice 15 und Jenišev Ûjezd 106, *Památky archeologické* supplementum 13, 361–369.

Schwappach, F. 1974. Zu einigen Tierdarstellungen der Frühlatènekunst, *Hamburger Beiträge zur Archäologie* 4, 103–140.

Spratling, M. 1970. Bronze shield-mount, in L. Alcock, Excavations at South Cadbury Castle, 1969: a summary report, *Antiquaries Journal* 50, 21–22 (14–25).

Spratling, M. 1972. The smiths of South Cadbury, *Current Archaeology* 2, 188–191.

Stary, P.F. 1981. Ursprung und Ausbreitung der eisenzeitlichen Ovalschilde mit spindelförmigem Schildbuckel, *Germania* 59, 287–306.

Stary, P. 1986–7. Die militärische Rückwirkungen der keltischen Invasion auf die Appenin-Halbinsel, *Hamburger Beiträge zur Archäologie* 13–14, 65–117.

Stead, I.M. 1967. A La Tène III burial at Welwyn Garden City, *Archaeologia* 101, 1–62.

Stead, I.M. 1979. *The Arras Culture.* York: Yorkshire Philosophical Society.

Stead, I.M. 1984. Celtic dragons from the River Thames, *Antiquaries Journal* 64, 269–279.

Stead, I.M. 1985. *The Battersea Shield.* London: British Museum Press.

Stead, I.M. 1991a. *Iron Age Cemeteries in East Yorkshire.* London: English Heritage Archaeological Report 22.

Stead, I.M. 1991b. Many more shields from Iron Age Britain, *Antiquaries Journal* 71, 1–35.

Stead, I.M. 1995. The metalwork, in K. Parfitt, *Iron Age Burials from Mill Hill, Deal*, 58–111. London: British Museum Press.

Stead, I.M. 1996. *Celtic Art in Britain in Britain before the Roman Conquest* (2nd edn). London: British Museum Press.

Stead, I.M. 1998. *The Salisbury Hoard.* Stroud: Tempus.

Szabó, M. 1977. The origins of the Hungarian sword style, *Antiquity* 51, 211–220.

Szabó, M. 1989. Beiträge zur Geschichte des keltischen Drachenpaarmotivs, *Communicationes Archaeologicae Hungariae*, 119–128.

Szabó, M. 1991. Le monde celtique au IIIe siècle avant, *Études Celtiques* 28, 11–31.

Szabó, M. 1995. Umbro-celtica, in Raftery 1995, 157–162.

Szabó, M. and Petres, E.F. 1991. *Decorated Weapons of the La Tène Iron Age in the Carpathian Basin.* Budapest: Inventaria Praehistorica Hungariae 5.

Taylor, T. 1991. Celtic art, *Scottish Archaeological Review* 8, 129–132.

Van der Veen, M., Hall, A.J. and May, J. 1993. Woad and the Britons painted blue, *Oxford Journal of Archaeology* 12, 367–371.

Verger, S. 1987. La genèse celtique des rinceaux à triscèles, *Jahrbuch des Römisch-Germanischen Zentralmuseums Mainz* 34, 287–339.

Vitali, D. 1984. Un fodero celtico con decorazione a lira zoomorfa da Monte Bibele (Monterenzio, Provincia de Bologna), *Études Celtiques* 21, 35–43.

Vitali, D. 1987a. Monte Bibele tra Etruschi e Celti: data archeologici e interpretzione storica, in Vitali 1987b, 309–380.

Vitali, D. (ed.) 1987b. *Celti ed Etruschi nell'Italia centro-settentrionale dal V secolo a.C. alla romanizzazione (Atti del Colloquio Internazionale Bologna 12–14 aprile 1985).* Imola: Bologna University Press.

Watkins, J., Stead, I.M., Hook, D. and Palmer, S. 1996. A decorated shield-boss from the River Trent, near Ratcliffe-on-Soar, *Antiquaries Journal* 76, 17–30.

An archaeological investigation of Later Iron Age Norfolk: analysing hoarding patterns across the landscape

Natasha Hutcheson

Introduction

The Later Iron Age of northern East Anglia is famed for two things; the story of Boudica, and hoards of gold torcs. Boudica, the flame-haired warrior 'Queen' and tribal leader of the Iceni, is documented as having led the native British in a rebellion against the Romans in AD 60/61. The most commonly recounted version of the story, derived from Tacitus (*Annals* XIV, 31–38), is a compelling tale of abuse and warfare. In addition, this narrative on the events of AD 60/61 is one of the few detailed 'histories' we have pertaining to Iron Age Britain. As such, it has received a great deal of attention, not only in terms of dedicated research, but also in terms of its use in interpreting the Later Iron Age in the region (see for example, Hingley and Unwin 2005). For example, the hoarding of Icenian silver coins during the final Iron Age in northern East Anglia is often viewed as a response to the rebellion, i.e. people burying their wealth for safekeeping during a time of stress (e.g. Allen 1970, 19; Chadburn and Gurney 1991; Chadburn 1992, 82). This historical dimension has resulted in a tendency to use the archaeological evidence to demonstrate historical events. As a result, the material record has not been effectively exploited as a source of insight into Iron Age communities living in this region in the period before and immediately after the Roman conquest.

This study aims to redress the balance of study and explore Later Iron Age communities in northern East Anglia through their archaeological remains, rather than through an historical filter. To achieve this, the paper will focus on patterns in the deposition of torcs, coins, and items of horse equipment across and within the landscape of Norfolk, especially in hoards, and will summarise the principal results obtained from a recent in-depth study of these topics (Hutcheson 2004).

Why Norfolk?

In broad terms, it is understood that the Iceni occupied north Suffolk, Norfolk, and north-east Cambridgeshire. When approaching the Iron Age of this region it is generally expected that the Icenian territory as a whole should be investigated. However, such a geographical perspective presents a number of problems for the approach adopted here. My research focuses on three categories of metalwork found by chance or by metal detectorists, and relies on the detail of twelve figure grid references in order to investigate patterns in their deposition and distribution across the landscape, but there are significant differences in the way material has been recorded in the three counties concerned, so that the datasets are not easily comparable. Norfolk, however, has had a long, comprehensive, and detailed programme of recording metal items, using twelve figure grid references, with objects being identified and recorded over twenty-five years and more, by the same people, forming a coherently recorded dataset; for this reason, the paper is directed to Norfolk and not to the wider Icenian tribal area. Furthermore, exploring this county alone avoids the problem of research becoming preoccupied with where the boundaries of the Iceni might be, and thus following once again a historically-led agenda. Instead, Norfolk forms a case study whereby later Iron Age communities in a large part of northern East Anglia are investigated through their archaeological remains, although this does not preclude discussion of the Iceni and the Boudican rebellion.

Metalwork in the landscape

There is little well-known and excavated Iron Age settlement in Norfolk. Instead, metal artefacts, many of which have been recovered by metal detectorists, dominate the archaeological record, and this forms the main dataset through which to investigate Iron Age communities. Metal-detected material is often considered problematic to use in archaeological research as it lacks detailed contextual information. However, where there is a detailed grid reference, it is possible to consider artefacts or, as in this paper, hoards of artefacts in terms of their landscape location, and it is patterns in location upon which this research focuses. Firstly, the distribution and deposition of torcs will be discussed, followed by an investigation of patterns in the location of coin hoards, and then hoards of horse equipment. Finally, the trends observed will be discussed with regard to what they might tell us about later Iron Age society in the region.

Torcs

Gold torcs have been recovered from seven separate locations in Norfolk (Fig. 1). The most famous is the site at Ken Hill, Snettisham, in the north-west of the county, where eleven hoards of gold, silver, electrum, and bronze torcs have been recovered since 1948. A number of finds were discovered by chance during agricultural activity, but the site has also seen two campaigns of excavation. The first, directed by R. Rainbird Clarke, was undertaken in the early 1950s. Subsequently, in 1990, under the directorship of Dr Ian Stead, the British Museum undertook a series of excavations at Ken Hill. In the 1950s, three hoards of torcs were excavated (A, B, and C), comprising one collection of 'tubular' torcs (hoard A) and two collections of 'scrap' metal (hoards B and C) including coins, fragments of twisted wire, items fused together, fragments of torcs, ingot rings, and bracelets (Clarke 1954). Two further torcs were found during ploughing: the 'Great Torc' from hoard E and the torc from hoard D. In 1990 another hoard of 'scrap' (hoard F) was recovered by a metal detectorist (Stead 1991, 450–1). This led to the British Museum excavations which recovered a further five hoards comprising nests of complete torcs (G, H, J, K, L; *ibid.*).

Of the remaining six torc sites in Norfolk, Bawsey, Narford, and Sedgeford have yielded more than one torc or torc fragment. The finds from Bawsey comprise two complete twisted bar torcs with loop terminals, which were found by chance in 1941 and 1944 during ploughing (Wake 1942; Clarke 1954, 50–51). After a gap of over forty years, the site was metal detected and a number of fragments of silver and gold-silver alloy wire were recovered. After a wrangle in the courts, two decorated buffer terminals have also been provenanced to the same field in Bawsey (Stead 1998, 136–7). At Sedgeford, a near-complete torc made up of a series of twisted wires with a moulded terminal ring was recovered in the 1960s, at a spot several hundred metres away from the hoard of Gallo-Belgic E staters discussed later in this paper. In 2004, the missing terminal of the torc was recovered by metal-detector survey in the field above where the coins were found (Faulkner 2004). From Narford, part of a buffer terminal torc, which was partly melted and had fragments of twisted bar and loop terminal torcs fused to it, was recovered by metal detector in 1980–81. A complete elongated loop terminal torc was subsequently recovered, as were a number of other wire fragments (HER 3974). The final three sites, North Creake (Clarke 1951a), Marham (HER 4484), and East Winch (HER 12559) have each only produced one torc or torc fragment.

Due to a lack of associated material, only the artefacts from Snettisham have been closely analysed in terms of date, and over the years opinion has varied as to when they were deposited. In the 1950s, Rainbird Clarke dated the manufacture of the torcs and bracelets in hoards A, B/C, D, and E to between 100 BC and 25 BC, and suggested that they were deposited between 25 BC and AD 10 (Clarke 1954, 69). This date of deposition was pushed back to the first half of the first century BC (*c.* 70 BC) after the British Museum excavations (Stead 1991, 455; 1998, 146). However, recent research on the dating of Gallo-Belgic coinage suggests that the dating of some of the torc deposits could be even earlier. The two 'scrap' metal hoards (B/C and F) both contain Gallo-Belgic A and C coins (Dolley 1954, 72–86; Sealey 1979, 165–66; Stead 1991, 455), whilst an insular type of Gallo-Belgic D quarter stater was found in the terminal of the Great Torc from hoard E (Clarke 1954, 59). It is now thought that Gallo-Belgic A coins came into use in Britain in the earlier second century BC (Haselgrove 1999, 125–7; 165), whilst Gallo-Belgic C and D types date between the later second century BC and the early first century BC (*ibid.*, 134–36; 165). The later, Gallo-Belgic E staters, which succeeded Gallo-Belgic C, are conspicuously absent from Snettisham. By association, then, the deposition of the 'scrap' metal hoards B/C and F and the Great Torc from hoard E could have been as early as the late second century BC.

None of the other hoards of complete torcs from Snettisham and the rest of the county have been found in association with coins, so dating their deposition will never be straightforward. However, it is likely that they are related in terms of date. On the basis of their terminals, torcs from Norfolk can be grouped into five types: loop, ring, buffer, cage, and reel terminals (Stead 1991, 454). These types occur across the deposits from Norfolk, and are mixed within the collections of 'scrap' and complete artefacts at Snettisham. In essence, there are no appreciable typological differences between the collections of torcs that would assist in a simple seriation

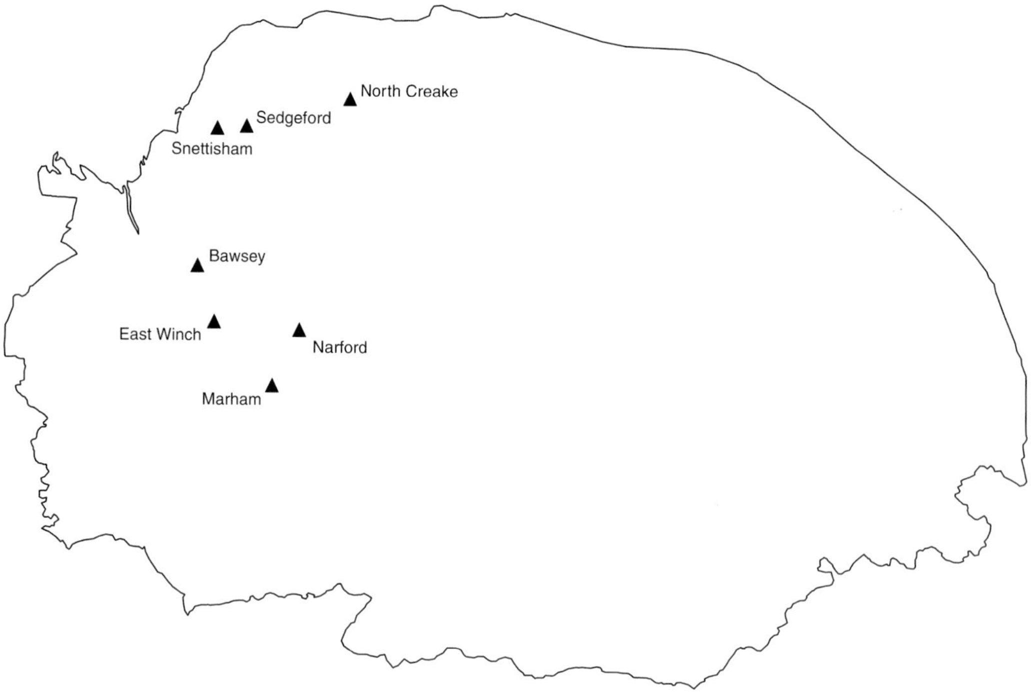

Fig. 1. Distribution of gold torcs in Norfolk.

Site name	*Location*
Snettisham 'Gold-field'	35 m OD *Highspot* On a spur of land
Bawsey	10 m OD *Highspot* Fen/estuary island
North Creake	63 m OD *Highspot* Hill top area
Sedgeford	58 m OD *Highspot* Hill top
East Winch	Approx. 35 m OD *Highspot*
Marham	22 m OD Gently undulating landscape
Narford	15 m OD Near base of Nar valley

Table 1. Location of torc deposits in Norfolk.

of the deposits. This implies that although not necessarily manufactured at the same time, the range of torcs from the county may have been deposited around the same time (*ibid.*). It is therefore possible that all the Norfolk torc deposits date to the second century BC, rather than to the first half of the first century BC. How long individual torcs were in use before deposition is, at present, unknowable.

To summarise, torcs have been recovered from seven locations in Norfolk, which have yielded varying quantities of artefacts ranging from over 175 complete examples at Snettisham, to single fragments, like that from North Creake. Finally, based on a recent reassessment of the dating of Gallo-Belgic coins, it is possible that at least some of the torc deposits date to the second century BC, rather than, as more usually suggested, the first century BC.

Distribution and deposition

As can be seen on Figure 1, there is a distinct pattern in the distribution of torcs across Norfolk: the findspots are all situated in the west of the county. In addition, it would seem that there was a preference for depositing torcs on prominent, high spots in the landscape (Table 1). For example, the site at Snettisham is located on a spur of land, and those at Sedgeford, East Winch, and North Creake are located in situations just off the top of the brow of a hill. These locations not only command a view, but by being situated off the brow of the hill they can be viewed from elsewhere in the landscape.

In contrast, the finds from Marham came from a low-lying 'valley' within a gently undulating landscape, and the Narford torcs were recovered near the base of another valley, within 200 m of the river Nar. In this respect, it is of interest that of the seven Norfolk torc finds, these two were recorded under the least convincing circumstances. The Narford torcs were recovered at night and sold on to an antiques dealer, so there is no full report. The Marham torc also bypassed the local museum, and although reported and described as being similar to the best Snettisham torc, it was thrown away! (HER 4484). Given the imprecise nature of the information regarding these two findspots and the impression that they do not fit the emerging landscape pattern of torc deposition, it is possible that the provenances are erroneous.

In addition to the preference for prominent high spots in the landscape, none of the Norfolk torc hoards are from places where other later Iron Age material is known, although the East Winch torc was discovered just to the north of an area of (undated) Iron Age activity, comprising pits and pottery (Hutcheson 2004, 45). Indeed, there appears to be clear dichotomy in north-west Norfolk between where metalwork entered the archaeological record and where other 'domestic' material did so. Metalwork hoards tend to be from high, 'secluded' places, whereas 'domestic' material is more often found at lower points, off the floodplains of the river valleys (Hutcheson 2003; 2004). Despite this emerging locational pattern, there is a great variation in the types of deposit encountered. In particular, Snettisham has produced a far greater number of torcs than any of the other sites. This site is exceptional; nowhere else in Britain has produced the same quantities of these artefacts. But is it possible that torcs recovered from elsewhere in Norfolk were interred in the ground as part of hoards like those at Snettisham, rather than as single items?

Whilst this is impossible to prove, there is nevertheless a relationship between the number of torcs and fragments recovered from any of the above sites and the nature and extent of archaeological investigation (Table 2). For example, the sites that have been metal detected (Bawsey, Narford, Sedgeford, and Snettisham) have produced more torcs than those that have not, and the sole site that has seen excavation as well as metal detecting (Snettisham) has produced the largest number of torcs and torc fragments. This pattern is paralleled in other parts of Britain, for example the single finds from Clevedon, Somerset and Glascote, Staffordshire (Ellis 1849; Leeds 1933; Painter 1970; Jope 2000, 254) were recovered by chance, and not excavated. Whether torcs are found as hoards or as single finds may be reflecting the method of recovery as much as the nature of deposition. It is possible, therefore, that all the torcs deposited in Norfolk entered the ground as hoards. Such an explanation would fit the distributional and depositional patterning of these artefacts, as it would seem that single finds and hoards are not treated differently in terms of landscape location.

The restriction of torcs to the west of the county might also suggest that their circulation, as well as their deposition, was controlled. In addition, if they were originally placed in the ground in hoards rather than singly, this implies a specific set of rules regarding their deposition. This is further expressed by the recurrent use of prominent locations in the landscape, implying that there was a 'correct' type of place for their deposition. As the Snettisham finds show, the torcs were also placed in the ground in a structured way. The hoards comprising complete torcs were described as nests (Stead 1991, 450) because of the way they were carefully placed one on top of another. As well as being carefully placed, each group was organised by metal type (*ibid.*,

Site name	*Number of torc finds*	*Method of recovery*
Snettisham	**175** complete torcs many hundreds of fragments	Chance find, metal-detecting, excavation
Bawsey	**2** buffer terminals **125** wire fragments **2** complete loop terminal torcs	Chance find, metal-detecting
Narford	**1** buffer terminal **8** torc fragments	Chance find, metal-detecting
Sedgeford	**1** torc in two fragments, found at different times	Chance find, metal-detecting
North Creake	**1** torc terminal	Chance find
Marham	**1** ?ring terminal torc	Chance find
Blackborough End Pits	**1** complete loop terminal torc	Chance find

Table 2. Number of torc finds and method of recovery.

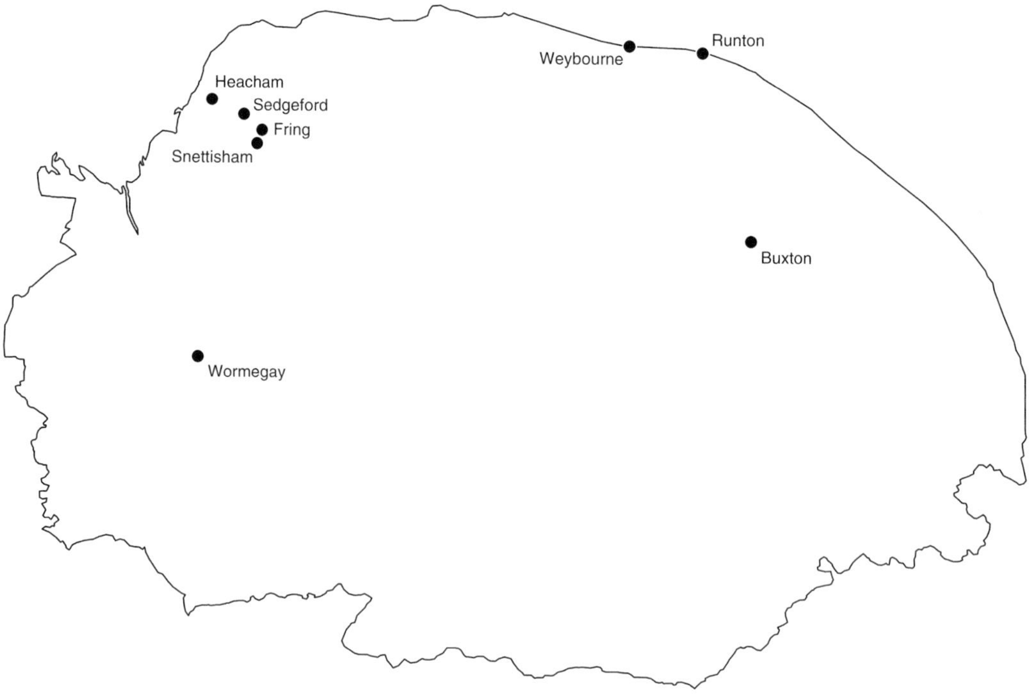

Fig. 2. Distribution of gold coin hoards in Norfolk.

451). The torcs with the highest silver content tend to be near the top of the hoards, with bronze and gold artefacts nearer the bottom. Stead (*ibid.*, 463) suggested that this reflected a desire to hide the most valuable torcs beneath less valuable 'decoys', but it could instead be argued that the deposits were organised around colour, the more silvery at the top, the more golden nearer the bottom (gold and bronze).

Coins

During the first century BC, a new type of hoard enters the archaeological record in this region: coins. These fall into two main groups, gold and silver. Gold coins can be further split into Gallo-Belgic and British types. The earliest of the hoards comprise five collections of Gallo-Belgic E and D types from Wormegay (HER 6459), Weybourne (HER 6264), Fring (HER 1661), Buxton-with-Lammas (HER 28394), and Sedgeford (HER 1607). The latest coins in these hoards are Gallo-Belgic E types, which can be broadly dated to the first half of the first century BC (although some would date them entirely to the middle of the century), thus post-dating the torc hoards with coins. Following the Gallo-Belgic coins, dating from around the mid first century BC through to the second half of the first century BC, are three hoards of British gold coins from Snettisham (Gregory 1992), Heacham (HER 28850), and Runton (HER 30894). Finally, seven well-provenanced hoards of Icenian silver coins have been recovered from the county: Honingham (Clarke 1956), Weston Longville (Roach-Smith 1853), Dereham (HER 31450), Forncett (HER 31949), Scole (Burnett and Bland 1986), North Creake (HER 25777), and Fring (Chadburn and Gurney 1991). The earliest silver coins minted in northern East Anglia date to the middle of the first century BC (Hobbs 1996, 31), although the majority of the hoards are later, dating to the first century AD (e.g. Creighton 1994). Essentially, then, the coin hoards post-date the torc hoards and run in a broad chronological sequence that starts with Gallo-Belgic types, followed by British gold types and then by Icenian silver units, which represent the latest and last phase of Iron Age coins in the region. Several of the late silver coin hoards also contain Roman coins.

Distribution and deposition: gold coins

Like torcs, Gallo-Belgic coin hoards and British gold coin hoards cluster in north-west Norfolk. From the second century BC through to the middle of the first century BC there is, then, a concentration of gold in the west of the county, first in the form of torcs, and then in the form of coins. However, this exclusive focus begins to break down during the first century BC, since, although concentrated in this area, later Gallo-Belgic and British gold hoards are also deposited elsewhere in the county (Fig. 2).

As well as having a broader cross-county distribution than torc deposits, gold coins were placed in a greater variety of 'landscape' locations. Within this range of locations, there is an emerging pattern: six of the eight gold coin hoards are from low-lying situations in close proximity to a water source (or overlooking the sea; Table 3). The first two of these, the collection of Gallo-Belgic E coins from Wormegay and the hoard of British gold staters from Heacham, are both located near the fen edge. The coins from Heacham lie on the northerly reaches of the salt fen, off the floodplain, and it is unlikely that they were originally placed in water. In contrast, the coins from Wormegay were located off the edge of a fen island at approximately 2 m above present day sea level. Given that water levels were higher in the Later Iron Age and that much of the present day fenland landscape is drained, this location may have been marshy or wet when the coins were deposited. Two hoards, both of Gallo-Belgic E staters, were found between 100 and 200 m from rivers, in both cases off the floodplain: Buxton-with-Lammas in the east of the county and Sedgeford in the west. Neither hoard seems likely to have been deposited in water.[1] The last two hoards were situated close to the sea: the find of Gallo-Belgic E and D coins from Weybourne and the hoard of Freckenham staters (a type of regional British gold coin) from Runton. Both hoards were found on the beach, having eroded out of the cliff. The coast in this region has receded, so these two hoards would originally have been deposited further inland than currently appears; however, it is probable that the depositional location would have commanded a view of the North Sea.

In contrast to the six hoards just discussed, the Gallo-Belgic E and D coins from Fring and the Snettisham hoard of British coin types, including Norfolk Wolf staters (Gregory 1992), come from prominent, 'high' spots in the landscape. The findspot of the Fring hoard is located at approximately 40 m above present day sea level, off the top of the hill overlooking the modern village of Fring, which is sited in the valley around a spring from which the Heacham river rises. The Snettisham hoard is located at approximately 60 m above present day sea level, again off the brow of the hill, again overlooking Fring. On current evidence, the gold coin hoards were not generally interred in close proximity to later Iron Age settlement.

It was proposed that torcs may all have been deposited in the ground in hoards and not singly. This is not, however, true of gold coins, since both Gallo-Belgic and British gold units are frequently recovered as single finds. However, the ratio of single coins to hoards changes through the first century BC. For example, of approximately 442 Gallo-Belgic E coins found in Norfolk up until 2001, only 20 (4%) were single finds, the rest from hoards. In contrast, of the 83 examples of Norfolk Wolf staters from the county, 30 were recovered as single finds (36%). During the first century BC, then, the ratio of single finds to hoard finds changes. In addition, single coins are distributed much more evenly across the region (Fig. 3), reflecting a shift away from the 'western-centric' deposition of gold in the second century BC.

Site name and coin type	*Landscape location*
Fring	40 m OD *Highspot* Overlooking river Heacham
Buxton-with-Lammas	12 m OD *Close to water* 200 m from river Bure
Wormegay	2 m OD *Close to water* Potentially wet in LIA
Weybourne	? m OD *Close to water* Cliff top – fallen onto beach
Sedgeford	15 m *Close to water* Valley bottom, 130 m from river
Snettisham	*60 m OD* Highspot
Heacham	5 m OD *Close to water* Edge of salt fen
Runton	? m OD *Close to water* Cliff – fallen onto beach

Table 3. Location of gold coin hoards.

As with torc deposits, patterns are emerging in the deposition of gold coins. It could be argued that the change in object type, from gold torc to gold coin, the greater variety of places in which coins were deposited, and the reduction in the proportion of material entering the ground in hoards, reflect a different depositional practice. However, the overriding tradition of purposeful deposition in the landscape away from obvious settlement locations continues. Indeed, the practice seems to expand geographically from what may have been a localised tradition in the second century BC. In addition, if single gold coins also represent 'deliberate deposits rather than accidental losses' (Haselgrove 1993, 50), it could be that the purposeful deposition of gold artefacts across the county increases during the first century BC.

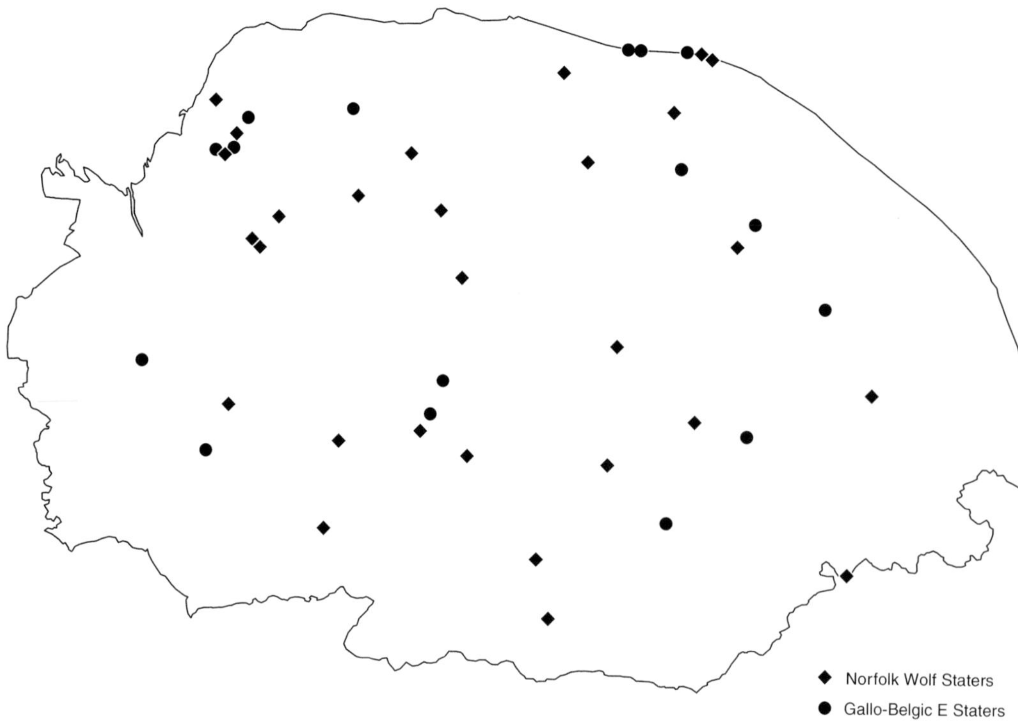

Fig. 3. Distribution of Gallo-Belgic E staters and Norfolk Wolf staters.

Fig. 4. Distribution of silver coin hoards in Norfolk.

Fig. 5. Distribution of silver coins in Norfolk.

Silver coins

After the mid first century BC, gold gives way to silver as the dominant coin metal. With the introduction of a different metal type, there is a distinct change in the distribution pattern of hoards across the county. Silver hoards are not concentrated in the west, indeed, of the seven under discussion, three are located centrally, two in the central south and only two in the north-west (Fig. 4). However, as with gold coins, the distribution of single silver coins is much more even across the county (Fig. 5).

Silver coin hoards appear to have been deposited in a variety of locations (Table 4). A number of sites occupy 'off-hilltop' locations. For example, the Weston Longville hoard was situated near the top of a steep slope approximately 35 m above present day sea level. The same is true of the Honingham hoard, which was situated near the top of the valley at a height of 44 m above sea level, overlooking the river Tudd. The location of the hoard from Dereham echoes that of Weston Longville and Honingham, being located at 55 m above sea level, in a gently rolling landscape. In contrast, the silver hoard from Fring came from near the base of the valley, overlooking the modern village, whilst those from North Creake and Scole were also placed in relatively low-lying positions within close proximity to waterways or water meadows. The Forncett hoard is located within 150 m of the nearest water source at a height of 40 m above sea level. The landscape in this part of the county is gently undulating.

Site name	*Landscape location*
Scole	25 m OD *Close to water* 150 m from the river Waveney
Fring	30 m Hillside location towards valley bottom
North Creake	25 m OD *Close to water* 40 m from the river Burn
Dereham	55 m OD *Highspot* High plateau
Forncett	40 m OD Gently undulating landscape
Honingham	44 m OD *Highspot* Off the top of the hill
Weston Longville	35 m OD *Highspot* Just off hilltop

Table 4. Location of silver coin hoards.

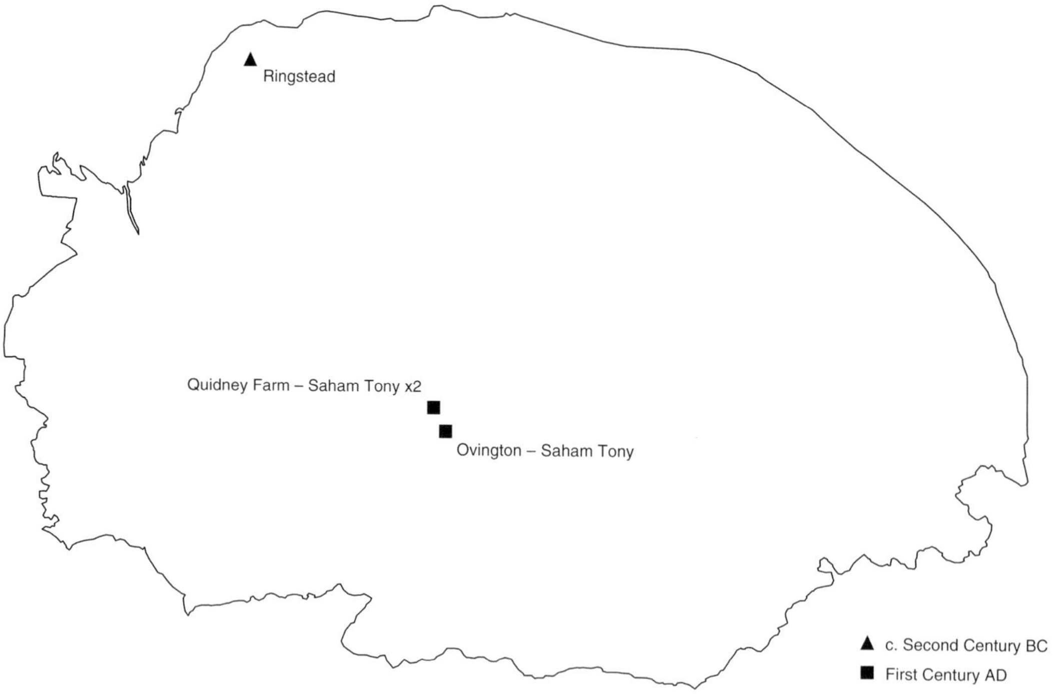

Fig. 6. Distribution of hoards of horse equipment in Norfolk.

Coin hoard	*Latest coin present*
Scole	AD 60/61 (Nero)
Forncett	AD 36/7 (Tiberius)
Dereham	AD 36/7 (Tiberius)
Fring	Pattern-horse SAENV (1st century AD)
Honingham	Pattern-horse SAENV (1st century AD)
Weston Longville	Pattern-horse AESV (1st century AD)
North Creake	Pattern-horse ECEN/EDN (?1st century AD)

Table 5. Date range of silver coin hoards.

On current evidence, five of the seven silver coin hoards (Weston Longville, Dereham, Honingham, Forncett, and Fring) are from places where no contemporary material has been recovered, and which show no sign of being settlements. The two remaining hoards, from Scole and North Creake, were however both found in locations where other later Iron Age and early Roman material has been recovered, suggesting a change in the 'seclusion' of hoard deposits in the first century AD.

The reduction in the quantities of artefacts taken out of circulation through hoarding noted for the first century BC gold coinage is also apparent in the silver coin record. Of approximately 1500 known and provenanced silver coins, 33% entered the archaeological record as single finds (Hutcheson 2004, 94). Clearly, hoards of silver coins represent purposeful or deliberate deposits of material culture. To what extent, however, are they related in terms of ongoing practice to torc hoards or hoards of gold coins?

At the start of the paper, it was noted that silver coin hoards are often associated with the Boudican rebellion. This assertion is founded on the dating of the latest (Roman) coin within a hoard. The evidence from Scole, for example, is particularly compelling as the latest coin dates to AD60/61, the date of the rebellion (Table 5). However, there is no reason why the hoards of silver coins should not continue the existing practice of deposition, as demonstrated by the finds from Snettisham. The torc hoards were followed first by a number of single gold Norfolk Wolf staters, and then by a hoard of silver coins, apparently a mix of Icenian and Corieltauvian types, although unfortunately this latter hoard was removed without record (Stead 1998, 147–8). There is, then, potentially a sequence of deposits from Snettisham spanning the period from the second century BC through to the first century AD. The silver coin hoard from this site may refer back to a tradition of deliberate deposition of metal artefacts rather than to the Boudican rebellion. In addition, a ditch dug around the base of the hill where the hoards were located can be shown to be open in the later first century AD (*ibid.*,

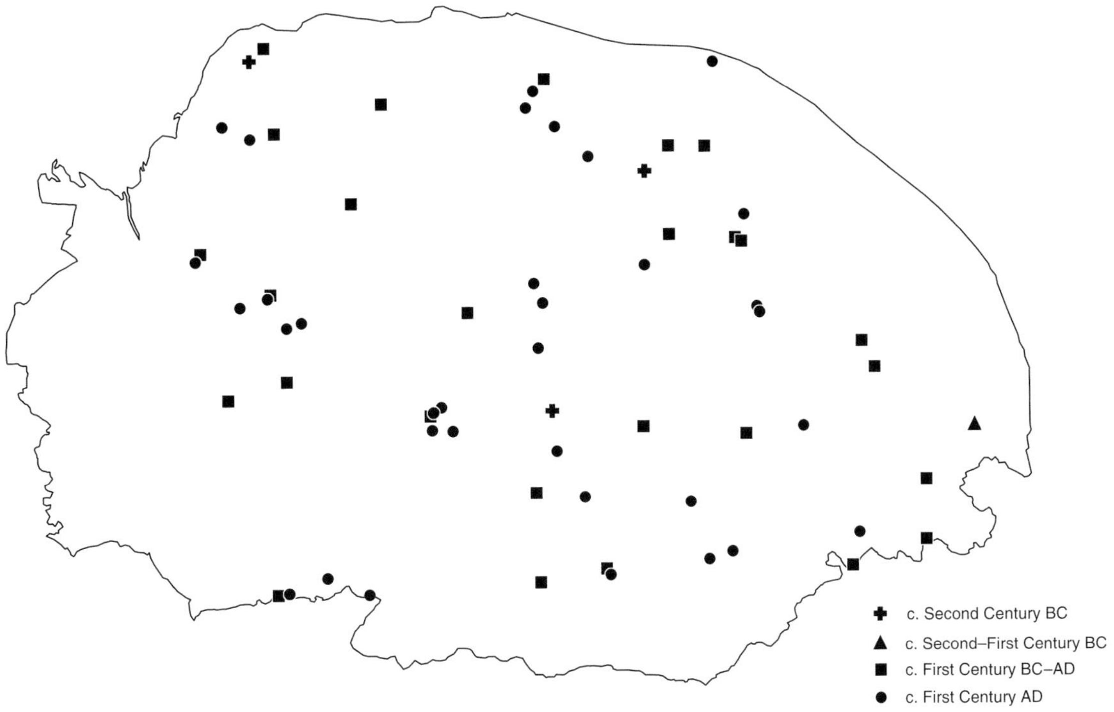

Fig. 7. Distribution of second-century BC to first-century AD horse equipment across Norfolk.

146), which would seem to signify the continuing importance of this site up to potentially 200 years after the deposits of torcs first took place.

The Snettisham complex is part of a whole series of finds that have been made at various locations within a 2 km radius of the modern village of Fring. These others include the hoard of Gallo-Belgic E coins and nearby gold torc from Sedgeford; the silver coin hoard from Fring itself; and a second hoard of Icenian silver coins found approximately 500 m south-east of the village (this latter deposit was not seen by local archaeologists). In addition, a Romano-Celtic temple is known through aerial photography and metal detecting in the valley where the modern village is situated. The temple is located in a position overlooked by the locations where the silver coin hoards and the British gold coin hoard from Snettisham were deposited. There is, then, a cluster of deliberate deposits of metalwork around this village. Again, it could be surmised that the silver coin hoards in Fring refer to a localised practice of deliberate deposition of metalwork in the landscape, rather than to the revolt of AD60/61.

Horse equipment

Far fewer hoards of horse equipment are known from Norfolk than of torcs and coins. They include the collections of material from Ringstead (Clarke 1951b), Quidney Farm, Saham Toney, hoards A & B (Bates 2000, 201), and Ovington, Saham Toney (Clarke 1939, 70). Despite the small number of hoards, Late Iron Age Norfolk has a strikingly high number of single finds of horse equipment dating to the first centuries BC and AD (Hutcheson 2004, 12–16). The low number of known hoards suggests that a smaller percentage of items of horse equipment was taken out of circulation through hoarding, particularly at the end of the Iron Age, mirroring the pattern noted for coins. It is possible that single finds of horse equipment were also 'special' deposits, but there is a striking relationship between road systems and Later Iron Age horse equipment (Hutcheson 2004, 86–7), which might suggest that such items fell from moving vehicles, rather than being deliberately buried.

The collection from Ringstead, with its 'Snettisham gold style' decoration, is the earliest of the four hoards of horse equipment found in Norfolk, potentially as early as the second century BC. The findspot is located in the north-west of the county in the same area as the torc hoards. In addition, the Ringstead hoard was located on a high-spot, overlooking the Wash in a place where no contemporary material is known (Clarke 1951b, 224). In terms of both date and location, it thus fits the emerging second/early first century BC 'landscape' pattern of hoarding in north-west Norfolk noted for torcs.

Although single items of horse equipment are evenly distributed across the county, the other three hoards were all found within the parish of Saham Toney, in the middle of the county (Figs 6 and 7). In each case, there is evidence of contemporary activity. At Quidney Farm,

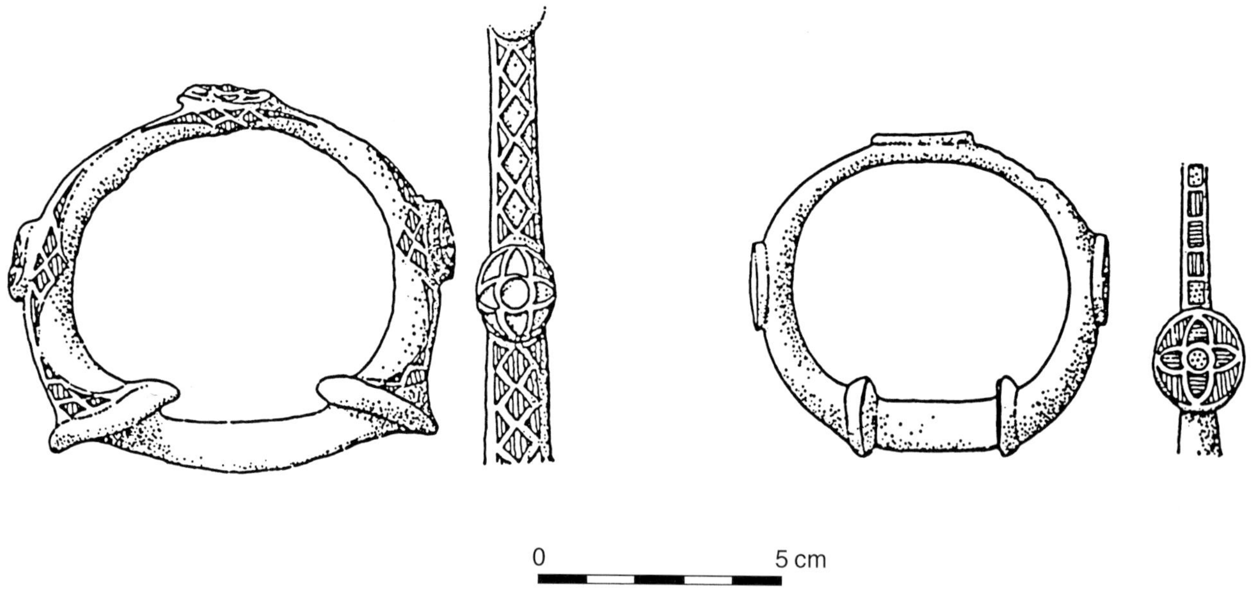

Fig. 8. Platform decorated terrets from the Ovington, Saham Toney, hoard (after MacGregor 1976).

there is evidence of later Iron Age metalworking, while the Ovington hoard was found within a small rectilinear enclosure, which has produced mainly Roman material, with a first century AD component.

It possible that these collections of horse equipment relate to the regional practice of purposeful metalwork deposition, although, like the silver coin hoards, they have tended to be linked with the Boudican rebellion, as for instance, in the case of the Ovington hoard (e.g. Hawkes and Hull 1947, 331; MacGregor 1976, 26). However, there is no independent evidence to support an AD60/61 date for its deposition, whilst it could be argued that the platform-decorated terrets in the hoard (Fig. 8) are later than the mid first century AD. The arrangement of geometric shapes (interlocking triangles and rows of squares) and the use of various colours of enamel, including blue and yellow on platform decorated terrets, is reminiscent of dragonesque brooches, which are generally dated to the post-conquest period (Hattatt 1985, 171; Johns 1996, 151–3; Jundi and Hill 1998; Megaw and Megaw 2001, 239). Headstud brooches, which date from the mid first to the second century AD, employ similar decorative techniques, including rows of enamelled interlocking triangles (Hattatt 1985, 100–5). Last but by no means least, all of the platform decorated terrets from Norfolk, bar one, derive from wholly Roman sites (two from Brampton Roman town, HER 1124; one each from Long Stratton, HER 12513; Tuttington, HER 33592; and Caistor St Edmund (*Venta Icenorum*). These examples were all found through metal detecting rather than excavation, so no direct associations exist, but their recovery from Roman sites and stylistic parallels with other post-conquest 'Roman' artefacts, points to a later date. It could, then, be argued that the hoard from Ovington, Saham Toney, post-dates the Boudican rebellion.

Discussion

At the start of this paper it was noted that there has been a tendency to explore the later Iron Age of northern East Anglia through a historical filter, fitting the archaeology to the historical record. By focusing on one part of this region, Norfolk, this paper has sought to investigate Iron Age communities through their archaeological remains. In particular, the distribution and deposition of metalwork hoards has been examined and a number of patterns have emerged.

Firstly, the practice of deliberately depositing metalwork and coins in the landscape occurs throughout the period under study (second century BC–first century AD). Within this broad pattern, there is a notable concentration of hoards in north-west Norfolk dating to the second and first century BC. All the torc deposits are located in this area, as is the only early hoard of horse equipment, along with the majority of gold coin hoards. North-west Norfolk is defined geographically by the Wash, with its links to the North Sea. It is possible that the means to acquire and concentrate gold in this region at this period reflects the control of exchange networks, with the Wash serving as a conduit for North Sea trade into this area of Britain. It is surely significant that Ken

Hill can be seen for many miles out into the Wash, and in a clump of trees in the field next to the 'gold field', there is a beacon which is marked on the 1828 Admiralty map, demonstrating that this hill continued to be important in terms of visibility beyond the Iron Age. The concentration of gold in north-west Norfolk may well reflect a specific social group or regional 'polity', overseeing the acquisition, circulation, and deposition of this metal in the region. If the depositional record is a reliable guide, little gold of a similar date made it further afield into northern East Anglia, or the 'land of the Iceni'. Only one hoard of torcs is known from the wider region (Owles 1969; 1970), and neither north-east Cambridgeshire nor north Suffolk have any great concentration of early, Gallo-Belgic gold coin hoards (Hutcheson 2004, 14, table 3) compared to Norfolk.

The western-centric focus of hoarding breaks down in the course of the first century BC. This is evidenced, in the first instance, by the location of three gold coin hoards elsewhere in the county, at Weybourne and Runton on the north Norfolk coast and Buxton-with-Lammas in the east of county. By the time silver coin hoards entered the archaeological record in the early first century AD, a different distribution pattern emerges: silver coins are generally located much more centrally within the county, although at least one hoard is also known from west Norfolk (Fring). The move away from a concentration of gold hoarding in the west of the county is coupled with other behavioural changes. Gold gives way to silver as the dominant metal for making coins, and there is a gradual decrease in the number of artefacts that are taken out of circulation in hoards. In essence, more metal artefacts are circulating, or are accessible to the population as a whole. These transformations potentially reflect the re-organisation of control over the acquisition, production, circulation, and deposition of metal artefacts and coins.

It could be surmised, then, that there was a change in the way that society was organised in this region in the later first century BC or first century AD. *Contra* Davies' suggestion (1999, 41), this apparent re-organisation of society, as reflected through changes in metalwork types, their circulation, distribution, and deposition, may have been related to the coming together of the tribe – or federation of tribes – that the Romans subsequently labelled the Iceni. The assemblage of latest Iron Age material culture from north Suffolk and north-east Cambridgeshire is not dissimilar to that from Norfolk, which supports this suggestion. In particular, Norfolk wolf staters, ornamented horse equipment, and silver coin hoards are found across the 'land of the Iceni'. Indeed, these items are used to plot the boundary between the Iceni and the Trinovantes (Martin 1999, 85).

Despite evidence of social change, hoarding does continue. However, there are changes in the relationship between the landscape and hoarding practice, which may again be reflecting broader social developments. In particular, there is a shift away from the distinctive types of 'right' location that torcs were placed in, to an apparently more fluid idea of what might comprise the appropriate location to hoard a group of material. A greater variety of locations within the landscape become 'suitable' for hoard deposits and, in the first century AD, there is a move away from 'isolated' or 'secluded' places for depositing hoards.

Conclusion

The Iron Age of northern East Anglia has not seen a great deal of research. Although 'that omnivorous dragon of Wessex' (Clarke 1939, 1) is beating a slow retreat, the region is still not well understood and there is, as yet, no great body of research upon which to build. It is, however, now possible to start commenting on apparent changes in social organisation. In particular, during the second and early first century BC, there is some evidence to suggest that sub-regional polities or communities existed. The restricted distribution of gold in the north-west of the county implies that a local community or group of people were able to acquire large amounts of gold. Patterns in hoarding, and the changes in the dominant material type (from gold to silver) in the first century BC and into the first century AD suggest that there was some kind of social upheaval at this time. Changes in the types of materials, and control over their distribution and deposition may reflect a change in social organisation at this point, perhaps even the formation of the Iceni.

Throughout these changes, the practice of hoarding continues, although it too alters, perhaps reflecting different perceptions of landscape through time. As already noted, Ringstead apart, hoards of horse equipment from Norfolk are late in date. This is also true of the only hoard of horse equipment known from the wider Iceni region, from Westhall in north Suffolk. If these later hoards are post-Boudican, as has been suggested, this implies that the practice of hoarding not only continued throughout the Later Iron Age, but also into the Romano-British period. The continuation of Iron Age practices into the Roman period counters the generally held belief that the Iceni were annihilated during the rebellion (e.g. Sealey 1997).

To conclude, by taking Norfolk as a case study, it is possible to start to situate our knowledge of the region in its archaeology, rather than in its history, and thus start to readdress some the assumptions about the Iron Age of northern East Anglia that derive from a research agenda that has until recently been historically led.

Acknowledgements

I would like to thank Andrew Hutcheson for reading and commenting on the text and helping with producing the maps. I would also like to thank Dr J.D. Hill for comments on my Ph.D. research, from which this paper derives, as well as the reader who commented on this paper before publication. Finally, I am indebted to the staff at Norfolk Landscape Archaeology, Union House, Gressenhall, Norfolk, for allowing me unrestricted access to the County Historic Environment Record. Any mistakes or misunderstandings are, however, my own.

Note

1. Since this paper was written, the original dispersed hoard of eight Gallo-Belgic E staters from Sedgeford used in the analysis here has been augmented by a further 31 staters discovered in excavation in 2003 (Faulkner 2004). These were found in a small pit, 20 of them still inside a cattle long bone, the rest in the surrounding soil. It is presumed by the excavators that the coins found previously originally formed part of the same deposit. The pit is in an area which is now waterlogged. A short distance away were two large Iron Age ditch terminals. For a detailed account of this find, see now Dennis and Faulkner (2005).

Bibliography

Allen, D. 1970. The coins of the Iceni, *Britannia* 1, 1–33.

Bates, S. 2000. Excavations at Quidney Farm, Saham Toney, Norfolk 1995, *Britannia* 31, 201–237.

Burnett, A.M and Bland R.F. (eds) 1986. *Coin Hoards from Roman Britain, Vol. VI.* London: British Museum.

Chadburn, A. 1992. A preliminary analysis of the hoard of Icenian coins from Field Baulk, March, Cambridgeshire, in Mays 1992, 73–82.

Chadburn, A. and Gurney, D. 1991. The Fring coin hoard, *Norfolk Archaeology* 41, 218–225.

Clarke R.R. 1939. The Iron Age in Norfolk and Suffolk, *Archaeological Journal* 96, 1–113.

Clarke R.R. 1951a. A Celtic torc-terminal from North Creake, Norfolk, *Archaeological Journal* 106, 59–61.

Clarke, R.R. 1951b. A hoard of metalwork of the Early Iron Age from Ringstead, Norfolk, *Proceedings of the Prehistoric Society* 10, 214–225.

Clarke, R.R. 1954. The early Iron Age treasure from Snettisham, Norfolk, *Proceedings of the Prehistoric Society* 20, 27–86.

Clarke, R.R. 1956. The hoard of silver coins of the Iceni from Honingham, Norfolk, *British Numismatic Journal* 28, 3–9.

Creighton, J. 1994. A time of change: the Iron Age to Roman monetary transition in East Anglia, *Oxford Journal of Archaeology* 13, 325–334.

Davies, J. 1999. Patterns, power and political progress in Iron Age Norfolk, in Davies and Williamson 1999, 14–43.

Davies, J. and Williamson, T. (eds) 1999. *Land of the Iceni: The Iron Age in Northern East Anglia.* Norwich: Centre for East Anglian Studies.

Dennis, M. and Faulkner, N. 2005. *The Sedgeford Hoard.* Stroud: Tempus.

Dolley, R.H.M. 1954. The speculum coins from Hoard C, in Clarke 1954, 72–86.

Ellis H. 1849. Account of a gold torquois found in Needwood Forest in Staffordshire, *Archaeologia* 33, 323–325.

Faulkner, N. 2004. Sedgeford, *Current Archaeology* 195, 533–539.

Gregory, T. 1992. Snettisham and Bury: some light on the earliest Icenian coinage, in Mays 1992, 47–71.

Haselgrove, C. 1993. The development of British Iron Age coinage, *Numismatic Chronicle* 153, 31–63.

Haselgrove, C. 1999. The development of Iron Age coinage in Belgic Gaul, *Numismatic Chronicle* 159, 111–168.

Hattatt, R. 1985. *Iron Age and Roman Brooches: A Second Selection of Brooches from the Author's Collection.* Oxford: Oxbow Books.

Hawkes, C.F.C. and Hull, M.R. 1947. *Camulodunum.* London: Report of the Research Committee of the Society of Antiquaries 14.

Hingley, R. and Unwin, C. 2005. *Boudica, Iron Age Warrior Queen.* London: Hambledon and London.

Hobbs, R. 1996. *British Iron Age Coins in the British Museum.* London: British Museum Press.

Hutcheson, N. 2003. Material culture in the landscape: a new approach to the Snettisham hoards, in J. Humphrey (ed.), *Re-searching the Iron Age*, 87–97. Leicester: Leicester Archaeology Monograph 11.

Hutcheson, N. 2004. *Later Iron Age Norfolk; Metal, Landscape and Society.* Oxford: British Archaeological Report 361.

Johns, C. 1996. *The Jewellery of Roman Britain: Celtic and Classical Traditions.* London: University College London Press.

Jope, E.M. 2000. *Early Celtic Art in the British Isles.* Oxford: Clarendon Press.

Jundi, S. and Hill, J.D. 1998. Brooches and identities in first century AD Britain: more than meets the eye?, in C. Forcey, J. Hawthorne and R. Witcher (eds), *TRAC 97. Proceedings of the Seventh Annual Theoretical Roman Archaeology Conference, Nottingham 1997*, 125–137. Oxford: Oxbow Books.

Leeds, E.T. 1933. Torcs of Early Iron Age Britain, *Antiquaries Journal* 13, 466–468.

MacGregor, M. 1976. *Early Celtic Art in North Britain.* Leicester: Leicester University Press.

Mays, M. (ed.) 1992. *Celtic Coinage: Britain and Beyond.* Oxford: British Archaeological Reports British Series 222.

Martin, E. 1999. Suffolk in the Iron Age, in Davies and Williamson 1999, 45–99.

Megaw, M.R. and Megaw, J.V.S. 2001. *Celtic Art from its Beginnings to the Book of Kells* (revised edn). London: Thames and Hudson.

Owles, E. 1969. The Ipswich gold torcs, *Antiquity* 43, 208–212.

Owles, E. 1970. The sixth Ipswich torc, *Antiquity* 45, 294–296.

Painter, K. 1970. An Iron Age gold-alloy torc from Glascote, Tamworth, Staffordshire, *Staffordshire Archaeological and Historical Society* 11, 1–6.

Roach-Smith C. 1853. British silver coins recently found at Weston in Norfolk, *Numismatic Chronicle* 58, 98–102.

Sealey, P.R. 1979. The later history of Icenian electrum torcs, *Proceedings of the Prehistoric Society* 45, 165–178.

Sealey, P. 1997. *The Boudican Revolt Against Rome.* Princes Risborough: Shire Publications.

Stead, I.M. 1991. The Snettisham treasure: excavations in 1990, *Antiquity* 65, 447–465.

Stead, I.M. 1998. *The Salisbury Hoard.* Stroud: Tempus.

Wake, T. 1942. Some recent archaeological discoveries in Norfolk, *Norfolk Archaeology* 28, 26–27.

Detecting the Later Iron Age: a view from the Portable Antiquities Scheme

Sally Worrell

This paper examines the Iron Age artefact data recorded by the Portable Antiquities Scheme (PAS) between autumn 1997 and October 2004. It presents a broad-brush preliminary analysis, which aims to highlight the real potential of this data by investigating some important general trends, as well as indicating areas that deserve further research. An attempt is made to assess the archaeological potential of the data as a resource in its own right and as a resource to be used in conjunction with information gained from more traditional archaeological methods.

To illustrate the potential of the data, studies examining Iron Age brooches and horse and vehicle equipment recorded by the PAS have been undertaken. These categories of artefact were chosen because both are reasonably well represented in the database and enjoy long traditions of study. In addition, a regional study comparing the Iron Age metallic artefacts from Hampshire recorded by the PAS against those discovered during archaeological fieldwork, or as earlier chance finds, was carried out. Hampshire was selected as a study area principally because its Iron Age archaeology has been well documented through excavation and research, providing an extensive context through which to analyse the PAS results.

The Iron Age background

The significance of regional variation within British Iron Age societies and, in turn, the contribution that these regional differences offer to the wider understanding of the British Iron Age has long been recognised (Cunliffe 1991; Davies 1996; Hill 1999). The study of material culture is key to the understanding of regional variations among Iron Age societies as well as for addressing questions of status, identity, and site function (Haselgrove *et al.* 2001, 17). Of particular interest for the purposes of this paper are local and regional variations in Iron Age material culture use and deposition through space and time, viewed through the data recorded by the PAS. In particular, the later part of the Iron Age is characterised by a very considerable increase in the volume of material culture in circulation, occurring in tandem with changes in settlement forms and burial rites (Fitzpatrick 1984; Hill 1995; 1997; Davies 1996; Haselgrove 1997; Haselgrove *et al.* 2001). Willis (1997) suggests that the visible increase in Late Iron Age artefacts may be the result of practices of artefact disposal and deposition, as well as increasing availability of metal, higher levels of manufacture, and population increase. This general picture has depended very much on excavated evidence, which is, of course, unevenly distributed across the country. In areas where less fieldwork and research has been undertaken, regional variation has been identified more on the basis of negative evidence in comparison to material from more intensively studied areas.

The use of unstratified artefacts to assess regionality is less established, although important studies using coins and harness equipment in particular have demonstrated the potential of such material for a fuller characterisation of Iron Age society in individual areas. Work in, for example, Kent, Norfolk, and Northamptonshire has exemplified the importance of such research when studying, on their own terms, regions previously perceived as 'marginal' in comparison to the well-studied landscapes represented by Wessex or

Hertfordshire (Curteis 1996; Davies 1996; Hill 1999; Holman 2000; Hutcheson 2004). A small number of important analyses of metal-detected assemblages have taken place (Brown 1986), but there is a need further to test unstratified artefactual data on a wider geographical basis in order to explore variations in the circulation and deposition of metallic artefacts (Haselgrove *et al.* 2001, 29). The study of metal-detected artefacts is, of course hampered by a lack of stratigraphic context, and it is often impossible to characterise the type of 'site' from which artefacts derive; indeed, many artefacts recovered by metal detectorists may well have been deposited away from settlements. However, the findspots of most artefacts are recorded with at least a six-figure NGR and thus distribution patterns (in a regional or national perspective) can be established with some precision.

One of the principal advantages of the PAS is that, since December 2003, its coverage has extended throughout England and Wales. It thus covers a very large and diverse zone, encompassing the most heavily studied 'heartland' areas of the Iron Age landscape, as well as – perhaps more significantly – regions which have been less intensively researched in the past. The PAS data have the potential to contribute to the 'regionality' debate in evaluating regional differences in the use and deposition of artefacts. Although not without problems, the national coverage by the PAS will increasingly allow patterns to be assessed both regionally and nationally. The creation of an ever-increasing national, as well as accessible, database of material is the real strength of the PAS.

Aims of the Portable Antiquities Scheme

Most of the data recorded by the PAS derive from metal detecting. This has been a popular pastime since the 1970s and its popularity shows no signs of abating. It is difficult to estimate the number of metal detectorists practising in England and Wales, but the CBA survey of metal detecting suggested that possibly up to 30,000 individuals were discovering perhaps as many as 400,000 archaeological objects every year (Dobinson and Denison 1994). It is now considered that the number of detectorists is considerably less, although establishing precise numbers of detectorists and objects is very difficult. There are approximately 6,500 members of the metal detecting clubs, which are affiliated to either the National Council for Metal Detecting (NCMD) or the Federation of Independent Detectorists (FID). However, not all members of these clubs record artefacts with the PAS. Estimating the number of individuals who operate independently of the clubs is very difficult. An estimated total of 10,000 is probably relatively realistic. According to the PAS Annual Report for the period April 2003–April 2004, 1726 detectorists recorded artefacts within the scheme and 26,600 metallic artefacts were recorded in that period. This suggests that many artefacts continue to be unrecorded and that the PAS may be only 'touching the tip of the iceberg'.

Prior to the introduction of the PAS, many archaeologists recognised the need to mitigate the information loss resulting from the lack of recording of unstratified artefacts. The recognition of the destructive effects on the archaeological record caused by intensive agriculture (Lambrick 1977; Hinchliffe and Schadla-Hall 1980; Geake 2002) also prompted some archaeologists to record artefacts discovered through metal detection. Indeed, the great majority of metal-detected finds come from archaeological sites, which have been damaged or destroyed by agriculture, and which continue to be intensively cultivated. As a consequence, the objects may often be the only surviving evidence of past activity at these sites. In areas such as Norfolk, Suffolk, and North Lincolnshire, relationships between finders and archaeologists were established and chance finds have been recorded since the 1970s and 1980s. Elsewhere, limitations in museum resources and staff time, coupled perhaps with a lesser inclination to develop positive relationships and contacts with detectorists, meant that finds were recorded on a sporadic and *ad hoc* basis, and in low quantities.

Following the passing of the Treasure Act in 1996, the first PAS projects were established in autumn 1997 in Kent, Norfolk, North Lincolnshire, the North-West, the West Midlands, and Yorkshire with the support of the Department of Culture, Media and Sport. They were followed in spring 1999 by projects funded by the Heritage Lottery Fund (HLF) in Hampshire, Northamptonshire, Somerset and Dorset, Suffolk, and Wales. A further successful bid to the HLF in 2002 saw the establishment of a further 21 Finds Liaison Officer posts so that by the end of 2003, the whole of England and Wales was covered by the PAS. Five specialist Finds Advisers, an IT Officer, and an Education Officer were also appointed. The different periods for which the PAS has been in operation in different counties, of course, has had an effect on the quantities of finds so far recorded there.

Working closely with metal detectorists and other finders, the PAS records artefacts and their findspots as accurately as possible. Full descriptions and images are made of the artefacts, since, unlike those in museum collections, there is no guarantee that it will be possible for researchers to examine them again in the future. The identification, description, and images of the artefact are passed to the finder and entered onto the PAS website, where the information is disseminated to a wide range of audiences. From April 2003, more standardised recording practices were adopted and it was intended that records would be validated by Finds Advisers before publication on the website. The vast quantity of finds currently being recorded has, however, led to a procedure whereby the records are made available immediately on

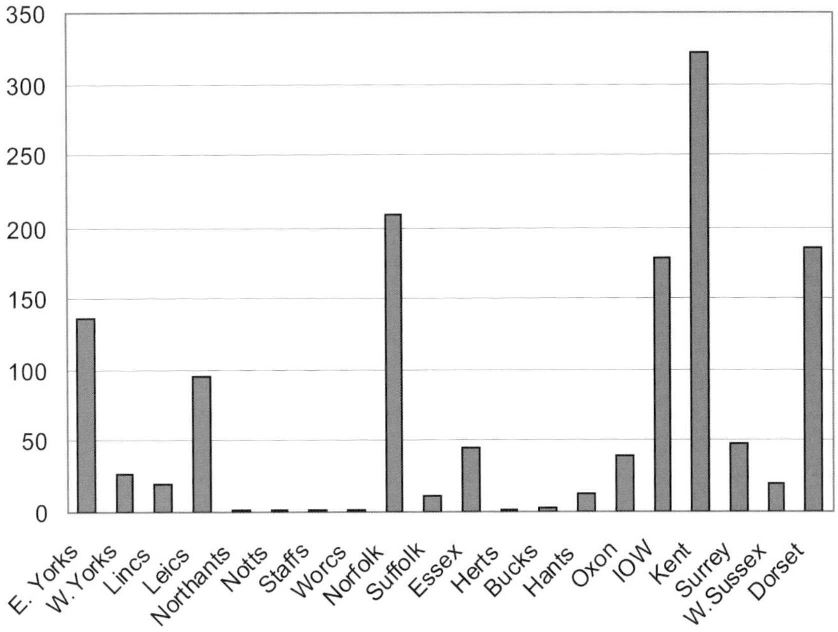

Fig. 1. Number of Iron Age coins recorded as Treasure, September 1998–December 2004.

the publicly accessible website, but indicate whether or not the find has yet been validated by the relevant Finds Adviser. The PAS, NCMD, and the Association of Local Government Archaeological Officers (ALGAO) have agreed the terms and conditions for the transfer of PAS data to Historic Environment Records (HERs).

Assessing data from metal detection

The volume of material recorded through the PAS varies enormously between counties. In the past, the level of co-operation between archaeologists and metal detectorists in different counties in England was far from uniform; consequently finds recording levels vary significantly. Good working relationships have existed in Norfolk, Suffolk, North Lincolnshire, and Kent for many years and these counties, particularly in East Anglia, are models of the benefits of co-operation and liaison. This is largely through the efforts of individuals who are aware of the value of recording unstratified artefacts and who have a personal interest in artefact-based research. In general, the greater quantities of finds recorded in these areas are likely to represent not only the intensity and character of human occupation, but also present land use, and variations in the intensity of metal detecting and finds being made available for recording. In other counties, proactive and effective liaison between archaeologists and metal detectorists through the PAS – which takes much time and effort to establish – is a new phenomenon. In counties where the PAS has only recently been established, the low number of recorded finds is therefore understandable. Elsewhere, it is unclear to what extent lower figures are a result of past and present variations in land use, variations in the intensity of metal detecting, or of the level of finds recording.

The PAS data

Between September 1997 and April 2003, the PAS pilot projects recorded a total of 174,640 artefacts found by members of the public (Fig. 1), and new records are constantly being added to the PAS database. This study is intended as a preliminary analysis of the data, which will benefit from re-working in the future. The range of material culture recorded by the PAS is extremely diverse, but non-ferrous metalwork dominates the data for all periods. The under-representation of iron objects is predictable due both to their poor survival in the ploughsoil, and to most metal detectorists discriminating against ferrous signals due to the frequency of recent iron objects in the ploughsoil. There is a similar absence of artefacts in bone and other organic materials, which might be expected in an excavated assemblage. Some of the individual finds are of national importance; others, whose individual archaeological value may be less obvious, when considered cumulatively, represent an important addition to the existing record.

The Iron Age data recorded by the PAS are sufficiently numerous to be quantitatively significant. This study is based on 3226 artefacts of Iron Age or possible Iron

Age date. Although the total number of artefacts varies significantly between the counties, the ratio of Iron Age artefacts to material of other periods is broadly similar. In most counties Iron Age finds account for ≤2% of all finds, except for Kent, where 9.73% of recorded finds date from the Iron Age. The figures include various artefact types that span the Roman conquest – for example, Colchester, Langton Down, and Rosette brooches, cosmetic articles, and some forms of terrets.

The objects have been subdivided into ten categories: coins, brooches, other personal ornaments, toggles/ fasteners, horse and vehicle equipment, cosmetic equipment, copper alloy vessels, other metallic finds, pottery sherds, and non-metallic 'other' finds. The number of finds per category are presented in Table 1 by county and ordered according to the regional PAS groupings. The data are derived from the records on the PAS website made between September 1997 and October 2004, with the exception of the Norfolk records. A separate survey of the Norfolk HER, which incorporates the PAS data recorded by the Norfolk Artefact Identification Unit, was undertaken. This includes all artefacts recorded between September 1997 and July 2003, although not all cosmetic articles and Aucissa brooches were recorded in the original survey. All Iron Age coins from Norfolk recorded between September 1997 and October 2004 have been included in this survey along with the sample of the Iron Age finds that have been entered on to the PAS database. This constitutes 25 records, but it is difficult to suggest what proportion of the total Iron Age artefacts this sample represents.

For this survey, all primary records were examined. Where a doubt existed concerning the identification, the record was excluded. A high proportion of artefacts recorded by the PAS before April 2003 are unfortunately not accompanied by images. Thus verifying identifications and refining classifications is occasionally problematical. Since April 2003, the proportion of records accompanied by images has risen to approximately 90%, thereby enabling the effective validation and checking of data by the Finds Advisers.

Table 1 highlights the variations between counties in terms of the quantity of artefacts recorded and proportions of different categories of artefact. As expected, the south-eastern counties are the richest in terms of the quantities and range of types of artefacts recorded. Although the data from Norfolk are incomplete, both Suffolk and Norfolk stand out as well-represented in all categories, particularly horse and vehicle equipment (Martin 1999). Judging from the quantities of artefacts recorded by the PAS, the patterns of material culture circulation and deposition in the eastern counties appears to be radically different (i.e. much higher) from areas of southern England, particularly Hampshire, Somerset, and Devon. This helps to confirm the results of recent work suggesting that attention should be diverted from the southern counties and their highly visible monuments, to the less visible settlement evidence but more visible material culture of the eastern counties (Davies 1996; Davies and Williamson 1999a).

Kent is outstanding in the number of coins recorded (734), but relatively poorly represented in other categories, for example brooches (34), and horse and vehicle equipment (6). Conversely, in Hampshire, a comparatively small number of coins (40) but a considerable number of brooches (70) have been recorded. The quantity of metallic artefacts recorded from Hampshire differs dramatically from the other south-western counties of Wiltshire, Dorset, and Somerset. The PAS has been established for the same period of time in Hampshire, Dorset, and Somerset, but was only established in Wiltshire in August 2003, which may account, in part, for the difference. The apparent disparity between the collective totals of unstratified artefacts from Dorset and Somerset when compared with Hampshire contrasts with the pattern from excavated south-western sites which are far richer in metallic finds than many excavated sites in Hampshire (Haselgrove 1997).

The very high number of Iron Age coins recorded from Kent, particularly east Kent, owes much to the establishment of the Kent Iron Age Coin Project in the early 1990s, and David Holman's work in recording single coins. All single coins are recorded on both the PAS and Celtic Coin Index (CCI) websites. The Kent data are now sufficiently numerous to have considerably altered the known distribution of some coin types, while confirming that of others (Holman 2000). Comparing the quantity of single coin finds reported to the CCI between 1992–2001 from the other 'high density' counties of Essex (608), West Sussex (449), and Hertfordshire (398) against the total of 1609 for Kent confirms the foremost position held by the latter (De Jersey 2003). This disparity is almost certainly due to Holman's work and demonstrates the regional variation apparent in the quantities of coins recorded, even within the 'core' area of south-east England (*ibid.*). The PAS was established in Essex and Hertfordshire in August 2003 and very similar quantities of coins have been recorded in these counties. However, it will take time – and quite possibly the presence of an individual with a particular interest in recording Iron Age coins, as in Kent – for patterns to emerge and for some of the differences in the South-East to balance out.

Artefacts that qualify as treasure under the terms of the Treasure Act 1996 and reported from September 1998–December 2004 have also been incorporated in this study. Non-coin treasure finds are included in Table 1. The total number of coins present in coin hoards by county is presented in Figure 1, and has not been included in the coins section of Table 1. Kent and Norfolk are the best represented, reflecting the pattern established through the single coin finds recorded by the PAS. However, East Yorkshire and Dorset, which had

	1	*2*	*3*	*4*	*5*	*6*	*7*	*8*	*9*	*10*	*Total*
Tyne and Wear	-	-	-	-	1	-	-	-	-	-	**1**
Durham	-	-	-	-	-	-	-	1	-	1	**2**
East Yorkshire (inc Humbs)	5	4	2	1	10	1	2	-	12	-	**37**
North Yorkshire	1	8	1	3	4	3	2	2	1	-	**25**
South Yorkshire	1	2	-	-	1	-	1	1	-	-	**6**
West Yorkshire	2	1	-	-	2	-	-	-	-	-	**5**
Leicestershire	8	6	-	2	3	2	2	-	1	-	**24**
Lincolnshire	59	98	8	9	24	12	3	1	2	1	**217**
Northamptonshire	58	22	2	-	9	-	-	1	4	1	**97**
Nottinghamshire	5	33	-	5	1	-	-	-	1	-	**45**
Derbyshire	-	-	-	-	-	-	-	1	-	-	**1**
Hereford & Worcestershire	20	7	1	2	2	4	-	2	10	-	**48**
Shropshire	-	1	-	-	1	-	1	1	-	-	**4**
Staffordshire	4	1	2	3	4	6	-	-	-	-	**20**
Warwickshire	18	8	-	-	12	5	1	-	17	-	**61**
West Midlands	1	-	-	-	2	-	-	-	2	-	**5**
Cheshire	3	-	-	-	4	3	2	1	-	-	**13**
Lancashire	-	1	-	-	-	-	-	-	-	-	**1**
Cumbria	-	-	-	-	1	-	-	-	-	-	**1**
Norfolk	227	142	10	13	57	11	7	10	169	-	**646**
Suffolk	123	90	5	11	37	35	4	9	15	1	**330**
Cambridgeshire	15	14	-	1	3	-	-	-	17	-	**50**
Essex	37	17	12	1	5	1	-	1	3	-	**77**
Hertfordshire	40	23	-	-	-	1	1	1	-	-	**66**
Bedfordshire	13	2	-	-	-	-	-	1	-	-	**16**
Kent	734	34	-	4	6	6	1	5	34		**824**
Hampshire	40	70	6	2	8	4	2	3	38	1	**174**
Buckinghamshire	17	5	-	-	-	-	-	-	-	-	**22**
Isle of Wight	18	3	-	-	-	-	-	-	1	-	**22**
Berkshire	3	2	-	-	-	-	-	-	-	-	**5**
Oxfordshire	-	1	-	-	1	-	-	-	-	-	**2**
Surrey	9	3	6	1	1	-	-	-	-	-	**20**
Greater London	11	4	-	-	-	-	-	-	-	-	**15**
Sussex	34	7	-	3	2	-	-	1	71	-	**118**
Somerset	11	12	-	-	1	1	-	2	79	1	**107**
Dorset	19	9	4	-	3	1	-	-	4	1	**41**
Gloucestershire	8	2	-	2	-	-	1	-	2	-	**15**
Avon	1	1	-	-	-	-	-	-	-	-	**2**
Wiltshire	17	13	1	2	3		1		1		**38**
Devon	-	-	-	-	1	1	-	-	-	-	**2**
Cornwall	1	-	-	-	1	-	-	-	-	-	**2**
Anglesey	-	-	1	-	1	-	-	-	-	-	**2**
Newport	2	-	-	-	1	-	-	-	-	-	**3**
Powys	-	-	-	-	-	1	-	-	-	-	**1**
Glamorgan	-	1	-	1	3	1	-	-	-	-	**6**
Wrexham	-	1	-	-	-	-	1	-	-	-	**2**
Monmouth	-	2	-	-	-	-	-	-	-	-	**2**
Torfn	-	1	-	-	-	-	-	-	-	-	**1**
Denbigh	-	-	-	-	-	-	1	-	-	-	**1**
Pembroke	-	-	-	-	-	-	1	-	-	-	**1**
Total	**1565**	**651**	**61**	**66**	**215**	**99**	**34**	**44**	**484**	**7**	**3226**

Table 1. Iron Age artefacts recorded by the PAS between September 1997 and April 2003. 1. Coins; 2. Brooches; 3. Other personal adornment; 4. Toggles/fasteners; 5. Horse and vehicle equipment; 6. Cosmetic implements; 7. Copper alloy vessels; 8. Other metalwork; 9. Pottery; 10. Non-metallic 'other'.

low numbers of single finds, both score highly in the number of hoard coins recorded in this period.

Case study 1: Brooches

In the context of the overall rise in material culture deposition during the Late Iron Age, Hill's so-called 'fibula event horizon' describes the massive increase in the quantity of brooches worn and deposited in the late pre-Roman Iron Age, particularly in southern and eastern Britain (Hill 1997). There is also a very noticeable increase in the range of types present during this period (Haselgrove 1997; Jundi and Hill 1998). Within the PAS data, Late Iron Age brooches massively outnumber those of the Early and Middle Iron Age, echoing the trend observed among brooches from excavated settlement contexts (Haselgrove 1997). The 52 La Tène I–II brooches recorded through the PAS since 1997 represent a valuable addition to the existing corpus of earlier types (Hull and Hawkes 1987). The distribution of early brooches follows that of brooches in general, with the exception of Somerset where the four Early Iron Age examples constitute one third of the total brooches recorded within a small corpus.

The 651 brooches recorded by the PAS comprise a sufficiently large dataset with which to examine regionality in the use and deposition of brooch types across England and Wales, and thus potentially to enhance our understanding of distributions based on excavated material. Any regional variations apparent in the distribution of the brooches recorded by the PAS are less likely to be an effect of the disparate level of recording between counties than is the case with coinage (see above). The brooches have been subdivided by type (Table 2): La Tène I, La Tène II, La Tène III (Boss-on-Bow, Birdlip, Lion Bow), Nauheim derivative, Colchester one-piece, Langton Down, Rosette, Strip, and Aucissa. Most of the simple wire brooches collectively known as 'Nauheim derivatives' probably date from the middle to the end of the first century AD, but examples are known from Late Iron Age contexts, as at Skeleton Green (Mackreth 1981).

Although the distribution is wide, the main concentration in terms of quantities and representation of types is very strongly biased to the eastern counties of Lincolnshire, Norfolk, and Suffolk, as with other artefact categories (see Table 1). This pattern is closely mirrored by the distribution of the Roman brooches recorded through the PAS. This may partly be explained by long established liaison between detectorists and archaeologists in these areas and the intensity of agriculture in this region, but a regional difference in costume is also likely to be a major factor.

Compared to various analyses of excavated first century AD brooch assemblages (Hull 1968; Creighton 1990; Haselgrove 1997), consideration of the pattern at county level and using PAS data remains a fairly crude measure. Nevertheless, the PAS distribution of individual types largely corresponds to established trends. When Haselgrove (1997) examined the relative proportion of 11 brooch types present in a sample of 2507 brooches from 20 assemblages derived from a variety of sites in the south and east of England, he found that Colchesters were the most common, followed by Nauheim derivatives, while Hull (1968) identified various distinctions in the distribution of different brooch types between eastern, southern, and western England.

In the PAS data, Colchesters are again the most common, particularly in the eastern counties, although not, up till now, in Hampshire, Kent, and Hertfordshire. The prevalence of the Nauheim derivative in central southern England (Hull 1971) is reflected in the Hampshire PAS records. The prevalence of the Strip bow, instead of the Colchester and the Nauheim derivatives, characterised the south-western counties, particularly Somerset and Dorset, in Hull's analysis; this too is reflected in the PAS data for Somerset and Dorset, where the Strip bow is dominant and both Colchester and Nauheim derivatives are absent.

The PAS data and analyses of excavated assemblages show a similar background distribution pattern as well as similar regional variations in the individual types represented.

Case study 2: Horse and vehicle equipment

The high incidence of Middle to Late Iron Age horse- and vehicle-related artefacts across Britain has been the subject of various studies based on excavated and chance finds (Spratling 1972; MacGregor 1976; Palk 1984; Taylor and Brailsford 1985; Cunliffe 1995; Davies 1996; Hutcheson 2004). The traditional view of Wessex and East Yorkshire as the Iron Age equine material culture 'hot-spots', is a result of particular biases in the archaeological record. Excavations of hillforts in Hampshire, particularly Bury Hill and Danebury; the settlement at Gussage All Saints, Dorset; and the Arras Culture cemeteries in East Yorkshire, have yielded considerable assemblages of horse gear (Stead 1979; 1991; Wainwright 1979; Cunliffe 1984; 1995; Cunliffe and Poole 1991). Recent studies of horse and vehicle equipment and other artefact types from Norfolk, however, suggest that a modification of this general view is timely and highlight the county's artefactual wealth (Davies 1996; Hutcheson 2004).

Within the PAS data, there are very marked differences in the types and proportions of horse and vehicle equipment between the regions (Fig. 2). In some important respects, the distribution of PAS data (Table 3) does not mirror the patterns of artefact deposition established on the basis of earlier chance finds and excavations. Terrets dominate the data, with a total of 131 recorded. On the basis of earlier research, linch pins

	A	*B*	*C*	*D*	*E*	*F*	*G*	*H*	*I*	***Total***
East Yorkshire (inc Humbs)	-	-	-	-	1	2	-	-	1	**4**
North Yorkshire	-	-	-	3	1	1	-	-	3	**8**
South Yorkshire	-	-	-	1	-	-	-	-	1	**2**
West Yorkshire	-	-	-	-	-	1	-	-	-	**1**
Leicestershire	1	-	-	2	2	-	1	-	-	**6**
Lincolnshire	1	1	12	18	36	14	3	-	13	**98**
Nottinghamshire	1	-	-	4	12	8	4	2	2	**33**
Northamptonshire	1	-	-	1	10	5	1	1	3	**22**
Hereford & Worcestershire	1	-	1	2	3	-	-	-	-	**7**
Shropshire	-	-	-	1	-	-	-	-	-	**1**
Staffordshire	-	-	-	-	-	1	-	-	-	**1**
Warwickshire	-	-	1	2	5	-	-	-	-	**8**
Lancashire	-	-	-	-	-	1	-	-	-	**1**
Norfolk	14	2	6	25	57	27	9	-	2	**142**
Suffolk	6	-	10	6	37	14	13	-	4	**90**
Cambridgeshire	1	1	1	1	7	3	-	-	-	**14**
Essex	-	-	1	2	6	3	4		1	**17**
Hertfordshire	-	-	1	4	4	13	1	-	-	**23**
Bedfordshire	-	1	-	1	-	-	-	-	-	**2**
Kent	5	1	2	11	7	1	6	-	1	**34**
Hampshire	3	1	5	22	14	15	5	1	4	**70**
Buckinghamshire	-	-	-	3	-	2	-	-	-	**5**
Isle of Wight	1	-	-	1	1	-	-	-	-	**3**
Berkshire	-	-	-	-	1	1	-	-	-	**2**
Oxfordshire	1	-	-	-	-	-	-	-	-	**1**
Surrey	2	-	1	-	-	-	-	-	-	**3**
Greater London	-	-	-	1	2	1	-	-	-	**4**
Sussex	-	-	-	3	3	1	-	-	-	**7**
Somerset	4	-	-	-	-	-	-	8	-	**12**
Dorset	1	-	-	2	-	-	1	4	1	**9**
Glos	-	-	-	1	-	1	-	-	-	**2**
Avon	-	-	-	-	1	-	-	-	-	**1**
Wilts	2	-	-	3	3	1	-	1	3	**13**
Wrexham	-	-	1	-	-	-	-	-	-	**1**
Glamorgan	-	-	-	-	-	-	-	1	-	**1**
Monmouth	-	-	-	-	-	1	-	-	1	**2**
Torfaen	-	-	-	-	-	1	-	-	-	**1**
Total	**45**	**7**	**42**	**120**	**213**	**118**	**48**	**18**	**40**	**651**

Table 2. Brooches according to type recorded by the PAS, September 1997–October 2004. A. La Tène I; B. La Tène II; C. La Tène III (Birdlip, Boss-on-Bow, Lion bow); D. Nauheim derivatives; E. Colchester; F. Langton Down; G. Rosette; H. Strip; I. Aucissa (not including all examples recorded by the Norfolk PAS project).

are a less common artefact type than strap-unions (Taylor and Brailsford 1985), but the PAS has recorded 24 linch pins to 16 strap-unions. In contrast to the excavated evidence, only a modest quantity of horse and vehicle equipment has been recorded by the PAS in Hampshire, Somerset and Dorset, and East Yorkshire. Kent is also poorly represented given the number of Iron Age coins recorded from the county. Perhaps iron linch pins – almost certainly under-represented in the PAS record – were more common in these regions. Examples of iron linch pins whose form closely follows that of the elaborate vase-headed ones with iron shanks and copper alloy terminals were found both at Danebury and Bury Hill (Selwood 1984; Cunliffe and Poole 2000a). Even so, it is interesting to contrast the apparent scarcity of archaeological evidence from south of the Thames with Caesar's description of the effectiveness of British chariot warfare and of very high numbers of charioteers:

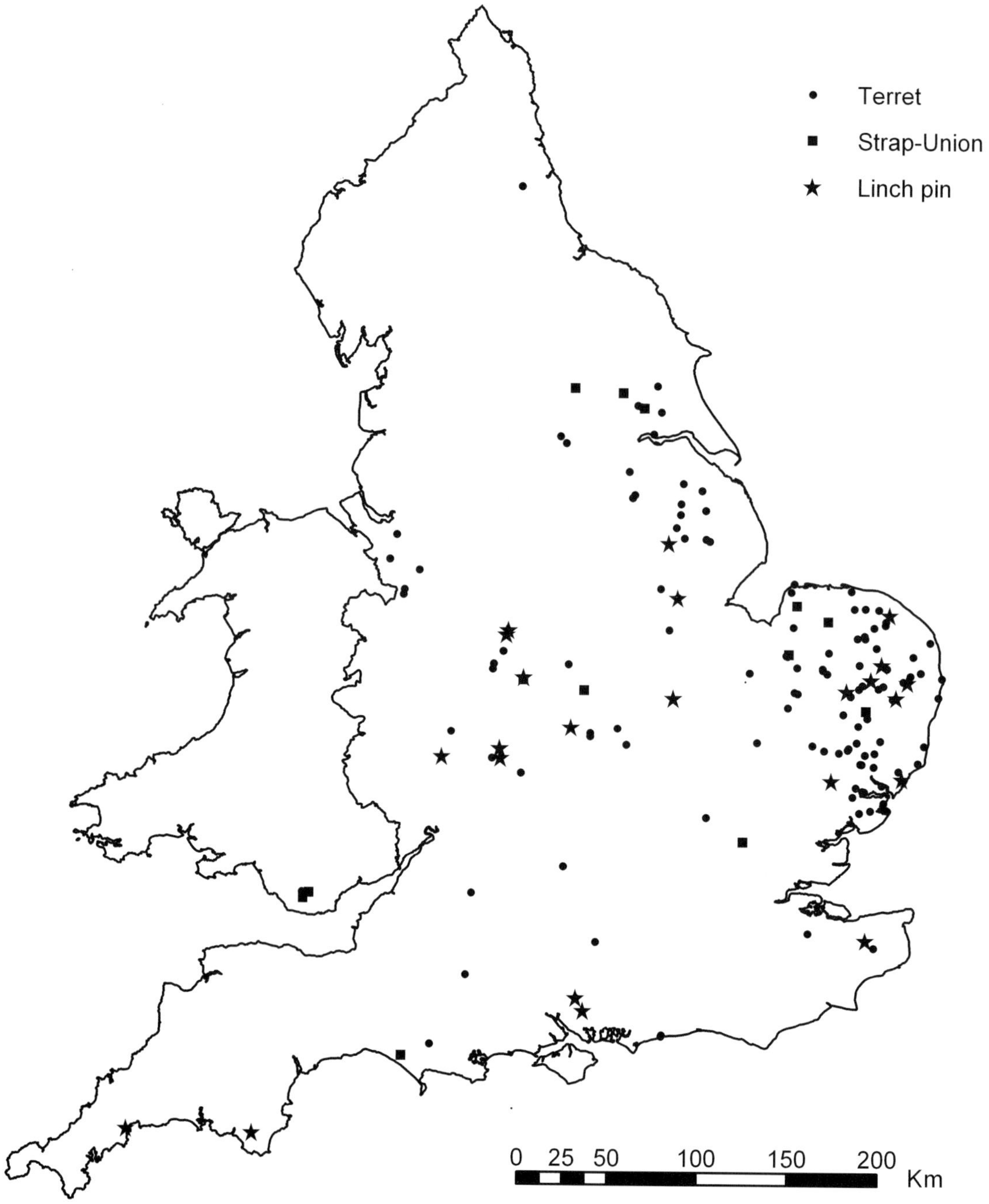

Fig. 2. Map showing the distribution of linch pins, terrets, and strap-unions recorded by the PAS, September 1999–October 2004.

'Cassivellaunus, as we have stated above, all hope [rising out] of battle being laid aside, the greater part of his forces being dismissed, and about 4,000 charioteers only being left…' (*Gallic War* IV, 33; V, 19).

By contrast, the eastern counties of Norfolk, Suffolk, and Lincolnshire have very considerable quantities of horse-related artefacts. The richness of horse and vehicle equipment in Norfolk and Suffolk has been identified in earlier studies (MacGregor 1976; Martin 1999; Hutcheson 2004; this volume). The PAS data, also used in Hutcheson's survey, confirms Norfolk and Suffolk as counties rich in the use and deposition of horse and vehicle equipment.

The horse and vehicle equipment, in particular linch pins, recorded through the PAS from the West Midlands counties of Warwickshire, Herefordshire and Worcestershire, and Staffordshire deserves emphasis. Among 21 artefacts in this category, seven linch pins have been

	Terret	*Linch pin*	*Strap-union*	*Bridle piece*	*Fitting/ mount*	*Total*
Tyne and Wear	1	-	-	-	-	**1**
East Yorkshire (inc Humbs)	7	-	2	-	1	**10**
North Yorkshire	1	-	1	1	1	**4**
South Yorkshire	-	-	-	-	1	**1**
WestYorkshire	2	-	-	-	-	**2**
Leicestershire	1	-	1	-	1	**3**
Lincolnshire	12	2	-	2	8	**24**
Northamptonshire	5	2	1	-	1	**9**
Nottinghamshire	-	-	-	-	2	**2**
Hereford& Worcestershire	1	1	-	-	-	**2**
Shropshire	1	-	-	-	-	**1**
Staffordshire	1	2	-	-	1	**4**
Warwickshire	2	4	2	-	4	**12**
West Midlands	2	-	-	-	-	**2**
Cumbria	1	-	-	-	-	**1**
Cheshire	4	-	-	-	-	**4**
Norfolk	40	5	3	3	6	**57**
Suffolk	28	3	1	1	4	**37**
Cambridgeshire	2	-	-	-	1	**3**
Essex	4	-	1	-	-	**5**
Kent	3	1	-	-	2	**6**
Hampshire	2	2	-	2	2	**8**
Oxfordshire	1	-	-	-	-	**1**
Surrey	-	-	1	-	-	**1**
Sussex	2	-	-	-	-	**2**
Somerset	-	-	1	-	-	**1**
Dorset	2	-	1	-	-	**3**
Wiltshire	3	-	-	-	-	**3**
Devon	-	1	-	-	-	**1**
Cornwall	-	1	-	-	-	**1**
Newport	1	-	-	-	-	**1**
Glamorgan	2	-	1	-	-	**3**
Total	**131**	**24**	**16**	**10**	**35**	**216**

Table 3. Horse and vehicle fittings recorded by the PAS September 1997–October 2004

recorded in an area which has yielded only four linch pins in the past: from Symond's Yat and Merlin's Cave in Herefordshire (Phillips 1931), Lapworth, Warwickshire (Webster 1990), and Wroxeter, Shropshire (Bushe-Fox 1916). In Staffordshire and Warwickshire, it is notable that twice as many linch pins as terrets have been recorded by the PAS. In the counties with higher numbers of horse and vehicle equipment, the number of terrets dramatically outnumbers that of linch pins: the pattern that might be expected.

Normally, the number of brooches recorded from a county exceeds that of horse and harness fittings, but in Staffordshire and Warwickshire the opposite is the case. Although the dataset from the West Midlands counties is comparatively small, the pattern is curious and highlights a possible regional trend in the Late Iron Age with horses and their trappings possibly being more decorated than people.

The very small PAS dataset for Devon and Cornwall does, however, include two linch pins, which represent important additions to our knowledge of linch pins outside the core distribution area. The linch pin found previously in Trevelgue, Cornwall, has been interpreted as evidence for gift exchange between elites, and the PAS data may help expand understanding of elite connections in the south-west (Ward Perkins 1941; Cunliffe 1995).

In contrast to the brooches, the distribution of horse and vehicle equipment recorded by the PAS offers a rather different perspective from that of the excavated data. It presents new evidence for the conspicuous consumption and deposition of metalwork in regions that are not within the traditional 'heartlands' of the Iron Age landscape, the social complexity of which in the Late Iron Age is increasingly acknowledged (Hill 1999).

Case Study 3: A regional distribution, Hampshire

The focus now shifts from national distribution patterns, to those in one region, the county of Hampshire. The Iron Age landscape of Hampshire is one of the most intensively investigated in Britain and excavations of sites in the county have been fundamental to the study of the British Iron Age, for example Danebury, Bury Hill, Balksbury Camp, Owslebury, Silchester and numerous sites in or near Winchester (Cunliffe 1964; 1984; 1991; 2000; Collis 1968; 1970; Davies 1981; Fasham 1985; Fasham *et al.* 1989; Cunliffe and Poole 1991; 2000a; Hill 1995; Wainwright and Davies 1995; Fulford and Timby 2000).

Unlike some eastern England counties, prior to the introduction of the PAS in 1999, Hampshire did not enjoy a long history of effective liaison between metal detectorists and archaeologists, although the well-known Iron Age sites in the county had undoubtedly received substantial attention from metal detectorists, at a level impossible to gauge. The best known and most spectacular Iron Age find recorded in Hampshire since the introduction of the PAS is the Winchester Treasure of two massive gold necklace torcs, two gold bracelets, and four gold brooches of Late Iron Age date (Hill *et al.* 2004). Overall, since 1999 a sample of 135 Iron Age non-ferrous metal artefacts has been recorded through the PAS, of which the categories and distribution can be compared to the dataset acquired through excavations and pre-PAS chance finds. The latter have been compiled from published and unpublished excavations, other archaeological fieldwork, HER records held by the Hampshire and Winchester District councils, Winchester Museums Service accessions, and other published and unpublished information (see Appendix).[1]

Since the majority of the finds recorded through the PAS are non-ferrous metal objects, this criterion was used to establish the second dataset in order to compare like with like. The second dataset therefore includes 'sites' from which non-ferrous metalwork has been found, but not all of the Iron Age 'sites' known from the HER. Many of the latter have been identified through aerial photography or surface finds of pottery sherds, for example through the East Hampshire survey (Shennan 1985). This approach therefore represents a selective comparison, but it is hoped that the PAS data will potentially offer information about the Iron Age in Hampshire from an alternative perspective. The results for each dataset are divided into five artefact classes: brooches, other items of personal adornment, harness equipment, a miscellaneous category of 'other' non-ferrous metal-work, and coins (Table 4). The number of coin hoards is represented in brackets after the total number of coins.

The great majority of the material in both datasets is of Late Iron Age date, but no attempt has been made to divide the results chronologically or by sub-classification within each category. As with the analyses at national level, some material is difficult to date more closely than the Late Iron Age to early Roman period and may post-date the Roman conquest. Of the Early and Middle Iron Age La Tène I–II brooches, there are 19 examples in the HER/published dataset compared to four examples from the PAS. Late first century BC brooches are the most frequently recorded non-coin artefact type in both datasets, although the relative proportions of brooch types differ. The quantities of Colchester, Langton Down, Rosette, and Aucissa brooches are broadly similar in the two datasets, although the PAS has recorded slightly more Langton Down and Rosette brooches, whereas the HER/published total of Colchesters is very slightly higher than the number recorded by the PAS. In both datasets, the Nauheim derivative type is best represented with 74 brooches recorded from excavations and previous chance finds, and 22 by the PAS. The general preponderance of this brooch type in central southern England has already been noted above.

The analysis of the PAS horse and vehicle equipment data revealed that fewer items have been recorded in Hampshire and other counties in Wessex than might have been expected, on the basis of the discovery at Gussage All Saints, Dorset, of bronze casting debris and clay moulds used in the production of linch pins, terrets, strap-unions, and other items of horse harness (Wainwright and Spratling 1973; Wainwright 1979), and of objects stylistically linked with the Gussage material

	Brooches	*Other personal adornment*	*Horse and vehicle equipment*	*Other non-ferrous*	*Coins (hoard)*	*Coins (non-hoard)*	*Total*
PAS/Treasure data	70	6	8	11	13 (1)	40	**148**
HER/published data	165	23	49	27	603 (21)	305	**1172**
Total	**235**	**29**	**57**	**38**	**616**	**345**	**1320**

Table 4. Quantity of artefacts from combined PAS and treasure since 1997 and HER/published data from Hampshire.

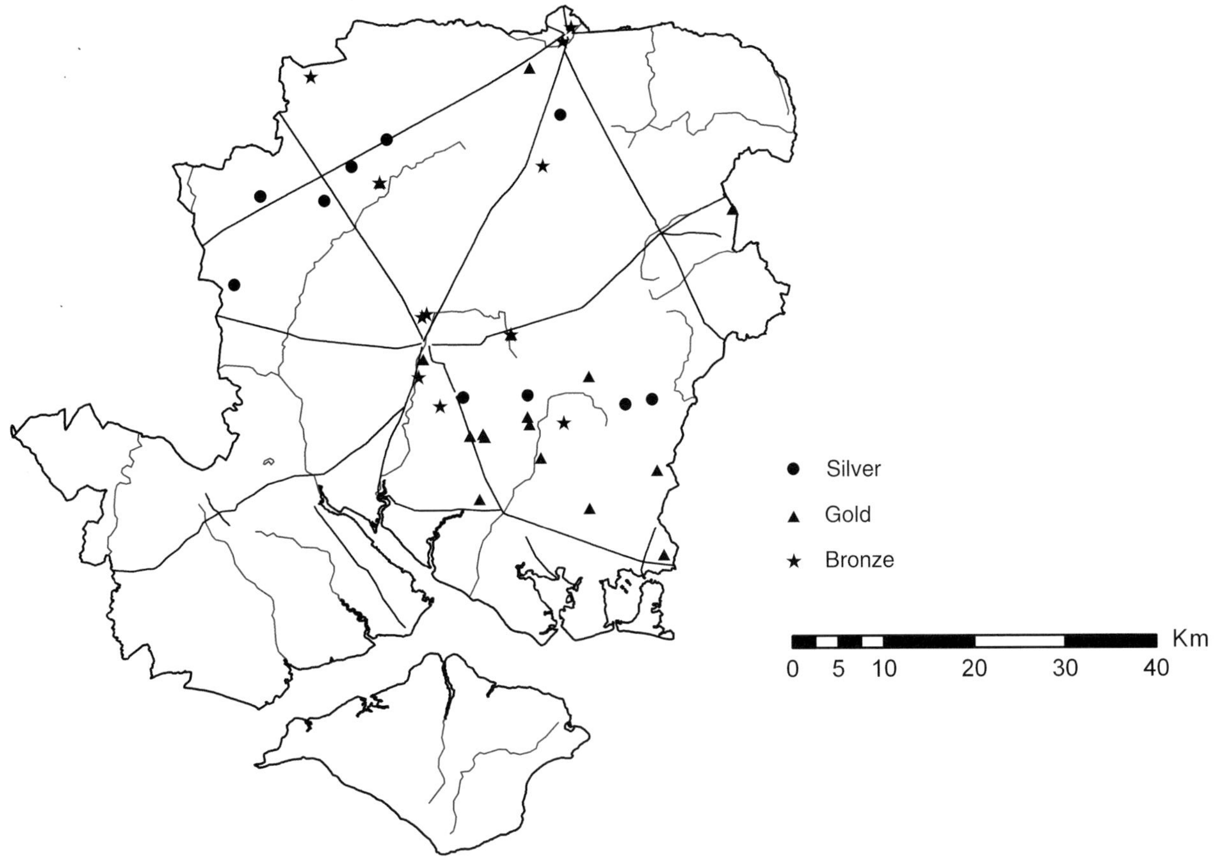

Fig. 3. Distribution of Iron Age coins by metal recorded by the PAS from Hampshire.

at several Wessex sites (Taylor and Brailsford 1985; Cunliffe 1995), in particular, Bury Hill (Hawkes 1940; Cunliffe and Poole 2000a). In particular, no strap-unions of the Bury Hill type have been recorded through the PAS. This might be explained by the fact that many items of excavated horse gear come from hillfort contexts, whereas the PAS examples are more likely to be associated with small farmsteads/lowland settlements, or to represent off-site finds. Alternatively, the dearth of horse gear recorded by the PAS in Hampshire and other southern counties compared to the apparent concentrations in eastern England and the West Midlands, may indicate that the use of horse gear with elaborate metal fittings has previously been exaggerated within Wessex, and underestimated elsewhere.

The small number of Iron Age coins from Hampshire reported through the PAS and as treasure cases since 1999 is a little surprising. Only one coin hoard, comprising 13 base metal 'Durotrigan' staters, found near Silchester, contrasts with the high number of hoards included in the other dataset, although this of course has accumulated over a much longer period of time (cf. Haselgrove 1987). The data do not include hoards recorded by the CCI. CCI records summarised by Hutcheson (2004, 13) reveal that 27 coin hoards are known from Hampshire, which has the highest number of recorded hoards of any county. This compares to Essex (14), Kent (14), Norfolk (16), and Suffolk (11). Excluding the hoard of Iron Age coins recorded by the PAS, 11 are base metal, 17 are gold, and 12 are silver. An analysis of the findspots of the gold coins reveals that, on the basis of current information, 65% are single finds with no other contemporary artefacts found nearby and recorded. This is a characteristic noted by Haselgrove (1987; 1996, 76), who established that excluding coin hoards, less than 30% of gold coins were found on 'sites' and that single gold coins were not accidental losses but should be interpreted as 'deliberate ritual or social acts of deposition' (Haselgrove 1992, 128). The distribution of these coins is shown in Figure 3 and discussed below.

A comparison of the Iron Age coinage from Hampshire recorded through the CCI and by the PAS over a similar period of time suggests that the existence of the PAS pilot projects has not led to a significant change in the quantity of coins reported to the CCI (De Jersey 2003). Ninety-two Iron Age coins, mostly found by metal detectorists, were recorded by the CCI between

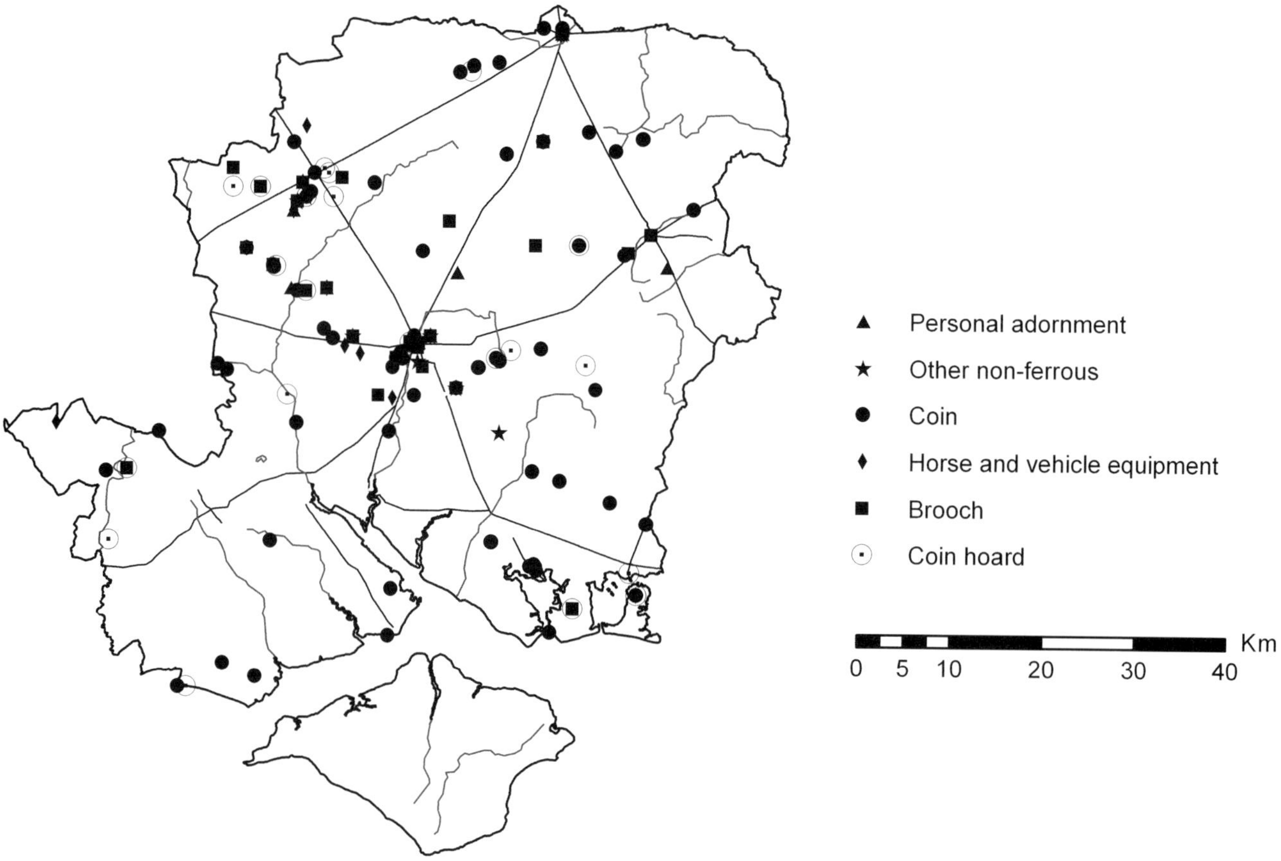

Fig. 4. Distribution of findspots of metallic Iron Age artefacts in Hampshire using HER/published data.

1999 and 2001 (*ibid.*), compared with 40 coins recorded through the PAS from January 1999 to October 2004. De Jersey's examination of the PAS database of records entered before 2003 confirms that most coins are also recorded on the CCI. Clearly, in Hampshire at least, the converse is not the case. The discrepancy in the quantities recorded must have much to do with the differences in the amount of time that the two projects have been in existence, but may also reflect the fact that the CCI includes coins in old collections, as well as those reported by dealers, often with sparse location information. In addition, when visiting metal detecting clubs, some finders have admitted reporting their finds to the CCI before selling a coin and before giving the PAS the opportunity to record it. It is hoped that better integration can be achieved between the two datasets in the future and that finders can be directed to the PAS to record coins and findspots.

The distribution of metallic artefacts in Hampshire

Figures 4 and 5 plot the findspots of metallic artefacts recorded respectively through HER/excavated finds and the PAS. A number of interesting preliminary observations can be made. The distribution of both datasets occurs in a broad swathe running diagonally across north-west, central, and south Hampshire. This general distribution coincides with the central chalk belt of predominantly arable land. The north Hampshire lowland and heath, comprising wooded acid soils and gravel in the north-east of the county, is poorly represented by finds from both datasets. The clustering of PAS findspots in river valleys, particular those of the Test and Meon rivers is a pattern not recognised from the HER/published dataset, presumably on account of the general lack of fieldwork in this setting within Hampshire (Champion and Champion 1981).

The distribution of non-PAS data is biased significantly to the areas that have had most excavations, in particular around Andover, Danebury, and Winchester. Elsewhere in the county, non-PAS findspots are generally distributed more evenly than those of the PAS data and extend into the New Forest. Apart from findspots generally following the line of the Roman roads from Winchester to Bitterne and Winchester to Old Sarum, and at the junction of roads close to Andover, there is not a significant link between findspots and the location of the Roman road network.

The distribution of the PAS findspots exhibits several features of interest. First, there is a significant clustering of findspots on or close to the line of the Roman roads,

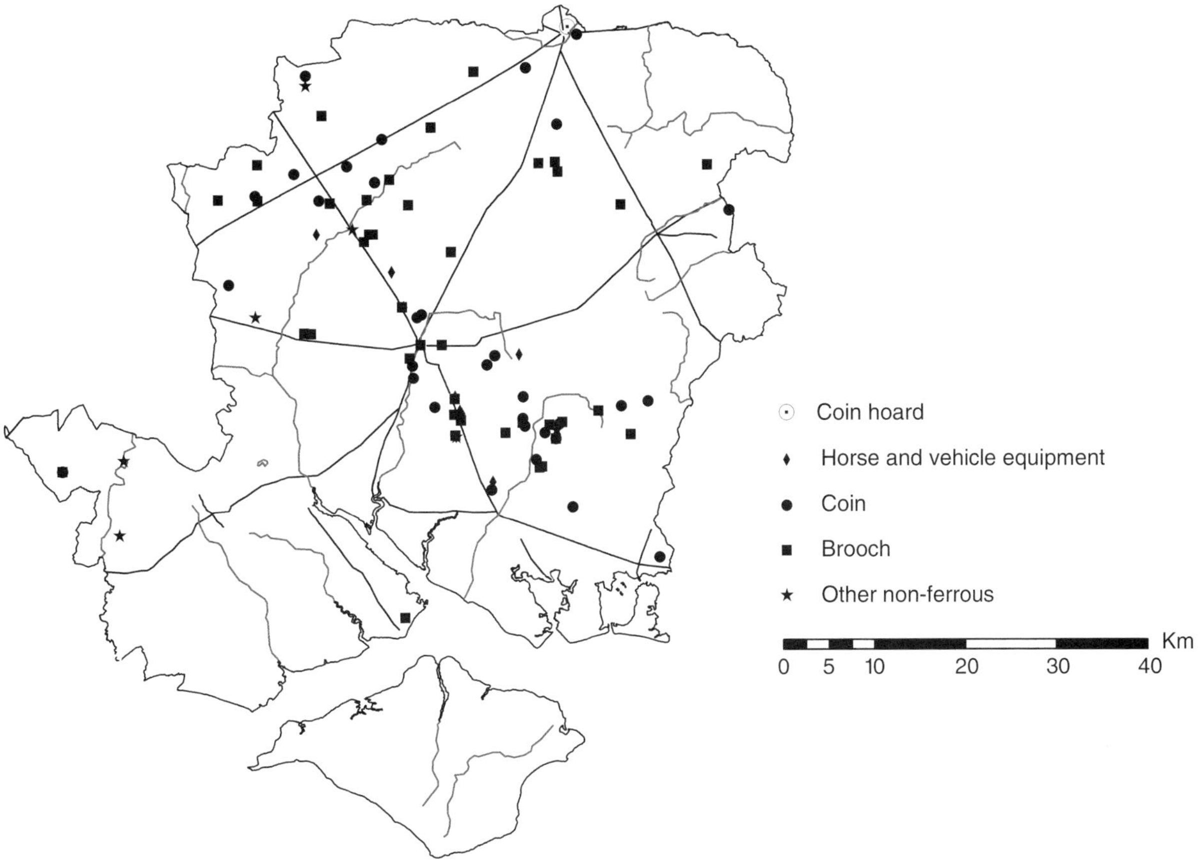

Fig. 5. Distribution of findspots of Iron Age metallic artefacts in Hampshire recorded by the PAS, September 1999–October 2004.

especially those connecting Winchester with Andover and Chichester. In part, this may reflect the targeting of areas close to Roman roads as potential attractive sites for metal detection. A general association between Iron Age coin findspots and Roman roads in central southern England has already been noted (Hodder and Orton 1976, fig. 7.1), with possible implications for the influence of pre-Roman settlement location on the Roman road network (Haselgrove 1996, 74). Similarly, Hutcheson's study of the location of Iron Age coins, torcs, and horse equipment in Norfolk reveals that single finds of Late Iron Age/early Roman horse equipment, in particular, tend to be found close to Roman roads and ancient routeways (Hutcheson 2004, 86; this volume). Although the amount of horse equipment found through metal detection in Hampshire is small, most of the artefacts were found close to the Roman road network, like the linch pin from Waltham Chase (Fig. 6). The line of the possibly ancient east–west communication route represented by the South Downs ridgeway may also be significant when evaluating the location of single coin finds in this area.

Second, the majority of the finds recorded by the PAS were found in the Winchester and Test valley districts. This not only reflects the archaeological wealth of these

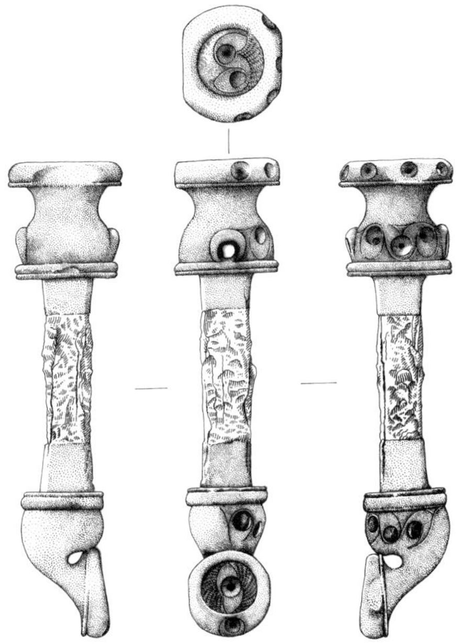

Fig. 6. Iron and copper alloy vase-headed linch pin inlaid with red glass from Waltham Chase, Hampshire. Scale 1:2.

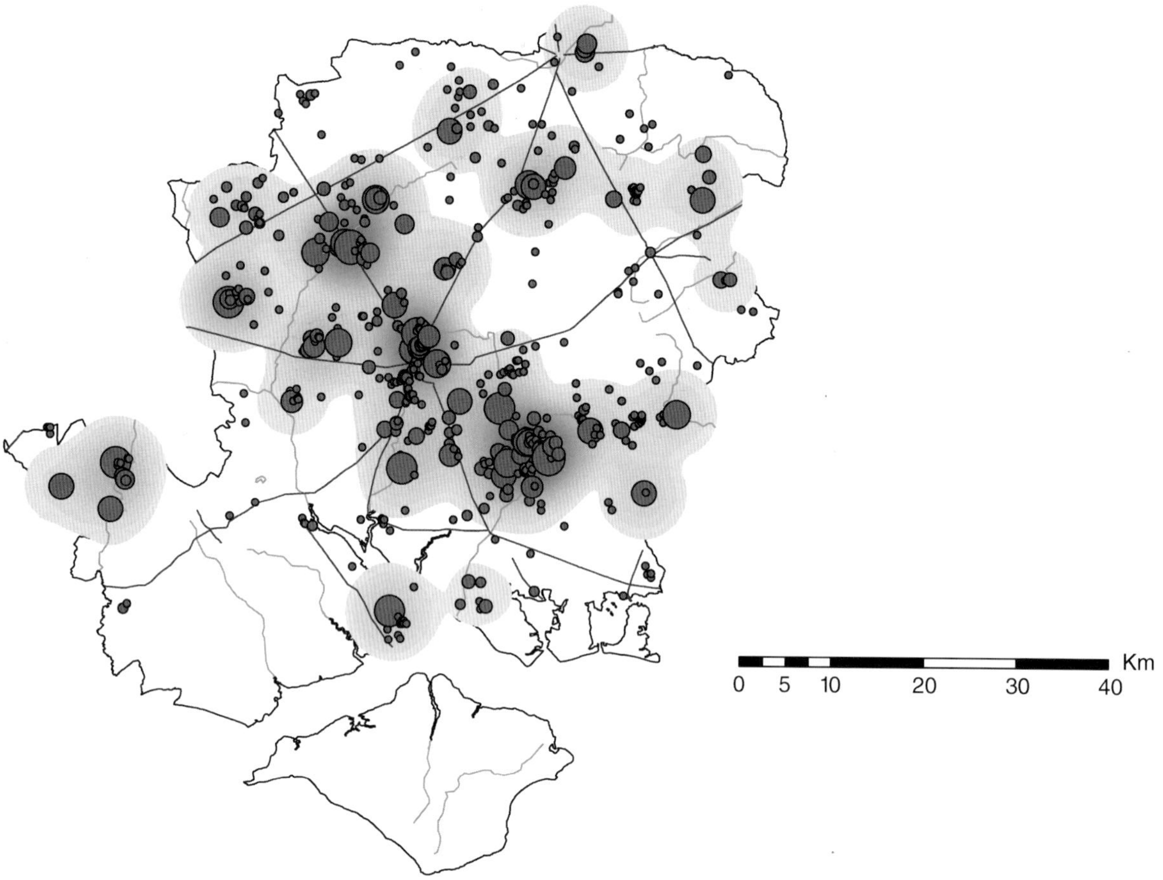

Fig. 7. Density of artefacts of all periods recorded by the PAS 1999–October 2004.

areas, but it is also likely to be influenced by the fact that the Finds Liaison Officer is based in Winchester and is therefore perhaps more accessible to local detectorists. This is especially apparent when recording those objects found by independent detectorists with whom it is more difficult to make initial contact than members of clubs. In Hampshire independent metal detectorists in fact record more artefacts than club members: 65% of the artefacts included in this study were reported either by independent detectorists or by detectorists who, although members of detecting clubs, discovered these artefacts on 'independent' sites. There are significant differences in the distribution of findspots in the Test valley between the two datasets. The majority of the findspots recorded by the HER/published data lie south and south-east of Andover largely as a result of the excavations undertaken by the Danebury Environs Programme, particularly at Danebury and Bury Hill. In contrast, this area is poorly represented by PAS findspots, which instead cluster along the line of the Roman roads running north-east and south-east from Andover and close to the River Test in the area between the two roads.

Finally, there is a concentration of findspots in the PAS corpus in the Meon valley, centred on the parishes of Corhampton, Meonstoke, Exton, and Warnford. This pattern is not replicated in the HER/published data and only a small number of single Iron Age coins have been recorded in that dataset from this general area. This part of the Hampshire landscape has been less investigated archaeologically than areas close to Winchester and in the Test valley. The PAS data, especially coins and brooches, suggest therefore that in the Late Iron Age this area may have been characterised by a relatively dense distribution of lowland settlements and small farmsteads. In addition, off-site deposition within the landscape must be considered in any interpretation of findspots in this area.

Alternatively, does this distribution reflect a higher level of metal detecting and reporting of artefacts? In order to assess the distribution of metal detection throughout the county, the density of findspots of metal-detected artefacts of all periods reported through the Hampshire PAS project was plotted (Fig. 7). The distribution of this data reveals three principal concentrations located on the line of the Roman road south of Andover in the Test valley, at Winchester, and in the Meon valley parishes mentioned above, all of which have the highest densities of Iron Age artefacts. The Meon valley concentration is the most prolific, suggesting that the quantity of Iron Age artefacts in this area also reflects the intensity of metal detecting and the level of finds reporting.

Conclusion

This study is a preliminary analysis, but nevertheless some significant observations can be made regarding the circulation and deposition of metalwork in the Iron Age across England and Wales as viewed through the PAS data.

The quantity of artefacts of Late Iron Age date documented by the PAS massively exceeds that of earlier periods, a pattern expected on the basis of excavated assemblages. Quantities of finds in all categories recorded in East Anglia are much larger than in other areas, with the exception of Kent, where coin finds massively outnumber those from other counties, in part a reflection of the Kent Iron Age coin project. Analysis of two artefact categories in greater detail gave contrasting results in relation to earlier studies. The distribution and frequency of brooch types is broadly consistent with that identified by Hull (1968) and Haselgrove (1997), but that of horse gear differed from expectations based on excavated data, with concentrations in East Anglia and parts of the West Midlands. Analysis of evidence from Hampshire showed that the PAS data represent a significant addition (13%) to the corpus of non-ferrous metalwork from the county, although not in all categories: brooches for example, are much better represented in the PAS data than coin finds. The distribution of PAS data is broadly similar to the excavated/HER data, but reveals a previously unidentified concentration of Iron Age settlement in south-east Hampshire in the Meon valley.

Insights from the PAS can be argued to contribute to the general reassessment of regional social trajectories during the Iron Age. This reconsideration has been increasingly argued in studies of Iron Age Norfolk (see case studies 1 and 2), but can be extended to a larger area of eastern England and, on the basis of horse gear, to the West Midlands. Less archaeological fieldwork has taken place in these areas, there are few surviving landscape monuments, and these regions have previously been considered as less socially complex than, and peripheral to, the core areas of south-east England. These areas are, however, better represented in terms of metallic artefacts than those which have been the traditional focus of Iron Age archaeology. At a local level, too, the Hampshire case study reveals that the PAS data can identify under-explored areas and offer a new view of intra-regional variability.

This study has only examined very general patterns based on data collected in a comparatively short period of time and over uneven periods of time across the country. At both local and national levels, variations in the intensity of recording have affected the patterns presented here. Further attention must be paid to the biases affecting the interpretation of metal-detected finds. Nevertheless, now that the PAS is established on a national basis, differences in regional reporting traditions should become less significant. The data now being recorded offer the potential of changing important aspects of our perceptions of the archaeology of England and Wales and of building an ever-increasing potential research resource.

Acknowledgements

My thanks to the following for providing HER information: Bruce Howard (formerly Hampshire County Council), Tracy Matthews (Winchester Museums Service), Martin Horlock and Alice Catermole (Norfolk Museums and Archaeology Service). Philip de Jersey, Winchester Excavations Committee, and Winchester Museums Service kindly gave me access to unpublished work. I am grateful to Chris Lyes for his help with distribution maps, and to J.D. Hill and Roger Bland for their encouragement and helpful comments on a draft. John Pearce provided much advice and support during the long gestation of this paper. Tom Moore's and Colin Haselgrove's encouragement and patience (!) are also much appreciated as are Colin's comments and advice.

Notes

1. Unfortunately, it was not possible to include details of the unpublished non-coin metallic artefacts from Hayling Island; nor does this survey include coins recorded in the CCI, other than those recorded by the Danebury Environs Programme (De Jersey 2000).

Appendix: Publication references for Hampshire non-PAS non-ferrous artefacts

Brooches

Balksbury Camp (Wainwright and Davies 1995); Danebury (Jope 1984; Jope 1991); Kimpton (Osgood 2000); Middle Wallop (Cunliffe and Poole 2000c); Neatham (Hull 1986); Old Down Farm (Davies 1981); Owslebury (Collis 1968); Otterbourne (Mackreth 1993); Silchester (Boon 1957; Corney 2000); Stockbridge (Cunliffe and Poole 2000a); Tinker's Hill (Osgood 2000); Winchester (Crummy 2004; forthcoming; Cunliffe 1964; Hawkes *et al.* 1930; Mackreth 1985; Winham 1985); Winchester Museums Service (unpublished archive); Winchester Research Unit (unpublished archive).
Brooches from sites in Hampshire are catalogued by Hull and Hawkes (1987).

Other personal adornment

Balksbury Camp (Wainwright and Davies 1995); Bury Hill (Cunliffe and Poole 2000b); Danebury (Cunliffe *et al.* 1991; Jope and Cunliffe 1984); Meon Hill (Liddell 1935); Micheldever (Winham 1987); Old Down Farm (Davies 1981); Stockbridge (Jope and Cunliffe 1984; Cunliffe and Poole 2000a); Winchester (Winham 1985).

Horse and vehicle equipment

Balksbury (Wainwright and Davies 1995); Bury Hill (Hawkes 1940; Cunliffe and Poole 2000b); Danebury (Cunliffe *et al.* 1991; Palk 1991); Hayling Island (Downey *et al.* 1979; Palk 1984; Taylor and Brailsford 1985); Middle Wallop (Cunliffe and Poole 2000c); Old Down Farm (Davies 1981); Otterbourne (Denford 1993); Owslebury (Collis 1968; 1970); Stockbridge (Cunliffe and Poolc 2000a); Winchester (Winham 1985).

Other non-ferrous

Andover (Osgood 2000); Balksbury Camp (Wainwright and Davies 1995); Danebury (Cunliffe *et al.* 1991; Jope and Cunliffe 1984); Hayling Island (Downey *et al.* 1979); Owslebury (Collis 1968); Otterbourne (Denford 1993); nr Silchester (Fulford and Creighton 1998); Winchester (Hawkes *et al.* 1930; Winham 1985).

Coins

Danebury Environs (De Jersey 2000); Owslebury (Collis 1968); Silchester (Boon 2000).
Coins from sites in Hampshire are listed in Haselgrove (1987).

Bibliography

Boon, G.C. 1957. *Roman Silchester: the Archaeology of a Romano-British Town*. London: Max Parrish.

Boon, G.C. 2000. The coins, in Fulford and Timby 2000, 127–170.

Brown, R.A. 1986. The Iron Age and Romano-British settlement at Woodcock Hall, Saham Toney, Norfolk, *Britannia* 17, 1–58.

Bushe-Fox, J.P. 1916. *Third report on the Excavations on the Site of the Roman Town at Wroxeter Shropshire, 1914*. Oxford: Reports of the Research Committee of the Society of Antiquaries of London 4.

Champion, T.C. and Champion, S. 1981. The Iron Age in Hampshire, in S. Shennan and R.T. Schadla-Hall (eds), *The Archaeology of Hampshire from the Palaeolithic to the Industrial Revolution,* 37–45. Winchester: Hampshire Field Club and Archaeology Society Monograph 1.

Collis, J.R. 1968. Excavations at Owslebury, Hants: an interim report, *Antiquaries Journal* 48, 18–31.

Collis, J.R. 1970. Excavations at Owslebury, Hants: a second interim report, *Antiquaries Journal* 50, 246–261.

Corney, M. 1984. Objects of copper alloy, in M.G. Fulford, *Silchester: Excavations on the Defences, 1974–80 and a Field Survey of the Extra-Mural Territory*, 110–112. London: Britannia Monograph 5.

Corney, M. 2000. The brooches, in Fulford and Timby 2000, 322–328.

Creighton, J. 1990. The Humber frontier in the first century AD, in S. Ellis and D. Crowther (eds), *Humber Perspectives: A Region through the Ages,* 182–198. Hull: Hull University Press.

Crummy, N. 2004. A La Tène II brooch, in K.E. Qualmann, H. Rees, G. Scobie and R. Whinney, *Oram's Arbour: The Iron Age Enclosure at Winchester, Vol. 1. Investigations 1950–99,* 67–68. Winchester: Winchester Museums Service.

Crummy, N. forthcoming. Objects of personal adornment and dress, in N. Crummy, P. Ottaway and H. Rees, *Small Finds from the Suburbs and City Defences.* Winchester: Winchester City Museum Publication 6.

Cunliffe, B. 1964. Roman small finds, in B. Cunliffe, *Winchester Excavations 1949–1960, Vol. I, Part III. Staple Gardens,* 179. Winchester: City of Winchester Museums and Libraries Committee.

Cunliffe, B. 1984. *Danebury: An Iron Age Hillfort in Hampshire. The Excavations 1969–78, Vol. 1: The Site; Vol. 2: The Finds.* London: Council for British Archaeology Research Report 52.

Cunliffe, B. 1991. *Iron Age Communities in Britain* (3rd edn). London: Routledge.

Cunliffe, B. 1995. The Celtic chariot: a footnote, in B. Raftery (ed.), *Sites and Sights of the Iron Age Essays on Fieldwork and Museum Research presented to Ian Mathieson Stead*, 31–39. Oxford: Oxbow Monograph 56.

Cunliffe, B. 2000. *The Danebury Environs Programme: the Prehistory of a Wessex Landscape, Vol. 1: Introduction.* Oxford: Oxford University Committee for Archaeology Monograph 48.

Cunliffe, B. and Poole, C. 1991. *Danebury: An Iron Age Hillfort in Hampshire, Vol. 5. The Excavations, 1979–1988: the Finds.* London: Council for British Archaeology Research Report 73.

Cunliffe, B. and Poole, C. 2000a. Objects of copper alloy, in B. Cunliffe and C. Poole, *Bury Hill, Upper Clatford, Hants, 1990. The Danebury Environs Programme: the Prehistory of a Wessex Landscape, Vol. 2 – Part 2,* 47–51. Oxford: Oxford University Committee for Archaeology Monograph 49.

Cunliffe, B. and Poole, C. 2000b. Objects of copper alloy, in B. Cunliffe and C. Poole, *The Danebury Environs Programme: the Prehistory of a Wessex Landscape, Vol. 2 – Part 1. Woolbury and Stockbridge Down, Stockbridge, Hants 1989,* 57–59. Oxford: Oxford University Committee for Archaeology Monograph 49.

Cunliffe, B. and Poole, C. 2000c. Objects of copper alloy, in B. Cunliffe and C. Poole, *The Danebury Environs Programme: the Prehistory of a Wessex Landscape, Vol. 2 – Part 3. Suddern Farm, Middle Wallop, Hants, 1991 and 1996,* 116–117. Oxford: Oxford University Committee for Archaeology Monograph 49.

Cunliffe, B., Jope, E.M. and Palk, N. 1991. Other objects of copper alloy, in Cunliffe and Poole 1991, 328–333.

Curteis, M. 1996. An analysis of the circulation patterns from Northamptonshire, *Britannia* 27, 17–42.

Davies, J. 1996. Where Eagles Dare: the Iron Age of Norfolk. *Proceedings of the Prehistoric Society* 62, 63–92.

Davies, J. and Williamson, T. 1999a. Introduction: studying the Iron Age, in Davies and Williamson 1999b, 1–14.

Davies, J. and Williamson, T. (eds) 1999b. *Land of the Iceni. The Iron Age in Northern East Anglia.* Norwich: Studies in East Anglia History 4.

Davies, S.M. 1981. Excavations at Old Down Farm, Andover, Part II: Prehistoric and Roman, *Proceedings of the Hampshire Field Club and Archaeological Society* 37, 81–163.

De Jersey, P. 2000. Iron Age coins from the Danebury Environs, in Cunliffe 2000, 215–218.

De Jersey, P. 2003. *Spatial Variation in the Recording of Celtic Coins.* Unpublished report for English Heritage.

Dobinson, C. and Denison, S. 1995. *Metal Detecting and Archaeology in England.* London: Council for British Archaeology/English Heritage.

Downey, R., King, A. and Soffe, G. 1979. *The Hayling Island Temple Third Interim Report on the Excavation of the Iron Age and Roman Temple 1976–78.* London: Privately printed.

Fasham, P.J. 1985. *The Prehistoric Settlement at Winnall Down, Winchester.* Winchester: Hampshire Field Club Monograph 2.

Fasham, P.J., Farwell, D. and Whinney, D.W. 1989. *The Archaeological Site at Easton Lane, Winchester.* Winchester: Hampshire Field Club Monograph 6.

Fitzpatrick, A.P. 1984. The deposition of La Tène Iron Age metalwork in watery contexts in southern England, in B. Cunliffe and D. Miles (eds), *Aspects of the Iron Age in Central Southern Britain*, 178–190. Oxford: Oxford University Committee for Archaeology Monograph 2.

Fulford, M.G. and Creighton, J. 1998. A Late Iron Age Mirror Burial from Latchmere Green, near Silchester, Hampshire, *Proceedings of the Prehistoric Society* 64, 331–342.

Fulford, M. and Timby, J. 2000. *Late Iron Age and Roman Silchester. Excavations on the Site of the Forum-Basilica 1977, 1980–86.* London: Britannia Monograph 15.

Geake, H. 2002. Further response to 'Time please', *Antiquity* 76, 386–388.

Gwilt, A. and Haselgrove, C. (eds) 1997. *Reconstructing Iron Age Societies.* Oxford: Oxbow Monograph 71.

Haselgrove, C. 1987. *Iron Age Coinage in South-East England: The Archaeological Context.* Oxford: British Archaeological Reports British Series 174.

Haselgrove, C. 1992. Iron Age coinage and archaeology, in M. Mays (ed.), *Celtic Coinage: Britain and Beyond. The Eleventh Oxford Symposium on Coinage and Monetary History,* 123–139. Oxford: British Archaeological Reports British Series 222.

Haselgrove, C. 1996. Iron Age coinage: recent work, in T.C. Champion and J.R. Collis (eds), *The Iron Age in Britain and Ireland: Recent Trends,* 67–85. Sheffield: J.R. Collis Publications.

Haselgrove, C. 1997. Iron Age brooch deposition and chronology, in Gwilt and Haselgrove 1997, 51–73.

Haselgrove, C., Armit, I., Champion, T., Creighton, J., Gwilt, A., Hill, J.D., Hunter, F., and Woodward, A. 2001. *Understanding the British Iron Age: An Agenda for Action.* Salisbury: Wessex Archaeology.

Hawkes, C.F.C. 1940. The excavations at Bury Hill, 1939, *Proceedings of the Hampshire Field Club and Archaeological Society* 14, 291–337.

Hawkes, C.F.C., Myres, J.N.L. and Stevens, G.C. 1930. St Catharine's Hill Winchester, *Proceedings of the Hampshire Field Club and Archaeological Society* 11, 1–286.

Hill, J.D. 1995. *Ritual and Rubbish in the Iron Age of Wessex.* Oxford: British Archaeological Reports British Series 242.

Hill, J.D. 1997. 'The end of one kind of body and the beginning of another kind of body?' Toilet instruments and Romanisation, in Gwilt and Haselgrove 1997, 96–108.

Hill, J.D. 1999. Settlement, landscape and regionality: Norfolk and Suffolk in the pre-Roman Iron Age of Britain and Beyond, in Davies and Williamson 1999b, 185–207.

Hill, J.D., Spence, A.J., La Niece, S. and Worrell, S. 2004. The Winchester Hoard: A find of unique Iron Age gold jewellery from southern England, *Antiquaries Journal* 84, 1–23.

Hinchliffe, J. and Schadla-Hall, R.T. (eds) 1980. *The Past under the Plough: Papers Presented at the Seminar on Plough Damage and Archaeology held at Salisbury, February 1977.* London: Department of the Environment.

Hodder, I.R. and Orton, C. 1976. *Spatial Analysis in Archaeology.* Cambridge: Cambridge University Press.

Holman, D.J. 2000. Iron Age coinage in Kent: a review of current knowledge, *Archaeologia Cantiana* 120, 205–233.

Hull, M.R. 1968. The brooches, in B. Cunliffe, *Excavation of the Roman fort at Richborough, Kent,* 74–93. Oxford: Report of the Research Committee of the Society of Antiquaries of London 23.

Hull, M.R. 1971. The brooches, in B. Cunliffe, *Excavations at Fishbourne, 1961–9,* 100–107. Oxford: Report of the Research Committee of the Society of Antiquaries of London 27.

Hull, M.R. 1986. The brooches, in M. Millett and D. Graham, *Excavations on the Romano-British Small Town at Neatham, Hampshire, 1969–1979,* 101–111. Winchester: Hampshire Field Club and Archaeological Society Monograph 3.

Hull, M.R. and Hawkes, C.F.C. 1987. *Corpus of Ancient Brooches in Britain.* Oxford: British Archaeological Reports British Series 168.

Hutcheson, N. 2004. *Later Iron Age Norfolk: Metalwork, Landscape and Society.* Oxford: British Archaeological Reports British Series 361.

Jope, E.M. 1984. Brooches, in Cunliffe 1984, Vol. 2, 340–343.

Jope, E.M. 1991. Brooches, in Cunliffe and Poole 1991, 328–331.

Jope, E.M. and Cunliffe, B. 1984. Other objects of copper alloy, in Cunliffe 1984, Vol. 2, 343–346.

Jundi, S. and Hill, J.D. 1998. Brooches and identities in first century AD Britain: more than meets the eye? in C. Forcey, J. Hawthorne and R. Witcher (eds), *TRAC 97. Proceedings of the Seventh Annual Theoretical Roman Archaeology Conference, Nottingham 1997,* 125–137. Oxford: Oxbow Books.

Lambrick, G. 1977. *Archaeology and Agriculture.* London: Council for British Archaeology.

Liddell, D.M. 1935. Metal. Report of excavations at Meon Hill, second season 1933, *Proceedings of the Hampshire Field Club and Archaeological Society* 13, 35–37.

MacGregor, M. 1976. *Early Celtic Art in North Britain.* Leicester: Leicester University Press.

Mackreth, D.F. 1981. The brooches, in C. Partridge, *Skeleton Green, a Late Iron Age and Romano-British Site*, 130–151. London: Britannia Monograph 2.

Mackreth, D.F. 1985. Brooches, in Fasham 1985, 46–47.

Mackreth, D.F. 1993. Iron Age brooch, in G.T. Denford, Some exotic discoveries at Silkstead Sandpit, Otterbourne, and the possible site of an ancient temple, *Proceedings of the Hampshire Field Club and Archaeological Society* 48, 46 (27–54).

Martin, E. 1999. Suffolk in the Iron Age, in Davies and Williamson 1999b, 45–100.

Osgood, R. 2000. Gazetteer of prehistoric sites and finds in the Danebury region, in Cunliffe 2000, 209–215.

Palk, N.A. 1984. *Iron Age Bridle Bits from Britain.* Edinburgh: Edinburgh University Occasional Paper 10.

Palk, N.A. 1991. Bronze fittings probably for horse harness, in Cunliffe and Poole 1991, 332–333.

Phillips, C.W. 1931. Final report on the Excavations at Merlin's Cave, *Proceedings of Bristol University Spelaeological Society* 4, 11–33.

Portable Antiquities Scheme. *Finds Database*, http://www.finds.org.uk

Selwood, L. 1984. Objects of iron, in Cunliffe 1984, Vol. 2, 346–371.

Selwood, L., Mays, M. and Taylor, J.W. 1984. Coins, in Cunliffe 1984, Vol. 2, 332–335.

Shennan, S. 1985. *Experiments in the Collection and Analysis of Archaeological Survey Data: The East Hampshire Survey.* Sheffield: Department of Archaeology and Prehistory, University of Sheffield.

Spratling, M.G. 1972. *Southern British Decorated Bronzes of the Late Pre-Roman Iron Age.* Unpublished Ph.D. thesis, University of London.

Stead, I.M. 1979. *The Arras Culture.* York: Yorkshire Philosophical Society.

Stead, I.M. 1991. *Iron Age Cemeteries in East Yorkshire.* London: English Heritage Archaeological Report 22.

Taylor, R.J. and Brailsford, J.W. 1985. British Iron Age strap-unions, *Proceedings of the Prehistoric Society* 51, 247–272.

Wainwright, G.J. 1979. *Gussage All Saints: An Iron Age Settlement in Dorset.* London: Department of the Environment Archaeological Report 10.

Wainwright, G.J. and Davies, S.M. 1995. The finds: copper alloy, in G.J. Wainwright and S.M. Davies, *Balksbury Camp, Hampshire: Excavations 1973 and 1981,* 31–36. London: English Heritage Archaeological Report 4.

Wainwright, G.J. and Spratling, M.G. 1973. The Iron Age settlement of Gussage All Saints, *Antiquity* 47, 109–130.

Ward-Perkins 1941. An Iron Age linch-pin of Yorkshire type from Cornwall, *Antiquaries Journal* 21, 64–67.

Webster, G. 1990. Part of a Celtic linch-pin, *Britannia* 21, 293–294.

Willis, S.H. 1997. Settlement, materiality and landscape in the Iron Age of the East Midlands: evidence, interpretation and wider resonance, in Gwilt and Haselgrove 1997, 205–216.

Winham, R.P. 1985. Other bronze objects, in Fasham 1985, 47–49.

Winham, R.P. 1987. Metal finds, in P.J. Fasham, *A 'Banjo' Enclosure in Micheldever Wood, Hampshire,* 21–24. Winchester: Hampshire Field Club Monograph 5.

The end of the Sheep Age: people and animals in the Late Iron Age

Umberto Albarella

At a conference in Sheffield a few years ago, I suggested that if the three age system had been created by a British zooarchaeologist, we might today be talking of a Cattle Age (the Early Neolithic), a Pig Age (the Late Neolithic), and a Sheep Age (the Bronze and Iron Ages; Albarella 2000). It goes without saying that this is a complete caricature of the reality, but perhaps no more so than the characterisation of a particular phase of human evolution on the basis of the most common material used to make tools. Of course, just as we find that some Iron Age societies barely used iron, there are also cases of populations of that period for whom sheep were less important than other livestock. Despite the obvious exceptions to any generalisation, it is worth bearing in mind that animals can be as representative of a society as any other elements of material culture.

In this paper I will discuss the relationship between people and animals in a period that ranges from approximately the mid second century BC to the first century AD (i.e. the Late Iron Age). We will see that this is a phase that especially deserves to be called the Sheep Age and anticipates the return to the Cattle Age prompted by the Roman invasion in AD 43. The paper is general enough in its aims not to require a precise definition of the area under investigation, but broadly speaking I will be writing about central and southern Britain.

The interest of the Late Iron Age for our understanding of past (and present) human cultures cannot be overestimated. This period pre-dates an important invasion, which is historically well documented. It therefore provides us with an excellent opportunity to analyse the effects of acculturation, or at least attempted acculturation. We have little chance of properly understanding the effects of the Roman conquest of Britain, if we do not have at least some idea of the lifestyle and customs of the British population before that event. The Late Iron Age is not just of historical interest *per se*, but it also provides us with the opportunity to analyse the mechanisms of cultural contact. This interest is enhanced by the fact that archaeology works at its best when it can be used comparatively, and the study of this period offers us the opportunity to compare life in Britain before and after this major historical event. It would, however, be a mistake to compare the Late Iron Age exclusively with the Roman period, as its characteristics depend equally on what occurred before its onset. A comparison with the Early and Middle Iron Ages – although the boundaries are not as clear cut as those with the Roman period – is therefore also appropriate.

The chief aim of this paper is to investigate to what extent the evidence of animal bones from archaeological sites can help us in characterising the Late Iron Age. To do so we will have to analyse differences and similarities with earlier and later periods. A full review of the available data is beyond the scope of the paper, so I will select the elements which are central to the question of how distinctive was Late Iron Age exploitation of animals. I will not discuss the intriguing dearth of aquatic resources – particularly fish – at many sites of this period, as this is dealt with in another contribution (Dobney and Ervynck this volume). Equally, I will not deal with the frequent and widespread presence of skeletons or partial skeletons of animals on Iron Age sites. This phenomenon has already generated much debate (e.g. Grant 1984a; Wilson 1992; Hill 1995a), and it would not be very useful to revisit the issue here. This is not to say that this paper will focus exclusively on economic aspects of Iron Age societies. That 'faunal... remains on Iron Age sites are very much "cultural" in the nature of their deposition' (Parker Pearson 1996,

128) is a truism, but it is probably still worth mentioning. Any dump of bone material on an archaeological site has cultural implications, which are connected with the organisation of the society and its beliefs. These characteristics are not exclusive to the so-called 'structured depositions' – a much-abused term in British archaeology (see Albarella and Serjeantson 2002).

Previous studies

It is often pointed out that our view of the Iron Age is strongly biased towards central southern Britain (e.g. Bevan 1999a, 1). This bias also applies to the study of animal bones. Although zooarchaeological studies of Late Iron Age faunal assemblages have been undertaken from sites across Britain, their frequency tends to diminish from south to north. A difficult balance therefore needs to be struck between using the evidence from the south as an interesting case study, but at the same time avoiding the trap of applying it uncritically to the rest of the country.

To draw truly convincing results about past ways of life, zooarchaeologists need to deal with at least a number of large assemblages of bones, which will permit the analysis of aspects of animal exploitation that go well beyond a mere list of exploited species. The reality of the present evidence is that the sites that have produced some of the largest animal bone assemblages tend to be in the same region (Wessex and neighbouring areas).

The study of the largest animal bone assemblage ever recovered from an Iron Age site was that carried out by Grant (1984b; 1991; but see Jones 1995 for a final comment) on the material from the famous hillfort of Danebury (Hampshire). The assemblage included bones from all Iron Age phases, but there was no Roman material. Another important Late Iron Age assemblage, also from Hampshire, is that from Owslebury. Regrettably the full study of the bones has never been published, but an Ancient Monuments Laboratory report is available (Maltby 1987). Unlike Danebury, Owslebury did not have any material from the Earlier Iron Age, but provided the opportunity for comparing the Late Iron Age with the Roman period.

Bob Wilson has studied several Late Iron Age assemblages, mainly from the upper Thames valley, but his key contribution is probably his work on the horizontal distribution of animal bones, which has made us aware of how different context types may produce assemblages with different biases (for a compendium of this evidence see Wilson 1996). Wilson's approach was also applied to the animal bones from Owslebury, where Maltby (1987) highlighted patterns and differences not only in the vertical, but also in the horizontal distribution of the bones. More recently, Hambleton (1999) has produced a very useful review of the relative frequency and age patterns of the three main domesticates (cattle, sheep, and pig) on British Iron Age sites. There are many other works, but this is the key evidence we must consider in studying the relation between people and animals in the Iron Age.

Historical sources

Although we have no direct written accounts of the British Late Iron Age, several Greek and Roman writers provide some information about life in Britain in this period, but for the most part this includes only a few vague references to the use of animals. The one source that provides more that a passing reference to agricultural practices and the use of animals in Britain is Caesar's account of the Gallic war. First he mentions the customs of Belgic populations, who had moved from the Continent to the maritime part of Britain. According to Caesar, these people cultivated the fields and owned vast amounts of livestock, and in general led a lifestyle not dissimilar from that of their land of origin. Apparently they restrained from eating hares, domestic fowl, and geese, but liked to keep some of these animals (*Gallic War* V, 12). In addition, Caesar states that the coastal populations were far more civilised than those living inland, who did not practice agriculture, lived entirely on milk and meat, and dressed in leather (*ibid.* V, 14).

Writing at the end of the first century AD (i.e. after the Roman conquest) Tacitus is disappointingly uninformative about British life in that period. Apart from mentioning the unpleasantness of the climate and the fertility of the soil, which produces many crops but neither olives nor vines (*Agricola* 12), he is silent about the relationship between indigenous people and their landscape. This lack of detail is particularly lamentable if we compare the *Agricola* with Tacitus' account of German populations (*Germania*), with its wealth of information about the local exploitation of natural resources. Among other sources it is worth noting that the Greek Strabo (late first century BC) mentions in his *Geography* (IV, 5, 4) that Britain exported to the Continent, among other things, grain, cattle, hides, and hunting dogs.

One word of comment is necessary. We must bear in mind that classical writers had a biased view of the world, which they tended to interpret as having its central place in Rome (Bevan 1999, 3). For instance Caesar's view of British life in inland areas – which can easily be discounted on the basis of archaeological evidence – tends to reflect the idea that the level of civilisation decreased when moving further from the area of Roman influence. A similar approach can be detected in Tacitus' account of Germanic populations. In addition, the reliability of these sources cannot be taken for granted. Caesar in particular seems to be rather fanciful in many of his descriptions – see for instance the imaginary animals supposed to live in the forested areas between Gaul and Germany (*Gallic War* VI, 25–28).

It is therefore possible that these brief descriptions tell us more about Roman ideology than about the reality of the people living in north-west Europe. Yet – however biased – these words represent our only opportunity to hear a direct account of the people from this distant past, and we should therefore not ignore them.

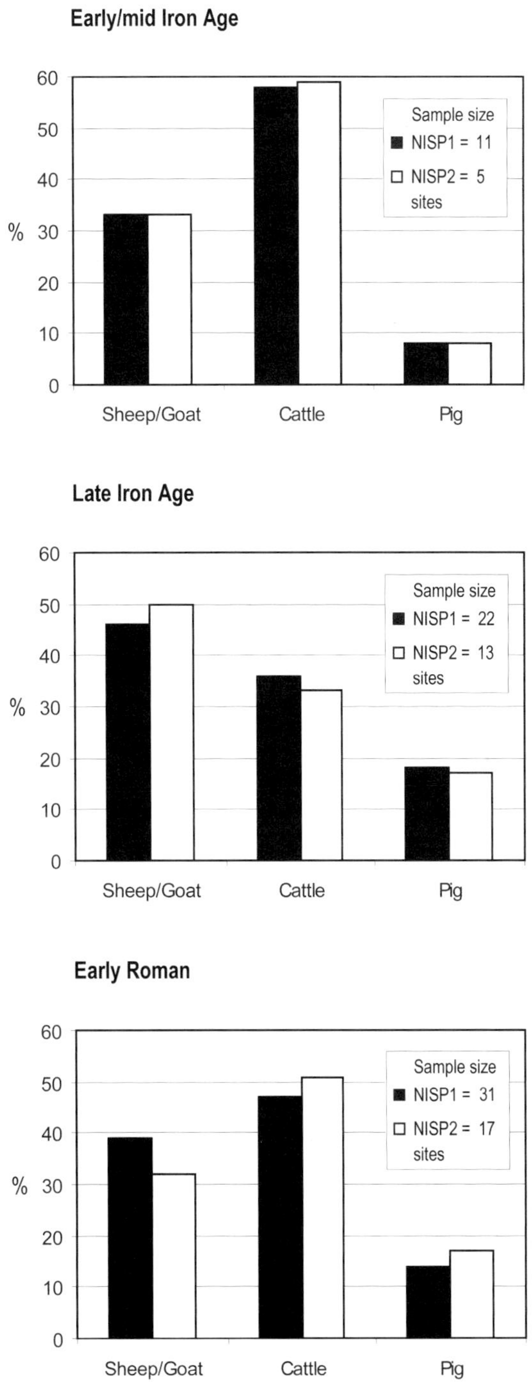

Fig. 1. Average frequency of the main domestic mammals at Iron Age and early Roman sites in the Midlands and East Anglia (see Table 1). NISP = Number of identified specimens; NISP 1 = mean of the percentages calculated for each site; NISP 2 = percentage of the total NISP for all sites. Despite small variations, the two calculations (NISP1 and NISP2) show similar trends.

The Late Iron Age and before

A starting date for the Late Iron Age cannot easily be established. Cunliffe (1991, 107) and Haselgrove (1999a, 130) place this around 150 BC, while other authors propose a somewhat later date (see Hill 1995b, 74). What is more important for this paper, however, is to pinpoint what criteria have been adopted to discriminate the Late Iron Age from previous periods.

The classic subdivision of the Iron Age is based on pottery typology. The Late Iron Age, in particular, is characterised by the appearance of new pottery forms, which seem to have been influenced by French and Roman originals (Hill 1995b, 79). Among other elements used to identify this period it is worth mentioning the suggested intensification not only in pottery making, but also in salt extraction, ironworking and in general in the trade with the Continent (Cunliffe 1991, 157; Haselgrove 1999a, 128–32). This last phenomenon seems also to have been associated with an increased consumption of exotic foodstuffs and drink, probably used as a means of social distinction (Hill 2002). Even more relevant here is that the period seems to be typified by an intensification in agricultural activity witnessed by the increased clearance of forests and the colonisation of areas with heavier and damper soils (Haselgrove 1999b, 271). This phenomenon is probably linked with the increased use of spelt (*Triticum spelta*), a type of wheat better suited to heavy soils, for which there is evidence from the Tees lowlands and other areas in northern England (Van der Veen 1992, 77).

Are any of these aspects of the Late Iron Age also reflected in the faunal record? The slight relative increase in sheep in the latest phases that seem to characterise the flagship site of the British Iron Age – Danebury – and a few other sites in Wessex (Grant 1984b; 1984c, 116), has led to the suggestion that in the south of the country sheep numbers increased 'throughout the first millennium' (Cunliffe 1991, 380). Maltby (1996, 21) refutes this suggestion, as he regards it to be based on insufficient evidence and not supported by data from other Wessex sites. Hambleton (1999) reinstates Grant and Cunliffe's assumption of a relative increase of sheep on the downland sites of southern England, but fails to identify any similar trend in other British regions.

A review that I carried out on sites located in the Midlands and East Anglia, however, suggests that the Wessex situation may not be unique. Figure 1 shows that the frequency of sheep bones is much greater at Late Iron Age sites than at those of Early and Middle Iron Age date. Details of the sites can be found in Table 1. Hambleton (1999) has already highlighted the fact that Iron Age sites in eastern Britain tend to have a large number of cattle bones. This certainly seems to apply to

Site	*County*	*Date*	*Type*	*Sheep NISP*	*%*	*Cattle NISP*	*%*	*Pig NISP*	*%*	*Reference*
Blackhorse Road	Hertfordshire	EIA	Enclosure	48		98		11		Legge *et al.* 1989
Harborough Rocks	Derbyshire	EIA	Open settlement	26		30		8		Bishop 1991
Ivinghoe Beacon	Buckinghamshire	EIA	Hillfort	658	32	1243	61	140	7	Westley 1970
Moles Farm	Hertfordshire	EIA	Pit cluster	11		54		0		Ashdown and Merlen 1970
Tallington	Lincolnshire	EIA	Enclosure	37		63		13		Harman 1993
Pennylands	Buckinghamshire	EIA/MIA	Open settlement	341	30	710	62	94	8	Holmes 1993
Scole-Dickleburgh	Norfolk	EIA/MIA	Unknown	231	34	351	56	58	9	Baker 1998
Ardale	Essex	MIA	Unknown	6		102		1		Luff 1988a
Aston Mill Farm	Hereford & Worcs	MIA	Enclosure	276	44	279	44	74	12	Lovett 1990
Blackhorse Road	Hertfordshire	MIA	Enclosure	130	26	330	67	31	6	Legge *et al.* 1989
Coldharbour Farm	Buckinghamshire	MIA	Open settlement	72		63		7		Sadler 1990
TOTAL				1836		3323		437		
Beckford	Hereford & Worcs	LIA	Enclosure	115		134		27		Gilmore 1972
Bierton	Buckinghamshire	LIA	Pit cluster	607	45	445	33	304	22	Jones 1988
Blackthorn	Northamptonshire	LIA	Enclosure	74		68		6		Orr 1974
Braughing Bath House	Hertfordshire	LIA	Village	91		84		89		Ashdown and Evans 1977
Burgh	Suffolk	LIA	Enclosure	692	48	585	40	178	12	Jones *et al.* 1987
Clay Lane	Northamptonshire	LIA	Enclosure	516	42	642	53	64	5	Jones *et al.* 1985
Cowbit Wash	Lincolnshire	LIA	Saltern	28		94		2		Albarella 2001
Dragonby	Lincolnshire	LIA	Open settlement	2922	58	1415	28	658	13	Harman 1996
Dragonby	Lincolnshire	LIA	Open settlement	3945	58	1944	29	879	13	Harman 1996
Elms Farm (Heybridge)	Essex	LIA	Open settlement	216	18	780	65	196	16	Johnstone and Albarella 2002
Edix Hill (Barrington)	Cambridgeshire	LIA	Open settlement	337	55	177	29	102	17	Davis 1995
Edmundsoles	Cambridgeshire	LIA	Pit cluster	78		24		41		Miller and Miller 1978
Hardingstone	Northamptonshire	LIA	Industrial	473	48	379	38	140	14	Gilmore 1969
Harlow Temple	Essex	LIA	Temple	1777	89	55	3	155	8	Legge and Dorrington 1985
Moulton Park	Northamptonshire	LIA	Enclosure	192	30	364	57	79	12	Orr 1974
Nazeingbury	Essex	LIA	Farm	40		142		15		Huggins 1978
Old Bowling Green	Hereford & Worcs	LIA	Industrial	147		94		10		Locker 1992
Puckeridge and Braughing	Hertfordshire	LIA	Open settlement	446	35	396	31	445	35	Croft 1979
Rainham Moor Hall Farm	Essex	LIA	Unknown	12		91		10		Locker 1985
Skeleton Green	Hertfordshire	LIA	Open settlement	449	18	786	32	1202	49	Ashdown and Evans 1981
Tort Hill West	Cambridgeshire	LIA	Open settlement	39		64		14		Albarella 1998
Wardy Hill	Cambridgeshire	LIA	Enclosure	708	56	371	29	183	15	Davis 2003
TOTAL				13904		9134		4799		

Table 1. (above and right) List of sites with frequencies of the main domestic mammals used to create Fig. 1. NISP = Number of identified specimens. Percentages have only been calculated for sites whose total NISP for the three species was greater than 500. Only these sites have been used to calculate NISP 2, while all sites contribute to NISP 1 (see Fig. 1). EIA = Early Iron Age; MIA = Middle Iron Age; LIA = Late Iron Age; ER = Early Roman. These are all hand-collected assemblages. Sites where the hand-collected and sieved samples had been combined have been excluded as they are not comparable with the others.

Site	*County*	*Date*	*Type*	*Sheep NISP*	*Cattle %*	*Pig NISP*	*Reference %*	*Site*	*County*	*Date*
Buckingham Street	Buckinghamshire	ER	Urban	9		15		2		Jones 1982
Caesaromagus	Essex	ER	Temple	1255	70	384	22	146	8	Luff 1992
Caesaromagus	Essex	ER	Local centre	130		152		36		Luff 1988b
Castle Hill (East Bridgeford)	Nottinghamshire	ER	Fort	126		65		6		Harman 1969
Causeway Lane	Leicestershire	ER	Urban	1475	36	1983	48	675	16	Gidney 1999
Colchester	Essex	ER	Urban	3206	23	7838	57	2761	20	Luff 1993
Dodder Hill	Hereford & Worcester	ER	Fort	74		141		10		Davis 1988
Dragonby	Lincolnshire	ER	Open settlement	413	51	284	35	111	14	Harman 1996
Dunstable	Bedfordshire	ER	Burials	102		86		1		Jones and Horne 1981
Elms Farm (Heybridge)	Essex	ER	Open settlement	462	26	1231	69	101	6	Johnstone and Albarella 2002
Grandford	Cambridgeshire	ER	Village	461	60	218	28	91	12	Stalllibrass 1982
Harlow Temple	Essex	ER	Temple	563	84	24	4	81	12	Legge and Dorrington 1985
Hockwold-cum-Wilton	Norfolk	ER	Villa + Vicus	112		115		10		Cram 1967
Kelvedon	Essex	ER	Unknown	68		96		33		Luff 1988c
Lincoln	Lincolnshire	ER	Urban	40		79		12		Scott 1988
Lincoln	Lincolnshire	ER	Urban	132	22	386	65	77	13	Dobney *et al.* 1996
Longthorpe	Cambridgeshire	ER	Fort	596	30	1123	56	276	14	Marples 1974
Longthorpe	Cambridgeshire	ER	Military	772	36	1221	58	120	6	King 1987
New Cemetery	Staffordshire	ER	Fort	66	14	306	65	101	21	Levitan 1996
Old Bowling Green	Hereford & Worcs	ER	Industrial	195		88		14		Locker 1992
Orton's Pasture	Staffordshire	ER	Enclosure	45		129		28		Hammon 1998
Park Street	Northamptonshire	ER	Urban	167		149		52		Payne 1980
Puckeridge–Braughing	Hertfordshire	ER	Town	701	55	366	29	215	17	Fifield 1988
Rainham Moor Hall Farm	Essex	ER	Unknown	10		67		0		Locker 1985
Sheepen	Essex	ER	Industrial	1188	20	3107	52	1714	29	Luff 1985
Sidbury	Hereford & Worcs	ER	Roadside settlement	451	47	431	45	71	7	Scott 1992
St Peters School	Essex	ER	Enclosure	18		166		0		Bedwin 1988
The Shires	Leicestershire	ER	Urban	525	32	749	46	360	22	Gidney 1991
Wavendon Gate	Buckinghamshire	ER	Unknown	171	21	611	75	35	4	Dobney and Jaques 1996
West Stow	Suffolk	ER	Industrial	279	44	257	41	97	15	Crabtree 1990
Whitwell	Leicestershire	ER	Farm	50		15		5		Harman 1981
TOTAL				13862		21882		7241		

the group of chosen sites from the earlier period – when cattle is even more frequent than it was to be in the Roman period – but not to the Later Iron Age sites.

Of course a number of difficulties have to be borne in mind in this comparison. Inter-site analysis is notoriously complex and full of potential pitfalls. Firstly, none of the sites considered has an Early or Middle Iron Age *and* a Late Iron Age phase. In other words, the two chronological groups include completely different sites and there is no opportunity to observe progression through time at the same site (as was possible at Danebury). This means that, beside chronological changes, factors like different geographical location and type of settlement may affect the frequency of species. In addition, different bone assemblages have probably been subject to different levels of taphonomic modification and quality of recovery during excavation, and derived from different types of contexts. Strictly speaking the two groups of sites are not directly comparable.

However, if we consider that no clear correlation has been found between settlement types (with the exception of banjo enclosures that tend to have more sheep), geological location, altitude, and species frequency (Hambleton 1999), we can be more confident that the difference between the two periods is genuine. Preservation and recovery factors will probably also have acted randomly in the two groups and whilst they certainly play a role in affecting the representation of species in individual sites they are unlikely to be the main factor behind this general trend. A less crude comparison should probably be carried out, but in the meantime the evidence points rather convincingly towards an increase in the importance of sheep in the Late Iron Age in central England.

To sum up the situation across the country, we should mention that on the downland of southern England there is a strong predominance of sheep throughout the Iron Age – probably reflecting the fact that this is a rather dry area and hence less suitable for cattle breeding. In this area sheep increase further in the later part of the period. In the upper Thames valley the frequency of cattle is much higher, and this predominance remains in place until the end of the period. The damper conditions of this region would not favour sheep husbandry (Grant 1984c, 104). In central England (the Midlands and East Anglia), there is also a predominance of cattle, but this situation is reversed in the Late Iron Age. In all other regions the evidence is too scanty to identify any clear chronological change (see Hambleton 1999, 59–60).

The trend, observed in some regions, of an increase in the importance of sheep, is not matched by any parallel change in strategies of sheep husbandry, at least as far as we can tell from the available evidence. There is a hint that the Late Iron Age witnessed an increase in mutton production at some southern sites (Maltby 1987, part 6; 1996, 23), but the general pattern indicates continuity rather than change (Hambleton 1999, 88). In most Iron Age sites – early and late – a large proportion of sheep was culled when relatively young, before they reached their optimum size in terms of meat production. This has led Grant (1984c, 107) and other authors to suggest that Iron Age sheep husbandry was more oriented towards wool than meat production. However, a comparison of three Iron Age sites, all displaying a quite typical mortality curve for the period, with a medieval site, where there is almost certainly an emphasis on wool production, shows striking differences between the Iron Age and medieval profiles (Fig. 2).

The killing of sheep at such an early age is likely to be connected with the difficulty of keeping and feeding large numbers of animals over the winter. Many yearlings would therefore be slaughtered in the late autumn before they start losing weight (Hambleton 1999, 70). A detailed analysis of the distribution of sheep tooth wear stages at the Mid/Late Iron Age site of Market Deeping (Lincolnshire) has highlighted the presence of a seasonal peak, probably corresponding to the period immediately preceding the coldest part of the year (Albarella 1997). Autumn killing has also been suggested for Edix Hill, Barrington (Davis 1995), and the Puckeridge sites of Station Road (Croft 1979) and Skeleton Green (Ashdown and Evans 1981).

Sheep were probably numerous, otherwise such a high rate of juvenile killings would have been difficult to sustain. However, management of the flocks may have been difficult, particularly over the winter. Meat, wool and milk were probably all used, with no specialisation in any particular production. Sheep must also have been important as sacrificial animals, as indicated by zooarchaeological work at the temple of Harlow (Legge and Dorrington 1985). The sacrifices sensibly occurred in autumn, to avoid any clash of economic and religious needs.

There seems to be a greater variation in cattle husbandry strategies between different sites. Some – like Danebury (Grant 1984a) and Cowbit Wash (Albarella 2001) – have large numbers of young calves, perhaps an indication of an emphasis upon milk production, although Hambleton (1999) suggests that this – at least in the case of Danebury – may represent the effect of a preservation bias. Others have large amounts of immature animals (Maltby 1996, 21), probably an indication of a particular interest in meat production. There are, however, also sites where most cattle are fully adult (Hambleton 1999, 78), which is probably a consequence of their use for traction. All in all there seems to be little evidence of specialisation, with the possible exception of a few individual sites. Most importantly, the evidence does not show any sign of a chronological trend, with the Late Iron Age similar in character to the earlier periods.

The only detectable element of animal husbandry that seems to differentiate the Late Iron Age from the previous period is the increase in sheep numbers (relative to cattle) that occurs in some regions. Can we relate this with the hypothesised agricultural intensification mentioned above? Both Cunliffe (1991, 380) and Hambleton (1999, 59) emphasise the importance of sheep manure for increasing soil fertility. Sheep were certainly folded onto the fields on a regular basis, and perhaps they were more suitable than cattle for this purpose, as they cause less damage and also – in many environmental conditions – they could have been easier to keep. Since crops can provide a higher yield of food per unit area than animal products, it is possible that a population expansion may have brought about the need to intensify agricultural activity, with the main purpose of animal keeping being their service to cultivation. In this respect an increase in sheep may be a by-product of farming intensification. There are, however, still obscure areas in this hypothesis, as cattle, though probably not as efficient as sheep in manuring the land, have the great advantage of providing traction power – a key factor in crop production. The clarification of this problem is frustrated by the dearth of sites that have Middle *and* Late Iron Age phases. As usual, more work is needed, both on the available data and in uncovering new evidence.

It has also been suggested that cattle, being more expensive to keep, may be indicators of wealth (Haselgrove 1999b, 268). It is therefore possible that their reduction in number in the Late Iron Age caused – or was a consequence – of some re-organisation of Iron Age society. If cattle were really a status symbol, then the fact they had become rarer (relatively to sheep) must have made them even more valuable. We should consequently consider the possibility of linking cattle frequency with the higher status of particular sites. Once again economy cannot be completely disconnected from social issues.

Pigs are consistently the third commonest species found on Iron Age sites, although a few exceptions occur, like Skeleton Green (Ashdown and Evans 1981). There is a slight trend towards increased pig frequency in the Late Iron Age (Fig. 1 – although not at Danebury where the opposite is the case), but it is hard to say to what extent this is significant. Perhaps more interesting is the consideration that relatively low numbers of pig bones are a characteristic of the British Iron Age, as sites in continental Europe tend to have much higher frequencies of this species (Grant 1984c, 112; Hambleton 1999; cf. Méniel 1987). Since pig is solely a meat-producing species, it is possible that this implies lesser consumption of meat on British sites, which may have relied to a greater extent on crop production.

Hunting (particularly of deer) may have been of social importance in the Iron Age (Grant 1981), but had little impact on the diet. Bones of wild animals are found quite regularly on British sites, but always in small numbers. Even in this respect the Late Iron Age does not seem to differ from the earlier periods.

The Iron Age faunal record provides little evidence of trade intensification in this period. However, one species, the domestic fowl (*Gallus gallus*) – although it had probably found its way to this country a little earlier – turns up with some regularity only from this period

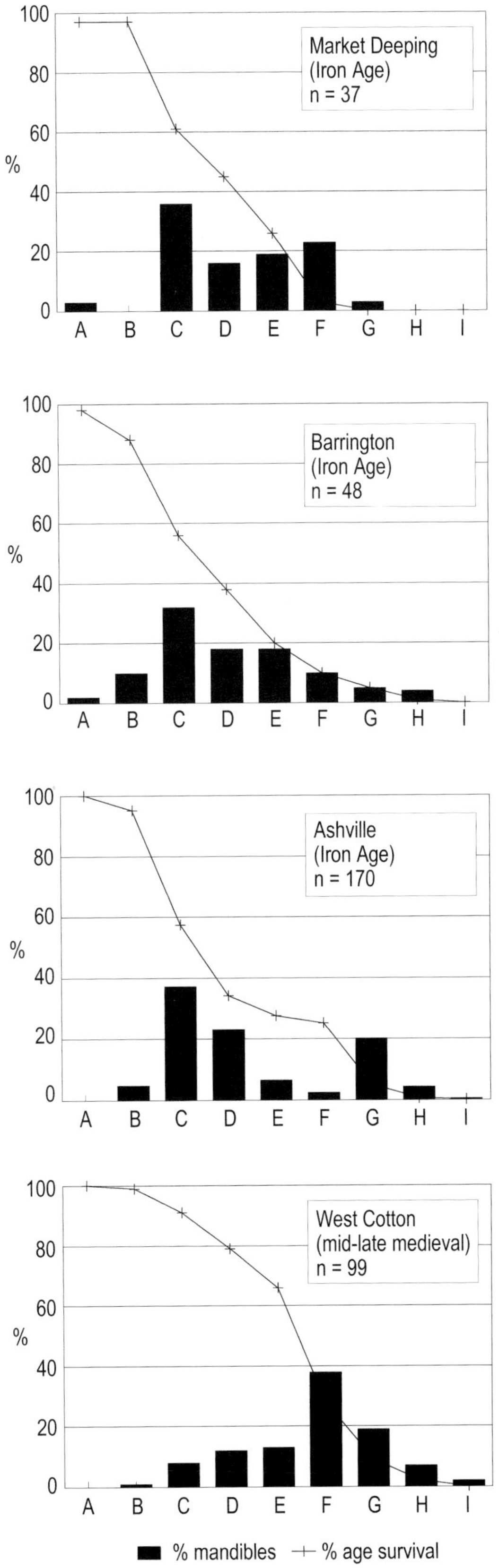

Fig. 2. Relative percentages of sheep mandibles by age-stage at the Iron Age sites of Market Deeping (Albarella 1997), Barrington (Davis 1995), and Ashville (Hamilton 1978). To emphasise the contrast, the kill-off pattern at the medieval site of West Cotton (Albarella and Davis 1994) is also shown.

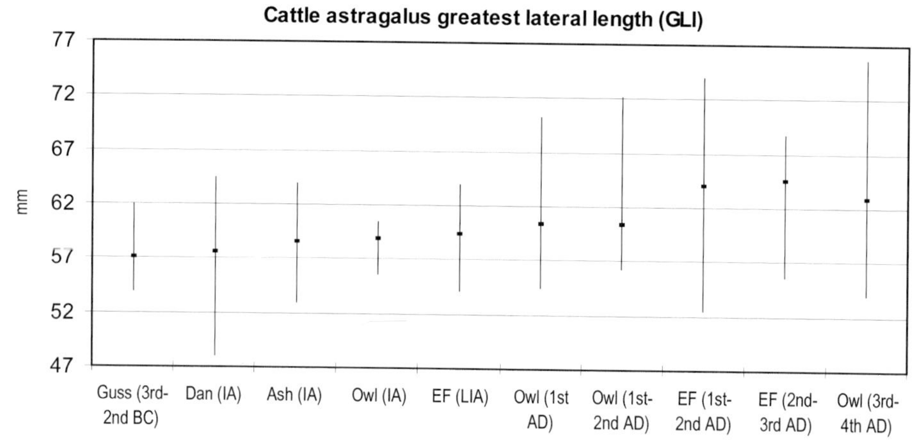

Fig. 3. Cattle size (range and mean) at various Iron Age and Roman sites in Britain. Guss = Gussage All Saints (Harcourt 1979); Dan = Danebury (Grant 1991); Ash = Ashville (Wilson et al. 1978); Owl = Owslebury (Maltby 1987); EF = Elms Farm (Johnstone and Albarella 2002).

onwards. In central England domestic fowl are found in Early Iron Age levels at Blackhorse Road, Hertfordshire (Legge *et al.* 1989), and in the Early/Mid Iron Age phase at Scole-Dickleburgh, Norfolk (Baker 1998), but at many more Late Iron Age sites. At Danebury, which has the full Iron Age sequence, it is not found before the latest part of the period (Grant 1984c, 114). The record therefore confirms Caesar's claim (see above) that British people kept domestic fowl, but there are more doubts about his assertion that these birds were not eaten. Large numbers of chicken bones were found in the Late Iron Age levels at Skeleton Green, Puckeridge (Ashdown 1981), and butchery marks were noted on domestic fowl bones from Station Road (Ashdown 1979). Admittedly both assemblages probably slightly post-date Caesar's visit to Britain, yet it is likely that the practice of eating fowl meat had a longer history.

One very important aspect of zooarchaeological analysis that has been neglected for the Iron Age is the examination of the size and shape of the animals, which can be so informative about cultural contact, introductions, and farming intensification. At Danebury a full biometrical study was not undertaken, but preliminary information indicates no change in cattle size over time and only a slight decrease in sheep size (Grant 1991); no comments are provided about pig size over time. Maltby (1996, 22) also believes that cattle were subject to no improvement throughout the Iron Age. The information from most sites (see Fig. 3) is, however, frustratingly approximate in terms of chronology, hampering any opportunity to clarify the question of whether there were any attempts to improve livestock, perhaps triggered by the economic and social changes that were taking place in the Later Iron Age. A frequent comment in reports on Late Iron Age sites is that the livestock was of a small size (e.g. at Burgh, Dragonby, Skeleton Green), but this is an area where more work is badly needed.

The Late Iron Age and beyond

The end of the Late Iron Age can quite conveniently be associated with the Roman invasion of AD 43. Obviously an Iron Age style of life did not abruptly end that year, which is why we tend to talk of a late pre-Roman Iron Age, but the Roman conquest undoubtedly brought about significant modifications in the organisation of society and in the use of the countryside. It is, however, debatable to what extent such changes were sudden and revolutionary, or merely represented an acceleration of forces that were already under way. It is therefore necessary to investigate how the animal evidence can contribute to the clarification of this question.

Unlike the Middle to Late Iron Age transition, the beginning of the Roman period saw a change in the frequency of the main domestic species that was widespread and is relatively well documented. The increased importance of cattle, mainly at the expense of sheep, is attested at most sites where both Late Iron Age and early Roman phases are represented. This is the case at Owslebury (Maltby 1987), Dragonby (Harman 1996), and Elms Farm, Heybridge (Johnstone and Albarella 2002), where large bone assemblages were analysed. A review of species frequency at a number of sites in East Anglia and the English Midlands is also consistent with this trend (Fig. 1). The earlier warning concerning the difficulties of inter-site comparison applies to this analysis as well, although the larger number of early Roman assemblages makes the results more reliable.

Such a clear change in the proportion of the species of greatest economic importance indicates a substantial re-organisation of at least some elements of the farming system. The increased emphasis in cattle husbandry may be related to a number of phenomena:

- the need to feed the Roman army with meat rapidly

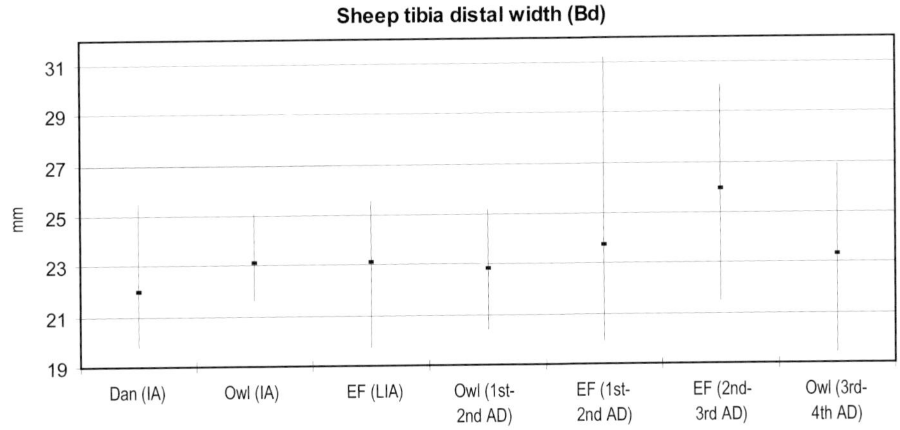

Fig 4. Sheep size (range and mean) at various Iron Age and Roman sites in Britain. Dan = Danebury (Grant 1991); Owl = Owslebury (Maltby 1987); EF = Elms Farm (Johnstone and Albarella 2002).

produced by improved cattle breeds imported from the Continent;

- the cultural preference for beef, which could have been imported by central European legionaries associated with the Roman army (see King 1978);
- a need to increase agricultural production through intensive ploughing of heavy soils aided by the use of large and powerful oxen.

The fact that at most early Roman sites cattle seem to have been slaughtered when adult would support the last suggestion. It is, however, worth mentioning that, while there is no substantial change in the age at slaughter of cattle between the Late Iron Age and the early Roman period at Heybridge, a larger proportion of adult animals is found in later periods (mid second century AD onwards). It is therefore possible that the need to produce meat (perhaps for the army) prompted the change, but this was eventually replaced by a shift to more crop production and the use of cattle for ploughing.

There is no indication that pigs – the most common animal at Roman sites in Italy – increased in importance after the arrival of the Romans. If farming practices were being modified, this was not a phenomenon prompted by Mediterranean cultural preferences.

It has been suggested that the dearth of Late Iron Age data prevents us from understanding whether large breeds of animals were introduced to Britain in that period, or as a consequence of the Roman arrival (Millett 1990, 11). Despite the unsatisfactory level of biometrical analysis for the whole of the Iron Age, this is fortunately no longer the case. There is clear evidence of increase in cattle size in the 'Belgic/early Roman' period at the site of Bancroft, Buckinghamshire (Holmes and Rielly 1994, table 55). At Owslebury too, larger cattle (and possibly horses, but the sample is small) are found from the beginning of the Roman period, although further increase occurred later (Maltby 1987, part 5). The most convincing evidence of all comes from the site of Elms Farm, Heybridge, where in the early Roman period cattle are not only more numerous but also considerably larger than their Late Iron Age counterparts (Johnstone and Albarella 2002).

Cattle seems to be the only species to have been improved so rapidly. At Elms Farm there is evidence that most other domestic species, including sheep, pig, horse, and domestic fowl also became larger, but not for at least another century after the arrival of the Romans. This evidence suggests that the Essex coast, rather than that of Wessex, probably acted as the main interface between Britain and the rest of the Roman empire (cf. Cunliffe 1991, 545). Since Belgic tribes had settled in central southern England, it is unlikely that they represented the main agent of innovation in agriculture and husbandry. The waves of change were more probably arriving from the South-East.

A wider comparison of the metric data is frustrated by the fact that most animal bone reports do not include individual measurements. Not even the six volume report on Owslebury (Maltby 1987) includes the metric data. Consequently any comparison between sites has to rely on ranges and means. Yet, even this crude analysis manages to highlight the increase in cattle size occurring after the end of the Iron Age (Fig. 3). Unfortunately, measurements from different Iron Age phases at Danebury and Ashville were combined, so that it is not possible to demonstrate a lack of size change between the earlier and later part of the period, which is likely to have been the case.

Fewer data for sheep are available (Fig. 4), but what little evidence there is indicates a lack of size increase in the early Roman period at both Owslebury and Elms Farm. As mentioned above, sheep improvement eventually occurred at Elms Farm, but not at Owslebury, where the local farmers seem to have been content to carry on breeding the same small type of animals, which had been present since the Iron Age.

The increase in size that occurs after the end of the Iron Age – immediately for cattle, later on for other species – is accompanied by a general increase in variation (e.g. Johnstone and Albarella 2002, Figs. 38–40). Small livestock of the Iron Age type are still present, but alongside larger animals, which contribute to increased mean values. Due to their rather sudden size increase it is likely that some cattle were imported from the Continent, although some local improvement may have also occurred.

The importance of livestock improvement, as part of a more general phenomenon of acculturation, should not be underestimated. The ancient Latin sources make it abundantly clear that this was a significant element of cultural differentiation for both the Romans and the indigenous populations of north-western Europe. Caesar (*Gallic War* IV, 2), for instance, compares the Gauls, who were prepared to spend large sums of money to procure improved animals, with the Germans, who preferred to keep local livestock, despite this being small and ungraceful. There is an implicit verdict here of cultural backwardness on the German populations. Tacitus claims that for the Germans it is only important to have large numbers of livestock, and they do not care about the fact that their cattle are short, ugly, and hornless (*Germania* 5). Unfortunately, we do not have comparable accounts for Britain, but it is likely that the Romans regarded its inhabitants in a similar fashion. In Roman eyes, the keeping of unimproved livestock was a sign of primitiveness, but for the local population they could have represented a way to maintain their cultural identity, as suggested by the difference in attitude between Gauls and Germans described by Caesar.

If we accept this point, it is not surprising that no evidence of livestock improvement exists throughout the Iron Age. Even in a period of frequent cultural contact with the Continent – as the Late Iron Age must have been – local populations may have been reluctant to give up their traditional systems of husbandry. Only a massive event like the Roman invasion seems to have brought about a significant change. Large animals are not necessarily better than small ones. Improved livestock can produce a greater meat output, perhaps better quality wool and greater traction power, and is therefore more suitable for intensive agriculture and an economy strongly oriented towards the market. However, the small, ungracious native animals could have been more resilient in local environmental conditions, and were probably maintained at less expense and with a lower labour input.

Among other elements that help to differentiate between the use of animals in the Late Iron Age and the early Roman period, it is worth mentioning some butchery patterns that seem to have been introduced by the Romans soon after their arrival. Two types in particular seem to have been typically Roman. One is represented by perforations in cattle scapulae, probably caused by hook damage, and generally associated with the brining or smoking of meat joints (Schmid 1972; Dobney 2001). The other is a pattern of intensive butchery on cattle post-cranial bones, which are normally reduced to small, clearly chopped, pieces. This type of assemblage (normally not much else is found in these groups of bones) has become known as a 'soup-kitchen' deposit, as it was originally interpreted as the result of the preparation of soup or broth (Van Mensch 1974). However, we cannot exclude the possibility that it represents waste from intensive fat extraction, or the making of glue. Both types of butchery have been identified at Elms Farm in the early Roman levels, but not earlier. One Late Iron Age site in Britain – Bierton, in Buckinghamshire (Jones 1988) – has produced evidence of hooked scapulae but the relevant assemblage is dated to the first century BC/AD and may therefore include post-conquest material. Both hooked scapulae and 'soup-kitchen' deposits are known from continental Europe but they are not found on Italian sites.

While different regions must have been affected in different ways, the animal bone evidence supports Cunliffe's view (1991, 200) of a rapid process of Romanisation, although further changes did occur at a later stage. What is difficult to establish is whether these changes in farming practices were the result of dietary and economic causes, or were cultural preferences imposed upon a reluctant population. Probably both elements, difficult to disentangle in the archaeological record, played a role.

Conclusions

The above discussion can lead to a number of different interpretations of Late Iron Age animal husbandry, according to which line of evidence is considered to be of the greatest importance.

- One possibility is to see the Late Iron Age as a period of *transition*, which prepares and anticipates the greater changes that occurred after the Roman conquest. The evidence for this viewpoint is, however, rather slim and can probably be confined to the appearance of the domestic fowl in the faunal record and the occasional case of a small pet dog or Roman style of butchery found on Late Iron Age sites.
- Conversely, we could interpret the Late Iron Age on the basis of its *distinctiveness,* as perhaps suggested by the increased emphasis in sheep husbandry noted in some regions. This is at odds with what subsequently occurred in the Roman period, and also distinguishes the Late Iron Age from the previous period.

- Finally, we may emphasise the degree of *continuity* between the Late Iron Age and earlier times. This hypothesis is supported by the fact that differences in animal husbandry seem to have been much greater between the Roman period and the Late Iron Age, than between this and the Earlier Iron Age.

In reality, the two centuries preceding the Roman conquest are characterised by all the elements described above, with a different emphasis at particular times and places. Yet, the overriding impression is one of *continuity*. However important the episodes of agricultural intensification that took place in the Late Iron Age, they are overshadowed by the massive changes that occur throughout the Roman period.

The strong emphasis placed on innovations brought about by the arrival of the Romans does raise the concern that such an interpretation may simply be the consequence of adopting a core–periphery view of the Roman area of influence, which will inevitably portray the periphery as backwards and rather static in its social and economic developments. In reaction, some authors have emphasised the fact that some changes in farming practices may have taken place in Britain *before* the Roman conquest (e.g. Millett 1990). We have, however, seen that – as far as the faunal record is concerned – there is little evidence that this was really the case.

Perhaps attempts to play down the effects of Romanisation, and indeed of getting rid of the term altogether, suffer from the problem of regarding the move towards intensification and market economy as necessary and inevitable, and indeed a sign of civilisation. The difference with more traditional views of the Roman conquest, influenced by the words of sources such as Caesar and Tacitus, is simply that this change is suggested to have occurred at an earlier date.

An alternative way to look at this question is to interpret the reluctance of British Iron Age populations to adopt elements of the Roman economy, and in particular strategies of animal husbandry, as a sign of vitality rather than backwardness. Haselgrove (1999b, 255), for instance, has pointed out that 'failure of material to enter the record on Iron Age settlements might reflect cultural choices on the part of the inhabitants rather than material impoverishment'. That there was a widespread resistance to adopt a Roman style of life can also be detected in the words of the ancient writers. It has already been mentioned that German populations were content with livestock of small stature despite the availability of larger animals through trade. At the same time some of them – according to Caesar – refused to drink wine as this would weaken the men (*Gallic War* IV, 2). Apart from avoiding the less pleasant physical effects of some of these imports, it is likely that the Germans were also trying to preserve their cultural identity, threatened by the expansion of Rome.

A similar situation may have occurred in Britain, where trade contact was certainly already intense in the first century BC (Cunliffe 1991; Hill 1995b). That this does not seem to have been followed by widespread changes in the economic system may be due to attempts of cultural self-preservation. The Iron Age animal economy seems to have continued for many centuries without an apparent need for substantial modification. The system was probably relatively sustainable and did not need the support of imported goods.

Eventually the British population gave in, and, as Tacitus notoriously reports, 'were led to things which dispose to vice, the lounge, the bath, the elegant banquet. All this in their ignorance they called civilisation, when it was but a part of their servitude' (*Agricola* 21). The evidence of the animal bones, however, suggests that the process was long and that, in order to be accomplished, it had to await the physical occupation of the island by the Romans. The final period of the Iron Age therefore saw not only the end of prehistory, but also of political freedom and cultural independence for the British populations. As herds of large imported cattle replaced flocks of small native sheep it was clear that the Sheep Age too had come to an end.

Acknowledgements

I would like to thank Colin Haselgrove and Tom Moore for inviting me to contribute to this volume, and Marina Ciaraldi, Simon Davis, and an anonymous referee for comments on an earlier draft.

Bibliography

Albarella, U. 1997. *The Iron Age Animal Bone Excavated in 1991 from Outgang Road, Market Deeping (MAD 91), Lincolnshire.* London: English Heritage Ancient Monuments Laboratory Report 5/97.

Albarella, U. 1998. The animal bones, in P. Ellis, G. Hughes, P. Leach, C. Mould and J. Sterenberg, *Excavations alongside Roman Ermine Street, Cambridgeshire 1996*, 99–104. Oxford: British Archaeological Reports British Series 276.

Albarella, U. 2000. The Pig Age: people and animals at the Neolithic–Bronze Age boundary in Britain. Paper presented at the conference *Food, Identity and Culture in the Neolithic and early Bronze Age*, Sheffield.

Albarella, U. 2001. Animal bone and mammal and bird remains, in T. Lane and E.L. Morris (eds), *A Millennium of Saltmaking: Prehistoric and Romano-British Salt Production in the Fenland*, 75–77; 151; 237; 383–385; 445–449. Heckington: Lincolnshire Archaeology and Heritage Reports 4.

Albarella, U. and Davis, S. 1994. *The Saxon and Medieval Animal Bones Excavated 1985–1989 from West Cotton, Northamptonshire.* London: English Heritage Ancient Monuments Laboratory Report 17/94.

Albarella, U. and Serjeantson, D. 2002. A passion for pork: meat consumption at the British late Neolithic site of Durrington Walls, in P. Miracle and N. Milner (eds), *Consuming Passions and Patterns of*

Consumption, 33–49. Cambridge: Monographs of the McDonald Institute.

Ashdown, R. 1979. The avian bones from Station Road, Puckering, in Partridge 1979, 92–96.

Ashdown, R. 1981. Avian bones, in Partridge 1981, 235–242.

Ashdown, R. and Evans, D.C. 1977. Animal remains, in C. Partridge, Excavations and fieldwork at Braughing, 1968–73, *Hertfordshire Archaeology* 5, 58–62 (22–108).

Ashdown, R. and Evans, C. 1981. Mammalian bones, in Partridge 1981, 205–235.

Ashdown, R. and Merlen, R. 1970. The bones, in R.J. Kiln, An early Iron Age site at Moles Farm, Thundridge, *Hertfordshire Archaeology* 2, 20–22 (10–22).

Baker, P. 1998. *The Vertebrate Remains from Scole-Dickleburgh, Excavated in 1993 (Norfolk and Suffolk), A140 and A143 Road Improvement Project.* London: English Heritage Ancient Monuments Laboratory Report 29/98.

Bedwin, O. 1988. The animal bone, in C. Clarke, Roman Coggeshall: excavations 1984–85, *Essex Archaeology and History* 19, 66 (47–90).

Bevan, B. 1999a. Northern Exposure: Interpretative Devolution and the Iron Ages in Britain, in Bevan 1999b, 1–19.

Bevan, B. (ed.) 1999b. *Northern Exposure: Interpretative Devolution and the Iron Ages in Britain.* Leicester: Leicester Archaeology Monograph 4.

Bishop, M. 1991. The bones, in G.A. Makepeace, An early Iron Age settlement at Harborough Rocks, Brassington, *Derbyshire Archaeological Journal* 110, 28 (24–29).

Champion, T.C. and Collis, J.R. (eds) 1996. *The Iron Age in Britain and Ireland: Recent Trends.* Sheffield: J.R. Collis Publications

Crabtree, P. 1990. Faunal remains from Iron Age and Romano-British features, in S. West, *West Stow, Suffolk: the prehistoric and Romano-British occupations*, 101–105. Bury St Edmunds: East Anglian Archaeology Report 48.

Cram, C. 1967. Report on the animal bones from Hockwell, in P. Salway, Excavations at Hockwold-cum-Wilton, Norfolk, *Proceedings of the Cambridge Antiquarian Society* 60, 75–80 (39–80).

Croft, P. 1979. The mammalian bones from Feature 1, in Partridge 1979, 73–92.

Cunliffe, B. 1991. *Iron Age Communities in Britain* (3rd edn). London: Routledge.

Davis, S. 1988. *Animal Bones from Dodder Hill, a Roman Fort near Droitwich (Hereford and Worcester), Excavated in 1977.* London: English Heritage Ancient Monuments Laboratory Report 140/88.

Davis, S. 1995. *Animal Bones from the Iron Age Site at Edix Hill, Barrington, Cambridgeshire, 1989–1991 Excavations.* London: English Heritage Ancient Monuments Laboratory Report 54/95.

Davis, S. 2003. Animal bone, in C. Evans, *Power and Island Communities: Excavations at the Wardy Hill Ringwork, Coveney, Ely*, 122–131. Cambridge: East Anglian Archaeology Report 103.

Dobney, K. 2001. A place at the table: the role of vertebrate zooarchaeology within a Roman research agenda for Britain, in S.T. James and M. Millett (eds), *Britons and Romans: Advancing an Archaeological Agenda*, 36–45. York: Council for British Archaeology Research Report 125.

Dobney, K. and Jaques, D. 1996. The mammal bones, in R. Williams, P. Hart and A. Williams, *Wavendon Gate: A Late Iron Age and Roman Settlement in Milton Keynes*, 203–230. Milton Keynes: Buckinghamshire Archaeological Society Monograph 10.

Dobney, K., Jaques, D. and Irving, B. 1996. *Of Butchers and Breeds. Report on Vertebrate Remains from Various Sites in the City of Lincoln.* Lincoln: Lincoln Archaeological Studies 5.

Fifield, P. 1988. The faunal remains, in T. Potter and S. Trow, *Puckeridge–Braughing, Hertfordshire: The Ermine Street Excavations 1971–72. The Late Iron Age and Roman Settlement* (*Hertfordshire Archaeology* 10), 148–153.

Gidney, L. 1991. *Leicester, The Shires 1988 Excavations. The Animal Bones from the Roman Deposits at Little Lane.* London: English Heritage Ancient Monuments Laboratory Report 56/91.

Gidney, L. 1999. The animal bones, in A. Connor and R. Buckley, *Roman and Medieval Occupation at Causeway Lane, Leicester*, 310–329. Leicester: Leicester Archaeology Monograph 5.

Gilmore, F. 1969. The animal and human skeletal remains, in P.J. Woods, *Excavations at Hardingstone, Northampton, 1967–8*, 43–55. Northampton: Northamptonshire County Council.

Gilmore, F. 1972. Animal remains, in A. Oswald, Excavations at Beckford, *Transactions of the Worcestershire Archaeological Society* (Ser. 3) 3, 18–27 (7–54).

Grant, A. 1981. The significance of deer remains at occupation sites of the Iron Age to the Anglo-Saxon period, in M. Jones and G. Dimbleby (eds), *The Environment of Man: the Iron Age to the Anglo-Saxon Period*, 205–212. Oxford: British Archaeological Reports British Series 87.

Grant, A. 1984a. Survival or sacrifice? A critical appraisal of animal burials in Britain in the Iron Age, in C. Grigson and J. Clutton-Brock (eds), *Animals and Archaeology 4: Husbandry in Europe*, 221–227. Oxford: British Archaeological Reports International Series 227.

Grant, A. 1984b. Animal husbandry, in B. Cunliffe, *Danebury: an Iron Age Hillfort in Hampshire, Vol. 2. The Excavations, 1969–1978: the Finds*, 496–548. London: Council for British Archaeology Research Report 42.

Grant, A. 1984c. Animal husbandry in Wessex and the Thames valley, in B. Cunliffe and D. Miles (eds), *Aspects of the Iron Age in Central Southern Britain*, 102–119. Oxford: Oxford University Committee for Archaeology Monograph 2.

Grant, A. 1991. Animal husbandry, in B. Cunliffe and C. Poole, *Danebury: an Iron Age Hillfort in Hampshire, Vol. 5. The Excavations, 1979–1988: the Finds*, 447–487. London: Council for British Archaeology Research Report 73.

Hambleton, E. 1999. *Animal Husbandry Regimes in Iron Age Britain. A Comparative Study of Faunal Assemblages from British Iron Age sites.* Oxford: British Archaeological Reports British Series 282.

Hamilton, J. 1978. A comparison of the age structure at mortality of some Iron Age and Romano-British sheep and cattle, in Parrington 1978, 126–133.

Hammon, A. 1998. *Orton's Pasture, Rocester, Staffordshire. Report on the Animal Bones.* Unpublished report, Birmingham University Field Archaeological Unit.

Harcourt, R. 1979. The animal bones, in G.J. Wainwright, *Gussage All Saints. An Iron Age Settlement in Dorset*, 150–60. London: Department of the Environment Archaeological Report 10.

Harman, M. 1969. The animal bones, in M. Todd, *The Roman Settlement at Margidunum: The Excavations of 1966–8* (*Transactions of the Thoroton Society* 73), 96–103.

Harman, M. 1981. The mammalian bones, in M. Todd, *The Iron Age and Roman Settlement at Whitwell, Leicestershire*, 40–42. Leicester: Leicestershire Museums, Art Galleries and Records Service Archaeological Report 1.

Harman, M. 1993. The mammalian bones, in C.A.I. French, D.A. Gurney, F.M.M. Pryor and W.G.A. Simpson, A double pit-alignment and other features at field OS29, Tallington, Lincs, in W.G. Simpson, D.A. Gurney, J. Neve, and F.M.M. Pryor, *The Fenland Project, No. 7, Excavations in Peterborough and the Lower Welland Valley 1960–1969*, 64–65 and fiche C4–5 (29–68). Peterborough: East Anglian Archaeology Report 61.

Harman, M. 1996. Mammalian bones, in J. May, *Dragonby. Report on Excavations at an Iron Age and Romano-British Settlement in North Lincolnshire*, 141–161. Oxford: Oxbow Monograph 61.

Haselgrove, C. 1999a. The Iron Age, in J. Hunter and I.B.M. Ralston (eds), *The Archaeology of Britain: An Introduction from the Palaeolithic to the Industrial Revolution*, 113–134. London: Routledge.

Haselgrove, C. 1999b. Iron Age Societies in Central Britain: retrospect and prospect, in Bevan 1999b, 253–278.

Hill, J.D. 1995a. *Ritual and Rubbish in the Iron Age of Wessex*. Oxford: British Archaeological Reports British Series 242.

Hill, J.D. 1995b. The Pre-Roman Iron Age in Britain and Ireland (ca. 800 B.C. to A.D. 100): an overview, *Journal of World Prehistory* 9, 47–98.

Hill, J.D. 2002. Just about the potter's wheel? Using, making and depositing Middle and Late Iron Age pots in East Anglia, in A. Woodward and J.D. Hill (eds), *Prehistoric Britain: the Ceramic Basis*, 143–160. Oxford: Prehistoric Ceramics Research Group Occasional Publication 3.

Holmes, J.M. 1993. Animal bones, in R.J. Williams, *Pennyland and Hartigans: Two Iron Age Sites in Milton Keynes*, 133–54. Aylesbury: Buckinghamshire Archaeological Society Monograph 4.

Holmes, J. and Rielly, K. 1994. Animal bone from the 'Mausoleum' site, in R.J. Williams and R.J. Zeepvat, *Bancroft. A Late Bronze Age/Iron Age Settlement, Roman Villa and Temple Mausoleum. Vol. 2: Finds and Environmental Evidence*, 515–549. Aylesbury: Buckinghamshire Archaeological Society Monograph 7.

Huggins, P.J. 1978. Appendix 9. Animal bones, mollusca and egg, in P.J. Huggins, Excavation of Belgic and Romano-British Farm with Middle Saxon Cemetery and Churches at Nazeingbury, Essex, 1975–6, *Essex Archaeology and History* 10, 108–114 (29–118).

Johnstone, C. and Albarella, U. 2002. *The Late Iron Age and Romano-British Mammal and Bird Bone Assemblage from Elms Farm, Heybridge, Essex*. Portsmouth: Centre for Archaeology Report 45/2002.

Jones, E. and Horne, B. 1981. Analysis of skeletal material, in C. Matthews, A Romano-British inhumation cemetery at Dunstable. Appendix: a Roman cesspit with skeletons, *Bedfordshire Archaeological Journal* 15, 69–72 (63–72).

Jones, G. 1982. The animal bones, in D. Allen, Salvage excavations at 13–19 Buckingham Street and the Bull's Head redevelopment site, Aylesbury, in 1979 and 1980, 94–5, *Records of Buckinghamshire* 24, 81–100.

Jones, G. 1988. The Iron Age animal bones, in D. Allen, Excavations at Bierton, a late Iron Age 'Belgic' settlement, Roman Villa and 12th–18th century manorial complex, *Records of Buckinghamshire* 28, 32–39 (1–120).

Jones, M. 1995. Aspects of animal husbandry, in B. Cunliffe, *Danebury: An Iron Age Hillfort in Hampshire, Vol. 6. A Hillfort Community in Perspective*, 50–53. London: Council for British Archaeology Research Report 102.

Jones, R., Levitan, B., Stevens, P. and Malim, T. 1985. *Clay Lane, Northamptonshire. The Vertebrate Remains*. London: English Heritage Ancient Monuments Laboratory Report 4811.

Jones, R., Sly, J. and Beech, M. 1987. *Burgh, Suffolk: the Vertebrate Remains 1987*. London: English Heritage Ancient Monuments Laboratory Report 14/87.

King, A. 1978. A comparative survey of bone assemblages from Roman sites in Britain, *Bulletin of the Institute of Archaeology London* 15, 207–232.

King, J. 1987. The animal bones, in G. Dannell and J. Wild, *Longthorpe II. The Military Works-Depot: an Episode in Landscape History*, 184–194. London: Britannia Monograph 8.

Legge, A.J. and Dorrington, E.J. 1985. The animal bones, in N.E. France and B.M. Gobel, *The Romano-British Temple at Harlow, Essex*, 122–133. Harlow: West Essex Archaeological Group.

Legge, A.J., Williams, J. and Williams, P. 1989. Animal remains from Blackhorse Road, Letchworth, in J. Moss-Eccardt, Archaeological investigations in the Letchworth area, 1958–1974, *Proceedings of the Cambridge Antiquarian Society* 77, 90–95 (35–103).

Levitan, B. 1996. Vertebrate remains, in S. Esmonde Cleary and I. Ferris, *Excavations at the New Cemetery, Rocester, Staffordshire, 1985–1987* (Transactions of the Staffordshire Archaeological and Historical Society 35 for 1993–94), 186–205.

Locker, A. 1985. *Rainham Moor Hall Farm – animal bones*. London: English Heritage Ancient Monuments Laboratory Report 4577.

Locker, A. 1992. Animal bone, in S. Woodiwiss (ed.), *Iron Age and Roman Salt Production and the Medieval Town of Droitwich*, 84–92. London: Council for British Archaeology Research Report 81.

Lovett, J. 1990. Animal bone, in J. Dinn and J. Evans, Aston Mill Farm, Kemerton: Excavation of a ring-ditch, Middle Iron Age enclosures and a Grubenhaus, *Transactions of the Worcestershire Archaeological Society* (Ser. 3) 12, 48–53 (5–66).

Luff, R. 1985. The fauna, in R. Niblett, *Sheepen: an Early Roman Industrial Site at Camulodunum*, 143–150; Fiche 4:A2–E7. London: Council for British Archaeology Research Report 57.

Luff, R. 1988a. The animal bones, in T.J. Wilkinson, *Archaeology and Environment in South Essex: Rescue Archaeology along the Grays By-pass, 1979/80*, 99. Chelmsford: East Anglian Archaeology 42.

Luff, R. 1988b. The faunal remains, in P.J. Drury 1988, *The Mansio and other Sites in the South-Eastern Sector of Caesaromagus*, 118–122; Fiche 2D–E. London: Council for British Archaeology Research Report 66.

Luff, R. 1988c. The animal bone, in K. Rodwell, *The Prehistoric and Roman Settlement at Kelvedon, Essex*, 89–91. London: Council for British Archaeology Research Report 63.

Luff, R. 1992. The faunal remains, in N.P. Wickenden, *The Temple and Other Sites in the North-Eastern Sector of Caesaromagus*, 116–24. London: Council for British Archaeology Research Report 75.

Luff, R. 1993. *Animal Bones from Excavations in Colchester, 1971–85*. Colchester: Colchester Archaeological Report 12.

Maltby, M. 1987. *The Animal Bones from the Excavations at Owslebury, Hants. An Iron Age and Early Romano-British Settlement*. London: English Heritage Ancient Monuments Laboratory Report 6/87.

Maltby, M. 1996. The exploitation of animals in the Iron Age: the archaeozoological evidence, in Champion and Collis 1996, 17–27.

Marples, B. 1974. Animal bones from the Roman fort at Longthorpe, near Peterborough, in S.S. Frere and J.K. St Joseph, The Roman fortress at Longthorpe, *Britannia* 5, 122–128 (1–129).

Méniel, P. 1987. *Chasse et élevage chez les Gaulois*. Paris: Editions Errance.

Miller, T.E. and Miller, M. 1978. The M11 western by-pass: three sites near Cambridge. 3. Edmundsoles, Haslingfield, *Proceedings of the Cambridge Antiquarian Society* 71, 41–73.

Millett, M. 1990. *The Romanization of Britain*. Cambridge: Cambridge University Press.

Orr, C. 1974. The animal bones, in J.H. Williams, *Two Iron Age Sites in Northampton*, 62. Northampton: Northampton Development Corporation Archaeological Monograph 1.

Parker Pearson, M. 1996. Food, fertility and front doors in the first millennium BC, in Champion and Collis 1996, 117–132.

Parrington M. 1978. *The Excavation of an Iron Age Settlement, Bronze Age Ring-Ditches and Roman Features at Ashville Trading Estate, Abingdon (Oxfordshire) 1974–76*. London: Council for British Archaeology Research Report 28.

Partridge, C. 1979. Excavations at Puckeridge and Braughing 1975–9, *Hertfordshire Archaeology* 7, 28–132.

Partridge, C. 1981. *Skeleton Green. A Late Iron Age and Romano-British Site*. London: Britannia Monograph 2.

Payne, S. 1980. The animal bones, in G. Lambrick, Excavations in Park Street, Towcester, *Northamptonshire Archaeology* 15, 105–112 (35–118).

Sadler, P. 1990. The animal bone from the Iron Age ditch, in I.J. Stewart, Coldharbour Farm, Aylesbury, an archaeological excavation 1990, *Records of Buckinghamshire* 30, 100–103 (91–105).

Schmid, E. 1972. *Atlas of Animal Bones*. London: Elsevier.

Scott, S. 1988. The animal bones, in M. Darling and M. Jones, The early settlement of Lincoln, *Britannia* 19, 43–45 (1–57).

Scott, S. 1992. The animal bone, in J. Darlington and J. Evans, Roman Sidbury, Worcester: Excavations 1959–1989, *Transactions of the Worcestershire Archaeological Society* 13, 88–92 (5–104).

Stallibrass, S. 1982. Faunal remains, in T. Potter and C. Potter, *A Romano-British Village at Grandford, March, Cambridgeshire*, 98–122. London: British Museum Occasional Paper 35.

Van der Veen, M. 1992. *Crop Husbandry Regimes. An Archaeobotanical Study of Farming in Northern England 1000 BC – AD 500*. Sheffield: Sheffield Archaeological Monograph 3.

Van Mensch, P.J.A. 1974. A Roman soup-kitchen at Zwammerdam? *Berichten van de Rijksdienst voor Oudheidkundig Bodemonderzoek* 24, 159–165.

Westley, B. 1970. App II. Bones from Ivinghoe Beacon, in M.A. Cotton and S.S. Frere, Ivinghoe Beacon excavations 1963–5, *Records of Buckinghamshire* 18, 252–260 (187–260).

Wilson, R. 1992. Considerations for the identifications of ritual deposits of animal bones in Iron Age pits, *International Journal of Osteoarchaeology* 2/4, 341–349.

Wilson, R. 1996. *Spatial Patterning among Animal Bones in Settlement Archaeology. An English Regional Exploration*. Oxford: British Archaeological Reports British Series 251.

Wilson, R., Hamilton, J., Bramwell, D. and Armitage, P. 1978. The animal bones, in Parrington 1978, 110–139.

To fish or not to fish? Evidence for the possible avoidance of fish consumption during the Iron Age around the North Sea

Keith Dobney and Anton Ervynck

Introduction

Accounts of the Late Iron Age economy of the areas around the southern part of the North Sea typically do not refer to fishing as an important contribution to subsistence (e.g. Bloemers and Van Dorp 1991; Green 1992; Van Heeringen 1992; Cunliffe 1995; Champion and Collis 1996). In the case of freshwater fishing, most texts seem to assume implicitly (by referring to older periods and common sense) that some food procurement did occur in inland waters, but how important this activity was remains unclear. The evaluation of marine resource exploitation is even more problematic for the Late Iron Age. We do not really know to what extent people were fishing in the sea, and, when they did, whether this fishing was practised in the estuaries, along the coast, or in open waters. In any case, the evidence is very scarce, but whether this is proof for a lack of interest in marine and freshwater resources needs to be more fully evaluated.

If some Late Iron Age peoples in north-west Europe did not incorporate aquatic resources as a significant part of their subsistence strategies, it remains unclear why this would have been the case. Was this because of ecological conditions, different economic options, a lack of economic specialisation, a lack of technology, or other reasons? The following paper reviews the Iron Age zooarchaeological record for three countries bordering the North Sea (England, Belgium, and the Netherlands) in order to evaluate more fully the possible nature and extent of fish exploitation.

England: the absence of evidence

The pre-Roman Iron Age in Britain is generally seen as a period characterised by a hierarchical society, where the control of agricultural production, surplus, storage, and distribution are central to its understanding (e.g. Cunliffe 1995). International links were also of manifest importance during this period (particularly for the Mid to Late Iron Age) and the scene is also set for the beginnings of Roman influence. Archaeological evidence indicates a high level of continuity in settlement and land use and, by implication, in social and economic organisation, between the Late Iron Age and Romano-British periods, as well as contemporary regional variations. Zooarchaeological research for these periods has traditionally focused upon economic systems, particularly in terms of intensification or extensification of agricultural production, but in recent years, a growing interest in using bioarchaeological evidence to explore broader social systems (for example ritualistic and religious practices) has led to a number of zooarchaeological studies that have a direct bearing on the issues to be explored in this paper.

Several authors reporting on Iron Age vertebrate assemblages from the south of England have noted the rarity or often complete absence of evidence for the exploitation of fish at the sites in question (e.g. Gregory 1978; Grant 1984; Hill 1995). Although this may be heavily influenced by the often poor preservation of vertebrate remains from the shallow deposits associated with rural settlements (e.g. through acid soils and the comminution of fragile remains by scavengers), or by the fact that many assemblages of this date have not been systematically sampled and sieved, this pattern may in fact still represent a real phenomenon.

There are wide regional variations in the number of Iron Age animal bone assemblages available for study. This results from a variety of factors, such as the effect of the underlying geology on preservation, differences in recovery techniques, site visibility, disparate scales of urban and rural development affecting the focus of rescue excavations, and differing regional research agendas to name but a few. The vast majority of published assemblages are from southern England and the Midlands, with far fewer collections having been excavated and published from northern England. A previous survey of zooarchaeological work found that only 20 Iron Age vertebrate assemblages were available for northern England (the vast majority of those being small evaluation or assessment reports) compared to a total of 79 from the Midlands (Albarella and Dobney, unpublished data). Iron Age animal bone assemblages are also much less well represented than Roman ones. For example, 94 Roman assemblages have been published from the north of England and 174 from the Midlands (*ibid.*). A comparable survey of archaeo-zoological assemblages for the south of England has unfortunately not yet been completed, but this paper includes as much of the available information as possible (e.g. Hambleton 1999).

In terms of broad topographic location, few Iron Age animal bone assemblages (or Roman ones for that matter) in England are from coastal settlements, which significantly limits our understanding of the possible scale and scope of marine exploitation during these periods, unless trade in marine fish from the coast to more inland locations regularly occurred (as it certainly did during medieval and later times). Thus a more realistic and balanced view of the role of fish and fishing in the Iron Age of England may perhaps only be addressed by reference to freshwater and estuarine resources. Although the many and varied potential biasing factors in the datasets should be borne in mind whenever such broad synthetic overviews are attempted, some interesting results have nonetheless been forthcoming.

A total of 117 published vertebrate reports from sites of broad Iron Age date throughout England were surveyed to assess the evidence for fish exploitation and consumption (see Appendix for details and references). Initial analysis showed that those sites where fish remains had been recorded were clearly in the minority (Fig. 1), with over 90% of the 117 sites yielding no remains at all. If we compare the frequency of Roman assemblages containing fish bones (from the Midlands and the north of England, where we have directly comparable datasets) to Iron Age ones (Fig. 2), it is clear that more Roman assemblages contain fish bones (7% of sites for the Midlands, 9% for the North) than Iron Age ones (2% for the Midlands, 0% for the North).

What is also very apparent is that at the 11 Iron Age sites where fish remains have been identified (see Appendix), the fish bone collections are both extremely small in terms of numbers of fragments (most less than six) and restricted in the variety of taxa identified, except one: the Late Iron Age nucleated settlement at Skeleton Green, Puckeridge–Braughing, Hertfordshire (Partridge 1981; see also Bryant this volume). At this site, six taxa and 46 identifiable fragments of fish were found, forming an unusual and distinctive collection, which does not follow the general patterns of the other Iron Age assemblages where fish remains are present; the possible significance of this is further discussed below.

Apart from differential preservation of fish remains, one of the most obvious possible explanations to account for this potentially interesting phenomenon is the lack of systematic sieving and recovery at many sites. Fish bone assemblages tend to be comprised of species whose individual skeletal elements are small. In fact, many of these remains would be completely overlooked during excavation (as indeed would small birds and mammals) if representative sediment samples were not sieved through a <5mm mesh. As Wilson (1993, 172) remarked in his analysis of the animal bones from Mingies Ditch, Oxfordshire, 'the absence of small species on other local Iron Age sites may result from a virtual absence of soil sieving'.

Whilst this argument must be a significant factor affecting the frequency of fish remains in many of the assemblages included in this survey, it surely cannot wholly account for their consistent absence. At least 22 (18%) of the assemblages included here were originally subjected to varying degrees and types of sampling, sieving, and systematic recovery during excavation (see Appendix). There appears, however, to be no correlation between those that were sieved and those that produced fish bone: only two of the 22 sieved assemblages contained fish bones, while a far larger number produced varying quantities of other small bones also often missed when sieving is not undertaken.

Thus, Mid–Late Iron Age deposits from Balksbury camp produced numerous small mammal and amphibian remains, but fish bones were lacking. Numerous small mammal taxa were recovered from Maiden Castle and Little Sombourne, sites again characterised by an absence of fish remains. Charcoal, seeds, snails, and a range of small mammals, amphibians and birds were present in wet-sieved samples from Micheldever Wood, but no fish bones were reported. Many small mammal bones were recorded from an Iron Age pit at Ructstalls Hill, where it was deemed notable that no bird or fish bones were recovered (Gregory 1978). Finally, at Winklebury, targetted sampling and subsequent sieving of sediment samples produced many small mammal bones, but once again no fish remains.

Bones from small taxa other than fish were also recovered at a number of sites where sieving was not apparently undertaken. For example, the bones of birds, small mammals, and amphibians have been recovered in moderate quantities from Iron Age deposits at Gussage All Saints, Danebury, Uley, and Winnall Down. At the religious site at Uley, it was notable that although no fish were recovered from prehistoric deposits, they were relatively plentiful in Roman contexts.

It is therefore clear that the remains of numerous

small vertebrate taxa other than fish were present in a variety of Iron Age animal bone assemblages, from both sieved and unsieved deposits. In this light – and given the diversity of geographical locations represented by the sites in the survey – it is difficult to argue that recovery and preservation are the principal and sole reasons why fish remains are largely absent from English Iron Age assemblages. Another explanation must be sought.

As previously noted, a single Iron Age site in the survey had a modest fish bone assemblage, which includes a broad range of taxa. The lower deposits of a Late Iron Age well at Skeleton Green yielded a total of 46 fish bones, including the remains of species such as eel (*Anguilla anguilla*), roach (*Rutilus rutilus*), chub (*Leuciscus cephalus*), and cyprinids (Cyprinidae sp.), all of which could have been caught in nearby rivers. However, the presence of estuarine species – plaice (*Pleuronectes platessa*) and flounder (*Platichtys flesus*) – at an inland site suggests a link with fisheries, perhaps in the Thames estuary, whilst the single marine species, Spanish mackerel (*Scombrus japonicus*), caught today off the coast of southern Europe, indicates foreign trade (Wheeler 1981). Pre-Roman import of culinary luxuries from the Mediterranean region is implicit in the ceramic containers found at Skeleton Green and other major Late Iron Age centres (Fitzpatrick and Timby 2002), but is more commonly associated with the Roman period (Dobney 2001). Finds have included the remains of Mediterranean fish species such as red mullet (*Mullus surmuletus*; Stallibrass 1997), Spanish mackerel (Murphy *et al.* 2000), and even Nile catfish (*Clarias* sp.; Jones 1996), which would have been imported as cured/dried specimens, or in sealed jars of oil as *salsamenta* (Van Neer and Lentacker 1994).

At Romano-British urban centres such as York (A. Jones 1988), Lincoln (Dobney *et al.* 1996), and London (Bateman and Locker 1982), concentrated deposits of small marine fish bones have been interpreted as remains from the preparation of fish sauce such as *garum*, *allec,* or *liquamen.* Direct evidence for the import of fish sauce into early Roman Britain is at present ambiguous. Possible finds from York (Kenward *et al.* 1986, O'Connor 1988) have not yet been studied sufficiently. Another potential example comes from Winchester Palace, Southwark, where the remains of six heads of Spanish mackerel were found in a first century AD amphora (Yule 1989; Locker 1994), on which the inscription described the contents as *liquamen*, and the property of one Lucius Tettius Africanus from Antipolis (modern-day Antibes). However, the heads are more likely to be the residue of imported pickled/ preserved fish present in a re-used container (Van Neer and Lentacker 1994), just like the examples cited above. There is also evidence for local fish sauce production in the later Roman period, since the species identified from some so-called 'fish sauce contexts', namely clupeids (Clupeidae sp.) and sand eels (Ammodytidae sp.), are

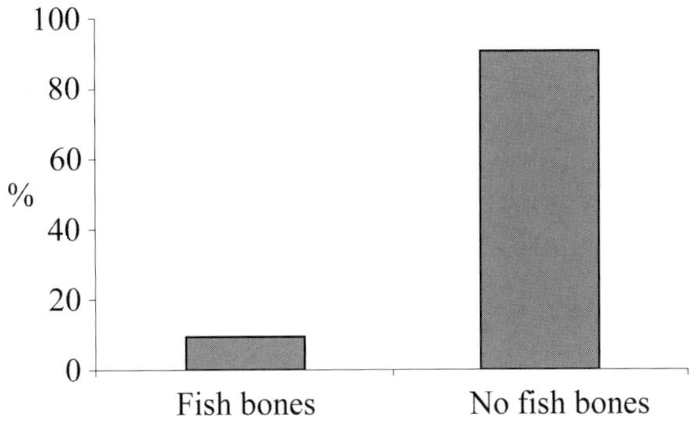

Fig. 1. Frequency of English Iron Age sites, with and without fish bones, surveyed for this study (n = 117).

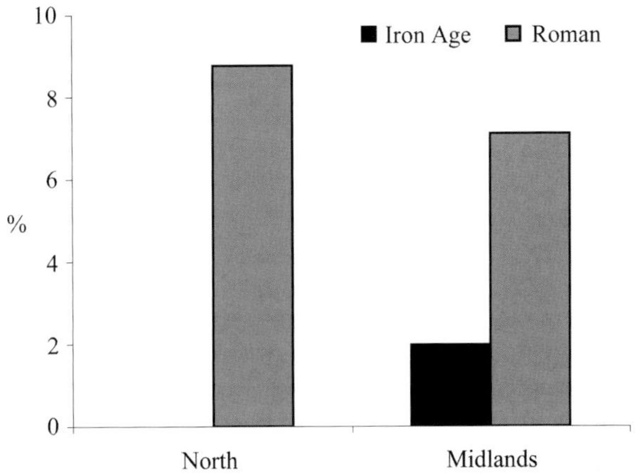

Fig 2. Percentage of sites with fish bones from Northern England (total Iron Age = 20, total Roman = 94) and the Midlands (total Iron Age = 79, total Roman = 174) (source: Albarella and Dobney unpublished data).

commonly available in the North Sea. This local British production appears to have developed to cater for a growing and characteristically 'Roman' culinary taste, and was not the continuation of an earlier Iron Age tradition (Dobney 2001, 38).

Along with other exceptional features of the site, including the unusually high incidence of pig and domestic fowl (Albarella this volume; Bryant this volume), the Spanish mackerel bones from Late Iron Age deposits at Skeleton Green evidently indicate pre-conquest Roman/Mediterranean contact, and the probable adoption of aspects of high-status Roman culinary tastes. This conclusion helps to explain the somewhat anomalous status of the fish bone assemblage compared to the vast majority of Iron Age sites.

The other Iron Age sites with fish bone finds exhibit no obvious patterns, although given the small sample size, this was not particularly to be expected. Only two were associated with significant expanses of water: Rookery Hill, Bishopstone, overlooks the English Channel and the estuary of the River Ouse, whilst Wardy Hill, Coveney, occupies a prominent spur on the north side of the Isle of Ely, dominating a former marsh embayment. Four are hillforts (Aylesbury, Balksbury, Danebury, Maiden Castle); one an extensive open settlement (Dragonby); and the rest smaller, enclosed and/or open settlements (Bishopstone, Gussage All Saints, Wardy Hill, Wavendon Gate, and Winnall Down). The hillforts and Winnall Down were occupied primarily in the Early and Middle Iron Age, whereas Dragonby and Wavendon Gate – like Skeleton Green – were Later Iron Age foundations. The other three sites span both the earlier and later parts of the period. None of these other sites have yielded continental imports on anything like the scale of Skeleton Green.

With regard to the Roman period, it is noteworthy that where there is evidence for the increasing development of mainly freshwater fisheries, with some utilisation of estuarine and inshore marine species, this seems to be associated more with high-status settlements. In contrast, the pattern of fish consumption at indigenous Romano-British settlements, not heavily influenced by Roman traditions, was very similar to that of their Iron Age counterparts (Dobney 2001).

Belgium: a lost heritage

The Iron Age zooarchaeological record for Belgium is very poor (Ervynck 1994), the result of hostile preservation conditions at many sites, particularly within the area of sandy soils (i.e. inland Flanders and the Campine area). Decalcified loess soils, occurring in areas such as Brabant, also form environments that are not conducive for bone survival. In contrast, one often finds Roman and medieval sites in these same regions that do contain significant numbers of animal remains. This pattern cannot be explained by differences in chronology alone, but must be related to the fact that Roman and medieval sites often have deeper and more elaborate structures than their Iron Age predecessors; equally, on sites of these periods, fragments of limestone and mortar are present in most archaeological deposits, neutralising percolating, acid rainwater. The Iron Age sites have no stone buildings and often no deep refuse pits, and are typically devoid of animal bones. As in England, inadequate recovery techniques have also been a characteristic of excavations on protohistoric sites in Belgium (*ibid.*); sieving was seldom practised and hand-collection performed in a non-systematic manner. Consequently, fish bones may have been consistently overlooked on many earlier excavations.

Despite the poverty of the zooarchaeological record for Belgium, it is generally assumed that people fished inland waters during the Late Iron Age. They certainly did so at earlier periods. This is proven by finds from four locations: a special activity site of the Early Neolithic *Swifterbant* culture excavated in northern Flanders (Van Neer *et al.* 2001); a Neolithic site at Oudenaarde, on the River Schelde (Van Neer, unpublished data); a number of prehistoric caves in the Ardennes (Van Neer 1999); and a *Linearbandkeramik* site at Liège (Desse 1983). In contrast, the remains of freshwater fish are mostly absent from the often rich archaeozoological record of Belgian Gallo-Roman sites. However, exceptions are found at the Veemarkt site in Tongeren, and at Namur, where in both cases a large number of very small freshwater fish have been found, assemblages of which the possible culinary meaning remains obscure (Vanderhoeven *et al.* 1993; Van Neer and Ervynck 1994; 2004).

During a large ritual banquet held at the temple of Mithras at Tienen, a few freshwater fishes were consumed (Lentacker *et al.* 2004); they were also prepared for a meal at one of the rich town houses in Tongeren (Van Neer and Ervynck, unpublished data). In general, these few examples from clearly 'Romanised' contexts seem to be no more than exceptions to the rule. Of course, the consumption patterns found at Gallo-Roman sites were basically part of an autochthonous (Iron Age) tradition, only slightly changed by southern European, Roman influence. Thus, if preservation conditions are not responsible for the pattern found, the consumption of freshwater fish appears not to have been a very important part of the food economy of the indigenous people living in northern Gaul.

With regard to the exploitation of the sea, the Belgian archaeological record also provides little information, simply because all protohistoric coastal settlements have vanished due to rising sea level during the Holocene (see Thoen 1987, 104–5). The Late Iron Age coastline is situated some 5 km from the present day coast and the only Iron Age economic activity that can be traced along the coast is salt production (*ibid.*, 50–3; De Ceunynck and Termote 1987), but there is no indication for fish having been exploited at these sites. At inland Iron Age sites, marine fish are completely absent (Ervynck *et al.* 2004), a pattern that could be linked to poor preservation and inadequate recovery methods, but could also reflect the absence of a trade in food products between the coast and inland sites.

One Late Iron Age site in the Benelux area which does possess evidence for the import of marine fish is the *oppidum* on the Titelberg in Luxembourg, where the remains of albacore tuna (*Thunnus alalunga*) have been found in a context dating to the first century BC (Desse-Berset 1993). This cannot, however, be seen as evidence of a specific focus on marine products within Iron Age society, but more likely reflects a trade in culinary luxuries, associated with Roman or Mediterranean cultural influence on the Iron Age elite in northern Gaul. In this respect, the Titelberg can be directly compared to the important Late Iron Age trading settlement at Skeleton Green, discussed above.

Marine fish are also almost completely absent from inland Gallo-Roman sites. The exceptions are a single find of a flatfish bone from Nevele (Ervynck *et al.* 1997); some more flatfish remains excavated at Tournai (Lentacker *et al.* forthcoming); and the common presence of salted products imported from southern Europe (*garum* and *salsamenta*) (Van Neer and Ervynck 2004), and of the remains of a local variety of fish sauce produced along the North Sea coast (Van Neer and Lentacker 1994). The local manufacture of fish sauce only appears to begin during the second century AD (Van Neer and Ervynck 2004) and thus cannot be regarded as the continuation of a previously established Iron Age tradition. The limited archaeological evidence does not indicate that Iron Age salt factories produced fish sauce and, to date, no Gallo-Roman North Sea fish sauce production sites have been found.

It must not however be forgotten that, as with the protohistoric coast, the Roman beach and dune belt have disappeared into the sea (Thoen 1987, 104–5), hampering all investigations of economic activities in coastal settlements. At the present day coastal sites of De Panne, Raversijde, Bredene, Wenduine, Blankenberge, and Zeebrugge, traces of Roman activity have been found, with some of these sites being described as salt production centres (Thoen 1987), but animal remains from these sites are, unfortunately, rare. At De Panne, a single fish bone (identified as from a ray, Rajidae sp.) was found (*ibid.*, 67), whilst amongst the finds from Bredene, only one skeletal element of a gadid (Gadidae sp.) was recognised (Peters 1987). It remains possible that intensive fishing was practised off the Flemish coast during Roman times but so far archaeological evidence is lacking.

The previous remarks also hold for marine fish, but the situation may perhaps be slightly different for molluscs. Fragments of mussel (*Mytilus edulis*) and oyster (*Ostrea edulis*) shells have been found at a number of inland Gallo-Roman sites (e.g. Vanderhoeven *et al.* 1992; Van Impe *et al.* forthcoming), which may indicate a link between the gathering of shellfish and inland trade. This does not however prove that a similar pattern existed in the preceding period. The interest in molluscs may have been another 'Roman' addition to the consumption pattern at Gallo-Roman sites, not an indigenous trait.

The Netherlands: subsistence along the coast

In contrast to Belgium, a certain number of Iron Age coastal sites where animal remains are preserved have been found in the Netherlands. They show that marine fish were caught, at least by line fishing but possibly in open waters, and consumed as part of the subsistence strategy of some Late Iron Age groups. For example, bones of cod (*Gadus morhua*) have been found in the Iron Age occupation phase at Velsen-Hoogovens (Therkorn 1984), at Leiden-Stevenshofjespolder (IJzereef *et al.* 1992), and at Midden-Delfland-Foppenpolder (Van Dijk 1992). Bones of haddock (*Melanogrammus aeglefinus*) have also been found, but only in the Late Iron Age to Roman occupation phase at Velsen-Hoogovens (Therkorn 1984).

Strangely enough, no flatfish remains – plaice, dab (*Limanda limanda*), and flounder – have yet been found (e.g. IJzereef *et al.* 1992), although these species can easily be fished in coastal waters. The absence of herring bones (*Clupea harengus*) is perhaps explained by the lack of floating net technology, which was apparently not introduced until around – or shortly before – AD 1000 in Flanders and northern England (Jones 1981; Ervynck *et al.* 2004). In general, the absence of evidence for the capture of smaller species, such as whiting (*Merlangius merlangus*) or herring, is difficult to evaluate, since once again, systematic sampling and recovery methods were not generally employed at the sites discussed (IJzereef *et al.* 1992).

The evidence from coastal Iron Age sites in the Netherlands can be better assessed through comparison with the fish remains from Neolithic sites. Indeed, a number of Dutch sites of this period show a remarkable variety of marine taxa. At Hoogwoud-Mienakker, for example, thin-lipped grey mullet (*Liza ramada*), turbot (*Scophthalmus maximus*), plaice, flounder, thornback ray (*Raja clavata*), cod, whiting, haddock, grey gurnard (*Eutrigla gurnardus*), and bass (*Dicentrarchus labrax*) were all found (Beerenhout 1991). The particularly abundant remains of mature haddock imply that fishing was also practised in deeper waters (Beerenhout 1994a; Lauwerier 2001), although we should bear in mind that the ecological characteristics of the original North Sea haddock population were different, or at least more variable, compared to the situation today (Beerenhout 1994a; De Vries 2001), so it is possible that, in prehistoric times, haddock occurred closer to the coast.

Other Neolithic sites with large numbers of marine fish bones (albeit with a lower species variety), are Winkel-Zeewijk (De Vries 2001), Aartswoud-Braakweg (Gehasse 2001), Kolhorn-Waardpolder (Brinkhuizen 1979), and Voorschoten-De Donk (Deckers 1991). Clearly, the exploitation of marine waters had already begun long before the Iron Age; indeed, it appears that the Neolithic population of the Netherlands explored open waters more than the Iron Age inhabitants.

In Roman times, marine fishing appears to have continued. The harbour site of Velsen yielded a wide range of species, including haddock (Brinkhuizen 1989; Beerenhout 1994b), and marine fish have also been found at Assendelver-Polders 'site F' (IJzereef *et al.* 1992), Castricum-Oosterbuurt (Lauwerier and Laarman 1999), Schagen-Witte, Paal III (Zeiler 1996), 's Gravenhage-Scheveningseweg (Carmiggelt *et al.* 1998), and Valkenburg-Marktveld (Gehasse 1997). All these sites are located close to the coast and thus cannot be taken as evidence of large-scale trade in North Sea products.

There is no evidence that the marine fish caught by the inhabitants of the Iron Age coastal sites was traded inland. There are, however, plentiful remains of freshwater fish from inland settlements, which prove that the catch in inland waters was rewarding. Due no doubt partly to its large, firmly-built bony skeletal elements, sturgeon (*Acipenser sturio*) is attested at several sites (IJzereef *et al.* 1992), but there is also evidence for the consumption of eel and cyprinids, for example, at Kesteren-De Woerd (Zeiler 2001). This pattern continued into the Gallo-Roman period, for example at sites such as Assendelver-Polders, 's Gravenhage, Valkenburg, and Velsen, as previously mentioned. Additional examples of Roman sites with freshwater fish remains are Nijmegen (Lauwerier 1988), Houten (Laarman 1996), and Leiden-Roomburg (Robeerst 2000). This apparent consumption of freshwater fish at sites in the Netherlands appears to contrast strikingly with the picture for Belgium.

Taphonomy and recovery, ecology or ideology?

On the basis of the evidence outlined above, a number of possible conclusions can be drawn. Firstly, during the Iron Age the exploitation of marine fish may have been an important economic activity for coastal settlements. This is suggested by the data from the Netherlands, but owing to the limitations of the archaeological and zooarchaeological record cannot be readily corroborated or contradicted by data from Belgium or England. In the case of freshwater fish, information is again lacking for Belgium, but is available for England and the Netherlands. In England, it seems that Iron Age interest in freshwater fish was extremely low, and that this has little to do with the vagaries of preservation and/or sampling and recovery, whereas in the Netherlands, there is plentiful evidence for their consumption at inland settlements.

In Roman times, freshwater fish consumption appears to have increased in inland England, and to have remained significant in the Netherlands. Roman sites in Belgium display no evidence, however, for exploitation of freshwater resources, apart for some puzzling contexts which contained only very small freshwater fishes, and the remains of two rich, 'Romanised' banquets. This implies that, in Belgium, fish consumption was equally negligible during the Iron Age. Where fish consumption seems to increase in Roman times, it appears to be in 'Romanised' contexts.

The overall conclusion must be that fishing and the eating of fish (both freshwater and marine) played little or no part in the lives of Iron Age peoples from England and the southern Low Countries (Belgium), in contrast to the Netherlands, where a more significant role for aquatic resources is implied. In fact, this division between the northern and the southern halves of the Low Countries may well be mirrored in the British Isles. Although an overview of the archaeozoological record for Scotland was beyond the scope of this paper, a relatively recent review of the north-eastern Scottish mainland, Orkney, and Shetland (Barrett *et al.* 1999) indicates that marine fisheries have always been important, from Neolithic times onward. It should, however, be noted that all the sites discussed in that review are located along the coasts.

The main challenge is now to explain the patterns highlighted. They certainly cannot be attributed to particular differences in ecological conditions between, on the one hand, Belgium and England, and, on the other hand, the Netherlands. There is little doubt that fish would have been plentiful in the rivers, estuaries, and shallow inshore coastal waters of all these areas during the Iron Age and Roman periods. However, Grant (1984, 513) notes in her discussion of the virtual absence of fish remains from the site of Danebury, 'the availability of a resource does not necessarily imply that the resource was exploited.' An example of this, from a very different part of the world, can be found in the case of the Tasman Aborigines, who at the time of European contact, were reported to have viewed the consumption of fish as abhorrent, despite the fact that they were surrounded by plentiful supplies, and even exploited a variety of other marine resources such as crustaceans (Simoons 1994, 253).

Food avoidances of all kinds are still widespread throughout the world today and must also have occurred in the past. Fish eating is – and always has been – one of the more common taboos, although the reasons why this should be so in different parts of the world are far from clear. In his survey of food taboos past and present, Simoons (1994) suggests that one possible reason for avoiding fish is the medium in which they live. Many groups and cultures considered water sacred. The Zuni and Hopi of the American South-West, along with the Navajo and Apache, avoided eating fish and all water creatures for this reason, whilst the Yezidis of Kurdistan regard all fountains and springs as sacred and regarded fish as blessed because of their association with these waters.

Numerous ponds or other bodies of water containing inviolable fish can still be found today in Turkey, Syria, and the Lebanon (Simoons 1994, 270). In classical accounts from Asia, fish were associated with Assyrian deities of fertility and life-giving water, and people bathed in ponds containing sacred fish (*ibid.* 269). Xenophon writes of a river in Syria where the fish are large and quite tame and considered by people as deities not to be harmed (*Anabasis* 1. 4. 9). These ancient south-west Asian deities (or versions of them) may have continued to have had cult followings in the Hellenistic period and even under the Roman empire, resulting in fish consumption being prohibited during sacred rites and at particular times of the year (Simoons 1994, 272).

Another major factor in fish avoidance appears to be

the fact that, in some quarters, they are considered to be 'unclean' or 'impure' creatures. This is most common, today, in arid and semi-arid parts of Africa and Asia and amongst pastoralist peoples, who may have passed on the taboo to some agricultural communities (Simoons 1994, 296). Fish-avoiding groups often view those who eat or even catch fish to be of poor or lower status, and this is often reflected in a difference between the caste or class of these individuals.

Returning to Iron Age England, there certainly appears to be clear evidence placing animals beyond the mere functional and economic sphere of human interaction into one of social and even symbolic value. Several researchers have highlighted the presence and possible significance of articulated and semi-articulated domestic animal remains in Iron Age deposits, usually in ditches and pits, and current consensus is that many do indeed represent some form of ritual activity. Grant (1984; 1991), in her analysis of these so-called 'special deposits' from Danebury, discussed a possible hierarchy of ritual activities on the basis of differential deposition of various domestic animal species and parts of the skeleton. Subsequently, in his detailed study of waste disposal at Iron Age sites in Wessex, Hill (1995) observed that hunting and fishing appeared to have played only a minor role in the subsistence economy. However, where the remains of wild mammals and birds were deposited on sites, they often appear to have been treated differently from the majority of recovered bone (mainly of domestic animals); indeed, 'the smaller a species' contribution to the overall total number of bone fragments, the more marked its *treatment*' in deposits (*ibid.*, 104, our emphasis). By implication, although of little calorific value, wild animals were probably of considerable social and symbolic value, and thus may provide important evidence of 'past emic ethnobiological classifications' (*ibid.*, 65).

As a result of his contextual analysis, Hill (1995, 104) concluded that a culture/nature division was of central importance in Iron Age Wessex and that dominant cultural symbols were articulated through the practices of ritual deposition and special treatment of elements of the wild fauna. The absence of wild resources from Iron Age diets was not due to a lack of time to hunt, or the availability of prey; instead they were probably surrounded by prohibitions, so that their occasional hunting, the use of their feathers and skins, and their consumption were all probably heavily regulated or proscribed. The almost complete absence of fish remains from the English sites surveyed in this paper can thus be taken to suggest that their capture and consumption was indeed forbidden, a result of their symbolic or possibly even unclean status. Hill (*ibid.*, 105) briefly noted the absence of otter remains from his sites in Wessex, postulating that their absence (along with fish) perhaps indicated that all creatures that lived in water were proscribed in Iron Age classifications.

In the context of the present review, we have noted that marine fishing was important in Neolithic times in the Netherlands. No information is available for Belgium, but in Britain stable isotope data from human skeletons reveal that a sharp shift in diet occurred at the onset of the Neolithic, consisting of a sudden lack of marine foods (Richards and Hedges 1999; Thomas 2003). Could this have been the origin of a dietary pattern that persisted into the Iron Age? Strikingly, Thomas notes that such a sudden shift in diet could have been accompanied by a cultural prohibition (*ibid.*, 70). Perhaps a whole new view on the aquatic environment of the earth had become widely accepted, linking water with the realm of death. The deposition of the dead in rivers could be another sign of this concept (Bradley and Gordon 1988; Parker Pearson 2000). Alternatively, fish avoidance could have been considered part of a new cultural identity, i.e. of 'being Neolithic' (Thomas 2003, 70). In that case, too, it must be investigated whether this cultural phenomenon has a link with fish avoidance during the English Iron Age.

Conclusion

From this brief review it appears that the absence of fish on many Iron Age sites in England and perhaps also across the North Sea in Belgium is a real phenomenon, not merely an artefact of various taphonomic processes. We have argued that the probable reasons for this pattern lie beyond the realm of mere economic and subsistence practices, instead perhaps providing evidence of how certain Iron Age communities perceived and classified the natural world. Fish, it would seem, were hardly exploited (despite the fact that certain species would have been both plentiful and relatively easy to catch), and we can but conclude that they were for some reason proscribed within Iron Age society.

Whether fish were perceived as unclean, or in some way divine, of course remains a moot point, but it is tempting to pursue the answer through what we understand about prehistoric people's views of water or wet places (see also Willis this volume). Interestingly, the situation appears to have differed in the Netherlands, where Iron Age coastal and inland sites appear to have exploited a wider range of both freshwater and marine fish species. Does this mean that the ideological explanations proposed for Belgium and England were not valid there? The present contribution is only the beginning of the discussion.

Acknowledgements

The authors wish to thank Umberto Albarella (University of Sheffield) for the use of unpublished data. Keith Dobney acknowledges the support of a Wellcome Trust Bioarchaeology Research Fellowship.

Appendix: English Iron Age sites used in this study.

Indicated are the site locations, dating, broad site classification, presence (yes/no) of fish remains, whether sieving was applied (yes/no), and the relevant references in the literature.

Site Name	*Date*	*Site Type*	*Fish bones?*	*Sieved?*	*Reference*
Abingdon, Wyndyke Furlong	Early–Mid Iron Age	open settlement	n	n	Wilson 1999
Andover, Old Down Farm	Early–Late Iron Age	enclosed settlement	n	n	Maltby 1981
Appleford	Early–Mid Iron Age	open settlement	n	n	Wilson 1980
Aslockton	Iron Age	defended settlement	n	n	Hamshaw-Thomas 1992
Aylesbury, Coldharbour Farm	Mid Iron Age	open settlement	n	n	Sadler 1990
Aylesbury, County Museum	Iron Age	hillfort?	y	n	Sadler 1998
Aylesbury, George Street	Iron Age	hillfort?	n	n	Jones 1983
Baldock	Late Iron Age	open settlement	n	n	Chaplin and McCormick 1986
Balksbury Camp	Early–Late Iron Age	hillfort	y	y	Maltby 1995
Bancroft (mausoleum)	Iron Age/Roman	settlement	n	n	Holmes and Rielly 1994
Barholm	Iron Age	open settlement	n	n	Harman 1993a
Barley, Aldwick	Iron Age	open settlement	n	n	Cra'ster 1961
Barnham 1	Iron Age	enclosure	n	n	Martin 1993
Barnham 2	Iron Age	enclosure	n	n	Martin 1993
Barrington, Edix Hill	Late Iron Age	open settlement	n	n	Davis 1995
Basingstoke, Ructstalls Hill	Early–Mid Iron Age	enclosed settlement	n	y	Gregory 1978
Beckford	Late Iron Age	enclosure complex	n	n	Gilmore 1970–72
Bierton	Late Iron Age	cluster of pits and ditches	n	n	G. Jones 1988
Bishopstone	Mid–Late Iron Age	enclosed settlement	y	n	Gebbels 1977
Blackthorn	Late Iron Age	enclosed settlement	n	n	Orr 1974
Bledlow	Iron Age	farmstead	n	n	Fraser 1946
Boreham, Bulls Lodge Farm	Iron Age/Roman	farmstead	n	n	Bedwin 1993
Brancaster	Iron Age	settlement	n	y	Jones *et al.* 1985
Brassington, Harborough Rocks	Early Iron Age	open settlement	n	n	Bishop 1991
Breedon-on-the-Hill	Iron Age	hillfort	n	n	Jackson 1950; Higgs 1964
Brigg	Bronze Age/Iron Age transition	deposit near trackway	n	n	Jope 1958
Brigstock	Iron Age	enclosed settlement	n	n	Field 1983
Burgh	Late Iron Age	enclosed settlement	n	n	Jones *et al.* 1987; 1988
Burton Fleming	Iron Age	burial, cemetery	n	n	Legge 1991
Catcote	Late Iron Age/Roman	open settlement	n	n	Hodgson 1968
Cherry Hinton, War Ditches	Iron Age	hillfort	n	n	Phillipson 1963
Chevington	Late Iron Age	settlement	n	y	Stallibrass 1998
Colchester	Late Iron Age	*oppidum*	n	n	Bate 1947; Jackson 1947
Costa Beck	Iron Age	settlement	n	n?	Hayes 1988
Cottingham, Creyke Beck	Iron Age	open settlement	n	y	Stallibrass 1997
Cowbit Wash	Iron Age	industrial	n	y	Albarella 2001
Coxhoe, West House	Iron Age	enclosure	n	n?	Rackham 1982
Croft Ambrey	Iron Age	hillfort	n	n	Whitehouse and Whitehouse 1974
Culworth, Berry Hill Close	Mid Iron Age	enclosure	n	n	Davis 1993–94

Site Name	*Date*	*Site Type*	*Fish bones?*	*Sieved?*	*Reference*
Danebury	Early–Late Iron Age	hillfort	y	n	Grant 1984; 1991
Dod Law West	Iron Age	small hillfort	n	n?	Smith 1990
Dragonby	Late Iron Age	open settlement	y	n	Harman 1996; Jones 1996
Droitwich, Friar Street	Iron Age	industrial	n	n	Locker 1992
Droitwich, Old Bowling Green	Late Iron Age	industrial	n	n	Locker 1992
Earls Barton, Clay Lane	Late Iron Age	enclosure	n	n	Jones, Levitan *et al.* 1985
Easingwold by-pass Crankleys Lane,	Mid-Late Iron Age	open settlement	n	y	Carrott *et al.* 1993
Edmundsoles	Late Iron Age	cluster of pits and ditches	n	n	Miller and Miller 1981
Enderby, Grove Farm	Mid–Late Iron Age	farm	n	y	Gouldwell 1992
Gamston	Iron Age	open/enclosed settlement	n	n	Levitan 1992
Garton Slack	Iron Age	cluster of pits and ditches	n	n	Noddle 1979
Gorhambury	Late Iron Age	enclosure	n	y	Locker 1990
Great Chesterford, Ickleton Road	Late Iron Age	burial, cemetery	n	n	Smoothy 1990
Grimthorpe	Iron Age	hillfort	n	n	Jarman *et al.* 1968
Gussage All Saints	Early–Late Iron Age	enclosed settlement	y	y	Harcourt 1979
Haddenham, Upper Delphs,	Mid Iron Age	enclosure	n	y	Evans and Serjeantson 1988
Hardingstone	Iron Age	enclosure/industrial	n	n	Gilmore 1969
Hardwick, Mingies Ditch	Mid–Late Iron Age	enclosed settlement	n	y	Wilson 1993
Harlow	Late Iron Age	temple	n	n	Legge and Dorrington 1985
Hartigans	Iron Age	open settlement	n	n	Burnett 1993
Hasholme Logboat	Late Iron Age	boat	n	n?	Stallibrass 1987
Hawks Hill	Iron Age	banjo	n	n	Carter *et al.* 1965
Hayton Fort	Iron Age	settlement	n	n	Monk 1978
Ivinghoe Beacon	Early Iron Age	hillfort	n	n	Westley 1970
Kemerton, Aston Mill Farm	Mid Iron Age	enclosure	n	n	Lovett 1990
Kennel Hall Knowe	Late Iron Age	enclosure	n	n?	Rackham 1978
Kirkburn	Mid Iron Age	cemetery	n	n	Legge 1991
Letchworth, Blackhorse Road	Early–Mid Iron Age	enclosed settlement	n	n	Legge *et al.* 1988
Leven-Brandesburton	Iron Age	settlement	n	y	Hall *et al.* 1994
Lincoln	Late Iron Age	settlement	n	n	Scott 1988
Little Sombourne	Iron Age	settlement	n	y	Locker 1979
Little Waltham	Iron Age	open settlement	n	n	Gebbels 1978
Longthorpe II	Iron Age	settlement	n	n	King 1987
Maiden Castle	Early–Late Iron Age	hillfort	y	y	Armour-Chelu 1991
Market Deeping, Outgang Road	Mid–Late Iron Age	open settlement	n	y	Albarella 1997a
Meare Village East	Late Iron Age	open settlement	n	n	Backway 1986; Levine 1986
Meare Village West	Late Iron Age	open settlement	n	n	Bailey *et al.* 1981
Melton	Late Iron Age/Roman	ladder settlement	n	y	Gidney 1994a
Micheldever Wood	Mid–Late Iron Age	banjo	n	y	Coy 1987
Nazeingbury	Late Iron Age	farmstead	n	n	Huggins 1978
Northampton, Moulton Park	Late Iron Age	enclosure	n	n	Orr 1974
North Stifford, Ardale School	Mid–Late Iron Age	enclosure	n	n	Luff 1988

Site Name	*Date*	*Site Type*	*Fish bones?*	*Sieved?*	*Reference*
Oakham, Stamford Road	Iron Age	cluster of pits and ditches	n	n	Hammon 1998
Pennyland	Early/Mid Iron Age	open settlement	n	n	Ashdown 1993; Holmes 1993
Puckeridge–Braughing, Bath House	Late Iron Age	nucleated settlement	n	n	Ashdown and Evans 1977
Puckeridge–Braughing, Ermine Street	Late Iron Age–Early Roman	nucleated settlement	n	n	Fifield 1988
Puckeridge–Braughing, Skeleton Green	Late Iron Age	nucleated settlement	y	n	Ashdown 1981; Ashdown and Evans 1981; Wheeler 1981
Puckeridge–Braughing, Station Road	Late Iron Age	nucleated settlement	n	n	Ashdown 1979; Croft 1979
Rainham Moor Hall Farm	Late Iron Age	settlement	n	n	Locker 1985
Rainsborough	Early Iron Age	hillfort	n	n	Banks 1967
Ravenstone	Iron Age	enclosure	n	n	Millard 1970
Rock Castle	Mid–Late Iron Age	enclosed settlement	n	n	Gidney 1994b
Roxby	Iron Age	open settlement	n	n	Inman *et al.* 1985
Rudston	Iron Age	burial, cemetery	n	n	Legge 1991
St Albans, King Harry Lane	Late Iron Age–Early Roman	cemetery	n	n	Davis 1989
Scole-Dickleburgh	Early–Mid Iron Age	settlement	n	y	Baker 1998
Slonk Hill	Early–Mid Iron Age	open settlement	n	n	Sheppard 1978
Stanwick, The Tofts	Late Iron Age–Early Roman	*oppidum*	n	n	Rackham forthcoming
Stifford Clays	Mid–Late Iron Age	enclosure	n	n	Luff 1988
Sutton Walls	Iron Age	enclosure	n	n	Cornwall and Bennet-Clark 1953
Tallington	Early Iron Age	enclosure	n	n	Harman 1993b
Thorpe Thewles	Iron Age	enclosed/open settlement	n	n	Rackham 1987
Thundridge, Moles Farm	Early Iron Age	cluster of pits and ditches	n	n	Ashdown and Merlen 1970
Tort Hill West	Late Iron Age	open settlement	n	n	Albarella 1997b
Trumpington	Iron Age	enclosure	n	n	Davidson and Curtis 1973
Twywell	Early Iron Age	open settlement	n	n	Harcourt 1975
Uley	Iron Age	temple	n	y	Levitan 1983
Wakerley	Iron Age	enclosure	n	n	Jones 1978
Wardy Hill, Coveney	Late Iron Age	enclosure	y	n	Davis 2003
Wavendon Gate	Iron Age	open/enclosed settlement	y	y	Dobney and Jaques 1996
Wendens Ambo	Iron Age	Farm	n	n	Halstead 1982
West Harling	Early Iron Age	enclosure	n	n	Clarke and Fell 1953
West Stow	Iron Age	open settlement	n	n	Crabtree 1990
Whitwell	Iron Age	open settlement	n	n	Harman 1981
Wighton	Iron Age/Roman	enclosure	n	n	Lawrence 1986
Willington, Plantation Quarry	Iron Age	enclosure	n	n	Clark and Hutchins 1996
Winlklebury Camp	Early–Mid Iron Age	hillfort	n	y	Jones 1977
Winnall Down	Early–Mid Iron Age	enclosed/open settlement	y	n?	Maltby 1985

Bibliography

Albarella, U. 1997a. *The Iron Age Animal Bones Excavated in 1991 from Outgang Road, Market Deeping (MAD91), Lincolnshire*. London: English Heritage Ancient Monuments Laboratory Report 5/97.

Albarella, U. 1997b. *Iron Age and Roman Animal Bones Excavated in 1996 from Norman Cross, Tort Hill East, Tort Hill West and Vinegar Hill, Cambridgeshire*. London: English Heritage Ancient Monuments Laboratory Report 108/97.

Albarella, U. 2001. Animal bone and mammal and bird remains, in T. Lane and E.L. Morris (eds), *A Millennium of Saltmaking: Prehistoric and Romano-British Salt Production in the Fenland*, 75–77; 151; 237; 383–385; 445–449. Heckington: Lincolnshire Archaeology and Heritage Report 4.

Armour-Chelu, M. 1991. The faunal remains, in N. Sharples, *Maiden Castle: Excavations and Field Survey 1985–1986,* 139–151. London: English Heritage Archaeological Report 19.

Ashdown, R. 1979. The avian bones from Station Road, Puckering, in Partridge 1979, 92–96.

Ashdown, R. 1981. Avian bones, in Partridge 1981, 235–242.

Ashdown, R. 1993. Avian bones, in Williams 1993, 154–158.

Ashdown, R. and Evans, D.C. 1977. Animal remains, in C. Partridge, Excavations and fieldwork at Braughing, 1968–73, *Hertfordshire Archaeology* 5, 58–62 (22–108).

Ashdown, R. and Evans, D.C. 1981. Mammalian bones, in Partridge 1981, 205–235.

Ashdown, R.R. and Merlen, R.H.A. 1970. The bones, in R.J. Kiln, An early Iron Age site at Moles Farm, Thundridge, *Hertfordshire Archaeology* 2, 20–22 (10– 22).

Backway, C. 1986. The animal bones, in B.J. Coles, S.E. Rouillard and C. Backway, *The 1984 Excavations at Meare*, 42–49. Cambridge: Somerset Levels Papers 12.

Bailey, G.N., Levine, M.A. and Rogers, S.J.Q. 1981. The faunal remains, in B.J. Orme, J.M. Coles, A.E. Caseldine and G.N. Bailey, *Meare Village West 1979*, 38–44. Cambridge: Somerset Levels Papers 7.

Baker, P. 1998. *The Vertebrate Remains from Scole-Dickleburgh, Excavated in 1993 (Norfolk and Suffolk), A140 and A143 Road Improvement Project*. London: English Heritage Ancient Monuments Laboratory Report 29/98.

Banks, J.W. 1967. Human and animal bones, in M. Avery, J.E.G. Sutton and J.W. Banks, Rainsborough, Northants, England: Excavations 1961–5, *Proceedings of the Prehistoric Society* 33, 302–305.

Barrett, J.H., Nicholson, R.A. and Cerón-Carrasco, R. 1999. Archaeo-ichthyological evidence for long-term socioeconomic trends in northern Scotland: 3500 BC to AD 1500, *Journal of Archaeological Science* 26, 353–388.

Bate, D.M.A. 1947. Bird remains, in Hawkes and Hull 1947, 354–5.

Bateman, N. and Locker, A. 1982. The sauce of the Thames, *London Archaeologist* 4 (8), 204–207.

Bedwin, O. 1993. Animal bone, in N.J.A. Lavender, '*Principia*' at Boreham, near Chelmsford, Essex: excavations 1990, *Essex Archaeology and History* 24, 18 (1–22).

Beerenhout, B. 1991. *Mienakker; Verslag van het onderzoek aan de visresten*. Amersfoort: Interne Rapporten van de Rijkdienst voor het Oudheidkundig Bodemonderzoek.

Beerenhout, B. 1994a. Paleoecology and faunal history: What conclusions can be drawn from mature haddock bones in a neolithic site in the Netherlands?, *Offa* 51, 341–347.

Beerenhout, B. 1994b. Velsen-1: Indications for water-pollution in the harbour of a Roman castellum in the Netherlands, *Archaeofauna* 3, 127–130.

Bishop M. 1991. The bones, in G.A. Makepeace, An early Iron Age settlement at Harborough Rocks, Brassington, Derbyshire, *Archaeological Journal* 110, 28 (24–29).

Bloemers, J.H.F. and Van Dorp, T. 1991. *Pre- and Protohistorie van de Lage Landen*. De Haan: Open Universiteit.

Bradley, R.J. and Gordon, F. 1988. Human skulls from the river Thames, their dating and significance, *Antiquity* 62, 503–509.

Brinkhuizen, D.C. 1979. Preliminary notes on fish remains from archaeological sites in the Netherlands, *Palaeohistoria* 21, 84–90.

Brinkhuizen, D.C. 1989. *Ichthyo-archeologisch onderzoek: Methoden en toepassing aan de hand van Romeins vismateriaal uit Velsen (Nederland)*. Unpublished Ph.D. thesis, University of Groningen.

Burnett, D.P. 1993. Animal bone from MK19, in Williams 1993, 199–205.

Carmiggelt, A., Laarman, F.J. and Waasdorp, J.A. 1998. Het archeozoologisch onderzoek, in A. Carmiggelt (ed.), *Romeinse vondsten van de Scheveningseweg te Den Haag. De dieren- en plantenresten*, 11–37. Den Haag: Haagse Oudheidkundige Publicaties 4.

Carrott, J., Dobney, K., Hall, A., Kenward, H., Jaques, D., Large, F. and Milles A. 1993. *An Assessment of Environmental Samples from Excavations in Crankleys Lane, on the Easingwold By-pass*. York: Reports from the Environmental Archaeology Unit, York 93/32.

Carter, P.L., Phillipson, D. and Higgs, E.S. 1965. Faunal Report, in F.A. Hastings, Excavations of an Iron Age farmstead at Hawks Hill, Leatherhead, *Surrey Archaeological Collections* 62, 40–42 (1–43).

Champion, T.C. and Collis, J.R. 1996. *The Iron Age in Britain and Ireland: Recent Trends*. Sheffield: J.R. Collis Publications.

Chaplin, R.E. and McCormick, F. 1986. The animal bones, in I.M. Stead and V. Rigby, *Baldock: The Excavation of a Roman and Pre-Roman Settlement 1968–72,* 396–415. London: Britannia Monograph 7.

Clark, R. and Hutchins, E. 1996. Animal bone, in M. Dawson, Plantation Quarry, Willington: excavations 1988–1991, *Bedfordshire Archaeology* 22, 30–31 (2–50).

Clarke, J.G.D. and Fell, C.I. 1953. The Early Iron Age site at Micklemoor Hill, West Harling, Norfolk, and its pottery, *Proceedings of the Prehistoric Society* 19, 1–36.

Cornwall, I.W. and Bennet-Clark, M. 1953. Animal bones, in K.M. Kenyon, Excavations at Sutton Walls, Herefordshire, 1948–51, *Archaeological Journal* 110, 79–83 (1–87).

Coy, J. 1987. Animal bones, in P.J. Fasham, *A Banjo Enclosure in Micheldever Wood, Hampshire*, 45–53. Winchester: Hampshire Field Club Monograph 5.

Crabtree, P.J. 1990. Faunal remains from Iron Age and Romano-British features, in S. West, *West Stow, Suffolk: the Prehistoric and Romano-British Occupations*, 101–105. Ipswich: East Anglian Archaeology Report 48.

Cra'ster, M.D. 1961. The Aldwick Iron Age settlement, Barley, Hertfordshire, *Proceedings of the Cambridge Antiquarian Society* 54, 22–46.

Croft, P. 1979. The mammalian bones from Feature 1, in Partridge 1979, 73–92.

Cunliffe, B. 1995. *Iron Age Britain*. London: English Heritage.

Davidson, I. and Curtis, G. 1973. An Iron Age site in the land of the

Plant Breeding Institute, Trumpington, *Proceedings of the Cambridgeshire Antiquarian Society* 64, 1–14.

Davis, S.J.M. 1989. Animal remains from the Iron Age cemetery, in I.M. Stead and V. Rigby, *Verulamium: the King Harry Lane Site*, 250–259. London: English Heritage Archaeological Report 12.

Davis, S.J.M. 1993–4. The animal bones, in M. Audouy, Excavations at Berry Hill Close, Culworth, Northamptonshire, *Northamptonshire Archaeology* 25, 59 (47–62).

Davis, S.J.M. 1995. *Animal bones from the Iron Age site at Edix Hill, Barrington, Cambridgeshire, 1989–1991 excavations*. London: English Heritage Ancient Monuments Laboratory Report 54/95.

Davis, S.J.M. 2003. Animal bone, in C. Evans, *Power and Island Communities: Excavations at the Wardy Hill Ringwork, Coveney, Ely*,122–137. Cambridge: East Anglian Archaeology Report 103.

De Ceunynck, R. and Termote, J. 1987. Een zoutwinningssite uit de Midden-Laat La Tène-periode te Veurne, *Westvlaamse Archaeologica* 3, 73–82.

Deckers, M.J.C. 1991. *Leven op een strandwal; Een zooarcheologische studie van de Vlaardingen-site: Voorschoten–De Donk*. Amsterdam: Bijvakscriptie Instituut voor Pre- en Protohistorische Archeologie A.E. van Giffen, Universiteit van Amsterdam.

Desse, J. 1983. Les restes de poissons dans les fosses omaliennes, in *Les fouilles de la Place Saint-Lambert à Liège*, 22–23. Liège: Centre Interdisciplinaire de Recherches Archéologiques de l'Université de Liège.

Desse-Berset, N. 1993. Analyse d'un échantillon d'ichthyofaune provenant de l'oppidum du Titelberg (Luxembourg), *Archaeologia Mosellana* 2, 407–409.

De Vries, L.S. 2001. De faunaresten van Zeewijk, een laat-neolithische nederzetting in de Groetpolder (N.H.), in Van Heeringen and Theunissen 2001, 281–332.

Dobney, K. 2001. A place at the table: the role of zooarchaeology within a Roman research agenda, in S.T. James and M. Millett (eds), *Britons and Romans: Advancing an Archaeological Agenda*, 36–45. York: Council for British Archaeology Research Report 125.

Dobney, K. and Jaques, D. 1996. The mammal bones, in R.J. Williams, P.J. Hart and A.T.L. Williams, *Wavendon Gate: a Late Iron Age and Roman Settlement in Milton Keynes*, 203–230. Aylesbury: Buckinghamshire Archaeology Society Monograph 10.

Dobney, K., Jaques, D. and Irving, B. 1996. *Of Butchers and Breeds. Report on Vertebrate Remains from Various Sites in the City of Lincoln*. Lincoln: Lincoln Archaeological Studies 5.

Ervynck, A. 1994. L'archéozoologie de l'âge du Fer: un bilan pour la Belgique, *Lunula. Archaeologia protohistorica* II, 38–41.

Ervynck, A., Gautier, A. and Van Neer, W. 1997. Import van schelpdieren en vis in een Romeinse nederzetting te Nevele, *VOBOV-info. Tijdschrift van het Verbond voor Oudheidkundig Bodemonderzoek in Oost-Vlaanderen* 46, 24–28.

Ervynck, A., Van Neer, W. and Pieters, M. 2004. How the North was won (and lost again). Historical and archaeological data on the exploitation of the North Atlantic by the Flemish fishery, in R.A. Housley and G.M. Coles (eds), *Atlantic Connections and Adaptations: Economies, Environments and Subsistence in Lands Bordering the North Atlantic*, 230–239. Oxford: Oxbow Books.

Evans, C. and Serjeantson, D. 1988. The backwater economy of a fen-edge community in the Iron Age: the Upper Delphs, Haddenham, *Antiquity* 62, 360–370.

Field, D. 1983. The animal bones, in D.A. Jackson, The excavation of an Iron Age site at Brigstock, Northants., *Northamptonshire Archaeology* 18, 28–29 (7–32).

Fifield, P.W. 1988. The faunal remains, in T.W. Potter and S.D. Trow, *Puckeridge–Braughing, Hertfordshire: The Ermine Street Excavations 1971–72. The Late Iron Age and Roman Settlement* (*Hertfordshire Archaeology* 10), 148–153.

Fitzpatrick, A. and Timby, J. 2002. Roman pottery in Iron Age Britain, in A. Woodward and J.D. Hill (eds), *Prehistoric Britain: the Ceramic Basis*, 161–172. Oxford: Oxbow Books.

Fraser, F.C. 1946. Bones from Iron Age site at Bedlow, Bucks, in J.F. Head and C.M. Piggott, An Iron Age site at Bledlow, Bucks., *Records of Buckinghamshire* 14, 208–209 (189–209).

Gebbels, A. 1977. The animal bones, in M. Bell, *Excavations at Bishopstone* (*Sussex Archaeological Collections* 115), 277–284.

Gebbels, A. 1978. Animal bone, in P.J. Drury, *Excavations at Little Waltham 1970–1971*, 116. London: Council for British Archaeology Research Report 26.

Gehasse, E.F. 1997. *Valkenburg: Het botmateriaal uit de Marktveld-geul 1985–1988*. Amsterdam/Amersfoort: Intern rapport/manuscript IPP/ROB.

Gehasse, E.F. 2001. Aartswoud: an environmental approach of a Late Neolithic site, in Van Heeringen and Theunissen 2001, 161–201.

Gidney, L.J. 1994a. *Melton, Humberside: MEL94. An assessment of the animal bones*. Durham: Durham Environmental Archaeology Report 32/94.

Gidney, L.J. 1994b. The animal bone, in R.L. Fitts, C.C. Haselgrove, P.C. Lowther and P. Turnbull, An Iron Age farmstead at Rock Castle, Gilling West, North Yorkshire, *Durham Archaeological Journal* 10, 31 (13–42).

Gilmore, F. 1969. The animal and human skeletal remains, in P.J. Woods, *Excavations at Hardingstone, Northampton, 1967–8*, 43–55. Northampton: Northamptonshire County Council.

Gilmore, F. 1970–72. Animal remains, in A. Oswald, Excavations at Beckford, *Transactions of the Worcestershire Archaeological Society* (Ser. 3) 3, 18–27 (7–47).

Gouldwell, A.J. 1992. The animal bone, in P. Clay, An Iron Age farmstead at Grove Farm, Enderby, Leicestershire, *Transactions of the Leicestershire Archaeology Society* 66, 58–69 (1–82).

Grant, A. 1984. Animal bones, in B. Cunliffe, *Danebury: an Iron Age Hillfort in Hampshire, Vol. 2. The Excavations 1969–78: The Finds*, 496–547. London: Council for British Archaeology Research Report 52.

Grant, A. 1991. Animal bones, in B. Cunliffe and C. Poole, *Danebury: an Iron Age Hillfort in Hampshire, Vol. 5. The Excavations 1979–88: The Finds*, 47–87. London: Council for British Archaeology Research Report 73.

Green, M. 1992. *Animals in Celtic Life and Myth*. London: Routledge.

Gregory, I. 1978. Animal bones, in M. Oliver and B. Applin, Excavations at Ructstalls Hill, Basingstoke, Hampshire 1972–75, *Proceedings of the Hampshire Field Club and Archaeological Society* 35, 82–86 (41–92).

Hall, A., Kenward, H., Hill, M., Large, F., Jaques, D., Dobney, K., Issitt, M. and Lancaster, S. 1994. *Technical Report: Biological Remains from Excavations on the Leven-Brandesburton By-pass, N. Humberside*. York: Environmental Archaeology Unit Report 94/15.

Halstead, P. 1982. The animal bones, in I. Hodder, *Wendens Ambo: The*

Excavation of an Iron Age and Romano-British Settlement, 44–49. London: The Archaeology of the M11, Vol. 2.

Hambleton, E. 1999. *Animal Husbandry Regimes in Iron Age Britain. A Comparative Study of Faunal Assemblages from British Iron Age Sites.* Oxford: British Archaeological Reports British Series 282.

Hammon, A. 1998. *Stamford Road, Oakham, Leicestershire. Report on the Animal Bones.* Unpublished report, Birmingham University Field Archaeology Unit.

Hamshaw-Thomas, J. 1992. *Aslockton, Nottinghamshire: Faunal Analysis.* Unpublished report, Trent and Peak Archaeological Trust.

Harcourt, R.A. 1975. The animal bones, in D.A. Jackson, An Iron Age site at Twywell, Northamptonshire, *Northamptonshire Archaeology* 10, 88–89 (31–93).

Harcourt, R. 1979. The animal bones, in G.J. Wainwright, *Gussage All Saints: An Iron Age Settlement in Dorset*, 150–160. London: Department of Environment Archaeological Report 10.

Harman, M. 1981. The mammalian bones, in M. Todd, *The Iron Age and Roman Settlement at Whitwell, Leicestershire*, 40–42. Leicester: Leicestershire Museums, Art Galleries and Records Service Archaeological Report 1.

Harman, M. 1993a. The mammalian bones, in W.G. Simpson, The excavation of a Late Neolithic settlement at Barholm, Lincs, in W.G. Simpson *et al.* 1993, 24–5.

Harman, M. 1993b. The mammalian bones, in C.A.I. French, D.A. Gurney, F.M.M. Pryor and W.G. Simpson, A double pit-alignment and other features at field OS29, Tallington, Lincs, in Simpson *et al.* 1993, 64–65.

Harman, M. 1996. Birds, in May 1996, 163–164.

Hawkes C.F.C. and Hull M.R. 1947. *Camulodunum. First Report on Excavations at Colchester 1930–1939.* London: Report of the Research Committee of the Society of Antiquaries of London 14.

Hayes, R.H. 1988. *North East Yorkshire Studies: Archaeological Papers Edited by P.R. Wilson.* Leeds: Yorkshire Archaeological Society, Roman Antiquities Section.

Higgs, E.S. 1964. Report on fauna, in J.S. Wacher, Excavations at Breedon-on-the-Hill, Leicestershire, 1957, *Antiquaries Journal* 44, 138–141 (122–142).

Hill, J.D. 1995. *Ritual and Rubbish in the Iron Age of Wessex.* Oxford: British Archaeological Reports British Series 242.

Hodgson, G. 1968. A comparative account of the animal remains from Corstopitum and the Iron Age site of Catcote near Hartlepool, County Durham, *Archaeology Aeliana* (Ser. 4) 46, 127–162.

Holmes, J.M. 1993. Animal bones, in Williams 1993, 133–154.

Holmes, J. and Rielly, K. 1994. Animal bone from the 'mausoleum' site, in R. Williams and R. Zeepvat, *Bancroft. A late Bronze Age/Iron Age Settlement, Roman Villa and Temple Mausoleum, Vol. 2. Finds and Environmental Evidence*, 515–536. Aylesbury: Buckinghamshire Archaeology Society Monograph Series 7.

Huggins, P J. 1978. Animal bones, mollusca and egg, in P.J. Huggins, Excavation of a Belgic and Romano-British farm with middle Saxon cemetery and churches at Nazeingbury, Essex, 1975–6, *Essex Archaeology and History* 10, 108–114 (29–117).

IJzereef, G.F., Laarman, F.J. and Lauwerier, R.C.G.M. 1992. Animal remains from the Late Bronze Age and the Iron Age found in the Western Netherlands, in R.M. van Heeringen (ed.), The Iron Age in the Western Netherlands, *Berichten van de Rijksdienst voor het Oudheidkundig Bodemonderzoek* 39, 257–267.

Inman, R., Brown, D.R., Goddard, R.E. and Spratt, D.A. 1985. Roxby Iron Age settlement and the Iron Age in north-east Yorkshire, *Proceedings of the Prehistoric Society* 51, 181–213.

Jackson, J.W. 1947. Mammalian remains, in Hawkes and Hull, 350–354.

Jackson, J.W. 1950. Report on the bones from the 1946 excavations, in K.M. Kenyon, Excavations at Breedon-on-the-Hill, 1946, *Transactions of the Leicestershire Archaeological and Historical Society* 26, 73–75 (37–82).

Jarman, M., Fagg, A. and Higgs, E.S. 1968. Animal bones, in I.M. Stead, An Iron Age hillfort at Grimthorpe, Yorkshire, England, *Proceedings of the Prehistoric Society* 34, 182–189 (148–190).

Jones, A. 1981. Reconstruction of fishing techniques from assemblages of fish bones, in I. Bodker-Enghoff, J. Richter and K. Rosenlund (eds), *Fish Osteo-archaeology Meeting, Copenhagen 28th-29th August 1981*, 4–5. Copenhagen: ICAZ Fish Remains Working Group.

Jones, A. 1988. Fish bones from excavations in the cemetery of St Mary Bishophill Junior, in O'Connor 1988, 126–131.

Jones, A. 1996. Fishes, in May 1996, 164–165.

Jones, G.G. 1983. The medieval animal bones, in D. Allen and C.H. Dalwood, Iron Age occupation, a middle Saxon cemetery, and 12th to 19th century urban occupation: excavations in George Street, Aylesbury, 1981, *Records of Buckinghamshire* 25, 31–44 (1–60).

Jones, G.G. 1988. The Iron Age animal bones, in D. Allen, Excavations at Bierton, a late Iron Age 'Belgic' settlement, Roman Villa and 12th-18th century manorial complex, *Records of Buckinghamshire* 28, 32–39 (1–120).

Jones, R. 1977. Animal bones, in K. Smith, The excavation of Winklebury Camp, Basingstoke, Hampshire, *Proceedings of the Prehistoric Society* 43, 58–69 (31–129).

Jones, R. 1978. The animal bones, in D.A. Jackson and T.M. Ambrose, Excavations at Wakerley, Northants, 1972–75, *Britannia* 9, 235–241 (115–242).

Jones, R., Langley, P. and Wall, S. 1985. The animal bones from the 1977 excavations, in J. Hinchliffe and C.S. Green, *Excavations at Brancaster 1974 and 1977*, 132–174. Dereham: East Anglian Archaeology Report 23.

Jones, R., Levitan, B., Stevens, P. and Malim, T. 1985. *Clay Lane, Northamptonshire. The Vertebrate Remains.* London: English Heritage Ancient Monuments Laboratory Report 4811.

Jones, R., Sly, J., Beech, M. and Parfitt, S. 1987. *Burgh, Suffolk: The Vertebrate Remains.* London: English Heritage Ancient Monuments Laboratory Report 14/87.

Jones, R., Sly, J., Beech, M. and Parfitt, S. 1988. The animal bones, in E. Martin, *Burgh: The Iron Age and Roman Enclosure*, 66–67. Ipswich: East Anglian Archaeology Report 40.

Jope, M. 1958. The animal remains from the late Bronze Age-early Iron Age level at Brigg Brickyard, Lincolnshire, in A.G. Smith, The context of some late Bronze Age and early Iron Age remains from Lincolnshire, *Proceedings of the Prehistoric Society* 24, 84 (78–84).

Kenward, H., Hall, A. and Jones, A. 1986. *Environmental evidence from a Roman well and Anglian pits in the legionary fortress.* London: The Archaeology of York 14/5.

King, J.M. 1987. The animal bones, in G.B. Dannell and J.P. Wild,

Longthorpe II. The Military Works-Depot: an Episode in Landscape History, 184–194. London: Britannia Monograph 8.

Laarman, F.J. 1996. The zoological remains, in L.I. Kooistra (ed.), *Borderland Farming. Possibilities and Limitations of Farming in the Roman Period and Early Middle Ages between the Rhine and Meuse*, 343–357. Unpublished Ph.D. thesis, University of Leiden.

Lauwerier, R.C.G.M. 1988. *Animals in Roman times in the Dutch eastern river area.* 's-Gravenhage: Nederlandse Oudheden 12.

Lauwerier, R.C.G.M. 2001. Archeozoologie, in R.M. van Heeringen and E.M. Theunissen (eds), *Kwaliteitsbepalend onderzoek ten behoeve van het duurzaam behoud van neolithische terreinen in West-Friesland en de Kop van Noord-Holland*, 174–210. Amersfoort: Nederlandse Archeologische Rapporten 21–1.

Lauwerier, R.C.G.M. and Laarman, F.J. 1999. Dierlijk botmateriaal, in J.K.A. Hagers and M.M. Sier (eds), *Castricum-Oosterbuurt, bewoningssporen uit de Romeinse tijd en middeleeuwen*, 129–151, 226–251. Amersfoort: Rapportage Archeologische Monumentenzorg 53.

Lawrence, P. 1986. Zoological evidence. Animal bones, in T. Gregory and D. Gurney (eds), *Excavations at Thornham, Wareham, Wighton and Caistor St Edmund, Norfolk*, 31. Dereham: East Anglian Archaeology Report 30.

Legge, A.J. 1991. The animal bones, in I.M. Stead, *Iron Age Cemeteries in East Yorkshire*, 140–147. London: English Heritage Archaeological Report 22.

Legge, A.J. and Dorrington, E.J. 1985. The animal bones, in N.E. France and B.M. Gobel, *The Romano-British Temple at Harlow, Essex*, 122–133. Harlow: West Essex Archaeological Group.

Legge, A, Williams, J. and Williams, P. 1988. Animal remains from Blackhorse Road, Letchworth, in J. Moss-Eccardt, Archaeological investigations in the Letchworth area, 1958–1974, *Proceedings of the Cambridge Antiquarian Society* 77, 90–95 (35–105).

Lentacker, A., Ervynck, A. and Van Neer, W. 2004. The symbolic meaning of the cock. The animal remains from the *mithraeum* at Tienen, in M. Martens and G. De Boe (eds), *Roman Mithraism: the Evidence of the Small Finds*, 57–80. Brussels and Tienen: Archeologie in Vlaanderen Monografie 4.

Lentacker, A., Van Neer, W. and Pigière, F. forthcoming. L'étude archéozoologique du site du quai Marché-aux-poissons/CV 12 à Tournai, in R. Brulet and L. Verslype (eds), *L'Escaut à Tournai au fil du temps. Les fouilles et surveillances archéologiques de travaux de pose de collecteurs d'eaux usées le long de l'Escaut à Tournai.* Louvain-la-Neuve: Publications d'Histoire de l'Art et d'Archéologie de l'Université Catholique de Louvain, Collection d'Archéologie Joseph Mertens XIV.

Levine, M.A. 1986. The vertebrate fauna from Meare East 1982, *Somerset Levels Papers* 12, 61–71.

Levitan, B. 1983. The animal remains, in A. Saville, *Uley Bury and Norbury Hillforts*, Fiche C6–D5. Bristol: Western Archaeological Trust Monograph 5.

Levitan, B. 1992. The vertebrate remains, in D. Knight, Excavations of an Iron Age settlement at Gamston, Nottinghamshire, *Transactions of the Thoroton Society* 96, 79 (16–90).

Locker, A. 1979. Animal bones, in D.S. Neale, Excavations at Little Somborne and Ashley, *Proceedings of the Hampshire Field Club and Archaeological Society* 36, 141 (91–144).

Locker, A. 1985. *Rainham Moor Hall Farm – animal bones.* London: English Heritage Ancient Monuments Laboratory Report 4577.

Locker, A. 1990. The mammal, bird and fish bones, in D.S. Neal, A. Wardle and J. Hunn, *Excavation of the Iron Age, Roman and Medieval Settlement at Gorhambury, St Albans*, 205–212. London: English Heritage Archaeological Report 14.

Locker, A. 1992. Animal bone, in S. Woodiwiss (ed.), *Iron Age and Roman Salt Production and the Medieval Town of Droitwich*, 172–181. London: Council for British Archaeology Research Report 81.

Locker, A. 1994. *The Fish Bones from Excavation at Winchester Palace, Southwark, 1983.* Unpublished report, Southwark and Lambeth Excavation Committee.

Lovett, J. 1990. Animal bone, in J. Dinn and J. Evans, Aston Mill Farm, Kemerton: excavation of a ring-ditch, Middle Iron Age enclosures and a Grubenhaus, *Transactions of the Worcestershire Archaeology Society* (Ser. 3) 12, 48–53 (5–66).

Luff, R. 1988. The animal bones, in T.J. Wilkinson (ed.), *Archaeology and Environment in South Essex: Rescue Archaeology along the Grays By-pass, 1979/80*, 99. Chelmsford: East Anglian Archaeology Report 42.

Maltby, J.M. 1981. Animal bone, in S.M. Davies, Excavations at Old Down Farm, Andover, *Proceedings of the Hampshire Field Club Archaeological Society* 37, 147–153 (81–163).

Maltby, J.M. 1985. The animal bones, in P.J. Fasham, *The Prehistoric Settlement at Winnall Down, Winchester*, 97–112. Winchester: Hampshire Field Club Monograph 2.

Maltby, J.M. 1995. Animal bone, in G. Wainwright and M. Davies, *Balksbury Camp, Hampshire: excavations 1973 and 1981*, 83–87. London: English Heritage Archaeological Report 4.

Martin, E. 1993. *Settlements on Hill-tops: Seven Prehistoric Sites in Suffolk.* Ipswich: East Anglian Archaeology Report 65.

May, J. 1996. *Dragonby. Report on Excavations at an Iron Age and Romano-British Settlement in North Lincolnshire.* Oxford: Oxbow Monograph 61.

Millard, L. 1970. Animal bones, in D. Mynard, An Iron Age enclosure at Ravenstone, Buckinghamshire, *Records of Buckinghamshire* 18, 410–411 (393–413).

Miller, T.E. and Miller, M. 1981. The M11 western by-pass: three sites near Cambridge, 3. Edmundsoles, Haslingfield, *Proceedings of the Cambridge Antiquarian Society* 71, 41–73.

Monk, J. 1978. The animal bone, in S. Johnson, Excavations at Hayton Roman Fort, 1975, *Britannia* 9, 99–103 (57–114).

Murphy, P., Albarella, U., Germany, M. and Locker, A. 2000. Production, import and status: biological remains from a late Roman farm a Great Holts Farm, Boreham, Essex, UK, *Environmental Archaeology* 5, 35–48.

Noddle B. 1979. *Animal bones from Garton Slack.* London: English Heritage Ancient Monuments Laboratory Report 2754.

O'Connor, T.P. 1988. *Bones from the General Accident Site, Tanner Row.* York: The Archaeology of York 15/2.

Orr, C. 1974. The animal bones, in J.H. Williams (ed.), *Two Iron Age sites in Northampton*, 43. Northampton: Northampton Development Corporation Archaeological Monograph 1.

Partridge, C. 1979. Excavations at Puckeridge and Braughing 1975–9, *Hertfordshire Archaeology* 7, 28–132.

Partridge, C. 1981. *Skeleton Green. A Late Iron Age Romano-British Site.* London: Britannia Monograph 2.

Parker Pearson, M. 2000. Ancestors, bones and stones in Neolithic and early Bronze Age Britain and Ireland, in A. Ritchie (ed.),

Neolithic Orkney in its European Context, 203–214. Cambridge: McDonald Institute.

Peters, J. 1987. De dierlijke resten uit de Romeinse nederzetting van Bredene II, in H. Thoen (ed.), *De Romeinen langs de Vlaamse kust*, 67–69. Brussel: Gemeentekrediet.

Phillipson, D.W. 1963. Faunal report, in D.A. White, Excavations at the War Ditches, Cherry Hinton, 1961–2, *Proceedings of the Cambridge Antiquarian Society* 56, 29 (9–29).

Rackham, D.J. 1978. Skeletal material, in G. Jobey, Iron Age and Romano-British settlements on Kennel Hall Knowe, North Tynedale, Northumberland, *Archaeology Aeliana* (Ser. 5) 6, 22–23 (1–28).

Rackham, D.J. 1987. The animal bone, in D.H. Heslop, *The Excavation of an Iron Age Settlement at Thorpe Thewles, Cleveland, 1980–82*, 99–109. London: Council for British Archaeology Research Report 65.

Rackham, D.J. 1982. Faunal remains, in C.C. Haselgrove and V.L. Allon, An Iron Age settlement at West House, Coxhoe, County Durham, *Archaeology Aeliana* (Ser. 5) 10, 43–44 (25–51).

Rackham, D.J. forthcoming. The animal bones, in C. Haselgrove (ed.), *Cartimandua's Capital? The 1984–89 Excavations and Related Research on the Iron Age and Early Roman Site at Stanwick, North Yorkshire.*

Richards, M.P. and Hedges, R.E.M. 1999. A Neolithic revolution? New evidence of diet in the British Neolithic, *Antiquity* 73, 891–897.

Robeerst, J.M.M. 2000. Onderzoek naar de archeozoölogische resten van Roomburg, in T. Hazenberg (ed.), *Leiden-Roomburg 1995–1997. Archeologisch onderzoek naar het kanaal van Corbulo en de vicus van het castellum Matilo*. Amersfoort: Rapportage Archeologische Monumentenzorg 77.

Sadler, P. 1990. The animal bone from the Iron Age ditch, in I.J. Stewart, Coldharbour Farm, Aylesbury, an archaeological excavation 1990, *Records of Buckinghamshire* 30, 100–103 (91–105).

Sadler, P. 1998. Animal remains, in D. Bonner, Investigations at the County Museum, Aylesbury, *Records of Buckinghamshire* 38, 64–78 (1–89).

Scott, S.A. 1988. The animal bones, in M.J. Darling and M.J. Jones, The early settlement of Lincoln, *Britannia* 19, 43–45 (1–57).

Sheppard, P. 1978. Animal remains, in R. Hartridge, Excavations at the prehistoric and Romano-British site on Slonk Hill, Shoreham, Sussex, *Sussex Archaeological Collections* 116, 133–140 (69–142).

Simoons, F.J. 1994. *Eat Not this Flesh* (2nd edn). Wisconsin: University of Wisconsin Press.

Simpson, W.G., Gurney, D.A., Neve, J. and Pryor, F.M.M. 1993. *The Fenland Project, No. 7: Excavations in Peterborough and the Lower Welland Valley 1960–1969*. Peterborough: East Anglian Archaeology Report 61.

Smith, C. 1990. Excavations at Dod Law West hillfort, Northumberland, *Northern Archaeology* 9, 1–55.

Smoothy, M. 1990. The human and animal remains, in C. Crossan, M. Smoothy and C. Wallace, Salvage recording of Iron Age and Roman remains at Ickleton Road, Great Chesterford, Essex, *Essex Archaeology and History* 21, 16 (11–18).

Stallibrass, S. 1987. The animal bones, in M. Millet and S. McGrail, The archaeology of the Hasholme logboat, *Archaeological Journal* 144, 139–144 (69–155).

Stallibrass, S. 1997. *Creyke Beck, Cottingham, North Yorks, Yorkshire CBC97. Assessment of Animal Bone Recovered from Evaluation Trenches at an Iron Age Settlement Site.* Durham: Durham Environmental Archaeology Reports 38/97.

Stallibrass, S. 1998. *Chevington Chapel, Northumberland. Vertebrate Remains from Prehistoric (late Iron Age/native Romano British), Medieval and Post-medieval Deposits.* Durham: Durham Environmental Archaeology Report 2/98.

Therkorn, L.L. 1984. *A Report on the Faunal Remains from Velsen Hoogovens (Excavations 1963–1968) and some Methodological Considerations.* Amsterdam: A.E. van Giffen Instituut voor Prae- en Protohistorie, Universiteit van Amsterdam.

Thoen, H. 1987. *De Romeinen langs de Vlaamse kust.* Brussels: Gemeentekrediet.

Thomas, J. 2003. Thoughts on the 'repacked' Neolithic revolution, *Antiquity* 77, 67–74.

Vanderhoeven, A., Ervynck, A. and Van Neer, W. 1993. De dierlijke en menselijke resten, in A. Vanderhoeven, G. Vynckier and P. Vynckier, Het oudheidkundig bodemonderzoek aan de Veemarkt te Tongeren (prov. Limburg). Eindverslag 1988, *Archeologie in Vlaanderen* 3, 177–186.

Vanderhoeven, A., Vynckier, G., Ervynck, A. and Cooremans, B. 1992. Het oudheidkundig bodemonderzoek aan de Kielenstraat te Tongeren (prov. Limburg). Interimverslag 1990–1993. Deel 1. De vóór-Flavische bewoning, *Archeologie in Vlaanderen* 2, 89–145.

Van Dijk, J. 1992. *Melkboeren in Midden Delfland; Het zooarcheologisch onderzoek van botmateriaal uit de Midden IJzertijd van de vindplaatsen M.D. 15.04 en M.D. 16.59.* Amsterdam: Bijvakscriptie oecologische archeologie, A.E. van Giffen Instituut voor Prae- en Protohistorie, Universiteit van Amsterdam.

Van Heeringen, R.M. 1992. The Iron Age in the Western Netherlands, V. Synthesis, *Berichten van de Rijksdienst voor het Oudheidkundig Bodemonderzoek* 39, 157–268.

Van Heeringen, R.M. and Theunissen, E.M. (eds) 2001. *Kwaliteitsbepalend onderzoek ten behoeve van het duurzaam behoud van neolithische terreinen in West-Friesland en de Kop van Noord-Holland.* Amersfoort: Nederlandse Archeologische Rapporten 21–3.

Van Impe, L., In 't Ven, I., De Paepe, P., Ervynck, A. and Desender, K. forthcoming. Invading tribes, advancing forests. A witness to the decline of economic activity in Flanders, circa 200 AD, *Studien zur Sachsenforschung* 15.

Van Neer, W. 1999. Fish remains at Abri du Pape, in J.-M. Léotard, L.G. Straus and M. Otte (eds), *L'Abri du Pape. Bivouacs, enterrements et cachettes sur la Haute Meuse belge: du Mésolithique au Bas Empire Romain*, 129–140. Liège: Études et Recherches Archéologiques de l'Université de Liège 88.

Van Neer, W. and Ervynck, A. 1994. New data on fish remains from Belgian archaeological sites, in W. Van Neer (ed.), *Fish Exploitation in the Past (Proceedings of the 7th Meeting of the ICAZ Fish Remains Working Group)*, 217–229. Tervuren: Annalen van het Koninklijk Museum voor Midden-Afrika, Tervuren, België. Zoologische Wetenschappen n° 274.

Van Neer, W. and Ervynck, A. 2004. Remains of traded fish in archaeological sites: indicators of status, or bulk food? in S.J. O'Day, W. Van Neer and A. Ervynck (eds), *Behaviour Behind Bones. The Zooarchaeology of Ritual, Religion, Status and Identity*, 203–214. Oxford: Oxbow Books.

Van Neer, W., Ervynck, A., Lentacker, A., Crombé, P., Sergant, J.,

Perdaen, Y., Van Strydonck, M. and Van Roeyen, J.-P. 2001. Dierenresten uit een vroege Swifterbant-nederzetting te Doel-Deurganckdok (Vlaanderen, België): jachtwild, maar vooral veel vis, *Notae Praehistoricae* 21, 85–96.

Van Neer, W. and Lentacker, A. 1994. New archaeozoological evidence for the consumption of locally-produced fish sauce in the northern provinces of the Roman Empire, *Archaeofauna* 3, 53–62.

Westley, B. 1970. App II. Bones from Ivinghoe Beacon, in M.A. Cotton and S.S. Frere, Ivinghoe Beacon excavations 1963–5, *Records of Buckinghamshire* 18 (3), 252–260 (187–260).

Wheeler, A. 1981. Fish bones, in Partridge 1981, 242–243.

Williams, R.J. 1993. *Pennyland and Hartigans: two Iron Age sites in Milton Keynes*. Aylesbury: Buckinghamshire Archaeological Society Monograph 4.

Wilson, R. 1980. Bone and shell report, in J. Hinchcliffe and R. Thomas, Archaeological investigations at Appleford, *Oxoniensia* 45, 84–89 (9–111).

Wilson, R. 1993. Reports on the bones and oyster shell, in T.G. Allen and M. Robinson, *The Prehistoric Landscape and Iron Age Enclosed Settlement at Mingies Ditch, Hardwick-with-Yelford, Oxon.*, 123–145. Oxford: Thames Valley Landscapes Monograph 2.

Wilson, R. 1999. The animal bone and shell, in J. Muir and M. Roberts, *Excavations at Wyndyke Furlong, Abingdon, Oxfordshire, 1994*, 58–60. Oxford: Oxford Archaeological Unit.

Whitehouse, R. and Whitehouse, D. 1974. Fauna, in S.C. Stanford, *Croft Ambrey, Hereford*, 215–222. Leominster: Privately published.

Yule, B. 1989. Excavations at Winchester Palace, Southwark, *London Archaeologist* 6 (2), 31–39.

Zeiler, J.T. 1996. *De faunaresten van Schagen Witte Paal III (1e-3e eeuw n. Chr.). Tussentijdse rapportage van het archeozoologisch onderzoek*. Groningen: ArchaeoBone Rapport 8.

Zeiler, J.T. 2001. Archeozoologie, in M.M. Sier and C.W. Koot (eds), *Archeologie in de Betuweroute Kesteren-De Woerd. Bewoningssporen uit de IJzertijd en de Romeinse tijd*, 217–293. Amersfoort: Rapportage Archeologische Monumentenzorg 82.

The production and consumption of cereals: a question of scale

Marijke van der Veen and Glynis Jones

Introduction

In their paper *Understanding The British Iron Age: An Agenda for Action*, Haselgrove *et al.* (2001, iv) identify regionality and the nature of socio-economic changes as two of the five key areas of future research on the British Iron Age. As farming formed the basis of all societies in this period, and as most settlements were farmsteads and most people were farmers (*ibid.*, 10), any assessment of regional differences and socio-economic change will have to include an assessment of farming practices. At a basic level this concerns an assessment of the scale of agricultural production (e.g. ability to produce a surplus, intensive/extensive cultivation regimes) and of the level of specialisation (e.g. crops versus animals, farming versus non-farming settlements). It goes without saying that the success of such assessments hinges on choosing the right methodology and the right scale of analysis and interpretation.

To date, much discussion of intra- and inter-regional variation in Iron Age crop production has focussed on the level of specialisation, namely the identification of producer and consumer sites. A model developed by M. Jones (1985) and applied to sites in the upper Thames valley was the first apparently successful attempt to identify settlements which produced their own crops (arable or producer sites) and those which received crops that had been grown elsewhere (pastoral or consumer sites). This pioneering work brought archaeobotanical data into the forefront of mainstream archaeological debate and has stimulated much of the more recent research in this area. The model aimed to facilitate easy comparison between sites and monitor the movement of arable produce across the landscape, and the results allowed M. Jones (1996, 35) to suggest the existence of 'neighbourhood groups of agrarian sites engaged in a common network of plant production and consumption'. While the main assumptions underlying the model and the method of constructing the diagrams were criticised early on (G. Jones 1987; Van der Veen 1987; 1991; 1992, chapter 8), the model, and the conclusions drawn from it, are still widely used.

In this paper we argue that the problems associated with M. Jones' model are such that it cannot be used to distinguish between producer and consumer sites, and that recent explanations of differences between archaeobotanical assemblages at sites in the upper Thames valley (Campbell 2000; Stevens 2003) are also flawed. Here we briefly summarise M. Jones' model, and the criticisms it has received, and review the more recent interpretations of the observed site differences. We then approach the problem from a different angle, proposing levels of analysis and interpretation more appropriate to the data available and the questions posed. Finally, we put forward our own interpretation of the patterning observed.

As the model is based on the interpretation of charred plant remains, our arguments inevitably involve detailed consideration of the formation processes at work. In this paper we try to put our case without recourse to complex archaeobotanical jargon, to keep the paper accessible to a wider readership. Some basic features of cereals and relevant terminology do, however, need to be explained first.

Cereal types and terminology

In the following discussions, we make a distinction between emmer and spelt wheat on the one hand and bread wheat and barley on the other. The first two cereals are 'glume' wheats, which, when threshed, break up into individual segments (spikelets) with the grain still tightly enclosed by the surrounding chaff (glumes). The last two are 'free-threshing' cereals, the ears of which, when threshed, disintegrate into free grain and chaff (Fig. 1). The glume wheats therefore require a further 'dehusking' operation to release the grain from the glumes, which is not necessary for the free-threshing cereals. Furthermore, for the glume wheats, the chaff elements most likely to survive archaeologically (because of their robustness) are the glume bases, while similarly, for free-threshing cereals, the central 'stalk' (rachis) is the part of the ear most likely to survive.

When we use the term 'producer site', we follow M. Jones' original definition (1985) of a site growing and harvesting its own crops. This is effectively the same as his later definition of 'biological' production (the production of grain by the plant itself), rather than his definition of 'economic' production, which includes all crop processing activities including the later grain cleaning stages (M. Jones 1996, 34), and which tends to blur his earlier distinction between consumer and producer sites. By consumption we mean the use of these crops, mostly their consumption as food, as opposed to 'everything that humans do' (*ibid.*). For the purposes of this paper, therefore, the inhabitants of producer sites are cultivators (as well as consumers of crops), who may or may not export part of their produce, whereas consumer sites import their crops from elsewhere, although they may process them further to obtain clean grain (especially with the glume wheats).

Throughout the paper we will use the terms grain-rich, chaff-rich and weed-rich to refer to the *relative* quantities of grain, chaff and weed seeds. Where large *absolute* quantities are indicated we have described these as 'large'. Furthermore, the term 'assemblage' will be used to indicate a site assemblage of archaeobotanical remains, while the term 'sample' will be used to refer to the plant remains recovered from a *single* archaeobotanical sample.

M. Jones' archaeobotanical model of production and consumption

The model

The model relies on the interpretation of 'triangular diagrams' which display the broad characteristics of charred plant assemblages from individual sites (M. Jones 1985). M. Jones made the convincing case that the occurrence of grain-rich samples required an explanation, as grain is that part of the harvest least likely to be wasted, and argued that the 'most likely place for this unlikely event to occur is at its place of production' (*ibid.*, 120). By plotting the relative proportions of cereal grain, chaff, and weed seeds onto triangular diagrams, on a sample-by-sample basis, and giving a measure of seed density, the overall assemblage from each site could be characterised. Grain-rich sites (i.e. Ashville and Mount Farm) were interpreted as producer sites, and sites poor in grain (but rich in weeds and/or chaff) as consumer sites (i.e. Smith's Field and Claydon Pike). Danebury is different from both of these categories in terms of both composition and density, and was interpreted as being engaged in a 'broad range of agricultural activities' (*ibid.*, 121). Finally, sites where the samples are concentrated in the centre of the diagram (with approximately equal proportions of grains, chaff and weeds; e.g. Iron Age sites north of the Tyne) were seen as 'self-contained units' (M. Jones 1996, 35).

The critique

While the aspiration of the model was widely welcomed, three aspects were criticised from the start. Firstly, in the construction of the diagrams the content of each sample is summarised without regard for context or species composition. With regard to the latter, any variation in the abundance of glume wheats (emmer or spelt wheat) versus free-threshing cereals (bread wheat or barley) affects the location of samples in the diagram (G. Jones 1987; Van der Veen 1991; 1992, 98). This is due to differences in the likelihood of chaff from these two types of cereal being found archaeologically. The chaff of free-threshing cereals is largely represented by rachis remains which are removed early in the processing sequence, often off-site, and is thus relatively rarely represented in archaeobotanical assemblages. The chaff of glume wheats, on the other hand, is largely composed of glume bases which are removed at a later stage of processing, often on a day-to-day basis in a household context. Thus, variations in the proportion of chaff as indicated in a triangular diagram may reflect variations in the relative importance of emmer and spelt wheat versus bread wheat and barley, rather than variations in subsistence strategy. Secondly, the assertion that grain is wasted more frequently on producer sites than on consumer sites is questionable (G. Jones 1987; Van der Veen 1991; 1992, 98). It has been argued that, on the contrary, producer sites are characterised by the waste from early stages of crop processing (straw and rachis) and consumption by grain-rich samples (Hillman 1981; 1984a). The burning of grain usually represents an accident, and accidents can occur on all types of site (G. Jones 2000). Finally, the diagrams make no reference to context or crop processing stage: variations between sites in the contexts or stages sampled (e.g. storage areas versus ditch fills and/or products versus by-products)

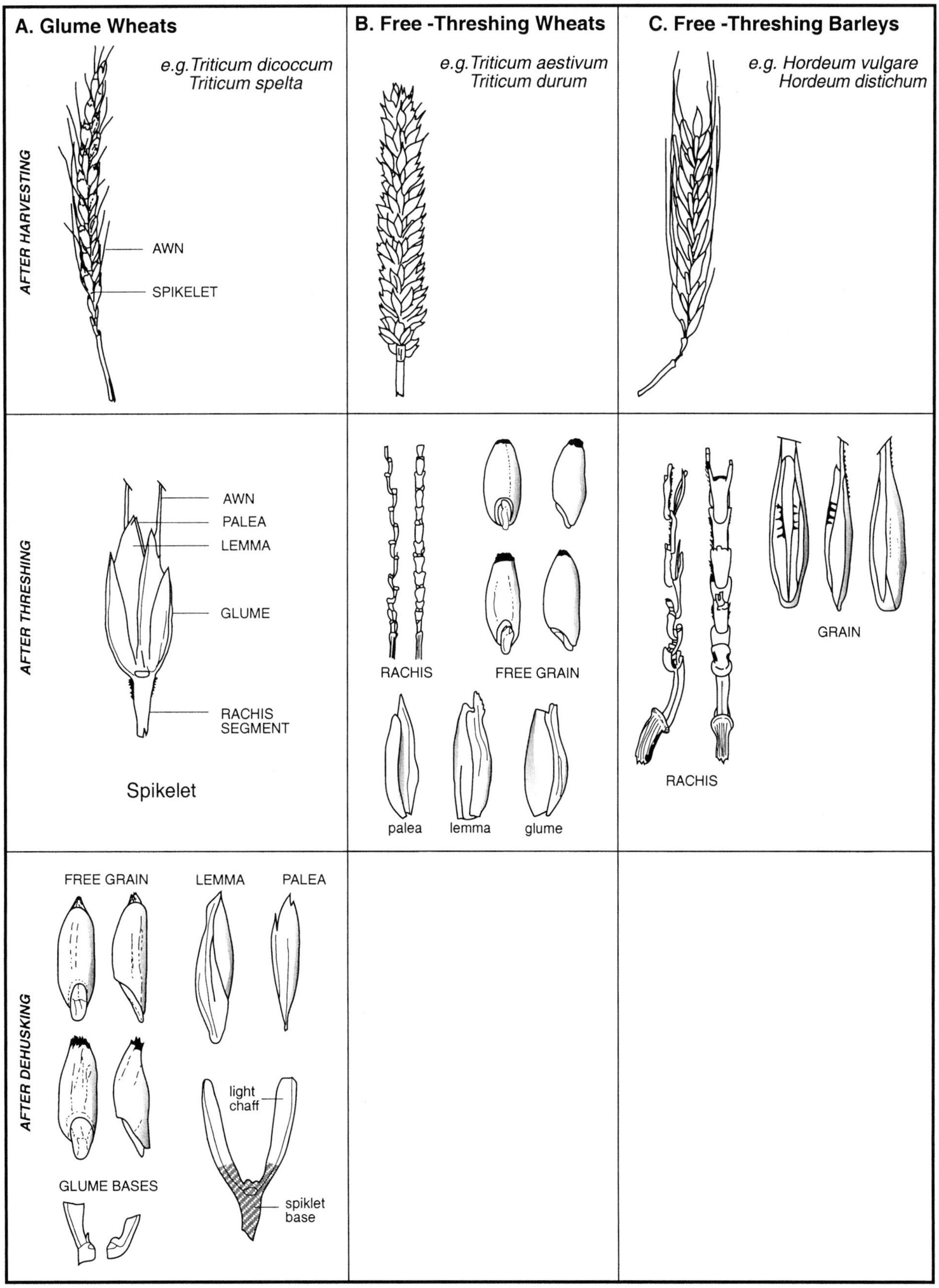

Fig. 1. Effects of crop processing on glume wheats and free-threshing cereals (after Charles 1984). Note that hulled barley is a free-threshing cereal; it behaves in the same way as bread wheat during threshing (the 'hulls' refer to the lemma and palea which are fused with the grain, not the glumes).

Model		Samples rich in grain	Samples rich in chaff/weed
M. Jones 1985	*interpretation*	producer site	consumer site
	reason	grain wasted at harvest time	grain carefully conserved
Campbell 2000	*interpretation*	fodder scarce	fodder plentiful
	reason	chaff used as fodder	chaff used as fuel
Stevens 2003	*interpretation*	communal storage	household storage
	reason	storage as 'semi-clean spikelets'	storage as 'partially threshed ears'
Van der Veen and Jones	*interpretation*	large scale	small scale
	reason	accidental charring of products	by-products of day-to-day processing

Table 1. Alternative interpretations of grain and chaff/weed-rich assemblages.

may affect the position of samples in the diagram; for example, storage areas house the cleaned products of crop processing and so are likely to be richer in grain than ditch fills receiving waste mainly from the by-products of crop cleaning (Van der Veen 1992, 98).

Problems with the application of the model

Whenever the model has been applied to other sites, analysts have struggled to interpret the patterns found. The classification provided by the model frequently did not match the expectation based on other information. M. Jones encountered such a situation himself at Maiden Castle, where the assemblage was dominated by chaff (especially glumes) and to a lesser extent weeds, even though grain-rich samples might reasonably have been expected, given the type of the site: a hillfort, like Danebury, with ample storage facilities (Palmer and Jones 1991). This discrepancy was explained by: (1) a sampling factor (the area excavated was small and grain-rich deposits might have lain outside this area); (2) a taphonomic factor (locally poor preservation of grain); and (3) a cultural factor (scale of storage smaller than at Danebury) (*ibid.*, 1991, 136). In fact, in the original study, the evidence that Danebury was a site supplied with crops from various parts of its territory was based primarily on the presence of weed species representing a mixture of ecological types (M. Jones 1985), rather than on the relative proportions of grain, chaff and weed. The suggestion that this grain would then leave Danebury in a clean state, introduces a methodological problem. The sites receiving this grain would be characterised by clean grain only, similar to the grain-rich assemblages considered by M. Jones to be typical of producer sites, making the two types of site difficult to distinguish.

Similarly, the application of the model to Iron Age settlements in north-east England led to all sites south of the Tyne being classified as consumer sites, which would have resulted in a complete absence of producer sites in that region (Van der Veen 1992, chapter 8). Conversely, the Roman fort at South Shields was classified as a producer site, even though the assemblage was derived from a granary destroyed by fire at a classic consumer site (Van der Veen 1992, chapter 8).

Alternative interpretations of variation in archaeobotanical site assemblages

Recently, two researchers have offered interesting alternative interpretations of the patterns observed by M. Jones, which provide new insights into the possible nature and organisation of Iron Age settlement and stimulate further debate. We review both of these interpretations here.

Use of chaff as fodder

Campbell (2000) applied the model to several Iron Age sites excavated as part of the Danebury Environs Project and reviewed the evidence from the upper Thames valley. She suggests that M. Jones' producer and consumer sites may, in fact, all be growing their own crops, and relates some of the observed differences to variations in the need for fodder (Table 1). The inhabitants of the second gravel terrace, where pasture was thought to be scarce, may have used chaff as fodder rather than as fuel, and hence created charred assemblages low in chaff. Moreover, high-status sites with more animals to feed over the winter (she mentions Danebury and Suddern Farm as examples) may also have used all the available chaff as fodder, rather than fuel.

This interpretation is attractive in that it offers a possible explanation for the lack of chaff at some sites, in particular at M. Jones' producer sites, which – if they were producing (and presumably partly consuming) their own crops – would be expected to generate considerable quantities of chaff. It does not, however, explain why some samples are dominated by large quantities of grain, a commodity that should not, in the normal course of events, be deliberately burnt. If grain cleaning by-products were used as fodder, any grain that was inadvertently removed in this way would be consumed by the animals along with the chaff. This explanation is therefore partial, at best, and some other explanation must be sought for the presence of grain-rich assemblages.

Communal versus household storage

Stevens (2003) reinterpreted the assemblages used in M. Jones' original model alongside some newly studied sites from the upper Thames valley, and related the differences to the stage at which crops were put into storage which, in turn, may reflect storage at a communal or household level (Table 1). He argued that cleaning waste from wheat stored as 'clean or semi-clean spikelets' led to assemblages rich in grain compared to weed seeds (as at M. Jones' producer sites), and were characteristic of communal storage. Conversely, cleaning waste from wheat stored as 'unsieved spikelets'[1] led to assemblages poor in grain compared to weed (as at M. Jones' consumer sites), and were characteristic of household storage. While the concept of storing sieved versus unsieved spikelets is an interesting one to explore (and could indeed have some connection with household or communal storage practices), it does not explain the pattern observed. Both forms of storage involve whole spikelets, and the quantity of grain relative to chaff (glumes) would therefore be the same in both cases.

Stevens maintains that the samples from his sites consist primarily of the processing waste associated with the routine, day-to-day dehusking and cleaning of glume wheat spikelets, after these have been taken out of storage (and that samples rich in grain result from a bias against the preservation of chaff in this type of processing waste; cf. Boardman and Jones 1990). However, contrary to what Stevens says, this would generate samples rich in weed seeds relative to chaff at sites where unsieved spikelets were stored (i.e. samples in the bottom left corner of a triangular diagram; see Fig. 2b), and samples rich in chaff relative to weed seeds where sieved spikelets were stored (i.e. samples in the bottom right corner of a triangular diagram; see Fig. 2c). If there were a bias against chaff, because it is preferentially destroyed compared to grain, some of the chaff-rich samples would appear higher in the triangle. In fact, however, neither of the sites (Ashville and Mount Farm) that Stevens classifies as storing cleaned spikelets (indicating communal storage, the equivalent of M. Jones' 'producer' sites) have samples rich in chaff compared to weed seeds whereas some of the samples from sites (e.g. Gravelly Guy and Yarnton) classified as storing unsieved spikelets (indicating 'household' storage, the equivalent of M. Jones' 'consumer' sites) do (Stevens 2003, fig. 3). This is the opposite of expectations based on his model.

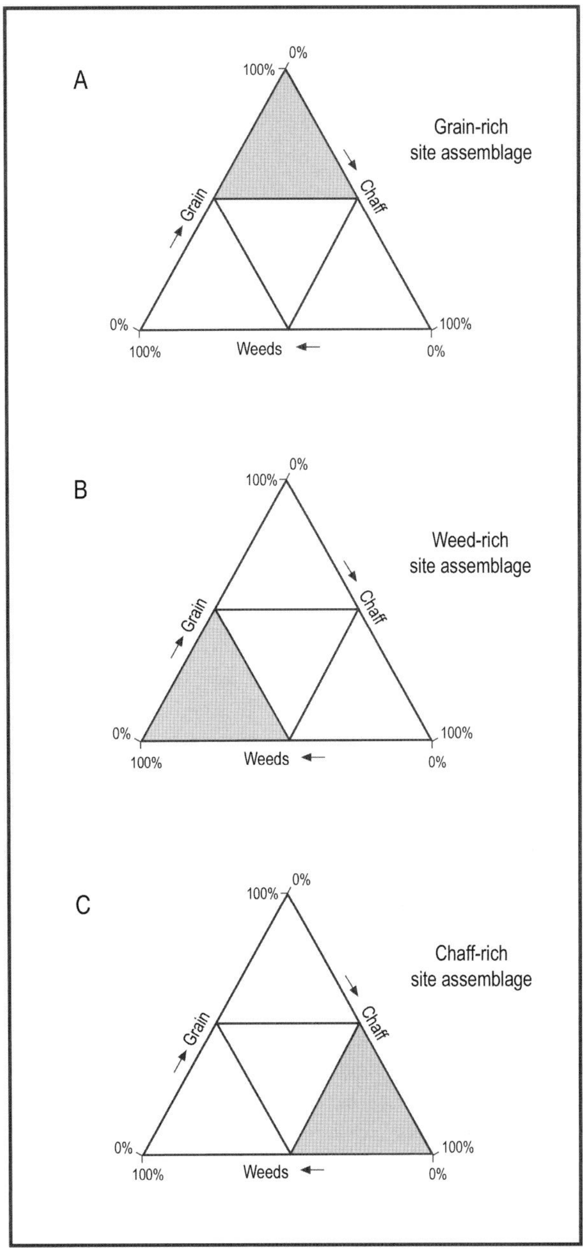

Fig. 2. Different types of charred plant assemblages. Shaded areas indicate the position (in the plot) of the majority of samples in each type of assemblage.

Formation of the archaeobotanical record and the scale of agricultural production/ consumption

It will be clear from the above discussion that we cannot expect a simple relationship between the observed patterning in the charred seed assemblage and the status of the sites in terms of production or consumption, nor do the alternative interpretations put forward by Campbell (2000) and Stevens (2003) explain the observed differences between sites. Nevertheless, patterning in the crop, chaff, and weed components exists in the archaeological record and the desire to interpret its meaning remains. We contend that an appreciation of the formation processes underlying the charred archaeobotanical record will help in understanding the patterning.

With the exception of deliberate offerings or destruction due to conflict, charring events occur in one of three circumstances: (1) when the by-products of grain dehusking and cleaning are deliberately burnt as either fuel or waste; (2) when an accident occurs during some process involving fire, e.g. during parching, drying or cooking; and (3) when a building containing stored produce catches fire. The first circumstance mostly arises from day-to-day processing immediately prior to consumption and is likely to yield samples rich in chaff and/or weed seeds rather than grain. Cooking will often involve 'processed' grain (e.g. cracked wheat or flour) or cooking with water, neither of which is likely to generate whole, charred grains. Drying/parching and destruction in store therefore remain the most likely events leading to samples rich in charred grain, and more likely (at least for large grain-rich samples) than either the 'wastage' of grain proposed by M. Jones or the preservation bias against chaff in processing waste proposed by Stevens (above). Thus, although most archaeobotanical material is probably generated during the day-to-day processing of cereals, some is generated during infrequent accidents.

The day-to-day processing of cereals takes place at all sites (producers and consumers), and the presence of samples consisting primarily of chaff and/or weed seeds is, therefore, to be expected at all sites. In contrast, the occurrence of large grain-rich deposits (as M. Jones 1985 says) needs explanation The answer to the question, 'where are accidents involving parching, drying and storage most likely to occur?' is that they will tend to occur in places where these activities are regularly carried out, i.e. where grain is handled in bulk. Hillman (1984a) suggested that quantities of charred grain most commonly occur on large sites, whether large producers (e.g. for a later period, manorial farms) or large consumers, since there is more opportunity at these sites for accidents such as the destruction of a store by fire (or for large scale parching/drying accidents).

A possible exception to this association of grain-rich deposits with accidental charring is the cleaning of storage pits through the deliberate burning of pit linings. This activity could generate grain-rich deposits that were not created by accident. As these pits tend to be associated with the large-scale handling of cereal produce (see below), however, they also point to sites engaged in the bulk handling of grain.

In other words, a predominance of grain-rich samples (interpreted as accidental charring of cleaned products or the deliberate cleaning of storage pits by fire), is far more likely to be an indicator of the *scale* of production and consumption than a means of distinguishing between the two (see also Van der Veen 1987; 1991; 1992, chapter 8). The upper Thames valley 'producer' sites may therefore represent large-scale production and/or consumption, and the 'consumer' sites may represent settlements engaged in small-scale activity relating to cereals.[2] Whether the sites are producers or merely consumers of cereal grain may not be reflected in the chaff : grain ratios because sites that import grain in bulk, and then store and dry it, might well produce plant assemblages very like large-scale producers, and small producers may be indistinguishable from small consumers (Van der Veen 1991).

Levels of archaeobotanical analysis and interpretation

The fact that some archaeobotanical samples are generated during routine activities while others occur primarily by accident also has implications for the level at which archaeobotanical remains should be analysed and interpreted (cf. G. Jones 1991).

Level of analysis

A critical drawback of M. Jones' model is that it interprets a site assemblage 'mechanically' on the basis of broad botanical composition. As we have indicated above, the complexity of the archaeobotanical record is such that only an analysis that takes this into account can hope to succeed. This means that we need to understand the taphonomic pathways of individual samples, primarily from botanical composition but also taking into account archaeological context (Dennell 1974; 1976; Hillman 1981; 1984a; G. Jones 1984; 1987). Only through this type of analysis can a distinction be made between regular, routine activities, of a particular type, and rare accidents, with their likely cause. While at the level of the sample this may be seen as rather mundane in itself, bringing together samples which have first been interpreted individually ultimately provides a more reliable interpretation at the site level and above than does the broad botanical site composition.

We suggest therefore that, rather than using a triangular diagram to summarise the botanical composition of a whole site, methods are first applied to determine the origin of individual samples. This can be achieved through a combined consideration of the ratios of major plant components (grain, chaff, straw and weeds), the *types* of weed accompanying crops, and the circumstances of deposition (see Table 2). Another advantage of this approach is that it allows the calculation of separate chaff : grain ratios for free threshing cereals (rachis internodes : grains) and glume wheats (glume bases : grains), while still allowing the calculation of weed : grain ratios, as it is not possible to determine the association of particular weeds with a

Sample variable	***Sample origin***	
Ratio	*High value*	*Low value*
cereal straw nodes : grains	by-product from early processing stage	grain product
free-threshing rachis internodes : grains	by-product from early processing stage	grain product
glume wheat glume bases : grains	by-product from late processing stage	grain product
weed seeds : cereal grains	by-product from late processing stage	grain product
small : large weed seeds	by-product from sieving	product from sieving or by-product of hand cleaning
number of crop items per litre of deposit	rapid/single deposition (usually result of accident)	slow/repeated deposition (usually day-to-day activity)

Table 2. Variables useful for the identification of crop processing stage, and their likely meaning. For the first three variables, the terms 'high' and 'low' value refer to the degree to which they differ from the ratio in the cereal plant; for the last three variables, they refer to the relative values within the site/region.

particular crop type in a mixed sample (Hillman 1981; 1984a; G. Jones 1984; for applications see G. Jones 1987; Van der Veen 1992; Campbell 2000; Hodgson *et al.* 2001). As different types of weed are removed at each stage of processing, this provides a complementary way of assessing processing stage and is applicable to both glume wheats and free-threshing cereals. This can be achieved through multivariate statistical methods (G. Jones 1984; for applications see G. Jones 1987; Van der Veen 1992; Charles and Bogaard 2001) or, more simply but less conclusively, by calculating ratios, e.g. of small weed seeds : large weed seeds. Circumstances of deposition can be assessed through: (1) the 'density' of crop remains (number of items per litre of deposit), which gives a broad indication of the rate of deposition; and (2) archaeological context, which may provide a clear indication of the nature of the deposit (e.g. a granary) or simply indicate a secondary or tertiary context (e.g. a refuse pit). This method will also help to distinguish between finds of very mixed origin and those derived primarily from one type of activity.

Level of interpretation

If it is accepted that differences between sites in the amount of grain charred are largely due to chance accidents, then the implication is that one cannot expect all sites to provide evidence for such accidents. On a *probabilistic* level, site assemblages dominated by grain may be an indication of large-scale agricultural activity. The assumption that this would inevitably be the case, however, will result in the misinterpretation of some individual sites, such as a site with small-scale storage totally destroyed by fire; or a site with large-scale storage, which happened never to have suffered any fire damage, or where the area excavated lay outside that where grain-rich deposits were dumped (as is suggested for Maiden Castle). To overcome this chance element, it is necessary to interpret charred archaeobotanical site assemblages at a regional level where individual sites make only a limited contribution to the overall pattern. The most useful levels of analysis and interpretation may therefore be those of the individual sample and the broad geographic region, respectively.

Iron Age Britain – scale, regionality, and change

Returning to regionality and socio-economic change, an examination, at a regional level, of the likely reasons for the presence of grain-rich assemblages may tell us more about the nature of early agriculture than whether individual sites were importing grain or producing their own. Grain-rich samples in the Iron Age, for example, have been contrasted with the relative lack of charred grain from Neolithic deposits, and used to suggest that cereals were not an important source of food in the Neolithic period (e.g. Moffett *et al.* 1989; Thomas 1991; Barrett 1994; Edmonds 1997). This has been questioned by several authors (e.g. Cooney 1997; G. Jones 2000; Monk 2000; Rowley-Conwy 2000), who attribute the lack of charred grain in the Neolithic to taphonomic causes and contextual differences; indeed recent evidence suggests that the quantity of cereal grain from Neolithic sites is not substantially less than that from the Iron Age (Jones and Rowley-Conwy forthcoming). If we are correct in interpreting accidentally charred grain-rich samples as representing large-scale production and/or consumption – rather than simply reflecting the relative contribution of cereals to the diet – then any evidence indicating greater quantities of grain in the

Iron Age suggests that arable production in some parts of Britain had moved beyond subsistence and included a considerable degree of surplus production.

The regular occurrences of grain-rich deposits in Iron Age Britain, representing visible surplus production of grain, are, to date, restricted to central and southern Britain (see, for example, M. Jones 1984a; 1985; 1996; Stevens 2003). This distribution is not dissimilar to that of grain storage facilities such as pits and, to a lesser extent, four-post structures (Gent 1983; Cunliffe 1992). While it is true that the geographical distribution of these storage pits is mostly conditioned by the underlying geology (Bradley 1978; Fenton 1983; Cunliffe 1992), and that there are alternative forms of grain storage that leave few if any archaeological traces (Fenton 1983), it is not just their geographical distribution, but also their chronological spread (*c.* 800–100 BC in Britain, *c.* 900–20 BC in northern France; Cunliffe 1992; Gransar 2000) that is strongly suggestive of a link with a particular agricultural or social system. Furthermore, ethnographic evidence suggests that underground grain silos are used for the storage of surplus grain (Fenton 1983), rather than seed corn, although the latter is still the widely held assumption amongst archaeologists (e.g. Reynolds 1974; M. Jones 1984b; Cunliffe 1992; 2000, 130). The short time-span between harvest and sowing for autumn-sown crops such as spelt wheat makes the storage of seed corn in such pits an unlikely investment, other than in periods of major unrest. Moreover, once opened, the grain from these pits needs to be used quickly. The fact that such storage facilities predominate in a certain type of site, i.e. hillforts (Gent 1983; Cunliffe 1992), and that the amount of storage available here often exceeds the needs of the individual site, also points to the practice of surplus production and some form of centralised storage (cf. Sharples 1991; Cunliffe 1992), at least in the earlier Iron Age. By the Middle Iron Age the situation is a little different, as the bulk of the population is then apparently nucleated into the 'developed' hillforts like Danebury and Maiden Castle, rather than dispersed in the immediate environs (see below), but even then storage appears to exceed need.

The unusual plant assemblage (very high density of deposition; grain-rich samples; weeds originating from wide region) and the exceptionally large storage facilities at one of these hillforts (Danebury), led originally to the suggestion that these sites functioned as central places, from which surplus grain was redistributed (Cunliffe 1984, 556–559; M. Jones 1984b; 1985), along the lines of the classic redistributive chiefdoms. Problems with this model were outlined by Hill (1995a), who pointed out that hillforts such as Danebury did not necessarily represent the peak of the social and settlement hierarchy (given the absence of status indicators and presence of storage facilities at non-hillfort sites, amongst other factors). We can now add to this the nature of the plant assemblages at sites in the Danebury region. The nature of the archaeobotanical assemblage at Danebury had originally led M. Jones to suggest that part of the crops found there derived from other settlements within its territory, which were then stored and processed into fully clean grain at the hillfort. The grain would then leave the hillfort in a fully cleaned state; and settlements receiving this grain should thus be characterised by assemblages with little or no chaff or weeds (M. Jones 1984b; 1985, 122).

No such settlements have however been found, either in the Danebury region, or for that matter anywhere else in Iron Age Britain. The recent results from the Danebury Environs Programme make it clear that the grain thought to have left Danebury did not go to settlements within the region. The plant assemblages from the five Iron Age sites investigated within the Danebury region all contain clear evidence for the dehusking and cleaning of grain (Campbell 2000), that is precisely the activities that were carried out at Danebury. Thus, the grain cleaned at Danebury apparently did not go (or return) to sites in the region, but instead was consumed in the hillfort itself or traded outside the region (possible scenarios already envisaged by M. Jones; 1985, 122). There is no real evidence for the latter, in that Danebury does not have the greater quantities of elite goods compared to surrounding settlements that one might expect from such trade (Hill 1995a). The most likely explanation for the large quantities of grain brought to the hillfort is, therefore, that this grain was consumed there. The evidence for dehusking and cleaning of the grain at Danebury also points to consumption, as this processing tends to take place immediately before consumption. Such grain is unlikely to have been used for seed corn as the dehusking damages the embryo of the grains and thus reduces their germination rate (glume wheats are usually sown as spikelets, not clean grain; Nesbitt *et al.* 1996). The evidence from Danebury thus points to large-scale consumption, possibly during large communal feasts.

This interpretation would fit comfortably within current models of social and economic change put forward for the Iron Age (e.g. Sharples 1991; Haselgrove 1999; Cunliffe 2000, chapter 4). Such models have identified the demise of the position of the elites in the Late Bronze Age caused by the development of the new iron technology and consequent reduced role of long-distance trade of precious metals. This led to an increased reliance on the creation of – and control over – agrarian surpluses during the Iron Age. A possible scenario is that many communities in southern Britain worked to achieve grain surpluses, which were stored in pits and used for occasional feasts. Some of these feasts may have been small domestic feasts, others large communal ones; the latter taking place at the regional hillforts. Both Sharples (1991) and Hill (1995a) see these hillforts as communal sites, and Hill (1995a) has suggested that Danebury may initially not have been occupied permanently (many of the storage pits at Danebury appear to have been left open for longer periods than those at non-hillfort sites). At both types of site some pits receive 'special deposits', offerings to the deities associated with fertility rituals, after the grain was removed (Grant 1984; 1991; Cunliffe 1992; 2000, 130; Hill 1995b).

By *c.* 300 BC the leaders of certain communities appear to have succeeded in enhancing their status and prestige to such an extent that they could move into the (developed) hillforts and raise the required manpower to enhance their encircling earthworks, possibly by using corvée labour (and involving further large-scale feasting). This would explain the evidence for increased occupation at these sites, the reduction in settlements around them, the increased storage facilities at such sites, and the concentration of shrines and increased evidence for ritual. Finally, by the Late Iron Age the hillforts are abandoned, settlement disperses again, storage pits disappear from the record and towards the very end of the period long-distance trade (re-)emerges. One of several explanations for this pattern is that instead of surpluses being stored for feasts, they now leave the region in exchange for new consumer goods: Roman ceramics, glass, and exotic foods such as wine and figs (Haselgrove 1999; Cunliffe 2000, 191–2).

What we appear to observe is a classic change in the way food is used either to homogenise or 'heterogenise' the participants in the meal (cf. Appadurai 1981; Dietler 1996; Van der Veen 2003). During the Early Iron Age grain surpluses may have been accumulated for celebratory feasts. Such feasts serve to enhance social bonds in societies with little social inequality. Over time certain communities or individuals manage to increase their standing and prestige by hosting more feasts and, by eating the food, the guests accept the obligation to give something in return, either deference or labour. The shift towards the developed hillforts around 300 BC may point to these communities or individuals having achieved special status, and commensal hospitality may now have been used to reiterate and legitimise growing differences in status and power. Leaders of these communities would have been expected to host lavish parties, whilst participants were expected to pay tribute and/or offer labour. Then, by the very end of the Iron Age, we see a move away from the use of food to maintain and enhance social bonds, towards the use of food to create distance. The emphasis is no longer on the consumption of the same foods (common staples), but on the consumption of different foods (Van der Veen forthcoming). The elite starts to consume wine and other exotics (such as the figs found at Hengistbury Head (M. Robinson pers. comm.); and to use imported ceramics and glass to enhance the display component of the meal. Thus, we see a move from communal feasts to exclusive dining; in the latter there is no longer any element of reciprocity; the 'audience' no longer participates ('diacritic' feasts; Dietler 1996).

Conclusion

In this paper we have drawn attention to two aspects of archaeobotanical analysis and interpretation, one methodological, the other concerning the meaning of charred plant assemblages. First, the fact that grain-rich samples are generated primarily through accidents has two major methodological implications: (a) we need to understand the taphonomic pathway of individual samples, which means that the sample is the most useful level of analysis; and (b) we need to allow for the 'chance' element in archaeobotanical preservation, which means that the region is the most useful level of interpretation. This is in contrast to the more usual approach where the site constitutes the unit of both analysis and interpretation.

Secondly, we argue that, although the use of chaff as either fodder or fuel provides a partial explanation in some cases, the relative proportions of grain, chaff, and weeds at archaeological sites tell us more about the scale of agricultural activity than about whether individual sites were consumers or producers, or whether storage was at the household or community level. These latter interpretations are based on the erroneous assumption that grain-rich samples are generated through charring of the waste from routine activities rather than as a result of relatively rare accidents involving fire. We have argued that such accidents are most likely to happen at sites where cereals are handled in bulk (be they producer or consumer sites), and that grain-rich samples thus point to large-scale production and/or consumption (adding an additional criterion to those discussed by Bakels (1996) for the detection of surplus production). We regard this ability to assess the scale of the agricultural system, with its implication for the presence of surplus production and its consumption, as an exciting new development – it will greatly facilitate the study of both regionality and socio-economic change.

Finally, we have interpreted the evidence for the production and consumption of grain surpluses in southern Britain as surpluses that may have been produced for – and consumed during – feasts. These may initially have functioned to maintain the social bonds within and between communities, but may over time have been increasingly used by the leaders of certain communities to enhance their own prestige and status, resulting in particular hillforts becoming centres of power. By the end of the period we see a major change: the grain surpluses are apparently no longer stored and consumed within the region, but possibly exported out of the region in return for items of elite display. Thus, during the Iron Age grain surpluses in southern Britain were used to mobilise prestige and status through local large-scale feasting; by the Late Iron Age we start to see the mobilisation of grain surpluses across the landscape, something that became increasingly common during the Roman period. To conclude, during the Iron Age grain surplus (the economic capital) was used to acquire social power (prestige, status); by the end of the period it started to be used to acquire cultural power (exclusivity, elitism).

Acknowledgements

We would like to thank Debbie Miles-Williams and Joe Skinner for preparing the figures.

Notes

1. In fact Stevens uses the term 'partially threshed ears' here but, as glume wheat ears inevitably break up into individual spikelets when threshed (Hillman 1981, 1984a, 1984b), it is not clear how 'partially threshed ears' would ever be generated. As Stevens himself implies that both types of storage product are still in a state where the glumes (chaff) tightly invest the grain (i.e. they have not undergone the dehusking process), the term 'unsieved spikelets' is used here in place of 'partially threshed ears'.
2. We agree with Stevens (2003) that it is unlikely that M. Jones' 'consumer' sites in the upper Thames valley are purely 'pastoralist' sites, as this would imply a level of agricultural specialisation (in crops or animals) not known in Britain until after World War II. Non-farming pastoralists are rare, and are typically found only in extreme environments (e.g. deserts). Instead, we interpret these sites as having little emphasis on arable production, or as occupied for a short period of time only. Indeed, the concept of consumer sites of cereals is one we would see as having little relevance for rural settlements in Iron Age Britain, with the possible exception of 'special' sites such as the port-of-trade at Hengistbury Head.

Bibliography

Appadurai, A. 1981. Gastropolitics in Hindu South Asia, *American Ethnologist* 8, 494–511.

Bakels, C. 1996. Growing grain for others or how to detect surplus production?, *Journal of European Archaeology* 4, 329–336.

Barrett, J. 1994. *Fragments from Antiquity*. Oxford: Blackwell.

Boardman, S. and Jones. G. 1990. Experiments on the effects of charring on cereal plant components, *Journal of Archaeological Science* 17, 1–11.

Bradley, R. 1978. *The Prehistoric Settlement of Britain*. London: Routledge and Kegan Paul.

Campbell, G. 2000. Plant utilization: the evidence from charred plant remains, in Cunliffe 2000, 45–59.

Charles, M. and Bogaard, A. 2001. Third millennium B.C. charred plant remains from Tell Brak, in D.Oates, J. Oates and H. McDonald (eds), *Excavations at Tell Brak, Vol. 2*, 301–326. Cambridge: McDonald Institute.

Cooney, G. 1997. Images of settlement and the landscape in the Neolithic, in P. Topping (ed.), *Neolithic Landscapes,* 23–31. Oxford: Oxbow Books.

Cunliffe, B. 1984. *Danebury: an Iron Age Hillfort in Hampshire, Vol. 2.* London: Council for British Archaeology Research Report 52.

Cunliffe, B. 1992. Pits, preconceptions and propitiation in the British Iron Age, *Oxford Journal of Archaeology* 11, 69–83.

Cunliffe, B. 2000. *The Danebury Environs Programme. The Prehistory of a Wessex Landscape, Vol. I: Introduction*. London: Oxford University Committee for Archaeology Monograph 48

Dennell, R.W. 1974. Prehistoric crop processing activities, *Journal of Archaeological Science* 1, 275–284.

Dennell, R.W. 1976. The economic importance of plant resources represented on archaeological sites, *Journal of Archaeological Science* 3, 229–247.

Dietler, M. 1996. Feasts and commensal politics in the political economy: food, power and status in prehistoric Europe, in P. Wiessner and W. Schiefenhövel (eds), *Food and the Status Quest. An Interdisciplinary Perspective*, 87–125. Providence: Berghahn.

Edmonds, M. 1997. Taskscape, technology and tradition, *Analecta Praehistorica Leidensia* 29, 99–110.

Fenton, A. 1983. Grain storage in pits: experiment and fact, in A. O'Connor and D.V. Clarke (eds), *From the Stone Age to the 'Forty-Five'*, 567–588. Edinburgh: John Donald Publications.

Gent, H. 1983. Centralized storage in later prehistoric Britain, *Proceedings of the Prehistoric Society* 49, 243–267.

Gransar, F. 2000. Le stockage alimentaire sur les établissements ruraux de l'âge du Fer en France septentrionale: complémentarité des structures et tendances évolutives, in S. Marion and G. Blancqaert (eds), *Les Installations Agricoles de l'Âge du Fer en France Septentrionale*, 277–297. Paris: École Normale Supérieure, Études d'Histoire et d'Archéologie 6.

Grant, A. 1984. Survival or sacrifice? A critical appraisal of animal burials in the Iron Age, in J. Clutton-Brock and C. Grigson (eds), *Animals and Archaeology 4. Husbandry in Europe*, 221–227. Oxford: British Archaeological Reports International Series 227.

Grant, A. 1991. Economic or symbolic? Animals in ritual behaviour, in P. Garwood, D. Jennings, R. Skeates and J. Toms (eds), *Sacred and Profane*, 109–114. Oxford: Oxford University Committee for Archaeology Monograph 32.

Haselgrove, C. 1999. The Iron Age, in J. Hunter and I. Ralston (eds), *The Archaeology of Britain*, 113–134. London: Routledge.

Haselgrove, C., Armit, I., Champion, T., Creighton, J., Gwilt, A., Hill, J.D., Hunter, F. and Woodward, A. 2001. *Understanding the British Iron Age: an Agenda for Action*. Salisbury: Trust for Wessex Archaeology.

Hill, J.D. 1995a. How should we understand Iron Age societies and hillforts? A contextual study from southern Britain, in J.D. Hill and C.G. Cumberpatch (eds), *Different Iron Ages. Studies on the Iron Age in Temperate Europe,* 45–66. Oxford: British Archaeological Reports International Series 602.

Hill, J.D. 1995b. *Ritual and Rubbish in the Iron Age of Wessex*. Oxford: British Archaeological Reports British Series 242.

Hillman, G. 1981. Reconstructing crop husbandry practices from charred remains of crops, in R. Mercer (ed.), *Farming Practice in British Prehistory*, 123–162. Edinburgh: Edinburgh University Press.

Hillman, G. 1984a. Interpretation of archaeological plant remains: the application of ethnographic models from Turkey, in Van Zeist and Casparie 1984, 1–41.

Hillman, G. 1984b. Traditional husbandry and processing of archaic cereals in modern times: part I, the glume wheats, *Bulletin on Sumerian Agriculture* 1, 114–152.

Hodgson, N., Stobbs, G.C. and Van der Veen, M. 2001. An Iron Age settlement and remains of earlier prehistoric date beneath South Shields Roman Fort, Tyne and Wear, *Archaeological Journal* 158, 62–160.

Jones, G. 1984. Interpretation of archaeological plant remains:

ethnographic models from Greece, in Van Zeist and Casparie 1984, 43–61.

Jones, G. 1987. A statistical approach to the archaeological identification of crop processing, *Journal of Archaeological Science* 14, 311–323.

Jones, G. 1991. Numerical analysis in archaeobotany, in W. van Zeist, K. Wasylikowa and K.E. Behre (eds), *Progress in Old World Palaeoethnobotany*, 63–80. Rotterdam: Balkema.

Jones, G. 2000. Evaluating the importance of cultivation and collecting in Neolithic Britain, in A.S. Fairbairn (ed.), *Plants in Neolithic Britain and Beyond*, 79–84. Oxford: Neolithic Studies Group Seminar Papers 5.

Jones, G. and Rowley-Conwy, P. forthcoming. On the importance of cereal cultivation in the British Neolithic, in S. Colledge and J. Conolly (eds), *The Origin and Spread of Domestic Plants in South-West Asia and Europe*. London: University College London Press.

Jones, M. 1984a. Regional patterns in crop production, in B. Cunliffe and D. Miles (eds), *Aspects of the Iron Age in Central Southern Britain*, 120–125. Oxford: Oxford University Committee for Archaeology Monograph 2.

Jones, M. 1984b. The plant remains, in Cunliffe 1984, 483–495.

Jones, M. 1985. Archaeobotany beyond subsistence reconstruction, in G. Barker and C. Gamble (eds), *Beyond Domestication in Prehistoric Europe*, 107–128. London: Academic Press.

Jones, M.1996. Plant Exploitation, in T.C. Champion and J.R. Collis (eds), *The Iron Age in Britain and Ireland. Recent Trends*, 29–40. Sheffield: J.R. Collis Publications.

Moffett, L., Robinson, M. A. and Straker, V. 1989. Cereals, fruits and nuts: charred plant remains from Neolithic sites in England and Wales and the Neolithic economy, in A. Milles, D. Williams and N. Gardner (eds), *The Beginnings of Agriculture*, 243–261. Oxford: British Archaeological Reports International Series 496.

Monk, M. 2000. Seeds and soils of discontent: an environmental archaeological contribution to the nature of the early Neolithic, in A. Desmond, G. Johnson, M. McCarthy, J. Sheehan and E. Shee Twohig (eds), *New Agendas in Irish Prehistory: Papers in Commemoration of Liz Anderson*, 67–87. Wicklow: Wordwell.

Nesbitt, M., Hillman, G., Pena-Chocarro, L., Samuel, S. and Szabo, A.T. 1996. Checklist for recording the cultivation and uses of hulled wheats, in S. Padulosi, K. Hammer and J. Heller (eds), *Hulled Wheats. Proceedings of the First International Workshop on Hulled Wheats, 21–22 July 1995, Castelvecchio Pascoli, Tuscany, Italy*, 234–245. Rome: International Plant Genetic Resources Institute, Promoting the Conservation and Use of Underutilized and Neglected Crops 4.

Palmer, C. and Jones, M. 1991. Plant resources, in Sharples 1991, 129–139.

Reynolds, P.J. 1974. Experimental Iron Age storage pits: an interim report, *Proceedings of the Prehistoric Society* 40, 118–131.

Rowley-Conwy, P. 2000. Through a taphonomic glass, darkly: the importance of cereal cultivation in prehistoric Britain, in J. Huntley and S. Stallibrass (eds), *Taphonomy and Interpretation*, 43–53. Oxford: Oxbow Books.

Sharples, N. 1991. *Maiden Castle: Excavations and Field Survey 1985–6*. London: English Heritage Archaeological Report 19.

Stevens, C.J. 2003. An investigation of agricultural consumption and production: models for prehistoric and Roman Britain, *Environmental Archaeology* 8 (1), 61–76.

Thomas, J. 1991. *Rethinking the Neolithic*. Cambridge: Cambridge University Press.

Van der Veen, M. 1987. The plant remains, in D.H. Heslop, *The Excavation of an Iron Age Settlement at Thorpe Thewles, Cleveland, 1980–1982*, 93–99. London: Council for British Archaeology Research Report 65.

Van der Veen, M. 1991. Consumption or production? Agriculture in the Cambridgeshire Fens, in J.M. Renfrew (ed.), *New Light on Early Farming. Recent Developments in Palaeoethnobotany*, 349–361. Edinburgh: Edinburgh University Press.

Van der Veen, M. 1992. *Crop Husbandry Regimes. An Archaeobotanical Study of Farming in Northern England, 1000 BC–AD 500*. Sheffield: Sheffield Archaeological Monograph 3.

Van der Veen, M. 2003. When is food a luxury? *World Archaeology* 34 (3), 405–427.

Van der Veen, M. forthcoming. Food as an instrument of social change: feasting in Iron Age and early Roman southern Britain, in K. Twiss (ed.), *We Were What We Ate: The Archaeology of Food and Identity*. Carbondale: Southern Illinois University Center for Archaeological Investigations Occasional Paper 34.

Van Zeist, W. and Casparie, W.A. (eds) 1984. *Plants and Ancient Man*. Rotterdam: Balkema.

Making magic: later prehistoric and early Roman salt production in the Lincolnshire fenland

Elaine L. Morris

Introduction

For many years researchers have known that there were numerous Iron Age and Roman salt production sites, or salterns, in the Lincolnshire fenland region (Fig. 1) including the Fens and the Fen edge (Swinnerton 1932; Baker 1960; 1975; Hallam 1960; Simmons 1975, fig. 18; May 1976, 143–55). Quantities of briquetage, the ceramic material associated with salt production, have been recovered from over 300 Iron Age and Roman salt making sites during fieldwalking as part of the Fenland Survey alone (Fig. 2; Hayes and Lane 1992; Lane 1993). Recent excavations, funded by English Heritage, as part of the Fenland Management Project, and by developers, have revealed the nature of production sites dating from the Middle and Late Iron Age and early Roman periods (Lane and Morris 2001), whilst previous excavations have now been published, presenting additional information about production in the Early Iron Age (Chowne *et al.* 2001) and in the Iron Age and early Roman periods (Bell *et al.* 1999). In addition, traces of Middle Bronze Age and Late Bronze Age salt making have been suggested from evidence at three sites in the area (Gurney 1980; Pryor 1980; Cleal and Bacon 2001). This enormous quantity of information, predominantly ceramic in nature, has provided an unparalleled opportunity to demonstrate that the production of salt was a dynamic system, and clearly one of considerable significance to the people of this region for over a millennium.

Evidence for the intensification of salt production during this period will be presented through a chronological review of the associated ceramic debris and by assessing the details about technological variation revealed through the analysis of these material remains. An interpretation of who the salt makers might have been and why they were so keen to make salt will be attempted. The distribution of salt during the later Iron Age specifically will be discussed briefly in relation to the distribution of salt from other regional sources, both coastal and inland.

Briquetage

There are three principal ceramic components, or classes of briquetage, in the Lincolnshire fenland salt production system: *containers*, *supports*, and *heating structures*. All of the evidence from the controlled excavations is extremely fragmented in nature. The interpretations presented here derive from this evidence alone; a great deal of experimental work needs to be conducted to assist in understanding exactly how the process of salt production was conducted, and to verify or challenge these interpretations. Examination of the range of briquetage from sites in France and Belgium and the reconstructions suggested by the excavators through experimentation (Daire 1994; Olivier 2000; Prilaux 2000) reveal that there are many different ways of creating containers, supports, and heating structures for drying brine to create salt crystals.

Containers

Containers are hand-made, gutter-shaped ceramic troughs (Fig. 3, 1–9; Fig. 4, 1–3; Fig. 5, 1–5), or wide, shallow, slightly curved but mainly flat pans (Crosby 2001a). The troughs appear to have been made by taking coil- or collar-built cylinders and slicing them from top

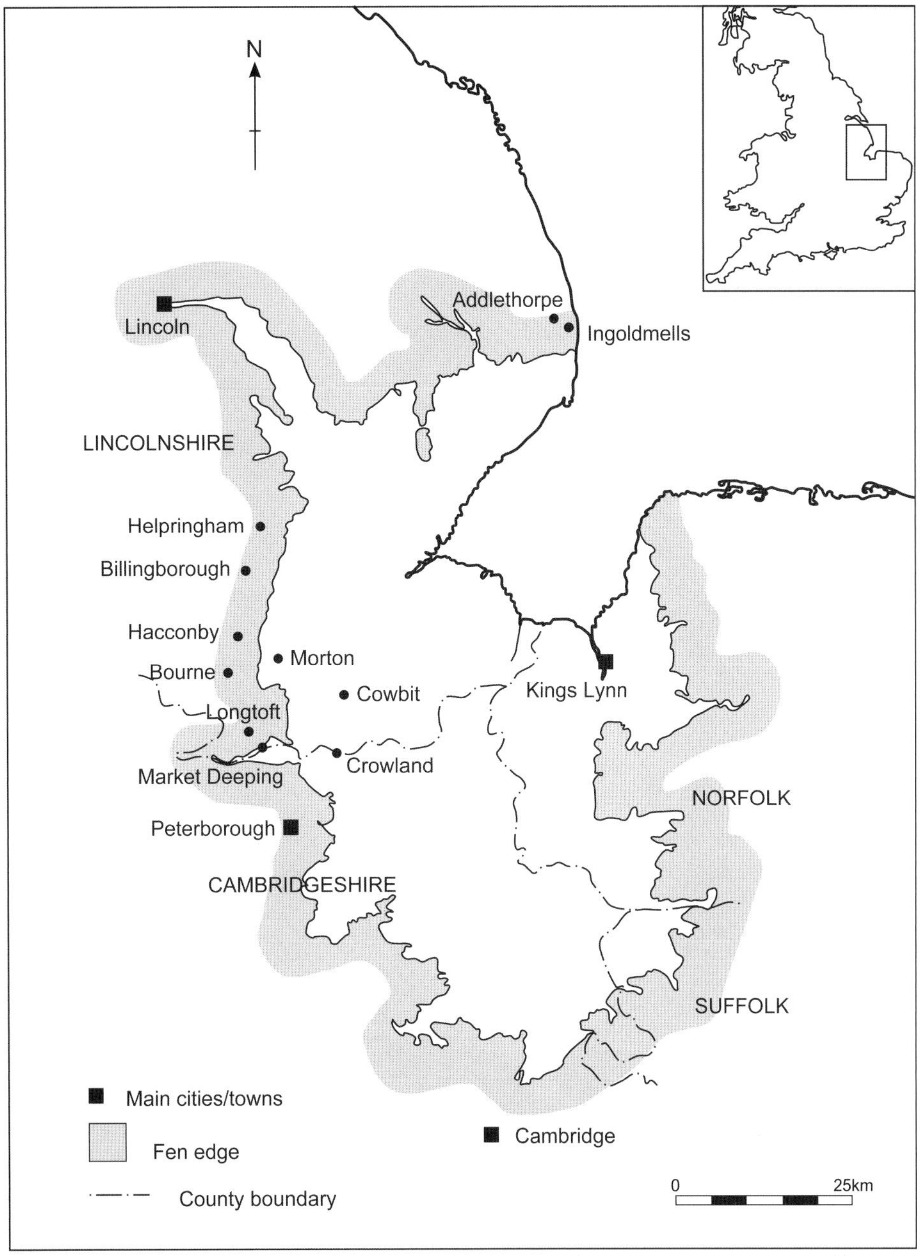

Fig. 1. Location of the fenland region in Britain (after Lane and Morris 2001, fig. 1).

to bottom to create two containers with distinctive cut rims. Half-moon pieces of clay would then have been added to the open ends to provide completed troughs for holding brine (Fig. 6). The pans show many signs that at least some were made over a mould (*ibid.*). The containers have been so fragmented in antiquity that there are no indications of the size of troughs, but we are fortunate to have four partially complete examples of Late Iron Age–early Roman pans from salvage excavations at Ingoldmells on the north side of the Fens; these measure >33 cm long, *c.* 15–23 cm. wide and *c.* 6–8 cm. deep (*ibid.*, figs. 126–131).

Supports

The containers were placed above the heating source on a variety of different supports, secured by stabilisers. The most distinctive, and probably most famous, of these supports are the hand-squeezed pedestals (Figs 4, 11–18; Fig. 5, 11–14), onto which the troughs were placed or pressed. The hand-made nature of these pedestals results in a great variety of sizes and shapes within the broad definition. In addition, substantial pyramidal pedestals (Fig. 3, 11–17), bars and rods (Fig. 5, 19–20), bricks (Fig. 5, 18), wedges, and platforms (Fig. 4, 16–18) are also found in briquetage assemblages.

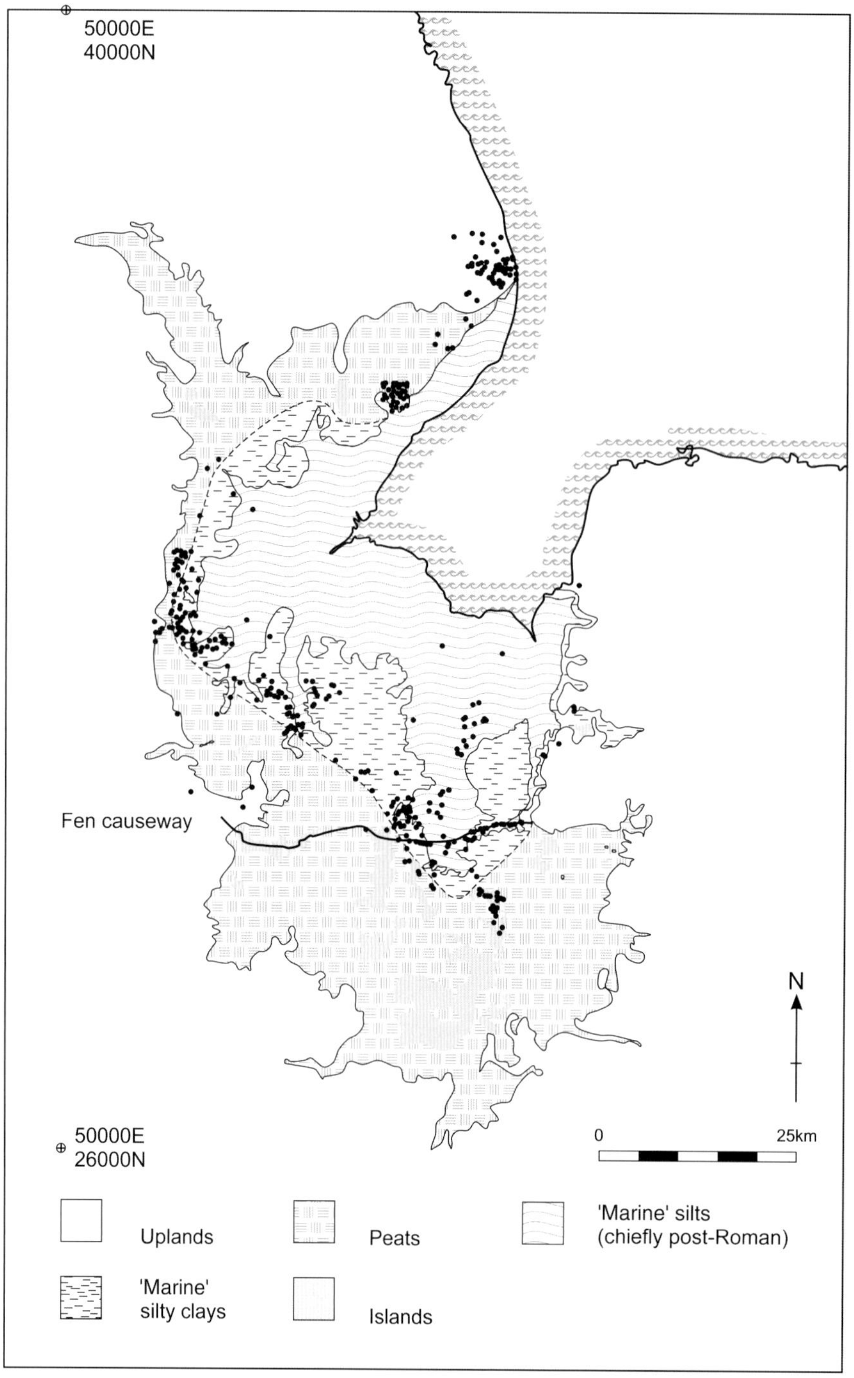

Fig. 2. Location of Iron Age and Roman salterns in the fenland (after Lane and Morris 2001, fig. 2).

Platforms are usually flat: two parallel-sided ceramic boards, which are definitely smoothed on both sides. They have evidence of salty brine splashes on both sides, which indicates that they must have been free-standing within the saltern complex. The curved profile of the troughs required them to be stabilised or balanced securely on top of the hand-squeezed pedestals. A series of mini-pedestals, or spacers, turned on their sides were pressed between the walls of the troughs (Fig. 4, 4–6), and lumps of clay were pinched over the rims of troughs and pans creating what look, once fired, like ceramic clips (Figs. 4, 7–10; Fig. 5, 6–11).

Structural material

At some salterns, chunks of broken-up heating structures identified as drying ovens were also recovered. Some of the structural material is interpreted as walls

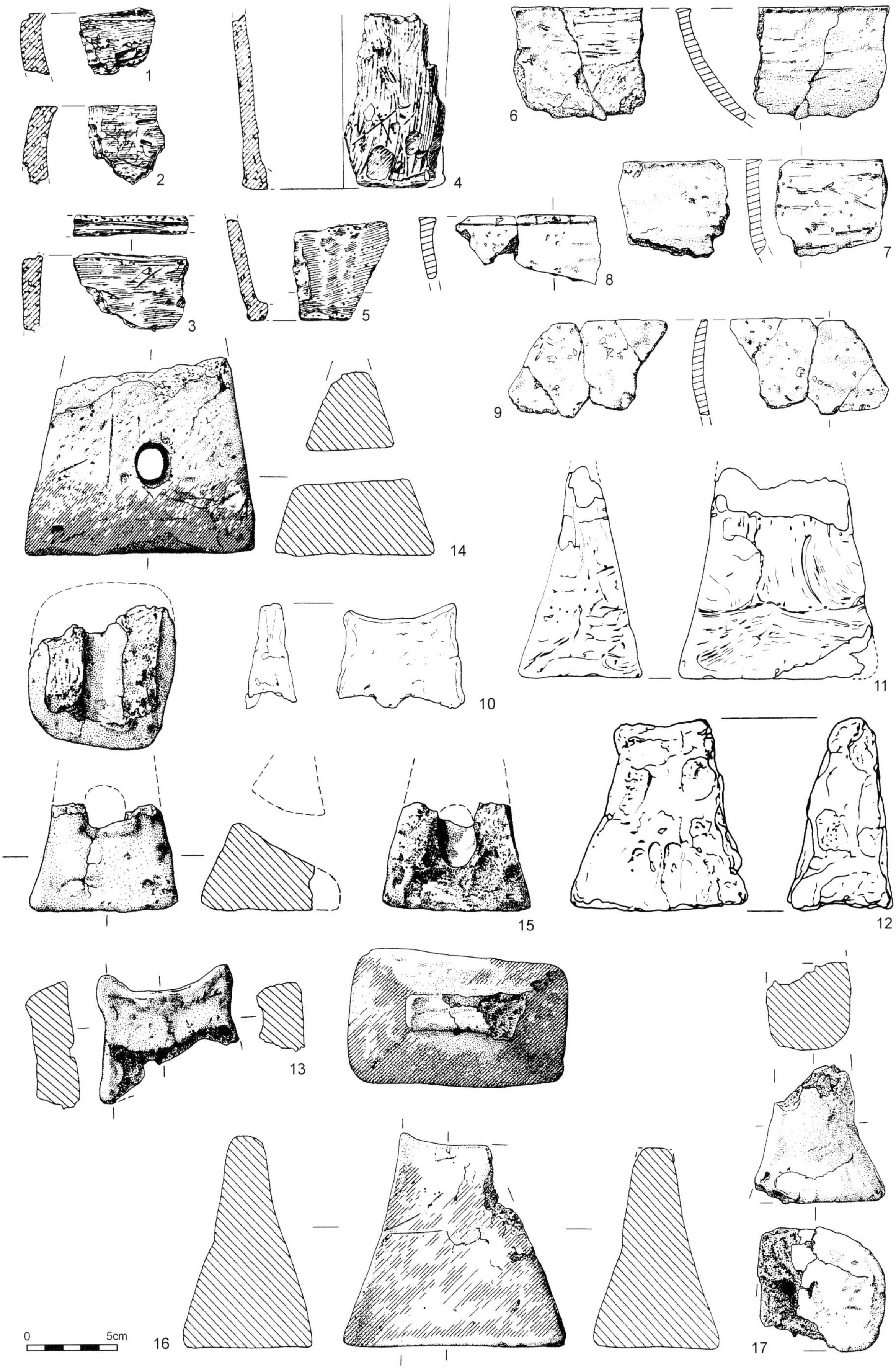

Fig. 3. Briquetage Phase 1 (Middle Bronze Age–Middle Iron Age) material by class: 1–9 containers; 10–17 supports (after Cleal and Bacon 2001, figs. 29, 32 and 34; Morris 2001b, figs. 88 and 90; 2001c, figs. 93–96).

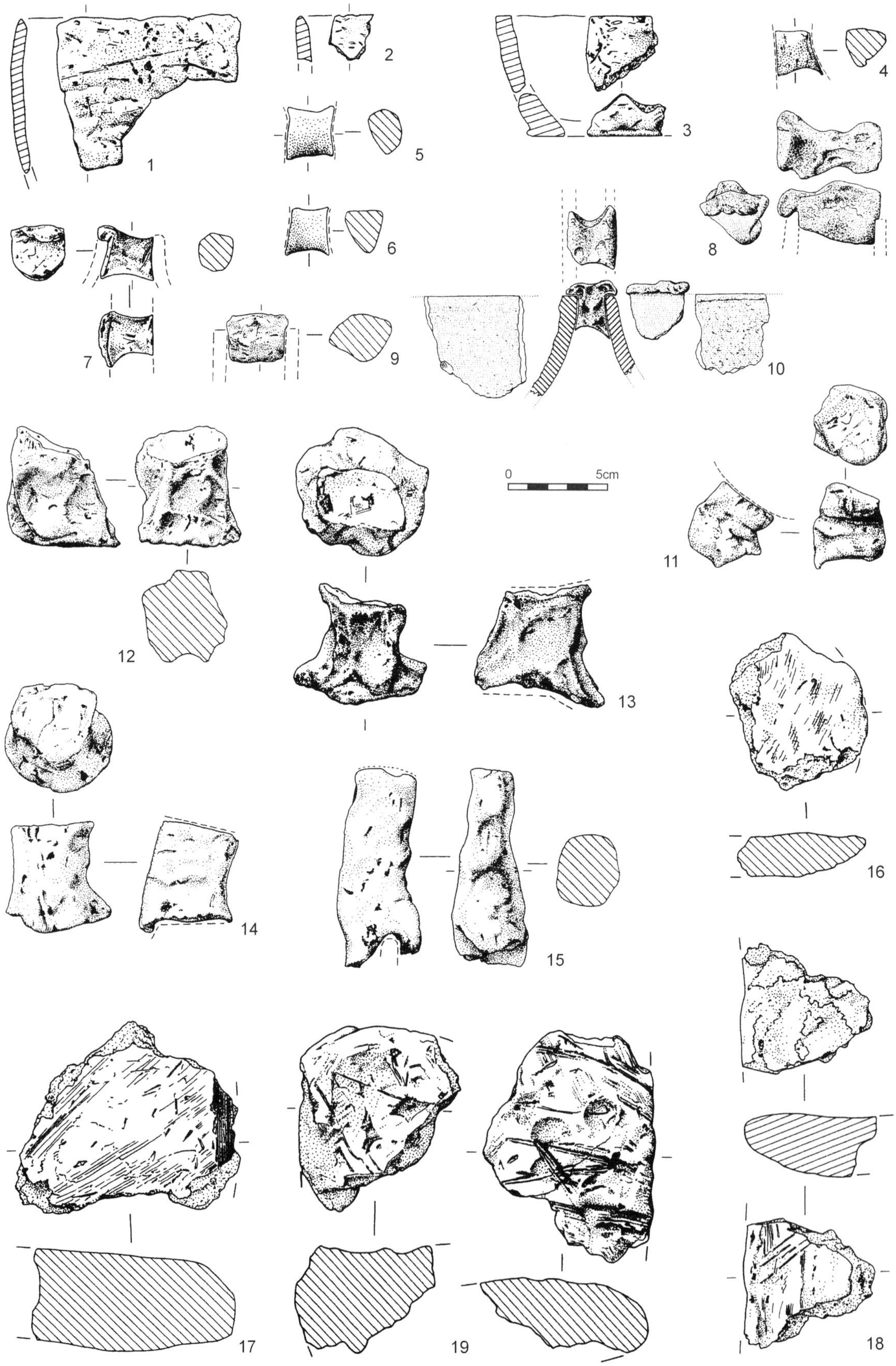

Fig. 4. Briquetage Phase 2 (Later Iron Age; c. mid second–first century BC) material by class: 1–3 containers; 4–18 supports; 19 structural material (after Morris 2001d, figs. 17–21).

and other segments as flooring. Flooring slabs are similar in many respects to the platforms described above, but they are much thicker and have only one smoothed surface, with the underside being irregular, rather than parallel to the top surface, and undulating (Fig. 4, 19). Examples of these slabs include corner pieces and perforated types (Fig. 5, 20). The surfaces of flooring slabs are often extremely well fired to a variety of pink, lavender, and purple shades, and can display a white top surface resulting from brine dribbles during the boiling procedures. Structural wall material has little of this salt effect but is identified due to the thickness of the fragments and the extremely high firing conditions during the use of the facility.

Miscellaneous

Many briquetage assemblages have numerous unidentifiable fired clay fragments which display different characteristics, but which cannot with confidence be assigned to either support piece types or structural material remains.

Chronological review of salt production evidence

There are distinct chronological components to the range of briquetage material recovered in the fenland region from the Bronze Age through to the Roman period. These can be divided into four principal phases.

Briquetage Phase 1

During the Late Bronze Age to Middle Iron Age, production sites are located along the Fen edge. The predominant class of briquetage (Fig. 3) consists of sherds of cut-rim, gutter-shaped troughs made from the same type of clays bearing fragments of naturally-occurring fossil shell as were used to make domestic pottery vessels at that time. These shelly clays are available at or very near to the production sites. The rims of the containers are nearly always 'cut' since two troughs could be made by slicing through a hand-made, collar- or coil-built ceramic cylinder, and the bases were actually the end pieces of the gutter (Fig. 6). The containers were quite thin-walled, with between 70–100% of them measuring less than 10 mm thick (Morris 2001a, table 91). There is a possibility that Middle Bronze Age salt production also occurred in the area at Billingborough, which has grog-tempered cut-rim containers (Cleal and Bacon 2001, 58, fig. 24, 49–50), and at Northey, which has a shell-gritted container (Pryor 1980, 18, 181, fig. 13, 1). In both cases, the possible briquetage is made from the same general fabric type as the contemporary pottery.

In addition to container fragments, there are large fragments of distinctive horned, pyramid-like pedestals, which are similar in form to triangular clay loomweights, and have well-smoothed surfaces, like pottery vessels. Their base footprint is rectangular, rising up to a much narrower top, which is curved or scooped and similar to a pair of horns, or a 'fishtail' (Cleal and Bacon 2001). The cupped tops of these solid pedestals held the containers over the hearth, and must have performed this role admirably because no clips or spacers are found at sites of this date.

The only other ceramic material directly associated with salt making in this early phase are fired clay fragments which appear to derive from hearths, although some may simply be general baked clay which has become affected by association with salt-water. There is no evidence for walls or floors for ovens with flues. It is therefore inferred that simple, flat hearths were the most likely heating system employed and that this provided a direct method of evaporation to produce salt crystals.

Excavated assemblages of ceramic salt making debris from this period have been found at Billingborough in Early Iron Age deposits (Cleal and Bacon 2001); at Langtoft in association with Middle Iron Age pottery (Morris 2001b; Knight 2001); and redeposited at Market Deeping (Morris 2001c). Fieldwalking collections assigned to this phase of salt production have been recovered from several different locations at Bourne, Morton, and Hacconby along the Lincolnshire Fen edge (Hayes and Lane 1992; Lane 1993; Morris and Percival 2001, table 85).

Briquetage Phase 2

A radical series of changes took place during the second century BC and later. At present, this date is based solely on two radiocarbon determinations of 185–95 cal. BC and 170–50 cal. BC (UB-4027; UB-4026) from deposits within a heating structure at Cowbit, Lincolnshire (Bayliss and McCormac 2001), and needs to be confirmed by more excavations and absolute dates.

Significantly, containers and supports were made from organic-tempered fabrics during this phase. The clays are naturally silty in texture, and chopped chaff, waste from grain production, was added to provide strength to the containers and supports during manufacture as well as porosity required during open firing and use. The containers are similar to those of Briquetage Phase 1, frequently displaying cut rims, but smoother, rounded rims are also found, suggesting that not all of the containers are trough-like in morphology (Fig. 4); either these represent shallow pans made using other manufacturing methods, or the rim edges could simply be smoothed over. The sherds of these containers display an additional difference from those of Phase 1 because they have more frequent evidence of salt splashes, or a white, skin-like effect on their exterior surfaces (Morris 2001d, plate 4a). Some assemblages have container sherds which are white throughout, with the original orange-red colour of the iron-rich clays being completely transformed by use.

A second, significant development is that the pedestals were made with much less effort – they were simply lumps of clay, squeezed by hand, revealing the shapes of several fingers; the containers were then pressed onto rows of pedestals during a soft stage to create the curved top edge effect to the pedestals. The flimsier footprint of these pedestals compared to the substantial pyramidal types of Briquetage Phase 1 appear to have required additional stabilisers such as clips or spacers to make the system rigid during use. Other types of supports such as bars or rods and platforms are also found at this time. Some assemblages assigned to this period have very hard-fired, bloated, or cracked examples of hand-squeezed pedestals as a result of extreme firing through the use of intense heat. Many pedestal fragments are very brittle and harsh to touch and appear purple or purple-grey in colour. This condition is possible with the porosity created through the use of organic temper.

The third major change during this period was the development of an indirect method of heating, by the construction of ovens with flues, floors, and walls, which allowed greater control of the heating of brine. If the mid second century BC date for the beginning of these changes is upheld by further research, this is likely to be nearly a century before the use of kilns in pottery production in eastern England (Swan 1984). In a kiln, the actual source of heat is not anywhere near the vessels, but is located at the flue end, with the structure drawing the heat through the flue. It appears that this indirect heating method was used during the second century BC and later for evaporating brine to produce salt. If a briquetage assemblage includes the extremely hard-fired pedestals mentioned above, then the same firing evidence is witnessed amongst the structural fragments, with very hard-fired wall and floor fragments which can also be deep reddish-purple to purple-grey in colour.

Thus, Briquetage Phase 2 encompassed several significant changes. Production sites are now found in the Fens as well as along the Fen edge: the salt makers were moving into the Fens to make salt. The geology is different in the Fens: the local clays are silty, rather than naturally shell-gritted as along the Fen edge. As the salt makers changed from using the shelly clays of the Fen edge to silty clays from the Fens, they needed to add a tempering agent to improve the porosity of the very dense silty clays during firing and provide strength during manufacture. They chose organic temper in the form of wheat chaff, but this chaff could not be a local resource because wheat cannot be raised in the Fens as it was at that time intolerant to brackish, salty soils (Murphy 2001). Therefore, the chaff was transported from the Fen edge, where wheat could be grown, into the Fens, so that the making of the various briquetage containers and supports could be conducted quickly. The closest possible sources of chaff may be as far as 2–10 km from the salt production sites.

Only one published, excavated assemblage of ceramic salt making debris dates from this period – Cowbit, Lincolnshire (Morris 2001d) – but several fieldwalking collections have been assigned to this phase of salt production from various locations near Cowbit, Crowland, Deeping St Nicholas, Hacconby, Morton, Pinchbeck, Pointon, and Weston in Lincolnshire (Hayes and Lane 1992; Lane 1993; Morris and Percival 2001, table 85) and have the potential to provide further important information about this significant period of salt production. In addition, a recently excavated assemblage from Addlethorpe, just inland from Ingoldmells on the north side of the Fens, may be dated to this phase (Morris 2002).

Briquetage Phase 3

This phase is often, but not always, characterised by the presence of Roman pottery of late first- to second-century AD date (Precious 2001, 142). The briquetage (Fig. 5) is once again dominated by organic-tempered fabrics, with rare pieces made from silty or sandy fabrics (Crosby 2001b; Percival 2001a). The types of container still include cut-rim troughs but other rim types are also represented, with rounded, pointed, or wavy top edges. This period is most likely to have both troughs and pans amongst the range of container profiles, although the reasons for such variation are not fully understood. Again, the white skin effect and the presence of all-white container sherds are common.

Clips change shape from very supportive types to slighter or simpler ones, and hand-squeezed pedestals are much less frequent; upright bricks are the most common type of support (Crosby 2001b, table 26) and the most distinctive briquetage characteristic of the phase. Large quantities of structural material and miscellaneous fired clay fragments probably representing oven structures suggest that once again ovens were employed to dry the brine using an indirect heating system based on the presence of flooring slabs (Gurney 1999).

Excavated sites of this phase include Morton Fen (Crosby 2001b), Bourne–Morton Canal (Crosby 2001c) and Holbeach St John (Gurney 1999), as well as Nordelph and Downham West in Norfolk (Percival 2001a). Many sites are identified from fieldwalking collections (Morris and Percival 2001, table 85).

Briquetage Phase 4

Late Roman salt production sites have yet to be firmly identified in Lincolnshire, but a major complex has been excavated at Middleton in Norfolk (Crowson 2001). It consists of three phases of large ovens, settling tanks, and brine channels. Briquetage is confined to massive

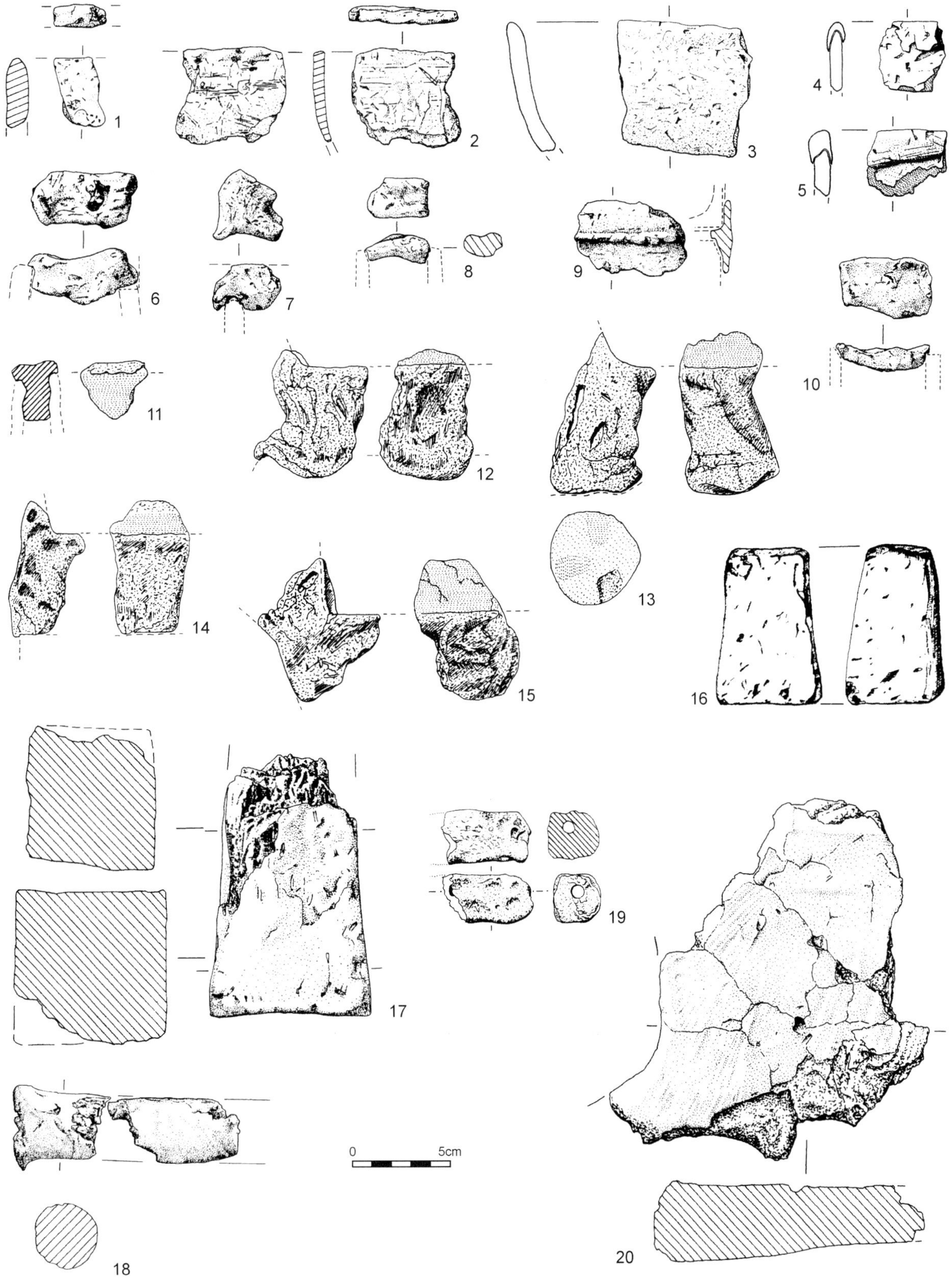

Fig. 5. Briquetage Phase 3 (first century AD/early Roman) material by class: 1–5 containers; 6–19 supports; 20 structural material (after Morris and Percival 2001, figs. 112–113 and 115; Gurney 1999, fig. 40; Lane 1993, fig. 84; Healey 1999, fig. 8; Crosby 2001a, figs. 34–35).

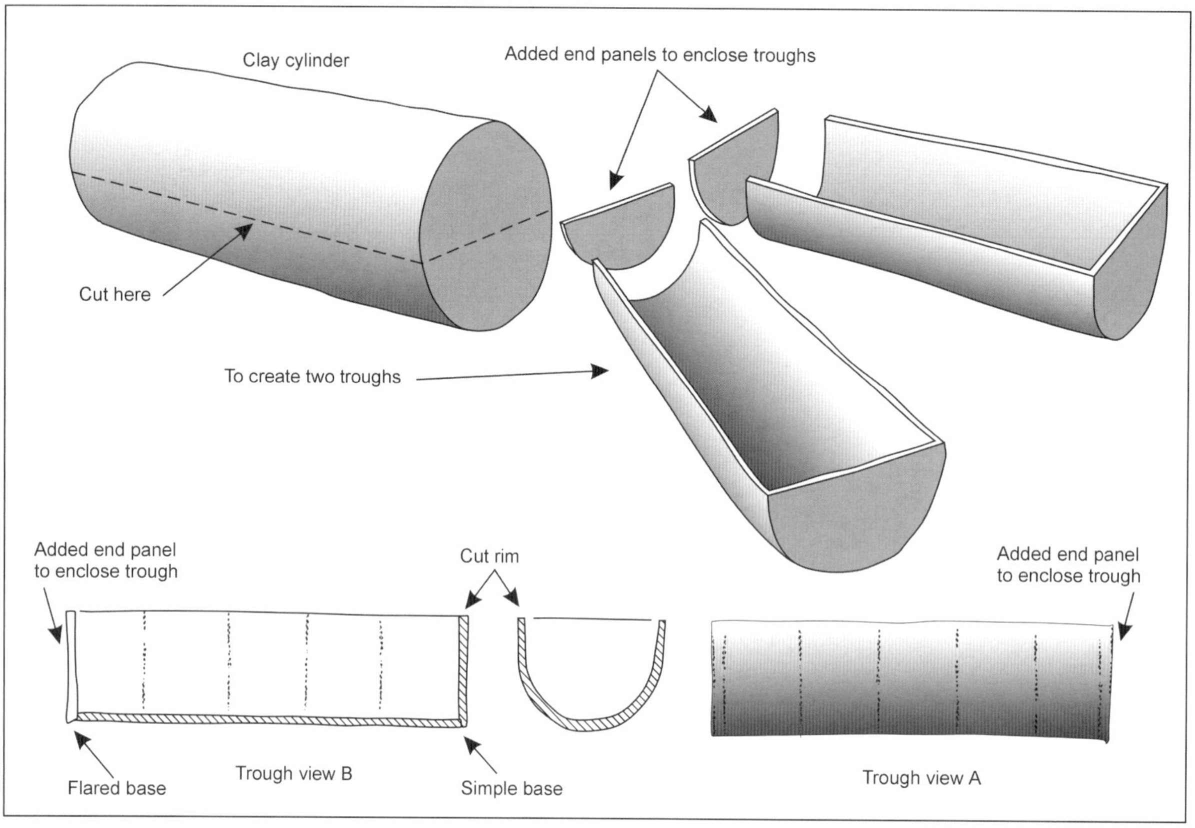

Fig. 6. Manufacturing technique for hand-made cut-rim troughs (after Morris 2001c, fig. 92).

supports and structural debris (Percival 2001a). The brine must have been boiled in lead pans. Possible sites of this production phase from fieldwalking include several from the Wrangle area in Lincolnshire (Morris and Percival 2001, table 85).

Intensification

Several aspects of the nature of the briquetage – its manufacture, use, and quantity – appear to indicate an escalation of changes signifying rapid intensification in production after the Middle Iron Age. Possibly a millennium of salt production took place from the Middle Bronze Age to the Middle Iron Age with hardly any noticeable differences amongst the ceramic debris from this industry. The same types of containers and pedestals were used, the fabrics employed were identical to those used to make common pottery, and simple hearths were constructed for direct heating of the brine. Very few sites of this date bearing briquetage have been found and these are inevitably located on the Fen edge. However, from the mid second century BC onwards little of this system remained.

The quantitative evidence points towards intensification of salt production during the Later Iron Age and early Roman periods. There are many more sites of this date than of the Middle Iron Age or earlier (Hayes and Lane 1992; Lane 1993; 2001; Morris and Percival 2001, table 53). Secondly there is a greater amount of briquetage debris at the later saltern sites. Fieldwalking results indicate that sites of this date display a great deal more evidence of salt production (compare Morris and Percival 2001, tables 84 and 85).

The manufacture of briquetage was altered significantly by the use of organic temper and the abandonment of care and attention to detail lavished on the Briquetage Phase 1 pyramidal pedestals. Gone are the days of well-finished surfaces on pedestals. Instead there was a rough-and-ready, rapid approach to the manufacture of hand-squeezed pedestals and clips, which was successful due to the use of organic temper. Shelly limestone fabric containers and pedestals were replaced during Briquetage Phases 2 and 3 by organic-tempered fabrics apparently for specific technological reasons. The salt makers may have appreciated that organic temper can increase the ease of manufacture, strength, and porosity of ceramics, as well as reduce their overall weight (Rye 1981, 33; Skibo, *et al.* 1989). In addition, there would have been a need to find a suitable temper once salt production took place actually in the Fens using silty Fen clays, rather than the naturally-

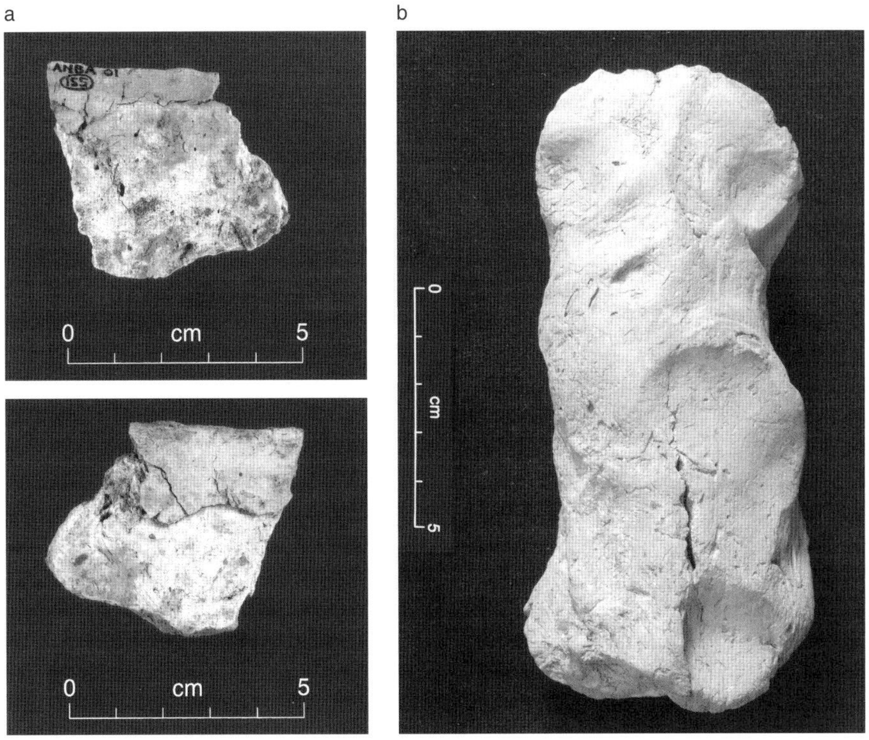

Fig. 7. Briquetage from Addlethorpe, Lincolnshire: a. example of repaired container rim with white-effect layer beneath the unaffected repair, above: exterior view, below: interior view (photo: Andy Vowles); b. hand-squeezed pedestal showing deep finger impressions (photo: Penny Copeland).

gritted, shelly limestone clays of the Fen edge. If chaff from grain production was available from farming along the Fen edge, this lightweight potential temper could have been easily transported to the salt production sites, as was demonstrated at Cowbit during the Later Iron Age and at Morton during the early Roman period (Fig. 1). The discovery that locally unavailable wheat production chaff was brought into the Fens and used to temper the local silty fenland clays to make briquetage for salt production is a new element to concepts of resource procurement and ceramic production (cf. Arnold 1985, 35–60; Morris 1994, 371–374).

Another manufacturing characteristic which suggests intensification is the making of pedestals which show that two layers of containers were in use rather than simply one layer as indicated by the flat-based pyramidal pedestals of Briquetage Phase 1. One pedestal type has a base that hooks over the rim of a container, and at the same time has its own flat top (Fig. 4, 15).

Thirdly, there are visible aspects of the use of the briquetage, which indicate repeated employment of the material in Briquetage Phases 2 and 3, which was not apparent earlier. These are the white colouring effect to the exterior surface of container sherds during the mid second to early first century BC; the deepening of this effect on later material, resulting in the complete whitening of the entire thickness of most container sherds, possibly during the first century BC and definitely later during the first–second century AD; and the repairing of rims, indicating the re-use of containers during this latest period, coinciding with much of Briquetage Phase 2 and all of Phase 3. It is uncertain precisely when the repairing of container rims first took place but this did not occur at Cowbit, dated to the mid second century to early first century BC, but did take place at Morton, dated to the late first century AD onwards, and at Addlethorpe, which unfortunately is undated but generally associated with early Roman pottery (T. Lane pers. comm.). Most striking is the evidence from Addlethorpe where is it easy to see that many containers were used frequently, damaged, and then repaired, because repairs were made from orange-red firing clays which cover the white layer on old container surfaces (Fig. 7a).

What exactly is this whitening effect? Previous discussions have suggested that it might be the result of an accumulation of salts or various minerals left in the slightly calcareous clay matrix of the ceramics as a result of association with salt-water during the heating process (Peacock 1984; Morris 2001d). However, there is also a distinct possibility that it is the effect of salt bleaching the otherwise orange-red firing clays utilised (D. Hurst pers. comm.). There is chlorine in salt ($NaCl_2$), and if containers were used over and over again, as suggested by the repaired rims, it is likely that bleaching would have occurred. What is important is that: (1) this effect was extremely rare during Briquetage Phase 1; (2) it was observed more often on briquetage from mid second century BC salt production; and (3) was extremely common thereafter. This whitening effect on containers is consistently viewed on hand-squeezed pedestals of Late Iron Age and early Roman date, and also on the platform fragments, walling debris and flooring material in these assemblages. The bleaching could be viewed as salt saturation of the briquetage.

It is possible to use this bleaching effect on the hand-squeezed pedestals in particular to show how the pedestals were positioned in the oven. Hand-squeezed pedestals are white down one half of their length where you can imagine the brine was dribbling all over with splashing from constant addition of brine to the pans. The other half of the pedestals would have been tucked underneath the trough/pans. These pedestals and the wall fragments and flooring of the ovens also display a range of extraordinary colours: pinks, purples, and lavenders. These are colours which emerge from high temperature firing (Matson 1971). The pedestals are in many cases very brittle, distorted, bloated, and cracked; they are harsh to touch. These same effects can be seen on the wall fragments, which are often deep purple in colour. The flooring fragments have a thick layer of white coloured clay on the upper surface while the rest of the irregularly thick pieces, which may have rested on the sides of the fire pits, are typically orange-red. In some assemblages, particularly Addlethorpe (Morris 2002), the thick oven walling is salt glazed, overfired, cracked, and crazed like the pedestals. All of this contrasts considerably with the pyramidal pedestals from Briquetage Phase 1 sites, which only occasionally show 'salty' patches and are never overfired. Clearly, the use of heat and the intensity of heating were different between the direct heating system of an open hearth and the controlled, indirect heating system of flued saltern ovens.

The quantity of salt made during this intensification of production would have been several times greater than that of the earlier phase. The number of salterns increased very dramatically during the Later Iron Age and early Roman periods. The tempering of briquetage with organic matter allowed for greater porosity of the material which would have aided construction and use with greater heat. The intensity of use evidenced by the bleaching and repairing of containers and similar evidence on supports, as well as the use of indirect heating systems which could be better controlled through the construction of flues, all point towards the production of more salt. This increase in salt production was taken to an even greater degree during the late Roman period in Norfolk with the use of lead pans, enormous pedestals (Percival 2001b), vast settling tanks and ovens with double, opposing flue systems (Crowson 2001, figs. 54 and 61).

Distribution and function

If there was a significant intensification of production during the Later Iron Age and early Roman periods, how can we identify the distance to which this salt was transported, since these shallow troughs and pans were clearly not appropriate for use as transportation vessels? They are obviously not salt transport packs, based on their broad, shallow forms, and sherds from briquetage containers have never been found on settlement sites in the East Midlands away from the coast.

During the Later Iron Age, salt was also produced from inland brine springs sources, and the distributions of ceramic packs transporting salt both from Droitwich in Worcestershire and from a source or sources in Cheshire to settlements in the wider Midlands area (Morris 1985, figs. 6 and 10; 1994, 384–386), and from other coastal locations inland (e.g. Bradley 1975; Poole 1984; 1991), is well documented. Comparison of the distributions of these different sources reveals that there is a vacant area of similar size inland from the Fens (Fig. 8). It is, therefore, likely that the fenland salt was being transported in non-ceramic, perishable containers such as bags or baskets to settlements in the East Midlands (Morris 2001e).

What was the salt used for in these various regions? There are the obvious uses for preservation of foodstuffs, principally meat and cheese, as well as for the processing of animal hides. Human health requirements for salt in a temperate environment would have been easily achieved via this food intake. The use of salt as currency and bridewealth cannot be ruled out (Godelier 1971; 1977), particularly prior to the common use of money as currency. Recently, Maltby (2006) has argued that an increased demand for salt used for curing meat may have been a major factor in the intensification in salt production during the Late Iron Age.

Who were the salt makers?

It is possible that the earliest salt makers in Britain were women – this is based on the modes of production established by Peacock (1982, 6–11) and Van der Leeuw (1977) for the manufacture of pottery through studies of ethnographic examples, and adapted for textile production by DeRoche (1997). Peacock and Van der Leeuw recognised that it is most likely that the production of hand-made, bonfired pottery was universally the realm of women potters if everyday pottery was being produced; it is only when there is a serious investment in structures, equipment, and scale of output that men appear to conduct production. Exceptions to this are known to occur if the pottery is being made for non-daily use, such as for special events when men are known to make pots (Marshall 1985). If the scale of production is modest, as for domestic use and for some trading outside the local community

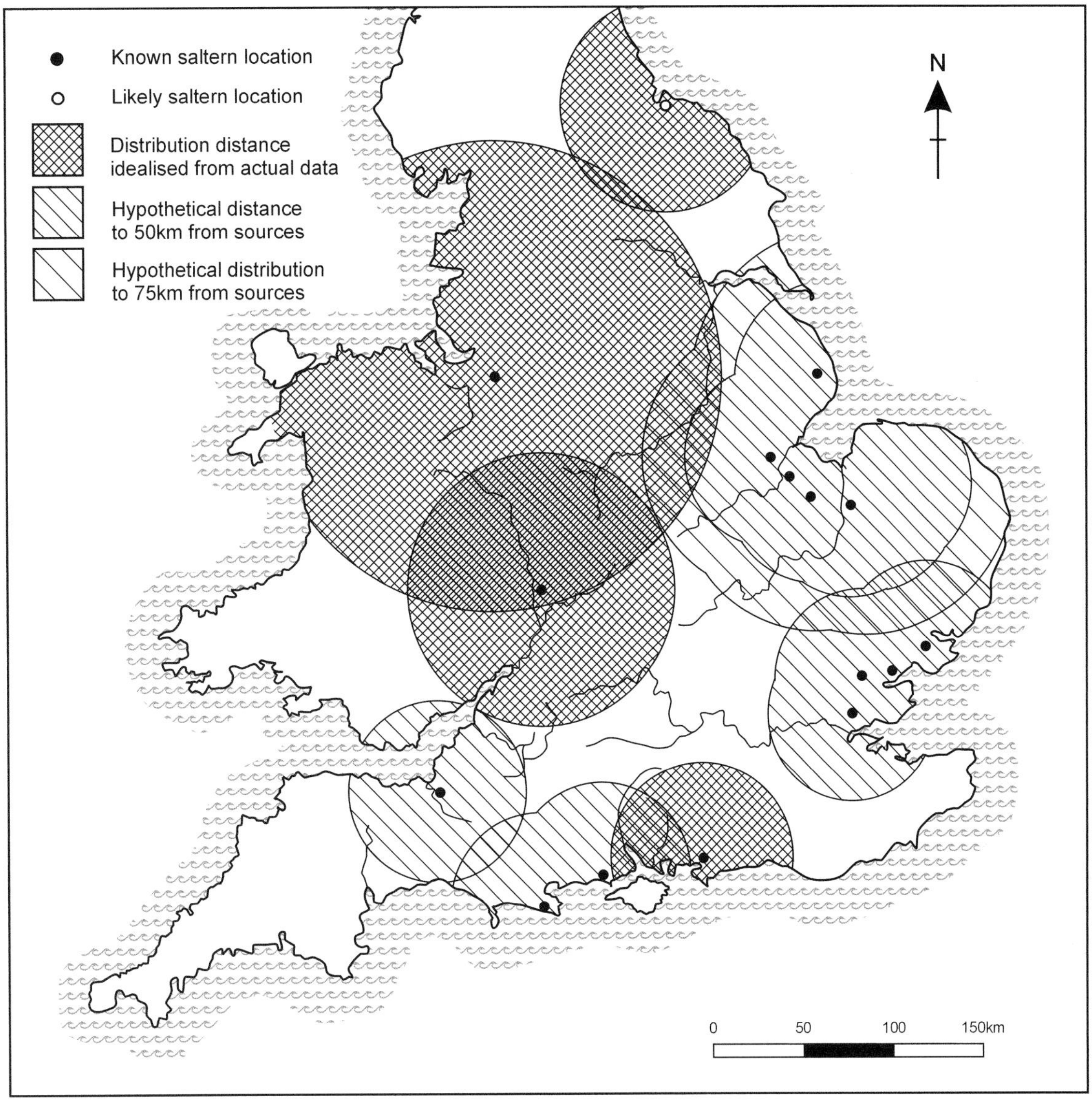

Fig. 8. The distribution of salt in England during the Later Iron Age based on actual and suggestive data (after Morris 2001e, fig. 123).

(domestic or household production; household industry), then production tends to be run by women. Larger-scale production is conducted by men when potmaking becomes a major source of family income (individual workshops; nucleated workshops).

The earlier briquetage is very much like pottery, particularly the pyramidal pedestals which are smoothed, well made, and similar to the surfaces of pots and very much like clay loomweights in form. Investment of effort beyond that which might be expected for a coarse industrial ceramic is clearly evident. The fossil shell-bearing clays for making the contemporary pots are the same as the clays for making the briquetage. The locations of salt making are near the settlements on the Fen edge, i.e. women salt makers would have been able to be close to their homes and families if necessary. There are only simple hearth-like structures in use – there are no specific structures (i.e. no investment in plant) designed to assist in the salt making process.

However, during the Later Iron Age changes begin to occur. Salterns are found away from the settlements, deep in the Fens, and the temper is carried to the clays found at the locations of the salterns. Intensity of production begins to develop with the building of oven structures; more production sites are known to exist; and then there is the bleaching of the ceramic material suggesting considerable intensification by the first century AD, which suggests that the briquetage was used for several salt making sessions at any one time or continuously for many days – rather than for short periods of time. Lots of salt was being made – more salt than could possibly have been used domestically by local communities.

It is possible then that during the intensification period, men took over the production of salt. However, many aspects suggest that this might not be the case. Although during the second century BC (Briquetage Phase 2), there is expansion into the Fens to make salt and an increase in the number of locations, the actual saturation of the briquetage containers and pedestals is not as intense as in the first-century AD and later assemblages (Briquetage Phase 3). Total wall saturation bleaching was not observed amongst the Cowbit container sherds. The presence of settlements of this date without salt working debris actually in the Fens is non-existent. The amount of domestic pottery and food remains at salterns indicate that they were not locations of long occupation. Therefore it is possible that women could have been the salt makers during Briquetage Phase 2, the beginning of intensification in production. During Briquetage Phase 3, salterns with Roman pottery present in the assemblages were often located near settlements of similar date in the Fens (Hayes and Lane 1992; Lane 1993), allowing for the possibility that some domestic chores and salt production may have been conducted in tandem.

The gender of later prehistoric and early Roman period salt makers in England is uncertain at present. A programme of research and experimental reconstruction is planned to investigate the number of salt workers at hand-squeezed pedestal-bearing salterns due to the individuality apparent on these objects (Fig. 7b). If it proves possible to identify individuals and determine their laterality and hand-size, this could add important information to this exploration of salt makers and modes of production.

Salt magic

Although there are distinct economic reasons why salt production appears to have been an important task for prehistoric and early Roman people in the Fenland, what did they actually think about salt and the sea? The sea does not appear to have been a food resource for later prehistoric people in the area (Serjeantson *et al.* 1994; see also Dobney and Ervynck this volume) – no fish or oyster shells have been found on Middle Bronze Age to Late Iron Age sites in this region. But salt was won from it.

The sea is water with a salty taste. It can be transformed into steam through the magic of heating by fire. The creation of steam and the disappearance of the water leaves behind white crystals. This is the world of magicians. It must have been even more mysterious for salt makers using salt-water which rises out of the earth at inland brine spring sources (Woodiwiss 1992). Were these locations magical places for prehistoric people? Undoubtedly such locations were recognised as unusual because the salt-water would have poisoned the soils, and normal plants would have been unable to grow in such environments. Similarly these would have been places that attracted wild animals, with the salt and associated minerals having a magnet-like effect.

The capability of salt to transform the world – to delay decomposition and preserve food for some time – may have been viewed as something very special. Reversing the natural trend of the world to decay must have been powerful magic in prehistory.

Acknowledgements

Many thanks go to the excellent team of Tom Lane, Andrew Crosby, and Sarah Percival for helping to make the Salt volume so successful – their enthusiasm for fenland briquetage made it all great fun, despite the hard work. The revised illustrations used here were prepared by Penny Copeland, whom I would like to thank for her persistence and patience. The preparation for the current article revealed a few mistakes in the original illustrations in Lane and Morris (2001), for which I would like to apologise, as they were my responsibility at the time. Finally, special thanks to Tom for allowing me to use information from the unpublished Addlethorpe assemblage.

Bibliography

Arnold, D.E. 1985. *Ceramic Theory and Cultural Process.* Cambridge: Cambridge University Press.

Baker, F.T. 1960. The Iron Age salt industry in Lincolnshire, *Lincolnshire Architectural and Archaeological Society* 8, 26–34.

Baker, F.T. 1975. Salt making sites on the Lincolnshire coast before the Romans, in De Brisay and Evans 1975, 31–32.

Bayliss, A. and McCormac, G. 2001. Radiocarbon dates from Cowbit, in Lane and Morris 2001, 89–90.

Bradley, R. 1975. Salt and settlement in the Hampshire Sussex border, in De Brisay and Evans 1975, 20–25.

Bell, A., Gurney, D. and Healey, H. 1999. *Lincolnshire Salterns: Excavations at Helpringham, Holbeach St Johns and Bicker Haven.* Sleaford: East Anglian Archaeology Report 89.

De Brisay, K.W. and Evans, K.A. (eds). 1975. *Salt, the Study of an Ancient Industry.* Colchester: Colchester Archaeological Group.

Chowne, P., Cleal, R.M.J. and Fitzpatrick, A.P. with Andrews, P. 2001. *Excavations at Billingborough, Lincolnshire, 1975–8: a Bronze–Iron Age Settlement and Salt-working Site.* Salisbury: East Anglian Archaeology Report 94.

Cleal, R.M.J. and Bacon, J.K.F. 2001. Briquetage, in Chowne *et al.* 2001, 56–65.

Crosby, A. 2001a. Briquetage containers from Ingoldmells Beach, in Lane and Morris 2001, 410–424.

Crosby, A. 2001b. Briquetage (Morton Fen, Lincolnshire), in Lane and Morris 2001, 106–133.

Crosby, A. 2001c. Briquetage (Bourne–Morton Canal), in Lane and Morris 2001, 290–302.

Crowson, A. 2001. Excavation of a late Roman saltern at Blackborough End, Middleton, Norfolk, in Lane and Morris 2001, 162–182.

Daire, M.-Y. (ed). 1994. *Le Sel Gaulois: Bouilleurs de sel et ateliers de briquetages armoricains à l'Age du Fer.* Saint-Malo: Dossiers du Centre Régional d'Archéologie d'Alet.

DeRoche, C.D. 1997. Studying Iron Age production, in A. Gwilt and C. Haselgrove (eds), *Reconstructing Iron Age Societies*, 19–25. Oxford: Oxbow Monograph 71.

Godelier, M. 1971. 'Salt Currency' and the circulation of commodities among the Baruya of New Guinea, in G. Dalton (ed.), *Studies in Economic Anthropology*, 52–73. Washington: American Anthropological Association Studies 7.

Godelier, M. 1977. 'Salt Money' and the circulation of commodities among the Baruya of New Guinea, in M. Godelier, *Perspectives in Marxist Anthropology*, 127–151. Cambridge: University of Cambridge Press.

Gurney, D. 1980. Evidence of Bronze Age salt-production at Northey, Peterborough, *Northamptonshire Archaeology* 15, 1–11.

Gurney, D. 1999. A Romano-British salt-making site at Shell Bridge, Holbeach St Johns: Excavations by Ernest Greenfield, 1961, in Bell *et al.* 1999, 70–81.

Hallam, S.J. 1960. Romano-British salt industry in south Lincolnshire, *Lincolnshire Architectural and Archaeological Society* 8, 35–75.

Hayes, P.P. and Lane, T. 1992. *The Fenland Project Number 5: Lincolnshire Survey, the South-West Fens*. Sleaford: East Anglian Archaeology Report 55.

Healey, H. 1999. An Iron Age Salt-making site at Helpringham Fen, in Bell *et al.* 1999, 1–19.

Knight, D. 2001. Iron Age Pottery (Langtoft, Lincolnshire), in Lane and Morris 2001, 261–262.

Lane, T. 1993. *The Fenland Project Number 8: Lincolnshire Survey, the Northern Fen-Edge*. Sleaford: East Anglian Archaeology Report 66.

Lane, T. 2001. Fenland survey briquetage: the landscape setting, in Lane and Morris 2001, 341–348.

Lane, T. and Morris, E.L. (eds) 2001. *A Millennium of Saltmaking; Prehistoric and Roman Salt Production in the Fenland*. Sleaford: Lincolnshire Archaeology and Heritage Reports 4.

Maltby, M. 2006. Salt and animal products: linking production and use in Iron Age Britain, in M. Maltby (ed.), *Integrating Zooarchaeology*, 117–122. Oxford: Oxbow Books.

Marshall, Y. 1985. Who made the Lapita pots? A case study in gender archaeology, *Journal of the Polynesian Society* 95.3, 205–233.

Matson, F.R. 1971. A study of temperatures used in firing ancient Mesopotamian pottery, in R. Brill (ed.), *Science and Archaeology*, 65–79. Cambridge (MA): Massachusetts Institute of Technology Press.

May, J. 1976. *Prehistoric Lincolnshire*. Lincoln: History of Lincolnshire Committee.

Morris, E.L. 1985. Prehistoric salt distributions: two case studies from western Britain, *Bulletin of the Board of Celtic Studies* 32, 336–379.

Morris, E.L. 1994. Production and distribution of pottery and salt in Iron Age Britain: a review, *Proceedings of the Prehistoric Society* 60, 371–393.

Morris, E.L. 2001a. The Fenland Project evidence: summaries, discussions and a model – briquetage, in Lane and Morris 2001, 351–376.

Morris, E.L. 2001b. Briquetage (Langtoft, Lincolnshire), in Lane and Morris 2001, 252–261.

Morris, E.L. 2001c. Briquetage (Market Deeping, Lincolnshire), in Lane and Morris 2001, 265–279.

Morris, E.L. 2001d. Briquetage (Cowbit, Lincolnshire), in Lane and Morris 2001, 33–63.

Morris, E.L. 2001e. Briquetage and salt production and distribution systems: a comparative study, in Lane and Morris 2001, 389–404.

Morris, E.L. 2002. *Briquetage from Excavations along the Addlethorpe Bypass*. Heckington: APS Archaeology/Heritage Trust for Lincolnshire archive client report.

Morris, E.L. and Percival, S. 2001. The Fenland Survey: a reassessment – briquetage, in Lane and Morris 2001, 323–341.

Murphy, P. 2001. Impressions and other plant material in briquetage, in Lane and Morris 2001, 37–38.

Olivier, L. 2000. Le "Briquetage de la Seille" (Moselle): nouvelles recherches sur une exploitation proto-industrielle du sel à l'âge du Fer, *Bulletin des Antiquités Nationales* 32, 143–171.

Peacock, D.P.S. 1982. *Pottery in the Roman World.* London: Longman.

Peacock, D.P.S. 1984. Seawater, salt and ceramics, in M.G. Fulford and D.P.S. Peacock, *Excavations at Carthage: The British Mission, Vol. 1.2. The Pottery and other Ceramic Objects from the Site*, 263–264. Sheffield: Department of Archaeology and Prehistory.

Percival, S. 2001a. Briquetage from Downham West. in Lane and Morris 2001, 314–318.

Percival, S. 2001b. Briquetage (Middleton, Norfolk), in Lane and Morris 2001, 182–202.

Poole, C. 1984. Briquetage containers, in B. Cunliffe, *Danebury, An Iron Age Hillfort in Hampshire, Vol. 2. The Excavations 1969–1978: The Finds*, 426–430. London: Council for British Archaeology Research Report 52.

Poole, C. 1991. Briquetage containers, in B. Cunliffe and C. Poole. *Danebury, An Iron Age Hillfort in Hampshire, Vol. 5. The Excavations 1979–1988: The Finds*, 404–407. London: Council for British Archaeology Research Report 73.

Precious, B. 2001. Roman pottery (Morton Fen saltern), in Lane and Morris 2001, 133–145.

Prilaux, G. 2000. *La Production du Sel à l'Age du Fer.* Montagnac: Protohistoire Européenne 5.

Pryor, F.M.M. 1980. *Excavation at Fengate, Peterborough, England: the Third Report.* Peterborough: Northamptonshire Archaeological Society Monograph 2/Royal Ontario Museum Archaeological Monograph 6.

Rye, O.S. 1981. *Pottery Technology; Principles and Reconstruction.* Washington: Taraxacum Manuals in Archaeology 4.

Serjeantson, D., Wales, S. and Evans, J. 1994. Fish in later prehistoric Britain, *Offa* 51, 332–339.

Simmons, B.B. 1975. Salt making in the silt fens of Lincolnshire in the Iron Age and Roman periods, in De Brisay and Evans 1975, 33–36.

Skibo, J.M., Schiffer, M.B. and Reid, K.C. 1989. Organic-tempered pottery: an experimental study, *American Antiquity* 54, 122–146.

Swan, V.G. 1984. *The Pottery Kilns of Roman Britain.* London: HMSO.

Swinnerton, H.H. 1932. The prehistoric pottery sites of the Lincolnshire coast, *Antiquaries Journal* 12, 239–253.

Van der Leeuw, S.E. 1977. Towards a study of the economics of pottery making, in B.L. van Beek, R.W. Brandt and W. Groenman-van Waateringe (eds), *Ex Horreo*, 68–77. Amsterdam: University of Amsterdam.

Woodiwiss, S. (ed.) 1992. *Iron Age and Roman Salt Production and the Medieval Town of Droitwich.* London: Council for British Archaeology Research Report 81.

Excarnation to cremation: continuity or change?

Gillian Carr

Introduction

Iron Age burial is very rare in many parts of Britain. Indeed, most of the regional burial traditions catalogued to date were minority rites; that is to say, most of the population was disposed of in archaeologically unrecoverable (or as yet unrecovered) ways. The aim of this paper is to discuss two of those rites, excarnation (literally 'defleshing') and cremation, and to explore the idea that the change from the former to the latter, where it occurred, represented a less radical shift than we might imagine.

Before discussing these two practices in more detail, a brief description of the variety of burial rites that are apparent in Iron Age Britain is appropriate. Whimster (1981) divides inhumation practices as follows: the central southern English tradition (including what was then termed 'pit burial', although some of these 'burials' might now be better seen as excarnations); 'Durotrigian' inhumation in southern Dorset; inhumation in cists in south-west England; La Tène inhumation in eastern Yorkshire; and 'peripheral practices' in northern and western zones. Inhumation of skeletally-sexed males with weapons and females with mirrors was another choice of burial rite for certain individuals in the Late Iron Age (e.g. Collis 1973; Farley 1983), although these attributions of sex were not necessarily related to the gender of these individuals in life, as the grave from Bryher, Isles of Scilly, combining sword and mirror shows (Johns 2002). Since Whimster wrote, inhumation cemeteries have been found in other areas, as at Mill Hill, Deal, in Kent (Parfitt 1995), Thetford, Norfolk (Gregory 1992), or Yarnton, Oxfordshire (Hey *et al.* 1999), but the overall pattern has not radically altered.

This brief review provides a backdrop to two of the arguably more interesting rites found in southern Britain: excarnation, hitherto seen as an Early and Middle Iron Age rite, and cremation, which was first practised in the Late Iron Age. Along with the weapon and mirror inhumations mentioned above, the adoption of cremation can be seen as part of the emergence of a visible, separate burial rite for the individual. Geographically, excarnation and cremation overlap in central southern England, an area where excarnation was relatively common (Carr and Knüsel 1997). Examples of cremation are seen in east Hampshire at sites such as Alton, Neatham, and Owslebury (Collis 1977; Millett 1987), and in West Sussex, at Westhampnett (Fitzpatrick 1997a). Excarnation is also (albeit rarely) found in parts of south-east England, the 'heartland' of cremation. Disarticulated human remains have been found in Kent at Dumpton Gap, Broadstairs; Crundale Limeworks, near Godmersham; and on a site at the foot of Castle Hill, Folkestone (P. Bennett pers. comm.). In other parts of south-east England, such as Essex, funerary rituals left little or no discernible trace until the later pre-Roman Iron Age (Sealey 1996, 57). We are thus discussing a minority of minority practices.

Excarnation and cremation

Some years ago, Chris Knüsel and I argued that for much of the Iron Age, excarnation was one of the commonest ways of disposing of the dead in southern Britain (Carr and Knüsel 1997). Indeed, it seems that this practice was performed from the Late Bronze Age onwards (Brück 1995). We argued that some corpses were exposed, possibly on platforms, until the flesh had partially decayed, or had been picked clean by animals and birds. As we find many partially and completely disarticulated bodies in the Iron Age, it is likely that the deceased were left to decay for varying periods. At some ritually specified time, bodies or body parts were brought back onto the settlement and deposited in pits and ditches. The archaeological signature for such a rite comprises elements such as animal gnawing and weathering on bones, and absent small bones, such as phalanges, which would have been among the first skeletal elements to drop off a decomposing body. These features, of course, would vary depending on the *method* of excarnation, which may not always have occurred through exposure in the open air.

In the Later Iron Age, a cremation burial rite, broadly similar to that of northern France, was introduced to parts of southern and south-eastern Britain (Fitzpatrick 1997a; see also Hamilton this volume). These cremations were often placed in grave pits, complete with (sometimes imported) grave goods, generally in cemeteries not settlements. Cremation is often seen as a foreign introduction transplanted wholesale to Britain in the early first century BC. This view has been recently reformulated by Creighton (2000, 19–20), in a discussion of the emergence or intrusion of new leaders with their *comitates* (bands of warriors/horsemen) during the Middle to Late Iron Age transition. For Creighton, these people instigated many of the changes we see in the archaeological record at this time, such as the move from hillforts to *oppida*, the use of gold and new types of pottery, and the imitation of Gallic rites of burial.

Creighton also speculates that, later on, elite Britons, who were raised in Rome as *obsides* (loosely 'hostages') and had returned to Britain as Roman client rulers, employed the same kinds of strategies for displaying power and authority as their patron, the eventual emperor Augustus, even constructing mounds above some of their burials in emulation of his mausoleum (*ibid.*, 188). Creighton implies that the congruence of burial rites in Britain and Gaul is a result of similar strategies among the elite of those areas, rather than a spread of the rite from one to the other. He considers that we should not necessarily see cremation as a 'foreign' rite, with the Channel as a divide, creating our own 'here' and 'there' which may not have been relevant then (J. Creighton pers. comm.).

However the rite reached Britain, I argue here that it was reformulated and reinterpreted by native Britons in a way that made sense to them and incorporated important Middle Iron Age concerns. Focussing on central southern and south-eastern Britain, I will ask whether the change from excarnation to cremation was as fundamental as many have imagined, or whether there is evidence for continuity of, and similarity in, practice. I will also ask whether there was a clear distinction between the two rites, or whether this became blurred towards the end of the Iron Age.

I have selected three main sites to illustrate my argument – King Harry Lane (Stead and Rigby 1989) and Folly Lane (Niblett 1999) in St Albans, and Westhampnett in West Sussex (Fitzpatrick 1997a) – supplementing them with data from other sites where appropriate. These three were chosen because they were excavated using modern techniques and are extensively published. It could be argued that they are atypical, but, given that cremation was a minority rite, I would suggest that all cremation cemeteries are, to a certain extent, atypical. In addition to the occasional large cemeteries like Westhampnett and King Harry Lane, cremation is represented by isolated burials of the un-urned, high-status Welwyn type (such as Lexden and Welwyn), and by the Aylesford cemeteries, comprising groups or clusters of urned graves, often described as 'family circles', and containing few artefacts. These types are part of the same rite and have been described as 'different ends of a spectrum' (Creighton 2000, 191).

Variation in practice

It is increasingly apparent that there was no single way of carrying out excarnation or cremation. There were many variations on a theme; we need only compare the cemeteries and sequences of ritual at Westhampnett (Fitzpatrick 1997a) and King Harry Lane (Pearce 1997; 1998). In the case of excarnation, there was variation in the method, period, and place of exposure, for example, in whether it took place above or below ground, or inside or outside the settlement. New research also suggests that, at least at Danebury, exposure was for the purposes of displaying the mutilated and denigrated dead, possibly captives brought in from elsewhere (Craig *et al.* 2005).

Not only can we see variations in mortuary ritual at each site (e.g. Fitzpatrick 1997a, 241), but it can also be observed that the change from excarnation to cremation, where it occurred, was not clear-cut. As we shall see below, disarticulated remains of exposed bodies of Later Iron Age or early Roman date are beginning to be recognised (e.g. Fulford 2001), whilst there is evidence that some cremated bodies underwent some excarnation through exposure, or were laid out for long periods of time, before burning. We now realise that we must be site-specific in our analyses of the treatment of the dead, even if there were shared aspects of practice in neighbouring settlements. With such a contextual approach, we can better understand variations in mortuary ritual. It is becoming increasingly apparent that heterogeneity, not homogeneity, was the norm for Late Iron Age burial practices.

The blurring of mortuary rituals

Excarnation in the Late Iron Age and Roman period

Evidence is now emerging that excarnation did not simply die out at the start of the Late Iron Age, but, in fact, continued into the Roman period. As Fitzpatrick (2000) notes in his discussion of the Westhampnett cemetery, unburnt human remains have been found at several nearby Late Iron Age sites, including the temple on Hayling Island and the settlements at Copse Farm, Oving, and North Bersted, leading him to observe that 'the excarnation of corpses, with some parts of the dead eventually being brought back to the settlement, appears to have continued to be practised... in the Late Iron Age cremation burial was not necessarily adopted by all communities' (*ibid.*, 25). Human remains were found in two Late Iron Age pits at Suddern Farm, Hampshire (Cunliffe and Poole 2000, 152).

In some cases, people were cremating and excarnating their dead at the same time, as parallel practices. Elsewhere, some people may have excarnated their dead while their neighbours cremated theirs. At Hinxton Rings in Cambridgeshire, a few inhumations were found next to the first century BC cremations (Hill *et al.* 1999). The report argues that 'the group burying (some of?) their dead were possibly living close to, working and feasting with and may even have been related to, others still practising earlier burial traditions' (ibid., 269). In the earlier of two mortuary enclosures at Owslebury, the primary burial was that of an inhumed individual accompanied by weapons and surrounded by cremations (Collis 1994). Assuming that the gap between the central burial and the earliest cremations was not great, this represents another example of parallel rites within one site.

Other possible evidence for the mixing of rites at the same site comes from Rushey Mead in Leicester, where the remains of a man were found in a pit thought to date to the Late Iron Age (although an earlier date could not be discounted). Because several elements of the pit fill (the grain, antler, and pottery) were charred, but not the skeleton, Pollard (2001, 28) argued that this find represented a 'hybridisation' of the 'pit burial' inhumation and Aylesford–Swarling cremation rites. It would appear that a 'blurring' of burial rites is perhaps more 'normal' than we have previously acknowledged.

Disarticulated bones have been recorded on several Roman sites. At Folly Lane, a number were found in ritual shafts and enclosure ditches dating from the early second to late third centuries AD, to the south and east of the Late Iron Age ditch; at least one bone showed evidence of animal gnawing (Niblett 1999, 323; 404). At Silchester, a pit from Insula XXI contained human remains including a femur, other leg bones, and part of a skull of an adult male (Hope and Fox 1900, 111), whilst at Baldock, stray human remains were found in a range of Late Roman contexts (Henderson 1986, 391; Stead and Rigby 1986, 45). Although some of the finds from the sites may be from disturbed graves, for example at Folly Lane, the other examples may suggest that excarnation continued into the Roman period alongside, and sometimes on the same site as, cremation.

In the second century AD, a large number of apparently ritual pits were dug within, and peripheral to, cremation cemeteries (Niblett 2000, 102). Forty-one are known from St Albans, 15 of which contained 'stray' human bones, including one second century AD skull that had been defleshed, as shown by the cut marks and perforations (Mays and Steele 1996; Niblett 1999, 307). As the teeth and mandible were missing, it was suggested that the skull had been exposed before it was incorporated into the pit, whilst the cut marks were thought to be mutilations visited upon a lifeless but still fairly fresh corpse. Since the area around the foramen magnum was lacking, the skull was probably mounted on a pole in antiquity and displayed (cf. Craig *et al.* 2005). Niblett (2000, 103) sees the stray bones from St Albans as evidence for the continuation of excarnation in the Roman period, with pits as places where the dead were placed temporarily.

Fulford (2001) has recently brought together the evidence for ritual deposits in Roman pits, wells, and shafts in Silchester, London, Neatham, Baldock, St Albans, and Portchester. Human (and animal) burials, and articulated and disarticulated remains, including single bones, occur frequently in these kinds of archaeological features. Esmonde Cleary (2000) also lists numerous features of Roman date where bodies and body parts are found in southern and eastern Roman Britain, including temples, wet places, wells, shafts, pits, and prehistoric monuments. Whilst only a minority of the Late Iron Age and early Roman population was cremated in Britain – or at least can be accounted for by archaeologists – these disarticulated bones may well represent some of the rest of the population.

'Exposure' before cremation

The area with the most potential for similarity in funerary practice between the Early and Middle Iron Ages and Late Iron Age/early Roman period is in the period of waiting after death. With excarnation, it is necessary to wait for the flesh to decay before the remains are further manipulated as part of the mortuary ritual. With cremation, the deceased often 'lies in state' or is 'laid out', waiting for the mourners to arrive and the funerary feast to be assembled. Niblett (1999, 58) lists four reasons why it might have been necessary for the deceased to lie in state in the shaft, which was used as a mortuary chamber at Folly Lane:

1. To house the body until an auspicious year or season in which the funeral could take place.

2. To allow time, and possibly a place, for initiation rites for a successor to be carried out.
3. To house the body while the whole tribe or *pagus* gathered together, and where visiting dignitaries and family members could pay their respects (or perhaps lay their claims).
4. To provide a place for the excarnation of the body before the final cremation.

It is not known for how long the dead person was kept in the shaft before cremation, as the small quantity of bone that survived was not sufficiently well preserved to determine whether it was already 'dry' when burnt (Niblett 2000, 99), but the mortuary chamber was hypothesised to have been robust enough to have stood for twenty years or more (Niblett 1999, 58). The upcast mound on which the cremation took place was low, unimpressive, and somewhat irregular, which Niblett (*ibid.*) suggests could have been due to five, ten, or even twenty years of weathering before the cremation took place. Folly Lane may, however, have been atypical compared to other cremations. Creighton (2000, 219–20) suggests that the deceased may have been Cunobelin, who died some time between AD 40 and 43, and even might have lain in state until a successor was anointed after the Claudian annexation of his territory. If Late Iron Age people were used to the concept and sight of corpses waiting for a long period before final mortuary rites were carried out, they would not presumably have objected to an extended period of 'lying in state' for Cunobelin.

It is, however, worth asking whether others also waited a significant amount of time before cremation; generally speaking, the period of waiting is not assumed to be particularly long. It is possible, however, that, in some places, the waiting *was* long enough for some defleshing caused by natural decay processes to occur. This would represent an example of (albeit perhaps unintentional) 'blurring' of mortuary practices.

Commenting on the other pre-Flavian cemeteries at St Albans, Niblett (2000, 101) proposes an alternative explanation for 32 inhumations associated with mid first-century AD cremation enclosures, of which 28 were within, or aligned upon, the ditches of the enclosures. These people are buried with no sign of a grave cut and without any grave goods, and are generally seen as the poor retainers of the individuals buried in the enclosures. Niblett suggests, however, that these people may actually be dead who were 'exposed' on the banks or in the ditches surrounding the cremation cemeteries prior to cremation, and who were never 'retrieved' for cremation, although she gives no osteological evidence to support this hypothesis.

How can we tell archaeologically whether a body was exposed for a significant length of time before cremation? It is possible to differentiate between the cremated remains of an excarnated and 'dry' individual, and those of a partly or fully fleshed 'green' one, as green bone shows dehydration fissuring after burning (J. McKinley pers. comm.), although distinguishing between fresh and partly decomposed individuals is less straightforward, as fully fleshed and partially fleshed bone both burn well, and would turn white or creamy yellow (depending on whether it is cortical or trabecular bone). Entirely dry bone, on the other hand, would burn poorly and would turn blue-black, as it is the body fats that burn (Stirland 1989, 241). However, as incomplete burning can also be due to the body's position in the pyre, other, more conclusive archaeological indicators of excarnation should be sought, such as signs of animal gnawing on bones; such marks can survive on cremated bone (J. McKinley pers. comm.)

Evidence from Late Iron Age cremations in Luxembourg and the Champagne-Ardennes region of north-east France suggests that, in some cases, the human bone was already dry and brittle by the time it was cremated (Lambot *et al.* 1994, 135–41). At the Lamadelaine cemetery, outside the Titelberg, in Luxembourg, the excavators noted various other indicators suggesting that a protracted period of exposure took place before the funeral. These included the corrosion and fragmentation of iron fibulae and other personal effects *before* they were placed on the pyre, implying that they had been exposed in the open air for a period of time (Metzler-Zens *et al.* 1999, 408–9; 460). Exposure can be read as either lying in state, or excarnation by exposure – both are different practices, but are difficult to distinguish archaeologically. Similar evidence was seen at Thugny-Trugny, in the Ardennes department (Lambot *et al.* 1994). This emphasises the importance for continued osteoarchaeological examination of cremated bone for evidence of prior exposure. Because the differences between fully- and partly-fleshed cremated bones are not easily identifiable, such evidence may be easily missed, even by a specialist.

Four-posters, shrines, and pyres

Having argued that in the Late Iron Age, some bodies were exposed for a period of time prior to cremation, we may consider the locations that were potentially used for exposure earlier in the Iron Age. Carr and Knüsel (1997) favoured excarnation on four-post platforms, either on or off the settlement, although acknowledging that it would not have happened in the same place or by the same method at every site. Interestingly, there are now hints of what some of those alternative methods may have been. In a Late Bronze Age–Early Iron Age house at Cladh Hallan on South Uist, Parker Pearson found evidence of corpses that had been wrapped in a tight shroud and kept in the roof space (Parker Pearson *et al.* 2002). At Suddern Farm in Hampshire, an Early–Middle Iron Age cemetery of 60 people was excavated in a quarry outside the later enclosed settlement (Cunliffe and Poole 2000, 152–70). As many of the skeletons were incomplete or had missing elements, it is possible that they were excarnated before burial, or that the graves were the primary but temporary locations for burial before bones were removed for secondary burial in pits and ditches, although they may simply have been disturbed.

Keeping in mind the original hypothesis of excarnation on four-post platforms, let us consider the postulated link between exposure before secondary burial, and prolonged lying in state or 'laying out' before cremation. The common factor linking the two was the period of *waiting*. Where did the dead wait before cremation? At Folly Lane, the suggested place of exposure was the mortuary shaft. At Westhampnett, Fitzpatrick (1997a) proposes that the dead waited in shrines, citing parallels from the Continent. At Clemency, in Luxembourg, some 8 km from the Titelberg, a single well-furnished cremation of a man was found (Metzler *et al.* 1991). Just outside the ditch which enclosed the tumulus was a five-post structure, which might have been used for the lying in state of the corpse. Fitzpatrick (2000, 20–25) also draws attention to the 'shrine' in the centre of the cemetery enclosure at Acy-Romance, La Croizette (Ardennes), which Lambot *et al.* (1994) suggest may have been used for exposing the deceased before cremation.

Can we postulate a link between four-posters and shrines? The division between the two in Iron Age Britain is not always obvious (cf. Downes 1997, 146–8). However, if there was a link, this might explain why many shrines (if that is what they were) were square, when houses were round. The shape of the shrine may have deliberately echoed the shape of the excarnation platform, as both may have been used, at times and amongst other things, for display and exposure of the dead. Just as building roundhouses started in earnest after the construction of stone circles and henges ceased and echoed their shape (Fitzpatrick 1997b, 77), so we might suggest that shrines, which are primarily a Late Iron Age phenomenon, took the shape of the primarily Early and Middle Iron Age four-poster. Just as exposing the dead on a four-poster similar to those used as granaries may have been making links with regeneration and the renewal of agricultural fertility and between the living and the dead of the settlement, so exposure in a shrine may have been referring back to such beliefs, making links with, and paying homage to, an older tradition.

The percentage of the dead represented by excarnation and cremation

Another feature of both excarnation and cremation is that we have accounted for only a very small percentage of the living population, although partial explanations for this have already been given here. John Pearce (pers. comm.) calculates that *c.* 0.03% of the population is accounted for from known burials during the Roman period as a whole (a figure biased to late towns – Pearce calculates that known rural burials comprise less than 0.01% of the estimated rural population). These figures represent cremated and inhumed individuals taken together – the figures for cremation alone would be even smaller – and are based on a number of assumptions relating to the estimated population as a whole and mortality rates (Pearce 1999, chapter 2).

Based on the human remains from 22 Iron Age sites over a period of seven centuries, Wait (1985, 90) calculated that some 5% of the Iron Age population of central southern Britain as a whole was represented on sites and around 6% of all deaths at Danebury – although the size of the hillfort population is itself controversial, which would affect Wait's calculations. Further, the demographic profile does not reflect a 'normal' distribution (Wait 1985, 90); adults are far too common, and infants and adolescents too few, for all periods on hillforts. With Pearce's figures in mind, we might well therefore wish to lower both estimates significantly.

As Carr and Knüsel (1997) noted, the effect of agencies such as weathering and the action of scavenging animals and birds on a corpse should not be underestimated. Andrews and Cook (1985) looked at the modification of cow bones in Somerset and showed that skeletal disarticulation and disappearance of some elements occurred within six months. They found that dispersal was quite rapid for lighter elements, and that after eight years even excavation could not recover a complete record of dispersal. Other agencies included trampling by animals combined with gravitational movement down a nearby slope and scavenging by small carnivores. Complete destruction is possible in a small space of time, although the season when – as well as where – exposure took place will influence how fully a corpse is chewed and consumed, especially if the availability of prey varies seasonally.

That 5% or less of the southern British Iron Age population survives should not be considered surprising. They were the ones who were deposited in features that enabled them to survive archaeologically. If other bodies were exposed, particularly above ground, but not brought back onto the settlement for a secondary rite, we should not underestimate the capabilities of natural agencies for destroying or scattering the rest of the population. In temperate climates, soft tissues usually persist for a year or two, the ligaments and tendons around the joints being the most durable. If a body is exposed in autumn or winter, it will last longer than if exposed in summer. While most bodies will become skeletonised within a year or two, this can happen within weeks during the summer if aided by animal predators (Knight 1991).

It has been argued that we should not necessarily see

the 5% of the population represented on settlements as 'special' categories of people (*contra* Craig *et al.* 2005). It could simply be that, at a culturally prescribed time, perhaps in the course of the same ceremonies or rites of passage that special deposits were made in pits and ditches, remains from the area of excarnation were gathered up for secondary burial. If these remains had been subject to animal scavenging, weathering, and other natural agents of modification for up to ten years – Hill (1995, table 1.1) suggests that special deposits may have been made in pits only once a decade – then it is to be expected that only a small number of body parts survived and were available for deposition in pits and ditches.

Not only is the percentage of the total population accounted for low, but even this percentage rarely represents whole bodies. Just as we usually only find partial bodies, articulated limbs, and single bone elements on Early and Middle Iron Age settlements, in the Late Iron Age only a small percentage of the cremated body is generally represented in the grave pit. McKinley (2000, 41) found that, on average, only 40–60% of the expected bone weight is recovered from a cremation pyre and put in the grave; this is not particular to the Late Iron Age or Roman period. Although the time-consuming nature of recovery may be factor, it is not a particularly difficult task: indeed, at Westhampnett, Fitzpatrick (1997a, 213) suggested that the lack of general pyre debris mixed with cremated bone reflected the relative ease with which the latter can be retrieved from the ashes of the pyre.

Perhaps the inclusion of all the bone was not considered a pre-requisite. Most, if not all, cremation burials are effectively token (McKinley 2000, 42). Collis (1977, 26) describes the amount of bone from some of the less disturbed cremations at Owslebury as meagre. Less than a quarter of the maximum possible amount of ash (1.5–3 kg; McKinley 1989) was recovered from 65% of the burials at King Harry Lane, a weight that included animal bone (Pearce 1997, 177), whilst at Westhampnett, 70% of the graves contained less than 200 g of human bone, and 35% of them had less than 50 g (Fitzpatrick 1997a, 213–4). Cremated remains are, however, very fragmentary by nature, and often crumble as soon as they are lifted from the ground (J. McKinley pers. comm.), which may well have influenced the recovery percentages.

We can again see continuity and similarities in both excarnation and cremation. It would seem that Iron Age people were concerned with representing only a portion of the body in the pit or ditch on a settlement, or in the grave pit in the cemetery. Perhaps this was all that was deemed necessary.

Ancestors or individuals?

As only a small percentage of the excarnated population was brought back to a settlement, we have often speculated on their identity. Why were they chosen, and who were they? Hill (1995) has argued that we should interpret Iron Age human and animal remains in the same way, as parallels exist in their treatment, which may have included sacrifice. Others have argued that the human remains represent those who died an unnatural or unclean death, or were outcasts, whilst complete skulls were the result of 'Celtic' head hunting (Cunliffe 1983, 164). More recently, Cunliffe (1992) suggested that the bones relate to various types of death, including ritual killing or sacrifice, warfare trophies, and massacres. More generally, he sees them as the bones of the ancestors. It should be noted here, as an aside, that sacrifice is a problematic concept and difficult to prove from skeletal remains.

Others also view the human remains from Late Bronze Age and Iron Age settlements as 'ancestors'. Brück (1995, 262) links the deposition of human remains on middens, in pits and other features on Late Bronze Age settlements that may once have been agricultural installations, with the renewal of agricultural fertility, whilst Fitzpatrick (1997b, 83) argues that the placement of ancestors in pits and ditches ensured tradition and continuity by reproducing the tradition. Placement of older relatives at the boundary of the settlement may have helped to reaffirm the differences between the 'social' and the 'natural' worlds. Parker Pearson (1996, 123) also suggests that the occurrence of loose human bone in enclosure ditches implied a concern with place and ancestral claims to it. It is commonly assumed that the excarnated people brought back to the settlement for secondary burial were not individually known, recognised and commemorated, but were, instead, undifferentiated generic ancestors.

As Whitley (2002) has noted, however, 'the ancestors' have become omnipresent in British prehistory and are invoked too frequently and readily as the object of veneration or the legitimators of land claims or group rights. He argues that we need to be more contextual in our interpretations. Especially on smaller settlements, it is difficult to imagine that inhabitants did not know the identity of the deceased, whether they were from excarnation platforms or other locations of primary burial, and whether one year or ten had elapsed between their death and final deposition in the ground. It is difficult to believe that the deceased were simply anonymous 'ancestors'. Even though they may not have been buried in single graves with grave goods which commemorated their individual identity, as the later, cremated, dead were, they are likely to have been known as individuals. As such, rather than talking about the excarnated dead as 'ancestors', I believe that we can think of them as known individuals, just as the ordinary non-elite cremated dead were, and remembered for just as long.

Interestingly, new research on the excarnated dead from Danebury argues that some of those chosen for exposure were also known and named (probably powerful and high-status) individuals (Craig *et al.* 2005). The perimortem injuries and mutilation seen on some skeletons are compatible with their interpretation as the remains of warrior enemies, who were exposed and denigrated after death. In all, 91 (7.9%) out of 1151 specimens studied from Danebury displayed evidence of possible perimortem fragmentation. Such treatment of the dead may help us to understand other enigmatic finds such as the 'massacre' deposit at Cadbury Castle (Barrett *et al.* 2000). As James (2007) reminds us, most current interpretations of Iron Age society almost certainly understate the incidence of warfare and other forms of communal violence in the period.

The similarities between humans and animals

There are yet other examples of continuity between excarnation and cremation. As I have mentioned, Hill (1995, 105) has discussed some of the similarities in treatment of the human and animal remains found in special deposits and proposed that they derive from similar ritual processes of feasting and sacrifice. He also suggests that there was no distinction in the way that humans and animals were perceived and manipulated in these practices. With reference to the Danebury remains, Chris Knüsel (pers. comm.) disagrees with this, arguing that animals were neatly and regularly butchered, whereas humans were not.

Fulford's discussion (2001) of pervasive ritual behaviour in Roman Britain emphasises the number of wells, pits, and ditches, which contain articulated and disarticulated human and animal skeletons that had been treated in the same way, or at least underwent similar depositional practices. While Fulford did not compare, for example, element frequencies, disarticulation sequences, or degrees of preservation in any detail, it is possible at a general level to argue that humans and animals shared these depositional contexts in articulated and disarticulated states.

Do we see the same parallels in the treatment of human and animal remains in cremation? Animal and human bones were often cremated together. At Folly Lane, for example, no attempt was made to sort out the cremated animal and human bone before final deposition in the burial pit (Niblett 2000, 100). Animal and/or bird remains were found in 6% of the cremations at King Harry Lane, and in 50% (14/28) of the Late Iron Age and early Roman graves with pyre goods (Fitzpatrick 2000, 16). Cremated pig and/or chicken were present in one in five graves (87/445). At Westhampnett, 36 of the 44 contexts that yielded cremated animal bones were graves (Fitzpatrick 1997a, 73). While these animal remains could be interpreted as feasting material thrown on the pyre, the fact that cremated human and animal remains were carefully collected and deposited together does suggest a similarity in treatment, although in practical terms it may have been difficult to distinguish between them.

It must be acknowledged that the species of animals deposited or burned did not remain the same between the Middle and Late Iron Age. In the earlier part of the Iron Age, cattle, sheep, horses, and dogs were the most common species to be deposited in burials (Wait 1985, 137), but with the introduction of cremation, pig – along with domestic fowl at King Harry Lane (Davis 1989, 240) and sheep/goat at Westhampnett (McKinley *et al.* 1997, 73) – became the most common species. Pig was also the most numerous species selected for cremation in continental Europe (Méniel 1993, table 6). In addition, while particular units of animals were chosen for cremation at both King Harry Lane and Westhampnett, there was no indication that specific human body parts were selected (e.g. McKinley 1997, 68). I would suggest that it is not necessary for there to be total continuity in terms of body parts and animal species in order for the hypothesis to hold. Continuity can be seen in other ways, and is apparent in the deposition of humans together with animals, first in pits and ditches and later in cremation burials.

Similarities in patterning in pits/grave pits

One last similarity between the rites concerns the patterning of body parts and cremated bones. As Hill (1994), Oswald (1997) and others have demonstrated, the Iron Age population were very concerned with the orientation of entrances to houses, shrines, and enclosed settlements. This concern with cosmological order extended to deposition on sites, with varied articulations of human remains being positioned in pits and ditches in particular parts of the site, as at Winnall Down in Hampshire (Hill 1994, 8). Different age groups were also sometimes positioned in different places (Hill 1995, 107)

This concern with orientation also applied at the level of the pit itself. At Suddern Farm, special deposits in pits overall favoured the south-east and south-west sectors (Cunliffe and Poole 2000, 149). Whole bodies on pit bases appeared to prefer the western half of the pit, but higher up, had a focus on the sector from north-east to south. The patterning of pots and animals also reflected certain favoured areas. Whimster, too, observed that pit burials had 'a relatively strong concentration within the sector of the arc between the north and east and a correspondingly thin scatter between south and north-west' (Whimster 1981, 14).

This concern with patterning is also found in Late Iron Age cremation cemeteries. If the 46 published plans at King Harry Lane are an accurate guide, there was a preference for placing the cremated bone in the western and northern part of the grave (Pearce 1998, 104–5). At Westhampnett, 11 of the 16 burials (69%) that contained both cremated bone and grave goods, had the cremation deposits placed between the north-west and north-east of the grave (Powell and Fitzpatrick 1997, 281). Thus, whilst we must not necessarily expect to see the same orientation through time or even from site to site, the important point to note here is that orientation *continued* to be a concern.

Conclusion

Although I have sought to highlight the potential similarity between the two mortuary rites of excarnation and cremation, I do not deny that obvious differences exist, and that it is these that have previously been emphasised. For example, Hill (1995, 122) argues that the change represents 'a deliberate rejection of the dominant authoritative symbols of the use of the excarnated body and the use of its parts', or perhaps 'purification' in contrast to the 'prolonged physical decay of the corpse' – i.e. human intervention in the process of decay. This, however, assumes that the choice was 'either/or' and that one made a statement depending on the choice. I argue here, however, that the choice often may *not* have been one of 'either/or'. As Table 1 shows, many of the supposed distinctions between the rites were blurred; they were not on opposite poles, but formed a sliding scale of similarities; a continuity of concerns. The choice was sometimes neither one nor the other, but both.

In arguing that the change from excarnation to cremation should not be seen as an abrupt break, I have highlighted various aspects of the archaeological record. First, we must not assume that cremation followed excarnation at every site. In many cases there is an overlap of funerary practices, sometimes with several occurring at the same time (cf. Fitzpatrick 1997a, 227). At some sites, cremated individuals may first have been exposed or 'lain in state', albeit for an unknown and, probably, variable period of time, and not long enough to have become skeletonised.

In the earlier part of the Iron Age, excarnation probably took place, *inter alia*, on four-poster structures (Carr and Knüsel 1997). In the Late Iron Age, it has been argued that the dead of Westhampnett and other cemeteries were exposed in shrines before cremation. I have suggested that the square form of many shrines echoed the shape of the excarnation platform of earlier periods. As both were structures on or in which the dead waited before the next stage of the mortuary ritual, we can again see continuity in the burial rite.

A further similarity concerns the small percentage of the excarnated population that we find on settlements and the even lower proportion of the cremated population represented in cemeteries. An analogy can also be drawn between the many partial bodies and loose bones found on settlements and the small percentage of the total weight of the cremated deceased represented in a grave. Equally, while it is often suggested that the cremation rite reflects a new concern with individual identity, a reinterpretation of the Danebury evidence challenges this by arguing that many of the remains put on display in the hillfort were those of known individuals (Craig *et al.* 2005). Other points of convergence concern the similar treatment of humans and animals in death, and the concern for particular orientations and patterning of human remains within pits and graves.

In conclusion, whilst many see the adoption of cremation as a radical break (e.g. Hill 1995, 122; Creighton 2000, 189–90), there is a significant amount of evidence to suggest that this may not be the case. At the same time, we must continue to be site-specific in our interpretations since, although the wider picture suggests that the 'change' from excarnation to cremation was more about continuity, local traditions still varied enormously.

Acknowledgements

This paper has been improved by comments from the audience at the Durham Seminar; at a research seminar at Bradford University; at the 2002 BABAO meeting at Sheffield University; and at a conference on Later Iron Age burial practices in Chelmsford. I would also like to thank Chris Knüsel for his comments; Jacqueline McKinley, John Pearce and Paul Bennett for their advice; and the editors and anonymous referees of this volume for their helpful comments. All errors that remain are my own.

EXCARNATION	*CREMATION*
Period of waiting before secondary burial	Potential period of waiting before cremation
Minority of excarnated population deposited	Minority of population cremated
Small portion of body placed in pits/ditches	Small portion of body placed in grave pit
The dead as individuals	The dead as individuals
Deposited in the same contexts as animals	Deposited in the same contexts as animals
Concern with patterning of bones in pit	Concern with patterning of cremation in grave

Table 1. Potential blurring/mixing of Middle and Late Iron Age mortuary practices.

Bibliography

Andrews, P. and Cook, J. 1985. Natural modifications to bones in a temperate setting, *Man* (NS) 20, 675–691.

Barrett, J., Freeman, P. and Woodward, A. 2000. *Cadbury Castle, Somerset: the Later Prehistoric and Early Historic Archaeology.* London: English Heritage Archaeological Report 20.

Brück, J. 1995. A place for the dead: the role of human remains in Late Bronze Age Britain, *Proceedings of the Prehistoric Society* 61, 245–277.

Carr, G. and Knüsel, C. 1997. The ritual framework of excarnation by exposure as the mortuary practice of the early and middle Iron Ages of central southern Britain, in Gwilt and Haselgrove 1997, 167–173.

Collis, J.R. 1973. Burials with weapons in Iron Age Britain, *Germania* 51, 121–133.

Collis, J.R. 1977. Owslebury (Hants) and the problem of burials on rural settlements, in R. Reece (ed), *Burial in the Roman World*, 26–34. London: Council for British Archaeology Research Report 22.

Collis, J.R. 1994. An Iron Age and Roman cemetery at Owslebury, Hampshire, in Fitzpatrick and Morris 1994, 4–8.

Craig, R., Knüsel, C. and Carr, G. 2005. Fragmentation, mutilation and dismemberment: an interpretation of human remains in Iron Age sites, in M. Parker Pearson and N. Thorpe (eds), *Warfare, Violence and Slavery in Prehistory*, 165–180. Oxford: British Archaeological Reports International Series 1374.

Creighton, J. 2000. *Coins and Power in Late Iron Age Britain.* Cambridge: Cambridge University Press.

Cunliffe, B. 1983. *Danebury: The Anatomy of an Iron Age Hillfort.* London: Batsford.

Cunliffe, B. 1992. Pits, preconceptions and propitiation in the British Iron Age, *Oxford Journal of Archaeology* 11, 69–83.

Cunliffe, B. and Poole, C. 2000. *The Danebury Environs Programme: the Prehistory of a Wessex Landscape, Vol.2 – Part 3. Suddern Farm, Middle Wallop, Hants, 1991 and 1996.* Oxford: Oxford University Committee for Archaeology Monograph 49.

Davis, S. 1989. Animal remains from the Iron Age cemetery, in Stead and Rigby 1989, 240–259.

Downes, J. 1997. The shrine at Cadbury Castle: belief enshrined? in Gwilt and Haselgrove 1997, 145–152.

Esmonde Cleary, S. 2000. Putting the dead in their place: burial location in Roman Britain, in Pearce *et al.* 2000, 127–142.

Farley, M. 1983. A mirror burial at Dorton, Bucks, *Proceedings of the Prehistoric Society* 49, 269–302.

Fitzpatrick, A.P. 1997a. *Archaeological Excavations on the Route of the A27 Westhampnett Bypass, West Sussex, 1992, Vol. 2. The Late Iron Age, Romano-British, and Anglo-Saxon Cemeteries.* Salisbury: Wessex Archaeology Report 12.

Fitzpatrick, A.P. 1997b. Everyday life in Iron Age Wessex, in Gwilt and Haselgrove 1997, 73–86.

Fitzpatrick, A.P. 2000. Ritual, sequence and structure in Late Iron Age mortuary practices in north-west Europe, in Pearce *et al.* 2000, 15–29.

Fitzpatrick, A.P. and Morris E.L. (eds.) 1994. *The Iron Age in Wessex: Recent Work.* Salisbury: Trust for Wessex Archaeology.

Fulford, M. 2001. Links with the past: pervasive 'ritual' behaviour in Roman Britain, *Britannia* 32, 199–218.

Gregory, T. 1992. *Excavations in Thetford, 1980–1982: Fison Way.* Norwich: East Anglian Archaeology Report 53.

Gwilt, A. and Haselgrove, C. (eds.) 1997. *Reconstructing Iron Age Societies.* Oxford: Oxbow Monograph 71.

Henderson, J. 1986. The human bones, in Stead and Rigby 1986, 390–396.

Hey, G., Bayliss, A. and Boyle A. 1999. Iron Age inhumation burials at Yarnton, Oxfordshire, *Antiquity* 73, 551–562.

Hill, J.D. 1994. Why we should not take the data from Iron Age settlements for granted: recent studies of intra-settlement patterning, in Fitzpatrick and Morris 1994, 4–8.

Hill, J.D. 1995. *Ritual and Rubbish in the Iron Age of Wessex.* Oxford: British Archaeological Report British Series 242.

Hill, J.D., Evans, C. and Alexander, M. 1999. The Hinxton Rings – a Late Iron Age cemetery at Hinxton, Cambridgeshire, with a reconsideration of northern Aylesford–Swarling distributions, *Proceedings of the Prehistoric Society* 65, 243–273.

Hope, W.H. St J. and Fox, G.E. 1900. Excavations on the site of the Roman city at Silchester, Hants, in 1899, *Archaeologia* 57 (1), 87–112.

James, S. 2007. A bloodless past: the pacification of Early Iron Age Britain, in C. Haselgrove and R. Pope (eds), *The Earlier Iron Age in Britain and the Near Continent*, 160–173. Oxford: Oxbow Books.

Johns, C. 2002. A sword and mirror grave from Scilly, *The Archaeologist* 44, 16.

Knight, B. 1991. *Simpson's Forensic Medicine* (10th edn.). London: Edward Arnold.

Lambot, B., Friboulet, M. and Méniel, P. 1994. *Le site protohistorique d'Acy Romance (Ardennes) II. Les nécropoles dans leur contexte régional 1986–1988–1989.* Reims: Mémoire de la Société Archéologique Champenoise 8.

Mays, J. and Steele, J. 1996. A mutilated skull from Roman St Albans, *Antiquity* 70, 155–160.

McKinley, J. 1989. Cremations: expectations, methodologies and realities, in C. Roberts, F. Lee and J. Bintliff (eds.), *Burial Archaeology: Current Research, Methods and Developments*, 65–77. Oxford: British Archaeological Report British Series 211.

McKinley, J. 1997. The cremated human bone from burial and cremation-related contexts, in Fitzpatrick 1997a, 55–73.

McKinley, J. 2000. Phoenix rising: aspects of cremation in Roman Britain, in Pearce *et al.* 2000, 38–44.

McKinley, J., Smith, P. and Fitzpatrick, A.P. 1997. Animal bone from burials and other cremation-related contexts, in Fitzpatrick 1997a, 73–77.

Méniel, P. 1993. Les animaux dans les pratiques funeraires des Gaulois, in D. Cliquet, M.Remy-Watte, V. Guichard and M. Vaginay (eds), *Les Celtes en Normandie. Les Rites Funéraires en Gaul (IIIème–Ier siècle avant J.-C.) (Actes du 14ème Colloque de l'AFEAF, Evreux, mai 1990)*, 285–290. Rennes: Revue Archéologique de l'Ouest Supplément 6.

Metzler, J., Waringo, R., Bis, R. and Metzler-Zens, N. 1991. *Clemency et les tombes de l'aristocratie en Gaule Belgique.* Luxembourg: Dossiers d'Archéologie du Musée National d'Histoire et d'Art 1.

Metzler-Zens, N., Metzler-Zens, J., Méniel, P., Bis, R., Gaeng, C. and Villemeur, I. 1999. *Lamadelaine: Une Nécropole de l'Oppidum du Titelberg.* Luxembourg: Dossiers d'Archeologie du Musée National d'Histoire et d'Art 6.

Millett, M. 1987. An early Roman burial tradition in central southern England, *Oxford Journal of Archaeology* 6, 63–68.

Niblett, R. 1999. *The Excavation of a Ceremonial Site at Folly Lane, Verulamium*. London: Britannia Monograph 14.

Niblett, R. 2000. Funerary rites in Verulamium during the early Roman period, in Pearce *et al.* 2000, 97–104.

Oswald, A. 1997. A doorway on the past: practical and mystic concerns in the orientation of roundhouse doorways, in Gwilt and Haselgrove 1997, 87–95.

Parfitt, K. 1995. *Iron Age Burials from Mill Hill, Deal*. London: British Museum Press.

Parker Pearson, M. 1996. Food, fertility and front doors in the first millennium BC, in T.C. Champion and J.R. Collis (eds), *The Iron Age in Britain and Ireland: Recent Trends*, 117–132. Sheffield: J.R. Collis Publications.

Parker Pearson, M., Marshall, P., Mulville, J. and Smith, H. 2002. The dead beneath their feet: housewarming *c.* 1000 BC – roundhouse rituals at Cladh Hallan, *PAST* 40, 1–2.

Pearce, J. 1997. Death and time: the structure of late Iron Age mortuary ritual, in Gwilt and Haselgrove 1997, 174–180.

Pearce, J. 1998. From death to deposition: the sequence of ritual in cremation burials of the Roman period, in C. Forcey, J. Hawthorne and R. Witcher (eds), *TRAC 97. Proceedings of the Seventh Annual Theoretical Roman Archaeology Conference, Nottingham 1997*, 99–111. Oxford: Oxbow Books.

Pearce, J. 1999. *Contextual Archaeology of Burial Practice: Case Studies from Roman Britain*. Unpublished Ph.D. thesis, University of Durham.

Pearce, J., Millett, M. and Struck, M. (eds.) 2000. *Burial, Society and Context in the Roman World*. Oxford: Oxbow Books.

Pollard, R. 2001. An Iron Age inhumation from Rushey Mead, Leicester, *Transactions of the Leicestershire Archaeological and Historical Society* 75, 20–35.

Powell, A.B. and Fitzpatrick, A.P. 1997. Analyses, in Fitzpatrick 1997a, 280–283.

Sealey, P. 1996. The Iron Age of Essex, in O. Bedwin (ed.), *The Archaeology of Essex: Proceedings of the 1993 Writtle Conference*, 46–68. Chelmsford: Essex County Council.

Stead, I.M. and Rigby, V. 1986. *Baldock: the Excavation of a Roman and pre-Roman Settlement, 1968–72*. London: Britannia Monograph 7.

Stead, I.M. and Rigby, V. 1989. *Verulamium: the King Harry Lane Site*. London: English Heritage Archaeological Report 12.

Stirland, A. 1989. The cremations from the Iron Age cemetery, in Stead and Rigby 1989, 240–244.

Wait, G. 1985. *Ritual and Religion in Iron Age Britain*. Oxford: British Archaeological Reports British Series 149.

Whimster, R. 1981. *Burial Practices in Iron Age Britain: A Discussion and Gazetteer of the Evidence c. 700 B.C.–A.D. 43*. Oxford: British Archaeological Reports British Series 90.

Whitley, J. 2002. Too many ancestors, *Antiquity* 76, 119–126.

Households and social change in Jutland, 500 BC–AD 200

Leo Webley

Introduction

The Iron Age archaeology of many parts of northern Europe is dominated by settlements and the artefacts used in everyday domestic practice. Despite this, critical investigation of the nature and internal organisation of domestic groups is a relatively underdeveloped area in the study of the period. This paper attempts to address these issues using a case study from southern Scandinavia.[1]

As several authors have recently argued, archaeologists have often failed adequately to consider domestic practice and relations. There is an unfortunate tendency to regard the domestic sphere as understood, as timeless rather than historically contingent (Brück and Goodman 1999). This conflicts with abundant ethnographic and historical evidence for radical differences from culture to culture in the membership of the household, the relationships between these members, and the activities they carry out. The 'household' has tended to be portrayed as an undifferentiated unit of production and consumption, ignoring the existence of social differences and conflicting interests within it (Tringham 1991; Hendon 1996; Allison 1999a). In neglecting intra-household relationships, researchers fall into the trap of assuming that these have little relevance to wider social systems or social change. This is fallacious, for as Hendon states, 'domestic action and relations… are of larger political significance precisely because they are not separable from the relationships and processes that make up the "public domain"' (1996, 47). Household relations are not insulated from the external social world, nor do they respond passively to externally imposed changes. Rather, they can themselves play an important, active role in maintaining or renegotiating wider social relations (Yanagisako 1979; Hendon 1996).

Research on Iron Age Europe that explicitly engages with domestic relations has been sporadic to say the least. One notable example is Clarke's (1972) classic study of the pre-Roman Iron Age settlement at Glastonbury in southern England. This proposed the existence of a recurring 'modular' household unit, with various internal socio-spatial divisions, including a major contrast between a 'familial' area with multiple activities, and a largely female area for domestic chores. Clarke's conclusions are unfortunately undermined by erroneous interpretations of the structural remains and stratigraphic sequence of the site (Coles and Minnitt 1995).

After a lull following Clarke's work, interest in the socio-spatial organisation of the household in Iron Age Britain has recently been revived, notably by Hingley (1990), who proposed a distinction between male and female associated areas within the roundhouse. On the Continent, Therkorn (1987) has provided an important study of the Iron Age household in Noord-Holland in the Netherlands. She argues that the house was divided into male and female activity areas, a distinction that became starker as part of the wider social changes bound up with 'Romanisation'. Elsewhere in northern continental Europe, however, it is still the case that 'analysis has primarily been at the level of hamlets/villages, as units in themselves, and of the social hierarchies and economic specialisation within them. There is therefore no framework for the relations at the intra-household level' (*ibid.*, 103).

The rich settlement evidence from Jutland provides an excellent yet neglected dataset for exploring the nature of domestic life during the Iron Age. This paper provides an introductory overview of the evidence for the character and internal organisation of the household in this region. It will be shown that from around 250 BC the household underwent a series of changes in terms of its place within the community, its role in systems of land tenure and inheritance, and its internal social relations. Analysis of the use of space within the farmstead indicates an increase through time in the expression of social distinctions within the domestic group. These changes have significant implications for our understanding of the nature of social change in 'Barbarian' Europe.

Contexts for the study: geography, chronology, and archaeology

The Jutland peninsula comprises the majority of modern Denmark. It has a low-lying landscape and a temperate climate. Iron Age settlement evidence is abundant across Jutland, but the longest research history and the most well-preserved sites are to be found in the north and west of the region, and this area provides the main focus for the present paper (Fig. 1). In terms of chronology, we are concerned with the time-span from 500 BC to AD 200, a period referred to in Danish archaeology as the Early Iron Age. Following Martens (1997), the Early Iron Age can be divided into three phases: the early pre-Roman period (500–250 BC), the late pre-Roman period (250–1 BC) and the early Roman Iron Age (AD 1–200).

English language accounts of the Danish Early Iron Age are provided by Jensen (1982) and Hedeager (1992). Early Iron Age communities were rural in character, with a subsistence base of mixed agriculture, supplemented by fishing in coastal areas. By the latter part of the period at least, much of the landscape seems to have been densely occupied. In terms of social organisation, most previous authors have characterised the first part of the Early Iron Age as relatively egalitarian, but have argued for a growth in social hierarchy as the period progressed, leading up to the emergence after AD 200 of the 'aristocratic' societies of the Late Iron Age (Parker Pearson 1984; Hedeager 1992). This issue will be returned to below.

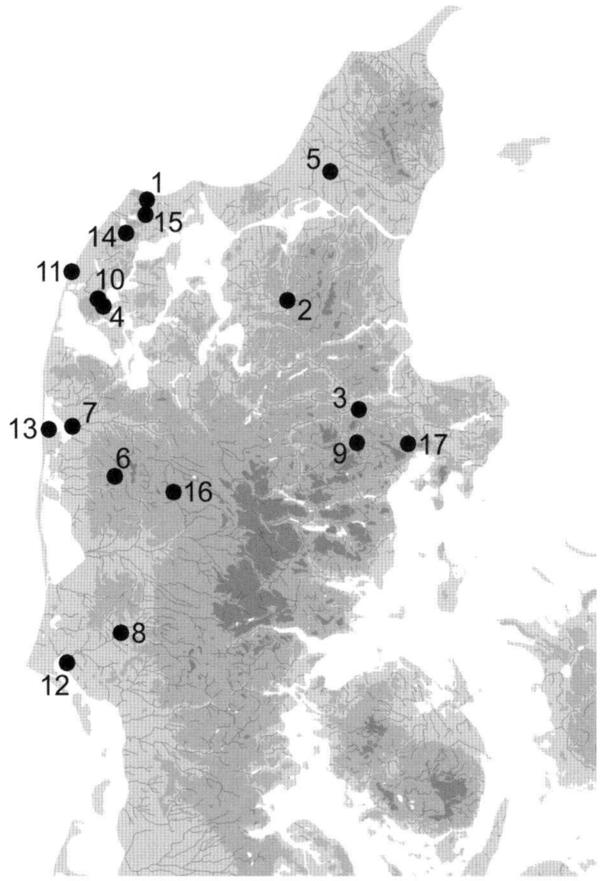

Fig. 1. Map of Jutland, showing sites mentioned in the text. The background map shows the coastline in the late eighteenth to early nineteenth centuries AD. Contours are at 30 m and 80 m above sea level. 1. Bjerre; 2. Borremose; 3. Frederiksdalvej; 4. Ginnerup; 5. Grishøjgårds Krat; 6. Grøntoft; 7. Gørding; 8. Hodde; 9. Holkærvej; 10. Hurup; 11. Lodbjerg; 12. Myrtue; 13. Nørre Fjand; 14. Skårup; 15. Smedegård; 16. Stenbjergkvarteret; 17. Vendehøj (background map courtesy of the Settlement and Cultural Landscape Project).

Defining the Early Iron Age household

The problems of applying the modern western concept of the 'household' to other societies have been well rehearsed elsewhere (e.g. Yanagisako 1979). Nevertheless, the archaeological evidence from Early Iron Age Denmark suggests the existence of a fundamental social unit for which the term 'household' is a reasonable label. The locus for this group was a 'farmstead' that forms the basic settlement module of the period. This farmstead takes the form of a longhouse, combining a dwelling room and an animal stall under one roof, often accompanied by one or more smaller outbuildings or granaries. The association of animal stalls and granaries with the individual farmstead, along with the fact that agricultural implements and fishing nets have occasionally been found within burned down longhouses (see below), suggests that the household had a fair degree of control over its own means of production.

The pattern of settlement in the landscape provides further evidence for the social position of the household. At the start of the Early Iron Age, farmsteads tended to be relatively dispersed, as for example at the site of Grøntoft in west Jutland (Fig. 2; Rindel 1999). Later there was a trend to increased

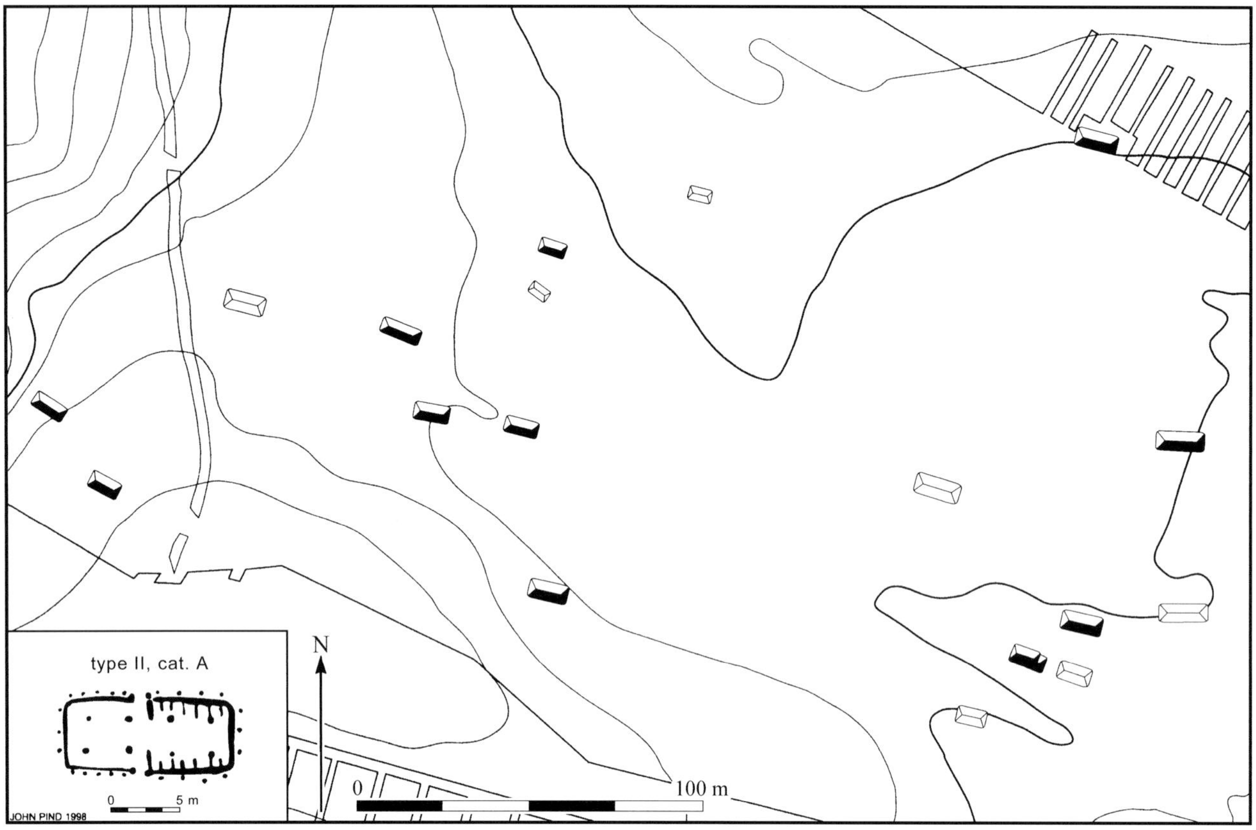

Fig. 2. Early pre-Roman Iron Age settlement at Grøntoft. Inset shows a typical longhouse of the period. Not all houses need be contemporary, and hence the settlement pattern here can be characterised as relatively dispersed (source: Rindel 1999).

nucleation and substantial 'villages' appeared, well-published examples including Hodde (Hvass 1985) and Vendehøj (Ejstrud and Jensen 2000). This change occurred in the late pre-Roman period in most areas, though it had already begun during the course of the early pre-Roman period in parts of north-west Jutland. In some places at least, nucleation appears to have involved a process of settlement contraction (e.g. Siemen and Stoumann 1995, 48). As people came to live closer together, the relationship between the household and the wider community would have changed. If nothing else, an increased intensity of interaction with one's neighbours would have given a different sense of community in terms of daily experience. However, the individual household did not simply surrender its independence to the collective. While early pre-Roman farmsteads were unenclosed (Fig. 2), fences appear around many farmsteads during the late pre-Roman period (Fig. 3), at the same time as the shift to more nucleated settlement. In this way households expressed their distinctiveness despite the loss of distance from their neighbours.

Households, land tenure, and inheritance

The trend to increased settlement nucleation was accompanied by greater settlement stability. The farmsteads of the early pre-Roman Iron Age tend to show only a single phase of building, which means that they must have shifted to a different plot after a relatively short period, perhaps only a single generation in many cases. This pattern of so-called 'wandering' settlement is typical of many areas of north-west Europe during the early part of the Iron Age (Kossack *et al.* 1984). With the transition to more nucleated settlement, farmsteads became more stable in location, and often show one or more phases of rebuilding on the same plot. This was taken to extremes in parts of north-west Jutland, where some farmsteads remained stationary for up to five centuries, with one example at Smedegård reportedly rebuilt thirteen times on the spot (Nielsen 1996, 52). Several other parts of north-west Europe show a similar trend to increased settlement stability during the final centuries BC, or around the time of Christ, with particularly clear evidence from southern Sweden (e.g. Tesch 1993) and the Low Countries (e.g. Gerritsen 1999; 2007. How are we to explain this striking and widespread change?

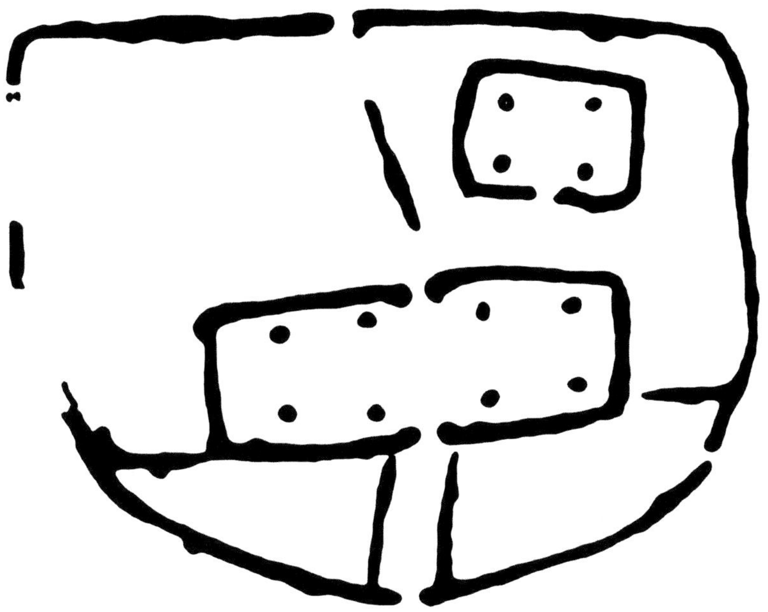

Fig. 3. Late pre-Roman farmstead from Frederiksdalvej. The farmstead consists of a longhouse and an outbuilding enclosed by a fence. Further fences within the enclosure divided domestic space and channelled movement. Scale 1:250 (source: Christiansen 1995).

One promising avenue is the role of the household in land tenure and inheritance systems. This was first mooted over sixty years ago by Hatt (1939), who tried to explain the distinction perceived at the time between a pattern of shifting settlement in Bronze Age Jutland and one of more stable settlement in the Iron Age. Hatt argued that during the Bronze Age there was no enduring ownership of land, which returned to the community when cultivation had ceased. In the Iron Age, as settlement and cultivation became more permanent so did land rights. Land was now inheritable and could be passed down through the generations, although it was not 'private property' in the modern sense. Drawing on ethnographic analogy, Hatt suggested a situation in which there was a complex interplay between individual and community rights to land.

Hatt's ideas were developed by Steffan Stumann Hansen (1979; 1984). By this time it had become clear that the shift away from 'wandering' settlement had in fact occurred around the middle of the pre-Roman Iron Age, and Hansen modified Hatt's theory accordingly, by placing the 'privatisation' of land at this later point. Some Dutch archaeologists have recently used a similar argument to that developed by Hatt and Hansen, by suggesting that the appearance of more stable settlement in the Netherlands from the first century BC onwards was connected with a rise in private claims to land (Gerritsen 1999; Roymans and Theuws 1999).

A crucial point here is the dating of the so-called 'Celtic' field systems, which are found across much of Denmark as well as in many other parts of northern Europe (Fries 1995). Hansen's theory of land 'privatisation' around the middle of the pre-Roman Iron Age was based on the contention that Celtic fields first appeared in Jutland at this time, and continued to be used into the early Roman period. This notion must now be rejected. Much of our knowledge of Celtic field systems in Jutland comes from Hatt's (1949) survey work prior to the Second World War, when many still survived as upstanding earthworks. The artefactual material collected by Hatt from in and around the field banks varies in date, but the majority of it appears to come from the *early* pre-Roman Iron Age. An association between Celtic fields and early pre-Roman 'wandering' settlement was shown through excavation by Hatt (*ibid.*, 92–108) at Øster Lem and later by Becker (1972) at Grøntoft. All more recent excavations of Celtic fields in western Denmark have also yielded dates prior to the late pre-Roman Iron Age. At both Lodbjerg (Liversage *et al.* 1987) and Grishøjgårds Krat (Nielsen 1993), it has been categorically shown that the fields were established in the early pre-Roman period but did not continue in use into the late pre-Roman period. Meanwhile, Celtic fields that had a use-life restricted to the latter part of the Late Bronze Age have been found at Bjerre (Bech and Mikkelsen 1999).

It can thus be argued that Hansen's theory should be turned on its head. The evidence available at present suggests that in Jutland, Celtic fields were essentially a phenomenon of a period stretching from the last stages of the Bronze Age through to the middle of the pre-Roman Iron Age. Perhaps, then, the transition to more stable settlement around 250 BC was associated with a move *away* from the Celtic field mode of land division. By this, it is not necessarily implied that the areas of land covered by Celtic fields were abandoned, but simply that the system of land *use* associated with this form of field division waned or ended. This model receives some support from observations in some other parts of north-west continental Europe, where a similar 'package' of changes seems to have occurred, although the dating of this seems to vary slightly from place to place. The clearest example is Flögeln in north-west Germany, where a shift from a 'wandering' and dispersed settlement pattern to a more stable and nucleated 'village' is associated with the abandonment of the neighbouring Celtic field system in the first century AD (Schmid 1984). There are also grounds to suggest that the appearance of more stable settlement in the late pre-Roman Iron Age in the Netherlands was associated with the demise of Celtic field systems (Roymans and Theuws 1999).

This might at first sight seem to contradict the theory that the shift to stable settlement was associated with the growth of private claims to land. However, the supposition that Celtic fields imply permanent private possession of land may be incorrect. They could instead have facilitated the distribution and redistribution of use-rights to land, the control of which remained in the hands of the community (Hedeager 1988). We can thus propose the following scenario for social change in Jutland and neighbouring regions of northern continental Europe. During the early pre-Roman period, the fact that the farmstead was relatively short-lived suggests that the individual domestic group was itself an ephemeral unit, rather than an institution that was maintained through the generations. When the life cycle of the domestic group ended, it was replaced or outlived by one or more successor households that were construed as new social units. At the end of the domestic cycle, the property and use-rights of the household were dispersed among the successor households, or redistributed within the kin group or community in some other way.

This social system ended with the shift to more stable settlement. As the individual farmstead could be occupied through several generations, the individual domestic group now formed only one stage of a body that had a longer lifespan. Continuity was carried to extremes in parts of northern Jutland, where, as we have seen, some farmsteads were occupied for four centuries or more. This transformation implies changes in systems of property and inheritance, with possessions and use-rights now passed down from one generation to another within the same domestic unit. The suggestion that there were significant changes in property and inheritance systems is supported by the apparent end to the use of Celtic fields around this time. While no firm conclusions are possible so long as we lack evidence for the forms of field division that followed, it seems logical to suggest that there was a shift in emphasis away from community control and towards the possession of land by individual households, although the existence of true land *ownership* in the modern sense is unlikely (cf. Hatt 1939; Hansen 1979; Gerritsen 1999).

The socio-spatial organisation of the household

We have seen that the role of the household within society underwent a significant transformation in the middle of the pre-Roman period, around 250 BC. It is therefore valid to inquire whether this was accompanied by changes in social relationships *within* the household group. This question will be investigated below, through an examination of the use of space in the farmstead. The architectural layout of the farmstead will be considered first, before a more detailed examination of the evidence for the distribution of everyday practices.

The architectural layout of the farmstead

The architectural plan of the longhouse remained fairly standardised throughout the Early Iron Age. The width of the longhouse remained constant at 5–6 m, but the length varied widely, normally within the range of 8–25 m. There were generally two entrances, situated opposite one another in the middle of the house. Internal space was divided into two rooms on either side of the 'cross passage' between the opposed entrances. Normally one end of the house was an animal stall, while the other was a dwelling room with a central hearth (Figs. 5 and 6).

The layout of the farmstead as a whole underwent a process of development through the Early Iron Age, involving trends towards increased size and greater structuring of space. The farmsteads of the early pre-Roman period consisted of a longhouse, about 13 m long on average, occasionally accompanied by a small outbuilding. The total roofed area of the farmstead was normally within the range of 40–100 m^2. In the late pre-Roman period, average longhouse length increased to about 15 m, and outbuildings were more common and often larger in size. By the early Roman period, average longhouse length had grown to about 18 m, and some of the larger farmsteads had three or more outbuildings, giving them a total roofed area in excess of 200 m^2. Thus as domestic space increased in extent, it also became more structured and divided by architecture, with the appearance of multi-building units.

Space also became more structured in other ways. As noted above, while early pre-Roman farmsteads are almost always unenclosed, later farmsteads were frequently surrounded by a palisade or fence. In a few cases, further fences *within* the enclosure divided up domestic space, as in the illustrated example from Frederiksdalvej, east Jutland (Fig. 3). Paved paths also

Type	*Description*	*Traces of use*	*Suggested functions*
1	Jar / vase over 32 cm high	Food remains	Storage, especially grain, also water and other liquids; malt production and brewing
2	Jar / vase 22–31 cm high	Food remains	Medium term storage, including cleaned/processed grain
3	Jar with restricted mouth, less than 22 cm high	Food remains	Short term storage; processing, cooking and serving of food and liquids
4	Vessel 10–21 cm high, in form of a cup or deep bowl, often with a single handle	Food remains	Short term storage; processing, cooking and serving of food; storage / processing of dyestuffs or medicinal plants
5	Cup or bowl less than 10 cm high, rim diameter less than 20 cm	–	Eating and drinking
6	Cup or bowl with foot	–	Receptacle for food or drink on occasions where display was important
7	Large dish / bowl, rim diameter more than double the height of the vessel and over 20 cm	–	Processing and serving food
7a	As above, with internal or 'swallow's nest' handles	Sooting	Cooking, processing, and serving food
8	Dish with large circular perforation in base	–	Cheese production, straining
9	Vessel with many small perforations in base	–	Sieving, straining

Table 1. Scheme of vessel types used in analysis of burned house assemblages.

appeared within settlements at this time, which together with the fences suggests a heightened concern with guiding and controlling axes of movement within the domestic sphere. In the context of this increased architectural division of domestic space, it is striking that keys make their first appearance in the archaeological record in Denmark during the first century AD (mainly occurring in graves; Levinsen 1984).

These changes are potentially significant to our understanding of domestic relations, but it would be a mistake to view architecture as a straightforward representation of social arrangements. While architecture may embody *ideals* of the proper use of space, it cannot directly tell us how people actually behaved in everyday practice (Allison 1999). In order to investigate that issue, the evidence of small finds patterning must be introduced.

Small finds patterning and everyday practice

Numerous sites in northern and western Jutland have yielded very well-preserved house remains with intact floors. This is thanks to two factors. Firstly, agriculture in this area remained relatively underdeveloped until the mid twentieth century, so that early excavations between the 1920s and 1950s often encountered sites untouched by modern ploughing. Secondly, the very stable settlement pattern that arose in the Early Iron Age in parts of north Jutland (see above) led to tell-like 'settlement mounds', up to 2.5 m high, formed by the build-up of culture layers over an extended period of time. Such sites can to this day retain well-preserved house remains, in their lower levels at least.

There has, however, been a surprising lack of interest in investigating the distribution of finds from within these houses. Of course, one should usually expect that the finds patterning from within a house would be strongly influenced by abandonment and post-abandonment activities rather than being a direct reflection of the use of space during the lifetime of the building (LaMotta and Schiffer 1999). However, possible exceptions to this principle are houses that were destroyed by fire. Burned houses are not uncommon in the well-preserved Early Iron Age settlements of north and west Jutland, which is unsurprising given the flammable nature of these structures (Boye 1996). There is nothing to suggest that any of these buildings were burned deliberately in an 'abandonment ritual', and it is therefore reasonable to assume that they were destroyed in a catastrophe unforeseen by their inhabitants, resulting either from mishap or arson. We may thus cautiously use the artefact distributions from these houses as evidence for the location of domestic activities at the time of the fire.

In order to do this, we must gain some impression of what the various artefact types were used for. The dominant class of artefact from house assemblages is pottery, and thus it is here that the main potential lies. In order to categorise the pottery from the burned buildings, a scheme of nine types has been created, based on simple differences in vessel form and dimensions (Table 1). These differences help to suggest the main functions that may have been associated with each type, but we also have evidence of vessel contents from some burned houses. Thus large jars (types 1 and 2) have been found which contain caches of pure grain, indicating a role in

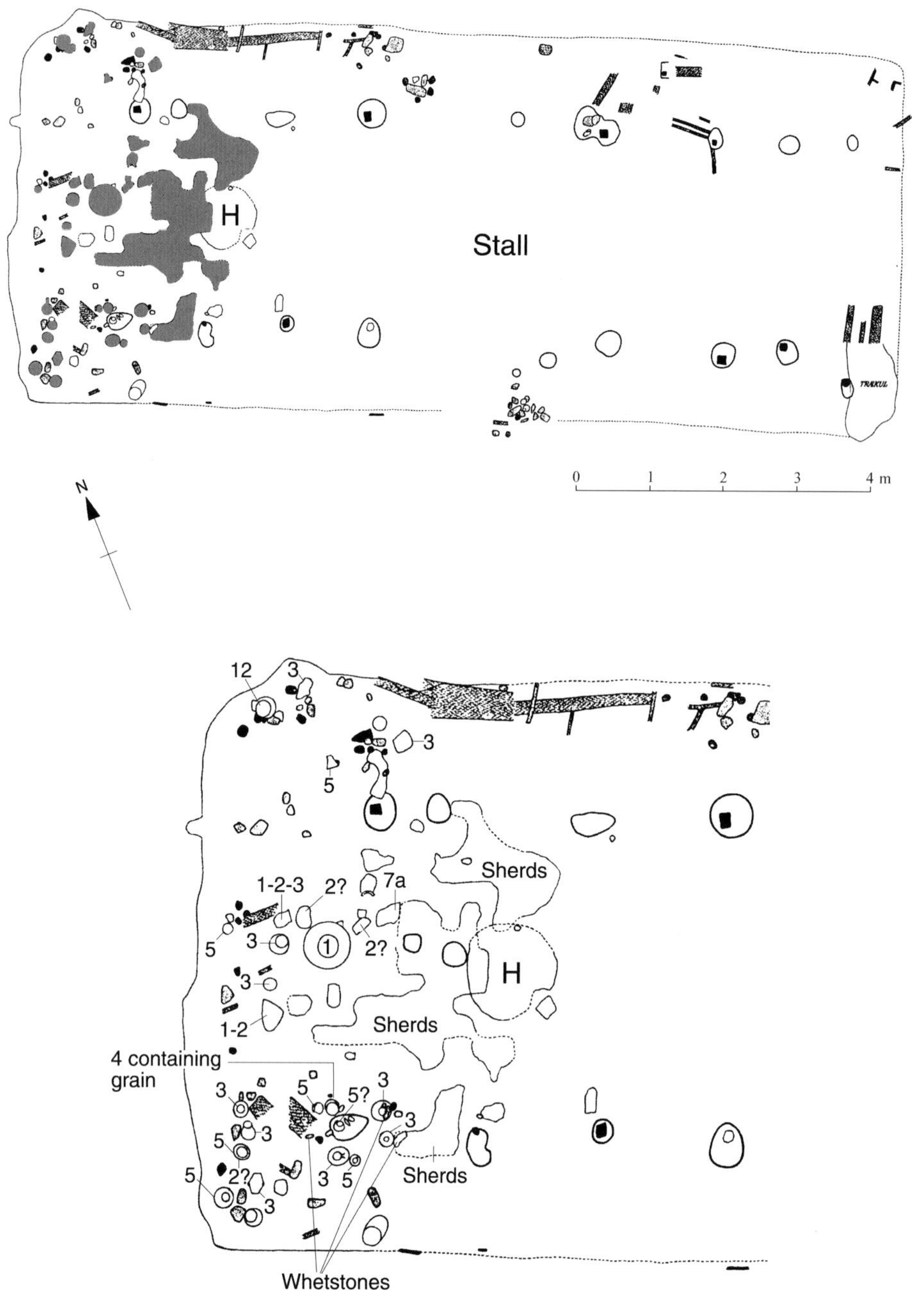

Fig. 4. Burned early pre-Roman longhouse from Gørding, west Jutland, showing a concentration of pottery between the hearth and rear wall. A. Plan of house, with pottery marked in grey. H = hearth. B. Detail of dwelling, showing distribution of vessel types. No clear patterning in the placing of different types can be seen (source: Becker 1961).

food storage, while medium-sized vessels (types 3 and 4) have been found that contain the apparent remains of meals, implying a role in food processing, cooking, and serving. Some other vessels show sooting to their exteriors (especially type 7a), again suggesting a use in cooking. I shall first consider the artefact patterning within longhouses, before moving on to the evidence from outbuildings.

Everyday practice within the longhouse

Information has been collated on 37 burned longhouses with intact floors from north and west Jutland. I intend to publish my analysis of these houses in full at a later date, but the salient results can be summarised here. The activities within the house for which the evidence is best are those involving food storage, processing, and consumption. No less than 30 of the 37 burned houses

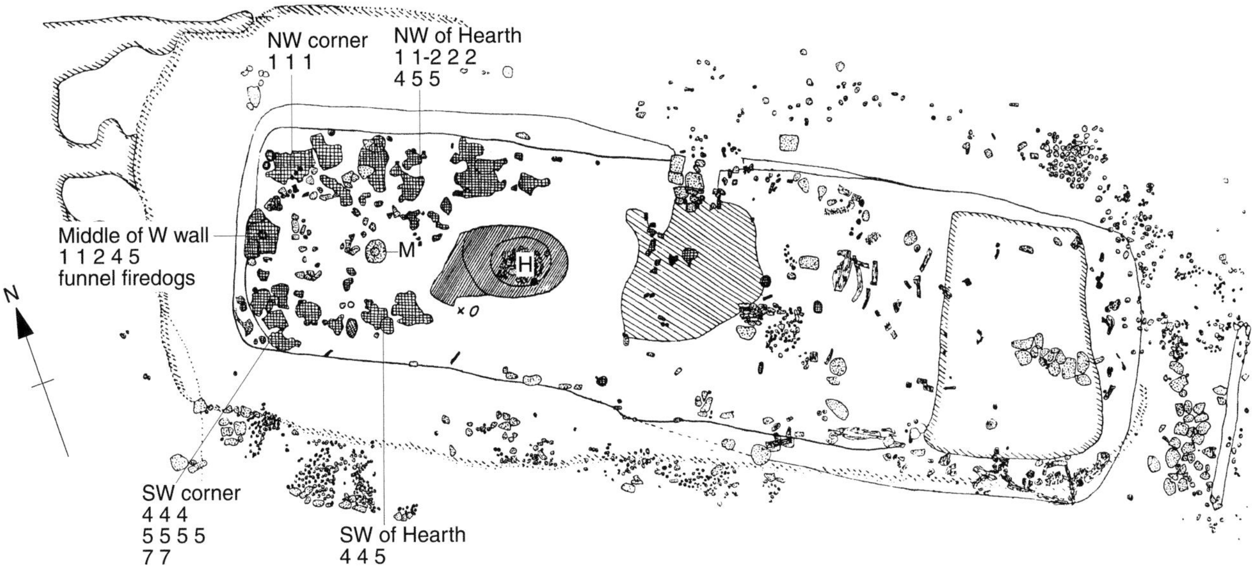

Fig. 5. Burned early Roman longhouse (house 9) from Nørre Fjand, showing a concentration of pottery in the rear of the dwelling. Pottery is marked in grey; M = mortar set in floor; H = Hearth. The approximate location of different vessel types is indicated. A concentration of vessels possibly associated with food serving and consumption (types 4, 5 and 7) can be seen in the southern rear part of the dwelling, while the assemblages from other areas are more varied (source: Hatt 1957).

show, to a greater or lesser degree, the same basic pattern in the location of these activities, which took place in the rear of the dwelling, behind the hearth. This is most commonly evinced by pottery distributions. Pottery was concentrated between the hearth and the rear wall in the majority of the houses; this typically included vessels of a range of sizes and forms, from large jars probably used for food storage, to medium-sized vessels perhaps used for the processing and cooking of food, and small vessels presumably used for eating and drinking. In nine houses, a large storage vessel was set into the floor by the rear wall. In twelve houses, grain or other foodstuffs were found in the same area, often within ceramic vessels. Food processing is also evinced by saddle querns and mortar stones, which were found in the rear of the dwelling in seven cases each. The mortars were set into the floor and were generally placed directly behind the hearth.

The fact that the distributions of portable items correspond to the locations of immovable vessels and mortars seems to confirm that we are dealing with evidence for activities during the lifetime of the house, rather than just at the time of its abandonment. Published houses that illustrate this custom of confining food-related activities to the rear of the dwelling include examples from Borremose (Martens 1988, 165), Gørding (Fig. 4; Becker 1961, 87–90), Nørre Fjand (Hatt 1957), and Skårup (Olesen 1982, 253). Normally, no pattern can be seen in the distribution of different vessel types within this rear area (Fig. 4b). However, a couple of houses from the early Roman period do show some evidence for the spatial separation of vessel types. Thus in one house at Nørre Fjand, the southern part of the rear of the dwelling is characterised by vessels associated with the serving and consumption of food, while a more varied ceramic assemblage is seen in the central and northern parts of this area (Fig. 5).

This custom in the use of space stretched throughout the Early Iron Age and is found in all areas of Jutland where well-preserved house remains exist. The strength of the adherence to this method of organising domestic activities seems remarkable, though it should be pointed out that at least five burned houses diverged markedly from the identified 'norm' in the distribution of pottery (see e.g. Gørding house 2; Becker 1961, 82–7). This shows that norms were not blindly followed, but could be rejected, subverted, or ignored in certain circumstances.

Evidence for other types of activity within longhouses is sparser, although craftwork or the storage of tools is evinced by occasional finds of whetstones, burnishing stones, iron knives and axe-heads, agricultural implements, and fishing net sinkers. Although the numbers of each type of find are small, it is notable that none seems to show any recurring pattern in location within the house. From this it may be tentatively concluded that while the location of food storage, preparation and consumption activities was circumscribed by social norms, the location of other craft and storage activities was not.

I have shown elsewhere that these patterns in the use of space differ from those that can be seen in architecturally similar longhouses from sites in the Netherlands and northern Germany, where food storage

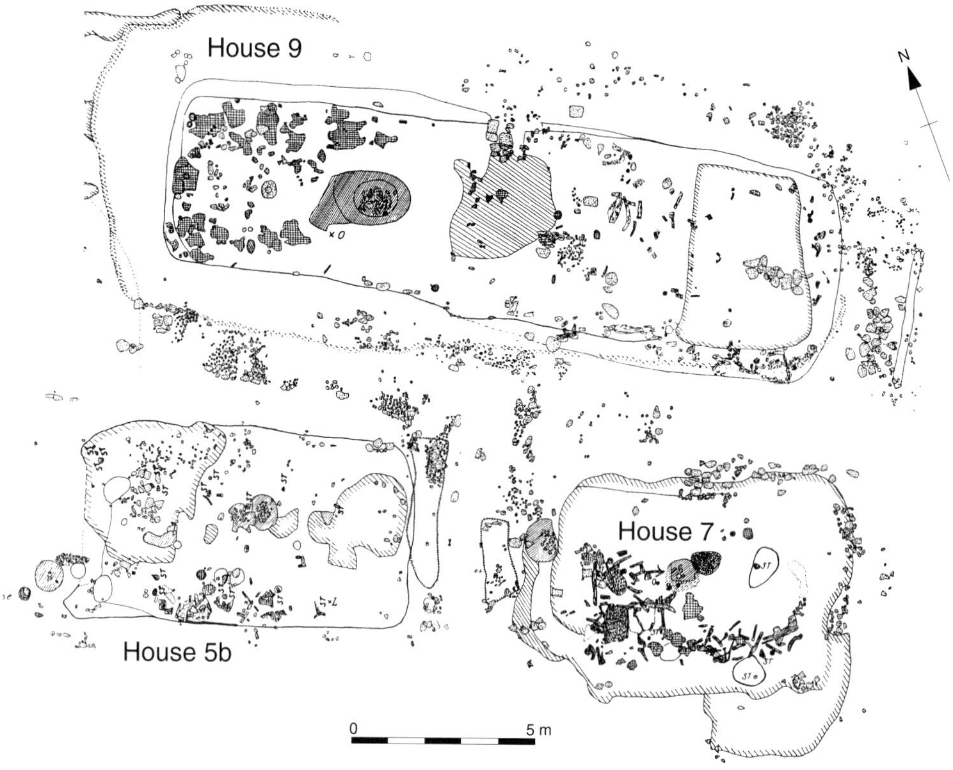

Fig. 6. Section of the early Roman 'village' at Nørre Fjand, showing houses 7 and 9 (source: Hatt 1957).

and preparation seems to have occurred in the *front* part of the living space (Webley 2003, 63–4). Thus the architectural tradition of the longhouse, common to a wide area of northern Europe, was interpreted in differing ways from one set of communities to another. It is valid to ask what implications these differences may have had for domestic relations. We have seen that the Jutland houses show an emphasis on confining food-related activities to the rear, while other practices were not regulated in this way. This is notable given the cross-culturally recurring importance of the preparation and consumption of food in maintaining gender and status distinctions. Perhaps keeping food preparation to the rear in Jutland maintained a social distinction whereby those who carried out these activities were also 'kept in their place'. Care is needed here, as of course spatial segregation need not only have negative connotations, but can also have positive associations of privacy and independence. Those who were involved in food preparation and those that were not may well have had different ideas about the connotations of working at the back of the house.

Everyday practice within outbuildings

The interior of the longhouse therefore shows a basic continuity in socio-spatial arrangements throughout the Early Iron Age. However, change through time becomes more apparent when outbuildings are considered. As we have seen, during the early pre-Roman period outbuildings are not common and are always small (no more than about 20 m^2). None of these structures possessed hearths, and while we have no direct evidence for their function, a use as granaries or storehouses seems likely. The situation changed in the late pre-Roman period, when outbuildings became more common and showed a wider size range. It has normally been assumed that late pre-Roman and early Roman outbuildings played a specialised 'economic' role in craftwork or storage, but this has never been fully argued through.

The function of late pre-Roman and early Roman outbuildings can be investigated by considering the finds from structures that were destroyed by fire, or have *in situ* fixtures. This allows the outbuildings to be divided into three categories. Firstly, there is a group of small buildings, up to 22 m^2 in size, which appear to have served primarily as storehouses. A clear example is a burned building from Ginnerup, that lacked a hearth but contained many large storage vessels, along with substantial quantities of grain (Juhl 1995). Secondly, there is a group of buildings measuring between 22 and 35 m^2 that housed fixtures used for iron working. For example, an outbuilding from a recently excavated early Roman farmstead at Stenbjergkvarteret was found to

	Longhouse (house 9)		*Outbuilding (house 7)*	
Vessel Type	*Number*	*%*	*Number*	*%*
1	9–12	20–26	3–4	19–25
2	6–9	13–20	1–2	6–13
3	0	0	0–1	0–6
4	9–10*	20–22	6*	38
5	12	26	1	6
6	1	2	2	13
7	2–3	4–7	1	6
9	1	2	0	0
6 reworked as funnel	1	2	1	6
Miniature bowl	1	2	0	0
Total vessels	*46*	*100*	*16*	*100*
Artefact type	*Number*		*Number*	
Quern	Fragments only		2	
Mortar	1		0	
Net sinker	8		1 (+ 4 outside house)	
Firedog	2		0	

Table 2. Comparison of assemblages from houses 7 and 9 at Nørre Fjand.

contain a smelting furnace and associated working pit (Olesen 2000).

The remaining group of outbuildings consists of burned structures that do not seem to have had such a specialised 'economic' function. These buildings were relatively large (from 27 to 54 m^2), possessed hearths and contained a varied assemblage of pottery and other artefacts, indicating that they played host to a range of domestic activities. Some of the best evidence comes from two cases from the early Roman period where a longhouse and associated outbuilding appear to have burned down in the same conflagration. These two examples deserve closer attention.

The first example comes from Nørre Fjand in west Jutland. The site is published (Hatt 1957; Lewis 1985), but further information has been gleaned from the site archive held at the National Museum, Copenhagen. We are concerned here with the farmstead unit represented by longhouse 9 and its neighbouring outbuilding, house 7 (Fig. 6). House 9 has already been mentioned in the discussion of the use of space within longhouses. The outbuilding measured 9 by 6 m and had a hearth placed in the centre of the floor. Comparison of the assemblages from the two buildings gives some interesting results. The outbuilding contained substantial (although unspecified) quantities of grain, mainly barley and oats, while grain was absent from the longhouse. This might be taken to imply that the outbuilding served as a storehouse (Lewis 1985, 145). However, a large amount of fragmentary sheep and cattle bone was found amongst the pottery in the dwelling of the longhouse, while only a tiny scrap of bone was found in the outbuilding. Thus what was in fact occurring, it would seem, was a separation of meat and grain storage between the two buildings.

Turning to the artefactual assemblages, the frequency of large storage vessels is no higher in the outbuilding than in the longhouse, a further indication that the outbuilding should not simply be labelled a 'storehouse'. Differences between the two buildings become apparent when the frequencies of other vessels are compared (Table 2). The outbuilding has a clearly higher frequency of medium-sized vessels, perhaps used for food processing and cooking, and a lower frequency of small vessels probably used for eating and drinking. Moreover, two querns were recovered from the outbuilding while only a few quern fragments were found in the longhouse. This suggests that the outbuilding was particularly associated with the preparation of food while the longhouse was more associated with consumption.

The second example comes from Hurup in north Jutland. The site is unpublished apart from brief preliminary articles (e.g. Rasmussen 1968), but information on house assemblages is available from the site archive held at the National Museum. The outbuilding (house 8) was a well-preserved structure, measuring 7 by 4 m, with a central hearth. The neighbouring longhouse (house 13) was unfortunately much more poorly preserved, making comparison of the finds from the two buildings difficult. Nevertheless, some observations can be made. Notable finds from the outbuilding included substantial quantities of grain and some 'cakes' of clay mixed with straw. This suggests that the outbuilding played a particular role in food storage and pottery production. It was clearly not a mere storehouse-cum-workplace, however. The ceramic assemblage shows a relatively high ratio of medium and small vessels, suggesting that food preparation and consumption may well have taken place. However, not all forms of food preparation seem to have occurred within the outbuilding, as no querns were present. In contrast, two querns were found in the longhouse, suggesting that this was the locus for corn grinding.

At both Nørre Fjand and Hurup it would seem that domestic activities were divided up in complex ways between the different buildings of the farmstead, though the exact nature of this division differs between the two sites. This indicates that the appearance of multi-building farmsteads in the latter part of the Early Iron Age involved a significant re-negotiation of the everyday use of domestic space. During the early pre-Roman period, domestic activities were concentrated within a single building, but in the late pre-Roman period and especially during the early Roman period activities were often dispersed between two or more buildings.

A number of explanations could be put forward for this, but here I wish to focus on the possibility that increased spatial distinctions between activities could be associated with increased *social* distinctions within the household. Separating the daily paths of various sets of people within the household could have been a powerful means of reinforcing social difference. The case studies from Nørre Fjand and Hurup appear to show that different food-related activities were housed in separate buildings. Again, the probable links between food, gender and status make this significant. To take the example of Nørre Fjand, the contrast between an outbuilding showing an emphasis on food preparation and a longhouse with more evidence of consumption raises the possibility of a distinction between those who served food and those who were served. The fact that corn grinding appears to have occurred in the outbuilding is particularly significant in view of the substantial investment of time that this would have required each day. Whoever was allotted the task of kneeling at the saddle quern would have had to spend much of their working day in this outbuilding. The contrast between meat storage in the longhouse and grain storage in the outbuilding may also have had social connotations, in that meat would have been a luxury, perhaps not consumed by all within the household.

In summary, it can be suggested that the trend through the Early Iron Age to greater architectural division of space, and greater separation of different domestic activities, represents an increased expression of social distinctions within the household unit.

Depositional practices and identity display

Further evidence for social relationships within the household may come from a consideration of depositional practices. When discussing deposition on Early Iron Age settlements, Danish archaeologists have tended to explain finds within buildings in a very different way from those outside. Where buildings are well preserved, it is not uncommon to find vessels or other objects that had been deliberately buried in the foundations, either in post holes or beneath floors, hearths, walls, or entrances. Such objects have traditionally been interpreted as propitiatory 'offerings' intended to promote the well-being of the building and its inhabitants (Henriksen 1998). Meanwhile, material deposited outside buildings – mainly in pits – has normally been assumed to be casually discarded 'rubbish' (Nielsen 1987, 89–90). This interpretative dichotomy between 'ritual' and 'rubbish' should be regarded with suspicion, not least because closer investigation of pit fills (Webley 2002) shows patterning and 'odd' features that seem to have more in common with the traditions of structured deposition identified elsewhere in Iron Age Europe (e.g. Hill 1995) than with modern notions of refuse discard. Detailed discussion of depositional practices within settlements lies beyond the scope of this paper, but it is relevant to note those aspects that may shed light on intra-household relations.

Previous explanations of structured or ritual deposition within settlements across Iron Age Europe have tended to revolve around the notion that the deposits were intended to help secure the continued existence of the household or other social group, by promoting fertility or success, or warding off harm (e.g. Capelle 1987; Cunliffe 1992; Henriksen 1998). This is undoubtedly a useful way to view many of the practices attested in the archaeological record, but other possibilities should also be considered. Ethnographic evidence shows that 'ritual' within settlements, sometimes involving deposition, can play a significant role in helping to maintain or contest social relations *within* social groups. An example is provided by the Mura of northern Cameroon (Lyons 1998). Men hold much of the power in Mura society, but women can wield influence through the threat of witchcraft. To protect themselves from witchcraft attacks from their wives, and thus from assaults on their position of dominance, Mura men use various kinds of items as 'amulets' that are buried at the entrances to household compounds and men's houses. Depositional practices are thus employed in the negotiation of gender and power relations within the household.

Might something analogous have occurred in Early Iron Age Denmark? Consideration of the types of objects that were deposited in settlements may throw some light on the issue. The material found in supposed 'refuse' contexts consists primarily of pottery, with animal bone and stone implements such as querns also common. The items deposited as so-called 'house offerings' tend to be of the same 'domestic' character. The most common type of 'offering' is a pot buried beneath the hearth, or in a post hole (Henriksen 1998). Iron knives and remains of domestic animals are also found incorporated into house foundations in various locations.

Another group of deposits consists of fossil sea urchins and Neolithic stone axes, which were buried beneath house walls and entrances, probably as charms to ward off harm, as for example at Hodde (Hvass 1985, 80) and Myrtue (Thomsen 1965, 23). In contrast, artefacts strongly associated with personal identity or status – namely dress accessories, weaponry, exotic imports, and 'wealth' items – were very rarely deposited in settlements, their proper context of disposal being graves and votive bog sites (cf. Hedeager 1992). This may suggest that depositional rituals in the domestic sphere were not normally a valid arena for the overt display of personal identity or status during the Early Iron Age.

Having said that personal items of this kind are rare from settlements, their chronological distribution does deserve comment. Finds are entirely absent from the early pre-Roman Iron Age and are concentrated towards the end of the Early Iron Age. Some of these late finds could well be casual losses, for example in cases where only a single glass bead is found. However, deliberate deposition of personal or status-associated items at early Roman period settlements seems clear in a couple of instances at least. A good example comes from Holkærvej, where a gilt silver brooch dating to the second century AD was placed in a small pot and buried within a house, adjacent to a roof-supporting post hole (Berthelsen and Christiansen 1989, 35). The appearance of small numbers of personal items within settlements by the early Roman period can be seen as foreshadowing the much more radical changes that occurred in depositional practices at the transition to the Late Iron Age, around AD 200, when personal ornaments, weaponry, and wealth items became far more common in settlements.

Thus through most of the Early Iron Age, we have few ostensible signs that depositional 'rituals' within the farmstead were used to negotiate the social position of individuals. However, towards the end of the period, there are possible hints that this situation was beginning to change, with the appearance of slightly greater numbers of items associated with identity and status. Depositional practices in the domestic sphere may have started to become a valid arena for the playing out of concerns with the status or social position of individuals, something that became much more strongly expressed in the more overtly hierarchical societies of the Late Iron Age.

Conclusion

This paper has outlined a striking set of changes in the nature of the household and its internal relations that occurred in Jutland from around 250 BC onwards. Settlement nucleation took place in many areas in the late pre-Roman Iron Age, altering the relationship between the household and the community. At the same time, major changes occurred in systems of land tenure and inheritance, matching changes that can be seen more widely across northern continental Europe. More emphasis was placed on the rights to land of the household, rights that could now be retained through the generations. These developments in the social role of the household were accompanied by changes in the internal social relations of this group, which began in the late pre-Roman Iron Age and gathered pace in the early Roman Iron Age. The farmstead could be much larger than before, which *may* imply an increase in the size of the domestic group, though this does not necessarily follow. Whether the household was larger or not, it arguably shows greater expression of internal social distinctions. Architectural developments evince an increased emphasis on structuring and dividing domestic space, on restricting access and laying down 'proper' paths of movement.

These architectural changes are matched by the evidence for the distribution of everyday practices. While customs in the use of space within the longhouse remained fairly constant, significant developments took place in the use of outbuildings. Domestic practices that had previously been housed in a single building were now often dispersed among two or more buildings, indicating spatial separation of the daily paths of different individuals. This might suggest that gender and status distinctions were becoming more strongly marked. Meanwhile, there are hints by the end of the Early Iron Age that depositional practices in the domestic sphere had begun to be used to negotiate the social position of individuals.

The argument that gender and status distinctions became more clearly expressed within the household resonates with previous narratives of social change in Early Iron Age Denmark, which have described a process of increased social differentiation through the period. However, these narratives have almost exclusively concerned the development of political hierarchy, with the postulated emergence of chieftains and warrior elites in the late pre-Roman and early Roman periods (Parker Pearson 1984; Hedeager 1992). Much emphasis has been placed on the control of imported prestige goods – derived from central Europe during the late pre-Roman period, and from the Roman empire in the early Roman period – as a key means by which a ruling class established itself. This focus on prestige goods and on the activities of 'chiefly' and 'warrior' groups has led to a narrow view of social change, in which elite adult males appear to be the only significant social agents.

The emphasis placed here on routine practice and the everyday conditions of existence provides a different perspective on social change. The developments seen within the household arguably represent a significant renegotiation of social roles and relationships that is likely to have resonated beyond the bounds of the farmstead. In line with the arguments laid out at the start of this paper, we should expect that developments in the domestic sphere would have not merely reflected wider changes in social relations, but would have constituted a significant, active part of them. Attention to the evidence for domestic relations can thus help to give a broader and more nuanced view of the origins of 'differentiation' during the period.

Across northern Europe, there is now widespread dissatisfaction with paradigms that attribute change in the late pre-Roman Iron Age primarily to relations with supposedly 'core' areas further south. Constructing alternative explanations has proved more difficult, however. The implication of the evidence from Jutland is that we need to consider how social developments were articulated at the level of everyday practice. Social change during the Iron Age would have been firmly grounded in the everyday conditions of existence, and the key to understanding it may lie in the settlements and field systems which are so abundant across the Continent, and yet so often taken for granted.

Notes

1. This paper is a summary of part of the author's Ph.D. thesis (Webley 2002). Inevitably, much supporting evidence and argumentation has had to be omitted. The full work is to be published by Aarhus University Press.

Bibliography

Allison, P. 1999a. Introduction, in Allison 1999b, 1–18.

Allison, P. (ed.) 1999b. *The Archaeology of Household Activities*. London: Routledge.

Bech, J.-H. and Mikkelsen, M. 1999. Landscapes, settlement and subsistence in Bronze Age Thy, north-west Jutland, in Fabech and Ringtved (eds), 69–77.

Becker, C.-J. 1961. *Førromersk Jernalder i Syd- og Midtjylland*. Copenhagen: Nationalmuseets Skrifter 6.

Becker, C.-J. 1972. Früheisenzeitliche Dörfer bei Grøntoft, Westjütland. 3. Vorbericht: Die Ausgrabungen 1967–68, *Acta Archaeologica* 42, 79–110.

Berthelsen, S. and Christiansen, F. 1989. Bopladskompleks fra ældre jernalder ved Hadsten, *Arkæologiske Fund, Kulturhistorisk Museum Randers* 1987–88, 33–5.

Boye, L. 1996. Jernalderhus i flammer – et brandeksperiment med store perspektiver, in M. Meldgaard and M. Rasmussen (eds.), *Arkæologiske Eksperimenter i Lejre*, 57–64. Copenhagen: Rhodos.

Brück, J. and Goodman, M. 1999. Introduction: themes for a critical archaeology of prehistoric settlement, in J. Brück and M. Goodman (eds), *Making Places in the Prehistoric World*, 1–19. London: University College London Press.

Capelle, T. 1987. Eisenzeitliche Bauopfer, *Frühmittelalterliche Studien* 21, 182–205.

Christiansen, F. 1995. Frederiksdalvej – en boplads fra ældre jernalder, *Kulturhistorisk Museum Randers Årbog* 1995, 103–10.

Clarke, D.L. 1972. A provisional model of an Iron Age society and its settlement system, in D.L. Clarke (ed.), *Models in Archaeology*, 801–869. London: Methuen.

Coles, J. and Minnitt, S. 1995. *'Industrious and Fairly Civilised'. The Glastonbury Lake Village*. Taunton: Somerset Levels Project.

Cunliffe, B. 1992. Pits, preconceptions and propitiation in the British Iron Age, *Oxford Journal of Archaeology* 11, 69–83.

Ejstrud, B. and Jensen, C.K. 2000. *Vendehøj – Landsby og Gravplads*. Århus: Jysk Arkæologisk Selskab.

Fabech, C. and Ringtved, J. (eds) 1999. *Settlement and Landscape*. Århus: Jysk Arkæologisk Selskab.

Fries, J. 1995. *Vor- und frühgeschichtliche Agrartechnik auf den britischen Inseln und den Kontinent*. Espelkamp: Marie Leidorf.

Gerritsen, F. 1999. To build and to abandon. The cultural biography of late prehistoric houses and farmsteads in the southern Netherlands, *Archaeological Dialogues* 6, 78–114.

Gerritsen, F. 2007. Familar landscapes with unfamiliar pasts? Bronze Age barrows and Iron Age communities in the southern Netherlands, in C. Haselgrove and R. Pope (eds), *The Earlier Iron Age in Britain and the Near Continent*, 338–353. Oxford: Oxbow Books.

Hatt, G. 1939. *The Ownership of Cultivated Land*. Copenhagen: Munksgaard.

Hatt, G. 1949. *Oldtidsagre*. Copenhagen: Det Kongelige Danske Videnskabernes Selskab.

Hatt, G. 1957. *Nørre Fjand. An Early Iron Age Village Site in West Jutland*. Copenhagen: Det Kongelige Danske Videnskabernes Selskab.

Hedeager, L. 1988. Jernalderen, in C. Bjørn (ed.), *Det Danske Landbrugs Historie. 1. Oldtid og Middelalder*, 109–203. Odense: Landbohistorisk Selskab.

Hedeager, L. 1992. *Iron Age Societies*. Oxford: Blackwell.

Hendon, J. 1996. Archaeological approaches to domestic labor: household practice and domestic relations, *Annual Review of Anthropology* 25, 45–61.

Henriksen, M.B. 1998. Guden under gulvet – ofringer under fynske huse fra ældre jernalder, *Fynske Minder* 1998, 191–212.

Hill, J.D. 1995. How should we understand Iron Age societies and hillforts? A contextual study from Southern Britain. In J.D. Hill and C.G. Cumberpatch (eds), *Different Iron Ages: Studies on the Iron Age in Temperate Europe,* 45–66. Oxford: British Archaeological Reports International Series 602

Hingley, R. 1990. Domestic organisation and gender relations in Iron Age and Romano-British households, in R. Samson (ed.), *The Social Archaeology of Houses*, 125–149. Edinburgh: University Press.

Hvass, S. 1985. *Hodde. Et Vestjysk Landsbysamfund fra Ældre Jernalder*. Copenhagen: Akademisk Forlag.

Jensen, J. 1982. *The Prehistory of Denmark*. London: Methuen.

Juhl, K. 1995. *The Relation Between Vessel Form and Vessel Function – a Methodological Study*. Stavanger: Arkeologiske Museum.

Kossack, G., Behre, K.-E. and Schmid, P. 1984. *Archäologische und naturwissenschaftliche Untersuchungen an ländlichen und frühstädlichen Siedlungen im deutschen Küstengebiet vom 5. Jahrhundert v. Chr. bis zum 11. Jahrhundert n. Chr. Band 1: Ländliche Siedlungen.* Weinheim: Acta Humaniora.

LaMotta, V. and Schiffer, M. 1999. Formation processes of house floor assemblages, in Allison 1999b, 19–29.

Levinsen, K. 1984. En ældre romertids smedegrav fra Tolstrup ved Års, *Hikuin* 10, 199–206.

Lewis, B. 1985. Overbygård og Nørre Fjand. En analyse af nogle jernalderlandsbyers tilligender og økonomi, *Kuml* 1985, 123–63.

Liversage, D., Munro, M., Courty, M.-A. and Nørnberg, P. 1987. Studies of a buried Early Iron Age field, *Acta Archaeologica* 56, 55–84.

Lyons, D. 1998. Witchcraft, gender, power and intimate relations in Mura compounds in Déla, northern Cameroon, *World Archaeology* 29, 344–362.

Martens, J. 1988. Borremose reconsidered, *Journal of Danish Archaeology* 7, 159–188.

Martens, J. 1997. The pre-Roman Iron Age in north Jutland, in J. Martens (ed.), *Chronological Problems of the Pre-Roman Iron Age in Northern Europe*, 107–36. Copenhagen: Arkæologiske Skrifter 7.

Nielsen, B.H. 1996. Smedegård – en byhøj fra den ældre jernalder ved Nors, *Historisk Årbog for Thy og Vester Hanherred* 1996, 51–60.

Nielsen, S. 1987. Huller i jorden, in Rigsantikvarens Arkæologiske Sekretariat (ed.), *Danmarks Længste Udgravning,* 87–93. Herning: Poul Kristensen.

Nielsen, V. 1993. *Jernalderens Pløjning: Store Vildmose.* Hjørring: Vendsyssel Historiske Museum.

Olesen, L.H. 1982. Jernalder-brandtomter i Skårup, Thy, *Antikvariske Studier* 5, 253–254.

Olesen, M.W. 2000. Tre smedier fra Snejbjerg, *FRAM* (*Fra Ringkøbing Amts Museer*) 2000, 23–36.

Parker Pearson, M. 1984. Economic and ideological change: cyclical growth in the pre-state societies of Jutland, in D. Miller and C. Tilley (eds), *Ideology, Power and Prehistory*, 69–92. Cambridge: Cambridge University Press.

Rasmussen, A.K. 1968. En byhøj i Thyland, *Nationalmuseets Arbejdsmark* 1968, 137–144.

Rindel, P.O. 1999. Development of the village community 500 BC – 100 AD in west Jutland, Denmark, in Fabech and Ringtved 1999, 79–99.

Roymans, N. and Theuws, F. 1999. Long-term perspectives on man and landscape in the Meuse–Demer–Scheldt region. An introduction, in F. Theuws and N. Roymans (eds), *Land and Ancestors*, 1–32. Amsterdam: Amsterdam Archaeological Studies 4.

Schmid, P. 1984. Siedlungsstrukturen, in Kossack *et al.* 1984, 193–244.

Siemen, P. and Stoumann, I. 1996. Hus, gård og landsby, in V. Bruhn, P. Holm, S. Meyer, J.D. Rasmussen, and I. Stoumann (eds), *Esbjergs Historie. 1. Før Byen Kom*, 23–66. Esbjerg: Rosendahl.

Stummann Hansen, S. 1979. Nogle aspekter omkring ejendomsformer og social arbejdsdeling i Danmarks yngre broncealder og ældre jernalder, *Kontaktstencil* 16, 63–79.

Stummann Hansen, S. 1984. Aspekter omkring relationen mellem landbrug og bebyggelse i Danmarks yngre bronzealder og ældre jernalder, in H. Thrane (ed.), *Beretning fra et Symposium om Dansk Landbrug i Oldtid og Middelalder*, 41–50. Odense: Historisk Institut, Odense Universitet.

Tesch, S. 1993. *Houses, Farmsteads and Long-Term Change.* Uppsala: University of Uppsala Press.

Therkorn, L. 1987. The inter-relationships of materials and meanings: some suggestions on housing concerns within Iron Age Noord-Holland, in I. Hodder (ed.) *The Archaeology of Contextual Meanings*, 102–110. Cambridge: Cambridge University Press.

Thomsen, N. 1965. Myrthue, et gårdanlæg fra jernalder, *Kuml* 1964, 15–30.

Tringham, R. 1991. Households with faces: the challenge of gender in prehistoric architectural remains, in J. Gero and M. Conkey (eds), *Engendering Archaeology,* 93–131. Oxford: Blackwell.

Webley, L. 2002. *A Social Archaeology of the Iron Age Household. Domestic Space in Western Denmark, 500 BC–AD 200.* Unpublished Ph.D. thesis, University of Cambridge

Webley, L. 2003. Iron Age houses and social space. A case study of the three-aisled longhouses of northern Europe during the pre-Roman and Early Roman Iron Age, in J. Humphrey (ed.), *Researching the Iron Age*, 59–68. Leicester: Leicester Archaeology Monograph 11.

Yanagisako, S. J. 1979. Family and household: the analysis of domestic groups, *Annual Review of Anthropology* 8, 161–205.

Weapons, ritual, and communication in Late Iron Age Northern Europe

Peter S. Wells

From the fourth century BC onward, communities in northern regions of Europe deposited large quantities of weapons in the course of rituals related to military activity. In the final century BC, at the same time that Rome was expanding its conquests and political control northward into temperate Europe, increasing numbers of weapons were being deposited at large numbers of sites, some in water, some in pits in the ground, and some in connection with fires. In the second half of the final century BC, the practice of burying men with standardised sets of weapons spread throughout the regions east of the middle and lower Rhine. These uses of weapons as objects for ritual deposition and as means of linking warriors throughout the unconquered regions of northern Europe indicate that weapons served as media of communication – means of conveying feelings and ideas about militarism and resistance among peoples threatened by the expansion of Rome.

Mobility, weapons and warfare in the Late Iron Age

Although trade and migration have long been issues in archaeology, until recently there has been relatively little appreciation of just how mobile individuals and communities were in Bronze Age and Iron Age Europe and how significant this mobility was for linking communities and transmitting information. Too often the archaeological materials recovered from excavated settlements and cemeteries are analysed and interpreted as though the communities represented were largely autonomous, depending upon their own members and their local landscapes for subsistence, raw materials, and social and ritual interaction. Yet archaeological evidence for regular inter-community contact is clear at virtually all Bronze Age and Iron Age sites. The widespread distribution of materials such as bronze, amber, glass, and graphite (as decoration on pottery) shows that communities were interlinked and participated in regular systems of goods circulation. But investigators do not always consider the full implications of these connections. While the circulation of materials is clear in the archaeological record, the role of such networks in social, political, and ritual interaction is less evident, but clearly implied by the evidence.

Recently a number of studies (e.g. Jockenhövel 1991; see also Wells 2001, 42–5) have focused on the issue of mobility in later prehistoric Europe, but the full implications of such movement and communication have not yet been explored. The specific purposes of individuals and groups moving from place to place varied and included migration to new settlement areas, traders peddling their wares, specialised bronzeworkers bringing their skills to customers, religious pilgrims, and family members traveling to visit kin, but also less benign purposes, such as raiding and warfare between groups. All such movement included communication – the exchange and spread of information between individuals and communities.

At the end of the prehistoric Iron Age, roughly 75 BC–AD 25, a special kind of mobility is evident in large numbers of men's graves that share strikingly similar sets of weapons throughout northern and central regions of the European Continent. In this paper I argue that the communication and associated mobility between the individuals represented in these graves, and between the communities of which they were members, was a

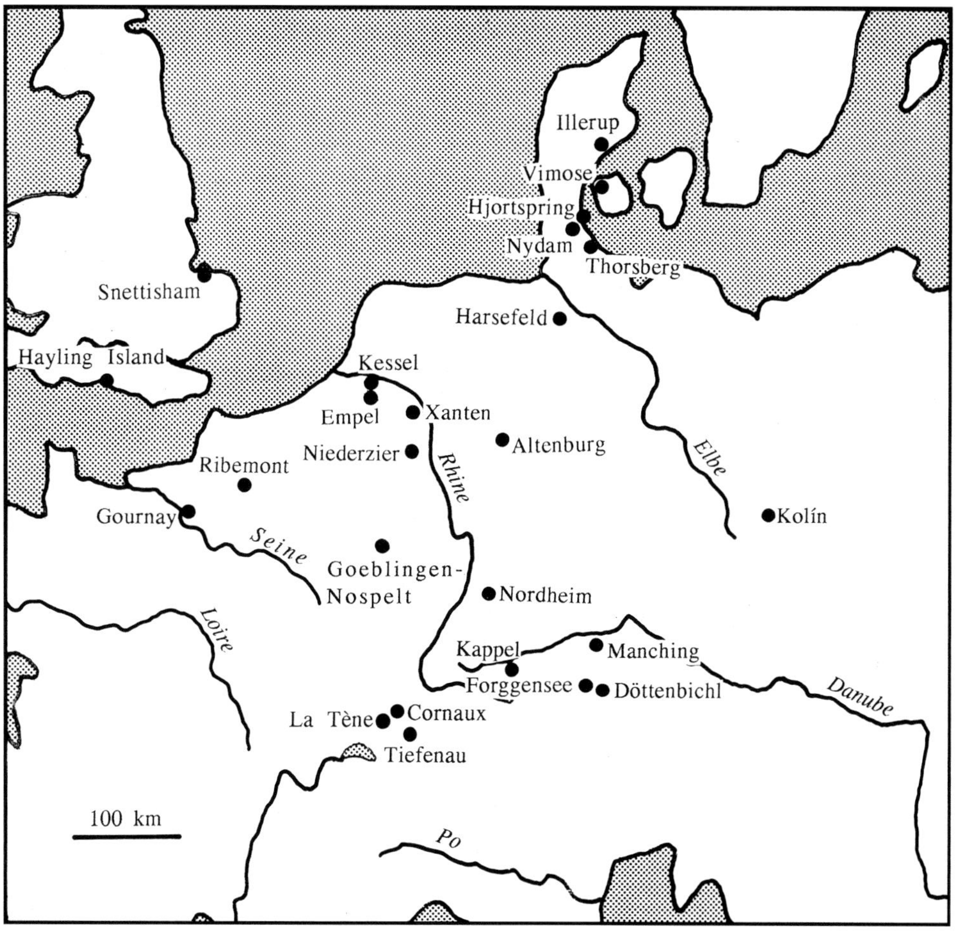

Fig. 1. Map showing locations of sites mentioned in the text.

key factor in determining the political configuration of Europe in the centuries just before and just after the Roman conquests. The weapons played special roles in these relationships, both as objects used in military action and as signs that had acquired powerful meanings in Bronze Age and Iron Age Europe. Relationships between people and their weapons changed in important ways during the latter part of the prehistoric Iron Age.

Weapons had long been special symbols of power and status in prehistoric Europe and thus often were included in burials of individuals of high status (Kristiansen 1998) and deposited in the course of rituals in places such as rivers, lakes, and caves (Torbrügge 1970–1). During the late fourth and third centuries BC, new ritual practices were developed that included the deposition of large quantities of weapons, many of them deliberately damaged in the process, in open places where large numbers of people – more than lived together in a single village community – could witness the proceedings. Among the best-documented sites of this period are Hjortspring in Denmark and Gournay-sur-Aronde and Ribemont-sur-Ancre in northern France. At Hjortspring (Randsborg 1995), a boat and weapons to outfit a force of some 80 warriors were deposited in a pond. At the two French sites, weapons, human bones, and remains of animals were placed in pits and ditches that formed parts of rectangular enclosures (Brunaux 1996; Arcelin and Brunaux 2003, 9–73). In these and other instances, the rituals involved a variety of actions that formed coordinated visual displays for participants and observers. At Hjortspring, the sinking of the large boat and weighing it down with stones, along with the depositing of hundreds of weapons, must have made a striking impression on viewers. At Gournay and Ribemont, the breaking and bending of weapons, the sacrifice of animals, and the deposition of human remains, whether the humans were sacrificed on the spot or not, were parts of public spectacles.

The site of La Tène in Switzerland, the interpretation of which has been a matter of much discussion and debate since its discovery in the nineteenth century, was probably principally a place where weapons, including 166 swords and 269 lance heads, were dropped into shallow water (Müller 1990; Bradley 1998, 158, fig. 36). Post remains indicate an elaborate structure built out into Lake Neuchâtel from which quantities of weapons and other objects were tossed into the water. Typological dating places most of the material from La Tène around the middle of the third century BC.

There is much evidence to indicate that during the fourth, third, and second centuries BC, warfare played an ever-increasing role in the political and social life of Europeans (Kristiansen 1998, chapter 7). The frequency of iron long-swords in men's graves of this period (La Tène B and C in the Reinecke chronology) supports the idea that systematic violence was an important factor in life at the time, and that the status of many individual men was significantly represented by their weapons. During the second and first centuries BC, great amounts of effort were devoted to the construction of the immense defensive walls around the *oppida*.

Greek texts refer to the martial prowess of warriors from temperate Europe (whom the Greek writers called 'Celts'), and to their service as mercenary troops in armies in the Mediterranean world during the fourth and third centuries BC (Szabó 1991). In the references to the migrations of the Cimbri and the Teutones toward the end of the second century BC (Last 1932), we find specific discussion of migration and violence among peoples north of the Alps, as it was understood by Mediterranean commentators. According to the accounts, the Cimbri, Teutones, and other groups who joined them along the way, migrated from northern regions of continental Europe southward, in 113 BC defeated a Roman army in battle at Noreia, thought to be in modern Austria or Slovenia, marauded westward into Gaul and southward, and finally into northern Italy, where they were defeated in 101 BC. It is not clear whether these migrations were unusual for the time and hence noted by Greek and Roman writers, or whether they were among many such movements that took place during the second and first centuries BC, and only because these groups reached Italy did they attract such special attention. Later, Julius Caesar refers to large-scale movements and warring between peoples in temperate Europe in the decades before his campaigns in Gaul.

Caesar also documents movements of warriors that may have been much more regular than we would conclude from the texts alone. He informs us of mercenaries serving in his army in Gaul who came not only from other parts of Gaul, but also from Germany across the Rhine (*Gallic War* VII, 65). The large number of graves east of the Rhine, especially in the lower Elbe region of Germany, which contain Roman bronze vessels together with iron swords and often with spurs, could be interpreted as burials of former mercenaries in Gaul, or perhaps in Caesar's or Pompey's armies during the subsequent Civil War (Erdrich 2001). In these burial contexts too, it is apparent that weapons played an important role as signs of status, power, and involvement in the geopolitical conflicts of the time.

New patterns and practices

The final two centuries BC were a time of great change in central and northern Europe with regard to settlement systems, military activity, and ritual practices. The *oppida* represented a need for defence on a much larger scale than before and constituted the first urban-type communities north of the Alps, with manufacturing and commerce growing to new levels of intensity (Colin 1998; Sievers 1999). Rectangular enclosures (*Viereckschanzen*) were constructed throughout much of temperate Europe (sharing some significant features with the earlier enclosures at Gournay and Ribemont in northern France), many of them with evidence of ritual activity performed in the enclosed areas or in the surrounding ditches (Wieland 1999). Throughout much of central and western Europe, practices for disposing of the dead changed from inhumation burial, abundantly represented during the preceding centuries, to other kinds of rituals. At present we do not understand much about those rituals, but an archaeologically apparent result of them is the large quantities of human bones, many showing signs of different kinds of manipulation, in settlement contexts. Among the best-studied assemblages is that from Manching (Hahn 1992). The manipulation and deposition of large numbers of human bones within settlements, rather than burying individuals in graves, imply more public, communal mortuary rites than the practices involved in inhumation burials.

At the same time that these changes in settlement character, ritual complexes, and treatment of the dead were taking place, we see a great increase in quantities of metal placed in what appear to be votive deposits, both on the Continent and in Britain (Bradley 1998). These include hoards of gold and silver coins; hoards that include gold coins together with sets of gold neck and arm rings, as at Niederzier (Göbel *et al.* 1991); pit deposits containing different metals in a variety of forms, of which the site at Snettisham is an example (Stead 1991); and deposits of iron tools, such as that at Kolín (Rybová and Motyková 1983), sometimes associated with bronze objects, as at Kappel (Fischer 1959). At the same time that these substantial quantities of wealth and metal equipment were being deposited in the ground, weapons came to play new roles in ritual display.

Weapons in archaeology and in tradition

The special ways in which weapons were often treated – as grave goods and as deposits – show that they played roles in human consciousness beyond their functional use as military implements. Mythological traditions indicate the special roles attributed to weapons – swords in particular, but others as well (Davidson 1988). Weapons were often regarded as magical and created by supernatural creatures. Heroes are distinguished by their abilities to use weapons in superhuman ways, as in the stories of Beowulf and of King Arthur. In some legends, specific weapons represent continuity of the social group, connecting heroic ancestors with their descendants.

From mythological and early historical traditions, it is apparent that weapons in general, and swords in particular, are associated with a variety of interrelated themes that we might call elite status, authority, power, and protection. Roymans (1996) has explored the role of weapons as emblems of a warrior class in late prehistoric and early historic contexts. Weapons were signs of an individual's ability to provide defence to the community. They were also means by which individuals and groups acquired wealth and power through conquest (Fitzpatrick 1984; Kurz 1995).

Historical background

The historical circumstances in the final two centuries BC provide the background to any consideration of the practice of depositing weapons during this period. Mercenary service in Mediterranean armies created a vehicle by which men from central and northern Europe could gain wealth and status, as well as adventure in and acquire knowledge of the wider world, by virtue of their skill with weapons. When those that survived returned to their homelands, they and other members of their communities must have held their weapons in high regard, as the means by which they had achieved their wealth and status. These experiences contributed to the ideas and feelings associated with weapons in second and first century BC Europe. Similarly, when native Europeans served as mercenaries in Caesar's army in Gaul, and in other situations with Roman generals, the status and material rewards they won derived from their skill with their weapons. Thus weapons were means towards the achievement of valued accomplishments.

Relations between indigenous peoples and the Roman army were complex and diverse, as Caesar and other Roman writers make clear. Some groups allied with Rome even before Caesar's campaigns in Gaul, some changed allegiances over time, and some remained resolutely anti-Roman. Among groups that set themselves against Roman expansion in Europe, weapons could serve as symbols of resistance to the imperial army. During and after the Gallic War, expansion of the practice of placing swords and other weapons in men's graves east of the Rhine (Schultze 1986) may reflect these two seemingly opposing ideas – weapon sets as signs of status gained through military service with Rome, and at the same time as signs of status as defenders of indigenous peoples against the Mediterranean aggressor. The common theme was weapons as media for display and communication of status and military effectiveness, or power.

Weapon deposits as displays

Within the general increase in the quantities of materials that people deposited during the final two centuries BC (see above), the increase in deposition of weapons is particularly marked (Torbrügge 1970–1, *Beilage* 24; Roymans 1996). We can distinguish at least three main categories of deposits (graves I treat separately below) that include weapons – water sites, dry land sites, and fire-place sites. These categories are, of course, ours and not necessarily the way that the people at the time thought about their world. Indeed, we find considerable 'mixing' of our categories among the actual deposits. Places where weapons were deposited in water during this period include Tiefenau and Cornaux in Switzerland, Kessel in the Netherlands, and the Thames in England. At Tiefenau at Bern, 80 swords and 30 lanceheads have been recovered, at Cornaux two swords and 14 lanceheads, along with human skeletal remains (Müller 1990). From Kessel on the Rhine, at least 27 Late Iron Age swords have been recovered, along with quantities of human bone (Roymans this volume). Much of the ornate metalwork from this period recovered from the Thames and other British rivers is likely to have been deposited under similar circumstances. The same practice of depositing weapons in water was carried out during the Roman period as well, for example at Xanten on the lower Rhine (Schalles 1996).

Examples of dry land weapon deposit sites include Altenburg in northern Hesse, where 40 fragments of swords, 20 lance points, and other iron objects were recovered at a shallow depth in an area of about 600 m^2 on a hilltop (Müller 1990, 82–3), and Hayling Island in Hampshire, where spearheads, parts of shields, chain mail, and metal pieces of horse and wheeled vehicle trappings have been found (King and Soffe 2001). The recently excavated site at Döttenbichl near Oberammergau, which includes the first direct archaeological evidence for the invasion of southern Bavaria by the armies of Tiberius and Drusus in 15 BC, appears to include a weapon deposit (Zanier 1997; 1999a). Besides these large weapon deposits that were created in the course of substantial public rituals, many small assemblages of weapons attest to practices on a much more modest scale. For example, recent excavations at a *Viereckschanze* at Nordheim in Wurttemberg recovered a deposit of eight iron shield bosses, together with a Roman ceramic amphora (Neth 1999). This discovery shows that small sites in the countryside, away from major centres and waterways, can also include deposits of weapons. This practice of depositing weapons at rectangular enclosures, including some that later became sites of Gallo-Roman temples, is demonstrated by the important finds at Empel in the Netherlands (Roymans and Derks 1994).

Third, the category of sites known as 'burned offering places' (*Brandopferplätze*), common throughout the

Alpine foothills and the central upland regions of Europe, contain weapons along with other metal objects, as Zanier's (1999b) recent publication of Forggensee illustrates. This site is an excellent example of the situation of many ritual deposits in places where visibility was exceptionally good. The land around the site is flat. It lay on the shore of a lake, affording people at considerable distance a view of the fires, and in the background rise the high Alps. The Forggensee fire-place site, like many others of this category, shows continuous use from the prehistoric Iron Age into the Roman period.

The ceremonies in which the large assemblages of weapons were deposited at all of the categories of sites mentioned here were performed in places where they could be viewed by sizeable numbers of people. The site at La Tène was in the shallows of a lake, that at Forggensee on a lake shore in a wide open landscape. The river site at Kessel is in a flat region with wide visibility, that at Altenburg on a hilltop. Such locations were apparently selected to enable a large number of people to see what was happening. At some sites, huge deposits were made, such as at the well-known deposits in northern Germany, Denmark, and Sweden, of which Illerup, Nydam, Thorsberg, and Vimose are among the best documented, where whole armies' outfits were dropped into lakes during the Roman Iron Age (Randsborg 1995). In other instances, sites and the rituals conducted at them were much smaller, involving smaller communities of participants and observers, as in the case of the enclosure at Nordheim.

In order to appreciate the process and impact of the rituals performed at these sites, we need to consider what the people who participated in these events experienced. At all of the sites, they witnessed the transformation of weapons from one state of being to another. All of the deposits involved removing objects from the world of the living and transmitting them into a different medium – earth, water, or, in the case of wooden weapons, in fire, air – such that they became invisible to the observers and irretrievable. Frequently, in addition to the process of transmission from one medium to another, the ritual involved rendering the weapons useless in the everyday world, by bending, breaking, or burning them, before the process of deposition.

In most cases, we do not have much information about the actual course of the ritual, although by examining the areas of ground around deposits, it should be possible to collect information about how the ritual was performed. At some recently excavated sites, archaeologists have paid close attention to such evidence. For example, at Illerup in Denmark, Ilkjaer and his colleagues have been able to show how some objects were broken, and others burned, before they were deposited, and also how they were deposited. Some were dropped from boats or rafts into the lake, others thrown from shore out into the water's depths (Ørsnes and Ilkjaer 1993).

Finally, I should mention an issue of interpretation of weapon deposits that, while important, is not central to the main point of this paper. The Danish and northern German weapon deposits are most often interpreted as sacrifices of weapons of defeated armies (Randsborg 1995), and Brunaux (1996) has suggested a similar interpretation for the weapons deposited at Gournay-sur-Aronde and Ribemont-sur-Ancre. Roman writers mention the practice of Iron Age peoples sacrificing the weapons of their enemies (e.g. Caesar, *Gallic War* VI, 17; Tacitus, *Annals* 13, 57), but there is little direct archaeological evidence to support this interpretation of the sites mentioned here. Perhaps the full publication of the deposit at Döttenbichl (Zanier 1997) will change this situation.

Weapons as grave goods: funerary ritual

The deposits of weapons discussed above, while often associated with human skeletal remains, were not primarily parts of burials. Weapons placed in graves played different, but related, roles from those deposited in the sites considered above. These roles were connected to the specific individuals with whom they were interred, whereas the large deposits considered above were related to entire communities.

Around the mid first century BC, the practice of weapon burial was adopted on a regular basis in regions east of the middle and lower Rhineland (Schultze 1986). Many of the burials share a strikingly similar set of grave goods that include a sword, in some cases of Roman manufacture, one or two spears, a shield, one or more spurs, one or more bronze vessels made in the Roman world (Italy or Gaul) that sometimes served as urns, and often a locally-made vessel in the form of a drinking horn. The regular occurrence of spurs in these graves, sometimes multiple sets and sometimes highly ornate, suggests that some of the buried individuals may have been among the cavalry troops Caesar (*Gallic War* VII, 65) mentions that he hired during the Gallic War from among the Germanic tribes. In any case, the widely-adopted practice of including weapons in graves in this region began around the time Caesar was fighting in Gaul. The regularity of the set of objects in large numbers of these graves raises important questions about the meaning of the weapons in these burial contexts.

Otto-Herman Frey (1986) has called attention to what has been called an 'international warrior elite'. This expression refers to the extensive series of burials across much of temperate Europe during the final century BC, from conquered Gaul in the west to as far east as Poland and north as Gotland in central Sweden. The similar combination of weapons over these great distances indicates a common set of ideas and practices, shared by elite men throughout much of northern and central Europe. Several investigators, most recently Böhme-Schönberger (1998), have drawn attention to a special subset of these weapon graves distinguished by a common pattern of bronze openwork ornament attached to the tops of scabbards that accompany the swords. These elaborate and labour-intensive decorations have no utilitarian purpose, but serve to distinguish the scabbard, and thereby the possessor of the weapon, from others. The top part of the exterior of the scabbard is a highly visible surface, and this space served as a place to display meaningful signs. These scabbard decorations have been identified in weapon graves throughout much of temperate Europe (Wells 1998, 278 fig. 7), from Luxembourg in the west to Sweden in the north, and as far south and east as Bulgaria. This broad distribution of graves with this particular form of ornamental detail indicates significant connections between the men represented in these burials, marked by these signs as different from the much larger group of men buried with sets of weapons that do not bear this distinctive ornament.

Spurs in these graves deserve special note. As Thomas Völling (1992) has shown, specific types of spurs occur only in the second half of the final century BC, in burials both within eastern areas of conquered Gaul and beyond the Rhine in the unconquered lands. Historical sources, including Caesar in his commentary on the Gallic War, cite the employment of native fighters – Caesar mentions both Gallic and Germanic warriors – as cavalry troops in the service of the Roman military. It is likely that many of the spurs recovered in weapon graves on both sides of the Rhine are signs of the buried individual's cavalry experience, perhaps in the service of the Roman army, perhaps on a different side. As I have suggested elsewhere (Wells 2001, 121), the rapid and wide spread of this practice of burying spurs in men's graves may indicate that many warriors created a particular identity for themselves, based on their military status and their role as cavalry. The practice of decorating spurs with gold and silver to draw special attention to them (e.g. Mangelsdorf and Schönfelder 2001) reinforces this interpretation of spurs as indicators of status and identity.

The wide geographical distribution of this common practice of warrior burial, frequently associated with signs of horseback riding, during the second half of the final century BC indicates a sharing of values and identity. These individuals had been in communication with one another, in some cases surely directly, probably in the majority of cases only indirectly. Some may have served together in auxiliary forces with the Roman legions, others in warrior bands who confronted the legions during various Roman campaigns east of the Rhine. In contrast to some burial practices in Gaul and elsewhere at the time, the mortuary rituals that preceded the burying of these individuals with their weapon sets were distinctly, we might say defiantly, un-Roman. The marked divergence from Roman-style burial is especially significant in the case of graves within conquered Gaul, such as the four at Goeblingen-Nospelt in Luxembourg (Metzler 1984). Certainly by the middle of the first century BC, indigenous groups, both within conquered Gaul and across the Rhine in the unconquered lands, were well aware of Roman burial traditions and practices. Some local people adopted Roman practices early after the conquest, while others did not (Wells 1999, 158–63). Many of the rituals may have been conducted in the context of resistance to practices introduced by Rome. The frequency of including weapons in the funerary rituals and burials of men east of the Rhine after the middle of the first century BC can be understood in terms of such resistance, along with other meanings that may be attributed to the popularity of the new practice (see below).

It is important to remind ourselves that these burials are the physical manifestations of a part of the funeral rituals that commemorated these men. While we do not have much archaeological evidence pertaining to the conduct of the rituals, it is reasonable to assume that the funerary ceremonies involving individuals who were buried in well-outfitted graves were public events attended by most, if not all, members of the community to which each man belonged, and perhaps by members of other communities as well. The mortuary rituals that resulted in the burials that archaeologists recover were focused on the single individual, in contrast to the deposits discussed in the preceding section, which were parts of rituals focused on whole communities.

Grave 157 in the large cemetery at Harsefeld in the lower Elbe region near Hamburg will serve as an example (Wegewitz 1984). In this grave, a bronze cauldron contained the cremated remains of the deceased along with the grave goods. These included sherds of ceramic vessels that may have been used in the funerary ritual. Remains of textile probably derive from clothing worn by the deceased at the time of cremation. A one-edged sword was bent to fit into the cauldron. A lance head and parts of a shield, including the boss and clamps, were recovered in the cauldron, indicating that the lance and shield had been broken up, dismantled, or burned before burial. A knife and its leather sheath were placed in the cauldron unburned and unbroken, along with a set of toilet implements. Two spurs with attached leather remains were found, indicating that shoes with spurs had been added to the assemblage after the cremation. The spurs are not identical, suggesting that each represents a pair, the matching spur of which is missing. A fibula that had served as a clothing attachment indicates a date for the burial in the second half of the final century BC.

We can only make educated guesses about how the earlier stages of the funerary ceremony were performed. The cremation of the body is likely to have been a component of the ceremony that was attended by the whole community. Reducing a body to ashes and small fragments of burned bone is not a simple matter (Zanier 1999b, 121). Substantial quantities of suitable wood must be amassed – at least two cubic metres for an adult corpse (Wahl 1981) – and a structure erected to hold the body and provide the requisite heat. The objects recovered in the cauldron that show fire damage must have been ceremonially arranged on or next to the body before the fire was lit. Sometime after the cremation process was complete, following two or three hours of intense burning, those conducting the ritual gathered together the ashes, burned bone fragments, and fire-damaged objects, and arranged them in the cauldron. Then the other objects – knife, toilet items, and shoes with spurs – were added, along with the ceramic vessels. The cauldron and its contents were then placed in the hole in the ground and covered with earth.

Grave 157 at Harsefeld illustrates the transformations of objects that made up such a significant part of the rituals that constituted the funerary ceremony. The weapons were burned with the body, destroying the wooden parts and changing the character of the iron pieces, thus transforming them from useful implements in military action to signs or representations of such objects. After the fire, the sword was bent into a small packet and placed in the urn, and the fire-damaged lance head and shield parts were added. The fire constituted one stage in the transformation of the weapons, and burial in the earth – permanent removal from the world of the living and from community visibility – was a second. We do not know what transpired before the creation and lighting of the funeral pyre.

Neither do we know who the personages were who conducted the different parts of the ceremony. It is likely that cultural rules stipulated that individuals in specific relationships with the deceased carried out the different processes – assembling the wood, building the pyre, arranging the corpse and preparing the objects, lighting the fire, collecting up the burned remains, digging the hole, placing the remains in the cauldron, placing the cauldron in the hole, and filling it in. In addition to these stages in the process of which we have direct physical evidence, much else probably happened as well, including processions, singing, saying of prayers, and other actions. From this period, we do not have much good data about the character of the sites at which the cremations were carried out (but see Schlott *et al.* 1985).

Weapons and agency

The special contexts in which we find weapons make it clear that they were signs of status and power, but we need to think about them in more dynamic ways. The evidence from the water and earth deposits, the fire-place sites, and the burials, indicates that people used weapons in active ways to communicate. We might think of the weapons we recover archaeologically in such contexts as the material components of the rituals in the course of which they were deposited – rituals that played central roles in creating and communicating relationships between people and ideas in Late Iron Age Europe. While at present we know little about the content of those rituals, the weapons survive as visible manifestations of them.

As recoverable components of the rituals, the weapons are critically important to us. But, to apply ideas recently presented by Knappett (2002), perhaps it was not the weapons themselves that were most important to the people who conducted and observed the ceremonies. The critical factor may have been the network of relationships between the weapons, the people who manipulated them in the rituals, and the feelings that participants experienced and ideas that the rituals communicated to them. But there are additional layers of complexity that need to be considered as well. The histories of specific weapons may have played important roles in the events – a sword that a leader used in a famous raid against an enemy, for example. But this kind of information is extremely difficult to recover.

Common to all of the categories of sites discussed above is deposition of weapons in the course of ceremonies that involved considerable display, to a community of participants and observers. Beyond that basic similarity, the specifics of weapon deposits vary. Regions in which there are large numbers of graves containing weapons in the final century BC (Völling 1995, 1, map 8) tend to have fewer weapon deposits in water or in pits in the earth (Müller 1990, 76, fig. 43). While no two graves are exactly alike, the recurrence, over a wide geographical range, of the specific set of weapons and other objects noted above is significant. Similarly, every water deposit, pit deposit, and *Brandopferplatz* is unique, but they share significant characteristics. Common to the sites I have discussed here and to the much larger universe of sites not mentioned are: (1) special role of weapons; (2) emphasis on display to a more-or-less sizeable audience; and (3) similarities in the composition of weapon sets included in graves throughout a large region of central and northern Europe.

Weapon display and the expansion of Roman power

The greater use of weapons – especially swords – in burials, and the more public display of weapons at votive offering ceremonies during this period suggest that the interrelationships between people, weapons, and the rituals in which they interacted were playing important roles. As noted in the first part of this paper, there are many indications that warfare was increasingly important to the peoples of central and northern Europe during the last few centuries BC, in terms of both their everyday lives and their ritual activity. The character of the weapon sets in graves indicates that weapons were also important media of communication.

In the final century BC, when the graves with swords proliferate and large numbers of swords and other weapons were deposited in water, in holes in the ground, and at fire-place sites, the expansion of Rome was a new threat, larger in scale than the conflicts between indigenous groups north of the Alps. As Rome's military and political power spread in southern Gaul, then in the mid first century BC into the whole of Gaul, with forays by Caesar and subsequent generals across the Channel to Britain and eastward across the Rhine, defence of communities, in the broadest sense – of land, community, and identity – became an increasingly important concern (Roymans 1996). This process was complex, and not all communities or all individuals viewed the Roman threat in the same way. Many groups east of the Rhine declared themselves allied to Rome, for example, and many individual warriors served as auxiliaries with Roman forces. We need to understand the rituals involving weapons not only in relation to feelings about the need to defend communities against Rome, but more generally in terms of the ever-greater role that weapons and military activity were playing in political and social life.

During this period, Rome also used weapons as powerful signs of military and political processes. For example, several series of coins issued when Caesar was in power show on the reverse side trophies of Gallic weapons, with prisoners set in the foreground (e.g. Wells 1999, 106, fig. 14). These ubiquitous media of propaganda relied on the association between images of weapons and ideas about conquest and political domination to convey messages about the progress of Roman expansion, and to draw special attention to the achievements of Rome's leaders. In imagery designed for consumption by Roman elites, similar themes were represented. On the *Gemma Augustea*, for example, made around AD 10, in the register below the scene of the enthroned Augustus crowned as Jupiter, with Tiberius approaching him, we see bound barbarian captives amidst a trophy of their captured weapons, mounted on a stand for display (Zanker 1988, 231, fig. 182). Thus both sides of the conflict – the imperial centre at Rome and the northern peoples under threat of conquest – were employing weapons in similar ways to communicate messages about conquest and defence, spreading imperial rule and protection of the community.

Communication and military action: an example

The mobility of and regular communication between weapon-bearing men in central and northern Europe at the end of the Iron Age created a vast network of individuals with a strongly developed martial ideology, who could respond quickly to demanding military circumstances. I close with an historical example that links the discussion above concerning the growing importance of weapons in the consciousness of Late Iron Age Europeans with a major, hitherto rather poorly understood event. When Rome's 17th, 18th, and 19th Legions under the command of Varus were destroyed in the Battle of the Teutoburg Forest in AD 9, the Emperor Augustus and the Roman commentators who recorded the event were not only horrified but also baffled (Schlüter and Wiegels 1999). How could the northern barbarians, described by Roman and Greek writers as simple peoples without towns, barely practising agriculture, with none of the centralised institutions that the Gauls possessed, not only defeat, but virtually annihilate some 20,000 men of the most powerful army in the world? This lack of understanding is apparent in the accounts written by the Roman and Greek writers who described the event, including Velleius Paterculus, Tacitus, and Cassius Dio.

But the archaeological evidence, in particular that discussed above relating to the increasing importance of weapons in rituals and as media for communication between warriors, enables us to understand how this event could have happened. The evidence shows that the native peoples were much more highly organised and mentally prepared to confront the legions than the Roman generals imagined. Rituals conducted around weapons and their various meanings had served to inculcate a military ideology in the communities east of the Rhine. For the rallying of the troops that confronted Varus' legions, the key element was communication. The Iron Age peoples east of the lower Rhine had no major centres such as the *oppida* of the Gauls, only farmsteads and small villages. Yet by drawing on fighters from hundreds of communities, who shared feelings about their roles as warriors and had been prepared materially and mentally to rally when called, the local leaders were able to mount a force of fighting men surpassing anything of which the Roman military officials thought them capable (Wells 2003, 141–60).

The common patterns of weapon burial are the material expressions of this organisation and of the shared ideas and goals that linked together hundreds of communities in the broad expanse of lands east of the Rhine. This system of communication that made possible rapid dissemination of information and quick response was a new creation at the end of the final century BC, developed in the context of the growing threat of Rome's armies. Such historically-recorded events as Caesar's forays across the Rhine in 55 and 53 BC, Drusus' campaigns between the lower Rhine and the Elbe between 12 and 9 BC, and subsequent incursions under Tiberius and other generals, made it clear to the indigenous peoples that conquest by Rome was a real possibility. The growth in military preparedness that took place over several decades during the final century BC, including the creation of a new appreciation of the value of military skill and power expressed in the deposits and graves examined above, was the critical factor that resulted in this outcome of the great battle in AD 9.

The archaeological evidence for the ways that people were manipulating and depositing weapons during the final two centuries BC gives us insight into the increasing roles that weapons and military activity came to play in the thinking of the Late Iron Age peoples of central and northern Europe. This material evidence provides us with an understanding of aspects of the military situation beyond the Roman frontier that was lacking among the planners of Roman policy east of the Rhine.

Acknowledgements

I thank Colin Haselgrove and Tom Moore for organising an excellent and highly stimulating conference at Durham and for inviting me to participate. For monographs and papers that were especially helpful in the preparation of this paper I thank Otto-Herman Frey, Kristian Kristiansen, Nico Roymans, and Werner Zanier.

Bibliography

Arcelin, E. and Brunaux, J.-L. 2003. Cultes et sanctuaires en France à l'âge du fer, *Gallia* 60, 1–268.

Böhme-Schönberger, A. 1998. Das Grab eines vornehmen Kriegers der Spätlatènezeit aus Badenheim, *Germania* 76, 217–256.

Bradley, R. 1998. *The Passage of Arms: An Archaeological Analysis of Prehistoric Hoards and Votive Deposits* (2nd edn). Oxford: Oxbow Books.

Brunaux, J.-L. 1996. *Les religions gauloises: rituels celtiques de la Gaule indépendante*. Paris: Errance.

Colin, A. 1998. *Chronologie des oppida de la Gaule non méditerranéenne*. Paris: Documents d'Archéologie Française 71.

Davidson, H.R.E. 1988. *Myths and Symbols in Pagan Europe*. Syracuse: Syracuse University Press.

Erdrich, M. 2001. *Rom und die Barbaren*. Mainz: Philipp von Zabern.

Fischer, F. 1959. *Der spätlatènezeitliche Depot-Fund von Kappel (Kreis Saulgau)*. Stuttgart: Silberburg.

Fitzpatrick, A.P. 1984. The deposition of La Tène Iron Age metalwork in watery contexts in southern England, in B. Cunliffe and D. Miles (eds), *Aspects of the Iron Age in Central Southern Britain*, 178–190. Oxford: Oxford University Committee for Archaeology Monograph 2.

Frey, O.-H. 1986. Einige Überlegungen zu den Beziehungen zwischen Kelten und Germanen in der Spätlatènezeit, *Marburger Studien zur Vor- und Frühgeschichte* 7, 45–79.

Göbel, J., Hartmann, A., Joachim, H.-E. and Zedelius V. 1991. Der spätkeltische Goldschatz von Niederzier, *Bonner Jahrbücher* 191, 27–84.

Hahn, E. 1992. Die menschlichen Skelettreste, in F. Maier, U. Geilenbrügge, E. Hahn, H.-J. Köhler and S. Sievers (eds), *Ergebnisse der Ausgrabungen 1984–1987 in Manching*, 214–234. Stuttgart: Ausgrabungen in Manching 15.

Jockenhövel, A. 1991. Räumliche Mobilität von Personen in der mittleren Bronzezeit des westlichen Mitteleuropa, *Germania* 69, 49–62.

King, A. and Soffe, G. 2001. Internal organisation and deposition at the Iron Age temple on Hayling Island, Hampshire, in J.R. Collis (ed.), *Society and Settlement in Iron Age Europe*, 111–123. Sheffield: Sheffield Archaeological Monograph 11.

Knappett, C. 2002. Photographs, skeuomorphs and marionettes: some thoughts on mind, agency and object, *Journal of Material Culture* 7, 97–117.

Kristiansen, K. 1998. *Europe before History*. Cambridge: Cambridge University Press.

Kurz, G. 1995. *Keltische Hort- und Gewässerfunde in Mitteleuropa*. Stuttgart: Theiss.

Last, H. 1932. The Cimbri and Teutoni, in S.A. Cook, F.E. Adcock and M.P. Charlesworth (eds), *The Cambridge Ancient History* IX, 139–151. Cambridge: Cambridge University Press.

Mangelsdorf, G. and Schönfelder, M. 2001. Zu den Gräbern mit Waffenbeigabe der jüngeren vorrömischen Eisenzeit im Steinkreis von Netzeband (Kr. Ostvorpommern), *Archäologisches Korrespondenzblatt* 31, 93–106.

Metzler, J. 1984. Treverische Reitergräber von Goeblingen-Nospelt, in H. Cüppers (ed.), *Trier: Augustusstadt der Treverer*, 87–99. Mainz: Philipp von Zabern.

Müller, F. 1990. *Der Massenfund von der Tiefenau bei Bern*. Basel: Schweizerische Gesellschaft für Ur- und Frühgeschichte.

Neth, A. 1999. Zum Fortgang der Ausgrabungen in der zweiten Viereckschanze bei Nordheim, Kreis Heilbronn, *Archäologische Ausgrabungen in Baden-Württemberg 1999*, 75–79.

Ørsnes, M. and Ilkjaer, J. 1993. Votive deposits, in S. Hvass and B. Storgaard (eds), *Digging into the Past*, 215–219. Copenhagen: Royal Society of Northern Antiquaries.

Randsborg, K. 1995. *Hjortspring: Warfare and Sacrifice in Early Europe*. Aarhus: Aarhus University Press.

Roymans, N. 1996. The sword or the plough, in N. Roymans (ed.), *From the Sword to the Plough*, 9–126. Amsterdam: Amsterdam Archaeological Studies 1.

Roymans, N. and Derks, T. (eds). 1994. *De Tempel van Empel*. 's-Hertogenbosch: Brabantse Regionale Geschiedbeoefening.

Rybová, A. and Motyková, K. 1983. Der Eisendepotfund der Latènezeit von Kolín, *Památky Archeologické* 74, 96–174.

Schalles, H.-J. 1996. *Römerschätze: Funde aus einem Xantener Altrheinarm*. Moers: Kulturstiftung Sparkasse Moers.

Schlott, C., Spennemann, D.R. and Weber G. 1985. Ein Verbrennungsplatz und Bestattungen am spätlatènezeitlichen Heidetränk-Oppidum im Taunus, *Germania* 63, 439–505.

Schlüter, W. and Wiegels R. (eds). 1999. *Rom, Germanien und die Ausgrabungen von Kalkriese*. Osnabrück: Rasch.

Schultze, E. 1986. Zur Verbreitung von Waffenbeigaben bei den germanischen Stämmen um den Beginn unserer Zeitrechnung, *Bodendenkmalpflege in Mecklenburg 1986*, 93–117.

Sievers, S. 1999. Manching: Aufstieg und Niedergang einer Keltenstadt, *Bericht der Römisch-Germanischen Kommission* 80, 5–24.

Stead, I.M. 1991. The Snettisham treasure, *Antiquity* 65, 447–464.

Szabó, M. 1991. Mercenary activity, in V. Kruta, O.-H. Frey, B. Raftery and M. Szabó (eds), *The Celts*, 333–336. London: Thames and Hudson.

Torbrügge, W. 1970–1. Vor- und frühgeschichtliche Flussfunde, *Bericht der Römisch-Germanischen Kommission* 51–52, 1–146.

Völling, T. 1992. Dreikreisplattensporen, *Archäologisches Korrespondenzblatt* 22, 393–402.

Völling, T. 1995. *Frühgermanische Gräber von Aubstadt im Grabfeldgau (Unterfranken)*. Kallmünz: Michael Lassleben.

Wahl, J. 1981. Beobachtungen zur Verbrennung menschlicher Leichnamen, *Archäologisches Korrespondenzblatt* 11, 271–279.

Wegewitz, W. 1984. Schuhwerk und Sporen im Totenritual, *Hammaburg* 6, 115–132.

Wells, P.S. 1998. Identity and material culture in the later prehistory of central Europe, *Journal of Archaeological Research* 6, 239–298.

Wells, P.S. 1999. *The Barbarians Speak: How the Conquered Peoples Shaped Roman Europe*. Princeton: Princeton University Press.

Wells, P.S. 2001. *Beyond Celts, Germans and Scythians: Archaeology and Identity in Iron Age Europe*. London: Duckworth.

Wells, P.S. 2003. *The Battle that Stopped Rome: Emperor Augustus, Arminius, and the Slaughter of the Legions in the Teutoburg Forest*. New York: W.W. Norton.

Wieland, G. (ed). 1999. *Keltische Viereckschanzen*. Stuttgart: Theiss.

Zanier, W. 1997. Ein einheimischer Opferplatz mit römischen Waffen der frühesten Okkupation (15–10 v. Chr.) bei Oberammergau, in W. Groenman-van Waateringe, B.L. van Beek, W. Willems and S.L. Wynia (eds), *Roman Frontier Studies 1995*, 47–52. Oxford: Oxbow Books.

Zanier, W. 1999a. Der Alpenfeldzug 15 v. Chr. und die Eroberung Vindelikiens, *Bayerische Vorgeschichtsblätter* 64, 99–132.

Zanier, W. 1999b. *Der spätlatènezeitliche und römerzeitliche Brandopferplatz im Forggensee (Gde. Schwangau)*. Munich: Beck.

Zanker, P. 1988. *The Power of Images in the Age of Augustus* (trans. A. Shapiro). Ann Arbor: University of Michigan Press.

Understanding social change in the Late Iron Age Lower Rhine region

Nico Roymans

Introduction

In recent decades the study of Late Iron Age societies in Gaul and the Rhineland has been at the forefront of discussion in both academic and popular archaeology. The primary focus has been the major social changes that occurred during that period, leading to more complex societies with a more highly developed social hierarchy and the first moves toward urbanisation. The most notable archaeological evidence is the appearance of major fortified settlements or *oppida*, a rapid rise in the use of coins, and the emergence of collective sanctuaries. Such changes are usually regarded as diagnostic of the La Tène cultural region, distinguishing it from regions to the north where they did not occur.

In the north-west European context, what picture do archaeological texts of today paint of Late Iron Age societies in the Lower Rhine region? The first response is that this region barely rates a mention in the international literature. It is viewed as part of the northern border zone of Gaul, as a region weak in La Tène cultural influences and which saw no structural social change in the Iron Age. Many publications reproduce a map showing the distribution of Late Iron Age *oppida*; the northern border runs through northern France, southern Belgium, and the German Middle Rhine region towards central Europe. The Lower Rhine region is thus usually seen as part of the northern zone of rather static societies with relatively egalitarian social structures. This picture stems chiefly from the Lower Rhine region's 'poor' material culture, in particular the weak presence of elements associated with elite power, such as major fortified settlements and rich metalwork. Characteristic are the simple burial ritual and the barely differentiated settlement pattern with an absence of *oppida*. Major social change, the texts suggest, would not occur there until after the Roman conquest. Some authors explain these regional differences by using core–periphery models (Haselgrove 1987) or social evolutionary perspectives (Roymans 1990). There is also a long and powerful tradition of explaining the differences in ethnic terms. The Lower Rhine region is regarded as part of the northern 'Germanic' world, the counterpart of a southern 'Celtic' world (e.g. Fichtl 1994, 104).

Some doubts have been raised in recent years about this stereotypical picture of the Lower Rhine region. Hiddink (1999, 42–82; 229–38) has argued that we chiefly owe this image of egalitarian, relatively undifferentiated communities to the lack of a tradition of depositing weapons and ornaments in graves. Gerritsen (2003a, ch. 1.2) has criticised the portrayal of Lower Rhine societies as static and traditional, by demonstrating that significant social changes occurred at a local level during the Iron Age, with the Late Iron Age in particular being a period of change. It is this latter picture which I wish to reinforce in this essay. Because recent archaeological studies of settlements, cult places, and coins have produced a more complex picture of Late Iron Age societies, a major reappraisal of traditional perceptions is called for. In this paper I shall first outline some of the areas where change is most evident, by looking at the adoption of coinage, the emergence of regional sanctuaries, the development of a major nucleated settlement, and the circulation of glass bracelets. These analyses are followed by a more general discussion on the interpretation of Late Iron Age social changes in the Lower Rhine region, the significance of external contacts, and the possible implications for our understanding of the substantial changes that occurred there after the Roman conquest.

My analysis will not only examine the changes in terms of broad, abstract processes such as social hierarchisation and the institutionalisation of new social relationships; I will also attempt to show how broad social changes in the political and religious spheres could interact with structural changes at the level of individual households and small local communities. My approach is primarily a regional one. Of course I recognise the importance of external influences, but their impact can only be understood in the context of the long-term social dynamics of Iron Age societies in this region.

Finally, I will briefly discuss a major methodological problem in the study of Late Iron Age societies in the Lower Rhine region and the Rhine/Meuse delta in particular, namely the absence of a sophisticated typochronological framework for archaeological data. This is due to the limited archaeological visibility of the material culture, given the near total absence of a tradition of depositing objects in graves. In large parts of the Lower Rhine region we encounter no formal cemeteries from this period; at most there are a few small groups of graves near farmsteads containing almost no finds (Roymans 1990, fig. 9.12; Gerritsen 2003a). We are therefore mainly dependent on material from settlements for drawing up typochronological surveys (Van den Broeke 1987; Van Heeringen 1989). However, the chronological resolution of settlement material (for the most part hand-made pottery) is rather approximate and metal finds are much under-represented. Awareness is only now beginning to dawn that the evidence from cult places and riverine deposition is essential for a balanced picture of Late Iron Age material culture. In addition, we need to give serious attention to the many small metal finds collected by detectorists at Late Iron Age sites. Creating a sophisticated regional typochronology of the Late Iron Age in the Lower Rhine region is a research priority for the near future. In the meantime, we are often obliged to work with a rather approximate chronological framework.[1]

The adoption of coinage

Two decades ago, pre-Roman coinage was generally thought to be a marginal phenomenon in the Lower Rhine region. With the advent of detector archaeology and a more systematic recording programme for coins, this picture has changed substantially. We see this most notably in the southern Netherlands, where there has been a ten- to twenty-fold increase in the main coin types found since 1980 (Roymans 2004a). This has given us a clearer picture of the process by which coinage was adopted and dispersed in the Lower Rhine region. The circulation of gold coins did not begin here until the middle of the second century BC, albeit on a modest scale and with 'imported' coins from neighbouring regions to the south. The chief evidence is the gold hoards of Beringen and Niederzier, both of which also contained torcs (Göbel *et al.* 1991; Van Impe *et al.* 1997–8). Circulation increased rapidly in the course of the first century BC (Fig. 1). From Haselgrove's (1999) phase 4 onwards (*c.* 60–30 BC), coins were also minted in the Lower Rhine region. We can distinguish two local emissions: the gold Scheers 31 staters, which can be ascribed to the Eburones (Roymans 2004a), and the silver and billon 'rainbow' staters of the *triquetrum* type (Fig. 2), which are probably linked to the Batavians (Roymans 2001). The first base metal coinages did not appear here until the mid Augustan period and in close association with the establishment of Roman army camps along the Rhine. These were bronze Scheers 217 types, the oldest of which were inscribed with the legend AVAVCIA (Van den Berg 2001).

In the pre-Augustan period, the coins circulating in the Lower Rhine region were almost exclusively gold issues in the stater tradition or series that developed from these. These coins were used primarily as a means of payment by tribal leaders to form and maintain clientship networks, in particular to establish *comitates*, or loyal bands of horsemen (Creighton 2000, 14ff). The frequent presence of gold and silver coins in settlement contexts suggests that rural populations were closely involved in these networks that were dominated by elites. Coinages were issued from a political centre; they imply the existence of authorities who used the emissions to establish power networks, albeit ones of limited stability.

The emergence of regional sanctuaries

Until recently we have assumed that sanctuaries supported by larger communities (tribes or sub-tribes) in the Lower Rhine region were a phenomenon of the period after the Roman conquest. We do know of open-air cult places in the form of rectangular, ditched enclosures from the third century BC; examples have been excavated at Oss, Mierlo-Hout, and Kontich (Annaert 1995–6; Fontijn 2002; Gerritsen 2003a, 150 ff.).[2] These rectangular cult places are often associated with small cemeteries, but they also occur in settlements independently from burial places. The relationship between cult places and graves has led various authors to suspect that the cult practised there was associated with ancestor worship. Gerritsen and others are probably correct in assuming that these cult sites functioned at a local level; there is nothing to suggest that they had a regional significance (Gerritsen 2003a, 167).

However, this picture should be revised in the light of recent research into Roman cult places with monumental podium temples at Empel, Elst, and Kessel in the Rhine delta (Fig. 3). They fall into the category of '*grands sanctuaires gallo-romains*', which undoubtedly had a

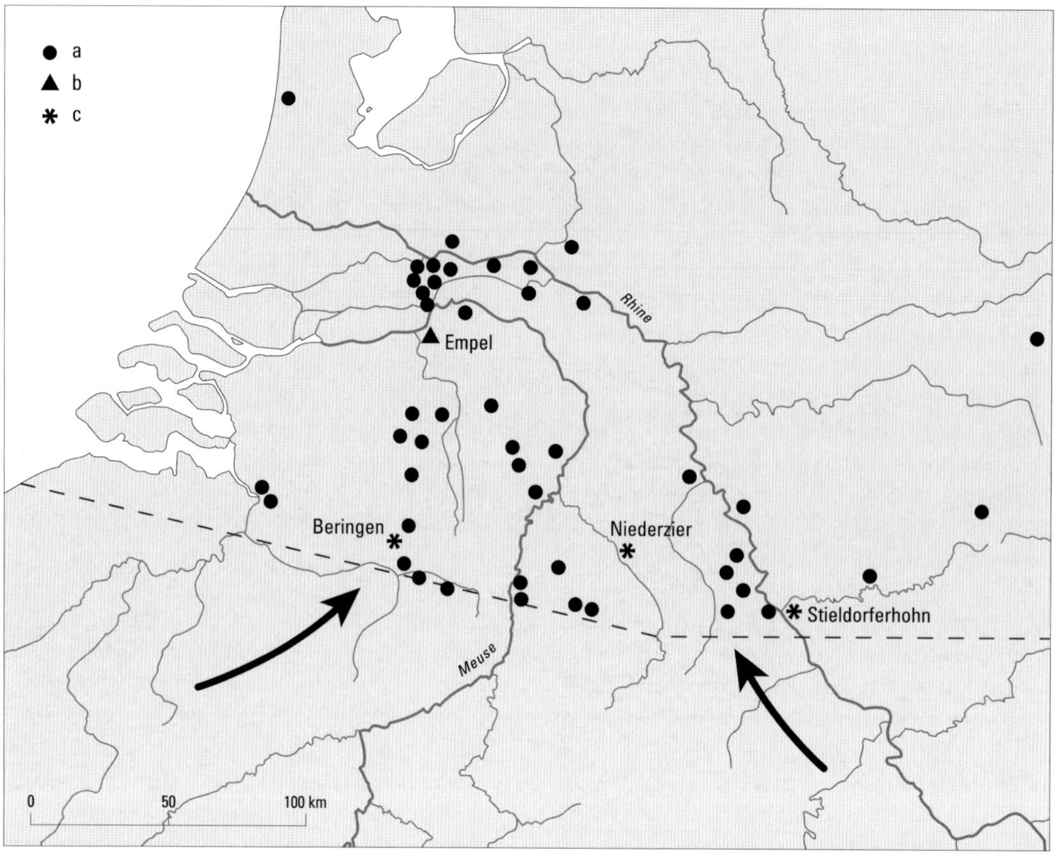

Fig. 1. Distribution of Late Iron Age gold coins in the Lower Rhine region. The approximate areas of origin of the imported coins are indicated by arrows. Key: a. isolated find, mostly from settlements; b. sanctuary; c. gold hoard.

public function in what was by then the *civitas Batavorum*. These monumental sanctuaries appear to have succeeded older open-air cult places. However, we know as yet very little about the spatial organisation of the earliest phases. Only at Empel do we have some clues as to the appearance of the cult place in the pre-temple phase (Roymans and Derks 1994). Traces were found of ritual post alignments and pits on a sandy elevation enclosed by fences. However, we owe most of our knowledge of the pre-temple phase to stray finds: pottery, animal bones, and in particular metal objects.

At Elst, a cultural layer was discovered, which extends over the entire cult site and pre-dates the building of the first stone temple around AD 50 (Bogaers 1955, 42, 59). The layer contained many cattle bones; the young age of slaughter of the animals, deviating from the regional pattern, suggests that they had been sacrificed (Lauwerier 1988, 120). It was assumed that the pre-temple phase corresponded to the earliest Roman period, but recent small-scale research has uncovered some Late Iron Age coins and a La Tène D2 brooch and sword fragment, which point to a pre-Roman origin.[3] In Kessel, the cult place is primarily known from an extensive ritual find complex from the edge of a fossil course of the Meuse, containing pottery, animal and human bone, and many Late Iron Age metal objects (Roymans 2004b). This ritual complex may be related to the remains of a monumental Roman temple found about 200 m to the south, used as *spolia* in a Late Roman fortification.

At Empel, Kessel, and Elst isolated metalwork finds are the primary source of information for establishing the earliest date of the cult places. The oldest material stems mainly from the La Tène D2 period, although La Tène D1 is also represented at both Empel and Kessel. The brooch chronology is particularly helpful here. Both sites have yielded fibulae of Middle La Tène type as well as early Nauheim brooches. We can therefore say that the regional cult places began a stage later than in north-west France, where they are known from La Tène C onward (Brunaux 1991; 2000).

Although the finds provide no hard evidence of collective rituals, there are good reasons for assuming that these sanctuaries already functioned at a regional level as cult centres of a larger community in the Late Iron Age.[4] Clues here are the rich metalwork assemblages found at Kessel and Empel, including coins, weapons, fibulae, and bronze cauldrons. Moreover, at both Empel and Elst, there were relatively large numbers of cattle

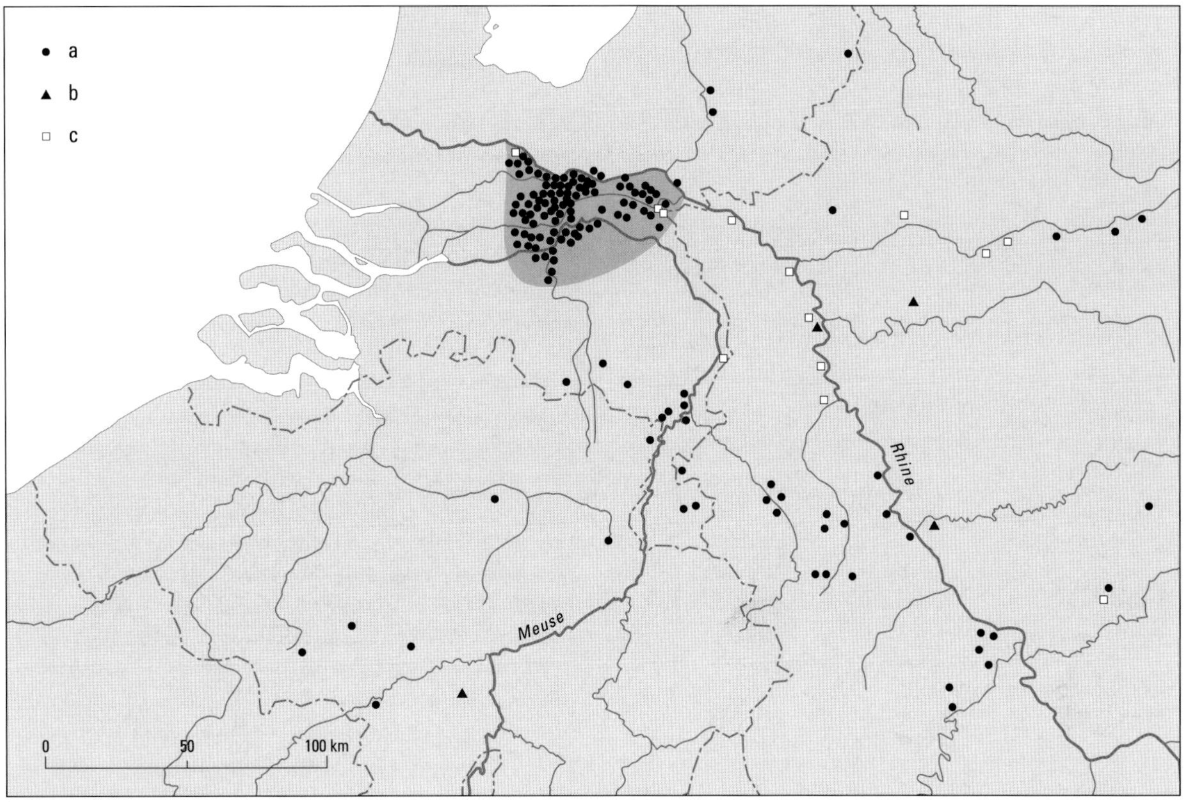

Fig. 2. Distribution of silver and billon 'rainbow' staters of the triquetrum type in the Lower Rhine region. Key: a. isolated find(s), mostly from settlements; b. hoards; c. finds from Roman army camps of the Augustan period (after Roymans 2001, fig. 2).

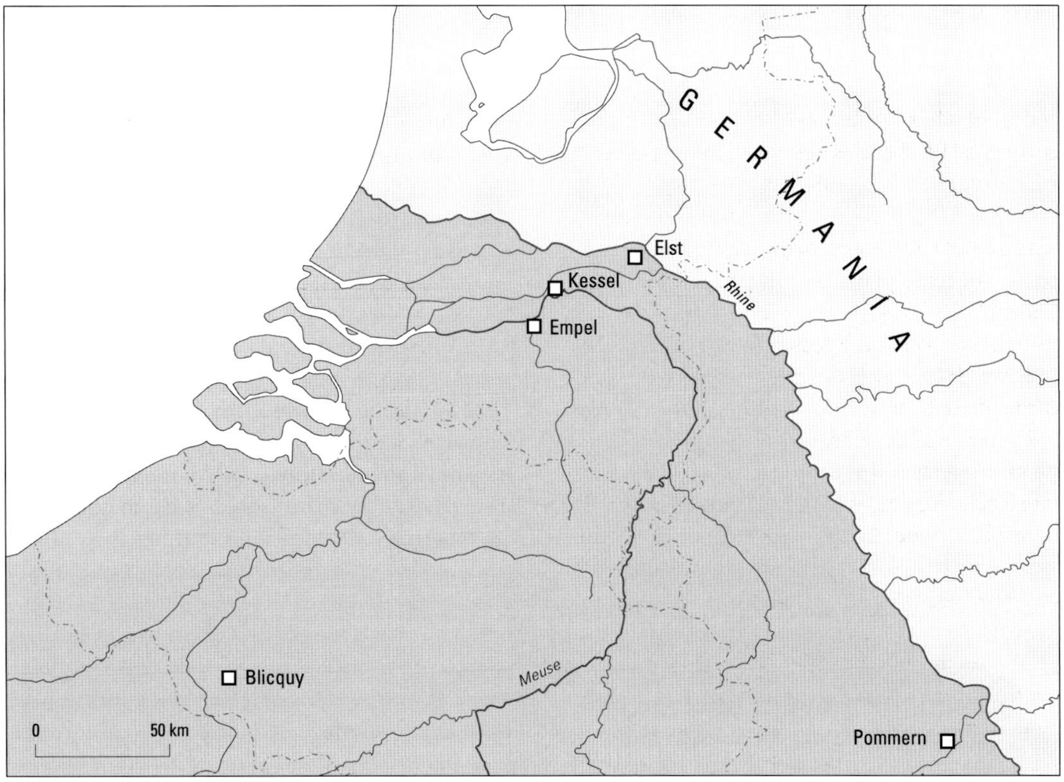

Fig. 3. Roman temples with Late La Tène forerunners in the Lower Rhine region.

among the animals that were sacrificed and then eaten (Lauwerier 1988; Seijnen 1994). The sacrifice of cattle would have been a rather expensive affair, probably carried out on behalf of a larger community during collective rituals rather than on an individual basis. Also notable is the large number of human bones dredged up at Kessel; they seem to be mainly those of adult males, some with clear indications that they met a violent death (Ter Schegget 1999). They too suggest collective rituals, carried out on behalf of a community. They are probably closely linked to the domain of warfare (remains of trophies?). Finally, we may point to the fact that these three cult sites went on to become the most important public sanctuaries of the *civitas Batavorum* in the late first century AD.

The sanctuaries had yet another characteristic in common in the Roman period. There is evidence to suggest that the popular deity Hercules Magusanus was worshipped there as the principal god. Hercules occupied a prominent place in the public cult of the Batavian *civitas* (Roymans 2004b); in the private sphere he was worshipped primarily by soldiers. It is unclear whether the sanctuaries' known link with Hercules Magusanus had pre-Roman roots. However, given the continuity in the use of the cult places from La Tène D2 to the early Roman period, it is tempting to link the Late La Tène cult places to Magusanus, the Lower Rhine deity whom the Batavian elite associated with the Roman Hercules, probably in the course of the Augustan era. A *terminus ante quem* for this syncretism is offered by the votive stone from St-Michielsgestel–'Ruimel', dedicated to Magusanus Hercules by a *summus magistratus* of the *civitas Batavorum* (*CIL* XIII, 8771); the stone is dated to around the middle of the first century AD.

Thanks to recent research into the cult places of Empel, Elst, and Kessel, we are now confronted in the Rhine delta with a phenomenon that – until recently – we associated mainly with northern France and the neighbouring middle Rhine area – namely, major Gallo-Roman sanctuaries that go back to pre-Roman cult places with a supra-local significance. The appearance of regional cult places went hand in hand with the introduction of new ritual practices of both an individual and collective nature: the offering of coins and weapons, and possibly human sacrifice as well. Futhermore, it was mainly cattle that were sacrificed and then subsequently eaten at collective meals. These discoveries open up possibilities for a host of new discussions. I will make a first attempt below.

The development of a major nucleated settlement at Kessel/Lith

The current picture of Late Iron Age habitation in the Lower Rhine region is one of an almost undifferentiated settlement landscape, wholly dominated by small villages and single farmsteads. This contrasts markedly with the settlement pattern further to the south in Gaul and in the Rhineland, which is characterised by increasing differentiation and hierarchisation (e.g. Haselgrove 1987; Roymans 1990; Fichtl 1994). There, the Late La Tène period saw the emergence of major defended settlements, or *oppida*, which in several ways fulfilled a central function in larger tribal communities.

However, recent research has produced a growing body of evidence to show that the settlement pattern in the Lower Rhine region was more complex and more differentiated than we have hitherto believed. I have already mentioned the development of central cult places from La Tène D1 onward. Still more significant is the settlement complex at Kessel/Lith on the Meuse, where an important complex of dredged and metal-detected finds has been collected in recent decades. As this site and the remains uncovered there have been described and interpreted in detail elsewhere (Roymans 2004b), I will confine myself here to the main points.

As is customary with finds dredged from rivers, we are poorly informed about the archaeological context and know only a small part of the total find complex. For this reason, the material from Kessel/Lith has to date attracted little attention from archaeologists. However, this find complex is relevant in that it forces us, by virtue of its sheer size and the wealth of metal objects, to modify our current perception of Late Iron Age communities and their material culture in the Lower Rhine region. There are indications that an extensive settlement was located at Kessel/Lith, one which fulfilled a religious and socio-political central function in the Rhine/Meuse delta.

Kessel/Lith is situated at a geographically strategic location in the Dutch river delta: on the southern bank of the Meuse river near the former confluence with the Waal, the main branch of the Rhine (Fig. 4). Until recently, the site (or cluster of sites?) lay in water meadows, covered by thick layers of clay and sand. Parts of the complex were affected by post-Roman river erosion, and what remained has been destroyed in recent decades by large-scale sand and gravel extraction. It was during these operations that dredger workers and local amateur archaeologists collected large quantities of Late Iron Age and Roman material. This consisted of pottery, bone, stone building remains, and metalwork, mainly in the form of isolated finds. Small-scale excavations were carried out at a few locations. By using the excavation results and the data and observations from the amateur archaeologists and dredger workers, as well as paleogeographical research, we can make a rough reconstruction of the find complex in the Late Iron Age and Early Roman period. The material we are dealing with originates firstly from the southern bank of the former Meuse. Typical settlement material (large quantities of hand-made pottery, mixed with spindlewhorls, loomweights, stone

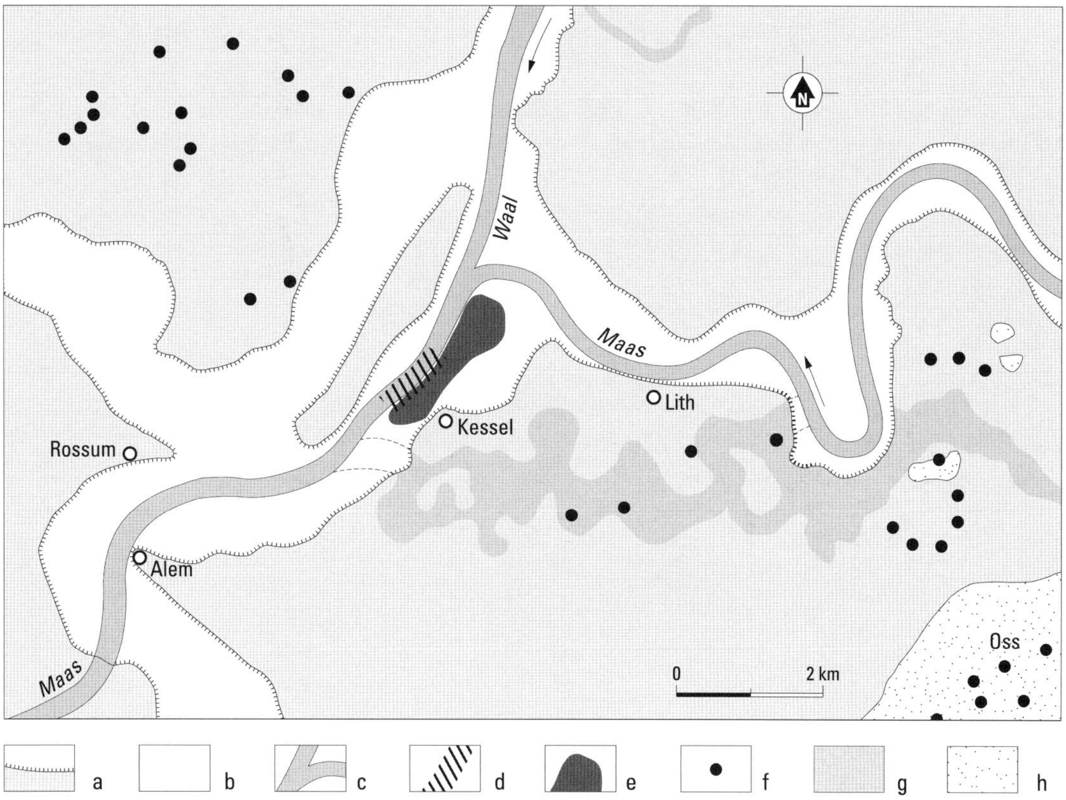

Fig. 4. Paleogeographical reconstruction of the river confluence at Kessel in the Late Iron Age and early Roman period (after Roymans 2004b, fig 7.13). Key: a. late medieval river embankments; b. (sub-)modern water meadows; c. presumed river course; d. zone with ritual deposits in river channel; e. Late Iron Age nucleated settlement or settlement cluster; f. rural settlement of Late Iron Age/Roman period; g. Early/Middle Iron Age channel belt; h. Pleistocene sand.

quern fragments, animal bone, and smaller numbers of metal objects) has been found over a distance of almost 2 km. The material comes secondly from a fossil bed of the Meuse, and consists of large quantities of pottery, animal and human bones, and metalwork, including many weapons. We must bear in mind, however, that only a fraction of the find material has been collected; the vast bulk has been lost without being documented.

The Kessel/Lith complex can be dated more precisely using the typochronology of the metal objects. Although the pottery suggests that habitation may have begun somewhat earlier, the metalwork indicates that the site did not acquire a supra-local significance until La Tène D1, the period of the early Nauheim fibulae.

So how should we interpret the complex? The almost complete lack of systematic excavations means that the information we have at our disposal is very fragmentary. With regard to the internal spatial structure and development of the settlement complex, we can do little more than roughly divide the material into two groups, as above. As already stated, the material from the riverbank zone should be viewed as mainly settlement remains; the finds from the bed of the Meuse, however, can best be seen as a ritual find complex. The main clues to this interpretation are the weapons and large quantities of human and animal bones. A sanctuary was probably located on the edge of the river, with the remains of votive gifts and sacrificial meals being regularly deposited in the adjacent river bed.

Kessel/Lith was a sizeable settlement or settlement cluster on the southern bank of the Meuse. Although we are no longer in a position to establish either the true density of habitation or habitation fluctuations within the complex, we are clearly dealing with a fundamentally different type of site from the many small villages and isolated farmsteads that characterised the settlement landscape of the Lower Rhine region. This is supported by the presence of an important ritual find complex in a former bed of the Meuse river, rich in weaponry, coins, cauldrons, pottery, and animal and human bones.

What then from our perspective is the significance of the find complex at Kessel/Lith when considered in a

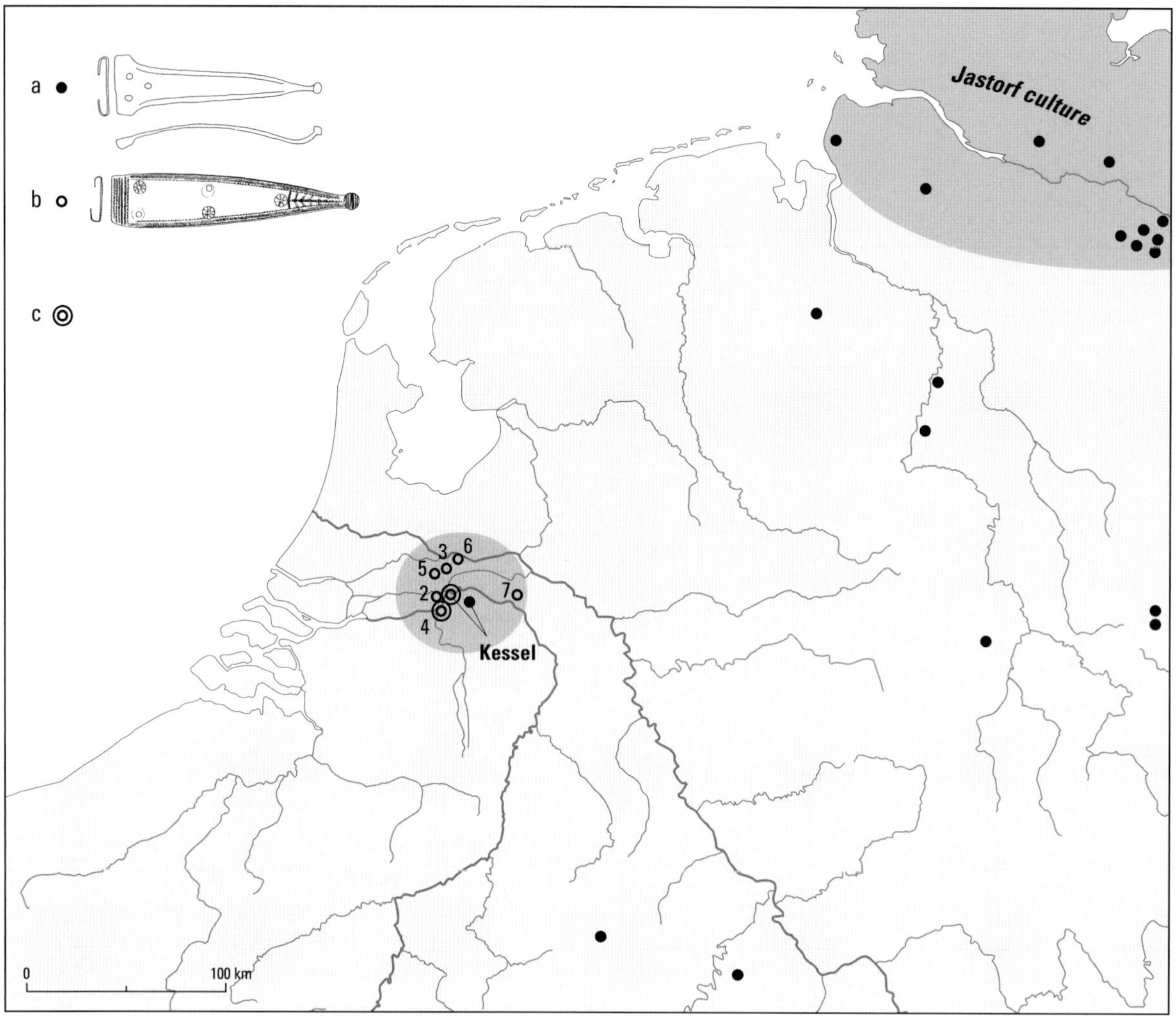

Fig. 5. Distribution of Late Iron Age bronze belt hooks of the Kessel type (b) in the Lower Rhine region and of related iron belt hooks of the Oitzmühle type (a), which have their origin in the north German Jastorf cultural area; (c) more than 5 pieces found (after Roymans 2004b, fig. 7.6).

north-west European context? Three points can be made:

1. Kessel/Lith is a key site for the study of metalwork circulation in the Lower Rhine area in La Tène D.
2. The artefact assemblage points to the existence of specialised metalworking in the region in La Tène D. We can identify certain artefact types (swords, bronze belt hooks, fibulae, coins) which seem to have been manufactured in the Rhine/Meuse delta. There is also indirect evidence for the extensive production of La Tène glass bracelets (see below). All of this suggests that important production sites for specialised crafts existed in this region, although such sites have yet to be located. Kessel/Lith, however, is the only serious candidate at present, as several distribution maps suggest (Fig. 5).
3. Kessel/Lith seems to have functioned as a central place from La Tène D1 onward. It may have been an important cult, craft, and political centre and have served as a symbol of a larger community. For the second half of the first century BC we could think of a link with the Batavian polity. It may have been a pre-Roman Batavian centre, which was transferred to Nijmegen in the Augustan period as part of the Roman reorganisation of the topography of power. Tacitus referred to this new centre as the *oppidum Batavorum* (*Histories* 5.19).

The above interpretation of Kessel/Lith has implications for current perceptions of the Late La Tène settlement pattern in the Lower Rhine area. This was more complex and more hierarchical than we have previously supposed. The region does not really fit within the simple dichotomy of a Celtic world dominated by *oppida* and a Germanic world consisting solely of small villages and farmsteads.

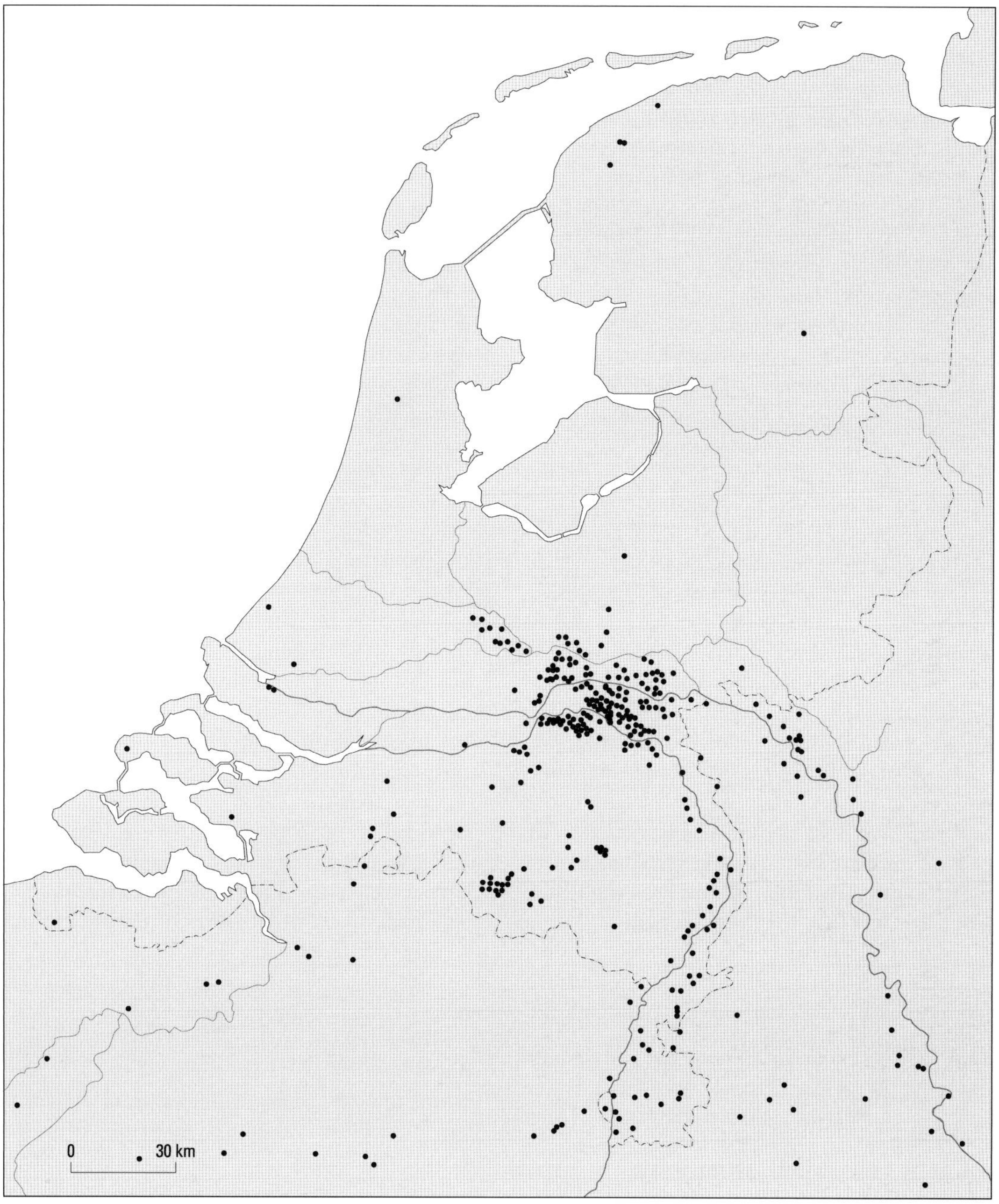

Fig. 6. Distribution of La Tène glass bracelets in the Lower Rhine region (after Roymans and Van Rooijen 1993, fig. 2).

The mass circulation of glass bracelets

Fragments of La Tène glass bracelets are undoubtedly among the commonest artefact types encountered on Late Iron Age settlements in the Lower Rhine region. Nowhere in the *oppida* zone of 'Celtic Europe' are they so densely distributed as in the eastern part of the Dutch river area, where more than three thousand items have now been found (Fig. 6). They occur on almost every settlement site, frequently in spectacular numbers; 25 sites have produced over 20 items, and seven sites more than 100 items (Roymans and Van Rooijen 1993). Although their period of circulation runs from the third century BC up to the early first century AD, almost nothing is known of their typochronological development (Lenz and Schuler 1998).

Of particular interest here is the production of glass bracelets, since there are good reasons for assuming large-scale manufacturing in the Lower Rhine region. The principal evidence, apart from the massive concentration of finds, is provided by typological study of the bracelets. They are characterised by regionally specific variations in form and colour, which makes large-scale importation from southern areas improbable

(Roymans and Van Rooijen 1993). Most items appear to have been produced in the Rhine delta. To some extent, imported raw materials or semi-manufactured products will have been utilised. However, as no concrete evidence for glass workshops has been found, we can say little about the social organisation of production. If we assume production was more or less centralised, as appears to have been the case in Central Europe, then Kessel/Lith is the main candidate.

Just as important are the social aspects of bracelet use. In the light of their presence in women's graves, they are generally considered a female attribute in the La Tène cultural region. Their mass presence in the Rhine delta suggests that almost every woman had one or more of them. This association with women has been confirmed in the excavated cemetery at Nederweert (Roymans 1996b), where the cremations have been investigated anthropologically. There the wearing of glass bracelets seems to be linked to adult women; they are absent from children's graves. We might hypothesise that the moment at which women began wearing bracelets was associated with a rite of passage, marking the entry of young girls into the group of adult women. The wearing of the first bracelets may have been the female equivalent of the girding on of the first weapons for men. These glass bracelets were the symbolic expression of sex and age–class identities within the Lower Rhine region, whose significance gained steadily in the course of the Late Iron Age. We also observe an interesting distribution pattern for bracelets in the Rhine delta, which suggests that they also functioned as a marker of cultural boundaries with outside groups. Significantly, they are almost totally absent in the western coastal region and in the region directly north of the Rhine (Fig. 6). The few bracelets in the latter two areas may indicate incidental marriage relationships.

Discussion: A new kind of society in the Lower Rhine region?

The changes in the Lower Rhine region suggest a considerable social dynamic in the Late Iron Age, involving processes of hierarchisation and increasing complexity. The issuing of coins, the rise of regional sanctuaries that were linked to the realm of warfare, and the emergence of specialised crafts, all point to the growing power of elite groups. This becomes even more marked if we compare it with the image we have of Early and Middle Iron Age societies in the same region. We have no evidence in these earlier periods of larger settlements with central functions, nor of cult places of regional significance, the use of coins, or increasing craft specialisation.[5] Although these phenomena did not appear until La Tène D1, that does not mean that the social changes underlying them could not have begun earlier. We should also take into account the considerable differences between regions. The changes occurred primarily in the eastern half of the river delta, running southwards via the Meuse and Rhine valleys, and scarcely seem to have affected the Holocene coastal zone and the region north of the Lower Rhine. Perhaps these changes should not be viewed separately from demographic developments in the Rhine/Meuse delta, even though their precise articulation is still far from clear. The Late Iron Age was a period of settlement expansion in Holocene as well as Pleistocene landscapes, often leading to a significant rise in population. However, in the peat landscapes of the Western Netherlands, the habitation was often of limited permanence because of their vulnerability to fluctuations in the water table (Van Heeringen 1989; Van den Broeke 1993).

In the light of these changes in the Lower Rhine region, we can first of all attempt to reconstruct the changes at the level of supra-local social formations. Historical sources provide us with some useful clues. Caesar's commentaries make reference to several large-scale tribal polities or *civitates*, namely the Menapii, the Eburones, the Tencteri and Usipetes, and the Sugambri (Fig. 7). They were headed by kings (the Eburones and Sugambri) or by *principes* (the Tencteri and Usipetes), and had a council of elders or tribal senate with considerable political influence (Roymans 1990, 29ff). The fact that the Eburones and, somewhat later, the Sugambri were in a position to triumph over Roman armies attests to the ability of groups and individuals in these societies to organise considerable energy, at least in periods of crisis. However, there are indications that the Lower Rhine *civitates* mentioned by Caesar should be seen as loosely structured, fluid confederations of smaller ethnic groups, each with their own leaders, who were bound together by alliances and clientship relations (Roymans 1990, 27; Creighton 2000, 13). Each of these groups retained their own cults. In view of this, we can best interpret the regional sanctuaries from the Rhine/Meuse delta as central cult places, not of the larger *civitates* to which Caesar refers, but of smaller polities which go almost unmentioned in the historical sources.

In addition, we should understand that the political geography of the Lower Rhine region described by Caesar was subject to constant change, which may have affected the ability of the *civitates* he mentions to establish any degree of permanence. However, what did have a far-reaching and destructive effect, certainly on the Lower Rhine region, were the direct consequences of the Roman conquest itself. Caesar refers to the genocide of the Eburones and the major part of the Tencteri and Usipetes. In the second half of the first century BC, as part of the reorganisation of the Roman frontier, new groups (Ubii, Batavi, Cugerni) made their appearance on the left bank of the Rhine. Migration played a key role, in combination with processes of ethnogenesis. However, the fluid, unstable nature of the political geography of the Lower Rhine region in the first century

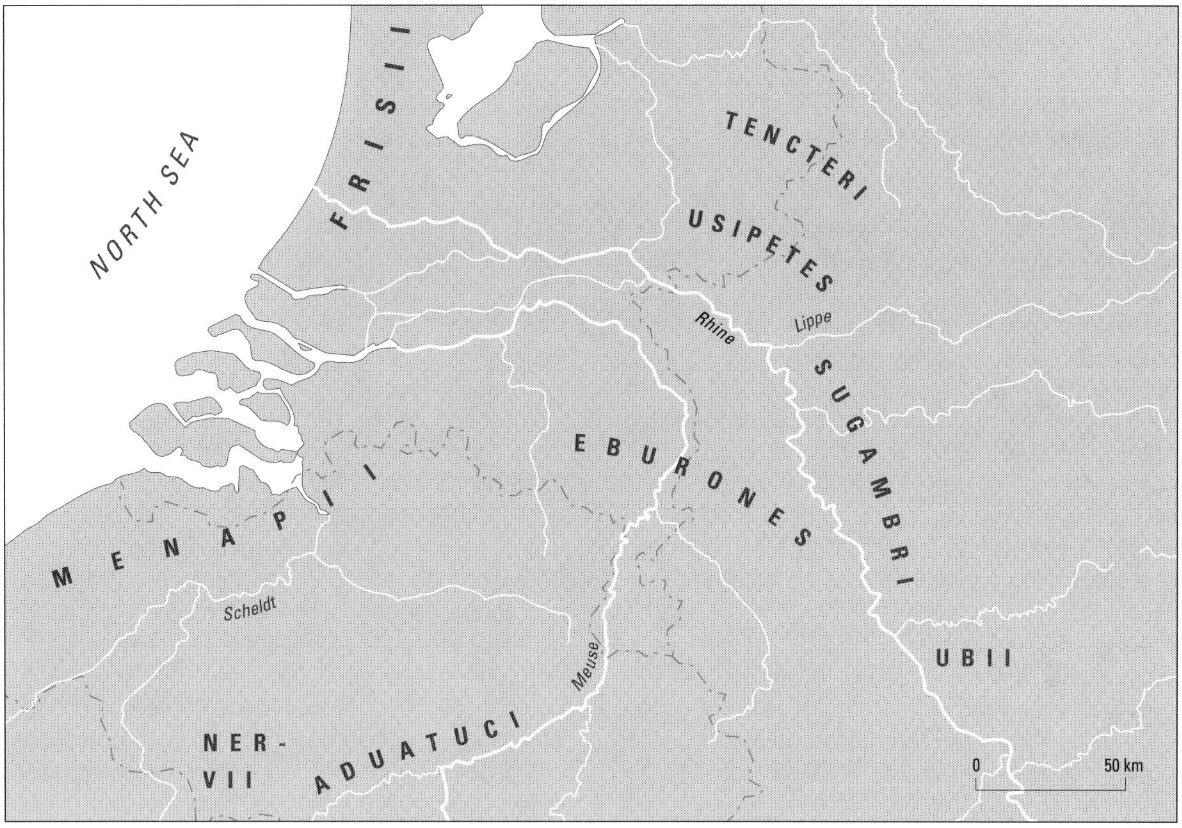

Fig. 7. Simplified tribal map of the Lower Rhine region at the time of Caesar's conquest.

BC should not suggest that the Late Iron Age saw few structural social changes.

Relying on historical data, Creighton (2000, 14ff.) refers to the emergence of warrior bands of picked horsemen (Tacitus calls them *comitates*) as one of the most important social innovations in Late Iron Age Western Europe. These retinues lay at the heart of the power and authority of individual leaders and they were the force behind the process of social hierarchisation. Warriors had a personal, semi-sacred bond of loyalty to their leader, who in turn offered protection and regular material rewards to his followers. Historical sources reveal that the *comitatus* had become a key social institution.

The *comitates* also appear to have been a phenomenon in the Late Iron Age Lower Rhine region, as evidenced by information on the prominence of horsemen in warfare and raiding. Caesar (*Gallic War* VI, 30; 43) reports that Ambiorix, the Eburonean leader, was flanked by a retinue of *equites* when he fled from the Roman troops. He also mentions a raid into Eburonean territory by 2000 Sugambrian horsemen (*ibid.*, 35), who made a surprise attack on a Roman army camp; they were probably the *comitatus* of a Sugambrian war leader, who is not mentioned by name. Elsewhere, Caesar refers to a raid carried out by a large group of Tencteri and Usipetes horsemen into the territory of the Ambivariti along the Meuse (*Gallic War* IV, 12); a smaller group of 800 horsemen is said to have stayed behind in their homeland. Caesar himself was personally acquainted with the qualities of the Germanic *comitatus*. His retinue included a band of 400 picked Germanic horsemen who functioned as his bodyguard. At the beginning of his Gallic campaigns, Caesar must have received this cavalry escort from an unspecified war leader of Ubian or Batavian origin (Speidel 1994, 12ff.). Even if the numbers were sometimes exaggerated, this historical information suggests a marked rise in horsemanship in the Lower Rhine region during the Late Iron Age. It also seems to indicate that the widespread fame of the Lower Rhine cavalry, and especially the Batavian cavalry, in the early Roman period was founded upon pre-Roman developments.

It is difficult to come up with direct archaeological evidence for the rise of the *comitates*. Nevertheless, the Lower Rhine region offers some clues. Firstly, there is archaeozoological evidence from the Rhine/Meuse delta, which shows that horses were kept in every Late Iron Age settlement (Roymans 1996a, table 5; IJzereef *et al.* 1989). If we assume that horsemen were organised in larger groups, then the increased occurrence of horse remains might indicate the significance of the *comitatus* system. Secondly, we can point to the extreme lengths of Late La Tène swords in this region (as well as in a much wider area), which suggests that they were primarily used as cavalry weapons. Thirdly, there is the introduction of gold in the form of coins and torcs from the middle of the second century BC. Gold opened up new possibilities for individuals to build up positions of power. According to Creighton (2000, 31), 'torcs were retained and worn to display the status of the leader, whereas coin could be distributed to articulate social relations'. Coins represented 'portable and transferable symbols of authority' and marked the involvement of individuals in supra-local networks. In addition, we should bear in mind that in the Lower Rhine region, where pastoral traditions had long played a key role, cattle and horses will also have been used as exchange items in the articulation of a range of social relationships (Roymans 1996a, 47).

It seems likely that there was a link between the emergence of new forms of authority – based on command of a *comitatus* – and the appearance of regional sanctuaries from La Tène D1 onward. In any event, the presence of weaponry suggests a connection with the domain of warfare and raiding, even if the precise nature of that association is still not clear. If we assume a close interrelationship between politics and religion in the public cult, the emergence of collective cult places can be linked to the process of social hierarchisation described above. The cult places may have provided new rituals and symbols through which social relationships could be redefined and ultimately institutionalised as relationships of inequality (Derks 1998, 183).

At the same time, the regional cult places may have played a role in the constitution of tribal groups with a shared identity. The approach of anthropologist Anthony Cohen (1985) may be helpful here. He views communities as symbolic constructs that can be manifested in many ways: through language, clothing, jewellery, oral traditions, shared day-to-day practices, and participation in collective rituals or festivities at cult sites. Sanctuaries such as those of Kessel, Empel, and Elst were probably key sites in the symbolic construction of smaller polities or ethnic groups on which Caesar's commentaries shed no light. Through their significance as centres for collective rituals and festivities, they could give expression to a community's identity and cohesion. Moreover, sanctuaries were often the places *par excellence* for commemorating collective origin myths and the ancestral histories of ethnic groups. One example is Tacitus' report (*Germania* 39) of the central sanctuary of the Germanic Suebi, where delegations of subtribes periodically gathered for the ritual celebration of the *initia gentis*.

How do these broad social developments relate to changes at the level of local communities? Gerritsen's recent study of changes in local habitation and land use structures in the southern Netherlands in the course of the first millennium BC is relevant here (Gerritsen 2003a; 2003b). He observes a specific structuring of the social and symbolic landscape of local communities in the Early Iron Age, with collective, stable urnfields as core elements, surrounded by diffuse habitation in isolated, single-phase farmsteads. This disposition symbolises a social organisation with a strong collective ideology at the local level, with the urnfields as central localities in the construction of local communities. Gerritsen notes a significant reordering of the social and symbolic landscape in the Middle and Late Iron Age. Houses and farmyards acquired greater permanence, while at the same time the traditional burial communities with their collective, stable cemeteries disintegrated. Collective urnfields were replaced by a system of dispersed clusters of graves within settlement territories, which were probably connected to single families. Other social practices and symbols were now used in the constitution of local communities; we can point to the use of local cult places, but in particular to a trend toward greater permanence in the location of individual farmsteads. This latter practice would have allowed more scope for inherited claims to land. The overall impression is that within local social organisation, the emphasis came to lie more on separate family groups than on communal ties based on co-residence.

The social changes that Gerritsen observes at the local level in the Lower Rhine region are consistent with the regional trends mentioned earlier. From the Middle Iron Age onward, membership of a local co-resident community was no longer the key factor that determined the identity of households and individuals. Gerritsen (2003a, 252) posits a certain degree of social fragmentation within local groups. He observes a greater emphasis on household or family groups within local social networks and sees the farmstead as the symbol that gave expression to the identity and permanence of a family group, and of its long-established link with the land surrounding the farmstead. His general conclusion is that family groups became more dominant in the social order at the expense of the collective identity of co-resident local communities. Nevertheless, he interprets this development not in terms of social disintegration or individualisation, but of a growing diversification of an individual's social identities. This term perhaps suggests too readily that a new set of identities was being created during this phase. It would be more appropriate to speak of major shifts in the relative importance of the various identities taken on by individuals. There seems to have been a greater emphasis on the expression of supra-local identities. We may think here primarily of ethnic identities and of identities – partly overlapping – that were connected with warriorship, clientship, and membership of regional cult communities. The greater importance of these supra-local identities arose from the growing involvement of individuals in supra-local social networks.

It should be emphasised that the Late Iron Age social changes in the Lower Rhine region cannot be understood without examining the role of external contacts. Artefact studies – for example of gold coins (Fig. 1 above) – point to an intensive interaction via the Rhine and Meuse valleys with northern France and central Belgium as well as with the Middle Rhine region. There were also dealings with the north German region, as evidenced by some categories of belt hooks (Fig. 5). Contacts over the North Sea with Britain seem to have been of no significance until the Augustan period, when some late British Iron Age coins are found in the Rhine delta. The social mechanisms behind these external contacts were very diverse. Elites became increasingly involved in inter-regional exchange networks, alliances, and clientship relations. The latter in particular were asymmetrical, as demonstrated by Caesar's comment that the Eburones were clients of the Treveri, and also paid tribute to the Aduatuci (*Gallic War* IV, 6; V, 27). Group migration may also have played a role. All these types of external contact resulted in the exchange of people, ideas and goods. However, it is still not clear precisely how the external relationships articulated with the internal changes in the domestic life of local communities in the Lower Rhine region.

It is interesting to note that Lower Rhine groups did not participate in the consumption of Mediterranean luxury goods, and wine in particular. There are almost no finds of Dressel 1 amphorae or imported bronze vessels associated with the consumption of wine. This may mean that Lower Rhine elites simply had no access to Mediterranean exchange networks or – as Caesar suggests for the Nervii and the transrhenine Suebi – that they were less motivated to accept, or even rejected, the consumption of Roman luxury items. However, the absence of goods imported from the Mediterranean does not preclude the possibility that Lower Rhine groups were involved in more indirect exchange relationships between Italy and Gaul. The north-west European plain may have been an important supply zone for slaves (a product of intertribal warfare and raiding), who were traded to Italy via intermediary groups in northern France or the middle Rhine region (Creighton 2000, 20). This trade may be related to the Late Iron Age 'importing' of gold into the Lower Rhine region from more southern parts.

In conclusion, we can say that Late Iron Age societies in the Lower Rhine region had an essentially different structure from those of the Early Iron Age. The Middle Iron Age appears to have been a period in which local social relationships and identities changed fundamentally. Instead of a strong collective ideology at the local level, a more open social system developed that allowed individuals and families more scope to construct supra-local networks and associated identities. In the Late Iron Age – and in particular from the mid second century BC onward, with the appearance of the Beringen and Niederzier gold hoards – polities emerged on this new social foundation, hierarchically structured around leaders who owed their positions of power to their ability to command a *Gefolgschaft* or *comitatus* of horsemen. Although these Lower Rhine polities certainly had less developed and less stable social hierarchies than most of the *civitates* in the interior of Gaul, the differences between the two appear less extreme than we have supposed until recently. The end of the second century BC saw the appearance of sanctuaries which went on to play a prominent role in the symbolic construction of polities and associated ethnic identities. These regional sanctuaries were also an expression of the process by which new social relationships and networks became institutionalised.

Finally, it should be noticed that in the above overview we have focussed on analysing a set of structural social changes operating in the Late Iron Age Lower Rhine region. A serious problem remains that the archaeological and historical evidence hardly informs us about the agency aspects of these changes. Here, we can only use our historical imagination and try to sketch a picture of the role agency has played at different levels of society (local, regional, supra-regional). Here, too, the *comitatus* system offers some important clues. Such bands of horsemen were raised and controlled by individual leaders who maintained personal ties with their retainers. Archaeological evidence from rural settlements (gold coins, horse bones) may illustrate how individuals within local communties of only a few farmsteads were integrated in this kind of network.

If we accept the interpretations proposed above, this in turn has implications for understanding developments in the early Roman period. I do not wish to detract here from the fundamental changes that rapidly succeeded one another in Roman times, following Drusus' reorganisation of the Lower Rhine frontier zone in *c.* 15/12 BC. However, several of these changes had their roots in the pre-Roman period. In many respects, the tribal *civitates* of the early first century AD built on existing institutions (*comitatus*, council of elders, tribal cult communities). The continued use of the Late Iron Age sanctuaries of Empel, Elst, and Kessel into the Roman period provides concrete proof of this.

Acknowledgements

This paper was written as part of the research programme *The Batavians. Ethnic identity in a frontier situation* based at the Archaeological Institute of the Free University, Amsterdam and supported by the Netherlands Organisation for Scientific Research (NWO). I would like to thank my colleagues Jan Slofstra, Ton Derks, Ivo Vossen, and Johan Nicolay, as well as Joris Aarts, for stimulating discussions on the topics raised in this paper. The drawings were undertaken by Bert Brouwenstijn (Figs 1 and 2). Annette Visser translated the text into English.

Notes

1. In Dutch archaeology a distinction is made between an Early Iron Age (*c.* 750–500 BC), a Middle Iron Age (*c.* 500–250 BC) and a Late Iron Age (250–12 BC).
2. Referring to the rectangular stone enclosure excavated at Nijmegen, Fontijn in a recent paper (2002) traces the origin of the rectangular cult places in the Lower Rhine region back to the Late Bronze Age. However, this still leaves a gap of half a millennium between the enclosure at Nijmegen, in many respects unique, and the first ditched cult places of the Middle Iron Age.
3. Unpublished excavations in 2002 by the Archaeological Institute of the Free University, Amsterdam. A publication is currently in preparation by Derks and Roymans.
4. We could speak here of 'public' cult places, although I am aware that we owe the distinction between a 'private' and 'public' cult to Roman religion, where it has specific legal connotations. Nevertheless, I am assuming that somewhat analogous structures existed in pre-Roman Gallic societies (cf. also Derks 2002).
5. Several elite graves dating to Hallstatt C and La Tène A, some of them under barrows, are known in the Lower Rhine region (Roymans 1991). There is nothing, however, to suggest that these burial places subsequently had a role as central locales in the construction of supra-local identity groups.

Bibliography

Annaert, R. 1995–6. De Alfsberg te Kontich (prov. Antwerpen). Eindrapport, *Archeologie in Vlaanderen* 5, 41–67.

Bogaers, J.E.A.T. 1955. *De Gallo-Romeinse tempels te Elst in de Over-Betuwe.* 's-Gravenhage: Nederlandse Oudheden 1.

Brunaux, J.-L. 1991. Les sanctuaires celtiques et leurs rapports avec le monde mediterraneen, in J.-L. Brunaux (ed.), *Les sanctuaires celtiques et le monde mediterranéen*, 7–13. Paris: Dossiers de Protohistoire 3.

Brunaux, J.-L. 2000. *Les religions gauloises (5ᵉ–1ᵉ siècles av. J.-C.).* Paris: Éditions Errance.

Cohen, A.P. 1985: *The Symbolic Construction of Community.* London/New York: Ellis Horwood.

Creighton, J. 2000. *Coins and Power in Late Iron Age Britain.* Cambridge: Cambridge University Press.

Derks, T. 1998. *Gods, Temples and Ritual Practices. The Transformation of Religious Ideas and Values in Roman Gaul.* Amsterdam: Amsterdam Archaeological Studies 2.

Derks, T. 2002. Roman imperialism and the sanctuaries of Roman Gaul, *Journal of Roman Archaeology* 15, 541–545.

Fichtl, S. 1994. *Les Gaulois du Nord de la Gaule (150–20 av. J.C.).* Paris: Éditions Errance.

Fontijn, D. 2002. Het ontstaan van rechthoekige 'cultusplaatsen', in H. Fokkens and R. Jansen (eds), *2000 jaar bewoningsdynamiek. Brons- en IJzertijdbewoning in het Maas–Demer–Scheldegebied*, 149–172. Leiden: Faculty of Archaeology.

Gerritsen, F. 2003a. *Local Identities. Landscape and Community in the Late Prehistoric Meuse–Demer–Scheldt Region.* Amsterdam: Amsterdam Archaeological Studies 9.

Gerritsen, F. 2003b. Archaeological perspectives on local communities, in J. Bintliff (ed.), *Blackwell Companion to Archaeology.* Oxford: Blackwell.

Göbel, J., Hartmann, A., Joachim, H.E. and Zedelius, V. 1991. Der spätkeltische Goldschatz von Niederzier, *Bonner Jahrbücher* 191, 27–84.

Haselgrove, C. 1987. Culture process on the periphery. Belgic Gaul and Rome during the late Republic and early Empire, in: M. Rowlands, M. Larsen and K. Kristiansen (eds), *Centre and Periphery in the Ancient World*, 104–124. Cambridge: Cambridge University Press.

Haselgrove, C. 1999. The development of Iron Age coinage in Belgic Gaul, *Numismatic Chronicle* 159, 111–168.

Hiddink, H.A. 1999. *Germaanse samenlevingen tussen Rijn en Weser. 1ste eeuw voor–4e eeuw na Chr.* Unpublished Ph.D. thesis, University of Amsterdam.

IJzereef, G.F., Laarman, F.J., and Lauwerier, R.C.G.M. 1989. Animal remains from the Late Bronze Age and the Iron Age found in the Western Netherlands, *Berichten van de Rijksdienst voor het Oudheidkundig Bodemonderzoek* 39, 257–267.

Lauwerier, R.C.G.M. 1988. *Animals in Roman Times in the Dutch Eastern River Area.* Amersfoort: Nederlandse Oudheden 12.

Lenz, K.H. and Schuler, A. 1998. Handgeformte Gefässkeramik der frühen römischen Kaiserzeit aus Bornheim-Sechtem, Rhein-Sieg-Kreis. Zum Übergang vom Spätlatène zur römischen Kaiserzeit im südlichen Niederrheingebiet, *Archäologisches Korrespondenzblatt* 28, 587–599.

Roymans, N. 1990. *Tribal Societies in Northern Gaul. An Anthropological Perspective.* Amsterdam: Cingula 12.

Roymans, N. 1991. Late Urnfield societies in the Northwest European Plain and the expanding networks of Central European Hallstatt groups, in N. Roymans and F. Theuws (eds), *Images of the Past. Studies on Ancient Societies in Northwestern Europe*, 9–89. Amsterdam: Studies in Pre- en Protohistorie 7.

Roymans, N. 1996a. The sword or the plough. Regional dynamics in the romanisation of Belgic Gaul and the Rhineland area, in N. Roymans (ed.), *From the Sword to the Plough. Three Studies on the Earliest Romanisation of Northern Gaul,* 9–126. Amsterdam: Amsterdam Archaeological Studies 1.

Roymans, N. 1996b. Vrouwendracht uit de IJzertijd. Glazen armbanden van de Weertse opgravingen, in N. Roymans and A. Tol (eds), *Opgravingen in Kampershoek en de Molenakker te Weert*, 57–61. Amsterdam: Zuidnederlandse Archeologische Rapporten 4.

Roymans, N. 2001. The Lower Rhine triquetrum coinages and the ethnogenesis of the Batavi, in T. Grünewald (ed.), *Germania inferior. Besiedlung, Gesellschaft und Wirtschaft an der Grenze der römisch-germanischen Welt*, 93–145. Berlin/New York: Walter de Gruyter.

Roymans, N. 2004a. Production, circulation and deposition of the Eburonean triskeles staters, in K. Strobel and R.H.M. Loscheider (eds), *Forschungen zur Monetarisierung und ökonomischen Funktionalisierung von Geld in den nordwestlichen provinzen des Imperium Romanum. Die Entstehung eines europäischen Wirtschaftsraumes (Akten des 2. Trierer Symposiums zur antiken Wirtschaftsgeschichte)*, 133–157. Trier: Trierer Historische Forschungen 49.

Roymans, N. 2004b. *Ethnic Identity and Imperial Power. The Batavians in the Early Roman Empire.* Amsterdam: Amsterdam Archaeological Studies 10.

Roymans, N. and Derks, T. (eds) 1994. *De tempel van Empel. Een*

Herculesheiligdom in het woongebied van de Bataven. 's-Hertogenbosch: Brabantse Regionale Geschiedbeoefening.

Roymans, N. and Van Rooijen, T. 1993. De voorromeinse glazen armbandproductie in het Nederrijnse gebied en haar culturele betekenis, *Vormen uit vuur* 1993/3, 2–10; 56–57.

Seijnen, M. 1994. Dierebotten en rituele maaltijden, in Roymans and Derks 1994, 162–173.

Speidel, M.P. 1994. *Riding for Caesar. The Roman Emperor's Horse Guards*. London: Batsford.

Ter Schegget, M. 1999. Late Iron Age human skeletal remains from the river Meuse at Kessel: a river cult place?, in F. Theuws and N. Roymans (eds), *Land and Ancestors. Cultural Dynamics in the Urnfield Period and the Middle Ages in the Southern Netherlands*, 199–240. Amsterdam: Amsterdam Archaeological Studies 4.

Van den Berg, F. 2002. *Productie, circulatie en depositie van AVAVCIA-munten in België en de Nederrijnse regio*. Unpublished M.A. thesis, Free University, Amsterdam.

Van den Broeke, P.W. 1987. De dateringsmiddelen van de IJzertijd van Zuid-Nederland, in W.A.B. van der Sanden and P.W. van den Broeke (eds), *Getekend zand: tien jaar archeologisch onderzoek in Oss-Ussen*, 23–43. Waalre: Bijdragen tot de studie van het Brabantse heem 31.

Van den Broeke, P.W. 1993. A crowded peat area: observations in Vlaardingen-West and the Iron Age habitation of southern Midden-Delfland, *Analecta Praehistorica Leidensia* 26, 59–82.

Van Heeringen, R.M. 1989. The Iron Age in the Western Netherlands, V. Synthesis, *Berichten van de Rijksdienst voor het Oudheidkundig Bodemonderzoek* 39, 157–255.

Van Impe, L., Creemers, G., Scheers, S., Van Laere, R., Wouters, H. and Ziegaus, B. 1997–8. De Keltische goudschat van Beringen (prov. Limburg), *Archeologie in Vlaanderen* 6, 9–132.

The age of enclosure: Later Iron Age settlement and society in northern France

Colin Haselgrove

Introduction

This paper reviews the nature of Later Iron Age settlement and society in northern France in the light of the new evidence, which has come to light in the last 30 years, much of it through rescue excavations in advance of modern development. My study area comprises the modern region of Picardy (the departments of Aisne, Oise and Somme), along with the parts of Artois (Pas-de-Calais), Champagne (Ardennes, Marne), and Upper Normandy (Seine-Maritime), which lie closest to its borders (Fig. 1). I have chosen this focus partly on account of the intrinsic interest of developments in the region during the Later Iron Age, and partly because, as Hawkes and Dunning (1930) established 75 years ago in a paper which set the agenda for the next two generations, the pottery, burial practices and coinage from this region have particularly close connections with south-east England.

Although these cultural links with northern France no longer play such a central role in our accounts of the Late Iron Age in south-east England (e.g. Hamilton; Hill this volume), they continue to influence our thinking about the period and certainly cannot be ignored. One way of enhancing our understanding of the changes in Britain is to look more closely at the context of related material on the far side of the Channel to see what similarities and differences emerge. For a long time, this was hindered by a lack of excavated settlements in northern France, but – as this paper will I hope show – there is now more than enough data. As in Britain, the critical obstacle to developing broader narratives of landscape and social change is simply the lack of time and resources to digest, analyse and synthesise the flood of material generated every year by new development projects.

The northern and western part of the study area, extending approximately 100 km inland from the Channel coast, is mostly chalk upland, divided up by the wide and winding valley of the River Somme and those of lesser rivers. Further inland, the study area is dominated by the limestone plateaux of the central Paris Basin, through which three major tributaries of the River Seine – the Aisne, the Marne and the Oise – have cut down to form broad alluvial valleys, whose sheltered gravel terraces present a marked contrast with the exposed plateau tops. Finally, at the south-east limit of the study area, on the boundary with Champagne, the chalk reappears as a vast, arid plain, where modern settlement is clustered around the main rivers and their tributaries like the Retourne and the Vesle (on which the modern city of Reims stands). A significant proportion of the chalk and limestone plateaux in the study area have retained a covering of loess, known locally as *limon*. Although as in Champagne, water supply is frequently a problem on the plateaux – causing the present-day villages to cluster along the spring lines at the edges and on the slopes below – the *limon* produces fertile, if heavy, loams, ideal for cereals and root crops, transforming what would otherwise be grass covered upland into some of the best agricultural land in France.

Caesar and Belgic Gaul

In dividing Gaul into three, Julius Caesar refers to the entire population of the area bounded by the Rivers Seine, Marne and Rhine as Belgae (*Gallic War* I, 1), but in a number of later passages, he appears to restrict the name *Belgium* to only part of this region (Hawkes and Dunning 1930, 241–2; Hawkes 1968; Fichtl 1994).

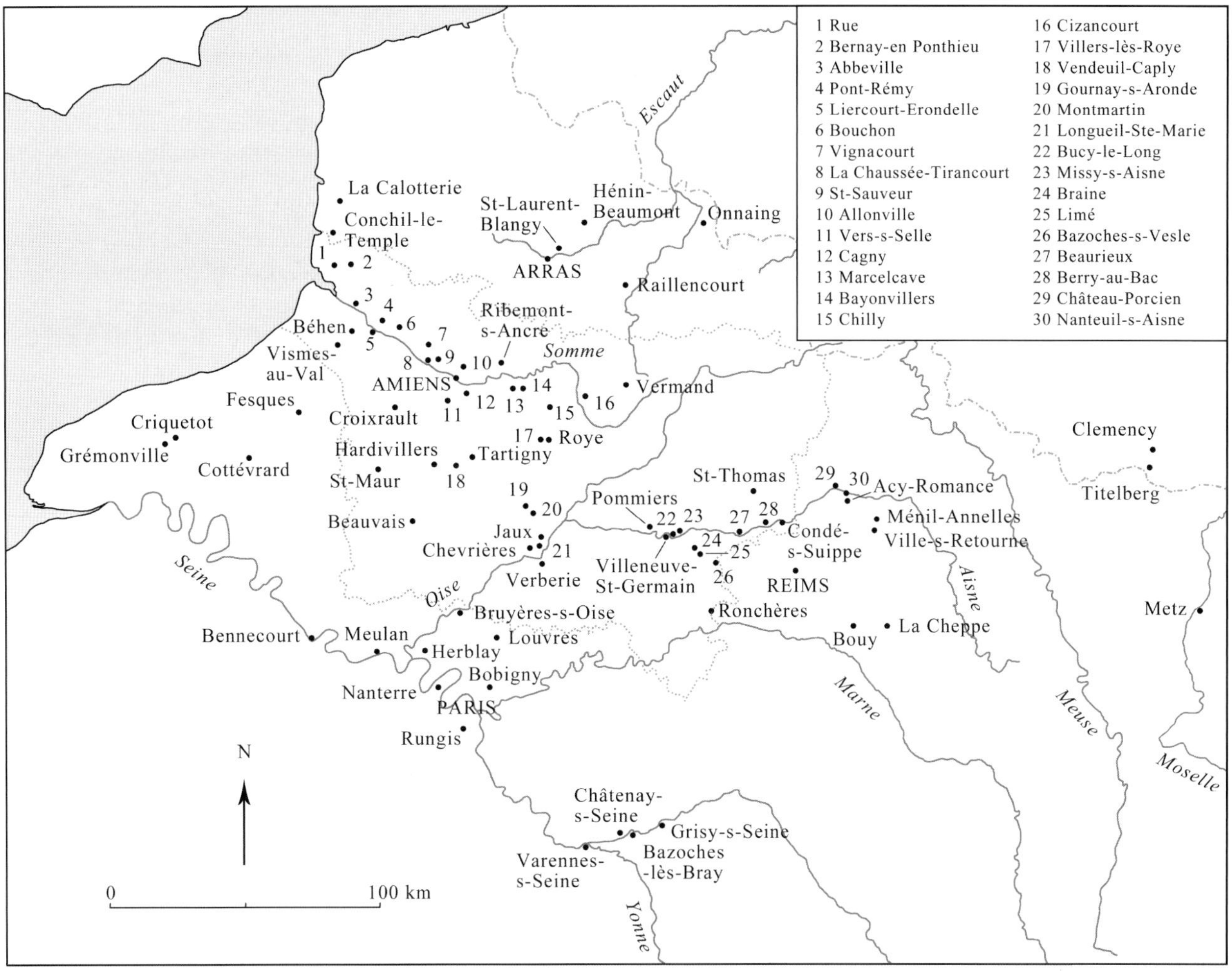

Fig. 1. Northern France, showing the principal Later Iron Age sites mentioned in the text.

Whilst the precise limits of this smaller core territory are uncertain, it appears in broad terms to correspond to the western half to two-thirds of the study area, and definitely included the groups known as the Ambiani, the Atrebates, and the Bellovaci amongst its inhabitants. They may also have included the Bellovaci's eastern neighbours, the Suessiones, whose lands straddled the lower Aisne and Marne valleys, but this latter group also had close ties with the Remi, who occupied the northern Champagne plain. The Remi do not seem to have been part of this core Belgic grouping, at least in Caesar's perception, and from 57 BC onwards, were to be his most constant allies in the region.[1]

Interesting though these insights into the identities of the different groups inhabiting the region in the mid first century BC are, attempting to project them back to an earlier period can only be a largely circular exercise and is best avoided. Most earlier coin types exhibit diffuse, overlapping distributions, difficult to reconcile with a strong degree of cultural or political stability (Haselgrove 1999; Gruel and Haselgrove 2006). Differences in other forms of material culture, such as pottery, do exist, but have yet to be mapped at a level of detail that might reveal the existence of meaningful long-lived groupings. Last but least, we know that the ethnic and political composition of northern Gaul underwent major changes in the 30 years between Caesar's conquest and the organisation of Belgic Gaul into *civitates* under Augustus; whilst the Roman presence was clearly an important ingredient in these changes (Roymans 2004; this volume), this is hardly the strongest argument for continuity in earlier periods.[2]

Much of the incidental information that Caesar provides about Belgic Gaul does seem to be fairly accurate, however. For instance, he mentions several fortified sites (*oppida*) in the south of the region – including the study area – but hardly any in the north, where the inhabitants allegedly took refuge in swamps, fens and forests (*Gallic War* III, 28–9). This south–north split accords well with the known distribution of *oppida* in northern Gaul (e.g. Fichtl 2005, 22–3). Similarly, there are still very few findspots of Republican wine amphorae in the far north of the region (e.g. Loughton 2003; Poux 2004), potentially supporting Caesar's claim that some groups refused to admit traders or import wine or other luxuries (*Gallic War* II, 15).[3]

From an archaeological perspective, these distinctions within Belgic Gaul appear far more significant than the supposed frontier along the rivers Marne and Seine. As Roymans (1990; 1996a) and others have shown, the longhouse building tradition, settlement pattern and subsistence economy in Flanders and the Low Countries are very different in character from most of northern France; the Iron Age inhabitants of the region had no coinage of their own until very late; and there is less overt evidence of social hierarchy or political complexity.[4] Throughout later prehistory, the cultural and ideological affinities of these groups are primarily with the north European plain to the east of the Rhine, whereas *Belgium* looks south, towards the rest of Gaul.

Later Iron Age archaeology in Picardy, 1974–2004

As in Britain, aerial survey has played a key role in the development of Later Iron Age settlement studies in Picardy. Between the 1960s and 1980s, systematic flying of the Somme chalklands by Roger Agache (1978) and of the limestone plateaux in Aisne by Michel Boureux (1974) led to the discovery of large numbers of probable Iron Age enclosed settlements.[5] To begin with, their research lacked follow-up on the ground, but in the late 1970s and 1980s this began to change as a growing number of the sites known from air photography came under threat, and the first large-scale excavations on Later Iron Age sites were carried out.

The initial driving factor was the growing pace of mineral extraction on the gravel terraces of the central Paris Basin. In 1974, a rescue programme led by Paris I University was formally instituted in the Aisne valley (Demoule and Ilett 1985) and the Centre de Recherche Archéologique de la Moyenne Vallée de l'Oise (CRAVO) was set up in Oise. Among the first major Iron Age sites to be excavated on the Aisne terraces were the two low-lying *oppida* at Villeneuve-Saint-Germain (Constantin *et al.* 1982; Debord 1982) and Condé-sur-Suippe (Pion 1987), transforming our knowledge of this type of site. Only Manching, in Germany, has been more extensively investigated. Rural settlements, too, began to be examined on a previously unthinkable scale, as, for instance, at Missy-sur-Aisne, Les Gardots (Aisne). In the ten years up to 1991, the number of excavated Later Iron Age sites in Picardy more than doubled, from 51 to 130 (Malrain *et al.* 2005), mainly as a result of gravel extraction.[6]

The 1990s saw the comprehensive investigation of several more settlements on the gravels of the Oise, the Aisne, and the Vesle (e.g. Malrain and Pinard 2000; Pommepuy *et al.* 2000). In retrospect, this will almost certainly be seen as the 'golden age' of gravel terrace archaeology in Picardy. Since 2002, wholesale stripping of the threatened areas has given way to a regime of evaluating 10% of the surface, and opening up only the most significant areas of archaeology for excavation, thereby limiting the possibility of recovering entire settlement plans or exploring the surrounding area.

In the last 15 years, other kinds of development have had an increasing impact on the archaeological record in northern France. Easily the most dramatic has been the building of hundreds of kilometres of new motorways and the TGV Nord and Est, whose routes have been subjected to comprehensive evaluation and follow-up excavations.[7] Most of this construction has been in the west of the region, complementing the evidence yielded by gravel extraction (Fig. 2). In Somme, as many as 77% of all excavated Later Iron Age sites are on new road and rail routes and 30% in Oise, compared to a mere 6% in Aisne – where gravel terrace sites account more than half (57%) of the total (Malrain *et al.* 2005).[8]

Unlike gravel extraction, the road building programme has affected the valley slopes and plateau tops as well as the river terraces so the data ought to be more representative of the overall settlement pattern in the zone most affected.[9] Interestingly, despite the number of enclosures already recorded by air photography on the chalk plateaux in western Picardy, most of the Later Iron Age sites found during motorway building were hitherto unrecorded, although this does include sites like cemeteries which are less susceptible to discovery from the air. All told, over a third of all excavated Later Iron Age sites in Picardy lie on the line of motorways and the TGV – as opposed to only a quarter linked to gravel extraction.

The other major new form of development, often closely linked to the transport network, has been the construction of new commercial and industrial parks (ZACs). These account for 12% of all excavations, again almost all in the last 15 years. Unlike excavations on the line of roads and railways, which are generally confined to the areas of sites directly affected, the construction of these parks has opened up the possibility of examining entire Iron Age landscapes, as at Saint-Laurent-Blangy (Pas-de-Calais), just outside Arras, where the Actiparc covers very nearly 300 ha. All told, 120 km of trial trenches were dug and 63 ha excavated, revealing the remains of five Later Iron Age enclosed settlements as well as three cemeteries, a stock enclosure, and a network of tracks (Jacques and Prilaux 2003).[10] On a similar scale, but outside the study area, is the Onnaing-Toyota development in Nord, where 237 ha were investigated, revealing nine Later Iron Age sites (Bretagne 1998).

Thanks to the boom in rescue archaeology, a staggering 263 Later Iron Age sites have been excavated in Picardy since 1992, a 200% increase on the previous

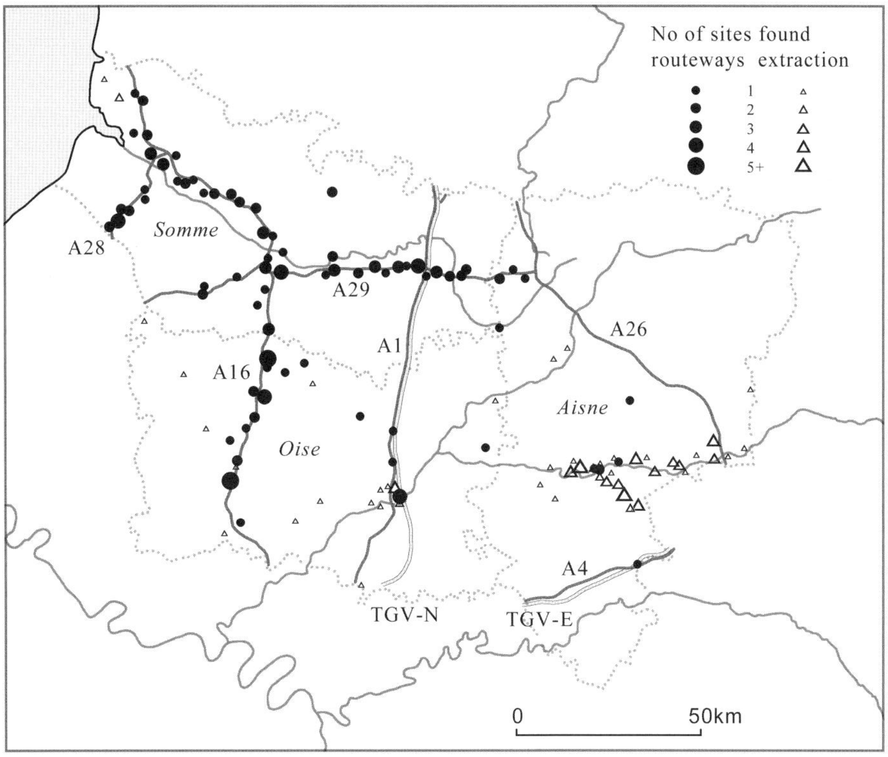

Fig. 2. Rescue archaeology in Picardy: Later Iron Age sites found building transport links and in gravel extraction (after Malrain et al. *2005).*

total (Malrain *et al.* 2005). The figure for neighbouring regions is unlikely to be significantly lower (e.g. Gouge and Séguier 1994; Desfossés 1996; Colin 2000; Geoffroy and Thoquenne 2000; Rougier 2000; Marion 2004). Around 70% of the sites can be classed as settlements, most of them apparently self-contained rural farmsteads and/or field systems, the other main category comprising sanctuaries and cemeteries. The latter are noticeably more common in the west of the region, accounting for as many as a third of the sites in Somme (34%), as opposed to less than one fifth in Aisne (18%).

In addition to the work already mentioned, our understanding of the Later Iron Age in and around Picardy has benefited from two outstanding research projects carried out in the last 30 years. Jean-Louis Brunaux's excavations from 1975–1984 (Brunaux *et al.* 1985) have made the sanctuary at Gournay-sur-Aronde (Oise) into one of the type-sites of the European Iron Age. Since then, many more have been investigated, among them Fesques in Seine-Maritime (Mantel 1997) and Ribemont-sur-Ancre in Somme (Cadoux 1984; Brunaux 1999). The other project, led by Bernard Lambot, is focused on the middle Aisne valley, where this enters the Champagne plain. Between 1988–2003, an agglomeration extending over several hectares at Acy-Romance (Ardennes) has been almost entirely excavated, along with its cemeteries, and a nearby sanctuary at Nanteuil-sur-Aisne (e.g. Lambot and Méniel 1992; 2000; Lambot *et al.* 1994), complementing the rich information available from the rescue programme lower down the valley

The sheer quantity of available evidence should not be allowed to conceal some important limitations in our knowledge. First, as Figure 2 shows only too graphically, there has been precious little work outside the archaeological 'hotspots' of the river valleys and the transport network. In between, the only information is generally from air photography, which, despite the clarity of much of the cropmark evidence, provides only partial coverage.[11] In addition, there are still important lacunae in our knowledge of specific types of site, notably *oppida.* In contrast to the valley-bottom sites at Condé-sur-Suippe and Villeneuve-Saint-German, none of the elevated *oppida* in the study area has seen extensive modern investigation. Knowledge of major sites like Reims, which underlie Gallo-Roman towns, is little better.

A further problem, hardly unique to France, is that relatively few sites are published in any detail. Although a structural report is produced for every excavation and deposited at the *Service Régional*, these may only be consulted in person; much of the time, it is necessary to rely on brief summaries and interim reports. Equally, whilst Picardy can justifiably claim to lead the rest of France in the comparative study of archaebotanical and faunal assemblages from Iron Age sites (e.g. Méniel 1987; 2001; Matterne 2001), analysis of the other material has lagged behind. Attention has tended to focus on specific types of objects (e.g. Brunaux and Rapin 1988; Lejars 1994; Pommepuy 1999), and there has been less integration and synthesis at regional or even site level. On a wider scale still, only weaponry (e.g. Lejars 1996) and coinage (Delestrée 1996; Haselgrove 1999; 2005; Sills 2003) have received much recent attention,[12] although a collective research project (PCR) on the pottery of the fourth to third centuries BC is in progress.

Absolute chronology

For the purposes of this paper, the Later Iron Age will be regarded as the period from the late fourth or early third centuries BC – when the first of a number of important changes begin to impact on the archaeological record in northern France – up until the decade *c.* 30–20 BC, after which Roman influence rapidly starts to manifest itself in the region. For subdividing the material, most French archaeologists have now adopted the chronology developed for the regions nearer the Rhine by Miron (1986; 1991) and Metzler (1995), drawing on the abundant burial evidence available in Luxembourg and Hunsrück–Eifel. A number of other schemes are in use locally in different parts of the Paris Basin (e.g. Lambot and Friboulet 1996; Malrain *et al.* 1996; Pion 1996a; 1996b; Marion 2004), each differing very slightly from the next; for simplicity, the Miron–Metzler terminology will be employed here.[13]

The approximate date ranges for the individual phases of the Later Iron Age are given in Table 1. On average, the absolute dating is now around 30 years earlier than it was two decades ago (Haselgrove 1996; Kaenel *et al.* 2004), with knock-on implications for the rate and timing of the different changes that characterise the period. On top of this, the long-running conflict between the archaeological and numismatic dating has finally been resolved (Guichard *et al.* 1993; Gruel and Haselgrove 2006). The early copying of Greek coins in northern France has been confirmed by recent finds at Ribemont-sur-Ancre (Delestrée 2001),[14] whilst potin coinage was certainly in widespread use by the end of La Tène C2 and may have been adopted in the Seine valley as early as the La Tène C1–C2 transition (Marion 2004) – as much as 150 years earlier than once thought. Silver coinage is relatively uncommon in northern France, but was used by some groups during La Tène D1b, much the same time as struck bronze was introduced (Haselgrove 1999).

Phase	*Date*
La Tène B2	325–270/250 BC
La Tène C1	270/250–200/180
La Tène C2	200/180–150/130 BC
La Tène D1a	150/130–120/110 BC
La Tène D1b	120/110–90/85 BC
La Tène D2a	90/85–60/50 BC
La Tène D2b	60/50–30/20 BC

Table 1. Later Iron Age chronology in northern France.

Burial, ritual and feasting: the rise of enclosure

The onset of the Later Iron Age in Picardy and the surrounding area is marked by significant changes in burial and ritual practice, and by the increased incidence of enclosure both in these spheres and to surround settlements. Within the study area, however, developments were less than uniform, the main split being once again an east–west one, between the areas nearer the coast, and those further inland.

For over two centuries in the mid first millennium BC, the Aisne valley formed the effective northern limit of the well-known Aisne–Marne culture, with its characteristic inhumation cemeteries and chariot burials (Demoule 1999). During La Tène B2, however, grave goods became noticeably more austere,[15] and the existing cemeteries were mostly abandoned. Those founded in their place were generally smaller than their predecessors, and quadrangular ditched enclosures were now often employed to define individual plots, or even the whole cemetery, although inhumation remained the normal burial practice in the area throughout the third century BC (Baray 2004).[16]

At the start of La Tène C2, however, we see a sudden switch to cremation, although inhumations still sometimes occur in settlements (below). The abrupt character of the transition is well illustrated by the small burial ground at Bucy-le-Long, Le Fond du Petit Marais (Fig. 3): all the La Tène C1 tombs are inhumations, whilst those dating to La Tène C2 and after are cremations (Pommepuy *et al.* 2000). Assuming the number of graves is a fair indicator, this new burial ground was apparently used by a rather smaller social group than the preceding Aisne–Marne cemeteries like the one at La Héronnière, only 1 km away, an observation that applies to other Later Iron Age cemeteries of the area.[17] At the same time, the existence in each phase of wealthier burials,

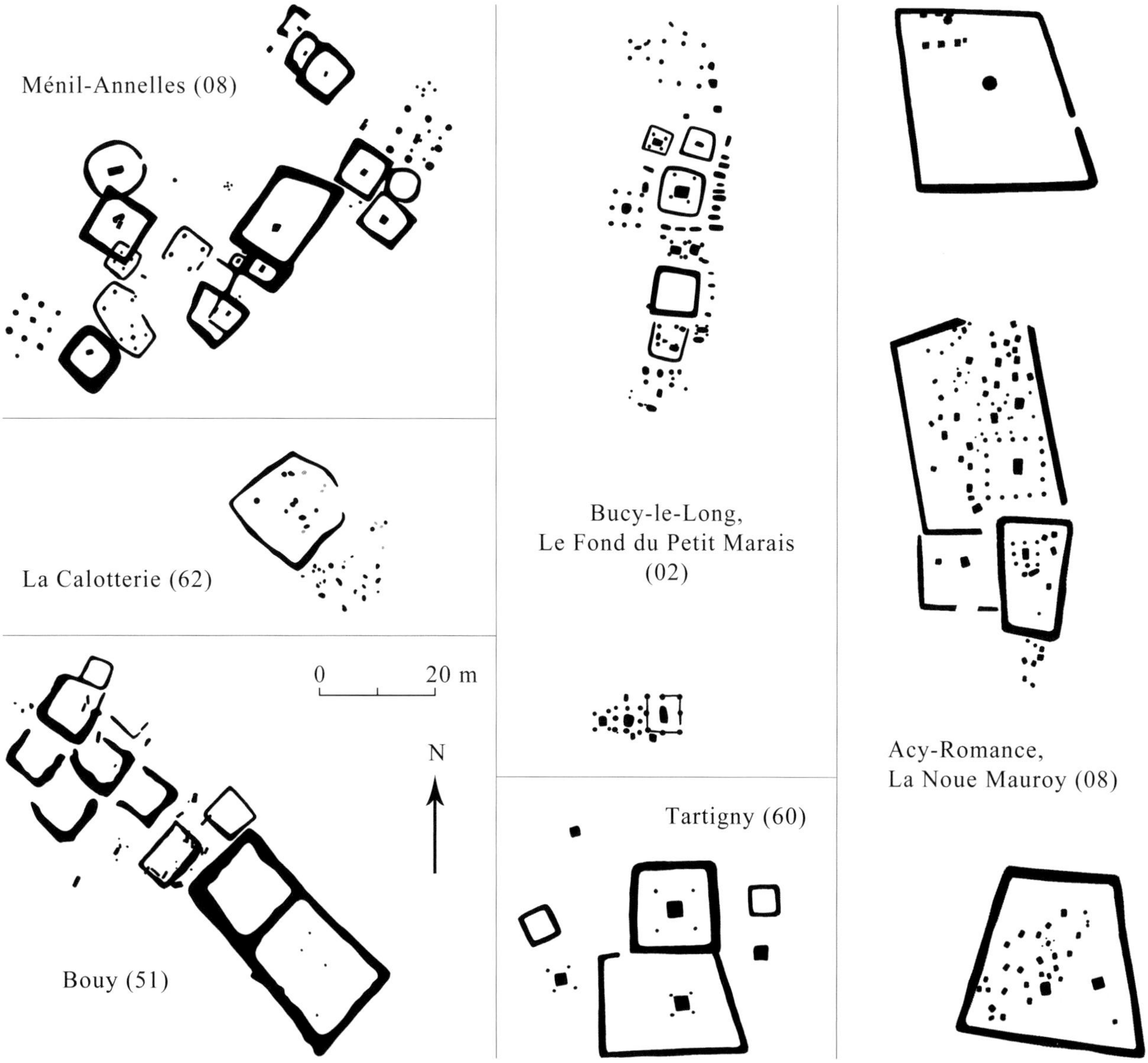

Fig. 3. Later Iron Age cremation cemeteries in northern France.

with simpler graves clustered round about, implies that these units were not socially homogeneous (Haselgrove 1996).

Although the earlier richer graves at Bucy-le-Long are delimited by enclosures, their successors tended instead to be surrounded by square timber structures, large or small. Similar structures, which may have been either open or – more likely – roofed, are common at excavated Later Iron Age cemeteries in the middle Aisne valley, including Acy-Romance, where nine separate mortuary enclosures have now been excavated around the settlement,[18] and Thugny-Trugny (Lambot *et al.* 1994). South of the river, however, and on the Champagne plain proper, the tendency is for individual graves to be within closely packed together square ditched enclosures, as at Ville-sur-Retourne, La-Neuville-en-Tourne-à-Fuy, and Ménil-Annelles, Le Montant de l'Obit – another cemetery spanning the transition from inhumation to cremation (Flouest and Stead 1979) – in Ardennes, or Bouy, Marne (Fig. 3; Chossenot 1997).

Unlike Bucy-le-Long or Ménil-Annelles, cemeteries founded in or after La Tène C2 consist entirely of cremations. The La Tène D1 period is especially well represented and there is some suggestion that the number of graves declines thereafter, although this may be partly a function of the cemeteries excavated. The earliest cremations tend to contain relatively few goods,[19] but later tombs are generally more abundantly furnished, sometimes richly so. Pottery, brooches and animal remains, especially pork (but also chicken and wild species like hare), are the commonest finds, together with items such as knives, razors, shears, and belt hooks.

More unusual goods accompanying individual burials include weapons and feasting equipment such as bronze bowls, wooden buckets with bronze fittings, and iron cooking grills. In all probability, the variation in mortuary assemblages evident within and between cemeteries reflects a range of social identities. At Acy-Romance, for instance, Lambot has suggested that three burials are those of the priests who presided over rituals in the nearly settlement (see below); as well as other unusual goods, the tombs contain a specific type of axe, apparently of identical type to that used to kill a young man buried with his wrists tied behind his back beside a cult building in the centre of the complex (Lambot and Méniel 2000, 114–20).

A further group of wealthy burials in the middle Aisne valley around Château-Porcien is marked out by the inclusion of imported Italian bronze serving and drinking equipment and/or Dressel 1 wine amphorae, alongside indigenous objects like swords or buckets (Roymans 1990; Lambot *et al.* 1994; Haselgrove 1996). Most are poorly recorded, but they seem to occur in isolated groups, as at Saint-Germainmont and Vieux-lès-Asfeld, or even on their own, as at Hannogne (Flouest and Stead 1977). None of them are earlier than La Tène D1 and they are best compared to the rich La Tène D2a burial excavated at Clemency in Luxembourg (Metzler *et al.* 1991); two of the three Vieux-lès-Asfeld burials were in very similar timber-lined chambers, presumably originally covered by a mound.[20] Dressel 1 amphorae occasionally occur in other rich cremations dating to La Tène D2, including at La Noue Mauroy, and Cuiry-lès-Chaudardes and Presles-Saint-Audebert in Aisne (Hénon and Auxiette 1997; Olivier and Schönfelder 2002).

The evolution of burial practices in western Picardy during the Later Iron Age shows both similarities and differences to the eastern part of the study area. In the fifth to fourth centuries BC, a degree of Aisne–Marne influence is apparent in the adjacent regions both in the settlements (e.g. Hurtrelle *et al.* 1990; Prilaux 2000a) and in the cemeteries, but whilst inhumation again predominated, a tradition of cremation also existed.[21] A minority of contemporary cremations occur at cemeteries like Chambly and Longueil-Sainte-Marie in Oise (Pinard 1997; Pinard *et al.* 2000), whilst smallish burial grounds apparently consisting only of cremations have been excavated at Milly-sur-Thérain and Saint-Martin-le-Noeud, both in Oise, and Oulchy-la-Ville in Aisne (Buchez *et al.* 2004). The few known burials of the period on the Somme chalklands include two rich La Tène B1 cremations at Thieulloy-l'Abbaye (Brun *et al.* 2005).

In the late fourth and early third centuries BC, cemeteries start to become commoner in the west of the study area. Almost all the graves were now cremations, although occasional inhumations do still occur, as at Cizancourt, La Sole des Galets in Somme (Lefèvre 2002), or Duisans and Gavrelle in Pas-de-Calais (Debliak *et al.* 1998).[22] The number of new cemeteries continued to rise rapidly during the later third century BC – no fewer than half the known Later Iron Age cemeteries in Somme were founded in La Tène C1 (Malrain *et al.* 2005) – after which numbers stabilized, only falling away again during La Tène D2, rather as happens further inland. Curiously, hardly any pyre sites have been identified, although there is a possible example at Villers-lès-Roye (Buchez and Dumont 1996).

Topographically, cemeteries show a definite bias to the slopes and plateau edges (*ibid.*, 141). This may simply reflect the overall distribution of settlement (below), but it could also reinforce the idea that cemeteries were one of the ways in which new settlers expressed claims to particular tracts of land at a time of rising population and settlement expansion (cf. Haselgrove 1996). At some sites on the A16, the cemeteries appear to pre-date the main phase of nearby settlements (see Baray 1998).[23] Another possibility is that cemeteries were used as territorial markers between different social groups (Gaudefroy *et al.* 2001), as has also been suggested for sanctuaries like Saint-Maur and Vendeuil-Caply and, not least, Gournay-sur-Aronde (Brunaux 1986).

From La Tène C1 onwards, quadrangular ditched enclosures were sometimes used to define individual rich graves, as at Allonville in Somme (Ferdière *et al.* 1973) and Tartigny in Oise (Massy *et al.* 1986); or whole burial grounds, as at Saint-Sauveur (Baray 1998) and Vismes-au-Val (Barbet and Bayard 1996) in Somme, although the practice is not as common as further inland. At La Calotterie, in Pas-de-Calais (Fig. 3), two tombs dating to the La Tène C1–C2 transition acted as twin foci for the subsequent burials on the site, only – whilst one of them lay within a square enclosure and was accompanied *inter alia* by a horse harness and a bucket – the other was unenclosed and contained only pottery (Desfossés 2000, 359–421).[24]

Very wealthy graves are comparatively uncommon on the chalk. Baray (2002) qualifies only seven out of nearly 200 graves excavated along the A16 in Somme as unusually rich: at Bouchon, Saint-Sauveur, and Vignacourt. Most of these wealthier graves were surrounded by post structures – these, too, are generally rarer and simpler than in the Aisne valley – and in just one case, at Vignacourt, by a small enclosure. None of these, however, is as rich as the La Tène C2–D1 burial excavated ahead of a gas pipeline at Marcelcave, Le Chemin d'Ignaucourt (Buchez *et al.* 1998). There, the rich array of grave goods included two firedogs, a bucket, a bronze cauldron, and a mass of other metal objects (Fig. 4). A second rich burial with a bucket and shears

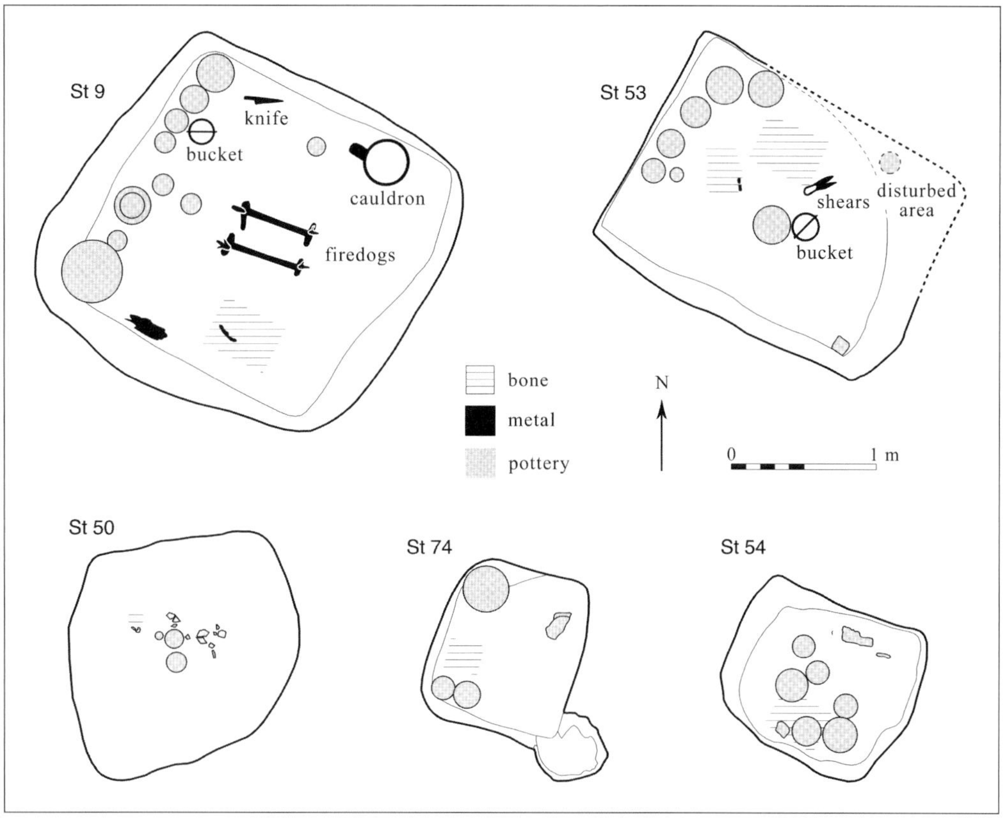

Fig. 4. Plans of later second-century BC cremation graves at Marcelcave, Somme (after Buchez et al. 1998).

and three other well-furnished cremations (one that of a child) were found nearby. All five burials were in timber chambers, although the form of construction differs from Clemency and Vieux-lès-Asfeld, or nearer at hand, tomb 15 at Bouchon (Baray 1997), all of which had upright posts. There is no sign, however, of a horizon of rich burials containing Italian imports in west of the study area to compare with the groups around Château-Porcien and in Luxembourg.[25]

Another difference from the former Aisne–Marne region is that more cemeteries in the west of the study area are directly associated with settlements.[26] Six of the nine cemeteries (67%) and six of the 13 settlements (46%) excavated along the A16 were definitely accompanied by the other (Baray 1998; Colin 2000). Given the narrowness of the corridor explored, the true incidence is probably even higher. At Bernay-en-Ponthieu, Pont-Rémy, and Conchil-le-Temple, La Commanderie (Lemaire and Rossignol 1996), the burial plots are integral with the settlement, albeit within an enclosure of their own, whereas at Bouchon, Francières, and Vignacourt, they are separated by 200–300 m.[27] Occasionally, two or three separate burial areas succeeded one another during the lifetime of the settlement, as at Cottévrard, La Plaine de la Bucaille, in Seine-Maritime (Blancquaert 1998), or Pont-Rémy, La Queute (Prilaux 2000a).

Not surprisingly, this close link between settlement and cemetery and the generally small size of the latter has led to the view that the plots belonged to family units (e.g. Malrain *et al.* 2005). In fact, they may be more selective still, as most cemeteries have fewer than 10 graves and hardly any over 40.[28] Moreover, most burials in Picardy appear to be of a single individual – in contrast to the middle Aisne valley, where it is not unusual for the remains of two or three people to be in a single grave (Lambot *et al.* 1994).[29] In many cemeteries, only adults and adolescents seem to be represented, whilst infants are almost unknown and children fairly rare – although at Cizancourt, the richest of the 15 cremations, containing similar status markers to adult graves, was that of a child aged between 7 and 13 years (Lefèvre 2002). As we have already seen, high status was apparently expressed primarily through the inclusion of goods connected with communal feasting and drinking, not by the carrying of arms – although weapons do sometimes occur, particularly nearer the coast – and by the manner in which the burial chamber and any superstructure were constructed.

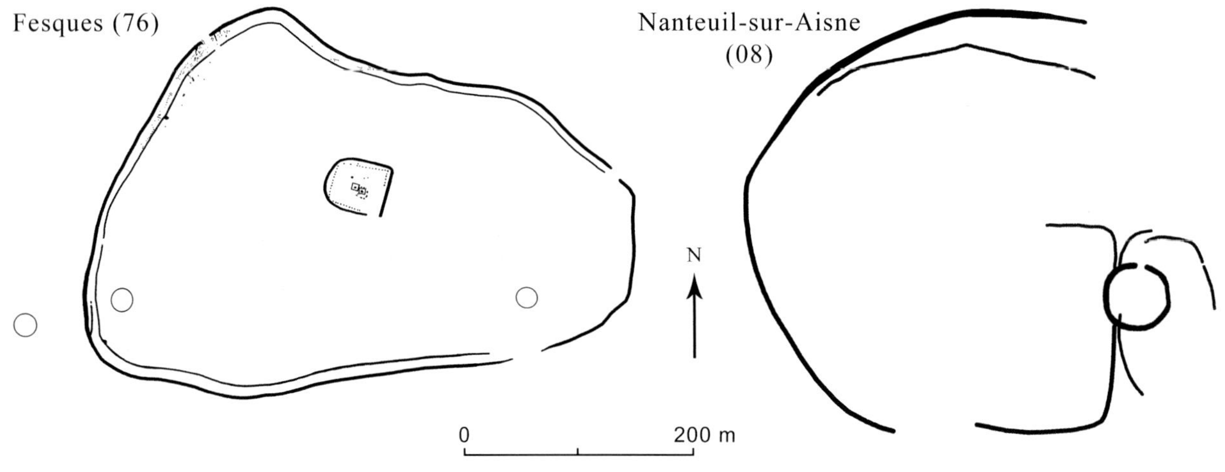

Fig. 5. Large sanctuary enclosures at Fesques, Seine-Maritime (after Mantel 1997), and Nanteuil-sur-Aisne, Ardennes (after Lambot and Méniel 2000).

Cult enclosures and sanctuaries

The second key change marking the start of the Later Iron Age in northern France – with a not unimportant role in the disposal of the dead – was the appearance of formal religious sanctuaries. Within the study area, there appears to be a particular concentration of sites in western Picardy and Seine-Maritime (Fichtl 1994). In many cases, the Iron Age phases have been severely disturbed by later Roman rebuilding, but enough sites have been investigated for the general character of the earliest structures and deposits to be apparent. Apart from Gournay-sur-Aronde, Fesques, and Ribemont-sur-Ancre, these include Chilly (Collart 1987), Estrées-Saint-Denis (Quérel and Woimant 2002), Morvillers-Saint-Saturnin (Delplace 1991), Saint-Maur-en-Chaussée (Brunaux and Lambot 1991), and Vendeuil-Caply (Piton and Dilly 1985), and, further afield, Bennecourt (Bourgeois 1999) in the Seine valley and Nanteuil-sur-Aisne (Lambot and Méniel 2000). From the finds, some sites at least saw activity from La Tène B2 onwards – although generally it is not until La Tène C1 that we can discern a clear structural context – implying that their development may be linked to the changes in burial practice which began at approximately the same period.

The character of these sites has been discussed elsewhere, most recently by Arcelin and Brunaux (2003). Most take the form of a simple rectangular enclosure defined by a ditch and/or palisade, with sides some 30–50 m long, and entrances pointing towards the midwinter or midsummer solstice, as at Gournay itself – which Brunaux suggests is when they were inaugurated. A few, however, are curvilinear or polygonal in shape, and/or associated with a still larger enclosure, as at Fesques or Nanteuil-sur-Aisne (Fig. 5). At several sites, the principal feature in the interior took the form of a large pit or hollow, surrounded by a horse-shoe arrangement of post pits (e.g. Gournay, Saint-Maur, Vendeuil-Caply), or as in the case of Fesques a square timber structure, which presumably formed the actual cult focus.

Up to the later second century BC, the main items found at sanctuaries are weaponry and animal and human bone. At Gournay, the main enclosure ditch yielded over 2500 scabbards, swords, shield bosses and lances, dating between La Tène B2 and C2, 3000 animal bone deposits, and a small amount of human bone (Brunaux *et al.* 1985). Many of the weapons had apparently been displayed as trophies and/or were ritually destroyed before they were buried (Brunaux and Rapin 1988; Lejars 1994). Ribemont is quite different: here human remains predominate and most of the weapons represent a very short period (La Tène C1; Lejars 1999). The dead were apparently all male.[30] Skulls are noticeable by their absence and three square ossuaries had been made out of long bones (Cadoux 1984); the best preserved one is estimated to contain the remains of 300 humans and 50 horses (Fercoq du Leslay 1996). Given these features, Brunaux (1999) has argued that Ribemont was not in fact a conventional sanctuary, but was instead a memorial to a major battle nearby, which gradually fell into decay.[31]

Some Belgic sanctuaries apparently served as focal sites for larger areas. At Fesques, for example, the sanctuary stood within a larger ditched enclosure (10 ha), around which there was a row of pits, containing the feet of a number of people, whose remains had been stood up in the pits or suspended over them, facing the interior (Mantel 1997). As Fichtl (2004) notes, the size of the site implies that it was used by the population of a large area, who presumably came there periodically to conduct communal business, make political decisions, exchange goods, and form alliances, as well as enact religious rituals. As at Gournay, large-scale feasting and drinking, for which there is abundant evidence, clearly accompanied these activities. Fichtl (2004) sees a clear link between the founding of these sanctuaries and the subsequent emergence of larger-scale polities, whilst Wells (2006) has suggested that the public performance of rituals at these sites in front of large numbers of people had a crucial role in bringing groups closer together during the third and second centuries BC.

In the course of La Tène C2–D1, the nature of sanctuary deposition began to change significantly, with other categories of material such as brooches, miniature wheels (rouelles), pottery, and coinage increasing in importance at the expense of weapons – although coinage was not deposited in large quantities until La Tène D2, when several sanctuaries apparently functioned as mints (Delestrée 1996). The overall number of cult sites also increased, although even at this late date, the focus is still very much on western Picardy and Seine-Maritime, and fewer examples are known in Aisne or Ardennes. One reason for this may be the early appearance of *oppida* in this area (Wellington 2005). As we shall see below, these fulfilled many of the same roles as sanctuaries, usually containing cult places of their own and providing a meeting place for peoples living over a larger area.

We also need to consider the various forms of ritual or ceremonial activity on rural settlements and on other sites that are categorised as domestic, but may have had a more specialised role.[32] They include two settlements with integral sanctuaries. The one at Montmartin (Oise) sits on the end of a promontory above the River Aronde, only 3 km from Gournay, separated by a ditch from the adjacent high-status settlement; it yielded the usual weapons and human remains (Brunaux and Méniel 1997). In contrast, the so-called 'sanctuary' at Acy-Romance occupied most of the south-west quarter of this 15 ha complex and was closely integrated with the rest of the settlement (Fig. 6). Its focus was a D-shaped enclosure, *c.* 90 by 55 m, on which several roads running through the site converged.[33] Lining the outside of the enclosure was a row of presumed shrines (one enclosing a square shaft); another group, accompanied by some storage pits, was located outside the north corner, along with 19 human burials in boxes – thought to be sacrificial victims (Lambot and Méniel 2000).

Apart from some iron tools and a scythe, the Acy-Romance shrines yielded few artefacts and the interior of the enclosure was largely clear of features. However, a mass of animal bone, nearly all cattle (70%) or horse (18%), was found in the surrounding ditch (which originally supported a palisade), whilst the finds outside the enclosure included four pits filled with sheep remains – one representing at least 150 individuals (*ibid.*, 93) – and the grave of the young man killed by an axe (see above). Both sets of faunal assemblages are highly selective and likely to represent a mixture of offerings and feasting debris. Like the settlement, the main use of the sanctuary dates to La Tène C2 and D1, after which the entire complex and its cemeteries were progressively abandoned.[34] This means that the sanctuary was frequented at exactly the same time as its neighbour at Nanteuil-sur-Aisne, also founded in La Tène C2 and only 1.5 km away (Lambot and Méniel 2000), implying different roles. In fact, this latter site resembles Fesques, the sanctuary linked to a much larger enclosure, 300 m across (Fig. 5 above), suggesting that it, too, drew in a non-resident population from a much larger area. The main development of the inner sanctuary in La Tène D2 might be linked to the decline of Acy-Romance, but the nature of the deposits changes at the same time, with weapons giving way to objects like coins or *rouelles*, so this could also reflect wider trends.

Ritual activity was not confined to the main sanctuary area at either Acy-Romance or Montmartin, as Bradley (2005) notes. *Inter alia*, this may reflect some kind of divide between rituals acted out at household level and those involving the community and/or specialists. At both sites, human remains occur in the living areas as well, along with various types of special deposit (Brunaux and Méniel 1997; Méniel 1998; Lambot and Méniel 2000).[35] At Acy-Romance and another nearby site, at Damary (Aisne), many coins – and other items such as brooches, blue glass ribbed armlets and lignite bracelets – were apparently deposited as part of closure rituals when living areas were abandoned (Haselgrove 2005). It seems likely that religious beliefs also had a strong influence on the overall plan of Acy-Romance, which Lambot (1999) believes was laid out with reference to a Bronze Age barrow at the heart of the complex.

As well as 'run-of-the-mill' structured deposits, which are a regular occurrence on Later Iron Age rural settlements throughout northern France (e.g. Gransar *et al.* forthcoming), certain enclosures in the study area have yielded the remains of larger-scale feasting and/or sacrificial offerings, whilst lacking some of the features habitually found on domestic sites. A good example is Braine, La Grange des Moines (Aisne), where very large quantities of animal bone (especially pig and sheep), pottery, wine amphorae and other high-status items were found in the ditches of a square enclosure and annexe dating to La Tène D1b (Auxiette *et al.* 2000; Poux 2004). The enclosure contained two large buildings, but no ancillary storage structures – although the number of querns indicates large-scale milling on site. In La Tène D2, it was replaced by a smaller ditched enclosure, placed at 45 degrees to its predecessor. This second enclosure also yielded significant deposits of animal bone and pottery – though not on quite the same scale as before – and had hardly any buildings. Potentially similar sites include Bruyères-sur-Oise (Toupet *et al.* 2005) – also with two main phases and containing several timber-lined shafts or wells full of offerings – and Beauvais, Les

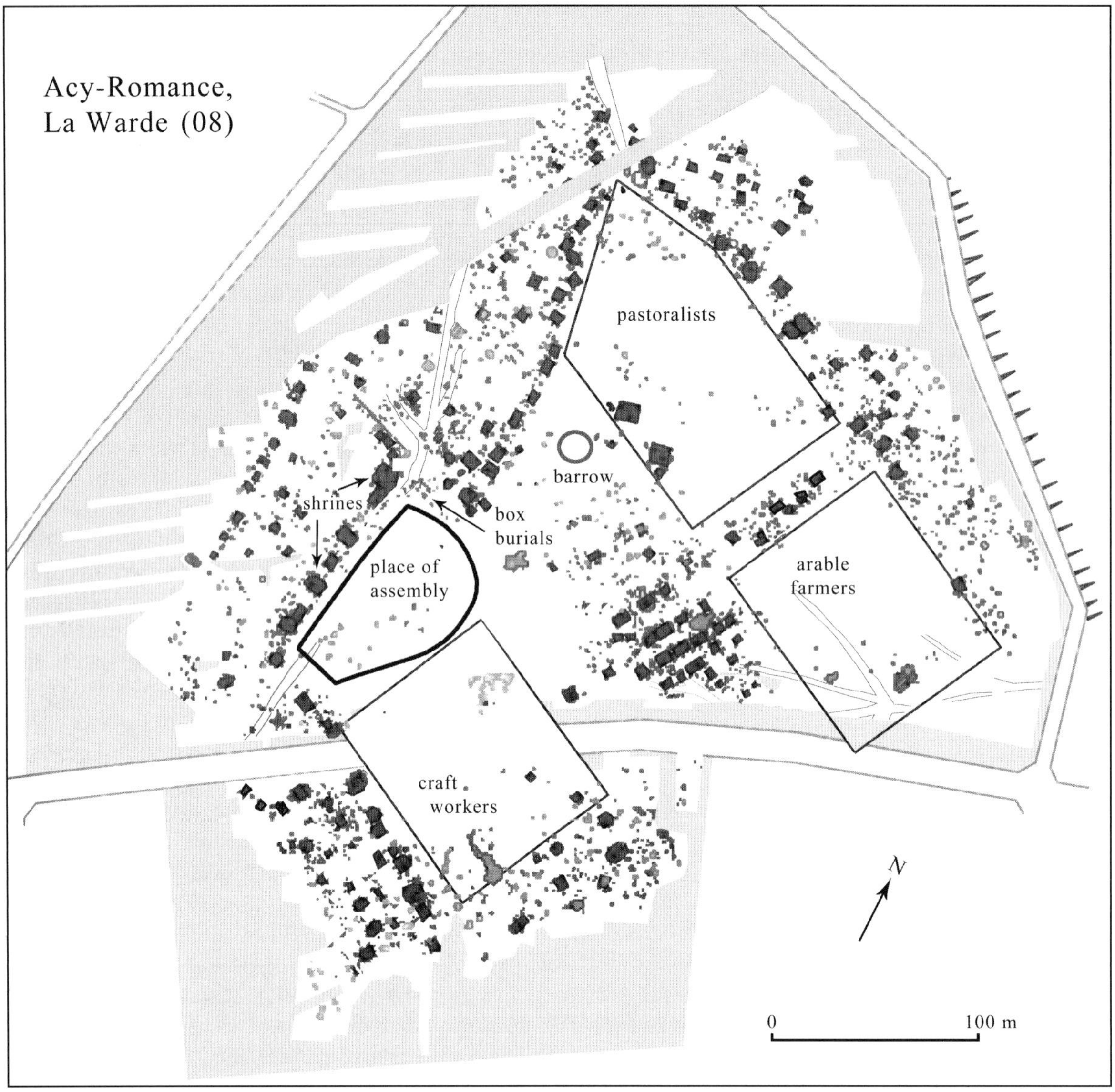

Fig. 6. The Iron Age agglomeration at Acy-Romance, Ardennes (after Lambot 2002b with additions).

Aulnes du Canada (Woimant 1990). There are a number of smaller quadrangular enclosures with structured deposits in the east of the study area, like Soupir (Aisne), which do not seem to have had a domestic or mortuary function, and might also be cult sites (Haselgrove and Lowther 2005).

Debris from what appear to be one-off feasts or banquets is occasionally found on 'ordinary' Later Iron Age settlements. For example, at Chevrières, La Plaine du Marais, one pit was filled with the remains of six young cattle and three pigs (Méniel 2001). At the larger settlement of Vermand, Champs des Lavoirs (Aisne), there were as many as five such pits full of animal remains, one of them containing no fewer than 13 sheep and 25 newly born lambs as well as several other species, in a combination implying both feasting and sacrifice (Lemaire 2000). It remains possible that the larger enclosures like Braine were also in fact settlements, but have lost the more insubstantial domestic structures through a combination of ploughing and over-deep stripping of topsoil prior to gravel extraction.

Rural settlement, economy and environment: the proliferation of enclosure

Like cemeteries, rural settlement numbers – and by implication the total population of the study area – seem to have grown continuously during the Later Iron Age until La Tène D2, when the trend was (temporarily) reversed, the number of sites abandoned now exceeding the number of new ones (Malrain *et al.* 2005). Based on the sharp increase in La Tène D1 sites on the limestone plateaux of the Aisne valley, I suggested fifteen years ago that this growth in population was closely linked to the opening up of the fertile soils on the plateau tops to intensive cultivation from the third century BC onward (Haselgrove 1990; 1996).[36] The data now available from other parts of Picardy strongly support this view, as well as providing more evidence of the hypothesised initial phase of colonisation of the slopes and plateau edges during La Tène C1–C2 (Gaudefroy *et al.* 2001; Malrain *et al.* 2005). As elsewhere, the availability of a mature iron technology for plough shares, axes and other agricultural tools, and of crops suited to cultivation on heavier soils were presumably key factors in this process of settlement expansion; the warmer climate (Magny and Richard 1992) will also have contributed.

Around the same period, linear ditches, enclosures, and field systems all start to become increasingly common on the river terraces and elsewhere (Malrain 1994; Marion 1994; Haselgrove 1996; Malrain and Pinard 2000). From their form and layout, it is clear that this process of enclosure was heavily influenced by agricultural concerns: to separate arable from pasture, and for stock management; to drain land that was otherwise too wet for permanent settlement;[37] and probably to mark property boundaries in a landscape that was fast filling up – for instance, in parts of the Aisne valley, farms were spaced no more than 1 km apart by La Tène D1b (Thouvenot *et al.* 2000). The cooperation and labour involved in digging and maintaining these ditch systems may also have served to integrate groups more closely.[38] Pollen analysis provides another indicator of the extent to which land use was now specialised. By the Later Iron Age, the floor of both the Aisne and Oise valleys was mostly grassland, with some woodland (Firmin *et al.* 1989; Malrain 2000). It appears that the land closest to the farms on the valley bottom was mostly used for pasture, whilst their arable fields were situated further away, on the lower slopes and on the plateau tops, only the steep upper slopes being left heavily wooded (Haselgrove 1990; Malrain 2000).

The nature of crop husbandry changed significantly during the Later Iron Age. Although emmer wheat and hulled barley were still the main cereals, both bread wheat and millet increased in importance, and monoculture became the rule, where previously additional species were often grown alongside the main crop (Bakels 1999; Matterne 2000; 2001). Another pointer to greater specialisation is the fall in the number of cultivated species present on many sites, although this trend is reversed during La Tène D1. Interestingly, spelt wheat – which had supplanted emmer in southern Britain by this period, and was grown in larger quantities in the Earlier Iron Age and in the Roman period – declined in significance on Later Iron Age sites in northern France.[39] Among the vegetable crops, peas and lentils also decreased in importance, whilst beans increased. The surviving woodland was presumably heavily managed for fuel and building materials; the main species represented (alder, hazel, oak, pine, and willow) are all valuable in this regard.

The methods of grain storage changed, with a reduction in the use of underground silos, the advent of large pottery storage vessels (*dolia*), and a general reduction in storage facilities at producer sites (Gransar 2000; 2002). Gransar interprets the latter as indicating that surplus cereal was taken elsewhere; it may also have been used in long-distance exchange. In addition, cereals were apparently no longer stored as grains, but on the ear or without the glumes having been removed (Gransar *et al.* 1999; Matterne 2000). The other major innovation was the adoption of the rotary quern in La Tène C2 (Pommepuy 1999), if not earlier.[40] In the eastern Paris Basin, these were mostly manufactured from local limestone, and probably by specialised workshops, as there is no evidence of on-site manufacture (*ibid.*; Robert and Landreat 2005). Only a tiny percentage of querns found in this area are from non-local sources, but it seems likely that systematic study of site assemblages in the chalk area will reveal a different pattern.

Changes in animal husbandry are less easy to evaluate, as there are substantial variations between sites even within quite small areas (e.g. Horard-Herbin *et al.* 2000). It is not always straightforward to decide which of these differences reflect site status or the local environment, and which are down to taphonomy.[41] Across Picardy as a whole, cattle generally lead in terms of crude numbers and meat weight, followed by pig, whilst sheep lags well behind (Malrain *et al.* 2005). This pattern is replicated at most larger settlements (including *oppida*) and a fair number of smaller ones. However, sheep are noticeably more important in certain areas, such as the Aisne valley, particularly when the data are converted to MNI (Auxiette 2000), and increased in frequency on many lesser rural farmsteads during the Later Iron Age and at some larger ones like Acy-Romance (Malrain *et al.* 2002, 191), a development which may well be connected with the process of arable intensification.

By the end of the period, the size of the indigenous domestic animals was on the increase, although this was probably under Roman influence. The arrival of large horses, thought to be imports from the south, is documented in La Tène D1 at certain sites, including Condé-sur-Suippe and Montmartin (Méniel 2001; Malrain *et al.* 2005), although no imported large cattle are known before La Tène D2, and then only at Varennes-sur-Seine, Le Marais de Pont (Seine-et-Marne) – an important nucleated settlement in the Seine valley – and other nearby sites, on the southern fringes of Belgic Gaul (Horard-Herbin *et al.* 2000). Other changes in the Later Iron Age included a general reduction in the consumption of both horse and dog – although, whether for cultural or other reasons, more horse was eaten in western Belgic Gaul than elsewhere in northern France – and a further diminution in the presence of wild species, which were now generally only found (mainly as hare and deer) on *oppida* and putatively high-status settlements (Méniel 1987; 2001).[42]

Although salt was produced from sea water in the coastal areas of Belgic Gaul throughout the first millennium BC, the industry underwent a major transformation from the third century BC onward (Weller 2000), almost certainly due to an increased demand for salt to preserve stored meat. This is reflected both in altered production methods and in the direct integration of workshops with permanent settlements. Three Later Iron Age sites on the A16 between the Rivers Somme and Canche yielded evidence of large-scale salt production (Desfossés 2000, 215–353; Prilaux 2000b), most spectacularly at Pont-Rémy, La Queute, on the fertile plateau which dominates the right bank of the Somme, where one of the largest furnaces for salt production known in France was built in La Tène D1 at the northern end of the settlement (Prilaux 2000a; 2000b). Another La Tène D1 settlement with its own salt oven, this time rather smaller, has since been excavated at Rue (Rougier and Blancquaert 2001). Late Iron Age briquetage for transporting salt has been found as far inland as the Aisne valley (Weller and Robert 1995).

Enclosed settlements

Prior to the third century BC, open settlements predominated throughout Picardy. From La Tène C1 onward, however, an increasing number of settlements on the chalk and as far inland as the Oise valley were enclosed by ditches (Fig. 7), although further east there is as yet little evidence of enclosed settlement until the later second century BC.[43] Not all 'ditches' were in fact open. At Bayonvillers (Somme), the ditches supported twin palisades (Prodeo 2000), whilst at Bazoches, Les Chantraines (Aisne), the ditch was later remodelled to contain a palisade (Gransar and Pommepuy 2005). At Vermand, they stood open beside the opposing entrances, but supported palisades elsewhere (Lemaire 2000). In size, the ditches around settlements vary from insignificant features no more than 1 m wide or 20–30 cm deep, to massive features some 3–4 m wide and over 1.5 m deep (Malrain and Pinard 2000). Occasionally, evidence of internal banks has been recovered: at Bazoches, where the bank had collapsed back into the ditch (Gransar and Pommepuy 2005), and at Ronchères, where – exceptionally – part of the bank still survived as an earthwork (Malrain 2003).[44] At Longueil-Sainte-Marie, Le Vivier des Grès, the remains of a probable stone revetment were found in the ditch, whilst at Pont-Rémy, La Queute, the bank was apparently faced with flint (Malrain *et al.* 2002, 147).

On the chalk plateaux in Somme, many enclosures appear to be double-ditched and were originally divided up by Agache (1978, 138), using the aerial survey evidence, into three principal classes. His Type I enclosures were generally irregular, often curvilinear, in form, as at Bernay-en-Ponthieu or Pont-Rémy on the A16 (Colin 2000). Type II sites comprised a more regular or rectilinear internal enclosure, often quite small, surrounded by an irregular external enclosure (for example, Blangy-Tronville, Bray-lès-Mareuil and Vers-sur-Selle), or sometimes conjoined (Cagny). Type III sites, many of which were also occupied in Roman times, consisted of concentric rectangular enclosures, generally longer than they are broad, like Abbeville, Arry, and Conchil-le-Temple, Le Fond de la Commanderie, on the A16 (Colin 2000); Behen and Bouillancourt-en-Séry on the A28 (Bayard 1996); and Croixrault on the A29 (Gaudefroy 2002).

Predictably, the motorway excavations have shown that the visible plan of many enclosed settlements is in fact a composite of various minor changes over time and occasional major reorganisations of the site layout (e.g. Collart 1996; Colin 2000; cf. Hamilton this volume), rendering Agache's typology in need of updating. In particular, it now seems that simple curvilinear or sub-rectangular enclosures with a single ditch were also common in the region during the Later Iron Age, exemplified by Bouchon (Colin 2000), the La Tène D1 phase at Roye, Le Puits-à-Marne (Collart 1996), or Trinquies (Bayard 1996). These often have few associated structures and may, in many cases, have been for stock, a role presumably performed by the outer enclosure at many double-ditched sites. The more regular double rectilinear enclosures seem to be a fairly late development, dating to La Tène D1b at the earliest (Colin 2000). Squared-off entrances are also a particular characteristic of the region, as at Arry or Conchil-le-Temple.

The motorway excavations seem to confirm Agache's (1978) view that Later Iron Age farms in Somme were preferentially located on the slopes and plateau margins, where they could exploit the resources of both valley and plateau, although virtually all areas have yielded some sites, implying that whole basin was densely inhabited by this period. Normally, the area enclosed is between 1–2 ha, although larger examples occur. Equally, most enclosures seem to be isolated, but they sometimes occur in groups of two, three, or four, a phenomenon which is paralleled in the Aisne valley and may reflect the nature of the colonisation process, or the existence of particular social networks, or both (Haselgrove 1996). Croixrault, L'Aérodrome (Malrain *et al.* 2005, fig. 18) is a good example. The first enclosure, which dates to La Tène C2, was rebuilt in more regular form at the start of La Tène D1. In La Tène D1b, a second enclosed settlement was constructed 400 m to the north-east (Gaudefroy 2002), and the two were linked together by a system of fields and ditches. Finally, in La Tène D2 or the early Roman period, a new trackway was built

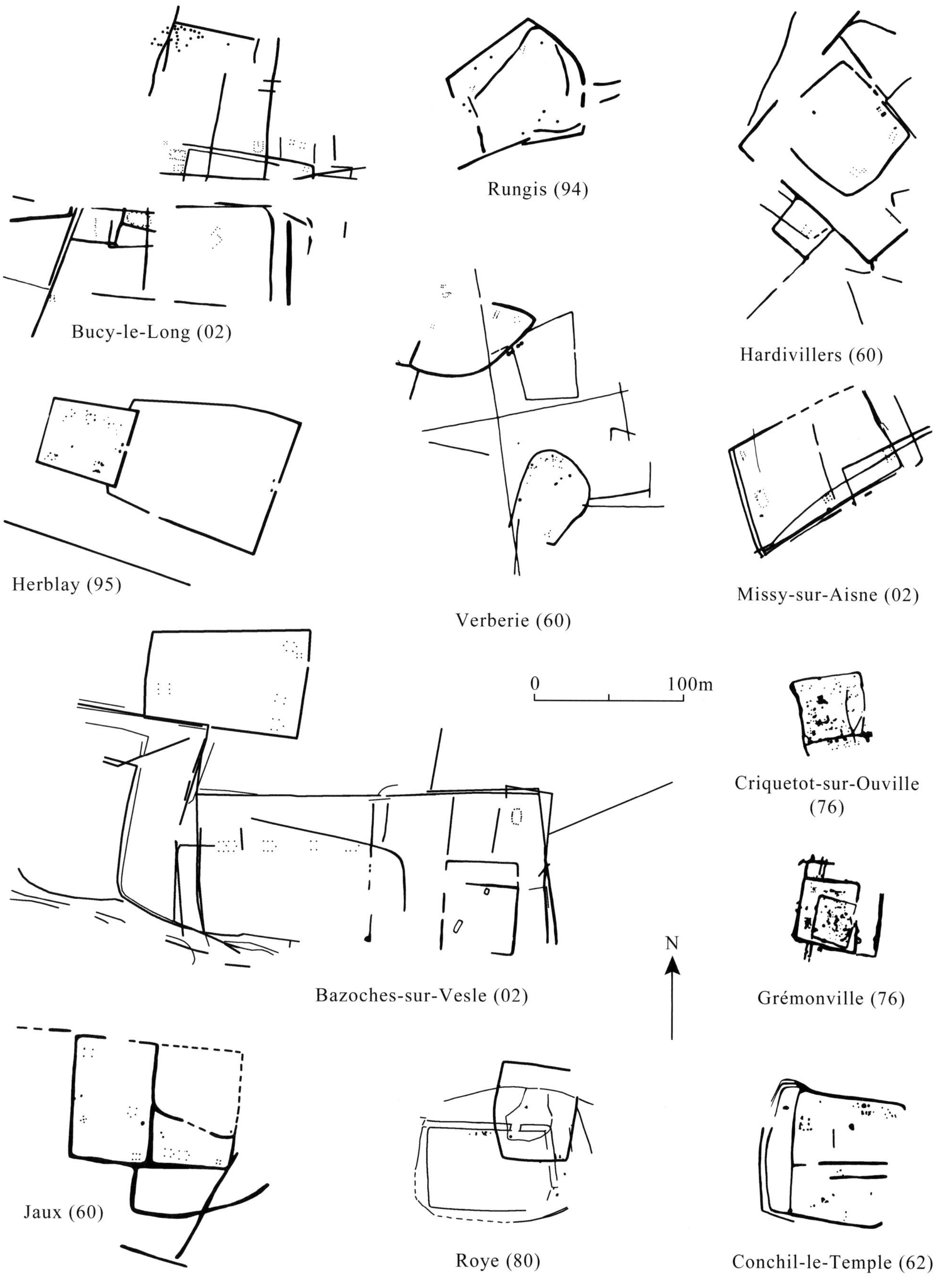

Fig. 7. Later Iron Age enclosed rural settlements in northern France.

through the western part of the field system, cutting through the middle of the original settlement.

Outside Somme, the character of Later Iron Age farmsteads varies from small, relatively compact rectilinear enclosures in the Pays de Caux, like Baons-le-Comte, Criquetot-sur-Ouville and Grémonville, Le Gal (Fig. 7; Desfossés 1996; Rougier 2000) to more heterogeneous enclosure complexes, as in Aisne and Oise, where ditch systems of sub-rectangular, trapezoidal, and curvilinear shape all occur (Haselgrove 1996; Malrain 1994). The mean enclosure size is smaller than in Somme, with no more than 10% of enclosures over 1 ha in extent (Malrain *et al.* 2002, 154), but small-scale shifts of location over time were a frequent occurrence on the gravel terraces – in effect carrying on a pattern which is already apparent during the Earlier Iron Age (Haselgrove 2007) – and many valley-bottom settlements consequently appear as palimpsests spreading over several hectares. Examples in Oise include Chevrières, La Plaine du Marais; and Verberie, La Plaine du Saint-Germain and Les Gats, each of which underwent various stages of enclosure and changes in location (Fémolant and Malrain 1996; Malrain *et al.* 1996; Malrain and Pinard 2000). Comparable complexes in Aisne include Bucy-le-Long, Le Fond du Petit Marais, where a settlement was founded beside the earlier cemetery during La Tène D2 (Pion 1996a); Bazoches, La Foulerie (Collart 1996); and Limé, Les Sables (cf. Soupart and Duvette 2005).

As in Somme, there is a clear tendency for enclosures to become more rectilinear in form in the course of the Later Iron Age (*ibid.*, 153), coupled with increased subdivision of the interior into discrete zones at certain sites (Pommepuy *et al.* 2000). The internal structures include various larger buildings, generally either rectangular or with rounded ends; most are post-built, although some structures of sleeper-beam construction or with continuous wall trenches do occur (Pion 1996a; Pinard *et al.* 1999). Many of these larger buildings were clearly residential, although macroscopic plant remains imply that some may have been barns or byres (Haselgrove 1996). There is no sign of buildings combining living quarters with byres or stables comparable to the aisled longhouse tradition of northern Belgic Gaul (Roymans 1996). The residential buildings are generally accompanied by smaller storage structures on four, six, or even nine posts, together with pits and wells. At Bucy-le-Long, Le Fond du Petit Marais, a battery of 30 storage pits was found outside the La Tène D2 enclosure complex (Gransar 2000), although this is the only such example known in the region at such a late date.[45]

Throughout Picardy, a common pattern in La Tène D1–D2 is for the principal buildings and ancillary structures on rural settlements to be ranged around the enclosure boundary looking onto a central open space. Examples include Bazoches, La Foulerie I, and Missy-sur-Aisne, in Aisne (Pommepuy *et al.* 2000); Bazoches-lès-Bray, La Voie Neuve, in Seine-et-Marne (Herbin-Horath *et al.* 2000); Conchil-le-Temple, La Frénésie, in Pas-de-Calais (Leman-Delerive and Piningre 1981); Chevrières, Hardivilliers and Villeneuve-les-Sablons, Le Bois des Saules, in Oise (Derbois 1994; Femolant and Malrain 1996); or Rungis in Val-de-Marne (Rimbault 1994). A not uncommon alternative, particularly on farms of La Tène C2–D1 date, is for the main enclosure to be subdivided into two, as at Bazoches, Les Chantraines; Bazoches-lès-Bray, Près le Tureau aux Chèvres (Herbin-Horath *et al.* 2000); Hénin-Beaumont 1 in Pas-de-Calais (Geoffroy and Thoquenne 2000); Rue in Somme (Rougier and Blancquaert 2001); and Jaux and Longueil-Sainte-Marie, L'Orméon, in Oise (Malrain and Pinard 2000).

Most farms are unlikely to have housed social units much larger than the extended family, but there is good reason to believe that their status varied. From a detailed analysis of various attributes, including the scale of the ditches, the types of building, the nature of the finds, and the quality of the meat eaten by the inhabitants, Malrain (2000; Malrain and Pinard 2000; Malrain *et al.* 2002, 143) has defined a fourfold hierarchy of rural sites in the Oise valley. At one end are a few higher-status settlements like Longueil-Sainte-Marie, Le Vivier des Grès and L'Orméon (ranks 1–2); at the other, rather more numerous low-status farms like Verberie, La Plaine d'Hermeuse I or Les Gats (ranks 3–4).[46] Whilst the fine detail can be argued over, Malrain's model does appear to reflect real differences between sites. Those at the bottom end of the spectrum like Les Gats were, at most, only partly enclosed, whereas at Le Vivier des Grès (rank 1), the main dwelling lay in its own compound, an arrangement also found at Herblay in Val-d'Oise (Fig. 7; Valais 1994).

Finally a group of larger enclosed settlements in the east of the region, including Bazoches, La Foulerie II; Beaurieux, Les Grèves (Aisne); and Verneuil-en-Hallatte (Oise), should be mentioned. These comprise a series of separate dwelling units with their own yards, pits and wells, laid out around a large open space in a manner that closely anticipates the well-known Roman courtyard villas of the region (Collard 1996; Haselgrove 1996).[47] In the present state of knowledge, these larger rural settlements appear to be a post-conquest development (La Tène D2b–Augustan), but their layout clearly has its roots in the smaller La Tène D1–D2 farmsteads and may even be directly presaged at one or two exceptional sites, such as Louvres, Le Vieux Moulin, in Val d'Oise (Casadéi and Leconte 2000), where a series of compounds are ranged round a central enclosure. Significantly, at both Bazoches and Verneuil, what appears to be the principal residence occupied a separate compound at one end of the courtyard – recalling the arrangement at Verberie and Herblay – the implication being that this was where the leading household lived, whilst the other dwelling units were occupied by their clients or social inferiors.

Open settlement

The proliferation of enclosed settlements in Picardy from La Tène C1 onwards should not blind us to the possibility that unenclosed sites continued to be a significant component of the settlement pattern during the Later Iron Age (particularly in the east of the region, where the process seems to begin significantly later), but are currently under-represented in our data owing to the greater difficulty of finding them. Open sites of La Tène D1–D2 date are not uncommon in the zone to the south, for the most part nucleated settlements such as La Cheppe, Camp de Mourmelon, in Marne (Chossenot 1997); Meulan, L'Île Belle; Nanterre, Les Guignons; and Varennes-sur-Seine along the Seine valley (Poux 2004); and far smaller farms like Châtenay-sur-Seine and Grisy-sur-Seine (Horard-Herbin *et al.* 2000).

As yet, very few Later Iron Age open settlements are known in the west of Picardy. Nevertheless, wherever systematic investigations have been carried out over a large area – for example along the A16 in Somme (Colin 2000) and in the Oise valley (Malrain 2000) – enough unenclosed sites have been found to imply that they were a regular feature of the Later Iron Age landscape, both on the chalk plateau and the gravel terraces.[48] It remains to be seen whether analysis of developer-funded sites will yield evidence of unenclosed phases pre-dating enclosed settlements – of which there are examples further south, like Rungis (Rimbault 1994) – or, for that matter, post-dating them.

The well-known La Tène C2 building found by Agache at Verberie, Le Buisson Campin (Blanchet *et al.* 1983), may similarly be part of an unenclosed settlement, since any enclosure might have been expected to show from the air, whilst equally large buildings are known at two other open settlements: one nearby at Longueuil-Sainte-Marie, Les Gros Grès, of La Tène D2 date (Malrain 2000); the other at Berry-au-Bac, Le Chemin de la Pêcherie, beside the river Aisne, which dates to La Tène D1a (Dubouloz and Plateaux 1983). A solitary late ditch at the latter site yielded a group of Italian amphorae (Hénon 1991) – amongst the earliest Roman imports known in the area – suggesting that, in the Aisne valley at least, the presence of a surrounding ditch was not (yet?) an essential status attribute.

In general, and as perhaps expected, there does seem to be rather more evidence of open settlement in the east of the region. Whilst these include some long-lived farmsteads like Berry-au-Bac, Le Vieux Tordoir and Juvincourt, Le Gué de Mauchamp, which were eventually abandoned at the end of La Tène C2 (Bayard 1989; Pommepuy *et al.* 2000), the majority are new sites – whether completely open like Le Chemin de la Pêcherie, Beaurieux, Les Grèves, and Damary (Haselgrove 1996), or partially enclosed like Ciry-Salsogne and Pontavert – which were mostly not occupied before La Tène D1.

All these sites appear to be fairly small, although not of low status – if the frequent presence of potin coins (largely absent from the Oise valley sites) and/or Dressel 1 amphorae is anything to go by. As a larger open settlement (as in nearly everything else), Acy-Romance remains unparalleled in the region, although Lambot believes he may have located a similar agglomeration on the chalk of the middle Aisne valley at Avançon, 8 km to the east (Lambot and Méniel 2000, 132).[49] Each of the three living quarters at Acy-Romance is ranged around a courtyard of about a hectare in extent. Many of the habitation units – comprising houses with accompanying barns and raised granaries, and in the case of the eastern courtyard, grain silos – were rebuilt up to three times on the same spot.

Based on their analysis of the buildings, associated finds and variations in meat consumption, Lambot (1999; 2002) and Méniel (1998; 1999) have suggested that each courtyard was the focus of a separate socio-occupational group (Fig. 6 above); within each of these groups, further internal gradations of status and wealth are apparent. In the northern court, which has the largest houses, the emphasis was on animal husbandry and secondary products; in the eastern court, the buildings are simpler, and it is here that the grain silos are found, suggesting more concern with arable cultivation; finally, the southern court, nearest the cult area, yielded a concentration of metalworking debris (*ibid.*). This industrial activity was not, however, on the scale that we find at the nucleated settlements that developed in many other regions of France in the century preceding the appearance of *oppida* (Buchsenschutz 2006), of which Levroux is the best known, and Bobigny the closest. Nor on current evidence were these other nucleated settlements divided up rigidly along ritual and social lines in the same way as Acy-Romance – at Bobigny, for example, the pattern of meat consumption and other activities appears fairly homogeneous throughout the occupied area (Marion *et al.* 2005) – although none of them of course has been excavated on anything approaching the same scale.

Late Iron Age settlement nucleation: the culmination of enclosure

As elsewhere in Gaul, the emergence of fortified *oppida* in Picardy (Fig. 8) in the latter part of La Tène D1 and above all during La Tène D2 was only one of a number of major changes in the archaeological record at this period. Many of these have already been mentioned, including the reappearance of individual rich burials; the altered nature of activity at religious sanctuaries; the minting of inscribed coinage; and the arrival of the first Italian imports. In Picardy at least, there is also clear evidence of increased instability in the rest of the settlement pattern in La Tène D2 when the occupation of *oppida* was at its peak (Haselgrove 1996). Many more

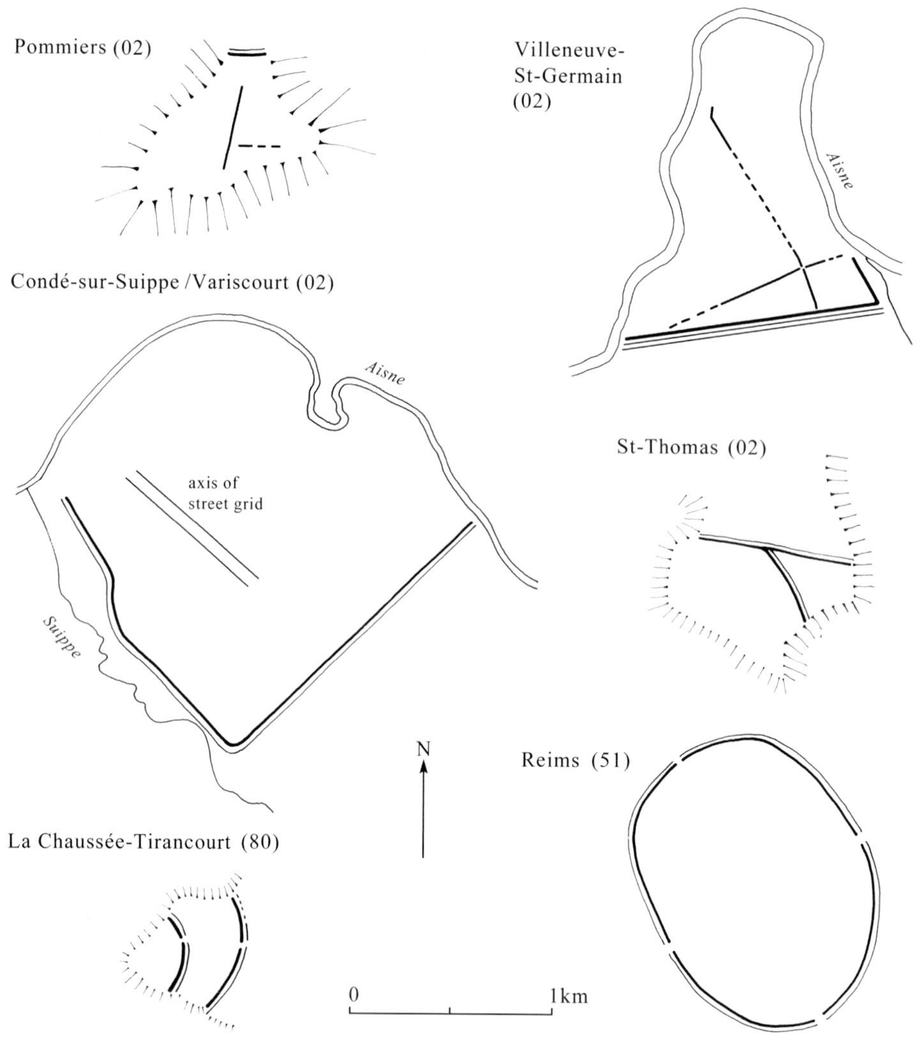

Fig. 8. Late Iron Age oppida in Picardy.

rural settlements were abandoned than were founded, apparently by a margin of four or five to one – the first time this had happened in the region since La Tène C1 and following a peak in La Tène D1 (Malrain *et al.* 2005) – resulting in a net reduction in the number of inhabited sites.

There is also remarkably little continuity at individual sites, even allowing for shifts to nearby locations. In the Aisne valley, not one farmstead can be certainly shown to have been continuously occupied from La Tène D1 or the start of La Tène D2 through to the early Roman period (Haselgrove 1996).[50] On the contrary, several sites including Bazoches, Beaurieux, Limé, and Pontavert experienced an apparent hiatus of one or two generations in the mid first century BC, before eventually being reoccupied at the end of La Tène D2 or in the early Augustan period (*ibid.*). Settlements occupied in La Tène D2b seem to be just as rare everywhere else. Rather than seeing *oppida* in evolutionary terms as signifying the emergence of a fully developed settlement hierarchy (e.g. Pion 1990), we therefore need to ask whether their appearance is bound up with the increased instability of rural sites.

This is not the place to review all the different explanations that have been suggested to explain the rise of fortified *oppida*. Many authors regard economic and political centralisation as the paramount factors, noting how the monumental defences and entrances often privilege display over defensive efficiency (e.g. Buchsenschutz 2004; Fichtl 2005). Others accord greater significance to internal or external crises and military contingencies (e.g. Collis 1984). It is not difficult to think of processes that might have led to increased instability in northern France at this time; they include intensified competition to control resources in a more densely populated landscape; upheavals linked to the formation of a more hierarchical society (as the burial evidence in some areas perhaps implies); increased raiding on neighbouring territories to obtain slaves and booty to exchange for newly-available Italian wine or luxuries; and renewed migration from across the Rhine by peoples searching for new land. In this latter context, the dendrochronological date of 114–112 BC for the building of the first ramparts at Metz in eastern Belgic Gaul (Faye *et al.* 1990) is highly suggestive, given Caesar's claim that the Belgae successfully prevented the Cimbri and Teutones from invading their territory (*Gallic War* II, 4). The Roman invasion certainly gave rise to further rampart building – shown by a further date of 55 BC for the refurbishment of the defences at Metz.

The majority of *oppida* in Picardy occupy elevated positions on promontories or the plateau tops, and enclose less than 50 ha,[51] but it is the two massive low-lying sites at Condé-sur-Suippe and Villeneuve-Saint-Germain, 40 km apart from one another in the Aisne valley, which have become the best known, thanks to the major excavations there in the 1970s and 1980s (Constantin *et al.* 1982; Debord 1982; Pion 1987).[52] Neither settlement had immediately antecedent occupation – although there was an earlier cult enclosure at Villeneuve-Saint-Germain (Debord 1981). Condé-sur-Suippe is the earlier of the two and was inhabited wholly within La Tène D1, whilst the main occupation at Villeneuve-Saint-Germain dates to La Tène D2a, although activity possibly carried on at a reduced scale for a while after this (Pion 1996b). Only 5 km from Villeneuve-Saint-Germain is the large promontory fort at Pommiers, which was extensively explored in the 1880s (Vauvillé 1903–4) and is thought to be its successor, whilst another major plateau-edge *oppidum* at Saint-Thomas, also known as Vieux-Laon, is only 13 km from Condé-sur-Suippe.

Both the valley-bottom *oppida* were evidently laid out according to a pre-conceived plan, implying they resulted from an individual or collective decision to regroup there, rather than a more gradual concentration of people at the site (Haselgrove 1996). At Condé-sur-Suippe, the street grid was traced over an area of more than 3 ha (Fig. 8), dividing the settlement up into a series of *insulae*, within which different craft activities were practised, in one case large-scale ironworking, in another bronze- and ironworking; there was also a large square or open space (Massy 1983; Pion *et al.* 1997). A second excavated area 350 m to the south-east yielded further evidence of streets, house compounds, and workshops (Cadoux 1981). At Villeneuve-Saint-Germain, the interior is subdivided by cruciform ditches into unequal quarters, each with distinct types of buildings and artefacts, and characterised by differing patterns of butchery and meat consumption (Auxiette 1996), very reminiscent of Acy-Romance; the three excavated zones are interpreted as being for living, agricultural storage, and industrial activity respectively (Debord 1990). A similar arrangement of ditches exists at Pommiers (Haselgrove 1990; 1996; Debord 2001, 15), implying that the site that succeeded Villeneuve-Saint-Germain was similarly subdivided. It is difficult to avoid the conclusion that like the inhabitants of Acy-Romance, the population of the two *oppida* was segregated along socio-occupational lines, with the clear implication that regional social organisation was based on some sort of caste system.

The partition ditches at both Pommiers and Villeneuve-Saint-Germain yielded large numbers of coins, brooches, and other finds like rouelles, whilst the ditches at the latter site were also covered by a large timber gallery of some kind (Debord *et al.* 1988). The coins were initially viewed as losses from commercial activity, but it is far more likely that the ditches had a symbolic role in addition to a functional one, and that the finds – many of which were in the upper fills – were offerings. This would be particularly apposite in a caste system, where the higher castes may be seen as being at risk of pollution by contact with the occupations of lower ones, but would still have had to cross the boundaries between them on account of the economic interdependence of the different groups.

Another suggestion – not incompatible with the view that the Villeneuve ditches were also important symbolic boundaries – is that the timber galleries above them were voting installations (Peyre 2000). A palisaded structure, which may have had this purpose, has recently been excavated at the *oppidum* of the Titelberg in Luxembourg (Metzler *et al.* 2006); it takes the form of a series of long parallel corridors and had apparently been erected and dismantled on more than one occasion. In consequence, the eastern end of the Titelberg has been reinterpreted as a vast public space, where the population of the area assembled for political and religious meetings, ceremonies, elections and fairs, and to muster to arms in times of war (*ibid.*), very much as is also suggested for larger sanctuaries like Fesques in western Belgic Gaul. Indeed, as Metzler *et al.* note, a palisaded structure resembling the one at the Titelberg, positioned right in front of the shrine, forms part of the final layout at Gournay-sur-Aronde (Brunaux *et al.* 1985, Phase V).

Both Condé-sur-Suippe and Villeneuve-Saint-Germain are in the kind of natural locations – the former at a confluence, the latter in a meander of the Aisne (Fig. 8) and just opposite the long-lived cemetery complex at Bucy-le-Long – which could well have been used as periodic meeting places before a decision was taken to occupy the sites permanently, as Metzler *et al.* (2006) have suggested was the case at the Titelberg and many other *oppida*. Either *oppidum* could also have been the site of a formal sanctuary, whether earlier in date, or contemporary with the main occupation. At Condé, the street grid leads towards the confluence of the Aisne and the Suippe, and geophysical survey has detected a possible ditched enclosure to the west of the main residential area, the rear of which would be formed by the confluence. At Villeneuve, Vauvillé (1907) identified a possible smaller enclosure at the northern extremity of the meander to add to the earlier cult enclosure excavated by Debord (1981). Numerous *oppida* in western Belgic Gaul are associated with earlier or contemporary sanctuaries (Fichtl 1994), most notably Gournay-sur-Aronde itself, where another unusually large *oppidum* (*c.* 100 ha) was constructed in La Tène D2 on the plateau beside the abandoned sanctuary, which was itself refurbished either then or in the early Augustan period when the *oppidum* was still intensively occupied (Brunaux *et al.* 1985).

Surprisingly in view of the investment of labour required to construct the enormous defences enclosing the two Aisne valley *oppida* – *c.* 3.5 km long at Condé-sur-Suippe, 1.5 km at Villeneuve-Saint-Germain – neither site was occupied for much more than a generation, as the homogeneity of the material and lack of intercutting features attests. Given the rarity of contemporary rural settlements near either site, it seems likely that most of the inhabitants were drawn from the immediate environs, whatever factors caused them to abandon their homes and live instead at these fortified sites, even if only temporarily. Indeed, a farm excavated at Les Étomelles, in 2001, only 800 m from Villeneuve-Saint-Germain, appears to have been abandoned at the end of La Tène D1, just as the *oppidum* was founded (Hénon 2001). Many of the craft activities at both sites were closely linked to agriculture – leather and textiles were particularly important – and none of them appear to be unique to the *oppida*, even the minting of coins, which is attested at several sanctuaries (see above). Apart from briquetage, evidence of long-distance exchange includes amphorae and a small number of other Roman imports.

Given the evidence of movement from low-lying sites to more defensible upland locations during the first century BC elsewhere in Gaul (e.g. Buchsenschutz 2004; Fichtl 2005), it seems likely that the rapid evacuation of these two valley-bottom *oppida* should be seen as part of a wider trend not confined to Belgic Gaul. As I have shown previously (Haselgrove 1995; 1996), the two plateau-edge forts each appear to follow on directly from their particular neighbour, Saint-Thomas being occupied during La Tène D2a, Pommiers from La Tène D2b to the early Augustan period, when it was in turn abandoned for the Roman foundation of *Augusta Suessionum* in the valley below. Limited excavations at Pommiers in the late 1980s identified two phases of building on the same alignment just behind the rampart (Brun and Robert 1988), whilst a recent geophysical survey at Saint-Thomas yielded evidence of intensive occupation in the interior, apparently adhering to a regular layout similar to the valley-bottom sites (Lambot *et al.* 1998).[53] Several other Belgic *oppida* in plateau locations also appear to have been founded in La Tène D2 (Fichtl 1994). Only two other major low-lying *oppida* are known in the area; one of these, the Camp d'Attila at La Cheppe (Marne), is contemporary with Condé-sur-Suippe (Chossenot 1997), whilst at Reims, the defences give the impression of being integral with the early Roman roads to Lyons and Trier (Neiss 1984) and may have been a later addition to an existing settlement.

Outside the Aisne valley, there has been little recent work on *oppida*. The only other sites investigated on any scale in the study area are Gournay-sur-Aronde and La Chaussée-Tirancourt (Fig. 8), above the Somme valley. Following excavations between 1983–90, the outer rampart at the latter site was interpreted as a Roman camp built by Gaulish auxiliaries between *c.* 40–20 BC (Brunaux *et al.* 1990). However, the assemblage has elements that go back to the start of La Tène D2b, so this might well be an instance of later military re-use of an existing site (Haselgrove 1996; 1999). Elsewhere, dating rests largely on older finds and on the character of the defences. All the principal Late Iron Age rampart types are represented in the study area, but once again there is a division between the west of the region and further inland. The Fécamp type of massive earthen bank and wide-bottomed ditch is concentrated in western Picardy and Upper Normandy, whereas further east, ramparts with horizontal or vertical timber-framing are commoner (Fichtl 1994; 2005). At Villeneuve-Saint-Germain, the rampart seems to be intermediate between a *Murus Gallicus* and the earlier, Ehrang variety (Debord 1995). Examples of the classic *Murus Gallicus* do occasionally occur, as at Montigny L'Engrain and Saint-Thomas in Aisne and Avesnelles in Nord, but are commoner on sites like Metz and the Titelberg further to the east

Many ramparts evidently went through major refurbishments, which cautions against adopting an over-simple classification based on surface remains alone. At La Chaussée-Tirancourt, for example, the first rampart phase was of true Fécamp type, whereas its successor was provided with internal framing and stone facing (Fichtl 1994), while at Gournay-sur-Aronde, a rampart of Fécamp type was replaced by a *Murus Gallicus* (Brunaux *et al.* 1985). At Saint-Thomas, however, it is the other way round: the principal earthwork is a *Murus Gallicus*, whereas the secondary rampart in the interior is of Fécamp construction. Inturned entrances are commonest, but overlapping and simple gap entrances also occur. The early rampart at the Titelberg was reconstructed no fewer than three times between La Tène D1 and D2, each time employing different methods of construction – the phase 4 *Murus Gallicus* is the most monumental of all (Metzler 1995) – providing a reminder that not all *oppida* in Belgic Gaul were used for such short periods as those in the Aisne valley.

In conclusion, the foundation of the two *oppida* in Picardy about which we know most, Condé-sur-Suippe and Villeneuve-Saint-Germain, appears to fit well with the kind of crisis model advocated by Collis (1984), although why (part of) their populations should apparently have decided to migrate to new sites on the plateau after only a generation is rather more obscure.[54] In the case of Pommiers, which was probably founded in the 50s BC, the Caesarian invasion might have been a factor – the same is true of La Chaussée-Tirancourt – but the other three Aisne valley sites are clearly too early for this to be the case. If any external threat was involved – and there is no particular reason why it should have been – it is more likely to have been the Cimbri and Teutones, although Roman expansion in southern Gaul may also have attracted notice.

As yet, none of the three major Belgic sites named by Caesar, which later became *civitas* capitals, has yielded incontrovertible evidence of mid first century BC occupation. The best candidate is *Durocortorum* (Reims), where Caesar convened a Gallic council in 53 BC (*Gallic War* VI, 44). As I indicated above, the earliest fortification of the site, an oval ditched enclosure of *c.* 110 ha, may be of early Roman date, but evidence of La Tène D2b occupation beneath the Roman city is gradually growing (e.g. Balmelle and Sindonino 2000; Delestrée 1996, 138) and there was an extensive La Tène D1 open settlement nearby, which could be a precursor.[55] Neither *Samarobriva* (Amiens), where Caesar convened a council in 54 BC and where he left his hostages, state papers, heavy baggage and entire winter grain supply in 54–53 BC, nor *Nemetocenna* (Arras), where he over-wintered in 51–50 BC (*Gallic War* V, 24, 47; VIII, 46), have yielded evidence of intensive occupation before the Augustan period, which appears to imply that the foci that preceded these Roman towns were not major settlements.

Three eventualities present themselves. First, these might have been places where periodic assemblies were held, but, whilst important in the political geography of Caesar's day, were not yet major settlements. The place-names offer some support for this idea: *Samarobriva* is literally 'the Somme river crossing', while *Nemetocenna* means 'the forest' (Wightman 1985). If this were the case, Caesar may simply have built a camp of his own nearby, rather like the undated legionary fortress at Folleville, overlooking the Gaulish sanctuary at Rouvroy-les-Merles in Oise (Agache 1978). A second possibility is that the place-name was transferred from a pre-Roman focus nearby; La Chaussée-Tirancourt is only 10 km from Amiens, Étrun less than 5 km outside Arras.

The third possibility, however, is that these 'central places' were more like British territorial *oppida*, such as *Camulodunum* or *Verlamion* (e.g. Bryant this volume). The latter have always seemed different from their European neighbours, extending as they do over large tracts of landscape and including multiple foci, separated by fields. There is no reason, however, why the landscape model of an *oppidum* should not also apply across the Channel. Where we may be going wrong is in thinking of all continental *oppida* as 'dots on the map' in the manner of plateau forts like Pommiers or La Chaussée-Tirancourt. The Gaulish mind could have conceived of an *oppidum* in terms of several elements dispersed over a larger territory, of which a permanent and/or fortified settlement was only one.[56]

Although this concept may seem most relevant to places like Amiens or Arras, it could be argued that the largest *oppida* like Condé-sur-Suippe share this tendency. They occupy significant natural locations; the defining earthworks were too long to defend against a sustained attack and must have been designed primarily to impress people coming to the site; and inside them were segregated living zones and other foci, as well as plenty of open space. The nearby plateau forts to which the population later moved might still have been regarded as part of the same overall complex, other elements of which will have continued to function as before. This is not something that is easy to document archaeologically, but it should not be discounted given the regularity with which shifts in settlement took place in the study area.

The coming of Rome

This leads to two final themes: the nature of early contacts between Belgic Gaul and the Roman world, and the degree to which the Gallic war itself is visible in the archaeological record. On present evidence, Italian wine started reaching southern Picardy in small quantities in the later second century BC (Loughton 2003; Poux 2004), as shown by the discovery of a handful of Graeco-Italic amphorae and vessels transitional between it and the succeeding Dressel 1A type in La Tène D1a contexts at sites such as Bazoches, Les Chantraines and Berry-au-Bac (Hénon 1995; Gransar and Pommepuy 2005). By the early first century BC, Dressel 1 wine amphorae were starting to reach the rest of Picardy as well as the Moselle valley (Haselgrove 1996). It is noticeable that the earliest finds of Italian bronze serving and drinking equipment come from the same area as the Graeco-Italic amphorae, which appears to confirm that the penetration of Belgic Gaul by Italian imports occurred in stages (Haselgrove 1996). Within the study area, however, the overall distribution of amphorae is still far from even, with the majority clustered in the Aisne, Oise, and Somme valleys, and along the upper reaches of the Scarpe, around Arras (Loughton 2003). Whilst this must be partly a function of the relative intensity of research, there has now been enough work on the plateaux to suggest that the clustering may also reflect the role of the river valleys as axes of communication.

As I have shown elsewhere (Haselgrove 1996, 168–73), although the number of Italian amphorae reaching the region rose steadily from La Tène D1b onward, the total amount of wine consumed was still quite small until the later first century BC, even at major settlements like Condé-sur-Suippe or Villeneuve-Saint-German. The implication is that prior to the conquest, imported wine was only drunk by a small section of Belgic society and

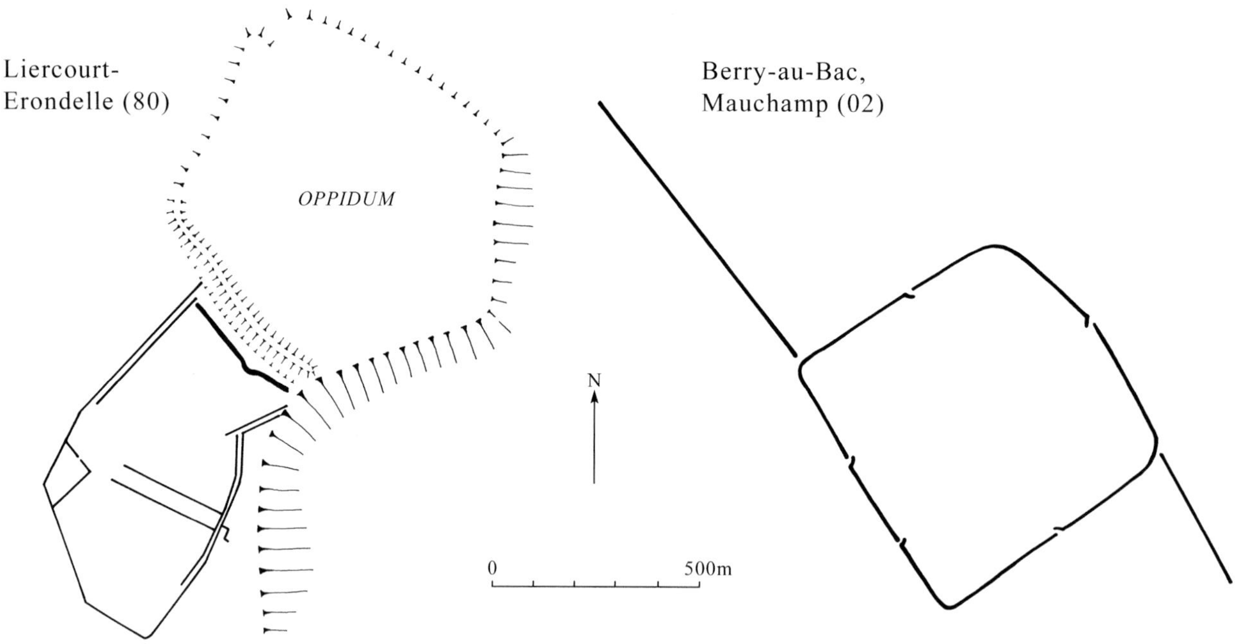

Fig. 9. Probable Caesarian forts at Liercourt-Érondelle, Somme (after Agache 1978) and Berry-au-Bac, Mauchamp Aisne.

probably mainly on special occasions such as banquets and feasts. Indeed, the quantity of Italian imports is sufficiently low compared to central Gaul for them to have been passed on via indigenous economic or social networks, with no Roman citizens involved in the trade until after Julius Caesar's invasion. If so, their presence cannot be taken as an index of early contacts between Belgic Gaul and the Roman world. We do not know whether the recipients even saw these goods as 'Roman'. Whilst their increasing availability must have impacted on indigenous society, this should not be confused with a process of 'becoming Roman', and the models that stress the role of trade with the Mediterranean world in the social and political changes of the period clearly need to be reviewed (*ibid.*, 173–5).

The conquest of Belgic Gaul was a long drawn out affair. Caesar campaigned there extensively every year but one between 57 and 51 BC, and the Romans had to suppress several more revolts over the next quarter century. In view of the suggestion that British archaeologists have been seriously underestimating the extent of warfare and violence in the Iron Age (James 2007), it is instructive briefly to consider the archaeological evidence which this protracted conflict has left behind – which is seemingly very little. As we have already seen, it is difficult enough even to pinpoint the sites mentioned by Caesar, let alone to show that they featured in the conflict. Villeneuve-Saint-Germain and Pommiers are a good example. Either could be the *Noviodunum* of the Suessiones, which Caesar besieged in 57 BC after he had defeated the Belgic coalition (*Gallic War* II, 12), but the dating is not good enough to decide which of the two sites was occupied at the time – indeed both could have been. Equally, both sites could theoretically answer to the name 'new fortification', whilst neither has produced definite evidence of a Roman assault.[57]

In the normal way, military installations are possibly the most obvious archaeological indication that we might expect to find of an ancient war of conquest. In Gaul, however, even these need not be particularly common, as we know of at least one case when Caesar quartered troops in native fortifications and buildings, at *Cenabum* (*Gallic War* VIII, 5). At least two *oppida* in Belgic Gaul, La Chaussée-Tirancourt and the Titelberg, certainly held Roman garrisons in the later first century BC. As the excavations at the former showed, a further complication is that fortifications built by Gaulish auxiliaries in Roman service may be indistinguishable from native ones; the refurbishment of the defences at Metz in 55 BC could just as well reflect Roman occupation, as preparations for defence.

The one fairly certain Caesarian site in the study area is the 41 ha fortification identified in the nineteeth century by archaeologists working for Napoleon III at Mauchamp (Aisne; Fig. 9). This exactly fits Caesar's description of the fortified camp and trenches, which his army constructed on the battlefield beside the river Aisne where he defeated the Belgae in 57 BC (*Gallic War* II, 8).[58] In all probability, the nearby plateau fort at Saint-Thomas is therefore *Bibrax*, the stronghold belonging to the Remi situated eight Roman miles away, which the

Belgic army attacked just before the battle (*ibid.*, II, 6), but here the evidence is suggestive rather than definitive.[59] Another contender for a Caesarian site is Liercourt-Érondelle (Somme), where a Roman fort of about 20 ha is attached to the outside of a 32 ha *oppidum* (Fig. 9). Small-scale trenching by Agache (1978) yielded coins and other material consistent with a mid first century BC date.[60] The complex at Nointel (Oise), which has *claviculae*, has been largely overlooked since the original publication (Matherat 1943), but might repay fresh work.

Most of the other alleged evidence of the Gallic war turns out, on closer inspection, to be a question of more or less hypothesis, and if pressed further, very easily leads to circular arguments. For instance, there were certainly major changes in the character of Belgic coinages in the mid first century BC, but not all of them need be directly linked to the war; indeed, some of them could well belong to the decades on either side (Haselgrove 1999). The same applies to other changes during La Tène D2 such as the reduction in rural settlements or the building of fortified sites, both of which probably have some links to the war, but may have other root causes as well. Attempts to link specific finds with recorded events are generally even more problematic, however tempting this sometimes is.[61] We would do well always to remember how our understanding of the Later Iron Age in Gaul was hampered for years by the refusal of numismatists to reconsider a chronology founded on historical hypothesis in the face of mounting archaeological evidence to the contrary. In short, whilst other finds from northern French sites like Ribemont-sur-Ancre and Gournay-sur-Aronde strongly suggest that we do need to find more room for violence and warfare in our narratives of the period, this will have to be in the abstract, not in terms of specific events.

Conclusion

Judging from the abundant material now available from excavations undertaken in advance of development and from a smaller number of long-term research projects, the principal changes in settlement and society during the Later Iron Age were relatively similar all over Picardy and the surrounding area, as I hope this survey has shown. In particular, from *c.* 300 BC onward, the enclosure of settlements and other types of site became the norm everywhere, and communities throughout the region developed broadly comparable ritual and burial practices, although these were often performed and interpreted somewhat differently at local level. Agricultural intensification is evident everywhere and, if site numbers are a reliable guide, went hand in hand with a steady rise in population, although in the first century BC, this trend was temporarily reversed, and site numbers – if not necessarily population levels – dipped for the first time in two centuries.

Other developments included the rapid spread of coinage and the emergence of various classes of communal or central sites. In many areas, fairly frequent shifts of settlement are apparent – this tendency is not, however, new to the period – and it was other classes of site like cemeteries and sanctuaries that provided the greater degree of permanency. In broad terms, the region shares in the developments evident elsewhere in Gaul at the same time, but there are differences; there is little sign, for example, of the more industrialised nucleated settlements that appeared in many other areas of Gaul in the century preceding the development of the *oppida*. The one large open settlement that has been fully excavated, at Acy-Romance, appears quite different from its contemporaries, a comment that might equally be applied to the large two valley-bottom *oppida* a little further downstream.

The spatial organisation of these sites strongly implies that – at least in the east of the area – Belgic society was founded on a caste system of some kind, or that one was in the process of forming in the Later Iron Age. It would be unwise, however, on present evidence to seek to extend this interpretation to the rest of Picardy, given the consistent differences that this study has revealed between the coastal regions and the area further inland. These concern both the substance of the record – such as the marked concentration of religious sanctuaries, but virtual lack of wealthy burials with Italian imports in western Picardy and Upper Normandy – and in the timing of specific developments, like the delayed adoption of cremation and onset of settlement enclosure, but earlier appearance of *oppida*, in the east. This distinction between western Belgic Gaul and area to the east is also apparent in other spheres of material culture only considered briefly here, such as coinage (Haselgrove 1999). In effect, the archaeological record seems to attest to the reality of the division between the *Belgium* of Caesar's time and the rest of 'Belgic' Gaul, and it is entirely plausible that its inhabitants saw themselves as sharing a common cultural identity distinct from neighbouring groups. There are some indications, too, that this distinction may owe something to the earlier split between Picardy and the Aisne–Marne culture, going back well into the Earlier Iron Age.

Many of the processes apparent in the study area during the Later Iron Age are broadly replicated on the English side of the Channel, although – with the arguable exception of the intensive salt production at settlements near the Somme coast – there are fewer signs, as yet, of the kind of niche specialisation in marginal environments observed in many different areas of lowland Britain at this time. In summer at least, it will often have been an easier journey in the Iron Age from the Thames estuary to the mouth of the

Somme than it was overland to many parts of Britain, a relative ease of communication clearly apparent both in the archaeology and in the few texts from the period (e.g. *Gallic War*, II, 4; V, 12–14). In our renewed quest to write more general narratives of social and cultural change for the Later Iron Age that pay due regard to both the unity and diversity of our material, it is time we abandoned our prevailing insularity, and followed Hawkes' and Dunning's lead and engage fully with the very similar – sometimes identical – archaeology of northern France.

Acknowledgements

Much of the initial research for this paper was undertaken whilst the author was the holder of a Sir Derman Christopherson Fellowship at the University of Durham. I am very grateful to Pam Lowther for many improvements to the text and for drawing the illustrations.

Notes

1. Caesar, of course, clearly elaborated various political or ethnic distinctions in his despatches to serve his own ends at Rome. The reason why he differentiated the Remi from their Belgic neighbours may simply be because they began the war as his allies.
2. In his recent study of the Gaulish *civitas*, Stefan Fichtl (2004) has argued that this was above all a political entity. Thus, whilst individual *civitates* had well-defined territorial limits – albeit in perpetual evolution over time – these cannot be expected to correspond to particular cultural indicators or coin circulation areas. This may be the case, but if so, merely underlines the futility of trying to reconstruct political divisions earlier in the Iron Age.
3. As Loughton (2003, 194) notes, new amphora finds around Arras and along the Somme have reduced the previous emphasis on southern Belgic Gaul noted by Haselgrove (1996) and Roymans (1996a), but larger assemblages of amphorae still appear to be confined to the southern region.
4. But see Roymans (this volume).
5. In the absence of definite dating evidence, these enclosed settlements are often known as *fermes indigènes* to distinguish them from villas and other overtly Roman rural sites.
6. Prior to 1972, only 27 Iron Age sites dating between the third and first centuries BC are recorded as having been excavated, many of them by nineteenth-century pioneers like Frédéric Moreau, who investigated a series of long-lived cemeteries in southern Aisne including Arcy-Sainte-Restitue and Caranda, and Octave Vauvillé, best known for his research on the *oppidum* at Pommiers. Between 1972–81, the number of excavated Later Iron Age sites very nearly doubled as archaeology began to react to the threat posed by gravel extraction and urban expansion, bringing the total to 51. For a detailed review of the impact of rescue archaeology in the three departments that make up modern Picardy, see Malrain *et al.* (2005).
7. The motorways constructed in Picardy since the 1980s are the A26 (between Laon and Reims); the A16 (which continues into Pas-de-Calais); and the A28 and A29 (both of which continue through Seine-Maritime). The first motorways in the region, the A1 and the A4, were built with next to no archaeological work.
8. Unusually, only one Late Iron Age rural settlement is recorded on the 45 km stretch of the TGV Est cutting through the southern tip of Aisne, at Ronchères, Le Bois de la Forge (Malrain 2003). Equally unusually for Late Iron Age rural sites it the region, this one had survived as an earthwork, as a result of its being in woodland, which had protected it from ploughing. This also resulted in exceptionally good preservation of the internal surfaces and of the surrounding bank and ditch; indeed, the latter – by then three-quarters full – was used as a German firing line during the First World War. The site appears to have been occupied continuously from the third century BC to the second century AD, with no significant changes in layout; one of the buildings adjacent to the ditch appears to have been a forge (*ibid.*).
9. If anything, the frequent bridging of wet and dry valleys has created a bias against the lower-lying land.
10. The westernmost enclosed settlement, which is significantly richer in finds than the others, is interpreted as belonging to the owner of the entire complex; it stands next to the stock enclosure and has its own cemetery plot, and is linked to main track running through the area by a separate spur.
11. As shown also by the results of fieldwalking in the Aisne valley, where, despite good aerial coverage (by Boureux), up to 20 new Later Iron Age sites were recorded, many of them on the adjoining slopes and plateaux, as well as numerous lesser scatters (Haselgrove 1996; Pichon 2002).
12. Quite apart from excavations, there have been large numbers of coin finds from metal detecting. The latter is illegal in France, other than as part of an authorised project, and reporting rates are consequently much lower than in Britain, apparently by at least 50% for gold (Haselgrove 2005, 137–8); for other metals, it could well be far more.
13. For a more detailed discussion of the Miron–Metzler chronology, see Haselgrove (1996), 135–8.
14. A group of coins belonging to the so-called Normandy 'sword' series were found in association with around 300 pieces of La Tène C1 weaponry (Delestrée 2001). These 'sword' coins appear to be two stages removed from the earliest *Philippus* imitations found north of the Loire (Sills 2003), in effect pushing the prototypes back into La Tène B2. Lambot (2004) has argued that the coins are intrusive, but this is firmly rejected by the excavator (Brunaux and Delestrée 2005). Two other early gold coins, one of them certainly a Picardy type, was found in later deposits, but were presumably deposited at the same time.
15. There are exceptions. At Orainville, La Croyère (Aisne), a small cemetery that spans the La Tène B2–C1 transition, one of the burials yielded a rich array of grave goods, including a torc (Desenne *et al.* 2005). A second inhumation was surrounded by a rectangular enclosure, but has fewer grave goods. All but one of the eight adult burials were female.
16. Enclosures are fairly rare in the earlier, Aisne–Marne cemeteries and are usually associated with chariot burials; these also tend to be circular or sometimes keyhole shaped, as at Bucy-le-Long, La Héronnière (Pommepuy *et al.*1998), rather than rectangular.
17. As Diepeveen-Jansen (2001, 147) rightly cautions, the actual size is known of only a few Aisne–Marne cemeteries, so the assumption may be erroneous. Only six of over 400 cemeteries listed by Demoule (1999) certainly possess more than 300 tombs; at most, fewer than 100 are recorded. A comparison of the two successive cemeteries at Bucy-le-Long is nevertheless instructive. Both cemeteries were in use for around 125 years: 233 graves are recorded at La Héronnière and an estimated 100–200 were

destroyed without record in the 1960s (Auxiette *et al.* 2002), whereas Le Fond du Petit Marais has only 68 (Pommepuy *et al.* 1998) and is near intact.

18. At La Croizette (one enclosure); La Noue de Barue (two enclosures); and La Noue Mauroy-La Prêle (four enclosures and one group without an enclosure). Only La Croisette and La Noue Mauroy-I are fully published (Lambot *et al.* 1994); for the rest see Lambot and Méniel (2000, 104–20).
19. It is possible that a relative lack of goods and the shallow depth of many early cremations have conspired to make the transition from inhumation seem more abrupt than it actually was. A number of sites have evidence of secondary burials in mounds over the wealthier graves, which will have been particularly vulnerable to destruction by ploughing.
20. The graves – the only ones excavated under modern conditions – were robbed in antiquity (Lambot *et al.* 1994), a continuation of the practice well attested in the earlier Aisne–Marne cemeteries.
21. Contemporary cremations very occasionally occur in the earlier Aisne–Marne cemeteries further east such as Bucy-le-Long (1 in 32 tombs) or Pernant (1 in 65), where they seem to denote important individuals (Pommepuy *et al.* 1998, 87).
22. There are signs that, as further inland, the transition from inhumation to cremation in the part of upper Normandy north of the Seine estuary, may have taken place rather later. At Cottévrard, La Plaine de la Bucaille (Seine-Maritime), for example, where two concentrations of burials associated with a settlement were excavated on the line of A29 (Blancquaert 1998), all the La Tène C1 burials are inhumations; cremation only appears in La Tène C2, recalling the sequence at Le Fond du Petit Marais.
23. At Bouchon, Le Rideau Miquet, for example, the cemetery dates to La Tène C2, whereas the main visible phase of settlement is La Tène D1 (Colin 2000). Care is necessary, however, as in many instances, the failure to find contemporary settlement may simply be due to the absence of work beyond the line of the motorway.
24. A somewhat similar situation is found at Vismes-au-Val (Somme), although there the two founder graves, both dating to La Tène C2–D1, lie within the same enclosure. Both graves contained swords and lances; in addition, what may be the slightly later of the pair was provided with a shield and a cooking grill (Barbet and Bayard 1996).
25. Another very rich burial was excavated in 2001 at Raillencourt-Sainte-Olle in Nord, some 28 km east-south-east of Arras (Bouche 2001), just north of the study area. As at Marcelcave, the grave goods included a bucket, a cauldron, and a pair of firedogs, but also other items such as a bronze basin and a pair of blacksmith's tongs. The burial occupied a substantial pit, around which was a rectangular timber structure with 14 posts. Three of six secondary burials also included buckets, and, in one instance, an Italian Aylesford type pan and another pair of firedogs. The whole ensemble occupied the northern half of a ditched rectangular enclosure. The poorly recorded vault burials containing Dressel 1 amphora and firedogs found in the Arras area in the nineteenth century were presumably similar to Raillencourt. The presence of Italian imports in these rich graves around Arras merely further highlights the absence of a similar horizon of burials in the west of the study area. Other rich Later Iron Age burials with firedogs have been found at Beine, Le Montéqueux (Marne); Bouchon, Le Rideau Miquet, grave 15 (Baray 1997); La Maillerie-sur-Seine (Seine-Maritime); and Poulainville-Amiens, Les Motellettes (Buchez 2003).
26. This may to a certain extent reflect differing histories of research in the two areas. In the middle Aisne valley, Lambot has noted several cemeteries close to unexcavated rural farmsteads known from cropmarks (to say nothing of the cemeteries ringing Acy-Romance). A good example is Bernicourt, La Louvière (Ardennes), where the cemetery is on a slope, 400 m south of the settlement and visible from it (Lambot 2002a). On the other hand, none of the rural settlements excavated further down the Aisne valley has an integral cemetery. In this region, most of the known cremation cemeteries are on the adjacent slopes and in side valleys (Haselgrove 1996), although small groups of burials are occasionally found on the gravels near contemporary settlements, as at Limé, Les Sables (Soupart *et al.* 2005).
27. Some cemeteries were connected to settlements by linear earthworks or trackways. At Jaux, Le Camp du Roi, in the Oise valley, an unenclosed burial ground was found 120 m along a boundary ditch leading from the settlement (Malrain *et al.* 1996). At Arras-Actiparc, one of the cemeteries was situated beside a track, which branched off the main route through the area (Jacques and Prilaux 2003), while at Acy-Romance one of the trackways radiating from the site leads directly to La Noue Mauroy (Lambot and Méniel 2000).
28. The cemetery at Abbeville, La Sole de Baillon (Baray 1998), which has 92 graves, is exceptional.
29. Apart from Allonne (Oise), where many of the tombs contain the remains of four or five individuals (Paris 1998).
30. The remains of over 120 individuals have been identified amongst the mass of bone lying on the ground beside the enclosure ditch, all adolescent or young adult males (Brunaux and Arcelin 2003, 67). At Gournay, three of the twelve individuals sexed were females (Brunaux *et al.* 1985).
31. Unlike Gournay, the overall interpretation of Ribemont and even the basic sequence have given rise to much debate (see also note 14). What were already complex deposits have been made even more difficult to understand by the overlying Roman remains, to say nothing of World War I trenches. Brunaux maintains that the main elements of the complex date to the third century BC, after which there was little activity until the Augustan period, when the later sanctuary was established (Brunaux and Arcelin 2003, 64–8). However, Fercoq du Leslay (2000) argues that the trapezoidal 'annexe' and a polygonal enclosure within it were added at the end of La Tène D1, when he thinks the sanctuary was founded. Without detailed publication, it is difficult to see how this can be resolved. The poorly recorded site at Moeuvres in Nord has some similarities to Ribemont (Arcelin and Brunaux 2003, 60–1). So, too, does Meaux, La Bauve (Seine-et-Marne), where a large collection of weapons was deposited in the late fourth century BC, but no structures have been yet been found pre-dating the first century AD (Marion 2005).
32. Further north, offerings of weapons and valuables in rivers and other significant natural locations remained the main visible form of ritual activity until after the Roman conquest (Roymans 1996a; this volume), but such activities are not especially prevalent in the Aisne–Ardennes area. It is however possible that, as in southern Champagne (Wellington 2005), a rather higher proportion of ritual activity was focused on cemetery enclosures than it was nearer the coast, and the higher level of conspicuous consumption represented by individual graves should also be borne in mind.
33. The enclosure occupies the highest point of the site, at the eastern edge of an area of higher ground (as at Montmartin). The residential quarters are situated on slightly sloping ground to the north and east of the sanctuary complex.
34. In the sanctuary area, the sheep pits are the only major features dating to the period of decline, implying that there was also a

dramatic change in the character of the activities performed here.

35. The human remains from the residential area at Acy-Romance amount to three sitting burials (in the northern quarter of the site) and the bones of over 50 individuals in other features. Finds in storage pits included four cremation burials, but no complete inhumations. Like grain silos themselves (Gransar 2000), pit burials are commoner in the Earlier Iron Age (Séguier and Delattre 2005), although a few Later Iron Age examples are known in the study area: one at Fresnes-Mazancourt (Somme) dating to La Tène C1 (Rougier *et al.* 2003); another at Baron, Le Buisson-Saint-Cyr (Oise), of La Tène D2 date, and associated with a large storage vessel or *dolium* (Fémolant 1997). Since such vessels increasingly supplanted storage pits in the Late Iron Age, this might be seen as supporting the widespread view that the pit burial tradition expressed a link between death and fertility (e.g. Delattre 2000). Unlike pit burials in Britain, those in northern France do not seem to follow particular alignments (Bradley 2005).
36. This hypothesis was founded entirely on aerial survey and fieldwalking data (Haselgrove 1996). However, the presence of Later Iron Age settlement on the plateau in Aisne has now been confirmed by excavation at Ploisy, a few kilometres south of Soissons, where three successive enclosures dating between La Tène C2 and La Tène D2 were recently found in an area of only 64 ha (Gransar 2003).
37. Shown by the frequency with which ditches were renewed at many sites beside palaeochannels, such as Missy-sur-Aisne, or Longueil-Sante-Marie, L'Orméon, and Verberie, La Plaine d'Hermeuse, in Oise (Malrain and Pinard 2000).
38. The large enclosure at Vermand, Champs des Lavoirs, was apparently constructed in separate segments, possibly by different groups (Malrain *et al.* 2002, 158).
39. Further to the east, the mix of cultivated cereals differs yet again (Buchsenschutz 2006), typical of the regionality apparent from one part of Europe to another.
40. In view of the lack of excavated settlements dating to the third century BC in Pommepuy's study area, and until more sites of this period in the west of Picardy have been published, it seems premature to conclude that rotary querns were not introduced until the early second century BC. The point is underlined by the recent discovery at Bobigny, La Vache à l'Aise (Seine-Saint-Denis), of no fewer than seven upper stones and three lower stones of well-made rotary querns in contexts attributed to Phase 2 – which Marion dates to La Tène C1–C2 (2004; Marion *et al.* 2005).
41. For instance, based on pit contents, sheep was the most important species at rural farmsteads, followed by pig and then cattle, but this trend is reversed in ditch assemblages (Méniel 1996).
42. Domestic fowl is widespread on Later Iron Age settlements and also increased noticeably in importance in burials during La Tène D1–D2 (Méniel 2001). Fish, on the other hand, is uncommon, as in Britain and Belgium at the same period (Dobney and Ervnyck this volume). Several of the sites where it is present, like Acy-Romance and Vermand, have yielded evidence of large-scale feasting, which might indicate that it was only eaten on special occasions (cf. Willis this volume).
43. Given the apparent avoidance of the alluvial terraces of the Aisne and Vesle valleys for settlement in La Tène C1, earlier enclosures may yet turn up on higher ground, where there has been little work; indeed the recent discovery of a La Tène C2 enclosed site on the plateau at Ploisy (note 36 above) points that way. Enclosures also seem to begin earlier on the chalk plateau in northern Aisne, as at Vermand (Lemaire 2000) and the ZAC A26–A28 at Saint-Quentin (Pichon 2002), where large enclosures dating to La Tène C1 have been excavated. So far, Bazoches, Les Chantraines, dating to La Tène D1a, is the earliest completely enclosed settlement known on the gravel terraces. A number of La Tène C2 sites are associated with shorter lengths of ditch, as at Berry-au-Bac, Le Vieux Tordoir or Ciry-Salsogne, Le Bruy (Pommepuy *et al.* 2000) and might have had their perimeters completed by banks or hedges, but, if so, the concept of enclosure differed significantly from that among communities nearer the coast.
44. See note 8 above. An external bank is attested for one of the funerary enclosures at Tartigny (Massy *et al.* 1986).
45. The practice is commoner in the Earlier Iron Age (Gransar 2000).
46. A total of 4 sites are assigned to ranks 1–2, as opposed to 13 to ranks 3–4 (Malrain and Pinard 2000, 182). Somewhat confusingly, in this article, rank 4 is used to denote sites at the top of the hierarchy and rank 1 for the sites of lowest status, whereas in other publications, it is the other way round (e.g. Malrain 2000; Malrain *et al.* 2002).
47. The other two sites in the group are Juvincourt, Le Gué de Mauchamp, and Limé, Les Terres Noires. Beaurieux and Verneuil-en-Hallatte subsequently developed into Roman villas, whilst at Limé the early Roman enclosure is just 600 m away from the well-known Villa d'Ancy.
48. Two of the 13 Later Iron Age settlements partially investigated on the A16 in Somme appear to be unenclosed: at Argoeuves and Saint-Vaast-en-Chaussée (Colin 2000). Unenclosed and/or partly enclosed settlements of La Tène D1–D2 date have been excavated on the Oise terraces at Longueil-Sainte-Marie, Les Gros Grès; Pont-Saint-Maxence, Le Jonquoire; and Verberie, Les Gats (Malrain 2000).
49. Lambot suggests there may have been another site of this kind accompanying the large cemetery at Thugny-Trugny, 8 km west of Acy-Romance. The large open settlement at La Cheppe, Camp de Mourmelon (Chossenot 1997) is another candidate. Other possibilities are Nizy-le-Comte (Aisne), where there is La Tène D1 occupation beneath the important Gallo-Roman sanctuary (Pion 1996a); and Reims (Marne), where traces of an extensive La Tène D1 open settlement have been found beneath the La Tène D2b *oppidum* and Gallo-Roman town (Delestrée 1996, 138).
50. This statement remains just as true a decade later as when it was written, despite the many new excavations in the intervening period. One possible exception to the general rule is the site at Mont-Notre-Dame, Vaudigny (Pion 1996a), which occupies a particularly circumscribed location beside the river Vesle; only a small area was excavated, so it is difficult to be certain. Pion also suggests that the settlement at Bucy-le-Long, Le Fond du Petit Marais, was occupied from the earlier first century BC, but the earliest published evidence is of La Tène D2b date.
51. There are also smaller promontory forts, between *c.* 8–15 ha, which many authors consider too small to classify as *oppida* (e.g. Collis 1984; Fichtl 2005), but were part of the Late Iron Age settlement pattern (e.g. Pion 1990).
52. Current estimates of the absolute dates of occupation are *c.* 125–85 BC for Condé-sur-Suippe and *c.* 90–50 BC for Villeneuve-Saint-Germain. For more detailed discussion of the dating of the sites and their relationship to the plateau-edge *oppida* at Saint-Thomas and Pommiers, see Haselgrove 1995; 1996.
53. The interior of Saint-Thomas is subdivided into unequal parts by a second massive rampart (Lobjois 1966). This is usually seen as a later reduction of the extent of the defended area, but could have been some other kind of boundary. From the large number of coin finds, it seems likely that there was also an important

sanctuary in the main/western enclosure (Delestrée 1996).

54. We may be wrong to stress the short-lived nature of occupation at the valley-bottom *oppida*. Small-scale shifts of location were, after all, a regular occurrence on the gravel terraces, and similar traditions of generational movement of settlements are well known elsewhere in the north of Gaul (e.g. Gerritsen 2003).
55. See note 48 above.
56. Poux (2005) has applied a similar idea to the complex of Late Iron Age sites on the Grande Limagne in the Auvergne, which he compares to the Classical city-state complete with territory.
57. Vauvillé's (1903–4) claim to have identified Roman siegeworks in front of Pommiers is difficult to verify nowadays as the area suffered badly during the First World War. For a recent discussion of the difficulties of identifying either *oppidum* as *Noviodunum*, see Debord 2001.
58. The identification was long disputed, both because the *claviculae* at the entrances were regarded as anachronistic (Wightman 1985), and because the nineteenth-century excavations produced second-century AD finds (Demoule and Ilett 1985). Both objections can now be set aside. *Claviculae* were used in 52 BC to defend Camp C at Alésia (Reddé and von Schnurbein 2001), while fieldwalking and aerial photography indicate that the supposed northern *castellum* trenched by Napoleon III is actually a Gallo-Roman settlement. The only finds from fieldwalking the interior of the fortress are a few sherds of Dressel 1 amphora, while Bayard's excavation of the southern lateral ditch down by the river Aisne yielded nothing which would be out of place in a mid first century BC context.
59. Lambot and Casagrande (1997) have suggested that a bronze coin of Ebusus (Ibiza) found in the interior of the *oppidum* was brought there by the Balearic slingers sent by Caesar to the aid of the garrison (*Gallic War* II, 70). The coin is the only known French find of an Ebusus issue north of the Rhone delta, but there are six from East Kent – where Caesar campaigned in 55 and 54 BC.
60. This could even have been one of Caesar's winter camps, with troops being quartered in the fort and in the *oppidum*. The site is only 35 km away from *Samarobriva*, around which three legions wintered in separate camps in 54–53 BC (*Gallic War* V, 53).
61. Interestingly, the finds at Liercourt-Érondelle include two Kentish potins (Delestrée 2003). British potins have turned up at seven other sites in northern France – mostly sanctuaries (including Fesques), but also in an early Roman fortlet in the ZI d'Actiparc (Jacques and Prilaux 2003) – with an intriguing outlier at Corent (Puy-de-Dôme), where four coins have been found. Corent is only 8 km from Gergovia, the site of Caesar's defeat by Vercingetorix in 52 BC, making one wonder whether Kentish potins were amongst the booty taken from Britain in 54 BC by Caesar's army. This is certainly not the only possible explanation for their presence in France, however, and at least three coins (all from Fesques) seem to be earlier exports.

Bibliography

Agache, R. 1978. *La Somme pré-romaine et romaine d'après les prospections aériennes*. Amiens: Mémoires de la Société des Antiquaires de Picardie 24.

Arcelin, P. and Brunaux, J.-L. 2003. Cultes et sanctuaires en France à l'âge du fer, *Gallia* 60, 1–268.

Auxiette, G. 1996. La faune de l'oppidum de Villeneuve-St-Germain (Aisne): quartiers résidentiels, quartiers artisanales, *Revue Archéologique de Picardie* 1996 1/2, 27–98.

Auxiette, G. 2000. Les rejets non domestiques des établissements ruraux du Hallstatt final à La Tène finale dans la vallée de l'Aisne et de la Vesle, in Marion and Blancquaert 2000, 169–180.

Auxiette, G. and Malrain, F. 2005. *Hommages à Claudine Pommepuy*. Amiens: Revue Archéologique de Picardie Numéro Spécial 22.

Auxiette, G., Desenne, S. and Pommepuy, C. 2002. Des viatiques et des banquets: alimentation des défunts, alimentation des vivants sur la nécropole de La Tène ancienne de Bucy-le-Long (Aisne), in Méniel and Lambot 2002, 317–336.

Auxiette, G., Desenne, S., Gransar, F. and Pommepuy, C. 2000. Structuration générale du site de Braine "La Grange des Moines" (Aisne) à La Tène finale et particularités: présentation présentation préliminaire, *Revue Archéologique de Picardie* 2000 1/2, 97–103.

Bakels, C. 1999. Archaeobotanical investigations in the Aisne valley, northern France, from the Neolithic up to the early Middle Ages, *Vegetation History and Archaeobotany* 8, 71–77.

Balmelle, A. and Sindonino, C. 2000. Reims, Médiathèque, *Bilan Scientifique Champagne-Ardenne 2000*, 116–117.

Baray, L. 1997. Les tombes aristocratiques de La Tène C2 de Bouchon "Le Rideau Miquet" (Somme), *Archäologisches Korrespondenzblatt* 27, 113–126.

Baray, L. 1998. Les cimitières à cremation de la basse vallée de la Somme d'après les découvertes de l'autoroute A16 nord, *Revue Archéologique de Picardie* 1998 1/2, 211–231.

Baray, L. 2002. Les tombes à cremation des cimitières de Saint-Sauveur, Bouchon et Vignacourt, in Guichard and Perrin 2002, 119–138.

Baray, L. 2004. *Pratiques funéraires et sociétés de l'âge du Fer dans le Bassin Parisien*. Paris: Gallia Supplément 56.

Barbet, P. and Bayard, D. 1996. Les tombes de Vismes-au-Val (Somme) dans le contexte du *Belgium*, *Revue Archéologique de Picardie* 1996 3/4, 177–188.

Bayard, D. 1989. Vestiges d'un village gaulois établi au bord de l'Aisne au "Gué de Mauchamp" à Juvincourt-et-Damary, in *Archéologie: grands travaux en Picardie: Autoroute A26*, 96–97. Amiens: Revue Archéologique de Picardie.

Bayard, D. 1996. La Romanisation des campagnes en Picardie à la lumière des fouilles récentes: problèmes d'échelles et de critères, in Bayard and Collart 1996, 157–184.

Bayard, D. and Collart, J.-L. (eds) 1996. *De la ferme indigène à la villa Romaine: la Romanisation des campagnes de la Gaule*. Amiens: Revue Archéologique de Picardie Numéro Spécial 11.

Blanchet, J.-C., Buchsenchutz, O. and Méniel, P. 1983. La maison de la Tène moyenne de Verberie (Oise), "Le Buisson-Campin", in *Les Celtes dans le nord du bassin Parisien*, 96–126. Amiens: Revue Archéologique de Picardie 1983 1.

Blancquaert, G. 1998. Cottévrard "La Plaine de la Bucaille" (Seine-Maritime). Présentation préliminaire de la nécropole laténienne, *Revue Archéologique de Picardie* 1998 1/2, 171–183.

Bouche, K. 2001. Raillencourt-Sainte-Olle, Extension Actipôle de l'A2, *Bilan Scientifique Nord–Pas-de-Calais 2001*, 68–71.

Boureux, M. 1974. Fermes de type indigene détectées d'avion dans le Laonnois et le Soissonais, *Septentrion* 4, 6–12.

Bourgeois, J., Cherretté, B. and Bourgeois, I. 2003. Bronze Age and Iron Age settlements in Belgium: an overview, in J. Bourgeois, I. Bourgeois and B. Cherretté (eds), *Bronze Age and Iron Age Communities in North-Western Europe*, 175–297. Brussels: Koninklijke Vlaamse Academie van Belgie.

Bourgeois, L. 1999. *Le sanctuaire rural de Bennecourt (Yvelines)*. Paris: Documents d'Archéologie Française 77.

Bradley, R. 2005. *Ritual and Domestic Life in Prehistoric Europe*. London: Routledge.

Braemer, F., Cleuziou, S. and Coudart, A. (eds) 1999. *Habitat et Société (XIXe Rencontres Internationales d'Archéologie et d'Histoire d'Antibes)*. Antibes: Éditions APDCA.

Bretagne, P. (ed.) 1998. Onnaing, L'opération Toyota, *Bilan Scientifique Nord–Pas-de-Calais* 1998, 71–100.

Brun. P. and Robert, B. 1988. *L'oppidum de Pommiers. Rapport de fouilles*. Amiens: Service Régional de l'Archéologie.

Brun, P., Buchez, N., Gaudefroy, S. and Talon, M. 2005. La protohistoire ancienne, *Revue Archéologique de Picardie* 2005 3/4, 99–126.

Brunaux, J.-L. 1986. *Les gaulois: sanctuaires et rites*. Paris: Éditions Errance.

Brunaux, J.-L. (ed.) 1991. *Les sanctuaires celtiques et leurs rapports avec le monde meditérranéen*. Paris: Dossiers de Protohistoire 3.

Brunaux, J.-L. (ed.) 1999. Ribemont-sur-Ancre (Somme), *Gallia* 56, 177–283.

Brunaux, J.-L. and Delestrée, L.-P. 2005. Les monnaies gauloises en or de Ribemont-sur-Ancre (Somme). Une mise en point sur leur datation, *Revue Archéologique de Picardie* 2005 1/2, 9–23.

Brunaux, J.-L. and Lambot, B. 1991. Le sanctuaire celtique et gallo-romain de Saint-Maur, in Brunaux 1991, 178–181.

Brunaux, J.-L. and Méniel, P. 1997. *La residence aristocratique de Montmartin (Oise) du IIIe au IIe siècle av. J.-C.* Paris: Documents d'Archéologie Française 64.

Brunaux, J.-L., and Rapin, A. 1988. *Gournay II. Boucliers et lances, dépôts et trophées*. Paris: Revue Archéologique de Picardie, Numéro Spécial.

Brunaux, J.-L., Fichtl, S. and Marchand, P. 1990. Die Ausgrabungen am Haupttor des "Camp César" bei La Chaussée-Tirancourt (Dept. Somme, Frankreich), *Saalburger Jahrbuch* 45, 5–23.

Brunaux, J.-L., Méniel, P. and Poplin, P. 1985. *Gournay I. Les fouilles sur le sanctuaire et l'oppidum*. Amiens: Revue Archéologique de Picardie, Numéro Spécial.

Buchez, N. 2003. Poulainville-Amiens, Les Motelettes, *Bilan Scientifique Picardie 2003*, 116–117.

Buchez, N. and Dumont, C. 1996. *Villers-lès-Roye "Les Longchamps" (Somme). Étude archéologique et anthropologique. Document de synthèse*. Amiens: Service Régional de l'Archéologie.

Buchez, N., Dumont, C., Ginoux, N. and Montaru, D. 1998. Les tombes à incineration de Villers-lès-Roye "Les Longs Champs" et de Marcelcave "Le Chemin d'Ignaucourt" (Somme), *Revue Archéologique de Picardie* 1998 1/2, 191–210.

Buchez, N., Le Goff, I. and Millerat, P. 2004. Les necropoles à incineration de La Tène ancienne de Milly-sur-Thérain et Saint-Martin-le-Noeud, *Revue Archéologique de Picardie* 2004 1/2, 19–32.

Buchsenchutz, O. 2004. Les Celtes et la formation de l'Empire romain, *Annales. Histoire, Sciences Sociales* 59, 337–361.

Buchsenchutz, O. 2006. Le monde rural et ses productions, in Haselgrove 2006, 55–65.

Buchsenschutz, O. and Méniel, P. 1994. *Les installations agricoles de l'Âge du Fer en Ile-de-France*. Paris: Études d'Histoire et d'Archéologie 4.

Buchsenchutz, O., Bulard, A. and Lejars, T. (eds) 2005. *L'âge du Fer en Ile-de-France (Actes du XXVIe Colloque de l'AFEAF, Paris et Saint-Denis 2002)*. Paris: Revue Archéologique du Centre de la France supplément 26.

Cadoux, J.-L. 1981. Variscourt, *Gallia* 39, 264–266.

Cadoux, J.-L. 1984. L'ossuaire Gaulois de Ribemont-sur-Ancre (Somme). Premières observations, premières questions, *Gallia* 42, 53–78.

Casadéi, D. and Leconte, L. 2000. Analyse spatiale d'un établissement rural de La Tène D1: Louvres, Le Vieux Moulin (Val d'Oise), in Marion and Blancquaert 2000, 37–73.

Chossenot, M. 1997. *Recherches sur La Tène moyenne et finale en Champagne*. Reims: Mémoire de la Société Archéologique Champenoise 12.

Colin, A. 2000. Les habitats ruraux de l'âge du Fer en Picardie nord-occidentale, d'après les fouilles de l'autoroute A16, in Marion and Blancquaert 2000, 445–462.

Collart, J.-L. 1987. Le contexte stratigraphique des monnaies gauloises découvertes à Chilly (Somme), in J.-L. Brunaux and K. Gruel (eds), *Monnaies Gauloises découvertes en fouilles*, 64–89. Paris: Dossiers de Protohistoire 1.

Collart, J.-L. 1996. La naissance de la villa en Picardie: la ferme Gallo-Romaine précoce, in Bayard and Collart 1996, 121–156.

Collis, J.R. 1984. *Oppida. Earliest towns north of the Alps*. Sheffield: Department of Prehistory and Archaeology.

Constantin, C., Coudart, A. and Demoule, J.-P. 1982. Villeneuve-Saint-Germain, Les Grandes Grèves – les bâtiments de La Tène III, in *Vallée de l'Aisne: Cinq Années de Fouilles Protohistoriques*, 195–205. Amiens: Revue Archéologique de Picardie Numéro Spécial.

Debiak, R., Gaillard, R., Jacques, A. and Rossignol, P. 1998. Le devenir des reste humains après la mort, en Artois, aux IVe et IIIe siècles av. J.-C., *Revue Archéologique de Picardie* 1998 1/2, 25–57.

Debord, J. 1981. Un enclos quadrangulaire à remplissage La Tène Ia à Villeneuve-Saint-Germain (Aisne), in *L'Âge du Fer en France Septentrionale*, 107–120. Reims: Mémoire de la Société Archéologique Champenoise 2.

Debord, J. 1982. Premier bilan de huit années de fouilles à Villeneuve-Saint-Germain (1973–1980), in *Vallée de l'Aisne: Cinq Années de Fouilles Protohistoriques*, 213–264. Amiens: Revue Archéologique de Picardie Numéro Spécial.

Debord, J. 1990. Les fouilles du site gaulois tardif de Villeneuve-Saint-Germain (Aisne), *Mémoires de la Fédération des Sociétés d'histoire et de l'archéologie de l'Aisne* 35, 137–170.

Debord, J. 1995. La fortification de l'oppidum de Villeneuve-Saint-Germain (Aisne), *Revue Archéologique de Picardie* 1995 1/2, 187–203.

Debord, J. 2001. *Noviodunum Suessionum*: Pommiers ou Villeneuve-Saint-Germain? *Mémoires du Soissonais* (sér. 5) 2, 7–30.

Debord, J., Lambot, B. and Buchsenschutz, O. 1988. Les fossés couverts du site gaulois tardif de Villeneuve-Saint-Germain (Aisne), in F. Audouze and O. Buchsenschutz (eds), *Architectures des âges des métaux: fouilles récentes*, 121–135. Paris: Dossiers de Protohistoire 2.

Delattre, V. 2000. Les inhumations en silos dans les habitats de l'âge du fer dans le Bassin Parisien, in Marion and Blancquaert 2000, 291–311.

Delestrée, L.-P. 1996. *Monnayages et peuples Gaulois du Nord-Ouest*. Paris: Éditions Errance.

Delestrée, L.-P. 2001. L'or du trophée laténien de Ribemont-sur-Ancre (Somme): témoin d'une bataille oubliée, *Revue Numismatique* 152, 177–215.

Delestrée, L.-P. 2003. 'Un nouveau bronze de l'île de Bretagne en Gaule Belgique', *Cahiers Numismatiques* 155, 39–40.

Delplace, C. 1991. La zone cultuelle de Morvillers-Saint-Saturnin (Somme), in Brunaux 1991, 196–198.

Demoule, J.-P. 1999. *Chronologie et société dans les nécropoles celtiques de la culture Aisne–Marne, du VIe au IIIe siècle avant notre ère.* Amiens: Revue Archéologique de Picardie Numéro Spécial 15.

Demoule, J.-P. and Ilett, M. 1985. First millennium settlement and society in northern France: a case study from the Aisne Valley, in T.C. Champion and J.V.S. Megaw (eds), *Settlement and Society: Aspects of West European Prehistory in the First Millennium BC*, 193–221. Leicester: Leicester University Press.

Derbois, M. 1994. Villeneuve-les-Sablons, Le Bois des Saules, *Bilan Scientifique Picardie 1994*, 122–123.

Desenne, S., Collart, J.-L., Auxiette, G., Martin, G. and Rapin, A. 2005. La nécropole d'Orainville "La Croyère" (Aisne). Un ensemble attributable au Aisne–Marne IV, in Auxiette and Malrain 2005, 233–287.

Desfossés, Y. 1996. L'évolution de la ferme indigène en Pays de Caux, in Bayard and Collart 1996, 203–208.

Desfossés, Y. (ed.) 2000. *Archéologie preventive en vallée de Canche. Les sites protohistoriques fouillés dans le cadre de la realisation de l'autoroute A16.* Berck-sur-Mer: Nord Ouest Archéologie 11.

Dubouloz, J. and Plateaux, M. 1983. Le site néolithique et de l'âge du fer de Berry-au-Bac (Chemin de la Pêcherie), *Fouilles Protohistoriques de la Vallée de l'Aisne* 11, 43–92.

Faye, O., Georges, M. and Thion, P. 1990. Des fortifications de La Tène à Metz (Moselle), *Trierer Zeitschrift* 53, 55–126.

Fémolant, J.-M. 1997. Les sépultures de La Tène D2 découvertes dans le Valois sur le tracé du TGV Nord, *Revue Archéologique de Picardie* 1997 1/2, 119–126.

Fémolant, J.-M. and Malrain, F. 1996. Les établissements ruraux du deuxième Âge du Fer et leur Romanisation dans le département de l'Oise, in Bayard and Collard 1996, 39–55.

Fercoq du Leslay, G. 1996. Chronologie et analyse spatiale à Ribemont-sur-Ancre (Somme), *Revue Archéologique de Picardie* 1996 3/4, 189–208.

Fercoq du Leslay, G. 2000. L'apport des fossés de Ribemont-sur-Ancre (Somme), à la chronologie et à l'interprétation du site, *Revue Archéologique de Picardie* 1996 1/2, 113–146.

Ferdière, A., Gaudefroy, R., Massy, J.-L., Marmoz, C., Mohen, J.-P. and Poplin, F. 1973. Les sépultures gauloises d'Allonville (Somme), *Bulletin de la Société Préhistorique Française* 70, 479–492.

Fichtl. S. 1994. *Les Gaulois du Nord de la Gaule.* Paris: Éditions Errance.

Fichtl, S. 2004. *Les peoples gaulois IIIe–Ier siècles av. J.-C.* Paris: Éditions Errance.

Fichtl, S. 2005. *La ville celtique (Les oppida de 150 av. J.-C. à 15 ap. J.-C.)* (2nd edn). Paris: Éditions Errance.

Firmin, G., Robert, B. and Thiébault, S. 1989. L'environnement floristique de Villeneuve-Saint-Germain (Aisne) à la Tène finale, *Revue Archéologique de Picardie* 1989, 123–130.

Flouest, J.-L. and Stead, I.M. 1977. Une tombe de la Tène III à Hannogne (Ardennes), *Mémoires de la Société Agriculture, Commerce, Sciences et Arts du département de la Marne* 92, 55–72.

Flouest, J.-L. and Stead, I.M. 1979. *Iron Age Cemeteries in Champagne.* London: British Museum Occasional Paper 6.

Gaudefroy, S. 2002. Croixrault-A29, L'Aérodrome, *Bilan Scientifique Picardie 2002*, 107–108.

Gaudefroy, S., Malrain, F. and Pinard, E. 2001. Département de l'Oise de La Tène I à La Tène III: approche micro-régionale, in J.R. Collis (ed.), *Society and Settlement in Iron Age Europe (Actes du XVIIIe Colloque de l'AFEAF, Winchester)*, 269–291. Sheffield: Sheffield Academic Press.

Geoffroy, J.-F. and Thoquenne, V. 2000. L'occupation du territoire à Hénin-Beaumont (Pas de Calais) à l'époque gauloise, in Marion and Blancquaert 2000, 371–394.

Gouge, P. and Séguier, J.-M. 1994. L'habitat rural de l'âge du Fer en Bassée et à la confluence Seine–Yonne (Seine-et-Marne), in Buchsenschutz and Méniel 1994, 45–69.

Gerritsen, F.A. 2003. *Local Identities. Landscape and Community in the Late Prehistoric Meuse–Demer–Scheldt Region.* Amsterdam: Amsterdam Archaeological Studies 9.

Gransar, F. 2000. Le stockage alimentaire sur l'établissements ruraux de l'âge du Fer en France septentrionale: complémentarité des structures et tendances évolutives, in Marion and Blancquaert 2000, 277–298.

Gransar, F. 2002. *Le stockage alimentaire à l'âge du Fer en Europe tempérée.* Unpublished Ph.D. thesis, University of Paris I.

Gransar, F. 2003. Ploisy, Le Bras de Fer – Zones 1 et 7, *Bilan Scientifique Picardie 2003*, 40–42.

Gransar, F. and Pommepuy, C. 2005. Bazoches-sur-Vesle "Les Chantraines" (Aisne). Présentation préliminaire de l'établissement rural aristocratique de La Tène D1, in Auxiette and Malrain 2005, 193–216.

Gransar, F., Auxiette, G., Desenne, S., Hénon, B., Malrain, F., Matterne, V., Pinard, E. and Ruby, P. forthcoming. Expressions symboliques, manifestations rituelles et cultuelles en contexte domestique au premier millénaire avant notre ère dans le nord de la France, in P. Barral, A. Daubigney, C. Dunning, G. Kaenel and M.-J. Lambert (eds), *L'âge du Fer dans l'arc jurassien et ses marges. Dépôts, lieux sacrés et territorialité à l'âge du Fer (Actes du XIXe Colloque de l'AFEAF, Bienne).* Besançon: Presses Universitaires de Franche-Comté.

Gransar, F., Matterne, V. and Pommepuy, C. 1999. Témoins archéologiques de la chaîne opératoire de traitment des cereals vêtues à l'âge du fer dans le nord de la France, in R. Buxó and E. Pons (eds), *Els Productes Alimentaris d'origen vegetal a l'Edat del Ferro de l'Europa Occidental: de la Producció al Consum*, 97–105. Girona: Museu d'Arqueologia de Catalunya Sèrie Monogràfica 18.

Gruel, K. and Haselgrove, C. 2006. Le développement de l'usage monétaire à l'âge du Fer en Gaule et dans les regions voisines, in Haselgrove 2006, 117–138.

Guichard, V., Pion, P., Malacher, F. and Collis, J.R. 1993. A propos de la circulation monétaire en Gaule chevelue au IIe et Ier siècles av. J-C, *Revue Archéologique du Centre de la France* 32, 26–55.

Haselgrove, C. 1990. Later Iron Age settlement in the Aisne Valley, in A. Duval, J.-P.Le Bihan and Y. Menez (eds), *Les Gaulois d'Armorique. La fin de l'âge du Fer en Europe Tempérée (Actes du XIIe colloque de l'AFEAF, Quimper 1988)*, 249–259. Rennes: Revue Archéologique de l'Ouest Supplément 3.

Haselgrove, C. 1995. Late Iron Age society in Britain and north-west Europe: structural transformation or superficial change? in B. Arnold and D.B. Gibson (eds), *Celtic Chiefdom, Celtic State*, 81–87. New York: Cambridge University Press.

Haselgrove, C. 1996. Roman impact on rural settlement and society in southern Picardy, in Roymans 1996b, 127–187.

Haselgrove, C. 1999. The development of Iron Age coinage in Belgic Gaul, *Numismatic Chronicle* 159, 111–168.

Haselgrove, C. 2005. A new approach to analysing the circulation of Iron Age coinage, *Numismatic Chronicle* 165, 129–174.

Haselgrove, C. (ed.) 2006. *Les mutations de la fin de l'âge du Fer.* Glux-en-Glenne: Collection Bibracte 12/4.

Haselgrove, C. 2007. Rethinking Earlier Iron Age settlement in the eastern Paris Basin, in Haselgrove and Pope 2007, 400–428.

Haselgrove, C. and Lowther, P. 2005. Bâtiment, enclos cultuel ou structure funéraire? Un petit enclos carré de La Tène C2 à Soupir "Le Parc" (Aisne), in Auxiette and Malrain 2005, 355–370.

Haselgrove, C. and Pope, R. (eds) 2007. *The Earlier Iron Age in Britain and the near Continent.* Oxford: Oxbow Books.

Hawkes, C.F.C. 1968. New thoughts on the Belgae, *Antiquity* 42, 6–16.

Hawkes, C.F.C. and Dunning, G.C. 1930. The Belgae of Gaul and Britain, *Archaeological Journal* 87, 150–335.

Hénon, B. 1995. Les amphores dans la Vallée de l'Aisne à La Tène finale, *Revue Archéologique de Picardie* 1995 1/2, 149–186.

Hénon, B. 2001. Villeneuve-Saint-Germain, Les Étomelles, *Bilan Scientifique Picardie 2001*, 51–52.

Hénon, B. and Auxiette, G. 1997. Une tombe de La Tène D2 à Cuiry-lès-Chaudardes (Aisne), *Revue Archéologique de Picardie* 1997 1/2, 107–114.

Horard-Herbin, M.-P., Méniel, P. and Séguier, J.-M. 2000. La faune de dix sites ruraux de la fin de l'âge du Fer de La Bassée, in Marion and Blancquaert 2000, 181–208.

Hurtrelle, J., Monchy, E., Roger, F., Rossignol, P. and Villes, A. 1990. *Les débuts du second âge du Fer dans le nord de la France.* Arras: Les Dossiers de Gauherier 1.

Jacques, A. and Prilaux, G. (eds) 2003. *Dans le sillage de César. Traces de romanisation d'un territoire, les fouilles d'Actiparc à Arras.* Arras: Service Archéologique de la Ville d'Arras/INRAP.

James, S. 2007. A bloodless past: the pacification of Early Iron Age Britain, in Haselgrove and Pope 2007, 160–173.

Kaenel, G., Curdy, P. and Carrard, F. 2004. *L'oppidum de Mont Vully: un bilan de recherché 1978–2003.* Fribourg: Archéologie Fribourgeoise 20.

Lambot, B. 1999. Organisation spatiale et sociale du village gaulois d'Acy-Romance (Ardennes), in Braemer *et al.* 1999, 383–405.

Lambot, B. 2002a. Noblesse, artistocratie et signes extérieures de richesse à La Tène finale en Champagne, in Guichard and Perrin 2002, 87–108.

Lambot, B. 2002b. Maisons et société à Acy-Romance (Ardennes), in Méniel and Lambot 2002, 115–124.

Lambot, B. 2004. Les monnaies gauloises en or de Ribemont-sur-Ancre (Somme). Réflexion sur leur datation, *Revue Archéologique de Picardie* 2004 1/2, 123–138.

Lambot, B. and Casagrande, P. 1997. Une monnaie d'Ebusus sur l'oppidum de "Vieux-Laon" à Saint-Thomas (Aisne), *Bulletin de la Société Archéologique Champenoise* 90, 15–29.

Lambot, B. and Friboulet, M. 1996. Essai de chronologie du site de La Tène finale d'Acy-Romance (Ardennes), *Revue Archéologique de Picardie* 1996 3/4, 123–151.

Lambot, B. and Méniel, P. 1992. *Le site protohistorique d'Acy-Romance (Ardennes), 1. L'habitat gaulois 1988–1990.* Reims: Mémoire de la Société Archéologique Champenoise 7.

Lambot, B. and Méniel, P. 2000. Le centre communautaire et cultuel du village gaulois d'Acy-Romance dans son contexte regional, in Verger 2000, 7–139.

Lambot, B., Friboulet, M. and Méniel, P. 1994. *Le site protohistorique d'Acy Romance (Ardennes), II. Les nécropoles dans leurs contexte régional 1986–1988–1989.* Reims: Mémoire de la Société Archéologique Champenoise 8.

Lambot, B., Haselgrove, C.C., Howard, P., James, S. and Lowther, P. 1998. Resistivity survey at St-Thomas (Aisne), northern France, *Universities of Durham and Newcastle-upon-Tyne Archaeological Reports for 1997*, 62–65.

Lemaire, F. and Rossignol, P. 1996. Un exemple exceptionnel d'établissement agricole romain précoce à Conchil-le-Temple "Le Fond de la Commanderie" (Pas-de-Calais): resultats préliminaires, in Bayard and Collart 1996, 185–202.

Lefèvre, P. 2002. La nécropole de Cizancourt (Somme): presentation des indices de hiérarchisation interne des tombes, in Guichard and Perrin 2002, 109–112.

Lejars, T. 1994. *Gournay III. Les fourreaux d'épée.* Paris: Éditions Errance.

Lejars, T. 1996. L'armement des celtes en Gaule du nord à la fin de l'époque gauloise, *Revue Archéologique de Picardie* 1996 3/4, 79–103.

Lejars, T. 1999. Le mobilier métallique d'époque gauloise, *Gallia* 56, 241–253.

Leman-Delrive, G. and Piningre, J.-F. 1981. Les structures d'habitat du deuxième âge du Fer de Conchil-le-Temple (Pas de Calais) – premiers résultats, in *L'Âge du Fer en France septentrionale*, 319–330. Reims: Mémoire de la Société Archéologique Champenoise 2.

Lobjois, G. 1966. Les fouilles de l'oppidum Gaulois "du Vieux Laon", *Celticum* 15, 1–33.

Loughton, M. 2003. The distribution of Republican amphorae in France, *Oxford Journal of Archaeology* 22, 177–207.

Magny, M. and Richard, H. 1992. Essai de synthèse vers une courbe de l'évolution du climat entre 500 BC et 500 AD, *Les Nouvelles de l'Archéologie* 50, 58–60.

Malrain, F. 1994. Les établissements ruraux du second Age du Fer dans les régions picarde et ardennaise d'après les fouilles et les prospections aériennes, in Buchsenschutz and Méniel 1994, 185–204.

Malrain, F. 2000. *Fonctionnement et hiérarchies des fermes dans la société Gauloise du IIIe siècle à la période Romaine: l'apport des sites de la moyenne vallée de l'Oise.* Unpublished Ph.D. thesis, University of Paris I.

Malrain, F. 2003. Le site artisanal de La Tène finale et du gallo-romain de Ronchères (Aisne) "Le Bois de Forge", *Bulletin de l'Association Française pour l'Étude de l'Age du Fer* 21, 2–3.

Malrain, F. and Pinard, E. 2000. Les enclos sur le territoire des Bellovaques et ses abords, *Revue Archéologique de Picardie* 2000 1/2, 179–195.

Malrain, F., Gransar, F., Matterne, V. and Le Goff, I. 1996. Une ferme gauloise de La Tène D1 et sa nécropole: Jaux "Le Camp du Roi" (Oise), *Revue Archéologique de Picardie* 1996 3/4, 245–306.

Malrain, F., Gaudefroy, S., Gransar, F., Auxiette, G. and Méniel, P. 2005. La protohistoire récente, *Revue Archéologique de Picardie* 2005 3/4, 127–176.

Malrain, F., Matterne, V. and Méniel, P. 2002. *Les paysans Gaulois (IIIe siècle–52 av. J.-C.).* Paris: Éditions Errance.

Mantel, E. (ed.) 1997. *Le sanctuaire de Fesques "Le Mont du Val aux Moines", Seine Maritime.* Berck-sur-Mer: Nord Ouest Archéologie 8.

Marion, S. 1994. Ensembles fossoyés à vocation agro-pastorale de la vallée de la Marne (Seine-et-Marne), in Buchsenschutz and Méniel 1994, 97–102.

Marion, S. 2004. *Recherches sur l'âge du fer en Ile-de-France*. Oxford: British Archaeological Reports International Series 1231.

Marion, S. 2005. Les occupations protohistoriques du sanctuaire de La Bauve à Meaux (Seine-et-Marne), in Buchsenchutz *et al.* 2005, 85–95.

Marion, S. and Blancquaert, G. (eds) 2000. *Les installations agricoles de l'âge du Fer en France septentrionale*. Paris: Études d'Histoire et d'Archéologie 6.

Marion, S., Métrot, P. and Le Béchennec, Y. 2005. L'occupation protohistorique de Bobigny (Seine-Saint-Denis), in Buchsenchutz *et al.* 2005, 97–126.

Massy, J.-L. 1983. Variscourt-Condé-sur-Suippe, *Gallia* 41, 236–238.

Massy, J.-L., Mantel, E., Meniel, P. and Rapin, A. 1986. La nécropole gauloise de Tartigny (Oise), *Revue Archéologique de Picardie* 1986 3/4, 13–81.

Matherat, M. 1943. La technique des retranchements de César à Nointel, *Gallia* 1, 6–127.

Matterne, V. 2000, Évolution des productions agricoles durant l'âge du Fer dans le nord de la France, in Marion and Blancquaert 2000, 129–146.

Matterne, V. 2001. *Agriculture et alimentation végétale durant l'âge du Fer et l'époque gallo-romaine en France septentrionale*. Montagnac: Archéologie des Plantes et des Animaux 1.

Méniel, P. 1987. *Chasse et élevage chez les Gaulois (450–52 av. J.-C)*. Paris: Éditions Errance.

Méniel, P. 1996. Les faunes des établissements ruraux de La Tène finale dans le Nord de la France, in Bayard and Collart 1996, 309–317.

Méniel, P. 1998. *Le site protohistorique d'Acy-Romance (Ardennes), III. Les animaux et l'histoire d'un village gaulois*. Reims: Mémoire de la Société Archéologique Champenoise 14.

Méniel, P. 1999. Histoire de l'alimentation carnée et de l'organisation sociale du village gaulois d'Acy-Romance (Ardennes, France), in Braemer *et al.* 1999, 405–418.

Meniel, P. 2001. *Les gaulois et les animaux: Élevage, repas et sacrifice*. Paris: Éditions Errance.

Méniel, P. and Lambot, B. 2002. *Repas des vivants et nourriture pour les morts en Gaule (Actes du XXVe colloque de l'AFEAF, Charleville-Mézières 2001)*. Reims: Mémoire de la Société Archéologique Champenoise 16.

Metzler, J. 1995. *Das Treverische Oppidum auf dem Titelberg*. Luxembourg: Dossiers d'Archéologie du Musée Nationale d'Histoire et d'Art 3.

Metzler, J., Méniel, P. and Gaeng, C. 2006. *Oppida* et espaces publics, in Haselgrove 2006, 201–224.

Metzler, J., Waringo, R., Bis, R. and Metzler-Zens, N. 1991. *Clemency et les tombes de l'aristocratie en gaule belgique*. Luxembourg: Dossiers d'Archéologie du Musée National d'Histoire et d'Art 1.

Miron, A. 1986. Das Gräberfeld von Horath: Untersuchungen zur Mittel- und Spätlatènezeit im Saar-Mosel-Raum, *Trierer Zeitschrift* 49, 7–198.

Miron, A. 1991. Die späte Eisenzeit im Hunsrück-Nahe-Raum: mittel- und spätlatènezeitliche Gräberfelder, in A. Haffner and A. Miron (eds), *Studien zur Eisenzeit im Hunsrück-Nahe-Raum*, 151–169. Trier: Trierer Zeitschrift Beiheft 13.

Neiss, R. 1984. La structure urbaine de Reims antique et son évolution du 1er au 3e siècle ap. JC, in *Les villes de la Gaule Belgique au haut empire*, 171–192. Amiens: Revue Archéologique de Picardie Numéro Spécial.

Olivier, L. and Schönfelder, M. 2002. Presles-et-Boves "Derrière-Saint-Audebert" (Aisne) – une tombe féminine à amphores de la période césarienne, in Guichard and Perrin 2002, 77–86.

Paris, P. 1998. Les sépultures à incineration de La Tène moyenne de la "ZAC de Ther" à Allonne (Oise), *Revue Archéologique de Picardie* 1998 1/2, 271–329.

Peyre, C. 2000. Documents sur l'organisation publique de l'espace dans la cité gauloise. Le site de Villeneuve-Saint-Germain et la bilingue de Verceil, in Verger 2000, 155–206.

Pichon, B. 2002. *Carte Archéologique de la Gaule: l'Aisne (02)*. Paris: Académie des Inscriptions et Belles Lettres.

Pinard, E. 1997. Étude anthropologique de la nécropole de Longueuil-Sainte-Marie "Pré des Grisards" (Oise) – La Tène ancienne, La Tène moyenne, *Revue Archéologique de Picardie* 1997 1/2, 57–88.

Pinard, E., Collart, J.-L., Malrain, F. and Maréchal, D. 1999. De l'architecture à la hiérarchisation sociale du Ve av. J.-C. au IIIe ap. J.-C. dans la moyenne vallée de l'Oise, in Braemer *et al.* 1999, 363–382.

Pinard, E., Delattre, V., Friboulet M., Breton, C. and Krier, V. 2000. Chambly "La Remise Ronde" (Oise), une nécropole de la Tène ancienne, *Revue Archéologique de Picardie* 2000 3/4, 3–75.

Pion, P. 1987. L'*oppidum* celtique du "Vieux-Reims" de Condé-sur-Suippe/Variscourt, *Fouilles Protohistoriques de la Vallée de l'Aisne* 15, 257–333.

Pion, P. 1990. De la chefferie à l'état? Territoires et organisation sociale dans la vallée de l'Aisne aux ages des métaux (2200–20 av. J.-C.), in *Archéologie et Espaces (Xe Rencontres Internationales d'Archéologie et d'Histoire d'Antibes)*, 183–260. Juan-les-Pins: Éditions APDCA.

Pion, P. 1996a. Les établissements ruraux dans la vallée de l'Aisne de la fin du second Âge du Fer au début du Haut-Empire Romain, in Bayard and Collart 1996, 55–108.

Pion, P. 1996b. *Les habitats Laténiens tardifs de la Vallée de l'Aisne: contribution à la périodisation de la fin du second Âge du Fer en Gaule nord-orientale*. Unpublished Ph.D. thesis, University of Paris I.

Pion, P., Pommepuy, C., Auxiette, G., Hénon, B. and Gransar, F. 1997. L'oppidum de Condé-sur-Suippe/Variscourt (Aisne) (fin IIe–début Ier s. av. J.-C.). Approche préliminaire de l'organisation fonctionnelle d'un quartier artisanale, in A. Bocquet (ed.), *Espaces physiques espaces sociaux dans l'analyse interne des sites du néolithique à l'âge du Fer*, 275–309. Paris : Éditions du CTHS.

Piton, D. and Dilly, G. 1985. Le *fanum* des Châtelets de Vendeuil-Caply (Oise), *Revue Archéologique de Picardie* 1985 1/2, 25–47.

Pommepuy, C. 1999. Le materiel de mouture de la vallée de l'Aisne de l'âge du Bronze à La Tène finale: formes et matériaux, *Revue Archéologique de Picardie* 1999 3/4, 115–141.

Pommepuy, C., Auxiette, G. and Desenne, S. 1998. Rupture et continuité dans les pratiques funéraires de La Tène ancienne et moyenne/finale à Bucy-le-Long (Aisne), *Revue Archéologique de Picardie* 1998 1/2, 85–98.

Pommepuy, C., Auxiette, G., Desenne, S., Gransar, F. and Hénon, B. 2000. Des enclos à l'âge du Fer dans la vallée de l'Aisne: le monde des vivants et le monde des morts, *Revue Archéologique de Picardie* 2000 1/2, 197–216.

Prilaux, G. 2000a. Une ferme gauloise spécialisée dans le travail du sel à Pont-Rémy "La Queute" et "Le Fond de Baraquin" (Somme). Évolution et particularités de l'espace enclos, *Revue Archéologique de Picardie* 2000 1/2, 233–254.

Prilaux, G. 2000b. *La production du sel à l'âge du Fer.* Montagnac: Protohistoire Européenne 5.

Prodéo, F. 2000. Bayonvillers "Chemin d'Harbonnière" (Somme). Un petit habitat fortifié de La Tène moyenne et finale, *Revue Archéologique de Picardie* 2000 1/2, 255–266.

Poux, M. 2004. *L'âge du vin. Rites de boisson, festins et libations en Gaule indépendante.* Montagnac: Protohistoire Européenne 8.

Poux, M. 2005. *Convergence et confrontation. Processus d'urbanisation et conquête romaine en territoire arverne (IIe–Ier s. av. J.-C.).* Mémoire d'Habilitation à Diriger des Recherches, Université d' Aix en Provence.

Querel, P. and Woimant, G.-P. (eds) 2002. *Le Site d'Estrées-Saint-Denis (Revue Archéologique de Picardie* 2002 3/4*).*

Reddé, M. and von Schnurbein, S. (eds) 2001. *Alésia: fouilles et recherches Franco-Allemands sur les Travaux militaires Romains autour du Mont-Auxois (1991–1997).* Paris: Mémoires de l'Académie des Inscriptions et Belles-Lettres 22.

Rimbault, S. 1994. L'occupation du second Âge du Fer à Rungis/Les Antes, in Buchsenschutz and Méniel 1994, 103–112.

Robert, B. and Landreat, J.-L. 2005. Les meules rotatives en calcaire à glauconie grossière et l'atelier de Vauxrezis (Aisne). Un état de la question, in Auxiette and Malrain 2005, 105–114.

Rougier, R. 2000. Les formes d'occupation du territoire à l'âge du Fer en Pays de Caux (Seine-Maritime) d'après les fouilles sur le tracé de l'autoroute A29, in Marion and Blancquaert 2000, 411–426.

Rougier, R. and Blancquaert, G. 2001. Un établissement rural de La Tène D1 à Rue "Le Chemin des Morts" (Somme), *Revue Archéologique de Picardie* 2001 3/4, 81–104.

Rougier, R., Watel, F. and Blondiaux, J. 2003. Deux inhumations en silo sur le tracé de l'autoroute A29 à Fresnes-Mazancourt and Framerville-Rainecourt (Somme), *Revue Archéologique de Picardie* 2003 3/4, 67–76.

Roymans, N. 1990. *Tribal Societies in Northern Gaul.* Amsterdam: Cingula 12.

Roymans, N. 1996a. The sword or the plough. Regional dynamics in the Romanization of Belgic Gaul and the Rhineland area, in Roymans 1996b, 9–126.

Roymans, N. (ed.) 1996b. *From the Sword to the Plough: Three Studies on the Earliest Romanization of Northern Gaul.* Amsterdam: Amsterdam Archaeological Studies 1.

Roymans, N. 2004. *Ethnic Identity and Imperial Power.* Amsterdam: Amsterdam Archaeological Studies 10.

Séguier, J.-M. and Delattre, V. 2005. Espaces funéraires et cultuels au confluent Seine-Yonne (Seine-et-Marne) de la fin du Vème au IIIème s. av. J.-C., in Buchsenschutz *et al.* 2005, 241–260.

Sills, J. 2003. *Gaulish and Early British Coinage.* London: Spink.

Soupart, N. and Duvette, L. 2005. Limé "Les Sables" (Aisne). Les sépultures et les depots de La Tène, in Auxiette and Malrain 2005, 289–326.

Thouvenot, S. and Gransar, F. 2000. La gestion du terroir des établissements ruraux de La Tène finale dans la vallée de l'Aisne, in Marion and Blancquaert 2000, 157–167.

Toupet, C., Méniel, P., Lemaître, P., Leconte, L. and Kohlmayer, C. 2005. Enclos quadrangulaires et puits à offrandes. Le cas de Bruyères-sur-Oise (Val d'Oise), in Buchsenschutz *et al.* 2005, 7–32.

Valais, A. 1994. La ferme des Fontaines à Herblay (Val-d'Oise), in Buchsenschutz and Méniel 1994, 113–124.

Vauvillé, O. 1903–4. L'enceinte de Pommiers (Aisne), *Bulletin de la Société Archéologique Historique Scientifique de Soissons* (ser. 3) 12, 321–361.

Vauvillé, O. 1907. L'enceinte antique de Villeneuve-Saint-Germain (Aisne), *Bulletin et Mémoires de la Société Nationale des Antiquaires de France* (sér. 7) 7, 1–5.

Verger, S. (ed.) 2000. *Rites et espaces en pays celte et méditerranéen.* Rome: Collection de l'École Française de Rome 276.

Weller, O. 2000. L'exploitation du sel marin dans le nord de la France durant le second âge du Fer. L'apport majeur des fouilles de l'autoroute A16, in Marion and Blancquaert 2000, 237–250.

Weller, O. and Robert, B. 1995. Le commerce du sel à La Tène final: une problématique enfin rélancée, *Revue Archéologique de Picardie* 1995 1/2, 87–96.

Wellington, I. 2005. Placing coinage and ritual in their archaeological contexts: the example of northern France, in C. Haselgrove and D. Wigg-Wolf (eds), *Iron Age Coinage and Ritual Practices*, 227–245. Mainz: Studien zu Fundmünzen der Antike 20.

Wells, P. 2006. Objects, meaning and ritual in the emergence of the *oppida*, in Haselgrove 2006, 139–153.

Wightman, E.M. 1985. *Gallia Belgica.* London: Batsford.

Woimant, G.-P. 1990. Beauvais "Les Aulnes du Canada": Viereckschanze ou enceinte quadrangulaire?, *Revue Archéologique de Picardie* 1990 3/4, 27–94.

The polities of Gaul, Britain, and Ireland in the Late Iron Age

John Collis

In the 1970s various of us were writing about the nature of Iron Age society in Britain and Gaul in the immediately pre-Roman period in reaction to two preconceptions then prevalent in the literature, both based on the colonialist and imperialist views which had dominated the first two thirds of the twentieth century. The first was the view of Roman archaeologists such as Richmond and Frere who largely saw the Roman invasion as the arrival of 'civilisation' in a 'barbaric' country with a previously low level of economic and social development. 'History' was written largely in terms of military campaigns, native revolts, and barbarian invasions; Roman forts would be discussed in terms of control of strategic locations, with little concern for the native settlement patterns; the population was divided into the cultured inhabitants of Roman villas and towns, in contrast to the uncultured peoples living on 'native settlements'.

The second preconception was of the immutable nature of pre-colonialist populations, in which change could only be instigated by invading groups with a higher level of technology and social organisation; left to themselves natives would only 'degenerate' (witness the development of Iron Age coinage in Britain, or the supposed devolution of the bases of Sussex pots from a high pedestal to a low ring-foot). This assumption meant that descriptions and reconstructions of Iron Age society could be extrapolated back from the Roman conquest to the time of Caesar, indeed to the 'arrival' of the Belgae (the previous supposed invasion), and so Cassivellaunus was transformed into a king like Cunobelin. At its worst this could lead to the conflation of evidence into timeless 'Celtic' warriors, societies, or religions, something which is, sadly, still rife in the literature (see the cover of *Current Archaeology* 191).

Social Anthropology in Britain, too, was bent to a colonialist agenda, that of recording native societies before they were transformed irrevocably by the march of western civilisation, and also to provide a better understanding of other cultures for colonial administrators. The school of Radcliffe-Brown and Evans Pritchard was primarily concerned with functional aspects of social and political systems, and deliberately rejected the evolutionary reconstructions of late nineteenth-century anthropologists and sociologists such as Morgan and Engels; thus Radcliffe-Brown interpreted the importance of the 'mother's brother' in strongly patrilineal societies as a functional escape mechanism rather than an archaic survival from an earlier 'matriarchal' society. Though Malinowski had laid the seeds of an economic approach to anthropology in his study of the Kula in the Trobriand Islands, such approaches, especially if they had a Marxist flavour, were not in the mainstream of the curricula of British universities. The teaching of 'Archaeology' and 'Anthropology' in the Faculty of that name in Cambridge was hardly a meeting of minds, though I personally remember the shock of a couple of supervisions with Maurice Bloch at the end of my first year which hinted at something different (he sent me off to read Marcel Mauss' (1954) *The Gift*).

In the late 1960s and early 1970s, a whole series of new influences hit British Archaeology: the re-introduction from American anthropology of ideas of social evolution (Service, Fried) and economic anthropology (Sahlins, Dalton, Carole Smith); the New Geography with its least effort models (Chisholm, Haggett); biology and statistical approaches to classification (Sokal and Sneath); from sociology, the pre-industrial city (Sjoberg); from economics, concepts of the Market, Ports-of-Trade and World Systems (Polanyi, Wallerstein). These opened up a whole series of new approaches, which characterised the 'New Archaeology'. Yet, at the recent Iron Age seminars it is precisely these approaches, which were under sustained attack by the 'Post-processualists', concepts such as the 'state', and 'core and periphery'. A lot has simply disappeared from the teaching of theory in our universities (e.g. 'least effort models'). Admittedly there were extremes in the New Archaeology which deserve to be forgotten, such as the hunt for 'universal laws' (which many of us rejected from the start), and there were many misapplications; models devised from the modern world which were simplistically applied without thought to the ancient world (the economic determinism of the Higgs Cambridge School, or the 'my chiefdom is older than your chiefdom', 'my site is a central place', 'my society is a state not a complex chiefdom' syndromes). But much of this mindless application was criticised at the time, indeed it seems that many of my own writings centred on attacking such follies!

Every new generation tends to caricature the failings of the previous, and then to reject its approaches in totality (e.g. the rejection of the concept of migration by some New Archaeologists, despite the historical evidence we have for it in the Iron Age and the early Medieval period). I feel very much that we are seeing the same with the rejection of the New Archaeology models by the present generation. In part it depends on what one wants to know. I personally still have great interest in social, economic, and environmental reconstruction, even though we must admit we cannot understand such matters without also trying to understand the ideology of the ancient peoples we are studying. Also our very nomenclature and the way in which we talk about ancient societies is tacitly based on concepts of social evolution; although we may recognise the special roles of base camps and assembly sites for cult and other activities in Palaeolithic and Mesolithic societies, we would never apply the term 'town' or 'city' to them as we would to medieval and modern sites. But even more, I feel it is a misunderstanding of archaeological process. Concepts like 'state' and 'centre–periphery' are not givens to impose on ancient societies, they are heuristic devices that allow us to explore the archaeological data and ask questions of them. There is always a danger of a theoretical totalitarianism being imposed by those who espouse the latest trendy ideas; I personally am an advocate of pluralism in our approaches.

The Iron Age state

The use of the term 'state' is justified for the Late Iron Age polities in Gaul and Britain as this is the term, *civitas*, used by the Latin writers who refer to them and had direct experience of them; the common translation into English, 'tribe', has unfortunate connotations in the anthropological literature, as it implies a lower level of social organisation. Also, we have small items of evidence hinting at the existence of features of a 'state' in some of the polities, especially the Aedui: the annual election of magistrates (e.g. the *vergobret*) and laws governing their election; the existence of state funds; an oligarchic assembly (*senatus*); and, among the Treveri, a decision-making popular assembly at which attendance by 'citizens' was compulsory.

But this does not mean that all of the 'tribal states' for which we have names had all of these features, or that they remained static through time, nor indeed that they were homogenous within themselves, as Alex Woolf (1998) reminds us in his study of the possible processes of language change in lineage-based segmentary societies in Ireland. The societies of central and northern Gaul, of Britain, and Ireland form something of a contrast with the polities of much of the Mediterranean world, where we can study from both documentary and archaeological sources the gradual development of the city state, and its transformation into larger entities through conquest or through local coalitions based on shared language, ethnicity and ritual, and eventually the emergence of empires. The city state was the typical form of polity in the Phoenician, Greek, and Etruscan worlds, and was exported widely around the coastal regions of the Mediterranean and the Black Sea through colonisation; indeed the process of colonisation may itself have formed a major factor in the development of the *polis*. But the city state may also have been the basic polity in other areas as well, such as southern France and eastern and southern Spain. Archaeologically, towns start as clusters of settlement and cemeteries around defensive sites (Athens, Rome, Veii, Cayla de Mailhac), which later become nucleated defended urban centres; but the city state is a worldwide phenomenon, and appears in many forms and varieties (Hansen 2000).

In contrast, for the 'tribal states' more typical of temperate Europe, we lack the documentary evidence of the processes of formation, although the equivalent polities also existed in Greece and Italy in the form of the *ethnos*, areas which were considered backward by the Greeks because of the late adoption of urban life and all its trappings (Snodgrass 1980). In terms of area, these tribal states were much larger than the city state, and when urbanisation appears, it is usually in the form of planned settlements (the process of synoecism in Greece, or the foundation of the *oppida* of central Gaul), and these deliberate foundations are often much larger in size and less densely spaced than the city states. The later history of these polities also often distinguishes them from the city state: coinage issued by city states usually bears the name of the city rather than the name of a ruler. Also in the city state it is the city that generally gives the name to the people (Athenians, Romans, Carthaginians), whereas in the tribal states the name of the city is usually replaced by the name of the tribe (*Lutetia*/Paris; *Avaricum*/Bourges, *Durocotorum*/Reims). As discussed below, it is often shared cult activity which gives us the first indication of the development of these polities. Under the Roman Empire it is generally the city state which provides the constitutional structure of the Roman *civitates*, but the tribal state which provides the model for the scale of the administered territory. So, in southern Gaul under the reforms of Augustus, the city states are grouped together to form tribal *civitates*, whereas in tribal states where urbanisation had not yet developed, urban settlements were imposed in the form of *civitas* capitals (Goudineau 1998).

For the Late Iron Age in both Gaul and in south-east Britain we are able to a fair degree to reconstruct the scale of the polities with which we are dealing. For Gaul we have documentary evidence of historical sources such as Caesar to tell us first-hand the 'names' of the *civitates* that he encountered, and secondly we have later sources such as Ptolemy or diocesan boundaries, as well as place-names such as '*Fines*' or '*Aequeranda*' (Iguerande), which we can project back, albeit with due caution, into pre-Roman times; the details may not be accurate, but the general outline is more or less acceptable. Some *civitates* had no obvious *oppidum* to act as a central place (especially in western France), one or two have a single major site (e.g. the Arverni), but others had several (e.g. the Bituriges Cubi and the Helvetii). Cult sites are equally unhelpful – some may be organised at *civitas* level, and others may be at *pagus* level (Roymans 1990; Collis 1995). Of the material culture, not even the coinage is very informative; it does not provide us with clear distributional boundaries, and the distributions of some coin types in the pre- and post-Conquest period seem to cover several polities (e.g. pre-conquest KALETEDOU and torc-bearer potins; post-conquest TOGIRIX, and GERMANVS INDVTILLI F.). The names of the centres of minting are not given on the coinage, and only a few of the names of individuals on the coins are mentioned in the historical sources (Colbert de Beaulieu 1962), so we do not know their status or tribal affiliations.

For south-east Britain the evidence is slightly different. We lack useful information from the first century BC, and it is not until the early Roman period that we have information from Tacitus, Ptolemy, etc. We do not have the diocesan boundaries, as there seems to be little or no continuity of Roman boundaries into early medieval times. On the other hand the coins give us names of known mint sites and of kings known from other historical sources (Cunobelin, Verica etc.). Although boundaries in coin distributions are not entirely as we might wish, they are more helpful than those in Gaul.

Four questions emanate from the discussion:

1. What evidence can we use to identify these polities further back in time, or indeed, to trace their inception?
2. Can we recognise polities outside the areas where documentation is relatively good, in areas where evidence is poor or non-existent (e.g. northern Britain, Ireland, central Europe)?
3. What is the range in the variety of the structure of these polities (e.g. what is the nature of less centralised polities)?
4. How much do they change over time both in terms of their size and nature, and can we detect this?

Central Gaul

The Gaulish *civitas* has recently been the subject of a new study by Stefan Fichtl (2004), which provides an up to date summary of the relevant archaeology and textual references. One element that we can trace back earlier than the first century BC is the name of tribes, but this does not, of course, imply that the state organisations, which bear the same names are equally early. The earliest contemporary classical author is Polybius writing in the mid second century BC, who mentions the Ardyes (presumably the Aedui) and the Allobroges in the context of Hannibal's and Hamilcar's crossings of southern France at the end of the third century. Contemporary with him is Apollodorus, who died around 144 BC, who mentions the alliance between the Aedui and the Romans, and the warlike nature of the Arverni. The Arverni also appear in Poseidonius' story of Luernios (Athenaeus IV, 37, 152 D-F), and this too takes us into the early to mid second century BC, as his son Bituitos was defeated by the Romans in 123 BC. We also have an early written source for the Helvetii, an Etruscan graffito with the name ELUVEITIE (Vitali and Kaenel 2000). The Campanian vessel and the stratigraphical context both date the find to around 300 BC, the earliest contemporary source we have for any Gallic tribal name.

However, we also have names mentioned in early contexts by much later authors. Pliny in the first century AD and Livy in the late first century BC, both relate events surrounding the Gallic invasion of northern Italy. The Helvetii appear in Pliny's story of Helico, the smith resident in Rome who returned home with tales of the wealth of the city, which Pliny explains as the cause of the invasion. This would place the events at the beginning of the fourth century, but there are, of course, alternative legends of the cause of the attack.

Livy is more problematic. He relates the involvement of a number of transalpine Gallic tribes in these events: the Bituriges Cubi, Arverni, Aedui, Cenomani, Senones, Lingones, and Boii, but dates them to around 600 BC rather than the date implied by other authors, the late fifth to early fourth centuries BC. The appearance of some of these names in later contexts in northern Italy, Cenomani, Boii, Lingones, and possibly the Senones (the Senones in Gaul have a short 'e' and short 'o', but they are long in the Italian name) would, however, tend to support the use of these names by at least the fifth century BC. Whether the tribes are to be located more or less where they are found in Caesar's *Commentaries* is also problematic, but Livy's story of the routes taken would only make sense if they were already located in central Gaul (see generally, Collis 2003). Also, if we accept a fifth century BC date, the importance of the Bituriges Cubi and their king Ambigatus would find support in the wealth of archaeological finds of this date in and around Bourges (Milcent 2004).

As already mentioned, assigning early dates to the tribal names does not necessarily imply early states. We can reject the idea that kingship represents an earlier form of Gallic society, as was assumed by many twentieth-century historians. Caesar's *Commentaries* imply that the first-century BC Gallic states, like their Greek and Italian counterparts, veered between monarchy and oligarchy; the Arverni had monarchy in the second century, oligarchy in the first, but one which was threatened by individuals seeking kingship, if we are to believe the story of Celtillus, father of Vercingetorix. In fact, from the written sources we know little of the political organisation of Gallic tribes before the first century BC. 'Kings' are mentioned in the case of the Arverni, with Luernios and his son Bituitos. However, the story of the way in which Luernios gained power, with his largesse of gold, wine, and food, implies that kingship was replacing some other form of political structure, and the general lack of the names of kings in both the historical and numismatic record might suggest that kingship, and especially dynastic kingship, was exceptional. Livy's story of Ambigatus, king of the Bituriges Cubi, suggests some sort of monarchy in the fifth century BC, and even some sort of suzerainty of patron-client relationship with other tribes in Gaul. However, the Latin term *rex* does not necessarily mean a 'king', and it could mean little more than a tribal chief or temporary leader.

The foundation of the Gallic *oppida* starts around 120 BC (Collis 2000). Some at least have urban characteristics from the start (e.g. Besançon). Although the act of founding them must itself had had a profound impact on the political development of the individual polities, I have argued elsewhere that their foundation implies the existence of a state level of organisation both at that time and before 120 BC (Collis 1995). Open urban-style settlements such as Levroux and Roanne can take us back earlier, but only to La Tène C2, that is the beginning of the second century BC. Earlier than that, there are specialised sites such as Paule in the Côte d'Armor (Menez and Arremond 1997), or La Grande Borne (part of the complex of sites at Aulnat near Clermont-Ferrand in the Auvergne), but nothing that one would consider a major 'central place' for a large polity. For that we have to go back to the fifth century BC and Bourges, a site which was unique in France at that time (Milcent 2004). Before that, in the sixth century BC, as well as Bourges, we have the *Fürstensitz* of Mont Lassois. There is thus a major gap in 'central places' in the fourth and third centuries BC. To fill this gap we have only one or two cult sites which start this early (e.g. Gournay-sur-Aronde in Picardy, and La Tène), but generally the mass deposition of weapons and other items on cult sites is mainly a late phenomenon, belonging to the later third and the second centuries BC.

The evidence that we have suggests that the tribal entities, which were to become the Roman *civitates*, already existed by the fifth century BC. As we have few or no names in the early sources that we do not have later, this can be interpreted as showing that their geographical extent had not changed much either. However, the archaeological evidence suggests that these early tribal polities functioned in a very different way from their late second- to first-century BC successors, and that the change may have started by the early second if not the third century BC in central Gaul, but perhaps later in the north and west.

South-eastern Britain

The information we have on tribal groupings in south-east Britain is very limited, and yet forms a considerable contrast with Gaul. Only one of the tribal names that Caesar gives us from his admittedly limited visits to Britain recurs in a later context, that of the Trinovantes, although the more general term Belgae also persists. Instead we hear of individuals, some of whom were called *rex* in the Roman literature, and they use this term themselves on their coins. The coin evidence tells us that we are dealing with dynasties. Nothing really comparable is found in pre-conquest Gaul; the closest we have is among the Arverni, with two cases of a father and son, Luernios and Bituitos in the second century BC, and Celtillus and Vercingetorix in the first.

We are more dependent on the archaeology to tell us about the pre-Roman polities in Britain, especially the coins – the dynastic relationships, the places where coins were minted, and, from the coin distributions, the possible size of the individual kingdoms, although many years ago I did suggest that power might be politically based (e.g. through clientship or descent groups) rather than territorially (Collis 1971). However, the evidence that we have suggests these 'kingdoms' crossed tribal boundaries, and were split up and re-organised at the time of the Roman organisation of the province. Cunobelin's power base included both the Trinovantes and the Catuvellauni, and Verica's kingdom the Atrebates, Regni, and Belgae.

In his recent book, John Creighton (2000) picks out the late second to early first century BC as the point when the later patterns of kingdoms may have started to evolve, with the abandonment of hillforts in Hampshire, the adoption of coinage and the rise of an elite warrior class, but to this we can add the first appearance of cult sites, as at Hayling Island and Harlow. Up to the time of Caesar's conquest of Gaul, south-east Britain and northern France had evolved more or less in tandem, but, although in both areas in the second half of the first century BC the coinage indicates the emergence of powerful individuals who we might wish to label as 'client kings', the evolution went further in Britain, where there was greater independence of action, whereas northern Gaul remained to some extent 'fossilised' with its structure of tribal states rather than client kingdoms, or at least reverted to that organisation under Augustus. To what extent the Roman *civitates* in south-eastern Britain also represent a reversion to an earlier order we can only conjecture.

Ireland

On the evidence of the historical sources and of coin inscriptions, kingship was a phenomenon of eastern England, and is not found in the west or north of Britain. It is therefore surprising to find that Ireland may have had 'kingdoms' in the Late Iron Age. The problem is that we have three disparate and disjointed sets of information: the Ulster Cycle; the geographical information of tribal names recorded by Ptolemy; and the political set-up of four or five kingdoms in the eighth century AD. The three are usually seen as a chronological succession, but with no obvious link between them.

However, the tendency is now to draw the curtain on Kenneth Jackson's 'window on the Iron Age' (1964), and see the Ulster Cycle not as reflecting the first century BC, but rather the political situation in the eighth century AD when the poems were first written down. The major centres of the Late Iron Age, Navan Fort and Dun Ailinne, are well dated by their dendrochronology or by their metalwork, and Tara is likely to be contemporary. It is interesting to note that the construction of these major centres, as well as major earthworks such as the Dorsey, seem to belong to a very short period of time (see also Armit this volume). The proposition is that the remains of the centres still survived in the landscape and something of their importance remained in folk memory, but this was then translated into eighth century terms, e.g. their role as kingly residences rather than as ceremonial or cult centres, with their circular enclosures being seen as some sort of 'super-rath'.

This alternative explanation means that we cannot take the existence of kingship for granted. Indeed the archaeological evidence supports an alternative explanation, as the sites show very little evidence for domestic occupation, royal or otherwise. However, we must accept the existence of some sort of authority capable of organising such large-scale works. Although the ceremonial centres may be nothing new (Early Bronze Age societies were capable of building monuments such as Stonehenge), and the same is true for the gold hoard from Broighter (the Late Bronze Age also had gold hoards), the two combined can best be interpreted as some sort of incipient state organisation, although it seems to have been very short-lived.

Archaeologically visible ostentatious burial rites are at present lacking, although, as in western Britain, some burials contain richer objects (the weapon burial at Lambay Island, the possible mirror burial at Kiltierney, or the bronze bowl from a burial at Fore), and some burials were placed in ring barrows (Raftery 1994). This general lack of rich grave goods should not surprise us, as it is fairly typical of western France, and western and northern Spain. The Auvergne again provides us with a cautionary tale. Rich burials here do not appear until after the Roman conquest, in the late first century BC. The documentary evidence, on the other hand, tells of Luernios' rise to power via the ostentatious use of gold and especially feasting. The enclosure set up by Luernios has its archaeological counterparts in the activities at Brézet (part of the Aulnat complex), where large quantities of amphorae and a horse burial with associated metalwork have been found. Amphorae are also a major feature, along with animal remains (several hundred sheep mandibles, for instance) at the slightly later ritual enclosure within the *oppidum* of Corent (Poux and Deberge 2002; Mennesier-Jouannet forthcoming).

If, in the case of Ireland, we are looking at a division of the island into polities comparable in size to those of the eighth century AD, this would not be exceptionally large for the Late Iron Age, be it the larger tribal states of Gaul or the multi-tribal kingdoms of south-eastern Britain. With the possible exception of the linear earthworks, in Ireland we have no indications of where the boundaries may have lain. The situation described by Ptolemy would be after the collapse of such polities, perhaps, as in Britain at the time of the Roman conquest, with the breaking up into pre-existing component parts.

Conclusions

Rather than reject many of the concepts adopted by the 'New Archaeology' such as states and chiefdoms, least-effort models, and centre–periphery relationships, I suggest that these provide very useful frameworks within which to pose questions of the archaeological record, as heuristic devices rather than models which provide ready-made answers to what was going on. I hope the thoughts presented here on the concept of the state in the Late Iron Age and the contrasting natures of the 'city state' and the 'tribal state', the contrast of their structures, their variability even as recognisable classes, and the problems of their origins, have made the point.

Bibliography

Colbert de Beaulieu, J.-B. 1962. Les monnaies gauloises au nom des chefs mentionnés dans les commentaires de César, *Latomus* 58, 419–446.

Collis, J.R. 1971. Functional and theoretical interpretations of British coinage, *World Archaeology* 3, 71–84.

Collis, J.R. 1995. States without centers? The Middle La Tène period in temperate Europe, in B. Arnold and D.B. Gibson (eds), *Celtic Chiefdom, Celtic State*, 75–80. Cambridge: Cambridge University Press.

Collis, J.R. 2000. Celtic Oppida, in M.H. Hansen 2000, 229–239.

Collis, J.R. 2003. *The Celts: Origins, Myths and Inventions.* Stroud: Tempus.

Creighton, J. 2000. *Coins and Power in Late Iron Age Britain.* Cambridge: Cambridge University Press.

Fichtl, S. 2004. *Les peoples Gaulois. IIIe – Ie siècles av. J-C.* Paris: Éditions Errance.

Goudineau, C. 1998. *Regard sur la Gaule.* Paris: Éditions Errance.

Hansen, M.H. (ed.) 2000. *A Comparative Study of Thirty City-State Cultures: an Investigation Conducted by the Copenhagen Polis Centre.* Copenhagen: Det Kongelige Danske Videnskabernes Selskab, Historiske-filosofiske Skrifter 21

Jackson, K.H. 1964. *The Oldest Irish Tradition. A Window on the Iron Age.* Cambridge: Cambridge University Press.

Menez, Y. and Arremond, J.-C. 1997. L'habitat aristocratique fortifié de Paule (Côtes d'Armor), *Gallia* 54, 119–155.

Mennesier-Jouannet, C. (ed.), forthcoming. *Actes du XXVIIe Colloque de l'AFEAF, Clermont-Ferrand, 2003.* Mélanges d'Archéologie Méridionale.

Mauss, M. 1954. *The Gift: Forms and Functions of Exchange in Archaic Societies.* London: Cohen and West.

Milcent, P.-Y. 2004. *Le premier âge du Fer en France centrale.* Paris: Société Préhistorique Française Mémoire 34.

Poux. M. and Deberge, Y. 2002. L'enclos cultuel de Corent (Puy-de-Dôme): festins et rites collectifs, *Revue Archéologique du Centre* 41, 57–110.

Raftery, B. 1994. *Pagan Celtic Ireland: the Enigma of the Irish Iron Age.* London: Thames and Hudson.

Roymans, N. 1990. *Tribal Societies in Northern Gaul: an Anthropological Perspective.* Amsterdam: Cingula 12.

Snodgrass, A.M. 1980. *Archaic Greece: the Age of Experiment.* Edinburgh: Edinburgh University Press.

Vitali, D. and Kaenel, G. 2000. Un Helvète chez les Etrusques vers 300 av. J.-C., *Archäologie in der Schweiz* 23/3, 115–122.

Woolf, A. 1998. Romancing the Celts: a segmentary approach to acculturation, in R. Lawrence and J. Berry (eds), *Cultural Identity in the Roman Empire*, 111–124. London: Routledge.

List of contributors

UMBERTO ALBARELLA, Department of Archaeology, University of Sheffield

IAN ARMIT, Department of Archaeological Sciences, University of Bradford

BILL BEVAN, Peak District National Park Authority, Bakewell, Derbyshire *and*
Department of Archaeology and Anthropology, The Australian National University, Canberra, Australia

STEWART BRYANT, Environment Department, Hertfordshire County Council, Hertford

GILLIAN CARR, Madingley Hall, Madingley, Cambridge

JOHN COLLIS, Department of Archaeology, University of Sheffield

LAURA CRIPPS, School of Archaeology and Ancient History, University of Leicester

MAIRI DAVIES, Historic Scotland, Edinburgh

KEITH DOBNEY, Department of Archaeology, University of Durham

ANTON ERVYNCK, Institute for the Archaeological Heritage of the Flemish Community, Brussels, Belgium

ANDREW FITZPATRICK, Wessex Archaeology, Salisbury, Wiltshire

PAUL FRODSHAM, Northumberland National Park Authority, Hexham, Northumberland

MELANIE GILES, School of Arts, Histories and Cultures, University of Manchester

ADAM GWILT, National Museum and Gallery, Cardiff

IAIN HEDLEY, Northumberland National Park Authority, Hexham, Northumberland

GILL HEY, Oxford Archaeology, Oxford

SUE HAMILTON, Institute of Archaeology, University College London

COLIN HASELGROVE, School of Archaeology and Ancient History, University of Leicester

J.D. HILL, Department of Prehistory and Europe, The British Museum, London

FRASER HUNTER, Department of Archaeology, National Museums of Scotland, Edinburgh

NATASHA HUTCHESON, Norfolk Museums and Archaeology Service, Gressenhall, Norfolk

GLYNIS JONES, Department of Archaeology, University of Sheffield

DAVID KNIGHT, Trent and Peak Archaeological Unit, University Park, Nottingham

PHILIP MACDONALD, Centre for Archaeological Fieldwork, School of Archaeology and Palaeoecology, Queen's University Belfast

TOM MOORE, Department of Archaeology, University of Durham

ELAINE MORRIS, Centre for Applied Archaeological Analyses, School of Humanities (Archaeology), University of Southampton

NICO ROYMANS, Archaeologisch Instituut, Vrije Universiteit, Amsterdam, The Netherlands

JIM RYLATT, 16 Carr Road, Walkley, Sheffield

MARIJKE VAN DER VEEN, School of Archaeology and Ancient History, University of Leicester

LEO WEBLEY, Oxford Archaeology, Osney Mead, Oxford

PETER WELLS, Department of Anthropology, University of Minnesota, Minneapolis, USA

STEVEN WILLIS, School of European Culture and Languages, University of Kent, Canterbury

ANDY WIGLEY, Sustainability Group, Economy and Environment Services, Shropshire County Council, Shrewsbury

SALLY WORRELL, Institute of Archaeology, University College London

ROB YOUNG, Northumberland National Park Authority, Hexham, Northumberland